HOUGHTON MIFFLIN HARCOURT

WRITE SOURCE

TEACHER'S EDITION

Grade 12

Authors

Dave Kemper, Patrick Sebranek, and Verne Meyer

Illustrator

Chris Krenzke

GREAT
SOURCE.

HOUGHTON MIFFLIN HARCOURT

Teacher Consultants

Patty Beckstead
St. George, Utah

Amy Goodman
Anchorage, Alaska

Debra McConnell
Williston, Vermont

Steve Mellen
Temple Hills, Maryland

Reviewers

Randolph C. Bernard
Lafayette Parish School System
Lafayette, LA

Beth Gaby
Carl Schurz High School
Chicago, IL

Susan Dinges
Mount Olive Public School
    District
Budd Lake, NJ

Shara W. Holt
St. Johns County School District
St. Augustine, FL

Guy M. Kinney
Orange County Public Schools
Orlando, FL

Raymond Klejmont
Desoto County
Arcadia, FL

Connie McGee
Miami-Dade County Public
    Schools
Miami, FL

Harriet Maher
Lafayette Parish School System
Lafayette, LA

Jenny R. May
Mason City Schools
Mason, OH

Pamela Miltenberger
J. C. Harmon High School
Kansas City, KS

Christine Neuner
Iberia Parish School System
New Iberia, LA

Marie T. Raduazzo
Arlington High School
Arlington, MA

Elizabeth Rehberger
Huntington Beach High School
Huntington Beach, CA

Stephanie Saltikov-Izabal
Huntington Beach Union High
    School District
Huntington Beach, CA

Ann Marie Seely
Henrico County Public Schools
Richmond, VA

www.hmheducation.com/writesource

Photo credits: TE-8 ©Mike Kemp/Getty Images; TE-10–11 ©Andrzej Tokarski/Alamy; TE-12 (bl) ©Image Source/Getty Images; TE-12 (cm, bm) ©Bananastock/Jupiterimages/Getty Images; TE-16–17 (teacher) ©Blend Images/Alamy; TE-16–17 (students) ©SuperStock RF/SuperStock.

Text credits: TE-61–68 Common Core State Standards © Copyright 2010. National Governors Association Center for Best Practices and Council of Chief State School Officers. All rights reserved.

Printed in the U.S.A.

ISBN 978-0-547-48468-6

3 4 5 6 7 8 9 10 0607 19 18 17

4500650629   B C D E F G

Program Overview

Professional Development for Writing

THE FORMS, THE PROCESS, AND THE TRAITS

WRITING WORKSHOP AND GRAMMAR

WRITING ACROSS THE CURRICULUM, ACADEMIC VOCABULARY, AND TEST PREPARATION

DIFFERENTIATION

RESEARCH

Teacher Resources

Contents

The Writing Process

The Forms of Writing

How does *Write Source* work?

Write Source is a complete language arts curriculum focused on writing and grammar in print and digital formats.

With writing instruction at the core, grammar, usage, and mechanics are taught in an authentic writing context.

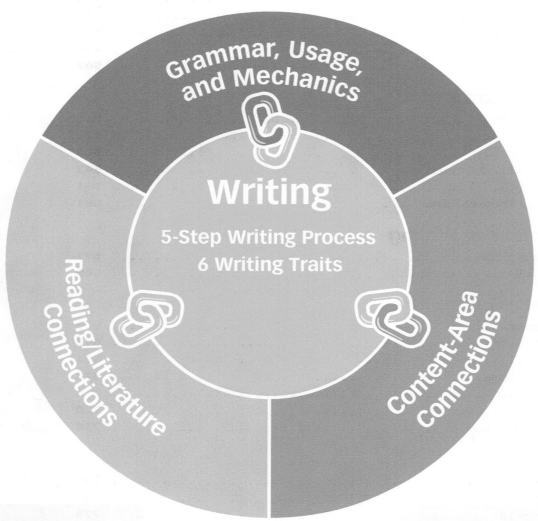

Grammar, Usage, and Mechanics

Writing
5-Step Writing Process
6 Writing Traits

Reading/Literature Connections

Content-Area Connections

The Six Traits of Effective Writing

- Ideas
- Organization
- Voice
- Word Choice
- Sentence Fluency
- Conventions

Steps of the Writing Process

- Prewriting
- Writing
- Revising
- Editing
- Publishing

Introduce the writing form:

- Preview the form by focusing on a key concept or skill.
- Analyze a model paragraph.
- Write a paragraph

Each core forms of writing unit follows the same instructional path—a consistent writing curriculum across all grade levels.

Explore the writing form:

- Read authentic, real-world fiction or nonfiction that models the writing form.
- Analyze a model story or essay.
- Use the writing process to write a story or essay.

- Use the six traits to revise and to edit for conventions.
- Repeat these steps for an addition writing assignment.

Write for the assessment:

- Write a piece in the same writing form for assessment.
- Read an essay or other response that models the form.

Write Source prepares students for success in the 21st century.

Write in other content areas:

- Write in a variety of forms across the major content areas—science, social studies, math, and the arts.

What are the main components of *Write Source*?

The *Write Source* **Student Edition** reflects the latest research on writing instruction. The **Teacher's Edition** has all the support you need to help students become confident, proficient writers.

The **SkillsBook** helps students practice and improve grammar, usage, and mechanics skills.

The **Assessment** book provides a pretest, progress tests, and a post-test.

The **Daily Language Workouts** build student grammar skills through quick, daily editing and proofreading activities.

Write Source Online
www.hmheducation.com/writesource

- Discover the power of writing instruction with **Net-text**, an interactive, collaborative online worktext.

- Engage students in grammar through **GrammarSnap**, the grammar practice Web application.

- Transform writing instruction through high-functioning **Interactive Whiteboard presentations**.

- Support instruction with a searchable **File Cabinet** teacher resource.

- Score essays accurately and efficiently with **Online Essay Scoring**.

How does the Teacher's Edition support instruction?

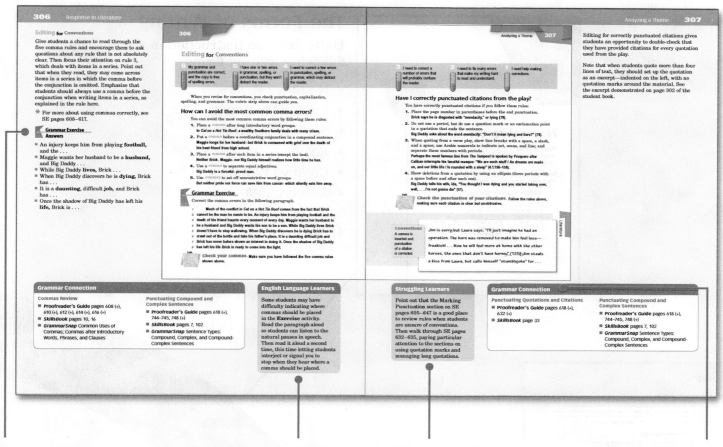

Teaching suggestions and activity answers provide the support you will need to implement writing instruction.

The Teacher's Edition provides consistent support for **English language learners**.

Differentiated Instruction for struggling learners and advanced learners is provided throughout the core instructional units.

Grammar Connections support grammar, usage, and mechanics instruction.

Additional Resources

- Common Core State Standards Correlation
- Yearlong Timetable
- Professional Development for Writing

- Reading-Writing Connection
- Benchmark Papers
- Copy Masters Resources

How is *Write Source* organized?

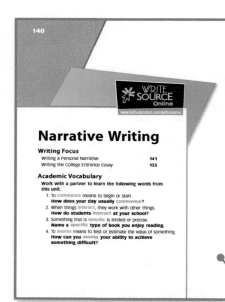

The Forms of Writing

Units focus on instruction in the following writing forms:

- Narrative Writing
- Expository Writing
- Persuasive Writing
- Response to Literature
- Creative Writing
- Research Writing

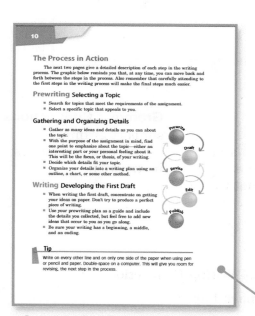

The Writing Process

This unit introduces students to the steps in the writing process and integrates instruction on the six traits of effective writing.

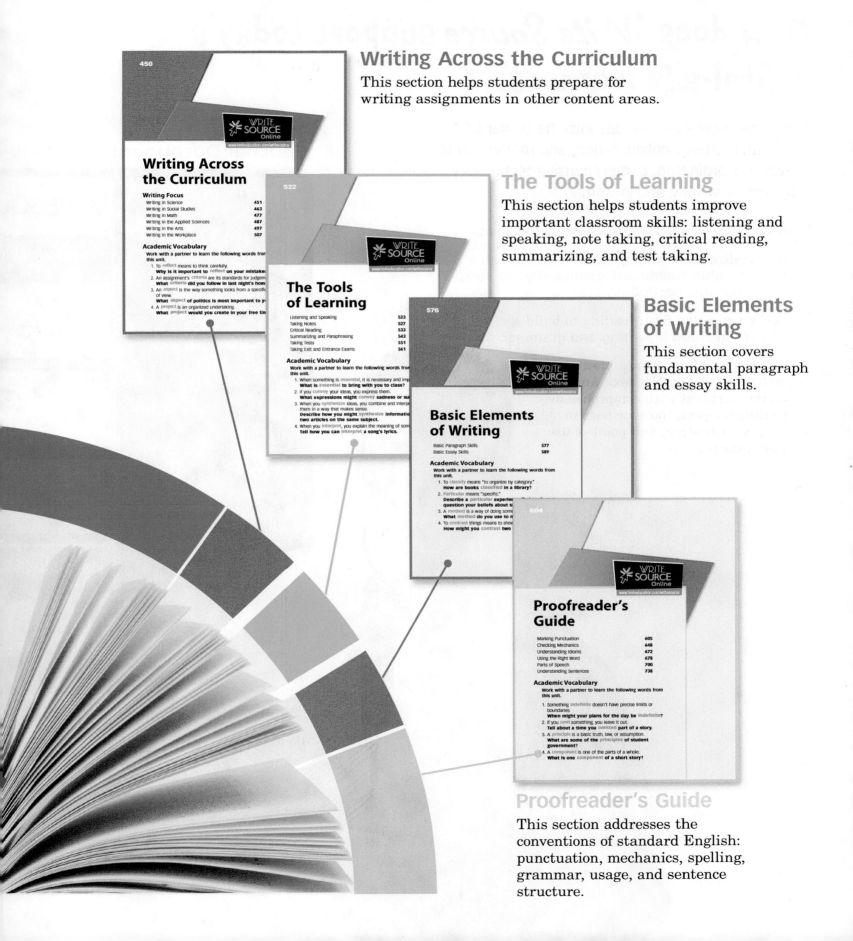

Writing Across the Curriculum

This section helps students prepare for writing assignments in other content areas.

The Tools of Learning

This section helps students improve important classroom skills: listening and speaking, note taking, critical reading, summarizing, and test taking.

Basic Elements of Writing

This section covers fundamental paragraph and essay skills.

Proofreader's Guide

This section addresses the conventions of standard English: punctuation, mechanics, spelling, grammar, usage, and sentence structure.

Writing Across the Curriculum

Writing Focus

Academic Vocabulary
Work with a partner to learn the following words from this unit.
1. To reflect means to think carefully.
   Why is it important to reflect on your mistakes?
2. An assignment's criteria are its standards for judgem...
   What criteria did you follow in last night's hom...
3. An aspect is the way something looks from a specific point of view.
   What aspect of politics is most important to yo...
4. A project is an organized undertaking.
   What project would you create in your free tim...

The Tools of Learning

Academic Vocabulary
Work with a partner to learn the following words from this unit.
1. When something is essential, it is necessary and imp...
   What is essential to bring with you to class?
2. If you convey your ideas, you express them.
   What expressions might convey sadness or su...
3. When you synthesize ideas, you combine and interp...
   them in a way that makes sense.
   Describe how you might synthesize information two articles on the same subject.
4. When you interpret, you explain the meaning of som...
   Tell how you can interpret a song's lyrics.

Basic Elements of Writing

Academic Vocabulary
Work with a partner to learn the following words from this unit.
1. To classify means "to organize by category."
   How are books classified in a library?
2. Particular means "specific."
   Describe a particular experien... question your beliefs about s...
3. A method is a way of doing some...
   What method do you use to m...
4. To contrast things means to show...
   How might you contrast two...

Proofreader's Guide

Academic Vocabulary
Work with a partner to learn the following words from this unit.

1. Something indefinite doesn't have precise limits or boundaries.
   When might your plans for the day be indefinite?
2. If you omit something, you leave it out.
   Tell about a time you omitted part of a story.
3. A principle is a basic truth, law, or assumption.
   What are some of the principles of student government?
4. A component is one of the parts of a whole.
   What is one component of a short story?

How does *Write Source* support today's digital-age learners?

*W*rite Source Online taps into the power of interactivity, collaboration, and motivation to deliver a coordinated, comprehensive technology program for writing and grammar.

With *Write Source Online*, teachers and students:

- personalize their writing experience through a **customizable dashboard**, **community network**, and **electronic portfolios**

- easily transition from reading to build a **solid foundation in writing and grammar**

- experience **interactive guided instruction** using Net-text, an online worktext with comprehensive writing support, tools for peer-to-peer collaboration, and point-of-use grammar practice

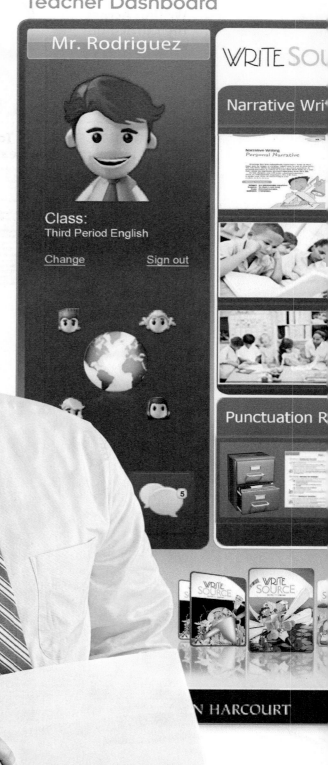

Teacher Dashboard

Mr. Rodriguez

Class:
Third Period English

Change   Sign out

WRITE SOU

Narrative Wri

Punctuation R

N HARCOURT

Write Source Online
www.hmheducation.com/writesource

Preparing students and teachers
for success in the 21st century

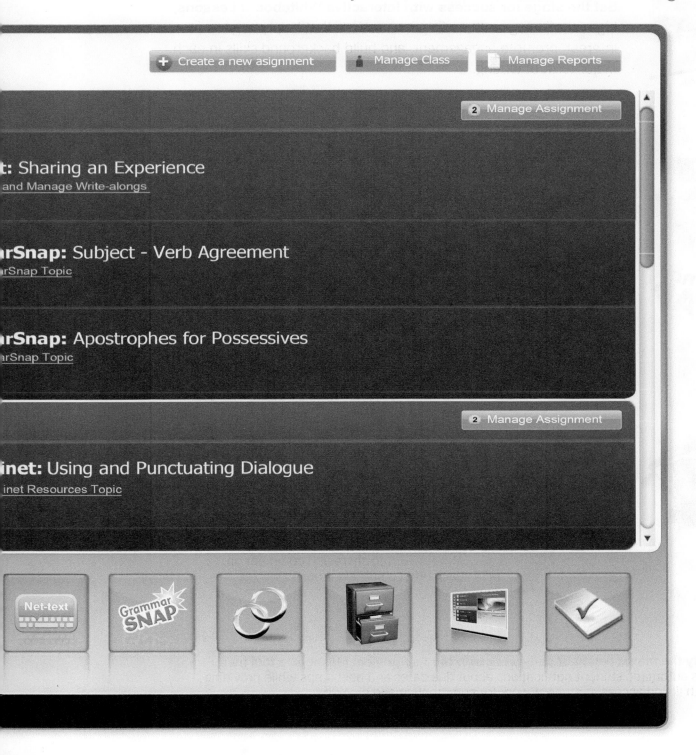

+ Create a new asignment   👤 Manage Class   📄 Manage Reports

2 Manage Assignment

t: Sharing an Experience
and Manage Write-alongs

rSnap: Subject - Verb Agreement
rSnap Topic

rSnap: Apostrophes for Possessives
rSnap Topic

2 Manage Assignment

inet: Using and Punctuating Dialogue
inet Resources Topic

Net-text   Grammar SNAP

What are the components of Write Source Online?

Set the stage for success with Interactive Whiteboard Lessons, high-functioning multimedia presentations that help you generate interest, promote engagement, and build background skills in each major form of writing.

Transform students into writers with Net-text, an innovative online worktext that features interactive instruction, online document creation, peer-to-peer commenting, and integrated grammar—all supported by tools that help you monitor progress and give feedback.

Engage students in grammar with GrammarSnap, a multimedia application that reinforces and extends understanding of key topics through videos, games, and quizzes that make learning about grammar fun.

Students are motivated to earn **SkillSnap points to unlock a variety of accessories** for their avatar character.

Tap into the power of publishing with the *Write Source Online* Portfolio, a customizable resource that gives students an authentic forum for sharing and reflecting on their writing.

Students and classrooms can connect in **My Network** to share and comment on each other's published portfolios.

Simplify the management of daily work with the Assignment Manager, a tool that delivers automatic student notifications about due dates and next steps while providing you with linked access to student work for commenting and grading.

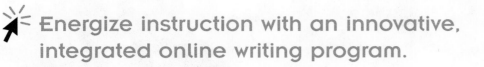

Energize instruction with an innovative, integrated online writing program.

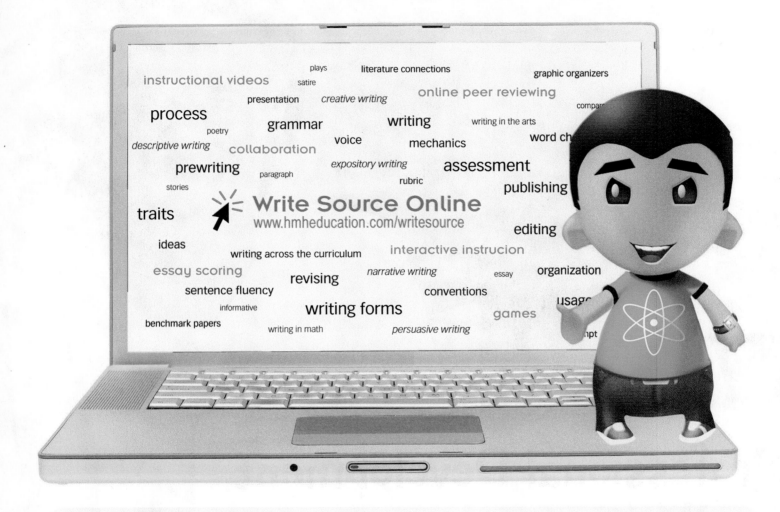

Additional Resources

- **Bookshelf** eBooks of *Write Source* print components
- **Essay Scoring** Prompts for additional writing practice with automatic scoring and evaluation

- **File Cabinet** Thousands of printable teacher resources, such as blackline masters and additional assessments, that help you minimize planning time and differentiate instruction.

Professional Development for Writing

This section of the *Write Source* Teacher's Edition provides information to help you make the most of *Write Source* in your classroom. The program's instructional design includes comprehensive support for the topics that matter most to teachers: grammar, writing workshops, academic vocabulary, test preparation, the use of technology, and so much more. Whether you are a new teacher or a veteran, the information in the following pages will show how *Write Source* can help you meet your classroom goals.

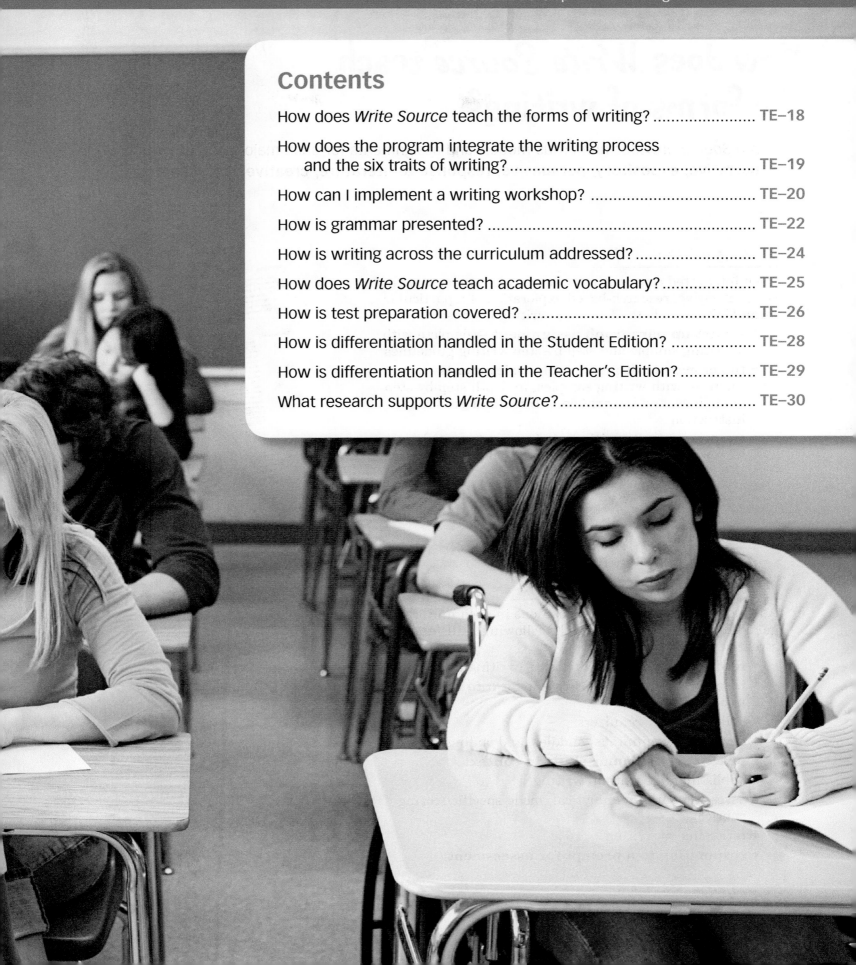

Contents

How does *Write Source* teach the forms of writing?

W*rite Source* provides numerous models and assignments for each major form of writing: **narrative**, **expository**, **persuasive**, **response to literature**, **creative**, and **research**.

Writing Assignments

Each integrated core writing unit provides students with a comprehensive, research-based exploration of a particular form. Units include the following writing lessons:

- a **start-up paragraph assignment**—complete with a writing sample and step-by-step writing guidelines
- two or more **multiparagraph assignments**—complete with writing samples, in-depth step-by-step guidelines, and integration of traits and grammar instruction
- one **assessment writing assignment**—complete with a sample response to a prompt plus writing tips

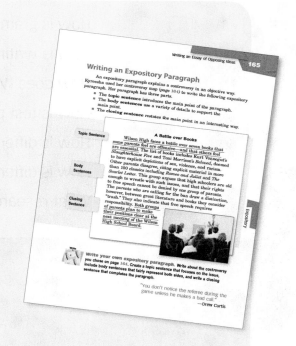

Writing Skills and Strategies

As students develop their compositions in each unit, they gain valuable experience with the following skills and strategies:

- reading and responding to texts (writing models)
- **integrating the traits of writing into the writing process**
- using graphic organizers
- developing beginnings, middles, and endings
- **practicing grammar skills in context**
- publishing (presenting) writing
- assessing with an analytical, mode-specific scoring rubric
- reflecting on writing
- **responding to a prompt for assessment**

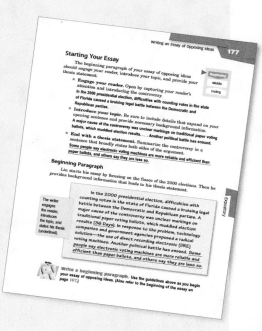

How does the program integrate the writing process and the traits?

Throughout each core forms of writing unit, the six traits of effective writing are integrated into the steps of the writing process. As students develop their writing, they develop an understanding of and appreciation for each trait of writing. In addition, checklists, guidelines, and activities are used to ensure that each piece of writing is completely traits-based.

The Process and the Traits in the Core Units

Understanding Your Goal

The beginning of each main assignment helps students understand the goal of their writing. A chart listing the traits of writing as they relate to the form helps students meet that goal.

Focus on the Traits

As students develop their writing, they will find valuable discussions of the six traits at different steps in the writing process.

Revising and Editing for the Traits

When students are ready to revise and edit, they will find step-by-step instruction, traits-based guidelines, strategies, and checklists to help them improve their writing.

Rubrics for the Core Units

A traits-based rubric concludes each major assignment. This rubric ties directly to the goal chart at the beginning of the unit and the rubric strips presented on the revising and editing pages.

Special Note: For more information about the writing traits, we recommend *Creating Writers Through 6-Trait Writing Assessment and Instruction*, 4th ed., by Vicki Spandel (Addison Wesley Longman, 2005) and *Write Traits®* by Vicki Spandel and Jeff Hicks (Houghton Mifflin Harcourt, 2011).

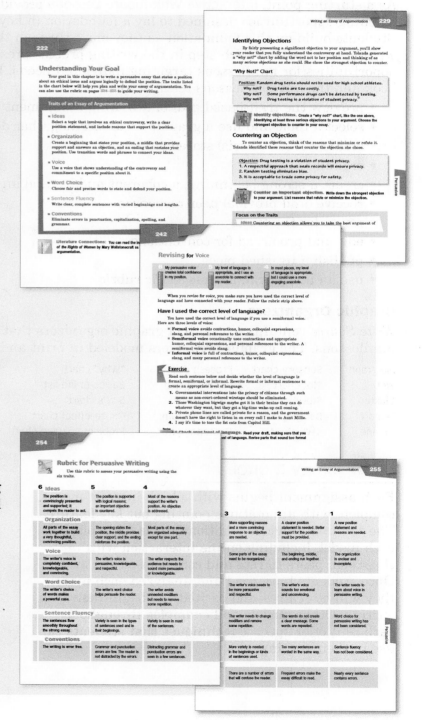

How can I implement a writing workshop?

Write Source complements implementation of a writing workshop through both print and technology resources. The program includes minilessons for instruction, high-quality models to encourage writing, support for whole-class sharing, and much more.

Integrated Minilessons

As a starting point, **Interactive Whiteboard Lessons** provide short, focused teaching opportunities designed to lay a foundation in key concepts. Students build on this foundation as they move through the core forms of writing units, where each step in the writing process presents additional opportunities for minilessons targeting individual needs. Both the print book and the **Net-text** lessons teach students to:

- preview the trait-based goal of a writing assignment
- select a topic and use a graphic organizer to gather details
- create a focus (thesis) statement
- organize ideas
- create a strong beginning, a coherent middle, and an effective ending
- receive (and provide) peer responses
- revise for the traits
- edit and proofread for conventions
- publish a finished piece
- use an analytical, mode-specific rubric

Mon	Tues	Wed	Thurs	Fri

Writing Minilessons
(10 minutes as needed)

Status Checks
(2 minutes)
Find out what students will work on for the day.

Individual Work
(30 minutes)
Writing, Revising, Editing, Conferencing, or Publishing

Whole-Class Sharing Session
(5 minutes)

Graphic Organizers

Write Source contains a wealth of graphic organizers that can serve as the subjects of minilessons. The graphic organizers modeled in print and technology include the following:

Pie graph	Sensory chart	Process diagram	"Why" chart	Topic list
Web	Plot chart	Venn diagram	Basics-of-life list	Character chart
Cluster	Storyboard	Circle graph	5 W's chart	Picture diagram
T-chart	Bar graph	Cycle diagram	Cause-effect chart	Comparison-contrast chart
Outline	KWL chart	Gathering grid	Problem-solution chart	Time line

High-Quality Models

Each assignment begins with a high-interest model, complete with annotations pointing out key features. The **Net-text** provides additional tools for exploring each model, including online interaction with classroom peers to rate and comment on the model. Once students have read and analyzed each model, they will be ready—and excited—to begin their own writing. Other models and examples throughout each unit offer specific techniques that students can use in their writing.

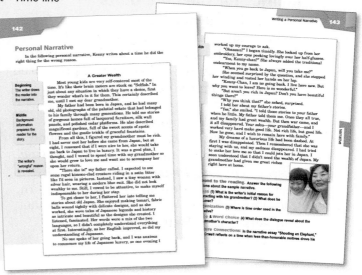

Individual Writing

Write Source makes it easy for writing-workshop students to work on their own. It also provides specific help whenever students have questions about their writing. Here are some of the areas that are addressed:

- catching the reader's interest
- providing background information
- developing strong paragraphs
- elaborating on ideas
- organizing ideas by time, location, importance, logic
- quoting, paraphrasing, and summarizing
- using transitions
- drawing conclusions
- calling the reader to act

In addition to supporting these and other key concepts from the print, the *Write Source* **Net-text** provides an extra layer of scaffolding for independent writing, including exercises with immediate feedback, at-a-click support for grammar and conventions concepts, ready access to resources such as a dictionary and thesaurus, and an application for creating and managing work online.

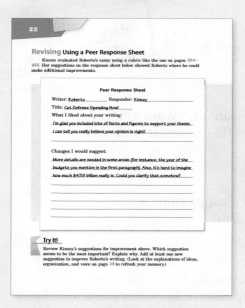

Peer and Teacher Response

Write Source reviews peer responding and provides a peer response sheet. Consistent integration of the traits into the writing process allows students and teachers to speak a common language as they conduct response sessions. Traits-based checklists help pinpoint just what is working—and what could work better—in each piece of writing. The *Write Source* **Net-text** provides additional support for teacher-to-student and student-to-student response, including a commenting tool and commenting notifications.

Whole-Class Sharing

Write Source helps students complete and prepare their work for whole-class sharing—whether in a traditional presentation or in the public section of the **Online Portfolio**. In addition, the program provides a wealth of suggestions for publishing work in a variety of forms and for a variety of audiences.

Most writing units include information on evaluating written compositions. Even the evaluation process is modeled with sample essays and assessments. A reflection sheet also helps students think about what they have learned an internalize the lessons to use in the future.

How is grammar presented?

If you follow the suggested yearlong timetable, you will cover all the key grammar skills, including those listed in state standards. Grammar instruction integrated into writing instruction allows students to learn about grammar in context when they are working on their own writing. If students have trouble with a particular concept, you can refer to a wealth of print and online resources for additional support.

Grammar in the Teacher's Edition

The yearlong timetable provides the big picture of grammar integration, and the unit overview at the beginning of each unit shows skills and concepts to teach while teaching writing. Grammar Connections at point of use help you pinpoint the time to present skills and concepts.

Grammar in the Student Edition

Forms of Writing

Each core forms of writing unit includes grammar instruction integrated into the revising and editing steps in the development of the main composition. Instruction on grammar skills includes examples and practice and application activities, and it links to students' writing.

Word Choice and Sentence Fluency

For more grammar in the context of writing, turn to the minilessons in "Word Choice" and "Sentence Fluency." Use these minilessons to workshop specific grammar and style issues that students can apply to their writing.

Proofreader's Guide

This section serves as a complete conventions guide, providing rules, examples, and activities for grammar, usage, punctuation, mechanics, and spelling.

☀ Write Source Online

The *Write Source* Net-text offers interactive instruction and practice for the grammar and conventions topics embedded in the core writing units. *Write Source* GrammarSnap provides additional instruction, practice, and basic skills reinforcement through videos, minilessons, games, and quizzes.

Grammar in Other Program Components

The *SkillsBook* provides more than 130 grammar, usage, punctuation, mechanics, sentence-construction, and spelling activities. The *Assessment* book contains pretests, benchmark tests, and post-tests for basic writing and editing skills. *Daily Language Workouts* includes a year's worth of sentences (daily) and paragraphs (weekly) for editing practice.

Planning Grammar Instruction

Should I implement *all* of the suggested basic grammar activities?

In the course of the year, if you assigned every grammar exercise listed in the daily lesson schedules (located in the unit overviews of your TE), your students would complete **all** of the "Proofreader's Guide," *SkillsBook*, and GrammarSnap activities.

Because the most effective teaching of grammar happens in context, grammar instruction appears at appropriate times during revising and editing in the core writing forms units. As the teacher, you must choose the type and number of activities that will best meet the needs of your students.

How are all the grammar resources related?

The *SkillsBook* grammar activities parallel and expand on the rules and exercises found in the "Proofreader's Guide" of the Student Edition. GrammarSnap offers additional support for key grammar topics in an engaging, interactive format.

How do I use the daily lesson schedule charts?

The sample below from the "Persuasive Writing" unit is followed by an explanation of how to read and use the charts.

Suggested Persuasive Writing Unit (Four Weeks)

| | Day | Writing and Skills Instruction | *Student Edition* | | *SkillsBook* | *Daily Language Workouts* | *Write Source Online* |
			Main Pages	Resource Units*			
WEEK 1	1–2	**Persuasive Paragraph**	219–221	583		46–49	*Interactive Whiteboard Lessons*
		Skills Activities:					
		• Punctuation		616 (+), 632 (+)	31		
		• Tense Shifts		718 (+), 722 (+)	176		*GrammarSnap*
	3–5	**Writing an Essay of Argumentation** (Model, Prewriting) Organization (Deductive, Inductive), Supporting Details, Audience, Diction ⓘ Literature Connections *A Vindication of the Rights of Women*	222–230, 62–63, 56–57, 108–109, 110, 69, 71				*Net-text*

1. The Resource Units column indicates the SE pages that cover rules, examples, and exercises for each "Skills Activity" item.
2. The *SkillsBook, Daily Language Workouts*, and Write Source Online columns indicate pages and information from those particular resources.

How do I use *Daily Language Workouts*?

Daily Language Workouts is a teacher resource that provides a high-interest sentence for each day of the year and weekly paragraphs for additional editing and proofreading practice. This regular practice helps students develop the objectivity they need to effectively edit their own writing.

How is writing across the curriculum addressed?

*W*rite Source provides a wide variety of cross-curricular activities and assignments. It promotes *writing to show learning, writing to learn new concepts,* and *writing to reflect on learning.*

Writing to Show Learning

Writing to show learning is the most common type of writing that content-area teachers assign. The following forms of writing covered in the program are commonly used for this purpose.

- Narrative paragraph and essay
- Expository paragraph and essay
- Persuasive paragraph and essay
- Response paragraph and essay
- Summary
- Research report

Sample Writing-Across-the-Curriculum Assignments

Specific content-area assignments let students show learning.

Writing in Science
- Cause-Effect Essay
- Directions
- Response to an Expository Prompt

Writing in Social Studies
- Informative Essay
- Response to an Editorial Cartoon
- Document-Based Essay

Writing in Math
- Article Summary
- Statistical Argument
- Response to a Math Prompt

Writing in the Applied Sciences
- Explanatory Essay
- Career Review
- Response to a Prompt

Writing in the Arts
- Research Report
- Performance Review
- Response to an Art Prompt

Writing in the Workplace
- Business Letters
- Letter of Application
- Résumé
- Proposal
- Memo
- E-Mail Message
- News Release

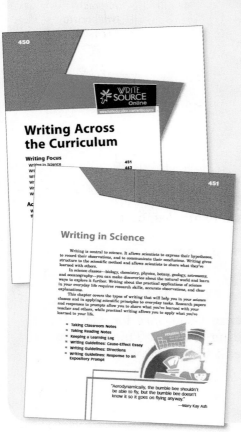

How does *Write Source* teach academic vocabulary?

Write *Source* gives students the opportunity to learn and use academic vocabulary terms so essential for success in school.

Academic Vocabulary in *Write Source*

Academic vocabulary refers to the words students must know in order to understand the concepts they encounter in school. Academic vocabulary terms such as *element, analyze, substantial*, and *consistent* are not specific to any one subject but rather denote key ideas and skills relevant to many subject areas. In a sense, academic vocabulary is the language of school. To be successful in school, students must understand and be able to use academic vocabulary as they write about and discuss what they learn in class.

The *Write Source* Academic Vocabulary feature gives students the opportunity to learn and practice using new academic vocabulary in a collaborative activity. This feature, which appears at the beginning of each unit of the Student Edition, provides a brief explanation of each academic vocabulary word, followed by a prompt that motivates students to practice using the term.

- Academic vocabulary is taken from words appearing in the unit.
- Students work with a partner to read the explanations of academic vocabulary words used in the unit.
- Each explanation is accompanied by an activity or question that prompts students to demonstrate their understanding of the new word.

Academic Vocabulary

With a partner, discuss the following words from this unit.

1. An element is one part of something, such as a play.
   Which element of books do you find most interesting?
2. A formula is a statement that describes a relationship.
   Describe a formula for success in school.
3. Something chosen to stand for something else is a symbol.
   What symbols represent the United States?
4. To integrate something, you bring parts together into a whole.
   How might you integrate quotations into your writing?

How is test preparation covered?

Each core forms of writing unit in the Student Edition prepares students for responding to testing prompts. **If students complete their work in each of the core units, they will have learned the skills necessary for success on any type of writing assessment.** Here are some of the main features in the Student Edition that address testing.

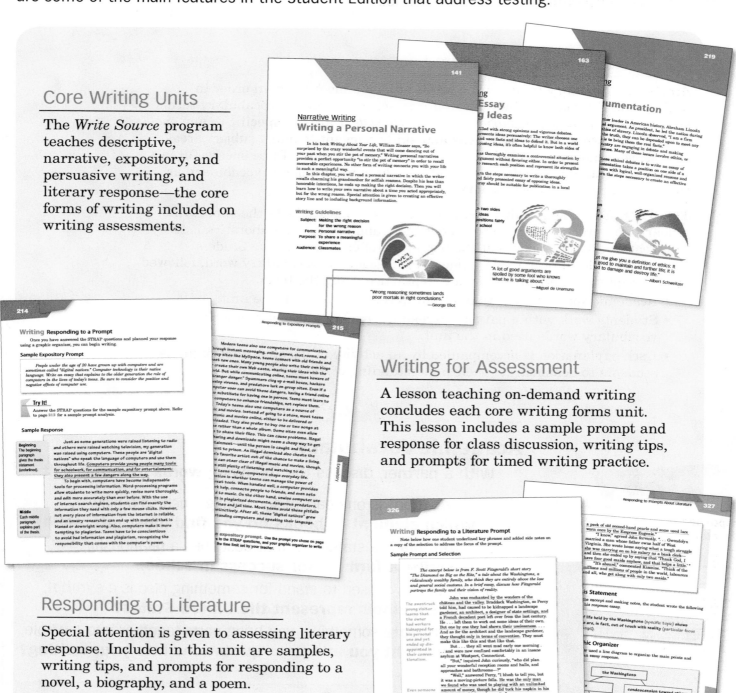

Core Writing Units

The *Write Source* program teaches descriptive, narrative, expository, and persuasive writing, and literary response—the core forms of writing included on writing assessments.

Writing for Assessment

A lesson teaching on-demand writing concludes each core writing forms unit. This lesson includes a sample prompt and response for class discussion, writing tips, and prompts for timed writing practice.

Responding to Literature

Special attention is given to assessing literary response. Included in this unit are samples, writing tips, and prompts for responding to a novel, a biography, and a poem.

Taking Classroom Tests

The chapter on test taking includes a section entitled "Taking Essay Tests" that helps students analyze the key words in writing prompts.

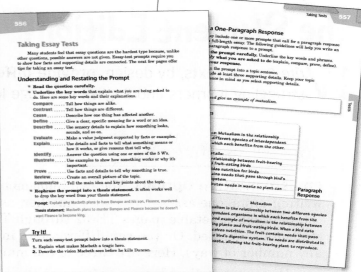

Writing Across the Curriculum

The writing-across-the-curriculum units help students prepare for on-demand writing on content-based tests.

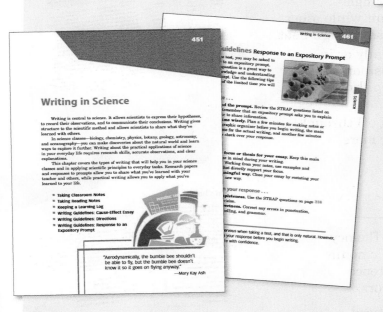

Test Prep for Grammar Skills

Tests at the end of each section in the "Proofreader's Guide" follow a standardized test format. Familiarity with this formatting will help students do their best on these important tests.

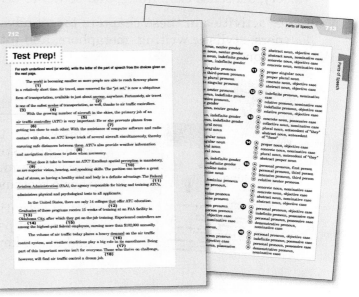

How is differentiation handled in the Student Edition?

Write *Source* texts, by design, **provide differentiation** in writing instruction—from struggling learners and English language learners to advanced, independent students.

Core Forms of Writing Units

Implementation Options: You can implement the forms of writing units, one assignment after another, as delineated in the yearlong timetable (pages TE-32 through TE-35), helping students as needed. Or you can differentiate instruction in any number of ways. Here are three of the many possibilities:

- Have **struggling learners** focus on the single-paragraph writing assignment in each unit while other students complete the multiparagraph essay assignment.
- Have **advanced learners** work individually or in small groups on a multiparagraph composition while you guide struggling learners step-by-step through the development of a composition.
- Conduct a **writing workshop** (pages TE-20 through TE-21), asking students to develop one or more

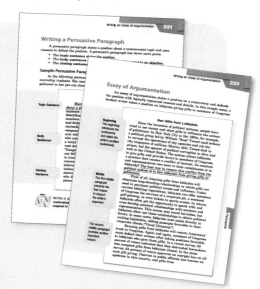

Word Choice and Sentence Fluency

Special chapters on word choice and sentence fluency teach the basics to struggling students: specific nouns and vivid verbs, problems with modifiers, sentence variety, sentence combining, and sentence errors.

Other activities in these chapters target advanced learners: stylistic writing, metaphors, and intentional repetition.

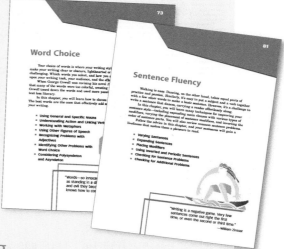

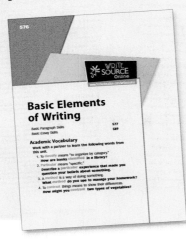

Basic Elements of Writing

This section teaches paragraph and essay basics to struggling students: the parts of a paragraph, basic paragraph modes, the parts of an essay, and outlines and thesis statements.

Other activities teach high-level skills to advanced students: patterns of paragraph organization, perfecting essay parts, and using key writing terms and techniques.

How is differentiation handled in the Teacher's Edition?

The Teacher's Edition provides point-of-use differentiation for struggling learners, English language learners, and advanced learners.

Struggling Learners

The Struggling Learners notes allow you to customize lessons to meet the needs of students who may have difficulty completing the work. These notes provide alternative approaches, extra practice, or additional insights.

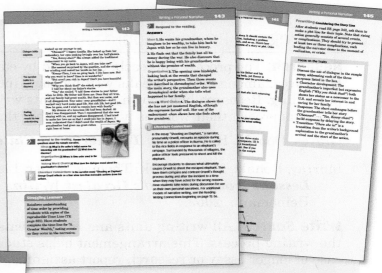

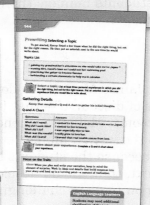

English Language Learners

The English Language Learners notes help you to guide students with limited language skills through the lessons. These notes provide extra practice, alternative approaches, connections to first languages, glossaries of new terms, demonstration ideas, and more.

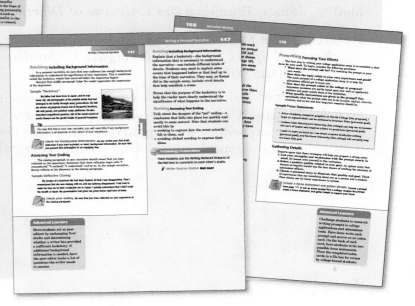

Advanced Learners

The Advanced Learners notes help you enhance the lessons for students who need to be challenged. Some of the notes extend the lessons.

What research supports the *Write Source* program?

Write Source reflects the best thinking and research on writing instruction.

Applying the Process Approach to Writing

Research: The process approach, discussed by educators Donald M. Murray and Donald H. Graves, among others, breaks writing down into a series of steps—prewriting through publishing. Research has shown that students write more effectively and more thoughtfully, if they approach their work as a process rather than as an end product.

Graves, Donald. H. ***Writing: Teachers and Children at Work.*** Heinemann, 2003.

Murray, Donald. M.; Newkirk, Thomas; Miller, Lisa C. ***The Essential Don Murray: Lessons from America's Greatest Writing Teacher.*** Boynton/Cook Heinemann, 2009.

Write Source: All writing units and assignments are arranged according to the steps in the writing process. This arrangement helps students manage their work, especially in the case of longer essay or research report assignments.

Sequencing Assignments

Research: Writing instructor and researcher James Moffett developed a sequence of writing assignments—known as the "universe of discourse"—that has over the years, served countless English/language arts classrooms. Moffett sequences the modes of writing according to their connection or immediacy to the writer. Moffett suggests that students first develop descriptive and narrative pieces because the students have an immediate, personal connection to this type of writing. Next, they should develop informational pieces that require some investigation before moving on to more challenging, reflective writing, such as persuasive essays and position papers.

Moffett, James. ***Teaching the Universe of Discourse.*** Boynton/Cook, 1987.

Related Title: Fleischer, Cathy; Andrew-Vaughn, Sarah. ***Writing Outside Your Comfort Zone: Helping Students Navigate Unfamiliar Genres.*** Heinemann, 2009.

Write Source: The writing units and assignments in the *Write Source* texts are arranged according to the "Universe of Discourse," starting with descriptive and narrative writing, moving on to expository writing, and so on. These assignments are designed to be used in a sequence that supports an existing writing curriculum or integrated reading/language arts program.

Implementing a Writing Workshop

Research: Countless respected writing instructors and researchers have touted the importance of establishing a community of writers in the classroom. Teachers can establish such a community by implementing a writing workshop. In a writing workshop, students are immersed in all aspects of writing, including sharing their work with their peers.

Atwell, Nancie. *In the Middle: New Understandings About Writing, Reading, and Learning.* Heinemann, 1998.

Write Source: The instruction in *Write Source* is clearly presented so that most students can work independently on their writing in a workshop. In addition, the core forms of writing units contain innumerable opportunities for workshop minilessons.

Producing Writing with Detail

Research: Rebekah Caplan learned through her teaching experience that students don't automatically know how to add details to their personal, informational, and persuasive writing. She discovered with her students that adding detail to writing is a skill that must be practiced regularly. To address this problem, Caplan came up with the "show-me" sentence strategy, in which students begin with a basic idea—"My locker is messy"—and create a brief paragraph that shows rather than tells the idea.

Caplan, Rebekah. *Writers in Training: A Guide to Developing a Composition Program.* Dale Seymour Publications, 1984.

Related Title: Bernabi, Gretchen S.; Hover, Jayne; Candler, Cynthia. *Crunchtime: Lessons to Help Students Blow the Roof Off Writing Tests—and Become Better Writers in the Process.* Heinemann, 2009.

Write Source: *Daily Language Workouts* contains a series of show-me sentences that teachers can implement as a regular classroom warm-up.

Meeting Students' Diverse Needs

Research: Many students in today's classrooms struggle with writing and learning. For struggling students, following the writing process is not enough. According to the research done by James L. Collins, struggling students need specific strategies and aids to help them become better writers. Collins found that these students benefit from the following: *skills instruction integrated into the process of writing, color coding and signposts in the presentation of instructional material, the use of graphic organizers, instructions presented in discreet chunks of copy,* and so on.

Collins, James L. *Strategies for Struggling Writers.* Guilford Press, 1998.

Write Source: The core writing forms units contain all the key features from Collins' work. As a result, the units are well suited to struggling learners and English language learners.

Yearlong Timetable

This suggested yearlong timetable presents **one possible sequence** of writing and language skills units based on a five-days-per-week writing class. The sequence can support an existing writing curriculum or integrated reading/language arts program.

First Quarter

Week	Writing Lessons	*Write Source*	Grammar and Writing Skills
1	Getting Started (TE pages 828–830) **Why Write?** **Understanding Writing** **One Writer's Process**	1–5 7–12 13–32	**Skills Assessment:** Using the Right Word Test Prep 698–699 Marking Punctuation Test Prep 622–623, 646–647
2	**Using a Rubric** **Understanding the Traits of Writing**	33–45 47–95	
3	**Exploring the Writing Process** **Listening and Speaking**	97–139 523–526	**Skills Assessment:** Checking Mechanics Test Prep 670–671
4	**Writing a Personal Narrative** (Model, Prewriting, Writing, Revising, Editing, Publishing, Assessing, Reflecting) **Peer Responding**	141–154 121–126	**Skills Assessment:** Understanding Sentences Test Prep 758–759 Verbs, verbals, sentence lengths, punctuating dialogue, pronoun-antecedent agreement, plurals
5	**Writing the College Entrance Essay**	155–161	Transitions, conjunctions, prepositions, interjections, pronouns, end punctuation, usage, pronoun shifts, commas
6	**Summarizing and Paraphrasing** **Expository Warm-Up Paragraph** **Writing an Essay of Opposing Ideas: A Controversy with Two Sides** (Model, Prewriting)	543–550 163–165 166–174	**Skills Assessment:** Spelling Test *SkillsBook* pages 47–48 Parallelism, using the right word, subjects and predicates
7	**Essay of Opposing Ideas** *(cont'd)* (Writing, Revising) **Peer Responding**	175–192 121–126	**Skills Assessment:** Parts of Speech Test Prep 736–737 Parallelism, active and passive voice, rambling sentences, commas, compound and complex sentences
8	**Essay of Opposing Ideas** *(cont'd)* (Editing, Publishing, Assessing, Reflecting)	192–202	Adjectives, run-on sentences, comma splices, pronouns
9	Portfolio Review *SkillsBook* Posttests		

Second Quarter

Week	Writing Lessons	*Write Source*	Grammar and Writing Skills
1	**Writing an Essay of Speculation** (Model, Prewriting, Writing, Revising)	203–209	Specific nouns, verbals
2	**Essay of Speculation** *(cont'd)* (Editing, Publishing) **Taking Tests** **Responding to Expository Prompts**	210 551–560 211–217	Verb forms, capitalization, semicolons, colons
3	**Persuasive Writing: Warm-Up Paragraph** **Writing an Essay of Argumentation** (Model, Prewriting)	219–221 222–230	Direct quotation, shifts in verb tense
4	**Essay of Argumentation** *(cont'd)* (Writing, Revising) **Peer Responding**	231–248 121–126	Complete sentences, sentence types, modifiers
5	**Essay of Argumentation** *(cont'd)* (Editing, Publishing, Assessing, Reflecting)	249–258	Spelling, hyphens and dashes, subject-verb agreement, tenses and irregular verbs, commas after introductory phrases and clauses, pronoun-antecedent agreement
6	**Responding to Persuasive Prompts** **Writing Across the Curriculum** (Teacher's Choice)	267–273 451–506	
7	**Critical Reading** **Response to Literature: Paragraph** **Analyzing a Theme: Literary Analysis of a Play** (Model, Prewriting)	533–542 275–277 278–286	Punctuating titles
8	**Analyzing a Theme** *(cont'd)* (Writing, Revising)	287–304	Figures of speech, sentence rhythm, integrating quotations
9	**Analyzing a Theme** *(cont'd)* (Editing, Publishing, Assessing, Reflecting)	305–314	Commas review, punctuating compound and complex sentences, punctuating quotations and citations, capitalization
	Responding to Prompts About Literature (Fiction) Portfolio Review *SkillsBook* Posttests	323–335, 339	

Third Quarter

Week	Writing Lessons	*Write Source*	Grammar and Writing Skills
1	**Persuasive Writing: An Essay of Evaluation** (Model, Prewriting, Writing, Revising, Editing, Publishing) **Peer Responding**	259–266 121–126	Sentence combining, adjectives, wordiness and deadwood, using the right word, and punctuation review
2	**Writing Stories: A Short Story** (Model, Prewriting, Writing)	341–348	
3	**Writing Stories** *(cont'd)* (Revising, Editing, Publishing) **Writing Plays: Facing a Personal Dilemma** (Model, Prewriting, Writing)	349–350 351–358	Punctuating dialogue; direct and indirect objects; modeling, expanding, and combining sentences; plurals and spelling review; using the right word; commas
4	**Writing Plays** *(cont'd)* (Revising, Editing, Publishing)	359–360	Punctuating dialogue, adverbs, pronouns, apostrophes
5	**Taking Entrance and Exit Exams**	561–575	
6	**Writing in the Workplace** (Teacher's Choice)	507–521	
7	**Response to Literature: Analyzing a Novel**	315–322	Sentence variety, voice, punctuating quotations, pronoun-antecedent agreement, subject-verb agreement, using the right word
8	**Responding to Prompts About Literature** (Nonfiction)	332–339	
9	**Writing Across the Curriculum** (Teacher's Choice) *SkillsBook* Posttests	405–461	

Fourth Quarter

Week	Writing Lessons	*Write Source*	Grammar and Writing Skills
1	**Writing Poems: Sonnet About Man and Machine** (Model, Prewriting, Writing, Revising, Editing, Publishing)	361–365	Prepositional and appositive phrases, parts of speech review, adverbs, absolute phrases, basic sentence patterns, clauses, spelling, capitalization
	Free Verse, Cinquains	366–369	
2	**Research Writing Skills** **Documenting Research** **Taking Notes** **Summarizing and Paraphrasing**	371–382 425–438 527–531 543–550	
3	**MLA Research Report— A Presidential Policy** (Model)	383–392	
4	**Research Report** (cont'd) (Prewriting)	393–401	
5	**Research Report** (cont'd) (Writing) **Writing Responsibly**	402–407 417–424	
6	**Research Report** (cont'd.) (Revising)	408–411	Active and passive verbs, mood of verbs, punctuating a research paper, sentences review, brackets, ellipses, parentheses
7	**Research Report** (cont'd) (Editing, Publishing) **Documenting Research**	412–416 425–438	Subjects and predicates review, sentence problems review, subject-verb agreement and pronoun-antecedent agreement review, using the right word review, shifts in construction
8	**Making Oral Presentations**	439–449	Spelling review, proofreading review
9	**Freestyle Writing Project** (Student's choice) **Journal and Portfolio Review** **Final Reflection Essay** *SkillsBook* Posttests		

Reading-Writing Connection

The literary works listed on pages TE-36 through TE-43 provide high-interest **mentor texts** that you can use to inspire your students as you teach the different forms of writing. Use these texts to accentuate **writer's craft**:

- Read **strong beginnings** or **strong endings** to inspire students as they create their own beginnings and endings.
- Read paragraphs that **elaborate ideas** or demonstrate **strong organization**.
- Read from two different examples to **contrast voice** and **word choice**.
- Read from different authors to examine their **sentence fluency**.

Narrative Books for Grades 11–12

The Perks of Being a Wallflower
Stephen Chbosky, 1999

The Body of Christopher Creed
Carol Plum-Ucci, 2001

A Door Near Here
Heather Quarles, 1998

Crazy as Chocolate
Elisabeth Hyde, 2002

Diamond Dogs
Alan Watt, 2000

A Long Way Gone: Memoirs of a Boy Soldier
Ishmael Beah, 2007

Born Again
Kelly Kerney, 2006

Fruit of the Lemon
Andrea Levy, 2007

The Discomfort Zone: A Personal History
Jonathan Franzen, 2006

The Syringa Tree
Pamela Gien, 2006

The Marsh Birds
Eva Sallis, 2006

Perfect, Once Removed: When Baseball Was All the World to Me
Phillip Hoose, 2006

Holdup
Terri Fields, 2007

A Novel Idea
Aimee Friedman, 2006

Monkey Town: The Summer of the Scopes Trial
Ronald Kidd, 2006

The Book Thief
Markus Zusak, 2006

Saint Iggy
K. L. Going, 2006

The Braid
Helen Frost, 2006

Harlem Hustle
Janet McDonald, 2006

A Summer Life
Gary Soto, 1990

Growing Up
Russell Baker, 1982

Story of a Girl
Sara Zarr, 2007

I Know Why the Caged Bird Sings
Maya Angelou, 1969

The Awakening
Kate Chopin, 1899

The Bean Trees
Barbara Kingsolver, 1997

Tuesdays with Morrie
Mitch Albom, 1997

Angela's Ashes
Frank McCourt, 1996

A Yellow Raft in Blue Water
Michael Dorris, 1987

A Tree Grows in Brooklyn
Betty Smith, 1943

Survival in Auschwitz
Primo Levi, 1961

Rocket Boys
Homer Hickam, 1998

Long Walk to Freedom: The Autobiography of Nelson Mandela
Nelson Mandela, 1994

The First Part Last
Angela Johnson, 2003

A River Runs Through It
Norman Maclean, 1976

Black Like Me
John H. Griffin, 1969

Oldest Living Confederate Widow Tells All: A Novel
Allan Gurganus, 1989

In the Time of the Butterflies
Julia Alvarez, 1994

The Last Shot: City Streets, Basketball Dreams
Darcy Frey, 1994

Travels with Charley
John Steinbeck, 1962

The Beet Queen
Louise Erdrich, 1986

Expository Books for Grades 11–12

Electric Universe
David Bodanis, 2005

Silent Snow: The Slow Poisoning of the Arctic
Marla Cone, 2005

And Still We Rise
Miles Corwin, 2001

Chronicles: Volume One
Bob Dylan, 2004

Nickle and Dimed: On (Not) Getting by in America
Barbara Ehrenreich, 2001

The Tipping Point: How Little Things Can Make a Difference
Malcolm Gladwell, 2002

The Modern American Presidency
Lewis Gould, 2003

Will in the World: How Shakespeare Became Shakespeare
Stephen Greenblatt, 2004

A Brief History of Time: From the Big Bang to Black Holes
Stephen Hawking, 1998

On Writing: A Memoir of the Craft
Stephen King, 2000

Founding Mothers: The Women Who Raised Our Nation
Cokie Roberts, 2004

Fast Food Nation
Eric Schlosser, 2001

Scourge: The Once and Future Threat of Smallpox
Jonathan B. Tucker, 2001

The Future of Life
Edward O. Wilson, 2002

Think
Simon Blackburn, 1999

Influenza: The Next Pandemic?
Connie Goldsmith, 2006

Extrasolar Planets
Ron Miller, 2002

The Gatekeepers: Inside the Admissions Process of a Premier College
Jacques Steinberg, 2002

Patterns of Culture
Ruth Benedict, 1989

The Sea Around Us
Rachel Carson, 1953

Requiem
Horst Faas, Tim Page, 1997

Gideon's Trumpet
Anthony Lewis, 1964

Moneyball: The Art of Winning an Unfair Game
Michael Lewis, 2003

The Rise of the Indian Rope Trick: How a Spectacular Hoax Became History
Peter Lamont, 2004

Finding Atlantis: A True Story of Genius, Madness, and an Extraordinary Quest for a Lost World
David King, 2005

There Are No Children Here: The Story of Two Boys Growing Up in the Other America
Alex Kotlowitz, 1991

Last Days of Democracy: How Big Media and Power-Hungry Government Are Turning America into a Dictatorship
Elliott D. Cohen, Bruce W. Fraser, 2007

Island of the Lost
Joan Druett, 2007

Webslinger: Unauthorized Essays on Your Friendly Neighborhood Spider-Man
Glenn Yeffeth, 2007

The Secret Family: Twenty-Four Hours Inside the Mysterious Worlds of Our Minds and Bodies
David Bodanis, 1997

School of Dreams: Making the Grade at a Top American High School
Edward Humes, 2003

Freedom Writers Diary: How a Teacher and 150 Teens Used Writing to Change Themselves and the World Around Them
The Freedom Writers, 1999

With Their Eyes: September 11th—The View from a High School at Ground Zero
Annie Thoms, 2002

What Color Is Your Parachute? For Teens
Richard Nelson Bolles, Carol Christen, 2006

Rock the SAT
Michael Moshan, 2006

Teenage Investor: How to Start Early, Invest Often, and Build Wealth
Timothy Olsen, 2003

Harriers: The Making of a Championship Cross Country Team
Joseph P. Shivers, Paul Shivers, 2006

Firestarters: 100 Job Profiles to Inspire Young Women
Kelly Beatty, 2006

The 7 Simple Truths of Acting for the Teen Actor
Larry Silverberg, 2006

High School Journalism
Homer L. Hall, Logan H. Aimone, 2002

Persuasive Books for Grades 11–12

Examples of Satire:

Animal Farm
George Orwell, 1946

Cat's Cradle
Kurt Vonnegut, 1963

Fahrenheit 451
Ray Bradbury, 1953

American Satire: An Anthology of Writings from Colonial Times to the Present
Nicholas Bakalar, 1997

Thank You for Smoking
Christopher Buckley, 1994

The View from the Upper Deck: Sportspickle Presents the Funniest Collection of Sports Satire Ever
D. J. Gallo, 2007

Devil's Dictionary
Ambrose Bierce, 2006 (reprint)

Santa Lives! Five Conclusive Arguments for the Existence of Santa Claus
Ellis Weiner, 2005

Ever Wonder Why? And Other Controversial Essays
Thomas Sowell, 2006

Our Endangered Values: America's Moral Crisis
Jimmy Carter, 2005

The JFK Assassination Debates: Lone Gunman Versus Conspiracy
Michael L. Kurtz, 2006

The Unaborted Socrates: A Dramatic Debate on the Issues Surrounding Abortion
Peter Kreeft, 1983

Debating the Death Penalty
Hugo Adam Bedau, 2005

Four Arguments for the Elimination of Television
Jerry Mander, 1978

The Vaccine Controversy: The History, Use, and Safety of Vaccinations
Kurt Link, 2005

Garbage and Waste (Current Controversies Series)
Charles P. Cozic, 1997

Censorship (Current Controversies Series)
Laura K. Egendorf, 2000

Civil Liberties (Current Controversies Series)
James D. Torr, 2003

Afghanistan (Current Controversies Series)
Jann Einfeld, 2005

Team Spirits: The Native American Mascots Controversy
C. Richard King, 2001

The Extreme Future: The Top Trends That Will Reshape the World for the Next 5, 10, and 20 Years
James M. Canton, 2006

Clicking: 17 Trends That Drive America
Faith Popcorn, 1998

Gun Control (Opposing Viewpoints)
Tamara L. Roleff, 2002

Ethics (Opposing Viewpoints)
Laurie Demauro, 2006

The Patriot Act (Opposing Viewpoints)
Louise I. Gerdes, 2005

Books About Literary Response for Grades 11–12

Understanding Of Mice and Men
Bradley Steffens, 2002

Understanding The Canterbury Tales
Clarice Swisher, 2003

Understanding Literature: An Introduction to Reading and Writing
Walter Kalaidjian, 2004

Understanding Frankenstein
Don Nardo, 2003

Understanding The Adventures of Huckleberry Finn
Gary Wiener, 2001

Understanding Pride and Prejudice: A Student Casebook to Issues, Sources, and Historical Documents
Debra Teachman, 1997

Understanding The Tempest: A Student Casebook to Issues, Sources, and Historical Documents
Faith Nostbakken, 2004

A Student's Guide to F. Scott Fitzgerald
Eva Weisbrod, 2004

Young Adult Poetry: A Survey and Theme Guide
Rachel Schwedt, Janice DeLong, 2001

When Text Meets Text: Helping High School Readers Make Connections in Literature
Barbara King-Shaver, 2005

Theme-Sets for Secondary Students: How to Scaffold Core Literature
Jeannine D. Richison, Anita C. Hernandez, Marcia J. Carter, 2006

A Student's Guide to Robert Frost
Connie Ann Kirk, 2006

A Student's Guide to Emily Dickinson
Audrey Borus, 2005

How to Read a Poem: And Fall in Love with Poetry
Edward Hirsch, 1999

Sleeping on the Wing: An Anthology of Modern Poetry with Essays on Reading and Writing
Kenneth Koch, Kate Farrell, 1982

A Grain of Poetry: How to Read Contemporary Poems and Make Them a Part of Your Life
Herbert R. Kohl, 2000

Born Storytellers: Readers Theatre Celebrates the Lives and Literature of Classic Authors
Ann N. Black, 2005

Novels into Film: The Encyclopedia of Movies Adapted from Books
John C. Tibbetts, James Michael Welsh, 1999

The Book Lover's Cookbook: Recipes Inspired by Celebrated Works of Literature, and the Passages That Feature Them
Shaunda Kennedy Wenger, Janet Jensen, 2005

Making Books by Hand
Peter Thomas, Donna Thomas, 2005

The Ideals Guide to Literary Places in the U.S.
Michelle Prater Burke, 1998

The Book That Changed My Life: 71 Remarkable Writers Celebrate the Books That Matter Most to Them
Roxanne J. Coady, Joy Johannessen, 2006

The Young Actor's Book of Improvisation: Dramatic Situations Based on Literature, Plays, and Films: Ages 12–16
Sandra Caruso, Susan Kosoff, 1998

Poet's Bookshelf: Contemporary Poets on Books That Shaped Their Art
Peter Davis, 2005

Books About Creative Writing for Grades 11–12

Twice Told: Original Stories Inspired by Original Artwork
Scott Hunt, 2006

Teen Ink: Written in the Dirt: A Collection of Short Stories, Poetry, Art and Photography
Stephanie H. Meyer, John Meyer, 2004

The Struggle to Be Strong: True Stories by Teens About Overcoming Tough Times
Al Desetta, Sybil Wolin, 2000

On the Fringe: Stories
Various authors, 2003

Blood on the Forehead: What I Know About Writing
M. E. Kerr, 1998

Turning Life into Fiction: Finding Character, Plot, Setting and Other Elements of Novel and Short Story Writing in the Everyday World
Robin Hemley, 1997

Points of View: An Anthology of Short Stories (Revised Edition)
James Moffett, Kenneth R. McElheny, 1995

Kennedy Center Presents: Award-Winning Plays from the American College Theater Festival
Gary Garrison, 2006

Stage Writing: A Practical Guide
Val Taylor, 2002

Twenty 10-Minute Plays for Teens (Volume I)
Kristen Dabrowski, 2004

Take Ten II: More Ten-Minute Plays
Eric Lane, 2003

Scenes for Young Actors
Lorraine Cohen, 1990

Doodlebug: A Selection of Plays Written by Wahoo High School Students for the Enersen Playwriting Contest 1995–2001
Larry Fangman, 2001

Just People & Paper/Pen/Poem: A Young Writer's Way to Begin
Kathi Appelt, Kenneth Appelt, 1997

Paint Me Like I Am: Teen Poems from WritersCorps
Bill Aguado, 2003

Shifting Sands
Weslynn McCallister, 2004

Complete Collected Poems of Maya Angelou
Maya Angelou, 1995

The Complete Sonnets and Poems (Oxford World's Classics)
William Shakespeare, Colin Burrow, 2002

Writing Sonnets for Your Friends and Soul Mates
Vee Bdosa, 2001

Sonnets: 150 Contemporary Sonnets
William Baer, 2005

A Teen's Guide to Getting Published: Publishing for Profit, Recognition and Academic Success
Jessica Dunn, Danielle Dunn, 2006

Luna, Luna: Creative Writing Ideas from Spanish & Latino Literature
Julio Marzan, 1997

Making a Winning Short: How to Write, Direct, Edit, and Produce a Short Film
Edmond Levy, 1994

The Practice of Poetry: Writing Exercises from Poets Who Teach
Robin Behn, 1992

Reference Books for Grades 11–12

The American Heritage High School Dictionary (Fourth Edition)
Houghton Mifflin, 2007

The American Heritage Essential Student Thesaurus
Houghton Mifflin, 2003

100 Research Topic Guides for Students
Barbara Wood Borne, 1996

100 More Research Topic Guides for Students
Dana McDougald, 1999

Encyclopedia of Genocide and Crimes Against Humanity
Dinah Shelton, 2005

The Greenhaven Encyclopedia of Capital Punishment
Bruce E. R. Thompson, 2005

Tobacco in History and Culture: An Encyclopedia
Jordan Goodman, 2005

Encyclopedia of Science, Technology and Ethics
Carl Mitcham, 2005

Encyclopedia of the American Presidency
Michael A. Genovese, 2004

Major Acts of Congress
Brian K. Landsberg (editor), 2003

Historical Encyclopedia of U.S. Presidential Use of Force, 1789–2000
Karl R. DeRouen Jr., 2000

My Fellow Americans: Presidential Addresses That Shaped History
James C. Humes, 1992

Social Issues in America: An Encyclopedia (8-Volume Set)
James Ciment, 2006

Encyclopedia of American Civil Rights & Liberties
Otis H. Stephens, 2006

The Executive Branch of State Government: People, Process, and Politics
Margaret R. Ferguson, 2006

Writing Research Papers 2001: Your Complete Guide to the Process of Writing a Research Paper, from Finding a Topic to Preparing the Final Manuscript
Houghton Mifflin, 2000

The Facts on File Guide to Research
Jeff Lenburg, 2005

Internet Research Illustrated, Third Edition (Illustrated Series)
Donald I. Barker, Carol D. Terry, 2006

Words You Should Know in High School: 1000 Essential Words to Build Vocabulary, Improve Standardized Test Scores, and Write Successful Papers
Burton Jay Nadler, Jordan Nadler, Justin Nadler, 2005

National Geographic Atlas of the World
National Geographic, 2005

Scientific American Inventions and Discoveries: All the Milestones in Ingenuity—From the Discovery of Fire to the Invention of the Microwave Oven
Rodney P. Carlisle, 2004

The Facts on File Dictionary of Proverbs
Martin H. Manser, Rosalind Fergusson, David Pickering, 2007

Scope and Sequence

Skills taught and/or reviewed in the *Write Source* program, grades 10–12, are featured in the following scope and sequence chart.

FORMS OF WRITING — Grades	10	11	12
Narrative Writing			
historical narrative	■		
narrative prompts	■		■
paragraph	■		
personal essay (college entrance essay)			■
personal narrative essay		■	■
phase autobiography essay	■		
reflective narrative essay		■	
Expository Writing			
cause-effect essay	■		
comparison-contrast essay		■	
essay of definition	■		
essay of opposing ideas			■
essay of speculation			■
expository prompts	■	■	■
informative article		■	
paragraph	■	■	■
Persuasive Writing			
editorial essay	■		
essay of argumentation			■
essay of evaluation			■
paragraph	■	■	■
persuasive prompts	■	■	■
position essay		■	
problem-solution essay	■		
satire		■	
Response to Literature			
analyzing a theme (essay)	■	■	■
analyzing a novel	■		■
analyzing a poem		■	
paragraph	■	■	■
response prompts	■	■	■

	Grades 10	11	12
Creative Writing			
bouts-rimés poem		■	
character's inner feelings (story)			■
cinquain			■
conflict within character (story)	■		
facing a personal dilemma (play)		■	■
free-verse poem	■	■	■
learning a lesson (play)	■		
life challenge (story)		■	
lune poem	■		
quatrain		■	
skeltonic verse	■		
sonnet			■
Research Writing			
engineering report	■		
multimedia presentation	■	■	■
oral presentation	■	■	■
presidential-policy research paper			■
social-issue research paper		■	
Tools of Learning			
business letters	■		
critical reading	■	■	■
improving vocabulary	■		
note taking	■	■	■
paraphrase paragraph	■	■	■
summary paragraph	■	■	■
taking exit and entrance exams		■	■
taking tests	■	■	■
understanding writing assignments	■		

THE WRITING PROCESS

	Grades 10	11	12
Prewriting			
Selecting a Topic			
character grid		■	
charts	■	■	■
cluster	■	■	
focus statement	■		
freewriting	■	■	■

Selecting a Topic (Continued)	Grades 10	11	12
list	■	■	■
sentence starters	■		
T-chart		■	
web		■	
Gathering Details			
answer questions			■
avoid plagiarism	■	■	■
charts	■	■	■
counter an objection	■	■	■
directed writing		■	
five W's and H		■	
freewrite	■	■	
gathering grid	■		■
gather objections	■	■	■
list	■	■	■
note cards	■	■	■
play map			■
quotations	■	■	
research		■	■
T-chart		■	■
tracking sources		■	■
Organizing Details			
charts			■
gathering grid	■	■	■
list		■	■
narrative map		■	
note cards	■	■	■
outline ideas	■	■	■
thesis statement		■	■
time line	■	■	
topic sentences	■	■	■
Sizing Up Your Topic			
list key details		■	■
research	■	■	■

Writing

	Grades 10	11	12
Beginning Paragraph			
anecdote			■
ask a question	■	■	
background information	■	■	■
connect with current events		■	
dialogue	■	■	■
dramatic opening sentence		■	■
engage the reader			■
exciting action		■	
historical context		■	
interesting fact	■	■	■
introduce main character and conflict	■	■	■
introduce topic and thesis	■	■	■
middle of action	■	■	
personal story		■	■
surprising statement	■	■	■
thesis statement	■	■	■
time and place	■		■
Middle Paragraphs			
action words	■	■	■
anecdotes		■	■
background information	■		
build to high point	■	■	■
cite sources	■		
comparisons		■	
counter an objection	■	■	■
dialogue	■	■	■
examples		■	■
explain terms	■	■	
facts	■	■	■
intensify conflict		■	■
key actions	■		
main points	■		■
order of importance		■	■
paraphrase information	■	■	
personal feelings	■		

Middle Paragraphs (Continued)	Grades 10	11	12
quotations	■	■	■
repeating key words		■	
sarcasm and exaggeration		■	
sensory details	■	■	
show, don't *tell*	■		
specific details	■	■	■
statistics	■	■	■
supporting details	■	■	■
suspense	■		■
topic sentences	■	■	■
transitions	■	■	■

Ending Paragraph

	10	11	12
call to action	■	■	
connect theme to life		■	■
final scene		■	
final thought/insight	■	■	■
historical context		■	
key idea/points	■		■
make the reader think		■	■
new information	■		
quotation	■	■	
refer back to beginning	■	■	
reflect on experience	■	■	■
restate position		■	■
restate thesis	■	■	■
satirical statement		■	
show how character is changed	■	■	■
solution to problem	■		
strong quotation		■	■
summarize	■	■	■

Revising

Ideas

	10	11	12
accurate facts	■		
answer objection		■	
background information			■
clear message		■	■
compelling reasons	■		■

	Grades 10	11	12
conflict	■	■	■
dialogue			■
fair presentation			■
historical context		■	
interesting/important details	■	■	
opinion statement	■		
quotations			■
sensory details	■	■	
show, don't *tell*	■		
sources	■		
specific reasons	■	■	■
support for opinion	■		
supporting details		■	■
thesis statement	■	■	■
unnecessary details	■		
variety of details		■	■

Organization

	10	11	12
beginning grabs reader's attention	■	■	■
build to high point	■	■	■
check overall organization		■	■
chronological order		■	
clear beginning, middle, and ending	■	■	■
clearly connected details/paragraphs	■		■
connect beginning and ending	■		■
ending reflects on experience		■	■
ending relates to real life		■	
evaluate unity	■	■	
final thought			■
key word or idea	■		■
line breaks and indents	■		
logical order	■		■
middle develops focus			■
revisit focus statement			■
signal words			■
supporting details	■		
topic sentences	■	■	
transition words	■	■	■

	Grades 10	11	12
Peer Response	■	■	■
Voice			
active			■
adjectives		■	
analytical			■
appropriate for topic	■	■	
compelling			■
confident	■		■
connect with audience			■
consistent point of view	■	■	
convincing	■		■
dialogue	■	■	■
engaging	■	■	■
enthusiastic	■		
interested	■	■	
knowledgeable	■	■	■
level of language		■	■
natural		■	■
personal			■
positive			■
serious		■	
third person			■
tone		■	
Word Choice			
active voice	■		
cliches			■
colloquialisms		■	
connotation	■		■
denotation			■
descriptive words		■	■
figures of speech	■	■	
helping verbs	■		
humor, exaggeration, and sarcasm		■	
literary terms	■		
modifiers		■	■
poetic techniques		■	
precise terms	■		
repeated words	■		■

	Grades 10	11	12
sensory words	■		
show rather than *tell*	■		
specific action verbs	■	■	■
specific nouns	■	■	■
technical terms	■	■	
"trapped" verbs		■	
unfair words	■		
unfamiliar terms		■	■
unnecessary modifiers	■		
vivid verbs	■	■	
wordy intensifiers		■	

Sentence Fluency

	Grades 10	11	12
balanced sentences	■		
clear comparisons			■
combining sentences	■		
expanding sentences	■		
long sentences	■		■
parallel series			■
rambling sentences	■	■	
rhythm	■	■	■
sentence fragments		■	
short sentences	■		■
smooth flow	■	■	■
transitions		■	
variety of beginnings	■	■	■
variety of lengths	■	■	■
variety of types	■	■	■

Editing

Capitalization

	Grades 10	11	12
beginning of sentences	■	■	■
proper adjectives	■	■	■
proper nouns	■	■	■
speaker's first word in quoted dialogue	■	■	

Grammar

	Grades 10	11	12
case of pronouns			■
correct comparative and superlative forms			■
correct forms of adjectives	■	■	
correct forms of verbs	■	■	■

Grammar (Continued)	Grades 10	11	12
double subjects	■		■
numbers and numerals		■	
pronoun-antecedent agreement	■	■	■
subject-verb agreement	■	■	■
using the right word	■	■	■

Punctuation

	10	11	12
apostrophes to show possession	■	■	
commas after introductory phrases and clauses	■	■	■
commas in compound sentences	■	■	■
commas, semicolons, colons			■
end punctuation	■	■	■
hyphenating compound adjectives		■	
parentheses to set off page numbers			■
punctuating complex sentences	■	■	■
punctuating dialogue	■	■	■
punctuating titles	■		
punctuating works-cited page	■	■	
quotation marks around direct quotations	■	■	■

Spelling

	10	11	12
catching errors spell-checker missed	■	■	■
double-checking words	■	■	■

WRITING ACROSS THE CURRICULUM

Writing in Science

	10	11	12
article summary	■		
cause-effect essay	■	■	■
classification essay	■		
classroom notes	■	■	■
definition essay	■		
directions			■
lab report	■		
learning-log entry	■	■	■
opposing-views essay	■		
position essay	■		
problem-solution essay	■		
process essay	■		

	Grades 10	11	12
procedure document		■	■
reading notes	■	■	■
response to an expository prompt		■	■

Writing in Social Studies

	10	11	12
biographical essay		■	
classroom notes	■	■	■
descriptive report	■		
document-based essay	■	■	■
editorial-cartoon response	■	■	■
informative essay			■
learning-log entry	■	■	■

Writing in Math

	10	11	12
article summary	■		■
classification paragraph or essay	■	■	
classroom notes	■	■	■
compare and contrast			■
definition paragraph or essay	■	■	■
descriptive paragraph or essay	■	■	
learning-log entry	■	■	■
math-prompt response	■	■	■
narrative paragraph or essay	■	■	■
position essay	■		■
problem analysis		■	
process paragraph or essay	■	■	■
research report	■	■	■
statistical argument	■		■
written estimate	■		

Writing in the Applied Sciences/Practical Writing

	10	11	12
career review			■
classification essay	■	■	■
classroom notes	■	■	■
comparison-contrast essay	■		■
descriptive essay	■		
essay of analysis	■	■	■
essay of explanation		■	■
learning-log entry	■	■	■

Writing in the Applied Sciences/ Practical Writing (Continued)	Grades 10	11	12
letter of application	■		
letter of complaint		■	
narrative essay	■	■	
persuasive essay		■	■
problem-solution essay	■	■	■
project proposal	■		
process essay	■	■	■
response to a prompt		■	■
restaurant review		■	

Writing in the Arts

	10	11	12
classroom notes	■	■	■
creative writing	■		
descriptive writing	■		
expository writing	■		
learning-log entry	■	■	■
narrative writing	■		
performance review		■	■
persuasive writing	■		
research report	■	■	■
response to an art prompt	■	■	■

Writing in the Workplace

	10	11	12
brochure		■	
business letters		■	■
e-mail message		■	■
memo		■	■
news release			■
proposal		■	■
report		■	
résumé			■

GRAMMAR

Understanding Sentences

	10	11	12
agreement of pronoun and antecedent	■	■	■
agreement of subject and verb	■	■	■
arrangements of sentences	■	■	■
clauses	■	■	■
diagramming sentences	■	■	■
direct objects	■		
kinds of sentences	■	■	■

	Grades 10	11	12
phrases	■	■	■
subjects and predicates	■	■	■
types of sentence constructions	■	■	■

Using the Parts of Speech

Adjectives

	10	11	12
articles	■	■	■
forms of adjectives	■	■	■
types of adjectives	■	■	■

Adverbs

	10	11	12
forms of adverbs	■	■	■
types of adverbs	■	■	■

Conjunctions

	10	11	12
coordinating conjunctions	■	■	■
correlative conjunctions	■	■	■
subordinating conjunctions	■	■	■

Interjections

	10	11	12
	■	■	■

Nouns

	10	11	12
abstract nouns	■	■	■
case of nouns	■	■	■
collective nouns	■	■	■
common nouns	■	■	■
concrete nouns	■	■	■
gender of nouns	■	■	■
proper nouns	■	■	■
singular and plural nouns	■	■	■

Prepositions

	10	11	12
common prepositions	■	■	■
prepositional phrases	■	■	■

Pronouns

	10	11	12
antecedents	■	■	■
case of pronouns	■	■	■
classes of pronouns	■	■	■
demonstrative pronouns	■	■	■
gender of pronouns	■	■	■
indefinite pronouns	■	■	■
interrogative pronouns	■	■	■
person of pronouns	■	■	■
personal pronouns	■	■	■
relative pronouns	■	■	■

Pronouns (Continued)	Grades	10	11	12
singular and plural pronouns		■	■	■
subject pronouns		■	■	■

Verbs

	10	11	12
active and passive voice	■	■	■
auxiliary verbs	■	■	■
irregular verbs	■	■	■
linking verbs	■	■	■
mood of a verb	■	■	■
person of a verb	■	■	■
singular and plural verbs	■	■	■
tenses of verbs	■	■	■
transitive and intransitive verbs	■	■	■

Verbals

	10	11	12
Verbals	■	■	■

Mechanics

Abbreviations

	10	11	12
acronyms	■	■	■
common abbreviations	■	■	■
correspondence abbreviations	■	■	■
initialisms	■	■	■

Capitalization

	10	11	12
abbreviations	■	■	■
days, months, holidays	■	■	■
first words	■	■	■
geographical names	■	■	■
historical events	■	■	■
letters	■	■	■
names of people	■	■	■
official names	■	■	■
organizations	■	■	■
particular sections of the country	■	■	■
proper nouns and adjectives	■	■	■
races, languages, nationalities, religions, certain religious words	■	■	■
sentences following colons	■	■	■

	Grades	10	11	12
sentences in parentheses		■	■	■
titles		■	■	■
titles of courses		■	■	■
titles used with names		■	■	■
words used as names		■	■	■

Numbers

	10	11	12
numbers in compound modifiers	■	■	
numerals only	■	■	■
numerals or words	■	■	■
time and money	■	■	■
very large numbers	■	■	
words only	■		■

Plurals

	10	11	12
adding an *s*	■	■	■
collective nouns	■	■	■
compound nouns	■	■	■
irregular spelling	■	■	■
nouns ending in *ch, sh, s, x,* and *z*	■	■	■
nouns ending in *f* or *fe*	■	■	■
nouns ending in *ful*	■	■	■
nouns ending in *o*	■	■	■
nouns ending in *y*	■	■	■
words discussed as words	■	■	■

Punctuation

Apostrophes

	10	11	12
in contractions	■	■	■
to express time or amount	■	■	■
to form certain plurals	■	■	■
to form plural possessives	■	■	■
to form possessives with compound nouns	■	■	■
to form possessives with indefinite pronouns	■	■	■
to form singular possessives	■	■	■
to show shared possession	■	■	■

	Grades	10	11	12
Brackets				
around an editorial correction		■	■	■
to set off added words		■	■	■
to set off clarifying information		■	■	■
Colons				
after salutations		■	■	■
between numerals in time		■	■	■
between titles and subtitles		■	■	■
for emphasis		■	■	■
to introduce lists		■	■	■
to introduce sentences or quotations		■	■	■
Commas				
after conjunctive adverbs and transitional phrases			■	■
before tags			■	■
between independent clauses		■	■	■
between items in a series		■	■	■
for clarity or emphasis		■	■	■
in compound sentences		■	■	■
in dates and addresses		■	■	■
in direct address		■	■	■
to enclose parenthetical elements		■	■	■
to keep numbers clear		■	■	■
to separate contrasted elements		■	■	■
to separate equal adjectives		■	■	■
to separate introductory clauses and phrases		■	■	■
to set off appositives		■	■	■
to set off dialogue		■	■	■
to set off interjections		■	■	■
to set off interruptions		■	■	■
to set off nonrestrictive phrases and clauses		■	■	■
to set off titles or initials		■	■	■
Dashes				
for emphasis		■	■	■
to indicate interrupted speech		■	■	■
to indicate a sudden break		■	■	■
to set off an introductory series		■	■	■
to set off parenthetical material		■	■	■

	Grades 10	11	12
Diagonals			
to show a choice	■	■	■
when quoting poetry	■	■	■
Ellipses			
at the end of a sentence	■	■	■
to show omitted words	■	■	■
to show pauses	■	■	■
Exclamation Points			
to express strong feelings	■	■	■
Hyphens			
between numbers in a fraction	■	■	■
in a special series	■	■	■
in compound words	■	■	■
to avoid confusion	■	■	■
to create new words	■	■	■
to divide words	■	■	■
to form adjectives	■	■	■
to join letters to words	■	■	■
to join numbers	■	■	
Italics and Underlining			
for emphasis		■	■
for scientific and foreign words	■	■	■
for special uses	■	■	■
in handwritten material	■	■	■
in printed material	■	■	■
in titles	■	■	■
Parentheses			
to set off explanatory or added information	■	■	■
with full sentences	■	■	■
Periods			
after abbreviations	■	■	■
after initials	■	■	■
as decimal points	■	■	■
at end of sentences	■	■	■

	Grades 10	11	12
Question Marks			
at end of direct questions	■	■	■
at end of indirect questions	■	■	■
short question within a sentence	■	■	■
to show uncertainty	■	■	■
Quotation Marks			
for quotations within quotations	■	■	■
for special words	■	■	■
placement of punctuation	■	■	■
to punctuate titles	■	■	■
to set off long quoted material	■	■	■
to set off quoted material	■	■	■
to set off a speaker's exact words		■	■
Semicolons			
to join two independent clauses	■	■	■
to separate groups that contain commas	■	■	■
with conjunctive adverbs	■	■	■
with transitional phrases		■	■

Usage

	10	11	12
Spelling			
consonant endings	■	■	■
i before *e*	■	■	■
silent *e*	■	■	■
words ending in *y*	■	■	■
Understanding Idioms	■	■	■
Using the Right Word	■	■	■

Meeting the Common Core State Standards

The following correlation clearly shows how the *Write Source* program helps you meet grade-specific **Common Core State Standards for English Language Arts,** along with their companion **College and Career Readiness (CCR)** standards. Students are expected to meet grade-specific standards by the end of the school year, thereby working steadily toward meeting the more general expectations described by the CCR standards.

Pages referenced below appear in the Teacher's Edition as well as the Student Edition.

Writing Standards

Text Types and Purposes

College and Career Readiness Standard 1. Write arguments to support claims in an analysis of substantive topics or texts, using valid reasoning and relevant and sufficient evidence.

Grade 12 Standard 1. Write arguments to support claims in an analysis of substantive topics or texts, using valid reasoning and relevant and sufficient evidence.

a. Introduce precise, knowledgeable claim(s), establish the significance of the claim(s), distinguish the claim(s) from alternate or opposing claims, and create an organization that logically sequences claim(s), counterclaims, reasons, and evidence.	**Student Edition pages:** 221, 223–224, 228–229, 232–236, 240–241, 260–261, 264, 270–271, 482–483, 494–495, 508–509, 510, 514–515, 570–571, 583 **Net-text:** Persuasive Writing
b. Develop claim(s) and counterclaims fairly and thoroughly, supplying the most relevant evidence for each while pointing out the strengths and limitations of both in a manner that anticipates the audience's knowledge level, concerns, values, and possible biases.	**Student Edition pages:** 221, 223–224, 228–229, 232–236, 238–239, 260–261, 264, 270–271, 273, 482–483, 494–495, 508–509, 510, 514–515 **Net-text:** Persuasive Writing

Text Types and Purposes (continued)

c. Use words, phrases, and clauses as well as varied syntax to link the major sections of the text, create cohesion, and clarify the relationships between claim(s) and reasons, between reasons and evidence, and between claim(s) and counterclaims.

Student Edition pages: 234–235, 240–241, 595–596
Net-text: Persuasive Writing

d. Establish and maintain a formal style and objective tone while attending to the norms and conventions of the discipline in which they are writing.

Student Edition pages: 71, 242–243
Net-text: Persuasive Writing

e. Provide a concluding statement or section that follows from and supports the argument presented.

Student Edition pages: 221, 224, 236, 261, 264, 271, 273, 483, 493, 495, 508–509, 510, 515, 571, 583, 597
Net-text: Persuasive Writing

College and Career Readiness Standard 2. Write informative/explanatory texts to examine and convey complex ideas and information clearly and accurately through the effective selection, organization, and analysis of content.

Grade 12 Standard 2. Write informative/explanatory texts to examine and convey complex ideas, concepts, and information clearly and accurately through the effective selection, organization, and analysis of content.

a. Introduce a topic; organize complex ideas, concepts, and information so that each new element builds on that which precedes it to create a unified whole; include formatting (e.g., headings), graphics (e.g., figures, tables), and multimedia when useful to aiding comprehension.

Student Edition pages: 165, 167–168, 173, 174, 176–180, 184–185, 204–205, 208, 214–215, 217, 277, 279–280, 285, 286, 288–292, 296–297, 316–317, 320, 328–329, 334–335, 339, 401, 403–406, 456–458, 459–460, 461–462, 466–467, 468–469, 470, 475–476, 480–481, 490–491, 492–493, 500–502, 512–513, 545–546, 582, 590, 592–594, 597
Net-text: Expository Writing, Response to Literature, Research Writing

b. Develop the topic thoroughly by selecting the most significant and relevant facts, extended definitions, concrete details, quotations, or other information and examples appropriate to the audience's knowledge of the topic.

Student Edition pages: 165, 167–168, 172, 176, 178–179, 182, 204–205, 208, 214–215, 217, 277, 279–280, 284–285, 286, 288, 290–291, 294–295, 316–317, 318–319, 320, 328–329, 334–335, 339, 401, 404–405, 456–458, 459–460, 461–462, 466–467, 468–469, 470, 475–476, 480, 490–491, 492–493, 500–502, 512–513, 582
Net-text: Expository Writing, Response to Literature, Research Writing

Text Types and Purposes (continued)

c. Use appropriate and varied transitions and syntax to link the major sections of the text, create cohesion, and clarify the relationships among complex ideas and concepts.	**Student Edition pages:** 296, 409, 595–596 **Net-text:** Response to Literature, Research Writing
d. Use precise language, domain-specific vocabulary, and techniques such as metaphor, simile, and analogy to manage the complexity of the topic.	**Student Edition pages:** 76–77, 188–189, 244–245, 300–301 **Net-text:** Expository Writing, Persuasive Writing, Response to Literature
e. Establish and maintain a formal style and objective tone while attending to the norms and conventions of the discipline in which they are writing.	**Student Edition pages:** 186–187, 298–299 **Net-text:** Expository Writing, Response to Literature
f. Provide a concluding statement or section that follows from and supports the information or explanation presented (e.g., articulating implications or the significance of the topic).	**Student Edition pages:** 165, 168, 176, 180, 205, 208, 215, 217, 277, 280, 292, 318, 320, 329, 335, 339 **Net-text:** Expository Writing, Response to Literature

College and Career Readiness Standard 3. Write narratives to develop real or imagined experiences or events using effective technique, well-chosen details, and well-structured event sequences.

Grade 12 Standard 3. Write narratives to develop real or imagined experiences or events using effective technique, well-chosen details, and well-structured event sequences.

a. Engage and orient the reader by setting out a problem, situation, or observation and its significance, establishing one or multiple point(s) of view, and introducing a narrator and/or characters; create a smooth progression of experiences or events.	**Student Edition pages:** 142–143, 146, 156–157, 159, 342–345, 348, 580 **Net-text:** Narrative Writing, Creative Writing
b. Use narrative techniques, such as dialogue, pacing, description, reflection, and multiple plot lines, to develop experiences, events, and/or characters.	**Student Edition pages:** 146, 147, 159, 346–347, 348, 580 **Net-text:** Narrative Writing, Creative Writing

Text Types and Purposes (continued)

c. Use a variety of techniques to sequence events so that they build on one another to create a coherent whole and build toward a particular tone and outcome (e.g., a sense of mystery, suspense, growth, or resolution).	**Student Edition pages:** 142–143, 145, 146, 156–157, 159 **Net-text:** Narrative Writing
d. Use precise words and phrases, telling details, and sensory language to convey a vivid picture of the experiences, events, setting, and/or characters.	**Student Edition pages:** 159, 363, 366 **Net-text:** Narrative Writing, Creative Writing
e. Provide a conclusion that follows from and reflects on what is experienced, observed, or resolved over the course of the narrative.	**Student Edition pages:** 143, 146, 147, 156, 159, 342, 345, 348, 354, 357, 366, 580 **Net-text:** Narrative Writing, Creative Writing

Production and Distribution of Writing

College and Career Readiness Standard 4. Produce clear and coherent writing in which the development, organization, and style are appropriate to task, purpose, and audience.

Grade 12 Standard 4. Produce clear and coherent writing in which the development, organization, and style are appropriate to task, purpose, and audience. (Grade-specific expectations for writing types are defined in standards 1–3 above.)	**Student Edition pages:** 15–19, 24–25, 60–66, 69, 70, 71, 80, 97–112, 142–146, 156–159, 165, 167–180, 182–183, 184–185, 188–189, 190–191, 204–208, 212–215, 217, 221, 223–236, 238–239, 240–241, 244–245, 246–247, 260–264, 268–271, 273, 277, 279–292, 294–295, 296–297, 300–301, 302–303, 317–320, 324–337, 339, 343–348, 352–358, 366, 367, 360, 363–364, 385–406, 456–458, 459–460, 461–462, 466–467, 468–469, 470, 475–476, 480–481, 482–483, 484, 490–491, 492–493, 494–495, 500–502, 503–504, 505–506, 512–513, 514–515, 516–517, 518–519, 520–521, 545–546, 580–583, 584–588
	Interactive Whiteboard Lessons: Narrative Writing, Expository Writing, Persuasive Writing, Response to Literature, Creative Writing, Research Writing
	Net-text: Narrative Writing, Expository Writing, Persuasive Writing, Response to Literature, Creative Writing, Research Writing

Production and Distribution of Writing (continued)

College and Career Readiness Standard 5. Develop and strengthen writing as needed by planning, revising, editing, rewriting, or trying a new approach.

Grade 12 Standard 5. Develop and strengthen writing as needed by planning, revising, editing, rewriting, or trying a new approach, focusing on addressing what is most significant for a specific purpose and audience.	**Student Edition pages:** 9, 10–11, 15–27, 97–120, 127–132, 144–149, 158–161, 169–196, 206–210, 212–216, 217, 225–252, 262–266, 268–272, 273, 281–308, 318–322, 324–338, 339, 346–349, 355–359, 363–365, 366, 367, 393–415, 456, 459, 461, 466, 468, 470, 480, 482, 484, 490, 492, 494, 500, 503, 505, 512, 514, 516, 518, 520, 546 **Interactive Whiteboard Lessons:** Narrative Writing, Expository Writing, Persuasive Writing, Response to Literature, Creative Writing, Research Writing **Net-text:** Narrative Writing, Expository Writing, Persuasive Writing, Response to Literature, Creative Writing, Research Writing

College and Career Readiness Standard 6. Use technology, including the Internet, to produce and publish writing and to interact and collaborate with others.

Grade 12 Standard 6. Use technology, including the Internet, to produce, publish, and update individual or shared writing products in response to ongoing feedback, including new arguments or information.	**Student Edition pages:** 28, 92–95, 139, 149, 197, 210, 253, 309, 322, 359, 365, 444, 448, 508–509, 510–511, 512–513, 514–515, 516–517, 518–519, 520–521 **Interactive Whiteboard Lessons:** Narrative Writing, Expository Writing, Persuasive Writing, Response to Literature, Creative Writing, Research Writing **Net-text:** Narrative Writing, Expository Writing, Persuasive Writing, Response to Literature, Creative Writing

Research to Build and Present Knowledge

College and Career Readiness Standard 7. Conduct short as well as more sustained research projects based on focused questions, demonstrating understanding of the subject under investigation.

Grade 12 Standard 7. Conduct short as well as more sustained research projects to answer a question (including a self-generated question) or solve a problem; narrow or broaden the inquiry when appropriate; synthesize multiple sources on the subject, demonstrating understanding of the subject under investigation.	**Student Edition pages:** 170–180, 204–208, 226–236, 284, 394–407, 418–424, 456–458, 466–467, 482, 470–476, 500–502 **Net-text:** Expository Writing, Persuasive Writing, Response to Literature, Research Writing

Research to Build and Present Knowledge (continued)

College and Career Readiness Standard 8. Gather relevant information from multiple print and digital sources, assess the credibility and accuracy of each source, and integrate the information while avoiding plagiarism.

Grade 12 Standard 8. Gather relevant information from multiple authoritative print and digital sources, using advanced searches effectively; assess the strengths and limitations of each source in terms of the task, purpose, and audience; integrate information into the text selectively to maintain the flow of ideas, avoiding plagiarism and overreliance on any one source and following a standard format for citation.	**Student Edition pages:** 16, 101, 111, 171–172, 227, 284, 372–382, 395–399, 407, 418–424, 426–438, 466, 482, 500 **Net-text:** Expository Writing, Persuasive Writing, Response to Literature, Research Writing

College and Career Readiness Standard 9. Draw evidence from literary or informational texts to support analysis, reflection, and research.

Grade 12 Standard 9. Draw evidence from literary or informational texts to support analysis, reflection, and research.

a. Apply *grades 11–12 Reading standards* to literature (e.g., "Demonstrate knowledge of eighteenth-, nineteenth- and early-twentieth-century foundational works of American literature, including how two or more texts from the same period treat similar themes or topics").	**Student Edition pages:** 276–277, 278–280, 283, 288–292, 316–318, 320, 326–329, 539–540, 541–542, 572–574 **Net-text:** Response to Literature
b. Apply *grades 11–12 Reading standards* to literary nonfiction (e.g., "Delineate and evaluate the reasoning in seminal U.S. texts, including the application of constitutional principles and use of legal reasoning [e.g., in U.S. Supreme Court Case majority opinions and dissents] and the premises, purposes, and arguments in works of public advocacy [e.g., *The Federalist,* presidential addresses]").	**Student Edition pages:** 332–337, 395–396, 403–406, 456–458, 470–476, 480–481, 482–483, 490–491, 500–502, 537 **Net-text:** Research Writing

Range of Writing

College and Career Readiness Standard 10. Write routinely over extended time frames (time for research, reflection, and revision) and shorter time frames (a single sitting or a day or two) for a range of tasks, purposes, and audiences.

Grade 12 Standard 10. Write routinely over extended time frames (time for research, reflection, and revision) and shorter time frames (a single sitting or a day or two) for a range of tasks, purposes, and audiences.	**Student Edition pages:** 3, 4, 8, 9, 11, 37, 39, 49, 57, 58, 62, 68, 69, 70, 72, 74, 77, 78, 82, 86, 112, 123, 124, 125, 131, 138, 144–149, 161, 165, 169–196, 206–210, 212–216, 217, 221, 225–252, 262–266, 268–272, 273, 277, 281–308, 318–322, 324–338, 339, 346–349, 355–359, 360, 363–365, 366, 367, 393–415, 440, 442, 452, 453, 454, 456, 458, 459, 461, 462, 464, 465, 466, 468, 469, 470, 478, 479, 480, 482, 484, 485, 488, 489, 490, 491, 492, 493, 494, 495, 499, 500, 503, 505, 506, 512, 514, 516, 517, 518, 520, 524, 531, 537, 538, 542, 546, 547, 548, 550, 556, 559, 571, 575, 578, 580, 581, 582, 583, 657 **Interactive Whiteboard Lessons:** Narrative Writing, Expository Writing, Persuasive Writing, Response to Literature, Creative Writing, Research Writing **Net-text:** Narrative Writing, Expository Writing, Persuasive Writing, Response to Literature, Creative Writing, Research Writing

Language Standards

Conventions of Standard English

College and Career Readiness Standard 1. Demonstrate command of the conventions of standard English grammar and usage when writing or speaking.

Grade 12 Standard 1. Demonstrate command of the conventions of standard English grammar and usage when writing or speaking.

a. Apply the understanding that usage is a matter of convention, can change over time, and is sometimes contested.	**File Cabinet:** Understanding Grammar Conventions
b. Resolve issues of complex or contested usage, consulting references (e.g., *Merriam-Webster's Dictionary of English Usage, Garner's Modern American Usage*) as needed.	**Student Edition pages:** 188–189, 250–251, 624–625, 626–627, 630–631, 752–753, 754 **Net-text:** Expository Writing, Persuasive Writing

Conventions of Standard English (continued)

College and Career Readiness Standard 2. Demonstrate command of the conventions of standard English capitalization, punctuation, and spelling when writing.

Grade 12 Standard 2. Demonstrate command of the conventions of standard English capitalization, punctuation, and spelling when writing.

a. Observe hyphenation conventions.	**Student Edition pages:** 624–627
b. Spell correctly.	**Student Edition pages:** 380–381, 664–671, 678–699 **Net-text:** Research Writing

Knowledge of Language

College and Career Readiness Standard 3. Apply knowledge of language to understand how language functions in different contexts, to make effective choices for meaning or style, and to comprehend more fully when reading or listening.

Grade 12 Standard 3. Apply knowledge of language to understand how language functions in different contexts, to make effective choices for meaning or style, and to comprehend more fully when reading or listening.

a. Vary syntax for effect, consulting references (e.g., Tufte's *Artful Sentences*) for guidance as needed; apply an understanding of syntax to the study of complex texts when reading.	**Student Edition pages:** 80, 82–85, 246–247, 303, 746–750 **Net-text:** Persuasive Writing, Response to Literature

Getting-Started Activities

The *Write Source* Student Edition is full of helpful resources that students can access throughout the year while they are developing their writing skills. Getting-started activities are provided as copy masters on TE pages 828–830. They will

- help students discover the kinds of information available in different sections of the book,
- teach students how to access that information,
- familiarize students with the layout of the book.

The more familiar students are with the text, the more proficient they will be in using its resources.

Scavenger Hunts

Students enjoy using scavenger hunts to become familiar with a book. The scavenger hunts we provide can be done in small groups or as a class. They are designed for oral answers, but you may want to photocopy the pages for students to write on. Also, you may want to vary the procedure, first having students take turns finding the items and then, on the next scavenger hunt, challenging students to "race" for the answers.

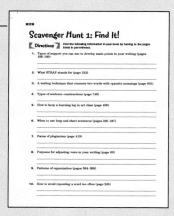

After your students have done each scavenger hunt, you can challenge them to create their own versions. For example, small groups can work together to create "Find It!" scavenger hunts and then exchange their "hunts" with other groups.

Special Challenge: Develop questions that teams of students try to answer using the book. Pattern this activity after a popular game show.

Other Activities

- Give students the following assignment: Across the top of a sheet of paper, write down three things you find difficult about school (e.g., taking notes, taking tests, writing essays, spelling, using commas). Then explore your book to find chapters, sections, examples, and so on, that might help you with your problem area. Under each problem, write the titles or headings and the page numbers where you can find help. Keep this sheet to use throughout the year.

- A variation on the above activity is to have students write down all the subject areas they study and list, under each heading, the parts of the book that might help them in that subject.

- Have students write a thought-trap poem: After reviewing the book, close it. The first line of your poem will be the title of the book. Then list thoughts and feelings about the book, line by line. When you have listed everything you want to say, "trap" your thoughts by repeating the title.

- Have pairs of students create poster-size advertisements for the book. Each ad should have a headline, list important features (what is in the book) and benefits (whom it can help and how), show an example of illustrations (made by tracing or copying), and urge readers of the ad to get their books now!

- Have students imagine they are going to send a copy of *Write Source* to a pen pal in another state. Have each student write a letter to send along with it to tell the pen pal about the book.

HOUGHTON MIFFLIN HARCOURT

WRITE SOURCE

Authors
Dave Kemper, Patrick Sebranek, and Verne Meyer

Illustrator
Chris Krenzke

GREAT
SOURCE.

HOUGHTON MIFFLIN HARCOURT

Welcome to the Teacher's Edition!

Strong writing brings success throughout high school—and beyond.

The Student Edition demystifies writing for your students. Using step-by-step instruction and concrete writing strategies, *Write Source* helps every student succeed at writing.

In the same way, the Teacher's Edition demystifies teaching writing. Simply have your class turn to any writing chapter—narrative, expository, persuasive, response to literature, creative, or research—and begin teaching. It's that simple. Of course, the Teacher's Edition also provides plenty of support to help you customize the instruction:

- Writing Traits Tips
- Teaching Tips
- Integrated Grammar, Literature, Writer's Craft, and Technology
- Assessment Options and Test Prep
- Notes for English Language Learners
- Accommodations and Modifications for Struggling Students
- Enrichments for Advanced Students

Thanks to the Teachers!

This program would not have been possible without the input of many teachers and administrators from across the nation. As we originally developed this K–12 series, we surveyed hundreds of teaching professionals, and as we revised this series, we implemented the feedback of even more. Our thanks goes out to each of you. We couldn't have done it without you!

Reviewers

Randolph C. Bernard
Lafayette Parish School System
Lafayette, LA

Jeanne Hackett Brakefield
Collier District
Naples, FL

Beth Gaby
Carl Schurz High School
Chicago, IL

Susan Dinges
Mt. Olive Public School District
Budd Lake, NJ

Shara W. Holt
St. Johns County School District
St. Augustine, FL

Guy M. Kinney
Orange County Public Schools
Orlando, FL

Raymond Klejmont
Desoto County
Arcadia, FL

Connie McGee
Miami-Dade County Public
   Schools
Miami, FL

Harriet Maher
Lafayette Parish School System
Lafayette, LA

Jenny R. May
Mason City Schools
Mason, OH

Pamela Miltenberger
J. C. Harmon High School
Kansas City, KS

Christine Neuner
Iberia Parish School System
New Iberia, LA

Marie T. Raduazzo
Arlington High School
Arlington, MA

Marianne Raver
William R. Boone High School
Orlando, FL

Elizabeth Rehberger
Huntington Beach High School
Huntington Beach, CA

Stephanie Sahikov-Izabal
Huntington Beach Union High
   School District
Huntington Beach, CA

Ann Marie Seely
Henrico County Public Schools
Richmond, VA

WRITE SOURCE Online
www.hmheducation.com/writesource

Quick Guide

The *Write Source* Voice

For over 30 years, our books have spoken directly to students. We see ourselves as writers speaking to other writers.

As a result, the *Write Source* voice is always encouraging, like a mentor who genuinely wants another student to succeed. We believe that every student can learn to write and that every writer can improve. Throughout this book, your students will hear a voice that says, "You can do it!"

In the same way, the material in the wraparound text speaks directly to you. After all, we are simply teachers speaking to other teachers, and so we use the same encouraging voice.

Whether you're a seasoned writing teacher or a fresh new face, we are certain that these materials in your hands can make a big difference for your students. We hope you agree!

Getting to Know *Write Source*

Just as we helped you learn about *Write Source* in the TE pages entitled "Professional Development," you can use these pages to help orient your students.

Here are suggestions for pointing out the key features of the program:

- **Writing guidelines:** "How many of you get writer's block? *Write Source* is designed to be a writer's block buster. This book breaks down the writing process into simple, concrete steps so you never get stuck."
- **Checklists:** "How many of you like to revise? *Write Source* makes the process much easier. Revising checklists help you decide what changes will improve your writing, and specific revising strategies don't leave you guessing as to what to do."
- **Rubrics:** "How many of you have an easy time judging writing? *Write Source* uses rubrics throughout the writing process to help you know what your goals are as you write and how to improve your work as you revise and edit. Rubrics also help you respond to the writing of your peers."

A Quick Tour of *Write Source*

Write Source contains many key features that will help you improve your writing and language skills. Once you become familiar with this book, you will begin to understand how helpful these features can be.

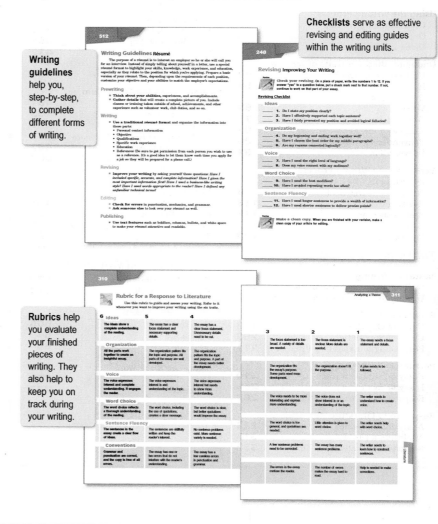

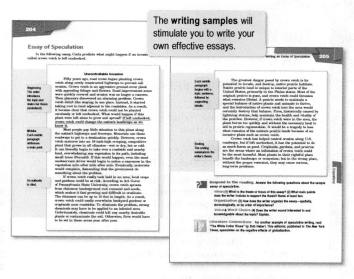

The **writing samples** will stimulate you to write your own effective essays.

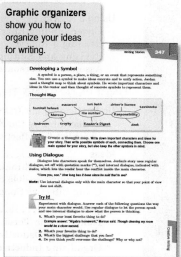

Graphic organizers show you how to organize your ideas for writing.

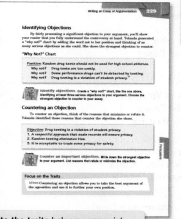

Links to the traits help you appreciate the importance of different traits at different points in the writing process.

- **Writing samples:** "In basketball, you have a net to shoot for. In football, you have the goal line and the goal post. In writing, you should also look at your goal before you begin. *Write Source* provides many models to help you know just what you are shooting for."
- **Graphic organizers:** "Have you ever heard that writing is thinking on paper? Well, graphic organizers are ways to draw out your thoughts. Graphic organizers help you think and sort out your ideas. They're just another way to make writing clear and easy."
- **Links to the traits:** "The traits of writing give us a common language for talking about what makes writing strong. As we go through the writing units in this book, we'll be talking a lot about ideas, organization, voice, word choice, sentence fluency, and conventions."

The Process and the Traits

The first section of the book gives an overview of the writing process, showing how the traits are integrated into it.

■ **Prewriting** and **writing** focus on *ideas, organization,* and *voice.*

■ **Revising** improves these traits and also *word choice* and *sentence fluency.*

■ **Editing** focuses on checking *conventions.*

The next section introduces the traits of writing and goes into depth with each trait, providing models and activities. Use these pages as minilessons in whole-class or small-group discussions.

Wraparound Feature

Focus on the Traits

Organization
Throughout the teacher's edition, trait boxes give you special tips for using the traits to help your students evaluate, discuss, and improve their writing.

Review, Reinforce, and Explore

When we developed this text, we knew that some of your students would be struggling to write, while others would be getting ready for college. That's why this book is set up to provide the basics for those who need to review them, reinforcement activities for those who are progressing at grade level, and extension activities for students who are ready to explore on their own.

For example, the chapter "Word Choice" starts with the basics—specific nouns and vivid verbs—but moves on to issues of style, such as using words with strong connotations and writing metaphorically.

Wraparound Features

Teaching Tip

Throughout the wraparound, you'll find special strategies for making the lesson come alive for your students.

Creating the Forms of Writing

The writing units in *Write Source* focus on creating the fundamental forms of writing:

- Narrative
- Expository
- Persuasive
- Response to Literature
- Creative
- Research

Each writing assignment includes instruction, models, and activities that lead students through the writing process. The material works well for whole-class instruction, writing workshop minilessons, and self-paced individual work time.

viii

contents

The Forms of Writing

NARRATIVE WRITING

Wraparound Features

Copy Masters

These features tell you what classroom presentation aids exist to help you deliver the lesson.

Benchmark Papers

Check this feature to find out what benchmark papers you can use to show your students a range of performance.

Teaching the Core Units

The core writing units focus on the forms that
are most often tested—expository, persuasive,
and response to literature.

Each unit begins with an accessible model with
response questions, helping students make the
reading-writing connection.

Afterward, the text leads students step-by-step
through the process of creating a similar piece
of writing. Concrete activities help students do
the following:

- Select a topic.
- Gather details.
- Organize details.
- Create a focus statement.
- Write a strong beginning.
- Build a solid middle.
- Create an effective ending.
- Revise for ideas, organization, voice, word
  choice, and sentence fluency.
- Edit for conventions.
- Publish work with polished presentation.
- Assess writing using traits-based rubrics.

Each unit ends with an invitation for reflection,
the point at which students internalize what
they have learned.

Wraparound Features

Grammar Connection

Each unit overview suggests grammar activities
to cover in the unit. Grammar Connection boxes
then help you pinpoint the places to integrate
instruction.

Using Rubrics Throughout the Process

You'll find that the traits-based rubrics in *Write Source* help guide your students throughout the process. Each core writing unit begins with a goal rubric that helps your students think about what they are trying to accomplish. Then, as your students revise and edit, rubric strips guide their work, helping them improve their writing in ways large and small.

Preparing for Assessment

Every core unit teaches students process-based strategies, which they internalize as "thinking moves" that will help them in on-demand writing situations. Each unit also ends with a sample on-demand writing prompt and response, as well as additional prompts for practice with high-stakes writing situations.

Efficacy studies from around the United States have demonstrated significant improvements from pretest to posttest scores for students using the *Write Source* series.

contents

Wraparound Feature

Test Prep!
These features give suggestions for preparing your students for high- and low-stakes writing and grammar tests.

RESPONSE TO LITERATURE

Literature Connections

Each unit contains numerous student models. By reading them and responding to them, students tune their minds to a given genre before beginning to write in it.

Also, the response to literature unit focuses on plays, novels, poems, short stories, and biographies that your students may have read—or may want to read. Student models analyze these works of literature:

Sisters by Marsha A. Jackson
The Glass Menagerie by Tennessee Williams
The Tempest by William Shakespeare
The Curious Incident of the Dog in the Night-Time by Mark Haddon
"The Diamond as Big as the Ritz" by F. Scott Fitzgerald
"The Second Coming" by William Butler Yeats
The Story of My Life by Helen Keller

Writing Workshop

If you use the writing workshop approach, note how each activity in the core writing units can function as a minilesson. You can use these minilesson activities . . .

■ to direct the whole class before individual writing time,

■ to instruct a group of writers who are ready to learn a new skill, or

■ to provide scaffolding for an individual writer who gets stuck.

Wraparound Feature

 Literature Connections

These features help you use literary works to teach students special writing techniques. You'll find interesting insights into the works and lives of favorite writers as well as fresh ways to use literature to teach writing.

Tapping Creativity

The *Write Source* series promotes creativity even in academic writing assignments. However, this section allows you and your students to develop forms that are especially inventive:

- Short Story
- Play
- Radio Play
- Sonnet
- Free-Verse Poem
- Cinquain

Research shows a direct connection between enjoyment and learning. Think how quickly a student masters a favorite video game or learns all the words to a favorite song. By letting students write for the joy of it, you can awaken in them a lifelong love of writing.

The Craft of Writing

Writing is an art. Art teachers teach techniques for creating perspective or formulas for the proportions of a human face, but then art students must internalize these techniques and use them to craft something new.

Writing teachers need to do the same. In the wraparound, you'll find suggestions for helping students develop their writing style and voice, going beyond concrete skills to discover writer's craft.

Wraparound Feature

 Writer's Craft

These features help you inspire students to write the way professional writers do. They feature techniques used by the masters as well as interesting anecdotes and quotations.

RESEARCH WRITING

Training Researchers

In this Internet age, strong research skills are more important than ever. Students must be able to evaluate sources and avoid the lure of plagiarism. This section equips students to succeed using traditional and digital source materials.

The step-by-step instructions in the "Research Writing" section help students learn to do the following:

- Use the library.
- Use the Internet.
- Evaluate sources.
- Summarize, paraphrase, and quote.
- Avoid plagiarism.
- Cite sources (according to MLA style).
- Use a gathering grid and create note cards.
- Outline a research report.
- Create a works-cited page.

The section also helps students present their material in a traditional report form—or as a multimedia presentation!

Wraparound Feature

 **Technology Connections**

In these features, you'll see connections to *Write Source Online* (www.hmheducation.com/writesource). *Write Source Online* includes *Interactive Whiteboard Lessons*, *Net-text*, *Bookshelf*, *GrammarSnap*, *Portfolio*, *File Cabinet*, and *Essay Scoring*.

Writing Across the Curriculum

Special chapters help your students write in their content areas: science, social studies, math, the applied sciences, and the arts. These sections help you partner with content-area teachers to make sure that students can use writing to show knowledge, to think through difficult concepts, and to succeed throughout the school day.

Chapters feature note taking, learning logs, and a number of subject-specific assignments. The social studies chapter culminates in instruction for answering document-based questions—a type of on-demand writing that is often required on social studies tests.

Differentiating Instruction

Throughout the teacher's edition, you'll find useful hints for modifications and accommodations to help all students learn. Watch for the wraparound features shown below. Also, because the *Write Source* series follows a consistent format throughout its K-12 line, students who need further differentiation can work at a grade below (or above) their classmates.

Wraparound Features

English Language Learners

These boxes provide differentiation tips to help English language learners.

Struggling Learners

Consult this feature to adjust the lesson for those who are struggling.

Advanced Learners

These boxes feature tips for challenging students who excel.

Workplace Writing

Whether students are preparing for the working world or for the world of academia, they need workplace writing. A well-written business letter can help a student get a job or get into college. A well-written proposal or report can lead to a promotion or a scholarship.

Teach from this section, and direct your students to refer to it whenever they need to get through a writing gateway.

Note: For more writing help to get out of high school or to get into college, see the chapter entitled "Taking Exit and Entrance Exams."

Equipping Students to Learn

This section focuses on crucial skills for academic success: oral language use, note taking, critical reading, summarizing, paraphrasing, taking tests, and taking exit and entrance exams.

Organized topically, these chapters can be taught as minilessons when your students most need them. Here are some suggested applications:

- **Use "Listening and Speaking"** when setting up a writing workshop so that students understand the ground rules for group discussion.
- **Present "Taking Notes"** at the beginning of the year to help students write to learn in all their classes.
- **Use "Critical Reading"** to equip students with the crucial study habits they need to succeed in all of their course work.
- **Present "Summarizing and Paraphrasing"** in tandem with the "Research Report" chapter.
- **Use "Taking Tests"** to help students improve their performance on low- or high-stakes assessments.
- **Teach "Taking Exit and Entrance Exams"** to help students succeed on these all-important tests.

The Tools of Learning

Basic Elements of Writing

Teaching Basic Writing Skills

This section equips students with specific strategies that they will use over and over during the writing process. Students will find strategies for getting started, for gathering and organizing ideas, for connecting their thoughts, and for strengthening their essays.

These chapters progress from basic paragraph and essay skills for struggling students to advanced techniques for students who are always a couple steps ahead.

With clear rules, simple explanations, high-interest models, and engaging activities, "Basic Paragraph Skills" and "Basic Essay Skills" have something for everyone.

Perfecting Conventions

The "Proofreader's Guide" includes the rules of punctuation, mechanics, idioms, usage, parts of speech, and sentence creation. The rules are accompanied by engaging example text and activities to test knowledge.

Also, as the "Test Prep!" box indicates, the major sections end with test-prep pages to help students study for grammar tests.

Cross-references in this TE connect to activities in the *SkillsBook* and *Write Source Online* GrammarSnap.

Proofreader's Guide

Test Prep!
A review test in standardized-test format follows each of the six sections in the "Proofreader's Guide."

Why Write?

1

You write essays, develop research papers, and respond to writing prompts. These are important *practical* types of writing that you do in school. Be prepared. You'll continue to do a lot of practical writing when your schooling is completed. As writer Patricia T. O'Conner states, "Because of computers, we're suddenly a nation of writers." Engineers, mechanics, lawyers, health-care workers, fitness trainers—everyone is "wired in" and writing reports, requests, proposals, news briefs, and so on.

You may also keep a writer's notebook, write about your course work in a learning log, and e-mail your friends and family members. These are important *personal* types of writing that help you figure things out and determine where you fit in. Writer Natalie Goldberg says that personal writing "allows you to penetrate your life and learn to trust your own mind." If you're not already doing personal writing, get started as soon as possible.

- **Using a Writer's Notebook**
- **Writing in Action**

"It is by sitting down to write every morning that one becomes a writer."

—Gerald Brenan

Why Write?

Ask students to talk about the kinds of personal writing they already do. In addition to the personal writing mentioned on the page, they might

- write poetry or fiction,
- compose song lyrics,
- maintain a personal blog or Web page, or
- exchange frequent text messages with friends.

Encourage students who already write on their own to talk about how they got started and how they stay inspired.

- When do they write?
- How often do they write?
- Do they set goals for themselves—such as getting down a certain number of words or pages—when they write?
- Do they have any plans to publish their work, or do they keep their writing private?

If you require students to keep a **writer's notebook** *(see below)*, have them begin their journal at the start of the school year, so they will have a number of entries by the time the grading period or the semester ends.

Teaching Tip: Writer's Notebook

Explain that you will be reviewing notebook entries periodically, but that students will have the option of keeping certain entries private. This will encourage students to write freely. Inform students of what you will expect. For example:

- Students should write an average of three pages per week.

- They will submit their journals for review once a month.
- Your review will consist of spot readings in the notebook. They may keep any entry private by folding the page in half vertically.

Using a Writer's Notebook

Point out that students do not necessarily have to handwrite their entries. Many of them may feel that their ideas flow more freely when they use a keyboard. If they have a computer, they should use it instead.

- This can make it easier for students who have their own Web site to cut and paste text from their journals onto the Web page when they want to share.
- Correspondingly, it also becomes easier to cut and paste text from e-mails and other documents into the journal. (Students may find that the information they include in e-mails to friends makes valuable journal entries.)
- Special journaling software exists, but students can also use a word processing program to organize their electronic journal entries in an electronic file. They should use a password to lock the file.
- Remind students that it is important to back up their journal regularly to make sure the contents are preserved, should the computer malfunction.

Using a Writer's Notebook

A writer's notebook (also called a journal) is a place to record your thoughts on any topic. As you do so, you will make countless discoveries about your world. You may also find yourself inspired to create more polished forms of writing—stories, poems, and narratives.

Getting started may not be easy for you, but if you keep at it, you will find that writing in a notebook will become part of your regular routine. As writer Thomas Mallon states, "There comes a point when, like a marathon runner, you get through some sort of 'wall' and start running on automatic." To find out if this is true, write every day—no excuses!

Ensuring Success

To make sure that your writer's notebook is a success, consider the approach, quality, and variety of your entries.

- **Approach:** Begin each entry with a high level of enthusiasm. Write about things that matter to you and develop your ideas fully.
- **Quality:** Focus on exploring and developing your ideas, not on producing perfect copy. Your notebook is your place to experiment, take risks, and make mistakes.
- **Variety:** Write some of your entries from different points of view. For example, after a disagreement with a family member, write about the experience from the other person's point of view, or from the perspective of someone who overheard the discussion.

Rules for Notebook Writing

1. Date each entry. The date on an entry helps you find it later and places it in a context with other entries and experiences.

2. Write freely. Push to keep your pen moving or your fingers keyboarding. Continuous writing helps you make discoveries.

3. Write regularly. Develop the habit of writing daily. Then reread your entries to consider what you've discovered. Those ideas may prompt additional writing.

Struggling Learners

Model the concept of different points of view by placing an object in the center of the room. Have students describe what they observe when standing directly in front of the object, behind the object, or on either side of the object. Guide students to recognize that the viewer's position, even the time of day, may highlight or mask certain traits of the object.

Advanced Learners

Explain that observing a situation from various points of view often helps opposing parties resolve a conflict. Ask students to reflect on a recent local, national, or world conflict and write about it from two different points of view. Then challenge them to describe a way the parties can resolve the conflict through compromise.

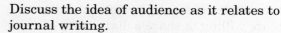

"Have fun. Your sense of freedom and play will infuse your writing with energy, and that energy will make your words enjoyable to read."

—Jack Heffron

Writing About Anything—and Everything

There are no limits to what you can write about—just as long as each of your entries connects with you personally. Write about people, places, and things; delve into your hopes, dreams, and memories; explore snippets of conversations that you overhear. Your notebook is the perfect place to explore these topics and form new understandings.

When you can't think of something to write about, refer to the following questions for ideas.

- **Observations:** What is happening around you right now? What are your thoughts and feelings about what's happening?

- **Memories:** What was the best moment of your day? The week? The year? What was the worst moment?

- **Hopes and dreams:** What do you want in life? What do you hope for in the future?

- **People:** What person means the most to you? What person do you most admire? What sort of person do you think you are or wish you were?

- **Places:** Where are you right now? Where do you wish you were? Where do you never want to be again?

- **Things:** What is your favorite possession? Your least favorite? What one thing most closely links you to your past?

- **Thoughts:** What is the most peculiar thing you've learned recently? What is the best piece of advice you've given or received?

Try It!

Find inspiration. Write freely for 8 to 10 minutes. The topic is you. Begin with *I wish I were . . .* and see where your writing takes you. Afterward, underline at least two discoveries that you made in this writing.

Discuss the idea of audience as it relates to journal writing.

- The primary—often the only—audience for a journal is the person who owns it. Keeping a journal private is a good way to free oneself to delve deeply into important issues.

- Some people who keep journals don't reread them. Instead, they write to free themselves from troublesome thoughts, in order to move beyond them.

- Some writers find it helpful to imagine another person as their audience. A writer might, for example, write directly to a person they're upset with to describe the problem from the writer's viewpoint. The writer may or may not decide to let that person read the entry later.

Share examples of diaries by famous writers. If you are willing to share a diary entry of your own, read it to the class. Showing them how others have used this medium will help students begin their own journaling. Among well-known published journals are those by the following writers:

- Anne Frank
- Louisa May Alcott
- James Boswell
- Anaïs Nin
- Samuel Pepys
- Virginia Woolf

Books that may yield useful readings include the following:

- *A Book of One's Own: People and Their Diaries,* by Thomas Mallon
- *The Assassin's Cloak: An Anthology of the World's Greatest Diarists,* edited by Irene and Alan Taylor
- *A Day at a Time: The Diary Literature of American Women Writers from 1764 to the Present,* edited by Margo Culley
- *Revelations: Diaries of Women,* edited by Mary Jane Moffat and Charlotte Painter

4

Taking It Personally

Here is a page from a student writer's notebook. This powerful entry focuses on the writer's future and does several important things. It . . .

- shows the depth of the writer's feelings,
- captures a time in her life,
- describes a place, and
- makes colorful comparisons.

Sample Notebook Entry

April 3, 2011

When I came home from school I headed right down to the lakefront. It had been a rough day, and it's always been easier to think when I'm looking at that big, blank expanse of water.

My guidance counselor was really upset with me when I told him I wasn't going to college next year. He kept going on about my good science grades, my potential, my future. But that's just it. It's my future, and I just don't see college as part of it—at least not right now. My parents aren't thrilled about my decision, either, but it's too late to do anything about it now. I missed all the application deadlines.

Tomorrow I'm going down to enlist in the navy. I know it's kind of weird for a girl, but I want to experience those big ships, to spend time out on the ocean. I can study oceanography and meteorology in the navy better than at any school. There's always been something pulling me to the water. My biology teacher used to talk about how we all came from the sea, and I laughed and said I always thought I had seawater in my veins. I just know this is the right decision, and that I am finally steering the right course.

Note: Keeping a writer's notebook lets you look at ordinary things in new ways, describe your feelings, choose good descriptive words, and practice writing until you feel confident.

Try It!

Write freely for 5 to 10 minutes about an obstacle in your life. Reflect on how you felt as you faced it.

Writing in Action

A notebook can be a useful tool for sorting out your thoughts. Below are passages that show how three different students use their notebooks.

Examining Feelings

This student uses her notebook to sort out her feelings about her aunt.

> I still can't believe Aunt Tanya is gone, even though I was right there when she slipped away. It's not fair! She wasn't that old! That cancer worked so fast, and she was suffering so much, but at least she was fighting! She was so brave. Two weeks ago, she joked that she'd found a foolproof way to lose weight! Then the regression, and today she's gone. But she's out of pain now. Mom's a basket case, and I guess I can be strong for her. Strong like Aunt Tanya.

Reliving an Experience

Here a student reflects on a memorable time.

> Visiting New York with the choir was the best! I've never seen so many people or so much traffic! When Alex and I asked directions from a pushcart owner, he gave us free hot dogs and said, "See, New Yorkers aren't so unfriendly!" We even got to sing on the steps of Lincoln Center. My favorite part was riding the ferry to see the Statue of Liberty. Suddenly someone started singing "America the Beautiful," and we all joined in. What an awesome moment! I'll always remember that feeling.

Questioning/Solidifying a Belief

This student explores her mistaken impression about a classmate.

> I don't know why I didn't like Luke. I guess I just figured he was this big popular jock. Then we got paired for this calculus lab. I thought I'd end up doing everything, but surprise! He really worked hard. He's actually had to help me with stuff I didn't understand, but he's been really nice about it. I liked working with him, and I think we can even be friends. I guess I shouldn't have judged him so quickly.

Writing in Action

Point out that one of the possible benefits of keeping a journal is to capture inspirations that help students in their daily lives. Students may find that as they write, they will think of ideas for poems, stories, school assignments, and letters. They may even stumble across the solution to a problem that has been on their mind—say, exactly the right way to start a difficult conversation with a friend.

Suggest that students devise a method for making these ideas stand out so they are easy to find again later if need be. Students might "bookmark" an idea by placing an asterisk in the margin next to the beginning of relevant information or by highlighting the beginning of an entry.

The Writing Process Overview

Common Core Standards Focus

Writing 5: Develop and strengthen writing as needed by planning, revising, editing, rewriting, or trying a new approach, focusing on addressing what is most significant for a specific purpose and audience.

Writing 6: Use technology, including the Internet, to produce, publish, and update individual or shared writing products in response to ongoing feedback, including new arguments or information.

Language 1: Demonstrate command of the conventions of standard English grammar and usage when writing or speaking.

Language 2: Demonstrate command of the conventions of standard English capitalization, punctuation, and spelling when writing.

Writing Process

- **Prewriting** Select a specific topic, and gather and organize details into a writing plan.
- **Writing** Complete a first draft using the prewriting plan as a guide to getting ideas down on paper.
- **Revising** Review the first draft for five key traits of effective writing; then delete, move, add to, and rewrite parts of the text.
- **Editing** Check revised writing for conventions and proofread the final copy.
- **Publishing** Share the work with others.

Focus on the Traits

- **Ideas** Selecting a timely topic, forming an opinion, and using specific reasons and details to defend the position
- **Organization** Creating a beginning that states the opinion, a middle that includes facts and examples to support the opinion, and an ending that gives a call to action
- **Voice** Using a confident, knowledgeable voice and maintaining an appropriate tone for the topic and the audience
- **Word Choice** Choosing fair and precise words and explaining important terms that might be unfamiliar to the audience
- **Sentence Fluency** Using varied sentence beginnings and transitions that guide the reader smoothly through the writing
- **Conventions** Checking for errors in punctuation, capitalization, spelling, and grammar

Technology Connections

 Write Source Online
www.hmheducation.com/writesource

- *Net-text*
- *Bookshelf*
- *GrammarSnap*
- *Portfolio*
- *Essay Scoring*
- *Writing Network features*
- *File Cabinet*

 Interactive Whiteboard Lessons

Suggested Writing Process Unit (Three Weeks)

	Day	Writing and Skills Instruction	Student Edition		SkillsBook	Daily Language Workouts
			Main Pages	Resource Units*		
WEEK 1	1–2	**Getting Started** (Activities, page TE-69) **Why Write?**	1–5	678–696 and Test Prep, 698–699	Skills assessment— Using the right word (57)	6–9
	3	**Understanding Writing**	7–12			
	4–5	**One Writer's Process**	13–32	605–644 and Test Prep, 622–623, 646–647	Skills assessment— Punctuation (3–4)	
WEEK 2	6	**Using a Rubric**	33–45			10–13
	7–10	**Understanding the Traits of Writing**	47–95	648–668 and Test Prep, 670–671	Skills assessment— Mechanics (39-40)	
WEEK 3	11–14	**Exploring the Writing Process**	97–139	738–756 and Test Prep, 758–759	Skills assessment— Sentences, 117, 121, 127, 132, 140, 144, 149, 157, 175	14–17
	15	**Listening and Speaking**	523–526	700–734 and Test Prep, 712–713, 736–737	Assessment— Parts of Speech, 69, 76, 84, 96, 107	

* These units are also located in the back of the *Teacher's Edition*. Resource Units include "Basic Elements of Writing" and "Proofreader's Guide."
(+) This activity is located in a different section of the *Write Source Student Edition*. If students have already completed this activity, you may wish to review it at this time.

Teacher's Notes for the Writing Process

This overview of the writing process includes some specific teaching suggestions for the unit. The description of each chapter will help you decide which parts of the unit to teach.

Writing Focus

Understanding Writing (pages 7–12)

A person's best writing almost always comes out of starting, stopping, beginning again, revising, editing, and proofreading. There are times when students must write on demand (tests, for example), but as a rule, students are given enough time to work through the writing process. When they do that, they will more likely create a pleasing essay, an interesting report, or a moving poem. The steps in the writing process are introduced in this chapter.

One Writer's Process (pages 13–32)

The student writer in this chapter follows the steps of the writing process to plan, develop, write, revise and edit, and publish a persuasive essay. Each step of the writing process is clearly presented.

Using a Rubric (pages 33–45)

The rubrics presented in this chapter are guidelines. Just as a pilot pays attention to the plane's instrumentation in order to negotiate the challenges of weather, similarly, accepted writing standards (rubrics) act as instruments by which student writers can negotiate the challenges of writing.

Academic Vocabulary

Read aloud the academic terms, as well as the descriptions and questions. Model for students how to read one question and answer it. Have partners monitor their understanding and seek clarification of the terms by working through the meanings and questions together.

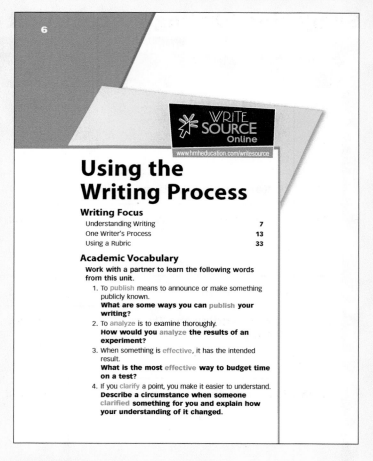

WRITE SOURCE Online
www.hmheducation.com/writesource

Using the Writing Process

Writing Focus

Academic Vocabulary

Work with a partner to learn the following words from this unit.

1. To publish means to announce or make something publicly known.
   What are some ways you can publish your writing?
2. To analyze is to examine thoroughly.
   How would you analyze the results of an experiment?
3. When something is effective, it has the intended result.
   What is the most effective way to budget time on a test?
4. If you clarify a point, you make it easier to understand.
   Describe a circumstance when someone clarified something for you and explain how your understanding of it changed.

Minilessons

Quoting Writers
Understanding Writing

- **READ** the quotations on page 1 of your textbook. **THINK** about what the writer meant. Then **WRITE** your own quotation about writing. **COLLECT** everyone's quotations in a class.

Reflections
One Writer's Process

- **READ** the "Reflecting on the Topic" section on SE page 15 of your textbook. **CHOOSE** a major issue in the world (population, food supplies, transportation, diseases). Then follow Roberto's example and **MAKE** a pros and cons list. **CHOOSE** a topic from that list you would like to defend. **SAVE** the list and your chosen topic for a future writing assignment.

A Blue Ribbon
Using a Rubric

- **STUDY** the rubric on SE pages 254–255 and the rubric checklist on SE page 31. On a separate sheet of paper, **REFER** to a rubric checklist and **SCORE** one of your previous essays. What was your best category? Which category needed the most work?

Understanding Writing

Writing is mind traveling, destination unknown. Let this statement be a reminder that when you write, you may be engaged in uncharted thinking, mind traveling, so to speak. As you go along, you may stumble upon old memories, face realities of the present, and speculate on what might be. You won't necessarily know where your writing will take you, at least not at the beginning. Your destination will only become clear as you travel further and further into your writing.

This is why writing may frustrate you. You feel you must know exactly where you are going before you start each journey. But effective writing seldom works that way. Instead, writing often works best when it is the product of an unexpected detour, a surprising thought burst, an ordinary idea gone haywire. That is why writing is thought of as a process; it can't be rushed, and it can't be fully scripted beforehand. In other words, it requires some mind traveling.

- **Becoming a Good Writer**
- **Understanding the Writing Process**
- **The Process in Action**
- **Learning from the Pros**

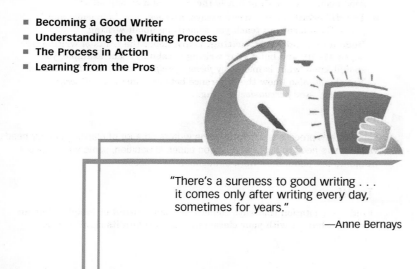

"There's a sureness to good writing . . . it comes only after writing every day, sometimes for years."

—Anne Bernays

Copy Masters

Sensory Chart (TE p. 10)

Understanding Writing

Objectives
- build good writing habits
- understand the five steps in the writing process
- learn the six traits of effective writing

Discuss mind-traveling—not knowing at the outset of a writing project where the journey will end. Assure students that although this may sound daunting, they will not be traveling without a map. The purpose of the information on the following pages is to provide guidance along the way by

- breaking the writing process down into five steps (prewriting, writing, revising, editing, and publishing) and
- identifying the six component parts, or traits, of writing (ideas, organization, voice, word choice, sentence fluency, and conventions), so they can be considered separately.

Each of these smaller, more manageable elements can function as a stepping-stone along the way to creating a finished essay.

Becoming a Good Writer

Discuss the idea in the FYI box that each writer approaches the writing process differently.

- Have students share their past experiences with writing—what methods have worked best for them?
- Encourage students who like to discuss ideas with others during the writing process to form a writing group with like-minded classmates.
- Students who feel they do their best planning in their heads need to make certain that this is true. Sometimes people convince themselves early in the process that they can remember their plans well enough, hoping to save themselves the trouble of having to write everything down.
- Note that while different writers do spend different amounts of time on the stages of the writing process described in this section, few of them skip a stage entirely. Encourage students to give each stage as much attention as they can, thinking about how each one best fits into their personal writing style.

8

"The way around writer's block is to write every day and to give up judging. Just write the novel or story or essay or poem and keep writing."

—Ron Koertge

Becoming a Good Writer

To become a good writer, you should act like one, which means that you should follow this advice:

- **Make reading an important part of your life.** Read anything and everything—books, magazines, and newspapers. Reading helps you internalize the traits of effective writing. Unless you become a regular reader, you can't expect to do your best as a writer.
- **Make writing an important part of your life.** Get into a regular writing routine, and stick to it! When writing becomes something that you want to do, rather than something that you have to do, you will begin to see improvement. (See pages **2–5** for more information.)
- **Explore meaningful topics.** In your personal writing, address your foremost thoughts, feelings, and experiences. In your assignments, write about topics that have special meaning to you. You will do your best work if you write about topics that truly interest you.
- **Set high standards.** If a first draft does not seem inviting, add more detail or voice to the writing. If the nouns and verbs in your writing are too general, replace them with more specific ones. Writer William Zinsser says, "Quality is its own reward." In other words, you will feel good about your writing if it is the result of a strong effort.
- **Try different forms.** Write essays, articles, stories, poems, and plays. Each form can teach you something about writing.
- **Become a student of writing.** Learn about the traits of writing (see pages **47–50**) and build your writing vocabulary. For example, you should know what is meant by *focus, specific details,* and *transitions.* You should also know the difference between *narrative, descriptive, expository,* and *persuasive* writing.

FYI

Each writer's process is different. Some writers do a lot of planning in their heads, while others need to put everything on paper. In addition, some writers find it helpful to talk about their work throughout the process.

Try It!

Find one quotation that says something inspirational or insightful about writing. Share it with your classmates and explain its significance.

Understanding the Writing Process

You should develop a piece of writing through a series of steps called the *writing process* before you share it. This page briefly describes these steps.

The Steps in the Writing Process

Prewriting

 The first step in the writing process involves selecting a specific topic, gathering details about it, and organizing those details into a writing plan.

Writing

 During this step, the writer completes the first draft using the prewriting plan as a guide. This draft is a writer's *first* chance to get everything on paper.

Revising

 During revising, the writer reviews the draft for five key traits: *ideas, organization, voice, word choice,* and *sentence fluency.* After deciding what changes to make, the writer deletes, moves, adds to, and rewrites parts of the text.

Editing

 Then the writer edits the revised draft for the *conventions* of punctuation, capitalization, spelling, and grammar and proofreads the final copy before sharing it.

Publishing

 Finally, the writer publishes the work by preparing a final copy and sharing it with others.

 Analyze your own process. Are you a slow writer or a fast one? Do you do a lot of planning? Do you make many changes in a first draft? Explain.

Writing

Understanding the Writing Process

After students have had time to think about the questions posed in the activity at the bottom of the page, have them share their answers with the class. Start by responding to the questions yourself. As the discussion progresses, make sure that students give detailed explanations for their answers. Ask additional questions to help them with this, as needed.

- What makes you a slower writer? (for example, liking to write and rewrite each sentence until it sounds just right before moving-on)
- What kind of planning works best for you? (for example, annotated notes, detailed outlines, note cards)
- What kinds of changes do you find yourself making as you revise a first draft? (for example, substantial organizational changes that involve changing the order of the details, or more subtle changes to improve word choice and sentence structure)

The Process in Action

Prewriting Selecting a Topic

Discuss the notion of an appealing topic. Note that many writers—such as students and journalists—are assigned topics to write about that may not interest them at first. Emphasize, though, that some aspect of nearly any subject can be fascinating once you learn more about it, but it is necessary to do some research. While choosing an already interesting topic is great, learning to figure out what's interesting about an assigned topic is a valuable skill.

Prewriting Gathering and Organizing Details

Emphasize that this step is when writers decide what to say and when to say it. Note that although the arrows on the graphic show the writer progressing from stage to stage, students may find themselves needing to circle back from a later stage to add more details or even to create a different organization method to strengthen their thesis.

Writing Developing the First Draft

Note that the key to this step is *getting all ideas down on paper*. A writer who does this successfully can spend the rest of the process arranging those ideas into the most effective presentation.

The Process in Action

The next two pages give a detailed description of each step in the writing process. The graphic below reminds you that, at any time, you can move back and forth between the steps in the process. Also remember that carefully attending to the first steps in the writing process will make the final steps much easier.

Prewriting Selecting a Topic

- Search for topics that meet the requirements of the assignment.
- Select a specific topic that appeals to you.

Gathering and Organizing Details

- Gather as many ideas and details as you can about the topic.
- With the purpose of the assignment in mind, find one point to emphasize about the topic—either an interesting part or your personal feeling about it. This will be the focus, or thesis, of your writing.
- Decide which details fit your topic.
- Organize your details into a writing plan using an outline, a chart, or some other method.

Writing Developing the First Draft

- When writing the first draft, concentrate on getting your ideas on paper. Don't try to produce a perfect piece of writing.
- Use your prewriting plan as a guide and include the details you collected, but feel free to add new ideas that occur to you as you go along.
- Be sure your writing has a beginning, a middle, and an ending.

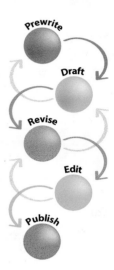

Tip

Write on every other line and on only one side of the paper when using pen or pencil and paper. Double-space on a computer. This will give you room for revising, the next step in the process.

English Language Learners

To help students sharpen their skills for the prewriting stage, distribute copies of the reproducible Sensory Chart (TE page 825). Have them complete the graphic organizer about their first day attending your school. Then have students review their completed charts, circling the details they would include in an essay titled "A Typical Day in an American High School."

Revising **Improving Your Writing**

- Set aside your first draft for a while so you can return to it with a fresh perspective.
- Read your first draft slowly and critically.
- Use these questions as a revising guide:
  - Is my topic interesting for the reader?
  - Does the beginning catch the reader's attention?
  - Are the ideas in order and easy to understand?
  - Have I included enough details to support my central idea?
  - Does the ending leave the reader with something to think about?
  - Do I sound interested in and knowledgeable about the topic?
  - Are the nouns specific and the verbs active?
  - Are the modifiers (adjectives and adverbs) clear and descriptive?
  - Does the whole piece read smoothly?
- Ask at least one person to review your writing and offer suggestions.
- Make as many changes as necessary to improve your writing.

Editing **Checking for Conventions**

- Check for errors in punctuation, capitalization, spelling, and grammar.
- Have another person check your writing for errors.
- Prepare a neat final copy.
- Proofread the final copy before publishing it.

Publishing **Sharing Your Writing**

- Share your writing with friends, classmates, and family.
- Consider submitting your writing to a newspaper or other publication.
- Include the writing in your portfolio.

Tip

For assignments, save all your work. Refer to the earlier drafts and to the teacher's comments on each graded piece for ideas and inspiration for future writing projects.

Consider the process. Some experts say that revising is the most important step in the writing process. Explain why this may be true.

Revising Improving Your Writing

Suggest that students provide a copy of the revising questions to their reader/reviewer. Acknowledge that it can be difficult to answer these questions objectively about your own writing and that their reader's responses can be very helpful.

Editing Checking for Conventions

Have students study the Proofreader's Guide in the back of the book (SE pages 604–763) so they can become as familiar as possible with the helpful information. Encourage them to use the resource regularly. The more it becomes second nature for students to write using correct punctuation, capitalization, spelling, and, grammar, the less work they will have to do in the editing stage of the writing process.

Publishing Sharing Your Writing

Note that ideas for sharing writing are offered in most units of the student edition. Suggest that students use the index to find this information for the forms of writing they will be using.

Struggling Learners

Students may feel editing for punctuation, capitalization, spelling, and grammar at the same time is demanding. Suggest that students edit their essays for each convention individually. While this involves multiple reviews, it increases the likelihood that they will catch more errors than they would with one review.

Learning from the Pros

Provide writing samples by some or all of the writers whose quotations are on the page.

- Ask students to read the samples, keeping in mind what that author says about revising.
- Is it possible to see the ideas expressed in the quotations directly in the samples? (sometimes)
- What do students like best about the samples? (useful for modeling and imitating techniques)
- Does reading extensively revised writing make it seem any less fresh? (Most should agree that it does not.)

Learning from the Pros

Keep the following thoughts in mind as you develop your writing. They come from experienced authors who appreciate writing as a process of discovery.

"I don't pick subjects so much as they pick me."

—Andy Rooney

"When I speak to students about writing, I hold myself up as an example of that ancient axiom—write about what you know."

—Robert Cormier

"The inspiration comes while you write."

—Madeleine L'Engle

"Writing comes more easily if you have something to say."

—Sholem Asch

"I think one is constantly startled by the things that appear before you on the page while you write."

—Shirley Hazzard

"By the time I reach a fifth version, my writing begins to have its own voice."

—Ashley Bryan

"Half of my life is an act of revision."

—John Irving

"I am an obsessive rewriter, doing one draft and then another and another, usually five. In a way, I have nothing to say but a great deal to add."

—Gore Vidal

"I believe in impulse and naturalness, but followed by discipline in the cutting."

—Anaïs Nin

"Write visually, write clearly, and make every word count."

—Gloria D. Miklowitz

Try It!

Create two of your own quotations that reflect your own experience as a writer. Share those quotations with your classmates, explaining their significance.

English Language Learners

Students may hesitate during the **Try It!** activity because they are uncomfortable forming quotations about a process that is still new and difficult. Have them celebrate their successes to this point by relating their most recent positive writing experience.

13

One Writer's Process

At your age, you probably know quite a lot about the steps in the writing process: prewriting, writing, revising, editing, and publishing. You also probably know that using the process helps you to produce your best work, an effective finished piece of writing. Since you already understand this, there's no real need to read further, is there?

Well, yes—in fact, refamiliarizing yourself with the steps in the writing process is always a good idea. As you become a better writer, it may be tempting to slack off, take it easy, skip a step or two. But *every* step in the process is essential to doing your best work. This chapter, which chronicles student writer Roberto Salazar's process for a persuasive essay, will serve as a simple reminder of that fact.

- **Previewing the Goals**
- **Prewriting**
- **Writing**
- **Revising**
- **Editing**
- **Publishing**
- **Assessing the Final Copy**
- **Reflecting on Your Writing**

"If you want to write, or really to create anything, you have to risk falling on your face."

—Allegra Goodman

One Writer's Process

Objectives
- examine the goals for persuasive writing
- evaluate one writer's work step-by-step through the writing process
- review one writer's final essay and self-assessment.

Encourage students to work through the unit as if they were learning about the writing process for the first time—even if they are very familiar with it.

To illustrate the idea that what one believes to be familiar can include new and interesting elements, try an observation activity such as the following:
- Ask students to close their eyes and visualize the classroom (ceiling, walls, bulletin boards, bookshelves, desks, windows, doorway, floor, and so on).
- Then ask students to open their eyes and closely observe their surroundings. Is everything exactly as they imagined it? Is there anything in the room that they never noticed before?
- Afterward, have students talk about their observations and recollections of details.

Previewing the Goals

To help students focus on the information, ask volunteers to read the traits out loud to classmates. **Discuss each trait** (*see below*), inviting students to add their observations, based on prior writing experience.

Try It!
Answers

Possible Answers

Topic—smoking in public places (should it or should it not be legal?); **tone**—semiformal/serious; **important terms**—*lung cancer, emphysema, secondhand smoke, passive smoking, personal freedom, self-determination*

Topic—the death penalty (should it be allowed or not?); **tone**—semiformal/serious; **important terms**—*capital punishment, criminal law, execution, retribution, human rights, deterrent*

Topic—a theme for the senior prom (propose a specific theme); **tone**—semiformal, could be fairly informal in tone; **important terms** would vary.

14

Previewing the Goals

Before Roberto Salazar began writing his essay, he previewed the goals for persuasive writing, which are shown below. He also looked over the rubric for persuasive writing on pages 254–255. Both of these activities helped him get started.

Traits of Persuasive Writing

- **Ideas**

  Select a timely topic, a controversial issue that you care about. Form your opinion and use specific reasons and details to defend your position.

- **Organization**

  State your opinion in the beginning, use facts and examples to support your opinion in the middle, and end with a call for action.

- **Voice**

  Use a confident voice that balances facts and feelings, and maintain an appropriate tone for your topic and audience.

- **Word Choice**

  Choose fair and precise words to state and defend your position. Explain important terms that may be unfamiliar to your audience.

- **Sentence Fluency**

  Write clear, complete sentences with varied beginnings and transitions that guide the reader smoothly through your argument.

- **Conventions**

  Follow rules of punctuation, capitalization, spelling, and grammar.

Try It!

List two or three topics that would be suitable for a persuasive essay. Considering voice, what tone would be appropriate for each topic? What important terms would you need to explain for each?

Teaching Tip: Discuss the Traits

Extend the information on the page by noting that the ideas of the ancient Greek philosopher and teacher Aristotle complement the information in the student edition. He identified the three types of appeals (convincing arguments):

- *logos* (logic)—An opinion must be supported by strong, logical reasons, such as facts and statistics.

- *ethos* (ethics)—An appeal to ethics shows that the writer is fair. This is conveyed primarily by how ideas are expressed: A confident voice that avoids loaded, insulting words wins readers' trust.

- *pathos* (emotion)—A controlled emotional argument backed up by strong, logical reasons is convincing—but too much emotion weakens the writer's position.

English Language Learners

Before students respond to the **Try It!** activity, explain that *tone of voice* refers to the feeling an author's writing (or a speaker's words) conveys. Model various tones, such as confident, enthusiastic, and negative. Then invite volunteers to share their own examples of different tones of voice.

Prewriting Selecting a Topic

Roberto's economics teacher assigned the following topic.

> Recently we've discussed the government's obligations in a market economy—providing for national defense, overseeing health-care initiatives, addressing environmental concerns, among others. Based on what you've learned about the federal budget process, do you support reductions in defense spending, or is the current spending level necessary? Support your position in a persuasive essay.

Reflecting on the Topic

Roberto made a list of pros and cons on the issue.

YES to reductions	NO to reductions
• Other issues that affect our citizens should be addressed before spending more on defense.	• Our military should be the best in the world.
• Another country won't attack us on our soil, so why worry about defense?	• We need to keep up with other countries.
• Having a strong military may lead to unwise involvement in conflicts.	• Lots of industries provide for defense and have a big effect on the economy.
• One day, armed conflict will be a thing of the past.	• There will always be conflict in the world; we have to be ready.

Roberto found that he still had some questions. He wrote them down and researched them before forming his opinion.

> • How much does our military spend, especially in relation to other countries?
> • What do we spend on the nation's health and education?
> • Is there public support for reducing defense spending?

Try It!

Which of Roberto's reasons (pro or con) is strongest? Weakest? Which of the opposing viewpoints would you address in a persuasive essay? Explain.

Prewriting Selecting a Topic

Note that Roberto's teacher has specified the topic, but sometimes students will be free to decide on their own topic. Remind them that a "Basics of Life" list (see SE page 99) can be a good way to start: The general categories listed, such as rules/laws and community, can help them think of controversies that apply to them.

Prewriting Reflecting on the Topic

Distribute photocopies of the reproducible T-chart (TE page 823). Remind students that this format can help them organize ideas about two aspects of a topic.

Note that the list represents Roberto's understanding of the topic before doing research (see SE page 16). It is a starting point. He will refine his ideas as he learns more.

Try It! Answers

Answers will vary. Consider using the activity as the basis for a class discussion about how to get started thinking about a topic. Ask students to explain their choices for strong and weak reasons, identify related ideas that occur to them, and tell how they would confirm the reasons before using them in an essay.

English Language Learners

Provide the following definitions before reading the page:

• obligations (responsibilities)
• market economy (system in which goods and services are distributed in free markets with free pricing)
• initiatives (actions to establish laws or policies)

Prewriting Gathering Details

Have students read through the information about research skills (SE pages 370–382) for more details about Roberto's process.

Remind students that genuinely controversial topics will generate a lot of opinionated writing. In fact, it may be difficult to find objective information, so students must remain alert to the biases of their sources. They should not mistake opinions for facts. And they should try to consult sources that support both sides of the argument.

Emphasize that students should always choose reliable sources. These might include the following:

- books published by established companies
- major periodicals
- credible reviews, essays, and interviews with experts
- facts and statistics gathered by governmental departments, polling organizations such as Gallup, and nonprofit research agencies

✱ For more about evaluating sources, see SE page 373.

Prewriting Gathering Details

Roberto went to the library and looked for information about defense spending; he also looked on the Internet. He recorded his source information on note cards.

Sources of Information

> Stockholm International Peace
> Research Institute. SIPRI
> Yearbook 2009: Armaments,
> Disarmament and International
> Security. Oxford:
> Oxford UP, 2009. Print.

> Peña, Charles. "Record Defense
> Spending, Less Security." Houston
> Chronicle 13 Nov. 2008: 28. Print.

> "Department of Defense." Office of
> Management and Budget. The White
> House, 27 Feb. 2010. Web. 20 Feb.
> 2010.

Quotations and Paraphrases

Roberto used note cards to record quotations and paraphrases, too. He was sure to include the source for each.

Quotation

> "The reality is: The United States
> would be just as secure if we
> reduced military spending, perhaps
> more so."
>
> Source: Peña

Paraphrase

> Worldwide military spending reached
> 1.2 trillion dollars in 2006, and the
> United States was responsible for a
> large portion of that amount.
>
> Source: Stockholm

Try It!

Find some sources that would answer Roberto's questions from page 15.

Struggling Learners

Discuss the specific information that each note card contains. Provide students with index cards, and help them make templates that detail what should be recorded on a book card, a magazine card, and so on. Encourage them to use their templates when gathering source information.

Forming a Thesis Statement

Once Roberto had formed his opinion and had enough information to support it, he was ready to write the *thesis statement* for his essay. An effective thesis statement consists of two parts: a specific topic plus a particular feeling or opinion about it. Roberto wrote this thesis statement:

Writing

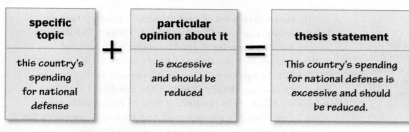

specific topic		particular opinion about it		thesis statement
this country's spending for national defense	**+**	is excessive and should be reduced	**=**	This country's spending for national defense is excessive and should be reduced.

Organizing the Essay

Next, Roberto wrote a topic outline for his essay. This step organized the details that supported his thesis.

> I. Introduction
> II. Background
>   A. Explanation of how federal budget is distributed
>   B. National defense as half of discretionary budget
>   C. Comparison to budgets for education and health
> III. Key Supporting Points
>   A. Other countries' spending on defense far less than U.S.'s
>   B. U.S. current level of preparedness
>   C. Widespread public support to reduce defense spending
> IV. Concession
>   A. Defense contractors benefiting from large budget
>   B. Economic impact of losing some defense contracts not great
> V. Conclusion

Try It!

Imagine that you had taken the opposite side of the issue. Write a thesis statement that reflects that opinion; then create an outline like the one above.

Prewriting Forming a Thesis Statement

Remind students that the thesis statement is a guide to their research and writing, but it can be changed at any time.

Prewriting Organizing the Essay

Remind students that they may instead create a detailed sentence outline, if they prefer.

✱ For more about sentence outlines, see SE page 401.

 Try It!
Answers

Possible Answers

Thesis: *This country's spending for national defense must remain at current levels in order to provide adequate protection.*
I. Introduction
II. Background
A. Explanation of federal budget distribution;
B. National defense half of discretionary budget; C. How the defense budget is spent
III. Key Supporting Points
A. Equipment must be kept in good repair; B. Military personnel must get fair pay, housing, and benefits; C. New security threats call for continued spending
IV. Concession
A. Domestic issues such as education and health need more funding; B. The benefits of keeping the country safe justify the expense

---

English Language Learners

Students may have difficulty identifying the opposite side of the issue for the **Try It!** activity. Write Roberto's specific topic, an addition sign, and *is* _____ *and should be* _____ . Help them complete the blanks with antonyms for *excessive* and *reduced*. Students then combine the two parts to form a thesis statement.

Encourage students to retain the format and headings of Roberto's outline. Help them replace the key supporting points, labeled *A*, *B*, and *C*, with statements that support the opposing view.

Writing Developing Your First Draft

Note that many ideas for improvement will occur to students as they read the first draft. Remind them that the writer will focus on these areas during the revision and editing stages.

For the moment, encourage students to look beyond the problems and focus on the draft's strengths.

- Ask them to compare the sample to the topic outline shown on SE page 17. Did the writer address all the ideas he listed in the outline? (They should agree that he does.)
- Draw their attention to the many details the writer used to support the information from his outline. Point out that even though there is not enough space in the student edition to show Roberto's research notes, these details came from extensive notes he took—likely on note cards—during the prewriting stage.

Writing Developing Your First Draft

Roberto referred to his outline as he wrote his first draft. At this point, he wanted to get all his ideas down on paper without worrying about writing the perfect essay.

> The first paragraph states the issue and ends with the thesis statement.

It sure takes a lot of cash to make a country feel secure. The defense budget for China was $62.5 billion. The defense budget for 11 countries in the European Union totaled $185.8 billion. But the United States spent $420.7 billion ("U.S. Military Spending"). That's 43 percent of the world's total. Worldwide military spending had reached 1.2 trillion dollars by 2006, with the United States responsible for a lopsided amount. It's obvious that this country's spending for national defense is excessive and should be reduced.

> The first middle paragraph covers the background.

In the United States, the federal budget is classified in two ways. National defense falls under a category of the federal budget called "discretionary" spending. Congress decides on the level of resources set aside for any specific area. Congress decides where to increase or decrease funds. Congress earmarks the other two-thirds of the budget for programs where the level of funding is decided by the number of people who is qualified for entitlements. Funding for the Department of Defense currently accounts for fully half of the federal discretionary budget. The president's request for 2007 was $439.3 billion for the Department of Defense ("Dept. of Defense"). Besides this, the departments' budget does not include outlays for ongoing military operations in the Middle East. The Department of Education meritted a request of $56.8 billion—about an eighth of the defense budget; and the amount budgeted for health was $53.1 billion ("FY '07"). Also, the 2007 defense budget had increased 14 percent over the 2005 budget ("Dept. of Defense"), while the education and health budgets decreased 9 and 5 percent ("Education Dept.," "Budget"). Priorities seam a bit skewed here.

> The next three paragraphs support the thesis.

As the U.S. military gobbles up more and more of the world's military spending pie, here is a logicle thought: decreasing the amount spent on national defense would have

English Language Learners

Define the following terms before students read Roberto's essay:

- lopsided (uneven)
- discretionary (able to be used as desired without stipulations)
- relative (in relation to)
- deficit (amount by which money or funding falls short of the desired or expected amount)
- contractor (company or individual that supplies goods or services to an organization)
- hawkish (favoring the use of military force)
- humanitarian (designed to promote human welfare)

Writing

little affect on U.S. military capability. Especially relative to other countries' military power. Even if the defense budget were cut in half, the next 2 big spenders combined wouldn't come near our level.

Further, the U.S. doesn't need the level of military preparedness it currently has. We're surrounded by friendly neighbors! An attack by another country on our soil is unlikely. Second, in the words of Charles Peña, "The real threat to the United States no longer consists of nation states, but the terrorist threat represented by al-Qaeda, which is relatively undeterred by the U.S. military" ("More"). In other words, continuously increasing military funding will do little to prevent terrorism. A change in terrorist thinking will come only with international cooperation to address poor conditions.

For another thing, there are lots of public support to reduce military spending. A 2005 poll by the University of Maryland's Program on International Policy Attitudes showed 65 percent of the respondents cutting defense spending (Soto). And another 2005 poll, conducted by the Pew Research Center, showed that 36% of respondents think lowering defense and military spending is a top priority in reducing the budget deficit ("Federal"). And there are dozens of organizations and Web sites that support decreased defense spending. Congress's leaders should take note.

While it is true that the current level of spending benefits many defense contractors and other businesses to the tune of $230 billion (Borgen), their impact on the economy isn't important. If these businesses could no longer rely on government contracts, they could evolve to the market (convert their production to non-military use). This is exactly what many defense contractors did following WWII.

It is not crazy to believe that huge military budgets are outdated. Humanitarian efforts make a huge difference. And contrary to "hawkish" thinking, when conflict does arise, peaceful resolutions are possible. It's time to start taking apart the military machine and spend that money better.

Sources are identified throughout.

An opposing argument is addressed.

The closing paragraph restates the thesis and ends with a call to action.

Review the margin notes for the draft. Ask students to look for other strong points in the draft. Possible responses:

- The writer uses statistics to back up the statements made. For example, to support the assertion that the public is in favor of cutting defense spending, the writer presents two different polls—a convincing strategy.
- The writer includes an expert quotation and cites reliable sources.
- The writer uses and explains specialized terms, such as *discretionary* and *evolve to the market.*
- The writer uses vivid nouns and modifiers (*skewed, military spending pie, hawkish, military machine*).

Struggling Learners

To provide additional instruction in how to address an opposing argument, direct students to the next-to-last paragraph of Roberto's essay. Ask them to identify the opposing argument. (The current level of spending benefits many defense contractors and other businesses.) Then ask them to explain how the author rebuffs this argument. (The survival of these businesses is not dependent on government contracts. They could convert their operations to nonmilitary ventures.) Ask students to tell in their own words how the author supports this point. (The author uses a historical reference, noting that defense contractors made a similar switch following World War II.)

Revising
Focusing on Ideas, Organization, and Voice

Point out that Roberto's strategy to focus first on ideas, organization, and voice, and then focus on style (word choice and sentence fluency—see SE page 24) is a good strategy. That way, he is not reading for too many traits at once, and he is reviewing the essay at least twice instead of once.

Revising Focusing on Ideas, Organization, and Voice

Roberto set his essay aside for a while before giving it a fresh look. When he did review it, he rechecked the goals on page **14**. Then he wrote down some changes he planned to make in terms of ideas, organization, and voice.

Ideas

"I should make the opening sentence more interesting. I need to beef up details in some places and delete one or two details that aren't really necessary."

Organization

"I should separate the second paragraph into two paragraphs to improve the organization. I need to be sure my ending is a strong finish for this essay."

Voice

"I should add more precise words to show how strongly I feel about this topic."

Roberto's First Revision

Here are some of the revisions that Roberto made in his essay.

The opening sentence is made into a question to increase interest.	How much cash does it take ~~It sure takes a lot of cash~~ to make a country feel secure. The defense budget for China was $62.5 billion. The defense budget for 11 countries in the European Union totaled $185.8 billion. But the United States spent $420.7 —close to half— billion ("U.S. Military Spending"). That's 43 percent of the world's total. Worldwide military spending had reached 1.2 trillion dollars by 2006, with the United States responsible
An explanation emphasizes an important point.	

One Writer's Process **21**

Writing

for a lopsided amount. It's obvious that this country's spending for national defense is excessive and should be reduced.

In the United States, ~~the federal budget is classified in two ways,~~ National defense falls under a category of the federal budget called "discretionary" spending. Congress decides on the level of resources set aside for any specific area. Congress decides where to increase or decrease funds. Congress earmarks the other two-thirds of the budget for "mandatory" spending: programs where the level of funding is decided by the number of people who is qualified for entitlements. ¶ Funding for the Department of Defense currently accounts for fully half of the federal discretionary budget. The president's request for 2007 was $439.3 billion for the Department of Defense ("Dept. of Defense"). Besides this, the departments' budget does not include ~~outlays for~~ ongoing military costs ~~operations~~ in the Middle East. The Department of Education meritted a request of just $56.8 billion—about an eighth of the defense budget; and the amount budgeted for health was even less: $53.1 billion ("FY '07"). Also, the 2007 . . .

An unnecessary idea is deleted.

An added detail completes the explanation.

A new paragraph improves the organization.

A few well-placed words intensify the voice and clarify the statistics.

Try It!

Review the changes Roberto made to the first few paragraphs of his essay. Make similar revisions to the rest of the essay, suggesting at least one revision in the area of ideas, one in organization, and one in voice.

Try It! Answers

Possible Answers

Ideas

Paragraph 3—Tell who the *next 2 big spenders* are.

Paragraph 4—Give facts to support the assertion that *an attack by another country on our soil is unlikely*; explain who Charles Peña is.

Paragraph 5—Give examples of *organizations and Web sites that support decreased defense spending.*

Paragraph 6—Give examples of nonmilitary companies that were defense contractors during WWII.

Paragraph 7—Give examples of peaceful resolutions that prevented wars.

Organization

Paragraph 4—Swap the last two sentences in the paragraph.

Paragraph 5—Reverse the order of the polls (giving the largest number of supporters last will make the point more convincingly).

Voice—Establish a more formal voice throughout by replacing casual words (*gobbles, crazy, huge*); avoid using an exclamatory sentence in paragraph 4.

Revising Using a Peer Response Sheet

Encourage students to make their peer responses as precise, polite, and helpful as possible. Note that one way to improve their response is to become familiar with terms related to writing. For example, persuasive writing depends heavily on presenting sound reasoning, so it is helpful for students to know about the kinds of flawed logic that can weaken an argument.

✳ For more about logical fallacies, see SE page 238.

Try It!
Answers

Possible Answers

1. Adding supporting details is most important. This will strengthen the writer's argument.
2. The logic used at the end of sentence 1 in paragraph 3 is flawed (it is an example of oversimplification). Dramatically decreasing military spending would have to affect the military more than just a little—the writer should instead focus on the idea that even a military that is half as powerful as the current one would still be stronger than any other country's military.

Revising Using a Peer Response Sheet

Kinsey evaluated Roberto's essay using a rubric like the one on pages 254–255. Her suggestions on the response sheet below showed Roberto where he could make additional improvements.

Peer Response Sheet

Writer: _Roberto_   Responder: _Kinsey_

Title: _Cut Defense Spending Now!_

What I liked about your writing:

I'm glad you included lots of facts and figures to support your thesis.

I can tell you really believe your opinion is right!

_____

Changes I would suggest:

More details are needed in some areas (for instance, the year of the

budgets you mention in the first paragraph). Also, it's hard to imagine

how much $439 billion really is. Could you clarify that somehow?

_____

_____

_____

_____

_____

Try It!

Review Kinsey's suggestions for improvement above. Which suggestion seems to be the most important? Explain why. Add at least one new suggestion to improve Roberto's writing. (Look at the explanations of ideas, organization, and voice on page 14 to refresh your memory.)

Struggling Learners

Before students begin the **Try It!** activity, have them revisit the boxed copy on SE page 14. Have student pairs find examples in Roberto's essay of the criteria described under *Ideas*, *Organization*, and *Voice*. Criteria omitted from the essay can form the basis of students' responses to the **Try It!** activity.

Roberto's Revision Using a Peer Response

Here are some revisions Roberto made, using Kinsey's comments.

> How much cash does it take to make a country feel secure?
>
> The defense budget for China was $62.5 billion. The defense
> ^2005^
> budget for 11 countries in the European Union totaled $185.8
> billion. But the United States spent $420.7 billion ("U.S.
> Military Spending"). That's 43 percent—close to half—of the
> world's total. Worldwide military spending had reached 1.2
> trillion dollars by 2006, with the United States responsible for
> (Stockholm)
> a lopsided amount. It's obvious that this country's spending for
> national defense is excessive and should be reduced.
>
> In the United States, national defense falls under
> a category of the federal budget called "discretionary"
> spending. Congress decides on the level of resources
> set aside for any specific area. Congress decides where
> to increase or decrease funds. Congress earmarks the
> other two-thirds of the budget for "mandatory" spending:
> (such as social security)
> programs ^where the level of funding is decided by the
> number of people who is qualified for entitlements.
>
> Funding for the Department of Defense currently
> accounts for fully half of the federal discretionary budget.
> The president's request for 2007 was $439.3 billion for the
> To give some perspective on how much $439.3
> Department of Defense ("Dept. of Defense"). Besides this,
> billion is, a mere four percent of that budget, or $19 billion,
> the departments' budget does not include ongoing military
> could cut global poverty by half in just 10 years (Borgen.)
> costs in the Middle East. . . .

The year of the budget is added.

A statistic is placed earlier in the paragraph for more impact, and the source of the figure is stated.

An example that improves the definition of the term is added.

A comparison helps the reader understand the enormity of a figure.

English Language Learners

Direct students' attention to the citations added to the first and last paragraphs: (Stockholm) and (Borgen.) Explain that the writer correctly places the citations within parentheses. Although it is not included here, the full entry for each source would appear in a "Works Cited" page at the end of the paper.

Revising

Roberto's Revision Using a Peer Response

While reviewing the sample revision with the class, ask students to note Roberto's use of editing marks and strategies to make the changes recommended by the peer responder.

- The writer, Roberto, used a different color ink so that his changes stand out from the original.
- He drew a circle with an arrow around text that will be moved.
- He used an editor's symbol (the caret) to indicate where citations and text will be inserted.

Have students refer to the inside back cover of their book for a list of editing and proofreading marks. Require students to become familiar with and use the symbols. They will use the editing and proofreading marks in both academic and professional settings.

Revising **Focusing on Style**

Suggesting changes for another writer's draft can give students a better idea of how others may comment on their work. Draw their attention to the quotation by Sue Grafton. As they complete the **Try It!** activity, have them remember to look at the text "with a dispassionate eye." Because they're not the writer, they have the advantage of reading objectively and suggesting improvements. Encourage students to remember this when they consider a response to their writing.

Try It!
Answers

Possible Answers

1. **Word Choice** Change *cash* to *money* in the opening sentence, and change *lopsided* to *uneven* in the new second sentence (formal language). In the second paragraph, change *who is qualified* to *who are qualified* (subject-verb agreement), and consider using another word for *entitlements* (connotation).
2. **Sentence Fluency** Vary sentence beginnings in the second paragraph or combine ideas (*Congress* begins three consecutive sentences).

24

Revising **Focusing on Style**

Roberto also reviewed his writing for its flow and style. His thoughts below tell you what changes he planned to make.

Word Choice

"I can use more formal language in some spots. I need to change some words that might have the wrong connotation. These changes will help me better defend my position."

Sentence Fluency

"I could combine related sentences to improve the flow. The reader will then be able to follow my argument from one point to the next. I could also expand a sentence here and there."

Try It!

Review the second revision of Roberto's essay (page 23). What two or three changes would you make in his word choice? Name two ways in which you would improve his sentence fluency. Compare your ideas to Roberto's revisions on the next page.

"Learn to evaluate your own work with a dispassionate eye. . . . The lessons you acquire will be all the more valuable because you've mastered your craft from within."

—Sue Grafton

English Language Learners

Some students will benefit from a review of connotation, or shades of meaning. Read aloud each pair of synonyms and have students compare the feelings each term evokes:

- inspect, observe
- excessive, unreasonable
- difference, discrepancy
- guard, protect
- blend, combine

Roberto's Revisions for Style

After reviewing the style and sound of his writing, Roberto focused on improving his word choice and sentence fluency.

Writing

> money
> How much ~~cash~~ does it take to make a country feel
>
> secure? Worldwide military spending had reached 1.2 trillion
>
> dollars by 2006, with the United States responsible for a
> disproportionate   While
> ~~lopsided~~ amount (Stockholm). ~~The~~ 2005 defense budget for
>   and
> China was $62.5 billion, ~~The~~ defense budget for 11 countries
>
> in the European Union totaled $185.8 billion. ~~But~~ the United
>
> States spent $420.7 billion ("U.S. Military Spending").
>   With the numbers telling the story,
> That's 43 percent—close to half—of the world's total. It's
>
> obvious that this country's spending for national defense is
>
> excessive and should be reduced.
>
> In the United States, national defense falls under
>
> a category of the federal budget called "discretionary"
>
> spending. Congress decides on the level of resources
> allocated to   and
> ~~set aside for~~ any specific area, ~~Congress decides~~ where
>
> to increase or decrease funds. ~~Congress earmarks~~ the
>   is earmarked
> other two-thirds of the budget for "mandatory" spending:
>
> programs (such as social security) where the level of funding
> determined   eligible
> ~~is decided~~ by the number of people who ~~is~~ qualified for
> benefits
> ~~entitlements~~.
>
> Funding for the Department of Defense currently
>
> accounts for fully half of the federal discretionary budget.
>
> The president's request for 2007 was $439.3 billion for the
>
> Department of Defense ("Dept. of Defense"). To give . . .

Sentences are combined to improve sentence fluency.

A phrase is added to further support the writer's thesis.

Sentence beginnings are varied.

Word choice is improved throughout the essay.

Revising Roberto's Revisions for Style

Focus on the idea mentioned in the third margin note—varying sentence beginnings. Note that writers sometimes inadvertently write too many sentences in the same form. This can make the prose sound choppy and singsong. Varying sentence beginnings is a good way to make sure that the sentences are varied all the way through, in length and form especially. Suggest that students

- turn ahead to the information on SE page 82 about varying sentence beginnings;
- read Roberto's draft aloud, listening to the rhythm and keeping alert for repeated words and phrases;
- watch for too many compound sentences joined by the same coordinating conjunction (usually *and*); and
- compare the beginnings of each paragraph to make sure they are varied as well.

Editing Checking for Conventions

Remind students that probably the most effective way to catch errors in their draft is to enlist the help of an outside reader. A thoughtful reader is more likely to find mistakes than the writer who made the errors.

Remind them also to make any changes in a different color ink so they stand out. This way a correction is easy to spot when finalizing the essay.

Try It!
Answers

All conventions errors from the excerpt are marked on SE page 27.

Editing Checking for Conventions

Roberto's last step in the process was to check for punctuation, capitalization, spelling, and grammar errors. He used the "Proofreader's Guide" in the back of his *Write Source* textbook and the checklist below.

Conventions

"I'll look carefully at my essay for punctuation, capitalization, spelling, and grammar errors."

PUNCTUATION

_____ **1.** Do I use end punctuation correctly?

_____ **2.** Do I use commas correctly?

_____ **3.** Do I correctly italicize or use quotation marks for titles?

_____ **4.** Do I use apostrophes correctly?

MECHANICS (CAPITALIZATION AND SPELLING)

_____ **5.** Have I capitalized all the proper nouns and adjectives?

_____ **6.** Have I spelled words correctly?

_____ **7.** Have I used the spell-checker on my computer?

_____ **8.** Have I used abbreviations correctly?

GRAMMAR

_____ **9.** Do I use the proper tense and voice for my verbs?

_____ **10.** Do my subjects and verbs agree in number?

_____ **11.** Do my pronouns clearly agree with their antecedents?

_____ **12.** Do I use the right words *(there, their, they're)*?

DOCUMENTATION

_____ **13.** Are sources properly presented and documented?

Try It!

Find two errors in Roberto's revised draft on page 25. Did you find the same errors as he found? (See page 27.)

English Language Learners

Students can confuse *their, there,* and *they're* in writing. Reinforce understanding of these terms by reviewing their definitions.

- *their* (possessive form of personal pronoun *they*): The campers unloaded their sleeping bags from the van.
- *there* (adverb tells where): Tom left his briefcase there.
- *they're* (contraction of *they are*): They're picking me up after the game.

Have students complete the following sentences with *their, there,* or *they're.*

1. They met _____. *(there)*
2. _____ reading each other's essay. *(They're)*
3. After class, _____ essays will be collected. *(their)*
4. Did they decide when _____ meeting again? *(they're)*
5. A teacher can be _____ to help them. *(there)*

Writing

Roberto's Editing

Here is a sample of Roberto's editing. (See the inside back cover of this textbook for common editing and proofreading marks.)

> A proper noun is capitalized, and subject-verb agreement is corrected.

> A numeric expression is corrected, and a misplaced apostrophe is fixed.

> Misspelled and misused words are corrected.

. . . Congress decides on the level of resources allocated to any specific area and where to increase or decrease funds. The other two-thirds of the budget is earmarked for "mandatory" spending: programs (such as ~~s~~ocial ~~s~~ecurity) where the level of funding is determined by the number of people who ~~is~~ ^are^ eligible for benefits.

Funding for the Department of Defense currently accounts for fully half of the federal discretionary budget. The president's request for 2007 was $439.3 billion for the Department of Defense ("Dept. of Defense"). To give some perspective on how much $439.3 billion is, a mere ^4^ ~~four~~ percent of that budget, or $19 billion, could cut global poverty by half in just 10 years (Borgen). Besides this, the department's budget does not include ongoing military costs in the Middle East. The Department of Education ^merited^ ~~meritted~~ a request of just $56.8 billion—about an eighth of the defense budget; and the amount budgeted for health was even less: $53.1 billion ("FY '07"). Moreover, the 2007 defense budget had increased 14 percent over the 2005 budget ("Dept. of Defense"), while the education and health budgets decreased 9 and 5 percent respectively ("Education Dept.," "Budget"). Priorities ^seem^ ~~seam~~ a bit skewed here.

English Language Learners

Explain that the subject-verb agreement error in the last line of paragraph 1 occurred because the noun and verb did not agree in number. Point out that the misplaced apostrophe in paragraph 2 would have been correct if referring to more than one department.

Editing Roberto's Editing

Discuss the way that Roberto presents statistics. Note that this is a matter of making a style choice. The goal is to be consistent. Point out examples such as the following:

- Numbers below 10, even fractions, that are used in a general way, are spelled out *(two-thirds of the budget)*.
- Numbers 10 and above are written as numerals *(in just 10 years)*. Note, though, that a number that begins a sentence must be spelled out.
- Years are given as numerals *(the 2007 defense budget)*.
- Large dollar amounts are given as numerals. Note also that the symbol *$* is used instead of the word *dollar ($493.3 billion)*—however, amounts below $10 would be spelled out *(a five-dollar bill)*.
- Percents are written as numerals, but the percent symbol *(%)* is *not* used in formal writing.

✱ For more on styles for writing numbers, see SE page 658.

Publishing Sharing Your Writing

Note that Roberto's persuasive essay is an opinion piece about an important current topic, like the essays published in the editorial section of the newspaper. One way of publishing his essay would be to submit it to his school or local newspaper.

Publishing Sharing Your Writing

Roberto used the information below to produce a clean and effective copy of his final essay. Then he shared his essay with his class.

Tips for Handwritten Copies

- Use blue or black ink and write clearly.
- Write your name according to your teacher's instructions.
- Skip a line and center your title on the first page; skip another line and begin your essay.
- Indent each paragraph and leave a one-inch margin on all four sides.

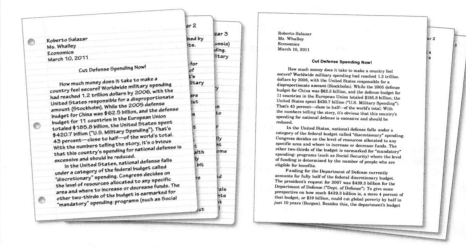

Tips for Computer Copies

- Use an easy-to-read font set at 12-point type size.
- Double-space the text and set your margins so that you have a one-inch space around the outside of each page.
- For more tips on using a computer, see pages 91–95.

Roberto's Final Copy

Roberto submitted his final essay with confidence. He felt that his writing met his goals and satisfied the terms of the assignment.

Roberto Salazar
Ms. Whalley
Economics
March 10, 2011

Cut Defense Spending Now!

How much money does it take to make a country feel secure? Worldwide military spending had reached 1.2 trillion dollars by 2006, with the United States responsible for a disproportionate amount (Stockholm). While the 2005 defense budget for China was $62.5 billion, and the defense budget for 11 countries in the European Union totaled $185.8 billion, the United States spent $420.7 billion ("U.S. Military Spending"). That's 43 percent—close to half—of the world's total. With the numbers telling the story, it's obvious that this country's spending for national defense is excessive and should be reduced.

In the United States, national defense falls under a category of the federal budget called "discretionary" spending. Congress decides on the level of resources allocated to any specific area and where to increase or decrease funds. The other two-thirds of the budget is earmarked for "mandatory" spending: programs (such as Social Security) where the level of funding is determined by the number of people who are eligible for benefits.

Funding for the Department of Defense currently accounts for fully half of the federal discretionary budget. The president's request for 2007 was $439.3 billion for the Department of Defense ("Dept. of Defense"). To give some perspective on how much $439.3 billion is, a mere 4 percent of that budget, or $19 billion, could cut global poverty by half in just 10 years (Borgen). Besides this, the department's budget does not include

Publishing Roberto's Final Copy

Focus on the title Roberto chose for his essay. What strategy would students say he used? (The title serves as a call to action.) Challenge students to think of other possible titles and to identify the strategy they used in devising them. For example:

- Take a position: It's Time to Reduce Military Spending
- Be creative: We Can Get By with a Smaller Piece of the Pie
- Use a line from the essay: Dismantle the Military Behemoth
- Be clever: Just Say "Less"

Have students respond to these questions about choosing a title:

- How important it is to give a clue to the content of an essay in its title?
- Is it more important to draw readers in with something catchy?
- Is it possible to do both?

✳ For more about choosing a title, see SE pages 252 and 265.

To demonstrate how much the essay changed between the first draft (SE pages 18–19) and the final, compare the two versions by having volunteers read each one aloud to the class, paragraph by paragraph.

Emphasize that different types of writing require different amounts of revision—depending both on the writer's experience and the complexity of the topic. Students may find that at times they need to make extensive changes to their first draft based on the information they learn about the topic and the requirements of the assignment.

Salazar 2

ongoing military costs in the Middle East. The Department of Education merited a request of just $56.8 billion—about an eighth of the defense budget; and the amount budgeted for health was even less: $53.1 billion ("FY '07"). Moreover, the 2007 defense budget had increased 14 percent over the 2005 budget ("Dept. of Defense"), while the education and health budgets decreased 9 and 5 percent respectively ("Education Dept.," "Budget"). Priorities seem a bit skewed here.

As the U.S. military devours more and more of the world's military spending pie, it is clear that decreasing our defense budget would have little effect on our military capability relative to that of other countries. Even if the defense budget were cut in half, the next two big spenders combined—China and Russia—wouldn't come near our level of spending. The U.S. would still have the richest military in the world.

Further, the need for our current level of military preparedness is questionable. First, the U.S. is surrounded by friendly neighbors. The likelihood of being attacked on our soil is slim. Second, Charles Peña of the Coalition for a Realistic Foreign Policy and an analyst for MSNBC television says, "The real threat to the United States no longer consists of nation states, but the terrorist threat represented by al-Qaeda, which is relatively undeterred by the U.S. military" ("More"). In other words, increased military funding will not prevent terrorism. The terrorist legacy will change only as the world addresses conditions that generate unrest.

Additionally, the public widely supports reduced military spending. A 2005 poll by the University of Maryland showed 65 percent of respondents would cut defense spending (Soto). Another 2005 poll by the Pew Research Center showed that 36 percent of respondents strongly favor lower military spending as a way to reduce the budget deficit ("Federal"). There are also many organizations and Web sites that support decreased defense spending. Congress should take note. Although defense spending benefits the defense contractors and other

Salazar 3

businesses to the tune of $230 billion (Borgen), these businesses do not make or break the economy. If they lost some government contracts, they could adapt to the market (convert their production to nonmilitary use). Many defense contractors had to do this after WWII.

It is not idealistic to believe that huge military budgets are an antiquated way of dealing with potential conflict. Humanitarian efforts can make a huge difference in the very need for defense, and, contrary to "hawkish" thinking, when conflict does arise, peaceful resolutions are possible. It's time to dismantle the military behemoth and put those funds to better use.

Assessing the Final Copy

The teacher used a rubric like the one found on pages 254–255 to assess Roberto's final copy. (A **6** is the best score for each trait.) The teacher wrote comments under each trait.

Rubric Checklist

__4__ **Ideas**
Your reasoning is clear, and your choice of details makes your argument very convincing. The answer to an opposing argument could be stronger.

__5__ **Organization**
You clearly state your position in the beginning, in each middle paragraph you offer background and support your opinion, and you make a call to action in the ending.

__5__ **Voice**
You obviously care about this issue. Your voice conveys a sense of urgency that fits the topic.

__5__ **Word Choice**
You use precise, formal language and explain unfamiliar terms.

__5__ **Sentence Fluency**
You use a wide variety of sentences. Your sentences read smoothly from one idea to the next.

__6__ **Conventions**
Your writing follows the rules of writing and is free of careless errors.

Assessing the Final Copy

If students are familiar with rubrics, provide practice using the rubric.

■ Distribute photocopies of the reproducible Assessment Sheet (TE page 766).

■ Ask students to cover the Rubric Checklist on the page before reviewing the final copy.

■ Have students review the goals for persuasive writing (SE page 14), and use the rubric (SE pages 254–255) to fill out the assessment sheet, assigning the score they think is appropriate for each trait.

■ Then have students compare their own assessments to the teacher's assessment.

■ Discuss their scores as a group. In what ways do they agree with the sample assessment? In what ways do they disagree?

Advanced Learners

To stimulate a deeper evaluation of the final copy, have pairs of students review each other's checklists. Where do they agree? Where do they differ? Can they reach a consensus for each score?

Reflecting on Your Writing

Emphasize the importance of taking the time to reflect on a completed essay. Note that the amount of time students will spend on reflecting will vary, depending on their preferences. Students might

- complete just the sentence starters shown on the reflection sheet;
- complete the sentence starters *and* add other thoughts about their experience; or
- write their reflections in the form of a journal entry (either as part of their writer's notebook or on a separate page that they can file with the finished essay).

Encourage students to look back at their reflections from previous assignments before beginning a new essay. The reflections will remind them of the skills they need to work harder on and techniques that were especially helpful.

Finally, for their future reference, have students answer the sample question 6. (Yes, it is best to cite a source that provided the statistics the writer used to calculate more statistics.)

Reflecting on Your Writing

Roberto filled out a reflection sheet after he completed his essay. This helped him think about the assignment and plan for future writing tasks.

Roberto Salazar
Ms. Whalley
Economics
March 13, 2011

Persuasive Essay: *Cut Defense Spending Now!*

1. **The best part of my essay is . . .**
   the ending. It expresses my feelings concisely and powerfully.

2. **The part that still needs work is . . .**
   the opposing argument. It's a little weak.

3. **The most important part of my prewriting and planning was . . .**
   my fact finding. I was alarmed at what I found, and I think this came through in my voice.

4. **During revising, I spent a lot of time dealing with . . .**
   adding details and refining word choice.

5. **What I've learned about this type of essay is . . .**
   that it's important to care about my topic. Without that, it would be difficult to convince others to support my position.

6. **Here is one question I still have . . .**
   If I derive a figure, fact, or detail from a source's statistics, do I cite that source?

Advanced Learners

Roberto's response to item 6 shows that he is uncertain about how to cite a particular source. Have partners research the rules and procedures for citing various types of sources. Each pair can cover one type of source, for example, statistics, quotations, and so on. Then have them compile the findings in a chart. Display the charts in the classroom so that students can use them to check their citations.

Using a Rubric

The rubrics in this book are graphic representations of accepted standards for the six traits of good writing (ideas, organization, voice, word choice, sentence fluency, and conventions). In other words, they help writers evaluate their writing according to a given scale.

Using a rubric throughout the process of your formal writing will result in a better paragraph, essay, or report. During prewriting, review the rubric so you know what's expected. During writing and revising, compare your writing to the ratings in the rubric. When you finish writing, check the rubric once more. Use a rubric throughout the process, and your writing will be the best it can be.

- **Understanding Rubrics**
- **Reading a Rubric**
- **Getting Started with a Rubric**
- **Revising and Editing with a Rubric**
- **Assessing with a Rubric**
- **Assessing in Action**
- **Assessing a Persuasive Essay**

"It is only through evaluation that value exists: and without evaluation the nut of existence would be hollow."

—Friedrich Nietzsche

Using a Rubric

Objectives
- understand the rating scale on a rubric
- learn how to read a rubric
- use a rubric to assess writing

Note that the following pages focus on the rubric for persuasive writing and refer students to the full rubric (SE pages 254–255). Have students compare and contrast the persuasive rubric with the other three rubrics included in the book: narrative (SE pages 150–151), expository (SE pages 198–199), and response to literature (SE pages 310–311). Note that even though each rubric varies slightly from the others, the rubrics are strongly related, so that becoming familiar with the wording on one will help students read all rubrics.

Understanding Rubrics

Without a rubric to guide them, students (and teachers) would probably assign one overall rating to a piece of writing, based on content and correctness. Explain that perhaps the biggest advantage to the rubric system is that it is designed as the writer's tool. A rubric allows the writer (and teacher) to assess and talk about writing in a deeper, more productive way. Assure students that the more they use the rubric system with their own writing, the easier it will become to pinpoint strengths and weaknesses in all writing, thereby helping them to improve their skills as a writer. In addition to getting better grades on their written work, they will spend less time revising, too.

Understanding Rubrics

A **rubric** is simply a rating scale. Have you ever rated the popularity of something on a scale of 1 (terrible) to 10 (fantastic)? With rubrics, you can rate your writing—in this case, on a scale of 6 (amazing) to 1 (incomplete).

| 6 Amazing | 5 Strong | 4 Good | 3 Okay | 2 Poor | 1 Incomplete |

The quality of any piece of writing can be rated on the basis of six traits: *ideas, organization, voice, word choice, sentence fluency,* and *conventions.* (For an introduction to these traits, see pages **46–90**.) An essay may be well organized (score of 5) but have repetitive, general word choice (score of 3).

Rating Guide

Here's a brief description of the rating scale.

A **6** means that the writing is **amazing**.
It far exceeds expectations for a certain trait.

A **5** means that the writing is very **strong**.
It clearly meets the requirements for a trait.

A **4** means that the writing is **good**.
It meets most of the requirements for a trait.

A **3** means that the writing is **okay**.
It needs work to meet the main requirements for a trait.

A **2** means that the writing is **poor**.
It needs a lot of work to meet the requirements of a trait.

A **1** means that the writing is **incomplete**.
The writing is not yet ready to be assessed for a trait.

English Language Learners

Help students conceptualize the term *trait* by explaining that it means "features or characteristics that are unique and revealing." Point out that traits such as honesty, kindness, and loyalty are important traits to look for in a friend. Have students discuss why organization is an essential trait for any piece of writing.

Reading a Rubric

Rubrics in this book are color coded according to the trait. *Idea* ratings appear in a green strip, *organization* in a pink strip, and so forth. There is a description for each rating to help you assess your writing for a particular trait.

Rubric for Persuasive Writing

6 Ideas	5	4
The position is convincingly presented and supported; it compels the reader to act.	The position is supported with logical reasons; an important objection is countered.	Most of the reasons support the writer's position. An objection is addressed.
Organization		
All parts of the essay work together to build a very thoughtful, convincing position.	The opening states the position, the middle provides clear support, and the ending reinforces the position.	Most parts of the essay are organized adequately except for one part.
Voice		
The writer's voice is completely confident, knowledgeable, and convincing.	The writer's voice is persuasive, knowledgeable, and respectful.	The writer respects the audience but needs to sound more persuasive or knowledgeable.

Guiding Your Writing

A rubric helps you . . .

- **plan your work**—knowing what is expected;
- **create a strong first draft**—focusing on *ideas, organization,* and *voice;*
- **revise and edit your work**—considering each trait; and
- **assess your final draft**—rating the traits throughout the whole piece of writing.

 Think about the rubric. Read the level 5 descriptions above and consider what they have to say about ideas, organization, and voice in persuasive writing. What should the essay include? What should each part of the writing do? How should the writer's voice sound?

Reading a Rubric

Acknowledge that while it can be difficult to assess one's own writing objectively, students who use rubrics discover that the objective quality of the rubric helps them identify their strengths along with areas of weakness. When students ask an outside reader to evaluate any piece of writing, it can confirm what the writer believes is good about the piece and provide a bonus—the reader's ideas for improving it. Receiving this guidance during the rather lonely task of writing will benefit the writer who sincerely wants to improve.

 Think about the rubric.

Answers

1. The essay should include a clear position statement and logical reasons to support it, as well as a response to an objection.
2. The opening describes the writer's position, the middle gives reasons to support the position, and the end sums up the argument.
3. persuasive, knowledgeable, respectful

Getting Started with a Rubric

Have students turn to the persuasive rubric (SE pages 254–255) and compare it with the goals—the Traits of Persuasive Writing—shown on this page. Point out that the goals essentially correspond to the rubric's description of a strong score of 5.

Point out that the rubrics in the student edition are designed to be used in conjunction with the advice and samples of writing in the book. Also point out that the descriptions of lower-scoring traits can be helpful in describing what to avoid. Explain that the following pages discuss each trait in detail. Further information is available throughout the other units. Encourage students to make use of the index and to use the book as their writing guide. They may find immediate information to help them with writing assignments for other classes.

Getting Started with a Rubric

Each of the writing units in this book includes a page like the one below. This page, which is arranged according to the traits of writing, explains the main requirements for developing the essay in the unit. Studying the "goals" page will help you get started with your planning.

222

Understanding Your Goal

Your goal in this chapter is to write a persuasive essay that states a position about an ethical issue and argues logically to defend the position. The traits listed in the chart below will help you plan and write your essay of argumentation. You can also use the rubric on pages 254–255 to guide your writing.

Traits of an Essay of Argumentation

- **Ideas**
  Select a topic that involves an ethical controversy, write a clear position statement, and include reasons that support the position.

- **Organization**
  Create a beginning that states your position, a middle that provides support and answers an objection, and an ending that restates your position. Use transition words and phrases to connect your ideas.

- **Voice**
  Use a voice that shows understanding of the controversy and commitment to a specific position about it.

- **Word Choice**
  Choose fair and precise words to state and defend your position.

- **Sentence Fluency**
  Write clear, complete sentences with varied beginnings and lengths.

- **Conventions**
  Eliminate errors in punctuation, capitalization, spelling, and grammar.

 Literature Connections: You can read the introduction to *A Vindication of the Rights of Women* by Mary Wollstonecraft as an example of an essay of argumentation.

A Closer Look at Understanding Your Goal

The following steps will help you get an overview of the assignment in each writing unit.

1. **Read through the traits chart** to familiarize yourself with the unit's goals.
2. **Focus on ideas, organization, and voice** at the start of the project, when you are prewriting and writing. These traits form the foundation of good writing.
3. **Identify specific requirements** for each trait (such as using "reasons and supporting facts" and "a confident, positive, and convincing voice").
4. **Ask questions** if you aren't sure about any part of the assignment.

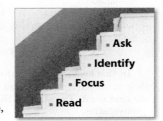

- Ask
- Identify
- Focus
- Read

A Special Note About the Traits

Different traits are important at different stages of the writing process. The following chart shows when the specific traits are important.

During **prewriting** and **writing**, focus on the *ideas, organization,* and *voice* in your work.

During **revising**, focus on *ideas, organization, voice, word choice,* and *sentence fluency.* (For some assignments, your teacher may ask you to pay particular attention to one or two of these traits.)

During **editing** and **proofreading**, concentrate on *conventions*— spelling, punctuation, capitalization, and grammar.

When you are **assessing** your final copy, consider all six traits. (For some assignments, your teacher may ask you to assess the writing for just a few of the traits.)

Exercise

Review the goals on page **36**. Then write a persuasive paragraph defending a position. Keep the traits in mind as you write.

Before students begin writing the paragraph for the **Exercise** activity, review the basic skills for writing a paragraph. Remind them that a single-paragraph work should

- begin with a topic sentence that presents the main idea,
- continue with body sentences that include solid supporting details, and
- close with a statement that sums up the position.

Have students read the sample persuasive paragraph on SE page 583 to get a sense of the structure.

✳ For more about basic paragraph skills, see SE pages 577–588.

Revising and Editing with a Rubric

38

Try It!
Answers

Possible Answers

The writing merits a score of 4 for the trait of "ideas."

- It clearly states the writer's position: More people should use E85 fuel.
- It presents three arguments in support of the position:
  (1) Corn is a renewable resource.
  (2) It can be grown domestically instead of having to be drilled for abroad.
  (3) It burns cleaner than gas.
- One argument does not support the position: Farmers also use corn to feed animals.
- An objection is addressed: the claim that it takes more energy to produce ethanol than the fuel saves.

Revising and Editing with a Rubric

6 The position is convincingly presented and supported; it compels the reader to act.

5 The position is supported with logical reasons; an important objection is countered.

4 Most of the reasons support the writer's position. An objection is addressed.

In this book, the pages that deal with revising and editing begin with a rubric strip. Each strip focuses on one trait of writing and will help you improve your first draft. The strip on these two pages focuses on the *ideas* for an essay of argumentation.

How do I use these rubric strips?

A rubric strip can help you look objectively at your writing. Focus on one trait (or strip) at a time.

- Begin by reading the goal for that specific trait and then read your writing with that in mind.
- Look at the description for writing that rates a 5 (strong). Does your writing match the description? If not, check the other rating descriptions until you find a match.
- If you're not satisfied with that rating, try to strengthen that trait in your writing.

Try It!

Review the persuasive paragraph below. Rate it for its ideas, using the rubric strip above, and give reasons for your rating.

> There are a lot of benefits to be realized if more people used E85, a blend of 85 percent ethanol and 15 percent gasoline, in their vehicles. Ethanol is a fuel made from corn, a renewable resource. We could grow our fuel here instead of drilling for it in other countries. Farmers would certainly benefit if demand for ethanol increased; their corn feeds animals, too. Finally, ethanol burns cleaner than gas, so it benefits the environment, as well. Some people think that it takes more energy to produce ethanol than it saves, but recent studies have refuted that notion. It's clear that ethanol is a winner all around.

Struggling Learners

Have writing partners work together to complete the **Try It!** activity. Encourage them to use a graphic organizer, such as a concept map, to note the position statement, supporting reasons, objection, and counter to the objection. They should base their rating on the completeness of the organizer.

Advanced Learners

Challenge students to expand the persuasive paragraph on ethanol into a short essay. Have writing partners research additional pros and cons of using the fuel and share their findings with the group. Then have students write first drafts of their essay independently. Afterward, have students discuss whether they incorporated the findings effectively.

Using a Rubric **39**

3 More supporting reasons and a more convincing response to an objection are needed.	**2** A clearer position statement is needed. Better support for the position must be provided.	**1** A new position statement and reasons are needed.

Writing

How can rubric strips help me revise and edit?

Once you have rated your writing for a given trait, you will see ways to improve your score. The writer of the paragraph on page 38 gave his ideas a score of 4, meaning that the writing meets *most* of the requirements for the trait. The score description told him just what he needed to do to improve his work: make *every* reason support his position. (Scores of 4 or lower offer suggestions for improving your writing.)

In the main writing units, each rubric strip is followed by brief lessons that will help you revise or edit your writing to improve that trait. There are separate rubric strips and lessons for each trait—ideas, organization, voice, word choice, sentence fluency, and conventions.

Making Changes

The writer decided to delete a reason that didn't really support his position and add another that did. He made the following changes.

An idea that doesn't support the writer's position is replaced with one that does.

. . . Farmers would certainly benefit if demand for ethanol
~~consumers would benefit, too, because ethanol blends are~~
increased; ~~their corn feeds animals, too.~~ Finally, ethanol
~~less expensive than pure gasoline.~~
burns cleaner than gas, so it benefits the environment,

as well. Some people think that it takes more energy to

produce ethanol than it saves, . . .

 Revise your paragraph for ideas. Revise the paragraph you wrote for the exercise on page 37, using the strip on these two pages as a guide.

Note one pitfall that writers may encounter: They may *think* they have clearly explained why a reason supports their argument without realizing that they have left something out and that readers won't interpret their reasoning the same way.

- For instance, in the sample, the detail that does not support the topic is *Farmers would certainly benefit . . . their corn feeds animals, too.*
- The writer might have meant to say: *Farmers would certainly benefit. They already grow corn to feed animals, so they could just increase their crop to provide corn for ethanol, too.*

Encourage students to make meaningful revisions by reading the draft out loud and asking themselves the following questions:
- Does every sentence say exactly what I mean it to say?
- Does everything I say support the topic?

Advanced Learners

Assign one student or pairs of students each a section of the persuasive rubric (SE pages 254–255) to review. Have them draft a description of how that section can be used while prewriting, writing a first draft, and revising. Have students share their drafts and comment on other students' work. Compile finished copies into a classroom reference.

Assessing with a Rubric

Remind students that they should use the rubric *as* they are writing also. It can be helpful to fill out an assessment sheet at any stage of writing if students want to take an in-depth look at how they are doing at any given point. So they don't forget when they wrote a particular assessment, remind students to write the following information at the top of the assessment:

- the date,
- the title of the paper (or the "working title"—a temporary title used to refer to it until they choose a final one), and
- what part they're working on.

Note that it can be helpful to compare assessments to make sure the desired improvements are made. (If they have written enough, it can also be helpful to ask an outside reader to review it.)

Assessing with a Rubric

Follow these four steps when you use a rubric to assess a piece of writing.

1. **Create an assessment sheet.** On your own paper, write each of the key traits from the rubric, preceded by a short line. Under each trait, leave two or three lines to allow for comments.
2. **Read the final copy.** First, get an overall feeling for the writing. Then read more carefully, paying attention to each trait.
3. **Assess the writing.** Use the rubric to rate each trait. Check the level 5 rubric description first and then go up or down the scale until you find the correct rating. Write the score next to the trait on your assessment sheet.
4. **Provide comments.** Under each trait, make whatever comments would be helpful for improving the writing.

Assessment Sheet	Title: _____
____ Ideas	
____ Organization	
____ Voice	
____ Word Choice	
____ Sentence Fluency	
____ Conventions	
	Evaluator: _____

Exercise

Assess your persuasive paragraph. Make an assessment sheet like the one above. Evaluate your paragraph using the rubric on pages 254–255. For each trait, write a comment about something you did well and something you'd like to improve. (See the sample on page 43.)

English Language Learners

Monitor students' use of the rubric by having them assess only one trait at a time. After students have made their initial assessment and changes, meet as a group so they can share how they improved their writing for that trait.

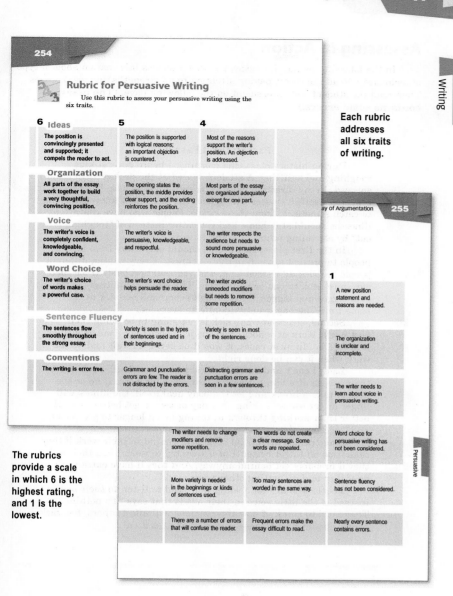

Using a Rubric **41**

Writing

254

Rubric for Persuasive Writing

Use this rubric to assess your persuasive writing using the six traits.

Each rubric addresses all six traits of writing.

6 Ideas	**5**	**4**
The position is convincingly presented and supported; it compels the reader to act.	The position is supported with logical reasons; an important objection is countered.	Most of the reasons support the writer's position. An objection is addressed.
Organization		
All parts of the essay work together to build a very thoughtful, convincing position.	The opening states the position, the middle provides clear support, and the ending reinforces the position.	Most parts of the essay are organized adequately except for one part.
Voice		
The writer's voice is completely confident, knowledgeable, and convincing.	The writer's voice is persuasive, knowledgeable, and respectful.	The writer respects the audience but needs to sound more persuasive or knowledgeable.
Word Choice		
The writer's choice of words makes a powerful case.	The writer's word choice helps persuade the reader.	The writer avoids unneeded modifiers but needs to remove some repetition.
Sentence Fluency		
The sentences flow smoothly throughout the strong essay.	Variety is seen in the types of sentences used and in their beginnings.	Variety is seen in most of the sentences.
Conventions		
The writing is error free.	Grammar and punctuation errors are few. The reader is not distracted by the errors.	Distracting grammar and punctuation errors are seen in a few sentences.

ay of Argumentation   **255**

1		
A new position statement and reasons are needed.		
The organization is unclear and incomplete.		
The writer needs to learn about voice in persuasive writing.		
The writer needs to change modifiers and remove some repetition.	The words do not create a clear message. Some words are repeated.	Word choice for persuasive writing has not been considered.
More variety is needed in the beginnings or kinds of sentences used.	Too many sentences are worded in the same way.	Sentence fluency has not been considered.
There are a number of errors that will confuse the reader.	Frequent errors make the essay difficult to read.	Nearly every sentence contains errors.

Persuasive

The rubrics provide a scale in which 6 is the highest rating, and 1 is the lowest.

Ask students to read and assess an editorial, a review, or another kind of persuasive article. Afterward, have students share their articles and assessment rubric with the class.

■ What were the strongest parts of the article?
■ Were there any weak points?
■ What was the average score for the article they chose?
■ Do they feel that reading the article with the six traits in mind helped them to understand it better than they would have without thinking about the traits? In which ways?

✷ The complete six-point rubric for persuasive writing is found on SE pages 254–255. Reproducible six-, five-, and four-point rubrics for persuasive writing are available on TE pages 769, 773, and 777.

Assessing in Action

Use the sample essay as the basis for a discussion of the way the writer has expressed emphasis. Note that the sample contains

- three exclamation points (one in the title, and one each at the end of the last two paragraphs) and
- two examples of italics for emphasis (in the last two paragraphs).

While these methods do give the reader a sense of how the writer imagines the words being read out loud, they are not characteristically used in serious informational writing (the tone for an essay such as this one). Encourage students to avoid using informal conventions when they need to maintain a more formal tone. Instead they should focus on making powerful word choices and using sentence structures to express emphasis.

✳ For more about exclamation points and italics for emphasis, see SE pages 605 and 636, respectively.

Assessing in Action

In the following persuasive essay, the writer shares information about a type of technology. Read the essay, paying attention to its strengths and weaknesses. Then read the student self-assessment on the following page. (**The essay contains some errors.**)

Psssst: Don't Pass It On!

During history class this morning, I heard several kids coughing and sniffling. A student seated at the desk next to mine sneezed. In my direction, without covering her mouth. This scene repeated itself in classes throughout the day. I just know I'm going to catch something from these sickos. People who have contagious illnesses should stay home and get better instead of "toughing it out" by attending school or going to work.

In the first place, sick people should stay away from healthy people to prevent spreading their sickness. Every winter, different people are sick all season long, and you could probably trace their exposure back to one or two people. The circle of infected people gets bigger and bigger. Even though everyone's not sick at the same time, the bug eventually affects everyone.

Second, someone who's sick is not going to be doing their best work. Work at school or on the job doesn't get done as well as it should be. In most cases, it would be better to wait and do the work when it can be done right.

Last, I can't understand why someone who is ill would place their health at a lower priority than school or work. If he or she doesn't take a break and let the body heal itself, the illness will linger or get worse. Taking off a day or two to get better is much better than working through it, taking much longer to get better, and infecting others.

Some people are afraid of getting behind in their work if they take time off to get better. But if they try to work when their sick, they'll probably get behind anyway. *And* they'll have extra work to do if they end up getting other people sick!

People who are not feeling well need to listen to their bodies instead of the little voice in their heads that says "it's nothing." They need to think of how their actions will affect others, too. Sick people should stay home—so they *don't* pass it on!

English Language Learners

Note that the essay uses the word *affects* at the end of paragraph 2. Clarify the easily confused words *affect* and *effect*. As a verb, *affect* means "to act on," as in *How does the new rule affect you?* As a noun, it means "feeling" or "emotion" and the stress is placed on the first syllable. As a verb, *effect* means "to bring about," as in *effect change.* As a noun, it means "the result." Mention that *affect* is most used as a verb, and *effect* as a noun. Tell students to remember to pair *affect* with *act*; both begin with the letter *a*.

Writing

Sample Self-Assessment

The student who wrote "Psssst: Don't Pass It On!" created the following assessment sheet to evaluate his essay. He used the persuasive rubric on pages 254–255 as his assessment guide. Under each trait, he wrote comments about the strengths and weaknesses of his writing.

Assessment Sheet   Title: _Psssst: Don't Pass It On!_

5   Ideas
My position is clear.
The essay could use a few more supporting facts.

4   Organization
My essay provides support for my position
in each middle paragraph.
The last reason might not be too convincing.

3   Voice
I sound interested.
The voice should be more formal.

4   Word Choice
My words help support my position.
I could have used more powerful words.

4   Sentence Fluency
I used different sentence structures.
I need to correct a fragment.

5   Conventions
I caught most errors.
I used "their" instead of "they're" in one sentence.

Evaluator: _Rueben_

Exercise

Review the assessment. On your own paper, explain why you agree with the responses above (or why you don't). Consider each trait carefully.

Exercise Answers

Possible Answers

Ideas **(4)**—There are not many specific details to support the arguments. There are no statistics, no quotations, no experts named or examples of specific illnesses.

Organization **(5)**—The beginning states the position, the middle supports the position, the ending sums up the argument and includes a call to action. Transition words and phrases are used.

Voice **(3)**—The voice is too casual and needs to be more persuasive and respectful. Note the attacking tone in words such as _sickos_ and _I can't understand why someone would_ . . .

Word choice **(4)**—The writer needs to include specialized terms to avoid repeating words, such as _sick, work,_ and _people._

Sentence fluency **(4)**—In addition to the sentence fragment, switching to the first-person point of view is jarring and works against the establishment of a knowledgeable tone.

Conventions **(5)**—The exclamation marks convey emotion without reason.

Assessing a Persuasive Essay

Note: For the narrative, expository, persuasive, and response to literature units, there are two additional writing samples that teachers can use with students for further assessment practice (TE pages 783–819). Copy Masters of the writing samples are available for students so that you can work together as a group. A reproducible, blank assessment sheet, based on the traits of writing, and genre-specific checklists allow you and students to rate the writing samples. Finally, a completed assessment sheet is provided to guide you through the assessment.

Assessing a Persuasive Essay

Read the essay below, focusing on its strengths and weaknesses. Then follow the directions at the bottom of the following page. (**The essay may contain errors.**)

Naomi Badalamenti
Ms. Sharp
English III
February 24, 2011

Make Financial Literacy Mandatory

A few months ago, an Arlington student named Damon started a job at a local grocery store. He gets paid by direct deposit. He opened a checking account and got a debit card. Within a month, Damon got a notice in the mail that he had overdrawn his account and the bank was charging him $29. Obviously, Damon mismanaged his money, but this really isn't a surprise since he was never taught how to plan a budget or use money from a bank account. His education, and that of all juniors and seniors at Arlington High, would be better if it included a mandatory course in money management.

Students should be taught how to plan their spending to help control expenses. They should develop 'practice' budgets that account for food, clothing, transportation, entertainment, computer, and communications expenses. This would help them understand that their income must cover their outlays (or cuts must be made!) They also need to know what will happen if they don't pay their bills on time.

Teachers could help students understand the maze of bank accounts. They could explain how to balance a checkbook and how to record every single transaction in order to do so. If someone doesn't tell students that an unpaid bounced check will result in their names being placed in a national database, preventing them from opening another checking account for five years ("Talking"), how will they know? They might think they're being smart and thrifty to hang on to a paycheck for months—but they'd certainly be disappointed to find that they couldn't cash it after only three or six months.

English Language Learners

Define the following terms for students and have them write out the definitions to refer to as they read the persuasive essay:

- direct deposit (a salary check that an employer places into their employees' bank accounts, usually electronically)

- overdrawn (more money withdrawn or debited from an account than is credited to it)
- outlays (monies spent)
- transaction (any action made to an account, such as a deposit or a withdrawal)
- interest (additional money that a borrower pays on a loan)
- compounds (interest that accumulates on loans or savings)

Badalamenti 2

And what about those offers for credit cards that they're already getting? Young adults don't understand how interest compounds. They are falling deep into debt because of credit cards, according to figures such as the following from Nellie Mae. Of undergraduate college students in 2008, 76% had at least one card; nearly half of those carried balances more than $1,000; and only 21% paid their balances in full each month ("Undergraduate"). High school is a good time for students to learn that although good credit is important to many aspects of their later lives, they have to manage their first credit card accounts well. Otherwise, they risk damaged credit or even bankruptcy.

Is financial literacy something that students should learn from their parents? Perhaps, and many parents are able to provide that education. Some, however, don't know enough about it themselves. Some don't have time. Some think it's a school's responsibility. In any case, a teacher, it seems, could devote more time to these important issues than parents or other adults could. High school students also may be more inclined to listen to a teacher.

A good number of students will be leaving home after high school, and they don't want to be dependent on their parents. There are many reasons why young people get in financial trouble; it would be great for them to know something about budgets and credit before they're faced with it head-on. Arlington should develop such a course to help students better prepare for their real-world futures.

Exercise

Assess this persuasive essay, using the rubric on pages 254–255 as your guide. To get started, create an assessment sheet like the one on page 40. Remember: After each trait, try to write one comment about a strength and one about a weakness.

Writing

Exercise Answers

Possible Answers

Ideas (5)—Strengths: The thesis is clear and supported; an objection is addressed. Weaknesses: The writer could add quotations; some things could be explained better (for example, at the end of paragraph 2, what happens if bills aren't paid?).

Organization (5)—Strengths: The essay starts with an interesting anecdote. Weakness: In paragraph 3, the detail about paychecks that expire doesn't support the topic.

Voice (4)—Strength: The voice is natural and interested. Weakness: The tone, partly because of the use of first person, is a little informal.

Word Choice (4)—Strength: The words support the thesis. Weaknesses: The writer should explain specialized terms (*outlays, balance, bounced check, interest, Nellie Mae*) and replace casual choices (*obviously, really, every single*).

Sentence Fluency (5)—Strength: Sentence forms vary. Weakness: In paragraph 4, end sentence 3 with a colon to introduce the statistics.

Conventions (4)—Strength: Few errors. Weaknesses: In paragraph 2, the word *practice* should be enclosed by double quotation marks, and end punctuation is required after (*or cuts must be made!*).

Teacher's Notes for Understanding the Traits

This overview of the traits includes some specific teaching suggestions for the unit. The description of each chapter will help you decide which parts of the unit to teach.

Writing Focus

Understanding the Traits of Writing (pages 47–50)

This chapter features a quick review of the six traits, a checklist for effective writing, and a chart showing how the traits can be applied to the writing process. A chapter is devoted to each of the six traits in this section of the text.

Ideas (pages 51–58)

This chapter encourages thinking and creativity in finding a topic, a focus, and a variety of supporting details.

Organization (pages 59–66)

This chapter includes deductive and inductive organization, and it offers several graphic organizers that can simplify organizing.

Voice (pages 67–72)

Voice has to do with writing style, word usage, approach to a topic, and so on. This chapter explores various aspects of voice.

Word Choice (pages 73–80)

This chapter helps students watch out for word choice problems such as unnecessary adjectives, redundancy, and clichés.

Sentence Fluency (pages 81–88)

This chapter provides examples to help students use a combination of short and long sentences, as well as a variety of sentence beginnings.

Conventions (pages 89–90)

This chapter provides tips for polishing the conventions of writing.

Presentation (pages 91–95)

This chapter examines effective design including the use of graphics.

Minilessons

Inductive Organization

■ **READ** "Organizing Inductively," on SE page 63. **USE** "Sardine School" as a guide and **OUTLINE** an essay on renewable energy. **READ** about organizing deductively on SE page 62. Then **WRITE** a deductive outline for the same topic.

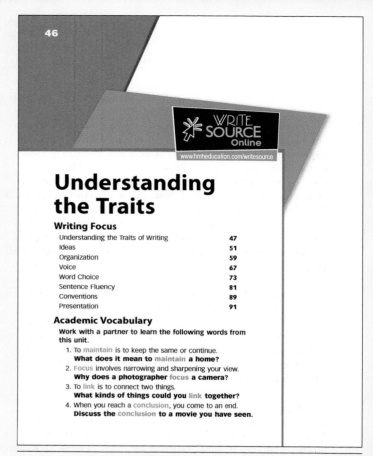

Academic Vocabulary

Work with a partner to learn the following words from this unit.

1. To maintain is to keep the same or continue.
   What does it mean to maintain a home?
2. Focus involves narrowing and sharpening your view.
   Why does a photographer focus a camera?
3. To link is to connect two things.
   What kinds of things could you link together?
4. When you reach a conclusion, you come to an end.
   Discuss the conclusion to a movie you have seen.

Levels of Diction Voice

■ **STUDY** the three "Other Forms of Diction" on PE page 71. Then **REWRITE** an article from a local or student newspaper in one of the three forms (your choice).

Ball or Batter? Word Choice

■ **CHOOSE** a sport that involves hitting, kicking, or throwing a ball. **WRITE** a paragraph describing a scene of intense action in that sport from a player's (doer of the action) point of view. **USE** active verbs. **REWRITE** the paragraph from the point of view of the ball (receiving action). **USE** passive verbs.

Check That! Conventions

■ **REVIEW** several papers you have written recently. What are some of your typical errors? **CHECK** the index in your textbook to find the pages that deal with those errors. **STUDY** those pages the next time you proofread a paper in order to avoid such errors.

47

Understanding the Traits of Writing

When a doctor does a physical examination, he or she checks a patient's blood pressure, height, weight, posture, circulation, breathing, and so on. When someone is in good health, all of these elements are in good working order. If, on the other hand, any of the elements are "out of order," the patient's health will suffer.

Similarly, a piece of writing can be evaluated by reviewing six key traits: *ideas, organization, voice, word choice, sentence fluency,* and *conventions.* If all six of these traits are strong, then the piece of writing will be effective. However, if there are problems with any of these traits, then the essay or article will not be as effective as it could be.

In this chapter, you'll get a quick overview of the six traits of writing, and you'll see how these traits fit into the writing process.

- ■ **Understanding the Six Traits**
- ■ **Using the Traits**
- ■ **Checklist for Effective Writing**

"What is written without effort is in general read without pleasure."

—Samuel Johnson

Understanding the Traits of Writing

Objectives
- understand each of the six traits of effective writing
- learn about specific concepts related to the traits
- practice applying the traits to writing

Discuss the idea that the six traits of writing can just as easily be considered the six traits of effective *reading.* Encourage students to remember that anything they read was—or should have been—written with the traits in mind. Therefore, they can look for the traits whenever they evaluate a piece of writing, whether for school or personal reading. Applying the traits can help students to

- ■ pinpoint what information the author thinks is most important;
- ■ decide whether the author argued a position effectively and, if so, observe how this was done;
- ■ see strong word choices in action; and
- ■ get ideas for writing techniques they can try.

Academic Vocabulary

Read aloud the academic terms, as well as the descriptions and questions. Model for students how to read one question and answer it. Have partners monitor their understanding and seek clarification of the terms by working through the meanings and questions together.

Understanding the Six Traits

Suggest that students tab this page so that they can quickly refer to it whenever they need a reminder of what to look for in each trait.

After students have completed the **Try It!** activity, invite them to share their answers. Be sure to solicit comments on both sides for each trait—after one student talks about her or his strongest trait, invite someone to share why that same trait is their weakest trait. Share your own thoughts about writing with the traits as well.

Understanding the Six Traits

Throughout this book, you'll use the six traits to make your writing the best it can be. Here is a brief description of each trait.

Ideas

The **ideas** in your writing include the topic, the focus (thesis), and the main supporting points and details. Ideas are the heart of writing—the message you want to communicate to your reader.

Organization

Organization refers to the way your writing begins, the order of the ideas in the middle, and the way your writing ends. By using logic and transitions, you can lead your reader step-by-step through your ideas.

Voice

Your writing **voice** reflects your personality, your feelings about the topic, your purpose in writing, and your relationship with the reader. Voice can be bubbly or angry, hopeful or sarcastic, formal or casual.

Word Choice

Word choice considers the quality of the nouns, verbs, and modifiers in your writing. Writers work with words the way jewelers work with gems.

Sentence Fluency

Sentence fluency refers to the flow of sentences and the rhythm of phrases and clauses. Some sentences meander like a melody. Others crack like a rim shot. Fluid sentences can make your writing memorable.

Conventions

Conventions are the rules of punctuation, capitalization, spelling, and grammar. Once upon a time, the rules of writing were taught as writing itself. Now, the rules are a separate consideration, especially important near the end of the writing process.

 Try It!

Reflect on the traits by answering the following questions:

1. Which trait challenges me the most? Explain.
2. Which trait is strongest in my writing? Explain.

Advanced Learners

Use student responses to the **Try It!** activity to form writing partners in the class. Pair a student who believes, for example, that sentence fluency is his or her strongest trait with a learner who identifies the trait as his or her weakest. Provide time for pairs to engage in dialogue as each new writing task is introduced here.

Using the Traits

Since no one can focus on all six traits at once, different traits are important at different stages in the writing process.

Prewriting

Ideas	Select a topic, gather details, choose your focus (thesis), and decide on main points.
Organization	Write your thesis statement and topic sentences, decide on a method of organization, and create a list or an outline.

Writing

Ideas	Connect all your ideas and details.
Organization	Write a beginning, a middle, and an ending, using the plan you have made.
Voice	Use a voice appropriate to your personality, topic, purpose, and reader.

Revising

Ideas	Revise your focus, main points, and details.
Organization	Check the order and unity of your paragraphs.
Voice	Adjust your voice as needed.
Word Choice	Make sure you use precise nouns, active verbs, and appropriate modifiers.
Sentence Fluency	Check your sentences for varied beginnings and lengths.

Editing, Proofreading, and Publishing

Conventions	Edit your work for punctuation, capitalization, spelling, grammar, and format.

Try It!

Write a notebook entry explaining which traits are most important early in the writing process and which are most important toward the end.

Using the Traits

Note that the ideas depicted in the graphic give only a general idea of when to focus on specific traits. For example, writers use conventions throughout the whole process—not just at the end. If they didn't use them, they would have trouble reading their drafts.

Individual writers may also find that they use slightly different strategies from the ones in the graphic. Some writers may spend time on word choice early in the process and focus on sentence fluency later.

Also note that the trait of voice develops as a writer gets more practice. A veteran writer tends to develop a consistent, unique voice. On the board, list the names of well-known writers such as Mark Twain, S. E. Hinton, Toni Morrison, and Ray Bradbury. Read aloud excerpts from their writing. Challenge students to match the excerpt with its author.

English Language Learners

Point out that this page is a more-detailed version of the box on SE page 37. Suggest that students tab this page or copy the information in their writer's notebook as a reference to use during the assessment process.

Checklist for Effective Writing

Have students compare the checklist, trait-by-trait, with the detailed explanation of each trait provided on SE page 48.

Note that this checklist relates to all writing and that students will find similar checklists geared to specific types or stages of writing throughout their book. Encourage them to consult the index whenever necessary to find the checklist that best suits their writing goals.

50

Checklist for Effective Writing

If a piece of writing meets the following standards, it exhibits the traits of effective writing. Check your work using these standards.

Traits Checklist

Ideas

_____ **1.** Is the topic interesting?
_____ **2.** Is there a specific focus and purpose?
_____ **3.** Do a variety of details support the focus?

Organization

_____ **4.** Is there a clear beginning, middle, and ending?
_____ **5.** Are the details arranged in the best order to support the focus?
_____ **6.** Do transitions and key words connect the ideas?

Voice

_____ **7.** Does the writing sound natural?
_____ **8.** Does the voice fit the topic and the purpose?
_____ **9.** Is the voice appropriate for the audience?

Word Choice

_____ **10.** Are the nouns specific and the verbs active?
_____ **11.** Are the modifiers colorful and necessary?

Sentence Fluency

_____ **12.** Do the sentences have rhythm and flow?
_____ **13.** Do the sentence beginnings and lengths vary?

Conventions

_____ **14.** Does the work follow the rules of punctuation, capitalization, spelling, and grammar?
_____ **15.** Is the work presented in a clear, correct format?

Struggling Learners

Provide students with guided practice on how to use the Traits Checklist. Distribute copies of a short letter from the editorial page of a local newspaper. Have students work together to assess the letter using the traits checklist. Afterward, have students share and explain their assessment.

51

Ideas

When writing, there is nothing more intimidating than staring at a blank piece of paper or an empty computer screen and waiting for an idea to come along. "Every writer I know has trouble writing," said Joseph Heller, author of *Catch-22*. Finding ideas is often the hardest part of the writing process. You need not only a topic and a main idea but also a number of supporting details.

Selecting a topic that interests you is the key to effective writing. "Write what you care about and understand," said writer Richard North Patterson. Being passionate about a topic creates stronger and more dynamic writing.

If, after staring at the computer screen for hours, an idea doesn't materialize, some creative thinking can often supply one. This chapter will help you generate ideas by developing a thinking attitude. You will also learn about the different types of supporting details and about using crots in writing.

- **Developing a Thinking Attitude**
- **The Creative Mind in Action**
- **Reviewing Possible Starting Points**
- **Using Effective Supporting Details**
- **Using Crots in Writing**

"Writing became such a process of discovery that I couldn't wait to get to work in the morning: I wanted to know what I was going to say."

—Sharon O'Brien

Objectives
- learn how to develop a thinking attitude
- understand what makes an effective supporting detail
- learn about the technique of using crots (small, essentially autonomous fragments, sentences, or paragraphs) to link ideas in writing

Discuss the quote by Sharon O'Brien and the idea that writing can be a "process of discovery." Note that this concept is helpful because it considers the existence of good ideas to be a given—the writer just needs to discover them.

Encourage students not only to take note of the methods for combating writer's block that are suggested in this section, but also to be alert to other helpful ideas they come across. As they find or think of the ideas, students should write them down in their writer's notebook (see SE pages 2–5) for a growing list of writing ideas and techniques to explore.

English Language Learners

Stress the importance of getting an idea down in writing, even if it isn't completely developed. Encourage students to jot down ideas as they come to mind. Suggest that they label each idea with a subject keyword, which can jog their memory later when they have time to expand the idea.

Copy Masters

Sensory Chart (TE p. 54)

Developing a Thinking Attitude

Reassure students that the idea of integrated thinking does not mean you expect them to be equally good at both styles of thinking. Still, those who believe they are right-brain thinkers shouldn't consider it hopeless to learn detail- and system-oriented thinking skills. Those who believe they are left-brain thinkers shouldn't consider it impossible to think creatively. All learners can use writing to develop their thinking skills. Not only will this help a writer communicate effectively, but also it will generate new ways to think about and solve problems in writing. On a practical level, analyzing one's mode of thinking can help students to know when to seek assistance.

"Always make room for the unexpected in yourself."
—Steve Martin

Developing a Thinking Attitude

It's a common myth that people use only 10 percent of their brains. In fact, you use 100 percent of your brain throughout the day, whether you're studying physics, writing an essay, watching TV, or eating a bowl of cereal. Thinking takes place even when you are asleep, and in both halves of your brain.

While some people may use one half of their brain more than the other, to be a complete thinker, you need to be "whole brained." The more balanced your thinking, the easier it is to develop effective ideas.

Learning About the Brain

Here is a short comparison of how the left and right parts of the brain operate.

Left Part	Right Part
■ processes information logically	■ processes information randomly
■ sees parts and arranges them into big picture	■ sees big picture first, then the details
■ completes tasks in order	■ jumps from one task to another
■ understands symbols easily	■ understands real objects easily
■ prefers using words	■ prefers using visuals
■ likes to make lists and schedules	■ *has to* make lists and schedules

Thinking to Write

There is no magic formula for forming and developing writing ideas. Whether you are a student writer or a professional writer, you use the same thinking skills. You observe, compare, analyze, evaluate, and solve.

Part of developing a thinking attitude is simply to have an open mind. Writer Robertson Davies said, "I don't get my ideas, they get me." This thought has been expressed by other writers who believe that ideas find them by chance instead of through any systematic thinking process.

Try It!

Try to become a balanced thinker. Decide which part of the brain you use more. Then find someone in class who uses the other half of his or her brain more. Discuss how each of you thinks as you carry out a big project like a research paper. How are your processes similar or different?

Advanced Learners

Have students spend a class period role-playing. If the student is primarily a left-brain thinker, have her or him role-play a right-brained thinker—and vice versa. Propose a problem—something that needs attention in school or in the community—and have students begin working on solutions. Then have students compare and contrast the methods they used with the ones they would use to approach the problem when thinking from their usual side of the brain.

Considering the Traits of Good Thinking

Having a thinking attitude will help you think more consistently and thoroughly. It will also help you complete any type of writing that you may be assigned. To develop a thinking attitude, you need to consider the following traits.

Thinking Traits

Endurance

Thinking can be a sprint or a marathon. If a good idea pops up right away, great. If it doesn't, be prepared to go the distance. Don't worry about time.

Curiosity

Curiosity may have killed the cat, but a lack of curiosity kills great ideas. Be curious, explore, and ask "Why" and "What if."

Concentration

Pick a comfortable place that is conducive to thinking. Noise and distractions often can't be avoided. Learn how to tune them out and stay focused on your goal.

Support

Look for detailed, accurate evidence to support an idea. Don't be satisfied with generalizations. The more support an idea has, the stronger it is.

Skepticism

Having a bit of skepticism is healthy when thinking. Look at an idea from all sides to test its validity. Question evidence and sources.

Openness

Be open to new or opposing viewpoints. Use them to test your own idea for weaknesses. Also be ready to change your ideas if research or discussion changes your opinion.

Try It!

Practice your thinking in a small group. Think of a problem at school or in your community and suggest a solution. Be sure to use all of the qualities described above. Have one member of the group record any examples of the thinking traits employed in the discussion.

Advanced Learners

Invite students to research the life of a famous educator. Have them focus their research on how the individual demonstrated the traits that make up a thinking attitude. Invite students to publish their findings on the class Web site.

Before students complete the **Try It!** activity, remind them that the member of the group who records examples from the discussion is basically *taking minutes*. Review what is involved in taking minutes for a meeting. Then, to give all students practice with this note-taking skill, divide the class into groups of three for the **Try It!** activity, and assign each person two thinking traits to focus on in their notes.

After students have completed the activity, have the groups review the minutes for accuracy. End by discussing students' experiences as a class.

- What problem did the group discuss?
- What is the proposed solution?
- Which thinking trait or traits were used to arrive at this conclusion?
- Which traits played the most influential part in the discussion?

✳ For more about taking meeting minutes, see SE page 532.

The Creative Mind in Action

Distribute photocopies of the reproducible Sensory Chart (TE page 825) for students to use as they do the activity.

Suggest that students expand on the **Try It!** activity on their own time:

- Once students have created a detailed list of questions about their chosen object, ask them to come up with the answers to those questions.
- Have them use that information as the basis for a written portrait of the object.
- Tell students they will not be graded for their work—rather, the purpose is for them to let themselves take the description in any direction they like. They can be meticulous and realistic or wild and impressionistic.
- When students have finished the portraits, have them read their work aloud to others and show the object (or a picture of the object) that inspired the work.

54

The Creative Mind in Action

When confronted with the word *creative*, many people panic, saying, "I'm not creative." Being creative doesn't mean you have to write a novel or develop something from nothing. "Creative" means *being imaginative,* and when applied to thinking, it means looking at something in a new way.

Use your mind creatively by making sensory observations: see, hear, taste, smell, and touch. Examining an object with your senses can get the creative process started. The resulting perceptions can trigger memories, which may develop into creative ideas. As the process continues, you explore, gather, shape, and fine-tune your ideas.

Thinking Creatively

Imagine you find a baseball cap. Notice the cap's parts: bill, crown, logo, and button. Then look closely at each part by asking yourself these questions.

A Creative Look at a Baseball Hat

- Has the bill been bent into a curve? Is it short, long, a different color than the crown?
- Is the crown striped or multicolored? Does it have a furry animal, cheese, or spinning propeller attached to it? Does it have a saying on it? Is the sweatband stained? Are there holes in it?
- Does the cap adjust with Velcro, a metal buckle, or plastic band? Is it sized small, medium, or large?
- Does its logo represent a college, a professional sports team, a special event, or an attraction? Is it custom printed?
- Does the cap smell new? Can you smell hair products, sweat, or oil?
- Rub the bill or wave the cap in the air. What sounds does it make?
- Bite the bill and crown. What does it taste like?
- Feel the fabric. Is it soft, stiff, scratchy? Is it wool or cotton?
- In which country was it made? What comes to mind when you think of that country?
- Imagine the process of how the cap was made, from raw materials to finished product.
- If the cap could tell you its story, what would it be?
- Imagine the cap was a gift. What was the occasion?
- What other creative ways are there to look at a cap?

Try It!

Put your creative mind in action. Focus on another common object and look at it in a variety of new ways. Record all of the questions that come to mind about it.

Struggling Learners

Using the sensory chart, work with the group to list the attributes of an object you display. Work especially with students who are having difficulty using descriptive words and those who are having difficulty forming questions.

Reviewing Possible Starting Points

During the year, you encounter a number of people, places, experiences, activities, trends, and beliefs. By applying a thinking attitude, many could be turned into writing topics. Listed below are a number of starting points organized according to the basic modes of writing. Just reviewing these ideas should prompt you to uncover interesting starting points for your own writing.

Traits

Expository

- Discuss one impact of the Iraq war on society in the United States.
- Explain how to make the perfect pizza.
- Explore the evolution of the personal computer.
- Explain the popularity of a particular novel or movie.
- Compare the presidencies of _____ and _____.
- Discuss global warming.

Persuasive

- Convince your school board to initiate an open-campus policy.
- Persuade a doubter of the reasons your favorite sports team will win.
- Identify the country's biggest problem and convince Congress to solve it using your recommendations.
- Argue for or against the increased use of public transportation.
- Persuade a postsecondary school to accept you.
- Persuade your state's governor to ban cell-phone use while driving.

Narrative

- Write about the worst day of work you have ever had.
- Recall the first day you met a good friend.
- Tell about an unforgettable family gathering.
- Write about a vacation horror story.
- Tell about a favorite concert you attended.

Descriptive

- Describe a place you go to get away from it all.
- Describe an influential teacher.
- Describe a popular music style.
- Describe a national park, forest, or monument.
- Describe your perfect job or career.

Try It!

Uncover four writing ideas that interest you by examining the people, experiences, and activities you come across each day. Try to find an idea for each of the writing modes listed above.

English Language Learners

Have students work in pairs and choose one starting point from each of the writing modes. Then have them brainstorm ideas for each starting point, using a cluster organizer.

Have all pairs meet to compare notes. Display their "thinking on paper" to remind them of this strategy when they write.

Reviewing Possible Starting Points

Refer students to the "Basics of Life" list (SE page 99) for an additional way to spark ideas for starting points.

Encourage students to use their work for the **Try It!** activity as the beginning of an ongoing list (in their writer's notebook or an electronic file) of ideas for future writing projects. Whenever they think of a promising topic, they can add it to the list for future reference.

Using Effective Supporting Details

Note that an effective piece of writing always **uses several different kinds of details** (*see below*). Talk with the class about why this is important. Possible responses include that effective writing should

- demonstrate the writer's thinking about the issue;
- show the writer's depth of knowledge about and interest in the topic; and
- convince a reader, if not by one reason, then perhaps by another.

Using Effective Supporting Details

There are many types of details you can use when writing about your topic. Your main idea, along with the purpose of your writing, determines which details are most effective. The key types of details are explained below and on the next page.

Facts are *details* that can be proven.

> In 1966, for the first time ever, five African Americans started for the Texas Western Miners in the NCAA basketball championship.

> When faced with impeachment as a result of his role in Watergate, President Richard Nixon resigned on August 9, 1974.

Statistics present *numerical information* about a specific topic.

> Making the *Lord of the Rings* films was an epic filmmaking process that included shooting more than 600 million feet of film, using 2,700 special-effects shots, and creating 1,600 pairs of Hobbit feet.

> With more than 900 wins and a winning percentage over .800, Tennessee coach Pat Summitt is the winningest coach in college basketball history.

Examples are statements that *illustrate a main point*.

> During the Victorian period of architecture, the Stick style was often overshadowed by other styles, but it had its own unique characteristics (main point). As its name suggests, the Stick style is known for its stickwork, the decorative patterns of boards on a house's exterior. Stick houses were always clad with wood siding. The stickwork created horizontal, vertical, or diagonal patterns on the siding, which imitated architecture from medieval Europe.

Anecdotes are *brief stories* that help to make a point about an idea. They are usually interesting and entertaining and can be more effective than a static list of details.

> Sometimes people's minds play tricks on them, and they need to take the time to look up information that they think they know. Explaining his embarrassing "potatoe" spelling incident, former vice president Dan Quayle admitted, "I should have caught the mistake on that spelling bee card, but as Mark Twain once said, 'You should never trust a man who has only one way to spell a word.'" When told that it was actually President Andrew Jackson and not Mark Twain he quoted, Quayle said, "I should have remembered that was Andrew Jackson who said that since he got his nickname 'Stonewall' by vetoing bills passed by Congress." Quayle was wrong again. He had confused Andrew Jackson with the Confederate general Thomas Jackson, who received the nickname "Stonewall" during the Civil War.

Teaching Tip: Use Several Different Kinds of Details

Advise students to get in the habit of marking their research notes with the types of details that are represented. Have them abbreviate the types, such as "STAT" for statistics, and so on. This way, when they are using their notes to plan their writing, they will see at a glance whether they have gathered a variety of details.

Quotations are *people's statements* repeated word for word. They usually offer powerful supporting evidence.

> Sometimes a comic observation can make a person think about an important topic. For example, comedian Jay London observed, "I told my therapist I was having nightmares about nuclear explosions. He said, 'Don't worry, it's not the end of the world.'" People may laugh at the idea, but when they actually think about it, the statement does remind them that they live in the nuclear age.

Definitions present the *meaning* of unfamiliar terms. Defining technical terms can be beneficial for the reader and clarify your writing.

> Greener vehicles may run on biodiesel, a renewable fuel derived from vegetable oil or animal fat.

Reasons answer *why* and can explain or justify ideas.

> Filmmakers should not be allowed to make sequels, especially ones with successive numbers in the titles. Producers should know that sequels lose money. Although these movies are made to capitalize on the success of the first film, no sequel has topped an original at the box office. With few exceptions, such as *Godfather II* and *Godfather III*, sequels almost never approach the quality of the original film. With each increasing title number, the film's originality decreases. Did moviegoers really need Jason X when Friday the 13th was enough? Most importantly, each sequel loses one or more "A" stars from the one before it. This clearly makes each movie less watchable.

Comparisons address the similarities or differences between two ideas or things. It is especially helpful to compare something new or unknown to something your reader understands.

> Although they were fought about 40 years apart, the war in Iraq is still similar to the Vietnam War. Most United States citizens did not know where Vietnam was in 1966. In 2006, after three years of war, 63 percent of U.S. citizens ages 18–24 could not find Iraq on a map. The U.S. entered both wars because of a perceived threat: Vietnam because of Communism and Iraq because of terrorism. Both wars were fought against a stubborn enemy that used guerrilla tactics. Early in each war, both Lyndon Johnson and George W. Bush declared that the mission was accomplished. They then saw their approval ratings plummet as the wars continued.

Try It!

Find an article that shows four of the detail types explained on this page and the previous one. On your own paper, write the examples that you find.

Traits

Remind students that using facts, statistics, and the ideas of others goes hand in hand with using them responsibly. For example, they must make sure to

- use the most current facts and statistics, unless drawing a "then and now" comparison;
- copy the details correctly from their sources (numbers and quotations are especially likely to contain errors and must be double-checked when copying);
- interpret the information correctly to avoid false reasoning;
- use quotations only in context;
- acknowledge and address the opposing viewpoint;
- reject the use of loaded or oversimplified language to influence the reader.

✱ More information about common logical fallacies is available on SE page 238.

Struggling Learners

Provide practice identifying key types of details. Have students select partners. Depending on the number of pairs, assign each pair one or more types of detail. Then ask them to search for examples of their details in newspaper or magazine articles. Have them label and display their examples in the classroom for reference while writing.

Using Crots in Writing

Point out that although the term *crots* may be unfamiliar, students are likely to have encountered the technique in poetry—and may even have used it in their own creative writing. Discuss reactions to the sample. Possible responses:

- The writing feels more immediate, as if the reader is sharing the writer's experience.
- The writing has a strong sensory effect. The sample evokes sight, sound, and touch (*too heavy to carry*).
- The sounds of the words take on greater importance.

Acknowledge that this form is better suited to narrative or creative writing than to academic writing. Have students use their observation skills to generate ideas and use the technique for their next journal entry or personal writing topic. Have them share their writing with a partner to see if it engages the reader's imagination. If they later use crots in expository or persuasive writing, students will need to revise for transitions later in the process.

"As each crot breaks off, it tends to make one's mind search for some point that has just been made—presque vu!—almost seen!"
—Tom Wolfe

Using Crots in Writing

Crot is an obsolete, odd-sounding word that means "*bit*" or "*fragment*." Writer Tom Wolfe revitalized crots as a writing technique during the 1970s. According to writer and teacher Winston Weathers, a crot "is fundamentally an autonomous unit characterized by the absence of any transitional devices that might relate it to preceding or subsequent crots." An entire essay can be a series of crots that are connected almost randomly. The ideas can be fragments, sentences, or paragraphs, and they are presented without traditional order or transitions.

Reading an essay that includes crots is like viewing the slides of a computer-generated presentation out of order and without graphics. "It will have you making crazy leaps of logic, leaps you never dreamed of before," Wolfe said. An effective series of crots can be a powerful form of writing that jolts the reader from one idea or image to the next.

Sample Essay

Read the following brief essay containing a series of crots and see if you can make the "crazy leaps of logic."

The Big Easy

Riding on the City of New Orleans. This train has got the disappearing railroad blues.

Mardi Gras 2008. Tons of plastic beads, green, gold, purple. Too heavy to carry, dropped and broken, lying in the road.

Long line for Mother's mountain-sized po' boy piled high with debris. Debris floating after the levees broke. Drove my Chevy to the levee, but the levee was dry.

Preservation Hall, dirty and small. Old gentlemanly trombonist with gnarled hands, lips permanently indented from mouthpiece, spit flying. When the saints go marching in. It's hard to be a saint in the city.

Now the boss singing—them who's got out of town, and them who ain't got left to drown, tell me, how can a poor man stand such times and live?

Try It!

Think about your time in high school and write a brief essay of crots about it. Don't worry about trying to connect or explain your ideas too deeply. Leave that to the imagination of the reader.

Organization

Once you have discovered an interesting writing idea and gathered supporting details, you must decide on an organizational pattern. Without clear organization, great ideas just get lost.

Often a topic fits easily into a particular pattern. For example, writing about the first time you met a friend would naturally fall into a narrative or storytelling pattern with a chronological order. Describing how to make the perfect pizza would fit the process pattern. A topic may fit more than one pattern, and it is up to you to determine the best method for presenting your ideas.

At times, an idea deserves a more creative approach. (See "Using Crots in Writing" on page 58.) Writing that breaks out of an organizational pattern and takes its own path is often more exciting and dynamic. Do not be afraid to experiment.

This chapter provides background information about organizing ideas effectively. It will help you learn different ways to structure your writing.

- **Understanding the Big Picture**
- **Following the Thesis Statement's Lead**
- **Organizing Deductively**
- **Organizing Inductively**
- **Using Graphic Organizers**
- **Using the Question-and-Answer Format**

"Complicated outlines tempt you to think too much about the fine points of organization, at a time when you should be blocking out the overall structure."

—Donald Hall

Organization

Objectives
- learn the basic structure of informational writing
- learn how a thesis statement affects the rest of the essay
- understand both inductive and deductive organization
- become familiar with graphic organizers
- consider the question-and-answer format as an alternative approach

Focus on the idea of breaking out of standard organizational patterns by discussing quotations such as the following:
- *Writing is an adventure . . .* (Winston Churchill)
- *The Brain—is wider than the sky—. . .* (Emily Dickinson)

Encourage students not to be afraid to experiment and push the envelope—the only way a writer becomes a better writer.

Understanding the Big Picture

Rather than using a sample essay from their book, have students apply the information on the page to outside examples of published writing for the **Try It!** activity. This will demonstrate that the organizing principles are used consistently by professional writers in all disciplines. Alert students to the possibility—even the probability—that they will need more than a single paragraph to create the opening or the ending of a well-written piece.

After students have completed the activity, have them share their example and outline in class.

Understanding the Big Picture

The basic structure of informational writing is simple. Essays, articles, and reports contain three main parts: the beginning, the middle, and the ending. Each part plays an equally important role in an effective piece of writing.

Beginning The opening paragraph should capture the reader's attention and state your thesis. Here are some ways to capture your reader's attention:

- Tell a dramatic or exciting story (anecdote) about the topic.
- Ask an intriguing question or two.
- Provide a few surprising facts or statistics.
- Provide an interesting quotation.
- Explain your personal experiences or involvement with the topic.

> Beginning
> Middle
> Ending

Middle The middle paragraphs should support your thesis statement. For example, in an essay about improved safety in NASCAR racing, each middle paragraph would focus on one main aspect of improved safety. (An outline can help you write this section.)

> Beginning
> Middle
> Ending

Ending The closing paragraph should summarize your thesis and leave the reader with a final thought. Here are some strategies for creating a strong closing:

- Review your main points.
- Emphasize the special importance of one main point.
- Answer any questions the reader may still have.
- Draw a conclusion and put the information in perspective.
- Provide a final significant thought for the reader.

> Beginning
> Middle
> Ending

Try It!

Select an essay from this book or an article from a magazine. Outline the three parts of the essay or article to show how it is organized.

Following the Thesis Statement's Lead

An organizing pattern may be built into your essay assignment. For example, you may be asked specifically to develop an argument or to write a process paper. When a pattern is not assigned, one may still evolve quite naturally during your initial thinking and planning. If this doesn't happen, take a careful look at your thesis statement (and supporting information). An effective thesis will almost always suggest an organizing pattern; if it doesn't provide this "controlling vision," consider rewriting it.

Review the following thesis statements and notice how they present the writer's focus and tell how the topic will be developed.

Traits

Sample Thesis

> Frodo Baggins and Harry Potter are both called upon to save their worlds but have different attitudes toward magic, friendship, and battling evil.

Discussion: This thesis shows how the writer will compare two literary characters on three points: magic, friendship, and battling evil. The middle of the essay will discuss each point in a separate paragraph.

Sample Thesis

> Applying for college has become a complicated, stressful process.

Discussion: This thesis indicates that the writer will explain a process. Information must be presented in a logical order, describing each step from beginning to end. The statement also suggests that besides describing each step in this complicated process, the writer will discuss the stress involved.

Sample Thesis

> The National Parks Service can reduce damage to Yellowstone National Park by limiting automobile traffic, increasing fees, and hiring additional staff.

Discussion: The writer of this thesis presents a problem and suggests ways to solve it. The statement suggests that after describing the problem the writer will explain each solution.

Try It!

List the thesis statements for two different essays in this book. Explain how each thesis suggests an organizing pattern for the essay. Discuss your findings with your classmates.

Following the Thesis Statement's Lead

Before students begin the activity, remind them that a thesis statement can be more than one sentence long and isn't always at the very end of the first paragraph.

Encourage students to identify the thesis whenever they read informational writing. If they find a particularly interesting example, they can model it.

Try It! Answers

Possible Answers

SE page 119, thesis: *CGI allows filmmakers to show things on-screen that people could only imagine before.* Organization: Suggests the writer will use process order to explain how CGI works. The writer will also give examples of imaginary things portrayed through CGI.

SE page 129, thesis: *The 73-year search for the* Titanic, *which went down in what is considered the world's greatest sea disaster, was a challenging one. It concluded finally in September 1985.* Organization: Suggests the writer will present events chronologically to describe the *Titanic* disaster, failed efforts to find it, and, last, the successful discovery mission.

English Language Learners

After discussing the second sample thesis, refresh students' memories about the structure of an essay that describes a process. Remind students that transitions that indicate time are used to link the steps. Direct them to the steps listed under *A Closer Look at Understanding Your Goal* (SE page 37). Have them use transition words that show time (SE page 595), and the steps to write a paragraph titled *Identifying the Goal of an Assignment.*

Organizing Deductively

Emphasize that the most important aspect of strong deductive reasoning is using known facts as supporting details in such a way that the writer convinces readers to agree with the thesis. For example, if a writer argues *We must find an alternative to gasoline to power our cars,* he or she might use the following as supporting details for part of the essay:

- Gasoline is made from petroleum.
- Scientists have discovered that petroleum is produced by the decomposition of the bodies of living organisms, a process that takes millions of years.
- Therefore, we are using petroleum much faster than it can possibly be produced.

Confronted with these fact-based points, the reader must concur that petroleum supplies will run out, and an alternative is needed.

Note that the kinds of details (see SE pages 56–57) that best accommodate deductive reasoning are facts, statistics, definitions, and reasons.

"It is a capital mistake to theorize before one has data.
—Sherlock Holmes

Organizing Deductively

Most people are familiar with Sherlock Holmes and his extraordinary powers of deduction. Holmes would make a surprising statement, back it up with many supporting details, and leave Dr. Watson in awe of his conclusion. For example, here is how Holmes deduced Watson had returned from Afghanistan at their first meeting in *A Study in Scarlet:*

> "I *knew* you came from Afghanistan. . . . The train of reasoning ran, 'Here is a gentleman of a medical type, but with the air of a military man. Clearly an army doctor, then. He has just come from the tropics, for his face is dark, and that is not the natural tint of his skin, for his wrists are fair. He has undergone hardship and sickness, as his haggard face says clearly. His left arm has been injured. He holds it in a stiff and unnatural manner. Where in the tropics could an English army doctor have seen much hardship and got his arm wounded? Clearly in Afghanistan.'"

Confronted with all that evidence, Watson can only say, "It is simple enough as you explain it." That is the same reaction you want from your readers, especially when you are trying to persuade them with your ideas.

Most of your academic writing should be organized deductively. *Induction* and *deduction* come from a Latin word meaning "to lead." When writing deductively, you lead the reader to your conclusion by presenting a main idea, or thesis, and then supporting it with specific details. The organizational pattern looks like this:

> **Deductive Arrangement**
> • Start with the main idea or thesis.
> • Present supporting details and examples.
> • Conclude by restating the thesis and/or summarizing the key support.

Deductive writing presents an idea and leads the reader smoothly through the evidence. Supporting details either define the idea, expand it, or illustrate it.

 Try It!

Study a building, house, or vehicle. Write down your observations and see what you can deduce from them. *When was it built? What was it used for previously? What condition is it in?* Then write a deductive paragraph about your findings.

Organizing Inductively

Inductive organization—providing details that lead up to the thesis—is not as common in academic writing as deductive organization. However, inductive organization works well in problem-solution essays and in essays of argumentation.

> **Inductive Arrangement**
> - Set the scene.
> - Provide examples and details.
> - Conclude with the main point or thesis.

Reviewing Excerpts from an Inductive Essay

In excerpts from this sample essay, the main point is stated in the closing paragraph. (The middle of the essay is represented here by topic sentences alone.)

Sardine School

Let's explore a typical school day for the 1,250 students that attend Harding High School.

At this urban school, most students arrive at the same time and enter through one main set of doors. . . .

If you survive entering the building, you must then navigate the crowded halls. . . .

Some classrooms, especially those in the old wing, are packed. . . .

It's almost impossible to move in the crowded physical education classes. . . .

The overcrowded conditions make Harding High School uncomfortable and unsafe. Harding is an older school that should serve 800 students, but it is 50 percent over capacity. The school needs to be remodeled and expanded by next year if the school population remains at its current level. More importantly, plans should be in process to construct a new high school to facilitate learning.

Organizing Inductively

Emphasize that using inductive reasoning involves drawing conclusions based on the writer's personal observation and experience. The kinds of details often used in inductive reasoning include examples, details, and anecdotes. Have students note that the sample uses this organizing method.

On the other hand, using deductive reasoning to make the case for a new high school, the writer could inform readers of the amount of square footage recommended to accommodate 1,250 students in order to lead readers to the conclusion that Harding High is overcrowded.

Struggling Learners

Clarify the difference between deductive and inductive reasoning. Point out that with deductive reasoning, the basic premise is made clear at the beginning of the essay, and with inductive reasoning, the basic premise is not stated until the end of the essay. Explain that sometimes organizing an argument inductively can make a stronger case for the final conclusion because by leading the reader through the presentation of facts, the writer lets the reader draw the same conclusion.

Using Graphic Organizers

Note that some graphic organizers can be applied to most any topic. The choice of which one to use can be based on personal preference.

■ A **5 W's chart** (*see below*) uses questions that should be answered in nearly every kind of writing. The chart helps writers focus their research and organize details.

■ A line diagram can help writers list ideas for most types of essays. Although similar to an outline, some writers prefer its visual impact.

■ A cluster diagram is a writer's tool for brainstorming ideas. Students who like to map out their ideas on paper can use it to help them evaluate possible essay topics or explore related ideas for supporting details.

Encourage students to experiment with many types of graphic organizers and to use them whenever they need to clarify their ideas for writing. They may find using more than one organizer helpful in the course of planning an essay or a research paper.

64

Using Graphic Organizers

Graphic organizers can help you gather and organize details for your writing. Clustering is one method (see page 98); the next two pages list and model other useful organizers. (Re-create the organizer on your own paper to gather details for an essay.)

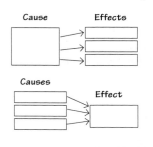

Cause-Effect Organizer

Use to collect and organize details for cause/effect essays.

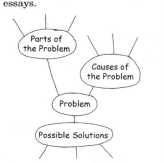

Problem-Solution Web

Use to map out problem-solution essays.

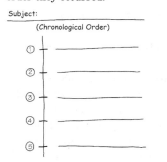

Time Line

Use for personal narratives to list actions or events in the order they occurred.

Evaluation Collection Grid

Use to collect supporting details for essays of evaluation.

Teaching Tip: The 5 W's Chart

Remind students that whenever possible they should also answer a sixth question—*How?*—along with the 5 W's. Note that these six questions are taught to journalism students. In a newspaper, space is limited, so the information provided must give readers a full and accurate picture. Using the 5 W's and H chart is an efficient way to be certain that everything is covered. Have students look for articles in newspapers that demonstrate how consistently journalists use this organizing method.

Traits

Venn Diagram

Use to collect details to compare and contrast two topics.

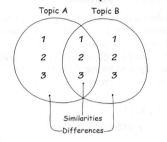

Line Diagram

Use to collect and organize details for academic essays.

Process (Cycle) Diagram

Use to collect details for science-related writing, such as how a process or cycle works.

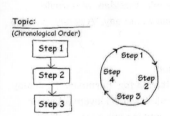

5 W's Chart

Use to collect the *who? what? when? where?* and *why?* details for personal narratives and news stories.

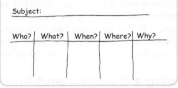

Definition Diagram

Use to gather information for extended-definition essays.

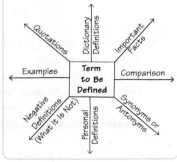

Sensory Chart

Use to collect details for descriptive essays and observation reports.

Have students turn back to the suggested topics on SE page 55. Ask them to tell which graphic organizers might work best for each topic and explain why. Possible responses:

- *Discuss one impact of the Iraq war*: cause-effect organizer
- *Explain how to make a pizza:* time line or process diagram
- *Compare the presidencies of George H. W. Bush and George W. Bush*: Venn diagram
- *Identify the country's biggest problem and convince Congress to solve it:* problem-solution web
- *Argue for or against increased use of public transportation*: evaluation collection grid
- *Write about the worst day of work you have ever had:* time line
- *Describe a place you go to get away from it all*: sensory chart
- *Describe a popular music style*: definition diagram

Using the Question-and-Answer Format

Note that the question-and-answer format suits topics that invite a less-formal, humorous treatment. Since the form requires the writer to take on someone else's persona and to imagine the answers that person might give to questions, it involves a significant amount of creative writing, even if a great deal of factual information is provided.

Note that creative writing techniques might provide students with other interesting ideas for unique ways to address a topic (see "Creative Writing," SE pages 340–369).

"Start with something interesting and promising; wind up with something the reader will remember."

—Rudolf Flesch

Using the Question-and-Answer Format

In general, you can organize your writing deductively or inductively (see pages 62–63). More specifically, you can employ one of these methods: classification, cause-effect, comparison-contrast, problem-solution, and so on. (See pages 584–588.)

There will also be times that your ideas will not fit logically into one of the common methods of organization. Then you must try something different. One unique organization pattern is the question-and-answer format.

Reviewing a Question-and-Answer Essay

Here is a portion of a humorous essay about a well-known figure.

Poor Richard

Q: Mr. Franklin, why did you call your book of essays <u>Poor Richard's Almanack</u>?

A: People were tired of the headlines I was getting, especially Tom Jefferson. Anyway, "Ben Franklin Invents Electricity," "Ben Franklin Invents Stove," "Ben Franklin Signs Declaration of Independence" all sound too self-serving.

Q: As an inventor, a printer, and a statesman, you weren't poor. So why did you use the name Poor Richard?

A: No one likes to listen to rich people. Besides, who would believe that a wealthy gentleman would say, "A penny saved is a penny earned"?

Q: What was your favorite invention?

A: I do like the armonica, which is Italian for "harmony." I can play really sweet tunes on the armonica, which I invented after noting the sounds produced by rubbing the rims of glasses filled with water.

Voice

Voice is what distinguishes one writer from another. It is how your writing expresses your personality; it is who the reader hears. Everyone's speaking voice is unique and almost instantly recognizable. Writers try to make their writing voice distinct as well.

A reader only has a writer's words to react to, which is why a writer's voice is so important. When you use your own natural voice, the reader senses this, and your words feel real and connect with the reader. Developing a writing voice takes time, but it will make your writing more effective. "Voice separates writing that is not read from writing that is read," says writing teacher Donald Murray. This chapter suggests ways to develop and adjust your voice. It also explains how to use dialogue, understand diction, and write like your favorite author.

- **Developing Voice**
- **Adjusting Voice**
- **Using Dialogue**
- **Understanding Diction**
- **Learning from the Masters**

"Writers should use their own voices as much as possible, for their own voices have power, control, and courage."

—Peter Elbow

Voice

Objectives

- think about how voice projects the personality of the writer or of the speakers of dialogue
- learn to adjust voice to suit the audience
- understand different levels of diction

Note that one of the best ways for students to establish their writer's voice is to keep a writer's notebook (see SE pages 2–5) and use it often. As they record their thoughts, students will practice all the elements that make up their voice:

- topics that interest them,
- details they notice,
- styles of reasoning that come naturally,
- specific words they choose, and
- the rhythm of the sentences.

Keeping a personal journal allows students to experiment until they are happy with the voice they project in writing. All that practice will help them start using their own natural-sounding voice from the start of the writing process.

Developing Voice

After students have completed the **Try It!** activity, read some of the revisions aloud to the class. (You may want to include your own.) Without revealing the authors, ask students to guess who wrote each passage. If the writer of a passage is not named, have that student reread the passage aloud so the audience can connect the author with the writing voice.

Developing Voice

Your speaking voice is filled with your personality, and your writing voice should reflect your true self as well. Writing often, whether in a notebook or in class assignments, will help you develop your voice. Here are some other tips for developing your voice:

- **Write about a topic that interests you.** Your interests help make you the person you are.
- **Be passionate.** If you feel strongly about your writing, these feelings will permeate your voice.
- **Be honest and genuine.** Don't try to be someone else to impress readers.
- **Write freely.** Don't edit your voice out of your writing.
- **Read your writing out loud.** Does it sound like you?

Read the following notebook entry. The thoughts and feelings reflect the writer's personality.

Sample Notebook Entry

> I don't know why cops got such a bad rap around here. Jaci and I were walking home yesterday, and a cop car zipped by, flashers and siren and all, and Jaci said, "Yeah, they must need donuts pretty bad." She laughed, but I didn't think it was funny. I mean, they were probably going to help someone. I didn't tell Jaci, but I think I want to be a cop. When my little brother Luis wandered away from Mom, a cop helped find him, and he was really nice. When Tia Bonita got hit by the cab and broke her leg, a cop got to her in a couple of minutes, and he sat and talked to her until the paramedics got there. And I've seen cops working at fires and accidents. I mean, they don't just hand out tickets and arrest people. They help people, and I think that must feel pretty good.

Try It!

Becoming familiar with other writers' voices may help you discover your own voice. Read the following quotation and then rewrite it in your voice, trying to express a comparable thought.

> "The sun escaping from the breaking clouds, as it sank toward the hills they had left, was now shining brightly again. Their fear left them, though they still felt uneasy."
>
> —J. R. R. Tolkien, *The Fellowship of the Ring*

Adjusting Voice

You adjust your speaking voice to the audience you are addressing and to your purpose. The same is true of your writing voice.

Adjusting for Audience

A personal, informal writing voice is closest to your usual way of talking. You should use it for writing narratives, sending e-mail to friends, or writing personal letters. It is often colorful and visual. To the reader, it is friendly and familiar.

On the other hand, you wouldn't use this voice when you are applying for a job, writing a research paper, or petitioning your senator. For those readers, you would adopt a more formal voice, but without losing your personality.

Adjusting for Purpose

You can adjust your writing voice to match your purpose—to relate an experience, to share information, or to persuade a reader.

- **Relating an experience:** When you describe an experience, your writing voice should be engaging, animated, and personal, similar to the way you sound when talking to a group of friends.

  Jack Smith gave a speech at our school yesterday that really got us pumped up. I would like to see him elected, but he's a third-party candidate with about as much chance of winning as I have of being named captain of the football team.

- **Sharing information:** Writing to inform demands an interested, knowledgeable voice that tells the reader you know your topic well.

  The electoral college favors a two-party system, as shown by Ross Perot's receiving 18 percent of the popular vote, but not a single electoral vote, in the 1992 presidential election.

- **Persuading a reader:** Think of how you tried to persuade your parents to let you use the family car, or a teacher to extend an assignment deadline. To persuade the reader, your writing voice must be convincing and informed.

  With the death-hold grip the electoral college has on elections, third-party candidates should not throw their candidates into the ring with the two main parties.

Try It!

Select a topic, choose one of the purposes above, and write a sentence or two that fits this purpose. Then adjust your voice and rewrite the passage to fit each of the other two purposes.

Adjusting Voice

Assemble a variety of examples of writing targeted to different audiences. Have volunteers read excerpts from them out loud in class, and then discuss how each one suits its intended purpose.

Good examples of different writing types might include the following:

- an article from a scientific journal (expository writing intended for an audience that is knowledgeable about a complex subject)
- a picture book (narrative writing intended for children who aren't yet able to read)
- a newspaper editorial (persuasive writing intended for an interested general audience)
- a personal letter (various styles of writing, intended for one particular reader)

English Language Learners

Help students recognize the difference between personal and formal voice. Read aloud the first sentence in each pair below, and have students write another sentence that conveys the same message, using a formal writing voice.

- We beat them by a mile! (Our team won by a wide margin.)

- I'd really love working with your people. (I would be pleased to become a member of your organization.)
- I'm dying to find out if they'll let me attend the school. (I am eagerly awaiting a response from the school.)

Using Dialogue

Note that examples of good dialogue writing are everywhere—in novels, short stories, plays, movies, and television series. Ask students to begin to notice how these various dialogues are crafted, and how well each speaker's personality is revealed in what they say.

Before students begin the **Try It!** activity, talk a little bit about speaker tags.

- Explain that speaker tags are the narrative portions of dialogue that identify who is speaking and sometimes describe how they talk or actions they perform while speaking.
- Have students point out all the speaker tags in the sample.
- Note that, as long as it is clear who is talking, a speaker tag isn't needed.
- Suggest that students keep the tags as simple as possible to avoid distracting readers from the dialogue. Often a plain *she* or *he said* is all that's needed.

✳ For more about creating dialogue, see SE page 347.

Using Dialogue

In creative writing, dialogue is used to give the reader information and to advance the story. Dialogue also breaks up the wall of text, making a story easier to read.

Writing realistic dialogue requires more than just copying what people say. Real speech is not planned or precise. People repeat phrases, add unnecessary words, contract words, and leave out words. They talk at the same time and interrupt each other. As a writer, you need to make use of these characteristics while keeping dialogue interesting and to the point.

When writing dialogue . . .
- mix in some narrative description to help describe a speaker's tone,
- be sure every line has a purpose, and
- read it out loud to be sure it sounds realistic.

Read the following sample. See how the dialogue adds information and develops the personalities of the speakers.

Sample Dialogue

While waiting in line to audition for <u>The Last Great Average American Survival Race</u>, Jack hands Dana the application. "Here. We have to pretend to be a couple for a few minutes. All you have to do is memorize these answers. I made a few changes to fit your . . ."

"Favorite food, spaghetti?" Shaking her head, Dana scowled. "No way, I hate spaghetti. It's a disgusting mess of slimy . . ."

"You don't have to eat any. You just have to say you like it. We need to show them that we're a happy, average, compatible couple."

"Why?"

"Why? Because that's what they're looking for," Jack replied, jabbing the clipboard with his finger. "It's in the name of the show. It's in the contest guidelines."

"Well, if the producers followed my guidelines, then I would be the next great pop diva," Dana said hotly.

Try It!

Record a conversation between yourself and one or more friends. Write it down as accurately as you can. Then rewrite the conversation as if it were dialogue for a story. Add descriptive phrases, keep it real, and give every line a purpose.

English Language Learners

For the **Try It!** activity, students may have difficulty maintaining an accurate record of their conversations. Provide student pairs with a tape recorder for a conversation. Then have them play back the tape to complete the activity.

Understanding Diction

Diction is the level of language you use based on your purpose and intended audience. Knowing about levels of diction will help you better understand your options for voice. You will use two basic levels of diction for most of your writing.

Formal English

Your essays, research papers, and business letters should meet the standards of formal English. This level of language pays careful attention to word choice, follows the conventions for grammar and usage, and maintains a serious, objective (factual) tone throughout.

> **Researchers are developing alternative fuels to decrease the world's dependency on fossil fuels. Automakers believe that re-forming ethanol into hydrogen will create the fuel of the future for flexible-fuel vehicles. Currently, one experimental ethanol re-former is able to produce 110 pounds of hydrogen per day, with its only by-product being one ounce of carbon dioxide per every four ounces of hydrogen.**

Tip

Generally, avoid using *I, we,* and *you* in academic writing. Instead, focus on the topic itself and let your attitude be revealed indirectly.

Informal English

You may write many other pieces, such as personal narratives and feature articles, using a more informal level of language. Informal English usually includes some personal references, a few popular expressions, and shorter sentences.

> **Almost two years ago, I passed my driver's test. I was so excited that day. Now, looking ahead, I wonder how much driving I will do. Gas prices are skyrocketing, and each trip I take pollutes the world a little more. Our government must help scientists find new sources of fuel that are less harmful.**

Other Forms of Diction

- **Colloquial language** refers to the expressions that are accepted in informal situations and certain locations: **You wanna shoot hoops or just hang?**
- **Slang** is language used by a particular group of people among themselves: **During rehearsal, I really got ticked off.**
- **Jargon** (technical diction) is the specialized language used by a specific group, such as those who use computers: **Hypertext, which is built in to HTML, can retrieve files over the Internet as long as a computer has the proper software.**

Traits

Understanding Diction

Suggest that one good way to get diction right in writing is for students to imagine talking or writing the information, especially for a typical member of that audience. For example,

- Formal English—imagine writing to someone with authority, such as a teacher, Congressperson, or potential employer.
- Informal English—imagine writing to a friend or family member.
- **Colloquial language / Slang** *(see below)*—imagine talking to close friends or sending a text message to them.
- Jargon—imagine talking to someone who is very knowledgeable about the topic.

Ask students to create writing samples using all the types of diction described. Challenge them to choose a single topic and approach it differently in each sample. Afterward, have volunteers read one or two of their writings out loud in class, and have the listeners identify the type of diction used.

Teaching Tip: Colloquial Language / Slang

Many students—as well as adults—use some form of slang in everyday conversation. Remind students that in their writing, they should strive to avoid slang unless they are reporting dialogue verbatim. If they are quoting one or two slang words out of context, they should indicate they are doing so by enclosing the words in quotation marks.

Struggling Learners

Have students search magazines in a specific field such as computers, automotives, or fashion for examples of jargon from that field. If they don't understand the jargon, have students look it up. Explain that if they are writing about such a topic to all but insiders, they will need to explain jargon that they use.

Learning from the Masters

Talk about the idea that emulating another's writing can help students develop their own voice. How is this different from plagiarizing the authors' ideas? Note that there are several reasons why the technique is helpful.

- Closely modeling sentences in a private forum such as a writer's notebook is like an athlete doing training exercises—the exercises develop a writer's ability to write for an outside audience.
- Practicing techniques used by the masters helps beginning writers get a sense of what it feels like to craft the sorts of sentences that speak to them. They can then try to achieve a similar feeling in their own work using their own voice.
- Writers express their personalities through the combination of authors they choose to emulate. As they practice using these authors' techniques, the writers create a unique style of their very own.

Learning from the Masters

Each of your favorite writers has a distinct writing voice. In all likelihood, this unique voice is one reason that you enjoy reading his or her books. When you come across sentences that have a voice, write them down. Then practice writing sentences of your own that follow the author's pattern of writing. This process is sometimes called modeling, and it can help you develop your own writing voice.

Modeling Your Favorite Authors

Follow these guidelines when you practice sentence modeling. You can also practice writing longer passages modeled after works by your favorite authors.

- **Copy the sentence** (or passage) in your writing notebook.
- **Think of a topic** for your practice writing.
- **Follow the pattern** of the sentence as you write about your own topic. (You don't have to follow the pattern exactly.)
- **Build each sentence** one small part at a time.
- **Save your writing.** Share it with your classmates.

Sample Sentences

Here are sentences by professional writers that exhibit an interesting voice.

"It was one of those days with which September is repeatedly cursed; hot and glaring, with slivers of dust in the wind."
—Dorothy Parker, "The Standard of Living"

"You squirrel away old stuff on the principle of its being useful and interesting someday; it's wonderful when the day finally arrives."
—Garrison Keillor, "Something from the Sixties"

"The winter we'd been waiting for arrived on New Year's Eve—a hard freeze followed by an enormous fall of snow the next day."
—Margaret Atwood, *The Blind Assassin*

"The master met him on the after-deck, looming up in the fog amongst the blurred shapes of the usual ship's fittings."
—Joseph Conrad, "The Tale"

Try It!

Reserve part of your writer's notebook for sentence modeling. To get started, try writing your own sentences modeled after any two of the sentences listed above.

Word Choice

Your choice of words is where your writing style begins. Word choice can make your writing clear or obscure, lighthearted or hard hitting, simple or challenging. Which words you select, and how you arrange them, will depend upon your writing task, your audience, and the effect you want to achieve.

When George Orwell was revising his novel *1984*, for example, he decided that many of the words were too colorful, creating the wrong feeling. As a result, Orwell toned down the words and used more passive constructions to make the text less literary.

In this chapter, you will learn how to choose the best words for your writing. The best words are the ones that effectively add meaning, feeling, and sound to your writing.

- **Using General and Specific Nouns**
- **Understanding Action and Linking Verbs**
- **Working with Metaphors**
- **Using Other Figures of Speech**
- **Recognizing Problems with Adjectives**
- **Identifying Other Problems with Word Choice**
- **Considering Polysyndeton and Asyndeton**

"Words—so innocent and powerless as they are, as standing in a dictionary, how potent for good and evil they become in the hands of one who knows how to combine them."

—Nathanial Hawthorne

Copy Masters

5 W's Chart (TE p. 74)

Word Choice

Objectives
- understand how effective nouns and verbs can make writing more interesting
- use figures of speech
- address common problems in word choice
- learn about expressing a series as a polysyndeton or an asyndeton

Note that the single most important way students can improve word choice is to expand their vocabulary. Suggest ways students might go about this, such as the following:
- Keep an ongoing list of interesting words and their definitions to use in conversation and writing.
- Take the time to look up unfamiliar words whenever they arise—in reading or conversation—or write them down to look up later.
- Browse through a dictionary and a thesaurus.
- Learn a specialized skill or a foreign language—both will provide students with new words to expand their vocabulary.

Using General and Specific Nouns

Have students work with a partner to complete the second **Try It!** activity.

- After students have completed the writing portion of the activity, have them trade papers with a partner.
- Ask students to read their partner's narrative and mark nouns that may be too general or unnecessarily specific.
- Encourage readers to suggest possible replacements for the marked nouns if they can think of them.
- Remind students before they begin to revise that any suggestion by the reader is just that—a suggestion. A writer should evaluate each one carefully before deciding how to proceed.

Using General and Specific Nouns

Your choice of nouns is your primary focusing tool. If all of your nouns are general, your message will be vague and unclear. On the other hand, if every noun is specific, some of them may actually compete against each other and weaken your paper. It is important, then, to understand the levels of specificity and to use them wisely.

General to Specific Nouns			
person	*place*	*thing*	*idea*
man	intersection	food	belief
humanitarian	landmark intersection	fruit	principle
Bono	Times Square	banana	honor

Try It!

Create your own chart showing four sets of nouns (*person, place, thing,* and *idea*) that become progressively more specific. Use the chart above as a guide.

Being Noun Smart

When developing your writing, make sure you have used the best nouns throughout. Use general nouns when giving a broad overview and specific nouns where detail is important. In the following paragraph, notice how the nouns help establish a broad idea, discuss its details, and then return to a broad conclusion.

> While art may shape history, it is even more certain that history shapes art. Consider the evolution of landscape painting in China. During the Tang dynasty (618–907 C.E.), landscape served merely as a sketchy background for human figures. At the cultural height of the Song dynasty (960–1279 C.E.), landscape itself became a symbol of order and unity in art. When intellectuals were barred from government service during the Yuan dynasty (1279–1368 C.E.), their landscape paintings became expressions of self-contemplation. The Ming dynasty (1368–1644 C.E.) brought a return of landscapes as images of cultured rule. Thus, historians can gauge a painting's place in history by its use of landscape.

Try It!

Write a brief narrative, recalling how you spent last weekend. Afterward, circle nouns that seem too general and underline specific nouns that might be redundant. Replace some of the nouns you have marked.

Struggling Learners

A graphic organizer may help students collect details regarding their weekend's activities. Provide students with photocopies of the reproducible 5 W's Chart (TE page 822) and encourage them to use their completed organizer to compose their narrative for the second **Try It!** activity.

Understanding Action and Linking Verbs

Verbs are among the most versatile words in our language. **Action** verbs—like *leap* and *snicker* and *negotiate*—convey the energy of a sentence. **Linking** verbs—like *be* and *seem* and *become*—serve as equal signs, equating the subject with its complement. Both types of verbs have their uses: Action verbs make a sentence dynamic; linking verbs convey certainty.

Use action verbs to . . .

- Write active, forward-moving sentences.
  At the snap of the ball, their lineman charged **forward, trying to crack the wall.**

- Add energy to your writing.
  Stan vibrated **with excitement.**

Use linking verbs to . . .

- State a definition.
  Physics is **the science of matter and energy.**

- Express a condition.
  The lake was **frozen.**

- Link an adjective to the subject.
  Curried chicken tastes **delicious.**

Using the Appropriate Verbs

Be sure you use the most appropriate verbs in your writing. In the revised version of the passage below, the writer changes the first three verbs to give the writing more energy. The linking verb *remains* works effectively, so she keeps it.

Original: **Consumer bankruptcy** grew **during the past two decades. It** was **nearly 92 percent in 1990. By 2000, it** was **over 97 percent. Unfortunately, consumer bankruptcy** remains **a critical problem in 2007.**

Revision: **Consumer bankruptcy** swelled **during the past two decades. It** reached **nearly 92 percent in 1990. By 2000, it** topped **97 percent. Unfortunately, consumer bankruptcy** remains **a critical problem in 2007.**

► Try It!

Review the verbs in an essay that you have recently completed. Improve at least three verbs in the writing using the information and examples above as a guide.

Traits

Understanding Action and Linking Verbs

Expand on the information given by discussing other issues related to verb use.

- Avoid the unnecessary use of the passive voice. Students should try to rephrase a passive sentence in the active voice wherever it makes sense. Overuse of the passive voice can make sentences wordy and sound distant from the topic. (Example: *His voice was filled with nervousness as he spoke.* Direct: *His voice quavered* or *He spoke nervously*.)

- Reserve continuous verb tenses for expressing action that *is*, *was*, or *will be* ongoing. Otherwise they add an extra word or two; lend a colloquial, stilted sound to the writing; and interfere with the vigor of the sentence. (Example: *She was planning to invite her daughter.* Direct: *She planned to invite her daughter*.)

✱ For more about the passive voice and continuous verb tenses, see the Proofreader's Guide, SE page 722.

Working with Metaphors

In reviewing the information on the page, remind students of a figure of speech related to the metaphor—the simile, a comparison that does make use of the words *like* or *as*. Note that a writer often has the choice of using either a simile or a metaphor.

Challenge students to rephrase the sample metaphors on the page as similes, if possible. For example:

- A conversation with Ignacio is substantial—like a meaty stew of politics, philosophy, and history.
- My brain felt like a boiling teakettle, shrieking with competing ideas.

Discuss the differences between metaphors and similes. Why do we choose one over the other? Possible responses:

- A metaphor increases the impact of a comparison by treating two ideas equally. It usually appeals strongly to the senses.
- The simile's use of *like* or *as* emphasizes the notion that a comparison is being made. It appeals to the reader's association of the two ideas.

Working with Metaphors

A metaphor is a figure of speech comparing two things without using the words *like* or *as*. Metaphors invite new ways of thinking about key ideas, and they do so in a very stylistic way. There are many ways to develop metaphors, including the three explained below.

Creating Metaphors with Nouns

The usual way to develop a metaphor is to compare two nouns: **A conversation with Ignacio is a meaty stew of politics, philosophy, and history.** In this example, the reader understands that a conversation with Ignacio is stimulating and challenging.

Creating Metaphors with Verbs

Another way to develop a metaphor is to use a verb: **My brain boiled over with competing ideas.** In this example, the verb *boiled over* metaphorically compares an agitated mind (brain) to a boiling pot of liquid.

It is also possible to enhance a comparison of two nouns with a participial phrase. A participial phrase begins with a participle, a verb form ending in *ing* or *ed*. (See page 742.) Note the following example: **My brain was a boiling teakettle, shrieking with competing ideas.**

Using Extended Metaphors

A metaphor doesn't have to be expressed in a single sentence. Sometimes it can serve as a unifying element throughout a series of sentences. Extending a metaphor in this way helps you expand or clarify an idea in your writing.

> The whole of human understanding **is an intricate spider's web of thought.** Each filament of insight **connects discrete bits of knowledge. Where much knowledge has been accumulated,** the dense netting **snags increasingly finer details and adds to the richness of our understanding. But oh, the gaps remaining in that web!**

Note: Be careful with extended metaphors. Your writing may sound forced or unnatural if you extend a metaphor through too many sentences.

Try It!

Find two or three effective metaphors in an article or a novel. Then write your own metaphors modeled after the examples that you have found. Be original! Afterward, share your work with your classmates.

Using Other Figures of Speech

Have you ever assembled something from a kit? If so, you know that clear, exact instructions make the job easier to complete. You wouldn't necessarily expect the same level of exactness in more imaginative forms of writing. Fiction and personal essays often include *figures of speech,* which are used to communicate ideas more indirectly or symbolically. The information below covers three common figures of speech.

Personification

Personification is a figure of speech in which an animal, object, or idea is given human characteristics. (This makes personification a form of metaphor.) When used effectively, personification can create a powerful image and help establish the voice in a piece of writing.

Example: **That car had it in for her. It always waited to break down until she absolutely had to be somewhere important, and whenever she worked on it, it always managed to draw blood. Even when she filled the gas tank, it would be sure to spit some back on her shoes.**

Hyperbole

Hyperbole is an extreme form of exaggeration used to make a point by drawing special attention to the subject. Often, the result is humorous.

Example: **You think you have a lot of brothers and sisters? I have so many siblings that when we were growing up, the U.S. government gave our house its own ZIP code.**

Understatement

Like hyperbole, understatement draws special attention to a subject in order to make a point. But whereas hyperbole exaggerates, understatement does the opposite, using overly restrained language. Its effect is typically ironic or sarcastic.

Example: **He [our new dog] turned out to be a good traveler, and except for an interruption caused by my wife's falling out of the car, the journey went very well.**

—E. B. White, "A Report in Spring"

Try It!

Write one brief passage about a topic of interest using personification, another passage about the topic using hyperbole, and a last passage about the topic using understatement.

Traits

Using Other Figures of Speech

Note that while personification, hyperbole, and understatement are often found in creative writing, especially **humorous writing** *(see-below)*, they play less of a role in academic writing.

Alert students to one type of personification (sometimes also called anthropomorphism) that commonly arises as a mistake in formal writing, especially in the sciences. A writer may unintentionally ascribe human traits to an inanimate object or process. For example, the writer of a lab report might state, *This experiment will attempt to demonstrate that lemons can be used as batteries.* The experiment itself cannot *attempt* anything. The writer should rephrase the sentence: *In performing this experiment, we will attempt to demonstrate . . .*

✳ For more information about figures of speech, see SE page 368.

Teaching Tip: Humorous Writing

Have students read several short excerpts from humorous writing to see the use of the figures of speech in action. Provide handouts of humorous sentences or paragraphs that include figures of speech, or have students find some on their own to share in class. Humor writers whose work may provide good examples include the following:

- Dave Barry
- Jerry Seinfeld
- Robert Benchley
- Samuel Clemens (Mark Twain)
- Sandra Tsing Loh
- David Sedaris
- James Thurber
- Sarah Vowell

English Language Learners

Have students show their understanding of hyperbole by restating the following:

1. My parents will kill me when they see my grades.
2. My bedroom is such a mess that the Board of Health is ready to shut it down.
3. Faced with the expense of prom necessities, I can either go to college or attend the prom.

Recognizing Problems with Adjectives

Note that much of the advice on this page can be applied equally to adverbs. Challenge students to suggest examples for each problem, using adverbs instead of adjectives. For example:

- Unnecessary adverbs (use a more specific verb): *He was <u>awfully glad</u> to go back to school.* Improved: *He was <u>thrilled</u> to go back to school.*
- Empty adverbs: *He clumped noisily across the floor.* Improved: *He clumped across the floor.*
- Overused adverbs: *They did really well on the algebra test.* Improved: *They scored top grades on the algebra test.*
- Multiple adverbs: *She ate the meat <u>hungrily</u> and drank the milk <u>thirstily</u>.* Improved: *She wolfed down the meat and guzzled the milk.*

Try It!
Answers

Possible Answer

Our adorable kitten rubbed its fur against my cheek. Chirping like a bird, it reminded me it was hungry. I poured some milk into a bowl and watched as the kitten happily lapped it up. I marveled at the beauty of its tortoiseshell coat.

Recognizing Problems with Adjectives

Mark Twain wrote, "When you catch an adjective, kill it. No, I don't mean utterly, but kill most of them—then the rest will be valuable." Obviously, adjectives have their purpose, and when used properly, they can clarify the nouns that they modify. But used carelessly, adjectives can bloat a text, muddying its meaning and effectiveness.

Knowing What to Look For

Watch for the following types of problems in your writing.

- **Unnecessary adjectives:** Don't add an adjective to modify a noun when a more specific noun would serve.
  Original: An awful smell **rose from the pit.**
  Improved: A stench **rose from the pit.**
- **Empty adjectives:** Remove adjectives that add no real meaning to your sentence.
  Original: The slow turtle **crept across the sidewalk.**
  Improved: The turtle **crept across the sidewalk.**
- **Overused adjectives:** At times, the first adjective that comes to mind will be overused. Replace these worn-out adjectives with fresh ones.
  Original: We strained to see in the pitch-black **darkness.**
  Improved: We strained to see in the relentless **darkness.**

Note: These overused adjectives contain little meaning: *neat, big, pretty, small, cute, fun, bad, nice, good, funny,* and so on.

- **Multiple adjectives:** Avoid stringing together multiple adjectives before a noun; very often a single adjective can effectively express the meaning that you are looking for.
  Original: **Dionne bit into a** juicy, runny, soggy **barbecue sandwich.**
  Improved: **Dionne bit into a** sloppy **barbecue sandwich.**

Try It!

Rewrite the following passage addressing any problems with the use of adjectives. Consider unnecessary, empty, overused, and multiple adjectives. Use the information above as a guide.

Our adorable, cute, cuddly kitten rubbed its downy fur against my cheek. Its little cries reminded me it was hungry. I poured some creamy milk into a bowl and watched as the tiny feline happily lapped it up. I marveled at the beauty of its brown, tortoiseshell coat.

Students may benefit from additional practice with adjectives. Have students revise the following sentences and explain how the revision is an improvement.

1. An *extremely loud* boom sounded from the garage. (A *thunderous* boom sounded from the garage.)
2. The *yelling, screaming, cheering* crowd showed support for the team. (The *boisterous* crowd showed support for the team.)
3. A *short, fat, round* worm inched along the sidewalk. (A *plump* worm inched along the sidewalk.)
4. Ali wore a *very colorful* costume to the dance. (Ali wore a *vibrant* costume to the dance.)

Identifying Other Problems with Word Choice

The best writing is always clear and interesting. Careful word choice ensures this outcome. When you revise and edit your writing, it is important to evaluate your words for clarity and freshness.

Checking for Problems

Listed below are common problems related to word choice. Check with your teacher for other problems to address.

- **Redundancy** occurs when words or phrases are used together but mean the same thing.
  Original version: **My grandfather stood more than six feet tall in height.**
  Revised version: **My grandfather stood more than six feet tall.**

- **Repetition** occurs when words or phrases are unnecessarily repeated.
  Original version: **When it comes to intelligent people, Louetta is just about the most intelligent person I know.**
  Revised version: **Louetta is just about the most intelligent person I know.**

- **Jargon** refers to specialized words that are not adequately explained.
  Original version: **The enlarged photo was too pixelated to use in our yearbook.**
  Revised version: **The enlarged photo was too pixelated—broken into large dots—to use in our yearbook.**

- **Cliches** are overused phrases that give the reader nothing new.
  Original version: **Advice for freshman: Put your best foot forward!**
  Revised version: **Advice for freshman: Have confidence that you can succeed!**

Try It!

Identify and correct the word problem in each of the following sentences. (Corrections may vary.)

1. A bird-rescue organization in California made a mint by auctioning bird prints.
2. In Spain, a Spanish court recently ruled that divorced couples in Spain cannot demand visitation rights with their dogs.
3. A teenage spelunker in Israel has discovered eight new species including four new crustaceans.
4. Don't drive through the construction site, and be sure to pick a different route if you want to avoid driving over nails.

Traits

Identifying Other Problems with Word Choice

Note that there can be a fine line between a writing problem and effective use of language.

- Repetition is a problem, but intentional echoes can add emphasis. For instance: *When the conversation turns to intelligent people, I think of Louetta. She's about the most intelligent person I know.*
- Note that it isn't necessary to avoid all jargon. The key is to explain it. Using and defining specialized terms help create a knowledgeable tone.

Try It!
Answers

Possible Answers

1. (cliche) A bird-rescue organization in California raised a lot of money by auctioning bird prints.
2. (repetition) A Spanish court recently ruled that divorced couples cannot demand visitation rights with their dogs.
3. (jargon, redundancy) A teenage spelunker—cave explorer—in Israel has discovered eight species, four of them crustaceans.
4. (redundancy) Be sure to pick a different route to avoid driving over nails at the construction site.

English Language Learners

Students may have difficulty finding all of the problems in the **Try It!** sentences. Have students work with a cooperative partner who reads each sentence aloud, emphasizing the word problem. If students cannot figure out how to address the problem, suggest improvements so they can choose the best one.

Considering Polysyndeton and Asyndeton

To help students remember the meaning of these specialized terms, break them down into component parts and discuss the etymologies.

- The prefix *poly-* means "many." (Example: a *polygon* is a *many*-sided shape.)
- The prefix *a-* means "without." (An *amoral* person is *without* morals.)
- The prefix *syn-* means "together." (*Synthesis* is the result of putting ideas *together*.)
- The Greek verb *dein* means "to bind," which is what conjunctions do in sentences.

Challenge students to combine the parts into the words. (*Polysyndeton*: "with many conjunctions" and *asyndeton*: "without conjunctions.")

Try It!
Answers

Possible Answers

Polysyndeton: *Making a choice at the ice cream store can be difficult—are you in the mood for decadent triple fudge, or a tart lemon sorbet, or classic butter pecan, or simple, elegant vanilla?*

Asyndeton: *The kaleidoscope revealed a gemlike mosaic in motion, constantly shifting facets of ruby, emerald, sapphire, amber, amethyst.*

Considering Polysyndeton and Asyndeton

Writing style is more than the words you choose. It is also the way you put those words together. Consider, for instance, the use of conjunctions in a series of items. In a normal series, commas separate the individual items, and a conjunction signals the last one. Benny's *"emergency kit" contained a flashlight, an old comic book, and a box of raisins.* There are other ways of presenting a series, however, which can dramatically affect the style of your writing.

Polysyndeton

When a series of words is linked together by multiple conjunctions, this is called *polysyndeton (pŏl-ē-sĭn′dĭ-tŏn)*. Here are three reasons to use this technique.

- **Emphasize each item** in a series.
  Example: Their ace pitcher can throw curveballs and sliders and cutters; he will be tough to hit.

- **Slow the pace** of a sentence by methodical attention to detail.
  Example: Sylvia came home from the factory every day and fixed dinner and helped the kids and straightened the apartment before falling exhausted into bed.

- **Or quicken the pace** of a sentence by building a sense of momentum.
  Example: She squeezed the clutch and downshifted and leaned hard into the curve before flying out of the corner like a stone from a sling.

Asyndeton

A different effect is achieved by *asyndeton (ə-sĭn′dĭ-tŏn)*, which means "presenting a series with no conjunctions at all." Here are three reasons to use this technique.

- **Suggest incompletion,** that something more should follow.
  Example: Jonathan blinked, coughed, wheezed, trembled.

- **Suggest simultaneous or random action.**
  Example: Like windup toys, the dancers spun, dipped, leapt, twirled.

- **Emphasize the finality** of the last item.
  Example: One last chord wavered in the night air, faded, died.

Try It!

Write one example each of polysyndeton and asyndeton. Use the information above as a guide.

Sentence Fluency

Walking is easy. Dancing, on the other hand, takes equal parts of practice and passion. Similarly, it's easy to put a subject and a verb together with a few other words to make a basic sentence. However, it's a challenge to write a sentence that dances, carrying a reader effortlessly along.

In this chapter, you will learn many techniques for improving your sentence style—including expanding main clauses with various types of modifiers, varying the placement of sentence modifiers, and inverting the order of sentence parts. You will also review common sentence problems.

Follow the advice in this chapter, and your sentences will gain a liveliness that makes them a pleasure to read.

- **Varying Sentences**
- **Expanding Sentences**
- **Placing Modifiers**
- **Using Inverted and Periodic Sentences**
- **Checking for Sentence Problems**
- **Checking for Additional Problems**

"Writing is a negative game. Very few sentences come out right the first time, or even the second or third time."

—William Zinsser

Sentence Fluency

Objectives
- learn how to vary and expand sentences
- learn where to place modifying phrases and clauses
- understand what inverted and periodic sentences are
- learn about common sentence fluency problems

Talk about the quotation by William Zinsser. What do students think he means by "negative game"? Possible responses:
- Writing involves taking away words as much as adding them.
- You "win" the writing game—create a successful piece—not by constantly moving forward but often by revisiting the writing.
- The goal of writing is to use only as many words as are needed to express an idea the right way.

Refer students to Zinsser's book *On Writing Well* for a detailed and well-written discussion of the writing process.

Varying Sentences

Besides beginning sentences with the subject, point out other common patterns of sentence beginnings that writers often use:

- Start with short introductory words or phrases: *In the early 1800s, travelers were given the chance to ride on trains. Before this, they could go no faster than a horse, or their own feet, could take them. Finally, they could cover long distances quickly.*
- Start with introductory clauses: *For travelers who had a long way to go, the chance to ride a train was a blessing. Now that they weren't limited by the speed of their horse or their own feet, people could cover distances quickly. Since trains zoomed along at speeds never before experienced, many travelers felt overwhelmed by the experience.*
- Start with the same word (often *the*): *The chance to ride on trains became available in the early 1800s. The speed of one's journey was no longer determined by how fast your horse or your feet could go. The railroad changed travel forever.*

82

Varying Sentences

If all of your sentences follow the same basic pattern, your writing will be lifeless. By varying your sentences in different ways, you can spice up your writing and increase your reader's enjoyment.

Varying Sentence Beginnings

Sentences that begin the same way start to plod along. To avoid this problem, vary the way you start them.

Starting with the Main Subject

Original version: Many European countries have megalithic stone monuments. England has the famous Stonehenge circle. France has the Cordon des Druides. Italy has the site near Fossa in Abruzzo. Europe also has many more examples.

Varied Beginnings

Revised version: Megalithic stone monuments can be found in many places in Europe. The famous Stonehenge circle stands in England. In France, there is the Cordon des Druides. Italy has the site near Fossa in Abruzzo. These are only three examples of Europe's many ancient stone structures.

Varying Sentence Lengths

To avoid plodding sentences, combine some of them to vary their lengths.

Similar Length

Original version: Today, students take the electronic calculator for granted. Until about 50 years ago, there was no such thing. Before then, people used pencil and paper or a slide rule. A slide rule helps a person multiply and divide large numbers. It adds or subtracts logarithmic distances to do this.

Varied Lengths

Revised version: Today, students take the electronic calculator for granted, but it was not invented until about 50 years ago. Before then, people used pencil and paper or a slide rule. A slide rule helps people to multiply and divide large numbers by adding or subtracting logarithmic distances.

Try It!

Find a passage in one of your essays in which many sentences begin in the same way or are close in length. Rewrite the passage, varying the sentences.

Struggling Learners

Provide students with additional practice combining sentences. Have students rewrite each of the following sentence pairs as a single sentence.

1. The player streaked across the end zone with the ball in his hands. The crowd roared its approval.
2. Della clumsily searched through her purse. It was hard to find things in the oversized bag.
3. Alex tossed his test paper into the basket. He was certain it would earn an *A*.
4. Ted had worked two jobs all summer. He needed $800 for his senior trip.

Sentence Fluency **83**

"A good writer can express an extremely complicated idea clearly and make the job look effortless."

—Patricia T. O'Conner

Traits

Expanding Sentences

Details seem to spill out of accomplished writers' minds naturally. Readers marvel at how effectively these authors can expand a basic idea with engaging details. Maybe you envy good writers because of this special ability and wish you could write in the same way. The truth is you can by writing *cumulative sentences,* or sentences with modifying clauses and phrases coming before and after the main clause. (See page 750.) In the following cumulative sentence, the main clause (in blue) precedes the modifying phrases.

Tony is laughing, **halfheartedly, with his hands on his face, looking puzzled.**

In the cumulative sentence below, modifiers are placed both before and after the main clause (in blue).

As the storm continued, the river rose, **rapidly overflowing its banks and sending waves of dirty water over the field.**

FYI

Below are six ways to expand your sentences.

1. With **individual words**: *halfheartedly*
2. With **prepositional phrases**: *with his hands on his face*
3. With **participial (-ing or -ed) phrases**: *looking puzzled*
4. With **infinitive phrases**: *to hide his embarrassment*
5. With **subordinate clauses**: *while his friend talks*
6. With **relative clauses**: *who isn't laughing at all*

Try It!

Expand each of these main clauses by adding at least two modifying words, phrases, or clauses.

1. A dog howled.
2. Junie started the car.
3. The moon cast an eerie glow.
4. My father tried to fix the bike.
5. The leaves blew.

Expanding Sentences

Before students begin the **Try It!** activity, tell them to not only expand the sentences but also list the techniques they use. Note that students may come up with **other expanding techniques** *(see below)* in addition to those listed on the page.

Try It! Answers

Possible Answers

1. In the distance, a dog howled, reminding Elsie of that creepy story "The Hound of the Baskervilles." (added prepositional and participial phrases)
2. Tired of talking, Junie started the car to signal that Aaron should step back from the open window and let her go. (added participial and infinitive phrases and a relative clause)
3. The moon, which was low and full, cast an eerie glow when the cloud passed in front of it. (added relative and subordinate clauses)
4. My father, who isn't what you'd call "handy," tried to fix the bike but did more harm than good. (added a relative clause and a verb phrase)
5. The leaves blew around the yard in a spiral, like a crackling, yellow and red tornado. (added prepositional phrases)

Teaching Tip: Other Expanding Techniques

Challenge students to think of other ways to expand sentences.

- Use an appositive to add a detail about a noun: *Tony, one of our oldest friends, is laughing . . .*
- Add a series (remind students about polysyndeton and asyndeton, SE page 80): *. . . looking not only puzzled but also worried, hurt, and a little angry*

- Add another independent clause: *Tony is laughing halfheartedly, but Phyllis is guffawing outright, barely able to contain her glee.*

❋ For more about appositives and independent clauses, see SE pages 742 and 744, respectively.

English Language Learners

Provide practice expanding sentences. Have students work as partners, with each student writing the same unadorned sentence, such as *The baby howled*. Have them exchange papers and expand the sentence in one way. Continue having them exchange and expand the sentence as much as possible without its becoming unwieldy.

Placing Modifiers

Expand on the purpose of using well-placed modifiers.

- First, modifiers help to vary sentences and clarify the writer's thoughts for the reader (see SE page 88).
- Second, sentence interrupters add qualifying information the writer believes is necessary to enhance or support ideas. For example,
  - ☐ commas are used to set off additional information within a sentence;
  - ☐ dashes are commonly used to provide a definition, to repeat or clarify an idea, or to introduce a new thought; and
  - ☐ parenthetical information is used to enclose a short message from the writer to the reader, written inside parentheses.

✳ For more about parentheses and dashes, see SE pages 638–641.

84

Placing Modifiers

Sentence modifiers add information to the sentence. One way to vary the rhythm of your writing is to vary the placement of sentence modifiers.

Using Trailing Modifiers

The most common placement for a sentence modifier is after the main clause. In this pattern, the main clause provides basic information, and the sentence modifiers add detail. In the following sentence, the main clause (in blue) is followed by a long modifying phrase.

> Some people take high doses of vitamin E, **hoping to combat free radicals (molecules) that have been blamed for damaging cells and promoting illnesses.**

Note: The main clause in the sentence above serves as a foundation for the information that follows it.

Trying Sentence Anticipators

It is also possible to place sentence modifiers before the main clause, in which case the modifiers lead up to the main point of the sentence. In the following sentence, the modifying phrases are in black.

> **Having reexamined studies of 136,000 people and finding no evidence of beneficial effects,** scientists now warn against taking megadoses of any vitamin.

Note: The introductory modifiers in the sentence above build support for the concluding thought in the main clause.

Including Sentence Interrupters

Finally, sentence modifiers can interrupt the main clause, giving additional information and adding emphasis or drama to the second part of the clause. Consider the phrases in black in the following example.

> Vitamin C, vitamin E, selenium, and beta carotene, **the four most popular antioxidants that many people have assumed to be life extenders,** can cause severe illness in megadoses.

Try It!

Review one of your textbooks for examples of sentences with trailing modifiers, sentence anticipators, and sentence interrupters. (Find at least one of each.) Then rewrite each sentence by placing the modifier or modifiers in a different position. Notice the effect this has on the meaning.

Using Inverted and Periodic Sentences

Another way to add style to your writing is to include inverted and periodic sentences. These types of sentences delay the main information until the end, giving it added emphasis. Like spices in cooking, however, it is best to use inverted and periodic sentences *sparingly* for effect.

Using Inverted Sentences

Usually, in English, the subject of a sentence comes before the verb. In an inverted sentence, however, the subject comes after the verb. (Inverted sentences sometimes begin with *there is.*) Compare these sample sentences:

> Normal: **Traffic is lighter in a gated community.**
> Inverted: **In a gated community, there is less traffic.**

Note: The second sentence above ends with the subject to give added emphasis to the main point: *less traffic.*

> Normal: **A nervous Ray Brown stood on the free throw line with two seconds left.**
> Inverted: **On the free throw line, with two seconds left, stood Ray Brown.**

Note: The second sentence above gives emphasis to the subject: *Ray Brown.*

Including Periodic Sentences

In most sentences, the main clause comes first. Once the reader has this information, additional clauses and phrases add detail. In a periodic sentence, however, the main clause is delayed until the end. This helps to build a sense of suspense and expectation. Consider the following example sentences.

> Normal: **A gated community may bring more harm than good to a city, restricting public access to parks, depressing adjacent property values, and shifting crime to other neighborhoods.**
> Periodic: **By restricting public access to parks, depressing adjacent property values, and shifting crime to other neighborhoods,** a gated community may bring more harm than good to a city.

Note: In the second sentence, the main clause (in blue) becomes a summation to the argument rather than an introduction.

 Try It!

Review an essay you have recently written and mark sentences that could be revised as inverted or periodic sentences. Change a few of these sentences and evaluate the overall effect on the essay.

(side tab) Traits

Using Inverted and Periodic Sentences

Share the following points with students as needed.

- Questions are often examples of inversion, for example: *Are you my friend?*
- In the first example, the inverted sentence could have read *In a gated community, traffic is lighter.* Point out that the word *there* is not the subject of the sentence but is a word that serves the grammatical function of getting the independent clause started. (In formal grammatical terms, it is called an *expletive.)*
- Refer to the introduction on the page, telling students to use these two types of sentences sparingly. Also note that, in the case of periodic sentences, this caution refers to long sentences, as in the example. Shorter ones—say, those with a single introductory phrase followed by a main clause—do not need to be avoided.

Struggling Learners

Have students revise the following to form inverted sentences:

1. The concerned parent waited at the bus stop on the first day of school.
2. The tuxedo shop is busiest during the prom season.
3. Sales of snowblowers increase after a snowstorm.

Checking for Sentence Problems

Note that since students need to use complete sentences in their school writing (except for the types of fragments mentioned in the FYI box), point out that most fragments are caused by

- omitting either the subject or predicate to complete the sentence, or
- using a period instead of a comma after an introductory phrase or clause.

The best way to prevent such errors is to read the draft aloud, pausing after each period. Any fragments will stand out vividly.

Try It!
Answers

Possible Rewrite

Last weekend, my mom asked me to clean out the walk-in closet in our living room. It reaches under our attic stairs and is so huge that we have stored many boxes in there. In one of the boxes I found a bunch of old videocassette tapes. We always watch DVD's—I forgot we even owned any VCR tapes. I suppose that someday, even DVD's will seem old-fashioned.

Checking for Sentence Problems

Complete, correct sentences may be made up of several ideas. The trick is getting those ideas to work together to carry your intended meaning. Presenting sentence elements incorrectly disrupts the flow and continuity of ideas in your writing. The most common errors are fragments, comma splices, run-ons, and rambling sentences.

Watching for Fragments

A sentence fragment lacks a subject, a verb, or some other essential part. Because of the missing part, the thought is incomplete.

Fragment: **Business transactions in colonial America. (This fragment lacks a verb.)**

Sentence: **Business transactions in colonial America often did not involve actual money.**

Fragment: **Because so many dealings were recorded as "book debt." (This fragment does not express a complete thought. We need to know the significance of recording transactions as book debt.)**

Sentence: **Because so many dealings were recorded as "book debt," colonial courts had to evaluate accounting records when disputes occurred.**

FYI

Sometimes writers use fragments for a good reason. For instance, you can use fragments when you write dialogue. It is also okay to use single words or phrases as sentences for dramatic effect. Note the following example from an article about the Stone Age.

> What's the main difference between the Mesolithic and Neolithic lifestyles? Farming. Without a doubt.

Try It!

Rewrite the following passage, correcting any fragments that you find.

> Last weekend, my mom asked me to clean out the closet. This huge walk-in closet in our living room. Reaches under our attic stairs. We have been storing many boxes in there. In one of the boxes, I found a bunch of old videocassette tapes. Because we always watch DVD's. I forgot we even owned any VCR tapes. Someday, even DVD's will seem old-fashioned.

English Language Learners

Provide students with extra practice revising sentence fragments. Have them read the following sentences aloud, identify what is missing, and then revise the fragment.

1. Because Marco did not make a car payment
2. Whenever I feel bored
3. Into the night, the stray cat
4. As the concert tickets were sold
5. The number of students who own cell phones
6. Living away at college
7. Without hesitation, Lila said
8. Since my computer crashed

Sentence Fluency **87**

Traits

Checking for Comma Splices

A comma splice results when two independent clauses are connected with only a comma. A period, semicolon, or conjunction is needed to correct this error.

Comma splice: Countless writers and artists since Aristotle's time have believed that creativity and madness are linked, experts today say that isn't quite the case.

Corrected: Countless writers and artists since Aristotle's time have believed that creativity and madness are linked, but experts today say that isn't quite the case. (A coordinating conjunction has been added.)

Corrected: Countless writers and artists since Aristotle's time have believed that creativity and madness are linked; experts today say that isn't quite the case. (A semicolon replaces the comma.)

Watching for Run-On Sentences

A run-on is two (or more) sentences joined without adequate punctuation or a connecting word. To correct this error, turn the run-on into two sentences or into a compound sentence.

Run-on: A creative mind-set and bipolar disorder share certain characteristics such as independence and nonconformity both lead to thinking "outside the box."

Corrected: A creative mind-set and bipolar disorder share certain characteristics such as independence and nonconformity. Both lead to thinking "outside the box."

Corrected: A creative mind-set and bipolar disorder share certain characteristics such as independence and nonconformity, and both lead to thinking "outside the box."

Try It!

Rewrite the following sentences, correcting the comma splices and run-ons.

1. The commuters had been bottlenecked on the freeway for two hours, some of the commuters had a crazed look in their eyes, the others were napping.

2. I thought the test would never end I had a classic case of finger cramps. In addition, I had severe brain-drain complications only a long nap would restore me.

Note: Be on the alert for a related sentence error—the rambling sentence, one that goes on and on because it contains too many *and*'s.

Point out that most comma splices and run-ons are caused by using conjunctive adverbs such as *however, otherwise,* and *therefore* to join closely related clauses, as in this example: *I wanted to go to the concert, however, I had promised to baby-sit.* A semicolon or a period should be used to end the first clause.

Try It!
Answers

Possible Answers

1. The commuters had been bottlenecked on the freeway for two hours. Some had a crazed look in their eyes; the others were napping.

2. I thought the test would never end. I had a classic case of finger cramps and severe brain-drain complications. Only a long nap would restore me.

English Language Learners

Students may benefit from additional practice in revising run-on sentences. Provide the following examples. First have students read them aloud. Then have them rewrite each as a compound sentence and then as two sentences.

1. The plane landed two hours late this caused many travelers to miss their connecting flights and spend the night in the airport.

2. The frisky puppy entered the waiting room filled with assorted animals he caused an uproar by jumping onto a coffee table, scattering magazines in every direction.

Checking for Additional Problems

Note that misplaced and dangling modifiers can be quite serious because modifier placement plays a crucial role in the meaning of a sentence. A misplaced modifier distracts or confuses the reader (for example, *We saw a herd of horses taking a Sunday stroll*). To demonstrate how modifier placement affects meaning, provide another version of the first example, such as

The clown with the balloon poodle entertained the child.

This doesn't imply that the balloon is entertaining the child.

Try It!
Answers

Possible Answers

1. The pool staff offers towels marked with ID numbers to the students.
2. The chef did not mean to sprinkle pepper on your potatoes.
3. As Jacque positioned himself to make the winning goal, his father yelled from the sideline.
4. The physics teacher gave the students, who were still confused about the concept, a special study guide.
5. After the drill, Coach James met with the team.

Checking for Additional Problems

The errors that follow could confuse a reader. Avoid them to make your sentences clear and readable.

Checking for Misplaced Modifiers

Misplaced modifiers are modifiers that have been placed incorrectly, leaving the meaning of the sentence unclear.

Misplaced: **The clown entertained the child with a balloon poodle.**
(Who has the balloon poodle, the child or the clown?)

Corrected: **The clown used a balloon poodle to entertain the child.**

Looking for Dangling Modifiers

Dangling modifiers are modifiers that appear to modify the wrong word or a word that isn't in the sentence.

Dangling: **Having unexpectedly turned red, I had to brake suddenly for the stoplight.**
(Who or what turned red?)

Corrected: **I had to brake suddenly for the stoplight, which had unexpectedly turned red.**

Correcting Double Negatives

A double negative is the improper use of two negative words to perform the same function in a sentence. (Using *hardly, barely,* or *scarcely* with *no* or *not* also results in a double negative.)

Double negative: **There were hardly no mistakes on her paper.**
Corrected: **There were almost no mistakes on her paper.**

Try It!

Rewrite each of the following sentences, correcting the misplaced modifier, the dangling modifier, or the double negative.

1. The pool staff offers towels to the students marked with ID numbers.
2. The chef did not mean to sprinkle no pepper on your potatoes.
3. Positioning himself to make the winning goal, Jacque's father yelled from the sideline.
4. Still confused about the concept, the physics teacher gave the students a special study guide.
5. After finishing the drill, Coach James met with the team.

Struggling Learners

If necessary, provide additional practice revising modifiers and double negatives by having students correct such sentences as the following. If they need more practice, consider sprinkling it throughout the year.

1. Mae has barely no money.
2. The woman was walking her dog in the red dress.
3. Lying in the road, I found a wallet.
4. Tess didn't say nothing.
5. Perched on a branch, I saw a nest.
6. We bought a used car from a dealer with low mileage.
7. The pan belongs to the chef with the red handle.
8. We couldn't hardly hear the music.

Conventions

A piece of writing with errors in grammar, punctuation, or spelling is like a news commentator with a piece of spinach stuck between his or her teeth. No matter how interesting the subject, the reader or listener has difficulty concentrating. Careless errors, in particular, can rob your message of its impact, suggesting to the reader that the quality of ideas may be less than trustworthy. Before you present your work, it is important, then, for you and a trusted classmate to check for conventions. Professional writers rely on editors and proofreaders for just these reasons.

There are many ways to improve your mastery of the conventions. One is to review the rules from time to time. For example, you can browse the "Proofreader's Guide" in the back of this book to remind yourself of the rules for using punctuation. It also helps to keep a list of errors that you commonly make. Then refer to this list whenever you are editing a piece of writing. The next page serves as a helpful guide for checking the conventions in your writing.

■ **A Quick Guide to Conventions**

"Ignorant people think it is the noise which fighting cats make that is so aggravating, but it ain't so; it is the sickening grammar that they use."

—Mark Twain

Copy Masters

Sample Draft Essay (TE p. 90)

Conventions

Objectives
- understand the importance of checking for conventions errors
- learn strategies for proofreading

Invite students to talk about
■ the conventions errors they make most often,
■ helpful ways they have found to find and correct errors, and
■ conventions they still have questions about.

Contribute your own experiences with learning (and teaching) the rules of writing. Have students consult the Proofreader's Guide to find answers to the questions they have about conventions. Encourage students to write down any information from the discussion that might help the next time they need to proofread.

A Quick Guide to Conventions

Make a transparency using a sample draft essay with numerous conventions errors, and work through it as a group. During this process,

- review the correct use of editing and proofreading marks (have students use the chart on the inside back cover);
- discuss individual conventions errors; and
- allow students to suggest one or two alternative ways to fix errors, where appropriate.

"I work on a word processor for the first draft, but for revisions, I always print out a copy and do my corrections by hand."

—Betsy Byars

A Quick Guide to Conventions

Checking to be sure that your work is free of errors becomes especially important near the end of a writing project.

Starting Point: You're ready to check for conventions once you . . .

- complete your major revisions—adding, cutting, rewriting, or rearranging the ideas in your writing;
- make a clean copy of your revised writing; and
- set your writing aside for a day or two (if time permits).

When you check for conventions, try to focus on one type of error at a time. This will help you edit more carefully and thoroughly. (See page 128 for a checklist.)

Tip

Have someone else check your work as well. You're too close to your writing to spot everything that needs to be changed.

Form: If you're working with pen and paper, do your editing with a different color of ink on a neat copy of your revised writing. Then complete a final copy of your work.

If you're working on a computer, do your editing on a printed copy of your writing and key in the changes. Save the edited copy so you have a record of your changes.

The Big Picture: When you check for conventions, remember that you are looking for punctuation, mechanics, spelling, or grammar errors.

- **Punctuation:** Review your work for all forms of punctuation; however, the most common errors involve commas and apostrophes. (See pages 130–131, 608–617, and 628–631.)
- **Mechanics and spelling:** Check your writing for capitalization, the use of numbers, and spelling. (See pages 648–653 and 656–668.)
- **Grammar:** Review your work for grammar errors. Pay special attention to subject-verb agreement, pronoun-antecedent agreement, and usage errors. (See pages 130–131 and 678–763.)

91

Presentation

What's the main difference between a banquet and a picnic? It isn't just the food or the setting. A banquet may serve chicken in a tent, and a picnic may include candlelight and caviar. The main difference is a matter of presentation: A banquet usually involves formal place settings, linen tablecloths and napkins, and silver utensils, while a picnic requires little more than a basket and some paper plates. When it comes to food, presentation plays a very important role, adding dignity or fun to what is otherwise just a necessity of life.

Presentation is important for writing, too. Your choice of typestyle and layout makes an immediate impression on your reader, before he or she reads a word. Taking care with your document design shows that you value your writing and respect your reader. Through effective use of headings, graphics, and white space, you can help your reader follow your ideas. This chapter will help you to understand the elements of good document design.

- Designing Your Writing
- Effective Design in Action
- Adding Graphics

"Writing well is at one and the same time good thinking, good feeling, and good expression; it is having wit, soul, and taste, all together."
—George-Louis Leclerc de Buffon

Presentation

Objectives
- learn what makes an effective design for writing
- understand how graphics can contribute to writing

Note that a good essay design doesn't have to be complicated. In fact, an elaborate design can distract readers from what the writing says—and the message should be the focus.

Computers have simplified many aspects of formatting essays that used to be time-consuming or complicated to attempt. Using a computer, a writer can easily experiment with formatting and adding graphic elements to enhance their work. Encourage students to try different variables, but not to get carried away. In the end, they should always opt for simplicity over complexity, which can distract from the content.

Designing Your Writing

Create handouts demonstrating the strategies described on the page so students can evaluate their different effects. For example, using the same block of text, print out samples that demonstrate various
- font types and sizes,
- kinds of titles and headings,
- margins and spacing, and
- graphics.

Have students examine the samples and discuss their advantages and disadvantages. Which ones are easiest to read? Why?

Designing Your Writing

The test of a good page design is that your writing is clear and easy to follow. Consider these guidelines for creating clean, attractive essays and articles.

Selecting an Appropriate Font

- **Choose an easy-to-read font for the main text.** In most cases, a serif typestyle is best for the text, and a sans serif style works for any headings. For most forms of writing, use a 12-point type size. Use **boldface** for headings if they seem to get lost on the paper.

  The letters of serif fonts have "tails"—as in this sentence.

  The letters of sans serif fonts are plain, without tails—as in this sentence.

- **Make titles and headings short and to the point.** Headings of equal importance should be stated in the same way. Follow the basic rules for capitalizing titles and headings. (See page **650**.)

Using Consistent Spacing and Margins

- **Set clear margins.** Use a one-inch margin around each page (top, bottom, left, and right).
- **Hit the tab key to indent the first line of each paragraph.** This key should be set at five spaces.
- **Leave one space after every period.** This will improve the readability of your paper.
- **Avoid placing headings, hyphenated words, and first lines of new paragraphs at the bottom of a page.** Also avoid single-word lines at either the bottom or the top of a page.

Including Graphic Elements

- **Use lists if appropriate.** Use numbered lists if your points have a clear number order. Otherwise, use bulleted lists (like the ones on this page).
- **Include graphics.** Use tables, charts, or illustrations to help make a point. Keep graphics small within the text. If a graphic is complex and needs to be large, display it on its own page. (See page **95**.)

Try It!

Compare an article from a newsmagazine like *Time* or *Newsweek* with a chapter in your history text. Which design elements are the same? Which are different? Explain how the design of each piece of writing fits the intended audience.

Advanced Learners

Have students create a pamphlet that explains the steps to follow when creating various graphic elements on a computer. Assign the following topics to pairs of students: table, pie graph, line graph, bar graph, and illustration. Have pairs write a set of directions that explain how to use a school computer to create the assigned graphic. Then have pairs check each other's work by trading directions and following the steps as written. Compile the completed sets of directions in a pamphlet for easy reference.

Effective Design in Action

The following essay by Terence Hatcher demonstrates effective design elements. The side notes highlight important design features.

Presentation **93**

Traits

Terence Hatcher
Ms. Brackett
Economics
May 9, 2011

The title is 18-point sans serif type.

Avoiding the Crunch

Let's say that someone decides to buy three CD's that are $10 each, and the cashier says, "That will be $30, please. If you don't have $30, just pay a little each month for the next 17 years." Sound ridiculous? Teenagers do it every day, creating credit card debt that will follow them into adulthood.

The main text is 12-point serif type.

Credit card companies are hoping to cash in by targeting students. Plush toys, T-shirts, and snacks are "freebies" intended to lure potential card users. Sociologist Robert Manning states, "The credit card marketers sign high school kids at college fairs. They get paid by the number of applications they turn in." Many students sign up without considering the fine print. For example, while most cards offer an introductory rate of 0 percent, the rate rises to 15 percent after the six-month promotional period. If an individual defaults or fails to pay, the rate skyrockets to 30 percent!

Subheadings are 14-point sans serif.

Doing the Math

What does this really mean? Let's say a new cardholder spends $2,000 during the first six months. Then the interest rate zooms up to 15 percent. The person decides to start paying off the balance, but doesn't have enough money to pay the whole thing. So he or she pays the monthly minimum of 2 percent or at least $25 a month. How long would it take to pay off the original $2,000 balance? Not only would it take almost 12 years, but the person would also end up spending about $4,000! As radio talk show host Clark Howard says, " . . . what you really need to know is that you are ripping yourself off because you are not paying off that balance."

Effective Design in Action

Note that students are usually not entirely free to customize the format of their essays. They usually must conform to a given standard, either specified by their instructor or the MLA (or APA) style manual. Examples of elements that students may be required to address in a specific way include the following:

- placement of their name, class, instructor's name, and date
- font style and margin requirements
- position of page numbers

Early in the course, encourage students who use computers to create a template of the format that meets your requirements. This way, they can use it for all written assignments.

Discuss the student writer's use of the line graph and bulleted list for this essay. Did she make good choices? (Students should agree that she did.) What works best?

- The soaring "total paid line" on the graph vividly depicts how much more money is required to pay off the debt.
- The choice of red—a color associated with danger—for the "total paid line" also emphasizes the writer's point.
- The list breaks up the block of text on the page and draws the eye through each guideline. Since the list is introduced with the phrase *four key guidelines,* she could also have used a numbered list.

Hatcher 2

The chart that follows illustrates the problem with making minimum monthly payments.

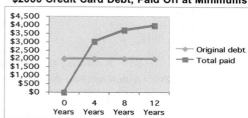

$2000 Credit Card Debt, Paid Off at Minimums

A chart adds impact and visual appeal.

Keeping a Clean Record

"Your credit report is often called your second résumé," according to Dr. Flora J. Williams in her book *Steps to Financial Success.* A credit report covers an individual's history of borrowing, bill payment, and debt owed. If someone uses a credit card irresponsibly, the credit card company will make negative comments on the credit report. Banks, college loan officers, employers, and landlords can request a credit report.

So how does someone maintain a positive credit report? Here are four key guidelines:

A bulleted list adds clarity to important points.

- People should use a credit card wisely. They should keep track of what they are buying and know how long it will take to pay for each item.
- They should also know their credit limit. Going over the limit may result in fines or even cancellation of an account.
- It is also wise to pay off the balance, or at least more than the minimum.
- Cardholders should pay on time to avoid late fees, increased interest rates, and credit damage.

What is the lesson here? It takes common sense and hard work to avoid the pitfalls of credit card debt. If people read the fine print, spend wisely, and pay promptly, they'll be on their way to building a solid financial foundation.

Adding Graphics

When adding graphics to your writing, make sure you aren't simply "dressing up" the words. Instead, include graphics to add information or enhance the reader's understanding. Follow these guidelines:

Use tables to provide statistics in a compact form. Clearly label rows and columns so that the reader can quickly grasp the information.

COMPARING COUNTRIES			
	Canada	Mexico	United States
Size (Sq. Miles)	3.85 million	759,000	3.8 million
Type of Government	Parliamentary	Republic	Republic
Voting Age	18	18	18
Literacy	99%	87%	98%

Traits

Use graphs to show statistics visually. Line graphs show how quantities change over time. Bar graphs compare and contrast amounts. Pie graphs show the parts of a whole. Be sure to provide a clear title, labels, and a legend (if needed).

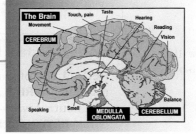

Sources of Carbon Monoxide Emissions, 2006

Transportation 82%
9% Miscellaneous
5% Industrial Processes
4% Other Fuel Combustion

Use diagrams to show the parts of something. Include labels or arrows to inform the reader about the parts being shown.

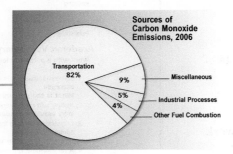

The Brain
Movement · Touch, pain · Taste · Hearing · Reading · Vision
CEREBRUM
Speaking · Smell · MEDULLA OBLONGATA · CEREBELLUM · Balance

Try It!

Review essays you have written and select one that could include a table, graph, or diagram. Create a graphic that demonstrates important ideas or statistics in the essay.

Struggling Learners

Reinforce the way graphics enhance writing by having students find tables, graphs, and diagrams in newspaper and magazine articles. Display the examples, and discuss the purpose of each visual.

Adding Graphics

If computers are available for students, show them how to create each of the different kinds of graphics shown. For example, many word-processing programs include

- a table-making function that allows students to create data tables;
- automatic graph makers that convert numerical data entered into the chosen style of chart or graph; and
- drawing features that allow students to superimpose labels and arrows on a digital image.

Teacher's Notes for Exploring the Writing Process

This overview of the writing process includes some specific teaching suggestions for the unit. The description of each chapter will help you decide which parts of the unit to teach.

Writing Focus

Prewriting (pages 97–104)

This chapter reviews choosing a topic, gathering details, writing a thesis statement, and organizing details.

Writing the First Draft (pages 105–112)

This chapter will take students through the process of drafting a beginning, a middle, and an ending.

Revising (pages 113–120)

Guidelines, a strategy, and a checklist are some of the elements of revising covered in this chapter.

Peer Responding (pages 121–126)

Students have a chance to see their role as a writer having work reviewed by classmates and their role as peer responders for fellow classmates.

Editing (pages 127–132)

The checklist for editing and proofreading on SE page 128 will help students with the editing process. Typical errors are also highlighted.

Publishing (pages 133–139)

Several publishing options (including writing contests) are listed in this chapter.

Academic Vocabulary

Read aloud the academic terms, as well as the descriptions and questions. Model for students how to read one question and answer it. Have partners monitor their understanding and seek clarification of the terms by working through the meanings and questions together.

Minilessons

Clustering   Prewriting

- **STUDY** the cluster shown on SE page 98. **MAKE** your own cluster for one of the following general subjects: space travel, ocean exploration, mountain climbing, or a general subject of your choice. **CHOOSE** a topic you would like to write about from your finished cluster.

Exploring the Writing Process

Writing Focus

Academic Vocabulary

Work with a partner to learn these words from this unit.

1. Something that is primary is the first or most important.
   What is the primary way you read books?
2. Redundant means repetitive.
   Why would redundant ideas weaken an essay?
3. Constrain means to force something into or hold something back.
   Describe how your writing can be constrained?
4. A requirement is a necessity or something you are obligated to do.
   What is a requirement for graduation?

Firm, Pigheaded, Resolute   Writing and Revising

- **RECALL** the plot of a movie or a recent event you attended. **WRITE** about the plot or what happened in a neutral way—matter-of-fact, objective view point. **REWRITE** the information first from a strong negative perspective and then from a highly positive point of view. **UNDERLINE** the words that you changed or added to create each version.

I Think That . . .   Peer Responding

- **CHOOSE** one of your recent essays. In a small group of classmates, **TAKE** turns assessing each other's essays using the checklist on SE page 126. **DISCUSS** the results. Did you gain some new insights about your writing?

Insert, Delete, Change   Editing

- **FREEWRITE** a paragraph on a topic of your choice. **INCLUDE** several spelling, usage, punctuation, and grammar errors. **REVIEW** the editing and proofreading marks on the inside back cover of your textbook. **EXCHANGE** paragraphs with a partner. **MARK** your partner's paragraph using the editing and proofreading marks. Finally, **WRITE** a final copy of your paragraph based on your partner's marks.

Prewriting

Author Barry Lane says writers "continually move back and forth between the sea and the mountain" during a writing project. As Lane explains it, writing begins in the "sea of experience," which contains the memories, experiences, and information that writers work with. When they actually write, writers begin to climb the "mountain of perception," forming new understandings, linking ideas, and drawing conclusions. If they need more details, they head back to the sea.

Prewriting refers to the beginning of a writing project—when you're still at sea—selecting a topic, gathering information about it, and so on. Prewriting also refers to trips back to the sea—when you need to carry out additional research and planning in the middle of a writing project. If you give prewriting the proper attention, you've laid a solid foundation for all of the other steps in the writing process.

- Selecting a Topic
- Gathering Details
- Finding Additional Information
- A Closer Look at Prewriting
- Forming Your Thesis Statement
- Organizing Your Details

"Writing is an exploration. You start from nothing and learn as you go."
—E. L. Doctorow

Prewriting

Objectives
- identify strategies to help choose writing topics
- examine the process of gathering details
- learn the thought processes that take place during prewriting
- understand the parts of a thesis statement
- learn how to make a writing plan

Note that the prewriting stage involves more different parts than any other stage of the writing process. During this stage, writers
- choose a topic,
- research it,
- draft a thesis statement, and
- plan the basic structure.

By contrast, all the other stages—writing, revising, editing, publishing—have a more single-minded focus.

Encourage students to keep in mind the various tasks they must complete as part of prewriting and to allow ample time to do them.

Selecting a Topic

Note that students should do research about the topics they're considering in order to answer their initial questions about them. Doing preliminary research will enable them to make a more informed decision about a topic. Remind them, however, that research can become time-consuming (one finding leads to another); they should not commit themselves to researching topics too thoroughly at this stage. Suggest that they dedicate one hour to do some research online, surfing reliable Web sites to answer their basic questions, and then to proceed with one of the strategies suggested in their book.

✱ For more about evaluating sources and Web sites for reliability, see SE pages 373–374.

Selecting a Topic

Your teacher may provide you with a general subject and ask that you narrow it to a specific topic.

General Subject: **The Endocrine System**

Specific Topic: **Glands and Hormones of the Endocrine System**

Depending on the assignment, use one of the following strategies to select an effective, specific writing topic.

Keeping a Writer's Notebook

Write on a regular basis in a personal notebook (journal), exploring your experiences and thoughts. Review your entries on occasion and underline ideas that you could explore in writing assignments. (See pages **1–5** for more information.)

Developing a Cluster

Begin a cluster with a nucleus word, usually a general term or idea related to your writing assignment. Then cluster related words around it.

Sample Cluster

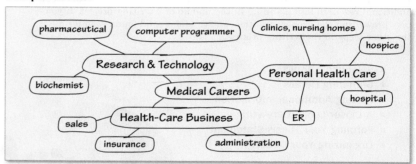

Note: After 3 or 4 minutes, scan your cluster for a word or an idea that interests you. Write nonstop about that idea for 5 to 8 minutes. A few writing topics should begin to occur to you.

Making a List

Begin with a thought or a key word related to your assignment and simply start listing words and ideas. Listing ideas with a group of classmates (brainstorming) is also an effective way to search for writing topics.

Trying Freewriting

Begin writing with a particular focus in mind—one that is related to your assignment. Write nonstop for 5 to 10 minutes to discover possible writing topics.

- Don't stop to judge, edit, or correct your writing.
- Keep writing even when you seem to be drawing a blank. If necessary, write "I'm drawing a blank" until a new idea comes to mind.
- Review your writing and underline ideas you like.
- Continue freewriting about ideas you want to explore further.

Sample Freewriting

> Most people think of doctors and nurses when they hear you're interested in a medical career. It's really amazing, the kinds of jobs there are in health care. With some medical careers, people don't even have to see or touch another human being. In others, that's what they do all day. And think about how important computers are to health care now! . . .

Considering the "Basics of Life" List

Below you will find a list of the essential elements in our lives. The list provides an endless variety of topic possibilities. For example, the category *education* led to the following writing ideas:

- internships for high school students
- community service requirements
- open campus vs. closed campus

Basics of Life

clothing	education	love	entertainment
communication	machines	rules/laws	health/medicine
exercise/training	faith/religion	science/technology	recreation
housing	family	energy	literature/books
community	trade/money	land/property	tools/utensils
food	agriculture	work/occupation	freedom/rights
arts/music	heat/fuel		

Try It!

List four or five possible writing ideas for any two categories in the "Basics of Life" list. (For your next writing assignment, use one of the strategies above to identify possible topics.)

Process

Advanced Learners

Ask students to create a file of writing topics for the "Basics of Life" list. Have students form a team and choose a column from the box. Their challenge is to generate a list of writing topics for each item in the column over a few weeks. Have teams record their lists on index cards to save in a *Writing Ideas* file for the class.

Suggest that students keep their freewriting or other notes they make while considering possible topics. This, like their writer's notebook, can serve as a sort of "idea bank" they can refer to from time to time when they need ideas. They may discover that a topic that did not appeal to them for one assignment is suitable for another, later project.

Gathering Details

Note that the amount of time students will need to spend gathering their thoughts will vary from topic to topic. If they are planning a research paper, they will jot down their ideas, but then move on to collecting the details that will form the bulk of the essay. If they are planning a personal narrative, most of their time may be spent on this step.

This is a good time to
- think of personal anecdotes or examples that might apply to the topic;
- document their opinions about the topic— keeping in mind that these might change substantially after they learn more details;
- write down questions about what they would like to investigate as they research the topic.

100

Gathering Details

In most cases, it's a good idea to first collect your initial thoughts about the topic you've selected, including personal experience and past knowledge. Then, if necessary, do research to find more information.

Gathering Your Thoughts

These strategies will help you to recall what you already know and establish how you feel about your topic.

- **Freewriting:** Approach freewriting in one of two ways. (1) Do a focused freewriting, exploring your topic from a number of different angles. (2) Approach freewriting as if it were a quick version of the actual paper.
- **Audience appeal:** Address a specific audience as you write. Consider a group of parents, a television audience, or the readers of a popular teen magazine.
- **Questioning:** Ask questions to gather information about your topic. If your topic falls into the categories of *problems, policies,* or *concepts,* you can use the questions in this chart.

	Description	Function	History	Value
Problems	What is the problem?	Who or what is affected by it?	What is the current status of the problem?	Why is it important?
Policies	What type of policy is it? What are its features?	What is the policy designed to do?	What brought this policy about?	Is the policy working? Why or why not?
Concepts	What type of concept is it? Who or what is related to it?	Who has been influenced by this concept?	When did it originate? How has it changed?	What value does it hold? What is its social worth?

Try It!

Gather your thoughts. Use one of these strategies to collect your own thoughts about a writing topic.

English Language Learners

Before beginning the **Try It!** activity, encourage students to chose a familiar topic. Pair students with cooperative partners and have them take turns explaining their topic, with details, before writing.

Finding Additional Information

For most writing assignments, it won't suffice to simply gather your own thoughts about a topic. Expository and persuasive essays, for example, will almost always require that you consult other sources for information. These sources can be divided into two categories—*primary* and *secondary*.

Exploring a Variety of Sources

- **Primary sources** include interviews, personal observations, firsthand experiences, surveys, experiments, and so on. A primary source informs you directly, not through another person's explanation or interpretation.
- **Secondary sources** include periodicals, books, references, Web sites, and so on. A secondary source is one that contains information other people have gathered and interpreted. It is at least once removed from the original.

Tips for Gathering Information

- Whenever possible, use both primary and secondary sources to get a thorough understanding of your topic.
- Read secondary sources with a critical eye, always evaluating the quality and the purpose of the information. (See page 373.)
- Take careful notes, writing down important facts, opinions, and quotations. Record any source information you will need to cite. (See page 399.)
- Consider using a graphic organizer such as a gathering grid (page 396) to keep track of the facts and details your research uncovers.
- Consult librarians and teachers if you have trouble finding information.

Try It!

Imagine that you've been assigned to write an essay about immigration in the United States. Identify each of the following sources of information as primary or secondary.

1. An e-mail message from a member of the National Immigration Forum, responding to your questions from a previous e-mail
2. An interview concerning immigration in *In Motion,* an online magazine
3. Your participation in an immigration-rights rally
4. A newspaper report, reviewing new immigration legislation

Process

Finding Additional Information

Suggest that one good way to distinguish between a primary and a secondary source is to ask the following:

- Are these the thoughts and observations of a person who was directly involved? (If yes, it is a primary source.)
- Were these ideas created after the fact by someone who was not involved? (If yes, it is a secondary source.)

Note that sources can include both kinds of information. In general, a documentary is a secondary source. However, it may contain information from primary sources: interviews with **eyewitnesses** *(see below),* photographs, recordings, the text of journals or letters.

* For more about primary and secondary sources, see SE page 372.

Try It! Answers

1. primary
2. Depends on the interview. For example, an interview with an immigrant or immigration worker would be primary; an interview with a historian about the events that led up to the present-day situation would be secondary.
3. primary
4. secondary

Teaching Tip: Eyewitnesses

Remind students that involvement in an event doesn't guarantee that a person fully understands all of the causes and implications of what happened, or that their view is unbiased. Emphasize that this is the reason the researcher must regard *all* sources with a critical eye and use a variety of sources.

- Primary accounts will recreate a sense of how the situation was experienced at the time.
- Secondary sources will show how different experts analyzed what happened.

English Language Learners

Students may have difficulty making a distinction between primary and secondary sources. Explain that primary sources have firsthand experiences with the topic. To help students understand this, have them brainstorm a list of events for which they would serve as primary sources.

A Closer Look at Prewriting

Acknowledge that students may not always have time to make a strong personal connection with their topic—that is the ideal, but sometimes it isn't practicable. Instead, they may be asked to write about something they are not invested in because of the focus of a particular assignment or writing prompt. They can, however, create a stronger essay by using the inventory.

Remind students that most of the questions are designed

- to make sure they have not strayed from the focus of the assignment and
- to help them make decisions about how to plan their writing.

Encourage those who feel they haven't quite connected with their topic to find something about it that does appeal to them and to concentrate on that. They may discover they are more interested than they had thought at first.

"As soon as you connect with your true subject, you will write."
—Rachel Carson

A Closer Look at Prewriting

After you've selected a topic and gathered details about it, you can plan and write your first draft, or you can consider how well you match up with your topic before you go any further.

Taking Inventory of Your Thoughts

After carefully considering the questions that follow, you will be ready to (1) move ahead with your writing or (2) change your topic.

Purpose

- Does my topic meet the requirements of the assignment?
- Am I writing to explain, persuade, describe, entertain, or retell?

Self

- How do I feel about the topic? Have I made a personal connection with it?
- Do I have enough time to develop it?

Topic

- How much more do I need to know about this topic?
- Has my research changed my thinking about the topic?
- What part of the topic will I focus on?

Audience

- Who are my readers?
- How much do they already know about my topic?
- How can I keep them interested in my ideas?

Form

- How should I present my ideas—in a story, an essay, a report, a multimedia presentation?
- What form of writing should I use—narrative, descriptive, persuasive, expository?

Forming Your Thesis Statement

After you have explored the topic and collected information, you should begin to develop a more focused interest in your topic. If all goes well, this interest will become the thesis of your writing. **A thesis statement identifies the focus of an academic essay.** It usually highlights a particular condition, feature, or feeling about the topic or takes a stand.

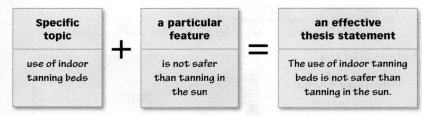

Specific topic		a particular feature		an effective thesis statement
use of indoor tanning beds	**+**	is not safer than tanning in the sun	**=**	The use of indoor tanning beds is not safer than tanning in the sun.

Sample Thesis Statements

Writing Assignment: Essay on some aspect of the '60s generation
Specific Topic: Social issues of the decade
Thesis Statement: The social issues of the 1960s (**specific topic**) continue to play a role in our current culture (**particular feature**).

Writing Assignment: Essay about the introduction of new species into the ecosystem
Specific Topic: The Asian carp in the Great Lakes
Thesis Statement: The introduction of the Asian carp into the Great Lakes (**specific topic**) could lead to a radical change in the lakes' ecosystem (**particular feature**).

 Try It!

Write thesis statements. Listed below are specific topics students have used for essays. For two of them, write a thesis statement that focuses on a particular feature of the topic.

General Subject:	Specific Topic:
the Internet	peer-to-peer sharing programs
a nineteenth-century author	Edgar Allan Poe
"helpful" insects	butterflies and dragonflies
a natural disaster	the 2010 earthquake in Haiti

Process

Forming Your Thesis Statement

Remind students that the thesis statement they create at this point is intended to get them started. Many writers' ideas change during the course of planning a piece.

 Try It! Answers

Possible Answers

Peer-to-peer file sharing programs, especially those that facilitate the free exchange of music, are on the rise, despite questions from the recording industry about how to protect their right to profit from the music they produce and distribute.

Although the events in stories by **Edgar Allan Poe** aren't precisely autobiographical, his tales do present a psychological portrait of a man haunted by personal demons and material hardship.

In addition to being beautiful, **butterflies and dragonflies** represent two types of "helpful" insect: predators (who eat pests such as flies and mosquitoes) and pollinators (who help propagate flowers and fruits).

The events following **the 2010 earthquake in Haiti** emphasized the need to strengthen relief and long-term aid strategies for devastated areas.

Organizing Your Details

Encourage students to experiment with different kinds of writing plans in order to figure out which ones work best for them. Discuss possibilities such as the following:

- Sentence outlines will appeal to writers who like to make detailed plans; the headings consist of draft topic sentences for the middle paragraphs.
- Topic outlines are made up of quick notes— writers who like this format prefer to work out the fine points during the writing stage.
- Students who think in terms of pictures might prefer to use one or more graphic organizers for their plan; refer them to the organizers shown on SE pages 64–65.
- Some students find it helpful to write their ideas on note cards, which they can then arrange and rearrange until they discover the order they like best.

✳ For more about sentence and topic outlines, see SE page 591.

Organizing Your Details

After forming a thesis statement, you may need to design a writing plan before you start your first draft. Your plan can be anything from a brief list of ideas to a detailed sentence outline. Use the guidelines that follow to help organize your details for writing.

1. Study your thesis statement. It may suggest a logical method of organization for your essay.
2. Review the details you have gathered.
3. Decide which basic pattern of organization fits your essay topic.

Sample Brief List

Topic: Hunger in Africa

- Natural resources
- India as an example
- The "Harare Declaration"

Sample Sentence Outline

Topic: Hunger in Africa

  I. Africa is a land of many valuable resources.
    A. It contains great areas of unused land, water, and minerals.
    B. There are enough resources to feed all of Africa.
    C. Developing these resources will take time and cooperation.
 II. India should give African countries hope.
    A. It experienced a similar hunger problem.
    B. The government began producing enough food for its people.
    C. Today, India is in much better shape than it was 25 years ago.

105

Writing the First Draft

Once you have chosen your topic, gathered details, and organized your details, you're ready to write your first draft. This is your first attempt at developing your prewriting into a complete, cohesive unit of writing.

Writing a first draft can be exciting and satisfying as you see your initial thinking about a topic take shape. Try to write your first draft freely without being overly concerned about correctness. Your goal is to get all your ideas on paper in a form that is easy to follow. Use the planning you've done (outline) as a basic guide, but be open to new ideas that come to mind as you write.

If you are writing an essay or a research paper, develop each of your main points in a separate paragraph. Also connect the paragraphs with linking words or transitions. The information in this chapter provides additional drafting tips and strategies for writing your first draft.

- Considering the Big Picture
- Writing the Beginning
- Developing the Middle
- Writing the Ending

"The first draft is the down draft—
you just get it down. The second
draft is the up draft—you fix it up."

—Anne Lamott

Writing the First Draft

Objectives

- understand the process of creating a first draft with a beginning, a middle, and an ending
- learn about the various types of support and levels of detail that make up a strong argument

Note that the following pages will offer detailed and practical suggestions for students to follow as they write. Discuss strategies they can use to help themselves establish "creative flow"—a state of mind in which a creative endeavor comes easily.

- Set aside a good amount of time to write. There should be enough time in a single session—at least an hour—to immerse oneself in the project.
- Find a place to write that is conducive to concentration. It may be helpful to create a working space that can be left undisturbed during the process and generous enough to hold writing accouterments and planning notes.

English Language Learners

Point out that in the quotation, the writer makes puns—plays on words—on *down, up,* and *draft*. Tell students a *downdraft* is an air current that sweeps downward—the equivalent of a writer putting down his or her ideas—and that an *updraft* is one that sweeps upward—the equivalent of a writer fixing *up* his or her work.

Considering the Big Picture

Assure students that it isn't necessary for them to work on the parts of the draft in order, unless they want to. They may discover that one part is much clearer in their minds (often this is a portion of the middle section). If so, they should feel free to get those ideas down on paper first. Writing what they know will very likely lead students to another part, and then another—possibly until all their ideas have been addressed. Then, during the revision stage, they can focus on making sure the parts flow smoothly from one to the next.

Considering the Big Picture

As you prepare to write a first draft, keep in mind these three traits of good writing: *ideas, organization,* and *voice.*

Ideas Start with a specific focus. Then develop the main supporting points you gathered in your prewriting. Write freely and add new ideas as they come to you.

Organization Use your planning as a guide and try to get all of your thoughts on paper. Be sure to include a beginning, a middle, and an ending. (See below.)

Voice Let your words flow naturally and freely, as if you were in a conversation with the reader.

Drafting Hints

- Review your prewriting materials before you begin. This will help you get started.
- If you are drafting by hand, write on every other line; if you are using a computer, double-space your work so you will have room to revise.
- Focus on the writing and don't be overly concerned about being neat and avoiding errors. You can make corrections later on.

Organizing Your Writing

As you write, keep in mind the three parts of any piece of writing: the beginning, the middle, and the ending.

The Beginning

- Gets the reader's attention.
- Identifies the thesis or purpose of your writing.

The Middle

- Presents the main points that support the thesis.
- Includes details that develop the main points.

The Ending

- Restates the thesis.
- Presents a final insight about the topic.

Try It!

Be sure to review this page before you write your next first draft. Afterward, assess your results. *Did you write naturally and freely? Did you get all of your ideas on paper? Did you include all three parts—beginning, middle, and ending?*

Struggling Learners

The notion of working out of order may fly in the face of what students have thought they should be doing, and it may make them feel disorganized. Point out that it is often much easier to write the middle section first because it contains most of the main points that support the writer's thesis. It isn't until a writer finishes these that she or he might figure out the best way to get the reader's attention and state the thesis. The beginning of an essay, as well as the ending, may not fully emerge until the revising stage.

Writing the First Draft **107**

Writing the Beginning

Your opening paragraph, informative and interesting, must hook the reader.

Grabbing Your Reader's Attention

Develop an opening statement that reflects the focus and tone of your writing. Here are some ways to attract the reader's interest.

- Give a surprising fact or statement.
  Although the wild dogs called dingoes are generally considered Australian natives, they originated in and still roam Southeast Asia.

- Ask a question.
  When is a dog not a dog? When it is a dingo: part wolf, part dog, and all danger.

- Use a relevant quotation.
  "They're the devil in fur, that's what they are." That's how an angry sheep rancher refers to dingoes, the wild dogs of the Australian outback.

- Present an interesting detail about the topic.
  Dingoes, often considered pests, play an important role in Australia's ecosystem.

Shaping Your Beginning Paragraph

The first part of your opening paragraph should identify your topic and hook the reader. Follow with any necessary background information. End with your thesis statement, identifying the specific part of the topic you plan to emphasize.

Attention-getting opening	*"They're the devil in fur, that's what they are!" That's how an angry sheep rancher refers to dingoes, the wild dogs of the Australian outback.* **Descended from wolves, these lean, shrewd creatures roam northern Australia, living off their wits and whatever small animals they can find. Farmers who suffer the loss of chickens or sheep to these predators consider dingoes little more than a headache.** *Yet these long-legged interlopers are actually an important part of the Australian ecosystem.*
Background information	
Thesis statement	

Try It!

Analyze the beginning paragraph you are writing for a current assignment. Experiment with different openings to grab the reader's attention.

Process

Writing the Beginning

Suggest that students look back at essays they wrote earlier to see what styles of beginnings they have favored in the past.

- What strategies have they used?
- Do they feel their beginnings have generally been effective?
- Do they have ideas for how to improve any of their less-effective beginnings?
- Have they relied on one strategy more than others?

If students usually rely on one strategy, suggest that they try another for their next essay. The goal is to try all of the approaches so they can create the beginning that best suits their topic.

Struggling Learners

Review with students the four bulleted methods of attracting a reader's interest. Then have students find articles in newspapers or magazines that demonstrate each type of opening. Have pairs of students work together to select one article and rewrite the opening using a different technique.

Developing the Middle

To demonstrate that an effective argument requires a number of methods to be used, ask students to look at each sample paragraph, identify exactly how it demonstrates the concept associated with it, and point out one or more additional types of support that are used in the paragraph. Possible responses:

- Paragraph 1 *explains* the lengths farmers went to protect their animals; it also *describes* the Dingo Fence and *reflects* on the magnitude of the project.
- Paragraph 2 *describes* what dingoes look like; it also *compares* them with dogs.
- Paragraph 3 *argues* that dingoes help maintain ecological balance; it also *explains* that they keep the rabbit population under control and *compares* the situations on either side of the fence.

108

Developing the Middle

Your middle paragraphs should provide the details that support your thesis. Use your planning materials to arrange your support in a logical order. Here are some ways to support your thesis:

Explain: Provide important facts, details, and examples.
Narrate: Share a brief story (anecdote) to illustrate or clarify an idea.
Describe: Tell how someone appears or how something works.
Summarize: Present only the most important ideas.
Define: Identify or clarify the meaning of a specific term or idea.
Argue: Use logic and evidence to prove something is true.
Compare: Show how two things are alike or different.
Analyze: Examine the parts of something to better understand the whole.
Reflect: Express your thoughts or feelings about something.

 FYI

Most essays, articles, and research papers require a number of these methods to thoroughly develop their theses. For example, an essay of definition may contain two or more definitions, a comparison, a brief story, and so on.

Using Various Types of Support

Below and on the next page are some examples of how one student used various types of support in his paper about dingoes, wild dogs of Australia.

Explain: Provide important facts, details, and examples.

> Dingoes have proven a real menace to Australian sheep and cattle farmers, who have gone to great lengths to protect their animals by building the Dingo Fence. Built in the 1880s, the fence stretches across New South Wales and southern Queensland, the country's major farming area. It effectively separates the cattle and sheep areas from dingoes. At six feet high, it is also sunk nearly a foot below ground to prevent the predators from digging underneath. At the time this 3,000-mile-long fence was built, it was the longest man-made structure in the world, showing just how far some people will go to protect their investments.

Describe: Create a mental picture of your subject.

> Although dingoes look somewhat like dogs, they have physical characteristics that link them to wolves. Their coats are generally ginger colored but may vary in color from sandy to dark red to black, with white markings on their feet, throats, and bushy tails. There

Advanced Learners

Provide the opening paragraph to an essay that doesn't require any or much research. Assign each student one or two (depending on the size of the group) types of support listed at the top of SE page 108. Have each student write a middle paragraph that illustrates one of the assigned techniques. Have students share their paragraphs with the group and offer each other comments and suggestions. Have them reach a consensus on which types of paragraphs help develop the topic the most.

are even white dingoes found in the Australian Alps. Dingoes stand about one and a half to two feet high at the shoulder, and are about five feet long. They are long legged and lean with long, pointed muzzles and pointed ears that stick straight up at the tops of their heads. Although related to dogs, dingoes have larger teeth and do not bark but howl instead, much like wolves and coyotes. Once considered close relatives to domestic dogs *(Canus familiaris)*, dingoes have been given feral status and their own scientific name, *Canus dingo*.

Argue: Present a case for or against a topic.

Ironically, the Dingo Fence has shown that although dingoes may seem like pests, they are an important part of the Australian ecosystem. As predators, dingoes help control the rabbit population. An unchecked rabbit population decimates grazing lands, negatively affecting sheep and cattle ranching. In fact, on the protected side of the Dingo Fence, rabbit and kangaroo populations have depleted grass and water. On the dingo side of the fence, these populations have been effectively reduced, allowing for more luxuriant grasslands. This indicates that dingoes help maintain an ecological balance.

Reflect: Consider the impact of your topic.

Dingoes have been considered pests—ostracized by special fences and overcome by poison, traps, and shooting. Scientists worry about the possible extinction of these animals, so they have set up conservation areas. However, a threat that is less easily controlled is that of dingoes interbreeding with domestic dogs. Scientists fear that in the not-too-distant future, the pure dingo strain may disappear forever.

Analyze: Examine the parts of something to better understand the whole.

Ever since the cry "Dingoes ate my baby!" appeared in a sensationalist tabloid newspaper, people have been concerned about dingo attacks. Scientists exploring the phenomena suggest that attacks on humans are not characteristic of purebred dingoes. The problem comes from offspring of dingoes and domestic dogs. The resulting hybrid pups are larger and more aggressive with characteristics of a dog and a dingo. Whereas a pure dingo might eat whatever bugs or lizards it finds, a hybrid craves meat, leading to more and more attacks on sheep, cattle, and even humans.

Try It!

Analyze the middle paragraphs in one of the essays in this book. Tell which method of support is used to develop each main point (explaining, comparing, analyzing, and so on).

Process

Try It!
Answers

Possible Answer

Essay on SE pages 29–31:

Middle paragraph 1 **explains** how the national budget is distributed by **defining** the terms *discretionary spending* and *mandatory spending*.

Paragraph 2 **explains** how much of the federal budget is devoted to defense, **compares** that amount to how much is allocated to education and health, and **reflects** on the implications of the statistics (priorities are skewed). This paragraph could also be considered an **analysis** of the budget.

Paragraph 3 **argues** that the defense budget could be cut and the U.S. military would still be the world's most powerful. Also, it **compares** the military power of China and Russia with that of the United States.

Paragraph 4 **argues** it is unlikely the U.S. will be attacked by another country and the greater threat is from terrorist groups.

Paragraph 5 **argues** that the public supports defense budget cuts and that the economy will not suffer. It also **defines**, a term *(adapt to the market)*.

Developing the Middle
Using Different Levels of Detail

Note that the levels of detail described correspond directly to the three familiar parts of the paragraph: the topic sentence, body sentences, and closing sentence.

✳ For more about the parts of a paragraph, see SE pages 578–579.

Try It!
Answers

Level 1: first sentence (lines 1–2)
Level 2: sentences 2–5 (lines 2–9)
Level 3: last sentence (lines 9–12)

Developing the Middle Using Different Levels of Detail

In most cases each main point is developed in a separate paragraph. Remember that specific details add meaning to your writing and make it worth reading, while writing that lacks effective detail leaves the reader with an incomplete picture and questions about the topic. A well-written paragraph often contains three levels of detail.

Level 1: A controlling sentence names the topic.

> Ironically, the Dingo Fence has shown that although dingoes may seem like pests, they are an important part of the Australian ecosystem.

Level 2: Clarifying sentences provide supporting points.

> As predators, dingoes help control the rabbit population. An unchecked rabbit population decimates grazing lands, negatively affecting sheep and cattle ranching. In fact, on the protected side of the Dingo Fence, rabbit and kangaroo populations have depleted grass and water. On the dingo side of the fence, these populations have been effectively reduced, allowing for more luxuriant grasslands.

Level 3: A completing sentence adds details to conclude the idea.

> This indicates that dingoes help maintain an ecological balance.

Try It!

Identify one set of sentences that show the three levels of detail in the paragraph below. Label each sentence after writing it down. (The topic sentence is the one controlling sentence in the paragraph.)

1. Until a few years ago, dingo watching was a popular tourist attraction on
2. Fraser Island, Australia's top vacation spot. Dingoes have traditionally displayed
3. a mild temperament around humans, but aggressive behaviors began appearing
4. in 2001, with a fatal attack on a child. Since that
5. time, another 20 attacks have been documented. It
6. appears that through continued contact with tourists,
7. the dingoes have lost their innate fear of humans.
8. Because the animals are by nature carnivores, this
9. newfound aggression poses obvious dangers. While
10. dingo watching is not discouraged, it now comes
11. with governmental warnings and regulations.

Integrating Quotations

Always choose quotations that are appropriate for your writing. Quotations should support your ideas, not replace them.

Strategies for Using Quotations

Use the strategies below to make the most effective use of quoted material in your writing.

- **Use quotations to support your own thoughts and ideas.**
  Effective quotations can back up your main points or support your arguments.

  > Even in the early twentieth century, pollution was a growing concern, as shown in this comment by Franklin D. Roosevelt: "Government cannot close its eyes to the pollution of waters, to the erosion of soil, to the slashing of forests any more than it can close its eyes to the need for slum clearance and schools."

- **Use quotations to lend authority to your writing.**
  Quoting an expert shows that you have researched your topic and understand its significance.

  > Despite vociferous opposition to the arms race, the development of the bomb was an important part of world peace. As nuclear physicist Edward Teller explained, "We had a wonderful record on the hydrogen bomb. We tested it, perfected it, and never used it—and that served to win the Cold War."

- **Use quotations that are succinct and powerful.**
  Distinctive quotations add value to your writing.

  > Country music's power doesn't come from complicated structures or deep political undertones; it is popular simply because it touches people's lives. As legendary songwriter Harlan Howard once put it, "Country music is three chords and the truth."

Common Quotation Problems to Avoid

Avoid these problems as you choose quotations.

- **Plagiarism**
  Cite sources for all quotations (and paraphrases).
- **Long quotations**
  Keep quotations brief and to the point.
- **Overused quotations**
  Use a quotation only when you cannot share its message as powerfully or effectively in another way.

Process

Developing the Middle

Integrating Quotations

Review how to punctuate quotations when integrating them in text.

- Where a quotation is part of the sentence, the quotation is either preceded by a comma or, if more emphasis is needed, a colon (first bullet).
- Where partial quotations can be embedded in the structure of the sentence, no comma is used before the quoted words, unless it is required by the structure of the sentence (third bullet).
- Ellipsis points are used to represent words that are left out: *"We had a wonderful record on the hydrogen bomb. We . . . perfected it, and never used it . . ."*

* For more about punctuating quotations and using ellipses, see SE page 632 and 642, respectively.

Writing the Ending

Acknowledge that coming up with an effective ending is challenging for most writers. It is a double challenge to restate the thesis without sounding repetitive and to convey one final thought or insight, after including details in the middle section. Suggest ways that students might approach writing the ending.

- Set the draft aside for a day before writing the ending, in order to return to it with a fresher outlook.
- Review research notes to see if there are any interesting unused details. (A memorable quotation that connects to the thesis can close the essay effectively.)
- Do a little extra research to find the right closing detail.
- Talk with friends or family about the topic. Sometimes the act of explaining things inspires new ideas—or a conversation partner will express a point of view that the writer hasn't considered before.

Writing the Ending

Your ending paragraph allows you to tie together the most important ideas in your essay. Your ending should do at least two of the following things:

- Restate or revisit the thesis of your paper.
- Review the main points.
- Leave the reader with something to think about.

Connecting with the thesis	*The dingoes of Australia provide an interesting quandary for the government.* **The animals have been important to maintaining an ecological balance, even though they pose an increasing threat to domestic animals, and, more recently, to humans. Tourists still love watching dingoes, and scientists still worry about the pure dingo strain dying out due to mixed breeding.** *The dilemma remains: Will preserving the species be worth the growing danger?*
Reviewing the main points	
A final thought	

Forming a Final Thought

Here are three different ways to form a final thought.

A call to action directs the reader to do something.

> Only the city council can save Heathrow Park from the bulldozers. Call, e-mail, or write your representative to ask that our beautiful city park be preserved.

A lingering question encourages the reader to further examine the subject.

> Help save unwanted dogs and cats by having your pet spayed or neutered. Thousands of animals are put to death each year because people didn't take action. Don't you want to do your part to avoid these unnecessary deaths?

A good-or-bad conclusion suggests that your topic poses a possible benefit or threat the reader should be aware of.

> The Starlight Players is the only community theater group in the area. If people don't support it, the company could disband. That would give people another reason to find entertainment elsewhere, and a valuable family activity would be lost. It's your choice.

Try It!

Write an ending for a current writing assignment. Try reworking it using the suggestions above. Select the one you like best.

English Language Learners

Students may benefit from additional explanation of the phrase *a call to action*. Explain that this phrase invites readers to do something about a situation. Then have students scan essays in the persuasive writing unit (SE pages 218–273) for examples of this type of ending.

113

Revising

In a first draft, you communicate your initial sense of a topic. You do your best to connect all of your ideas. When you revisit a first draft, after setting it aside for a day or two, you will see different parts that you would like to change.

You may spot redundant information, which you need to cut. You may note places that would benefit from more details. You may detect weak arguments, which you can strengthen. You may also decide to reorder ideas to improve the logical flow. These are all the basic revising moves.

Revising may be the most important step in the writing process. It helps you improve the thoughts and details that carry your message. This chapter will give you a better understanding of this step, covering everything from a review of basic revising guidelines to an explanation of a valuable revising strategy.

- Basic Revising Guidelines
- A Revising Strategy that Works
- A Closer Look at Revising
- Revising Checklist
- Revising in Action
- Checking for Depth

"To the confident [change] is inspiring because the challenge exists to make things better."

—King Whitney, Jr.

Revising

Revising

Objectives

- understand what is involved in revising a first draft
- learn an effective revising strategy that works
- practice basic revising techniques

Discuss with students their experiences with revision.

- How many of them already make a habit of approaching revision as a separate writing step?
- How does revising help them create a better essay?
- How long does it generally take them, compared with the time they spend writing the first draft?
- What sorts of changes do they find they make to their draft?
- What advice do they have about revising?

Basic Revising Guidelines

To expand on the **Try It!** activity, have students practice consulting with a peer reader to evaluate the essay.

- Ask students to begin by reviewing the revision checklist on SE page 117.
- Have students read their essay aloud to their partner.
- Afterward, have not only the writer but also the partner consider the questions posed in the activity.
- Have students take notes about their thoughts and talk about what they each wrote. Did they have similar responses? Did the partner's reactions give the writer even more ideas for improvement?

114

Basic Revising Guidelines

No writer gets it right the first time. Few writers even get it right the second time. In fact, professional writers almost always carry out many revisions before they are satisfied with their work. As writer Virginia Hamilton says, "The real work comes in the rewriting stage." The following guidelines will help you make the best revising moves.

- **Set your writing aside.** Get away from it for a day or two. This will help you see your first draft more clearly when you are ready to revise.
- **Carefully review your draft.** Read it at least two times: once silently and once aloud. Also ask another person to react to your writing—someone whose opinion you trust.
- **Consider the big picture.** Decide if you've effectively developed your thesis.
- **Look at the specific parts.** Rewrite any parts that aren't clear or effective. Cut information that doesn't support your thesis, and add ideas if you think your reader needs more information.
- **Assess your opening and closing paragraphs.** Be sure that they effectively introduce and wrap up your writing.

Revising a Timed Writing

When you have little time to make changes, writer Peter Elbow recommends "cut and paste revising." For example, if you are responding to a writing prompt on a test or for an in-class assignment, you may have just 10 to 15 minutes to revise your writing. The steps that follow describe this quick revising strategy.

1. Don't add any new information.
2. Cut unnecessary details.
3. Check for basic organization.
4. Do whatever rewriting is necessary.

Try It!

Find an essay you wrote but haven't read in a while. Read it aloud, either alone or to someone else, paying careful attention to every word, every punctuation mark. *What trouble spots do you notice? Why do you notice them more when reading your work aloud? How would you fix these parts?*

English Language Learners

During the revision process, have students first read their essays aloud into a tape recorder. Then have them play back the recording and make the necessary corrections on their first drafts. Have students make a second tape that implements the corrections and listen to the recording to ensure all errors have been detected.

A Revising Strategy That Works

The strategy below covers everything from reading the first draft to improving specific ideas. Use this strategy when you have time for in-depth revising.

Read: Sometimes it's hard to keep an open mind when you read your first draft. It's good to put some distance between yourself and your writing.

- Whenever possible, put your writing aside for a day or two.
- When you return to it, read your first draft aloud.
- Ask others (peers, family members) to read it aloud to you.
- Listen to your writing: What does it say? How does it sound?

React: Use these questions to help you react to your writing:

- What parts of my writing work for me?
- Do all of these parts work together?
- Have I arranged the parts in the best possible order?
- What other revising should I do?

Rework: Make changes until all parts of your writing work equally well. There is usually plenty of reworking to do in the early stages of revising, when you are still trying to bring a clear focus to a topic and share it effectively.

Reflect: Write comments in the margins of your paper (or in a notebook) as you revise. Here are some guidelines for reflecting:

- Explore your reactions freely. Be honest about your writing.
- Note what you plan to cut, move, explain further, and so on.
- Reflect on the changes you make. (How do they work?)
- If you are unsure of what to do, write down a question to answer later.

Refine: Refining is checking specific ideas for logic, readability, and balance. Use these questions to help you refine your ideas:

- Will the reader be able to follow my train of thought from idea to idea?
- Do I use transitional words or phrases to link ideas?
- Have I overdeveloped or underdeveloped certain points?

Tip

Remember that revising is the process of improving the ideas and the details that carry the message in your writing. Don't pay undue attention to conventions too early in the process; just concentrate on improving your message.

Process

A Revising Strategy That Works

Note that in doing the **Try It!** activity on the previous page, students have read and reacted to a draft.

If possible, have them revise the essay so they can practice the remaining three steps in the process.

Instruct them to apply the ideas described in the following pages as they carry out their revisions.

Have students turn in their revised essay, along with all their work notes and the original version, for your review. If time permits, schedule conferences to discuss students' experiences with the revising strategy.

Struggling Learners

Students may need additional support comparing "cut and paste" revising and in-depth revising. Guide students in recognizing that the goal of both methods is to create a work that demonstrates the traits of effective writing detailed on SE page 50. The methods differ in the degree to which the writing is analyzed. Stress that time constraints are the major factor in determining which method is used. Then have students identify situations suited for each type of revision process.

A Closer Look at Revising

Note that while it is extremely important to revise, overworking a text can make it less lively. These questions are designed to help writers avoid dull writing. If students find trouble spots in their work, encourage them to start the repair process by checking an earlier version of the draft. Does the problem exist there? If not, they might be able to restore the wording they had earlier—or use it as the basis for their revision.

Try It!
Answers

Possible Answers

Consider substituting a livelier title to match the bustling scene described.

A couple of word choices are a bit stale and could be replaced (*sprawling city, cater to tourists*).

The writing sounds natural but is quite informal (use of exclamatory sentences and all capitals for emphasis) and may not be suitable for all purposes.

116

A Closer Look at Revising

The later stage of revising allows you to deal with those aspects of your writing that may make it seem boring. Use the questions that follow to check for any uninspired "badlands" in your writing.

- **Is your topic worn out?** An essay entitled "Lead Poisoning" sounds uninteresting. With a new twist, you can enliven it: "Get the Lead Out!"
- **Is your approach stale?** If you are writing primarily to please your teacher, start again. Try writing to learn something or to trigger a particular emotion within the reader.
- **Do you sound uninterested or unnatural?** If you do ("A good time was had by all"), try another approach. This time, be honest. Be real.
- **Do parts of your writing seem boring?** Maybe those parts are boring because they don't say enough, or they say too much. To rework these parts, think of them as a series of snapshots. Each picture needs the proper balance between its main idea and the supporting details.
- **Is your writing constrained by overly tight organization?** The structure of an essay provides you with a frame to build on. However, if the frame is followed too closely, your writing may become predictable. If the "formula" is obvious when you read your draft, change the structure in order to more freely present your ideas.

Try It!

As a class (or in a small group), evaluate these two paragraphs using the questions above as a guide.

Adventures in Cairo

Cairo is a sprawling city of 15.2 million people. Bazaars, small stalls or storefronts selling various goods, cater mostly to tourists. The prices are quite reasonable, but the vendors are pushy to the point of actually grabbing some people and pulling them into their shops. Adding to the commotion, many poor people beg for "bakshish" or tips (essentially for doing an unrequested "favor").

Traffic is just incredible—but it moves! Drivers are absolutely obsessed about getting where they want to go. There are no lanes; drivers just squeeze in and out of traffic however they can. The few traffic lights seem not to work. If there is too much traffic on one side of a divided highway, well, drivers go the wrong way on the other side. They make left turns from the middle lanes. There is a LOT of honking going on at all times. Also sharing the road are donkey-drawn carts. It's crazy! And although there are police everywhere, they do not seem very concerned about any of this.

English Language Learners

Students may be confused by the question, *Is your approach stale?* Tell them that the opposite of *stale* is *fresh*. Explain that it is often difficult for native speakers to think of an entirely fresh way to say something. Language learners may not realize that a word or an expression has been used over and over so that it has become a cliche. Suggest that each student partner with a language-proficient student. As they read through the draft together with revising in mind, have them stop at any word or phrase that they suspect might be overused. Have them circle it and then research cliches online. By placing *cliches* in their browser's search window, they will be directed to a number of sites that list hundreds and even thousands of overused wordings. Then have them brainstorm ways they can replaced the tired words with fresh-sounding ones.

"Any activity becomes creative when the doer cares about doing it right or doing it better."
—John Updike

Revising Checklist

Use this checklist as a guide when you revise your writing. *Remember:* When you revise, you improve the thoughts and details that carry your message.

Ideas

_____ **1.** Is my topic important and relevant?
_____ **2.** Have I developed a specific focus or thesis statement?
_____ **3.** Does each paragraph support my thesis?
_____ **4.** Have I included enough details to make my ideas clear?

Organization

_____ **5.** Does my writing follow a clear pattern of organization?
_____ **6.** Have I developed effective beginning, middle, and ending parts?
_____ **7.** Do I need to reorder any parts?

Voice

_____ **8.** Does my voice fit the purpose of my writing?
_____ **9.** Do I sound interested in and knowledgeable about my topic?

Word Choice

_____ **10.** Have I used an appropriate level of formality?
_____ **11.** Do I use specific nouns and vivid verbs?
_____ **12.** Do I avoid repetition and redundancy?

Sentence Fluency

_____ **13.** Are my sentences complete and clearly written?
_____ **14.** Do my sentences flow smoothly?
_____ **15.** Have I varied my sentence beginnings and lengths?

Process

Revising Checklist

Discuss the first item on the checklist, *Is my topic important and relevant?* Note that students will have asked themselves this important question in some form earlier in the writing process, both as they chose the topic (SE pages 98–99) and as they inventoried their thoughts before beginning the first draft (SE page 102). Acknowledge, however, that some people may worry unnecessarily about whether their topic will interest others. Remind students that

- they cannot know for certain what will interest other people;
- they cannot please everyone—people all have different interests; and
- the best approach to evaluating a topic is to decide whether they themselves would be interested in reading about it—a writer's obvious passion for a topic can make it interesting even to people who might not care about it otherwise.

Struggling Learners

Assure students—as with any checklist—that it may seem overwhelming to try to approach all the items on the first pass. Suggest that, while it may seem tedious to review a revision to an essay five times, it is preferable to facing the cumbersome task of dealing with five traits of the revising process at the same time.

Revising in Action

Explain that although students can use a computer to add, delete, move, or rework their drafts, making these changes electronically will not allow them to keep a complete record of how they have changed the text—and it can be very helpful to have earlier versions to refer to in case they change their mind about a revision. This is why they are advised to print out a draft before editing it and/or to rename the file that contains the revision, while maintaining the original in a separate file.

Note, however, that some word-processing programs have a special editing function that, when activated, saves a record of the changes made and shows additions and deletions on the page. Students may wish to use this as they work on the computer, in addition to printing out drafts for editing and keeping a separate file for the original. If desired, use a computer to show students how this editing function works.

Revising in Action

When you revise a first draft, focus on improving the writing overall. You can improve a piece by adding, deleting, moving, or reworking information. (See the next page for examples.)

Adding Information

Add information to your writing if you need to . . .

- share more details to make a point,
- clarify or complete an interesting idea, or
- link sentences or paragraphs to improve clarity and flow.

Deleting Information

Delete material from your draft when the ideas . . .

- do not support your focus or
- are redundant or repetitious.

Moving Material

Move material in your writing in order to . . .

- create a clear flow of ideas,
- present points in order, or
- make a dramatic impact.

Reworking Material

Rework material in your writing if it . . .

- is confusing or unclear,
- does not maintain the proper voice, or
- needs to be simplified.

Being Your Own Critic

When revising, try to anticipate your reader's concerns. Doing so will help you determine what changes to make. Here are some questions and concerns a reader may have:

- What is the main point of this essay?
- Is the writer's voice interested and authoritative?
- Can I follow the writer's ideas smoothly?
- Does the ending wrap up the essay in a clear way?

Sample Revision

The writer of this essay improved it by moving, adding, deleting, and reworking parts. (See the inside back cover of this text for editing and proofreading marks.)

A sentence is moved for clarity.

An interesting detail is added.

An unnecessary detail is deleted.

An important idea is reworded for appropriate voice.

The Sky's Not the Limit

Ever since movies began, filmmakers have tried to put imaginary things on film. Still, the effects never seemed real enough. People used model building, hand-drawn cartoons, or stop-motion animation. In the last 20 years, however, computer-generated imagery (CGI) has made it possible ^Anything that can be imagined can be put on-screen and look real. to create believable special effects in movies. CGI allows filmmakers to show things realistically on-screen that people could only imagine before.

CGI can create totally imaginary characters that look real. An early example is a knight leaping out of a stained-glass window in *Young Sherlock Holmes* (1985). ~~Dinosaurs are the most popular creatures for special effects over the years, starting with the stop-motion puppets of The Lost World (1925).~~ Later on, CGI showed us believable dinosaurs in *Jurassic Park* (1993). More recently, CGI and the voice and acting of Andy Serkis created the incredible character of Gollum (*Lord of the Rings: The Two Towers*, 2002). Today, CGI even replaces older special effects technologies like the Yoda puppet from The Empire Strikes Back (1980). ~~Even though I loved and believed in Yoda as a puppet in The Empire Strikes Back (1980), the technology is outmoded and too limited.~~ Many of the aliens in the newer *Star Wars* films are all CGI creations (*Revenge of the Sith*, 2005). Now, even the most fantastic creatures from folklore to science fiction can seem real on-screen.

Process

Sample Revision

Note that even though the revising changes are clearly marked on the page, it is a bit difficult to get a good sense of what the page now says when reading it silently—the inserted lines distract the reader's eye. Encourage students to test each of their revisions by reading the new versions aloud. Not only will doing so help them decide whether they have improved the essay as planned, but it will also help them identify any mistakes they may have made in the editing markup.

Checking for Depth

Focus on the idea that it's possible to include too many details as well as too few. Discuss examples of this, such as the following:

- Familiar terms or ideas are explained. This could create a patronizing tone or make readers feel the essay doesn't include new ideas.
- The main point is obscured by too many details.
- In narratives especially, the writer slows the action by dwelling on details that readers can imagine for themselves—for example, describing a character who unlocks a door by saying *She reached into her purse, pulled out the key, and then pushed it into the lock and turned it clockwise. The bolt slid back, and the door opened.*

Try It!
Answers

Possible Answers

The passage would be improved by adding details about how blood clots and providing a definition for the word *scab*.

Checking for Depth

One important consideration when revising an essay is to determine whether or not the level of detail is appropriate. Some ideas can be expressed perfectly well without a lot of specifics (and, in fact, may suffer from too many details). If, however, you realize during revision that a particular passage needs more support, the addition of specific details will help the reader better understand your writing.

Different types of writing require different types of details. For instance, facts, statistics, and examples support expository and persuasive writing, while narrative and creative writing benefit from sensory and memory details.

Adding Depth

As Alahandra was reviewing her essay about the process of digestion, she came upon these two sentences:

> In the mouth, saliva helps break down food. When someone swallows, a movement called peristalsis pushes the food down into the stomach.

Alahandra then added details to better explain the process.

> In the mouth, the chewing of food causes the exocrine glands to release saliva. Enzymes in saliva help break down food. Saliva also helps condense the chewed-up food into small balls that can pass into the esophagus when swallowed. In the esophagus, peristalsis, or contraction of the smooth muscle tissues, pushes the food down toward the stomach, where it enters through a one-way "gate" called the cardiac sphincter.

Try It!

The following passage is from a student essay about the body's healing process. Explain why the writer should or should not add details.

> As soon as you receive a minor cut, your body's healing process begins. Blood from tiny blood vessels fills the wound and begins to clot. Then a scab forms.

121

Peer Responding

If you had some poppy seeds stuck between your teeth, surely you'd want someone to politely and discreetly point out your little *faux pas*. Similarly, if there is a problem in your writing, you would appreciate a friend or classmate directing your attention to it. That's what peer responding is all about. When you ask your peers for their honest opinions about your writing, they can show you things you don't see yourself—good and bad. Once you have this feedback, you can decide on the best way to address any problem areas.

Feedback from your fellow writers is valuable throughout the writing process, but it is especially helpful during the early stages of revising when you are evaluating your first draft. Some experts go so far as to say that talking about your work will help you more than anything else you do during the writing process.

- **Peer-Responding Guidelines**
- **Using the Traits to Respond**
- **Trying a New Strategy**

"Criticism, like rain, should be gentle enough to nourish a man's growth without destroying his roots."

—Frank A. Clark

Peer Responding

Objectives
- understand the roles of the author and peer responder in peer responding
- learn how to give helpful responses
- practice reacting to or critiquing a peer's paper

Explain that many writers work with a writer's group through every stage of a project and consider the input of these peers to be indispensable to the creative process. Emphasize that it is not the same as having someone else do one's work.

Encourage students to consider forming an ongoing writer's group with other like-minded people. These could be friends from within or outside the class—or even from outside the school. The goal is to create a compatible group whose skills and interests are complementary and whose schedules permit regular meetings.

Peer-Responding Guidelines

As a class, discuss the quotation by Ken Macrorie in conjunction with the other information on the page. Why is his advice so important? Possible responses:

- **Reacting defensively** *(see below)* will sidetrack the conversation by making the topic of conversation become "why I was right" rather than staying focused on suggestions for ways to improve the writing.
- It can create tension in the discussion, changing the tone from constructive to unpleasant.
- A reader who gets a defensive reaction may become unwilling to respond honestly in future.

Remind students that not only can it be difficult to hear about weaknesses in their work, but it can also be difficult for a peer responder to decide how to "break the news" gently. The work students will do on these pages will give them a start at practicing both skills—they should be generous and patient in both roles as they learn how to proceed.

122

"The first rule in listening to comments about your work is 'Never defend yourself' unless you can tell that your critic has misunderstood something."

—Ken Macrorie

Peer-Responding Guidelines

The guidelines below will help you participate in peer-response sessions. (If you're just starting out, work in small groups of two or three classmates.)

Considering the Writer's Role

Come to the session with a meaningful piece of your writing—perhaps a recently completed first draft. Make a copy for each member of the group (if this is what the group usually does).

- **Introduce your writing.** Give a brief explanation of what your piece is about without going into too much detail.
- **Read your writing aloud.** If you don't feel comfortable reading aloud, ask group members to read your piece silently.
- **Ask for feedback.** Listen carefully and consider all suggestions. Don't be defensive, because this may stop some members from commenting honestly.
- **Take notes.** Record your classmates' comments on your copy so you can decide later what to change.
- **Answer questions.** If you're unsure of an answer, it's okay to say, "I don't know" or "I'll look into that."
- **Seek assistance.** If you have trouble with a specific part of your writing, ask for help.

Seeking Constructive Criticism

To get constructive criticism, you may need to ask the responders some direct questions. Consider your purpose, your intended audience, and the focus of your writing. Knowing these three things will help you form your questions.

 Try It!

Practice your role as the writer in a peer-responding session with a classmate, friend, or family member. First, share the information on the next page about the responder's role. Then follow the guidelines for the writer listed above. Afterward, assess the effectiveness of the session: *Did the session help you see parts of your writing that could be improved? Did the responder answer any questions that you had? Did he or she make any other helpful suggestions?*

Teaching Tip: Reacting Defensively

Some people struggle more than others with the urge to defend themselves when their work is critiqued. Reassure students who experience this that they are not alone in this feeling. Offer coping strategies to those who admit they are vulnerable to the problem. For example:

- Remind yourself that the responder's goal is to help you improve, not to insult you.

- Take care not to interrupt a responder—listen to all of what he or she has to say.
- Check to make sure you've understood the comment by asking "Are you saying that . . . ?"
- Find out whether other responders agree with the comment.
- In the longer term, seek out responders who express themselves in ways that don't make you feel anxious.

Peer Responding　**123**

Considering the Responder's Role

You need to be honest in your feedback without hurting the writer's feelings. Your comments should always be polite and constructive.

Giving Constructive Criticism	
Don't make demands . . . "Change the ending so the reader has something to think about."	**Do** make suggestions . . . "The ending could be stronger if you leave the reader with a question to think about."
Don't focus on the writer . . . "Nobody understands what you're trying to say in the middle part."	**Do** focus on the writing . . . "Don't you think your ideas would be easier to follow if you switched paragraphs two and three?"
Don't focus on the problem . . . "The beginning paragraph is boring."	**Do** focus on the solution . . . "Descriptive details might make the beginning more interesting."
Don't give general comments . . . "Your sentences aren't very interesting."	**Do** give specific advice . . . "Changing from passive to active voice in a few places could liven things up."

Responding Tips

- Listen carefully to the writer's reading and questions.
- Take notes in the margins of your copy.
- Ask questions. If you are not sure of something, ask for clarification.

Try It!

Using the tips above, write three strong criticisms about this paragraph.

> In the northwest part of Utah lie the remnants of a sizable lake from the Ice Age. All that remains of the ancient Lake Bonneville is salt—up to six feet deep in some areas. The Bonneville Salt Flats, which occupy approximately 160 square miles, are extremely flat and devoid of plant life. As such, the area is well suited for motor sports, and the state's highway department now maintains a part of the Flats known as the Bonneville Speedway. It was here that numerous land speed records were set, beginning in 1935 when Malcolm Campbell, driving a specially designed Rolls-Royce, passed the 300-mph mark for the first time. For the next 62 years, each of the world's land speed records was broken at the Bonneville Speedway, until Andy Green's rocket-powered record of 763 mph in October 1997 at Black Rock Desert in Nevada.

Process

Talk about word choices that help make criticism constructive rather than harsh.

- Phrase the comment as a question: *Do you think . . . ?*
- Phrase the comment as an idea: *I wonder if . . .*
- Use verbs that acknowledge that the writer has a choice, like *consider* or *think about*.
- Choose modifiers that express possibility— *maybe, perhaps, possibly.*
- Choose positive words over negative ones—*It might be more interesting if . . .* , rather than *It is boring when . . .*

Try It!
Answers

Possible Answers

- The first sentences suggest that the paragraph is going to be about the geology of the salt flats, rather than about land-speed records set at the speedway. Consider mentioning this earlier?
- Varying sentence lengths might improve fluency.
- More sensory details might add interest. For example, you could include details about how the salt flats look or sensory details about what it's like to go 763 mph.

Using the Traits to Respond

To expand on the information, have students look back at the revision checklist (SE page 117). Which of these questions do they find most difficult to judge for themselves in their own revisions? **A constructive way to respond** *(see below)* to a peer's work would be to help the writer determine the answers to the difficult questions.

 Try It!
Answers

Possible Answers

See the final middle paragraph of the essay on SE pages 44–45.

Ideas: Using a question to bring up the objection is a good strategy—but I wondered how common the idea is that parents should teach kids financial literacy. Consider adding details about this?

Ideas: I wonder if another objection might be that students should know to read the documents that come with their credit cards and bank accounts for themselves.

Organization: The topic and body sentences are well differentiated, but it might be good to have a more conclusive closing.

Voice: You might sound more knowledgeable if you quoted an expert or used statistics to support the arguments in this paragraph.

124

Using the Traits to Respond

Responders help writers rethink, refocus, and revise their writing. As a responder, you may find it helpful to base your responses on the traits of writing.

Addressing Ideas, Organization, and Voice Early in the Process

Ideas: Helping the Author Focus on Ideas
- Can you tell us the main idea of your writing?
- It seems like you're trying to say . . . . Is that right?
- Are these points the main ideas in your writing?
- The most convincing details are . . .
- A few details like . . . may make this part more interesting.
- In my opinion, details like . . . may distract from your main idea.
- Your writing left me thinking . . . . Is that what you intended?

Organization: Helping the Author Focus on Organization
- You got my attention in the beginning by . . .
- This sentence seems to state your focus. Is that correct?
- Are the middle paragraphs organized according to . . . ?
- Why did you place the information about . . . in the fourth paragraph?
- Is the purpose of your ending to . . . ?
- I wonder if a transition is needed between the second and third paragraphs.

Voice: Helping the Author Focus on Voice
- The sentences that most clearly show your personality are . . .
- How would you describe your attitude about this topic?
- What audience did you have in mind when you wrote this?
- The third paragraph sounds too formal to me. Do you think it fits in with the rest of your writing?
- The overall feeling I get from your writing is . . .
- The middle part of your essay might be too subjective.

Try It!

Find and read any student writer's paragraph in this book. Afterward, write two constructive criticisms based on the *ideas, organization,* and *voice* in the writing.

Teaching Tip: A Constructive Way to Respond

Reading letters written by editors to famous authors can be a good way to learn how to express criticism. Provide students with examples of such letters, and then discuss the language the editors used. Did students get ideas for how to construct their own responses? Sources of letters include the following:

- *Editor to Author: The Letters of Maxwell Perkins* (Perkins' authors included F. Scott Fitzgerald and Ernest Hemingway.)
- *Dear Genius: The Letters of Ursula Nordstrom,* edited by Leonard Marcus (Nordstrom edited many children's book writers, including E. B. White and Louise Fitzhugh.)
- *The Element of Lavishness: The Letters of Sylvia Townsend Warner and William Maxwell* (Maxwell was Warner's editor for decades.)

Peer Responding 125

Addressing Word Choice and Fluency Later in the Process

Word Choice: Helping the Author Focus on the Nouns, Verbs, and Modifiers

- The most powerful verbs in the writing are . . .
- I found these general nouns: . . . . What specific nouns could you use instead?
- Do you think there are too many modifiers in the first paragraph?
- I'm confused by the meaning of . . . . Can you define it, please?
- The words . . . feel wrong to me. You could use . . . instead.
- Have you used . . . too often in the first part of your writing?

Sentence Fluency: Helping the Author Focus on the Sentences

- I like the flow of the sentences in the beginning paragraph.
- Check your sentences in the middle part. Do you think too many of them begin the same way?
- It might add interest to vary the sentences in the closing paragraph.
- Could some of the sentences in the second paragraph be combined?
- For the most part, your sentences have a nice rhythm.

Process

Try It!

Read the following paragraph. Then write a few constructive criticisms about the *word choice* and *sentence fluency* in the writing.

When I was about six years old, my friend Barbie and I happily spent our summer afternoons exploring the world of our neighborhood. Venturing a block or two away, we'd find an orchard in someone's backyard and help ourselves to a fresh pear. Or we'd hunt for fossils in the stone landscaping near the church parking lot down the street. One afternoon Barbie and I found a caterpillar and brought it home to put in a jar with a branch. We let the caterpillar crawl up and down our little arms. Gradually I became aware that I wasn't feeling well, so I went home. When I reported to my mom, she lifted my shirt and looked at my back, proclaiming that I had chicken pox. For years after that, I believed there was a link between handling a caterpillar and feeling sick.

Reacting to Criticism

You don't have to incorporate all of your classmates' suggestions. The following tips will help you get the most out of response sessions.

- Trust your own judgment about your writing.
- Determine which issues are most important.
- Pay attention to comments made by more than one responder.
- Get another opinion if you are not sure about something.

English Language Learners

Assign student pairs, and have partners share writing samples. Have students use the bulleted statements as sentence frames for responding to their peer's writing. Encourage students to include comments on all five traits of writing in their responses.

Try It! Answers

Possible Answers

Word Choice: Would you consider making some of the details about the neighborhood more specific, to give a sense of how you were at home there? For example, instead of *someone's backyard,* say whose yard it was; and instead of *the church,* tell the name of the church.

You might be able to add words to provide more sensory details. For example, add description of what the caterpillar looked like and instead of saying you weren't *feeling well,* describe the symptoms (fever, itchiness, and the like).

Sentence Fluency: Two sentences begin with introductory phrases starting with *when*. Would you consider changing one of them so the pattern doesn't repeat?

Trying a New Strategy

Ask students to sum up the information on the page by describing the two strategies that are outlined. How do they differ? Possible responses:

- To *react* is to focus on reporting your personal responses to the piece as a reader.
- To *critique* is to comment more objectively on the piece, by comparing it to certain standards.

Note that students may discover that they prefer to use a combination of strategies when they comment on someone's work.

126

Trying a New Strategy

Provided on this page are two strategies for evaluating a piece of writing.

Reacting to Writing

Peter Elbow, in *Writing Without Teachers,* offers four types of reactions peer responders might have to a piece of writing:

- **Pointing** refers to a reaction in which a group member "points out" words, phrases, or ideas that impress him or her.
- **Summarizing** is a list of main ideas or a single sentence that sums up the work. It's a reader's general reaction to the writing.
- **Telling** involves the reader describing what happens in a piece of writing: first this happens, then that happens, and so on.
- **Showing** refers to speaking metaphorically about the piece. A reader might speak of a quality as if it were a voice, color, shape, or piece of clothing ("Your writing has a neat, tailored quality").

Critiquing a Paper

Use this checklist as a guide when you assess a piece of writing-in-progress.

_____ **Purpose:** Is it clear what the writer is trying to do—entertain, inform, persuade, describe? Explain.

_____ **Audience:** Does the writing address a specific audience? Will the reader understand and appreciate the subject? Why?

_____ **Ideas:** Does the writer develop the topic with enough information?

_____ **Organization:** Are the ideas arranged in the best way?

_____ **Voice:** Does the writer sound sincere and honest? Does the writer speak to his or her audience? Explain.

_____ **Word Choice:** Does the writer include any technical terms? Are these terms defined? Does the level of language fit the audience?

_____ **Sentence Fluency:** Do the sentences read smoothly?

_____ **Purpose Again:** Does the writing succeed in making the reader smile, nod, or react in some other way?

Try It!

Try one of these strategies the next time you respond to one of your peer's essays or papers. Afterward, assess the effectiveness of the strategy.

Advanced Learners

Challenge students to model the four types of reactions that peer responders might have to a piece of writing. Assign students or have them choose one of the four, making sure that you have a balanced representation.

Editing

Editing is the final step before publishing anything you've written. When you edit, you check your revised writing for errors in spelling, punctuation, and grammar. Your goal is to produce a clean, correct final draft—a necessity if you want the reader to take you seriously as a writer. Errors not only interrupt the reading; they also reduce the reader's confidence in your message.

Editing is most easily accomplished with the appropriate tools: a dictionary, a thesaurus, spell- and grammar-checkers, and the "Proofreader's Guide" in this book (pages 605–763). These resources will help as you prepare your writing for publication. The information in this chapter will help you improve your editing and proofreading skills.

- ■ **Checklist for Editing and Proofreading**
- ■ **Editing in Action**
- ■ **Errors to Watch For**
- ■ **Special Editing Problems**

"When something can be read without effort, great effort has gone into its writing."

—Enrique Jardiel Poncela

Editing

Editing

Objectives
- review the elements of checking a paper for conventions
- learn how to spot and correct common errors

Acknowledge that for some people, grammar and spelling errors stand out on the page, while other readers must work harder to spot the problems. Note that at this point in their writing experience, students probably already have a good sense of whether or not checking for conventions comes naturally. Assure those who struggle that they can greatly improve their skills by studying the information on the following pages and in the other editing sections of their book.

Encourage students also to keep a list of the types of errors that they make most often. This practice will
- ■ help them to be extra vigilant in the future, and
- ■ reassure them that they can identify their common errors.

In later units, when students work with peer editors, they will also see that many writers make the same kinds of mistakes.

Checklist for Editing and Proofreading

Advise students always to run the computer spell-check program and the **grammar-check program** *(see below)* before making a printout for editing. This way, as they read their printout, they can focus on catching errors the program has missed (see the last item under Mechanics). Challenge students to describe what sorts of mistakes these might be. Possible responses:

- homonyms spelled incorrectly (such as *their* for *there*)
- subject-verb agreement errors
- the omission of an important word, such as *not*
- small words not flagged by the spell-checker— for example, *on, or, of,* and *to*

✳ For a comprehensive list of words that commonly cause confusion, see Using the Right Word on SE pages 678–697.

"Grammar is a tricky, inconsistent thing. Being the backbone of speech and writing, it should, we think, be eminently logical, make perfect sense, like the human skeleton. But, of course, the skeleton is arbitrary, too."
—John Simon

Checklist for Editing and Proofreading

Use this checklist as a guide when you edit and proofread your revised writing. Also refer to "Errors to Watch For" on pages 130–131.

Tip

Always have a trusted friend or peer serve as a second editor. You're too close to your work to catch every error.

Conventions

PUNCTUATION (See pages 605–647.)
_____ Do my sentences end with the proper punctuation?
_____ Do I use commas correctly in compound sentences?
_____ Do I use commas correctly in a series and after long introductory phrases or clauses?
_____ Do I use apostrophes correctly?

MECHANICS (CAPITALIZATION AND SPELLING) (See pages 648–671.)
_____ Do I start my sentences with capital letters?
_____ Do I capitalize proper nouns?
_____ Have I checked for spelling errors (including those the spell-checker may have missed)?

GRAMMAR (See pages 678–763.)
_____ Do the subjects and verbs agree in my sentences?
_____ Do my sentences use correct and consistent verb tenses?
_____ Do my pronouns agree with their antecedents?
_____ Have I avoided any other usage errors?

PRESENTATION (See pages 91–95.)
_____ Does the title effectively lead into the writing?
_____ Are sources of information properly presented and documented?
_____ Does my writing meet the requirements for final presentation?

Teaching Tip: Grammar-Check Program

Remind students that the grammar-check program must be used even more cautiously than the spell-check program. They should never accept the program's suggested changes at face value—it has a limited ability to read words in context. Students can use it to initially scan text for

- passive verb usage,
- subject-verb agreement problems, and
- sentence fragments.

Writers should be aware that the grammar program may flag many problems in error, and worse yet, it may even miss obvious errors, including the types it is programmed to find.

Struggling Learners

As with other checklists, suggest that students focus on one thing at a time—in this case, a particular type of error in conventions. You may want students to participate in a round-robin, in which they pass their essay to three other people in a group. Each group member is assigned to check for a particular kind of error.

Editing in Action

Note the editing corrections made in these paragraphs from a student essay. See the inside back cover of this book for an explanation of the editing symbols used.

A comma is inserted after a long introductory phrase.

Apostrophe and spelling mistakes are corrected.

Abbreviations are spelled out.

Placement of punctuation with quotation marks is corrected.

The name of the ship is marked for italics.

Usage errors are corrected.

> About 450 miles off the coast of Newfoundland in 12,000 feet of water, scientists discovered the remains of the great ocean liner, the R.M.S. <u>Titanic</u>. The 73-year search for the <u>Titanic</u>, which went down in what is considered the world's greatest sea disaster, was a *challenging* one. It concluded finally in September 1985.
>
> When it was first launched in 1912, the British steamer was the largest ship in the world. An incredible 882 *feet* long and 175 *feet* high, the <u>Titanic</u> was proclaimed the most expensive and luxurious ship ever built. It was said to be "unsinkable." It was *equipped* with a double bottom, and the hull was divided into 16 separate watertight compartments.
>
> Despite its reputation, the mighty <u>Titanic</u> did sink—on its maiden voyage. Carrying *approximately* 2,200 passengers and over $420,000 worth of cargo, the <u>Titanic</u> set sail from England in April 1912, bound for New York. Just a few days out of port, however, on the night of April 14, the <u>Titanic</u> collided with an iceberg in the north Atlantic Ocean, damaging steel plates along its starboard side. The great "floating palace" sunk in a matter of 2 1/2 hours, taking with it all of its cargo and 1,522 of its passengers and crew.

Process

Editing in Action

Discuss conventions in the sample that are neither spelling nor grammar errors, precisely, but are instead a matter of an agreed-upon style. Provide the following examples:

- Numbers with four or more digits require commas *(12,000 feet of water)*.
- However, the numbers used for years do not include commas *(1912)*.
- Names of ships and aircraft are underlined or placed in italics (<u>Titanic</u>).
- In dates, if only the month and year are given, no comma is required *(September 1985)*. If the date is specified, the year is set off with a comma *(April 14, 1912)*.
- Dates are presented as cardinal numbers *(April 14,* not *April 14th)*.
- Units of measure with numbers are usually written out *(450 miles, 882 feet)*.

✳ For more about how to punctuate dates, how to write numbers, and when to use italics or underlining, see SE pages 614, 658, and 636, respectively.

Struggling Learners

When reviewing the editing corrections, reinforce students' understanding of apostrophes and the possessive case by pointing out the following:

- To form the possessive case of a singular noun, add an apostrophe and *s*.
- To form the possessive case of a plural noun, add an apostrophe after the final *s*, unless the word has an irregular plural *(children's)*.
- Personal pronouns in the possessive case *(hers, his, its, theirs)* do not take an apostrophe.

Then have students write sentences that illustrate the rules explained above.

Errors to Watch For

To help students master the grammatical principles listed, have them suggest additional sentences to illustrate each error and provide the necessary corrections.

Note that one of the most common causes of grammatical errors is a writer's lack of knowledge of the different parts of speech. Encourage students to familiarize themselves with the parts of speech. Give visual learners an overview of simple sentence diagramming to demonstrate how a sentence can be broken down into its constituent parts. If this strategy is helpful, encourage them to diagram sentences themselves.

✳ For information about diagramming sentences, see SE pages 760–763.

130

Errors to Watch For

These two pages show 10 common errors to check for in your writing.

1. **Problem: Missing Comma After Long Introductory Phrase**
   Solution: Place a comma after a long introductory phrase.

   > Growing up in suburban Chicago, I longed for a dog of my own.

2. **Problem: Confusing Pronoun Reference**
   Solution: Be sure the reader knows whom or what your pronoun refers to.

   > Although Ty pointed out the error to Hakeem, he didn't fix it. *Hakeem*

3. **Problem: Missing Comma in Compound Sentence**
   Solution: Use a comma between two independent clauses joined by a coordinating conjunction—*and, but, or, nor, so, for,* or *yet.*

   > Myra just turned 16 years old, yet she is starting her senior year.

4. **Problem: Missing Comma(s) with Nonrestrictive Phrases or Clauses**
   Solution: Use commas to set off a phrase or clause that is not needed to understand the sentence. (See page **612**.)

   > I ordered a tostada, which is my favorite Mexican food.

5. **Problem: Comma Splice**
   Solution: When only a comma separates two independent clauses, add a conjunction, replace the comma with a semicolon, or create two sentences.

   > First water the vegetable garden, then cut the front lawn.

6. **Problem: Subject-Verb Agreement Error**
   Solution: Verbs must agree in number with their subjects.

   > Tomatoes from the farmers' market ~~tastes~~ the best. *taste*

Provide additional practice editing for subject-verb agreement. Write the following sentences on the board. Have students read them aloud, one at a time, first identifying the subject and then making the necessary corrections so that the verb agrees with the subject.

1. Students from a nearby high school volunteers at the animal shelter. *(students/volunteer)*
2. One paper, which lacks a name, remain ungraded. *(paper/remains)*
3. Many of the employees in our company prefers flexible schedules. *(many/prefer)*

4. Each of my neighbors are on vacation. *(each/is)*
5. One of the players check the locker room every morning. *(one/checks)*

✳ For further information about subject-verb agreement, see SE pages 752–755.

7. **Problem: Missing Comma in a Series**
   Solution: Use commas to separate individual words, phrases, or clauses in a series.

   > Mr. Taneka was loaded down with balloons␣gifts␣and games.

8. **Problem: Pronoun-Antecedent Agreement Error**
   Solution: A pronoun must agree in number with the word that the pronoun refers to. (See page **756**.)

   > Either Tracy or her girlfriends left ~~her~~ *their* books on the bus.

9. **Problem: Missing Apostrophe to Show Ownership**
   Solution: Use an apostrophe after a noun to show possession.

   > Our school's mascot is a bulldog.

10. **Problem: Misusing *Its* and *It's***
    Solution: *Its* is a possessive pronoun meaning "belonging to it." *It's* is a contraction of "it is" or "it has."

    > The cute little sports car was missing one of ~~it's~~ *its* taillights.

Try It!

Find the errors in the passage below. Write the paragraph correctly on your paper.

> Kent wants to attend a four-year college but his family can't afford it. His parents who both work for the telephone company haven't been able to maintain a college savings fund. None of Kents cousins have attended college, either. Maybe Kent will get one or more of the scholarships he applied for, he deserves a chance to continue his education. Its not an easy time of life for him.

Process

Before students do the **Try It!** activity, tell them not only to correct the errors they find but also to explain why they are errors.

Try It! Answers

Kent wants to attend a four-year college, [missing comma in compound sentence] *but his family can't afford it. His parents, who both work for the telephone company,* [missing commas with a nonrestrictive clause] *haven't been able to maintain a college savings fund. None of Kent's* [missing apostrophe in a possessive] *cousins have attended college, either. Maybe Kent will get one or more of the scholarships he applied for. He* [comma splice] *deserves a chance to continue his education. It's* [misusing* its *and* it's] *not an easy time of life for him.*

Editing and Proofreading Mark's

Have students practice using the editing and proofreading marks. Invite them to create sentences modeled after the examples in the chart on SE page 132. Then have partners edit each other's sentences using the correct symbols.

132

Editing and Proofreading Marks

Use the symbols and letters below to show where and how your writing needs to be changed. Your teachers and peers may also use these symbols to point out errors in your writing or to suggest areas for improvement.

Symbols	Meaning	Example	Corrected Example
≡	Capitalize a letter.	George orwell wrote *1984*.	George Orwell wrote *1984*.
/	Make a capital letter lowercase.	His novel explores life without personal Freedom.	His novel explores life without personal freedom.
⊙	Insert (add) a period.	*1984* focuses on a parallel world in the future It is . . .	*1984* focuses on a parallel world in the future. It is . . .
⬭ or *sp.*	Correct spelling.	Winston Smith tries to escape the (tyrany.)	Winston Smith tries to escape the tyranny.
⟋	Delete (take out) or replace.	His every movement is scrutinized.	His every move is scrutinized.
∧	Insert here.	Winston and Julia create a plan.	Winston and Julia create a complicated plan.
∧ ∧ ∧	Insert a comma, a colon, or a semicolon.	Together they profess their allegiance against the Party.	Together, they profess their allegiance against the Party.
V V V	Insert an apostrophe or quotation marks.	O'Brien is not a member of the Brotherhood.	O'Brien is not a member of the Brotherhood.
? ! ∧ ∧	Insert a question mark or an exclamation point.	Broken, Winston screams, "Not me"	Broken, Winston screams, "Not me!"
¶	Start a new paragraph.	Winston is a changed man after he . . .	Winston is a changed man after he . . .
∼	Switch words or letters.	Julia admits ultimately her betrayal.	Julia ultimately admits her betrayal.

Publishing

According to *The American Heritage Dictionary*, the word *publish* means "to prepare and issue (printed material) for public distribution." What better destiny for your writing? This chapter offers guidelines for preparing to publish as well as suggestions on where you might submit your work.

This chapter also explains how to prepare a writing portfolio. A writing portfolio shows your teacher (and other readers of your work) your progress as a writer. It gives you yet another reason to put forth your best effort on writing assignments.

- **Preparing to Publish**
- **Places to Publish**
- **Preparing a Portfolio**
- **Parts of a Portfolio**
- **Creating Your Own Web Site**

"To write well, express yourself
like the common people,
but think like a wise man."

—Aristotle

Objectives

- understand how to prepare writing for publication
- learn how to put together a portfolio
- learn how to create a Web site

Point out that the word *publishing* covers a range of possibilities for sharing, from sharing a personal narrative with one of the people who inspired it, to reading a completed essay to a group of peers, to posting work on the Web, where it is accessible to many anonymous readers.

Talk with students about the ways they've published writing so far.
- Have any of them ever submitted work to the editors of a magazine or newspaper?
- Was it published?
- If so, ask them to describe the work and the publication and, if possible, to bring a copy to share with the class.

Encourage students to think about making their best writing available to an audience beyond the teacher who assigned it. Note that the following pages will get them started with the process.

Preparing to Publish

Focus on the first bulleted point and emphasize that its main message is that students must
- feel good about the piece,
- know that they have worked hard on it, and
- want to share it with others.

Note that many experienced writers never feel *completely* finished with a work. (Some even return to revising after a piece has been published and release it again in a new edition.) High standards can be good, but this kind of perfectionism can distract writers so they are tempted to revise endlessly and never publish. This should be avoided. Encourage students who might experience this cycle to be sure to seek the advice of someone they trust, so they can tell when it is time to move on.

Offer to read and evaluate any works students are considering **submitting for publication** *(see below).*

134

"An essential element for good writing is a good ear. One must listen to the sound of one's prose."
—Barbara Tuchman

Preparing to Publish

Publishing is the final step in the writing process, offering your readers a chance to enjoy your writing. The following guidelines will help you prepare your writing for publishing.

Tasks to Complete

- **Work with your writing** until you feel good about it from start to finish. If any parts still need work, then it isn't ready to publish.
- **Ask for input and advice** during the writing process. Your writing should answer any questions the reader may have about your topic. Confusing parts must be made clear.
- **Save all drafts for each writing project** so you can keep track of the changes you have made. If you are preparing a portfolio, you may be required to include early drafts as well as finished pieces. (See pages 136–138.)
- **Check for the traits of writing** to be sure that you have effectively addressed ideas, organization, voice, word choice, and sentence fluency in your work. (See pages 51–88.)
- **Carefully edit and proofread for conventions** after you have completed all of your revisions. (See pages 89–90.)
- **Prepare a neat final copy** to share with the reader. Use pen (blue or black ink) and one side of the paper if you are writing by hand. If you are using a computer, avoid fancy, hard-to-read fonts and odd margins. (See pages 91–95.)
- **Know your publishing options** since there are many ways to publish. (See page 135.)
- **Follow the requirements** indicated by the publisher. Each publisher has its own set of requirements, which must be followed exactly.

Try It!

Use these guidelines once you decide to publish a piece of writing. Be sure to ask your teacher for help if you have any questions about the publishing process.

Teaching Tip: Submitting for Publication

Discuss the idea that when students begin submitting their work for publication they are likely—nearly certain—to experience rejection. Provide advice such as the following:

- It is important not to get discouraged. Sometimes it takes time to find the right publisher for a piece; sometimes the work needs to be revised before it is ready.

- Many famous writers have had their work rejected. Sometimes a future best-seller will be rejected many times before finding a publisher.

- Students should be encouraged if they receive feedback along with a rejection. This shows that the reader was interested in the piece and may mean that revising it will result in publication.

Places to Publish

Think back to the day you started writing a particular piece. You decided what you would write about with two fundamental ideas in mind: a topic that interested you and a thesis or controlling idea about that topic. At this point, you've done a lot of work to perfect your writing. Peers and teachers probably reviewed it as you went along. Now it's time to share the finished product.

School Days

If you have written about a topic that interests or affects others in your age group, school publications provide some good publishing options.

- Your school's newspaper is a good choice for expository or persuasive writing about school-related topics.
- A student literary magazine offers publishing opportunities for a variety of writing forms, but especially for narrative writing, literary criticism, and poetry.

Your Own Backyard

The people in a community generally share some interests or background—that's what brought them together as a community in the first place. As a result, ideas that draw your attention may also appeal to your community as a whole. You may find that local publications are interested in publishing your writing.

- A local newspaper or newsletter may be interested in an insider's view of school events, or a young person's opinions on current issues.
- Depending on what you have written about, special-interest Web sites may provide a publishing opportunity. Look for clubs and organizations that have a connection to your writing topic.

Explore the Possibilities

Traditional publishers of magazines and books may also be an option to investigate. If you have a favorite national magazine, it may accept writing from outside writers on certain topics. A librarian can help you to research the possibilities. You can also look in the *Writer's Market* for more places to publish.

Tip

Before submitting your work to a publication, check the submission guidelines to be sure your writing is in an acceptable form and style. Include a self-addressed stamped envelope (SASE) when submitting your work to help ensure that you receive a response and that your work will be returned if that's what you want.

Process

Places to Publish

Note that in addition to the national publishers listed, students can look for ways to publish their work locally. Ideas include the following:

- Seek out a position on the school newspaper.
- Write letters to the editor of the local newspaper.
- Volunteer to write for a local, nonprofit organization's newsletter.

Warn students that as they research publishing opportunities, they may come across advertisements that solicit manuscripts and offer to publish them for a fee. Some legitimate contests do ask for a small reader's fee—but respected publishers and publications do not. Businesses that charge for publication are often known as "vanity presses." They will produce a book in exchange for the money, but it is usually of low quality (and without editing); they will not help the writer advertise or distribute the work; and they will often insist that the writer sign away all rights to the work. These "publishers" should be avoided.

English Language Learners

Encourage students to research publications that accept stories and articles written in their first language. They can check with publishers of high school writers to see if they publish in other languages. And they may find useful information from the appropriate foreign language department of a local college or university. Also, ask students to consider writing in both their first language and English for submissions.

Preparing a Portfolio

The process of looking through their collected work, choosing the items that best represent their skills and progress, and then explaining why they chose those items can be very beneficial to students. Consider having them work toward submitting a showcase portfolio for review.

Inform students at the start of the year that they will be expected to compile portfolios and tell them when they will be due. Inform them of who will review the portfolios, how the portfolios will be reviewed, and how they will be assessed. For example, the assessment might be based primarily on the care taken in assembling the portfolio and the quality of the opening letter, or it might be based on the entire contents. The variety of writing samples to be used might include

- a significant report from a science or social studies class,
- essays of various lengths from humanities classes,
- examples of creative writing,
- a multimedia presentation, or
- workplace writing.

If desired, schedule ongoing conferences to discuss each student's progress in selecting submissions and evaluating her or his developing skills.

136

Preparing a Portfolio

A writing portfolio is a collection of your work that shows your skill as a writer. Your teacher will probably ask you to compile a *showcase portfolio*—a collection of your best writing for a quarter or a semester. Compiling a showcase portfolio allows you to participate in the assessment process. You decide which writing samples to include, and you reflect upon your writing progress.

Working Smart

Use the following information as a guide when you compile a showcase portfolio. There are no shortcuts when it comes to putting together an effective portfolio, so don't skip any of these suggestions.

1. Organize and keep track of your writing (including planning notes and drafts).

2. Be sure that you understand all of the requirements for your portfolio. If you have any questions, ask your teacher for help.

3. Keep your work in a safe place. Use a good-quality expandable folder for your portfolio to avoid dog-eared or ripped pages.

4. Maintain a regular writing/compiling schedule. It will be impossible to create an effective portfolio if you approach it as a last-minute project.

5. Develop a feeling of pride in your portfolio. Make sure that it reflects a positive image of yourself. Look your best! (Remember that your teacher will be reviewing your portfolio for assessment.)

Try It!

Create a chart—similar to the one below—to help you keep track of writing you may want to include in a portfolio. For each piece, put a check next to each step you complete.

	Social Studies: "Urban Sprawl"	Literature: Great Gatsby
Prewriting Notes	✓	✓
First Draft	✓	✓
Revision	✓	
Edited Copy		
Final Draft	✓	
Cover Sheet		

English Language Learners

Have students create a showcase portfolio that includes all writing completed during the school year. Have them include an individual spelling log noting all spelling errors that occurred during the writing process. Encourage students to periodically review their logs.

Parts of a Portfolio

Check with your teacher about specific requirements for your portfolio. Most showcase portfolios contain the following parts:

- **A table of contents** listing the pieces included in the portfolio
- **An opening essay or letter** detailing the story behind your portfolio (how you organized it, what it represents to you, and so on)
- **Specific finished pieces** representing your best writing (Your teacher may ask you to include all of the planning, drafting, and revising for one or more of your writing samples.)
- **A best "other" piece** related to your work in another content area
- **A cover sheet** attached to each piece of writing, discussing the reason for its selection, the work that went into it, and so on
- **Evaluation sheets or checklists** charting the basic skills you have mastered as well as the skills you still need to work on (Your teacher will supply these sheets.)

Writing Your Opening Pages

The first two pages of a showcase portfolio are shown here.

Table of Contents

Showcase Portfolio
Jenna Bosworth

Table of Contents

Opening Letter

Dear Ms. _____

I first thought compiling a portfolio was just another assignment. However, as the semester progressed, I realized that I wanted to "show off" my writing. As a result, I put a lot of effort into the enclosed pieces of writing. You will be able to see that by looking at the different steps I took in writing them.

The first piece—"The U.S. Department of Peace: Why Not?"—is a persuasive essay that I wrote for my current-events class. The essay stems from a resolution by Senator Mark Dayton, who proposed that the United States have a Department of Peace. Writing about this resolution helped me feel more connected to the affairs of government. I paid careful attention to both sides of the argument when I crafted this essay. I am pleased to include it in my portfolio for all to read.

The second selection—"Misery in Missouri"—is a feature article I wrote in Honors Composition. It depicts a few summer days in hot, humid St. Louis and how various people cope with the heat. I enjoyed profiling the different personalities. Developing this piece certainly improved my interviewing skills.

My third piece is a letter to the editor that I submitted to the *Bugle-Call*. I was both surprised and happy when it was published. The letter expresses my displeasure with the new rules regarding Senior Prom. I discovered my civil-but-angry voice while writing this letter. This experience gave me new confidence in my writing ability.

Sincerely,
Jenna Bosworth

Process

Parts of a Portfolio

The more deeply students reflect on their skills and progress as writers, the more they will gain from the exercise of assembling and introducing the portfolio. The essay format will allow them to reflect in greater detail than the shorter letter format. Suggest that students consider the following questions as they write their introduction:

- How does this selection of writings represent my growth as a writer?
- Which sample am I proudest of? Why?
- How does my choice and treatment of topics express my preferences?
- What writing skills do I most need to work on in future projects?

Struggling Learners

Help students see improvement in their writing by having them put together a growth portfolio. After the pieces have been selected, place each one in a plastic sheet protector or tape an overhead transparency on top of it. Then have students use markers to track skills in their writing, such as circling specific details or underlining clear sentences so they can easily see their progress.

Note that it can be difficult to create an effective cover sheet for an essay that was written long ago if students don't have notes available to remind them of their experience. Encourage students from this point onward to

- include specific details and examples from their writing when they write self-assessments and reflections,
- reflect candidly on their writing experiences, and
- record details in their writer's notebook about every writing project.

✱ For information on reflections and self-assessments, see SE pages 32 and 43.

These strategies will save them time and trouble when they decide which essays to include in a showcase portfolio.

138

Creating a Cover Sheet

When you create your showcase portfolio, you should attach a cover sheet to each writing project you include. (See the sample below written for a student's persuasive essay.) Your cover sheet should do one or more of the following things:

- Explain why you chose the piece for your portfolio.
- Tell about the process of writing you used, including problems you encountered.
- Describe the strong points and the weak points in the writing.
- Reflect on the writing's importance to you.

Sample Cover Sheet

I chose this essay because I am proud of how I expressed myself about an important issue. Our assignment was to write a persuasive essay based on any of the issues we'd been discussing in Current Events. One issue, a resolution by Senator Mark Dayton to create a federal Department of Peace and Nonviolence, really struck me as a commonsense approach to preventing conflict. The resolution, unfortunately, never went anywhere in Congress, but I decided I would write an essay in support of it.

An article from *Time* magazine provided some background information. I researched the issue further using congressional sites on the Internet and the senator's own Web site. I did some personal research, as well, getting the opinions of friends and family members. Then I organized my information using a line diagram before writing my first draft.

The strongest point in this paper is my confident voice. I'm sure it's because I felt so strongly about the topic. The weakest point is probably the flow of my ideas. I was more concerned with presenting my thoughts than with sentence fluency.

Writing this essay helped me see that persuading someone to accept my viewpoint is more than being passionate about a particular issue. Being persuasive requires a logical presentation of an argument and paying careful attention to opposing points of view.

Try It!

Write a cover sheet for a piece of writing that you would like to include in your portfolio.

Creating Your Own Web Site

Creating a Web site is one way to showcase your work. Check with your Internet service provider to find out how to get started. If you are designing your page at school, ask your teacher for help. The questions and answers below will help you get started.

Q. How do I begin planning my site?

A. Think about the number of pages you want on your site. Do you want just one page to showcase a piece of your work, or do you want multiple pages (a home page, a page of poetry, a short-story page, a page of favorite links, and so on)? Check out other students' Web pages for ideas. Then sketch out your pages. Note how the pages will be linked by marking the "hot spots" on your sketches.

Q. How do I make the pages?

A. Each page is created as a separate file. Many word-processing programs let you save a file as a Web page. Otherwise, you may have to learn HTML (hypertext markup language). This is a code that allows you to add text and graphics to a page. Your teacher may be able to help you with it. If not, you can find instructions on the Internet.

Q. How do I know if my pages work?

A. You should always test your pages. Using your browser, open your first page. Then follow the links to make sure they work correctly.

Q. How do I get my pages on the Web?

A. You must upload your finished pages to your Internet provider's computer. Ask your provider how to do this. (If you're working on your home computer, get a parent's approval. If you're using a school computer, work with your teacher.) Your provider will tell you how to access the pages later, in case you want to make changes. After you upload a page, visit your site and make sure it still works.

Try It!

Get the word out about your site. E-mail your friends and ask them to visit your site. Your service provider can offer tips on how to get your site listed on various Web browsers.

Creating Your Own Web Site

In addition to discussing personal Web sites, discuss a related idea, the Web log, or blog.

- A blog consists of ongoing commentary arranged chronologically, with the most current entry serving as the page first seen by visitors to the site. Recent entries follow, and older ones are available as archived links.
- A comment link below each entry allows readers to respond.
- Web sites are available that provide "blogging" software to users at no cost.
- People have adapted the blogging format to many uses. Some use it as a public journal. Others focus on a specific topic. Many journalists discuss their work and field of expertise on their blog; and most major newspapers have added blogs to their Web site.

Ask students to share examples of Web sites and Web logs that they use and admire. Invite any students who already have a blog site to show their work.

Narrative Writing Overview

Common Core Standards Focus

Writing 3: Write narratives to develop real or imagined experiences or events using effective technique, well-chosen details, and well-structured event sequences.

Language 2: Demonstrate command of the conventions of standard English capitalization, punctuation, and spelling when writing.

Writing Forms

- personal narrative
- college entrance personal essay

Focus on the Traits

- **Ideas** Sharing a meaningful experience and including background information, specific details, and dialogue
- **Organization** Including an interesting beginning that draws the reader in; a middle that builds suspense through action, dialogue, and details; and an ending that explains what the writer has learned
- **Voice** Creating a narrative voice that sounds realistic and reflects the writer's feelings
- **Word Choice** Choosing specific nouns, active verbs, and descriptive modifiers to create clear images and feelings
- **Sentence Fluency** Using a variety of sentences to create a smooth flow
- **Conventions** Checking for errors in punctuation, capitalization, spelling, and grammar

 Literature Connections

- **"Shooting an Elephant"** by George Orwell
- **"Of Studies"** by Francis Bacon

 Technology Connections

 Write Source Online
www.hmheducation.com/writesource

- *Net-text*
- *Bookshelf*
- *GrammarSnap*
- *Portfolio*
- *Essay Scoring*
- *Writing Network features*
- *File Cabinet*

 Interactive Whiteboard Lessons

Suggested Narrative Writing Unit (Two Weeks)

Day	Writing and Skills Instruction	Student Edition		SkillsBook	Daily Language Workouts	Write Source Online
		Main Pages	Resource Units*			
1	**Narrative Essay: Making the Right Decision for the Wrong Reason** (Model, Prewriting) ⓛ Literature Connections "Shooting an Elephant"	141–145			18–21	*Interactive Whiteboard Lessons, Net-text*
2	(Writing) Crots Polysyndeton	146, 58, 80				*Net-text*

* These units are also located in the back of the *Teacher's Edition*. Resource Units include "Basic Elements of Writing" and "Proofreader's Guide."
(+) This activity is located in a different section of the *Write Source Student Edition.* If students have already completed this activity, you may wish to review it at this time.

Day	Writing and Skills Instruction	Student Edition		SkillsBook	Daily Language Workouts	Write Source Online
		Main Pages	Resource Units*			
WEEK 1 CONT. 3	(Revising)	147–148				Net-text
	Skills Activities:	75	714–715, 726–727, 742–743	85, 86, 87–88		
	• Verbs and Verbals					
	• Sentence Lengths and Beginnings	82	151–152			GrammarSnap
	Peer Responding	121–126				
4	(Editing and Publishing)	149				Portfolio, Net-text
	Skills Activities:					
	• Punctuating Dialogue		616–617, 632–633	30		
	• Pronoun-Antecedent Agreement		756–757	77, 145, 178		GrammarSnap
	• Plurals		654–655, 656–657	49, 50		
5	(Assessing, Reflecting)	150–154				
opt.	Speeches	439–447				
SECOND FORM WEEK 1 1–5	**Writing the College Entrance Essay** (Model) ⓛ Literature Connections "Of Studies"	155–157			22–25	
	(Prewriting)	158				Net-text
	(Writing)	159				Net-text
	(Revising)	160				Net-text
	Skills Activities:					
	• Transitions		595–596			
	• Conjunctions, Prepositions, Interjections		732–733, 734–735	108, 109, 110, 111, 112		GrammarSnap
	• Pronouns		704–705, 706–707, 708–709	80, 81, 82, 83		GrammarSnap
	(Editing)	160				Net-text
	Skills Activities:					
	• End Punctuation		605–607	5		
	• Using the Right Word		678–679, 680–681	58		
	• Pronoun Shifts		708 (+), 710 (+), 756 (+)	179		
	• Commas (In a Series, To Separate Adjectives)		608–609, 610–611	8, 11		GrammarSnap
	Example Prompts	161				

* These units are also located in the back of the *Teacher's Edition*. Resource Units include "Basic Elements of Writing" and "Proofreader's Guide."

(+) This activity is located in a different section of the *Write Source Student Edition*. If students have already completed this activity, you may wish to review it at this time.

Teacher's Notes for Narrative Writing

This overview of narrative writing includes some specific teaching suggestions for the unit. The description of each chapter will help you decide which parts of the unit to teach.

Writing Focus

Writing a Personal Narrative (pages 141–154)

Narrative writing invites the reader to share the writer's experiences. Students can learn to shape their experiences into stories that have effective beginnings, middles, and endings. Students are expected to create an engaging story by exploring dialogue, sensory details, specific action, and personal feelings. Easy-to-follow guidelines, tips, samples, revising and editing checklists, and a rubric for narrative writing are included in this chapter.

Writing the College Entrance Essay (pages 155–161)

Many colleges use the college entrance essay (along with grades, standardized-test scores, and other information) when they determine whom to admit. So, students wishing to go on to college need to be familiar with this important narrative writing task. A sample essay, directions for writing such an essay, and sample prompts are included.

Grammar Focus

For support with this unit's grammar topics, consult the resource units. (Basic Grammar and Writing, A Writer's Resource, and Proofreader's Guide).

Academic Vocabulary

Read aloud the academic terms, as well as the descriptions and questions. Model for students how to read one question and answer it. Have partners monitor their understanding and seek clarification of the terms by working through the meanings and questions together.

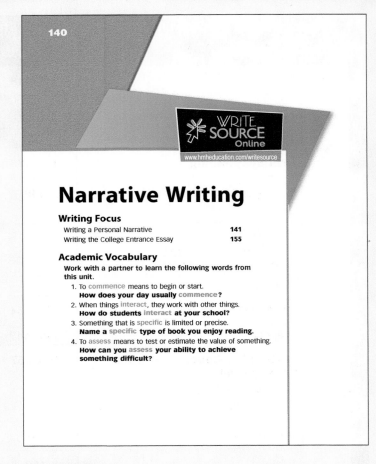

Narrative Writing

Writing Focus

Academic Vocabulary

Work with a partner to learn the following words from this unit.

1. To commence means to begin or start.
   How does your day usually commence?
2. When things interact, they work with other things.
   How do students interact at your school?
3. Something that is specific is limited or precise.
   Name a specific type of book you enjoy reading.
4. To assess means to test or estimate the value of something.
   How can you assess your ability to achieve something difficult?

Minilessons

Learning Something New
Writing a Personal Narrative

- **FREEWRITE** about one of your experiences during which you made an important decision. Consider the following questions as you write: *What would have been different if you hadn't made that decision? What did this decision teach you? Did the decision change who you are or how you treat others?*

Special Effects
Writing the College Entrance Essay

- **THINK** about all the people, circumstances, experiences, challenges, or achievements that have dramatically affected your life. **FREEWRITE** to discover one special effect and **EXPLORE** its meaning by writing the story surrounding how it affected you and why you feel it is significant.

141

Narrative Writing
Writing a Personal Narrative

In his book *Writing About Your Life*, William Zinsser says, "Be surprised by the crazy wonderful events that will come dancing out of your past when you stir the pot of memory." Writing personal narratives provides a perfect opportunity "to stir the pot of memory" in order to recall memorable experiences. No other form of writing connects you with your life in such a meaningful way.

In this chapter, you will read a personal narrative in which the writer recalls charming his grandmother for selfish reasons. Despite his less than honorable intentions, he ends up making the right decision. Then you will learn how to write your own narrative about a time you acted appropriately, but for the wrong reason. Special attention is given to creating an effective story line and to including background information.

Writing Guidelines

Subject: **Making the right decision for the wrong reason**
Form: **Personal narrative**
Purpose: **To share a meaningful experience**
Audience: **Classmates**

"Wrong reasoning sometimes lands poor mortals in right conclusions."

—George Eliot

Writing a Personal Narrative

Objectives
- understand the purpose, content, and form of a personal narrative
- choose a topic (making the right decision for the wrong reason) to write about
- plan, draft, revise, and edit a personal narrative

Point out that a personal narrative (often referred to as a *memoir*) focuses on a specific time or event in the writer's life. This section will briefly describe the process of writing a personal narrative.

 Literature Connections

Mentor texts: In addition to William Zinsser's *Writing About Your Life,* consider inspiring students with the following selections.
- *The Art of the Personal Essay,* an anthology edited by Phillip Lopate
- *The Book of Life,* an anthology of selections from memoirs, edited by Eve Claxton
- *The Situation and the Story: The Art of Personal Narrative,* by Vivian Gornick
- *Bird by Bird: Some Instructions on Writing and Life,* by Anne Lamott

 Technology Connections

Use this unit's Interactive Whiteboard Lesson to introduce narrative writing.

 Interactive Whiteboard Lessons

Copy Masters

Time Line (TE pp. 143, 146)

T-chart (TE p. 144)

Benchmark Papers

My Escape from Vietnam (excellent)
TE pp. 783–787

Learning to Express Our Love (fair)
TE pp. 788–792

Personal Narrative

Review the rubric on SE pages 150–151 before reading the essay.

Work through this sample essay with the class, pointing out the elements that make it a good personal narrative.

Ideas

- The experience shared is interesting.
- The writer explains how the event changed him.
- The writer uses interesting writing techniques.

Organization

- The beginning identifies the problem that the writer will explore and captures the reader's interest.
- The middle explores the relationship between the writer and his grandmother.
- The ending illustrates the writer's new understanding about himself and others.
- Transitions (*From all this, Instead, Still, At first*) are used effectively to link ideas.

Voice

- The writer's voice is casual and natural throughout.
- The dialogue sounds realistic and helps define the characters.

142

Personal Narrative

In the following personal narrative, Kenny writes about a time he did the right thing for the wrong reason.

Beginning
The writer draws the reader into the narrative.

Middle
Background information prepares the reader for the story.

The writer's "wrongful" reason is revealed.

A Greater Wealth

Most young kids are very self-centered most of the time. It's like their brain meters are stuck on "Selfish." In just about any situation in which they have a choice, first they wonder what's in it for them. This certainly described me, until I met my dear grandmother.

My father had been born in Japan, and he had many old, old photographs of the palatial estate that had belonged to his family through many generations. He told me stories of gorgeous homes full of lacquered furniture, silk wall panels, and polished cedar platforms. He also described magnificent gardens, full of the sweet scents of exotic flowers and the gentle trickle of graceful fountains.

From all this, I figured my grandmother must be rich. I had never met her before she came from Japan, but at eight, I reasoned that if I were nice to her, she would take me back to Japan to live in luxury. It was a good plan, I thought, and I vowed to spend time with my grandmother so she would grow to love me and want me to accompany her upon her return.

"There she is!" my father called. I expected to see some regal kimono-clad creature riding in a satin litter like I'd seen in pictures. Instead, I saw a tiny woman with silver hair, wearing a modern blue suit. She did not look wealthy to me. Still, I vowed to be attentive, to make myself indispensable to her during her stay.

To get closer to her, I flattered her into telling me stories about old Japan. She enjoyed making temari, fabric balls wound tightly with delicate designs, and as she worked, she wove tales of Japanese legends and history as intricate and beautiful as the designs she created. I listened, fascinated. Her words were a mix of the two languages, so I didn't completely understand everything at first. Interestingly, as her English improved, so did my understanding of Japanese.

No one spoke of her going back, and I was anxious to commence my life of Japanese luxury, so one evening I

English Language Learners

Define these terms before students read the narrative:

- palatial (spacious and ornate)
- lacquered (covered with a clear coating that produces a sleek, glossy finish)
- regal (wonderful, splendid)
- dashed (destroyed, ruined)

Dialogue builds suspense.

worked up my courage to ask.

"Obaasan?" I began timidly. She looked up from her embroidery, her eyes peeking lovingly over her half-glasses.

"Yes, Kenny-chan?" She always added the traditional endearment to my name.

"When you go back to Japan, will you take me?"

She seemed surprised by the question, and she stopped her winding and rested her hands on her lap.

The narrative builds to a moment of discovery.

"Kenny-Chan, I am no going back. I live here now. But why you want to leave? Here is so wonderful."

"But aren't you rich in Japan? Don't you have beautiful things there?"

"Why you think that?" she asked, surprised.

I told her about my father's stories.

"Yes," she smiled. "I told those stories to your father when he little. My father told them me. Once they all true, and my family had great wealth. But then war came, and it all disappeared. Your sohu—your grandfather—and I worked very hard make good life. Not rich life, but good life. Now he gone, and I wish to remain here with family."

Ending
The writer reveals his new understanding.

My dreams of a luxurious life had been dashed. At first I was disappointed. Then I remembered that she was staying with us, and my sadness disappeared. I had tried to make her love me so that I could join her in Japan. I soon understood that I didn't need the wealth of Japan. My grandmother had given me great riches right here at home.

Narrative

 Respond to the reading. Answer the following questions about the sample narrative.

Ideas (1) What is the writer's initial reason for interacting with his grandmother? (2) What does he discover?

Organization (3) Where is time order used in the narrative?

Voice & Word Choice (4) What does the dialogue reveal about the grandmother's character?

 Literature Connections: In the narrative essay "Shooting an Elephant," George Orwell reflects on a time when less-than-honorable motives drove his actions.

 Respond to the reading.

Answers

Ideas 1. He wants his grandmother, whom he imagines to be wealthy, to take him back to Japan with her so he can live in luxury.

2. He finds out that the family lost all its money during the war. He also discovers that he is happy being with his grandmother, even without the promise of wealth.

Organization 3. The opening uses hindsight, looking back at the events that changed the writer's perspective. Then those events are described in chronological order. Within the main story, the grandmother also uses chronological order when she tells what happened to her family.

Voice & Word Choice 4. The dialogue shows that she has not yet mastered English, although she expresses herself well. Her use of the endearment *-chan* shows how she feels about her grandson.

 Literature Connections

In the essay "Shooting an Elephant," a narrator, presumably Orwell, recounts an episode during his time as a police officer in Burma. He is called to the rice fields in response to an elephant's rampage. Surrounded by thousands of villagers, the police officer feels pressured to shoot and kill the elephant.

Encourage students to discuss what ultimately causes Orwell to shoot the escaped elephant. Then have them compare and contrast Orwell's thought process during and after the incident to a time when they may have acted for the wrong reasons. Have students take notes during discussion for use on their own personal narratives. For additional models of narrative writing, see the Reading-Writing Connections beginning on page TE-36.

Prewriting Selecting a Topic

Encourage students to think creatively about the assignment, considering serious situations and comic ones, as well as times when they were aware of the objective and times when the outcome was a complete surprise.

Prewriting Gathering Details

Distribute photocopies of the reproducible T-chart (TE page 823) for students to use for their Q-and-A chart.

Encourage students to use Kenny's questions in their chart, adding any other questions they think would contribute to the essay.

Focus on the Traits

Ideas

Note that, in practical terms, keeping readers in suspense requires withholding certain information in the beginning. Point out that the opening of the sample reveals that the writer's selfish attitude was changed when he met his grandmother, but that is all that the writer reveals. Without an explanation at this point, it keeps readers wondering, *What happened?*

Technology Connections

Students can use the added features of the Net-text as they explore this stage of the writing process.

 Write Source Online **Net-text**

144

Prewriting Selecting a Topic

To get started, Kenny listed a few times when he did the right thing, but not for the right reason. He then put an asterisk next to the one time he would write about.

Topics List

- gaining my grandmother's attention so she would take me to Japan *
- mowing Mrs. Havel's lawn so I could use her swimming pool
- practicing the guitar to become famous
- befriending a certain classmate to help me in calculus

 Select a topic. List at least three personal experiences in which you did the right thing, but not for the right reason. Put an asterisk next to the one experience that you would like to write about.

Gathering Details

Kenny then completed a Q-and-A chart to gather his initial thoughts.

Q-and-A Chart

Questions	Answers
What did I want?	I wanted to have my grandmother take me to Japan.
Why did I want this?	I wanted to live in luxury.
What did I do?	I was especially nice to her.
What was the result?	I really grew to love her.
What did I learn?	I learned that real wealth comes from love.

 Learn about your experience. Complete a Q-and-A chart about your experience.

Focus on the Traits

Ideas When you plan and write your narrative, keep in mind the element of surprise. Work in ideas and details that build suspense into your story and lead up to a turning point—a moment of realization.

English Language Learners

Students may need additional clarification of the topic. Explain that doing the "right thing for the wrong reason" in this case means doing something that benefits another person in the hope of gaining something personally. Provide examples such as returning a lost wallet in the hope of receiving a reward.

Considering the Story Line

Since a personal narrative is essentially a true story, it should contain the basic elements that create an effective story or plot line, including a problem to get things started, complications, a moment of truth, and so on. Here's how Kenny's narrative develops according to the base elements of a story or plot. (Also see page **342**.)

Determining the Problem

Kenny believes he would live a life of luxury in Japan, so he needs to convince his grandmother to take him back with her.

Working in Complications

Kenny learns a great deal about life in Japan from his father and his grandmother. No one talks about the grandmother going back, yet Kenny is anxious to start his new life. A conversation between Kenny and his grandmother builds to the moment of truth.

Identifying the Climax or Moment of Truth

Kenny discovers that his grandmother isn't rich and that she isn't returning to Japan.

Bringing the Story to a Close

In the resolution, Kenny discovers that living without luxury will be okay, and interacting with his grandmother is its own reward—one that is much more valuable than material wealth.

Prewrite

Develop your story line. Identify the main parts for your narrative: problem, complications, climax, and resolution. (During the actual writing, change or add to any part as needed.)

Focus on the Traits

Voice Dialogue is an essential feature in narratives. It has three main functions: (1) It helps develop the personalities of the participants. (2) It furthers the action and builds suspense. (3) It serves as a transitional device to move from one part of the experience to the next. See if you can find at least one example of each of these functions in the sample narrative.

Narrative

Prewriting **Considering the Story Line**

After students read SE page 342, ask them to make a plot line for their topic. Note that rising action generally consists of several events, or complications. They should try to present at least two or three complications, each leading the narrator closer to the moment of realization, or crisis.

Focus on the Traits

Voice

Discuss the use of dialogue in the sample essay, addressing each of the three purposes listed in the box.

- Character development: The grandmother's imperfect but expressive English (*"Why you think that?"*) both shows her status as a newcomer to the U.S. and reveals her interest in and caring for her family.
- Suspense: The short exchanges before the grandmother tells her story (*"Obaasan?"* . . . *"Yes, Kenny-chan?"*) build suspense by delaying the story.
- Transition: *"There she is!"* is a transition from the writer's background explanation to the grandmother's arrival and the start of the action.

Struggling Learners

Draw out the classic plot line and explain the following:
- The *problem* is introduced in the exposition.
- The *complications* create the rising action.
- The *moment of truth* is the climax.
- The *close* of the story is also called the denouement.

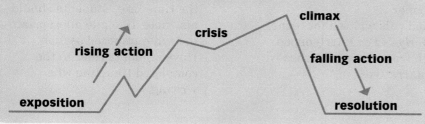

Writing Creating a Beginning, a Middle, and an Ending

Ask students to notice how the author constructs each paragraph in the narrative. How does he use transitions to make the writing flow smoothly and to advance the action?

 For information about basic paragraph skills, see SE pages 577–588; for a sample narrative paragraph, see SE page 580.

To see how other authors choose to begin, sustain, and end their personal narratives, ask students to work on their own to **find a published personal narrative** (see below) to discuss in class. They should be prepared to

- identify the technique used to grab readers' interest at the beginning,
- describe how the author builds suspense, and
- explain how the events change the author.

Technology Connections

Students can use the added features of the Net-text as they explore this stage of the writing process.

Write Source Online **Net-text**

"Your opening has to be good—or the rest of the story won't have a chance because nobody'll stick around to read it."
—Lawrence Block

Writing Creating a Beginning, a Middle, and an Ending

A personal narrative relates and reflects upon a pivotal moment in the writer's life. All narratives have a beginning, a middle, and an ending.

The Beginning   Draw the reader in. The beginning must hook the reader and introduce the situation. You can gain the reader's interest in several ways:

- Start with an interesting or surprising statement.
- Begin with dialogue to pull the reader into the action.
- Make a statement that piques the reader's curiosity.
- Share information that sets the scene.

Kenny selected the fourth technique. In his introduction, he discusses a common childhood condition—self-centeredness—that every reader can identify with.

The Middle   Build suspense through action, dialogue, and details. The middle develops the story line and supports the main idea of your narrative. In the sample narrative, Kenny works to make his grandmother love him; and at the moment of truth, he discovers that his grandmother is not returning to Japan.

The Ending   Explain what you learned from the situation. Wrap up your story and explain what you have learned. Remember that the purpose of your narrative is to explore a time when you made the right decision for the wrong reason. In his conclusion, Kenny explains that great wealth is not limited to money and luxury.

 Write

Develop your first draft. Catch your reader's interest, build suspense through actions and details, and reveal the lesson you learned.

Teaching Tip: Find a Published Personal Narrative

Point students to any of the personal narratives listed in the "Reading-Writing Connections" pages in the front of this book. Also suggest that students use the following techniques to find a narrative to analyze:

- Look through books in the classroom (see TE page 141).
- Search the library catalog or ask a librarian for advice.
- Find out if a favorite writer has published a memoir.
- Look for personal commentaries in the newspaper.
- Read periodicals written for teens, such as *Merlyn's Pen* (merlynspen.org), which frequently publishes personal narratives.

Struggling Learners

Distribute copies of the reproducible Time Line (TE page 821). Have students arrange the plot events of their personal narratives on the time line. Students should also note dialogue appropriate to each numbered section. Have students refer to the completed time line when writing.

Writing a Personal Narrative **147**

Revising Including Background Information

In a personal narrative, be sure that your audience has enough background information to understand the significance of your experience. This is sometimes called the *backstory,* events that occurred before the experience begins.

Kenny's first middle paragraph helps the reader appreciate the importance of the experience.

Sample "Backstory"

My father had been born in Japan, and he had many old, old photographs of the palatial estate that had belonged to his family through many generations. He told me stories of gorgeous homes full of lacquered furniture, silk wall panels, and polished cedar platforms. He also described magnificent gardens, full of the sweet scents of exotic flowers and the gentle trickle of graceful fountains.

Tip

You may find that in your own narrative, you will need little if any background information. It all depends on the nature of your experience.

Revise

Check for background information. As you review your first draft, determine if you have included, or need, background information. Be sure that you present this information in an engaging way.

Assessing Your Ending

The closing paragraph in your narrative should reveal that you have reflected on the experience. Sentences that show reflection begin with "I remembered," "I realized," "I understood," and so on. In the sample narrative, Kenny reflects on his discovery in the closing paragraph.

Sample Reflective Closing

My dreams of a luxurious life had been dashed. At first I was disappointed. Then I remembered that she was staying with us, and my sadness disappeared. I had tried to make her love me so that I could join her in Japan. I quickly understood that I didn't need the wealth of Japan. My grandmother had given me great riches right here at home.

Revise

Check your ending. Be sure that you have reflected on your experience in the closing paragraph.

Narrative

Revising Including Background Information

Explain that a backstory—the background information that is necessary to understand the narrative—can include different kinds of details. Students may need to explain some events that happened before or that lead up to the time of their narrative. They may, as Kenny did in the sample essay, include vivid details that help establish a scene.

Stress that the purpose of the backstory is to help the reader more clearly understand the significance of what happens in the narrative.

Revising Assessing Your Ending

Talk about the dangers of the "pat" ending—a conclusion that falls into place too quickly and neatly to seem natural. Note that students can avoid this by

- working to capture how the event actually felt to them, and
- avoiding cliched wording to express their ideas.

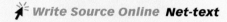

Technology Connections

Have students use the Writing Network features of the Net-text to comment on each other's drafts.

 Write Source Online **Net-text**

Revising Improving Your Writing

Have students work with partners to revise their first draft.

- Ask writers to read their personal narrative aloud to their partner.
- Note that the listener should focus only on the questions related to ideas, organization, and voice.
- Note that the writer should focus only on the questions related to word choice and sentence fluency.
- After the sharing, have students take a few minutes to jot down their responses and thoughts.
- Have the pair complete the checklist together.

148

Revising Improving Your Writing

Use a checklist. On your own paper, write the numbers 1 to 12. Put a check next to the number if you can answer "yes" to that question. If not, go back and revise that part of your personal narrative.

Revising Checklist

Ideas

_____ **1.** Do I identify the reason for my actions?
_____ **2.** Do I include essential background information?
_____ **3.** Do I include specific details and dialogue?

Organization

_____ **4.** Do I include an interesting opening that draws in the reader?
_____ **5.** Does the narrative build to a climax?
_____ **6.** Does my ending reflect on the experience?

Voice

_____ **7.** Does my dialogue sound realistic?
_____ **8.** Does my voice reflect my feelings about the event?

Word Choice

_____ **9.** Do I use specific nouns and active verbs?
_____ **10.** Do I use descriptive modifiers?

Sentence Fluency

_____ **11.** Do my sentences read smoothly throughout the narrative?
_____ **12.** Do I use a variety of sentence lengths?

Make a clean copy. After you've finished your revisions, make a fresh copy of your writing to edit.

Grammar Connection

Verbs and Verbals

- **Proofreader's Guide** pages 714–715, 726–727, 742–743
- *SkillsBook* pages 85, 86, 87–88

Sentence Lengths and Beginnings

- *SkillsBook* pages 151–152
- *GrammarSnap* Kinds of Sentences: Compound, Complex, and Compound-Complex Sentences

Advanced Learners

Reinforce understanding of active verbs by having students generate a list of dynamic verbs for the following overused verbs:

- walk slowly (shuffle, inch, crawl)
- grew (ballooned, skyrocketed, expanded)
- move forward (charge, plunge, leap)
- watch (look at, observe, inspect, analyze)
- eat quickly (consume, inhale, devour)
- yell (bellow, boom)
- request (implore, beseech)
- answer (reply, respond, retort)

Writing a Personal Narrative **149**

Editing Checking Your Writing

Use a checklist. On your own paper, write the numbers 1 to 12. For each of the questions below, put a check by the number if you can answer "yes" to that question. If not, go back and edit your narrative for that convention.

Editing Checklist

Conventions

PUNCTUATION

_____ **1.** Do I use punctuation after all my sentences?

_____ **2.** Do I use commas after long introductory word groups?

_____ **3.** Do I use commas correctly in compound and complex sentences?

_____ **4.** Do I punctuate dialogue correctly?

_____ **5.** Do I use apostrophes correctly?

CAPITALIZATION

_____ **6.** Do I begin all my sentences with capital letters?

_____ **7.** Do I capitalize all proper nouns?

SPELLING

_____ **8.** Have I spelled all my words correctly?

_____ **9.** Have I doubled-checked the words my spell-checker may have missed?

GRAMMAR

_____ **10.** Do I use correct forms of verbs?

_____ **11.** Do my pronouns agree with their antecedents?

_____ **12.** Do my verbs agree with their subjects?

Publishing Sharing Your Writing

There are several ways to publish your personal narrative.

- Read your story out loud to the class.
- Submit the story to your school's creative writing magazine.
- Send your story to a student-writing magazine. (See page **135**.)

Narrative

Editing Checking Your Writing

Focus on item 7, and have students think about how to determine when a word is a proper noun. The best way to check whether a word is used as a proper noun is to look up the word in a dictionary. Here are three other types of proper nouns to watch for.

- Titles used in place of names should be capitalized: _When Mom calls, I answer._ Note that a proper noun can replace _Mom_ in the example.
- Brand names should be capitalized: _While at the store, I decided to buy a box of Kleenex._
- Words used to name a region are capitalized: _I was born in the South._ Note that _south_ is not capitalized when used as a general direction: _I was born south of the capital._

✳ For more on proper nouns, see SE page 701; for more on capitalization, see SE page 648.

Publishing Sharing Your Writing

Consider posting students' work on the class or school Web site, if available. Invite students to include photographs or artwork with their essays. If the blog format is used on the site, a "Comments" link could allow readers to give feedback.

✳ For more about creating a Web site, see SE page 139.

Technology Connections

Remind students that they can use the Writing Network features of the Portfolio to share their work with peers.

➤ **Write Source Online** _Portfolio_

➤ **Write Source Online** _Net-text_

English Language Learners

Write the following sentences on the board and have students fill in each blank with an appropriate pronoun.

1. Everybody completed _____ homework assignments. (_everybody, their_)

2. One of my sisters thinks that _____ will become engaged soon. (_one, she_)

3. Several people left _____ umbrellas on the bus. (_people, their_)

Grammar Connection

Punctuating Dialogue

- **Proofreader's Guide** pages 616–617, 632–633
- _SkillsBook_ page 30

Pronoun-Antecedent Agreement

- **Proofreader's Guide** pages 756–757
- _SkillsBook_ pages 77, 145, 178
- _GrammarSnap_ Pronoun-Antecedent Agreement

Plurals

- **Proofreader's Guide** pages 654–655, 656–657
- _SkillsBook_ pages 49, 50

Rubric for Narrative Writing

Remind students that a rubric is a chart that they can use to evaluate their writing.

- The rubrics in this book are based on a six-point scale, in which a score of 6 indicates an amazing piece of writing and a score of 1 means the writing is incomplete and not ready to be assessed.
- Explain that the rubric is designed to help students break down the assessment process by evaluating each of the six traits of writing individually—ideas, organization, voice, word choice, sentence fluency, and conventions.
- Point out that a rubric can also be helpful during the writing process. It can guide students whenever they write because it tells which elements to include and how to present each effectively.
- Stress that honest self-assessment is the best way to identify what needs improvement.

✱ Reproducible six-, five-, and four-point rubrics for narrative writing can be found on pages 767, 771, and 775.

Rubric for Narrative Writing

Use the following rubric as a guide for assessing your personal narrative. Refer to it whenever you want to improve your writing.

	6	**5**	**4**
Ideas	The narrative shares a memorable event. Details bring the essay to life.	The writer shares an interesting experience. Specific details help maintain interest.	The writer tells about an interesting experience. Details should show, not tell.
Organization	The structure of the narrative makes it enjoyable and easy to read.	The narrative has a clear beginning, middle, and ending. Transitions are helpful.	For the most part, the narrative is organized. Most of the transitions are helpful.
Voice	The writer's voice captures the experience for the reader.	The writer's voice sounds natural. Dialogue helps hold the reader's interest.	The writer's voice creates interest in the essay, but dialogue should sound more natural.
Word Choice	The writer's excellent word choice creates a vivid picture of the event.	Specific nouns, verbs, and modifiers create clear images and feelings.	Some stronger nouns, verbs, and/or modifiers would create a clearer picture.
Sentence Fluency	The sentences are skillfully written to hold the reader's interest.	The sentences show variety and are easy to understand.	The sentences are varied, but some should flow more smoothly.
Conventions	The narrative has no errors in spelling, grammar, or punctuation.	The narrative has a few minor errors in punctuation, grammar, or spelling.	The narrative has some errors that may distract the reader.

English Language Learners

Students may be overwhelmed by the scope of the rubric. To alleviate their concerns, narrow the focus of the rubric by having students concentrate on evaluating only the ideas, organization, sentence fluency, and conventions categories.

Narrative

3	2	1
The writer should focus on one event. Some details do not relate to the essay.	The writer should focus on one experience. More details are needed.	The writer should select an experience and provide details.
The order of events must be corrected. More transitions are needed.	The beginning, middle, and ending all run together. The order is unclear.	The narrative must be better organized.
The writer's voice usually can be heard. More dialogue is needed.	The voice is weak. Dialogue is needed.	The writer sounds uninvolved or disinterested in the essay.
More specific nouns, verbs, and modifiers would paint a clearer picture of the event.	Better words are needed. Many are overused or too general to paint a clear picture.	The writer has not considered word choice or has used words incorrectly.
A better variety of sentences is needed. Sentences do not flow smoothly.	Many incomplete or short sentences make the writing choppy.	Few sentences are written well. Help is needed.
The narrative has several errors.	Numerous errors make the narrative hard to read and confusing.	Help is needed to find errors and make corrections.

Test Prep!

The six traits of writing were first identified in the 1960s by Paul Diederich and a group of 50 professionals who reviewed student papers and brainstormed the qualities that made writing strong. In 1983, a group of educators in Beaverton, Oregon, learned of Diederich's work and replicated it, settling on a similar set of six traits. A separate team in Missoula, Montana, simultaneously ran a study that identified the same basic group of traits.

Put simply, the six traits provide a universal set of criteria for strong writing. They correlate very well to the rubrics used in most state testing. Using the traits throughout the writing process, therefore, prepares students for any writing test they will face.

Evaluating a Personal Narrative

Ask students if they agree with the sample self-assessment on SE page 153. If they agree with the overall comments, ask them to suggest improvements based on the comments. If they disagree with any comment, ask them to explain why.

Ideas—It's not clear how the writer made the right decision for the wrong reason.

Organization—The beginning, middle, and ending are clear. If, however, the writer included one or two more significant actions in the middle, that section might build more effectively to the climax.

Voice—The writer could consider trying to express each character's individual personality a little more through dialogue.

Word Choice—Casual or slang expressions may not be clear to every reader (*chick flick; a little hyper*)

Sentence Fluency—The writer could have varied the sentence structure a bit more. The sentence that begins *Not a gym that reeked . . .* is incomplete.

152

Evaluating a Personal Narrative

As you read the narrative below, focus on the strengths and weaknesses in the writing. (**The essay may contain errors.**) Then read the self-assessment on page 153.

Girls' Night Out

"I'll pick you up at 6:30!" Greg's voice on the phone was excited. "Great! I can't wait!" I said and hung up.

I lied. It wasn't great. I wanted to go to a new chick flick with the girls, not sit in the bleachers watching bulky guys getting their faces smooshed into a wrestling mat. The things we do for our boyfriends! I sighed and called my friend Carly.

"What do you mean, you can't go?" Carly nearly shrieked, and I held the phone away from my ear. She did tend to be a little hyper sometimes. "What about me and Shandra and Kate? Friday night is always Girls' Night Out!" I explained that I felt I had to support Greg during his tournament.

"Well, I suppose that's noble of you," she admitted. "But really, Jan, you must become your own person."

"I'm sorry. I'll make it next week!" I said.

"Yeah, unless Mr. Wonderful wants to drag you to a fly-fishing festival or something!"

I hung up, mentally kicking myself. It had been a rough week. I had really been looking forward to our weekly evening of girly giggles. Not a gym that reeked of sweat.

At the gym, Greg and I parted; he disappeared into the locker room. I picked my way up through the crowded bleachers to get a good spot. I settled onto a hard wooden seat. I was glad I had brought along a novel to read in between matches.

The meet began. I cheered when Greg won his match with a late takedown, even though I winced at the painful-looking contortions he had to go through to do it. The team did pretty well, coming in second, and the coach announced a pizza party at his house. I must have looked pretty unhappy because Greg hugged me.

"You don't have to go, Jan!" he said. "It's just the guys, and I know it won't be much fun for you."

"You mean you'd go without me? Greg, I gave up Girls' Night Out for you!" He seemed genuinely surprised.

"Jan, you didn't have to do that!"

"I wanted to show you how much I support your stuff!" I blinked hard to stop the stinging in my eyes.

English Language Learners

Review the following terms with students before reading the essay:

- chick flick (movie with a story line that primarily appeals to females)
- hyper (high-strung, nervous)
- meet (organized competition, contest, game)
- contortions (actions that twist the body out of shape)

"Look, I know that sometimes my 'stuff' is boring for you, and that's okay! We don't have to do everything together. Sometimes you need your friends, just like I need mine."

He was right. We liked each other for who we are. Not who we might try to be. I, in fact, felt even closer to Greg after what he said. I realized that he had a very mature attitude about our relationship, far more mature than my own attitude.

Student Self-Assessment

Narrative Rubric Checklist

Title: _Girls' Night Out_

Writer: _Jan Harrison_

4 Ideas
- Is the narrative about making the right decision for the wrong reason?
- Is background information provided?
- Does the narrative include specific details and dialogue?

5 Organization
- Does the beginning interest the reader?
- Does the middle include a series of actions that build to the climax?
- Does the ending show what was learned?

5 Voice
- Does the writing sound natural?
- Does the dialogue sound realistic?

4 Word Choice
- Does the writing contain vivid verbs and specific nouns?
- Does it contain descriptive modifiers?

3 Sentence Fluency
- Do the sentences flow smoothly?
- Is the writing free of fragments and rambling sentences?

6 Conventions
- Does the narrative avoid careless errors?
- Is the dialogue correctly punctuated?

OVERALL COMMENTS:

I like how I started right in the middle of the action. I also think that my dialogue sounds very real.

My closing paragraph could show more thought and reflection.

Some of my sentences sound choppy. I also have to watch for sentence fragments.

Review your narrative.
Rate your narrative and write comments that explain why you gave yourself the scores you did.

Narrative

Student Self-Assessment

To give students additional practice with evaluating a narrative essay, use a reproducible Assessment Sheet (TE page 766), the Narrative Rubric Checklist (TE page 779), and one or both of the benchmark papers listed in the Benchmark Papers box below.

For your reference, a completed checklist and a comments sheet are provided for each benchmark paper.

Suggest that students fill out their self-assessment sheet and turn it in with their essay. Then, when you return their work, they can compare your comments to their own.

Struggling Learners

Form two groups, and assign each the trait *Word Choice* or *Sentence Fluency*. Have each group use the rubric to explain why the essay received a low score for the assigned trait. Then have students suggest changes so the essay could earn a score of 5 or 6 for that trait.

Advanced Learners

Provide students with opportunities to assess examples of personal writing. (Student samples are often available online.) Provide copies, and have students reach agreement on the score for each trait.

Benchmark Papers

My Escape from Vietnam (excellent)
- TE pp. 783–787

Learning to Express Our Love (fair)
- TE pp. 788–792

Reflecting on Your Writing

Students may not at first understand the distinction between the self-assessments they did on the previous page and the reflections. Point out that the assessment requires them to pinpoint specific aspects of a particular essay, whereas the reflection asks them to think about their writing process *as a whole*. Explain that doing so can help them integrate what they have learned into their overall knowledge of the writing process.

Some students may think of questions about their writing (item 5) later on. A mailbox in the room in which students can deposit written questions can keep the dialogue going. Address these queries anonymously as part of class discussions on writing.

Reflecting on Your Writing

You've worked hard to write a personal narrative that your classmates will enjoy. Now take some time to think about your writing. Finish each of the sentence starters below on your own paper. Thinking about your writing will help you see how you are growing as a writer.

My Narrative

1. The strongest part of my personal narrative is . . .

2. The part that still needs work is . . .

3. The main thing I learned about writing a personal narrative is . . .

4. In my next personal narrative, I would like to . . .

5. One question I still have about writing personal narratives is . . .

Struggling Learners

Schedule individual writing conferences to review the reflections. Adding your own comments to theirs will help students build a writing vocabulary to evaluate their writing more deeply. Encourage students to complete the last item so that they are clear on how to improve their writing.

155

Writing the College Entrance Essay

For some college applications, you will be asked to write a personal essay in response to a given prompt. Your goal in this essay is to address the prompt specifically, while at the same time telling something about yourself—how you think and why you are drawn to the particular school or program.

Before you begin your essay, be sure that you understand what you are being asked to write about and why. Remember that the reader is trying to gain a better understanding of you, the student and the person; so be sure to present your ideas honestly and sincerely.

This chapter includes a sample entrance essay, writing guidelines, and a list of typical writing prompts you might see on applications. Also refer to online sources that provide additional tips for writing entrance essays.

Writing Guidelines

Subject: Application prompt
Form: Personal essay
Purpose: To reveal something about you as a student and as a person
Audience: School admissions officer

"Be honest with yourself and your readers. Don't try to write only what you think readers want to hear."

—Verne Meyer

Objectives

- choose a topic for a college entrance essay
- plan, draft, revise, and edit a practice college entrance essay
- learn about the types of prompts that colleges often use for entrance essays

If appropriate and feasible, have students work on their actual college entrance applications as they go through this section.

Test Prep!

Writing is a gateway skill. A well-written essay can open the doors of a college, and during the college years, well-written papers can lead to solid grades and strong work potential. A well-written résumé and cover letter can open the doors of a workplace, and on the job, well-written memos, letters, reports, and proposals can help an employee get ahead.

Some students may feel awkward writing about their lives and abilities, but assure them that this skill will pay dividends throughout life.

Struggling Learners

Students who intend to apply to a trade or technical school may think that this section is irrelevant to them. Explain that applications to most post-secondary schools or programs require a writing sample and that working through this section will aid that process.

College Entrance Essay

Have students examine the sample carefully. How does the writer express his individuality while addressing the question in the prompt? Possible responses:

- The opening captures the reader's interest (How will this anecdote influence the writer?). It also informs the reader (college admissions committee) that the writer is a student council member, a definite plus for a college applicant.
- The writer crafts and sustains an interesting beginning that leads to his main point (to study filmmaking), which isn't stated until the fifth paragraph.
- The final paragraph provides details that show he seeks advice of mentors, and he is open to exploring various options.

 Writer's Craft

Modes: The writer combines a number of modes of writing:

- an opening anecdote *(narrative)*
- a paragraph of explanation *(expository)*
- an allusion to an important work *(response to literature)*
- further explanations and examples *(expository)*

Often the most effective writing draws on multiple modes to achieve a single purpose.

156

College Entrance Essay

As part of his college application, David Schaap was asked to write a personal essay in response to this prompt: "In 500 words or less, explain what you want to study at Burnley College and why."

In his response, David uses an anecdote from his own experience to introduce his goal and then relates the goal to a particular program at the college. Margin notes point out important features in his essay.

A New World of Cinema

Beginning The writer uses a personal experience to get the reader's attention.

As one of my duties as a student council member, I help new students learn about our school. Earlier this year, I was doing this by introducing Anastasia Korkoff (a foreign-exchange student from Moscow) to other students. As we talked, a picture of a woman taped on the inside of a locker door caught Anastasia's eye. "Rachel McAdams!" she said. "I loved *The Notebook!*"

"You saw that?" I replied. I was shocked. This girl from Russia had seen a movie that was not a blockbuster, liked it, and even knew the name of the actress—not even a major celebrity. That conversation stuck in my mind for days.

Middle The writer explains the point of the experience.

From events like this, I came to realize that film is a major source of shared experience—not just with my friends or with others in this country, but also with people throughout the world. While I had always enjoyed movies as a form of entertainment, I had never realized before how broadly they shape culture—from Miami to Moscow.

A few weeks later, I explained these ideas to Ms. Crane, my English teacher. She listened, smiled, and suggested that I read the essay "Cinema Is the New Cathedral." As I read the piece, suddenly everything clicked. The writer argued that movies have replaced many other forms of communal experience, and even serve a religious-like function. At that point, I knew that understanding film was critical to understanding culture—both culture in this country and in others.

Introductory phrases link the paragraphs.

Ever since then, understanding film and filmmaking has been my goal. Entering the film program at Burnley

---

Invite students to find articles about what college admissions committees look for when assessing entrance essays. Have students compare their findings to the sample and then compile their findings in a booklet titled *A Guide to Writing an Entrance Essay*. Display the booklet for reference.

Provide the following definitions before students read the essay:

- blockbuster (movie that commands a vast audience, a "hit")
- clicked (suddenly fell into place or made sense)
- communal (belonging to a community; public)
- culture (arts, beliefs, and institutions characteristic of a society)
- achieve (reach a goal, attain)
- springboard (a factor that advances a career)

The writer offers details that explain his educational goal.

College will help me achieve that goal. I particularly want to study international film and the relationship between a film and its national culture. Also, because films have such a broad international audience, I want to study how Hollywood movies affect cultures outside the United States.

While I'm not sure yet where my film study might lead, I am sure that the trip will be interesting and worth the effort. For example, my mom suggests that I combine film study with communication and think about a career in journalism. My counselor says that the film-study program could be a springboard into the filmmaking industry. But Ms. Crane suggests that I study film and culture—and then teach the subject either in high school or in college. Wherever the film-study path leads, I'd like to start the journey at Burnley College.

Ending
In closing, the writer links the college with the career path he has chosen.

Narrative

 Respond to the reading. Answer the following questions about the sample college entrance essay.

Ideas (1) What field of study does the writer want to pursue? (2) Why does he find this field of study appealing?

Organization (3) In which paragraph does the author explain his goal? (4) What purpose is served by the paragraphs before that?

Voice & Word Choice (5) How would you describe the author's voice in this essay—enthusiastic, sincere, negative, confident? Explain. (6) What words or phrases stand out in the essay? Name two or three.

Literature Connections: Before writing your college entrance essay, read "Of Studies" by Francis Bacon for inspiration. It may help you think about the benefits of studying in a particular field.

 Respond to the reading.

Answers

Ideas 1. film and filmmaking **2.** Film is a global communication medium.

Organization 3. paragraph 5 **4.** to explain how he arrived at his goal—from being inspired by a comment from an exchange student to seeking advice from his teacher and reading an essay

Voice & Word Choice 5. enthusiastic and sincere, based on wording such as the following:

- That conversation stuck in my mind for days.
- . . . how broadly they shape culture . . .
- . . . suddenly everything clicked.
- I'd like to start the journey . . .

6. Answers will vary. Possible answers:

- *I was shocked.* (The writer was strongly affected by the shared experience.)
- *. . . understanding film was critical to understanding culture.* (He made an important connection.)
- *While I'm not sure yet where my film study might lead . . .* (He is sincere about not knowing which career path he will choose, and he is open to possibilities.)

Literature Connections

Sir Francis Bacon's "Of Studies" advises the reader of the benefits of studying. Bacon aims to inform the reader of the best methods of study so that the reader gains the most from what is read.

Have students discuss Bacon's thoughts on the uses of studies. What points do they find especially interesting? Encourage students to relate Bacon's discussion to their own college ambitions. For additional models of narrative writing, see the Reading-Writing Connections beginning on page TE-36.

Struggling Learners

To help students evaluate the author's voice, make sure they understand the adjectives (enthusiastic, sincere, negative, confident). Read key passages expressively to help students hear the writer's voice. Discuss how they know that the writer does not sound negative.

Prewriting Focusing Your Efforts

Explain that students will write a 500-word practice essay. They may use the same prompt as for the sample essay on SE page 156 and substitute the name of their college or choose a prompt from the examples on SE page 161. If they need to write an actual entrance essay later in the year, they will have their practice essay and these pages for guidance.

Prewriting Gathering Details

Encourage students not to rush through the detail-gathering steps. Each step prepares them to choose pertinent and interesting details that will shape and personalize their essay. Thinking of the best way to create a written self-portrait such as this can take time.

One good getting-started approach is for students to freewrite in response to the prompt they are using for practice. After several days of compiling ideas, students will find they have details to include in their essay.

✱ For more about freewriting, see SE pages 99–100.

 Technology Connections

Students can use the added features of the Net-text as they explore this stage of the writing process.

 Write Source Online **Net-text**

Prewriting Focusing Your Efforts

The first step in writing your college application essay is to establish a clear focus for your work. To begin, consider the following questions:

- **What does the prompt ask for?** Try restating the prompt in your own words.
- **How does the topic relate to your own experience and goals?** The main purpose of a college application essay is to help the admissions official get to know you.
- **How does the prompt relate to the college or program?** Admission decisions are partly based upon how well an applicant's abilities and goals match those of the institution.
- **What specific instructions are given in the prompt?** Note specifically what the prompt asks you to do (*analyze, explain, describe, evaluate*, and so on) and how long your response should be.

Sample Focus Statements

- After studying computer graphics at Norrid College (the program), I hope to expand what can be achieved in Internet films (personal goal).

- I believe that Waterworth University (the college) can help me to become the sort of leader who inspires others to greatness (personal goal).

- I want to learn as much as I can about creative nonfiction writing (personal goal), and Northern University (the college) will certainly help me meet this goal.

Gathering Details

Experts agree that these strategies will help you prepare a strong essay.
1. **List your strengths and weaknesses with the prompt clearly in mind.** Be honest with yourself in this evaluation.
2. **Select a positive quality related to your goal.** An upbeat essay that focuses on hopeful results has the best chance of catching the attention of admissions officers.
3. **Choose a personal story to illustrate that quality and goal.** Think of experiences that say something about you as a person and a student. Then choose one (or more) experiences to include.

 Prewrite

Create a focus statement and gather details. Choose a prompt from page **161** or use an actual prompt from a college. Analyze the prompt, create a focus statement, and gather details to support your focus.

Advanced Learners

Challenge students to research writing prompts in college applications and admissions tests. Have them write each prompt and source on an index card. On the back of each card, have students write two possible focus statements. Place the completed index cards in a file box for review by college-bound students.

Writing the College Entrance Essay **159**

Writing Creating Your First Draft

Admissions personnel face a staggering number of application essays each year. For yours to get the attention it deserves, it must be compelling, honest, and personal. As you write your first draft, be sure each section does its job well.

Beginning Paragraph

The beginning paragraph should catch the reader's interest and smoothly lead up to your focus. Here are different ways to begin your essay.

- **Open with a personal anecdote.** This is the approach that we recommend. Be sure that the anecdote reveals something positive about you and relates to the prompt. (Use dialogue to bring the anecdote to life.)
- **Start with a revealing quotation.** Select a quotation that truly reflects your thoughts and feelings about your goal and the school in question.
- **Begin with an eye-catching fact or statistic.** Of course, this statement should effectively introduce the rest of your essay.

Middle Paragraphs

As you develop the main part of your essay, use an honest, sincere voice. Also keep these tips in mind.

- **Develop your focus.** Each paragraph in your essay should advance or develop the main point of your response.
- **Include specific details.** Instead of stating *I grew up in the country near a medium-sized city,* write *I grew up on a huge dairy farm near Muncie, Indiana, a medium-sized city northeast of Indianapolis.*
- **Use transitional words and phrases.** To ensure that your essay flows smoothly, link paragraphs with connecting words or phrases such as "From events like this" and "A few weeks later."

Ending Paragraph

The ending part should bring the reader to a satisfying sense of closure and leave him or her with a favorable impression of you. Here are two ways to conclude your essay.

- **Revisit your focus.** Bring your reader back to the main point of your essay.
- **End positively.** State politely but confidently that you look forward to attending the college in question.

Write

Draft your college entrance essay. Write freely without worrying about length just yet. Get your ideas on paper. You will have time to revise later.

Narrative

Writing Creating Your First Draft

Although entrance essays are strictly limited in length, students should not worry about length as they write their first draft. Encourage students to write freely to get all their ideas on paper. The process of trimming the essay down to the right size can help ensure that they include only the most persuasive anecdote and details.

✳ For information on basic essay skills, see SE pages 589–603.

Technology Connections

Students can use the added features of the Net-text as they explore this stage of the writing process.

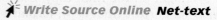

Write Source Online **Net-text**

English Language Learners

Students may need extra support when writing the first draft of a practice application essay. Have students identify the topic by restating the writing prompt in their own words. Then have them list the main point of the beginning, middle, and ending parts of their essay. Beneath each part, have students list supporting details. Encourage students to use the completed list to organize their draft.

Revising Improving Your First Draft

Encourage students to ask a close friend or family member to read their essay before they revise it. This might be a person who is mentioned in the essay. Students should ask the following questions:

- Does my beginning capture your attention?
- Do my details support my main point?
- Are the events organized chronologically?
- Does my voice sound natural and sincere?
- Is there a sentence you would change? Why?

Editing Checking for Conventions

Emphasize that since admissions personnel read so many good essays, the difference between getting to the next stage of the admissions process and being rejected could be due to one oversight on the final copy. Students should prepare a perfect final copy, formatted according to the college requirements for written work, and correct all mistakes in their essay. Students should not only edit it several times on their own, but also seek out another reader with proven proofreading skills.

✳ For more about the rules of punctuation, see the Proofreader's Guide (SE pages 604–647)

Technology Connections

Have students use the Writing Network features of the Net-text to comment on each other's drafts.

⚡ *Write Source Online* **Net-text**

160

Revising Improving Your First Draft

Once the first draft of your application essay is complete, review and revise it using the following questions as a guide:

- **Ideas** Is your main idea clear, fully developed, and well supported? Is the connection clear between your goal and the school or program?
- **Organization** Does your essay grab the reader's attention right from the beginning? Does the middle of your essay develop your focus? Does the ending revisit the focus statement and end on a positive note? Do you use transitions to lead the reader from idea to idea and from paragraph to paragraph?
- **Voice** Does your essay sound personal, sincere, and positive? Does it give the reader a sense of your personality? Does the dialogue, if you've used it, sound realistic?
- **Word Choice** Have you avoided cliches in your writing? Do you use specific nouns and verbs?
- **Sentence Fluency** Do your sentences flow smoothly?

Revise your essay. Use the questions above to guide your revision. Also ask a trusted classmate to read and respond to your essay, giving feedback to help you revise.

Editing Checking for Conventions

With an application essay, first impressions are critical. As a result, careful attention to punctuation, capitalization, spelling, and grammar is also critical. Take time to check your essay for errors and ask a trusted friend, teacher, or parent to check it as well. Then prepare a clean final copy to submit with your application.

Edit your work. Carefully check your punctuation, capitalization, spelling, and grammar.

 FYI

The Most Important Rule

The most important rule for a college application essay is this: **Be yourself.** Admissions readers must judge whether your goals, experiences, and abilities match well with their school. Your best chance of success overall is in letting them see who you really are. So don't try to impress them with words borrowed from a thesaurus or with grandiose statements. Instead, **focus on yourself and your goals.**

Grammar Connection

Transitions
- *Write Source* page 595–596

Conjunctions, Prepositions, Interjections
- **Proofreader's Guide** pages 732–733, 734–735
- *SkillsBook* pages 108, 109, 110, 111, 112
- *GrammarSnap* Subordinating Conjunctions, Prepositions

Pronouns
- **Proofreader's Guide** pages 704–705, 706–707, 708–709

- *SkillsBook* pages 80, 81, 82, 83
- *GrammarSnap* Nominative, Possessive, and Objective Cases of Pronouns

End Punctuation
- **Proofreader's Guide** pages 605–607
- *SkillsBook* page 5

Using the Right Word
- **Proofreader's Guide** pages 678–679, 680–681
- *SkillsBook* page 58

Pronoun Shifts
- **Proofreader's Guide** pages 708 (+), 710 (+), 756 (+)
- *SkillsBook* page 179

Commas (In a Series, to Separate Adjectives)
- **Proofreader's Guide** pages 608–609, 610–611
- *SkillsBook* pages 8, 11
- *GrammarSnap* Common Uses of Commas

Example Prompts

The following types of writing prompts are typically found on college applications. Most college application prompts also include the words "in one page or less" or a similar instruction about the length of your response.

Open-Ended Prompts

Prompts such as these leave a lot of leeway for possible answers. This means you will have to work extra hard to shape a focused response.

- Please include a personal statement with your application.
- Why is our college a good choice for you?
- Tell us your goals after college. How might our program contribute to those goals?

Influences in Your Life

Prompts like these ask you to write about people, places, and things that are important to you. Remember to relate their influence to your goals and to how the school can help you meet those goals.

- Describe a creative work in literature, art, music, or science that has had an effect on you, and explain that effect.
- Identify a person who has had a significant influence on your life, and describe that influence.

General Subject Prompts

These types of general subject prompts ask you to reflect on your thoughts, feelings, and beliefs.

- What is the value of community service in our society? Tell us how it relates to your life and plans.
- Do you believe there is a "generation gap"? Describe the differences between your generation and others.
- Think of a time when you have taken a risk: What was the effect (whether positive or negative) on your life?

Try It!

Choose one of the prompts above and write a one-page application essay in response. Carefully follow the steps outlined in this chapter. When you are finished, ask a friend, teacher, or parent for feedback. Then try again, using a prompt from a different category.

Narrative

Example Prompts

Divide the class into three groups, and assign each group one of the sample prompts under Open-Ended Prompts. Students in the group should work separately to write a focus statement for the prompt and come together as a group to talk about their ideas and respond to one another's work.

This practice will help students realize the broad range of responses possible in addressing an open-ended question. Students will also benefit from discussing their ideas about planning a response.

For additional practice in writing entrance essays, refer students to the **Try It!** on this page.

Technology Connections

Many schools provide their college-entrance essay prompts online. Have students log on to the colleges they hope to attend and search for essay prompts. This exercise can . . .

- provide authentic prompts to work with,
- allow students to write to an authentic audience, and
- give students more insight into the school.

Expository Writing Overview

Common Core Standards Focus

> **Writing 2:** Write informative/explanatory texts to examine and convey complex ideas, concepts, and information clearly and accurately through the effective selection, organization, and analysis of content.
>
> **Language 2:** Demonstrate command of the conventions of standard English capitalization, punctuation, and spelling when writing.

Writing Forms

- expository paragraph
- essay of speculation
- essay of opposing ideas
- writing for assessment

Focus on the Traits

- **Ideas** Stating the thesis clearly and including a variety of details that support the topic sentences
- **Organization** Beginning with a hook that captures the reader's attention, using the middle paragraphs to present both sides of the argument, and putting the debate in perspective in the ending
- **Voice** Using an informative voice that shows respect for both sides of the argument
- **Word Choice** Choosing words that explain the topic clearly, that have the right denotation, and that have an appropriate connotation
- **Sentence Fluency** Writing clear, complete sentences with varied beginnings and lengths
- **Conventions** Eliminating errors in punctuation, capitalization, spelling, and grammar

 Literature Connections

- **"Female Orations"** by Margaret Cavendish
- **"The White Collar Blues"** by Bob Herbert

 Technology Connections

 Write Source Online
www.hmheducation.com/writesource

- *Net-text*
- *Bookshelf*
- *GrammarSnap*
- *Portfolio*
- *Essay Scoring*
- *Writing Network features*
- *File Cabinet*

 *Interactive Whiteboard Lessons*

Suggested Expository Writing Unit (Five Weeks)

Day	Writing and Skills Instruction	Student Edition		SkillsBook	Daily Language Workouts	Write Source Online
		Main Pages	Resource Units*			
WEEK 1 1–3	**Expository Paragraph: Opposing Ideas**	163–165			26–29	*Interactive Whiteboard Lessons*
	Skills Activities:					
	• Parallelism		601, 762–763	169–170		*GrammarSnap*
	• Using the Right Word		682–683, 684–685	59		
	• Subjects and Predicates		738–739, 740–741	118		*GrammarSnap*
4–5	**Writing an Essay: Opposing Ideas** (Model, Prewriting) Thesis Statement, Supporting Details ⊕ Literature Connections "Female Orations"	166–174, 60, 61, 103, 56–57, 108–109	582			*Net-text*

* These units are also located in the back of the *Teacher's Edition*. Resource Units include "Basic Elements of Writing" and "Proofreader's Guide."
(+) This activity is located in a different section of the *Write Source Student Edition*. If students have already completed this activity, you may wish to review it at this time.

Day	Writing and Skills Instruction	Student Edition		SkillsBook	Daily Language Workouts	Write Source Online
		Main Pages	Resource Units*			
6–8	(Writing) Voice, Diction (Connotation), Quotations	175–180, 69, 71, 111			30–33	Net-text
9–10	(Revising)	181–192				Net-text
	Peer Responding	121–126				
	Skills Activities:					
	• Active and Passive Voice		722–723	91		GrammarSnap
	• Parallelism		601	171		GrammarSnap
	• Rambling Sentences			164		
	• Commas		612–613	12–13		GrammarSnap
	• Compound and Complex Sentences		748–749	128, 136		GrammarSnap
11–12	(Editing, Publishing)	193–197			34–37	Portfolio, Net-text
	Skills Activities:					
	• Pronouns (Case)		710–711	79		GrammarSnap
	• Adjectives	78	648–649, 728–729	97		GrammarSnap
	• Run-On Sentences and Comma Splices	87		159, 160, 161		
13–15	(Assessing, Reflecting)	198–202				
opt.	*Making Oral Presentations*	439–447				
1–5	**Writing an Essay of Speculation: A Timely Topic** (Model, Prewriting, Writing) Thesis Statement Supporting Details Diction 🌐 Literature Connections "The White Collar Blues"	203–208, 60–61, 56–57, 108–109, 110, 69			38–41	Net-text
6–7	(Revising, Editing, Publishing)	209–210			42–45	Portfolio, Net-text
	Skills Activities:					
	• Specific Nouns	74	701–703	70, 71, 72, 73, 74, 75		GrammarSnap
	• Verbals		726 (+)	122, 126		
	• Verb Forms		718–719, 720 (+), 722 (+)	93, 177		GrammarSnap
	• Capitalization		648 (+), 650–651, 652–653	41, 42		GrammarSnap
	• Semicolons, Colons		618–619, 620–621	17–18, 19, 20, 21		GrammarSnap
8	**Taking Tests**	551–560				
9–10	**Responding to Expository Prompts**	211–217				

Week 2 · Week 3 · Second Form Week 1 · Second Form Week 2

* These units are also located in the back of the *Teacher's Edition*. Resource Units include "Basic Elements of Writing" and "Proofreader's Guide."
(+) This activity is located in a different section of the *Write Source Student Edition*. If students have already completed this activity, you may wish to review it at this time.

Teacher's Notes for Expository Writing

This overview of expository writing includes some specific teaching suggestions for the unit. The description of each chapter will help you decide which parts of the unit to teach.

Writing Focus

Writing an Essay of Opposing Ideas (pages 163–202)

An essay of opposing ideas presents the value or strength of an important issue. When developing this type of essay, the writer's main task is to present the different points of view fairly and honestly. This chapter includes sample essays, a complete guide to the writing process for this type of essay, editing and revising checklists, and a rubric for expository writing. Television programs such as *Nightline* and *20/20* often present opposing views. Have students (as a class) watch one or two broadcasts and take notes on how the opposing viewpoint is presented.

Writing an Essay of Speculation (pages 203–210)

Students should regard the essay of speculation as a type of cause/effect writing in which the effects are not yet known. The effects will be the fruit of students' speculations—their reflections, projections, and educated guesses. *Reflections* involve deliberating, having a mental debate with yourself about a subject. *Projections* utilize current facts, trends, and information to predict the future. *Educated guesses* take into account as many variables as possible and consider what is already known to create logical theories about the future. The essay of speculation requires blending analysis and imagination. It's important for students to feel personal commitment to their topics.

Responding to Expository Prompts (page 211–217)

Classroom essay tests, state assessments, and college exams all require students to respond to prompts in a timely manner. Under such circumstances, writing a clear explanation can be challenging, but can be made easier if students know the steps to follow. These steps are part of this chapter. Students should work with the practice prompts provided.

Grammar Focus

For support with this unit's grammar topics, consult the resource units. (Basic Grammar and Writing, A Writer's Resource, and Proofreader's Guide).

Academic Vocabulary

Read aloud the academic terms, as well as the descriptions and questions. Model for students how to read one question and answer it. Have partners monitor their understanding and seek clarification of the terms by working through the meanings and questions together.

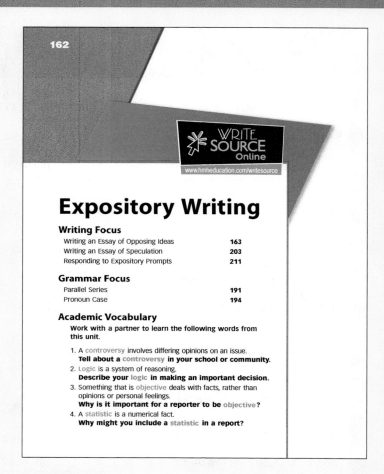

Academic Vocabulary

Work with a partner to learn the following words from this unit.

1. A controversy involves differing opinions on an issue.
   Tell about a controversy in your school or community.
2. Logic is a system of reasoning.
   Describe your logic in making an important decision.
3. Something that is objective deals with facts, rather than opinions or personal feelings.
   Why is it important for a reporter to be objective?
4. A statistic is a numerical fact.
   Why might you include a statistic in a report?

Minilessons

Pro/Con   Writing an Essay of Opposing Ideas

■ **MAKE** a list of controversial issues, whether local or international or things you would like to change. **COMPARE** lists with your classmates. **WRITE** two sentences for each issue or change—one presenting the position, the second presenting an opposing point of view.

**If This Continues,
Then . . . Disaster!**   Writing an Essay of Speculation

■ **LOOK** up some of the major predictions from the last 20 years. **CHOOSE** three of those predictions. Were the predictions accurate or did they wildly miss the mark? What evidence didn't they have or what evidence did they ignore?

163

Expository Writing
Writing an Essay of Opposing Ideas

The world of politics is filled with strong opinions and vigorous debates. Much writing about politics presents ideas persuasively: The writer chooses one side of a political argument and uses facts and ideas to defend it. But in a world full of strong opinions and opposing ideas, it's often helpful to know both sides of an argument.

An essay of opposing ideas thoroughly examines a controversial situation by presenting both sides of an argument without favoring either. In order to present both sides fairly, you'll need to research each position and represent its strengths and weaknesses.

In this chapter, you'll learn the steps necessary to write a thoroughly researched, well-organized, and fairly presented essay of opposing ideas. Your explanation of a controversy should be suitable for publication in a local or school newspaper.

Writing Guidelines

Subject:	A controversy with two sides
Form:	Essay of opposing ideas
Purpose:	To examine both positions fairly
Audience:	Readers of local or school newspapers

"A lot of good arguments are spoiled by some fool who knows what he is talking about."

—Miguel de Unamuno

Writing an Essay of Opposing Ideas

Objectives
- understand the elements of an essay of opposing ideas
- understand the form and content of an essay of opposing ideas
- plan, draft, revise, edit, and publish an essay of opposing ideas

An **essay of opposing ideas** examines both sides of a controversial issue. Such an essay presents facts, statistics, examples, and quotations that help explain the two major opposing positions. The essay may also explain points of agreement between the opposing sides.

The writer of an essay of opposing ideas should thoroughly research both sides of a controversy and present a fair, balanced, and unbiased explanation of each side's position.

 Technology Connections

Use this unit's Interactive Whiteboard Lesson to introduce expository writing.

 Interactive Whiteboard Lessons

Copy Masters
Assessment Sheet (TE p. 201)

Benchmark Papers
The Almond Story (good)
 TE pp. 793–797

Why Rome Fell (fair)
 TE pp. 798–801

Expository Writing Warm-Up

Mapping a Controversy

Brainstorm with the class a list of controversies and write them on the board. Keep the list posted so that students can refer to it when settling on topics for both their expository paragraph and their essay of opposing ideas. Emphasize the importance of considering controversies about which they are able to write objectively and so present a balanced argument.

By their nature, arguments have two or more sides. Students may, however, have some difficulty maintaining objectivity for both sides of certain controversies because one side of the argument appears to be so much stronger than the other or because one side appeals to their own thoughts and feelings about the issue.

For example, some people do not think that they should be forced to wear seat belts, yet statistics show that seat belts do save lives. This latter point is difficult to argue against. Presenting opposing sides of this controversy fairly would be challenging.

164

Expository Writing Warm-Up Mapping a Controversy

Controversies take place around you every day—in classroom debates, lunchroom conversations, or hallway arguments. To understand a controversy, you must understand both sides. A controversy map can help you. Kyreesha created the following map to understand a book-banning controversy at her high school.

Controversy Map

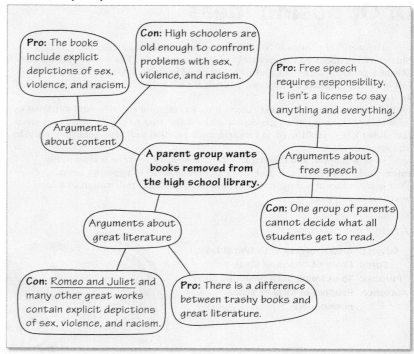

Try It!

Think of a controversy that you can be objective about. Create a map or cluster, writing the controversy in the center and creating branches for different arguments. Write down both sides of the argument and try to be fair to each position.

Advanced Learners

Challenge students to work collaboratively to develop a list of books or films that are about controversial topics. Have students share their results and add those topics to the class list.

English Language Learners

If students identify a controversial topic but have trouble articulating both sides of the issue, remind them that writers begin by asking questions. Have students generate a list of questions before they begin their research. Set aside in-class time to search for the answers. To ensure balanced arguments, have students use two sets of note cards: one set for one side of the argument and the second set for the other side, and to be sure they have equivalent numbers of cards.

Writing an Expository Paragraph

An expository paragraph explains a controversy in an objective way. Kyreesha used her controversy map (page 164) to write the following expository paragraph. Her paragraph has three parts.

- The **topic sentence** introduces the main point of the paragraph.
- The **body sentences** use a variety of details to support the main point.
- The **closing sentence** restates the main point in an interesting way.

A Battle over Books

Topic Sentence

Wilson High faces a battle over seven books that some parents feel are offensive—and that others feel are essential. The list of books includes Kurt Vonnegut's *Slaughterhouse Five* and Toni Morrison's *Beloved*, deemed to have explicit depictions of sex, violence, and racism.

Body Sentences

Other parents disagree, citing explicit material in more than 100 classics including *Romeo and Juliet* and *The Scarlet Letter*. This group argues that high schoolers are old enough to wrestle with such issues, and that their rights to free speech cannot be denied by one group of parents. The parents who are calling for the ban draw a distinction, however, between great literature and books they consider "trash." They also indicate that free speech requires responsibility.

Closing Sentence

Both groups of parents plan to make their positions clear at the next meeting of the Wilson High School Board.

Expository

Write

Write your own expository paragraph. Write about the controversy you chose on page 164. Create a topic sentence that focuses on the issue, include body sentences that fairly represent both sides, and write a closing sentence that completes the paragraph.

"You don't notice the referee during the game unless he makes a bad call."
—Drew Curtis

Writing an Essay of Opposing Ideas **165**

Writing an Expository Paragraph

Review the three main parts of an expository paragraph—topic sentence, body, and closing sentence. Have students use specific details from the sample expository paragraph to explain how the parts work together in the paragraph.

✳ For more information about the construction of an effective expository paragraph, see SE page 582. For more about basic paragraph skills, see SE pages 577–588.

Have students also note these elements of the sample paragraph.

The topic: The writer has chosen a controversy (a battle over banning specific books from a high school) that has two viable and supportable sides.

A balanced argument: The writer presents an equal number of reasons to support each side of the argument.

An objective tone: The writer presents the position of each side without bias. The writer avoids using inflammatory language to discredit either side.

Students should keep these elements in mind as they write their own paragraph.

Advanced Learners

Have students discuss the quotation by Drew Curtis at the bottom of the page and whether or not they agree with the statement. Ask the following questions as a springboard for discussion:

- Do you think noticing a referee's calls during a game is positive or negative? Why?

- In what way does the meaning of this quotation relate to writing about a controversy?
- What do you think readers of a controversial essay might consider a "bad call?"

Grammar Connection

Parallelism
- *Write Source* page 601
- **Proofreader's Guide** pages 762–763
- *SkillsBook* pages 169–170
- *GrammarSnap* Creating a Parallel Series

Using the Right Word
- **Proofreader's Guide** pages 682–683, 684–685
- *SkillsBook* page 59

Subjects and Predicates
- **Proofreader's Guide** pages 738–739, 740–741
- *SkillsBook* page 118
- *GrammarSnap* Complete Sentences and Sentence Fragments

Understanding Your Goal

Sometimes, the first three traits—ideas, organization, and voice—are referred to as the "global" traits. They focus on large-scale issues. That's why these three traits guide the prewriting and writing phase.

When the time comes to revise, students will review the first three traits and also check the next two: word choice and sentence fluency. These two traits have a more specific focus, on individual clauses, phrases, and words.

Only after these larger-scale issues are addressed should students check for conventions, making sure each letter and punctuation mark is correct. Polishing conventions is the job of the editing step.

❋ The six-point rubric on SE pages 198–199 is based on these traits. Reproducible six-, five-, and four-point rubrics for expository writing can be found on pages 768, 772, and 776.

Literature Connections

In her essay of opposing ideas "Female Orations," Margaret Cavendish presents seven points of view that comment on—and in some cases challenge—common attitudes toward women in 17th-century England. While some orators in the essay believe women should be good, submissive housewives, others take a strong stance against that notion.

Encourage students to discuss the essay's structure as well as the strengths and weaknesses of each debater's argument. Then have students comment on which argument they find most convincing and explain their position. For additional models of expository writing, see the Reading-Writing Connections beginning on page TE-36.

166

Understanding Your Goal

Your goal in this chapter is to write a well-organized essay of opposing ideas that fairly examines both sides of an argument. The traits listed in the chart below will help you plan and write your essay of opposing ideas. The rubric on pages 198–199 will also guide you.

Traits of an Essay of Opposing Ideas

- **Ideas**
  Choose a topic that will interest the reader, write a clear thesis statement, and include a variety of details that support your topic sentences.

- **Organization**
  Start with a hook that captures your reader's attention. Use middle paragraphs to fairly present both sides of the argument. End with a paragraph that puts the debate in perspective.

- **Voice**
  Use an informative voice that shows respect for both sides of the argument.

- **Word Choice**
  Choose words that explain your topic clearly, that have the right denotation (meaning), and that have an appropriate connotation (feeling).

- **Sentence Fluency**
  Write clear, complete sentences with varied beginnings and lengths.

- **Conventions**
  Eliminate errors in punctuation, capitalization, spelling, and grammar.

Literature Connections: For a historical example of opposing ideas, read Margaret Cavendish's "Female Orations." It takes the form of a debate between seven women, each with a different point of view on the same topic.

Essay of Opposing Ideas

An essay of opposing ideas fairly presents both sides of an argument. It uses facts, statistics, examples, and quotations to support each side. In this article, a student writer presents both sides of the argument about "third parties."

Beginning
The beginning introduces the topic and presents the thesis statement (underlined).

Middle
The first middle paragraphs present one side of the argument.

Writing an Essay of Opposing Ideas **167**

Are Third Parties Viable in U.S. Politics?

Since the Republican Party gained major party status in the 1850s, candidates from the Democratic or Republican parties have won the vast majority of United States elections ("Political"). Yet candidates from much smaller "third parties" have participated in many elections, and have even won local and state contests. Often, third-party platforms differ widely from the platforms of the two major parties. Perhaps for this reason, third parties have played a controversial role in U.S. politics. While proponents of third parties laud them for the new ideas they bring to the political arena, critics consider third parties an insignificant or damaging influence on U.S. politics.

Those who support third parties insist that the two-party system is one of the main reasons that new ideas are never tried. In an effort to win a majority vote, proponents say, the Democratic and Republican parties have often adopted watered-down platforms that will attract the necessary number of voters but won't solve society's problems. As long as Democrats and Republicans enjoy an unshakable hold on power, this situation is likely to continue. Third parties such as the Green Party, however, have offered bold solutions to society's problems, and their participation in the electoral system is invaluable ("Fresh Look").

Proponents also argue that the two major parties have created a system of money politics in which politicians are beholden to corporations and other wealthy donors instead of to the average citizen. Since third parties are generally more dependent on grassroots support, they are more likely to be responsive to the concerns of the voters. Third-party supporters also cite the success of third-party candidates in state, local, and even national elections as evidence that a significant number of U.S. voters want fresh ideas and grassroots activism.

Expository

Essay of Opposing Ideas

Work through the model essay with the class, pointing out the elements that make it a good expository essay.

Ideas

- The thesis statement identifies the opposing ideas of the controversy.
- The writer supports both sides of the argument with specific facts, statistics, and examples.

Organization

- The first two middle paragraphs explain one side of the argument, and the next two middle paragraphs explain the other side of the argument.
- The final middle paragraph identifies areas of agreement.
- The ending puts the controversy in perspective and summarizes its current status.

Voice & Word Choice

- The writer maintains an objective third-person point of view throughout the essay.
- The writer defines political terms in context to help readers understand ideas and uses words with appropriate connotations to make the essay informative and enjoyable.

English Language Learners

Before having students read the model essay, explain these unfamiliar words and phrases:

- third parties (political parties operating in a nation characterized by a two-party system)
- laud (praise)
- watered-down platforms (weak policies)

- unshakable hold (constant control)
- beholden to corporations (owing favors to large companies)
- grassroots (society at the local level, often rural areas)
- skewed (distorted; slanted)
- spoiler (a candidate who ruins the chances of another major candidate)

- Green Party (a political party that advocates social justice and environment protection)
- partisans (those who believe strongly in a political party's policies)
- brought to the forefront (emphasized)
- influx (a coming in)

Respond to the reading.

Answers

Ideas **1.** Proponents of third parties laud them for the new ideas they bring to the political arena. Critics consider third parties an insignificant or damaging influence on U.S. politics.

2. Both sides tend to agree that the U.S. political system needs an influx of new ideas, and both sides hope that new ideas capable of solving chronic problems will be brought to the forefront of our political process.

Organization **3.** The first two middle paragraphs present one side of the argument, and the next two middle paragraphs present the opposing side of the argument. The final middle paragraph identifies two areas of agreement between the two positions.

Voice **& Word Choice 4.** The writer uses comparison and contrast to show that third parties are smaller than and separate from the two major parties—the Democratic and Republican parties. The writer gives an example—the percentage of votes Ralph Nader received in the 2000 presidential election—to explain what a "spoiler" is.

Middle
The other side of the argument is presented next.

Those who oppose third parties insist that the participation of such parties more often results in skewed election results than in any kind of meaningful reform. Often, they cite the "spoiler" role of third-party candidates. In the 2000 presidential election, for example, Green Party candidate Ralph Nader received only 2.74 percent of the vote ("Election"). Yet many analysts believe that Nader's participation drew enough votes from Democrat Al Gore to deliver a victory to Republican George W. Bush.

In addition to the "spoiler" argument, those who oppose third-party candidacies insist that when people abandon major parties for third parties, they only reinforce the major parties' fear of new ideas. Without new ideas, these partisans argue, the major parties will remain stagnant, and the problem of an unresponsive, money-driven political system will remain.

Although both sides disagree on the effectiveness of third parties, they tend to agree that the U.S. political system needs an influx of new ideas. Chronic problems such as the health-care crisis, the national debt, poverty, and homelessness have resisted solution, despite a range of attempts by the major parties. People on both sides of the third-party debate hope that new ideas capable of solving these problems will be brought to the forefront of our political process.

Ending
The ending puts the arguments in perspective.

As major-party politics and pressing social problems remain a focus in U.S. politics, it's likely that third parties will also remain a part of the political system. Whether they will be able to effect meaningful change remains to be seen. Much of their effectiveness—or lack of effectiveness—results from the ability of those on either side of the debate to convince voters to either support or abandon third parties.

 Respond to the reading. Answer the following questions.

Ideas **(1)** What are the two positions about third parties? **(2)** What are the points of agreement between the two sides?

Organization **(3)** How do the middle paragraphs work to fairly present both sides of the argument?

Voice **& Word Choice (4)** How does the writer help the reader understand the terms "third party" and "spoiler"?

Writing an Essay of Opposing Ideas **169**

Prewriting

In the prewriting stage, you'll identify a controversial issue, explore both sides of the argument, and create an organizational structure for your essay.

Keys to Effective Prewriting

1. Choose a political controversy in which two major positions are in opposition.

2. Gather details that clearly present and support both sides of the argument.

3. Identify areas of agreement between the two positions.

4. Write a thesis statement that summarizes the controversy.

5. Plan your essay using a sentence outline, a topic outline, or an organized list.

Expository

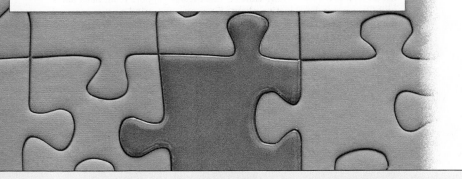

Prewriting

Keys to Effective Prewriting

Remind students of the purpose of the prewriting stage in the writing process. This is the stage during which the writer selects a topic, gathers details, and decides how to organize those details.

The Keys to Effective Prewriting list explains the process students will be guided through on SE pages 170–174.

Because students will be presenting two major positions in opposition to one another, they will have many opportunities to use such terms as *proponents*, *critics*, *support,* and *oppose*. (Have them note the use of these terms in the model essay on SE pages 167–168.) Explain to students that their writing will be more interesting and enjoyable to read if they can avoid excessive repetition of these terms in their essay. As part of their prewriting, encourage students to take some time to develop a list of appropriate **synonyms** *(see below)* to use in place of these terms for interest and variety in their essay.

Writing Workshop

Note that the pages in the prewriting, writing, revising, and editing sections can function as minilessons.

Technology Connections

Students can use the added features of the Net-text as they explore this stage of the writing process.

 Write Source Online **Net-text**

Teaching Tip: Synonyms

Encourage students to use a thesaurus and a dictionary to find synonyms for *proponents, support, opponents,* and *oppose* before writing. Suggest students make a list of synonyms to use in their essay.

Encourage students to suggest synonyms that the class can use, especially while revising. To get students started, offer two or three ideas.

- **proponents**—advocates, supporters, promoters, fans, allies, backers, exponents
- **support**—champion, defend, promote, back
- **critics**—opponents, detractors, challengers, rivals
- **oppose**—resist, disagree with, contest

Prewriting Selecting a Controversy

Work together to create a list of controversies suitable for an essay of opposing ideas. Have on hand several current editions of major and local newspapers and weekly news magazines. Encourage students to jot down ideas from local and national news broadcasts.

Ask students enrolled in debate class or club to list controversies they have considered for debate. Students can also include the nonstarred issues in the sample Controversies Chart.

Focus on the Traits

Ideas

Remind students that unlike writing a position paper in which they take a stand for or against an issue, when writing an essay of opposing ideas they should not reveal their personal views. Their goal is to present both sides of a controversy objectively. Therefore, they should choose a topic that will allow them to maintain a neutral stance.

Prewriting Selecting a Controversy

To create an effective essay of opposing ideas, you need to find a current controversial issue that will interest you and your classmates. Think of controversies at your school, in your community, in the nation, and in the world.

A student named Lin gathered topics by reading local and national newspapers and watching news shows. He made a controversies chart and put an asterisk next to the topic he wanted to write about.

Controversies Chart

School	Community	Nation	World
– funding for new gymnasium	– city council resignations	– congressional redistricting	– how to stop genocides in Africa
– MySpace.com limits	– community service requirement	– electronic voting *	– globalization and free trade
– special education overhaul	– subsidy for Klement Manufacturing	– congressional ethics reform	– third-world debt relief
			– global warming

 Prewrite

Create a controversies chart. Write "School," "Community," "Nation," and "World" at the top of a piece of paper. Then read local and national newspapers, looking for current controversies that interest you. Place an asterisk (*) next to the controversy you choose to write about.

Focus on the Traits

Ideas Select a controversy that (1) has strong support from both sides and (2) you can be objective about. Keep an open mind as you research, doing your best to understand each side of the argument. Think of yourself as a referee, watching closely, noting the strengths and weaknesses of both sides, but not favoring either one.

English Language Learners

Some students may have difficulty listing current controversies, due to language barriers or gaps in their knowledge of U.S. politics and culture.

Allow students to choose controversial subjects related to their country of origin. Invite them to ask family members for ideas.

Researching the Controversy

Once you have selected a controversy to write about, you need to conduct research to make sure you fully understand the issue. Solid research includes a variety of sources:

- **Print media** such as newspapers and newsmagazines provide in-depth articles on current crises and controversies. Current books can provide even more information. These resources tend to be well edited and reliable, though some publications have a bias.
- **Online media** can provide either authoritative and current information (government or university Web sites) or biased and outdated information (blogs and message threads). All online sources should be carefully double-checked to be sure the information is accurate, up to date, and nonbiased.
- **Primary sources** such as surveys and interviews allow you to ask questions and gather opinions from the "person in the street." Of course, the information you receive depends on your interviewing and surveying skills as well as on the knowledge of the people you approach.

Lin created the following list to be sure that he could research a variety of sources on his topic: electronic voting.

Sources List

<u>Print Media:</u>
  36 Days: The Complete Chronicle
    of the 2000 Election Crisis,
    New York Times correspondents
  "Is E-Voting Safe?" Paul Boutin, PC World
  Overtime! The Election 2000 Thriller,
    Larry J. Sabato

<u>Online Media:</u>
  Electronic Frontier Foundation Web site
  "Electronic Voting Raises New Issues," <u>washingtonpost.com</u>

<u>Primary Sources:</u>
  Betty Parks, District 7 voting coordinator

Prewrite

Create a sources list. Look for a variety of sources about your topic—print media, online media, and primary sources.

Expository

English Language Learners

To help students stay organized as they look for sources and research both sides of an issue, have them create one Sources List for each side of the controversy. Partner students with cooperative, English-proficient peers to conduct online searches, to locate reliable sources, and to record citations accurately.

Prewriting Researching the Controversy

Remind students that when they research a topic, they should look for as many primary sources as possible. Primary sources include

- diaries, journals, and letters;
- presentations;
- interviews;
- surveys and questionnaires; and
- personal observation and participation.

✳ For more about primary sources and how to evaluate all types of sources for dependability, see SE pages 372–373.

Encourage students to list at least two of each type of source: Print Media, Online Media, and Primary Sources. By doing so, they will have another resource to consult should one source prove unreliable or incomplete.

Literature Connections

Research: For more help with research, direct students to the following resources:

The Craft of Research by Wayne C. Booth et al.

The Curious Researcher: A Guide to writing Research Papers by Bruce Ballenger

Prewriting Gathering Details

Point out to students that the questions they have about their topic may come from their own thinking about the topic or may arise through **conducting research** *(see below)*.

- Sometimes, finding the answer to one question may lead to a new question. Point out the first two sample note cards in which the answer to the writer's first question probably led the writer to ask a question about problems in Florida on the second card.

- Then point out the last two sample note cards in which the writer asks about the benefits and problems related to the topic. Suggest to students that asking similar questions about their topic might be a useful strategy. Such questions can help them identify both sides of an issue and determine if they can represent both sides fairly.

Prewriting Gathering Details

As you conduct research, you need to keep track of many different facts, statistics, examples, and quotations. Note cards are a convenient way to record details and their source. Here are sample note cards that Lin prepared during his research.

Note Cards

> Why are people thinking about electronic voting?
> In 2000, problems with the Florida elections held up the decision for 36 days.
>
> "36 Days," The New York Times

> What problems happened in Florida?
> "Butterfly" ballots were confusing and some were miscounted or not counted because of "hanging chads."
>
> Overtime! The Election 2000 Thriller

> What are the benefits of electronic voting?
> • Quicker and easier
> • Can check results before submitting
> • Totaled faster
> • Counted more accurately
> "Electronic Voting Raises New Issues," washingtonpost.com

> What are the problems with electronic voting?
> • Errors occur
> • A power loss means data loss
> • No paper trail
> • Hacking
>
> "Is E-Voting Safe?" PC World

Prewrite

Research your controversy. Take notes on cards or in a notebook. Write questions you have, answers you find, and the sources that provide the answers.

Teaching Tip: Conducting Research

Remind students that they are planning to write a two-page, or approximately a seven-paragraph, essay. Although they should conduct enough research to develop and support their ideas, they should limit their sources list to what they will use in their essay. Emphasize, however, the importance of documenting all sources as they would for any research report, including complete online addresses.

✳ For more on documenting research sources, see SE pages 425–438.

Organizing Your Essay

Once you have completed your research, it is time to write a thesis statement.

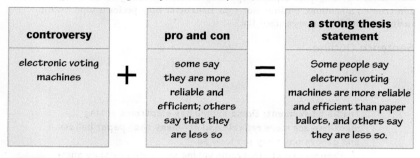

controversy		pro and con		a strong thesis statement
electronic voting machines	**+**	some say they are more reliable and efficient; others say that they are less so	**=**	Some people say electronic voting machines are more reliable and efficient than paper ballots, and others say they are less so.

Prewrite

Write your thesis statement. Use the model above to create a thesis statement for your essay. Try different versions until you are satisfied.

Writing Topic Sentences

Write topic sentences first for the "pro" side, then for the "con" side, and last for the common ground. Here are Lin's topic sentences.

Topic Sentences

Pro (convenience): Proponents of electronic voting systems say they allow people to vote quickly and easily.

Pro (accuracy): Proponents also point out that electronic voting makes vote counting faster and easier.

Con (unreliability): Opponents of electronic voting insist that such systems are unreliable.

Con (tampering): Opponents of electronic voting also fear that computer hackers could tamper with election results.

Common ground: While people disagree about the effectiveness of electronic voting, they agree that the fiasco of 2000 should not be repeated.

Prewrite

Write topic sentences. Focus first on the "pro" argument, then on the "con" argument, and finally on the common ground.

Expository

Prewriting Organizing Your Essay

Review the formula for creating a thesis statement: controversy + pro and con = a strong thesis statement. Point out to students that the benefit of creating a strong and effective thesis statement at this point is twofold:

- Students should be able to identify the opposing sides of the issue. If they can't, they have more research to do.
- A well-structured thesis statement will guide writing and help students decide which details to include and which to leave out of their essay.

✳ For more on writing effective thesis statements, see SE page 592.

Prewriting Writing Topic Sentences

Ask students to explain the purpose of the topic sentences shown. (The first four present the arguments for and against electronic voting, as expressed in the thesis statement, with both sides being represented equally. The last topic sentence expresses the point on which both sides agree.)

Point out that the thesis statement and topic sentences provide an organizational guide for writing their essay.

English Language Learners

Some students may not be familiar with the expression *common ground*. Explain that this expression means "shared opinion." Help students understand that the expression refers to the point on which both sides agree.

Prewriting Outlining Your Essay

Help students recognize that the outline consists of the sample thesis statement, the topic sentences, and details from their research notes.

✳ For more information about outlining, see SE page 591.

Some students may be in the habit of writing directly from their notes, without creating an organizing outline. Tell them that creating an outline ensures that they will have a visual plan to keep them on track. If you require an outline, clarify the kind of outline you prefer (sentence outline, topic outline, or organized list). Or, let students choose the type of outline they prefer to create, thereby allowing for different approaches to planning and writing.

Prewriting Outlining Your Essay

Before writing your essay of opposing ideas, organize your ideas and details. Lin created a sentence outline, but your instructor may prefer a topic outline (using phrases) or an organized list.

Sentence Outline

Thesis Statement: Some people say electronic voting machines are more reliable and efficient than paper ballots, and others say they are less so.

I. Proponents of electronic voting systems say they allow people to vote quickly and easily.
  A. Voters simply touch a certain candidate's name.
  B. Voters can review choices before submitting the ballot.

II. Proponents also point out that electronic voting makes vote counting faster and easier.
  A. The computer keeps a running tally.
  B. Election results are available sooner.

III. Opponents of electronic voting insist that such systems are unreliable.
  A. In 2004, electronic machines caused many errors.
  B. Some machines failed completely, losing votes forever.

IV. Opponents of electronic voting also fear that computer hackers could tamper with election results.
  A. Users can fool the machines to allow multiple votes.
  B. Hackers could cause skewed results.

V. While people disagree about the effectiveness of electronic voting, they agree that the fiasco of 2000 should not be repeated.
  A. The country endured 36 days of "hanging chads."
  B. Castro offered to send "election monitors" to sort out the chaos.

Prewrite

Organize your ideas. Create a sentence outline (as above), a topic outline (using phrases), or an organized list, whichever your instructor prefers.

Struggling Learners

Some students may have difficulty creating an outline or organized list of their ideas. Have students create a three-column chart (pro, con, and common ground) and fill it in with the information from their note cards.

Writing an Essay of Opposing Ideas **175**

Writing

Now that you have gathered and organized your ideas and details, you can begin writing the first draft of your essay.

Keys to Effective Writing

1. Use your outline or list as a writing guide.

2. Write on every other line or double-space if you are using a computer. This will allow room for changes.

3. Introduce the topic and state your thesis in the first paragraph.

4. Include your topic sentences in the middle paragraphs.

5. Use a variety of details to support each main idea (topic sentence).

6. End by putting the two opposing arguments in perspective.

Expository

Writing

Keys to Effective Writing

Remind students that the writing stage is when they get to write, or draft, their ideas on paper (or on the computer).

The Keys to Effective Writing list explains the process students will be guided through on SE pages 176–180.

Encourage students to review their outlines and their notes to verify that they can present a balanced picture of both sides of the argument. Explain that they should have close to the same number of details for the pros as for the cons. If students see a noticeable imbalance in one area, they should address the problem now, before they start to write their draft.

Writing Workshop

One of the key concepts of creating a writing community is to model writing for your students. You are one writer among many. When you lead your class through creating a strong opening, draft a few sentences of your own to demonstrate how you might start an essay. When you talk about transitions, write some sentences to show the concepts. Your students will be encouraged to see you writing and will be more ready to try their hands.

Technology Connections

Students can use the added features of the Net-text as they explore this stage of the writing process.

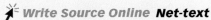 *Write Source Online* **Net-text**

Writing Getting the Big Picture

Help students see the connection between the sentence outline on SE page 174 and this graphic by pointing out that the thesis statement and topic sentences in the outline form the beginning and middle sections of the graphic.

Writer's Craft

Two-part organization: An essay of opposing ideas is one of many two-part essays: cause-effect, pro-con, compare-contrast, problem-solution. Because every two-part essay deals with two subjects, organization is key.

If students have followed the organizational pattern suggested in the prewriting assignments, their essays will have **subject-by-subject organization**: first one side is dealt with, and then the other side is dealt with. Students could also follow **point-by-point organization**: one point is addressed for both sides, then another point for both sides, and so on.

176

Writing Getting the Big Picture

The graphic below shows how the elements of an essay of opposing ideas work together to present a clear picture of a controversy. Use this graphic as a guide when preparing to write your first draft. (The examples are from the student essay on pages 177–180.)

Beginning

The **beginning** introduces the controversy and states the writer's thesis.

> **Thesis Statement**
> Some people say electronic voting machines are more reliable and efficient than paper ballots, and others say they are less so.

Middle

The **middle** paragraphs clearly explain both sides of the controversy.

> **Topic Sentences**
> Proponents of electronic voting systems say they allow people to vote quickly and easily.
>
> Proponents also point out that electronic voting makes vote counting faster and easier.
>
> Opponents of electronic voting insist that such systems are unreliable.
>
> Opponents of electronic voting also fear that computer hackers could tamper with election results.
>
> While people disagree about the effectiveness of electronic voting, they agree that the fiasco of 2000 should not be repeated.

Ending

The **ending** puts the controversy in perspective.

> **Closing Sentences**
> As the population of the United States and its dependence on technology grow, the debate over electronic voting will continue. However, many observers envision an eventual compromise between the parties on either side of the electronic voting debate.

English Language Learners

Students may not understand how the ending "puts the controversy into perspective." Explain that the ending of an essay of opposing ideas usually explains current developments related to the controversy and sometimes makes a prediction about what will happen in the future.

Starting Your Essay

The beginning paragraph of your essay of opposing ideas should engage your reader, introduce your topic, and provide your thesis statement.

Beginning

Middle

Ending

- **Engage your reader.** Open by capturing your reader's attention and introducing the controversy.

  In the 2000 presidential election, difficulties with counting votes in the state of Florida caused a bruising legal battle between the Democratic and Republican parties.

- **Introduce your topic.** Be sure to include details that expand on your opening sentence and provide necessary background information.

  A major cause of the controversy was unclear markings on traditional paper voting ballots, which muddled election results. . . . Another political battle has ensued.

- **End with a thesis statement.** Summarize the controversy in a sentence that broadly states both sides of the argument.

  Some people say electronic voting machines are more reliable and efficient than paper ballots, and others say they are less so.

Beginning Paragraph

Lin starts his essay by focusing on the fiasco of the 2000 elections. Then he provides background information that leads to his thesis statement.

Expository

> The writer engages the reader, introduces the topic, and states his thesis (underlined).

In the 2000 presidential election, difficulties with counting votes in the state of Florida caused a bruising legal battle between the Democratic and Republican parties. A major cause of the controversy was unclear markings on traditional paper voting ballots, which muddled election results (36 Days). In response to the problem, technology companies and government agencies proposed a radical solution—the use of direct recording electronic (DRE) voting machines. Another political battle has ensued. <u>Some people say electronic voting machines are more reliable and efficient than paper ballots, and others say they are less so.</u>

Write

Write a beginning paragraph. Use the guidelines above as you begin your essay of opposing ideas. (Also refer to the beginning of the essay on page 167.)

Writing Starting Your Essay

Although writing an engaging beginning is important, perfecting it at this point can slow or even halt the writing process. Remind students that the point of the writing stage is to draft the whole essay; that is, to get their ideas down on paper. Assure them that they will have time to refine their writing during the revision stage.

✱ If students cannot develop a beginning paragraph on their own, encourage them to follow the four-step beginning strategy explained on SE page 593. Doing so will help them get ideas down on paper so that they can move on to their middle paragraphs. Later, when they revise, they can add to or change ideas in their beginning to improve it.

English Language Learners

Some students may have difficulty understanding the term *bruising legal battle*. Explain that a legal battle is a dispute carried out by lawyers representing both sides of a controversy. Such disputes often become unpleasant, with each side accusing the other of some wrongdoing or crime. Such accusations may damage the public reputation of one or both sides. In this case, both sides (the Republican and Democratic parties) suffered damage to their reputations.

Writing Developing the Middle

Remind students that transitions help them create a smooth flow of ideas from one sentence to the next and from one paragraph to the next. This, in turn, makes following and understanding ideas easier for readers.

To help students recognize how they can use transitions to show time order, add extra information, make comparisons, and explain causes and effects, have students locate and discuss the use of transitions in the model essay on SE pages 167–168, and the sample middle paragraphs on SE pages 178–179.

✳ For a more extensive list of transition words and phrases, students can refer to SE pages 595–596.

178

Writing Developing the Middle

The middle part of your essay of opposing ideas should present each side of the argument fairly. The first middle paragraphs deal with the "pro" position, the next deal with the "con" position, and the last with common ground.

As you write your middle paragraphs, use transitions to connect your ideas. Lin used a variety of transitions to show different relationships between ideas.

Time	Extra Information	Compare/Contrast	Cause and Effect
after	in fact	both	thus
sometimes	also	even	as a result
during	in addition	while	consequently

Middle Paragraphs

Notice how Lin uses topic sentences, facts, statistics, examples, and quotations to build his middle paragraphs.

The first middle paragraphs present the "pro" side of the argument.

> Proponents of electronic voting systems say they allow people to vote quickly and easily. Most DRE systems use touch-screen computer monitors, which are now common across the United States. After choosing a slate of candidates, the user of a DRE machine can review and even change choices before submitting a final ballot—something that is possible but sometimes difficult with paper ballots.

Each paragraph begins with a topic sentence.

> Proponents also point out that electronic voting makes vote counting faster and easier. Most DRE machines are capable of compiling both ongoing and final vote counts immediately, thus eliminating human error from the vote count and allowing faster reporting of election results ("Electronic"). In the 2000 elections, many news anchors "called" state results when only a small percentage of the votes were tabulated—and reported inaccurate information. As a result, voters went to bed one night thinking that a specific candidate had won but woke up the next morning to

Beginning
Middle
Ending

English Language Learners

Students may understand the concept of transition words but have difficulty understanding the particular relationships established by using each. Have students identify transitions in the first two sample paragraphs. Then have them identify the category to which each transition belongs and explain how the transition helps them understand the ideas in the writing.

Paragraph 1: *After* at the beginning of sentence 3 (Time, makes sequence clear); *sometimes* near the end of the same sentence (Time, helps clarify the idea that changing choices is not always possible).

Paragraph 2: *also* in sentence 1 (Extra Information, tells reader that another issue has been introduced); *thus* in sentence 2 (Cause and Effect, shows that the cause has been stated in the first part of the sentence and that the effect is in the second half); *As a result* in sentence 4 (Cause and Effect, indicates that what follows is an effect).

discover something else—no one had won. Electronic voting machines would eliminate these errors.

Next, the writer explains the "con" side of the argument.

Opponents of electronic voting insist that such systems are unreliable. Studies have shown that in a number of elections, DRE machines produced errors in vote counts ("Accessibility"). In the presidential election of 2004, DRE machines in Ohio gave George W. Bush nearly 4,000 extra votes. In North Carolina, some machines failed totally: One county lost 4,500 votes ("Computer"). In addition, detractors point to another major factor in muddled elections—human error. Many of the same Floridians who found the paper "butterfly ballot" confusing would be even less comfortable poking a screen to indicate their choice. Consequently, voters would make errors in their selections, though this time there would be no paper trail for a recount.

Opponents of electronic voting also fear that computer hackers could tamper with election results. A skilled computer programmer could rewrite the code that controls electronic voting machines to skew the results toward a particular candidate. Since DRE machines do not offer a paper record of a voter's choices, there is no way to prove the validity of vote counts (Boutin 121).

The last middle paragraph covers the common ground between the two positions.

While people disagree about the effectiveness of electronic voting, they agree that the fiasco of 2000 should not be repeated. For 36 days, the outcome of the election was disputed, and the nation received an education in "butterfly ballots" and "hanging chads." In a particularly low point for democracy, Fidel Castro offered to send "election monitors" to Florida to help with the recount ("Stolen Elections"). No one, except perhaps Mr. Castro, would like a repeat of the 2000 debacle, and both sides recognize the problems with the butterfly and punch-card systems. They simply disagree about what should take their place.

Expository

Write

Write your middle paragraphs. Use your outline (page 174) to create paragraphs that present both sides of the controversy and explain the common ground. Include supporting facts, statistics, examples, and quotations.

Struggling Learners

Provide extra practice for students who have difficulty connecting the paragraphs in their essay. Using paragraphs from the sample essay, help students identify the transition words or key phrases that link the paragraphs. Then model the process for students, using paragraphs from their essay.

Point out that theoretically, if Lin has used reasonable facts, statistics, examples, and quotations in his middle paragraphs to support each side, readers should not be able to discern whether he is a proponent or an opponent of electronic voting. Ask students if they can tell from Lin's middle paragraphs which side of the argument he supports. Students should conclude that Lin has presented a fair, unbiased, and balanced picture of both sides of the controversy.

 Writer's Craft

Balance: Three features of Lin's essay create the sense of balanced reporting:
- Equal and diverse support for either side of the issue
- A focus on the opinions of either side (not those of the writer)
- Fair language in representing either position

These three features create a reliable voice that the reader trusts.

Writing Ending Your Essay

Have students analyze the paragraph to explain how the writer accomplishes the following:

■ **Puts the controversy in perspective:** In the first sentence, Lin says that the debate over this issue will continue as the population and its dependence on technology grow.

■ **Summarizes the current situation:** In the next few sentences, Lin states that observers envision an eventual compromise. Then Lin makes predictions about possible outcomes of this compromise.

■ **Includes an insight:** In the last sentence, Lin states that a candidate's best defense is to win by a landslide.

Test Prep!

After students finish the first drafts of their expository essays, point them to the on-demand expository essay on SE pages 214 and 215. The sort of writing the students have just completed is preparing them for the same sort of writing in high-stakes tests. By learning the process step by step, they are learning strategies they can apply in on-demand situations.

180

Writing Ending Your Essay

You have presented both sides of the political controversy, as well as outlined points on which both sides agree. Now that you have explained the controversy in detail, you are ready to write your ending paragraph. Follow these guidelines:

■ Put the controversy in perspective.
■ Summarize the current situation.
■ Include an insight that makes the reader think.

Ending Paragraph

In his final paragraph, Lin connects the ideas in his essay with current developments and predictions about the future of the controversy.

The writer creates a thoughtful ending for his essay.

> As the population of the United States and its dependence on technology grows, the debate over electronic voting will continue. However, many observers envision an eventual compromise between the parties on either side of the electronic voting debate. Such a compromise would allow electronic voting systems to be employed, but would produce paper "receipts" showing a voter's choices. This innovation would satisfy both parties by enabling rapid, accurate vote counts and ensuring accountability of results. Until then, though, a candidate's best defense against voting irregularities is to win not by a few percentage points, but by a landslide.

Write your ending paragraph. Put the controversy in perspective, summarize current ideas about the controversy, and leave your reader with something to think about.

Prepare a complete first draft. Double-space if you use a computer, or write on every other line if you write by hand. This makes the draft easier to review and gives you room to make revisions.

English Language Learners

Define the term *landslide* so students understand the metaphor. Explain that during a landslide, a massive amount of rock and earth suddenly moves down a hill or mountain, overwhelming anything in its path. Thus, the expression *winning by a landslide* means the winner received the vast majority of the votes.

Writing an Essay of Opposing Ideas **181**

Revising

Thorough revision helps ensure that the controversy you chose has been clearly explained. When you revise, you check your logic, rearrange parts of your writing, and create a more engaging, informative voice. You also check your word choice and improve sentence structure and variety.

> ### Keys to Effective Revising
>
> 1. Read your essay aloud to yourself or to a friend.
>
> 2. Be sure you have thoroughly analyzed the controversy.
>
> 3. Check your topic sentences and details to confirm that you have followed your outline.
>
> 4. Locate and eliminate any errors in logic.
>
> 5. Check your draft for strong word choice and variety in sentence length and structure.
>
> 6. To mark revisions on your draft copy, use the editing and proofreading marks found on the inside back cover of this book.

Expository

Revising

Keys to Effective Revising

Remind students that the revising stage provides them the opportunity to improve their first draft. At this stage they can think about refinements they might not have considered while drafting.

The Keys to Effective Revising list lays out the process students will be guided through on SE pages 182–192.

Encourage students to set aside their draft for a day or two before they begin revising. Point out that doing so enables them to look at their writing more objectively and with a fresh perspective.

Peer Responding

A constructive peer response at the beginning of the revision stage can help students discover what is working—and what is not—in their writing. (See pages 121–126 for a closer look at peer responding.) Armed with a thoughtful response, students can decide which revising strategies on the next pages will make the biggest improvement to their work.

Technology Connections

Have students use the Writing Network features of the Net-text to comment on each other's drafts.

Write Source Online **Net-text**

Revising **for** Ideas

The rubric strips that run across all of the revising pages (SE pages 182–191) are provided to help students focus their revising and are related to the full rubric on SE pages 198–199.

Exercise Answers

- "For more than a decade, Congress has debated the issue of funding for the Corporation of Public Broadcasting (CPB)." This fact helps to create a knowledgeable voice.
- "In 2006, a House budgetary . . . of the CPB." These details (facts, example, statistics) help explain the topic, make the information precise, and make the writing seem well informed.
- "Proponents of the cuts argue that the money would be better spent elsewhere . . . to market pressures." These facts and examples help explain the topic, add a knowledgeable voice, and make the writing concrete.
- The David Obey **quotation** *(see below)* about how Americans view public broadcasting shares an expert's knowledge of the situation.

182

Revising **for** Ideas

| **6** My essay brims with fascinating details that engage the reader. | **5** I have effectively used a variety of details to support my main points. | **4** I have used a variety of details, but some details do not support my main points. |

When you revise for *ideas*, you make sure you have used details effectively. The rubric strip above will help you revise.

Have I used different types of details effectively?

You have used different types of details effectively if you have used each for a specific purpose:

- **Facts** are details that can be proven. Use facts to clearly explain your topic and create a knowledgeable voice.
- **Statistics** are facts that include a numerical amount. Use statistics to make your information precise.
- **Examples** are specific events or situations that illustrate a general idea. Use examples to make your writing concrete.
- **Quotations** are the exact words of a speaker. Use quotations to share an expert's knowledge.

Exercise

Find different types of details in this paragraph and tell what effect each type has.

> For more than a decade, Congress has debated the issue of funding for the Corporation for Public Broadcasting (CPB). In 2006, a House budgetary subcommittee recommended 25-percent cuts to the 400-million-dollar budget of the CPB. Proponents of the cuts argue that the money would be better spent elsewhere, that the Public Broadcasting System has a liberal agenda, and that it is time for the stations to respond to market pressures. Opponents perceive a different agenda: Representative David Obey of Wisconsin said, "Americans overwhelmingly see public broadcasting as an unbiased information source. . . . [Conservatives] are trying to put their ideological stamp on public broadcasting." The next few years will determine whether viewer-supported television and radio are "voter supported" as well.

Check your details. Read your essay to review how you have used facts, statistics, examples, and quotations. Use each type of detail effectively.

Writing an Essay of Opposing Ideas **183**

3 I need to use a better variety of details and make sure they support my main points.

2 I need a variety of details and should remove many unneeded details.

1 I need help understanding how to effectively use details to support my main points.

Do my details support my main points?

Your details support your main points if you can answer "yes" to the following question about each one: *Does this detail pertain to the topic sentence?*

 Exercise

Read the following paragraph and check each detail by answering the question *Does this detail pertain to the topic sentence?* Indicate which details are not needed.

> The debate over federal funding of the CPB dates back more than 10 years. In 1994, Speaker of the House Newt Gingrich announced a plan to "zero out" funding for the CPB. Gingrich was born in 1943 in Harrisburg, Pennsylvania. Citing conservative grievances with the Corporation for Public Broadcasting and the National Endowment for the Arts and Humanities, Newt Gingrich said, "I personally would privatize them all." He felt conservatives should not have to pay tax money to support "liberal institutions" ("Gingrich"). Gingrich left office in 1998. His budget cuts were unsuccessful, but now, cuts are once again being considered.

Revise

Check your support. Be sure each detail pertains to the topic sentence of the paragraph in which it appears. If a detail does not, consider cutting it.

Ideas
Statistics make information more precise.

> In the presidential election of 2004, DRE machines in Ohio ~~gave George W. Bush nearly 4,000 extra votes.~~ made mistakes. In North Carolina, some machines failed
> ^ One county lost 4,500 votes ("Computer").
> totally. In addition, detractors point to another major
> factor in muddled elections—human error. Many of the
> same Floridians who found the paper "butterfly ballot" . . .

Expository

Revising for Organization

The Essay Structure Checklist can help writers perform self-evaluations of their essays or can help peers focus their responses on overall structure.

Peer Response

Ask students to evaluate each others' essays using the Essay Structure Checklist. A peer can provide the reader's perspective for questions 1 and 9 and can also help the writer think through the organizational pattern. The peer can also make suggestions to help the writer improve.

184

Revising for Organization

| **6** Each part of my essay does its job perfectly, providing engaging information. | **5** My essay has a solid structure, and I use signal words to make the structure clear. | **4** My essay has a solid structure, although I could use more signal words to make the structure clear. |

When you revise for *organization*, you check the overall structure of your essay to be sure that you have effectively arranged and connected your ideas. The rubric strip above can guide you.

How can I check the overall structure of my essay?

You can check the overall structure of your essay by using the essay structure checklist below.

Essay Structure Checklist

BEGINNING PARAGRAPH

_____ 1. Does my first sentence capture the reader's interest?

_____ 2. Do I provide background information that leads to my thesis statement?

MIDDLE PARAGRAPHS

_____ 3. Do my first middle paragraphs explain the "pro" position?

_____ 4. Do my next middle paragraphs explain the "con" position?

_____ 5. Does my last middle paragraph address the common ground?

_____ 6. Does each middle paragraph include a topic sentence?

_____ 7. Does each paragraph include details that support the topic sentence?

ENDING PARAGRAPH

_____ 8. Does my ending sum up my analysis?

_____ 9. Do I leave the reader with a final thought?

Revise

Check your overall structure. Write numbers 1 to 9 on a piece of paper. Then ask yourself the questions above. If you can answer "yes" to a question, check off the number. If not, revise until you can answer the question with a "yes."

Writing an Essay of Opposing Ideas **185**

3 My essay's structure is uncertain, and I should use signal words to connect the parts.

2 My essay has no clear structure and needs signal words.

1 I need to learn basic essay structure and how to use signal words.

How can signal words make my structure clear?

Signal words make your structure clear by reminding the reader where he or she is in your argument. Here are some sample signal words:

Proponents say . . .   Many people argue . . .   Those who favor . . .

Opponents contend . . .   Both sides agree . . .   Those who oppose . . .

Exercise

Read the following thesis statement and main points for an essay of opposing ideas. Add signal words to make the structure of the essay clear.

Thesis Statement: The proposal to drill for oil in the Arctic National Wildlife Refuge has inspired heated debate on Capitol Hill.

1. Drilling for oil would help alleviate U.S. dependence on foreign oil.
2. Drilling would create new jobs in Alaska and new revenue for the country.
3. The Arctic National Wildlife Refuge is meant for wildlife, not big oil companies.
4. The United States should search for alternative energies to decrease its oil dependence.
5. The question is "What is right for Alaska and for the nation?"

Revise

Check your topic sentences. Use signal words to help the reader know where she or he is in your argument.

Organization
Signal words help the reader keep track of the argument.

> Proponents of
> ⋀Electronic voting systems⋀allow people to vote quickly
>   say they
> and easily. Most DRE systems use touch-screen computer
> monitors, which are now common across the United States. . . .

Expository

Be sure that students understand the distinction between transitions and signal words. Point out to students that signal words remind readers what side of the argument they are reading about. Signal words are important not only to the structure of the essay but also to its sense.

Have students identify signal words in the sample expository paragraph on SE page 165 and the sample essays on SE pages 167–168 and 177–180.

Exercise
Answers

1. *Proponents say* drilling for oil would help alleviate U.S. dependence on foreign oil.
2. *Those who support* drilling argue that it would create new jobs in Alaska and new revenue for the country.
3. *Opponents contend* that the Arctic National Wildlife Refuge is meant for wildlife, not big oil companies.
4. *Those who oppose* drilling say that the United States should search for alternative energies to decrease its oil dependence.
5. *Both sides agree* that the question to be addressed is, "What is right for Alaska and for the nation?"

Revising for Voice

Explain to students that passive sentences tend to be longer and less direct than active sentences. Instead of performing the action, the subject is being acted upon. Often, the word *by* signals the noun that is doing the action.

No Child Left Behind was enacted *by Congress.*

To make the sentence active, make the noun after *by* into the subject.

Congress enacted No Child Left Behind.

Exercise
Answers

1. The No Child Left Behind law reformed the system for federal funding of schools.
2. The law requires schools to meet certain standards and show improvement.
3. Conservatives have praised the legislation.
4. Liberals have criticized the law.
5. The government has reformed public education almost continuously since its creation.
6. The government created the public school system to educate students and prepare them to be citizens.

186

Revising for Voice

6 My voice sounds professional and polished from start to finish.

5 I use active voice in most sentences and remain in third-person point of view.

4 I use active voice in most sentences but sometimes shift out of third-person point of view.

When you revise for *voice,* you make sure that most of your sentences are active and that you maintain the third-person point of view. The rubric strip will guide your revision.

How can I make a passive sentence active?

You can make a passive sentence active by rewriting it so that the subject of the sentence is doing the action of the verb. Active sentences are clearer, shorter, and more energetic than passive sentences. (See **722.2.**)

Passive Voice
All public schools have been affected by No Child Left Behind.
(The subject, *schools,* is not doing the action.)

Active Voice
No Child Left Behind has affected all public schools.
(The subject, *No Child Left Behind,* is doing the action.)

Exercise

Rewrite the passive sentences below to make them active.

1. The system for federal funding of schools was reformed by the No Child Left Behind law.
2. Schools are required by the law to meet certain standards and show improvement.
3. The legislation has been praised by conservatives.
4. The law has been criticized by liberals.
5. Since its creation, public education has been reformed almost continuously by the government.
6. The public school system was created by the government to educate students and prepare them to be citizens.

Revise

Check for active voice. Read your essay and watch for sentences in which the subject does not do the action of the verb. Rewrite these passive sentences to make them active.

Grammar Connection

Active and Passive Voice
- **Proofreader's Guide** pages 722–723
- *SkillsBook* page 91
- *GrammarSnap* Active and Passive Voice

Struggling Learners

Have students work in pairs or small groups to identify passive sentences in their essays. Then have them suggest ways to revise the sentences to see if the change will improve the writing.

Writing an Essay of Opposing Ideas **187**

3 Some of my sentences should be made active, and I need to be consistent in person.

2 Many passive sentences and shifts in person make my essay difficult to read.

1 I need help understanding active voice and third-person point of view.

How can I maintain the third-person point of view?

You can maintain the third-person point of view by using third-person pronouns and avoiding first- and second-person pronouns. (See **708.2**.)

Use: he, she, it, him, her, his, hers, its, they, them, their, theirs

Avoid: I, me, my, we, us, our, ours, you, your, yours

Exercise

Rewrite the following paragraph so that it maintains the third-person point of view.

> Students may feel that you take enough tests already, but the creators of No Child Left Behind legislation disagree. The law mandates tests that demonstrate basic proficiency and yearly advancement. These tests decide also whether our school gets the federal funding it needs to keep going. You need to do your best on these tests because they will determine the quality of your school in the future.

Revise

Check for third-person point of view. Read your essay and make sure you avoid using first- or second-person pronouns. If you find shifts in person, rewrite the material to remain consistently in third-person point of view.

Voice
Changes correct point of view to third person.

As a result, ~~you~~ ^voters^ went to bed one night and you thought that a specific candidate had won but ~~you woke up the~~ ^thinking^ next morning to discover something else — no one had won.

Electronic voting machines would eliminate these errors. . . .

Expository

Point out to students that using third-person pronouns in their essay will help them maintain objectivity throughout their essay. Using first-person pronouns, on the other hand, can lead them unwittingly to inject their own feelings and opinions into their writing. This is acceptable in a position essay in which students take a stand on a controversy; however, in an essay of opposing ideas, their goal is to remain objective.

✱ For more on personal pronouns, see SE pages 708–710.

Exercise Answers

Students may feel that they take enough tests already, but the creators of No Child Left Behind legislation disagree. The law mandates tests that demonstrate basic proficiency and yearly advancement. These tests decide whether schools get the federal funding they need to keep going. Students need to do their best on these tests because the results will determine the quality of their schools in the future.

Struggling Learners

Reread the beginning paragraphs of the essays in this unit. First, point out that their purpose is to engage and make readers want to continue reading. Second, point out that the writer chose the third-person point of view so that the essay does not take on a personal tone and maintains objectivity.

Revising for Word Choice

As students can see in the range of synonyms given for *passed*, synonyms with different connotations can often be arranged on a scale from friendly or neutral *(approved)* to negative or strong *(rubber-stamped, mandated)*. Deciding which word to use depends on what the writer wants the reader to feel about an idea. Remind students that in an essay of opposing ideas, they must maintain an objective tone.

Students may want to set aside a section of their writer's notebook for common synonyms with varying connotations. In addition to a dictionary, students should consider consulting a thesaurus for exploring the connotations of words as well as for completing the **Exercise.**

**Exercise
Answers**

Possible Answers

1. *swarmed*—unruly, disturbing
2. *watched over*—suspicious *throng*— disorganized
3. *seized*—forceful
4. *debated*—deliberate
5. *improvement*—positive
6. *rewards*—economic
7. *discriminatory*—loaded; inflammatory
8. *tentative*—hesitant; cautious

188

Revising for Word Choice

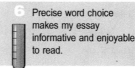

| 6 Precise word choice makes my essay informative and enjoyable to read. | 5 I use words with appropriate connotations and correct denotations throughout my essay. | 4 Most of my connotations are appropriate, but I should check the denotation of some words. |

When you revise for *word choice,* you check the connotation and denotation of your words. The rubric strip above can guide you.

How can I check the connotation of my words?

You can check the connotation of your words by making sure each word creates the feeling you intend. Not all synonyms are created equal. Note how the feeling of the following sentence changes as different synonyms are inserted:

Congress passed **the immigration reform bill.**

| approved | rubber-stamped | pushed through | mandated |
| *(friendly)* | *(jaded)* | *(aggressive)* | *(dictatorial)* |

Exercise

In the following sentences, choose a synonym for the italicized words, noting each synonym's connotation or feeling. Write down an adjective that describes the feeling of each word.

1. Protesters *gathered* outside the Capitol building.
2. Police *monitored* the *crowd*.
3. Security forces *detained* any unruly protestors.
4. Inside the Capitol, legislators *discussed* amendments to the bill.
5. The president welcomes the *reform*.
6. Some critics say the bill is costly without yielding many *results*.
7. Others feel that the bill is *unfair* to those who have already immigrated.
8. The new legislation faces an *uncertain* future.

Revise

Check your connotation. Read your essay and weigh the feeling created by each word. If you find a word that creates the wrong feeling, search for a synonym that has a more appropriate connotation.

Writing an Essay of Opposing Ideas 189

3 I use some words with the wrong connotation and others with the wrong denotation.

2 Many of my words have the wrong connotation and denotation.

1 I need help understanding how to use connotation and denotation effectively.

How can I check the denotation of my words?

You can check your denotation by making sure that you understand the precise dictionary definition for each technical term you use. Note the incorrect denotation of the words in blue:

National Guard troops enforce the new immigration bill.
(Troops enforce *laws*, not *bills*.)

They ticket **illegal immigrants crossing the border.**
(Troops *arrest* or *detain* illegal immigrants; they don't *ticket* them.)

Exercise

Replace each word in italics with a word that has the correct denotation. Use a dictionary if you need to.

1. Despite patrols, hundreds of immigrants cross the *state line* every day.
2. Many of them find work, though they don't have a *license*.
3. The new law allows some resident aliens to apply for *membership*.
4. Critics say the law lets illegal aliens remain, granting them *sanctuary*.

 Revise

Check your denotation. Read your essay and look up each technical term in a dictionary, making sure it has the right denotation. If you find words that have the wrong denotation, replace them with correct terms.

Word Choice
Changes improve connotation and correct denotation.

> Opponents of electronic voting also fear that computer
> hackers tamper with
> technicians could change election results. A skilled computer
> programmer code
> designer could rewrite the language that controls electronic
> voting machines to skew the results toward a particular . . .

Expository

Students should recognize from the examples given for the incorrect denotations that using words correctly is a combination of

- knowing the exact dictionary meaning of the word, and
- conveying ideas accurately.

For example, a bill establishes or is passed into law, and laws are enforced by the National Guard.

 Literature Connections

Word play: If some of your students are interested in wordplay, suggest the following titles:

Crazy English: The Ultimate Joy Ride Through Our Language by Richard Lederer

Forgotten English by Jeffrey Kacirk

 Exercise Answers

Possible Answers

1. border
2. work permit
3. citizenship
4. asylum or refuge

Struggling Learners

Have students get in the habit of checking both the denotations and connotations of words they choose from a thesaurus. Often students replace overused words with more specific or impressive words that do not have the proper denotation or connotation for the context. Point out that even though a thesaurus lists many synonyms for a particular word, not all the words will be suitable replacements.

Revising **for** Sentence Fluency

Point out to students that unclear comparisons often confuse readers.

- In the first example, readers could wonder if the writer meant that doctors care more about antibiotic overuse than they care about their patients.
- In the second example, readers could mentally complete the comparison in a variety of ways. (. . . than their predecessors did . . . than other drugs with fewer side effects.)

Exercise Answers

Possible Answers

1. It is more dangerous to overprescribe antibiotics than it is to overprescribe other, less powerful drugs.
2. "Superbugs"—or antibiotic-resistant bacteria created by overprescription—pose more threat to patients than viruses do.
3. More hospital patients than homebound patients get superbugs.
4. Doctors consider superbugs more dangerous than patients consider them.
5. Scientific studies show more concern about superbugs than opinion polls show.

190

Revising **for** Sentence Fluency

6 My sentences are skillfully written and easy to follow.

5 I use clear comparisons and parallel series.

4 My comparisons are clear, but I should make a few of my series more parallel.

When you revise for *sentence fluency,* you make sure your comparisons are clear and your series are parallel. The rubric strip above can guide you.

How can I fix unclear comparisons?

You can fix unclear comparisons by making sure you indicate what is being compared to what.

Unclear: Doctors care more about antibiotic overuse than patients.
Clear: Doctors care more about antibiotic overuse than patients do.
Clear: More doctors than patients care about antibiotic overuse.

Unclear: Doctors should prescribe antibiotics less.
Clear: Doctors should prescribe antibiotics less often than they currently do.

Exercise

Rewrite the unclear comparisons below to make them clear.

1. It is more dangerous to overprescribe antibiotics.
2. "Superbugs"—or antibiotic-resistant bacteria created by overprescription—pose more threat to patients than viruses.
3. More hospital patients get superbugs than homebound patients.
4. Doctors consider superbugs more dangerous than patients.
5. Scientific studies show more concern about superbugs than opinion polls.

Revise

Check for clear comparisons. Review your essay and make sure all of your comparisons are clear. Rewrite any that are not.

English Language Learners

Before students complete the **Exercise** activity, explain that the term *superbug* is relatively new and is used to describe an extremely harmful strain of bacteria that has become resistant to antibiotics. Explain that the antibiotics in use today kill most bacteria, but not all, and that the remaining bacteria can develop a super resistance to the drugs.

Writing an Essay of Opposing Ideas **191**

3 I need to make some comparisons clearer and some series parallel.

2 My comparisons are unclear, and my series aren't parallel.

1 I need help understanding how to create clear comparisons and parallel series.

How can I create parallel series?

You can create parallel series by making sure that each item in a group of three or more is the same kind of grammatical element: three present-tense verbs or three past-tense verbs or three participles, and so on.

Not Parallel: Superbugs are adapting, spreading, and kill thousands.

Parallel: Superbugs are adapting, spreading, and killing thousands.

Grammar Exercise

Rewrite each series below to make it parallel.

1. Researchers study superbugs, probe their weaknesses, and they hope to find new treatments.
2. The threat of superbugs is serious, a growing problem, and global.
3. Not prescribing antibiotics for viral infections, remaining watchful for hospital infections, and to wash hands are the best policies.

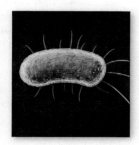

Revise

Check for parallel series. Make sure that each item in a series of three or more has the same grammatical structure.

Expository

Sentence Fluency
A comparison is made clear.

Many of the same Floridians who found the paper "butterfly ballot" confusing would be even less comfortable, *poking a screen to indicate their choice* Consequently, voters would make errors in their selections, though this time there would be no paper trail for a recount. . . .

English Language Learners

Some students may have difficulty creating a parallel series with past-tense verbs when one or more of the verbs are irregular. For example, *adapted, killed, fought,* and *spread* are parallel in tense, but do not all share the *-ed* ending. Help students study the list of irregular verbs on SE page 720, and have them use the list as a reference when they revise.

Grammar Connection

Parallelism
- *Write Source* page 601
- *SkillsBook* page 171
- *GrammarSnap* Creating a Parallel Series

Have students read the sample sentences. Point out that because two of the three words in the series were participles (verb forms that end in *-ing* or *-ed*), it makes sense to change *kill* to the participle *killing* to make a parallel series. Then ask students to suggest other ways to rewrite the sentence, using different verb forms and tenses. (Possible answers: Superbugs can adapt, spread, and kill thousands. Superbugs have adapted, spread, and killed thousands.)

✱ For more on participles, see SE page 726.

Grammar Exercise
Answers

1. Researchers study superbugs, probe their weaknesses, and hope to find new treatments.
2. The threat of superbugs is serious, growing, and global.
3. Not prescribing antibiotics for viral infections, remaining watchful for hospital infections, and washing hands are the best policies.

Have students discuss why they rewrote each sentence as they did. Point out to students that one way for them to check if a series is parallel is to read their writing aloud. Series that aren't parallel will usually stand out, be difficult to read, and make their writing sound uneven.

Revising Using a Checklist

Remind students that checklists like this one are only helpful if students take the time to think about each question and answer it honestly.

- Point out that students have already put a lot of effort into their work. They should not hurry through the checklist. By responding carefully to the checklist, they will produce a first-rate piece of writing.
- Encourage students to give more attention to questions that address an aspect of a trait with which they struggled as they drafted their essay. For example, if they had a difficult time structuring a balanced argument, then they should look over their draft one more time before they check off question 3.

192

Revising Using a Checklist

 Revise

Check your revising. On a piece of paper, write the numbers 1 to 12. If you answer "yes" to a question, put a check mark next to that number. If not, continue to work on that part of your essay.

Revising Checklist

Ideas

_____ **1.** Do I state my thesis clearly?

_____ **2.** Have I included a variety of details to support each topic sentence?

_____ **3.** Have I fairly represented each side of the argument?

Organization

_____ **4.** Does the overall structure of my essay work well?

_____ **5.** Have I used transitions to connect my ideas?

_____ **6.** Have I also used signal words to help my reader understand the argument?

Voice

_____ **7.** Have I used an active voice?

_____ **8.** Do I use third-person point of view consistently?

Word Choice

_____ **9.** Have I used words with the appropriate connotation?

_____ **10.** Have I used words with the correct denotation?

Sentence Fluency

_____ **11.** Have I fixed any unclear comparisons?

_____ **12.** Are all of my series parallel?

Revise

Make a clean copy. When you are finished with your revision, make a clean copy of your essay for editing.

Grammar Connection

Rambling Sentences
- **SkillsBook** page 164

Commas
- **Proofreader's Guide** pages 612–613
- **SkillsBook** pages 12–13
- **GrammarSnap** Common Uses of Commas

Compound and Complex Sentences
- **Proofreader's Guide** pages 748–749
- **SkillsBook** pages 128, 136
- **GrammarSnap** Sentence Types: Compound, Complex, and Compound-Complex Sentences

Writing an Essay of Opposing Ideas 193

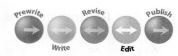

Prewrite Write Revise Edit Publish

Go Online!

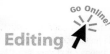

Editing

Now that you have finished revising your essay of opposing ideas, you are ready to edit for conventions: punctuation, capitalization, spelling, and grammar.

Keys to Effective Editing

1. Use a dictionary, a thesaurus, and the "Proofreader's Guide" in the back of this book as editing resources.
2. Check your writing for correctness of punctuation, capitalization, spelling, and grammar.
3. Edit on a clean revised copy of your essay. Then either enter the corrections on your computer file or write a new handwritten copy that includes the corrections.
4. Use the editing and proofreading marks on the inside back cover of this book.

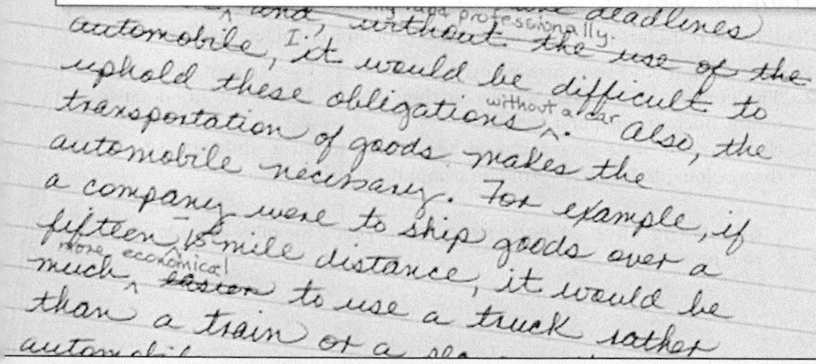

automobile, it would be difficult to
uphold these obligations without a car. Also, the
transportation of goods makes the
automobile necessary. For example, if
a company were to ship goods over a
fifteen-mile distance, it would be
much easier to use a truck rather
than a train or a

Expository

Go Online!

Editing

Keys to Effective Editing

Remind students that during the editing stage, they have a chance to find and correct errors in

- punctuation,
- capitalization,
- spelling, and
- grammar.

The Keys to Effective Editing list explains the process students will be guided through on SE pages 194–196.

To encourage students to edit on a new printed copy, have them submit their marked, revised, and edited copies with their final clean copy.

Technology Connections

Students can use the added features of the Net-text as they explore this stage of the writing process.

Write Source Online ***Net-text***

Struggling Learners

Remind students that the spell-check feature on a computer will not catch errors related to choosing the right word, such as *immigrant* or *emigrant,* or mistakes in spelling that result in another correctly spelled word, such as *stage* instead of *state.* Have students work with a peer editor to identify spelling errors.

Editing for Conventions

Students make mistakes with the case of pronouns (as well as with person and number) for several reasons: oversight, a lack of knowledge of the rules, or pronoun misuse in their speech. Share these tips:

- Consult the Proofreader's Guide (SE pages 604–763) when editing pronouns.
- Learn the rules governing pronouns in order to write and speak fluently.

✳ For more information about the case of pronouns, see 710.1 on SE page 710.

Grammar Exercise
Answers

1. Kim Jon-il said that <u>he</u> wanted Condoleezza Rice to pay <u>him</u> a visit.
2. The purpose of the visit was to let <u>them</u> discuss North Korea's defense and <u>its</u> nuclear weapons program.
3. Secretary of State Rice restated <u>her</u> desire to enter multilateral discussions, holding <u>them</u> in the company of other nations.

Grammar Connection

Pronouns (Case)

- **Proofreader's Guide** pages 710–711
- *SkillsBook* page 79
- *GrammarSnap* Nominative, Possessive, and Objective Cases of Pronouns

---

Editing for Conventions

6 My grammar and punctuation are correct, and the copy is free of spelling errors.

5 I have a few minor errors in grammar, spelling, or punctuation, but they won't distract the reader.

4 I must correct some errors in punctuation, spelling, or grammar that may distract the reader.

When you edit for *conventions,* you correct errors in punctuation, capitalization, spelling, and grammar. The rubric strip above will guide you.

How can I check the case of my pronouns?

You can check the case of your pronouns by paying attention to how each pronoun is used in the sentence. (See **710.1**.)

- Use **nominative case** for subjects and predicate nouns.

  he   she   it   they

  He told the secretary of state to refuse to negotiate with North Korea, but it was she who gave the reason for the denial.

- Use **possessive case** to show ownership.

  Before the noun: his   her   their   its
  After the noun: his   hers   theirs   its

  His policy prevented the meeting, but the language expressing that policy was hers.

- Use **objective case** for any objects (direct or indirect objects; objects of prepositions or infinitives).

  him   her   it   them

  The president told her that multilateral talks were acceptable to him.

Grammar Exercise

Replace each underlined pronoun with a pronoun of the correct case.

1. Kim Jong-il said that <u>him</u> wanted Condoleezza Rice to pay <u>his</u> a visit.
2. The purpose of the visit was to let <u>they</u> discuss North Korea's defense and <u>it</u> nuclear weapons program.
3. Secretary of State Rice restated <u>hers</u> desire to enter multilateral discussions, holding <u>they</u> in the company of other nations.

 Edit

Check the case of your pronouns. Follow the rules above to check your pronoun use.

Struggling Learners

Pronoun mistakes commonly occur when students use pronouns in a compound subject. Remind students to use the nominative case pronouns (I, you, he, she, it, we, they) for both pronouns in compound subjects.

Similarly, students should use the objective case pronouns (me, you, him, her, it, us, and them) when forming compound objects of prepositions, such as *between her and me.*

Writing an Essay of Opposing Ideas **195**

3 I need to correct a number of errors that will confuse my reader.

2 I need to fix many errors that make my writing hard to read and understand.

1 I need help finding errors and making corrections.

What adjectives should I capitalize?

Capitalize proper adjectives, which are created from proper nouns:

Britain ⟶ British   Arthur ⟶ Arthurian

Islam ⟶ Islamic   Newton ⟶ Newtonian

Capitalize geographic directions if they are part of a proper name, unit, or regional term.

South Carolina	South Pole	the East Coast (but the eastern U.S.)
North Dakota	Western Hemisphere	the Northwest Passage (but northwestern states)

Exercise

In the following paragraph, correct any errors in capitalizing adjectives.

> The people of north Korea live under totalitarian rule, while the people of south Korea live in a democracy. The korean War was fought because the Northern part of the country had fallen under a stalinist model of government, while the southern part aspired to a jeffersonian democracy.

Edit

Check your adjectives. Be sure your writing follows the capitalization rules above. Make any changes necessary to correct your work.

Expository *(side tab)*

Conventions
An error in pronoun case is corrected.

> While people disagree about the effectiveness of
>   *they*
> electrolic voting, ~~them~~ agree that the fiasco of 2000
> should not be repeated. For 36 days, the outcome of the . . .

Discuss problems students may have with rules of capitalization.

Emphasize that adjectives created from proper nouns are proper adjectives and should be capitalized.

■ Knowing when to capitalize geographic places and directions can be tricky, especially with words that have generic denotations such as *south* (direction) and *the South* (the region), *earth* (ground) and *Earth* (the planet).

Encourage students to use the Proofreader's Guide (SE pages 604–763) at the back of their book, or look in a dictionary whenever they are not sure whether or not to capitalize a word.

✳ For more on capitalization of adjectives and geographical names, see SE pages 648 and 728.

Exercise Answers

The people of North Korea live under totalitarian rule, while the people of South Korea live in a democracy. The Korean War was fought because the northern part of the country had fallen under a Stalinist model of government, while the southern part aspired to a Jeffersonian democracy.

English Language Learners

Students may not recognize proper adjectives because they are unfamiliar with the proper nouns. For example, students who do not know who Stalin was may not know to capitalize the adjective formed from his name. Before students attempt the **Exercise** activity, clarify any terms in the paragraph that are unfamiliar to them.

Grammar Connection

Adjectives
- ■ *Write Source* page 78
- ■ *Proofreader's Guide* pages 648–649, 728–729
- ■ *SkillsBook* page 97
- ■ *GrammarSnap* Adjectives, Comparative and Superlative

Editing Using a Checklist

Remind students to use the Proofreader's Guide (SE pages 604–763) whenever they edit. Throughout the year, they should refer to the instruction, rules, and examples to clarify any checklist items or to resolve questions about their own writing.

Remind students that they do not have to put quotation marks around ideas that they paraphrase from a reference source, but they do have to provide in-text citations. If necessary, review how to show source information using parentheses within the body of the text.

✳ For more on how to show in-text citations, see SE page 426–427.

Creating a Title

Besides trying the three strategies for creating a title shown here, suggest that students look for words and phrases in their essay that could be excerpted and used as a title.

196

Editing Using a Checklist

 Edit

Check your editing. On a piece of paper, write the numbers 1 to 11. If you can answer "yes," put a check mark after that number. If you can't, continue to edit for that convention.

Editing Checklist

Conventions

PUNCTUATION

_____ **1.** Do I use end punctuation after all my sentences?
_____ **2.** Do I use commas after long introductory phrases and clauses?
_____ **3.** Have I used quotation marks correctly for quotations?

CAPITALIZATION

_____ **4.** Do I start all of my sentences with capital letters?
_____ **5.** Do I capitalize all proper adjectives and nouns?

SPELLING

_____ **6.** Have I spelled all words correctly?
_____ **7.** Have I double-checked for errors my spell-checker may have missed?

GRAMMAR

_____ **8.** Have I checked the case of my pronouns?
_____ **9.** Do my pronouns agree with their antecedents?
_____ **10.** Do my subjects and verbs agree?
_____ **11.** Have I used the right words (*there, their, they're*)?

Creating a Title

After your editing is complete, add a title that engages your reader and sums up the content of your essay. Here are a few ways to create an effective title for your essay.

- Use a hook: **A Closer Look at Electronic Voting**
- Ask a question: **Does Electronic Voting Get the Job Done?**
- Identify the controversy: **The Battle over Electronic Voting**

Grammar Connection

Run-On Sentences and Commas Splices

- *Write Source* page 87
- *SkillsBook* pages 159, 160, 161

English Language Learners

Because the English language contains many irregular spellings, catching errors can be difficult. Assure students that all writers can easily miss their own spelling mistakes. Suggest that students read their essay backward from the last word to the first word. This strategy will allow them to concentrate on finding and correcting only spelling errors.

Writing an Essay of Opposing Ideas **197**

Publishing Sharing Your Essay

The purpose of your essay of opposing ideas is to present a clear, evenhanded examination of a political controversy. Now that you've completed your essay, share your ideas in a public forum. The following guidelines will help you publish your work.

Format your final copy. To format a handwritten essay, use the guidelines below or follow your teacher's instructions. (If you are using a computer, see pages 91–95.) Make a clean copy and carefully proofread it.

Focusing on Presentation

- Write neatly using blue or black ink.
- Place your name in the upper left corner of page 1.
- Skip a line and center your title; skip another line and start your essay.
- Indent every paragraph and leave a one-inch margin on all four sides.
- Write your last name and the page number in the upper right corner of every page after page 1.

Publish Your Essay
School and local newspapers often welcome writing that clearly examines political controversies. Send your article to a local or school-based newspaper using e-mail or postal mail. Before sending your article, make sure it conforms to the publication's submission guidelines and would interest the publication's audience.

Add It to a Blog
Many students have created Web logs, or blogs, to share their ideas in online forums. If you have a blog, consider publishing your article on it. You may also invite comments from your readers.

Post It in Public
If you are using a computer to format your essay, add photographs, charts, and other visual elements to support your ideas. Then post a printed copy of your essay on a school bulletin board or another prominent site. (Be sure to get permission first.)

Expository

Publishing
Sharing Your Essay

If your formatting requirements differ from those given here, make sure students are aware of them.

- Distribute a sheet with your manuscript preparation instructions for students to keep in their writer's notebook.
- Post your instructions in the classroom or on the school Web site, and encourage students to visit the site often for special instructions.
- Review the steps for electronic submissions of final drafts, if you accept them.

Technology Connections

Remind students that they can use the Writing Network features of the Portfolio to share their work with peers.

Write Source Online **Portfolio**

Write Source Online **Net-text**

Rubric for Expository Writing

Remind students that a rubric is a chart that helps them evaluate their writing.

- The rubrics in this book are based on a six-point scale, in which a score of 6 indicates an amazing piece of writing and a score of 1 means the writing is incomplete and not ready to be assessed.
- Explain to students that the purpose of the rubric is to help them break down the assessment process by evaluating each of the six traits individually—ideas, organization, voice, word choice, sentence fluency, and conventions.
- Point out that rubrics are also helpful during the writing process. Explain that a rubric can help guide them whenever they write because the rubric tells them which elements to include in their writing and how to present each element.
- Explain to students that they will most likely have different ratings for the traits. For example, they may give themselves a 5 for ideas but a 4 for organization.

✳ Reproducible six-, five-, and four-point rubrics for expository writing can be found on pages 768, 772, and 776.

Rubric for Expository Writing

The following rubric will help you assess your expository writing. Use it to improve your writing using the six traits.

6 Ideas	**5**	**4**
The ideas in the essay are compelling from start to finish.	The essay shows a clear relationship between thesis and supporting evidence.	The essay presents a clear topic and thesis. More support is needed.
Organization		
The essay shows thoughtful use of an organizational pattern. Transitions are strong.	The essay uses an effective organizational pattern. Transitions are appropriate.	The essay follows an organizational pattern. Transitions could be stronger.
Voice		
The writing voice is lively, engaging, and memorable.	Voice is appropriate for the topic, purpose, and audience and sounds knowledgeable.	Voice fits the audience and sounds knowledgeable in most places.
Word Choice		
Word choice is vivid and precise. Special terms are defined or explained.	Word choice is effective. Words are not repeated, and special terms are defined.	Word choice is adequate. Some overused words could be replaced.
Sentence Fluency		
Sentences are carefully crafted. Sentences flow naturally and vary in type and length.	Sentences flow well and are varied in type and length.	Sentences could use more variety in type and length.
Conventions		
Editing shows mastery of conventions. The essay is error free.	Editing is effective, but a few errors in grammar, spelling, or punctuation remain.	A few too many errors remain.

Writing an Essay of Opposing Ideas 199

3	2	1
The essay shows some understanding of the topic and thesis. More support is needed.	The topic and thesis should be more focused. The essay needs specific support that relates to the topic.	The topic should be reworked and a new thesis formed.
The essay does not follow an organizational pattern. Key points need separate paragraphs and transitions.	The beginning, middle, and ending parts need to be made clear.	The essay must be rewritten using an organizational plan.
Voice sounds uneven. It should match topic, purpose, and audience.	Voice sounds as if the writer does not have a good understanding of the subject.	Voice does not show confidence.
Word choice needs to be more precise, and overused words need to be replaced.	A thesaurus is needed to find more expressive words in many places.	The writer needs help choosing stronger words throughout.
Sentences are basic. More variety is needed in sentence type and length.	Too many sentences are simple and begin the same way.	Most sentences need to be rewritten.
Control of conventions is basic. Errors sometimes get in the way of understanding.	Many corrections are needed to make the essay less confusing.	The writer needs help to understand and edit conventions.

Expository

Evaluating an Essay of Opposing Ideas

Ask students if they agree with the sample self-assessment on SE page 201. If they agree with the overall comments, ask them to suggest improvements based on the comments in the self-assessment. If they disagree with any comment, ask them to explain why.

Ideas—The argument is fairly balanced, but the writer does not provide any point on which both sides agree.

Organization—The comment about most voters thinking they elect the president is intriguing, and will hook readers quickly. The writer could have tried harder to use a variety of signal words.

Voice—Third-person point of view is maintained throughout the essay, contributing to the objective, knowledgeable voice.

Word Choice—In the fifth paragraph, the phrase *tends to depress* may connote the wrong feeling to readers. Change to *tends to lower* or *to suppress* for a more accurate denotation.

Sentence Fluency—Sentences and paragraphs flow smoothly.

Conventions—Capitalize *Electoral College* throughout.

200

Evaluating an Essay of Opposing Ideas

Read the essay below and focus on its strengths and weaknesses. **(The essay contains some errors.)** Then read the student self-assessment on the next page.

The Best Route to the Presidency?

Every four years, a president is elected by U.S. voters—or at least most voters think this is the case. In fact, the President of the United States is chosen not by voters but by the roughly 530 members of the electoral college. In each state, members of the college agree to cast their ballots for the candidate who receives the most votes statewide ("Electoral"). While this system has been largely successful, it has created controversy. Some citizens support the Electoral College, but others feel that it should be replaced by a popular vote for the presidency.

Supporters of the electoral college point out that it was created to ensure the survival of U.S. democracy. As the founding fathers worked to create a plan for presidential elections, they worried that a charismatic and dishonest candidate might manipulate the public into voting against its best interests and then impose a dictatorship. So the framers of the Constitution created the electoral college to serve as a buffer against poor choices by the voters. Supporters of the college feel this is still necessary.

Supporters argue the electoral college provides stability by giving influence to sparsely populated states. In order to win the presidency, a candidate must show broad popularity, not just popularity in states with large populations. And for more than 200 years the electoral college has provided stability, resulting in elections decided within the rule of law—no small achievement for any government, democratic or otherwise.

Those who favor a direct election of the president insist that the electoral college system unfairly takes power from voters. They argue that citizens now directly elect every official in the nation except the president and vice president, and are capable of directly electing those officials as well. Supporters of direct election also cite numerous polls of voters, which universally favor election of the president by popular vote.

Another argument against the electoral college is the historical one. Under the electoral college system, three American presidents have won election despite losing the popular vote. This most recently happened in 2000, when George W. Bush was elected president despite losing the popular vote by a small margin ("Popular"). Third party candidates also tend to fare poorly in the electoral college. In the 1992 election, Ross Perot won 19 percent of the popular vote but did not get a single electoral vote ("1992"). Finally, say opponents, the electoral College tends to depress turnout in states in which one party enjoys clear dominance, because people who support the opposing party feel their votes don't count.

With voters largely split between the Democratic and Republican parties, it's likely that presidential elections in the near future will be decided by a relatively small margin. That means the debate over the Electoral College is likely to continue. No matter what turn the debate takes, the decision will just as likely be made using the democratic process—just as the founding fathers intended.

Student Self-Assessment

Expository Rubric Checklist

Title: _The Best Route to the Presidency?_

Writer: _Garret Honnecker_

 5 **Ideas**
- Does my essay include a clear thesis statement?
- Do I support my thesis with a variety of details?

 4 **Organization**
- Does my overall structure work well?
- Have I used signal words to make my structure clear?

4 **Voice**
- Are most of my sentences active?
- Do I use third-person point of view consistently?

 5 **Word Choice**
- Do I use words with the appropriate connotation?
- Do I use words with the correct denotation?

5 **Sentence Fluency**
- Are all my series parallel?
- Are my comparisons clear and complete?

4 **Conventions**
- Do I use correct punctuation, capitalization, spelling, and grammar?

OVERALL COMMENTS:

My essay does a good job addressing the controversy.

I forgot to write a paragraph about the common ground between the two positions.

I had a few problems with capitalization and should proofread more closely.

Expository

 Review your essay. Rate your essay and write comments that explain why you gave yourself the scores you did.

Advanced Learners

Have students read the overall comments about the essay. Discuss why including common ground, if it exists, is important. Challenge students to write a compelling common ground paragraph for the sample essay.

Benchmark Papers

The Almond Story (good)
- TE pp. 793–797

Why Rome Fell (fair)
- TE pp. 798–801

Student Self-Assessment

To give students additional practice with evaluating an expository essay, use a reproducible assessment sheet (TE page 766), the Expository Rubric Checklist (TE page 780), and one or both of the **benchmark papers** listed in the Benchmark Papers box below.

For your reference, a completed checklist and a comments sheet are provided for each benchmark paper.

Reflecting on Your Writing

Suggest that students review comments you and peers have provided during various stages of the writing process, including your comments on students' final essays, before they write their personal reflection. The added insights will make their reflection more valuable.

Encourage students to keep all their personal reflections in one place. For example, students might keep them in a section of their writer's notebook specifically for reflections, in a folder, or in a computer file. Tell them to be sure to date their reflections. Being able to flip through past and current reflections will make it easier for students to assess their writing progress with specific problems, as well as their overall progress.

Reflecting on Your Writing

Now that you have completed your essay of opposing ideas, take some time to reflect on the process of writing it. On a separate sheet of paper, complete each sentence below. This personal reflection will help reinforce what you've learned about writing an essay of opposing ideas.

My Essay of Opposing Ideas

1. The strongest part of my essay is . . .

2. The part that still needs work is . . .

3. The prewriting activity that worked best for me was . . .

4. The main thing I learned about writing an essay of opposing ideas is . . .

5. In my next essay of opposing ideas, I would like to . . .

6. One question I still have about writing an essay of opposing ideas is . . .

Struggling Learners

Some students may feel overwhelmed by the amount of work their paper may still need. Rephrase the second reflection to read: *The part that I improved the most is* . . . Tell them to identify one major improvement each time they write.

Expository Writing
Writing an Essay of Speculation

No one can be certain of what will happen in the future. The best anyone can do is to speculate on what the world might be like. By definition, *speculate* means "to engage in a course of reasoning based on inconclusive evidence." Effective speculation is far different from wild guessing. It involves careful research, logical thinking, common sense, and a touch of imagination.

In this chapter, you will read an essay of speculation about an invasive ground cover—crown vetch—that could cause serious problems in the future. Then you will be guided through the process of developing your own essay of speculation. *Remember:* For this type of essay, you must think carefully about something in the present and make an educated guess (speculate) about its future.

Writing Guidelines

Subject: A timely topic
Form: Essay of speculation
Purpose: To speculate on the future of the topic
Audience: Classmates

"Common sense in an uncommon degree is what the world calls wisdom."
—Samuel Taylor Coleridge

Writing an Essay of Speculation

Objectives
- understand the elements of an essay of speculation
- use what has been learned about the form and content of an expository essay to create an essay of speculation
- plan, draft, revise, edit, and share an essay of speculation

In an **essay of speculation,** a writer makes an informed prediction about what could take place in the future, based on research and careful analysis of the topic.

Explain to students that a speculation is, in effect, a guess. Although it cannot be proved true at the time it is made, an informed prediction, or speculation, about a current issue should be based on logic. It should rely on current facts and statistics, and not be merely a matter of opinion, an intuitive feeling, or a personal belief.

Essay of Speculation

As students read the model essay of speculation, have them note the elements that make this an effective expository essay. If students have recently completed an essay of opposing ideas (SE pages 166–202), have them point out similarities and differences between the two kinds of essays.

- Like the beginning of an essay of opposing ideas, the beginning paragraph of this essay identifies the topic (the invasive plant, crown vetch) and provides background information that leads up to the thesis, which is stated at the end of the first paragraph.
- Unlike the thesis statement in the essay of opposing ideas, which describes two sides of a controversy, this thesis statement makes a prediction about a current issue.
- Like the middle of other well-structured expository essays, the middle paragraphs of this essay of speculation explore the topic and support the thesis. The ending summarizes the main points of the essay and recalls the prediction made in the thesis statement.

204

Essay of Speculation

In the following essay, Carla predicts what might happen if an invasive plant called crown vetch is left unchecked.

Uncontrollable Invasion

Beginning
The writer introduces the topic and states her thesis (underlined).

Fifty years ago, road crews began planting crown vetch along newly constructed highways to prevent soil erosion. Crown vetch is an aggressive ground-cover plant with appealing foliage and flowers. Road improvement scars were quickly covered and erosion was no longer a concern. Then planners discovered an alarming problem. Crown vetch didn't like staying in one place. Instead, it started taking root in land adjacent to the roadsides. As a result, it became clear that crown vetch could not be planted carelessly or left unchecked. What would happen if this plant were left alone to grow and spread? If left unchecked, crown vetch could change the nation's landscape as we know it.

Middle
Each middle paragraph addresses a main point.

Most people pay little attention to this plant along the nation's highways and freeways. Motorists use these roadways to get to a destination quickly. However, crown vetch matures into an 18-inch-high creeping, competitive plant that grows in all climates—wet or dry, hot or cold. It can literally begin to take over a roadside and nearby land, overwhelming any vegetation in its path, including small trees (Fernald). If this would happen, even the most unobservant driver would begin to notice a sameness in the vegetation mile after mile after mile. Eventually, motorists would complain, demanding that the government do something about the problem.

An authority is cited.

If crown vetch really took hold in an area, local crops and gardens could be at risk. According to Art Gover of Pennsylvania State University, crown vetch sprouts from rhizomes (underground root runners) and seeds, which makes it fast growing and difficult to eradicate. The rhizomes can be up to 10 feet in length. As a result, crown vetch could easily overwhelm backyard gardens or croplands near roadsides. To eliminate the problem, strong chemicals may have to be applied to an infested area. Unfortunately, chemicals could kill any nearby desirable plants or contaminate the soil. Otherwise, fires would have to be set in these areas year after year.

English Language Learners

Before reading the model essay, explain unfamiliar terms:

- erosion (wearing away)
- road improvement scars (unsightly stretches of roadway caused by roadwork)
- adjacent (next to)
- root runners (long, extended roots that run underground)
- eradicate (wipe out)
- infested (diseased)
- contaminate (infect)

Writing an Essay of Speculation **205**

Each middle paragraph begins with a topic sentence, followed by supporting details.

The greatest danger posed by crown vetch is its potential to invade, and destroy, native prairie habitats. Native prairie land is unique to interior parts of the United States, primarily in the Plains states. Most of the original prairie is gone, and crown vetch could threaten what remains (Heim). A prairie needs to maintain a special balance of native plants and animals to thrive, and the introduction of crown vetch into the area would certainly destroy that balance. Fires, historically caused by lightning storms, help maintain the health and vitality of the prairies. However, if crown vetch were in the area, the plant burns too quickly and without the necessary heat to aid in prairie regeneration. It would be a tragedy to lose what remains of the nation's prairie lands because of an invasive plant such as crown vetch.

Crown vetch has helped control erosion along U.S. roadways, but if left unchecked, it has the potential to do as much harm as good. Croplands, gardens, and prairies are the areas where an infestation of crown vetch could be the most harmful. Most plants in their rightful place benefit the landscape or ecosystem; but in the wrong place, without the proper restraint, they may cause serious, long-term problems.

Ending
The ending summarizes the writer's thesis.

Expository

 Respond to the reading. Answer the following questions about the sample essay of speculation.

Ideas (1) What is the thesis or focus of this essay? (2) What main points does the writer include to support the thesis? Name at least two.

Organization (3) How does the writer organize the essay—spatially, chronologically, or by order of importance?

Voice & **Word Choice** (4) Does the writer sound interested in and knowledgeable about the topic? Explain.

 Literature Connections: For another example of speculative writing, read "The White Collar Blues" by Bob Hebert. This editorial, published in *The New York Times*, speculates on the negative effects of globalization.

English Language Learners

Students may benefit from further discussion of prairie regeneration to understand the final middle paragraph. Explain that controlled fires benefit prairies by helping to recycle certain valuable nutrients back into the soil. Point out that crown vetch, however, burns so quickly that this recycling of nutrients does not occur.

 Respond to the reading.

Answers

Ideas 1. If left unchecked, crown vetch could change the nation's landscape as we know it.

2. Possible answers:

- Crown vetch can begin to take over a roadside and nearby land, overwhelming any vegetation in its path, including small trees.
- If crown vetch really took hold in an area, local crops and gardens could be at risk because of how quickly it grows and spreads, and because it is difficult to eradicate.
- The greatest danger posed by crown vetch is its potential to invade, and destroy, native prairie habitats.

Organization 3. by order of importance, from least to most important

Voice & **Word Choice 4.** Yes. The writer uses language that conveys a sense of urgency about the problem, such as *alarming, overwhelming, risk, invade, destroy,* and *threaten.* She also uses facts and examples from a variety of sources, including information from an expert on the subject, Art Gover.

 Literature Connections

In the editorial "The White Collar Blues," Bob Herbert speculates on the negative effects of globalization. Herbert argues that government policies focus on what is best for corporations rather than what is best for American workers. Consequently, families and communities continue to face economic turmoil. Herbert believes that trade agreements and tax policies must be reconsidered in order to improve the quality of life in the United States.

Have students discuss Herbert's conclusion about globalization and what he suggests we do about it. Then encourage students to point out facts Herbert uses to support his opinions, and have students explain whether they agree with Herbert's stance. For additional models of expository writing, see the Reading-Writing Connections beginning on page TE-36.

Prewriting Considering Current Issues

Encourage students to think of current issues that affect their lives today and that will continue to affect them in the future. Choosing such a topic will engage their interest and provide greater motivation to make an informed prediction.

Prewriting Selecting a Specific Topic

If students have trouble generating a list of topics for their essay, have them try the following sources, which often deal with current issues and usually include predictions based on facts and expert opinions:

- environmental articles in news magazines
- in-depth coverage of consumer issues on nightly news programs
- documentaries on problems facing communities

 Technology Connections

Students can use the added features of the Net-text as they explore this stage of the writing process.

 Write Source Online **Net-text**

Focus on the Traits

Ideas

After students compile their topics list, suggest that they identify at least three topics that interest them, putting an asterisk next to their first choice. If they can't find enough information to write about their first choice, they can switch to one of the other topics.

Prewriting Considering Current Issues

The purpose of an essay of speculation is to make an informed prediction about a specific aspect of life. To get started, Carla made a list of current issues—national and global—that will affect life in the future.

Current-Issues List

technology in education	oil resources
urban sprawl	invasive plant species *
fresh water	global warming
voting apathy	the two-party system

 Prewrite

Think of current issues. Make a list of current issues that might affect life in the future. Then choose one to explore further for this assignment. Place an asterisk (*) next to the issue you choose.

Selecting a Specific Topic

Carla had discussed issues about invasive plant species in her botany class. She decided it would be interesting to investigate one of these species and speculate what effect it might have on future life. After reviewing her class notes and checking on the Internet, she came up with this list. Then she put an asterisk next to the species of plant she wanted to write about.

Topics List

Invasive Plants

pepper trees	hydrilla	kudzu
crown vetch *	leafy spurge	garlic mustard

Prewrite

Choose a topic. List specific topics related to the current issue that you chose above. Then put an asterisk (*) next to the topic that you would like to write about.

Ideas The goal of an essay of speculation is to make an informed prediction. In order to do that, you will need to research your topic so that you can base your speculations on solid information. If you can't find enough information about your topic, switch to another one.

Advanced Learners

As they generate their list of current issues, challenge students to think of not only national or global issues but also local and even school-related issues. Point out that issues closer to home can be just as important as national and global issues and also affect their lives in significant ways. Have them present their list to the class for all students to consider.

Writing a Thesis Statement

Once you have gained a thorough understanding of your topic, write a thesis statement expressing your topic's potential effect in the future. Here is Carla's thesis statement.

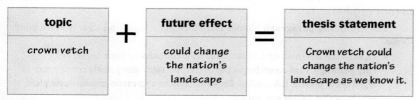

topic		future effect		thesis statement
crown vetch	**+**	could change the nation's landscape	**=**	Crown vetch could change the nation's landscape as we know it.

Learn about your topic. Research your topic to learn as much as you can about it. Then write a thesis statement that expresses its potential effect in the future. (Use the example above as a guide.)

Organizing Your Information

Organizing the facts and details that support your thesis statement is the next important step in the essay-writing process. Carla used a two-column chart to organize her main points and related details.

Two-Column Chart

Main Points	Related Details
dominates roadsides	• grows into dense cover • creates a disturbing sameness • overwhelms other vegetation
could put local crops and gardens at risk	• grows fast • needs strong chemicals or annual fires to eradicate
could destroy native prairie habitats	• destroys prairie unique to U.S. • upsets balance of native plants and animals • hinders prairie regeneration

Organize your support. Complete a two-column chart like the one above in which you list the main points and related details that support your thesis. List main points in the order that you will write about them.

Expository

Depending on the **prediction** *(see below)* they decide to make, students may not use all the facts and details they gather. Explain to them that, even if they find that they want to go in a new direction as they write, they will have all the information they need on hand.

✳ For more about constructing effective thesis statements, see SE page 592.

 Writer's Craft

Speculation: Science fiction writers speculate about the future by focusing on current "stress points." A stress point is a current crisis— whether political, economical, social, religious, environmental, artistic—that could be resolved in two or more ways. Then the writer predicts the most likely (or most interesting) resolution to write about.

Your students can do the same. After selecting a topic, the writer can list possible outcomes and select the most likely one.

Distribute photocopies of the reproducible T-chart (TE page 823) for students to use to organize facts and details for their essay.

Teaching Tip: Predictions

As students research their topic, tell them to weigh expert predictions against their own understanding. If, after careful consideration, they come to similar conclusions about what could occur in the future, they can choose one of these expert predictions for their thesis statement, using their own words and crediting the source within their statement.

Writing Creating Your First Draft

Have students use their thesis statements and T-charts, as well as the tips and examples on this page, to guide their writing.

✱ For more on basic essay skills, see SE pages 589–603.

Technology Connections

Students can use the added features of the Net-text as they explore this stage of the writing process.

Write Source Online **Net-text**

Writing Creating Your First Draft

The following tips will help you develop your first draft. Be sure to use your prewriting to guide your drafting.

Beginning Paragraph

The beginning paragraph should introduce your topic and clearly state your thesis.

- Open with interesting information that introduces your topic.
  Fifty years ago, road crews began planting crown vetch along newly constructed highways to prevent soil erosion. Crown vetch is an aggressive ground-cover plant with appealing foliage and flowers.

  Then planners discovered an alarming problem. Crown vetch didn't like staying in one place. Instead, it started taking root in land adjacent to the roadsides.

- End with your thesis statement.
  If left unchecked, crown vetch could change the nation's landscape as we know it.

Middle Paragraphs

The middle paragraphs explain the main points that support the thesis.

- Use an effective topic sentence at the start of each paragraph to state the paragraph's main idea.

  Most people pay little attention to this plant along the nation's highways and freeways.

- Include details to support each topic sentence.
  Motorists use these roadways to get to a destination quickly. However, crown vetch matures into an 18-inch-high creeping, competitive plant that grows in all climates— wet or dry, hot or cold. It can literally begin to take over a roadside and nearby land, overwhelming any vegetation in its path, including . . .

Ending Paragraph

The ending paragraph should restate the thesis and summarize the main supporting points.

- Restate your thesis.
  Crown vetch has helped control erosion along the U.S. roadways, but if left unchecked, it has the potential to do as much harm as good.

Write

Write your first draft. Write an initial draft of your essay, using the sample essay, your prewriting work, and the information above as a guide.

Struggling Learners

Have students who need extra support create an outline (see SE page 174) before they write their drafts. The outline can help them
- begin with a paragraph that includes the thesis statement,
- create topic sentences and supporting details for each middle paragraph, and
- end by restating the thesis.

Advanced Learners

Challenge students to rewrite the beginning paragraph about crown vetch on SE page 204 so that it immediately hooks the reader. Point out that the purpose of a strong opening is to capture the attention of a reader.

Revising Improving Your First Draft

As you revise, use the checklist below as a guide.

Revising Checklist

Ideas

_____ **1.** Do I clearly introduce my issue?
_____ **2.** Do I make an informed prediction about its future?
_____ **3.** Do I support my thesis with compelling main points?
_____ **4.** Do I effectively develop each middle paragraph?

Organization

_____ **5.** Does my essay have a strong beginning, middle, and ending?
_____ **6.** Have I presented my points in a logical order?

Voice

_____ **7.** Does my voice sound confident and knowledgeable?
_____ **8.** Does my voice show interest in the topic?

Word Choice

_____ **9.** Have I chosen words that clearly explain my ideas?

Sentence Fluency

_____ **10.** Are my sentences varied in type and length?

Revise

Revise your first draft. Read your essay carefully. Then use the checklist above to improve your first draft.

Creating a Title

- Draw on your thesis: **Uncontrollable Invasion**
- Ask a question: **Can Crown Vetch Be Contained?**
- Use your imagination: **A "Vetching" Problem**

Expository

Revising Improving Your First Draft

Explain to students that an effective way to create a lively flow in their writing is to use a variety of sentence types and to vary the lengths of their sentences. As students review for sentence fluency, have them jot down

- how many different types of sentences they use, including simple, compound, complex, and compound-complex; and
- how many sentences they have that are approximately the same length.

Students should be able to tell from these notes if their sentences are varied in type and length.

✱ For more information about sentence types, see SE page 748.

Creating a Title

Tell students that their first paragraph is a good place to look for ideas for a title. They may have already asked a question in the first paragraph that they could adapt for a title. They may also have already stated the problem in an imaginative way that they can use as a title.

 Technology Connections

Have students use the Writing Network features of the Net-text to comment on each other's drafts.

⚡ *Write Source Online* ***Net-text***

English Language Learners

The title "A 'Vetching' Problem" may be difficult for students to understand. Explain that *vetching* is a play on the word *vexing*, which means "troublesome" or "irritating." The writer changed the spelling slightly to form the memorable phrase from the plant's name.

Grammar Connection

Specific Nouns
- *Write Source* page 74
- **Proofreader's Guide** pages 701–703
- *SkillsBook* pages 70, 71, 72, 73, 74, 75
- *GrammarSnap* Nouns

Verbals
- **Proofreader's Guide** page 726 (+)
- *SkillsBook* page 122, 126

Editing **Checking for Conventions**

Focus attention on items 9 and 10 in the Editing Checklist, which address subject-verb agreement and pronoun agreement, respectively.

- Point out to students that subject-verb agreement errors are often made when phrases and clauses come between the subject and the verb. To check for subject-verb agreement, students should read the sentence aloud, omitting the words between the subject and the verb.
- Problems with pronouns and their antecedents often occur because pronouns may appear several words apart from the nouns they refer to. Students should check that each pronoun has an antecedent, and that the antecedent agrees in number and gender with the pronoun.

✳ For more on checking for subject-verb agreement, see SE page 250. For more on checking for pronoun–antecedent agreement, see SE page 251.

Publishing **Sharing Your Work**

If any students have chosen the same topic to write about, they may enjoy working together to conduct a debate or an open forum on the topic. To lead off the discussion, they can read their essays of speculation.

Technology Connections

Remind students that they can use the Writing Network features of the Portfolio to share their work with peers.

 Write Source Online **Portfolio**

Write Source Online **Net-Text**

210

Editing **Checking for Conventions**

After revising your essay, use the following checklist to edit your writing for punctuation, capitalization, spelling, and grammar errors.

Editing Checklist

Conventions

PUNCTUATION

_____ **1.** Have I ended my sentences with the correct punctuation?

_____ **2.** Have I used commas, semicolons, and colons correctly?

_____ **3.** Have I punctuated quotations correctly?

CAPITALIZATION

_____ **4.** Do I capitalize the first word in every sentence?

_____ **5.** Do I capitalize all proper nouns and adjectives?

SPELLING

_____ **6.** Have I spelled all my words correctly?

_____ **7.** Have I double-checked for easily confused words that my spell-checker would miss?

GRAMMAR

_____ **8.** Have I used the correct forms of verbs?

_____ **9.** Do my subjects and verbs agree in number?

_____ **10.** Do my pronouns agree with their antecedents?

 Edit

Edit your essay. Use the checklist above to edit for conventions. Also ask a partner to check your work for errors. Then prepare a final copy and proofread it.

Publishing **Sharing Your Work**

This final step accomplishes the purpose of sharing information with your audience.

 Publish

Publish your essay. Share your writing by reading it aloud in the classroom, followed by a question-and-answer session, or by posting it on a bulletin board. Also consider presenting it as a speech or uploading it to a Web site.

Grammar Connection

Verb Forms
- **Proofreader's Guide** pages 718–719, 720 (+), 722 (+)
- *SkillsBook* pages 93, 177
- *GrammarSnap* Verb Tense Overview

Capitalization
- **Proofreader's Guide** page 648 (+), 650–651, 652–653
- *SkillsBook* pages 41, 42

- *GrammarSnap* Capitalization of Proper Nouns and Adjectives

Semicolons, Colons
- **Proofreader's Guide** pages 618–619, 620–621
- *SkillsBook* pages 17–18, 19, 20, 21
- *GrammarSnap* Semicolons

Writing for Assessment
Responding to Expository Prompts

Expository writing is basically informational writing. Depending on the topic, you might summarize, illustrate, analyze, explain, classify, or compare. For most expository assignments, you will be given plenty of time to complete your work. However, when you are asked to respond to an expository prompt on an assessment test, you will have to complete your work within a set period of time.

When responding to an expository prompt, you will need to plan, write, and revise your writing quickly. In this chapter, you will learn how to analyze an expository prompt and create an effective, well-organized response—all within specific time constraints. Having the ability to write on demand is a valuable skill that you will use now and later—when you go on to college or enter the workplace.

Writing Guidelines

Subject: An expository prompt
Form: Response essay
Purpose: To demonstrate competence
Audience: Instructor

"I see only one rule: to be clear. If I am not clear, then my entire world crumbles into nothing."

—Stendhal

Copy Masters

Quick list, Time Line, T-chart, Venn Diagram (TE p. 213)

Responding to Expository Prompts

Objectives
- demonstrate an understanding of the elements of an expository prompt
- practice writing for assessment

If your students must take school, district, or state assessments this year, focus on the writing form on which they will be tested.

Discover students' general attitude toward responding to prompts in a timed setting. Use these questions to stimulate the discussion.
- What do you like or dislike about this kind of writing?
- What are some ways that you prepare yourselves mentally to complete a timed response?
- Do you think that being able to respond to a prompt within a specific time frame is a valuable skill? Why or why not?
- What do you think is the most important thing to do when responding to a prompt in a timed setting?

Prewriting Analyzing an Expository Prompt

If students are not familiar with the STRAP questions or with using the STRAP strategy for analyzing a prompt, provide them with several samples of expository prompts. Then work together to use the STRAP questions to analyze the prompts.

Try It!
Answers

Subject: personal definition of a hero
Type: letter (to Mark Twain)
Role: student responding to Mark Twain's writings
Audience: Mark Twain (or teacher, classmates)
Purpose: explain and inform

212

Prewriting Analyzing an Expository Prompt

To respond effectively to an expository prompt, you will first need to analyze it. If you do a thorough job of analyzing the prompt, you'll have a much better chance of producing a successful essay. To analyze a prompt, use the STRAP questions:

> **Subject:** What topic should I write about?
>
> **Type:** What form of writing should I create (essay, letter, editorial, article, report)?
>
> **Role:** What role should I assume as the writer (student, son or daughter, friend, employee, citizen)?
>
> **Audience:** Who (teacher, parents, classmates, employer, official) is the intended audience?
>
> **Purpose:** What is the goal of my writing (inform, summarize, illustrate, analyze, classify, compare)?

| Subject |
| Type |
| **Role** |
| Audience |
| Purpose |

Some people always stand out as individuals. These people don't follow trends; they set them. ***Assuming the role of a historian,*** write a brief __essay__ for your classmates about someone you admire for individuality. Explain what makes the person stand out in the crowd and how the person's unique traits make you admire him or her.

Note: One of the following key words or phrases is often found in an expository prompt: *outline, analyze, inform, compare and contrast, explain,* or *define.*

Try It!

Analyze this prompt by answering the STRAP questions. (Some answers may be implied or left open. Use your best judgment.)

> According to Mark Twain, "We find not much in ourselves to admire; we are always privately wanting to be like somebody else. If everybody was satisfied with himself there would be no heroes." Write a letter to Twain explaining your own definition of a hero, including examples of people you consider heroic.

English Language Learners

Have students work in small groups to complete a five-column STRAP chart for the **Try It!** activity. Have them take turns filling in the columns based on their discussions. Point out that this will make it easier for them to write the letter, which they will do on SE page 215.

Planning Your Response

After you have analyzed the prompt using the STRAP questions, it's time to start planning and organizing your response. One good way to do this is to use a graphic organizer. The organizers below all provide ways to organize an effective response to an expository prompt.

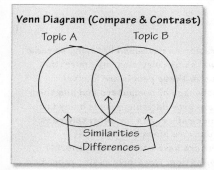

Quick List (Any Essay)

1. First Point
   —Detail 1
   —Detail 2
2. Second Point
   —Detail 1
   —Detail 2
3. Third Point
   —Detail 1
   —Detail 2

Time Line
(How-To/Process)

First
Next
Then
After
Last

T-Chart (Two-Part Essay)

Topic:

Part A	Part B
*	*
*	*
*	*
*	*

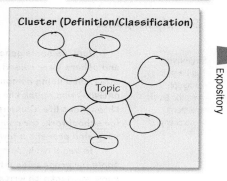

Venn Diagram (Compare & Contrast)

Topic A   Topic B

Similarities
Differences

Cluster (Definition/Classification)

Topic

Expository

Prewrite

Use a graphic organizer. Reread the expository prompts on page 212. Choose one and use a graphic organizer to plan and organize your response to the prompt. Keep the STRAP questions in mind as you work.

Tip

When it comes to responding to a prompt, good time management is critical. If you have 45 minutes to respond to a prompt, use the first 5 to 10 minutes to analyze the prompt and plan your response, the last 5 to 10 minutes to revise and edit your response, and the time in between for the actual writing.

Prewriting **Planning Your Response**

Students should be familiar with all of the graphic organizers shown and understand how and when to use each organizer. To check that they are familiar with the organizers, ask students which organizer they would use to prepare a response for the two prompts on SE page 212 and to explain why they think it would help them organize an effective response. Students will probably say that the quick list and the cluster would be the most appropriate organizers for these prompts.

To simulate a real test situation, set a timer for 5 to 10 minutes, and have students try to organize their response to the **Try It!** prompt on SE page 212, using one of these graphic organizers, before the timer goes off.

English Language Learners

Modify the planning activity by having pairs fill in one of the five graphic organizers on the page. Then have pairs take turns presenting their graphic organizer so that students have a clearer idea of how each one can help organize information.

Struggling Learners

Students may prefer using certain graphic organizers to others, but they may not understand that the same organizer will not work well with every prompt. Point out that answering the T question in STRAP (Type) will provide them with a good clue as to which graphic organizer may be most useful.

Writing Responding to a Prompt

Being able to recognize key words in a prompt is essential to answering the STRAP questions and to planning and writing a response. Before asking students to complete the **Try It!** activity, have them point out key words in the sample expository prompt that they could use to answer the STRAP questions and write a response. (Possible choices: "digital natives," essay, explains, to the older generation, role of computers in lives of today's teens, consider positive and negative effects of computer use)

Try It!
Answers

Subject: role of computers in the lives of today's teens
Type: expository essay
Role: teen (computer user, student)
Audience: older generation
Purpose: explain and inform

Writing Responding to a Prompt

Once you have answered the STRAP questions and planned your response using a graphic organizer, you can begin writing.

Sample Expository Prompt

> *People under the age of 20 have grown up with computers and are sometimes called "digital natives." Computer technology is their native language. Write an essay that explains to the older generation the role of computers in the lives of today's teens. Be sure to consider the positive and negative effects of computer use.*

Try It!

Answer the STRAP questions for the sample expository prompt above. Refer to page 212 for a sample prompt analysis.

Sample Response

Beginning
The beginning paragraph gives the thesis statement (underlined).

Just as some generations were raised listening to radio and others were raised watching television, my generation was raised using computers. These people are "digital natives" who speak the language of computers and use them throughout life. <u>Computers provide young people many tools for schoolwork, for communication, and for entertainment; they also present a few dangers along the way.</u>

Middle
Each middle paragraph explains part of the thesis.

To begin with, computers have become indispensable tools for processing information. Word-processing programs allow students to write more quickly, revise more thoroughly, and edit more accurately than ever before. With the use of Internet search engines, students can find exactly the information they need with only a few mouse clicks. However, not every piece of information from the Internet is reliable, and an unwary researcher can end up with material that is biased or downright wrong. Also, computers make it more tempting to plagiarize. Teens have to be conscientious to avoid bad information and plagiarism, recognizing the responsibility that comes with the computer's power.

Transitions connect the middle paragraphs.

Modern teens also use computers for communication. Through instant messaging, online games, chat rooms, and group sites like MySpace, teens connect with old friends and meet new ones. Many young people also write their own blogs or create their own Web casts, sharing their ideas with the world. But while communicating online, teens must beware of "stranger danger." Spammers clog up e-mail boxes, hackers develop viruses, and predators lurk on group sites. Even if a computer user can avoid these dangers, having a friend online is no substitute for having one in person. Teens must learn to use computers to enhance friendships, not replace them.

Today's teens also use computers as a source of music and movies. Instead of going to a store, most teens buy music and movies online, either to be delivered or downloaded. They also prefer to buy one or two songs at a time rather than a whole album. Some sites even allow teens to share their files. This can cause problems. Illegal file sharing and downloads might seem a cheap way to get entertainment—until the person is caught and fined, or even sent to prison. An illegal download also cheats the person's favorite artist out of the chance to make a living. If teens can steer clear of illegal music and movies, though, there is still plenty of listening and watching to do.

Ending
The ending sums up the essay and provides a final thought.

For teens today, computers shape everyday life. The question is whether teens can manage the power of these great tools. When handled well, a computer provides homework help, connects people to friends, and even sets the world to music. On the other hand, unwise computer use can result in plagiarized documents, dangerous predators, and even fines and jail time. Most teens avoid these pitfalls almost instinctively. After all, these "digital natives" grew up understanding computers and speaking their language.

Expository

Write

Respond to an expository prompt. Use the prompt you chose on page 212, your answers to the STRAP questions, and your graphic organizer to write a response within the time limit set by your teacher.

After students read the sample response, have them point out the elements of the response that make it similar to other expository essays they have read and written. Doing so can help reassure students that they are well prepared to write a response to an expository prompt.

- The writer engages the reader in the beginning paragraph, making a comparison that helps the audience (the older generation) connect with the writer (a teen and computer user).
- The beginning paragraph ends with an effective thesis statement that states the main points used in the rest of the response.
- The middle paragraphs contain details that support the topic sentence of each paragraph and help explain the topic.
- The writer uses specific computer terms throughout the response, which helps create a knowledgeable voice.
- A strong ending summarizes the main points made in the middle paragraphs of the essay.

Test Prep!
Have students respond to the prompt from page 212 within a specific time frame (perhaps 45 minutes). This gives them a chance to practice writing a response while the clock ticks.

Revising **Improving Your Response**

By using the STRAP questions both to analyze a prompt and to review the written essay, students insure that their work is on target. A well-written essay that is off topic or that does not accomplish the purpose will not score highly.

If students discover a deficiency, they should devise a quick solution. For example, the prompt on page 214 says, "Be sure to consider the positive and negative effects of computer use." If the student had not addressed negative effects, he or she could add a paragraph focusing on the problems of computer use—and score higher on the assessment.

Editing **Checking Your Response**

Tell students to check first for the errors in conventions they commonly make. This will eliminate most errors. If they have time remaining, they should also check the spelling and punctuation of words used from the prompt.

216

Revising **Improving Your Response**

Most writing tests allow you to make corrections to improve your work, though you should find out ahead of time how many changes are allowed. If changes are allowed, make them as neatly as possible. Use the STRAP questions to guide you.

Subject: Does my response focus on the prompt topic?
Do my main points support my thesis statement?

Type: Have I followed the correct form (essay, letter, article)?

Role: Have I assumed the role called for in the prompt?

Audience: Have I effectively addressed my audience?

Purpose: Does my response accomplish the goal of the prompt?

Revise

Improve your work. Using the STRAP questions above as your guide, revise your response within the allowed time period.

Editing **Checking Your Response**

Check your expository response for punctuation, capitalization, spelling, and grammar. You don't want any careless errors that confuse the reader.

Editing Checklist

Conventions

_____ **1.** Have I used end punctuation for every sentence?
_____ **2.** Have I capitalized all proper nouns and first words of sentences?
_____ **3.** Have I checked my spelling?
_____ **4.** Have I made sure my subjects and verbs agree?
_____ **5.** Have I used the right words (*their, they're, there*)?

Edit

Check for conventions. Review your response for any errors in punctuation, capitalization, spelling, and grammar. Make neat corrections.

Struggling Learners

If students have difficulty reading for spelling errors, have them circle words in their essay that look incorrect to them as they write. Then during the editing time, they can quickly find the circled words and decide on their final spelling.

Expository Writing on Tests

Before you write . . .

- **Study the prompt.**
  Use the STRAP questions listed on page 212. Remember that an expository prompt asks you to explain or inform.
- **Budget your time carefully.**
  Spend several minutes planning and organizing your response. Use the last few minutes to read over what you have written.

As you write . . .

- **Choose a clear focus or thesis for your response.**
  Keep your main idea or purpose in mind as you write.
- **Be selective.**
  Use examples that support your focus.
- **End in a meaningful way.**
  Remind the reader about the importance of the topic.

After you've written a first draft . . .

- **Check for completeness.**
  Use the STRAP questions on page 216 to revise your work.
- **Check for correctness.**
  Check your punctuation, capitalization, spelling, and grammar.

Try It!

Analyze one of the prompts below using the STRAP questions. Then plan and write a response. Complete your work within the time your teacher gives you.

- In recent years, political debate has often taken a negative, even angry tone. As someone concerned with the tone of political debate, write a set of guidelines to keep debates civil and focused on solving problems at hand.

- People spend their leisure time in a variety of ways. Some play team sports while others pursue pastimes such as cooking and playing music. Write a brief essay explaining one leisure-time activity that you find rewarding. Include details that provide a clear explanation for your classmates.

Expository

Expository Writing on Tests

Point out that students must approach writing-on-demand assignments differently from open-ended writing assignments and that timed writing creates pressures for everyone.

Test Prep!

To teach students who must take timed assessments how to approach their writing, allow them the same amount of time to write their response essay as they will be allotted on school, district, or state assessments. Break down each part of the process into clear chunks of time. For example, you might give students

- 10 minutes for note taking and planning,
- 25 minutes for writing, and
- 10 minutes for editing and proofreading.

Tell students when time is up for each section. Start the assignment at the top of the hour or at the half-hour to make it easier for students to keep track of the time.

If your state, district, or school requires students to create and submit graphic organizers along with their writing, instruct your students to do so as they practice.

English Language Learners

Some students may find it challenging to identify an expository prompt if it does not contain the word *explain*. Point out key words and phrases in the first prompt that identify it as expository, such as "a set of guidelines." Point out that guidelines are rules that explain how to perform a task.

Persuasive Writing Overview

Common Core Standards Focus

Writing 1: Write arguments to support claims in an analysis of substantive topics or texts, using valid reasoning and relevant and sufficient evidence.

Language 3a: Vary syntax for effect, consulting references (e.g., *Tufte's Artful Sentences*) for guidance as needed; apply an understanding of syntax to the study of complex texts when reading.

Writing Forms

- persuasive paragraph
- essay of argumentation
- essay of evaluation
- writing for assessment

Focus on the Traits

- **Ideas** Writing a clear position statement and including reasons that support the position
- **Organization** Creating a beginning that states the position, a middle that provides support and answers an objection, and an ending that restates the position
- **Voice** Using a voice that shows understanding of the controversy and commitment to the position
- **Word Choice** Choosing fair and precise words to state and defend the position
- **Sentence Fluency** Writing clear, complete sentences with varied beginnings and lengths
- **Conventions** Checking for errors in punctuation, capitalization, spelling, and grammar

 Literature Connections

- *A Vindication of the Rights of Women* by Mary Wollstonecraft
- "Another Renaissance" by Gary Fisher

 **Technology Connections**

 **Write Source Online**
www.hmheducation.com/writesource

- *Net-text*
- *Bookshelf*
- *GrammarSnap*
- *Portfolio*
- *Essay Scoring*
- *Writing Network features*
- *File Cabinet*

 Interactive Whiteboard Lessons

Suggested Persuasive Writing Unit (Four Weeks)

Day	Writing and Skills Instruction	Student Edition		SkillsBook	Daily Language Workouts	Write Source Online
		Main Pages	Resource Units*			
1–2	**Persuasive Paragraph**	219–221	583		46–49	*Interactive Whiteboard Lessons*
	Skills Activities:					
	• Punctuation		616 (+), 632 (+)	31		
	• Tense Shifts		718 (+), 722 (+)	176		*GrammarSnap*
3–5	**Writing an Essay of Argumentation** (Model, Prewriting) Organization (Deductive, Inductive), Supporting Details, Audience, Diction ⊙ Literature Connections *A Vindication of the Rights of Women*	222–230, 62–63, 56–57, 108–109, 110, 69, 71				*Net-text*

(WEEK 1)

* These units are also located in the back of the *Teacher's Edition*. Resource Units include "Basic Elements of Writing" and "Proofreader's Guide."
(+) This activity is located in a different section of the *Write Source Student Edition*. If students have already completed this activity, you may wish to review it at this time.

Day	Writing and Skills Instruction	Student Edition		SkillsBook	Daily Language Workouts	Write Source Online
		Main Pages	Resource Units*			
WEEK 2						
6–7	(Writing) Transitions	231–236	595–596		50–53	*Net-text*
8–10	(Revising)	237–248				*Net-text*
	Skills Activities: • Modifiers	84, 88	610 (+), 728 (+), 730–731	98, 99, 103, 166, 167		
	• Sentence Types		746 (+)	134		*GrammarSnap*
	• Complete Sentences	86	738 (+), 740 (+)	162–163		*GrammarSnap*
WEEK 3						
11–13	(Editing, Publishing)	249–253			54–57	*Portfolio, Net-text*
	Skills Activities: • Subject-Verb Agreement		738 (+), 740 (+), 752–753, 754–755	141–142		*GrammarSnap*
	• Pronoun-Antecedent Agreement		756 (+)	146		*GrammarSnap*
	• Commas		610 (+)	9		*GrammarSnap*
	• Tenses and Irregular Verbs		720–721, 722 (+)	89, 90, 94, 95		*GrammarSnap*
	• Hyphens and Dashes		624–625, 626–627, 640–641	22, 23, 24		
	• Spelling		664–665	51, 52		
14–15	(Assessing, Reflecting)	254–258				
opt.	*Making Oral Presentations*	439–447				
	Responding to Persuasive Prompts	267–273				
SECOND FORM WEEK 1						
1–5	**Writing an Essay of Evaluation: A Current Trend, Product, or Group** (Model) ⓛ Literature Connections "Another Renaissance"	259–261			58–61	
	(Prewriting, Writing) Supporting Details, Integrating Quotations	262–264, 56–57, 108–109, 110, 111				*Net-text*
	(Revising, Editing, Publishing)	265–266				*Portfolio, Net-text*
	Peer Responding	121–126				
	Skills Activities: • Sentence Combining	82	742 (+), 744 (+), 748 (+)	153–154		
	• Adjectives	78	728 (+)	100		*GrammarSnap*
	• Wordiness and Deadwood	79		168		
	• End Punctuation Review		605 (+), 606 (+)	6		
	• Using the Right Word		686–687, 688–689	60		

* These units are also located in the back of the *Teacher's Edition*. Resource Units include "Basic Elements of Writing" and "Proofreader's Guide."
(+) This activity is located in a different section of the *Write Source Student Edition*. If students have already completed this activity, you may wish to review it at this time.

Teacher's Notes for Persuasive Writing

This overview of persuasive writing includes some specific teaching suggestions for the unit. The description of each chapter will help you decide which parts of the unit to teach.

Writing Focus

Writing an Essay of Argumentation (pages 219–258)

Students who are able to form cogent and coherent arguments in favor of their own positions are better prepared to judge fairly the arguments presented to them by others. Students should work at becoming comfortable with logical argumentation so that testing the logic of their own reasoning and that of others will become second nature to them.

When writing their essays, students may not always use all of the elements of formal argumentation, but they should keep them in mind.

Writing an Essay of Evaluation (pages 259–266)

When writing essays of evaluation, students should think of themselves as roving critics, exploring and reviewing subjects that cover a wide range of areas, from personal incidents to casual observations, from important occasions to current trends, from memorable places to the latest gadgets or products. Impress upon your students that evaluating a subject generally means determining its value or worth.

Responding to Persuasive Prompts (pages 267–273)

Some state assessment tests expect students to take a position on an issue and write a solid argument (a persuasive essay) for or against that issue. This chapter encourages students to use the STRAP questions, to plan their responses with graphic organizers, and to write and revise as quickly as possible. Two persuasive prompts are included for practice.

Grammar Focus

For support with this unit's grammar topics, consult the resource units. (Basic Grammar and Writing, A Writer's Resource, and Proofreader's Guide).

Academic Vocabulary

Read aloud the academic terms, as well as the descriptions and questions. Model for students how to read one question and answer it. Have partners monitor their understanding and seek clarification of the terms by working through the meanings and questions together.

Academic Vocabulary

Learning these words will help you understand this unit.

1. A debate involves presenting opposing ideas on a subject. **Tell about a time when you saw a debate at school.**
2. To counter an argument, explain why it isn't the best idea. **How might you counter an argument for raising the voting age?**
3. Something chosen at random is chosen without a reason. **Why might raffle winners be chosen at random?**
4. Perspective is a person's way of thinking about something. **Is your perspective about school different from that of your teacher? How?**

Minilessons

That's Debatable.   Writing an Essay of Argumentation

■ **LIST** topics related to your academic experience (take-home exams, group-assignment projects). **CREATE** a T-chart to gather reasons for and against the issues in two columns. **ANSWER** these two questions: What is the position I wish to promote and support? How strongly do I feel about it? **CHOOSE** the topic about which you have the strongest feelings and the most facts to support your position. **WRITE** a position statement.

Soda Can Found in Mummy Case . . .   Writing an Essay of Evaluation

■ **STUDY** the logical fallacies on SE pages 238–239. **REVIEW** a copy of a tabloid-style newspaper (supplied by your teacher). **FIND** an article or advertisement in the paper that you find unconvincing. **EXAMINE** the logic used to sell the product or prove a point. **POINT OUT** to a partner any fallacies of thinking you detect. **EXPLAIN** what makes the logic false.

Persuasive Writing
Writing an Essay of Argumentation

219

Perhaps more than any other leader in American history, Abraham Lincoln understood the value of a logical argument. As president, he led the nation during many fierce debates over the ethics of slavery. Lincoln observed, "I am a firm believer in the people. If given the truth, they can be depended upon to meet any national crises. The great point is to bring them the real facts."

Today, the people of our country are engaging in debate and making decisions about any number of issues. Many of these issues involve ethics, or moral controversies.

One way to participate in these ethical debates is to write an essay of argumentation. An essay of argumentation takes a position on one side of a controversy and defends the position with logical, well-organized reasons and details. In this chapter, you'll learn the steps necessary to create an effective essay of argumentation.

Writing Guidelines

Subject: An ethical issue
Form: Essay of argumentation
Purpose: To argue for a position
Audience: Classmates, readers of a local newspaper

"Let me give you a definition of ethics: It is good to maintain and further life; it is bad to damage and destroy life."
—Albert Schweitzer

Objectives

- understand the form and content of an essay of argumentation
- take a position on an ethical issue
- use specific reasons to argue for that position
- plan, draft, revise, edit, and publish an essay of argumentation

Discuss the Albert Schweitzer quotation on the page and invite students to contribute their own definitions of the **concept of ethics** (see below).

To provide more examples of ethical questions, as a group read "The Ethicist," a weekly advice column by Randy Cohen, published in the *New York Times Magazine* (see www.nytimes.com):
- Read the letter describing the ethical dilemma.
- Have students tell what advice they would give this person and explain the reasons for their answer.
- Read the response provided by Randy Cohen.
- Discuss students' reactions to his response—do they agree with it?

 **Technology Connections**

Use this unit's Interactive Whiteboard Lesson to introduce persuasive writing.

 Interactive Whiteboard Lessons

Teaching Tip: The Concept of Ethics

To further broaden the class discussion, suggest that students look online for other quotations related to ethics, via www.bartleby.com (click on "Respectfully Quoted"). Have each student contribute a quotation, stating the ethical question it addresses, and encourage the rest of the class to offer observations.

Copy Masters

T-chart (TE p. 220)

5 W's Chart (TE p. 246)

Assessment Sheet (TE p. 257)

Benchmark Papers

Creatine Crazy (good)

TE pp. 802–806

Environmental Pollution (fair)

TE pp. 807–811

Persuasive Writing Warm-Up

Taking a Stand

Remind students that they cannot collect the details they need by consulting only one article; the prewriting stage involves research. They are looking for details that not only support their position but also those that express an opposing viewpoint. These should be strong, valid objections. Otherwise, their argument will not be as persuasive.

Note that four sources are cited on the sample chart. Suggest that students' research should include a variety of approaches, such as

- doing online searches and reading reliable Web sites;
- searching the library catalog to find periodical articles;
- listening to radio broadcasts (archived programs may be available online at radio stations' Web sites); and
- talking to friends and family members about their chosen controversy.

Distribute photocopies of the reproducible T-chart (TE page 823) for students to use when making their pro-con chart.

✳ For more about research skills, see SE pages 371–382.

220

Persuasive Writing Warm-Up Taking a Stand

When you take a stand, you give your position (opinion) on a controversial issue and support your position with solid reasons. Most current newspapers and magazines will present several issues to choose from. Once you have found a controversy, filling in a pro-con chart is one way to record facts that support each side.

Pro-Con Chart

Issue: Some people are getting microchip implants beneath their skin to provide identification, medical history, and even global tracking.

Pro	Con
– Microchip implants make photo ID's unnecessary.	– Microchip implants could be faked, just like photo ID's. ("Cybertalk")
– "By carrying complete medical history, an implant can save the person's life." ("Cybertalk")	– People with medical problems like diabetes can wear bracelets that identify the disease.
– Implants can give GPS locations, helping to foil kidnappings. ("Chips to Fight")	– GPS tracking can also allow governments and businesses to track anyone.
– Implants could hold credit card numbers, preventing theft and ensuring payment.	– "Companies will use implants to keep vast databases, trafficking in consumer profiles." ("Dangers")
– Different types of information could have different access codes.	– No laws exist about who can access the information.
– Each member of the Jacobs family was implanted because the son was interested in technology and the father requires 10 cancer medications. ("Chips to Keep")	– "The intimacy between technology and the flesh crosses a line. My instinct tells me this is an entirely unnecessary and dangerous technology." ("Chips to Fight")

My Position: Microchip implants may lead to some terrible abuses.

Try It!

Check out newspapers and magazines, looking for controversial issues. Select an issue, write it down, and create a pro-con chart to list arguments for each side. Then write your position.

English Language Learners

Students may be unfamiliar with the term *microchip*. Explain that a microchip is a miniaturized electronic circuit that can be as small as a grain of rice. Point out that the word begins with the prefix *micro-*, which is derived from the Greek word *micros*, meaning "small." The words *microscope* and *microwave* also contain this prefix.

Writing a Persuasive Paragraph

A persuasive paragraph states a position about a controversial topic and uses reasons to defend the position. A persuasive paragraph has three main parts:

- The **topic sentence** states the position.
- The **body sentences** support the position and respond to an objection.
- The **closing sentence** restates the position.

Sample Persuasive Paragraph

In the following persuasive paragraph, a writer expresses her position about microchip implants. She uses facts, statistics, examples, and quotations she has gathered in her pro-con chart.

A Chip in the Old Block

Topic Sentence

Microchip implants that carry crucial information about a person may lead to some terrible abuses. Already implants are used in some places in Europe to provide identification, medical information, and credit card numbers. Supporters point to the security, convenience, and foolproof nature of the implants. However, no laws currently exist to prevent unscrupulous people and companies from accessing this information. Imagine a chair arm with a hidden scanner, or a doorway that "knows" who enters at what time. Futurist Tom Dormant foresees a world in which "companies will use implants to keep vast databases, trafficking in consumer profiles" (qtd. in "Dangers"). Implants with global positioning technology can foil kidnappers, but they can also allow governments to track wearers at all times. These privacy issues deeply concern Simon Davies of Privacy International, who calls microchip implants "an entirely unnecessary and dangerous technology" ("Chips to Fight"). People who voluntarily get a microchip implant should be aware of the risks, and people who don't want to get one should make sure these little pieces of technology never become mandatory.

Body Sentences

Closing Sentence

Persuasive

Write

Write a persuasive paragraph. State your position about the controversy you chose (page 220), provide reasons from your pro-con chart, respond to an objection, and end by restating or reinforcing your position.

Writing a Persuasive Paragraph

After your students review the sample paragraph, lead a discussion about microchip implants. Ask, "Which of you would be willing to have a microchip with your personal information implanted in your skin?" Ask the students to give their reasons for or against this technology, and ask whether the paragraph has influenced their feelings.

✳ For more about basic paragraph skills, see SE pages 577–588; persuasive paragraphs are covered on SE page 583.

 Writer's Craft

Selectivity: Point out that the author of the paragraph did not use all the material she had gathered in her pro-con chart. The process of writing is a process of distilling—putting down on paper just the pieces that work best to make a strong argument. The American author Donald Barthelme put it this way:

"I write a lot—every day, seven days a week—and I throw a lot away. Sometimes I think I write to throw away; it's a process of distillation."

—Donald Barthelme

Understanding Your Goal

Sometimes, the first three traits—ideas, organization, and voice—are referred to as the "global" traits. They focus on large-scale issues. That's why these three traits guide the prewriting and writing phase.

When the time comes to revise, students will review the first three traits and also check the next two: word choice and sentence fluency. These two traits have a more specific focus, on individual clauses, phrases, and words.

Only after these larger-scale issues are addressed should students check for conventions, making sure each letter and punctuation mark is correct. Polishing conventions is the job of the editing step.

＊ The six-point rubric on SE pages 254–255 is based on these traits. Reproducible six-, five-, and four-point rubrics for persuasive writing are available on pages 769, 773, and 777.

Literature Connections

In her essay of argumentation *A Vindication of the Rights of Women,* Mary Wollstonecraft argues for the rights of women and calls for an end to the prevailing injustices against women in the 18th century.

Discuss with students the historical context that inspired Wollstonecraft's writing. Then have students discuss the organization of the piece, as well as strengths and any weaknesses in Wollstonecraft's arguments. Encourage students to comment on parts of the piece that surprise them. Ask which points seem self-evident today. For additional models of persuasive writing, see the Reading-Writing Connections beginning on page TE-36.

222

Understanding Your Goal

Your goal in this chapter is to write a persuasive essay that states a position about an ethical issue and argues logically to defend the position. The traits listed in the chart below will help you plan and write your essay of argumentation. You can also use the rubric on pages 254–255 to guide your writing.

Traits of an Essay of Argumentation

■ **Ideas**
Select a topic that involves an ethical controversy, write a clear position statement, and include reasons that support the position.

■ **Organization**
Create a beginning that states your position, a middle that provides support and answers an objection, and an ending that restates your position. Use transition words and phrases to connect your ideas.

■ **Voice**
Use a voice that shows understanding of the controversy and commitment to a specific position about it.

■ **Word Choice**
Choose fair and precise words to state and defend your position.

■ **Sentence Fluency**
Write clear, complete sentences with varied beginnings and lengths.

■ **Conventions**
Eliminate errors in punctuation, capitalization, spelling, and grammar.

Literature Connections: You can read the introduction to *A Vindication of the Rights of Women* by Mary Wollstonecraft as an example of an essay of argumentation.

English Language Learners

Discuss the word *objection.* Explain that an objection is a point raised in opposition. Point out that to include an objection is a good strategy because doing so will strengthen the position of the writer in the eyes of the reader.

Essay of Argumentation

An essay of argumentation states a position on a controversy and defends the position with logically organized reasons and details. In this sample essay, a student writer takes a position on lobbyists giving gifts to members of Congress.

Essay of Argumentation

Work through this sample essay with the class, pointing out the elements that make it a good persuasive essay.

Ideas
- The position statement clearly presents the writer's opinion.
- The writer provides several reasons in support of that position.

Organization
- The writer addresses a solid objection (see paragraph 5).
- The writer uses effective transitions to connect ideas, both to clarify the order of details (*First of all, Perhaps most important, In a recent survey, In the same survey*) and to express contrast or comparison (*but, however, in either case, not only . . . but also*).

Voice & Word Choice
- The writer's serious voice is appropriate for the topic.
- The writer uses special terms relating to the topic, such as *lobbyist, political corruption, conflict of interest, constituents, deterrent,* and *undue influence.*

Test Prep!
Point out to students that learning to write an essay of argumentation can help them respond to a persuasive prompt on a high-stakes test.

Beginning
The beginning introduces the controversy and states the writer's position (underlined).

Middle
The first middle paragraph presents the first reason to support the writer's argument.

The second middle paragraph provides another important reason.

Persuasive

Ban Gifts from Lobbyists

Since the invention of political systems, people have tried to use money and other gifts to influence the actions of politicians. In New York City in the 1800s, for example, a political group led by William "Boss" Tweed used bribery to corrupt the operations of city agencies and rob the city taxpayers of millions (Martin 434). Tweed died in prison, but the specter of political corruption is alive and well in the United States. The system allows lobbyists to give gifts and provide favors to members of Congress, a practice that creates a conflict of interest. Do senators and representatives owe more to their constituents or to lobbyists? The best way to remove this conflict from the political system is to ban lobbyists from giving gifts to politicians.

First of all, banning gifts from lobbyists will eliminate long-standing relationships in which gifts are used to purchase political access and influence. Under current lobbying regulations, lobbyists can offer members of Congress the services of a corporate jet, a weekend golf getaway, or even tickets to sports events. In return, lobbyists often get the opportunity to speak with and even develop personal relationships with senators and representatives. This access may sound harmless, but lobbyists often use these relationships to obtain political favors. In some cases, lobbyists even assist directly in writing legislation, adding passages favorable to their corporate clients ("Great Giveaway").

Banning gifts from lobbyists will restore Americans' trust in Congress. Again and again, members of Congress must defend their actions after taking positions favorable to lobbyists who gave them gifts. In a recent survey, 83 percent of voters indicated that they distrusted lawmakers who accepted gifts from lobbyists (Jones). In the same survey, 64 percent of voters approved an outright ban on all such gift giving. Distrust in public officials has become an epidemic in this country, and gifts from

Respond to the reading.

Answers

Ideas **1.** It should be banned.

2. It will end the practice of purchasing political favors; it will increase citizens' trust in Congress; it will give ordinary citizens better access to politicians.

Organization **3.** to present arguments in support of the writer's position

4. to address and refute an objection

Voice & Word Choice **5.** Responses include

- bribery
- political corruption
- conflict of interest
- ban lobbyists from giving gifts
- purchase political access
- political favors
- distrust
- epidemic
- buy influence

224

The third middle paragraph presents the writer's most important reason.

The final middle paragraph defends the position against a significant objection.

Ending
The ending restates the writer's position and adds perspective.

lobbyists to members of Congress contribute greatly to that distrust. Banning such gifts would create an honest, open environment in which respect for our leaders can grow.

Perhaps most important, banning gifts will give typical citizens of the United States more opportunity to be heard in Washington. In the 2004 presidential elections, more than one-third of eligible voters chose not to vote (FEC). When surveyed, many nonvoters explained that they felt their votes didn't count, and that the government did not consider their input. With lobbyists using gifts to influence the political process, it's little wonder. Because many lobbyists are former politicians, they already have much more access than common people. Making gifts from lobbyists illegal can help level the playing field in Washington so that regular voters can be heard.

Some people might argue that banning gifts from lobbyists will do little to reduce the buying of influence since such gifts can easily be hidden. However, the same could be said for any number of illegal activities. Banning such gifts forces those who wish to buy influence to break the law, and sets up a system of punishment for those who do. An outright ban would be a deterrent and help to prevent corruption.

When many voters look at Congress, they see an institution in which lobbyists are able to buy power and favorable treatment. Sometimes this is true, and sometimes it isn't. In either case, the ability of lobbyists to give gifts to politicians stirs controversy and contributes to an environment of mistrust that makes it easy for citizens to turn their backs on the political process. Banning these gifts will not only reduce the undue influence of lobbyists, but it will also bring ordinary citizens back into the political process—and that might improve life for everyone.

 Respond to the reading. Answer the following questions.

Ideas **(1)** What is the writer's position on gift giving by lobbyists? **(2)** What are the three main reasons that support the writer's position?

Organization **(3)** What is the purpose of the first three middle paragraphs? **(4)** What is the purpose of the final middle paragraph?

Voice & Word Choice **(5)** Find two or three examples of specific words that illustrate the author's unfavorable view on gifts from lobbyists.

Struggling Learners

Reinforce understanding of the organization of an essay of argumentation by copying this list of elements on the board and asking students to put them in the correct order. (The correct order is given in parentheses.)

- Defend against a significant objection (5)
- Use order of importance to organize supporting reasons (4)
- State the writer's position (2)
- Introduce the topic (1)
- Restate the writer's position (6)
- Present the first supporting reason in the position statement (3)

Advise students to follow this order when planning their essay.

Advanced Learners

Invite volunteers to research the positions that high-profile elected officials have taken on gifts from lobbyists. Then have students draw on these findings to add to the final middle paragraph, in which they use votes and/or quotations from an official or two to strengthen their position advocating a ban on lobbyists' gifts.

Writing an Essay of Argumentation **225**

Prewriting

Prewriting begins when you are still deciding what to write about and ends when you are ready to write your first draft. By breaking an essay project into small steps, you'll be well prepared to begin writing.

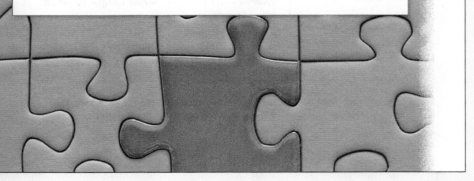

Keys to Effective Prewriting

1. Choose an ethical controversy that will be of interest to your audience.

2. Gather reasons and details to help form and support your position.

3. Write a position statement that focuses your thoughts.

4. Choose a significant objection to address in the middle part of your essay.

5. Create an outline or organized list to plan your essay.

Persuasive

Prewriting

Keys to Effective Prewriting

Remind students of the purpose of the prewriting stage in the writing process: It is when the writer selects a topic, gathers details, and decides how to organize those details.

The Keys to Effective Prewriting list explains the process students will be guided through on SE pages 226–230.

Writing Workshop

The activities on the following pages teach key prewriting strategies and are perfect to use as minilessons in a writing workshop. Present the material to the whole class prior to individual work time, use the activities with a small group that needs intervention, or assign the activities to guide students who are working independently.

Technology Connections

Students can use the added features of the Net-text as they explore this stage of the writing process.

Write Source Online *Net-text*

Prewriting Selecting a Controversy

This project provides an opportunity for students to keep up with news events. If possible, announce several weeks in advance that they will write an essay about an ethical controversy.

- Instruct students to pay attention to newspapers, magazines, broadcasts, and online news items for controversial stories.
- Encourage students to save articles and bookmark Internet items about interesting topics.
- Regularly set aside class time for students to discuss current events.
- When the time comes to choose topics, students will be able to generate a list of timely issues.

Prewriting Considering Sources

Note that personal experiences are a type of primary source. Acknowledge that students may not have personal experiences relating to the topic they choose. This is fine—but then they must be sure to **find primary sources** *(see below)* for their essays.

Prewriting Selecting a Controversy

To find an ethical controversy, Yolanda searched newspapers, magazines, and news shows. She listed controversies and put an asterisk beside her choice.

List of Political Controversies

Newspapers and Magazines	News Shows
right to privacy for criminals	wiretapping without warrants
drug testing for student athletes *	free speech for student newspapers
universal Internet access	mandatory sentencing laws
animal testing for cosmetics	high cost of prescription drugs
federal budget cuts for housing	carbon emissions laws

Prewrite

Select a controversy. Read national newspapers and magazines and watch news broadcasts, making a list of ethical controversies. Put an asterisk (*) next to the controversy you'd like to write about.

Considering Sources

Once you have selected a controversy to write about, you need to research it. Yolanda listed her own experiences and then primary (firsthand) and secondary (secondhand) sources.

Source List

Personal Experiences	Primary Sources	Secondary Sources
My cousin had to do drug testing to join track.	Interview with Coach Colton	Steroids: Silent Danger, Steven Smith
There was a creatine problem at the high school five years ago.	Interview with school nurse	Major League Baseball Web site
	Survey of student athletes at Millard Fillmore	"School Tackles Alarming Subject: Steroid Use," USA Today

Prewrite

List research sources. Make a source list like the one above. Then choose three or four sources to use as you research your controversy.

Challenge students to suggest ways of finding primary sources other than those that involve personal experience. These include the following:

- seeking out published interviews with or writings (letters, journals, articles) by people involved in or affected by the controversy;
- seeking out the texts of public speeches made about the topic by those who were involved or affected; and
- contacting someone involved in or affected by the controversy for an interview. E-mail or the telephone can be used for long-distance interviewing. If the telephone is used, be sure to ask for permission to tape the interview.

Students may have difficulty selecting a controversial topic. Provide students with newspapers and magazine articles at their reading level, especially ones with follow-up questions to help readers analyze the material. After choosing a topic, have pairs work together to create a list of suitable primary and secondary sources.

Conducting Research

A well-written essay of argumentation uses a variety of details.

■ **Facts** are bits of information that can be proven to be true. Use facts to lay the foundation of the controversy.

Major League Baseball has instituted strict standards for testing pro baseball players for the use of steroids. (Major League Baseball Web site)

■ **Statistics** are facts that include a numerical value. Use statistics to provide examples that help to illustrate the controversy.

Over a five-year period, steroid use among high school athletes in New Jersey rose from 3 percent to 6.2 percent. (*USA Today*)

■ **Quotations** are the exact words of people involved in the topic. Use quotations to let experts and authorities speak for themselves.

"Pro sports have, for a long while, forgotten the reason for competition—the love of the game, the pursuit of excellence. Instead of our high school athletes learning from drug-using pros, the pros ought to learn from our kids." (Coach Colton)

■ **Anecdotes** are brief stories that make a point. Use anecdotes to demonstrate an abstract idea in a concrete way.

When the high school had trouble with creatine use five years ago, strict school policies were implemented. At first athletes and parents complained about the invasion of privacy, but now they support the policy for healthy, fair competition.

Using Note Cards

Yolanda used note cards to gather her details. She wrote questions at the top and answers below, making sure to note the source.

> What are potential side effects of
> steroid use?
> – acne
> – liver damage
> – heart attacks
> – increased aggression
> – dependency and depression
>   (SportScience Web site)

Prewrite

Conduct research. Gather facts, statistics, quotations, and anecdotes. Write them down on note cards or in a notebook and be sure to keep track of sources.

Persuasive

Prewriting Conducting Research

Suggest that students clearly identify the different types of details as they take notes during research. (For example, they could write the type of detail in block letters—*FACT, STAT, QUOT, ANEC*—in the top right-hand corner or color-code each note card.) It will then be easier for them to see as they go along whether they are collecting a good variety of details.

Prewriting Using Note Cards

Emphasize the importance of keeping careful track of sources. This will ensure that students do not accidentally plagiarize or fail to acknowledge a source.

■ Suggest that they **keep a full list of sources** *(see below)* in the format required for the works-cited list. This way, they will get in the habit of using the MLA documentation style.

■ Write out citations fully on note cards to ensure a valid reference for each source.

✱ For more about writing responsibly, see SE pages 417–424.

Teaching Tip: Keep a Full List of Sources

Discuss students' options for making source lists. For example:

● Write information for each source on a separate note card. Cards are easy to sort into alphabetical order.

● Write the list on notebook paper, adding each source as they find it. This is a quick approach to use as they conduct their research.

● Type the source information into a computer. This requires the student to first write a list and then retype it at the end of a research session. Once created, though, an electronic document provides the information in a form that is easy to work with.

Prewriting **Stating Your Position**

Remind students that the purpose of creating the position statement at this early stage is to capture a strong, straightforward expression of their opinions as a starting point for writing. This is a first draft, however. Students may find as they proceed that they want to refine, or even drastically change, their position statement.

Prewriting **Supporting Your Position**

Make sure students understand that the two columns of the "Why?" Chart contain the reasons (left column) and basic details (right column) the writer intends to use to support the position statement. Note that students can make the information in the right column as detailed as they wish, according to the way that works best for them.

Literature Connections

Mentor texts: To deepen students' thinking about persuasive writing, suggest that they read books that deal with controversial issues. Here are three excellent examples:

Animal Rights by Herbert M. Levine

21st Century Earth: Opposing Viewpoints edited by O. W. Markley and Walter R. McCuan

Working Women: Opposing Viewpoints edited by Mary E. Williams

Prewriting **Stating Your Position**

The next step is writing a preliminary position statement. An effective position statement names the controversy and gives a specific stand or opinion about it.

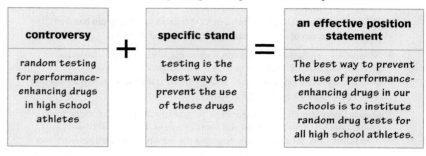

controversy		specific stand		an effective position statement
random testing for performance-enhancing drugs in high school athletes	**+**	testing is the best way to prevent the use of these drugs	**=**	The best way to prevent the use of performance-enhancing drugs in our schools is to institute random drug tests for all high school athletes.

Prewrite

Write a position statement. Use the formula above to create a position statement for your essay. Try two or three versions until you are satisfied.

Supporting Your Position

After taking a position, you need to offer reasons and supporting details from your research. Yolanda created the "why?" chart below to list her support.

"Why?" Chart

Position: Random drug tests should be used for high school athletes.		
Why?	Testing is the only sure way to detect steroids.	Muscles can be built naturally. Steroid use is illegal and secretive. Peer pressure makes people keep silent.
Why?	Testing makes it easy to resist steroids.	Athletes won't risk getting benched. Testing gives an excuse to say "no."
Why?	Athletes' health and well-being are at risk.	Drugs damage internal organs. Drugs cause mental-health issues.

Prewrite

Organize support for your position. Create a "why?" chart of your own. Write your position and three reasons that answer the question "Why?" Then add details that support each reason.

Identifying Objections

By fairly presenting a significant objection to your argument, you'll show your reader that you fully understand the controversy at hand. Yolanda generated a "why not?" chart by adding the word *not* to her position and thinking of as many serious objections as she could. She chose the strongest objection to counter.

"Why Not?" Chart

Position: Random drug tests should *not* be used for high school athletes.
  Why not?   Drug tests are too costly.
  Why not?   Some performance drugs can't be detected by testing.
  Why not?   Drug testing is a violation of student privacy.*

Identify objections. Create a "why not?" chart, like the one above, identifying at least three serious objections to your argument. Choose the strongest objection to counter in your essay.

Countering an Objection

To counter an objection, think of the reasons that minimize or refute it. Yolanda identified these reasons that counter the objection she chose.

Objection: Drug testing is a violation of student privacy.
1. A respectful approach that seals records will ensure privacy.
2. Random testing eliminates bias.
3. It is acceptable to trade some privacy for safety.

Counter an important objection. Write down the strongest objection to your argument. List reasons that refute or minimize the objection.

Focus on the Traits

Ideas Countering an objection allows you to take the best argument of the opposition and use it to further your own position.

Persuasive

Prewriting Identifying Objections

Encourage students to put themselves in the place of a person with an opposing viewpoint. Their goal is to understand and address the objection in order to strengthen their own viewpoint.

Have students choose partners, explain the controversy, and argue the *opposite* position from the one they plan to take. Is the partner convinced? Why or why not?

Prewriting Countering an Objection

Discuss strategies for countering the most important objection. Ideas include the following:

- Acknowledge the objection's validity but explain how or why another factor outweighs it. (For example: Privacy may be compromised, but safety will be ensured.)
- Explain how the objection can be overcome. (Privacy will not be sacrificed if records are sealed so names won't be made public.)
- Suggest another way of looking at the issue. (Instead of seeing all testing as a violation of privacy, remember that students will be selected at random—not for reasons having to do with personal information.)

Prewriting Outlining Your Essay

Note that in creating the "Why?" and "Why Not?" charts for SE pages 228–229, students have done much of the work of making an outline. To complete the outline, they need only refine and expand on the information in those charts.

Remind students to refer frequently to their research notes as they create their outlines. They may find it helpful to highlight or check off information in the notes as they incorporate it into their outline. Afterward, they can reread their notes to make sure they included all pertinent information.

✱ For more about outlining, see SE page 591.

Prewriting Outlining Your Essay

Before actually writing your essay, it is a good idea to organize your reasons and supporting details in an outline or a list. Yolanda created a sentence outline, but your teacher may prefer a topic outline (using phrases).

Sentence Outline

Position Statement: The best way to prevent the use of performance-enhancing drugs in our schools is to institute random drug tests for all high school athletes.

I. Random testing is needed because steroid use can be hard to detect.
   A. Big muscles don't always prove drug use.
   B. Student athletes hide their drug use.
   C. Drug tests can quickly and easily detect steroids.
II. Random testing makes it easier for young athletes to resist the temptation of performance-enhancing drugs.
   A. Athletes love their sports—and want the chance to play.
   B. Tests give students an incentive to not use drugs and an excuse to say "no."
III. Instituting testing can protect young athletes from physical and mental harm.
   A. Performance drugs can lead to major health problems.
   B. The drugs also affect mental health.
   C. Some effects can be reversed if drug use is stopped.
IV. Some civil rights advocates believe that random testing for performance-enhancing drugs violates student privacy rights.
   A. If testing is administered carefully, rights can be respected.
   B. Random testing will prevent bias against certain athletes.
   C. Testing tells kids that adults care about their private lives—and want to help them make good decisions.

Prewrite

Create an outline. Organize your reasons and supporting details in an outline or a list. (Follow your teacher's instructions.)

Writing an Essay of Argumentation **231**

Prewrite   Write   Revise   Edit   Publish

Writing

After selecting a topic, researching it, writing a position statement, and organizing your essay, you are ready to write your first draft.

Keys to Effective Writing

1. Use your outline or list as a writing guide, closely following it as you work.

2. Write on every other line or double-space if you are using a computer. This will allow room for changes.

3. In the first paragraph, introduce the ethical controversy and state your position.

4. Include topic sentences in each middle paragraph.

5. In the last middle paragraph, answer a significant objection.

6. End by restating your position and sharing an insight with the reader.

Persuasive

Writing

Keys to Effective Writing

Remind students that at the writing stage they write a draft, not the final version of their essay.

The Keys to Effective Writing list outlines the process students will be guided through on SE pages 232–236.

Draw students' attention to item number 5. Note that, while it is a solid strategy to address an objection in the last middle paragraph, writers may occasionally choose to address the objection first or in the middle of the essay.

Depending on the complexity of the issue, it is also acceptable for students to address more than one objection, as long as the argument is strong and balanced.

Technology Connections

Students can use the added features of the Net-text as they explore this stage of the writing process.

Write Source Online **Net-text**

Writing Getting the Big Picture

Have students compare the graphic to the sample outline on SE page 230, taking note of how they relate to each other.

- Ask students to double-check their own outlines against the graphic. Have they established a clear beginning and middle? If not, ask them to revisit the organization of their outline.
- Note that the main headings in the outline have been turned into topic sentences for the middle part of the graphic through the addition of transitional phrases. Suggest that students convert their outline headings into topic sentences.
- Ask students if they have any ideas for a closing sentence. Assure them that it is fine if they do not at this point. If they do, have them jot down their idea now for reference later.

Writing Getting the Big Picture

The graphic below shows how the elements of an essay of argumentation work together. Use this graphic as a guide to help you write your first draft. (The examples are from the student essay on pages **233–236**.)

Beginning

The **beginning** introduces the controversy and states the writer's position.

Position Statement
The best way to prevent the use of performance-enhancing drugs in our schools is to institute random drug tests for all high school athletes.

Middle

Each **middle** paragraph supports the writer's position.

Topic Sentences
To begin, random testing is needed because steroid use can be hard to detect.

Random testing also makes it easier for young athletes to resist the temptation of performance-enhancing drugs.

Most importantly, instituting testing can protect young athletes from physical and mental harm.

The last middle paragraph answers a major objection.

Of course, some civil rights advocates believe that random testing for performance-enhancing drugs violates student privacy rights.

Ending

The **ending** puts the controversy in perspective.

Closing Sentence
It's time to level the playing fields again, *without* steroids in the balance.

English Language Learners

Point out the expression *level the playing fields* in the closing sentence. Explain that as it is used here, it describes a situation in which every competitor has a fair and equitable chance of success.

Advanced Learners

Have students rewrite the essay from the point of view of a physician or sports trainer. Ask them to draw on current research on steroid use for the basis of the essay's supporting details.

Writing an Essay of Argumentation **233**

Starting Your Essay

The beginning paragraph of your essay should engage your reader, introduce your topic, and provide your position statement.

| Beginning |
| Middle |
| Ending |

- **Engage your reader.** Begin with a sentence that will capture your reader's interest and keep him or her reading.
  In 2005, scandal rocked the world of professional baseball as allegations of the use of steroids and other performance-enhancing drugs hit the headlines.

- **Introduce your topic.** Include details that expand on your opening.
  Steroids and other drugs that quickly build muscle mass and make athletes stronger and faster have permeated virtually all levels of athletics.

- **Provide your position statement.** The thesis statement clearly and concisely states your position on the controversy.
  The best way to prevent the use of performance-enhancing drugs in our schools is to institute random drug tests for all high school athletes.

Beginning Paragraph

> In 2005, scandal rocked the world of professional baseball as allegations of the use of steroids and other performance-enhancing drugs hit the headlines. Responding to pressure by Congress, Major League Baseball instituted standards for testing players for the use of these drugs ("Baseball Battles"). However, the controversy extends far beyond the baseball diamond. Steroids and other drugs that quickly build muscle mass and make athletes stronger and faster have permeated virtually all levels of athletics. For example, in the last five years, steroid use among high school athletes in New Jersey has doubled to 6 percent ("School Tackles" C3). That means a typical high school football team includes several users. <u>The best way to prevent the use of performance-enhancing drugs in our schools is to institute random drug tests for all high school athletes.</u>

The controversy is introduced.

The position statement is given (underlined).

Persuasive

Write

Write a beginning paragraph. Be sure to engage your reader, introduce your topic, and provide a clear position statement.

Writing **Starting Your Essay**

Note that the sample essay hooks readers with an anecdote. Discuss other strategies students might use to begin their essays. These include the following:

- Opening with a quotation: *"Pro sports have, for a long while, forgotten the reason for competition,"* argues Coach Carl Colton of the Fillmore High School wrestling team.
- Providing background: *Steroids are hormonal drugs that, when taken in pill form or injected, can cause rapid muscle growth and dramatically increase physical stamina. The side affects of taking steroids include acne, liver damage, aggression, and even death.*
- Asking a question: *How do athletes increase muscle and physical stamina, and perform so superbly? For most, it's a combination of talent and long, hard training, but some turn to a deadly shortcut—steroids.*

✳ For more about creating beginning sentences, see SE page 593.

Literature Connections

Great beginnings: Check out the series of anecdotes that begin John Allen Paulos' persuasive book, *Innumeracy: Mathematical Illiteracy and Its Consequences.*

Writing **Developing the Middle Part**

Note that using transitions effectively is an important part of sentence fluency. Ask volunteers to read the sample paragraphs out loud, and ask students to pay attention to how each sentence flows from one to the next.

Challenge students to find transitions used in the sample that are not already listed on this page and to identify them by type. For example:

- *Once* (expresses time passage)
- *Fortunately* (comments on the information associated with it)
- *Furthermore* (gives more information)

✱ For more about using transitions, see SE pages 595–596.

234

Writing Developing the Middle Part

The middle part of your essay supports your position with reasons and details. It also answers a significant objection to your position. Remember to refer to your outline or list (page 230) as you write.

Linking Your Ideas

Transition words and phrases help you connect your ideas. You can use transitions to connect your paragraphs, showing the order of importance of your reasons and signaling your answer to an objection.

Reason 1	Reason 2	Reason 3	Answer to Objection
First of all	Secondly	Most importantly	Even so, some people . . .
To begin	In addition	The biggest reason	Granted, opponents say . . .
For starters	Also	The main issue	Of course, critics allege . . .

You can also use transitions to show other relationships between ideas, such as time, cause and effect, comparison and contrast, and added information.

Time	Cause	Contrast	More Information
When	Consequently	Although	For example
After	As a result	However	Besides
At first	Because	Nevertheless	In addition

Middle Paragraphs

A topic sentence (underlined) introduces the main idea of each middle paragraph.

To begin, random testing is needed because steroid use can be hard to detect. When young people participate in sports, they build muscle mass naturally, so large muscles are not always recognized as a symptom. Also, because steroids and other performance-enhancing drugs are illegal, most student athletes realize that getting caught with them would mean immediate expulsion from sports. As a result, students will do everything they can to cover up their use. Peer pressure only reinforces the silence (Smith 26). However, drug tests can quickly and easily detect steroids in a minimally intrusive fashion. Once a student is identified as a user of performance-enhancing drugs, he or she can receive treatment and put an end to steroid use.

Struggling Learners

Remind students that a cause-and-effect relationship describes a pair of linked events. The first event that occurs, the cause, triggers a second event, or the effect, to happen. (*Because* the key had been forced into the lock, the door would not open.)

Have students brainstorm a list of transitions that indicate cause-and-effect relationships.

Guide them to recognize that certain terms generally precede a cause, while others precede an effect. Reinforce this concept by having students classify the listed terms. For example, *because*, *since*, and *due to* are "cause" terms, while *consequently*, *as a result*, and *therefore* are "effect" terms.

The body of each paragraph supports the paragraph's topic sentence.

>   Random testing also makes it easier for young athletes to resist the temptation of performance-enhancing drugs. Most student athletes participate in sports because they love them. If athletes know that testing positive could put them on the sidelines, they are more likely to resist the pressure to bulk up with performance-enhancing drugs. By acting as a deterrent, testing makes it easy for student athletes to resist peer pressure to use steroids and other enhancers. Athletes who do not want to risk their school sports careers are more likely to say "no" because of the random testing.

The middle paragraphs build to the most important reason.

>   Most importantly, instituting testing can protect young athletes from physical and mental harm. Performance-enhancing drugs can cause a broad range of serious health issues, from liver damage and heart attack to certain types of cancer. In addition, these drugs can affect mental health, causing unprovoked rage and violence among users. Sometimes the mood swings lead to depression and even suicide. That fact makes these drugs doubly deadly. Fortunately, if treatment is provided soon enough, most of these health issues can be avoided or reversed—another reason for supporting mandatory testing ("Anabolic").

The last middle paragraph responds to a significant objection.

>   Of course, some civil rights advocates believe that random testing for performance-enhancing drugs violates student privacy rights. However, if testing is conducted in a careful manner, students' rights can be respected. Furthermore, random testing eliminates potential bias against students. In a recent survey of track athletes at Fillmore High, 78 percent said they were not bothered by the privacy issues of drug testing. "It makes the sport fair for everyone," said junior Megan Krupinski. Random drug testing is a way of publicly telling athletes that adults care about what students do in their private lives and want to see them make good decisions.

Persuasive

Write

Write the middle. Using your outline (page 230), write middle paragraphs that effectively support your position and counter an objection.

Continue to address the trait of sentence fluency. Ask students to look at the essay, noting

- the different types of sentences (simple, compound, complex);
- the varied sentence lengths; and
- the ways that sentences can begin.

Remind students that making a point of using a wide variety of sentences keeps their writing from sounding dull and repetitive.

✳ For more about the trait of sentence fluency, see SE pages 81–88.

✳ For more about sentence variety, see SE pages 302–303.

Struggling Learners

Reinforce an understanding of sentence types by assigning partners paragraphs from SE pages 235–236. Have pairs work individually to classify the paragraph's sentences as simple, compound, or complex. Allow pairs to compare their findings. Invite volunteers to explain what they learned from the activity.

Writing Ending Your Essay

Challenge students to point out the final insight the writer includes in the ending paragraph: a quote expressing the idea that students can lead professional athletes by their example, instead of the reverse.

Reassure students that it is not unusual for a writer to need time to figure out the best way to end a work. **If they feel stuck** *(see below)*, suggest that they take a break between completing the middle of the essay and writing the ending, so they can look through their notes or even do a little extra research to find a final interesting fact or insight. Remind students that inspiration might strike at any time; they should be prepared to make notes, so they don't forget their idea.

✳ For creating great endings, see SE page 597.

236

Writing Ending Your Essay

You have stated your position, supported it with reasons and details, and responded to an objection. Now you are ready to write your ending paragraph. To do the job effectively, use the following guidelines:

- Restate your position clearly and concisely.
- Sum up the main reasons for supporting your position.
- Summarize your response to the significant objection.
- Include an insight for your reader.

Ending Paragraph

> The position is restated.

> The paragraph sums up the support and ends with a final thought.

Random testing for high school athletes is the best way to prevent kids from using steroids. Right now, all across the United States, thousands of kids are risking their lives for the sake of bigger muscles. Carl Colton, coach of the Fillmore High School wrestling team, said, "Pro sports have, for a long while, forgotten the reason for competition—the love of the game, the pursuit of excellence. Instead of our high school athletes learning from drug-using pros, the pros ought to learn from our kids." The best way to reverse the current trend is to make random drug testing of high school athletes—done in a way that protects civil rights—mandatory. It's time to level the playing fields again, without steroids in the balance.

Write your ending. Write an ending paragraph to summarize your position and your answer to an objection. Include a final thought or an insight for the reader.

Prepare a complete first draft. Write a copy of your entire essay. Double-space if you use a computer, or write on every other line if you write by hand, so that you have room to make revision notes.

Teaching Tip: If Students Feel Stuck

Remind students that a great strategy for breaking through writer's block is to freewrite. Suggest that they devote 10 or 15 minutes to writing down any ideas that come to them when they think about how to conclude their essay. Encourage them not to censor themselves—or even to stop writing for more than a moment or two during this time.

Afterward, as they read through their freewriting, students may come across the idea they need for their ending.

✳ For more about freewriting, see SE page 99.

English Language Learners

Explain to students that a final insight is a final thought about what they may have learned that is shared with the reader. Point out that a good final insight leaves the reader with something to think about and reflects the essence of the argument.

Revising

The revision process makes your initial draft better. When you revise, you add or delete details, reorganize parts of your writing, and improve your writing voice. You also check word choice and sentence style.

Keys to Effective Revising

1. **Read your essay aloud and note parts that sound unclear or unconvincing.**

2. **Make sure you have clearly stated your position.**

3. **Check the order and unity of your middle paragraphs.**

4. **Be sure you use an informed, confident, and persuasive voice.**

5. **Check your essay for strong word choice and sentence variety.**

6. **Use the editing and proofreading marks inside the back cover of this book.**

Persuasive

Revising

Keys to Effective Revising

Remind students that the revising stage is when writers have an opportunity to make improvements to their first drafts. At this stage they can think about refinements they might not have considered when they were drafting.

The Keys to Effective Revising list explains the process students will be guided through on SE pages 238–248.

Many students are tempted to skimp on revisions. After all, they feel, they have done the research, they have a complete draft—why review the whole piece again? Emphasize that conscientious revision can transform a mediocre paper into an outstanding one. Assure them that **famous writers revise** (see below). They often do not capture their ideas in a first draft, and it isn't until they go back to revise that they sculpt the work into what they had first imagined.

Peer Responding

Writers need the perspective of readers, so make sure that students have a chance to get (and give) a peer response.

Technology Connections

Have students use the Writing Network features of the Net-text to comment on each other's drafts.

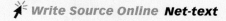
Write Source Online **Net-text**

Teaching Tip: Famous Writers Revise

Share with students some examples of revisions by famous writers. If possible, allow students to read both an early and the final version. The Library of Congress Web site may be helpful. For instance, the site's online exhibit about Thomas Jefferson shows marked-up drafts of the Declaration of Independence (www.loc.gov/exhibits/jefferson).

A few writers known for making extensive revisions are the following:

- F. Scott Fitzgerald
- Ernest Hemingway
- Henry James
- Edith Wharton
- Virginia Woolf
- William Wordsworth

Revising **for** Ideas

The rubric strips that run across all of the revising pages (SE pages 238–247) are provided to help students focus their revising and are related to the full rubric on SE pages 254–255.

Note also that, in addition to learning about logical fallacies so that they can avoid them in their own writing, students can use this knowledge to help them as they analyze their topic for this essay.

Can they find any logical fallacies in the arguments made for or against their topic's controversy? If so, pointing them out by name in the essay might help them sound rational and knowledgeable as they make their case.

Exercise Answers

Possible Answers

1. oversimplification
2. appeal to ignorance
3. bandwagoning
4. bandwagoning
5. oversimplification or appeal to ignorance
6. appeal to ignorance

238

Revising **for** Ideas

6 My position is clear and compelling, supported by a wide array of details.

5 My essay states and supports my position fairly and is fair to opposing positions.

4 I am fair when stating my position, but I'm sometimes unfair to opposing views.

When you revise for *ideas*, you make sure you have dealt fairly with your own position as well as with opposing views. The rubric strip above can guide you.

Have I presented my ideas fairly?

You have presented your ideas fairly if you avoided these logical fallacies:

- **Bandwagoning** implies that the reader should agree because most other people do.
  Most Europeans oppose testing cosmetics on animals, so we should, too.
  (A better argument would state why we should oppose it.)

- **Appeals to ignorance** use a lack of evidence to try to prove something.
  Animal testing facilities don't advertise, so there could be thousands of them.
  (A little research would tell how many facilities exist.)

- **Oversimplification** reduces complex situations to overly simple ones.
  Scientists should be curing cancer, not putting lipstick on rats.
  (Scientists who specialize in cosmetics are probably not experts on cancer.)

Exercise

Read the sentences below and identify the logical fallacy in each one.

1. If the government banned animal testing of cosmetics and drugs, all that would happen is that people wouldn't have such nice mascara.
2. Whenever you buy blush, imagine how many animals were tortured for it.
3. If you're like most attractive people, you won't mind giving up your makeup until animal testing is stopped.
4. Millions of caring people reject cosmetic testing on animals, and you should, too!
5. You don't put eyeliner on your cat, and neither should scientists.
6. Who knows how many animals die each year from testing?

Revise

Present your position fairly. As you present your views, avoid bandwagoning, appeals to ignorance, and oversimplification. If necessary, rewrite statements to eliminate errors in logic.

---

3 Sometimes logical fallacies make my essay unfair.

2 I need to remove many logical fallacies that make my essay unfair and confusing.

1 I need help recognizing and correcting logical fallacies.

Have I presented opposing ideas fairly?

You have presented opposing ideas fairly if you avoided these logical fallacies:

- **Either-or thinking** allows for no other viewpoints.
  Either we end all testing of cosmetics on animals, or we have no compassion.
  (It's unfair to assume opponents have no compassion.)

- **Slanted language** insults the person or position instead of arguing against it.
  Of course, the animal haters see no problem with cosmetics testing.
  (It's unfair to call opponents "animal haters.")

Exercise

Read the sentences below and identify the logical fallacy in each one.

1. People who support animal testing must love seeing chimps with rouge.
2. Either we ban cosmetics testing, or every animal in the world will be in danger.
3. If we don't stop animal testing right now, we'll face a "gorilla" war.
4. Heartless scientists should try to remember their childhoods—if they ever were children.

Revise

Be fair to opposing views. Read your essay and watch for either-or thinking and slanted language. Remove any you find.

Ideas
Slanted language is removed.

> *civil rights advocates*
> Of course, some ~~knee-jerk liberals~~ believe that random
> testing for performance-enhancing drugs violates student
> privacy rights. ~~These people care more about freedom than~~
> ~~about the health of the young people,~~ However, if testing . . .

Persuasive

Review the information about slanted language to provide an opportunity to discuss the role of word choice in logical fallacies. Note that as long as students take care to choose fair, intelligent words to express their ideas—not to insult or attack—they will probably avoid the fallacy of slanted language.

Note that scholars have identified other logical fallacies besides those listed. Mention others—or have students research them on their own and share their findings with the class. Two additional logical fallacies are the following:

- Stacking the Deck—trying to strengthen an argument by focusing on only one side of it. (This is why students must address objections.)
- Straw Man—focusing on a minor point of opposition rather than the best argument.

Exercise
Answers

1. slanted language
2. either-or thinking
3. either-or thinking
4. slanted language

English Language Learners

Explain to students that slanted language consists of terms that insult and offend. It "slants" an argument in one direction by attacking the opposition. Pair each student with a language-proficient classmate. Have pairs study magazine ads (the same ads from TE page 238 or new ones) to find and list examples of slanted language.

Revising **for** Organization

Make sure students understand that the beginning and ending should work as a team, employing the same basic strategy to persuade. That doesn't mean that the opinion statement should be withheld until the ending.

- To check the teamwork of their beginnings and endings, have students work as partners.
- The writer should read the beginning and ending aloud.
- The partner should indicate what strategy is used in each part. If it isn't one of the strategies on this page, the partner should suggest a different type of strategy.
- The team should then switch roles.

Exercise Answers

1. question and answer
2. problem and solution
3. problem and solution

240

Revising **for** Organization

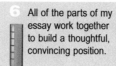

6 All of the parts of my essay work together to build a thoughtful, convincing position.

5 My beginning and ending work together, and my middle paragraphs are in the best order.

4 My beginning and ending work together, but my middle paragraphs need a clearer order.

When you revise for *organization*, you make sure your beginning and ending work together and your middle paragraphs are in the best possible order. The rubric strip above can guide your revision.

Do my beginning and ending work together?

Your beginning and ending work together if they use the same persuasive strategy to convince the reader. Here are three strategies to make your beginning and ending work as a team:

1. Begin with a **problem** and end with your **solution**.
2. Begin with a **question** and end with your **answer**.
3. Begin with a **common belief** and end with your **specific position**.

Exercise

For each beginning and ending, indicate which strategy (1, 2, or 3) is used.

1. **Beginning:** Aside from diet, exercise, and lifestyle, what other factor most affects longevity?
   Ending: The other factor that affects longevity is money—and the access it provides to health care. This situation is unfair, and it needs to change.

2. **Beginning:** Every person in the United States has a heart, a stomach, and a brain, but over 45 million of those people do not have health care coverage.
   Ending: Government of the people, by the people, and for the people must make sure that all the people receive adequate health care.

3. **Beginning:** Health insurance companies, in order to protect their profitability, are free to deny coverage to those who most need it.
   Ending: A government-sponsored health care program is a more equitable way to ensure adequate health care for everyone.

Revise

Check your beginning and ending. Make sure they work together persuasively. If they do not, revise using one of the strategies above.

Struggling Learners

To extend the practice, have students form three groups. Assign one strategy to each group, without revealing the strategy to the others. Have each group work together to write a beginning and an ending that illustrate their strategy. Allow the groups to exchange their completed writings and identify the strategy used.

3 My beginning and ending should work together better, and my middle paragraphs should be rearranged.

2 I need to create an effective beginning and ending and organize the middle paragraphs.

1 I need help understanding how to organize a persuasive essay.

Are my middle paragraphs in the best order?

Your middle paragraphs are in the best order if your reasons are organized by importance. Here are three strategies for organizing your middle paragraphs:

1. **Start strong.** Place your most important reason first, give other reasons next, and end with your answer to an objection.
2. **End strong.** Begin with your least important reason and build to the most important reason. Then answer an objection.
3. **Try 2-3-1.** Begin with your second most important reason, provide your least important reason, and finish with your strongest reason. Then answer an objection.

Exercise

Read the following four reasons for universal health care and decide on an order for them. Indicate which strategy you chose and why.

1. Lack of universal health care harms children most.
2. Though some people point to higher taxes for socialized medicine, U.S. citizens already pay exorbitant amounts for medical insurance.
3. Citizens of Western nations with socialized medicine live an average of five years longer than citizens of the United States.
4. Universal health care would reduce infant mortality rates.

Revise

Check the order of your reasons. If your reasons do not have a clear order, use one of the strategies above to reorganize them.

Persuasive

Organization
Changes ensure that the beginning and ending work together.

> ~~Random~~   the best
> ⌃Testing for high school athletes is ~~one~~ way to prevent kids
> from using steroids. Right now, all across the United . . .

Exercise Answers

Before students begin the **Exercise** activity, have them identify the position that the four reasons support: The United States should have universal health care. Note also that different people will have different opinions about which reasons are the most important.

Possible answer, using strategy 3: Try 2–3–1.

2—Begin with the second most important point: Children are the ones harmed most by the lack of universal health care (sentence 1). A paragraph could discuss how lack of medical attention leads to lifelong problems.

3—Then develop the third most important point: Infant mortality would be reduced by universal health care (sentence 4). This would be an extension of the first reason.

1—Present the strongest reason: Statistics suggest that socialized medicine extends lives (sentence 3). A paragraph could analyze and compare statistics to argue that all U.S. citizens deserve access to universal health care.

Finally, the answer to the objection (taxes would be higher) is that citizens already pay high prices for medical insurance (sentence 2).

Struggling Learners

If students have difficulty ranking the reasons in their own essays, ask them to list the supporting details for each reason. Tell them to consider not only the number but also the strength of the details. Point out that the reason supported by the greatest number of strong details is most likely the strongest reason.

Revising **for** Voice

Focus on the idea of colloquial expressions (expressions used in everyday conversation).

- Remind students that the difference between colloquialism and cliches—overused expressions—can be slight.
- Note also that idioms—expressions with special meanings—have often become cliches.
- Encourage students to choose fresh wording over something they've often heard before—unless using a cliche is the point.

✳ For more about cliches and idioms, see SE pages 79 and 672–677, respectively.

Exercise
Answers

Possible Answers

1. Formal. *The government shouldn't invade citizens' privacy with non-court-ordered wiretaps and other such actions.*
2. Informal. *Leaders in Washington may think they can ignore the law, but they are mistaken.*
3. Informal. *When I talk on the phone with a relative or a friend, I assume our conversation is private.*
4. Informal. *We should vote for new leaders in the next election.*

242

Revising **for** Voice

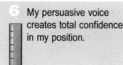

6 My persuasive voice creates total confidence in my position.

5 My level of language is appropriate, and I use an anecdote to connect with my reader.

4 In most places, my level of language is appropriate, but I could use a more engaging anecdote.

When you revise for *voice*, you make sure you have used the correct level of language and have connected with your reader. Follow the rubric strip above.

Have I used the correct level of language?

You have used the correct level of language if you use a semiformal voice. Here are three levels of voice:

- **Formal voice** avoids contractions, humor, colloquial expressions, slang, and personal references to the writer.
- **Semiformal voice** occasionally uses contractions and appropriate humor, colloquial expressions, and personal references to the writer. A semiformal voice avoids slang.
- **Informal voice** is full of contractions, humor, colloquial expressions, slang, and many personal references to the writer.

Exercise

Read each sentence below and decide whether the level of language is formal, semiformal, or informal. Rewrite formal or informal sentences to create an appropriate level of language.

1. Governmental interventions into the privacy of citizens through such means as non-court-ordered wiretaps should be eliminated.
2. Those Washington bigwigs maybe got it in their brains they can do whatever they want, but they got a big-time wake-up call coming.
3. Private phone lines are called private for a reason, and the government doesn't have the right to listen in on every call I make to Aunt Millie.
4. I say it's time to toss the fat cats from Capitol Hill.

Revise

Check your level of language. Read your draft, making sure that you have used a semiformal level of language. Revise parts that sound too formal or informal.

English Language Learners

People learning a new language have difficulty picking up and correctly using idiomatic expressions in speaking and writing. In light of the use of semiformal and informal language, review the difference between idioms and slang.

Then pair each student with a language-proficient student. Ask the language-proficient student to review the student's draft to see if the writer has used any idioms and, if so, whether she or he used them correctly. Have the reviewer make suggestions for places in which the language might sound more relaxed or natural if an idiom were used.

Advanced Learners

Challenge students to demonstrate understanding of the three levels of voice by writing three paragraphs conveying identical information. The first paragraph should use a formal voice; the second, a semiformal voice; and the third an informal voice. Post the paragraphs and have the class identify the voice of each.

Writing an Essay of Argumentation **243**

3 In a number of places, my writing sounds too formal or informal, and I need to add an anecdote.

2 My language level varies widely, and I should find an anecdote to include.

1 I need help understanding how to create an appropriate writing voice.

How can I connect with my audience?

One powerful way to connect with your audience is to use an anecdote. An anecdote is a little story that demonstrates a point. Anecdotes give the reader specific examples of the controversy's effects. To find an anecdote to include, ask yourself the following questions:

1. What experiences have I had that demonstrate the problem?
2. What experiences have people in my school or community had that show the effects of the controversy?
3. What stories in the news media provide examples that support my position?

Revise

Think of anecdotes. Consider adding a story to demonstrate your point in a way that connects with the reader.

Voice
An anecdote is added to connect with the reader.

In 2005, scandal rocked the world of professional baseball as allegations of the use of steroids and other performance-enhancing drugs hit the headlines. Responding to pressure by Congress, Major League Baseball instituted standards for testing players for the use of these drugs ("Baseball Battles"). However, the controversy extends far beyond the baseball diamond. ∧Steroids and other drugs that quickly build muscle mass and make athletes stronger and faster have permeated virtually all levels of athletics. For example, in the last five . . .

Persuasive

The reason anecdotes create a connection with the reader is that they are a form of "showing" instead of "telling." After reading an anecdote, the reader has vicariously experienced the issue firsthand.

Anecdotes abound. For issues that are local, students can think of their own experiences or ask friends and classmates about their experiences. For national or international stories, a little digging in current media or online will produce numerous anecdotes about the topic.

Struggling Learners

Read aloud several short pieces from the editorial or op-ed page of a local newspaper. Ask students to classify each one as either containing or lacking an anecdote. For the ones that do contain an anecdote, have students explain how the story enriches the writing for the reader. Help students decide if their topics lend themselves to anecdotes. If it seems possible to find anecdotes, help students brainstorm where they might find such stories.

Revising for Word Choice

Walk students through the process of evaluating the use of modifiers:

- Ask them to go through the draft and lightly circle every modifier with a pencil.
- Have students evaluate each adjective and eliminate unnecessary modifiers.
- Have students trade papers to evaluate the remaining modifiers in each other's essays. Do the modifiers help to clarify the meaning?

Exercise Answers

1. Congress passed legislation mandating the "least restrictive" environment for psychiatric patients.
2. The law emptied the nation's asylums since the least restrictive environment for people taking mental-health medications was not within the walls of asylums.
3. However, once the medicine ran out, homeless patients had a difficult time surviving on the streets.
4. Though some institutions have a bad reputation, others are well run and necessary.
5. When homelessness results from a psychological condition, the state should provide a home.

244

Revising for Word Choice

6 My word choice makes a powerful case for my position.

5 I have used only the best modifiers, and I have avoided overusing words.

4 I have a few unnecessary modifiers, and I may overuse a word or two.

When you revise for *word choice*, you check to make sure you have used only the best modifiers and have avoided repeating certain words too often. The rubric strip above can help you revise.

Have I used only the best modifiers?

You have used only the best modifiers if you have cut those that do not help to clarify your meaning. Here are types of modifiers that you should remove from your writing:

- "Waffle words" are modifiers that make your voice sound uncertain.
  It's kind of sad that government doesn't care very much about homelessness.

- Redundant modifiers are words that aren't needed.
  The desperate plight of the indigent homeless is terribly depressing.

- Strings of modifiers should be replaced with one strong modifier.
  The number of young, inexperienced, teenaged people who are homeless is rising.

Exercise

Rewrite each sentence below, removing the unnecessary modifiers.

1. Congressional legislators passed legal legislation mandating the "least restrictive" environment for mental psychiatric patients.
2. The law sort of emptied the nation's asylums since the least restrictive environment for people taking prescription mental-health medications was not within the walls of an asylum.
3. However, once the medicine ran out, the patients had a rough, difficult, troubling time surviving homeless on the streets.
4. Though some institutional asylums have gotten a bad, negative, unpleasant reputation, others are well run and kind of necessary.
5. Homelessness sometimes maybe results from a psychological mental condition, so the state should provide a home.

Revise

Check your modifiers. Read your essay, watching for "waffle words," redundant modifiers, and strings of modifiers. Cut any you find.

Grammar Connection

Modifiers

- *Write Source* pages 84, 88
- **Proofreader's Guide** pages 610 (+), 728 (+), 730–731
- *SkillsBook* pages 98, 99, 103, 166, 167

English Language Learners

Students may find the term *waffle words* confusing. Explain that the noun *waffle* names a breakfast food made from batter that is cooked evenly on both sides in a press. The verb *to waffle* means "to speak or write in a vague or misleading way." When writers use waffle words, they sound so unconvincing that they actually help the other side of the argument.

Writing an Essay of Argumentation **245**

3 I need to cut many unnecessary modifiers and remove repeated words.

2 My modifiers do not make my ideas clear, and I have repeated many words.

1 I need help understanding how to improve word choice.

How can I avoid repeating the same word too often?

You can avoid repeating the same word over and over by using one of the following strategies:

- Replace the word with an appropriate synonym.

  medicine   prescription   pharmaceutical   controlled substance

- Replace the word with a pronoun, making sure the antecedent is clear.

  it   they   he   she   one   some   many   few

- Rewrite sentences to avoid the word.

  Instead of . . . When there's no money to buy medications, people will stop taking their medications.

  Write . . . Without money to refill prescriptions, people will discontinue their medications.

Write

Replace overused words. Read your work, watching for overused words. Replace them with synonyms or pronouns, or rewrite the sentence to eliminate the repetition.

Word Choice
Sentences are reworked to avoid repetition.

> Also, because ~~student athletes know that~~ steroids and other performance-enhancing drugs are illegal, most student athletes realize that getting caught with ~~performance-enhancing drugs~~ them would mean immediate expulsion from sports. As a result, student athletes will do everything they can to cover up their use. Peer pressure only reinforces . . .

Persuasive

Note that one of the best ways for students to spot overused words is to read the draft aloud or have someone else read it to them. As students do more writing, they may discover that they have a tendency to overuse certain words, and they can learn to watch carefully for them. Mention some types of commonly overused words that students might notice.

- Intensifying modifiers such as *very* and *really*
- The conjunction *and:* This is especially common when a writer has many ideas and details to fit in.
- The word *that:* Because this word can serve as so many different parts of speech, it's easy to overuse. *(That man said that that book that he was reading wasn't all that interesting.)*
- Forms of *to be:* When *is* and *was*—and other forms of *to be*—are repeated too often, writing becomes bland and sluggish. Substituting active verbs will often strengthen the writing.

English Language Learners

Point out to students that in everyday conversation, people often use a plural pronoun with a singular antecedent: *Everybody has their textbook in class today. A student should be clear about their choice of subjects.* Tell students that in writing, they should make sure that the subject and the antecedent agree in number:

Everybody has his or her textbook in class today. Students should be clear about their choice of subjects.

Revising for Sentence Fluency

Review the 5 W's and H questions, reminding students that the answers to them make up the core—the basic meaning—of any information, written or spoken.

To make certain that students understand the grammatical terms used on the page, review the meanings of and provide additional examples of

■ prepositional phrases,
■ subordinate clauses,
■ infinitive phrases, and
■ cumulative sentences.

✳ For more about phrases and clauses, see SE pages 742–745.

✳ For more about prepositions, see SE page 732.

246

Revising for Sentence Fluency

6 My sentences spark the reader's interest in my position.

5 I have effectively used long and short sentences in my essay.

4 I have used some short sentences for effect, but I should expand some sentences.

When you revise for *sentence fluency,* you check to see whether you have used long and short sentences effectively. The rubric strip above can guide your revision.

When should I use long sentences?

You should use long sentences to convey a wealth of information about a complex issue. Consider this short sentence:

Stem-cell researchers conduct experiments.

This sentence answers *who* (stem-cell researchers) and *what* (conduct experiments), but it does not provide other details the reader needs, such as *where, why,* and *how*:

1. *Where?* in states where it is allowed (prepositional phrase and subordinate clause)
2. *How?* by injecting undifferentiated cells into damaged areas (prepositional phrases)
3. *Why?* to reconstruct tissues (infinitive phrase)

These answers can be added to the original sentence to create a cumulative sentence that is full of detail. (For more about cumulative sentences, see page 750.)

In states where it is allowed, stem-cell researchers conduct experiments by injecting undifferentiated cells into damaged areas to reconstruct tissues.

Revise

Create cumulative sentences. Read your writing and watch for short sentences that do not provide enough detail. For each sentence, answer the following questions, using prepositional phrases, infinitive phrases, and subordinate clauses.

1. Where?   **3.** How?
2. When?   **4.** Why?

Combine some of your answers with the original sentence to create a cumulative sentence.

Grammar Connection

Sentence Types

■ **Proofreader's Guide** page 746 (+)
■ *SkillsBook* page 134
■ *GrammarSnap* Sentence Types: Compound, Complex, and Compound-Complex Sentences

Struggling Learners

Students who have difficulty creating cumulative sentences may benefit from using a 5 W's chart. Distribute photocopies of the reproducible chart (TE page 822). Have them complete the graphic organizer for some of the shorter sentences in their writing. The completed organizer will highlight the type of details that could be incorporated to create a cumulative sentence.

Writing an Essay of Argumentation **247**

3 I need to expand a number of sentences and use short sentences to punctuate my ideas.

2 My sentences have little rhythm, and I need to use long and short sentences more effectively.

1 I need help understanding how to create sentence fluency.

When should I use short sentences?

You should use short sentences to make an important point. When constructed carefully, short sentences pack a punch—and improve sentence rhythm. Note the power of the short sentences in the following paragraph.

> Both sides of the stem-cell research controversy believe they hold the moral high ground. Those who oppose stem-cell research feel they are advocating for the tens of thousands of frozen embryos that scientists may use in their research. Those who favor stem-cell research feel they are advocating for the millions of people living with neuromuscular diseases. Both sides are correct. Albert Schweitzer once said, "It is good to maintain and further life; it is bad to damage and destroy life." These are wise words. The best use of stem-cell research maintains and furthers life on both ends of the scale—using adult instead of embryonic stem cells.

Revise

Employ short sentences. Read your work carefully, looking for places where you want to make a strong point. Insert a short sentence that makes the point.

Sentence Fluency

A cumulative sentence and a short sentence improve flow.

Persuasive

, causing unprovoked rage and violence among users

In addition, these drugs can affect mental health.

Sometimes the mood swings lead to depression and
~~That fact makes these drugs doubly deadly.~~
even suicide. Fortunately, if treatment is provided soon

enough, most of these health issues can be avoided or

reversed—another reason for supporting mandatory

testing ("Anabolic").

Of course, some civil rights advocates believe that

random testing for performance-enhancing drugs . . .

Draw attention to the way the writer's short sentences make the voice sound confident and knowledgeable. Because they are straightforward, declarative sentences, with few or no extra words to distract the reader, they convey a sense of certainty.

Note that overuse of short sentences, however, can lead to an undesirable choppy rhythm. Encourage students to think of short sentences as spice; they are a good way to impart tang to their writing, when purposefully and moderately used.

＊ For more ways to improve sentence fluency, see SE pages 81–88.

Revising **Improving Your Writing**

Note that most of the items on this checklist connect directly to the revising strategies provided on pages 237–247. The checklist, therefore, can help students pinpoint which strategies they need to use to complete their revisions. A student who can honestly answer "yes" to an item does not need to employ the revision strategy that connects to that item.

Writing Workshop

This revising checklist can help guide students during individual work time. You can assign each student to use the checklist to determine what areas need revision, and then choose two or three of the items to revise for. You can also use the checklist to group students so that those who need to work on ideas can meet for a minilesson with you, and then you present a separate minilesson for those who need to work on organization, and so forth.

Revising **Improving Your Writing**

 Check your revising. On a piece of paper, write the numbers 1 to 12. If you answer "yes" to a question below, put a check mark next to that number. If not, continue to work on that part of your essay.

Revising Checklist

Ideas

_____ **1.** Do I state my position clearly?

_____ **2.** Have I effectively supported each topic sentence?

_____ **3.** Have I fairly presented my position and avoided logical fallacies?

Organization

_____ **4.** Do my beginning and ending work together well?

_____ **5.** Have I chosen the best order for my middle paragraphs?

_____ **6.** Are my reasons connected logically?

Voice

_____ **7.** Have I used the right level of language?

_____ **8.** Does my voice connect with my audience?

Word Choice

_____ **9.** Have I used the best modifiers?

_____ **10.** Have I avoided repeating words too often?

Sentence Fluency

_____ **11.** Have I used longer sentences to provide a wealth of information?

_____ **12.** Have I used shorter sentences to deliver precise points?

Make a clean copy. When you are finished with your revision, make a clean copy of your article for editing.

Grammar Connection

Complete Sentences

- **Write Source** page 86
- **Proofreader's Guide** pages 738 (+), 740 (+)
- **SkillsBook** pages 162–163
- **GrammarSnap** Complete Sentences and Sentence Fragments

Struggling Learners

Refer students to SE pages 678–699. Point out that this section, which lists words alphabetically, is a quick reference to the right word as they write.

Editing

Now that you have finished revising your essay of argumentation, you are ready to edit for conventions: punctuation, capitalization, spelling, and grammar.

Keys to Effective Editing

1. Use a dictionary, a thesaurus, and the "Proofreader's Guide" in the back of this book to check your writing.

2. Check for errors in punctuation, capitalization, spelling, and grammar.

3. Edit on a clean revised copy of your essay. Then either enter the changes on your computer file or write a new handwritten copy that includes the changes.

4. Use the editing and proofreading marks on the inside back cover of this book.

Persuasive

Editing

Keys to Effective Editing

Remind students that during the editing stage, they have a chance to find and correct errors in

- punctuation,
- capitalization,
- spelling, and
- grammar.

The Keys to Effective Editing list explains the process students will be guided through on SE pages 250–252.

Remind students that it is a good idea, if possible, to take a day or two away from a draft before they edit. This helps them look at it with a fresh perspective.

Peer Responding

Suggest that each student **find a peer editor** *(see below)*—preferably a person who is good at spotting conventions errors.

Technology Connections

Students can use the added features of the Net-text as they explore this stage of the writing process.

Write Source Online Net-text

Teaching Tip: Find a Peer Editor

Suggest that students find a writing partner to work with for the long term. Peer editing can help students improve as writers. Advantages include

- having a partner who will double-check their work,

- working with a partner in the writing class or with someone who has to write regularly for another class, and
- learning another writer's strengths and weaknesses and tracking each other's progress.

Editing for Conventions

To expand on the information on the page, review compound predicates.

- Challenge students to define a compound predicate. (More than one verb that share the same subject, such as *Mary read* Beowulf *and wrote an essay about it.*)
- Note that the compound verbs must agree with the subject in number, but they don't have to have the same form. For example, one verb may be past tense and the other may be future tense: *Mary read* Beowulf *in twelfth grade and will read it again in college.*
- Remind students that they do not have to place a comma before the coordinating conjunction that connects compound predicates, unless they feel it is necessary for clarity or emphasis: *Mary read, and chose to write about,* Beowulf.

✳ For more information about the agreement of subject and verb, see SE pages 752–755.

✳ For more about compound predicates, see SE page 740.

250

Editing for Conventions

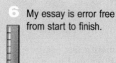

6 My essay is error free from start to finish.

5 I have one or two errors, but they don't distract the reader.

4 I need to correct a few errors in my paper that may distract the reader.

When you edit for *conventions,* you correct punctuation, capitalization, spelling, and grammar errors. The rubric strip above can guide your editing.

How can I check subject-verb agreement?

Check subject-verb agreement by making sure subjects and verbs have the same number. If the subject is singular, the verb must be singular. If the subject is plural, the verb must be plural.

> The doctrine of preemptive war has many detractors.
> Critics argue that preemptive war is like punishing a person before any crime has been committed.

Compound Subjects

If the compound subjects are joined by *and,* use a plural verb.

> The president *and* the secretary of defense contend that it is better to preempt an attack than retaliate after one has taken place.

If the subjects are joined by *or* or *nor,* match the verb to the nearest subject.

> Even so, neither diplomacy *nor* war has eliminated terrorism.

Indefinite Pronouns

Some indefinite pronouns are singular: *each, either, neither, one, everybody, another, anybody, everyone, nobody, everything, somebody,* and *someone.*

> Nobody wants war.

Some indefinite pronouns are plural: *both, few, many,* and *several.*

> Many believe that war is necessary to stop tyranny.

Some indefinite pronouns are singular or plural, depending on the object in the prepositional phrase that follows the pronoun: *all, any, most, none,* and *some.*

> Most of the world participates in the war on terrorism.
> Most of the nations, however, oppose the doctrine of preemptive war.

Edit

Check agreement. Read your position essay and check for the agreement of your subjects and verbs. Make any necessary corrections.

Writing an Essay of Argumentation **251**

3 I need to correct several errors in my paper because they confuse the reader.

2 I need to correct many errors because they make my essay difficult to read.

1 I need help finding errors and making corrections.

How can I check pronoun-antecedent agreement?

To check pronoun-antecedent agreement, make sure pronouns have the same number and gender as the nouns they replace.

Incorrect: Each politician should make their position clear.
(*Politician* is singular, but *their* is plural.)

Incorrect: Each politician should make his position clear.
(The word *his* makes a sexist assumption about the gender of the politician.)

Correct: Each politician should make his or her position clear.
(The singular *politician* needs singular male and female pronouns.)

Correct: Politicians should make their positions clear.
(*Politicians* and *their* are both plural.)

Grammar Exercise

Rewrite each sentence below, correcting the pronoun-antecedent errors.

1. Every member of Congress must vote his conscience.
2. Each voter must cherish their right to vote.
3. The representative from each district should tell where they stand.

Edit

Check pronoun-antecedent agreement. Read your essay carefully, checking to make sure that pronouns and antecedents agree in number and gender. Make any necessary corrections.

Conventions
Pronoun-antecedent errors are corrected.

> Random drug testing is a way of publicly telling athletes
> that adults care about what students do in ~~his or her~~ *their*
> private lives and want to see ~~him or her~~ *them* make good decisions.

Persuasive

Remind students to take care not to create ambiguity with their pronoun usage. The antecedent to which the pronoun refers must be clear. Provide examples of ambiguous pronouns and ask students to suggest revisions. For example: *Angela told Kendra that she couldn't go to the party.* (Who can't go to the party?)

■ Clarify: *Angela couldn't go to the party, and she told Kendra so;* or
■ Clarify: *Angela told Kendra that Kendra couldn't go to the party.*

✱ For more about the agreement of pronoun and antecedent, see SE page 756.

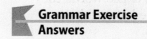
Grammar Exercise
Answers

Possible Answers

1. Every member of Congress must vote his or her conscience.
2. Voters must cherish their right to vote. (*Or omit pronoun:* Each voter must cherish the right to vote.)
3. The representative from each district should tell where he or she stands.

Struggling Learners

Some students will benefit from additional review of pronoun-antecedent agreement. Write the following sentences on the board. Invite volunteers to draw an arrow from the pronoun to its antecedent. Then have students rewrite the sentences, correcting the errors.

1. *Members* of the team should do *his* best to show good sportsmanship. (*Members* of the team should do *their* best to show good sportsmanship.)

2. Each *physician* will decide how *they* want to be introduced. (Each *physician* will decide how *she* or *he* wants to be introduced.)

3. Every *student* has the right to express *their* opinion. (Every *student* has the right to express *his* or *her* opinion.)

Grammar Connection

Subject-Verb Agreement
■ **Proofreader's Guide** pages 738 (+), 740 (+), 752–753, 754–755
■ *SkillsBook* pages 141–142
■ *GrammarSnap* Subject-Verb Agreement with Compound Sentences, Subject Verb Agreement with Indefinite Pronouns

Pronoun-Antecedent Agreement
■ **Proofreader's Guide** page 756 (+)
■ *SkillsBook* page 146
■ *GrammarSnap* Pronoun-Antecedent Agreement

Editing Checking for Conventions

Give students a few moments to look over the Proofreader's Guide (SE pages 604–763). Remind them that throughout the year, they can refer to the instruction, rules, and examples to clarify any checklist items or to resolve questions about their own writing.

Students will benefit from regular discussion of commonly misused words (see item 7). Consider focusing on a tricky word or word sets each day, showing how the words are misused and giving examples of correct usage. Encourage students also to keep a running list of the words they often confuse. Studying the list will help students master the words.

✳ For a long list of commonly misused word pairs, see SE pages 678–697.

Creating a Title

Suggest that students who haven't decided on a title take 10 minutes to brainstorm a list of ideas. Emphasize that the goal is to let ideas flow—without worrying whether any of them are usable. Afterward, have them exchange lists and have partners look through the list for the one that captures their interest.

252

Editing Checking for Conventions

 Check your editing. On a piece of paper, write the numbers 1 to 10. If you can answer "yes" to a question below, put a check mark after that number. If you can't, continue to edit for that convention.

Editing Checklist

Conventions

PUNCTUATION

_____ **1.** Do I use end punctuation after all my sentences?
_____ **2.** Do I use commas after long introductory phrases and clauses?
_____ **3.** Have I correctly punctuated quotations?

CAPITALIZATION

_____ **4.** Do I start all my sentences with capital letters?
_____ **5.** Do I capitalize all proper nouns and adjectives?

SPELLING

_____ **6.** Have I spelled all words correctly?
_____ **7.** Have I checked for commonly misused pairs?

GRAMMAR

_____ **8.** Do my subjects and verbs agree in number?
_____ **9.** Do my pronouns and antecedents agree in number and gender?
_____ **10.** Have I avoided double subjects?

Creating a Title

After your editing is complete, add a title that engages your reader and sums up the content of your essay. Here are a few ways to create an effective essay title.

- Call the reader to action: **Test for Performance Drugs Now**
- Take a position: **Performance Drug Testing Just Makes Sense**
- Be creative: **Stop Steroids Cold**

Grammar Connection

Commas
- **Proofreader's Guide** page 610 (+)
- *SkillsBook* page 9
- *GrammarSnap* Common Uses of Commas; Commas after Introductory Words, Phrases, and Clauses

Tenses and Irregular Verbs
- **Proofreader's Guide** pages 720–721, 722 (+)
- *SkillsBook* pages 89, 90, 94, 95

- *GrammarSnap* Verb Tense Overview

Hyphens and Dashes
- **Proofreader's Guide** pages 624–625, 626–627, 640–641
- *SkillsBook* pages 22, 23, 24

Spelling
- **Proofreader's Guide** pages 664–665
- *SkillsBook* pages 51, 52

Advanced Learners

After reviewing the strategies and sample titles at the bottom of the page, have students generate a list of interesting titles that demonstrate other ways to catch a reader's attention. Publish their list of titles in the classroom.

Writing an Essay of Argumentation **253**

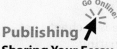

Publishing Sharing Your Essay

The purpose of an essay of argumentation is to take a position on a controversial issue and defend the position using ideas and details. Once you've done this, it's time to share what you've written.

Publish

Format your final copy. To format a handwritten essay, use the guidelines below or follow your teacher's instructions. (If you are using a computer, see pages **91–95**.) Make a clean copy and carefully proofread it.

Focusing on Presentation

- Write neatly using blue or black ink.
- Place your name in the upper left corner of page 1.
- Skip a line and center your title; then skip a line and start your essay.
- Indent every paragraph and leave a one-inch margin on all four sides.
- Write your last name and the page number in the upper right corner of every page after page 1.

Publish Your Essay

Check the guidelines of local newspapers to see which ones might be interested in your essay. Format your paper according to the guidelines, write a cover letter (or an e-mail message) introducing yourself, and send in your essay.

Self-Publish Your Work

Use a personal computer to format your essay. Add photographs or illustrations. Work with the layout and design until you feel your essay is clear and compelling. Then print copies of your work and mail them to relatives or post copies on school or library bulletin boards. (Get permission first.)

Stage a Debate

Find a classmate who takes the position opposite to the one expressed in your essay. Invite him or her to prepare an essay stating this position. Then stage a debate by reading your essays publicly. Invite a panel of students and teachers to judge which essay makes its point most effectively.

Persuasive

Publishing

Sharing Your Essay

Note that one of the best ways to get an essay of argumentation published is to revise it into the form of a letter to the editor of a newspaper.

Another possibility lies in the op-ed pages that some newspapers have. They accept essays on topics of interest to readers. If an essay is strong enough, it would generate its own stream of response letters.

Make sure that students inform the class when they have writing that is accepted for publication. If possible, obtain a copy of the published work for display in the classroom.

Technology Connections

Remind students that they can use the Writing Network features of the Portfolio to share their work with peers.

Write Source Online **Portfolio**

Write Source Online **Net-text**

Advanced Learners

Discuss the rules of a debate with students, focusing on ways to counter objections. Then have students work in small groups to plan and stage a debate. The debate topic should be a position a group member expressed in an essay of argumentation. Have students form two teams—pro and con. Have the "pro" team do additional research and revise the paper's position to strengthen the essay if necessary. Have the "con" team work together to prepare an essay that advocates the position opposite to the one expressed in the original essay. Stage the debate by having group members take turns reading the essays aloud with appropriate expression. Invite a panel of judges to assess which essay makes its point more effectively and why.

Rubric for Persuasive Writing

Remind students that a rubric is a chart that helps writers evaluate their writing.

- The rubrics in this book are based on a six-point scale, in which a score of 6 indicates an amazing piece of writing and a score of 1 means the writing is incomplete and not ready to be assessed.
- Explain to students that the purpose of the rubric is to help them break down the assessment process by evaluating each of the six traits individually—ideas, organization, voice, word choice, sentence fluency, and conventions.
- Point out that rubrics are also helpful during the writing process. Rubrics can guide writers whenever they write because they tell what elements to include in the writing and how to present them.
- Explain to students that they will most likely have different ratings for the traits. For example, they may give themselves a 5 for ideas but a 4 for organization.

✳ Reproducible six-, five-, and four-point rubrics for persuasive writing can be found on pages 769, 773, and 777.

254

Rubric for Persuasive Writing

Use this rubric to assess your persuasive writing using the six traits.

	6	**5**	**4**
Ideas	The position is convincingly presented and supported; it compels the reader to act.	The position is supported with logical reasons; an important objection is countered.	Most of the reasons support the writer's position. An objection is addressed.
Organization	All parts of the essay work together to build a very thoughtful, convincing position.	The opening states the position, the middle provides clear support, and the ending reinforces the position.	Most parts of the essay are organized adequately except for one part.
Voice	The writer's voice is completely confident, knowledgeable, and convincing.	The writer's voice is persuasive, knowledgeable, and respectful.	The writer respects the audience but needs to sound more persuasive or knowledgeable.
Word Choice	The writer's choice of words makes a powerful case.	The writer's word choice helps persuade the reader.	The writer avoids unneeded modifiers but needs to remove some repetition.
Sentence Fluency	The sentences flow smoothly throughout the strong essay.	Variety is seen in the types of sentences used and in their beginnings.	Variety is seen in most of the sentences.
Conventions	The writing is error free.	Grammar and punctuation errors are few. The reader is not distracted by the errors.	Distracting grammar and punctuation errors are seen in a few sentences.

Writing an Essay of Argumentation **255**

3	**2**	**1**
More supporting reasons and a more convincing response to an objection are needed.	A clearer position statement is needed. Better support for the position must be provided.	A new position statement and reasons are needed.
Some parts of the essay need to be reorganized.	The beginning, middle, and ending run together.	The organization is unclear and incomplete.
The writer's voice needs to be more persuasive and respectful.	The writer's voice sounds too emotional and unconvincing.	The writer needs to learn about voice in persuasive writing.
The writer needs to change modifiers and remove some repetition.	The words do not create a clear message. Some words are repeated.	Word choice for persuasive writing has not been considered.
More variety is needed in the beginnings or kinds of sentences used.	Too many sentences are worded in the same way.	Sentence fluency has not been considered.
There are a number of errors that will confuse the reader.	Frequent errors make the essay difficult to read.	Nearly every sentence contains errors.

Persuasive

Test Prep!

The six traits of writing were first identified in the 1960s by Paul Diederich and a group of 50 professionals who reviewed student papers and brainstormed the qualities that made writing strong. In 1983, a group of educators in Beaverton, Oregon, learned of Diederich's work and replicated it, settling on a similar set of six traits. A separate team in Missoula, Montana, simultaneously ran a study that identified the same basic group of traits.

Put simply, the six traits provide a universal set of criteria for strong writing. They correlate very well to the rubrics used in most state testing. Using the traits throughout the writing process, therefore, prepares students for any writing test they will face.

Evaluating an Essay of Argumentation

Ask students if they agree with the sample self-assessment on SE page 257. If they agree with the overall comments, ask them to suggest improvements based on the comments. If they disagree, ask them to explain why.

Ideas—The details used need to be stronger and more varied. The essay does not include facts such as dates, names, or specific examples; there are no statistics or quotes provided.

Voice—Without specific details, the voice sounds less authoritative.

Word Choice—The language should be trimmed to be stronger and more direct. For example:

- *news information* (paragraph 2) is redundant;
- the adverb is not needed in *directly affects* (paragraph 2);
- use of the passive voice in *while the war itself is prosecuted* (paragraph 3) weakens the sentence;
- extra words are included in *the freedom of the media is one on which our system of government was founded*—it could be *our government was founded on freedom of the press*.

Conventions—Errors include

- *war time* (instead of *wartime*) in paragraph 2 and
- *American* (instead of *America*) in paragraph 4.

Evaluating an Essay of Argumentation

Read the essay of argumentation below and focus on its strengths and weaknesses. Then read the student self-assessment on the next page. (**The student essay below contains some errors.**)

A Free Media Helps Us—Even in War Time

During recent years, the U.S. Government limited the ability of the media to report freely from the war zone. Instead, reporters were embedded, or placed within selected military units, where their movements were controlled. Free speech advocates decried the move to limit the reporters' access, but the government insisted that the efforts were necessary both to protect reporters' safety and to avoid leaking information that might be valuable to the enemy. However, even during wartime, the benefits of a free media outweigh the risks.

At a time of national crisis, people need to be able to trust the government. If government manipulates the media, then this trust can be lost. Any number of military secrets must be kept during war time, but the release of general news information does not compromise military intelligence. Denying citizens basic information about the conduct of the war not only denies them a right to information that directly affects them but creates a suspicion of the government that can weaken the country.

In addition, a free media helps deliver the information the citizens need to make decisions about the conduct of the war. While the war itself is prosecuted by our armed forces, those very forces are drawn from the ranks of citizens. And while the decision to go to war and even continue to fight is made by government, the government acts at the will of the people. If the people are denied the information they need, the input they provide to their representatives about the war will be inaccurate, and the government will not be able to express the people's will.

Most critically, the freedom of the media is one on which our system of government was founded. The media of colonial American helped create the uprising against tyranny that led to the formation of our free nation, and the Constitution guaranteed the free press in the First Amendment. Even today, media freedom helps protect the people against a government that may act in the best interests of a few instead of that of the vast majority.

Some might argue that during wartime, we must allow the government to decide what information we can see and hear, and that the free flow of information compromises our battlefield plans.

English Language Learners

Discuss the meanings of the following terms to aid students' comprehension of the essay.

- decried (expressed a low opinion)
- compromise (to make vulnerable or susceptible to harm)
- conduct (behavior or action)
- inaccurate (false or incorrect)
- tyranny (absolute power that is used unjustly)
- enable (to supply with the means, opportunity, or knowledge to do something)

However, there has been little evidence that the media has ever compromised a military operation. In fact, media has often informed the public of the results of military operations, providing the public with critical information about the conduct of the war.

Our soldiers fight to defend our freedoms, including freedom of the press. A free press during wartime gives citizens valuable information without compromising military secrecy. Free reporting on the war might even enable our nation to avoid some costly political and military mistakes. So support a free media during wartime—your actions might even save a soldier's life.

Student Self-Assessment

Persuasive Rubric Checklist

Title: _A Free Media Helps Us—Even in War Time_
Writer: _Cole Margolis_

 4 **Ideas**
- Does my essay include a clear position statement?
- Do I support my position with reasons and details?
- Do I avoid logic errors?

5 **Organization**
- Does the beginning introduce the topic and state the position?
- Does the middle support my position?
- Does my ending restate the position and offer a final thought?

 4 **Voice**
- Do I use the right level of language?
- Do I connect with the reader?

 4 **Word Choice**
- Have I used only necessary modifiers?
- Have I avoided repeating words too often?

 4 **Sentence Fluency**
- Do I use long sentences effectively?
- Do I use short sentences effectively?

 4 **Conventions**
- Have I avoided most errors in punctuation, capitalization, spelling, and grammar?

OVERALL COMMENTS:

I think my essay does a good job of explaining the controversy and arguing for my position.

I use the right language level and engage my reader. I should have included some synonyms for the word "media" and used more sentence variety.

I guess I used an appeal to ignorance in the last middle paragraph.

My essay includes a few errors, so I should have proofread one more time.

Persuasive

 Review your essay. Rate your essay and write comments that explain why you gave yourself the scores you did.

Advanced Learners

Divide students into four groups. Assign each group one of the following traits: Ideas, Voice, Word Choice, Sentence Fluency, and Conventions. Have group members work together to rewrite the essay so that it receives a score of 6 for the trait assigned. Encourage students to refer to the rubric on SE pages 254–255 when deciding how to improve the essay.

Benchmark Papers

Creatine Crazy (good)
- TE pp. 802–806

Environmental Pollution (fair)
- TE pp. 807–811

Student Self-Assessment

To give students practice with evaluating a persuasive essay, use a reproducible assessment sheet (TE page 766), the Persuasive Rubric Checklist (TE page 781), and one or both of the **benchmark papers** listed in the Benchmark Papers box below.

For your benefit, a completed checklist and a comments sheet are provided for each benchmark paper.

Acknowledge that it can be difficult for students to look at their own work objectively. To help them get a sense of how well they did, fill out the same checklist students use as part of your own evaluation of their essays. This will allow them to directly compare the scores.

Reflecting on Your Writing

Set aside class time for students to complete their reflection sheets. Encourage them not only to complete the suggested sentence starters but also to add any other thoughts they have about their essays.

Remind them to write the date and essay title on the page and to file it in their portfolio, along with

- the planning notes,
- drafts, and
- the final copy of the essay.

Encourage students to look back at their reflections from time to time. This practice will remind them of techniques they found helpful, problems they need to work on, and ideas for future projects.

258

Reflecting on Your Writing

Now that you have completed your essay of argumentation, take some time to reflect on your writing experience. On a separate sheet of paper, complete each sentence below.

My Essay of Argumentation

1. The strongest part of my essay is . . .

2. The part that still needs work is . . .

3. The prewriting activity that worked best for me was . . .

4. The main thing I learned about writing an essay of argumentation is . . .

5. In my next essay of argumentation, I would like to . . .

6. One question I still have about writing an essay of argumentation is . . .

259

Persuasive Writing
Writing an Essay of Evaluation

In popular magazines, you're sure to find articles that explore current trends, new products, businesses, organizations, and so on. An article in one magazine may explore a new trend in health and fitness. An article in another magazine may assess the effectiveness of a nonprofit group. These articles usually evaluate the topic's value and significance, its strengths and weaknesses, and its overall place in the scheme of things.

In this chapter, you will read a sample essay in which a student evaluates a particular elective class. Then you will write your own essay of evaluation. Remember to look at both the pros and cons of the topic so you can develop a thoughtful, convincing piece of writing.

Writing Guidelines

Subject: A current trend, product, or group
Form: Essay of evaluation
Purpose: To present a thoughtful assessment
Audience: Classmates

"Whatever is popular deserves attention."
—James Mackintosh

Copy Masters

T-chart (TE pp. 263, 266)

Writing an Essay of Evaluation

Objectives
- understand the form and content of an essay of evaluation
- use what has been learned about persuasive writing to write an essay of evaluation
- plan, draft, revise, edit, and share an essay of evaluation

Point out that when students read a review of a product, a book, or a performance, they are reading an essay of evaluation. The writer's goal is to convince them whether or not to try the product, read the book, or take in the performance.

Make available a selection of magazine and/ or newspaper reviews for students to examine before they begin their own essays. As they work through their essays, encourage students to look again at these articles (and to find new ones) to see how the writers address the topics under review.

Essay of Evaluation

Have students review the rubric for persuasive writing on SE pages 254–255. Ask them questions to help them focus on how well the writer accomplished the goals of the essay.

- *How does the writer begin the essay?* It begins with a humorous and engaging description of a few elements of the class.
- *How does the writer organize the middle section?* The first two paragraphs are organized chronologically and also describe two different approaches to the subject matter (analysis and practice). The second two paragraphs are devoted to the highlight of the course and a negative aspect, respectively.
- *How does the writer convey his interest in the topic?* The many details provided, as well as word choices such as *great horror stories*; *best feature of the class*; *wealth of knowledge*; and *terrific, fascinating course.*
- *How does the writer end the piece?* With an inspiring quotation from a play.

260

Essay of Evaluation

An essay of evaluation tells the value of something. It describes the subject and gives an opinion about its worth, providing details to support the opinion. The following essay evaluates a senior-level class.

Beginning
The beginning introduces the topic and provides a thesis statement (underlined).

Middle
Each middle paragraph describes part of the topic and tells what is good (and bad) about it.

To Act or Not to Act

Only one class at Greendale High School lets students dress up like singing candlesticks, carve rocks from foam, and play double-blind freeze. The class is Drama and Theater, which is taught by Mr. Maclay. But it isn't all fun and games. The course also includes a serious study of plays throughout time and analysis of how plays are put together. Drama and Theater begins by pouring knowledge into students' heads and ends by requiring students to pour out that knowledge onstage.

The first half of the course is devoted to drama, which is the study of the history, variety, and structure of plays. The course covers plays that range from ancient to modern, from classics by playwrights like Shakespeare and O'Neill to obscure and experimental plays. Students learn to interpret drama, which is an essential skill for anyone in theater. Actors and directors must interpret drama to give an authentic performance; technical people must interpret drama to design effective sets, lighting, and sound; and theater managers and promoters must interpret drama to schedule shows and attract audiences.

The second half of the course focuses on theater— which is the art of putting on a play. Students must complete projects in many areas of theater production: lighting, set and costume design, makeup, stage management, directing, and acting. This requirement means that everyone learns what it is like for the other people involved in a production. Often, actors and crews hang together and exclude other groups. Mr. Maclay told us some great horror stories about techie-actor wars from shows he was in. By the time of our final production, our class was a close-knit theater group that worked well together under stress.

The best feature of the class, though, is Mr. Maclay himself, whose philosophy of teaching and acting is expressed in the words of Polonius: "To thine own self be true" (*Hamlet* 1.3.78). Mr. Maclay has appeared in famous

English Language Learners

Before reading the essay, discuss the meanings of the following terms:
- obscure (hidden; not well-known, undistinguished)
- authentic (believable; real)
- prestigious (renowned, prominent)
- soliloquy (dramatic dialogue in which a character speaks to himself)

regional theaters like the Guthrie in Minneapolis and has performed with prestigious theater companies such as Steppenwolf in Chicago. He has a wealth of knowledge and stories that he uses as he teaches. For instance, instead of simply saying that mistakes happen onstage, Mr. Maclay tells how he once tripped on his coat and almost knocked Nicole Parker of *MAD TV* off the stage when they were in a summer production of *The Sound of Music*. His stories are educational, entertaining, and inspirational. Mr. Maclay expects a great deal of himself and of his students, and he inspires everyone to rise to the challenge.

Sometimes, however, Mr. Maclay's ambitions exceed his students' abilities. For example, he places too much emphasis on advanced acting techniques. Chekhov, Meisner, and Stanislavsky may have wonderful methods for acting, but, to rephrase Polonius: "Though this be method, yet there is madness in it" (*Hamlet* 2.2.206). Mr. Maclay requires each student to memorize a Shakespearean soliloquy and recite it for the class. After the students nervously deliver their speeches, Mr. Maclay calls them up again to redeliver the soliloquies in different ways: as fast as possible, as loud as possible, sarcastically, with gestures for each word, like cartoon characters. Few students can rise to this challenge.

Ending
The ending sums up the evaluation and leaves the reader with a final thought.

Overall, Drama and Theater is a fascinating course. Mr. Maclay expects great things of his students, and most often students surprise themselves by meeting or exceeding his expectations. Even when Mr. Maclay pushes students beyond their abilities, they realize how much they need to learn. He teaches his students that "We are such stuff as dreams are made on" (*The Tempest* 4.1.156).

Persuasive

 Respond to the reading. Answer the following questions.

> **Ideas** (1) What is the difference between drama and theater? (2) What sorts of details does the writer include to make the difference obvious?
>
> **Voice & Word Choice** (3) How do examples, anecdotes, and quotations affect the writer's voice?

 Literature Connections: For another example of an essay of evaluation, read "Another Renaissance" by Gary Fisher, published in *Electronic Engineering Times*.

 Respond to the reading.

Answers

Ideas **1.** Drama is the study of the history, variety, and structure of plays; theater is the art of putting on a play.

2. The writer uses examples of what topics were studied.

Voice & Word Choice **3.** They make the writer sound enthusiastic and knowledgeable about the topic.

 Literature Connections

In his essay of evaluation "Another Renaissance," Gary Fisher explores the value and significance of the Renaissance and suggests that we may be in the middle of another "Renaissance." Fisher argues that online communication and a widespread creative spirit have come together to provide people with the opportunity to quickly and efficiently share their ideas, work, and talents with millions worldwide.

Encourage students to discuss what the author means when he suggests that "the sum of human thought and knowledge . . . can be literally at the fingertips of anyone with the desire to master the skills and a little technology." Then have students review Fisher's main points and discuss whether they agree. For additional models of persuasive writing, see the Reading-Writing Connections beginning on page TE-36.

Advanced Learners

Invite volunteers to search Web sites of local or national newspapers or magazines to find a review of a TV show, a movie, a play, or an art exhibit that they have seen or a video game they have played. Have students use the first four of the six traits to evaluate the effectiveness of the reviewer's evaluation.

Prewriting Selecting a Topic

Point out that the word *evaluate* contains the word *value*. The process of evaluating something is indicating its worth. The traits-based rubrics used throughout this text are tools of evaluation.

In Bloom's taxonomy of thinking, evaluation is one of the highest functions of the human mind. An effective evaluation, therefore, assigns a value to something by considering numerous aspects of it and presenting diverse types of evidence to support the value.

Technology Connections

Students can use the added features of the Net-text as they explore this stage of the writing process.

 Write Source Online **Net-text**

Focus on the Traits

Ideas

Note that it is not uncommon in everyday conversation, when a person is asked if she or he liked something—a book, class, or movie, say—for the response to be a simple "yes" or "no," without further explanation. Suggest that students begin practicing giving more insightful answers to such questions, by addressing the 5 W's and H—and by considering both the pros and cons as they answer. They will not only find that this promotes interesting discussion, but they'll also reach a deeper understanding of their own opinions.

262

Prewriting Selecting a Topic

The purpose of an essay of evaluation is to assess the value or worth of a timely topic. Sam began by listing potential topics that interested him.

Topics List

School
- student council
- community service requirements
- drama skills class*
- language lab

Community
- Harbor Fest
- crime watch program
- Gritty Coffeehouse
- new supercenter

Popular Trends
- latest MP3 player
- blogging
- American Idol
- energy drinks

At first Sam thought he would assess the impact of the new supercenter in his community, but he wasn't sure that his classmates would be interested in this topic. So, instead, he decided to focus on a school-related topic—the drama skills class in his school.

 Choose your topic. List possible topics related to school, community, and popular trends. (Try to list at least three topics under each category.) Then put an asterisk next to the topic that you want to write about.

Focus on the Traits

Ideas The goal of an essay of evaluation is to present an insightful assessment of a topic. To be insightful, you will need to consider all aspects of your topic (significance, strengths, weaknesses, and so on).

Struggling Learners

Use the following prompts to help students generate a list of topics.

School
- What class or activity has benefited you the most?
- What school policy do you agree with most (or least), and why?
- What school policy should be changed and why?

Community
- What organization has the greatest impact on the members of your community?
- What are your reasons for wanting to stay in or leave your community?

Popular Trends
- If you could invent a product that helped disabled students, what might it be?
- If you designed a school campus, what would it look like, and why?

Writing an Essay of Evaluation **263**

Gathering and Organizing Details

Once you have chosen the topic, you need to gather and organize information for your essay. To plan his essay, Sam used a pro-con chart, listing the strengths (pluses) and weaknesses (minuses) of the Drama and Theater class.

Pro-Con Chart

Pro	Con
Learning about great plays throughout history	Too many methods of acting
Working in all areas of play production	Too challenging sometimes
Mr. Maclay's skills, stories, and challenges	

Collect your information. Use a pro-con chart to collect information for your essay. Try to include at least two or three main points under each label.

Writing a Thesis Statement

A thesis states the focus of your essay and guides your writing. An effective thesis statement usually takes a stand or expresses a specific feeling about or feature of your topic. Use the following formula to form your thesis.

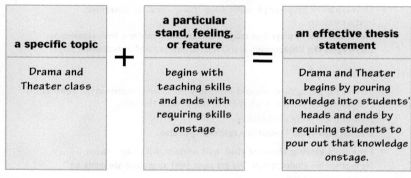

a specific topic	+	a particular stand, feeling, or feature	=	an effective thesis statement
Drama and Theater class		begins with teaching skills and ends with requiring skills onstage		Drama and Theater begins by pouring knowledge into students' heads and ends by requiring students to pour out that knowledge onstage.

Write your thesis statement. Use the information above as a guide to create your thesis.

Persuasive

Prewriting **Gathering and Organizing Details**

Point out that while the writer of the sample essay used only his own experiences as the basis for the essay, students may find that they need to do a bit of library or online research during the prewriting stage. For example, an essay about on-campus blogging might include a brief history of Web logging. Students should feel free to customize the topic with specific details that they find important to their own situation.

Distribute photocopies of the reproducible T-chart (TE page 823) for students to fill out as they gather details.

Prewriting **Writing a Thesis Statement**

Point out to students that although the thesis statement expresses Sam's belief, it does *not* read "*I think Drama and Theater begins . . .*" Note that an essay of evaluation is stronger when the writer uses the third-person point of view to examine the thesis. This is not to say the writer is not invested in the topic, but the distance created by the third-person voice is appropriate for evaluating an issue.

Writing Creating Your First Draft

Discuss how students should organize their essays. Point out that each paragraph might follow a different pattern of organization, according to its topic. For example:

- Generally, opening paragraphs contain a series of details leading up to an important summary statement—the thesis.
- If the topic is an event, such as a class or performance, description of what happens will be in chronological order.
- To compare the topic to a similar thing (for example, if the sample writer had mentioned another drama course he had taken), the writer might use comparison-contrast order.

✱ For more about patterns of organization within paragraphs, see SE pages 584–588.

✱ For information about basic essay skills, see SE pages 589–603.

✱ Refer students who need more guidance at this stage to Writing the First Draft, SE pages 105–112.

Technology Connections

Students can use the added features of the Net-text as they explore this stage of the writing process.

⚡ *Write Source Online* **Net-text**

Writing Creating Your First Draft

As you write your essay, use your planning from the previous page and refer to the following guidelines.

Beginning Paragraph

Your beginning paragraph should introduce your topic in an interesting way and state your thesis.

- Capture your reader's attention in the first sentence.
  Only one class at Greendale High School lets students dress up like singing candlesticks, carve rocks from foam, and play double-blind freeze.

- Provide background information and end with your thesis statement.
  Drama and Theater begins by pouring knowledge into students' heads and ends by requiring students to pour out that knowledge onstage.

Middle Paragraphs

The middle paragraphs should develop the main points in your evaluation. (See your pro-con chart.) Devote a separate paragraph to each main point. Organize these paragraphs in a logical way—perhaps starting with the "pros" and ending with the "cons."

- Provide a topic sentence for each paragraph.
  The first half of the course is devoted to drama, which is the study of the history, variety, and structure of plays.

- Develop each paragraph with supporting details, examples, and anecdotes.
  The course covers plays that range from ancient to modern, from classics by playwrights like Shakespeare and O'Neill to obscure and experimental plays.

Ending Paragraph

Your ending paragraph should restate your thesis, summarize your main points, and leave the reader with a final important thought.

- Summarize your evaluation.
  Overall, Drama and Theater is a fascinating course.

- Provide a closing thought that will remain with the reader.
  He teaches his students that "We are such stuff as dreams are made on" (*The Tempest* **4.1.156).**

Write your first draft. Use the guidelines above and your prewriting work to help you complete your first draft.

English Language Learners

After students write their thesis statements, pair students with language-proficient partners. Using the Pro-Con Chart, have them work together to write the first middle paragraphs of their essay.

Struggling Learners

Before students begin drafting the middle parts of their essays, have them rank the main points on their charts. They can follow the ranking to organize their middle paragraphs. Emphasize that each main point should be developed in a separate paragraph.

Revising Improving Your First Draft

Writing an Essay of Evaluation **265**

When you revise your first draft, you clarify your ideas, check your organization, and improve your voice. The guidelines below can help you revise.

Revising Checklist

Ideas

_____ **1.** Do I clearly introduce my topic?
_____ **2.** Have I stated a thesis about the topic?
_____ **3.** Have I effectively evaluated the topic?

Organization

_____ **4.** Does my essay have a strong beginning, middle, and ending?
_____ **5.** Have I presented my points in a logical order?

Voice

_____ **6.** Is my voice confident and convincing?
_____ **7.** Do I avoid being overly emotional?

Word Choice

_____ **8.** Do I clearly explain unfamiliar terms and concepts?

Sentence Fluency

_____ **9.** Do I use a variety of sentence lengths and beginnings?

Revise

Revise your first draft. Carefully review your essay using the checklist above. Make the necessary improvements.

Creating a Title

A good title introduces your topic and catches the reader's interest. Here are some different ways to approach writing a title.

- Use a line from the evaluation: **Pouring In and Pouring Out**
- Be clever: **To Act or Not to Act**
- Create an interesting rhythm: **Fun and Games and More**

Persuasive

Revising Improving Your First Draft

Focus on item 7, avoid using an overly emotional tone. This can happen when a writer uses slanted language or loaded words, such as

- "attack words" that create an insulting tone (*Lazy* readers won't make much headway with this book);
- "overblown modifiers" that appeal to emotion rather than logic (The *achingly gorgeous* prose *completely takes one's breath away*); and
- "extreme words," such as *always* or *never*, in situations that shouldn't be characterized so strongly (You will *never* read a better novel than this one).

Creating a Title

Briefly discuss the title chosen by the sample writer. Why is it a clever choice? (It not only summarizes the thesis, but it also refers to the opening line of a famous speech in Shakespeare's play *Hamlet:* "To be or not to be . . ." The title connects to the quotations from Shakespeare used in the essay.)

Technology Connections

Have students use the Writing Network features of the Net-text to comment on each other's drafts.

Write Source Online **Net-text**

English Language Learners

Remind students that a writer's voice should not sound overly emotional. Then read these sentences aloud. Have students restate each sentence to avoid a strong display of emotion.

- I am *begging* you to consider my position. (I urge you to consider my position.)

- I *absolutely love* the idea of an extended summer vacation. (I support the idea of an extended summer vacation.)
- I think it's *disgusting* to expect students to pay for summer school. (I think it's unfair to expect students to pay for summer school.)

Grammar Connection

Sentence Combining
- **Proofreader's Guide** pages 742 (+), 744 (+), 748 (+)
- *SkillsBook* pages 153–154

Adjectives
- **Proofreader's Guide** page 728 (+)
- *SkillsBook* page 100
- *GrammarSnap* Adjectives, Comparative and Superlative

Wordiness and Deadwood
- *Write Source* page 79
- *SkillsBook* page 168

Editing Checking for Conventions

All writers must remain vigilant when checking spelling, especially when writing with a computer. Remind students as they write to highlight or circle words they need to check when they edit.

Remind them also that the two best strategies for becoming a competent speller are to familiarize themselves with the rules of spelling and to keep a vocabulary list for every subject.

✳ For a list of spelling rules, see SE pages 664–669.

Publishing Sharing Your Work

Many Web sites invite reader reviews and may provide ways for students to publish their evaluations. For example,

■ online booksellers and other stores may allow readers to submit reviews of the titles or products for sale;

■ some movie sites offer a viewers' comments section; and

■ blogs (Web logs) often have a "Comments" link so readers can respond to the topic being discussed.

Students could also post their work on their own or a class Web site.

✳ For more about creating a Web site, see SE page 139.

Technology Connections

Remind students that they can use the Writing Network features of the Portfolio to share their work with peers.

➤ *Write Source Online* **Portfolio**

➤ *Write Source Online* **Net-text**

Grammar Connection

End Punctuation Review
■ **Proofreader's Guide** pages 605 (+), 606 (+)
■ *SkillsBook* page 6

Using the Right Word
■ **Proofreader's Guide** pages 686–687, 688–689
■ *SkillsBook* page 60

Editing Checking for Conventions

After revising your essay, you'll need to edit it for conventions: punctuation, capitalization, spelling, and grammar. If your conventions are correct, the reader will be more likely to respect your evaluation.

Editing Checklist

Conventions

PUNCTUATION

_____ 1. Have I ended my sentences with the correct punctuation?
_____ 2. Have I used commas, semicolons, and colons correctly?
_____ 3. Have I punctuated quotations correctly?

CAPITALIZATION

_____ 4. Did I capitalize the first word in every sentence?
_____ 5. Did I capitalize all proper nouns and adjectives?

SPELLING

_____ 6. Did I spell all my words correctly?
_____ 7. Did I double-check for words that my spell-checker might miss?

GRAMMAR

_____ 8. Did I use the correct forms of verbs (*he saw*, not *he seen*)?
_____ 9. Do my subjects and verbs agree in number?
_____ 10. Do my pronouns agree with their antecedents?

Edit your essay. Use the checklist above to edit for conventions. Then prepare a final copy of your essay of evaluation and proofread it.

Publishing Sharing Your Work

It's time to make your ideas public—by sharing them. Encourage readers to respond to your ideas.

Publish your essay of evaluation. Choose one of these methods.
■ Submit your essay to your school or local newspaper.
■ Post your essay on a Web site.

Struggling Learners

Distribute photocopies of the reproducible T-chart (TE page 823). To help students check for spelling errors, have them read their essay from the ending to the beginning so they focus on each word. Have them circle problem words, even if they are fairly sure of the correct spelling. Afterward, have them list the circled words in the first column on a T-chart. Then have a partner review the list and correct any misspelled words in the second column.

If students write on computers, have them make sure to use the spell-check feature after they've made their changes.

Writing for Assessment
Responding to Persuasive Prompts

Sometimes it's necessary to create and present a persuasive argument quickly. For example, imagine that you're trying to convince your parents to let you borrow their car to drive to the home of a friend in another town. Your parents are reluctant, but you feel you have good reasons to support your argument. Creating an organized argument quickly may mean the difference between visiting your friend and staying home for the evening.

Writing tests also require you to organize and present an argument in a relatively short period of time. After reading a prompt, you'll need to choose a position; structure your argument; and write, revise, and edit your response—all within a predetermined time limit. This chapter will show you how to respond to a persuasive writing prompt quickly and effectively.

Writing Guidelines

Subject:	**A persuasive prompt**
Form:	**Response essay**
Purpose:	**To demonstrate competence**
Audience:	**Instructor**

"Opinions cannot survive if one
has no chance to fight for them."

—Thomas Mann

Responding to Persuasive Prompts

Objectives
- understand the elements of a persuasive prompt
- apply what has been learned about writing persuasively to write the response
- practice writing for assessment

If your students must take school, district, or state assessments this year, focus on the writing forms on which they will be tested.

Students have probably already encountered persuasive prompts in tests during their time in high school. Talk about their experiences so far and share your own. Note that college professors often make use of essay prompts in examinations, so college-bound students have good reason to master this skill.

Prewriting Analyzing a Persuasive Prompt

Encourage students to devise a note-taking method similar to the one used in the sample (although they won't have colors or bold available) for marking the various STRAP questions directly on the prompt. For example,

- underline the subject once,
- underline the type twice,
- put parentheses around the role,
- use an asterisk for the audience, and
- circle the purpose.

Remind students to read the prompt all the way through before beginning to make any notes, so that they know they are taking the full question into account as they apply the STRAP questions.

Try It!
Answers

Subject: a mandatory bicycle helmet law for children under 12
Type: editorial
Role: a person with siblings or neighbors under 12
Audience: local newspaper readers
Purpose: support or oppose

268

Prewriting Analyzing a Persuasive Prompt

To respond to a persuasive prompt, begin by analyzing the prompt. A thorough analysis of the prompt will give you your topic, the form of your response, your role in writing, your expected audience, and your purpose for writing. To analyze a prompt quickly and effectively, use the STRAP questions:

Subject:	What topic should I write about (policy, proposal, decision)?
Type:	What form of writing should I create (essay, letter, editorial, article, report)?
Role:	What role should I assume as the writer (student, son or daughter, friend, employee, citizen)?
Audience:	To whom am I writing (teacher, parents, classmates, employer, official)?
Purpose:	What is the goal of my writing (persuade, respond, evaluate, tell, describe)?

Subject	In response to problems with traffic on the roads in your community, a
Type	council member has proposed assessing a $50 fee on each car. The
Role	money collected will be used to reduce the cost of local bus service. As an
Audience	**automobile owner who commutes to work by bus,** write a letter to the
Purpose	city council to persuade them to vote for or against this new fee.

Note: The following key words are often found in persuasive prompts: *convince, argue, defend, persuade.*

Try It!

Analyze this prompt by answering the STRAP questions.

A group of legislators in your state has proposed a new law that would require all children under the age of 12 to wear helmets while cycling. As someone with siblings or neighbors of that age, write an editorial for your local newspaper encouraging other legislators to support or oppose the law.

Planning Your Response

After answering the STRAP questions, you need to begin planning your persuasive response. One of the following graphic organizers can help you to plan your response quickly.

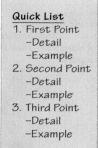
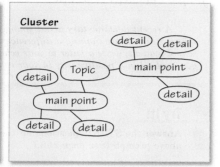

Choosing a Side

Persuasive prompts often ask you to choose one side or the other of an argument. In order to do this, you'll need to consider the ideas on both sides first, and then choose the side with the strongest reasons behind it.

One way to thoroughly examine both sides of an argument is to use a graphic organizer. Placing the "pros" and "cons" side by side will make it easier for you to determine the stronger side.

Considering both sides of an argument will also help you to find an important objection to respond to. By explaining how the objection is wrong or weak, you will demonstrate that you have considered both sides of the issue; this can strengthen your argument.

Prewrite

Use a graphic organizer. Reread the persuasive prompts on page 268. Choose one and use a graphic organizer to plan your response to the prompt.

Tip

One secret to success with writing prompts is careful time management. For example, if you have 45 minutes to respond, use the first 5 minutes to analyze the prompt and plan your response, the last 5 minutes to revise and edit your response, and the 35 minutes in between for writing your response.

Prewriting **Planning Your Response**

Instead of reproducing the T-chart and quick lists in the copy masters, have students generate their own graphic organizers. Few on-demand writing tests provide ready-made graphic organizers for students to use. By creating their own organizers, students are practicing a crucial skill for test day.

Prewriting **Choosing a Side**

Remind students that, for most persuasive questions, there is no "correct" answer. Their essay will be judged by how well they develop their position, not by whether the evaluator agrees with the position they take.

Remind them also that since the evaluator will be reading many responses to the same prompt—most of them written in a five- to seven-paragraph format—students should try as hard as they can to infuse their own voice into the piece. This, along with a well-developed argument, will make their work stand out.

Persuasive

Struggling Learners

Students may benefit from an example to see how the three graphic organizers represent the same information. Use the essay on SE pages 270–271 to fill in the three graphic organizers with student help. Then encourage students to fill in organizers about their own topics.

Writing Responding to a Prompt

To help students begin thinking about how to respond under time pressure, expand on the **Try It!** activity by having them answer the STRAP questions and also by asking them to plan what they would say in response. Give students 5 to 10 minutes to complete the activity.

After students have finished the activity, note that the purpose of the first sentence of the prompt is to set the tone only. Since students cannot know which documentary is meant, they do not have to refer to a documentary in their response. They can, instead, answer the STRAP questions by focusing on the second sentence in the prompt.

Try It!
Answers

Subject: students getting involved in the community
Type: letter to school newspaper
Role: a high school student
Audience: editor/fellow students
Purpose: call to action

270

Writing Responding to a Prompt

Once you have answered the STRAP questions and planned your response using a graphic organizer, you can begin writing.

Sample Persuasive Prompt

> *A recent documentary about young people highlighted ways that high school students are making a difference in their communities. As a high school student, write a letter to your school newspaper that invites students to get involved in a positive way in your community.*

Try It!

Answer the STRAP questions for the above prompt. (See page **268**.)

Sample Response

Dear Editor:

Beginning
The beginning paragraph draws the reader in to the letter.

How would you like to help save lives without spending years training to be a doctor, a nurse, or a firefighter? You can make a life-changing difference, and it won't take much of your time. I'm talking about giving blood.

While surgery, accidents, and illness can all bring someone to the point of death, a transfusion can change that outcome. In addition, modern medicine is able to separate blood into its components: platelets, plasma, stem cells, and so on. So someone who is a hemophiliac (a person whose blood lacks enough clotting potential) and a person being treated for cancer can both be helped. Stem-cell therapies are being used to treat a variety of illnesses. One donation of blood may actually save a number of lives because of the many ways blood can be used.

Middle
The first middle paragraphs express reasons for supporting the position.

The process of giving blood only takes about 20 minutes. Snacks and juice are provided at the donation site. You

---

English Language Learners

Before students read the essay, discuss the meanings of the following terms:

- transfusion (an injection of blood or another liquid into the bloodstream)
- restrictions (limits; barriers)
- sterile (free from bacteria and other microorganisms)
- surpass (to go beyond)

need a valid ID and a parental permission slip if you are under 18. Students must be at least 16 years old, weigh at least 110 pounds, and be in good health.

James Loclin, a senior, said, "I would like to give blood, but I am on medication." There are both tests and restrictions in place to keep the nation's blood supply safe. Those who have had a tattoo or a body piercing (not including ears) are not allowed to give blood for one year owing to the risk of blood infections with those activities. Those on medication or those who have traveled abroad should talk to the technicians to find out if they can safely donate blood.

You may be someone who would like to give blood, but you fear the process. You may worry about getting AIDS or just hate needles. You may think you'll feel faint or be at risk until your blood supply is back to normal. The donor program has anticipated all these concerns. The needles used are new and sterile, so you won't contract AIDS or any other blood-borne disease. The needles are also extremely sharp and generally cause little discomfort. Finally, about one pint of blood is taken, so your blood supply is not drastically reduced. Just remember, your discomfort will be outweighed by a lifesaving gift.

The student council supports the annual blood drive. Let's all turn out to surpass the goal of 150 pints. The donation center will be in the school gym on Friday, September 20, from 8:00 a.m. to 2:00 p.m. I gave last year. It felt great to help someone I didn't even know. Get in line early to give the gift of life.

Sincerely,

Veronica Heath

The final middle paragraph cites objections and responds to them.

Ending The ending restates the writer's position and makes a call to action.

Persuasive

Write

Respond to a persuasive prompt. Use the prompt you chose on page 268, your answers to the STRAP questions, and your graphic organizer to write a response. Finish your response in the time allotted by your teacher.

Ask students to point out the ways the writer successfully addresses the prompt. Possible answers:

- She focuses on a specific way of making a difference (giving blood), rather than trying to cover the broader topic of general volunteering in such a short space.
- She mentions not just one but two possible objections to the idea (the idea that you can't give blood because you're on medication, and the fear of giving blood), focusing on the strongest objection last.
- She creates a knowledgeable tone by including many informative and practical details.

Struggling Learners

Explain that the graphic organizers completed on TE page 269 provide a basic structure for their writing. Have students revisit the organizers they prepared and rank the main points listed in order of importance. Have them suggest two supporting details and one example for each point before they begin to write.

Revising Improving Your Response

Note that even when revisions are allowed on the test, students will not have time to make extensive changes. Encourage students who usually spend a lot of time on revising to think about ways they can compensate for this when they must take tests. Possible strategies:

- allowing a little more time during the planning stage to develop their ideas in more detail before writing; and
- practicing timed writing with a partner to adjust how much time they will have to improve their writing.

Editing Checking Your Response

Suggest that students use editing time to check for errors in conventions. These are the kinds of mistakes that may happen more frequently than usual when students are working quickly.

Revising Improving Your Response

Before you begin a writing test, find out if you are allowed to make changes to your draft copy. If changes are allowed, make them as clear and neat as possible. Use the STRAP questions to guide your revisions.

> **S**ubject: Have I responded to the topic of the prompt? Do all my main points support my position?
>
> **T**ype: Have I responded in the form requested (essay, letter, editorial, article, report)?
>
> **R**ole: Have I assumed the role called for in the prompt?
>
> **A**udience: Have I addressed the audience identified in the prompt?
>
> **P**urpose: Does my response accomplish the goal indicated in the prompt?

Revise

Improve your work. Carefully review your response, using the STRAP questions above as your guide. Within the time allowed, make changes to revise your response.

Editing Checking Your Response

After revising, be sure to read through your response one final time. Correct any errors in conventions: punctuation, capitalization, spelling, and grammar.

Editing Checklist

Conventions

_____ **1.** Have I used end punctuation for every sentence?

_____ **2.** Have I capitalized all proper nouns and the first word of every sentence?

_____ **3.** Have I spelled all words correctly?

_____ **4.** Have I made sure my subjects and verbs agree?

_____ **5.** Have I used the right words (*to, too, two; there, their, they're*)?

Edit

Check your conventions. Read through your response one final time. In the time allowed, neatly correct any errors in punctuation, capitalization, spelling, and grammar.

English Language Learners

Students may benefit from a quick review of the words *there, their,* and *they're.* Read the following sentences aloud. Have student respond by spelling the form of the word used.

1. Donna and Joe said *they're* going to meet me at the game.
2. My grandparents still dance to *their* favorite songs.
3. Are *there* any bandages in the first-aid kit?
4. Many students were excited about *their* upcoming prom.
5. Did the reporters describe the story *they're* working on?

Persuasive Writing on Tests

Before you write . . .

- **Analyze the prompt.**
  Use the STRAP questions. Remember that a persuasive prompt asks you to use facts and logical reasons to persuade or convince.
- **Plan your response.**
  Carefully allot the time you will spend on planning, writing, revising, and checking conventions. Use a graphic organizer to gather your details and organize your response.

As you write . . .

- **Stay focused.**
  Keep your main idea or argument in mind as you write. All your reasons should clearly support your argument.
- **Answer a significant objection.**
  Make your argument stronger by responding to a likely objection.
- **Summarize your argument.**
  In the final paragraph, summarize your opinion and supporting reasons to make a final plea to the reader.

After you've written a first draft . . .

- **Revise and edit.**
  Use the STRAP questions to revise your response. Correct any errors in punctuation, capitalization, spelling, and grammar.

Try It!

Choose one of the prompts below. First, analyze it using the STRAP questions. Then use a graphic organizer to gather details and plan. Finally, write, revise, and edit your response.

- Swordfish populations are declining due to overfishing. Local restaurants are campaigning for people to give swordfish a break by choosing other fish on the menu. Write a letter to the local newspaper editor asking people to support or oppose this campaign.

- Many people in this country do not get enough exercise. Yet exercise is known to help maintain an appropriate weight, reduce the risk of heart disease, and improve general health. As a health-care professional, write an essay for a fitness Web site that seeks to convince people to exercise more.

Persuasive

Persuasive Writing on Tests

Point out that students must approach writing-on-demand assignments differently from open-ended writing assignments and that timed writing creates pressures for everyone.

Test Prep!

To teach students who must take timed assessments how to approach their writing, allow them the same amount of time to write their response essay as they will be allotted on school, district, or state assessments. Break down each part of the process into clear chunks of time. For example, you might give students

- 10 minutes for note taking and planning,
- 25 minutes for writing, and
- 10 minutes for editing and proofreading.

Tell students when time is up for each section. Start the assignment at the top of the hour or at the half-hour to make it easier for students to keep track of the time.

If your state, district, or school requires students to use and submit a graphic organizer as part of their assessment, instruct students to do so in their practice.

Response to Literature Overview

Common Core Standards Focus

> **Writing 9:** Draw evidence from literary or informational texts to support analysis, reflection, and research.
>
> **Language 3a:** Vary syntax for effect, consulting references (e.g., *Tufte's Artful Sentences*) for guidance as needed; apply an understanding of syntax to the study of complex texts when reading.

Writing Forms

- analysis paragraph
- literary analysis (play) essay
- literary analysis (novel) essay
- writing for assessment

Focus on the Traits

- **Ideas** Developing a thesis statement that focuses on a main theme; analyzing the theme by connecting it to the characters, setting, and plot; and including textual evidence
- **Organization** Creating a beginning that introduces the theme, a middle that logically analyzes the theme, and an ending that reflects on the theme
- **Voice** Showing knowledge and understanding while creating a narrative flow
- **Word Choice** Choosing words that capture a precise meaning
- **Sentence Fluency** Writing sentences that flow smoothly and have a variety of lengths and beginnings
- **Conventions** Checking for errors in punctuation, capitalization, spelling, and grammar

  **Literature Connections**

- ***Riders to the Sea*** by J.M. Synge
- ***The Tragedy of Macbeth*** by William Shakespeare
- **"Bloody, Bold, and Resolute"** by Robert Hatch
- **"The Rime of the Ancient Mariner"** by Samuel Taylor Coleridge
- **"Coleridge's Dreamscape: The Rime of the Ancient Mariner"** by C. M. Bowra

 **Technology Connections**

 Write Source Online
www.hmheducation.com/writesource

- *Net-text*
- *Bookshelf*
- *GrammarSnap*
- *Portfolio*
- *Essay Scoring*
- *Writing Network features*
- *File Cabinet*

Interactive Whiteboard Lessons

Suggested Response to Literature Unit (Four Weeks)

Day	Writing and Skills Instruction	Student Edition		SkillsBook	Daily Language Workouts	Write Source Online
		Main Pages	Resource Units*			
1–3	**Response Paragraph: Literary Analysis of a Play** (Model)	275–277			62–65	*Interactive Whiteboard Lessons*
	Critical Reading	533–542				
	Skills Activities: • Punctuating Titles		634–635, 636–637	34		
4–5	**Literary Analysis: A Play** (Model) ⓛ Literature Connections *Riders to the Sea,* The Tragedy of Macbeth, "Bloody, Bold and Resolute"	278–280				
	Summarizing and Paraphrasing	543–550				
	(Prewriting) Outlining	281–286	591			*Net-text*

(Week 1 label appears vertically on the left side of the table.)

* These units are also located in the back of the *Teacher's Edition.* Resource Units include "Basic Elements of Writing" and "Proofreader's Guide."
(+) This activity is located in a different section of the *Write Source Student Edition.* If students have already completed this activity, you may wish to review it at this time.

Day	Writing and Skills Instruction	Student Edition		SkillsBook	Daily Language Workouts	Write Source Online
		Main Pages	Resource Units*			
6–7	(Writing) Thesis Statement	287–292, 61			66–69	*Net-text*
8–10	(Revising)	293–304				*Net-text*
	Skills Activities:					
	• Figures of Speech	76–77, 368	672–677 (+)			
	• Integrating Quotations	111	636 (+)	84–86		
	• Sentence Rhythm	88, 85	750–751	137, 138, 139		
11–12	(Editing)	305–308			70–73	*Net-text*
	Skills Activities:					
	• Commas Review		608 (+), 610 (+), 612 (+), 614 (+), 616 (+)	10, 16		*GrammarSnap*
	• Punctuating Compound and Complex Sentences		618 (+), 744–745, 748 (+)	7, 102		*GrammarSnap*
	• Punctuating Quotations and Citations		616 (+), 632(+)	33		
	• Capitalization		648 (+), 650 (+)	43		*GrammarSnap*
13	(Assessing, Publishing, Reflecting)	309–314				*Portfolio, Net-text*
opt.	*Making Oral Presentations*	439–447				
14–15	**Responding to Prompts About Literature**	323–339				
1–5	**Analyzing a Novel** (Model, Prewriting, Writing) Thesis Statement Integrating Quotations ☉ Literature Connections "The Rime of the Ancient Mariner," "Coleridge's Dreamscape: The Rime of the Ancient Mariner"	315–320, 61, 111			74–77	*Net-text*
	(Revising, Editing, Publishing)	321–322				*Portfolio, Net-text*
	Revising Activities:					
	• Sentence Variety (Flow)	82–85	744 (+), 748 (+), 750 (+)			
	• Voice (Diction and Terminology)	69, 71	598–601			
	Editing Activities:	322	616 (+), 632 (+)			
	• Punctuating Quotations					
	• Pronoun-Antecedent Agreement		756 (+)			*GrammarSnap*
	• Subject-Verb Agreement		752 (+), 754 (+)			*GrammarSnap*
	• Using the Right Word		694–695, 696–697	62		

* These units are also located in the back of the *Teacher's Edition*. Resource Units include "Basic Elements of Writing" and "Proofreader's Guide."
(+) This activity is located in a different section of the *Write Source Student Edition*. If students have already completed this activity, you may wish to review it at this time.

Teacher's Notes for Response to Literature

This overview of response to literature includes some specific teaching suggestions for the unit. The description of each chapter will help you decide which parts of the unit to teach.

Writing Focus

Analyzing a Theme (pages 275–314)

Playwrights such as Shakespeare, Chekhov, Miller, and so on write to explore a theme. This chapter shows students how to dig through the intricacies of a play to identify a theme and discuss it. Students will find in the chapter a thorough approach to writing an analysis of a theme.

Point out to students that the starting point (and foundation) for honest and meaningful analysis is the thoughts and feelings they establish in relation to a particular text. How students proceed with their writing, how they work with or explore an initial idea, is the real challenge to literary analysis. Students must base their ideas on the soundest reasoning they can muster and connect these ideas with evidence in the text.

The students' analysis in this activity should be limited to their own critical reading of and reaction to a text. Remind students that conscientious writers back up their statements with evidence to show that what they say is true.

Analyzing a Novel (pages 315–322)

This chapter parallels "Analyzing a Theme" (play). Students will see a model novel analysis and will write their own analysis of a novel.

Responding to Prompts About Literature (pages 323–339)

Since assessment tests and college-entrance tests often use literature prompts, students need to know the best way to plan and execute this demanding form of writing. This chapter takes students through that process. There are sample responses and practice prompts for both fiction and nonfiction.

Grammar Focus

For support with this unit's grammar topics, consult the resource units. (Basic Grammar and Writing, A Writer's Resource, and Proofreader's Guide).

Academic Vocabulary

Read aloud the academic terms, as well as the descriptions and questions. Model for students how to read one question and answer it. Have partners monitor their understanding and seek clarification of the terms by working through the meanings and questions together.

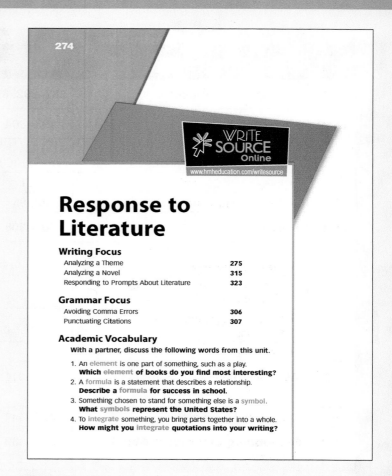

274

Response to Literature

Writing Focus

Grammar Focus

Academic Vocabulary

With a partner, discuss the following words from this unit.

1. An *element* is one part of something, such as a play.
   Which *element* of books do you find most interesting?
2. A *formula* is a statement that describes a relationship.
   Describe a *formula* for success in school.
3. Something chosen to stand for something else is a *symbol*.
   What *symbols* represent the United States?
4. To *integrate* something, you bring parts together into a whole.
   How might you *integrate* quotations into your writing?

Minilessons

Talking It Over — Analyzing a Theme

- **SELECT** a play that you have read recently. **DEVELOP** an imaginary dialogue between you and the playwright in which you talk about why the writer wrote the play. **DISCUSS** your dialogue with a partner.

A Novel Idea — Analyzing a Novel

- **LIST** a couple novels that you have read recently. **DESCRIBE** each one (main characters, setting, time frame) briefly. **ASK** yourself what insights you gained about life.

275

Response to Literature
Analyzing a Theme

Plays are among the earliest forms of art. Before television and film, before theaters and amphitheaters, before writing itself, plays fired the imagination of ancient people. The same cave dwellers who created charcoal murals of great hunts probably acted out those hunts around the campfire. Some plays entertained. Others enlightened. But almost all plays helped people to explain the meaning of life and how their world worked.

Plays have always had a profound effect on viewers. The ancient Greeks said that plays create *catharsis*—literally washing the soul. Tragedies allow audiences to experience terrible events without being destroyed, and comedies allow audiences to laugh and forget their troubles. People keep going to plays because they make life better.

In this chapter, you will learn how to analyze a play, beginning with the characters, setting, and plot. Through these basic elements, you will discover the meaning—or theme—of the play. Then you will write an analysis that will deepen your understanding of this ancient art form.

Writing Guidelines

Subject: A play
Form: Literary analysis
Purpose: To analyze a main theme
Audience: Classmates

"A good drama critic is one who perceives what is happening in the theater of his time. A great drama critic also perceives what is not happening."

—Kenneth Tynan

Analyzing a Theme

Analyzing a Theme

Objectives

- understand the content and form of a response essay that analyzes a theme
- plan, draft, revise, edit, and publish an analysis of a theme

An **analysis of a theme** is writing that explores how a writer expresses the theme, or central meaning, of a piece of literature through literary elements.

To analyze the main theme of a play, students have to

- understand the playwright and the background of the play;
- develop an understanding of the characters, setting, and plot of the play; and
- connect the characters, setting, and plot of the play to the theme.

Technology Connections

Use this unit's Interactive Whiteboard Lesson to introduce literature response writing.

Interactive Whiteboard Lessons

Copy Masters

Details Chart (TE p. 282)

Assessment Sheet (TE p. 313)

Benchmark Papers

The Beast of Fear (good)
● TE pp. 810–815

Huck Finn: The Relationship Between Huck and Jim (fair)
● TE pp. 816–819

Writing Warm-Up **Thinking About Drama**

Students' knowledge and recollection of plays may be limited. Before having them fill out a play map, work together to brainstorm a list of play titles students may recognize and may recall seeing or reading.

- If possible, have students refresh their memory by reading a summary of their play choice, which they can likely find online, or in an encyclopedia of literature.
- Since students will need topics for an analysis paragraph and for a response essay, display their list of play titles in the classroom, or post them on the classroom Web site as potential plays for students to analyze.
- If several students choose the same play, they will benefit from each other's ideas and interpretations of the play's meaning.

You can also consider having students respond to TV dramas. (See **TV analogies** below.)

276

Writing Warm-Up **Thinking About Drama**

Almost all plays contain the same elements: characters, conflict, action, dialogue, plot, and theme. Even TV dramas have these elements. To better understand the basic elements of one particular play, a student named Sa'id filled out a play map.

Play Map

Title: _Party at the End of the World_

Playwright: _Dedra Runningcloud_

Characters: _Jonas Jenkins (a drifter prophet), Sheriff Smith, Lyndsey Peck (owner of the Eel Creek General Store)_

Setting: _Eel Creek, Alaska, a remote village above the Arctic Circle_

Conflict: _Jonas Jenkins says the world will end, but most people won't believe him._

Plot:

Event 1: _Sheriff Smith tries but fails to run Jonas off._

Event 2: _Jonas meets Lindsey in the general store._

Event 3: _Jonas's dire predictions start to come true._

Climax: _Lyndsey holds an "End of the World Party" on the rooftop of the general store, and Jonas and the others who attend see a spectacular meteor shower. It seems the world is really coming to an end._

Resolution: _The sun rises on a new day, proving Jonas wrong, except that he had passed away during the party. He had predicted the end of the world for himself._

Theme: _Look at life through a wide-angle lens._

Write

Fill out a play map. Think of a play (or a TV drama—if your teacher allows it) you have recently seen or read and fill out a play map. Do your best to remember each element of the play.

English Language Learners

Some students may find it difficult to identify and understand the theme of a play. Assist students by helping them first identify the conflict of the story. Explain that the conflict often gives clues to the theme because the characters learn lessons through their struggles. Model the process using short, familiar TV dramas.

Teaching Tip: TV Analogies

Because the world of television is more familiar to most students than the world of plays, you can help students understand this assignment by comparing it to conversations they have had about favorite shows: "Did you see that rerun of (title) last night? It was the one in which (character) went to (setting), and (conflict). I loved the part when (climax). The ending was sad when (resolution). It's a great episode because it shows that you should (theme)."

Analyzing a Theme **277**

Writing an Analysis Paragraph

Using his play map, Sa'id wrote a one-paragraph analysis of the play. Note that his analysis has the following parts:

- The **topic sentence** names the play and playwright and summarizes the analysis.
- The **body sentences** describe the characters, setting, and plot and indicate the theme.
- The **closing sentence** provides a thoughtful conclusion.

Topic Sentence

Look Out for Jonas

In *Party at the End of the World,* playwright Dedra Runningcloud explores how different points of view bring people together—and drive them apart. The play centers on Jonas Jenkins, a "drifter prophet" who arrives in the small town of Eel Creek, Alaska, and proclaims that the world will end that night. Jenkins's predictions startle the people of the town. "Look out for Jonas!" a child cries. Sheriff Smith arrives to run Jonas out of town but can't find the prophet, who has wandered into the Eel Creek General Store. There, Jonas meets the storekeeper, Lyndsey Peck, and tells her the world will end that night. Instead of fearing him, Lyndsey joins in the fantasy and declares an "End of the World Party" on the store roof. Lyndsey hosts the celebration, and Jonas and an eclectic group of townsfolk lie in lawn chairs and watch a spectacular meteor shower. When the sun rises the next day, those who were partying discover that the world didn't end, but Jonas has had a heart attack. From his point of view, it really was the end of the world. Runningcloud contrasts the close-minded suspicion of Sheriff Smith with the open-minded acceptance of Lyndsey Peck. Both agree with the child—"Look out for Jonas!"—but in opposite ways. By accepting and even celebrating Jonas's point of view, Lyndsey brings the community together.

Body Sentences

Closing Sentence

Literature

Write

Write an analysis paragraph. Use the play map you created on page 276 to create a one-paragraph analysis of the play and its main theme.

Writing an Analysis Paragraph

Using the parts of a paragraph and the margin notes, discuss the role of each part of the paragraph in the sample analysis.

✱ For more information about basic paragraph skills, see SE pages 577–588.

Students should have a copy of the play they plan to analyze on hand for both the analysis paragraph and the response essay. If they have their own personal copies of the plays, they can highlight important elements and sections. Self-stick notes are useful for marking passages in borrowed books.

Understanding Your Goal

Sometimes, the first three traits—ideas, organization, and voice—are referred to as the "global" traits. They focus on large-scale issues. That's why these three traits guide the prewriting and writing phase.

When the time comes to revise, students will review the first three traits and also check the next two: word choice and sentence fluency. These two traits have a more specific focus, on individual clauses, phrases, and words.

Only after these larger-scale issues are addressed should students check for conventions, making sure each letter and punctuation mark is correct. Polishing conventions is the job of the editing step.

* The six-point rubric on SE pages 310–311 is based on these traits. Reproducible six-, five-, and four-point rubrics for responses to literature are available on pages 770, 774, and 778.

Literature Connections

Students should choose a play that is complex enough for close study and interpretation. Any play by William Shakespeare is a good choice. Other authors students might consider are J. M. Synge (*Riders to the Sea*), Thornton Wilder (*Our Town*), Samuel Beckett (*Waiting for Godot*), Tennessee Williams (*A Streetcar Named Desire*), and Arthur Miller (*The Crucible*). Students might also find that reading sample reviews, such as "Bloody, Bold, & Resolute," by Robert Hatch, is helpful as they prepare to analyze a play.

For additional pieces about responding to literature, see the Reading-Writing Connections beginning on page TE-36.

Understanding Your Goal

Your goal in this chapter is to write an essay that analyzes an important theme of a play. The chart below lists the key traits of a play analysis, with specific suggestions for this assignment. Consulting the chart, along with the rubric on pages 310–311, will help you write your essay.

Traits of a Play Analysis

■ **Ideas**

Write a thesis statement that names the play and focuses on a main theme. Then analyze that theme by connecting it to the characters, setting, and plot. Include textual evidence from the play.

■ **Organization**

Create a beginning that introduces the play and the thesis, a middle that logically analyzes the theme, and a closing that puts the play in perspective.

■ **Voice**

Show your knowledge and understanding of the play while also creating a narrative flow, allowing the reader to experience the play's action.

■ **Word Choice**

Correctly use play terminology in your analysis and choose words that capture a precise meaning.

■ **Sentence Fluency**

Write sentences that flow smoothly and have a variety of lengths and beginnings.

■ **Conventions**

Check your writing for punctuation, capitalization, spelling, and grammar errors.

 Literature Connections: Your interpretation can focus on a short play, such as J. M. Synge's *Riders to the Sea*, or a full-length play, such as Shakespeare's *Macbeth*. Both plays contain strong thematic elements. You can find a review of a film version of *Macbeth* in Robert Hatch's essay "Bloody, Bold, & Resolute."

English Language Learners

Simplify the task for students by having them focus on the ideas trait. Point out the underlined thesis statement in the essay on SE page 279. Tell students they can use this structure to help them write their own thesis statements. Create a sentence starter or write the following on the board:

In the play _____ (name of play), _____ (author's name) shows how _____
_____
_____ . (theme/message)

Play Analysis

In the following essay, Joelle analyzes *Sisters*—a play by Marsha A. Jackson.

Beginning
The beginning catches the reader's interest, introduces the play, and states the thesis (underlined).

Middle
The first middle paragraph sets the scene.

Stuck with Each Other

In the dark theater, children sing a haunting tune: "Don't Play with the Alley Children." It's a singsong chant that young Olivia Williams and her friends would sing in their upper-middle-class apartments while young Cassie Charles and her friends played among the garbage cans below. Though both girls are African Americans, they are divided by their social class, their experience, and their strategies for living in a white world. Then, one New Year's Eve, the grown-up Olivia is stranded in her ad-agency office along with the grown-up Cassie, a cleaning woman. In her play *Sisters,* Marsha A. Jackson contrasts the two women's lives, showing how color and gender make two very different women into true sisters.

The action of the play begins on New Year's Eve in Olivia's office at Peat, Montgriff, and Simon, an ad agency in Atlanta, Georgia. Olivia kneels on the floor among boxes and is packing up her office when Cassie arrives singing "I'm Every Woman" at the top of her lungs. The two women could not be more different. Olivia is 30, single, stiff, proper, and sad, listening to MUZAK as she packs up her life. Cassie is 40, a mom, loose and happy, listening to Whitney Houston. As Jackson points out in her notes before the play, "Both characters are intentionally broadly drawn in Act I, such that the laughter is the medium of entry into the complexity of each character and situation" (104). These two women begin as stereotypes, but when they get stuck together, both characters start to unfold.

A storm begins outside, lightning strikes, and the power in the building goes out. Olivia and Cassie, alone in the building, must rely on each other. They walk down twenty flights of stairs so that Olivia can drive Cassie home, but Olivia has forgotten her car keys, and the storm has turned to a blizzard. All traffic is stopped, and the trains that Cassie would ride aren't running because of the blackout.

The women climb back up the stairs, and Cassie reluctantly helps Olivia pack up her office while the two women unpack their lives. Olivia reveals that she is leaving because she has hit the "glass ceiling" and, despite her hard

Literature

Play Analysis

Work through this sample essay with the class, pointing out the elements that make it a good response to literature.

Ideas
- The thesis statement identifies the play's theme.
- The beginning starts with a strong image and provides background information that leads to the thesis statement.
- The writer analyzes how setting, characters, and plot reveal the theme.

Organization
- The opening names the theme, play title, and playwright.
- The middle paragraphs analyze the setting, characters, plot, and theme in that order.
- The ending expands on the theme.

Voice **&** Word Choice
- The writer effectively narrates the plot to help create a compelling voice.
- The analysis clearly shows how parts of the play relate to each other.
- The writer uses correct and precise play terminology to analyze the play.

Advanced Learners

Discuss why Joelle titled her response essay "Stuck with Each Other" and the meaning behind it. Challenge students to think of a clever title for their topic by using one of the following:

- oxymoron
- hyperbole
- metaphor
- irony
- pun
- symbol
- juxtaposition

Encourage students to look up any of these literary devices on SE pages 600–601 before creating their titles.

Respond to the reading.

Answers

Ideas 1. Color and gender make two very different women into sisters. **2.** The sharp contrast between the women's lives at the start of the play underscores the bond they eventually forge by the end of the play. The office setting where they both work becomes a common meeting ground for these two women from such different backgrounds. The plot reveals that both women have unfulfilled dreams, drawing them together as friends and sisters.

Organization 3. The middle paragraphs are organized systematically and chronologically. The first middle paragraph describes the characters and setting. The next two paragraphs describe events in order. The last middle paragraph discusses theme.

Voice & Word Choice 4. The voice is most analytical in the last middle paragraph where the writer connects the setting, characters, and events to the main theme. **5.** The writer's narrative voice comes out in the first three middle paragraphs. She describes the characters and uses dialogue to reveal their personalities.

280

work, is getting passed over for promotions. Cassie says that Olivia's ambition is a curse: "Being ungrateful for what you got, and wishing for things you can't have. If that ain't a curse, I ain't seen one" (134). Cassie has her own hang-ups. She has taken care of others her whole life: first her grandmother and now her son. Olivia points out, "Who's taking care of you, Cassie? You've been so busy working, trying to convince yourself you don't deserve a life, you didn't even feel it when you gave up" (144). As they talk, Olivia and Cassie grow to understand each other.

Jackson seems to be showing that the things that keep people apart—walls and alleys, work and money—aren't as powerful as the forces that draw them together. Simply by setting these two women in the same space, Jackson undoes the years and dollars that had kept them apart. Stuck with each other on New Year's Eve, Olivia and Cassie create their own celebration. They trade stories, listen to music, dance, and even make resolutions. Olivia resolves to find her way in a "white man's world" and have fun doing it. Cassie resolves to start her own cleaning business and move up in the world.

Ending
The ending paragraph reflects on the main theme of the play.

By the end of their time together, Olivia and Cassie are more than friends: They are sisters. Their theme song no longer is "Don't Play with the Alley Children" but "Blest Be the Tie That Binds." Marsha Jackson has brought two very different women together—two different aspects of the playwright herself. Jackson not only wrote the play but starred as Olivia during its run. As a classically trained playwright and a leading light in the theater scenes of Atlanta and Houston, Jackson is very much like Olivia. But the loving way in which she writes Cassie's part—and her own experience of being an "alley child" in a white world—show that part of Jackson is and always will be Cassie.

 Respond to the reading. Answer the following questions about the essay.

Ideas (1) What theme does Joelle focus on in her analysis? (2) How do the characters, the setting, and the plot demonstrate the theme?

Organization (3) How are the middle paragraphs organized?

Voice & Word Choice (4) Where does the writer's voice sound most analytical? Explain. (5) Where does the writer's voice sound most narrative? Explain.

Analyzing a Theme **281**

Prewriting

To get started on your analysis, you need to unlock the secrets of a play. The keys to prewriting can help you do so. Once you finish the activities on the next pages, you'll be ready to write.

Keys to Effective Prewriting

1. Select a play that interests you and contains a main theme to explore.

2. Reread the play and (if possible) see a performance of it.

3. Research the background of the play and the playwright.

4. Write a clear thesis statement that identifies the theme you will analyze. Develop topic sentences for the main points of your analysis.

5. Plan your essay using an outline or organized list.

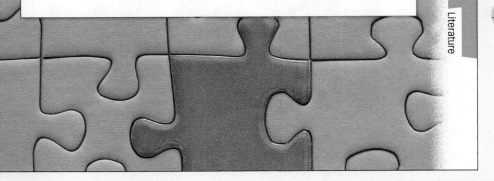

Literature

Prewriting

Keys to Effective Prewriting

Remind students of the purpose of the prewriting stage in the writing process: It is when the writer selects a topic, gathers details, and decides how to organize those details.

The Keys to Effective Prewriting list lays out the process students will be guided through on SE pages 282–286.

If possible, introduce this writing assignment soon after students have finished reading a play, or have attended a school play or a community or professional production of a play. Students are likely to have discussed these plays at length in class and on their own and will have lots of fresh ideas to draw on as they write their essay.

Writing Workshop

The activities in the prewriting, writing, revising, and editing sections of this chapter can function as minilessons to teach specific skills. These activities work for whole-class instruction, small-group lessons, or scaffolding for individual students.

 Technology Connections

Students can use the added features of the Net-text as they explore this stage of the writing process.

 Write Source Online **Net-text**

Prewriting Selecting a Play

Have on hand the following materials as students create their own topics list:

- Anthologies from different grade levels—Students can scan the tables of contents to recall plays they read this year and in past years.
- Playbills from school, community, and professional productions
- Teachers' suggestions

Provide photocopies of the reproducible Details Chart (TE page 826) for students to use for making their topics list.

Focus on the Traits

Ideas

Discuss the difference between visual recordings of stage performances and movies based on plays.

- The former do not change the script in any way, except perhaps to edit time between scene changes.
- A movie based on a play may be an **adaptation** (see below) that does not stay completely true to the original play.

Prewriting Selecting a Play

You may already know what play you would like to analyze. If not, follow the instructions on this page.

Think about plays you have read and plays that you have seen performed—in or out of school. Also consider famous plays that have been made into movies. To select a play, Julius created a topics list.

Topics List

Plays I've Read	Plays I've Seen	Plays Made into Movies
Romeo and Juliet	The Fantasticks	The Night of the Iguana
Julius Caesar	Godspell	Death of a Salesman
Inherit the Wind	The Lion King	Chicago
The Glass Menagerie*		

Prewrite

Brainstorm a topics list. Write "Plays I've Read," "Plays I've Seen," and "Plays Made into Movies" at the top of a piece of paper. Underneath, list topic ideas. Place an asterisk (*) next to the play you'd like to write about.

Focus on the Traits

Ideas To create a thorough analysis, try to select a play that you can both read and see onstage. If you've read but haven't seen a certain play, find the video of a performance. Also consider getting the script for a play you've seen performed locally.

Teaching Tip: Adaptation

Point out to students that producers may purchase the rights to adapt, or rewrite, a play for the screen.

- When filmmakers adapt a play and make it into a film, they may enhance or change important elements, including setting, characters, and dialogue.

- Although the main story line remains the same, these changes could affect the interpretation of the original theme.
- Reviews of the movie may tell how true the film has stayed to the original play, and what elements, if any, have been altered.

English Language Learners

Explain that a *menagerie* is a collection of live animals. Therefore, a "glass" menagerie refers to a collection of glass animals. Point out that titles are often keys to symbols and themes. Tell students to keep the title in mind as they read about the play.

Writing Down Main Events

After you have selected a play to write about, you need to read (or reread) it and, if possible, view it. Then consider the play's basic elements. Julius created the following play map for *The Glass Menagerie.*

Play Map

Title:	The Glass Menagerie
Playwright:	Tennessee Williams
Characters:	Amanda Wingfield (the mother), Laura Wingfield (the shy daughter), Tom Wingfield (the son), and Jim O'Connor (the gentleman caller)
Setting:	The Wingfield apartment in an overcrowded city tenement
Conflict:	Laura has withdrawn from life, and her mother and brother want to bring her out.
Plot:	
Event 1:	Amanda reminisces about her gentleman callers.
Event 2:	Amanda learns Laura has quit business school.
Event 3:	Tom arranges for a friend to come to dinner.
Climax:	The gentleman caller, Jim O'Connor, kisses Laura, but then reveals that he is already "going steady" with someone else.
Resolution:	Laura is left desolate, and Tom, tired of working to support his mother and sister, runs away, chasing his military dreams.
Theme:	Life may be fragile, but it can't be lived in a glass case, without risk.

Prewrite

Create a play map. Fill in the main elements of the play you have chosen to write about.

Prewriting Writing Down Main Events

Students may need extra time to reread and view the play they have chosen. Point out to students that reading (or rereading) the play will help them identify the basic elements of the play, which they will need to fill out a play map. However, viewing may help them grasp a deeper understanding of the theme because of the actors' unique interpretation of the characters and the director's emphasis on certain events, through creative staging and sound and lighting effects.

Writer's Craft

Auditory and visual media: One big difference between stage plays and screenplays is dialogue. Because stage plays are restricted to the settings and actions that can be shown on a stage, they often rely on dialogue to carry much of the meaning. Plays for the stage rely heavily on the auditory experience. Film, by contrast, is a visual medium. Much of the storytelling in a film occurs with images, actions, and special effects, de-emphasizing the importance of dialogue.

Prewriting Gathering Background Information

Point out to students that they should research a variety of materials to learn about a playwright and the background of a play.

- Anthologies usually introduce plays with brief author biographies. Students should look here first for information about an author's style and theme(s).
- Library databases such as *Biography Resource Center + Marquis Who's Who, Contemporary Authors Online,* and *Dictionary of Literary Biography* contain reliable information and are easy to access at school or home.
- Online sources, such as New York Theatre Experience (www.nyte.org), provide descriptions of current and recent plays, and interviews with the playwrights.

Prewriting Gathering Background Information

To fully understand a play, you need to understand the playwright and the background of the play. Often this information appears in the introduction, preface, or appendix of the published play. (You can also do some research at the library or online.) Julius formed a set of questions to investigate the background of *The Glass Menagerie.*

Background Questions

Who is the playwright, and when and where did the playwright live?
Tennessee Williams was born on March 26, 1914, in Columbus, Ohio. His real name was Thomas Lanier Williams.

What was the playwright's first produced play, and when was it performed?
Williams's first play was <u>Battle of Angels</u>, performed in 1940.

What are the playwright's most famous plays and awards?
Williams also wrote <u>A Streetcar Named Desire</u> and <u>Cat on a Hot Tin Roof</u>, both of which won the Pulitzer Prize and the Drama Critics Award.

When was the play first performed and where?
<u>The Glass Menagerie</u> was first performed at the Civic Theatre in Chicago, opening December 24, 1944.

What did audiences and critics think of the play?
Audiences and critics loved <u>The Glass Menagerie</u>, and its success made Tennessee Williams an overnight star. He talked about the success being a "catastrophe" for him because it was so sudden.

What did the playwright think of this play?
Tennessee Williams called <u>The Glass Menagerie</u> a "memory play," one that portrays life not with stark realism, but with "a closer approach, a more penetrating and vivid expression of things as they are."

Prewrite

Research the background of the play. Read the material printed with the play or do your own research. Write down answers to the questions above.

Note: If you are writing about an older play, such as a work by Shakespeare or Sophocles, you may not be able to answer all of the background questions. Answer those you can and add any others that occur to you.

Advanced Learners

Challenge students to work in pairs to find out more about Tennessee Williams or another author mentioned in this unit by conducting research in the library or online. Have them share their findings in an author/reporter interview format.

Analyzing a Theme 285

Writing a Thesis Statement

Your thesis statement should name the play and playwright and focus on the theme you plan to explore. The following formula can help you.

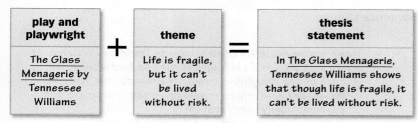

play and playwright		theme		thesis statement
The Glass Menagerie by Tennessee Williams	**+**	Life is fragile, but it can't be lived without risk.	**=**	In The Glass Menagerie, Tennessee Williams shows that though life is fragile, it can't be lived without risk.

Write your thesis statement. Use the formula above as you develop a thesis statement for your essay. Try two or three versions until you are satisfied.

Organizing the Middle of Your Essay

The middle of your essay should set the scene, highlight key actions in the plot, give insights into the characters' actions, and discuss the theme. Here are Julius's topic sentences.

Topic Sentence 1 (setting the scene)

Each of the Wingfields—mother Amanda, son Tom, and daughter Laura—lives physically in the apartment but psychologically very far from it.

Topic Sentence 2 (plot and characters)

Soon after the characters are introduced, Amanda is shocked to learn about the secret lives her two children are leading.

Topic Sentence 3 (plot and characters)

When the "gentleman caller," Jim O'Connor, arrives at the Wingfield apartment, he brings life to the whole place.

Topic Sentence 4 (theme)

Jim O'Connor seems to be everything the Wingfields need—romance, adventure, confidence, and risk.

Create topic sentences. Follow the pattern that Julius used above, or create your own pattern. Write a topic sentence for each middle paragraph, focusing on the basic elements of the play (page 283).

Literature

Prewriting **Writing a Thesis Statement**

Remind students that a strong and effective thesis statement can guide their writing, helping them to know which main points to make and which details to use to support those points.

✴ For more about writing effective thesis statements, see SE page 592.

During revising, students will learn that symbols are key to unlocking a play's theme. Suggest that students turn to SE page 301 now to learn more about symbols and how to discover them in their play. Encourage students to use these symbols to help focus on a theme for their thesis statement, and also to refer to these symbols in their analysis.

Prewriting **Organizing the Middle of Your Essay**

Although the text directions give students the option of creating their own organizational pattern, consider requiring students to follow the pattern shown on SE page 285. Having a set organizational plan to follow will help students concentrate on ideas.

Prewriting Planning Your Essay

Make sure students know whether they have to create a sentence outline, a topic outline, or a simple organized list, or if they can choose which way to plan their essay.

Explain the benefits of writing a full sentence outline when planning an essay:

- It provides a solid framework for the construction of each paragraph in the essay.
- You can clearly see how sentences and ideas in each paragraph will flow from one to the next.

Students can get a better idea of the benefits of a full sentence outline by comparing the organization of details in the sample Sentence Outline to those in the sample Middle Paragraphs on SE pages 290–291.

＊ For more about outlining ideas before writing, see SE page 591.

Schedule **writing conferences** *(see below)* with students to review their outline or list.

286

Prewriting Planning Your Essay

Julius planned his essay with a sentence outline, but if your teacher prefers, you can create a topic outline, or even a simple list.

Sentence Outline

Thesis Statement: In *The Glass Menagerie*, Tennessee Williams shows that though life is fragile, it can't be lived without risk.

I. Each of the Wingfields—mother Amanda, son Tom, and daughter Laura—lives physically in the apartment but psychologically very far from it.
   A. Amanda grew up with Southern gentility.
   B. Tom works at a factory to support the family but wants to be a poet.
   C. Laura collects glass animals and "attends" a business college.

II. Soon after the characters are introduced, Amanda is shocked to learn about the secret lives her two children are leading.
   A. Laura has dropped out of business college.
   B. Tom goes to movies, dreaming of adventure.
   C. Amanda gets Tom to invite a "gentleman caller" to meet Laura.

III. When the "gentleman caller," Jim O'Connor, arrives at the Wingfield apartment, he brings life to the whole place.
   A. He believes in adventure, just as Tom does.
   B. Jim represents the genteel past to Amanda.
   C. He is the boy Laura had a crush on in high school.

IV. Jim O'Connor seems to be everything the Wingfields need—romance, adventure, confidence, and risk.
   A. Jim remembers Laura as "Blue Roses."
   B. Jim accidentally breaks her glass unicorn.
   C. He kisses her, but then tells her he is "going steady" with another girl.

Prewrite

Plan your essay. Use your thesis statement and topic sentences to create an outline or list to plan your essay. Add details to support each topic sentence.

Teaching Tip: Writing Conferences

Most students will benefit from one-on-one discussions with you about their writing. Arrange a convenient time to meet with individual students to review their outline or list and to discuss their play analysis.

- Check to see that students have created a strong thesis statement

and clear topic sentences. Check that they have listed details to support their main points.
- Take this opportunity to discuss their interpretations of the theme.
- Have students explain to you how they figured out the theme. Students may have read reviews

and analyses of the play during prewriting. This is perfectly acceptable, so long as the research helped them formulate or confirm their own ideas. However, it is important that students have not simply adopted someone else's ideas.

Analyzing a Theme **287**

Writing

After thinking carefully about the elements of the play and planning your analysis, you are ready to start writing. By following your plan, you can get all of your ideas on paper.

Keys to Effective Writing

1. Use your outline or list to guide your writing.

2. Write on every other line or double-space if you are using a computer. This will allow room for changes.

3. Create a beginning that introduces the play and playwright and states your thesis.

4. In the middle paragraphs, support your topic sentences with quotations and paraphrases from the play.

5. Analyze the theme, focusing on characters, setting, and plot.

6. Write an ending that expands upon the theme.

Literature

Writing

Keys to Effective Writing

Remind students that the writing stage is when they get to write, or draft, their ideas on paper.

The Keys to Effective Writing list explains the process students will be guided through on SE pages 288–292.

Suggest that students take time now to highlight or flag the dialogue that they will quote and paraphrase as evidence to support their analysis. This will make it easier to find passages as they write. Students may also want to note in which middle paragraph they plan to use the evidence.

Remind students that, as they write, they may decide to detour from their outline, or they may want to use different evidence to support their ideas. If they decide to go in a totally new direction than they originally planned, tell them to come to you to discuss a revised outline and schedule for submitting work.

Writing Workshop

Model writing for your students. If your students see you composing sentences as examples, they will recognize you as a fellow writer and facilitator. This is a key concept for the writing workshop approach.

Technology Connections

Students can use the added features of the Net-text as they explore this stage of the writing process.

 Write Source Online **Net-text**

Writing Getting the Big Picture

Tell students that if they use their prewriting notes and follow the steps presented on SE pages 289–292, they should be able to see their own "big picture."

To see exactly how the three parts of their play analysis fit together, suggest to students that they create a chart similar to the one on the page. This will serve to highlight any major problems in the organization and the construction of their essay, which they can address when they revise.

Writing Getting the Big Picture

Your analysis should include three parts: a beginning, a middle, and an ending. The chart below shows how the three parts of a play analysis fit together. The examples are from the essay on pages 289–292.

Beginning

The **beginning** captures the reader's interest, names the play and playwright, and states the thesis.

Thesis Statement
In The Glass Menagerie, Tennessee Williams shows that though life is fragile, it can't be lived without risk.

Middle

The **middle** paragraphs analyze the theme by focusing on character, setting, and plot.

Topic Sentences
Each of the Wingfields—mother Amanda, son Tom, and daughter Laura—lives physically in the apartment but psychologically very far from it.

Soon after the characters are introduced, Amanda is shocked to learn about the secret lives her two children are leading.

When the "gentleman caller," Jim O'Connor, arrives at the Wingfield apartment, he brings life to the whole place.

Jim O'Connor seems to be everything the Wingfields need—romance, adventure, confidence, and risk.

Ending

The **ending** expands upon the main theme.

Closing Sentences
When Jim O'Connor leaves the apartment, he takes the newfound hope away with him. That's because he can't live life for the Wingfields. Everyone must take his or her own fragile soul out into the world and risk it—as Jim does.

Starting Your Essay

The opening of your analysis should capture the reader's interest, introduce the play and playwright, and state your thesis. Here are some strategies for capturing your reader's interest:

Beginning

Middle

Ending

- **Start with a strong image.**
  Aside from her mother and brother, Laura Wingfield's only companions in life are tiny, fragile glass creatures—her "glass menagerie."

- **Use a quotation from the play.**
  "The Wingfield apartment is in the rear of the building, one of those vast hive-like conglomerations of cellular living-units that flower as warty growths in overcrowded urban centers of lower middle-class population" (27). It's a location most people can imagine, a location many people can simply look around and see. . . .

- **Begin with an intriguing idea.**
  From the moment the curtain opens, the audience wonders about the smiling portrait of the sailor—the one Wingfield who no longer remains in the cramped apartment. . . .

Beginning Paragraph

Julius begins his essay with an intriguing idea and then provides background information before stating his thesis.

> The first paragraph catches the reader's interest and delivers the thesis statement (underlined).

From the moment the curtain opens, the audience wonders about the smiling portrait of the sailor—the one Wingfield who no longer remains in the cramped apartment. The father has escaped the claustrophobic world where the mother and her two grown children still live. The whole play takes place in this small space, with an occasional breath of fresh air out on the fire escape in the alley. The family has withdrawn to this apartment as if it is a safe haven from the world, but their unhappiness demonstrates that the apartment is anything but safe. The Wingfields aren't really living. In <u>The Glass Menagerie</u>, Tennessee Williams shows that though life is fragile, it can't be lived without risk.

Literature

Write

Write your beginning. Use one of the strategies above to capture the reader's interest. Then provide background information and present your thesis.

Writing Starting Your Essay

Discuss the three different strategies for starting an essay and the three examples. Ask students if they agree with the writer's choice (an intriguing idea), or if they would have used one of the other beginnings, and why.

Have students study the beginning paragraph carefully. Ask them to point out details that

- provide background information about the setting and characters (smiling portrait of sailor, cramped apartment, father has escaped, mother and two grown children, small space, fire escape in alley);

- identify the play and playwright (*The Glass Menagerie* by Tennessee Williams);

- state the main theme (life is fragile but it can't be lived without risk); and

- introduce **topics, or minor themes** (*see below*), that the play touches on, including disappointment and escape (the father has escaped . . . , the family has withdrawn . . . , their unhappiness demonstrates . . .).

Writing Developing the Middle Part

Have students read all the middle paragraphs on SE pages 290–291. Ask students to point out details the writer uses to connect the setting, characters, and plot to the theme.

Possible responses:

- Setting (The Wingfields live in the apartment physically, but they are psychologically far away from it.)
- Characters (Mother Amanda lives in a bygone age, ignoring its sad results. Tom works in a shoe factory, wants to be a poet, and escapes to the movies every night for adventure. Laura is crippled and shy, preferring to spend her time with a collection of glass animals than with people in the real world.)
- Plot (Tom's coworker, Jim O'Connor, visits Laura in the apartment. His vitality infuses life and hope into the characters and the setting. When Jim tries to teach Laura to dance, her prized glass unicorn falls and breaks. This event, combined with the kiss he steals and the revelation that he has a girlfriend, highlights the theme that life is indeed fragile, but people who are willing to risk "getting broken" lead fuller, happier lives.)

Writing Developing the Middle Part

In the middle part of your essay, you systematically analyze the theme. First, focus on major elements of the play—characters, setting, and plot—and show how each contributes to the theme. Then discuss the theme itself.

Beginning
Middle
Ending

Middle Paragraphs

The first middle paragraph uses characters and setting to analyze the theme.

Each of the Wingfields—mother Amanda, son Tom, and daughter Laura—lives physically in the apartment but psychologically very far from it. Amanda is an older woman brought up in the genteel traditions of the Old South, with lemonade on verandas and gentlemen callers. She lives in this bygone age and discusses her glory days of dating, even though they resulted in a broken marriage and single motherhood. Tom also feels trapped, working in a shoe factory, though he wishes to be a poet. Coworkers call him "Shakespeare" (92). Tom works simply to make money to support his mother and sister, though he spends nights at the movies, wishing for adventure. Laura is the most lost and fragile of them all. She had been a shy girl in high school, with a crippled leg and lungs weakened by "pleurosis." Laura has withdrawn from the world, spending her time with a collection of animal statues, her "glass menagerie." Her favorite is also the oldest, a unicorn that tries to fit in with a shelf full of horses. This unicorn symbolizes Laura, who doesn't fit in and is so very fragile.

The next middle paragraphs use plot to analyze the theme.

Soon after the characters are introduced, Amanda is shocked to learn about the secret lives her two children are leading. When Amanda stops at Rubicam's Business College, where her daughter is supposed to be taking classes, she learns that Laura became so nervous in the first week of class that she threw up and dropped out of school. She has been going to the library and wandering around town instead of going to class. Shortly afterward, Amanda learns of Tom's dreams of adventure and his plans to join the military. "Man is by instinct a lover, a hunter, a fighter, and none of those instincts are given much play at the warehouse," Tom

---

Struggling Learners

Students may have difficulty understanding how Julius's sentence outline was incorporated into his first draft. Review the four main points of the outline on SE page 286. Then direct students' attention to the first sentence of each middle paragraph.

Point out that these are topic sentences that match the main points of the outline and they also occur in the same order. Choose one paragraph for students to read. Tell them to note the lettered items from the outline as they read the paragraph. Point out that these are details that support the topic sentence.

tells his mother (64). Frustrated with both of her children, Amanda asks Tom to help Laura find a man. Tom at first says no, but then arranges for a gentleman caller.

When the "gentleman caller," Jim O'Connor, arrives at the Wingfield apartment, he brings life to the whole place. Jim is Tom's only friend and confidant at the factory, and he understands Tom's desire for adventure. Jim also enlivens Amanda, who redecorates the apartment to make ready for him. To Amanda, Jim represents the return of the gracious past. But Jim's strongest effect is on Laura, who has secretly loved him since his glory days in high school. Back then, she had been absent for a while, and Jim asked why. When Laura said "pleurosis," Jim heard "blue roses," and called her that name (112). The name is another symbol of Laura's odd and fragile beauty.

Jim O'Connor seems to be everything the Wingfields need—romance, adventure, confidence, and risk. Perhaps Amanda has found a way back to bygone days; perhaps Tom has found a coconspirator to help him escape the factory; perhaps Laura has found a gentleman who would lift her out of her fragile glass world and into life. Laura trusts Jim with the unicorn, and he gently sets it on a table. Later, as he tries to teach Laura to dance, they knock the unicorn off the table, and its horn is broken away. Jim is sorry, but Laura says, "I'll just imagine he had an operation. The horn was removed to make him feel less—freakish! . . . Now he will feel more at home with the other horses, the ones that don't have horns" (125). Jim steals a kiss from Laura, but calls himself "stumblejohn" for doing it, given that he has a steady girlfriend already. This is just what Laura needs—to take risks, even possibly to get broken, if only to fit in better with the rest of the world. The problem is that she isn't like her unicorn—she doesn't lose her horn or learn to fit in with the other horses.

> The last middle paragraph focuses directly on the theme.

Literature

Write

Write your middle paragraphs. Use your outline (page 286) as a guide. Add quotations from the play to support your analysis of the theme.

Point out the numbers in parenthesis throughout the middle paragraphs. Explain that these are the page numbers for the citations from the play. Students should remember to include the page numbers for their citations. Students will learn more about rules for punctuating citations during revising on SE page 307. However, before they write their middle paragraphs, they can turn to SE page 307 for a quick reference to these rules.

 Writer's Craft

Symbolism: Point out how the writer of this essay focuses on the symbol of the glass unicorn. Tennessee Williams uses the little statue to represent Laura—fragile and strange, kept in a glass case away from life. What happens to the unicorn represents what is happening to Laura. Symbolism is one way that playwrights can take an abstract idea and make it concrete—turn an invisible idea visible.

English Language Learners

Some students may find it difficult to generate ideas for writing while also incorporating important quotations and major plot elements. They may have in mind what they want to say but cannot think of or spell the English words they want to use.

Encourage them to do the following:
- Leave a blank or write similar words in their first language.
- Flag the words they want to change by circling or highlighting them.
- Revisit these words during the revising process and make necessary changes then.

Writing **Ending Your Essay**

Remind students that the theme of a play is the main message or the lesson learned about life that the playwright is conveying to the audience through the setting, characters, and plot. The playwright wants readers or the audience to come away from the play with a new perspective, a heightened awareness, and a deeper understanding of life in general. The ending of an effective play analysis should do the same thing—leave readers with the feeling that by understanding the specific theme of the play, they have a greater understanding of life in general.

Writing **Ending Your Essay**

The ending of your analysis should expand on the main theme of the play. Here are strategies you can try:

- **Connect the theme to life in general.**
  When Jim O'Connor leaves the apartment, he takes the newfound hope away with him. That's because he can't live life for the Wingfields. Everyone must take his or her own fragile soul out into the world and risk it—as Jim does.

- **Relate the theme of the play to the playwright's life.**
  When Tom Wingfield leaves home, abandoning his job at the shoe warehouse, Tennessee Williams is reliving his own escape from the shoe warehouse where he worked before becoming a successful playwright.

- **Provide a powerful quotation from the play.**
  After leaving home, Tom is haunted by thoughts of his sister and her glass menagerie: "The window is filled with pieces of colored glass . . . like bits of a shattered rainbow. . . . Oh, Laura, Laura, I tried to leave you behind me, but I am more faithful than I intended to be!" (137).

Ending Paragraph

In his final paragraph, Julius connects the play to life in general.

The ending paragraph expands upon the theme.

When Jim O'Connor leaves the apartment, he takes the newfound hope away with him. That's because he can't live life for the Wingfields. Everyone must take his or her own fragile soul out into the world and risk it—as Jim does. Amanda's hope that a gentleman caller would make her life perfect was dashed when her husband left, and now Laura's hope for a similar knight in shining armor is also dashed. Such rescuers don't exist. Only Tom escapes the apartment, but he can't be free either, because he knows his mother and sister are still there, waiting for their lives to begin.

Write

Write your ending and form a complete first draft. Develop the last paragraph of your essay, using one or more of the suggestions listed above. Make a complete copy of your essay, double-spacing or writing on every other line to leave room for revising.

Analyzing a Theme **293**

Revising

When you write, you allow your thoughts to pour out onto the page. When you revise, you reexamine those thoughts to improve your paper, deciding what to add, delete, move, or rework. The points below give you an overview of the revision process.

Keys to Effective Revising

1. Read your essay aloud to see whether it makes sense from start to finish.

2. Check your beginning and ending. To start, you must capture the reader's interest, introduce the play and playwright, and present the theme. To end, you must expand on the theme.

3. Review each middle paragraph for unity and organization.

4. Check your voice. It should be analytical and, when necessary, narrative.

5. Review your word choice and sentence fluency.

6. Use the editing and proofreading marks on the inside back cover of this book.

Literature

Revising

Keys to Effective Revising

Point out to students that at the revising stage they can think about refinements they might not have considered when they were drafting.

The Keys to Effective Revising list explains the process students will be guided through on SE pages 294–304.

Give students time to review the Keys to Effective Revising list and to note items that highlight areas in which they struggled during the writing stage or in previous assignments. Suggest that students focus extra attention on these particular elements during revising.

Peer Responding

Ask students to respond to each others' essays. A constructive peer response helps the writer know just what needs to be improved in an essay. For more on peer responding, see SE pages 121–126.

Writing Workshop

Instead of assigning all the following revision strategies, use them as minilessons to target specific problems. For example, gather a group of students who need to work on ideas, and present the ideas strategies. You'll know who needs to work on what after students have received peer responses.

Technology Connections

Have students use the Writing Network features of the Net-text to comment on each other's drafts.

Write Source Online **Net-text**

English Language Learners

Students may be distracted by the amount of information presented in the **Revising** section. Focus the task by selecting only one trait from SE pages 294–304 for students to focus on during the revising process.

Revising **for** Ideas

The rubric strips that run across all of the revising pages (SE pages 294–303) are provided to help students focus their revising and are related to the full rubric on SE pages 310–311.

Remind students that their audience is the class.

- If the writer chose a play the class members have read or attended, then it is likely the audience has prerequisite knowledge of the play. The writer should concentrate on details that relate to the theme.

- If the writer is analyzing a play that may be unfamiliar to most of the class, then the writer should provide more background information.

Exercise Answers

- **Unnecessary Details:** (line 4) A deaf-mute hangs out there. (line 7) They sing and dance, talking about good garbage and ugly garbage.

- **Missing Detail:** an explanation of faking uranium. (Some students might suggest that the writer should have included the playwright's name.)

294

Revising **for** Ideas

6 My ideas provide a complete and careful analysis of the play.

5 I have effectively summarized material and included appropriate quotations.

4 Most of my summaries are effective, but I should make better use of quotations.

When you revise for *ideas,* you check your thesis statement, topic sentences, and details. These two pages will also help you revise your summaries and include effective quotations. The rubric strip above will guide you as you revise for ideas.

Have I created effective summaries?

You have created effective summaries if you have included only the information the reader needs—but *all* the information the reader needs. Some summaries are puffed up with unnecessary details. Others are confusing because of missing details. Ask yourself the following questions:

1. What does my reader know about the play?
2. What does my reader need to know about the play?

Exercise

Read the summary that follows. Find two details that are not necessary and should be deleted. Also indicate which detail is missing. (Ask yourself: What do I still need to know?)

1   In *Dear World,* the madwomen of Paris battle rampant capitalism to save the
2   city they love. A prospector has discovered that a great deposit of oil stretches
3   beneath Café Francis in Paris, and so he, a lawyer, and a politician plot to blow
4   up the café. A deaf-mute hangs out there. The sinister plot is foiled when the
5   politician's servant drops the bomb in the Seine instead of placing it in the café's
6   flower box. The café patrons—led by the madwomen—band together to stop the
7   conspiracy. They sing and dance, talking about good garbage and ugly garbage. In
8   the end, the madwomen defeat the evil trio by faking uranium.

Revise

Check your summaries. Be sure you have included only the information the reader needs, but *all* the information the reader needs. Ask yourself the following questions:

1. What does my reader know about the play?
2. What does my reader need to know about the play?

Struggling Learners

Some students may mistakenly associate an effective summary analysis with a summary of the story's events. Point out that in an analysis, an effective summary must contain the necessary story events to support the analysis. Point out that the emphasis for a score point 6 in the rubric strip is a complete and careful analysis.

Analyzing a Theme **295**

 3 I need to improve my summaries and provide more helpful quotations.

 2 My summaries are unclear or confusing, and I need to quote from the play.

1 I need help to understand how to summarize and quote from a play.

Have I used effective quotations?

You have used effective quotations if you have quoted only those passages that make a strong, clear point. An analysis with too many quotations becomes cumbersome, while one with too few quotations gives the reader little insight into the play.

Exercise

In the following paragraph, decide which quotation should remain and which should be deleted. Give reasons for your decision.

1   The madwomen enlist the aid of the Sewerman who poles around the sewers
2 of Paris on a gondola. The Sewerman seems to have the same madness as the
3 ladies, reveling in garbage: "It used to be if garbage smelled a little strange, it was
4 only because it was a little confused. Everything was there: sardines, cologne,
5 iodine, roses. Ah! The feast you found floating by" (43). The Sewerman's madness
6 allows him to see beauty in everything, even garbage. A stark contrast is drawn
7 between the Sewerman's madness and the madness of rampant capitalism, which
8 sees beauty in nothing. As the politician sings: "There will be a sweet taste in the
9 air, of industrial waste in the air" (32).

 Revise

Check your quotations. Be sure that each one strongly supports your point and that you have not used too many or too few quotations.

Ideas
An ineffective quotation is deleted.

When Laura said "pleurosis," Jim heard "blue roses," and called her that name (112). The name is another symbol of Laura's odd and fragile beauty. ~~Jim apologizes about the nickname, saying, "I hope you didn't mind" (113).~~

To fill space, students sometimes rely on too many or exceedingly long quotations. Limit the number of long quotations, and provide these additional guidelines for checking quotations:

■ Am I able to connect this quotation directly to the theme for my readers? If not, delete it.

■ Is the quotation longer than four lines? If it's important to the analysis, consider using only part of it.

 To learn more about using quoted material, see SE page 424.

Exercise Answers

■ Retain the second quotation that begins on line 8. It exemplifies the personification of rampant capitalism as something, "which sees beauty in nothing."

■ Delete the first quotation that begins on line 3. The writer's phrase *reveling in garbage* paraphrases the same description.

Struggling Learners

Some students may have difficulty assessing whether their quotations are effective. Provide the following questions to help students evaluate the necessity of the quotations they have included:

● Does this quotation support my thesis statement?

● Is this quotation the strongest choice to support the information in this paragraph?

● Will this quotation make an impression on my reader?

Revising for Organization

Point out to students that transitions function for both the writer and the reader.

- Transitions help writers create unified, cohesive paragraphs in which the sentences and paragraphs flow naturally from one to the next.

- Transitions make it easier for readers to follow the flow of ideas from sentence to sentence and from paragraph to paragraph, and to quickly see how all the writer's ideas are connected, making the essay more enjoyable to read.

✳ For more about using transitions, see SE pages 595–596.

Exercise
Answers

1. Transition: By focusing on; Organization: point by point
2. Transition: In terms of plot; Organization: point by point
3. Transition: At the climax; Organization: time order
4. Transition: Looking at the theme; Organization: point by point
5. Transition: The theme of deception; Organization: point by point

296

Revising for Organization

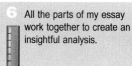

| 6 All the parts of my essay work together to create an insightful analysis. | 5 I use transitions to connect my paragraphs and key words to connect my sentences. | 4 I use transitions to connect my paragraphs, but I should use more key words to connect my sentences. |

When you revise for *organization,* you check the overall structure of your essay and the unity of each paragraph. The rubric strip above can guide your revision.

Have I clearly connected my paragraphs?

You have clearly connected your paragraphs if you have used transitions. Different types of organization use different transitional words and phrases.

Time Order	Point by Point	Logical Order
First	Considering the characters	To begin with
Soon	As to the plot	Furthermore
In the end	In the climactic scene	As a result

Exercise

Read the following thesis statement and topic sentences. Identify the transitional words and phrases used in the topic sentences and indicate the organizational pattern.

Thesis Statement: In *The Final Adventure,* playwright Stephen Dietz explores the uses of deception.

1. By focusing on two great deceivers—Sherlock Holmes and Professor Moriarty—Dietz differentiates between "good" and "bad" deception.
2. In terms of plot, the play is one grand spiderweb woven by Holmes.
3. At the climax, Dietz pits his two deceivers in a battle to the death atop Reichenbach Falls in Switzerland.
4. Looking at the theme in a larger context, Dietz himself is a "good deceiver," using actors, costumes, and sets to fool the audience.
5. The theme of deception expands, taking in the whole play and its many costumes, sets, and sound effects.

Revise

Review your paragraphs. Have you connected them with transitions that show the overall structure of the analysis? If not, consider adding transitional words and phrases to your topic sentences to make the structure clear.

English Language Learners

Some students may have difficulty using transition words and phrases. Before students begin revising for organization, have them practice using transition words with familiar topics, such as using time order transitions to summarize a schedule or using logical order transitions to explain steps in a process.

Analyzing a Theme 297

3 I need clearer transitions to connect my paragraphs and should use key words to connect my sentences.

2 My paragraphs and sentences show no connection, and I need to use transitions and key words.

1 I need to learn how to organize an analysis of a play.

Have I used key words to connect my sentences?

You have used key words if an important term from one sentence is repeated in another. Key words connect your ideas like the pieces of a jigsaw puzzle.

Watson himself is often the unwitting but **willing** victim of Holmes's deceptions.

The doctor's **willingness** comes from trust in his friend, which shows that deceivers can be heroic.

Holmes's **heroism**, despite his deceptions, is strongly contrasted with the villainy of the deceitful Moriarty.

Exercise

Identify the key words that connect the sentences below.

1   Holmes and Moriarty each weave webs of deception in *The Final Adventure.*
2   Holmes's web is, in fact, the larger of the two, constructed to slowly contract around
3   his prey. That prey, Moriarty, escapes the outer strands of the web only to be caught
4   in the center. He cannot escape the central strand because it is not a deception but
5   the truth—evidence to convict the crime boss and destroy his syndicate.

Revise

Check your sentences. Have you connected them with key words? If not, add some to clarify and improve the flow of your ideas.

Literature

Organization
Key words help connect the ideas in sentences.

Tom also feels trapped, working in a shoe factory, though

Coworkers
he wishes to be a poet. ~~Friends~~ call him "Shakespeare" (92).

works simply to
Tom makes money to support his mother and sister, though

he spends nights at the movies, wishing for adventure. . . .

Make sure students understand that they can use different forms of the words they repeat, such as those shown in the examples *willing* and *willingness*, and *heroic* and *heroism*.

Encourage students to read aloud their writing to themselves as they revise to make sure that they have used repetition effectively and to eliminate repetition of insignificant words.

Point out to students that they can also use **repetition between paragraphs** (*see below*) to clarify and improve the flow of ideas throughout their essay.

Exercise
Answers

lines 1, 2, 3: webs, web, web
lines 1, 4: deception
line 3: prey
lines 3, 4: strands, strand
line 4: center, central

Teaching Tip: Repetition Between Paragraphs

Explain to students that repeating a key word or phrase at the end of one paragraph and in the beginning of the next can help them achieve paragraph coherence and a unified essay. For an example, have students turn back to the sample Middle Paragraphs on SE page 291. Discuss the effect of the writer's repetition of the phrase "gentleman caller" at the end of the second paragraph and at the beginning of the first sentence of the third paragraph.

English Language Learners

Some students may have difficulty knowing which words to use for effective repetition. Point out that key words often come from one or more of the following:

- character traits
- character descriptions ("gentleman caller")
- theme/thesis statement
- dialogue
- tone

Revising **for** Voice

Remind students that in their analysis, they are not only telling the story of the play, but they are also conveying its theme. Readers will accept the writer's interpretation only if they feel they know the characters and their problem. Using a narrative voice to tell the story, one that engages the reader with sensory details and dialogue, will help readers

- get to know the characters and understand their experiences, and
- care about what happens to them.

Exercise
Answers

1. b; This sentence uses sensory details to describe Brad Bowers.

2. a; This sentence uses vivid verbs to show important action.

3. b; This sentence uses a quotation from the play to reveal Bower's vain personality.

298

Revising **for** Voice

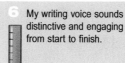 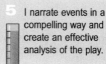 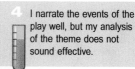

6 My writing voice sounds distinctive and engaging from start to finish.

5 I narrate events in a compelling way and create an effective analysis of the play.

4 I narrate the events of the play well, but my analysis of the theme does not sound effective.

When you revise your play analysis for *voice*, make sure you effectively narrate the plot and analyze the theme. The rubric strip above will guide your revision for voice.

Have I used a compelling narrative voice?

You have used a compelling narrative voice if your summary of the plot is vivid and inviting and your character descriptions are revealing. A compelling narrative voice does the following things:

1. **Describes** people, places, and things using sensory details
2. **Shows** important action with vivid verbs
3. **Provides** dialogue that reveals personalities

Exercise

For each pair of sentences, indicate which sentence has a better narrative voice and why.

1. a. The game show host, Brad Bowers, doesn't seem very genuine.
   b. The game show host, Brad Bowers, wears a perpetual plastic smile and an obvious toupee.

2. a. Brad Bowers bursts through the curtain opening, leaps down from the stage, and grabs audience members to join in the game show, *King of the Mountain*.
   b. Brad Bowers comes out on stage and then goes down in the audience and asks questions to see who knows the answers.

3. a. Bowers is so vain that he refuses to wear glasses, though he needs them.
   b. Bowers declares, "There's nothing wrong with my eyes," just before he runs into a couch and tumbles headlong.

Revise

Refine your narrative voice. Review the part of your essay that focuses on the plot and characters. Make sure you provide clear descriptions, use vivid verbs to describe action, and provide dialogue that reveals personality.

Analyzing a Theme **299**

3 My narration of events should be more compelling, and my analysis should be more effective.

2 Throughout my essay, my voice is flat and needs to be made effective.

1 I need help understanding how to create an effective voice for my play analysis.

Have I used an effective analytical voice?

You have used an effective analytical voice if your writing does the following things:

1. **Divides** a topic into parts
2. **Defines** each part
3. **Shows** how the parts relate to each other and to the whole

Exercise

Read the paragraph below and identify how the writer divides the theme into parts, defines each part, and shows the relationship between the parts.

1 All of the contestants in *Game Show* hope for a shot at the American Dream.
2 Ethel Tinsley wants to win enough money to publish her book. Dolly Perkins hopes
3 to be able to move out of the "retirement villa" where she lives. Kathy Burns and
4 Steve Nystrom both want to advance their film careers—and perhaps rekindle their
5 romance. Most of the contestants are destined not for the American Dream but for
6 the American Reality: that competition results in one winner and many losers.

Revise

Review your analytical voice. Read the part of your essay that analyzes the theme. Be sure you have divided the theme into parts and shown how the parts relate to each other.

Voice
The writer divides the topic into parts and defines each.

*Jim O'Connor seems to be everything the Wingfields need**—romance, adventure, confidence, and risk.*

Perhaps Amanda has found a way back to bygone days; perhaps Tom has found a coconspirator to help him escape the factory; perhaps Laura has found a gentleman who would lift her out of her fragile glass world and into life.

Literature

Reassure students that
■ if they have explained the characters, setting, and important plot events in order, using evidence from the play,
■ and they connected those elements to the central theme in a logical way,
■ then they have used an analytical voice.

If students are confused by the mention of two voices (narrative and analytical) in one piece of writing, point out that a narrative voice relates to what happens in the play (plot, characters, setting) while an analytical voice relates to the theme and structure of the writing.

Exercise Answers

■ In this paragraph, the writer analyzes the characters, who are contestants in the play *Game Show,* and who all want a shot at the American Dream.
■ The writer defines each contestant by describing his or her idea of the American Dream.
■ The writer shows how the contestants are related to each other and to the theme by pointing out that most of them are destined for the American Reality—one winner and many losers.

Revising for Word Choice

Remind students that precise and correct use of specialized terms—in this case, play terminology—helps to create an analytical voice. Readers trust writers who sound knowledgeable.

If students would like a more detailed definition of a particular play term, suggest that they consult a literary reference source, a list of which should be available in the library or on their library Web site.

Writer's Craft

Literary terminology: The terminology on SE page 300 focuses on theatrical terminology, but advanced students might also want to use terminology that refers to the writer's craft. Terms such as *metaphor, overstatement,* and *irony* are defined on SE pages 600–601.

Revising for Word Choice

6 My writing voice sounds distinctive and engaging from start to finish.	**5** I have correctly used theater terminology and have referred to symbols in the play.	**4** I have used most terminology correctly, but I should refer to symbols in the play.

When you revise for *word choice,* be sure you have used theater terminology correctly and referred to symbols in the play. Use the rubric strip above to help you revise for word choice.

How can I check my use of theater terminology?

You can check your theater terminology by reviewing these basic terms:

Act: A main part of a play; a group of scenes

Character: A person or an animal in a play

Climax: The moment when the main character confronts the conflict

Comedy: A play in which the hero is redeemed despite flaws

Conflict: The problem or clash between forces in a play

Dialogue: Characters speaking to each other

Drama: The study of plays and playwriting; a play that deals with serious themes

Monologue: One character speaking to the audience

Narrator: A person who speaks directly to the audience and connects the scenes

Plot: The series of events that intensify conflict and lead to a climax

Prop: A small item actors use and manipulate onstage

Scene: Part of an act happening in one place and time

Set: The arrangement of the stage to represent a specific place

Setting: The place and time where the action of the play occurs

Soliloquy: A speech delivered by one character

Stage: The main area of action for the play

Symbol: A person, a place, a thing, or an idea that stands for something else

Theme: The playwright's message about life or human nature

Tone: The playwright's attitude toward the subject

Tragedy: A play in which the hero's flaws cause his or her undoing

Revise

Check your theater terminology. Read through your essay and make sure you use correct and precise terminology when discussing your play.

Analyzing a Theme   **301**

3 Some of my theater terminology is incorrect, and I need to refer to symbols in the play.

2 I need to use theater terminology, and I need to refer to symbols in the play.

1 I need help understanding word choice in a play analysis.

How can I discover symbols in the play?

You can discover symbols in a play by paying close attention to words that the author gives special treatment to. Watch especially for these types of words:

■ **Words Used in Titles**
The title *The Glass Menagerie* hints at two symbols: glass, which stands for fragility and beauty (Laura), and menagerie, a collection of living things representing the Wingfields and people in general.

■ **Words Used Repeatedly**
In *The Glass Menagerie,* the character Tom is often associated with the word *movie,* which symbolizes adventure.

■ **Words That Describe Important Props**
In *The Glass Menagerie,* the unicorn is Laura's favorite glass animal, the one that doesn't fit in and is "freakish." It is a symbol of Laura herself.

Note: A symbol is a person, a place, a thing, or an idea that stands for something else. Symbols are keys to unlocking a play's themes.

Revise

Check your symbolism. Consider words that appear in the title of the play, words that are repeated in connection with one character or situation, and words that describe important props. Refer to these symbols in your analysis and show how they demonstrate the theme.

Literature

Word Choice
A symbol is explained.

This is just what Laura needs—to take risks, even possibly to get broken, if only to fit in better with the rest of the world.

The problem is that she isn't like her unicorn—she doesn't lose her horn or learn to fit in with the other horses.

English Language Learners

Some students may have difficulty identifying symbols or their special meanings. Have students practice identifying common symbols and discussing their importance:

- the Statue of Liberty as a symbol of freedom
- a heart as a symbol of love
- a flower as a symbol of beauty
- a bracelet as a symbol of friendship
- flags as symbols of countries
- a trophy as a symbol of victory

Tell students that understanding symbolism in any work of literature can be challenging and even controversial.

■ A symbol is used by the writer to represent another idea. A symbol has a literal meaning, such as a glass unicorn, and a figurative meaning, such as the fragile Laura.

■ Understanding a symbol requires a basic understanding of the work and a willingness to think beyond the literal meaning to why and how an author uses a symbol to connect to the theme.

■ Sometimes, people have different and contrary interpretations of the meaning of a symbol. Point out that if a student can support an interpretation of a symbol with solid evidence, either from the play or from an expert source, she or he can use it confidently.

Revising for Sentence Fluency

As students closely examine the three strategies for integrating quotations, tell them to pay particular attention to different punctuation used with each quotation. Noting the differences now can make the editing process on SE page 307 easier.

Suggest that students read to a partner the parts in their analysis that contain quoted text. The partner should listen specifically for how well the writer has integrated quotations. At the same time, the writer will have an opportunity to hear breaks in the flow, caused by poorly integrated quotations from the play.

 Literature Connections

Mentor texts: The examples on SE page 303 refer to a play entitled *The Complete Works of William Shakespeare (Abridged)* by Adam Long, Daniel Singer, and Jess Winfield. This fast-paced and hilarious play provides a fun introduction to the works of the bard. Showing the DVD version of this play to your class could help warm them up to a unit studying one of the Bard's works—especially *Romeo and Juliet* or *Hamlet*.

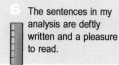 **302**

Revising for Sentence Fluency

6 The sentences in my analysis are deftly written and a pleasure to read.

5 I have smoothly integrated quotations in my analysis, and I have created an effective sentence rhythm.

4 Most of my quotations are smoothly included, but I should vary my sentence lengths to create a better rhythm.

When you revise for *sentence fluency,* be sure that you have smoothly integrated quotations in your analysis and that you have created an effective sentence rhythm. The rubric strip above will guide your revision for sentence fluency.

Have I smoothly integrated quotations?

You have smoothly integrated quotations if they fit naturally in the flow of your analysis. Here are three strategies for integrating quotations into your analysis:

- Make **short quotations** part of the sentence.
  Daniel begins the three-man play by pledging to "capture, in a single theatrical experience, the genius of *The Complete Works of William Shakespeare*" (8).

  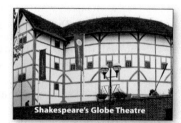
  Shakespeare's Globe Theatre

- Introduce **medium-length quotations** as you would dialogue. During the show, Adam often butchers famous lines, for example, reciting the following: "What's in a name, anyway? That which we call a nose / By any other name would still smell" (18).

- When **quoting four or more lines,** indent the material as an excerpt. Adam even turns an audience member into an actor, coaching her how to play the part of Ophelia from Hamlet:

  > Now your job as an actress is to take all of these elements, synthesize them within your soul, then, at that moment of truth, we're going to build everyone into a mighty frenzy, stop everything, all attention goes to you, and you let out with that scream that epitomizes Ophelia. (63)

 Revise

Check your quotations. If a quotation breaks the flow of thought, revise using one of the strategies above.

Grammar Connection

Integrating Quotations
- *Write Source* page 111
- **Proofreader's Guide** page 636 (+)

Sentence Rhythm
- *Write Source* pages 88, 85
- **Proofreader's Guide** pages 750–751
- *SkillsBook* pages 137, 138, 139

English Language Learners

Some students may not fully understand the humor in the second quotation because they are not familiar with the original line. Explain that in Shakespeare's *Romeo and Juliet*, the famous line is "What's in a name? That which we call a rose/ By any other name would smell as sweet."

Analyzing a Theme **303**

 3 Some of my quotations stop the flow of the analysis, and I need to vary my sentences.

2 I haven't smoothly integrated any quotations, and I need sentence rhythm.

1 I need help understanding how to quote from a play and how to create sentence rhythm.

Have I created an effective sentence rhythm?

You have created an effective rhythm if you have done the following:

- Used **medium sentences** (about 20 words) for most of your writing
- Used **long sentences** (30 words or more) to express complex ideas
- Used **short sentences** (10 words or fewer) to make a strong point

◀ Exercise

Count the number of words in each sentence below and label them medium, long, or short. What effect do the sentence lengths in this passage have on the rhythm?

> After the three-man troupe acts out a 20-minute version of *Hamlet*—complete with Hamlet's soliloquy, Ophelia's drowning, and the deaths of Gertrude, Claudias, and Hamlet himself—they notice they have some time left to do *Hamlet* "One more time" (72). They proceed to compact the whole play into two gory minutes that end with everyone dead onstage. Jess then suggests that they do the play "faster" (74). The three actors simply walk onstage and die. Lastly, Daniel suggests that they do the play "backwards," a crazy spectacle of characters coming back to life, reciting lines backward, and even depicting Ophelia's drowning. These four versions of Hamlet bring the crowd to its feet.

 Revise

Check your sentence lengths. Be sure to vary your sentences effectively, using different lengths for different purposes.

Sentence Fluency
Sentence variety is improved.

> Amanda's hope that a gentleman caller would make her life perfect
> was dashed when her husband left. *and* Now Laura's hope for a similar
> knight in shining armor is also dashed. Such rescuers don't exist,
> and only Tom escapes the apartment, but he can't be free . . .

Literature

Many students will associate rhythm with poetry, but not with prose. Explain that the rhythm of prose depends on the sound and arrangement of words in sentences and paragraphs. Using sentences of different lengths and types, and varying sentence beginnings help produce a rhythm that, like free-verse poetry, flows naturally and smoothly.

 Exercise Answers

- Sentence 1—long (39 words)
- Sentence 2—medium (17 words)
- Sentence 3—short (9 words)
- Sentence 4—short (8 words)
- Sentence 5—medium to long (26 words)
- Sentence 6—short (11 words)

Varying sentence length creates an effective sentence rhythm that sounds natural and is pleasing to read.

Revising Improving Your Writing

As students review the checklist, have them pay particular attention to questions that focus on elements that they struggled with during prewriting and writing. Emphasize the importance of reviewing their revised draft to make sure that they have improved the parts of the essay that may have been affected by these elements.

Peer Responding

Have students exchange their essays with a partner. Tell partners to review each other's writing for sentence fluency. Have them check their partner's use of

- coordinating conjunctions to connect ideas,
- appositives to add information,
- transitions to achieve coherence, and
- verbal phrases to modify.

✳ See the Proofreader's Guide (SE page 748) for more information on sentence construction.

304

Revising Improving Your Writing

Check your revising. On a piece of paper, write the numbers 1 to 13. If you can answer "yes" to a question, put a check mark after that number. If not, continue to work with that part of your essay.

Revising Checklist

Ideas

_____ **1.** Does my thesis statement focus on a major theme of the play?
_____ **2.** Have I analyzed the theme using character, setting, and plot?
_____ **3.** Have I created effective summaries and used appropriate quotations?

Organization

_____ **4.** Does my beginning catch the reader's attention and introduce the thesis?
_____ **5.** Are my middle paragraphs connected with transitions?
_____ **6.** Are the ideas in my sentences connected with key words?
_____ **7.** Does the ending expand upon the theme?

Voice

_____ **8.** Have I used an engaging narrative voice to summarize the play?
_____ **9.** Have I used a strong analytical voice to explain the theme?

Word Choice

_____ **10.** Do I use theater terminology correctly?
_____ **11.** Have I identified symbols in the play?

Sentence Fluency

_____ **12.** Have I integrated quotations smoothly?
_____ **13.** Have I varied the length of my sentences?

Make a clean copy. When you finish revising your essay, make a clean copy for editing.

English Language Learners

Students may have difficulty achieving an engaging narrative writing voice. To demonstrate, have students orally summarize a scene from their play for a partner. Explain that the narrative voice they used to describe the scene should be used to express their ideas in writing.

Analyzing a Theme   305

Editing

Once you have finished revising your work for its content, you need to edit it for punctuation, capitalization, spelling, and grammar.

Keys to Effective Editing

1. Use a dictionary, a thesaurus, and the "Proofreader's Guide" in the back of this book to check your writing.

2. Check your use of any comparative and superlative modifiers as well as your punctuation, capitalization, spelling, and grammar.

3. Edit on a clean revised copy of your essay. Then either enter your changes on the computer file or write a new handwritten copy that includes the corrections.

4. Use the editing and proofreading marks on the inside back cover of this book.

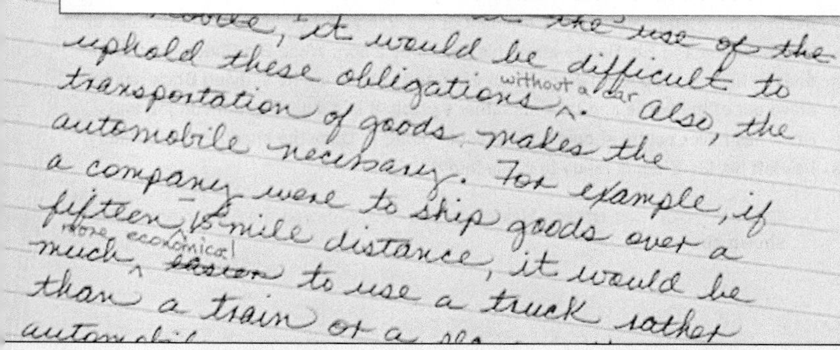

[handwritten essay text, partially legible]

Literature

Editing

Keys to Effective Editing

Tell students to be careful if they are using the spell-check function on their computer while editing. A word may be spelled correctly, but it may be the incorrect word to use. For example, you may have written a homophone, *knight* instead of *night*. Both words are spelled correctly, but have different meanings. A computer will catch only misspelled words. It is, therefore, important to read your writing to check that words are used correctly.

Technology Connections

Students can use the added features of the Net-text as they explore this stage of the writing process.

Write Source Online **Net-text**

Editing for Conventions

Give students a chance to read through the five comma rules and encourage them to ask questions about any rule that is not absolutely clear. Then focus their attention on rule 3, which deals with items in a series. Point out that when they read, they may come across items in a series in which the comma before the conjunction is omitted. Emphasize that students should always use a comma before the conjunction when writing items in a series, as explained in the rule here.

✱ For more about using commas correctly, see SE pages 608–617.

▶ Grammar Exercise
Answers

- An injury keeps him from playing **football, and** the . . .
- Maggie wants her husband to be a **husband, and** Big Daddy . . .
- While Big Daddy **lives,** Brick . . .
- When Big Daddy discovers he is **dying,** Brick has . . .
- It is a **daunting,** difficult **job, and** Brick has . . .
- Once the shadow of Big Daddy has left his **life,** Brick is . . .

306

Editing for Conventions

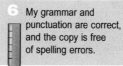

6 My grammar and punctuation are correct, and the copy is free of spelling errors.

5 I have one or two errors in grammar, spelling, or punctuation, but they won't distract the reader.

4 I need to correct a few errors in punctuation, spelling, or grammar, which may distract the reader.

When you revise for *conventions,* you check punctuation, capitalization, spelling, and grammar. The rubric strip above can guide you.

How can I avoid the most common comma errors?

You can avoid the most common comma errors by following these rules:

1. Place a comma after long introductory word groups.
   In *Cat on a Hot Tin Roof,* a wealthy Southern family deals with many crises.
2. Put a comma before a coordinating conjunction in a compound sentence.
   Maggie longs for her husband, but Brick is consumed with grief over the death of his best friend from high school.
3. Place a comma after each item in a series (except the last).
   Neither Brick, Maggie, nor Big Daddy himself realizes how little time he has.
4. Use a comma to separate equal adjectives.
   Big Daddy is a forceful, proud man.
5. Use commas to set off nonrestrictive word groups.
   But neither pride nor force can save him from cancer, which silently eats him away.

▶ Grammar Exercise

Correct the comma errors in the following paragraph.

1   Much of the conflict in *Cat on a Hot Tin Roof* comes from the fact that Brick
2 cannot be the man he needs to be. An injury keeps him from playing football and the
3 death of his friend haunts every moment of every day. Maggie wants her husband to
4 be a husband and Big Daddy wants his son to be a son. While Big Daddy lives Brick
5 doesn't have to stop wallowing. When Big Daddy discovers he is dying Brick has to
6 crawl out of the bottle and take his father's place. It is a daunting difficult job and
7 Brick has never before shown an interest in doing it. Once the shadow of Big Daddy
8 has left his life Brick is ready to come into the light.

Edit

Check your commas. Make sure you have followed the five comma rules shown above.

Grammar Connection

Commas Review

- **Proofreader's Guide** pages 608 (+), 610 (+), 612 (+), 614 (+), 616 (+)
- *SkillsBook* pages 10, 16
- *GrammarSnap* Common Uses of Commas; Commas after Introductory Words, Phrases, and Clauses

Punctuating Compound and Complex Sentences

- **Proofreader's Guide** pages 618 (+), 744–745, 748 (+)
- *SkillsBook* pages 7, 102
- *GrammarSnap* Sentence Types: Compound, Complex, and Compound-Complex Sentences

English Language Learners

Some students may have difficulty indicating where commas should be placed in the **Exercise** activity. Read the paragraph aloud so students can listen to the natural pauses in speech. Then read it aloud a second time, this time letting students interject or signal you to stop when they hear where a comma should be placed.

Analyzing a Theme **307**

3 I need to correct a number of errors that will probably confuse the reader.

2 I need to fix many errors that make my writing hard to read and understand.

1 I need help making corrections.

Have I correctly punctuated citations from the play?

You have correctly punctuated citations if you follow these rules:

1. Place the page number in parentheses before the end punctuation.

Brick says he is disgusted with "mendacity," or lying (79).

2. Do not use a period, but do use a question mark or an exclamation point in a quotation that ends the sentence.

Big Daddy asks about the word *mendacity*: **"Don't it mean lying and liars?" (79).**

3. When quoting from a verse play, show line breaks with a space, a slash, and a space; use Arabic numerals to indicate act, scene, and line; and separate these numbers with periods.

Perhaps the most famous line from *The Tempest* **is spoken by Prospero after Caliban interrupts his fanciful masque: "We are such stuff / As dreams are made on, and our little life / Is rounded with a sleep" (4.1.156–158).**

4. Show deletions from a quotation by using an ellipsis (three periods with a space before and after each one).

Big Daddy tells his wife, Ida, "You thought I was dying and you started taking over, well, . . . I'm not gonna die" (57).

Edit

Check the punctuation of your citations. Follow the rules above, making sure each citation is clear but unobtrusive.

Conventions
A comma is inserted and punctuation of a citation is corrected.

Jim is sorry, but Laura says, "I'll just imagine he had an operation. The horn was removed to make him feel less— freakish! . . . Now he will feel more at home with the other horses, the ones that don't have horns." (125) Jim steals a kiss from Laura, but calls himself "stumblejohn" for . . .

Literature

Editing for correctly punctuated citations gives students an opportunity to double-check that they have provided citations for every quotation used from the play.

Note that when students quote more than four lines of text, they should set up the quotation as an excerpt—indented on the left, with no quotation marks around the material. See the excerpt demonstrated on page 302 of the student book.

Struggling Learners

Point out that the Marking Punctuation section on SE pages 605–647 is a good place to review rules when students are unsure of conventions. Then walk through SE pages 632–635, paying particular attention to the sections on using quotation marks and managing long quotations.

Grammar Connection

Punctuating Quotations and Citations
- **Proofreader's Guide** pages 618 (+), 632 (+)
- *SkillsBook* page 33

Punctuating Compound and Complex Sentences
- **Proofreader's Guide** pages 618 (+), 744–745, 748 (+)
- *SkillsBook* pages 7, 102
- *GrammarSnap* Sentence Types: Compound, Complex, and Compound-Complex Sentences

Editing Checking for Conventions

Give students a few moments to look over the Proofreader's Guide (SE pages 604–763). Throughout the year, they can refer to the instruction, rules, and examples to clarify any checklist items or to resolve questions about their own writing.

Explain that compound adjectives (item 3 in the Editing Checklist) are often hyphenated, especially when they precede a noun. They are formed when two or more words that are usually written separately are combined to form one word that is then used to modify a noun:

- Amanda's request that Tom find a man for Laura may have been ill advised.
- Amanda's ill-advised request precipitated dramatic changes.

Creating a Title

Encourage students to try all three strategies. If they still cannot come up with a title they like, suggest that they

- skim the play looking for a piece of important dialogue that can be rephrased as a title, or
- scan the titles of professional reviews and articles about the play for ideas that could be adapted and reworded to suit their essay.

308

Editing Checking for Conventions

 Edit

Check your editing. On a piece of paper, write the numbers 1 to 12. Put a check by the number if you can answer "yes" to that question. If not, continue to edit your essay for that convention.

Editing Checklist

Conventions

PUNCTUATION

_____ **1.** Does each sentence have correct end punctuation?

_____ **2.** Have I used quotation marks and correctly cited direct quotations?

_____ **3.** Have I correctly hyphenated compound adjectives?

_____ **4.** Have I used parentheses to set off page numbers?

_____ **5.** Have I avoided comma errors?

CAPITALIZATION

_____ **6.** Do I start all my sentences with capital letters?

_____ **7.** Have I capitalized all proper nouns?

SPELLING

_____ **8.** Have I spelled all my words correctly?

_____ **9.** Have I double-checked the spelling of names and terms from the play?

GRAMMAR

_____ **10.** Have I used correct verb tenses throughout?

_____ **11.** Have I used the correct comparative and superlative forms?

_____ **12.** Have I used the right words *(its, it's)*?

Creating a Title

Be sure to give your analysis a title that attracts the reader's attention and represents your essay well. Try one of these strategies:

- Create a play on words: **Glass People**
- Use a common expression: **Those Who Live in Glass Apartments**
- Take a line from the essay: **Broken to Fit In**

Grammar Connection

Capitalization

- **Proofreader's Guide** pages 648 (+), 650 (+)
- *SkillsBook* page 43
- *GrammarSnap* Capitalization of Proper Nouns and Adjectives

---

English Language Learners

Students may benefit from reading their essays aloud or having them read aloud by a partner so that they can listen for places where they need to add punctuation. Have students listen for places where the voice naturally rises or stops, indicating a question mark or period, and where there are pauses, indicating commas.

Analyzing a Theme **309**

Publishing Sharing Your Essay

You're nearly done! You've selected a topic, gathered and organized details, written a first draft, revised it, and edited it. Now it's time to share your analysis with others.

Make a final copy. Follow your teacher's instructions or use the guidelines below to format your paper. (If you are using a computer, see pages 91–95.) Prepare a final copy of your essay and proofread it for errors.

Focusing on Presentation

- Use blue or black ink and write neatly.
- Write your name in the upper left corner of page 1.
- Skip a line and center your title; skip another line and start your essay.
- Indent every paragraph and leave a one-inch margin on all four sides.
- Write your last name and the page number in the upper right-hand corner of every page after page 1.

Perform a Dramatic Reading

Present your analysis as a speech. Use props that represent important symbols or ideas in the play. If you have access to a video performance of the play, show short excerpts to make a point.

Post Online

Search online for the title of the play, looking for sites that include chat rooms or bulletin boards. Post your essay where others interested in the play can see it and read it.

Stage a Scene

Choose your favorite scene from the play and perform it with fellow classmates. Either read the scene dramatically (this is called "reader's theater"), or perform it—memorizing lines, blocking the action, and devising costumes, sets, props, and lighting.

Literature

Publishing
Sharing Your Essay

Offer students two more ideas for publishing their essays.

- If the play is currently being performed in the area, have students submit their analyses to the editor of the local newspaper and ask if they could be published in the entertainment section of the paper, alongside any play reviews.
- If the play is in the library collection, students can provide copies of their analyses. Reading the essays can provide readers with extra insight into the meaning of the plays.

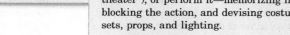

Remind students that they can use the Writing Network features of the Portfolio to share their work with peers.

Write Source Online **Portfolio**

Write Source Online **Net-text**

Struggling Learners

Allow time for students to complete their final copy over several sessions, if necessary. Some students may accidentally introduce errors if the recopying process becomes too tedious.

Rubric for a Response to Literature

Tell students the following about rubrics and how to use them:

■ The rubrics in this book are based on a six-point scale. A score of 6 indicates an amazing piece of writing. A score of 1 means the writing is incomplete and not ready to be assessed.

■ The purpose of the rubric is to help students break down the assessment process by evaluating each of the six traits individually—ideas, organization, voice, word choice, sentence fluency, and conventions.

■ Rubrics are also helpful during the writing process. They can guide you whenever you write because they tell you what elements to include in your writing and how to present them.

■ Explain to students that they will most likely have different ratings for the traits. For example, they may give themselves a 5 for ideas but a 4 for organization.

✱ Reproducible six-, five-, and four-point rubrics for responses to literature are available on pages 770, 774, and 778.

310

Rubric for a Response to Literature

Use this rubric to guide and assess your writing. Refer to it whenever you want to improve your writing using the six traits.

6 Ideas	**5**	**4**
The ideas show a complete understanding of the reading.	The essay has a clear focus statement and necessary supporting details.	The essay has a clear focus statement. Unnecessary details need to be cut.
Organization		
All the parts work together to create an insightful essay.	The organization pattern fits the topic and purpose. All parts of the essay are well developed.	The organization pattern fits the topic and purpose. A part of the essay needs better development.
Voice		
The voice expresses interest and complete understanding. It engages the reader.	The voice expresses interest in and understanding of the topic.	The voice expresses interest but needs to show more understanding.
Word Choice		
The word choice reflects a thorough understanding of the reading.	The word choice, including the use of quotations, creates a clear message.	The word choice is clear, but better quotations would improve the essay.
Sentence Fluency		
The sentences in the essay create a clear flow of ideas.	The sentences are skillfully written and keep the reader's interest.	No sentence problems exist. More sentence variety is needed.
Conventions		
Grammar and punctuation are correct, and the copy is free of all errors.	The essay has one or two errors that do not interfere with the reader's understanding.	The essay has a few careless errors in punctuation and grammar.

English Language Learners

Students may have difficulty checking their final copy for accidentally introduced mistakes. Pair students with cooperative, language-proficient partners and have them work together to review their changes.

3	**2**	**1**
The focus statement is too broad. A variety of details are needed.	The focus statement is unclear. More details are needed.	The essay needs a focus statement and details.
The organization fits the essay's purpose. Some parts need more development.	The organization doesn't fit the purpose.	A plan needs to be followed.
The voice needs to be more interesting and express more understanding.	The voice does not show interest in or an understanding of the topic.	The writer needs to understand how to create voice.
The word choice is too general, and quotations are needed.	Little attention is given to word choice.	The writer needs help with word choice.
A few sentence problems need to be corrected.	The essay has many sentence problems.	The writer needs to learn how to construct sentences.
The errors in the essay confuse the reader.	The number of errors makes the essay hard to read.	Help is needed to make corrections.

Literature

Evaluating a Play Analysis

Ask students if they agree with the sample self-assessment on SE page 313. If they agree with the overall comments, ask them to suggest improvements based on the comments in the self-assessment. If they disagree with any comment, ask them to explain why.

Many students will already be familiar with *The Tempest* and may have read it or seen it performed. Some students, however, may not know the play and will find it difficult to comment on elements of the response essay and the assessment that relate to ideas.

If possible, have students watch a video of a production of *The Tempest.* After viewing the play, have students address the writer's overall comments on SE page 313. Ask them to

- explain how and where the writer might add more depth to the analysis,
- suggest quotations from the play that would support the writer's theme, and
- identify symbols in the play that the writer could have discussed.

Evaluating a Play Analysis

Read the following analysis of Shakespeare's *The Tempest.* Then read the self-evaluation on the next page. (**There may be errors in the essay below.**)

Good Dreams and Evil Realities

Long before *The Poseidon Adventure, The Perfect Storm,* or *Titanic,* William Shakespeare wrote of another great shipwreck in *The Tempest.* A raging storm at sea batters the ship that carries King Alonso of Naples, Duke Antonio of Milan, and their retinue. These nobles and the ship's crew are "wracked" upon a strange and magical island. There, they all fall under the grand spell of Prospero, the rightful duke of Milan. In *The Tempest,* Shakespeare shows how good fantasies can transform evil realities.

Prospero's spell is meant to purge the bad blood in his family. Prospero's brother Antonio stole the throne of Milan from him and, with the help of the king of Naples, exiled Prospero and his young daughter, Miranda, to a desert island. There, Prospero discovered two strangely magical beings: Caliban, the monstrous man-fish, and Ariel, an airy spirit. Prospero takes charge of the brutish Caliban and the spiritual Ariel, using one to tame the island physically and the other to prepare his great spell.

The illusions begin with the tempest itself. Ariel and his spirit kin churn the sea and sky and make the ship seem to wreck on the shore. The usurping Antonio and the conniving Alonso stagger out of the ship along with their company. They have barely been on shore half an hour before Antonio and the brother to the king try to murder King Alonso and usurp his throne. Their plot, though, is broken up by Ariel, who sings to startle the conspirators and awaken the king. Throughout *The Tempest,* the illusions and magic that Prospero creates through Ariel perform this function—not destroying but saving.

As the play progresses, the shipwreck "survivors" split up and wander the island, each group experiencing illusions that suit their crimes. King Alonso thinks his son Ferdinand is dead—when in fact he is falling in love with Prospero's daughter, Miranda. Their marriage in the end will allow Prospero's daughter to gently "usurp" the rule of Naples. Meanwhile, Caliban falls in with the jester Trinculo and the drunken butler Stephano, and the three hatch a ridiculous plot to kill Prospero and take over his island. They end up hopelessly mired in mud and horse manure. Even Antonio must face up to what he has done. After presenting the usurper with an ethereal banquet, Ariel withdraws it before Antonio can eat and confronts him with his evil: "I and my fellows are ministers of fate," Ariel says, "But remember / (For that is my business to you) that you three from Milan / Did supplant good Prospero; . . . Upon your heads is nothing but heart's sorrow" (3.3.60-61, 68-70, 81).

Though Prospero might seem to be taking revenge, the purpose of these illusions isn't simply to punish, but to correct an evil reality. Alonso's son Ferdinand isn't truly dead. Nor is Antonio killed for his treason against his brother. In the end, a right relationship is created among them all. Prospero's wisdom, compassion, and maturity seem to reflect Shakespeare's own. *The Tempest* was one of the last plays Shakespeare ever wrote, and it has the feeling of a man putting his affairs in order. Prospero breaks his wand at the end of *The Tempest*, saying he will create no more illusions, and Shakespeare puts down his pen with the same result. In that way, *The Tempest* shows how Shakespeare believed that the good dream of theater has the power to correct the evil realities of the world outside.

Student Self-Assessment

Response Rubric Checklist

Title: *Good Dreams and Evil Realities*
Writer: *Dave Denoon*

4 Ideas
  • Do I have a clear thesis statement?
  • Do I use effective details?

4 Organization
  • Does the beginning state the thesis?
  • Does the middle focus on major elements?
  • Does the ending expand the theme?

5 Voice
  • Is my voice suitably analytical?
  • Is my voice compelling as I narrate the plot?

4 Word Choice
  • Have I used correct theater terminology?
  • Have I focused on symbols?

5 Sentence Fluency
  • Do my sentences read smoothly?

5 Conventions
  • Have I followed the rules of English?

OVERALL COMMENTS:

I love The Tempest, and I did a good job exploring the play.

I should have gone into more depth analyzing the theme, and I should have used more quotations.

I mentioned the wand, but I should have talked about other symbols.

Review your analysis. Rate your essay and write comments that explain why you gave yourself the scores you did.

Literature

To help students feel more comfortable using the traits to assess their essay, modify their self-assessment by

• focusing on two traits, such as voice and conventions, and

• having students read their essay first for strengths, and then for weaknesses in only those areas.

Benchmark Papers

The Beast of Fear (good)

● TE pp. 810–815

Huck Finn: The Relationship Between Huck and Jim (fair)

● TE pp. 816–819

Student Self-Assessment

To give students additional practice with evaluating a response essay, use a reproducible assessment sheet (TE page 766), the Response to Literature Rubric Checklist (TE page 782), and one or both of the **benchmark papers** listed in the Benchmark Papers box below. You can use an overhead transparency while students refer to their own copies made from the copy masters. For your reference, a completed checklist and a comments sheet are provided for each benchmark paper.

Reflecting on Your Writing

After students complete their reflection, ask them to compare the responses in this reflection to responses in earlier reflections. Remind students that they can use their reflections to monitor their progress as writers. If they don't see any improvement as the year progresses, encourage them to use their reflections to seek advice from you or their peers.

Reflecting on Your Writing

Take a few moments to think back on your experience of analyzing a play. Reflection helps you to retain what you have learned and prepare for future writing assignments.

My Play Analysis

1. The strongest part of my analysis is . . .

2. The part that most needs to be changed is . . .

3. The main thing I learned about analyzing a play is . . .

4. Next time I analyze a play or another work of literature, I would like to . . .

5. One question I still have about analyzing a play is . . .

6. Right now, I would describe my writing ability as (excellent, good, fair, poor) because . . .

English Language Learners

Before having students fill out the **My Play Analysis** sheet, offer them individual conferences, in which you discuss their strengths and the writing goals they have achieved. Then help them list their responses to the six questions.

315

Response to Literature
Analyzing a Novel

In a personal response, you explore your thoughts and feelings about a piece of literature. In a review, you discuss the merits of a particular literary work. In an analysis, you present your understanding or interpretation of a novel or a series of stories. Writing an effective literary analysis requires a high level of critical thinking on your part.

In this chapter, you will read a sample analysis of the novel *The Curious Incident of the Dog in the Night-Time* by Mark Haddon, tracing the theme of mystery that runs through the story. Then you will write your own analysis of a novel, focusing on a main theme or another key feature.

Base your literary analysis on a close and careful reading of the novel. Then present your ideas in a carefully planned essay, connecting all of your main points with specific references to the text.

Writing Guidelines

Subject: **A novel**
Form: **Literary analysis**
Purpose: **To analyze a main theme**
Audience: **Classmates**

"A good novel tells us the truth about its hero; but a bad novel tells us the truth about its author."

—G. K. Chesterton

Analyzing a Novel

Objectives
- understand how to analyze the main theme in a novel
- understand the content and form of a novel analysis
- plan, draft, revise, edit, and publish a novel analysis

A **novel analysis** examines how an author conveys the main theme (or another key feature) in the novel through literary elements.

- A novel may have more than one theme, although one dominant main theme usually runs throughout the story.
- The theme expresses a general lesson or insight about life that can be applied beyond the characters and events of the novel.
- The theme may be stated directly by the narrator or expressed through the setting, characters, plot, and effective use of symbolism.

Novel Analysis

Ask students to compare the structure of the Novel Analysis to that of the Response Essay on SE pages 279–280, using the margin notes for points of comparison.

- **Similar:** Introductory paragraph introduces the topic, provides vital background information, and ends with a strong, effective thesis statement that states the theme. The middle paragraphs show how the literary elements of the work connect to its main theme. The ending restates and expands the theme.
- **Different:** In the Response Essay, the four middle paragraphs describe setting, characters, plot events, and theme in systematic order. In the Novel Analysis, the writer summarizes the novel in the first middle paragraph and then analyzes the theme in the next three middle paragraphs, weaving details from the novel into the analysis.

Point out that the differences between the play and novel analyses are subtle. Recognizing them may help students when they write their novel analysis.

316

Novel Analysis

In the following analysis, Andrew examines a main theme in the novel *The Curious Incident of the Dog in the Night-Time*. The side notes highlight important features in the analysis.

Beginning
The beginning includes a quotation, background information, and the thesis statement (underlined).

Middle
The main characters, situations, and conflicts are summarized.

The writer analyzes the theme of mystery in the novel.

The Limits of Being Normal

Sherlock Holmes once asked Dr. Watson about "the curious incident of the dog in the night-time." When Watson pointed out that the dog did nothing in the night-time, Holmes responded, "That was the curious incident." In *The Curious Incident of the Dog in the Night-Time,* Mark Haddon introduces another detective obsessed with discovering the truth. Christopher John Francis Boone is a 15-year-old autistic savant who has trouble understanding other people but knows every prime number up to 7,057. As Christopher investigates the mysterious death of a neighborhood dog, Haddon uses the theme of mystery to explore the complexities of human interaction.

The story begins when Christopher discovers a crime scene across the street. A large black poodle named Wellington lies dead, and Christopher kneels to cradle the dog. When the dog's owner discovers him there, Christopher says he did not kill the dog, but he gets in a scuffle with the police and lands in jail. After his father comes to get him out, Christopher pledges to solve the mystery of Wellington's death.

As Christopher investigates the killing, he is directly confronted with a deeper mystery: other human beings. Like most people with autism, Christopher has trouble reading simple facial expressions. At one point, he says that people look at him when they speak, trying to see what he is thinking, but he can't see what they are thinking. People are confusing to Christopher. By contrast, he likes dogs because he can always tell what they are thinking; they have only four moods—"happy, sad, cross and concentrating"—and they don't lie since they can't talk (4). Christopher is alone in his social world. In fact, Christopher has a recurrent, favorite dream: "And in the dream nearly everyone on the earth is dead . . . and eventually there is no one left in the world" except people with autism (198).

Haddon deepens the theme of mystery by exploring the complexities of human language. For example, Christopher

Another elaboration on the theme is provided.

never lies. A lie means saying something happened that didn't happen, and Christopher cannot see the point of it. For him, the only things worth speaking about are facts and mathematics. Christopher also doesn't understand jokes and metaphors, such as "apple of my eye." He writes, "When I try and make a picture of the phrase in my head, it just confuses me because imagining an apple in someone's eye doesn't have anything to do with liking someone a lot . . . " (15).

The writer outlines the climactic part of the book.

Christopher's quest for truth leads him inevitably to discover even deeper mysteries. Two years before the beginning of the story, Christopher's mother died of a sudden heart attack. At that time, Mrs. Shears, the neighbor woman who owned Wellington, became a family friend who helped them deal with their grief. Her friendship with the Boones ended on the night that Wellington was killed—but the question is whether the friendship ended because of the dog's death, or the dog died because the friendship ended. As Christopher investigates, he strips away years' worth of lies and discovers the truth.

Ending
The ending gives the theme its final interpretation.

At the beginning of the book, Christopher writes, "This is a murder mystery novel" (4), but it is much more than that. Haddon uses the theme of mystery to show how deeply mysterious human expressions, language, and relationships are to a person with autism. At first, the book seems to show the limits of being autistic, but in the end, it shows the limits of being normal. Christopher himself describes it best in the final sentence of the book: "And I know I can do this because I went to London on my own, and because I solved the mystery of Who Killed Wellington? . . . and I was brave and I wrote a book and that means I can do anything" (221).

 Respond to the reading. Answer the following questions.

Ideas (1) What theme does the analysis explore? (2) What does the analysis reveal about people with autism? Name two things.

Voice & Word Choice (3) What section of the analysis shows the essay writer at his analytical best? Explain your choice.

 Literature Connections: Before reading and analyzing a full novel, you may find it helpful to read something shorter, such as a narrative poem. If you read Samuel Taylor Coleridge's "The Rime of the Ancient Mariner," you can also read "Coleridge's Dreamscape" by C. M. Bowra as an example of literary criticism.

Literature

 Respond to the reading.

Answers

Ideas **1.** The theme is the author's use of mystery to explore the complexities of human interaction. **2.** Possible choices: People with autism have trouble understanding other people. They can be savants—extremely knowledgeable or wise—in specific fields, for example, math. They can be compassionate. They are alone in a social world. They don't always understand the subtleties of facial expressions, or of language, for example, in jokes or metaphors.

Voice & Word Choice **3.** The ending is the most analytical. The writer expands on the theme by exploring it in a new light. The writer suggests that while Haddon was seemingly using the theme of mystery to show the limitations of autism, he was actually showing the limits of being normal. Ironically, Christopher's struggles with people and communication with them better prepared him to uncover lies and discover the final truth.

Literature Connections

Samuel Taylor Coleridge's poem "The Rime of the Ancient Mariner" is a narrative ballad that tells the story of a mariner who has returned from a long and transforming sea voyage. Encourage students to discuss the dreamlike and supernatural occurrences throughout the poem, and what they might mean in the larger context of the poem. After students read and discuss Coleridge's poem, they may benefit from reading C. M. Bowra's critical essay "Coleridge's Dreamscape." In it, Bowra praises Coleridge for presenting a series of incredible events in such a way that they seem convincing and authentic.

Encourage students to discuss the how the narrative is structured in Coleridge's poem, as well as how language affects the mood of the poem. Then have them respond to the poem along with Bowra's critical essay, noting whether they agree with Bowra and why. For additional pieces about responding to literature, see the Reading-Writing Connections beginning on page TE-36.

Prewriting Considering the Elements of a Novel

By answering the questions about characters, setting, conflict, and plot, students will in effect have created a story map of their novel. This will help them understand how these complex literary elements work together to tell the story. They can then use these elements to reveal and interpret the theme.

Point out to students that the main theme of a novel emerges from the events that show how the main character deals with the conflict. **Understanding conflict** (see below) is key to understanding and interpreting theme.

 Technology Connections

Students can use the added features of the Net-text as they explore this stage of the writing process.

 Write Source Online **Net-text**

Prewriting Considering the Elements of a Novel

Novels are complex, so if you try to consider a whole novel at once, you may feel overwhelmed. Instead, start your analysis by thinking about the novel's different elements. Andrew answered questions about the elements of *The Curious Incident of the Dog in the Night-Time* to clarify the book's complexities for himself.

Questions About Elements

Characters
- **Who is the main character?** Christopher Boone, a 15-year-old with autism
- **What other characters are in the novel?** Christopher's father, his counselor, the next-door neighbor, and Wellington, a black poodle

Setting
- **Where does the action take place?** Swindon and London, England
- **When does the action take place?** modern day

Conflict
- **What does the main character want?** to find out who killed Wellington
- **What obstacles does the character face?** his trouble understanding people

Plot
- **What happens at the beginning?** Christopher discovers that Wellington has been killed and pledges to find the killer.
- **What happens in the middle?** Christopher investigates and discovers a terrible secret. Then he runs away to London.
- **What happens in the ending?** Christopher solves the mystery of Wellington's death and determines to solve other deep mysteries about his own life.

Theme
- **What important idea about life is the author trying to convey?** the mystery of understanding other people and what it is like to be alone
- **What symbols represent the theme?** the dead dog, the drawer full of letters, red cars in a row, brown things, math problems

 Prewrite

Consider the elements. Choose a novel to analyze. Then answer the questions above about it. Consider your book's major themes and how they are demonstrated through the characters, setting, conflict, and so on.

Teaching Tip: Understanding Conflict

Remind students that conflict is what drives the plot of a story. Conflict is the main challenge, problem, or struggle between two forces in a novel, short story, or play. There are two basic types of conflict, internal and external.

- **Internal conflict:** The main character struggles within his or her mind to make a decision, usually between two extremely diverse and opposing things or feelings.
- **External conflict:** The main character struggles against some outside force, which might be another character, society, an idea, or nature.

Writing the Thesis Statement

Once you have analyzed the elements of your novel, write a thesis statement about the theme you wish to focus on. Andrew used the following formula to focus on one theme of *The Curious Incident of the Dog in the Night-Time*.

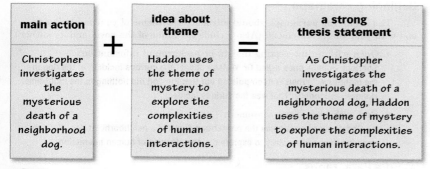

main action		idea about theme		a strong thesis statement
Christopher investigates the mysterious death of a neighborhood dog.	**+**	Haddon uses the theme of mystery to explore the complexities of human interactions.	**=**	As Christopher investigates the mysterious death of a neighborhood dog, Haddon uses the theme of mystery to explore the complexities of human interactions.

Write your thesis statement. Use the model above to meld the story and theme of your novel into a strong thesis statement. Try two or three versions if necessary.

Gathering Support

You should analyze the theme by showing how it is demonstrated through other elements of the story: characters, conflicts, and plot. Andrew used a gathering chart to list the ways these elements supported the theme of mystery.

Gathering Chart

Theme: The mystery of other people

Characters	Conflicts	Plot
Christopher has autism and doesn't understand others.	Christopher wants to solve the crime.	The police arrive and arrest Christopher.
The police officer doesn't understand Christopher's intentions.	When the police officer touches Christopher, he strikes back.	His father has to pick him up from lockup.

Support the theme. Create a chart like the one above, listing how characters, conflicts, and plot support the theme you have chosen to write about. Decide which details you would like to include in your analysis.

Literature

Prewriting **Writing the Thesis Statement**

Most students will find it a challenge to condense all the action in a novel into one succinct main action. Suggest that students look at the responses they wrote for the plot questions on SE page 318, which should summarize the action at the beginning, in the middle, and at the end of the story. By synthesizing, or putting together, their responses, they should be able to come up with one main action for their thesis statements.

✳ For more about writing effective thesis statements, see SE page 592.

Prewriting **Gathering Support**

Distribute photocopies of the reproducible details chart (TE page 826) for students to use to gather details for their analysis. Remind students that authors sometimes also use setting to convey the theme of a novel. If students feel that the setting is important to the analysis of the theme of their novel, they should include a section about setting in their gathering chart.

Writing **Creating Your First Draft**

Students may also want to take this opportunity to reread the sample Novel Analysis on SE pages 316–317 as an example of how the parts of an analysis of a novel fit together.

 For more about basic essay skills, see SE pages 589–603.

Technology Connections

Students can use the added features of the Net-text as they explore this stage of the writing process.

 Write Source Online **Net-text**

Writing **Creating Your First Draft**

As you write your analysis, use your planning from the previous page and refer to the following guidelines.

Beginning Paragraph

The beginning paragraph should introduce the theme of your analysis and end with your thesis statement. (Also include the name of the novel and its author.)

- Open with an interesting insight or background information.
  Sherlock Holmes once asked Dr. Watson about "the curious incident of the dog in the night-time." When Watson pointed out that the dog did nothing in the night-time, Holmes responded, "That was the curious incident."

- End with your thesis statement.
  As Christopher investigates the mysterious death of a neighborhood dog, Haddon uses the theme of mystery to explore the complexities of human interaction.

Middle Paragraphs

The middle paragraphs explain how the characters, conflicts, and plot of the novel present the theme. (Note: Provide background, but do not simply retell the story.)

- Provide a topic sentence for each paragraph.
  The story begins when Christopher discovers a crime scene across the street.

- Include details or quoted words from the novel to support each topic sentence.
  A large black poodle named Wellington lies dead, and Christopher kneels to cradle the dog.

Ending Paragraph

Your ending paragraph provides a final interpretation of the theme.

- Restate your thesis.
  . . . Haddon uses the theme of mystery to show how deeply mysterious human . . . relationships are to a person with autism.

- Give the reader something new to think about.
  At first, the book seems to show the limits of being autistic, but in the end, it shows the limits of being normal.

Write your first draft. Use the guidelines above and your prewriting work to help you complete the first draft of your analysis.

Revising **Improving Your First Draft**

After you have written a first draft, put it aside for a while to get a fresh perspective. Then revise your work for the first five traits.

Revise your analysis. Carefully review your writing using the checklist below. Make the necessary improvements.

Revising Checklist

Ideas

_____ **1.** Have I clearly stated the thesis for my analysis?
_____ **2.** Do I include elements from the novel as well as my own personal insights?

Organization

_____ **3.** Does my analysis include a beginning, a middle, and an ending?
_____ **4.** Are my ideas presented logically?
_____ **5.** Does each main point have its own paragraph with a focused topic sentence?
_____ **6.** Does my ending include a personal insight?

Voice

_____ **7.** Do I sound authoritative?
_____ **8.** Do I use quotations effectively without eliminating my personal voice?

Word Choice

_____ **9.** Do I use literary terms correctly?
_____ **10.** Do I avoid "loaded" words that bias my interpretation?

Sentence Fluency

_____ **11.** Do my sentences move naturally from one point to the next?
_____ **12.** Do I use a variety of sentence lengths and types?

Literature

Revising **Improving Your First Draft**

While students are often advised to put their writing aside for a while to get a fresh perspective, poor time management or overlapping deadlines of assignments in other subject areas often prevent them from following this advice. To encourage students to plan ahead so that they will have the time to set their work aside for a while, give students a deadline for turning in their first draft, and strongly encourage them not to use the revising checklist for at least a day or two.

Technology Connections

Have students use the Writing Network features of the Net-text to comment on each other's drafts.

 Write Source Online _Net-text_

Advanced Learners

Some students who naturally write well are reluctant to revise what they have written because their first drafts meet the criteria listed on the revising checklist. For these students, modify the revising activity so that they must rate themselves from 1 to 5 instead of answering yes or no, with 5 being the highest rating. Have them revise for any traits that score 4 or lower.

Grammar Connection

Sentence Variety
- _Write Source_ pages 82–85
- **Proofreader's Guide** pages 744 (+), 748 (+), 750

Editing Checking for Conventions

Besides checking for the seven general conventions listed in the Editing Checklist, remind students to also check specifically for

- commas for items in a series,
- words that they frequently misspell or misuse,
- the accuracy of quotations used from the novel, and
- the correct punctuation and placement of citations (see SE page 307).

Publishing Sharing Your Analysis

If your school or class publishes a literary magazine, students could choose to submit their essay for publication.

Technology Connections

Remind students that they can use the Writing Network features of the Portfolio to share their work with peers.

Write Source Online **Portfolio**

Write Source Online **Net-text**

Editing Checking for Conventions

After you have made the necessary improvements in your analysis, you should edit your work for punctuation, capitalization, spelling, and grammar errors.

Editing Checklist

Conventions

_____ 1. Have I used correct end punctuation after each sentence?

_____ 2. Have I used commas correctly?

_____ 3. Have I spelled all words correctly and checked any that I question?

_____ 4. Do my subjects and verbs agree in number?

_____ 5. Do my pronouns refer to clear antecedents and agree with them in number and gender?

_____ 6. Have I placed quotation marks around exact words quoted from the novel?

_____ 7. Have I included page numbers in parentheses after quoted material?

Edit

Edit your analysis. Use the checklist above to edit for conventions. Then prepare a final copy of your essay and proofread it.

Publishing Sharing Your Analysis

When you complete your analysis, it's time to share your ideas. Here are a number of options:

- **Send your analysis to a newspaper or magazine.** Check the submission guidelines and format the work as a review of a book.
- **Post your analysis at a library.** Ask your school or local librarian for permission.
- **E-mail your analysis to the publisher or author.** Search the Internet for a "contact us" link. Publishers and authors appreciate hearing from readers—especially those who like their books!

Publish

Publish your analysis. Choose one of the methods above, format your analysis accordingly, and share your work with others.

Grammar Connection

Punctuating Quotations

- *Write Source* page 322
- **Proofreader's Guide** pages 616 (+), 632 (+)

Pronoun-Antecedent Agreement

- **Proofreader's Guide** page 756 (+)
- *GrammarSnap* Pronoun-Antecedent Agreement

Subject-Verb Agreement

- **Proofreader's Guide** pages 752 (+), 754 (+)
- *GrammarSnap* Subject-Verb Agreement with Compound Subjects, Subject-Verb Agreement with Indefinite Pronouns

Using the Right Word

- **Proofreader's Guide** pages 694–695, 696–697
- *SkillsBook* page 62

Advanced Learners

If students publish their essay on the school or classroom Web site, encourage them to provide links to information relevant to the essay, such as

- brief author biographies,
- additional works by the author,
- lists of awards and prizes earned by the novels, and
- films and plays based on the novels.

Writing for Assessment
Responding to Prompts About Literature

Many assessment tests now include writing about literature. The test will typically include a prompt asking you to respond to one or two specific aspects of a given literary selection. For instance, you may be asked to focus on the plot of a novel, the theme of a poem, or a character in a story. Your writing will show how well you understand these elements of literature.

In this chapter, you are reminded of the value of using the writing process—even in a timed test situation. You'll read examples of effective fiction and nonfiction responses, and you'll get a chance to respond to some prompts on your own.

Writing Guidelines

Subject: Literature prompt
Form: Response to a prompt
Purpose: To demonstrate competence
Audience: Instructor

"To understand a literary style,
consider what it omits."

—Mason Cooley

Copy Masters

T-chart (TE pp. 325, 333)

Responding to Prompts About Literature

Responding to Prompts About Literature

Objectives
- apply what has been learned about writing literary analysis to other curriculum areas
- practice writing for assessment

If your students must take school, district, or state assessments this year, focus on the writing form on which they will be tested.

Test Prep!
Point out to students that since they may be asked to respond to a prompt about the elements of a novel or a short story, the best way for them to prepare for writing about literature on an assessment test is to
- complete all reading assignments when they are given;
- take notes during and after reading about setting, character, plot, and theme;
- read published analyses and evaluations of the work as well as the work itself; and
- keep a reader's response journal to record personal connections to a reading selection.

Try It!
Answers

Possible Answers

1. **Key words:** Southern family's move to Harlem, young John's struggle with his identity, essay that compares John's feelings about white people to those of Gabriel, to those of Richard, quote the characters.
   Supporting information needed: background information about the move and about the relationship among John, Gabriel, and Richard; dialogue and description of specific important plot events that help illustrate the attitudes of John, Gabriel, and Richard to white people

2. **Key words:** Esther, searches for values in 1950s America, suffers a nervous breakdown, essay, describe role that Esther's mother, Esther's attitude toward her, plays in the main character's breakdown
   Supporting information needed: description of Esther, of her mother, and of their relationship at start of novel; discussion of the conflicting values and attitudes toward women in 1950s America; list of events that lead to Esther's breakdown

"Surely that's the whole point about literature—that for a body of fiction to constitute literature, it must rise above its origins, its setting, even its language, to render accessible to a reader anywhere some insight into the human condition."

—Shashi Tharoor

Prewriting Analyzing a Literature Prompt

A prompt about literature asks you to respond to specific characteristics of a story, a poem, a novel, or a nonfiction selection. As you read a prompt, look for key words that tell you exactly what the prompt requires (such as *explain, describe,* or *compare*). In the sample prompt below, key words and phrases are underlined. The word discuss gives the main direction or focus for the response.

Sample Prompt

> John Milton's **Paradise Lost** follows <u>Adam and Eve's defiance and fall from grace</u>. In an essay, <u>discuss how Milton uses images of light and darkness to express other opposites</u> appearing throughout the poem. How does this <u>pattern</u> lead to your understanding of the epic poem's major theme? Support your thesis with examples from the text.

Try It!

Copy the following sample prompts on a sheet of paper. Underline key words and phrases for each prompt and make notes about the kinds of supporting information that you would need for a response.

1. *Go Tell It on the Mountain* is James Baldwin's account of a Southern family's move to Harlem and young John's struggle with his identity. Write an essay that compares John's feelings about white people to those of Gabriel (his stepfather) and to those of Richard (his natural father). Quote the characters in your response.

2. In Sylvia Plath's *The Ball Jar,* Esther, a smart, ambitious young woman, searches for values in 1950s America but eventually suffers a nervous breakdown. In an essay, describe the role that Esther's mother—and Esther's attitude toward her—plays in the main character's breakdown.

Planning Your Response

Once you analyze and understand a prompt, you are ready to plan your response. If a reading selection is provided, read it with the prompt in mind, picking out the information you need for your response. Then form your topic sentence and organize the details.

Sample Prompt and Selection

Responding to Prompts About Literature **325**

This excerpt from Thoreau's Walden *focuses on the author's surroundings. In a paragraph, describe the feeling or mood created in this passage.*

My nearest neighbor is a mile distant, and no house is visible from any place but the hill-tops within half a mile of my own. I have my horizon bounded by woods all to myself; a distant view of the railroad where it touches the pond on the one hand, and of the fence which skirts the woodland road on the other. But for the most part it is as solitary where I live as on the prairies. . . . I have, as it were, my own sun and moon and stars, and a little world all to myself.

> The underlined words connote solitude.

Writing a Topic Sentence

After reading the prompt and selection, one student wrote this topic sentence.

> **Thoreau's description of his surroundings** (specific topic) **creates a feeling of pleasing solitude** (focus related to the prompt).

Creating a Graphic Organizer

The student also used a graphic organizer to gather details.

Author's terms	Feeling created
nearest neighbor is distant	privacy
horizon bounded by woods	security
solitary as the prairies	isolation
little world all to myself	satisfaction

Literature

Prewriting **Writing a Topic Sentence**

To form an effective topic sentence for a response to a literature prompt, students can reword elements in the prompt itself. To illustrate, note that the sample topic sentence uses wording from the prompt *(Thoreau's description of his surroundings creates a feeling)* along with the student's analysis *(of pleasing solitude)*.

Some students may have an easier time formulating a topic sentence after they organize their details. Suggest that they follow the directions on the rest of the page before they try to write their topic sentence.

Prewriting **Creating a Graphic Organizer**

Provide photocopies of the reproducible T-chart (TE page 823) for students to use to gather details for a response to a literature prompt.

Writing **Responding to a Literature Prompt**

Tell students that if they are writing for a test, they should find out the test protocol before they begin. For example, they should know if they are allowed to underline and take notes directly on the test, or if they are required to show prewriting notes, including graphic organizers, on a separate piece of paper.

Use these questions for discussion of the sample prompt and selection:

- What kinds of details did the student underline? Why? (The details all relate to the family, their wealth, and their absurd vision of reality. The prompt asks students to discuss how Fitzgerald portrays the family and their vision of reality.)
- What is the purpose of the student's side notes? (They summarize information. They also analyze and interpret the characters and events.)
- What other details related to the prompt would you have underlined?
- What other side notes would you find helpful?

326

Writing **Responding to a Literature Prompt**

Note below how one student underlined key phrases and added side notes on a copy of the selection to address the focus of the prompt.

Sample Prompt and Selection

The excerpt below is from F. Scott Fitzgerald's short story "The Diamond as Big as the Ritz," a tale about the Washingtons, a ridiculously wealthy family, who think they are entirely above the law and general social customs. In a brief essay, discuss how Fitzgerald portrays the family and their vision of reality.

The awestruck young visitor learns that the owner had workers kidnapped for his personal use and yet ended up disappointed in their conventionalism.

John was enchanted by the wonders of the château and the valley. Braddock Washington, so Percy told him, had caused to be kidnapped a landscape gardener, an architect, a designer of state settings, and a French decadent poet left over from the last century. He . . . left them to work out some ideas of their own. But one by one they had shown their uselessness. . . . And as for the architect and the landscape gardener, they thought only in terms of convention. They must make this like this and that like that.

But . . . they all went mad early one morning . . . and were now confined comfortably in an insane asylum at Westport, Connecticut.

"But," inquired John curiously, "who did plan all your wonderful reception rooms and halls, and approaches and bathrooms—?"

"Well," answered Percy, "I blush to tell you, but it was a moving-picture fella. He was the only man we found who was used to playing with an unlimited amount of money, though he did tuck his napkin in his collar and couldn't read or write."

Even someone who met their standards in terms of being able to spend enough money comes up short in other ways.

As August drew to a close, John began to regret that he must soon go back to school. He and Kismine had decided to elope the following June.

"It would be nicer to be married here," Kismine confessed, "but of course I could never get father's permission to marry you at all. Next to that I'd rather elope. It's terrible for wealthy people to be married in America at present—they always have to send out bulletins to the press saying that they're going to be married in remnants, when what they mean is just

---

English Language Learners

Before reading the sample prompt and selection on SE pages 326–327, provide students with definitions of unfamiliar words and phrases:

- enchanted (charmed, delighted)
- chateau (French castle)
- a designer of state settings (someone who creates plans for grand buildings, such as palaces)

- decadent (extravagant)
- in terms of convention (rules and standards)
- went mad (became crazy)
- insane asylum (mental institution)
- approaches (accesses to places)
- tuck his napkin in his collar (so as not to get any food onto his clothes while eating)

- elope (run away to get married)
- remnants (old clothes)
- peck (unit of dry volume equal to 8 quarts)
- Empress Eugenie (1826–1920; wife of Napoleon III)
- fervently (passionately, intensely)

Responding to Prompts About Literature 327

The dialogue reveals how the speakers feel about what they see as the "struggle" of wealthy people.

a peck of old second-hand pearls and some used lace worn once by the Empress Eugenie."

"I know," agreed John fervently. ". . . Gwendolyn married a man whose father owns half of West Virginia. She wrote home saying what a tough struggle she was carrying on on his salary as a bank clerk— and then she ended up by saying that 'Thank God, I have four good maids anyhow, and that helps a little.' "

"It's absurd," commented Kismine. "Think of the millions and millions of people in the world, labourers and all, who get along with only two maids."

Writing a Thesis Statement

After reading the excerpt and making notes, the student wrote the following thesis statement for his response essay.

> The perception of life held by the Washingtons (specific topic) shows that these people are, in fact, out of touch with reality (particular focus related to the prompt).

Creating a Graphic Organizer

The student writer used a line diagram to organize the main points and supporting details for an essay response.

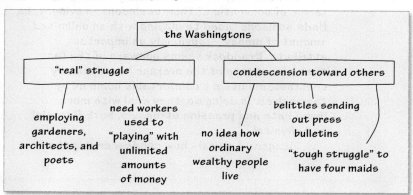

Literature

Right sidebar:

Writing **Writing a Thesis Statement**

Before discussing the sample thesis statement, have students work as a class to create their own thesis statement for a response to the prompt on SE page 326, using the prompt, underlined details, and side notes, and their discussion notes. Then have students compare their thesis statement to the sample on SE page 327. Which do they prefer? Why?

Writing **Creating a Graphic Organizer**

Remind students that they can use a line diagram like the one shown here to organize ideas for an essay response, or they may prefer another graphic organizer, such as an organized list, to help them arrange their main ideas and supporting details for their response.

Writing Student Response

Have students point out elements of the student response that are similar to their analyses of the play and the novel that they wrote earlier in this unit. Remind them that they are well prepared to write a response to a literature prompt. Students may point out these similarities:

- The beginning tells the title and author.
- A thesis statement focuses the direction of the essay.
- Each middle paragraph has a topic sentence that supports the thesis statement.
- Each middle paragraph addresses a separate main point in the analysis of the characters.
- Details and examples, including quotations from the novel, support the student's main points and help emphasize the thesis.
- The ending restates the thesis and offers a personal insight about the author's attitude toward his subject (or topic).

Student Response

In this student response to the excerpt from "The Diamond as Big as the Ritz," note how the writer used details from the story to support the thesis statement.

Whose Reality?

Beginning
The first paragraph leads up to the thesis statement (underlined).

This excerpt from F. Scott Fitzgerald's story "The Diamond as Big as the Ritz" elicits an ironic feeling about "poor rich people." Most individuals strive to improve their lives, but most people can only wish for what the Washingtons see as a burden or strain. <u>The perception of life held by the Washingtons shows that these people are, in fact, out of touch with reality.</u>

Middle
One paragraph focuses on the Washingtons' "struggles."

The characters in this story come off as somewhat pathetic as they describe what they perceive as real struggles in their lives. In the realm of extreme wealth portrayed here, there are chateaus and villas in which to employ gardeners and architects—and poets! It seems, however, such a burden for Braddock Washington to locate the workers, only to find that they think "only in terms of convention." Their uselessness evident, he finds someone "used to playing with an unlimited amount of money"—obviously an important attribute. Braddock seems unaware of the fact that inhabitants of the average household, by contrast, maintain a comfortable home all by themselves. In doing so, they deal with more immediate and pressing struggles, both financial and physical.

Fitzgerald reveals how condescending the

Struggling Learners

Some students may not understand the assertion in the first sentence. (For a definition and an example of irony, have students refer to SE page 600.) Discuss how the term *poor rich people* is ironic. Ask students what could make a rich person poor? (loss of family, friends, or reputation) Then read the essay together, asking students to list the "burdens" the rich family carry.

The other middle paragraph focuses on how condescending they are toward others.

Washingtons are toward those who aren't like them. The Washingtons don't have any idea how ordinary wealthy people live. Toward the end of the excerpt, Kismine relates how wealthy people feel obligated to "send out bulletins to the press" about their valuable wedding clothes, but then she goes on to belittle this practice: "what they mean is just a peck of old second-hand pearls and some used lace." And then John agrees with her, scoffing at the "tough struggle" of a wealthy family with four maids. Again, Kismine demeans such suffering as "absurd"; but then she betrays her ignorance by commenting on how well most people, "labourers and all," do with only two!

Ending
The closing restates the thesis and provides a final thought.

Fitzgerald does not say that wealthy people's perception of struggling is invalid. He acknowledges that wealthy people suffer, too, in their own little worlds, but he implies that their struggles are so far from the reality of most people as to make them almost laughable. This excerpt seems to add just one more aspect to a phrase famously attributed to Fitzgerald: "The very rich are different from you and me."

 Respond to the reading. Answer the following questions about the student response. Explain your answers.

Ideas (1) What is the focus of the student writer's thesis statement? (2) Does each middle paragraph clearly support the thesis statement? Explain.

Organization (3) Does the ending connect with the beginning? Explain.

Voice & Word Choice (4) Which verbs used by the student writer seem most effective? List three or four.

Literature

 Respond to the reading.

Answers

Ideas 1. The main characters of the novel, the Washingtons, are out of touch with reality.
2. Yes. Both middle paragraphs show how the Washingtons are out of touch with reality. The first middle paragraph explains how Braddock Washington considered it a real struggle to find workers for his chateau who could be unconventional and knew how to play with an unlimited amount of money. The second middle paragraph highlights the condescending attitude of the Washingtons toward the low- and middle-classes, emphasized by Kismine's ridiculous comment about "labourers and all" getting by with only two maids.

Organization 3. Yes. The writer says Fitzgerald was implying that the struggles of the wealthy are so far from the realities of ordinary people, that they can be perceived as laughable. The writer also provides a quotation by Fitzgerald that restates and expands the theme.

Voice & Word Choice 4. Possible choices: elicits, strive, perceive, portrayed, deal with, reveals, relates, belittle, scoffing, demeans, betrays, acknowledges, implies

Advanced Learners

Have students read the last sentence of the student response. Challenge students to debate Fitzgerald's statement, "The very rich are different from you and me." Provide ample time for students to prepare their arguments and cite examples from their experiences and readings.

Practice Literary Prompt

Before students read the selection, ask them to explain the steps they will follow to prepare and write a response. Have them

- point out key words in the prompt that they should keep in mind as they read the poem (state of humanity following World War I, explain how Yeats portrays the world, disturbing images throughout the poem); and

- explain what details they might underline and what notes they might make in the margin (underline details of disturbing images; make side notes that attempt to interpret these images and explain what Yeats was saying).

330

Practice Literary Prompt

Whenever you respond to a writing prompt, especially in a timed situation, begin by studying the prompt. Find the key word that indicates what you are to do in the response: *compare, explain, describe,* and so on.

In addition, be sure that you understand any specific points you need to address in your response before you read the selection. Of course, it is important to quote examples and specific details from the selection to support your thesis. However, it is equally important to share your own insights about the selection.

Practice Prompt and Selection

In the following poem, William Butler Yeats reacts to the state of humanity following World War I. Explain how Yeats portrays the world, paying careful attention to the disturbing images throughout the poem.

The Second Coming
by William Butler Yeats

Turning and turning in the widening gyre[1]
The falcon cannot hear the falconer;
Things fall apart; the centre cannot hold;
Mere anarchy is loosed upon the world,
The blood-dimmed tide is loosed, and everywhere
The ceremony of innocence is drowned;
The best lack all conviction, while the worst
Are full of passionate intensity.

Surely some revelation is at hand;
Surely the Second Coming is at hand.
The Second Coming! Hardly are those words out
When a vast image out of Spiritus Mundi[2]
Troubles my sight: somewhere in sands of the desert
A shape with lion body and the head of a man,

English Language Learners

Prior to a group discussion of the poem, explain unfamiliar terms that are not footnoted:

- falconer (a person who trains falcons)
- anarchy (chaos)
- a shape with lion body and the head of man (Sphinx)
- indignant (angry)

Advanced Learners

Explain to students that the meaning of Yeats' poem is widely debated. Have students conduct research online to find out about the author and the poem's different interpretations. Then have students discuss their findings as a group, including their own interpretations and opinions.

A gaze blank and pitiless as the sun,
Is moving its slow thighs, while all about it
Reel shadows of the indignant desert birds.
The darkness drops again; but now I know
That twenty centuries of stony sleep
Were vexed to nightmare by a rocking cradle,
And what rough beast, its hour come round at last,
Slouches towards Bethlehem to be born?

---

[1] gyre: spiral

[2] Spiritus Mundi: the collective
spirit of mankind

 Respond to a fiction prompt. Read Yeats's poem (above). After
reading through everything once, read the prompt again to make sure you
understand its focus. Then carefully reread the poem. Next, form a thesis
statement; quickly arrange your main supporting details in a graphic organizer;
and write your essay. When you're through, check your work for spelling,
mechanics, and punctuation errors.

Literature

This practice literary prompt is challenging
and may work best as a follow-up to a unit
studying poetry. Help students understand that
by reading the poem three times and writing
down especially strong images, they can quickly
assemble the raw material of a response. Once
they can answer the question "What is this
poem about?" they are ready to respond.

For struggling students, demonstrate this
process with a different poem. Read it aloud
three times and have the students volunteer
especially strong images. Then ask the question
"What is this poem about?" Organize the
response and details in a graphic organizer,
and then have the students write a response.

After this modeled run through, have students
respond to the poem on these pages.

Advanced Learners

Have students reread the last two
lines of the first stanza of Yeats'
poem:

> The best lack all conviction,
>   while the worst
> Are full of passionate intensity.

Ask students what they think Yeats
meant by these lines. Use questions
such as these to guide discussion:

- What seems contradictory in these
lines? (You might think that "the
best" would have all conviction and
passionate intensity, and that "the
worst" would have no conviction
and no passionate intensity.)
- Why might it be hard for "the best"
to have conviction? (It may be hard
to be clear and certain what to
believe in.)

- Why might "the worst" be full
of passionate intensity? (They
might be trying to convince others
of their point of view and to
manipulate them to action.)
- Remind students of the context
in which Yeats wrote the poem.
Discuss if the poem still has
relevance in today's world.

Writing **Responding to a Nonfiction Prompt**

Explain to students that they can follow the same steps to respond to a nonfiction prompt as they would to any writing prompt about literature.

- Analyze the prompt carefully to make sure you understand what it asks you to do. One way to analyze a prompt is to answer the **STRAP questions** (*see below*).
- Read the selection carefully and look for details, quotations, and ideas that you can use to respond to the prompt.
- When you write a thesis statement, use key words and ideas in the prompt and your own interpretation of ideas in the selection.
- Organize the details that support your thesis statement in a simple graphic organizer.
- Write organized, cohesive paragraphs that show your understanding of the ideas in the reading selection.

332

Writing **Responding to a Nonfiction Prompt**

The following prompt deals with a nonfiction selection. A student has underlined key words and phrases in the selection and added notes in the margin.

Sample Prompt and Selection

While very young, Helen Keller lost her sight and hearing. In this excerpt from her autobiography, **The Story of My Life,** *Keller describes several episodes from her early life. Explain in an essay why you think Ms. Keller shared these particular memories. What do they say about the youngster's resourcefulness?*

These memories, for different reasons, made impressions on Helen.

Many incidents of those early years are fixed in my memory, isolated, but clear and distinct, making the sense of that silent, aimless, dayless life all the more intense.

At five I learned to fold and put away the clean clothes when they were brought in from the laundry, and I distinguished my own from the rest. I knew by the way my mother and aunt dressed when they were going out, and I invariably begged to go with them. I was always sent for when there was company, and when the guests took their leave, I waved my hand to them, I think with a vague remembrance of the meaning of the gesture.

In one memory, she learns something the hard way.

One day I happened to spill water on my apron, and I spread it out to dry before the fire which was flickering on the sitting-room hearth. The apron did not dry quickly enough to suit me, so I drew nearer and threw it right over the hot ashes. The fire leaped into life; the flames encircled me so that in a moment my clothes were blazing. I made a terrified noise that brought Viny, my old nurse, to the rescue. Throwing a blanket over me, she almost suffocated me, but she put out the fire. Except for my hands and hair, I was not badly burned.

In this memory, she learns to her great satisfaction that she can have power over others.

About this time I found out the use of a key. One morning I locked my mother up in the pantry, where she . . . kept pounding on the door, while I sat outside on the porch steps and laughed with glee as I felt the jar of the pounding. This most naughty prank of mine convinced my parents that I must be taught as soon as possible. After my teacher, Miss Sullivan, came to me, I sought an early opportunity to lock her in her room. I went upstairs with something which my mother made

---

Teaching Tip: STRAP Questions

Even if students are familiar with using the STRAP questions to respond to a test prompt, review the meaning of the acronym and the questions that go with it.

- **Subject:** What topic should I write about?
- **Type:** What form of writing should I create?

- **Role:** What position should I assume as the writer?
- **Audience:** Who is the intended reader?
- **Purpose:** What is the goal of my writing?

Have students apply the strategy to the sample literature prompts they have examined in this unit. Remind

them that when using this strategy, they may not always find an answer to every question.

✳ For more about using the STRAP questions to respond to writing prompts, see SE pages 569–573.

me understand I was to give to Miss Sullivan; but no sooner had I given it to her than I slammed the door, locked it, and hid the key under the wardrobe in the hall. I could not be induced to tell where the key was. My father was obliged to get a ladder and take Miss Sullivan out through the window—much to my delight. Months after I produced the key.

Despite trying, she does not learn the reason for a mystery.

When I was about five years old we moved. . . . My earliest distinct recollection of my father is making my way through great drifts of newspapers to his side and finding him alone, holding a sheet of paper before his face. I was greatly puzzled to know what he was doing. I imitated this action, even wearing his spectacles, thinking they might help solve the mystery. But I did not find out the secret for several years. Then I learned what those papers were, and that my father edited one of them.

Writing a Thesis Statement

After reading the excerpt and making notes, the student wrote the following thesis statement for her essay.

> **Sharing these particular memories** (specific topic) **demonstrates that Ms. Keller didn't let her disabilities prevent her from trying to discover some things on her own** (particular focus related to the prompt).

Creating a Graphic Organizer

The student writer organized her details using a collection grid.

Memory	What she learned from it
Placing damp apron on fire	Getting too close to fire means you get burned.
Discovery of what a key does	She could lock people up, gaining control for a brief time.
Father with paper in front of his face	Sometimes you don't learn the reason for an action just by imitating it.

Literature

Writing **Writing a Thesis Statement**

Ask students to explain how the thesis statement shows that the student writer has understood the prompt. (The first part of the thesis statement rewords the part of the prompt that asks "why you think Ms. Keller shared these particular memories." The second part of the thesis statement answers the question at the end of the prompt. It explains what the writer believes the memories say about Ms. Keller's resourcefulness as a child.)

Writing **Creating a Graphic Organizer**

Discuss the organization of the details in the outline and how they relate to the writer's underlining and margin notes in the reading selection on SE pages 332–333.

Provide photocopies of the reproducible T-chart (TE page 823) for students to use to organize details for a response to a nonfiction prompt.

Struggling Learners

Point out that the student writer created her graphic organizer based on the prompt on SE page 332. Reread the prompt with students and ask them to suggest the focus for the essay (important memories in the life of Helen Keller and what she learned from these experiences).

Student Response

After students have read the essay response, have them work in small groups to evaluate it, using the following questions to guide their discussion.

- Does the response contain a clearly stated thesis statement that shows how the essay will answer the prompt on SE page 332 about the reading selection? Explain.
- Does the essay have a beginning, a middle, and an ending?
- Does each middle paragraph cover a main point that supports the thesis statement? What are these main points? What details does the writer use to support these main points?
- Does the writer support ideas with direct references to the text, using quotations and paraphrasing? Where?

334

Student Response

Having completed her planning, the student wrote the following essay in response to the prompt and excerpt from *The Story of My Life*.

Beginning
The first paragraph identifies the subject of the prompt and leads up to the thesis statement (underlined).

Middle
The middle paragraphs focus on the different memories.

Rising Above

This excerpt from Helen Keller's autobiography, *The Story of My Life*, focuses on a few key memories from her very early life, after she lost her ability to see or hear. It would be easy to believe that a child without these abilities would have no incentive to learn, living a "silent, aimless, dayless life." But by sharing these particular memories, Ms. Keller demonstrates that she didn't let her disabilities prevent her from trying to discover some things on her own.

She relates how she learned to use her sense of touch to distinguish her clothes from others in the laundry and to determine how her mother and aunt were dressed when they went out. She also recalls being summoned to wave to guests when they would leave, but with only "a vague remembrance of the meaning of the gesture." But from each of three specific memories, she appears to have learned something distinctly important.

First, she remembers placing a damp apron near the fire to dry. Her impatience leads her to draw closer to the hearth to put the apron directly on the hot ashes, where it promptly catches fire. Helen makes "a terrified noise" that brings help, preventing her from serious injury. The lesson learned from this encounter was a rather simple one about physical danger.

English Language Learners

Before reading the student response, provide students with definitions for unfamiliar words:

- incentive (reason)
- aimless (without direction)
- summoned (called)
- modicum (a small amount)
- innate (natural)

Specific references to the text are made.

The next memory she describes illustrates a more complex lesson. Helen not only learns how to use a key but also finds that this knowledge gives her a modicum of control over others. She locks up both her mother and her teacher and—despite her awareness that it's a "most naughty prank"—takes delight from it. She experiences the thrill of having power.

In the final memory, Ms. Keller admits to a degree of defeat in her effort to unravel a certain mystery. Imagine her frustration at finding her father "alone, holding a sheet of paper before his face" and not having a clue as to the reason for such an action! Of course, imitation doesn't reveal his motive. The child learns that she won't always be able to puzzle things out on her own; in this case, she doesn't uncover "the secret" until several years later.

Ending
The closing revisits the thesis statement.

Helen Keller's remarkable resourcefulness eventually led her to rise above her disabilities. Her innate intelligence and spirit come through in this excerpt as she relates these memories and what she learned from them. Sharing them is inspirational, giving hope to others who feel somehow limited.

Respond to the reading. Answer the following questions about the student response.

Ideas (1) What is the thesis of the student's response? (2) What details does the student use to support her thesis? Name three.

Organization (3) How does the writer organize her response? (4) Does each middle paragraph clearly support the thesis statement? Explain.

Voice & Word Choice (5) Which words or phrases quoted from the story are most effective? Name two.

Literature

Respond to the reading.

Answers

Ideas 1. By sharing her memories, Ms. Keller shows that she did not let her disabilities prevent her from discovering things on her own. **2.** The writer uses Ms. Keller's memories about learning to use her sense of touch to identify her own clothes, about physical danger when she accidentally started a fire by placing a damp apron near the fire, and about power when she used a key to lock up her mother and teacher.

Organization 3. The writer uses the order in which Helen Keller recalls these memories in the book. The transitions *first, next,* and *final* make this organization clear.

4. Yes. Each middle paragraph discusses a memory and explains how it illustrates Ms. Keller's ability to discover things on her own.

Voice & Word Choice 5. Possible choices: silent, aimless dayless life; a vague remembrance of the meaning of the gesture; a terrified noise; most naughty prank; alone, holding a sheet of paper before his face; the secret

Advanced Learners

Have students discuss the differences between the analysis of *The Glass Menagerie* by Tennessee Williams on SE pages 289–292 and the response "Rising Above" on SE pages 334–335. Have students use the following questions to get started:

- How are the thesis statements in both essays similar?
- How does each response support the idea that life must be lived to the fullest?
- What real-life examples can you think of that relate to this theme?

Practice Nonfiction Prompt

Before having students read the selection, ask them to

- point out key words in the prompt that they should keep in mind as they read (possible choices: Mark Twain; satirical essay in which Twain states that mankind falls short of its ideals and has become the lowest species on earth; do or do not agree with Twain's characterization); and
- explain what kinds of details they should look for as they read, and why (reasons Twain uses to support his claims; points that may be too satirical to be taken seriously). These kinds of details will help them write a successful response that answers the prompt.

Practice Nonfiction Prompt

Whether you are reading and responding to fiction or nonfiction, remember that the author of the selection carefully chose the words to describe a person, establish a setting, share information, arouse an emotion, and so on.

Practice Prompt and Selection

The following excerpt is from Mark Twain's "The Lowest Animal," a satirical essay in which Twain states that mankind falls short of its ideals and has become the lowest species on Earth. Write an essay that explains why you do or do not agree with Twain's characterization. Use examples from the text to support your thoughts.

I have been studying the traits and dispositions of the "lower animals" (so-called) and contrasting them with the traits and dispositions of man. I find the result humiliating for me. For it obliges me to renounce my allegiance to the Darwinian theory of the Ascent of Man from the Lower Animals, since it now seems plain to me that that theory ought to be vacated in favor of a new and truer one, this new and truer one to be named the Descent of Main from the Higher Animals.

Some of my experiments were quite curious. In the course of my reading, I had come across a case where, many years ago, some hunters on our Great Plains organized a buffalo hunt for the entertainment of an English earl—that, and to provide some fresh meat for his larder. They had charming sport. They killed seventy-two of those great animals and ate part of one of them and left the seventy-one to rot.

I was aware that many men who have accumulated more millions of money than they can ever use have shown a rabid hunger for more, and have not scrupled to cheat the ignorant and the helpless out of their poor servings in order to partially appease that appetite.

In the course of my experiments, I convinced myself that among the animals man is the only one that harbors insults and injuries, broods over them, waits till a chance offers, then takes revenge. The passion of revenge is unknown to the higher animals.

Indecency, vulgarity, obscenity—these are strictly confined to man; he invented them. Among the higher animals there is no trace of them.

Man is the only animal that robs his helpless fellow of his country—takes possession of it and drives him out of it or destroys him.

Read the practice prompt with students. Discuss the similarities between this prompt and the one on SE page 332 (they both discuss important events in the characters' lives as children and how these events shaped their adulthoods).

Have students note the organization of "Rising Above" on SE pages 334–335. If necessary, have students use this structure as a model when addressing the practice prompt on this page.

Man is the only Slave. And he is the only animal who enslaves. He has always been a slave in one form or another, and has always held other slaves in bondage under him in one way or another.

Man is the only Patriot. He sets himself apart in his own country, under his own flag, and sneers at the other nations, and keeps multitudinous uniformed assassins on hand at heavy expense to grab slices of other people's countries and keep them from grabbing slices of his.

Man is the Religious Animal. He is the only Religious Animal. He is the only animal that has the True Religion—several of them. He is the only animal that loves his neighbor as himself, and cuts his throat if his theology isn't straight.

Man is the Reasoning Animal. Such is the claim. I think it is open to dispute. Indeed, my experiments have proven to me that he is the Unreasoning Animal.

In truth, man is incurably foolish. Simple things which the other animals easily learn he is incapable of learning. Among my experiments was this: In an hour I taught a cat and a dog to be friends. I put them in a cage. In another hour I taught them to be friends with a rabbit. In the course of two days I was able to add a fox, a goose, a squirrel, and some doves. Finally a monkey. This lived together in peace, even affectionately.

Next, in another cage, I confined an Irish Catholic from Tipperary, and as soon as he seemed tame, I added a Scottish Presbyterian from Aberdeen. Next a Turk from Constantinople, a Greek Christian from Crete, an Armenian, a Methodist from the wilds of Arkansas, a Buddhist from China, a Brahman from Benares. Finally, a Salvation Army colonel from Wapping. Then I stayed away for two whole days. When I came back to note results, the cage of the Higher Animals was all right, but in the other there was but a chaos of gory odds and ends of turbans and plaids and bones and flesh—not a specimen left alive. These Reasoning Animals had disagreed on a theological detail and carried the matter to a higher court.

 Respond to a nonfiction prompt. Read the practice prompt on the previous page again to be sure that you understand its focus. Then carefully reread the selection. Next, form a thesis statement, quickly arrange your main supporting details in a graphic organizer, and write your essay. Use the revising and editing tips on the next page to check your response before turning it in.

Literature

Remind students that timed writing assignments create pressure. Tell students that they can ease some pressure by taking the time to make sure that they understand the prompt.

- To create an actual test experience for students, tell them how much time they will have to complete the response. Try to approximate the time that they will have on their next timed writing test.

- Suggest that students jot down how much time they will spend on prewriting, writing, revising, and editing. The bulk of the time should be given to planning and writing, but they should try to allow at least 10 minutes to revise and edit.

- Display several graphic organizers (TE pages 821–827) that students could use to organize details for their response. Encourage them to choose one that they think will work best to organize their response.

Revising Improving Your Response

Point out to students that in a real test situation, they won't have a checklist of traits. Have students jot down the following list in their writer's notebook:

- **Ideas**—Does my thesis statement address the prompt?
- **Organization**—Have I included a beginning, a middle, and an ending?
- **Voice**—Do I sound knowledgeable?
- **Word Choice**—Have I avoided unnecessary repetition?
- **Sentence Fluency**—Are my sentences complete?

Suggest that they commit the list to memory.

Remind students that retelling a selection in their own words does not answer the prompt, nor does it provide an insight about the piece of literature.

Editing Checking Your Response

Point out to students that they are more likely to make careless mistakes with punctuation, capitalization, spelling, and grammar during a timed test than in other, less-pressured writing situations. To ensure that students do not lose grade points because of careless mistakes, they should check their response for all types of errors, even the kinds that they usually avoid.

338

Revising Improving Your Response

Always review your response at the end of a writing test. Make any changes and corrections as neatly as possible. Use the following questions to help you revise your response.

- **Ideas** Does my thesis statement address the focus of the prompt? Do the details support the thesis?
- **Organization** Have I included a beginning, a middle, and an ending? Does each paragraph have a focus? Did I conclude with an insight about the literature selection?
- **Voice** Do I sound knowledgeable and confident?
- **Word Choice** Do the words that I use reflect a thorough understanding of the literature selection? Have I avoided any unnecessary repetition?
- **Sentence Fluency** Are all of my sentences complete? Do my sentences flow smoothly from one to the next?

Revise

Improve your work. Reread your practice response, asking yourself the questions above. Make any necessary changes neatly.

Editing Checking Your Response

In your final read-through, check your punctuation, capitalization, spelling, and grammar.

Editing Checklist

Conventions

_____ **1.** Have I used end punctuation for every sentence?
_____ **2.** Have I capitalized all proper nouns and first words of sentences?
_____ **3.** Have I checked the spelling in my work?
_____ **4.** Have I made sure my subjects and verbs agree?
_____ **5.** Have I put quotation marks around the exact words that I quoted from the selection?

Edit

Check your response. Read over your work, looking for errors in punctuation, capitalization, spelling, and grammar. Make corrections neatly.

English Language Learners

Because limited vocabulary leads many students to be visual learners, have students check for word choice by first reading their paragraph and highlighting or circling places where better words are needed or words are overused. Then have them go back and replace them with specific nouns and verbs to create clearer writing.

Responding to Literature on Tests

Use the following tips as a guide whenever you respond to a prompt about literature. These tips will help you respond to both fiction and nonfiction selections.

Before you write . . .

- **Be clear about the time limit.**
  Plan enough time for prewriting, writing, and revising.
- **Understand the prompt.**
  Be sure that you know what the prompt requires. Pay special attention to the key word that tells you what you need to do.
- **Read the selection with the focus of the prompt in mind.**
  Take notes that will help you form your thesis. If you're working on a copy of the selection, underline important details.
- **Form your thesis statement.**
  The thesis statement should identify the specific topic plus the focus of the prompt.
- **Fill in a graphic organizer.**
  Jot down main points and possible quotations for your essay.

As you write . . .

- **Maintain the focus of your essay.**
  Keep your thesis in mind as you write.
- **Be selective.** Use examples from your graphic organizer and the selection to support your thesis.
- **End in a meaningful way.**
  Start by revisiting the thesis. Then try to share a final insight about the topic with the reader.

After you've written a first draft . . .

- **Check for completeness and correctness.**
  Use the questions on page 338 to revise your essay. Then check for errors in punctuation, capitalization, spelling, and grammar.

Try It!

Read and analyze a prompt and literary selection your teacher supplies. Form a thesis statement that reflects the focus of the prompt, list supporting ideas in a graphic organizer, and write your essay. Then revise and edit your response.

Literature

Responding to Literature on Tests

Point out that students must approach writing-on-demand assignments differently from open-ended writing assignments and that timed writing creates pressures for everyone.

To teach students who must take timed assessments how to approach their writing, allow them the same amount of time to write their response essay as they will be allotted on school, district, or state assessments. Break down each part of the process into clear chunks of time. For example, you might give students

- 15 minutes for note taking and planning,
- 20 minutes for writing, and
- 10 minutes for editing and proofreading.

Tell students when time is up for each section. Start the assignment at the top of the hour or at the half-hour to make it easier for students to keep track of the time.

If your state, district, or school requires students to use and submit a graphic organizer as part of their assessment, refer students to SE pages 584–588.

Struggling Learners

Remind students that they will probably have only 5 to 10 minutes to revise. If they do not use the traits to improve their response, it is unlikely that they will have enough time to make meaningful revisions. Suggest that prior to presenting the prompt, students jot down one or two writing techniques that give them the most difficulty, such as using transitions or writing complete sentences. When students revise, they should check only the items on their list.

Creative Writing Overview

Common Core Standards Focus

> **Writing 3:** Write narratives to develop real or imagined experiences or events using effective technique, well-chosen details, and well-structured event sequences.
>
> **Language 2:** Demonstrate command of the conventions of standard English capitalization, punctuation, and spelling when writing.

Writing Forms

■ short story ■ play ■ poems

Focus on the Traits

- ■ **Ideas** Creating a protagonist who is believable, developing a clear conflict, and using a symbol to represent an important character
- ■ **Organization** Writing a beginning that introduces the main character, setting, and conflict; a middle that provides complications leading to the climax; and an ending that resolves the conflict
- ■ **Voice** Using dialogue (regular and internal) that sounds natural
- ■ **Word Choice** Choosing specific nouns and active verbs
- ■ **Sentence Fluency** Writing a variety of sentences that create an effective rhythm
- ■ **Conventions** Checking for errors in punctuation, capitalization, spelling, and grammar

Literature Connections

- • **"The Rocking-Horse Winner"** by D. H. Lawrence
- • *Come and Go* by Samuel Beckett
- • **Sonnets 18, 29, 116, and 130** by William Shakespeare
- • **"The Horses"** by Ted Hughes

Technology Connections

 *Write Source Online*
www.hmheducation.com/writesource

- • *Net-text*
- • *Bookshelf*
- • *GrammarSnap*
- • *Portfolio*
- • *Essay Scoring*
- • *Writing Network features*
- • *File Cabinet*

 *Interactive Whiteboard Lessons*

Suggested Creative Writing Unit (Five Weeks)

Day	Writing and Skills Instruction	Student Edition		SkillsBook	Daily Language Workouts	Write Source Online
		Main Pages	Resource Units*			
WEEK 1 1	**Writing Stories: A Character's Inner Feelings** (Model) Literature Connections "The Rocking-Horse Winner"	341–345			78–81	*Interactive Whiteboard Lessons*
2–5	(Prewriting, Writing) Dialogue	346–348, 70				*Net-text*
WEEK 2 6–10	(Revising, Editing)	349			82–85	*Net-text*
	Skills Activities:					
	• Punctuating Dialogue	70	616 (+), 632 (+)	32		
	• Direct and Indirect Objects		716–717	92		
	• Modeling, Expanding, and Combining Sentences	72, 83		155–156		*GrammarSnap*
	• Plurals and Spelling Review		654 (+), 656 (+), 664 (+)	55–56		
	• Using the Right Word		690–691, 692–693	61		
	• Commas		614–615, 616 (+)	14, 15		*GrammarSnap*

* These units are also located in the back of the *Teacher's Edition*. Resource Units include "Basic Elements of Writing" and "Proofreader's Guide."
(+) This activity is located in a different section of the *Write Source Student Edition*. If students have already completed this activity, you may wish to review it at this time.

	Day	Writing and Skills Instruction	Student Edition: Main Pages	Student Edition: Resource Units*	SkillsBook	Daily Language Workouts	Write Source Online
Second Form Week 1	1	**Writing Plays: Facing a Personal Dilemma** (Model) Literature Connections *Come and Go*	351–354			86–89	
	2–5	(Prewriting, Writing)	355–358				*Net-text*
Second Form Week 2	6–7	(Revising)	359			90–93	*Net-text*
		Skills Activities: • Punctuating Dialogue		616 (+), 632 (+)			
		• Adverbs		730 (+)	101		*GrammarSnap*
		• Pronouns		710 (+)	78		*GrammarSnap*
	8–9	(Editing, Publishing)	359				*Portfolio, Net-text*
		Skills Activities: • Apostrophes		628 (+), 629 (+)	29		
	10 opt.	*Writing a Radio Play*	360				
Third Form Week 1	1–2	**Writing Poems: Sonnet About Man and Machine** (Model, Prewriting) Literature Connections Sonnets 18, 29, 116, 130	361–363			94–97	*Net-text*
		(Writing) Prepositional and Appositive Phrases	364	732 (+)	123, 124		*Net-text*
	3–5	(Revising, Editing, Publishing)	365				*Portfolio, Net-text*
		Skills Activities: • Parts of Speech Review		700 (+), 701–734 (+)	113–114		
		• Adverbs		730 (+)	104, 105, 106		
		• Absolute Phrases		744 (+)	125		
		• Basic Sentence Patterns		760–761, 762 (+)			
		• Clauses		744 (+), 748 (+), 750 (+)	129, 130, 131, 132		*GrammarSnap*
		• Spelling		666–669	53		
		• Capitalization		648 (+), 650 (+), 652 (+)	44		*GrammarSnap*
	opt.	*Writing Free Verse, Cinquains* Literature Connections "The Horses"	366, 367				

* These units are also located in the back of the *Teacher's Edition*. Resource Units include "Basic Elements of Writing" and "Proofreader's Guide."

(+) This activity is located in a different section of the *Write Source Student Edition.* If students have already completed this activity, you may wish to review it at this time.

Teacher's Notes for Creative Writing

This overview of creative writing includes some specific teaching suggestions for the unit. The description of each chapter will help you decide which parts of the unit to teach.

Writing Focus

Writing Stories (pages 341–350)

Students writing short stories can explore fantasy, science fiction, mystery, and other genres. In this chapter, students will focus on an internal conflict. The sample story is about a boy whose world is suddenly changed. Point students to the "elements of fiction" on page 350.

Writing Plays (pages 351–360)

The nineteenth-century Frenchmen Eugene Scribe and Victorien Sardou developed a form for play writing called the "well-made play." You might want to begin your discussion by examining the following elements these men considered essential to play writing.

Exposition (in the opening scene) gives the *who, what, when,* and *where* of the story. Characters may divulge this information through dialogue, or it may be revealed through stage directions.

Rising action is the problem the characters struggle with during the play. The conflicts people experience in life (and in plays) are closely related to *who* they are. Rising action develops through a series of events until the action reaches a breaking point or **climax**.

Climax occurs when the conflict breaks, and the action moves toward a **resolution**.

Denouement, or resolution, is the portion of the play where the conflict or problem is solved.

Explain to students that play writing demands that they *get inside and know* their characters. The audience wants to know what motivates a character; they'll believe, and even consider heroic, a character they feel they understand, having watched that character struggle.

Writing Poetry (pages 361–369)

This chapter offers students the chance to write their own poetry, which should give deeper appreciation for what poetry is all about. A list of poetry techniques on SE pages 368–369 outlines the elements of poetry.

Academic Vocabulary

Read aloud the academic terms, as well as the descriptions and questions. Model for students how to read one question and answer it. Have partners monitor their understanding and seek clarification of the terms by working through the meanings and questions together.

340

Creative Writing

Writing Focus

Academic Vocabulary

Work with a partner to learn the following words from this unit.

1. A strategy is a plan to achieve a goal.
   What strategy would you use to improve your grades?
2. To indicate is to show or express.
   How would you indicate worry or surprise?
3. The significance of an object or idea is its importance or meaning.
   What is the significance of your favorite book?
4. Something is internal when it occurs on the inside, such as within your mind or body.
   What internal conflicts, or struggles, have you faced? Describe one.

Minilessons

Metaphor Stretches   Writing Stories

■ **WRITE** a one-sentence metaphor to describe a key aspect of a person (or your main character). Then **EXTEND** the metaphor into a paragraph. **ALLOW** your extended metaphor to color your writing about this character in your short story.

Speak Up!   Writing Plays

■ **ASK** two volunteers to carry on a brief, but animated, conversation (about the weather or another topic) in front of the class. **NOTICE** that they don't use complete sentences or complicated sentence structure. **TAKE** notes about any body language (a shoulder shrug), facial expressions (raised eyebrows), or gestures (hands on hips). **DISCUSS** how these elements can be incorporated into a play.

Poetic Musings   Writing Poetry

■ **CHOOSE** a poem that you enjoyed reading. **REVIEW** SE pages 368–369, and then **LIST** the poetry techniques that you find in your poem. **IDENTIFY** your favorite poetic elements. Then **WRITE** your own poem using some of those techniques. **SHARE** what you have written with a classmate (or the class).

Writing Stories

Stories can do many things. They can take us to faraway places and let us experience cultures other than our own. They can make us laugh or cry through exciting plots that keep us reading. But stories can offer more than just excitement or inventiveness. They also explore a character's inner feelings, sharing with us moments that can be very familiar, very similar to our own experiences. They allow us to examine those feelings and maybe understand ourselves a little better.

In this chapter, you will be writing a story that explores a character's inner feelings. You will establish a situation that tests a character's beliefs and examine the way that situation affects the person. You will also explore how to use a symbol to represent important characters or items in the story.

Writing Guidelines

Subject:	**A character's inner feelings**
Form:	**Short story**
Purpose:	**To engage and entertain**
Audience:	**Classmates**

"The American imagination releases itself very easily in the short story—and has done so since the beginning of our national history."

—Henry Seidel Canby

Copy Masters

Details Chart (TE p. 346)

Writing Stories

Objectives
- understand the content and structure of a short story
- choose a topic (a character's inner struggle) to write about
- plan, draft, revise, and edit a short story

A **short story** is a short work of fiction in which a main character faces an external or internal conflict. All short stories follow a basic pattern that includes the exposition, rising action, and falling action.

As preparation for writing their own stories, have students brainstorm situations that test a character's beliefs, and have them save their ideas for later.

To model, present the following situation:

Derek believes it is important to be kind and honest. He is directing a play. His friend Meg tried out for a part, but Derek doesn't think she can act well. This situation will test his beliefs. The internal conflict Derek has is how to be kind, and yet still be honest about Meg's audition. The external conflict he will have is how he will interact with her.

 Technology Connections

Use this unit's Interactive Whiteboard Lesson to introduce creative writing.

 Interactive Whiteboard Lessons

The Shape of Stories

To help students think about the shape of stories they have read, have them jot down a list of characters and conflicts in familiar stories. Then lead the class in plotting the pattern of a few of the stories on a chart.

Keep the chart posted in the classroom. During prewriting, when students are developing their own story ideas, they can refer to the chart for inspiration.

Have students do the **Try It!** activity independently, using one or more of the stories the class has not discussed. Applying the questions to each story will reveal how the story fits the basic pattern of a plot line.

342

The Shape of Stories

Most stories create dramatic tension by establishing a conflict, introducing complications, building to a climax, and so on. The graphic that follows shows the basic pattern that most fiction follows.

Plot Line

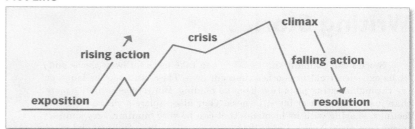

The **exposition** introduces the main character(s), the settings, and the conflict. It gives background information the reader needs to understand the story.

The **rising action** is a series of events, called *complications,* that build suspense. Each event develops the story line. During the rising action, the drama builds as the character faces complications that block his or her way.

The **crisis** is a moment of realization for the main character, when he or she comes to some decision or does something that will determine the outcome of the story. The crisis is not the climax but will lead to it.

The **climax** is the moment of truth, or the emotional high point of the story, when the main character either triumphs or fails. The climax should also somehow cause a change, either obvious or subtle, in the main character.

The **falling action** shows how the main character adjusts to the change.

The **resolution,** also called the *denouement,* is the ending. The falling action and resolution should be short, bringing the story to a satisfying close.

Try It!

Think about a story you read recently and answer these questions.

1. Who was the main character, and what was the setting? (exposition)
2. What challenges did the main character face? (rising action)
3. When did the main character make a difficult decision? (crisis)
4. What was the high point of the story? (climax)
5. What happened afterward? (falling action and resolution)

English Language Learners

Remind students that the exposition is at the beginning of a plot line, and the resolution is at the end. Write the word pairs *exposition/expository* and *resolution/resolve* on the board. Remind students that expository text is writing that explains or informs.

Likewise, exposition sets the stage of a story by explaining what the story will be about through the introduction of the characters, setting, and problems. Explain that *resolve* means "to solve or finish," so the resolution occurs at the end of the story.

Advanced Learners

Point out that the falling action occurs after the climax and brings the story to an end. Explain that the falling action provides a way for the main character (and the reader) to proceed from what they have learned. Challenge students to find a story in which the conflict is resolved in an unusual way, for example, the death of the main character.

Short Story

Every story has conflict, but sometimes that conflict is subtle. Some stories revolve around characters and the forces that motivate and change them. Jordan decided to write about how a single moment can change someone's life.

The **exposition** presents the central symbol—the bath—and the first step in the rising action.

The **rising action** adds complications and develops the central symbol.

Soaking

Marcus pulled into his driveway, shut off the engine, and sank back, exhausted. Football practice had been brutal, and every fiber of his being was calling out for a hot, soaking bath. Of course, Mom would have other ideas. She always wanted him to do homework before anything else—before watching TV or talking on the phone or even taking a bath. But tonight was different. It had to be. Marcus felt like one big bruise. *I'm going to take that bath,* Marcus thought, *no matter what.*

He dragged himself up to the back door and was surprised to find it locked. Odd. His mother usually left the door open. Digging around in the garden, he found the "secret" rock that hid the spare key and let himself in. The house was unusually quiet.

"Mom?" he called out, but got no answer. He shrugged. Strange. She always made it a point of being there when he and his sister Chelsea got home.

This is my golden opportunity. As long as Mom's not home, there won't be any nagging about homework.

Marcus went to the kitchen, opened the fridge, and crouched down, staring in. On the bottom shelf sat a plastic container with baby carrots in water, what Mom called the perfect after-school snack. She had a strange idea of perfection. If she were here, Marcus would be crunching carrots—but since she wasn't. . . . He reached to the cupboard above the fridge and pulled out some snack cakes and chips. Mom once kidded that she weighed the junk food to make sure nobody cheated, but Marcus doubted it. *She won't notice a little grazing. Besides, I've probably burned ten thousand calories at practice. It's not a problem.* Finishing his snack, Marcus hauled himself upstairs for a long, hot soak.

He stepped into the bathroom, leaned down to the tub, and grasped the porcelain handle. Twisting it brought out a gurgling column of water. Once it was hot, Marcus plugged the tub, pulled Mom's Epsom salts from the closet,

Creative Writing

Short Story

Work through the sample story with the class. Point out elements that make it a good short story.

Ideas
- The main character, Marcus, is a typical high-school athlete, making him believable.
- His inner feelings and conflict with his mother's rules are clearly conveyed through his thoughts.
- The use of an ordinary and concrete symbol, like a hot bath, connects the events in the story.
- The change in Marcus after receiving the news about his mother is obvious.

Organization
- The beginning introduces the main character, the setting, and his inner conflict.
- The middle presents a surprise complication that leads to the moment of truth for Marcus and begins to change him.
- The ending clearly shows that Marcus is changed.

Voice
- The character's internal dialogue sounds natural and emphasizes the conflict.
- Dialogue between Marcus and his dad is realistic.

Struggling Learners

Explain the significance of the title "Soaking" to students. Point out that the word has several meanings. It can mean "staying immersed in water," such as soaking in a tub of water. The word can also mean "taking in mentally, becoming absorbed mentally."

Point out that not only does Marcus want to soak in the tub after a rigorous football practice, but also he is soaking in new information. For example, direct students' attention to the point in the story where Marcus finds out that his mother was in an accident (SE page 344).

Explain that Marcus is taking in—trying to make sense of—the new information he hears from his dad. Then on SE page 345, point out that Marcus is absorbing the news and his new responsibilities as he folds the laundry and thinks about how he is going to take care of his mom as she recovers.

Remind students that one very obvious characteristic of a short story is that it is short.

- Unlike a novel, in which authors have the luxury of adding numerous important complications and a multitude of surprising twists and turns to the plot, short story writers are limited by space to one major complication and a few minor complications that build up to it.
- In a short story, the major complication leads directly to a climactic moment and the resolution. There are no other important events in between to complicate the story.

Have students summarize the major complication in the sample story and explain how it leads to the climax and ending. (The phone call from Marcus's dad about his mother's accident is the major complication. It immediately makes Marcus regret his rebellious attitude toward his mother's rules, which he then follows to show how much he loves her.)

and poured some in. *This is going to be good,* he thought, anticipating the joy of the warm water enveloping his body.

As the tub filled, Marcus went to his room to get some clean clothes. A pile of clean laundry waited on the bed. *I guess I'm supposed to fold these and put them away. Yeah, right. I've got my own system.* Marcus scooped up the pile of clothes, carried it to a big chair by the window, and dumped it atop last week's pile. Then he plucked a wrinkled T-shirt, sweats, underwear, and mismatched socks from the mess and carried them with him toward the bathroom.

Halfway there, his eye snagged on the books stacked on his desk. He could almost hear his mother say, "Homework first!" but the thought just made him snort. *Homework last. First a bath, and then the Packers, and then algebra—cramming for the test tomorrow. I can't do it right now anyway. I need Mom's help.*

The telephone rang. Marcus startled. "It's probably her, making sure I'm doing my homework." He went out into the hallway, grabbed the cordless, and went in to check on the bathwater.

"Marcus?" It was his father's voice.

"Hey, Dad! You gonna be home soon? The Packers are on TV tonight."

"Marcus, listen!" His father's sharp voice cut him off.

"Dad? What's wrong?" Marcus asked, quickly turning off the water.

"I'm at the hospital, son. Your mother's been in an accident. A drunk driver . . . " Marcus sat on the side of the tub, suddenly unable to breathe, as though he'd been dunked in a tank of ice water.

"Is she—okay?" he heard himself say.

"The doctors said she'll pull through, but she's pretty well banged up. Her leg's broken, she's got some cracked ribs, and her shoulder was crushed. She'll be in the hospital for a while, and then she'll have a long recovery period."

"I'll be right there," Marcus said.

"No, don't. She'll be asleep for a while. Besides, I need you to wait for Chelsea. When she gets home from her Scout meeting, you'll have to tell her. You can bring her here with you then."

Marcus couldn't speak, but finally managed to squeak out a sound. "Okay. Tell her I love her, will you?"

> New complications are presented through dialogue, leading up to a **crisis** for the main character.

English Language Learners

The figurative expression "his eye snagged on the books" may be confusing to some students. Explain that when your eyes snag on a thing, that thing is grabbing or catching your attention. Point out that when Marcus walked toward the bathroom, the books stacked on his desk grabbed or caught his attention. Provide other examples of using this expression, such as the following: Her eyes snagged on the shiny jewelry in the store window.

"I will," his father said, and then he started to cry. Marcus had never heard his father cry before.

"Dad? I love you, too," Marcus said. It was quiet on the other end.

"I love you, son." *How long has it been since he said that to me?*

He hung up, and Marcus sat numbly, phone in hand, for a long time. When he finally looked at his tub, the water had cooled. He opened the drain and went back into his room to change into clean clothes. Afterward, he sat down, feeling out of breath.

Sitting on his unmade bed, Marcus gazed around the room, so familiar and suddenly so strange. Clothes and books were everywhere—his hockey skates sitting in a corner, papers and junk cluttering the top of his dresser, CD cases everywhere but in their rack. His mother was always after him to pick up, and she usually just got disgusted and cleaned it for him. He'd never even thought about it, or the million other little things she was always doing for him and his sister. Now it would be his turn to take care of her as she recovered. It would be different, but he would handle it. He had to.

Marcus sat down on the floor by the big chair and slowly began folding his laundry. *After I finish this, I'll clean the rest of this dump. Then it'll be algebra until Chelsea gets home, and I'll make sure Chelsea brings her homework to the hospital, too.* . . . Marcus continued folding clothes, letting the eerie quiet of the empty house rise up around him. The only sound was the gentle gurgle of bathwater spiraling down the drain.

The cooling bathwater reflects a key change in the story line.

The climax comes when Marcus realizes his life has changed.

The final metaphor represents the change in the character's life.

 Respond to the reading. Answer the following questions.

Ideas & **Organization** (1) What is the conflict? (2) What is the significance of Marcus's room? (3) How does the story build in suspense?

Voice (4) How does the writer show us the character's thoughts? (5) How does the dialogue help create a feeling?

Literature Connections: Consider reading "The Rocking-Horse Winner" by D. H. Lawrence, a short story that includes a powerful symbol.

Creative Writing

 Respond to the reading.

Answers

Ideas & **Organization** **1.** Marcus is tired of having to follow his mother's strict rules. **2.** The things in Marcus's room (the unfolded laundry, his books on the desk) symbolize his mother's rules and Marcus's desire to defy them. At the end, they become symbolic of his desire to help his mother recover from her accident. **3.** Marcus's internal dialogue describes a series of events that build toward the climax. First, he discovers that the door is locked. Then his thoughts show him doing a series of things he would never be allowed to do if his mom were home (eat junk food, ignore the laundry and his homework, start a bath). Finally, the ring of the phone abruptly interrupts his thoughts.

Voice **4.** Marcus's inner dialogue appears in italicized type. **5.** The inner dialogue has a believable tone that helps define the character. The dialogue between Marcus and his father conveys Marcus's concern and real feelings for his parents.

 Literature Connections

D. H. Lawrence's short story "The Rocking-Horse Winner" explores the tenuous connection between money and happiness. The story describes a middle-class woman who feels she has no luck because she doesn't have enough money to support her family's lifestyle. When her young son Paul discovers that his rocking horse reveals advance knowledge of horse-race winners, he is determined to win as much money—or luck—as he can for his mother. Although his efforts are rewarded financially, he exhausts himself to the point of illness and finally death.

Encourage students to discuss the motivations of each character in the story. Then have them discuss the story's ending and explore how the rocking horse functions as a symbol throughout the story. Finally, encourage students to comment on whether luck was a positive or negative force for each of the story's main characters. For additional short story models, see the Reading-Writing Connections beginning on page TE-36.

Prewriting Finding Your Focus

Before asking students to create their story-elements chart, ask why they think male authors usually write stories with male main characters, and female writers write stories with female main characters. (Writers know and understand the feelings, thoughts, and experiences of people of their own gender best.) Explain that when writers follow the advice **"write what you know"** *(see below),* readers are more likely to believe in the characters, their conflicts, and settings.

Distribute photocopies of the reproducible Details Chart (TE page 826) for students to use to explore characters, conflicts, and settings for a short story.

Prewriting Building Complications

To understand how the complications can help provide a framework for the events in their story, it may help students to place the sample complications on a plot line to see how they help provide a shape for Jordan's story on SE pages 343–345. The first two complications would be part of the rising action. The third would be the crisis. The last is the climax.

Technology Connections

Students can use the added features of the Net-text as they explore this stage of the writing process.

 Write Source Online **Net-text**

346

Prewriting Finding Your Focus

You can develop a story idea by listing possibilities for the three basic elements: character, conflict, and setting. *Remember:* Your story will focus on a character whose views are tested and changed. Jordan generated this story-elements chart:

Story-Elements Chart

Characters	Conflicts	Settings
a track star	trying to find a job	a highway
the new kid	losing a game or contest	a run-down park
a linebacker	adopting a pet	a fast-food restaurant
the preacher's son	dealing with an injury	a car wash

By mixing and matching the different entries in the columns, Jordan came up with the following list of possible stories. He starred the one he decided to use.

- A track star adopts a pet greyhound and trains it in a run-down park.
- The preacher's son loses a fund-raising contest at a car wash.
- A linebacker deals with his mother's injury in a crash on the highway. *

Create a story-elements chart. List characters, conflicts, and settings. Then mix and match them to develop three story ideas and choose one.

Building Complications

Next, Jordan listed complications—events that would increase the conflict, leading toward the climax of the story.

First . . . the player's mom isn't home.
Then . . . he's glad she's not there to boss him around.
Next . . . he gets a phone call to say she's been in a car wreck.
After . . . he feels bad he took her for granted.

List complications. Write "First," "Then," "Next," and "After" on a piece of paper. Then write down how the conflict begins. Continue by writing events or details that make the conflict more serious, leading to a climax.

Teaching Tip: Write What You Know

A common piece of advice frequently offered to student writers by experienced writers is "write what you know." The problem is that the advice is often taken too literally. Explain to students that it is not necessary for writers to experience everything their characters experience. Writers are ordinary people who usually do not live extraordinarily exciting or adventurous lives. Writers can use their imagination about how someone would act and feel in a particular situation, based on their knowledge of human behavior.

When selecting characters and conflicts, students should explore ideas that relate to people their own age because they will write what they know, thereby creating a realistic story. They can draw on their experiences, feelings, and observations, making the writing process easier. Thus their writing will also be more believable to readers.

Developing a Symbol

A symbol is a person, a place, a thing, or an event that represents something else. You can use a symbol to make ideas concrete and to unify action. Jordan used a thought map to think about symbols. He wrote important characters and ideas in the center and then thought of concrete symbols to represent them.

Thought Map

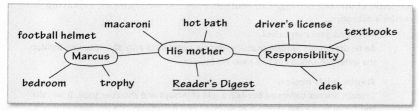

Create a thought map. Write down important characters and ideas for your story. Then write possible symbols of each, connecting them. Choose one main symbol for your story, but also keep the other symbols in mind.

Using Dialogue

Dialogue lets characters speak for themselves. Jordan's story uses regular dialogue, set off with quotation marks (" "), and internal dialogue, indicated with *italics,* which lets the reader hear the conflict inside the main character.

"I love you, son." *How long has it been since he said that to me?*

Note: Use internal dialogue only with the main character so that your point of view does not shift.

Try It!

Experiment with dialogue. Answer each of the following questions the way your main character would. Use regular dialogue to let the person speak and use internal dialogue to show what the person is thinking.

1. What's your least favorite thing to do?
   Example answer: "Algebra homework," Marcus said. *Though cleaning my room would be a close second.*

2. What's your favorite thing to do?
3. What's the biggest challenge that you face?
4. Do you think you'll overcome the challenge? Why or why not?

Creative Writing

Prewriting Developing a Symbol

Remind students that their main symbol will run through the whole story like an **extended metaphor** *(see below).*

- Have students turn back to Jordan's story on SE pages 343–345 to see how he incorporates the symbol of the *hot bath* throughout the story.
- Ask them to point out other symbols in the story and how they tie together (the laundry, homework, and Marcus's messy room). Discuss how they relate to his mother's rules, a symbol for her love and concern for Marcus.

Prewriting Using Dialogue

Remind students that the purpose of dialogue is threefold: (1) to reveal the character, (2) to move the action along and build suspense, and (3) to move from one part of the experience to the next. Explain that using italics for a character's inner thoughts eliminates the need for quotation marks and speaker tags, which can interrupt the flow of ideas. Emphasize, however, that quotation marks are always used for regular dialogue between two or more characters.

✳ For more information about using quotation marks to set off dialogue, see SE page 632.

Teacher Tip: Extended Metaphor

Remind students that a metaphor is a figure of speech that compares two things without using *like* or *as.* Extended metaphors are often found in poetry and plays, but writers use them in stories, too. Writers should keep in mind that their metaphor must work, without seeming contrived or forced, for the length of the story. Point out that Jordan does a good job of extending the bath metaphor throughout his story, even using it to symbolize his change of heart (gurgling water down the drain).

✳ For more about using metaphors, see SE page 76.

English Language Learners

Model internal dialogue by making statements such as "It's cloudy. Wonder if it will rain." Explain that internal dialogue remains in the thoughts of the character. In a story, it is used to reveal a character fully. Ask students to suggest scenarios, such as when a phone rings or when a dog growls, and share examples of internal dialogue.

Writing Developing the First Draft

Have students study the four sample beginnings. Ask them why they think Jordan settled on the fourth one, set the scene. Ask if they agree with his choice and to explain their reasoning. Encourage students to apply these strategies as they experiment with writing several story beginnings and decide on the best one.

Students should have a good idea of the following additional elements of their story before they begin to write. If they haven't taken time to figure these out, they should do so now.

- Setting (Limit setting to one main place, although other places may be mentioned. For example, in Jordan's story, the main setting is his home, but the highway and hospital are mentioned.)
- Minor characters (Limit minor characters to two and know their roles.)
- Resolution/Ending (Know how the main character will demonstrate a change in attitude or behavior.)

 Technology Connections

Students can use the added features of the Net-text as they explore this stage of the writing process.

 *Write Source Online* **Net-text**

348

Writing Developing the First Draft

Your story should include a beginning, a middle, and an ending that work together to show how the character changes.

Starting Strong

In your beginning, you should capture your reader's interest and introduce the main character, setting, and conflict. Here are strategies for capturing your reader's attention.

- **Present your symbol.**
  As he drove from football practice, Marcus could think only of a steaming bathtub, the water hot enough to boil away his bruises.

- **Begin with action.**
  Crunch! Marcus collapsed beneath a pile of jerseys and shoulder pads. It was the last tackle in the last skirmish of practice, and it made every bone and bruise ache.

- **Begin with dialogue.**
  "Hey, Mom," Marcus said, walking through the front door. "You home?"

- **Set the scene.**
  Marcus pulled into his driveway, shut off the engine, and sank back, exhausted.

Building the Action

In the middle of your story, provide complications that lead to the climax. Follow these tips:

- Use **action** that shows what the main character is experiencing.
- Use **dialogue** to let characters speak, and use **internal dialogue** to show the thoughts of your main character.
- Unify the middle of your story using a **symbol** for an important idea.
- Intensify the **conflict** as the character approaches the climax.

Bringing the Story to a Close

Show how the character is changed by the climax. Then, in the falling action and resolution, indicate how life will be different for him or her.

 Write

Write your first draft. Use your planning from pages 346–347 and the information above to guide your writing.

Writing Stories **349**

Revising Improving Your Writing

Use the following checklists as you revise and edit your story.

Revising Checklist

Ideas

_____ **1.** Is my main character believable?

_____ **2.** Is the conflict clear, and is the change obvious?

_____ **3.** Have I described the setting (place and time) clearly?

Organization

_____ **4.** Does my beginning capture the reader's interest and introduce the main character, setting, and conflict?

_____ **5.** Does my middle provide complications that lead to the climax?

_____ **6.** Does my ending resolve the conflict and show how the character changed?

Voice

_____ **7.** Does my dialogue (regular and internal) sound natural?

Word Choice

_____ **8.** Have I used specific nouns and active verbs?

Sentence Fluency

_____ **9.** Do I vary my sentence types to create an effective rhythm?

Editing Checking for Conventions

When you edit, check your _punctuation, capitalization, spelling,_ and _grammar._

Editing Checklist

Conventions

_____ **1.** Have I checked for easily confused words (_there, their, they're_)?

_____ **2.** Have I correctly punctuated dialogue (regular and internal)?

Creative Writing

Revising Improving Your Writing

Encourage students to make a copy of their draft and exchange stories with a writing partner. Have partners use the revising checklist and offer helpful comments.

✳ For more information on using the traits to respond, see SE page 124.

If you maintain a class Web site, give students the option of uploading their story to the Web site for interested students to print out for review. After students have responded to a story, writers can collect the completed checklists, evaluate the feedback, and decide what changes to make.

Editing Checking for Conventions

Remind students who are working on a computer that the spell-check feature will not catch words that are spelled correctly but used incorrectly. Students should print out a copy of their revised story and edit on paper to check that they have used the right words throughout their story.

✳ For more about using the right word, see SE pages 678–699.

 Technology Connections

Have students use the Writing Network features of the Net-text to comment on each other's drafts.

➤ **Write Source Online** **Net-text**

Grammar Connection

Punctuating Dialogue

- **Write Source** page 70
- **Proofreader's Guide** pages 616 (+), 632 (+)
- **SkillsBook** page 32

Direct and Indirect Objects

- **Proofreader's Guide** pages 716–717
- **SkillsBook** page 92

Modeling, Expanding, and Combining Sentences

- **Write Source** pages 72, 83

- **SkillsBook** pages 155–156
- **GrammarSnap** Sentence Types: Compound, Complex, and Compound-Complex Sentences; Restrictive/Nonrestrictive Clauses for Combining Sentences

Plurals and Spelling Review

- **Proofreader's Guide** pages 654 (+), 656 (+), 664 (+)
- **SkillsBook** pages 55–56

Using the Right Word

- **Proofreader's Guide** pages 690–691, 692–693
- **SkillsBook** page 61

Commas

- **Proofreader's Guide** pages 614–615, 616 (+)
- **SkillsBook** pages 14, 15
- **GrammarSnap** Common Uses of Commas

Elements of Fiction

Give students an opportunity to skim the elements of fiction and their definitions. Encourage students to ask questions about any element they find difficult or challenging when analyzing literature or when writing fiction.

To help students understand the different third-person points of view, ask students to identify the point of view they used in their own stories. Ask those who used one of the third-person points of view to read aloud a paragraph that exhibits that point of view. Have classmates identify the point of view and explain how they identified it.

Suggest to students that they bookmark SE page 350 and use it as a reference whenever they are discussing or writing about works of fiction.

Elements of Fiction

The following terms will help you write about and discuss literature.

Antagonist	The person or force that works against the hero of the story (See *protagonist*.)
Character	A person or an animal in a story
Climax	The moment of change when the protagonist either succeeds or fails and is somehow changed by the action
Conflict	A problem or clash between two forces in a story
	▪ **Person vs. person** A problem between characters
	▪ **Person vs. self** A problem within a character's own mind
	▪ **Person vs. society** A problem between a character and society, the law, or some tradition
	▪ **Person vs. nature** A problem with an element of nature, such as a blizzard or a hurricane
	▪ **Person vs. destiny** A problem or struggle that appears to be beyond a character's control
Narrator	The person or character who tells the story, gives background information, and fills in details between dialogue
Plot, Plot Line	See page 342.
Point of View	The angle from which a story is told
	▪ In **first-person point of view,** one character is telling the story.
	▪ In **third-person point of view,** someone outside the story, a narrator, is telling it.
	▪ In **omniscient point of view,** the narrator tells the thoughts and feelings of all the characters.
	▪ In **limited omniscient point of view,** the narrator tells the thoughts of only one character.
	▪ In **camera view** (objective), the narrator records the action from his or her own point of view, without any of the characters' thoughts.
Protagonist	The main character or hero in a story (See *antagonist*.)
Rising Action	A series of events that propel the story to the climax
Setting	The place and time period in which a story takes place
Theme	The author's message about life or human nature
Tone	The writer's attitude toward her or his subject (*angry, humorous,* and so on)

Struggling Learners

For extra practice with point of view, choose several short story or novel excerpts to read with students, and discuss the angle from which each story is told. For example, Ernest Hemingway uses first-person point of view in *The Sun Also Rises* and George Eliot uses third-person omniscient in *Silas Marner.*

Advanced Learners

Challenge students to analyze a movie they have recently seen and enjoyed. Have them identify the twelve elements of fiction in the movie and use the information to write a thorough movie analysis.

351

Writing Plays

A play is an exciting writing challenge. Because a play is intended to be watched rather than read, its story is told with action and speech rather than with long sections of description. Even so, the script must be clearly written, giving the reader an understanding of the characters and what happens to them.

In terms of plot, writing a play is like writing any other narrative. The main character desires something and meets with opposition before finally succeeding or failing. At the climax, the character changes in some way, realizing a universal truth about the world or about him- or herself.

In this chapter you will read a short play about a character who, faced with a personal dilemma, finally makes a decision. You will then write your own short play, creating a character who wants something or faces an obstacle and then comes to a decision to overcome the problem. You will also use stage directions to explain your characters' actions on stage.

Writing Guidelines

Subject: Facing a personal dilemma
Form: Brief play
Purpose: To entertain and enlighten
Audience: Classmates

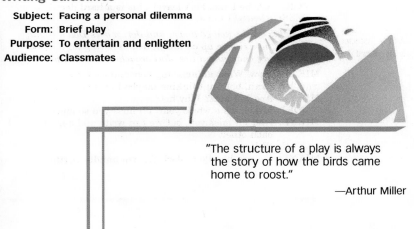

"The structure of a play is always the story of how the birds came home to roost."

—Arthur Miller

Writing Plays

Objectives
- understand the content and structure of a play, including stage directions and stage terminology
- choose a topic (a personal dilemma) for a play
- plan, draft, write, revise, and edit a play
- write a radio script about a conflict between two people

A **play** uses action and dialogue to tell a story. It is written to be
- performed on a stage,
- in front of an audience,
- by actors who assume the roles of the story characters.

A play script contains a cast of characters, usually with brief descriptions of their relationship to one another; dialogue for the actors to speak; and stage directions that tell the actors and stage crew what to do at specific moments in the play.

Discuss the Arthur Miller quote. You may need to explain the expression *the birds came home to roost*. (The birds coming home to roost refers to the consequences of characters' actions, the aftereffects of what they did.)

Brief Play

Many students will have some experience participating in school drama productions. Some students may belong to the school's drama club. Other students may have participated in community theater productions. Throughout this assignment, encourage knowledgeable students to draw on their experiences regarding

- reading play scripts,
- interpreting stage directions, and
- understanding stage terms.

Provide opportunities for students to share their acquired knowledge with those who have had limited or no exposure to stage productions.

To prepare all students to write their own play, review and discuss play terminology on SE page 300 and the stage diagram on SE page 358. Have students affix sticky notes on the pages for easy reference.

Brief Play

Deanna wrote the following play in which a character must make an important personal decision.

Exchange Rate

Characters: **Jori,** who wants to be an exchange student
Tess, her friend
Mikyl, Jori's boyfriend

(The stage is bare. The lights come up on Jori, Center, as Tess rushes in to her.)

> Background information is given and the conflict is suggested.

TESS: Jori, I can't believe you're going to France for a whole year!
JORI: Isn't it awesome! A whole year of traveling, learning a new culture, meeting new people . . .
TESS: Especially those French boys! Oo la la!
JORI: I don't care about that! After all, I have Mikyl.
TESS: Um, yeah, but you won't have him for a whole year! Aren't you worried about that?
JORI: We'll be okay. We can write and e-mail.
TESS: He can't take an e-mail to homecoming, the Holiday Ball, prom, or games. Come on, Jori. Mikyl, all alone, for a year? I don't think so!
JORI: I never thought of that. I mean, Mikyl and I—we're forever!
TESS: Jori, senior year is longer than forever.
JORI: Maybe I shouldn't leave! This is a hard decision.
TESS: *(Gently)* I know.

> A third character is introduced.

(The lights on the two go down, and Jori moves Down Right, where the lights come up on Mikyl, who is sitting on the floor pantomiming changing a tire. Jori crouches next to him.)

MIKYL: Wow. What an amazing opportunity for you.
JORI: Yeah, but I'm thinking maybe I shouldn't go.
MIKYL: Are you nuts? Why not?
JORI: Mikyl, it's a whole year. I'll miss you so much!
MIKYL: And I'll miss you, but we can write and e-mail each other.
JORI: Well . . .
MIKYL: We can handle it, Jori. We can handle anything.

English Language Learners

Some students may have difficulty understanding the term *exchange rate* and its meaning as the title of the play. Explain that an exchange rate is the value of money or goods to be traded, or the cost of an exchange, on any given day. Tell students that in Deanna's play, the exchange rate is the price that Jori is willing to pay to go to France. This is the conflict in the story. Point out that Jori must place a value on her relationship with Mikyl and decide whether the relationship is worth exchanging for a trip to France.

(The lights go down and Jori moves Stage Left, where the lights come up on Tess.)

> JORI: See? He's fine with it.
> TESS: Well, sure! He loves you and wants you to be happy. But don't you want the best for him?
> JORI: Of course I do.
> TESS: So you want him to put his life on hold for you?
> JORI: I don't want Mikyl to suffer, Tess! I really want to go, but I don't want to lose him!
> TESS: *(Gently)* I know.

A complication is presented.

(Their light goes down and Jori moves Center, where the lights come up on Mikyl, who is examining a fishing reel.)

> JORI: I'll be back in June. It's not so bad. You'll hardly know I'm gone. *(Casually)* And you'll be going out with other girls . . .
> MIKYL: Why would I do that?
> JORI: It's your senior year. You should have fun.
> MIKYL: You're wearing my ring. We're exclusive.
> JORI: Mikyl, I'm going to be gone a whole year. I don't want you to just freeze-dry yourself until I get back.
> MIKYL: Jori, I don't want to date anyone else.
> JORI: Oh. *(Hesitantly she walks away, thinking.)* Well . . . maybe I do.
> MIKYL: Huh?
> JORI: I mean, I'll be in Paris, Mikyl. Think of it! I'll be going to museums and the theater and parties . . .
> MIKYL: Jori, are you breaking up with me?
> JORI: *(It's painful for her to say this.)* I just thought, maybe we should take a little time off. See what's what.
> MIKYL: You ARE breaking up with me!
> JORI: Mikyl . . .
> MIKYL: Jori, I thought you loved me! We planned . . .
> JORI: *(Weakly)* People change.
> MIKYL: Yeah, so I see.
> JORI: I mean, *(Forcing a casual attitude)* I'm going to be traveling, changing, becoming worldly.
> MIKYL: Oh, I'll just be stagnating in the home pond, huh?
> JORI: Oh, I'm sure you'll be moving right along, too.

A new approach is used to solve the conflict.

Stage directions in parentheses reveal the character's feelings.

Creative Writing

Work through this sample play with the class, pointing out the elements that make it realistic and well written.

Ideas

- The main character has a believable conflict. Jori wants to go to France for a year, but she doesn't want to lose her boyfriend, Mikyl, because of it.
- The characters are believable, and the dialogue moves the action of the play along.

Organization

- The action moves logically between scenes.
- Each complication in the plot builds the story toward a logical and satisfying conclusion.

Voice

- The characters' language sounds natural for young adults.
- The tone of the play is serious yet not overly dramatic.
- The writer's stage directions help the reader to understand the story, and stage terminology is used appropriately.

English Language Learners

Review the following expressions before reading the play:

- exchange student (a student who studies in another country as part of a program between the schools or countries)

- freeze-dry (preserve in a frozen vacuum)
- becoming worldly (gaining life experiences)
- stagnating in the home pond (doing nothing, not moving)

Ask volunteers to read the parts of the characters, or have students form groups of three and assign the parts. Ask students to pay special attention to the conjunctions and interjections that help create the natural-sounding dialogue.

✳ For more about conjunctions and interjections, see SE page 734.

 Respond to the reading.

Answers

Ideas & Organization 1. Jori wants to go to France as an exchange student for a year. **2.** She has to leave her boyfriend behind. Because she'll be gone so long, his social life will come to a halt. **3.** The writer raises questions about whether Jori and Mikyl's relationship can last by switching back and forth between scenes with Jori and Tess, and Jori and Mikyl.

Voice & Word Choice 4. Possible choices: Gently, Casually, Hesitantly, It's painful for her, Weakly, Forcing a casual attitude, plastering a smile on her face, Softly, then checks herself **5.** Repeating this phrase at the end of each scene has two effects: First, it emphasizes Jori's emotional dilemma and internal conflict. Second, it helps to unify the play.

Literature Connections

Samuel Beckett's play "Come and Go" is part of a group of work that has come to be known as the "theater of the absurd." Beckett's play expresses the sentiment that human life has no ultimate purpose. There is little action, and the characters undergo no obvious changes.

Encourage students to discuss ways this play is similar to and different from plays they've read or seen before. Have students pay special attention to the stage directions throughout the play and discuss how they impact the play aesthetically and contribute to the play's meaning. For additional models of plays, see the Reading-Writing Connections beginning on page TE-36.

354

MIKYL: Darn right I will! Listen, why don't you just give me back my ring right now, before you depart for your new, better life.
JORI: Oh! Oh. Sure. *(Turns away and slowly slips off the ring. Stares at it a minute before plastering a smile on her face and turning back.)* Here! I feel lighter already.
MIKYL: I'll bet. Sorry it was weighing you down for so long. *(Softly)* It's still warm. *(Jori makes a move toward him, then checks herself.)*
JORI: Well! I guess that's that.
MIKYL: Yeah. Have fun in France, and don't waste a minute thinking about me. I'll be having a great life!
JORI: *(Softly)* That's all I ever wanted for you. *(Pause)*
MIKYL: You really are amazing, you know.
JORI: I don't have to go, Mikyl.
MIKYL: Yes, you do.
JORI: I can say no. I can stay here, with you. We'd have the best senior year . . .
MIKYL: You can't do that, Jori. You really want this. Maybe this will be a good test for us. If we can stand this, we're meant to be.
JORI: We are. I'm sure of it.
MIKYL: What about my ring? *(Holds it out to her.)*
JORI: Maybe you'll want to give it to someone else.
MIKYL: Maybe I'll hold on to it until June.
JORI: Maybe you will. *(Looks at him.)* Maybe you won't. Mikyl, I'm going to go to France. I have to go. *(Turns, then looks back.)* But I really do love you.
MIKYL: *(Softly)* I know.

(She runs to him, and they hug.)

The decision is made, the conflict overcome, and the play ends.

 Respond to the reading. Answer the following questions about the play.

Ideas & Organization (1) What does Jori want? **(2)** What is her obstacle? **(3)** How does the author build the suspense?

Voice & Word Choice (4) Find three stage directions that help you understand how the actor should say the line. **(5)** Why do you think the author repeats the phrase "I know"?

Literature Connections: To better understand the importance of stage directions, read *Come and Go*, a play by Samuel Beckett.

English Language Learners

Help students identify characters' internal conflicts by creating a dialogue t-chart. Have students reread the following dialogue. Have them record the dialogue on one side, and the character's feelings at that time on the other side.

● SE page 353 (ninth Jori entry) after Mikyl asks if Jori is breaking up with him, Jori painfully says, "I just thought, maybe we should take a little time off. See what's what." (Jori is saying this because she thinks it's best, not necessarily because she wants it.)

● SE page 354 (fourth Mikyl entry) when he says, "You really are amazing." (That could be read two different ways—sarcastically or heartfelt. He has been angry. This is a shift in his attitude. It's heartfelt here, and it makes for the resolution.)

Writing Plays **355**

Prewriting **Inventing a Main Character**

One way to start planning a play is to select a main character who wants something. That something is called the character's **objective**, and the reason the character wants it is called the **motivation**. Deanna wanted to write about a teenage girl, so she made a list of things her character might want.

- To have a car
- To host a surprise party for a friend
- To be an exchange student
- To be admitted to a prestigious college

Deanna decided to explore the idea of becoming an exchange student.

Invent your main character. Think about a possible character. Then explore potential objectives before deciding on your character's objective.

Choosing a Conflict

Conflict is the heart of drama. To write a good play, you must include an **obstacle** that prevents your character from achieving his or her goal. There are two types of conflict.

- **Internal conflict:** The main character struggles to make a decision.
- **External conflict:** The main character struggles against an outside force, either another person, society, an idea, or an element of nature.

Deanna made the following chart to look at the possible conflicts her character could face. She starred the one she decided to use.

Conflict Chart

External Conflicts	Internal Conflicts
– Her boyfriend/parents/gymnastics coach/friends ask her not to go.	– She doesn't want to leave her friends.
– She has to come up with money to pay for the trip.	✱ – She doesn't want to lose her boyfriend; neither does she want him to be unhappy.
– Her host family sounds unfriendly.	– She knows she will be homesick.
– She will probably have to repeat her senior year when she returns.	– She is afraid of flying.

Choose your character's conflict. Make a list of possible obstacles to your character's objective and select the one you would like to write about.

Creative Writing

Prewriting **Inventing a Main Character**

Make sure students understand the following concepts as they explore their main character.

The objective is *what* the character wants. In a short story, this would be the same as the character's goal. Ask students what Jori's objective is in the sample play on SE pages 352–354 (to go to France for a year).

The motivation is *why* the character wants this. The character's motivation has to be strong and transparent; otherwise, the audience won't understand the conflict that results. The motivation may be articulated through the dialogue, but it must also be conveyed by the actions of the actor playing the part. Ask students to identify Jori's motivation (the opportunity to travel for a year, learn a new culture, and meet new people).

Prewriting **Choosing a Conflict**

Provide photocopies of the reproducible T-chart (TE page 823) for students to use to explore internal and external conflicts for their main character.

 Technology Connections

Students can use the added features of the Net-text as they explore this stage of the writing process.

 Write Source Online **Net-text**

Struggling Learners

When working on their lists of possible obstacles that create conflict for a character, it may be helpful for students to work with partners to brainstorm and bounce ideas off each other. Students can then decide on their own which conflict interests them the most to write about.

Prewriting **Planning Your Resolution**

As students plan their resolution, ask them if they have ever seen a play or a movie with an ending in which everything worked out perfectly for all the characters. Remind students that in real life, problems seldom have perfect solutions that make everyone happy. Life leaves loose ends. Explain that in trying to make their resolution as realistic as possible, it is acceptable if their ending suggests these loose ends, such as the last option in the Resolution Chart, "wait and see what the future brings."

Prewriting **Developing Secondary Characters**

Have students examine the role of Tess in the sample play on SE pages 352–354 to see how a secondary character can be used to present complications and act as a sounding board for the main character in the play.

Prewriting **Considering Irony**

Many students are adept at using verbal irony, but **dramatic and situational irony** (see below) may be more difficult. Challenge students to share their ideas first with you or a writing partner to see if they will work in their play.

Prewriting **Planning Your Resolution**

In the sample play, Jori's obstacle to becoming an exchange student is her desire both to keep her boyfriend and to see him happy. To overcome her internal conflict, Jori tries several strategies.

Resolution Chart

Character	Options
Jori	– do not go to avoid separation – stay "together" but see other people – break up – wait and see what the future brings

Developing Secondary Characters

Secondary characters should be used selectively—especially in a short play. Each should have a specific role. Secondary characters can play the following roles:
- Give background information.
- Provide a sounding board for the main character.
- Introduce complications that block the main character's goal.

Prewrite

Create your secondary characters. Invent a few secondary characters and determine the purpose for each.

Considering Irony

Irony is the use of words to express something other than what is really meant. There are three kinds of dramatic irony:
- **Verbal:** A character says one thing but means another.
  "Oh, sure, I just love making a fool of myself in front of others!"

- **Dramatic:** The audience knows something the character does not.
  In *Romeo and Juliet,* Romeo thinks Juliet is dead so he kills himself, but we know Juliet is alive.

- **Situational:** What is expected to happen and what does happen are very different things.
  Willy Loman thinks his life insurance money will make his family happy, but his death just brings them sorrow.

In her play, Deanna utilizes dramatic irony when she has Jori tell Mikyl she wants to date others. The reader knows that's not so, but Mikyl does not know it.

Teaching Tip: Dramatic and Situational Irony

Share the following examples of irony with students and work with them to develop more.

Dramatic: People on a beach are relaxing and playing in the waves, not knowing that a shark is lurking in the waters.

Situational: Someone calls in sick from school and then runs into a teacher at the mall.

English Language Learners

Students may have difficulty with verbal irony because it requires comprehending the actual meaning of the words as well as recognizing what is really meant. Provide the following examples, and discuss the irony in each:
- A date shows up in dirty work clothes. "I see you really got dressed up for me tonight!" his friend remarks. (When you dress up, you wear nice, clean clothes, not dirty work clothes. The friend was making a point that the date did not go to much effort for the occasion.)
- "Harry is a lousy speller. He only knows how to spell half the words in the dictionary." (The dictionary is filled with hundreds of thousands of words. Knowing how to spell even half of the words would make a person a remarkable speller.)

Writing Plays **357**

Writing Writing Your First Draft

Remember to let your characters tell the story and reveal their personalities through what they say and do. Keep in mind the interplay of action and dialogue.

Beginning

1. **Give the opening stage directions.** Include any information that will help the reader visualize the scene.
2. **Introduce your characters and conflict.** Include enough background information to explain to the audience how the characters arrived at this opening situation.

Middle

3. **Use dialogue and action to move the play along.** Include complications to add suspense and keep the audience interested. Write stage directions that convey the subtext.
4. **Divide into scenes if necessary.** Use separate scenes to condense time or present a new development.
5. **Present the climax.** Bring the main character to a point where the conflict is resolved.

Ending

6. **Bring your play to a close.** Show how the character has changed and wrap up the action with a definite ending.

Building Scenes

A scene is like a mini-play with its own beginning, middle, and ending. Each scene should advance the action, build upon the character's objective, create complications, and move toward the resolution.

In the sample play, each of the scenes has a specific purpose:

Scene 1: To present background information and provide the conflict

Scene 2: To introduce Mikyl and provide one solution: That he and Jori "stay together" while she is gone

Scene 3: To build suspense as Tess suggests that Jori shouldn't try to tie Mikyl to a commitment

Scene 4: To present the final confrontation, the climax, and the end of the play

Write

Write your play. Write your play, using your prewriting as a guide. Use at least two scenes and work in new ideas that occur to you as you write.

Creative Writing

Writing Writing Your First Draft

Remind students that a play is a story. Readers should be able to enjoy and follow the story as easily as a theater audience would.

- Events should flow smoothly and logically from one to the next.
- Setting descriptions and the relationships between characters should be clear.
- Dialogue should be meaningful, as well as lively and natural. It should reveal a character's personality and help move the plot along.
- The actions and reactions of the characters should make sense.

Writing Building Scenes

Before students plan the rest of the play's actions, tell them that if their plays lend themselves to four scenes, students can consider using the same basic format to build scenes as outlined on SE page 357. After they have built their scenes, have them consider how lighting, sound, and changes of setting can help them transition from the beginning to the middle and end.

Technology Connections

Students can use the added features of the Net-text as they explore this stage of the writing process.

 Write Source Online **Net-text**

English Language Learners

Some students may have difficulty writing their first drafts because they are thinking about where to separate scenes. Have students write their first draft without worrying about the scenes. They can divide it into scenes later on. Have them read their drafts aloud or to a partner so they can locate places where time is condensed or new developments occur.

Writing Creating Subtext

Point out to students that because a play rarely has a narrator, subtext acts as a kind of narrator. It is important not only for helping the actor understand a character's motivation but also for helping readers or the audience understand the character's behavior.

Writing Thinking About Stage Directions

Encourage students to keep their stage directions simple and brief.

- Keep setting directions to two or three sentences, at most.
- Use single words, phrases, or short sentences to tell characters what emotions to express and how to move.

Students can look back at the sample play on SE pages 352–354 to recall examples of simple stage directions and how to incorporate them into the script.

Writing Creating Subtext

Subtext is the unspoken emotions of your characters—what they really think and feel, even while their actions suggest something else. Sometimes the playwright will include stage directions to help actors understand their character's motivation.

In the sample play, the subtext of the action is suggested through the stage directions. For example, when Jori removes Mikyl's ring, the dialogue suggests she is happy to break up. However, the stage directions present the subtext.

> JORI: Oh! Oh. Sure. (*Turns away and slowly slips off the ring. Stares at it a minute before plastering a smile on her face and turning back.*) Here! I feel lighter already.

These stage directions help the reader see that Jori does not want to give Mikyl his ring. We know that she is trying to make it easier for him when she leaves. That she still cares is further emphasized by the later stage directions.

> (*Jori makes a move toward him, then checks herself.*)

Thinking About Stage Directions

As you write stage directions, consider using stage shorthand to indicate the acting areas. The diagram below identifies the shorthand.

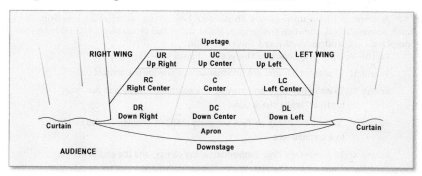

Advanced Learners

Point out the term *upstage* on the diagram. Ask students if they are familiar with the word *upstaged*; for example, "When Sasha performed at the recital, she upstaged the other piano students." Explain that when someone upstages another, she or he attracts attention and draws it away from the other person. Point out that when an actor performs upstage, he or she is standing on the back half of the stage and the other actors must turn their backs to the audience when they speak directly to the upstage actor. In this sense, the upstage actor naturally draws the audience's attention away from the others.

Have students research the origins of other theater expressions such as the following:

- curtain call
- in the limelight
- break a leg
- run that by me
- on the catwalk

Revising Improving Your Writing

Read your play out loud or have someone else read it to you. Change any lines that sound forced or unnatural. Use these questions to guide your revisions.

Revising Checklist

Ideas

_____ **1.** Is the conflict believable?
_____ **2.** Have I included complications?
_____ **3.** Do the characters seem real?

Organization

_____ **4.** Does my play move logically from one scene to the next?
_____ **5.** Does my play build to a logical conclusion?

Voice

_____ **6.** Does the dialogue sound natural?
_____ **7.** Does the tone convey the intended meaning and purpose of the play?

Sentence Fluency

_____ **8.** Does the dialogue move smoothly?
_____ **9.** Do the stage directions make sense?

Editing Checking for Conventions

Editing Checklist

_____ **1.** Does the play follow correct script form?
_____ **2.** Have I used parentheses for directions?
_____ **3.** Have I checked my punctuation?
_____ **4.** Have I checked for spelling errors?

Publishing Presenting Your Play

Share your play with an audience. Have some students act it out in class, or post it on your (or your school's) Web site.

Creative Writing

Revising Improving Your Writing

Encourage students to read aloud their play in front of a test audience of four of their classmates.

- Have each member of the audience review the play for a different trait (Ideas, Organization, Voice, and Sentence Fluency), using the questions in the checklist for that trait as a guide.
- Have reviewers provide feedback, telling what they think worked well, and what needs improvement.
- If reviewers point out a part of the play that needs to be improved, they should be ready to explain why and, if possible, offer a suggestion for how to improve that part.

Editing Checking for Conventions

Suggest that students use the sample play on SE pages 352–354 as a model for correct script form.

Publishing Presenting Your Play

If students will be presenting their play on a stage, make sure they are aware of its layout and the technology that is available to them. Encourage them to have at least one practice before they present their play to an audience.

Technology Connections

Remind students that they can use the Writing Network features of the Portfolio to share their work with peers.

⚡ *Write Source Online* **Portfolio**
⚡ *Write Source Online* **Net-text**

Struggling Learners

Students may have difficulty understanding tone. Point out that tone is the writer's attitude toward the subject. Point out that the connotations of words the writer chooses contributes to the tone. For example, a description of a character as a "shifty malcontent" communicates a distrustful tone while a description of a character as a "class clown" conveys a humorous tone.

Grammar Connection

Punctuating Dialogue
- **Proofreader's Guide** pages 616 (+), 632 (+)

Adverbs
- **Proofreader's Guide** page 730 (+)
- *SkillsBook* page 101
- *GrammarSnap* Adverb Clauses, Adverb Phrases

Pronouns
- **Proofreader's Guide** page 710 (+)
- *SkillsBook* page 78
- *GrammarSnap* Nominative, Possessive, and Objective Cases of Pronouns

Apostrophes
- **Proofreader's Guide** pages 628 (+), 629 (+)
- *SkillsBook* page 29

Writing a Radio Play

The sample radio play "Fireworks" uses a similar conflict as the sample play "Exchange Rate," but with a twist. Discuss the similarities and differences in the story line of both plays to give students an idea of how they might possibly rework the conflict that they used to write their play to write their radio play.

■ In the play "Exchange Rate," the girl doesn't want to break up with her boyfriend, but feels she should to make him happy. The boy and girl are in love and want what's best for each other. The setting is incidental to the story.

■ In the radio play "Fireworks," the girl wants to break up with the boy because she feels that there's no magic between them. He doesn't have a clue as to her feelings. The setting echoes the events, including using the sound of fireworks fizzling out to mimic the end of the relationship.

Writing a Radio Play

One of the best things about radio plays is that both the writer and the audience can really use their imaginations. The stories come to life entirely through the voices of the actors and the sound effects. With this in mind, Rahji developed a script.

Fireworks

(SCENE: A PARK, FOURTH OF JULY. WE HEAR FIREWORKS IN THE DISTANCE PUNCTUATED BY THE CROWD'S "OOOHS" AND "AAAHS.")

LUC: Wow, Cher! These are the best Fourth of July fireworks.
CHER: They're nice, Luc.

(SOUND: A LOUD BOOM AND THE CROWD'S OOOOH!)

LUC: Nice? They're spectacular!
CHER: Yes. Listen, Luc, we have to talk.

(SOUND: A CRACKLING NOISE AND THE CROWD'S AAAAH!)

LUC: That one was really cool! Talk about what?
CHER: About us, Luc. I mean, I think we should see other people.

(SOUND: A POP FOLLOWED BY SMALLER POPS, AND THE SOUND OF LAUGHTER AND APPLAUSE.)

LUC: Wow, that was—What?
CHER: I think we should break up.
LUC: But, Cher, we had the whole summer planned! We were going to go on nature hikes, go bird-watching, . . .
CHER: YOU had the whole summer planned!
LUC: I thought you'd like doing those things, too.
CHER: Listen, Luc, it's more than just the things we like to do.

(SOUND: BOOM AND AUDIENCE REACTION.)

LUC: What else is it, then?
CHER: It's us, Luc. We don't click. There's just no magic between us, no—fireworks. I'm really sorry, Luc.
LUC: But—
CHER: Goodbye, Luc.

(SOUND: A WHISTLING BUILDUP AND THEN A FIZZLE. AUDIENCE GROANS IN DISAPPOINTMENT.)

Try It!

Write a short radio play of your own, presenting a conflict between two people. Include important background noises or special sound effects.

Struggling Learners

Explain that the sound of fireworks is especially important in the radio play because the sound helps the reader "hear" the conflict. Point out that the fireworks are a symbol for the relationship and closely mirror Luc's feelings and reactions to the things that Cher has to say. Have students use Rahji's play as a model for writing their radio plays.

Writing Poetry

Some people think poetry is just for literature books. Others think it's mainly for greeting cards. But the earliest poetry was used for public performance, and much of the best modern poetry is written by everyday people for other everyday people.

In essence, a poem is "heightened" language—carefully chosen words with sounds and rhythms that are fun to hear, and with imagery and ideas that surprise or delight. In this chapter, you will find various examples of poetic forms along with definitions and demonstrations of common poetic techniques. As the examples show, poetry is for everybody!

By following the instructions in this chapter, you will learn to write your own sonnets, free-verse poems, and cinquains. We hope that you will return to this chapter often, whenever you have an idea that deserves to be expressed in a poem.

Writing Guidelines

Subject: Man and machine
Form: Sonnet
Purpose: To entertain
Audience: Friends, family, and classmates

"The future masters of technology will have to be lighthearted and intelligent. The machine easily masters the grim and the dumb."

—Marshall McLuhan

Writing Poetry

Objectives

- understand the content and structure of a sonnet and other forms of poetry
- choose a topic (man and machine) to inspire a poem
- use poetry techniques, including rhythm, rhyme, and enjambment in a poem
- plan, draft, revise, edit, and share a sonnet, a free verse poem, and a cinquain

Students may not be enthusiastic about writing in a genre they only read for class assignments. Acknowledge that students may find some poetry obscure and difficult to understand if little time is spent on reflection. However, if students can refrain from dismissing the whole genre, they may discover that most poetry is accessible and enjoyable to read. In addition, they will discover that poetry gives them freedom as writers to explore and express their ideas about everyday topics in unique and creative ways.

Understanding Sonnets

Point out to students that while a sonnet can be written about any topic, the sonnets of such famous poets as Shakespeare, Elizabeth Barrett Browning, Pablo Neruda, and others are love poems.

If there is time, read several examples of love sonnets by these and others poets. This will help students become familiar with the structure and rhythm of the traditional sonnet. Then ask them if they would call "Old Junker" a love poem. (It's not a classic love poem about two people, but the poet is writing about love for an object, a beloved car.)

 Respond to the reading.

Answers

Ideas & Organization 1. An old car goes unnoticed and unappreciated. **2.** Looks and age don't matter to the owner who loves the car just for itself.
Voice 3. casual and meant to be humorous

 Literature Connections

Encourage students to read Sonnets 18, 29, 116, and 130 by William Shakespeare. Each follows the structure students have been learning about and addresses love as its central theme.

Encourage students to discuss the meaning of each sonnet and compare and contrast how love is portrayed in each. Have them comment on lines and specific words and phrases that stand out to them in each sonnet. For additional poetry models, see the Reading-Writing Connections beginning on page TE-36.

362

Understanding Sonnets

The sonnet originated in Italy during the Middle Ages and then found its way into English poetry around the time of Shakespeare. A sonnet is 14 lines long, with a logical structure, a regular rhythm, and—usually—a rhyme scheme.

The English sonnet consists of three *quatrains* (four lines each) that present a theme, followed by a *couplet* (two lines) that responds to the theme. The Italian sonnet offers its theme in an *octave* (eight lines—often as two quatrains), followed by a *sestet* (six lines) of response.

The rhythm of English sonnets is generally iambic pentameter (see pages 364 and 369), and the most common rhyme scheme is *abab cdcd efef gg*. Italian sonnets usually present an *abababab* or *abbaabba* scheme in the octave and a *cdecde* or *cdccdc* scheme in the sestet. Other structures and rhyme schemes are possible. For an unrhymed sonnet, see W. H. Auden's "The Secret Agent."

A sonnet may be written about any topic. Boyce Pappan wrote about his car:

> This sonnet follows the Italian form of octave and sestet.
>
> The rhyme scheme is very loose (*abcbdefe ghihjh*).
>
> Most lines are iambic pentameter. Exceptions add emphasis to individual words and phrases.

Old Junker

My car is old as me—in car years, that's
middle-aged—an unappreciated
stretch of time between "brand new" and "classic"
when one's value is depreciated.
In other words, it's simply out of style,
so it doesn't get as much attention
as it once did. No one admires it. (I
never wash or wax it, I should mention.)

Still, I love this car and it's comfortable
as only an old car can be. No fear
of spilling something—the upholstery's
already stained. And you will never hear
me complain about gas mileage. Now if
I could only get the thing in gear!

 Respond to the reading. Reflect on the organization and voice of the sonnet above.

Ideas & Organization (1) What theme does the octave present? (2) What response does the sestet provide?

Voice (3) What is the writer's attitude or tone in the poem?

 Literature Connections: For more examples of sonnets, you may want to read Sonnets 18, 29, 116, and 130 by William Shakespeare.

English Language Learners

To help students understand the structure of sonnets, review the meanings of the following prefixes and provide examples.

- quad (four); quadrangle, quadrant
- oct (eight); octagon, octopus; octave
- ses (six); sextuplets; the Spanish words *seis* and *sesenta* (six; sixty)

Prewriting Choosing a Topic and a Focus

To decide on a topic, Boyce used freewriting. Here's part of what he wrote:

> What does "man and machine" mean to me? Machines are tools we use to enhance our abilities. Maybe I could write about a screwdriver or a hammer. Not a lot to say about something that simple. How about something more complex, like a car? Yeah! I could come up with lots of ideas about my car! I couldn't get by without my old . . .

Select a focus. Use freewriting to brainstorm for a topic related to "man and machine." Keep writing whatever comes to mind until you discover something exciting.

Gathering Details

Make a list of thoughts about your topic. List descriptive details as well as feelings or ideas you have. Your list may also include possible similes or metaphors to use in your poem. (See page 368.) Here's part of Boyce's list about his car:

> It's as old as I am.
> Ugly and rusty outside, but comfortable inside
> I never wash it!
> Not very powerful, but great gas mileage
> At that awkward age between new and classic
> Tricky to start on cold days
> It's my one private spot on the planet.
> Like my locker, it's full of books, old papers, clothes, and junk!
> In its day, it was "stylish"; what happened?
> Don't have to worry about scratching it (like I would a new car)

Organizing Details

Next, arrange the ideas in your list. Place similar ideas together. Think about what each section of your sonnet might cover. (*Remember:* Most sonnets are either three quatrains and an answering couplet or an octave and an answering sestet.) Review Boyce's sonnet on page 362 to see how he used his details.

Gather details. Make a list of descriptive details, feelings, and ideas about your topic. Include similes and metaphors that occur to you.

Creative Writing

Prewriting Choosing a Topic and a Focus

To give students a head start with their freewriting, have them work together to brainstorm a list of machines they have used. Encourage students to think in broad terms to include any kind of mechanical device. (Some ideas are bicycle, lawn mower, dishwasher, roller coaster, sewing machine, cash register, and so on.) Students can begin freewriting with the question about "man and machine" that Boyce used.

Prewriting Gathering Details

Have students study the definitions and examples of **similes** *(see below)* and metaphors, along with the other poetry techniques described on SE pages 368–369, before they begin to gather details.

Prewriting Organizing Details

Tell students to arrange ideas from their list in the order that they want them to come in the poem. Tell them not to be concerned with using poetic language here but to concentrate on the order.

 Technology Connections

Students can use the added features of the Net-text as they explore this stage of the writing process.

 Write Source Online Net-text

Teaching Tip: Similes

Remind students that just because the word *like* or *as* appears in a sentence, it does not necessarily mean the sentence contains a simile. For example, at the beginning of the poem "Old Junker" on SE page 362, the speaker says, "My car is old *as* me," and later, "it's comfortable *as* only an old car can be." Explain that neither of these is a simile. They simply state facts. Tell students to make sure that when they are writing similes that they are actually making a comparison between two unlike things, for example, "my car is *like* an old friend."

English Language Learners

Some students may find it difficult to generate ideas through freewriting. Point out other brainstorming techniques, such as using clusters and word webs, asking "what if" questions, and listing ideas in their response journal. If possible, allow an extra day or two for the lesson so students have time to let their ideas percolate.

Writing **Writing Your First Draft**

Assure students that except for rhythm and rhyme, they aren't required to incorporate any of the techniques on SE page 368–369 into their sonnet, but they may want to try.

Writing **Using Rhythm**

Explain that while using short, one-syllable words will make it easier to recreate the rhythm of iambic pentameter, students should not feel that they need to limit themselves to one-syllable words. (See Rhythm examples on SE page 369.)

Writing **Using Rhyme**

The simplest nursery rhymes have rhyme schemes, yet rhyme is one of the most difficult techniques to use well. Remind students that they will have to use a rhyme scheme in their sonnet. However, if they find that their first rhyme scheme is making their poem sound contrived, they should be willing to alter that scheme by choosing different rhyming pairs.

Writing **Using Enjambment**

Make it clear that the rhyme still has to come at the end of a line, but with enjambment the end of the line does not have to fall at the end of the sentence. Challenge students to find examples of enjambment in their favorite poems and share them in class.

Technology Connections

Students can use the added features of the Net-text as they explore this stage of the writing process.

✵ *Write Source Online* **Net-text**

364

Writing **Writing Your First Draft**

Write a first draft of your poem. Watch for opportunities to use the various poetic techniques described below and on pages 368–369.

Using Rhythm

The standard rhythm for a sonnet is iambic pentameter. (See page 369.) As you write, let this rhythm guide your phrases. But remember, it's okay to vary the rhythm, especially for emphasis.

> ᵕ ⁄ ᵕ ⁄ ᵕ ⁄ ᵕ ⁄ ᵕ ⁄
> My car is old as me. In car years, that's

Using Rhyme

While you are drafting your poem, a rhyme scheme may begin to suggest itself. If so, allow it to guide your word choice. However, don't work too hard at rhyming yet. Just focus on completing your first draft.

> In other words, it's simply out of style,
> so it doesn't get as much **attention**
> as it once did. No one admires it. (I
> never wash or wax it, I should **mention**.)

Using Enjambment

Poems with lines that always end on a rhyme can sometimes sound singsongy, like a nursery rhyme. When you use enjambment—carrying sentences from line to line and ending them inside a line—your poems will flow more naturally. Enjambment also makes rhyming simpler. (It's easier to fit a rhyme inside a sentence than at the end.)

> as only an old car can be. **No fear**
> of spilling something—the upholstery's
> already stained. And you will never hear

Write your first draft. Use your plan as a guide. Watch for opportunities to use poetic techniques such as rhythm, rhyme, and enjambment to make your sonnet read effectively.

English Language Learners

Correct pronunciation of words is key to using rhythm and rhyme. It may benefit students to partner with students proficient in English to help them to verify the pronunciation of words in their first drafts.

Writing Poetry **365**

Revising Improving Your Poem

After drafting a sonnet, let it sit for a while. Later, when you return to it with fresh eyes, you will notice which parts work and which parts could be improved. Also have a trusted friend respond to the poem. Then make any needed changes, based on the traits of good writing.

- **Ideas** Do I use effective details? Does my poem show my feelings without telling the reader what to think?
- **Organization** Does my poem follow a sonnet structure? Does it introduce an idea in the quatrains or octave and a response in the couplet or sestet?
- **Voice** Does my poem show inventiveness and personality?
- **Word Choice** Are my words precise and interesting? Do my rhymes work well? (See page 369.)
- **Sentence Fluency** Do my phrases and ideas flow smoothly? Are they—at least loosely—set in iambic pentameter?

Revise your poem. Using the questions above as a guide, keep revising until your poem is the best that it can be.

Editing Checking for Errors

Because poetry is a concise form, every word, every punctuation mark, is important. Careful editing is essential.

Edit your poem. Be sure that every element of your poem accomplishes the purpose you intend.

Publishing Sharing Your Poem

There are many ways in which you can share a sonnet. Here are a few ideas:

- **Post it.** Put it on a bulletin board or a Web site.
- **Submit it.** Send your poem to a contest or a magazine.
- **Perform it.** Have an "open-mike" poetry reading in your class.
- **Send it** to friends and family members in a card or by e-mail.

Publish your poem. Share your poem with others and discuss the ideas and feelings it presents. Ask your teacher for other publishing ideas.

Creative Writing

Revising Improving Your Poem

The best way for students to know if their rhymes work well and if their ideas flow smoothly is to read their sonnet aloud. Encourage students to read aloud their sonnet every time they make revisions to hear how those changes affect the sound.

Suggest that students try to tap out lightly the rhythm of their sonnet, listening for the beat. If it follows a repeated pattern of an unstressed syllable followed by a stressed syllable, then they have used standard iambic pentameter rhythm, or something close.

Editing Checking for Errors

As students edit their sonnets, they should pay particular attention to where they used enjambment to ensure that sentences that end inside a line have the correct end punctuation and that the sentence that follows starts with a capital letter.

Publishing Sharing Your Poem

Set aside class time for poetry readings. Students can read their sonnets and other original poetry they have written.

 Technology Connections

Remind students that they can use the Writing Network features of the Portfolio to share their work with peers.

Write Source Online **Portfolio**

Write Source Online **Net-text**

Grammar Connection

Parts of Speech Review
- **Proofreader's Guide** pages 700 (+), 701–734 (+)
- *SkillsBook* pages 113–114

Adverbs
- **Proofreader's Guide** page 730 (+)
- *SkillsBook* pages 104, 105, 106

Absolute Phrases
- **Proofreader's Guide** page 744 (+)
- *SkillsBook* page 125

Basic Sentence Patterns
- **Proofreader's Guide** pages 760–761, 762 (+)

Clauses
- **Proofreader's Guide** pages 744 (+), 748 (+), 750 (+)
- *SkillsBook* pages 129, 130, 131, 132
- *GrammarSnap* Noun Clauses, Adjective Clauses, Adverb Clauses

Spelling
- **Proofreader's Guide** pages 666–669
- *SkillsBook* page 53

Capitalization
- **Proofreader's Guide** pages 648 (+), 650 (+), 652 (+)
- *SkillsBook* page 44
- *GrammarSnap* Capitalization of Proper Nouns and Adjectives

Writing Free Verse

Have students read "Dear Aunt Janie." Then discuss the elements that make this a **free verse poem** (see below).

- There is no defined rhythm. It varies throughout the poem.
- The words flow in an uneven but lyrical pattern as a result of their arrangement.
- It has no set structure of lines.
- There is no rhyme scheme, but it does contain other poetic elements such as consonance, assonance, and repetition (spilling, spilled).

Ask students what Justine Fredrickson does not tell them in the poem, but expects them to fill in on their own. What words communicate this meaning? (Her dear Aunt Jamie has died. The words "My Aunt Jamie left me a typewriter" and "I'd shrug/and change the subject" suggest this meaning.)

The sample free verse poem and the two sample cinquains on SE page 367 are also about "man and machine." Remind students that their topic should have broad appeal.

 Literature Connections

Ted Hughes' free-verse poem "The Horses" begins with a bleak, dark tone that describes a "world cast in frost." The tone changes, however, as the speaker has a pre-dawn encounter with a herd of horses. The poignant meeting is romanticized and becomes an important memory for the speaker.

Encourage students to discuss the language and strong imagery in the poem. For additional poetry models, see the Reading-Writing Connections beginning on page TE-36.

366

Writing Free Verse

At first glance, free verse may seem to follow no rules at all. Actually, each free-verse poem creates its own form—using traditional poetic elements such as consonance, assonance, repetition, and rhythm. (See pages 368–369.) However, free verse almost never uses end rhymes.

Justine Fredrickson wrote the following free-verse poem about an old-fashioned typewriter. Notice the poetic techniques she used.

"Dear Aunt Janie"

My Aunt Janie
left me a typewriter—
a clunky machine

with which she wrote letters
starting, "Dear Niece"
and spilling her thoughts

It sat on my dresser for weeks
near the window,
just catching dust in the sun

When friends asked,
"Where'd you get
that clackety old thing?"

I'd shrug
and change the subject

This afternoon I came home
to find a white sheet of paper
waiting in the roller

As I touched the keys,
this poem spilled out

> Consonance is used in the repeated "t" of line 2.

> The words "Dear Niece" echo the poem's title. Assonance is used with the words "just," "dust," and "sun" in line 9.

> Periods are left out to avoid abrupt pauses at the ends of sentences.

> The ending recalls an earlier thought in the poem.

 Literature Connections: Consider reading "The Horses" by Ted Hughes, a free-verse poem about a poignant pre-dawn encounter.

 Write **Write a free-verse poem.** Follow the writing process to write a free-verse poem of your own. Use techniques such as consonance, assonance, repetition, and rhythm (see pages 368–369) to make your poem a work of art.

Teaching Tip: Writing A Free Verse Poem

Point out that some poets believe it is more difficult to write free verse than poems with strict rules for rhythm, rhyme, and the arrangement of lines and verses. With no rules to follow, the free-verse poet has to decide how many verses to write, where lines break, how long or short lines and verses will be, and so on.

English Language Learners

Some students may find writing free verse intimidating because they need more structure. Assist students by providing them with a formula, such as a sentence starter they can use to begin each sentence. After they have written their poems, have them delete the sentence starter and adapt their poem into a free verse poem.

Possible sentence starters are the following:

My favorite place to be is _____ where _____.

All I ever want to do is _____.

The funniest animal I ever saw was a _____ that _____.

Writing Cinquains

A cinquain (sometimes called a quintet) is a carefully structured poem of five lines. The first line has two syllables, the second has four, the third six, the fourth eight, and the final line just two again. Often the rhythm is iambic, although this is not a strict rule. Generally both syllables in the first and last lines are strongly accented. Most cinquains are unrhymed, although rhyme is sometimes used for humorous effect.

In a poem such as this, short, precise words are essential. It's important to make every syllable count—not just to fill the form. Also, a good cinquain delays its sense of closure until the very last line. Those final two syllables should feel like a climax to the poem.

Hammers

Hammers
are perfect for
driving nails or breaking
things: full piggy banks, geodes—and
silence.

—Avery Strattman

Mystery Machine

What does
this machine do?
I see levers and dials;
I hear gears whirring, smell something
burning!

—Marissa Troff

Write

Write a cinquain. Follow the prewriting activities on page 363 to generate a topic and gather details. Then write a cinquain in the form shown above.

Creative Writing

Writing Cinquains

Have students count out the syllables in each line of the sample poems, "Hammers" and "Mystery Machine," to see that they fit this carefully structured form.

Offer students these suggestions for writing a cinquain.

- Brainstorm a list of objects that have only two syllables, like *hammer,* and use that word to start the cinquain. Some ideas are *blender, jigsaw, grinder,* or *printer.*
- Write the following numbers in parentheses in a column along the left of a piece of paper: 2, 4, 6, 8, 2. Use the numbers as reminders of how many syllables each line should have.

English Language Learners

Writing a cinquain requires command of knowing syllables and how they are accented. This may present a challenge for students whose first language is not English. Invite these students to write a cinquain in their first language, and then have them read their poems aloud to the class. The class may not understand the meaning of the words, but they will appreciate the music in a cinquain, and that poetry communicates with sounds and rhythms, as well as word meanings. Students can provide a general translation of their poems afterwards.

Advanced Learners

Have students use a thesaurus to expand their vocabulary while creating their cinquain. Challenge them to use new descriptive, colorful, or humorous words and still keep to the 2-4-6-8-2 syllable structure.

Using Special Poetry Techniques

After students have had a chance to review the poetry techniques described on SE pages 368–369, ask them to select and read aloud an original poem or one by a poet who uses one or more of these techniques. Ask listeners to identify the different techniques they hear used in the poem.

368

Using Special Poetry Techniques

Poets use a variety of special techniques in their work. This page and the next define some of the most important ones.

Figures of Speech

- A **simile** (*sĭm´ə-lē*) compares two unlike things with the word *like* or *as*.

  The washing machine coughed
  like a dying stegosaurus.

- A **metaphor** (*mĕt´ə-fôr*) compares two unlike things without using *like* or *as*.

  That radio was more
  than tubes and speakers;
  it was the wide world come to visit
  in her parlor.

- **Personification** (*pər-sŏn´ə-fĭ-kā´shən*) is a technique that gives human traits to something that is nonhuman.

  The mailbox gaped
  with open mouth,
  speechless.

- **Hyperbole** (*hī-pûr´bə-lē*) is an exaggerated statement, often humorous.

  A bicycle sped past
  with a sonic boom!

Sounds of Poetry

- **Alliteration** (*ə-lĭt´ə-rā´shən*) is the repetition of consonant sounds at the beginning of words.

  I never wash or wax it, I should mention.

- **Assonance** (*ăs´ə-nəns*) is the repetition of vowel sounds anywhere in words.

  just catching dust in the sun

- **Consonance** (*kŏn´sə-nəns*) is the repetition of consonant sounds anywhere in words.

  No fear of spilling something—the upholstery's
  already stained.

Struggling Learners

To make figurative language more concrete, provide pairs with photographs and have them discuss the images and what they think the images represent. Have them consider similes, metaphors, personification, and hyperbole and then choose the figure of speech that best represents what they have discussed.

Advanced Learners

Have students create a multimedia presentation that explains the special poetry techniques. Pair students and assign each pair one or two of the special techniques to focus on for their part of the presentation. When pairs have finished their parts, have the group work together to create the slideshow.

Writing Poetry **369**

■ **Enjambment** (*ĕn-jăm´mənt*) is running a sentence across more than one line of verse or from one stanza to another.

> a clunky machine
> with which she wrote letters
> starting, "Dear Niece"

■ **Line breaks** help control the rhythm of a poem. The reader naturally pauses at the end of a line, the last word of which receives added emphasis.

> Branches reaching out,
> stretching,
> as though fingers yearning
> to strum the wind.

■ **Onomatopoeia** (*ŏn´ə-măt´ə-pē´ə*) is the use of words that sound like what they name.

> that clackety old thing?

■ **Repetition** (*rĕp´ĭ-tĭsh´ən*) uses the same word, phrase, or pattern of words more than once, for emphasis or for rhythm.

> What flames shot from the tailpipes!
> What smoke rolled from the spinning tires!
> What gasps rose from the crowd!

■ **Rhyme** (*rīm*) means using words whose endings sound alike. *End rhyme* happens at the end of lines.

> so it doesn't get as much attention
> as it once did. No one admires it. (I
> never wash or wax it, I should mention.)

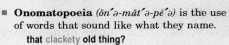

Internal rhyme happens within lines.

> Finding her way in blinding snow.

■ **Rhythm** (*rĭth´əm*) is the pattern of accented and unaccented syllables in a poem.

 ■ Iambic: an unstressed followed by a stressed syllable (*Ĭ am´*)
 ■ Trochaic: a stressed followed by an unstressed syllable (*la´-tĕr*)
 ■ Anapestic: two unstressed followed by a stressed syllable (*ĭo the moon´*)
 ■ Dactylic: a stressed followed by two unstressed syllables (*stealth´-ĭ-lў*)

The rhythm of free-verse poetry tends to flow naturally, like speaking. Traditional poetry follows a more regular pattern, as in the following example.

> Moon´ on snow´
> Evening glow´

Creative Writing

Arrange time for students to share their cinquain. Then hold a question-and-answer session about the techniques—described on SE pages 368–369—they used to write poetry. Remind students that they can use several of these techniques to enhance all their writing, not just their poetry. For example, they can use figures of speech to create stronger images in both fiction writing and nonfiction articles and essays. They can use repetition in all their writing to achieve unity between sentences and between paragraphs.

Encourage students to review writing assignments that they are currently working on to see if there are places where they could add a figure of speech or use repetition to enhance their writing.

✳ For writing techniques students can use in all their writing, see SE pages 600–601.

Research Writing Overview

Common Core Standards Focus

Writing 8: Gather relevant information from multiple authoritative print and digital sources, using advanced searches effectively; assess the strengths and limitations of each source in terms of the task, purpose, and audience; integrate information into the text selectively to maintain the flow of ideas, avoiding plagiarism and overreliance on any one source and following a standard format for citation.

Writing 9: Draw evidence from literary or informational texts to support analysis, reflection, and research.

Language 2: Demonstrate command of the conventions of standard English capitalization, punctuation, and spelling when writing.

Writing Forms

- MLA research paper
- oral presentation
- multimedia report

Focus on the Traits

- **Ideas** Stating the thesis clearly, supporting it with sufficient details, and crediting sources
- **Organization** Creating a sentence outline to organize topic sentences and details that support each topic sentence
- **Voice** Engaging the reader with a natural, knowledgeable voice
- **Word Choice** Choosing specific nouns and active verbs, and avoiding unnecessary modifiers
- **Sentence Fluency** Varying sentence lengths and constructions
- **Conventions** Checking for errors in punctuation, capitalization, spelling, and grammar

Technology Connections

 Write Source Online
www.hmheducation.com/writesource

- **Net-text**
- **Bookshelf**
- **GrammarSnap**
- **Portfolio**
- **Essay Scoring**
- **Writing Network features**
- **File Cabinet**

 Interactive Whiteboard Lessons

Suggested Research Writing Unit (Five Weeks)

Day	Writing and Skills Instruction	Student Edition		SkillsBook	Daily Language Workouts	Write Source Online
		Main Pages	Resource Units*			
WEEK 1 1–5	**Research Writing Skills**	371–382			98–101	
	Documenting Research	425–438				
	Taking Notes	527–531				
	Summarizing and Paraphrasing	543–550				
WEEK 2 6	**MLA Research Report: A Presidential Policy** (Model)	383–392			102–105	*Interactive Whiteboard Lessons*

* These units are also located in the back of the *Teacher's Edition*. Resource Units include "Basic Elements of Writing" and "Proofreader's Guide."
(+) This activity is located in a different section of the *Write Source Student Edition*. If students have already completed this activity, you may wish to review it at this time.

Day	Writing and Skills Instruction	Student Edition		SkillsBook	Daily Language Workouts	Write Source Online
		Main Pages	Resource Units*			
WEEK 2 (CONT.) 7–10	(Prewriting) Supporting Details	393–401, 56–57, 100, 108–109, 110			102–105	*Net-text*
	Beginnings, Middles, Endings	60, 107, 108, 109, 112, 120	590, 593, 594, 597			
	Outlines	104	591			
WEEK 3 11–15	(Writing)	402–407			106–109	*Net-text*
	Thesis Statements	61, 103	592			
	Integrating Quotations	111				
	Writing Responsibly	417–424				
WEEK 4 16–20	(Revising) Transitions	408–411	595–596		110–113	*Net-text*
	Skills Activities: • Active and Passive Verbs, Mood of Verbs		722 (+), 724–725			*GrammarSnap*
	• Punctuating a Research Paper			35–36, 37		
	• Sentence Review		738–757 (+)	181–184		*GrammarSnap*
	• Brackets, Ellipses, Parentheses		638–639, 642–643, 644–645			
WEEK 5 21–23	(Editing, Publishing)	412–416			114–117	*Portfolio, Net-text*
	Skills Activities: • Subjects and Predicates Review		738 (+), 740 (+)	120		
	• Sentence Problems Review			165, 173–174		
	• Subject-Verb Agreement and Pronoun-Antecedent Review		752–753 (+), 754–755 (+), 756–757 (+)	143, 147, 148		*GrammarSnap*
	• Using the Right Word Review		678–696 (+)	63–64		
	• Shifts in Construction			172, 180		
24–25 *opt.*	Multimedia Presentations	448–449				
	Skills Activities: • Spelling Review		644 (+)	54		
	• Proofreading Review			65–66		

* These units are also located in the back of the *Teacher's Edition*. Resource Units include "Basic Elements of Writing" and "Proofreader's Guide."
(+) This activity is located in a different section of the *Write Source Student Edition*. If students have already completed this activity, you may wish to review it at this time.

Teacher's Notes for Research Writing

This overview of research writing includes some specific suggestions for the unit. The description of each chapter will help you decide which parts of the unit to teach.

Writing Focus

Research Skills (pages 371–382)

Libraries are information centers that provide a variety of resource services. Students will find collecting information in a library easier once they understand how various resources are stored and accessed. Students are expected to use reference materials (such as a dictionary, an encyclopedia, an almanac, an atlas, and a thesaurus) as an aid to writing. They should understand and use tables of contents, chapter and section headings, glossaries, indexes, and appendices to locate information in reference books.

MLA Research Paper (pages 383–416)

This chapter presents the MLA approach to writing a research paper and documenting sources. Each step of the research writing process is illustrated using a model research paper, which examines the New Deal of President Roosevelt. Numerous checklists and suggestions will help students write their own research papers.

Writing Responsibly (pages 417–424)

This chapter provides examples to help students understand plagiarism. Some students think that if they put someone else's work in their own words it's acceptable. Of course, the use of quotations and paraphrases is acceptable, but proper credit must be given.

Documenting Research (pages 425–438)

Because documentation of resources in research writing is so important, this chapter reviews in-text citations, an MLA works-cited list, and an APA reference list.

Making Oral Presentations (pages 439–449)

Giving a speech is challenging for most people. This chapter provides the information students need to prepare for and present a speech or an oral report. Information about, (and a checklist for) a multimedia presentation are also included.

Academic Vocabulary

Read aloud the academic terms, as well as the descriptions and questions. Model for students how to read one question and answer it. Have partners monitor their understanding and seek clarification of the terms by working through the meanings and questions together.

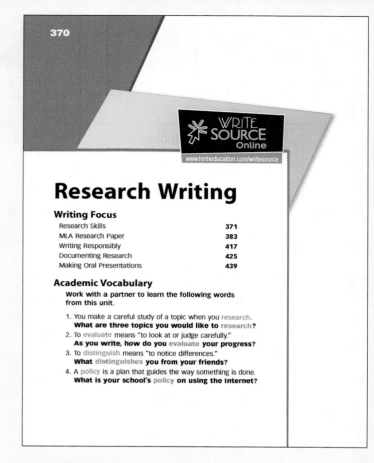

370

Research Writing

Writing Focus

Academic Vocabulary

Work with a partner to learn the following words from this unit.

1. You make a careful study of a topic when you research.
   What are three topics you would like to research?
2. To evaluate means "to look at or judge carefully."
   As you write, how do you evaluate your progress?
3. To distinguish means "to notice differences."
   What distinguishes you from your friends?
4. A policy is a plan that guides the way something is done.
   What is your school's policy on using the Internet?

Minilessons

Card Games   MLA Research Paper

- **READ** a featured essay at the end of *Time* or *Newsweek*. On one note card, **PARAPHRASE** the paragraph that best reveals the thesis of the essay. On another card, **QUOTE** the most memorable sentence in the essay. On a third card, **COMMENT** personally on what you've read.

Here's Your Citation!   Documenting Research

- **CHOOSE** an article from a magazine, a paragraph from a book, and a report from the Internet on a topic that interests you. **CHECK** SE pages 426–436 and then **WRITE** the correct documentation for each item assuming you have cited it in a research paper.

Love, Hate, Hope, Fear . . .   Making Oral Presentations

- **WRITE** notes for a one-minute impromptu speech on an abstract concept such as love, hate, hope, fear, and so on. **INCLUDE** a visual aid in your presentation. **TAKE** turns giving your speeches in small groups or for the class. **USE** the presentation evaluation sheet on SE page 447 to **EVALUATE** one another's presentations.

371

Research Writing
Research Skills

Doing research will help you in more ways than you know. If you begin with a topic that's too broad, research can help you narrow it. If you don't know which side of an issue to write about, research can help you take a position. Anyone who has ever done research knows that it can provide not only answers but also additional questions to consider.

That's why it's as important to know *how* to research as it is to know *what* to research. This chapter will serve as a guide to various sources of information, where to find them, and how to gauge their reliability.

- **Primary vs. Secondary Sources**
- **Evaluating Sources of Information**
- **Using the Internet**
- **Using the Library**
- **Using Reference Books**

"The outcome of any serious research can only be to make two questions grow where only one grew before."

—Thorstein Veblen

Research Skills

Objectives
- distinguish between primary and secondary sources
- learn to evaluate sources
- understand how to use the Internet to do research
- understand how to access and use library reference materials
- use the elements of a dictionary page
- review how to use periodical guides to find articles

As you begin this unit, have students share their experiences conducting research. Use these questions to initiate discussion:
- Have you researched a topic on your own to learn more about it? When? Did the results surprise you? Is your research ongoing?
- How would you describe the difference between personal research and research you do for a school assignment?
- What aspects about doing research or sharing the results of your research are enjoyable? Explain.
- How do you interpret the Thorstein Veblen quotation at the bottom of SE page 371?

Primary vs. Secondary Sources

Some students may not understand exactly how to distinguish between certain primary and secondary sources. For example, students might be confused about whether a book or magazine article written by an expert in a particular field is a primary source (because the author is an expert) or a secondary source (because the book represents a third-person account of information).

Explain that sources such as these are, strictly speaking, secondary sources. Point out, however, that secondary sources may provide the only reliable information. Knowing how to evaluate any source is the key to deciding whether to use the information in it. Students will learn more about evaluating sources on SE page 373.

Try It!
Answers

Possible Answers

- Primary Sources: Interview parents and parents of friends. Read a diary of someone who lived during the particular era.
- Secondary Sources: Read a book about the era. Watch a TV documentary about the era.

Primary vs. Secondary Sources

Primary sources are original sources (diaries, people, events, surveys). They inform you directly, not through a second person's explanation or interpretation. Ideally, when you research a topic, you should find as much primary information as possible.

Primary sources include . . .

- **Diaries, journals, and letters:** You can often find these in museums, in libraries, or at historic sites.
- **Presentations:** A speaker at a museum or a historic site can give you firsthand information, but be aware of the presenter's own interpretation of events.
- **Interviews:** Talk to an expert on your research topic. You can do this by phone, e-mail, or letter.
- **Surveys and questionnaires:** These tools help you gather a great deal of data from many people.
- **Observation and participation:** Your own observations of a person, a place, or an event provide excellent firsthand information. Participating in an event can give you insights that cannot be discovered through the reports of others.

Secondary sources are third-person accounts found in research done by other people. Much of the news *(television, radio, Internet, books, magazines)* can be considered a secondary source of information. Keep in mind that, by their very nature, secondary sources represent filtered information that may contain biases or misunderstandings.

Primary Sources	Secondary Sources
1. Reading the journal of a travel guide	**1.** Exploring a Web site about being a travel guide
2. Listening to a travel guide's presentation on-site	**2.** Reading a magazine about the site
3. Interviewing a shop owner in London	**3.** Watching a TV documentary about London's retail business

Try It!

List two primary and two secondary sources you might use to learn about the era of your parents' adolescence. Be as specific as you can be.

Evaluating Sources of Information

You may find a lot of information about your research topic. But before you use any of it, decide whether or not the information is dependable. Use the following questions to help you decide about the reliability of your sources.

Is the source a primary source or a secondary source?

You can usually trust any information you've collected yourself, but be careful with secondary sources. Although many of them are reliable, others may contain outdated or incorrect information.

Is the source an expert?

An expert knows more about a subject than other people. Using an expert's thoughts and opinions can make your paper more believable. If you aren't sure about a source's authority, ask a teacher or librarian what he or she thinks.

Is the information accurate?

Sources that people respect are usually very accurate. Big-city newspapers (*New York Times* or *Chicago Tribune*) and well-known Web sites (CNN or ESPN) are reliable sources of information. Little-known sources that do not support their facts or that contain errors are not reliable.

Tip

Be especially cautious about the accuracy of information on the Internet. While there is an incredible amount of information available on the Net, there is also a lot of misinformation.

Is the information fair and complete?

A reliable source should provide information fairly, covering all sides of a subject. If a source presents only one side of a subject, its information may not be accurate. To make themselves sound better, politicians and advertisers often present just their side of a subject. Avoid sources that are one sided; look for those that are balanced.

Is the information current?

Usually, you want to have the most up-to-date information about a subject. Sometimes information changes, and sources can become outdated quickly. Check the copyright page in a book, the issue date of a magazine, and the posting date of online information.

Research Skills 373

Research

Evaluating Sources of Information

Point out that publishers often employ people called fact-checkers, or researchers, whose job is to ensure that the facts in a book or an article are accurate. In a similar way, students can act as their own fact-checkers by following some basic procedures.

- Students should check the information they research against other sources. If they find the same fact in at least three different, reliable sources (for example, a reliable Web site, an encyclopedia article, and a book printed by an established publisher), students can assume the facts are correct. Later, if a fact is challenged or questioned, students will have additional supporting sources.

- Focus students' attention on the Tip. When checking facts found on the Internet, students should not rely solely on other Internet sites. People often copy and paste information from one site to another. One indication of this is finding the exact wording or details from one site on another. Tell students to be alert to this.

Struggling Learners

Point out that reliable Internet sources list their sources of information. Tell students that if they suspect that information on a site may not be reliable, they can research the sources listed on the site. Point out that sites that do not list their sources are less likely to be credible. Whenever students encounter such sites, they should look for more reliable sources.

Advanced Learners

Challenge students to create a source evaluation checklist the class can use to evaluate their different types of sources. Have the checklist include factors such as the following:

- primary or secondary source of information
- evidence of reliability
- accuracy of facts
- procedure to update facts
- use of outside sources

Using the Internet

Suggest that students work together to compile a master list of the most useful search engines they find.

- Tell students to list any new search engines they discover as they conduct research and use the Internet.
- Each listing should include the search engine's Web address and any advice students can offer for using the search engine.
- Students can add to the master list the Web sites they discover during the **Try It!** activity.
- Have a volunteer create an electronic file of the list and upload it to the classroom Web site for students to access.
- Because not every student will have access to the Internet at home, print copies of the list for students to keep in their writing notebooks.

374

Using the Internet

Because you can access many resources by surfing the Web, the Internet is a valuable research aid. You can find government publications, encyclopedia entries, business reports, and firsthand observations on the Internet.

Points to Remember

- **Use the Internet wisely.** Sites that include *.edu, .org,* and *.gov* in the Web address are often reliable. These sites are usually from educational, nonprofit, or government agencies. If you have questions about the reliability of a site, talk to your teacher. (See also page 373.) Remember to check the date of the Web site. Abandoned Web sites may contain outdated information.

- **Try several search engines.** When you type a term into a search engine's input box, the search engine scans its database for matching sites. Then the engine returns recommendations for you to explore. Because there is an enormous amount of information on the Web, no one search engine can handle it all. So employ at least two search engines when you surf the Web. Enter keywords to start your research or enter specific questions to zero in on your topic.

- **Take advantage of links.** When you read a page, watch for links to other sites. These may offer different perspectives or points of view on your topic.

- **Experiment with keywords.** Sometimes you must ask a number of different questions or use different keywords to find the information you need.

- **Ignore Web sites that advertise research papers for sale.** Using these sites is dishonest. Teachers and librarians can recognize and verify when a paper is someone else's work.

- **Learn your school's Internet policy.** Using the computer at school is a privilege. To maintain that privilege, follow your school's Internet policy and any guidelines your parents may have set.

Try It!

With a partner, make a list of all the search engines you know of. Then enter the keywords "search engine" into one of them and compare the results to your list. Is there one that you believe would yield the best results for a topic you are interested in?

English Language Learners

To facilitate students' Internet searches, do the following:

- Provide students with a list of student-friendly sites.
- Bookmark useful sites and search engines.
- Pair students with cooperative, English-proficient research partners.

Using the Library

The Internet may be a good place to initiate your research, but a library is often a more valuable place to continue your research. A library offers materials that are more in-depth and reliable than what you find on the Internet. Most libraries contain the following resources.

Books

- **Reference** books include encyclopedias, almanacs, dictionaries, atlases, and directories, plus other resources such as consumer information guides and car-repair manuals. Reference books provide a quick review or overview of research topics.
- **Nonfiction** texts are a good source of facts that can serve as a foundation for your research. Check the copyright dates to be sure you are reading reasonably up-to-date information. (Some libraries organize nonfiction using the Library of Congress system, but most use the Dewey decimal system as shown on page 377.)
- **Fiction** can sometimes aid or enhance your research. For example, a historical novel can reveal people's feelings about a particular time in history. (Fiction books are grouped together in alphabetical order by the authors' last names.)

Periodicals

Periodicals *(newspapers* and *magazines)* are grouped together in a library. Use the *Readers' Guide to Periodical Literature* to find articles in periodicals. (See page 382.) You will have to ask the librarian for older issues. Your library may subscribe to online databases of periodicals.

The Media Section

The media section of your library includes DVD's, CD-ROM's, CD's, cassettes, and videotapes. These resources can immerse you in an event. Keep in mind, however, that directors and screenwriters may present events in a way that accommodates their personal views.

Computers

Computers in most libraries are connected to the Internet, although there may be restrictions on their use.

 Try It!

Practice using the online *Readers' Guide to Periodical Literature* or another online database of periodicals. Think of several broad topics and look them up. Notice how this resource can help you narrow a broad topic.

Using the Library

Many libraries provide patrons with direct at-home access through the Internet to many of the libraries' resources, including articles and information from Web sites. Usually a user password is required. An actual trip to the library will provide additional benefits. Encourage students to explore their school or public library before they begin a research paper to learn what resources are available only at the library. If feasible, conduct a class trip to the public library in your area to meet with the **reference librarian** *(see below),* who can speak to students about the library's resources and how to access them.

For the **Try It!** activity, provide students with a list of several broad topics suggested by teachers in other curriculum areas and based on topics students are currently studying. Tell students to keep a record of their results as these ideas may prove useful when students write research papers for other classes.

Teaching Tip: Reference Librarians

Encourage students to introduce themselves to the reference librarian at their library. Point out that a reference librarian can be a researcher's best ally. It is the reference librarian's job to know where all the reference resources are located in the library. As a result, a reference librarian can

- locate materials in the reference sections of the library much faster than most patrons, and
- find with a few keystrokes information stored in the library's computer network much faster than most researchers.

Encourage students to become familiar with the electronic card catalog system utilized by the school library and the public library.

■ Prepare a list of book titles, authors' names, and subject-related topics students are studying in other classes. (Ask teachers in these classes for help compiling a list.)

■ Have students look up each item, using both the school library and the public library computer catalogs. (Note that both electronic catalogs may be available to students on home computers via the Internet.)

■ Invite volunteers to describe differences, if any, between the information available and how types of information are displayed on the two systems.

Since most public libraries belong to larger networks, their computer catalog often shows search results for all the library branches in the network. If the book is not available at their library branch, there is usually an option in the system software whereby a patron can request an interlibrary transfer from another branch. If students are not sure how to use this feature at their library, suggest that they ask their librarian for help.

376

Using the Computer Catalog

While some libraries still use a card catalog in a cabinet with drawers, most libraries keep their catalog on computer. Each system varies a bit, so ask for help if necessary. A **computer catalog** lists the books held in your library and affiliated systems. It lets you know if a book is available or if you must wait for it.

Various Search Methods

When you are using a computer catalog, you can find information about a book with any of the following methods:

■ If you know it, enter the **title** of the book.
■ If you know the **author** of the book, enter the first and last names.
■ A general search of your **subject** will also help you find books on your topic. Enter either the subject or a related keyword.

Sample Computer Catalog Screen

In the illustration below, the key to the right identifies the types of information provided for a particular resource, in this case, a book. Once you locate the book you need, make note of the call number. You will use this to find the book on the shelf.

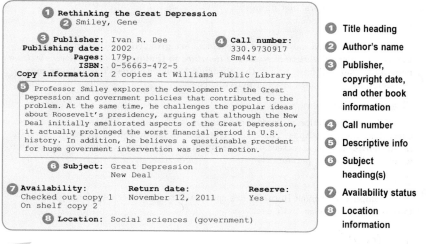

Try It!

Use the computer catalog to see what current newspapers your library subscribes to. Ask the librarian for help if necessary.

Research Skills **377**

Research

Understanding Call Numbers

All nonfiction books in the library have **call numbers**. The books are arranged on the shelves according to these numbers. Call numbers are usually based on the **Dewey decimal classification** system, which divides nonfiction books into 10 subject categories.

000–099	**General Works**	500–599	**Sciences**
100–199	**Philosophy**	600–699	**Technology**
200–299	**Religion**	700–799	**Arts and Recreation**
300–399	**Social Sciences**	800–899	**Literature**
400–499	**Languages**	900–999	**History and Geography**

A call number often has a decimal in it, followed by the first letter of an author's name. Note how the following call numbers are ordered on the shelves.

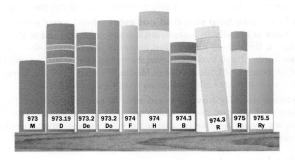

Try It!

Each subject category or class in the Dewey decimal classification system is divided into *divisions*. Identify the division for books listed in the 900's.
Note: Each division is further divided into *sections* and *subsections*.

Identifying the Parts of a Book

Each part of a book provides valuable information. The **title page** includes the title of the book, the author's name, and the publisher's name and city. The **copyright page** follows with the year the book was published. The **preface, foreword, or introduction** comes before the table of contents and tells why the book was written. The **table of contents** lists the names and page numbers of sections and chapters in the book. At the end of the book, you may find at least one **appendix,** containing various maps, tables, and lists. Finally, the **index** is an alphabetical list of important topics and their page numbers in the book.

Although students may not regularly refer to the term *Dewey decimal classification system*, most will have had experience using it.

- Make sure students understand that memorizing the ten subject categories and their call numbers is not required to find books. All libraries use this system to arrange books on the shelves. Knowing this makes finding materials much easier.
- Most libraries post maps of the layout of their resources at various locations throughout the library. These maps usually break down the nonfiction section into the ten subject categories of the Dewey decimal classification system and show the range of call numbers. Students can refer to these maps to find a book quickly. This can be especially helpful in a large library.

Try It!
Answers

Books with call numbers from 900 to 999 are in the History and Geography category.

Have students use their *Write Source* text to review identifying the parts of a book.

English Language Learners

Although students may have had experience using the Dewey decimal classification system, clarify the following categories and any unfamiliar terms:

- General Works includes encyclopedias and indexes that help you find general information.

- Philosophy—the study of how people think—includes works on logic, dreams, psychology, philosophy, and ethics.
- Social Sciences includes subjects that are concerned with the interaction of people, such as sociology, law, education, political science, economics, and anthropology.

Using Reference Books

In addition to determining which print encyclopedias are available at the library, encourage students to explore the library's online encyclopedias, which provide several benefits. Using these online resources, students can

- print articles or pertinent sections of articles, along with tables, illustrations, and maps, for easy reference while organizing a report;
- find complete citation information at the end of every article;
- use links within an article to find related subject matter in other online resources, including encyclopedias, magazines, newspapers, and reliable Web sites;
- utilize updated information; and
- access the encyclopedias on the library's Web site from any other computer.

Discuss any questions students have about using an **encyclopedia index** (see below).

Using Reference Books

A reference book is a special kind of nonfiction book that contains specific facts or background information. The reference section includes encyclopedias, dictionaries, almanacs, and so on. Usually, reference books cannot be checked out, so you must use them in the library.

Referring to Encyclopedias

An encyclopedia is a set of books (or a CD-ROM) that contains basic information on topics from A to Z. Topics are arranged alphabetically.

Tips for Using Encyclopedias

- **At the end of an article, there is often a list of related articles.** You can read these other articles to learn more about your topic.

- **The index can help you find out more about your topic.** The index is usually in a separate volume or at the end of the last volume. It lists every article that contains information about a topic. For example, if you look up "newspapers" in the index, you would find a list of articles—"United States Media," "Freedom of the Press," and so on—that include information on that topic. (See below.)

- **Libraries usually have several sets of encyclopedias.** Review each set and decide which one best serves your needs. (Always check with your teacher first to see if you can use an encyclopedia as a source for your research.)

Sample Encyclopedia Index

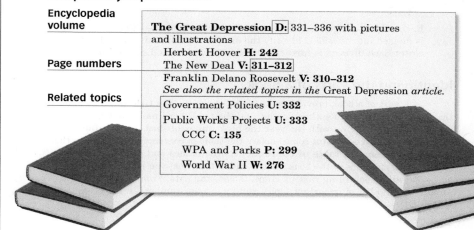

Encyclopedia volume	**The Great Depression** **D:** 331–336 with pictures and illustrations
	Herbert Hoover **H: 242**
Page numbers	The New Deal **V:** **311–312**
	Franklin Delano Roosevelt **V: 310–312**
	See also the related topics in the Great Depression *article.*
Related topics	Government Policies **U: 332**
	Public Works Projects **U: 333**
	CCC **C: 135**
	WPA and Parks **P: 299**
	World War II **W: 276**

Check students' understanding of an encyclopedia index. Have students use the sample index on SE page 378 to identify the volume and page(s) where they would find the following related information:

- a photograph of people lined up outside a soup kitchen during the Great Depression (volume D, pages 331–336)

- a list of events leading to the enactment of the New Deal (volume V, pages 311–312)
- general information about public works projects during the depression (volume U, page 333)
- President Hoover's reasons for refusing to extend public assistance to the nation's

unemployed during the Great Depression (volume H, page 242)
- a list of articles related to the topic, the Great Depression (after the Great Depression in volume D, pages 331–336)

Research

Consulting Other Reference Books

Most libraries contain several types of reference books in addition to encyclopedias.

Almanacs

Almanacs are books filled with facts and statistics about many different subjects. *The World Almanac and Book of Facts* contains celebrity profiles; statistics about politics, business, and sports; plus consumer information.

Atlases

Atlases contain detailed maps of the world, continents, countries, and so on. They also contain statistics and related information. Specialized atlases cover topics like outer space and the oceans.

Dictionaries

Dictionaries contain definitions of words and their origins. Biographical dictionaries focus on famous people. Specialized dictionaries deal with science, history, medicine, and other subjects.

Directories

Directories list information about groups of people, businesses, and organizations. The most widely used directories are telephone books.

Periodical Indexes

Periodical indexes list articles in magazines and newspapers. These indexes are arranged alphabetically by subject.

- The *Readers' Guide to Periodical Literature* lists articles from many publications. (See page 382.)
- The *New York Times Index* lists articles from the *New York Times* newspaper.

Other Reference Books

Some reference books do not fit into any one category but are recognized by their names:

- *Facts on File* includes thousands of short but informative facts about events, discoveries, people, and places.
- *Facts About the Presidents* presents information about all of the presidents of the United States.
- *Bartlett's Familiar Quotations* lists thousands of quotations from famous people.

Tell students that later in this unit they are going to be writing a research paper that analyzes the effectiveness of a presidential policy. Encourage students as they survey the list of references to jot down the types of books they might want to consult as they conduct research for their paper.

Encourage students to check out the availability and location of these types of reference books in their library in advance of their project. The more familiar they are with what is available and how to find it, the easier the research process will be for them.

English Language Learners

Explain that local print directories can be useful tools for contacting people in the area, should students want to include an interview as a primary source in a paper. Have small groups examine a local telephone directory. Check that students understand how to use it to find government offices, businesses, and organizations.

In addition to the **Try It!** activity, this variation of a dictionary game can encourage students to consult the resource regularly.

- List several challenging words from the dictionary or high-school "100 Words" lists on the board (for example, *expurgate, supercilious,* and *tautology*).
- On note cards, write out three different etymologies and definitions for each word, with only one being correct.
- Pronounce the first word, and read the definition cards.
- Have students vote on the correct origin and meaning.
- Then have students use a classroom dictionary to verify the correct information.

Keep the game informal so that all students are willing to participate. As students look forward to playing the game, they may want to form groups for competitive play.

380

Checking a Dictionary

A dictionary gives many types of information:

- **Guide words:** These are the first and last words on the page. Guide words show whether the word you are looking for will be found alphabetically on that page.
- **Entry words:** Each word defined in a dictionary is called an entry word. Entry words are listed alphabetically.
- **Etymology:** Many dictionaries give etymologies (word histories) for certain words. An etymology tells what language an English word came from, how the word entered our language, and when it was first used.
- **Syllable divisions:** A dictionary tells you where you may divide a word.
- **Pronunciation and accent marks:** A dictionary tells you how to pronounce a word and also provides a key to pronunciation symbols, usually at the bottom of each page.
- **Illustrations:** For some entries, an illustration, a photograph, or a drawing is provided.
- **Parts of speech:** A dictionary tells you what part(s) of speech a word is, using these abbreviations:

n.	**noun**	*tr. v.*	**transitive verb**
pron.	**pronoun**	*interj.*	**interjection**
intr. v.	**intransitive verb**	*conj.*	**conjunction**
adj.	**adjective**	*adv.*	**adverb**
prep.	**preposition**		

- **Spelling and capitalization:** The dictionary shows the acceptable spelling, as well as capitalization, for words. (For some words, more than one spelling is given.)
- **Definitions:** Some dictionaries are large enough to list all of the meanings for a word. Most standard-size dictionaries, however, will list only three or four of the most commonly accepted meanings. Take time to read all of the meanings to be sure that you are using the word correctly.

 Try It!

Find a word in a dictionary that is totally unfamiliar to you. Look at its pronunciation and say it out loud. Use it correctly in a sentence.

Advanced Learners

Challenge students to work with a partner to research etymologies of unfamiliar words. Have them create a three-column chart and label

- the first and second columns OE and ME for Old English and Middle English, and

- the third column "Languages Other Than English."

For languages other than English, have students note the language in parentheses next to the etymological part, using the abbreviations provided in the dictionary.

Sample Dictionary Page

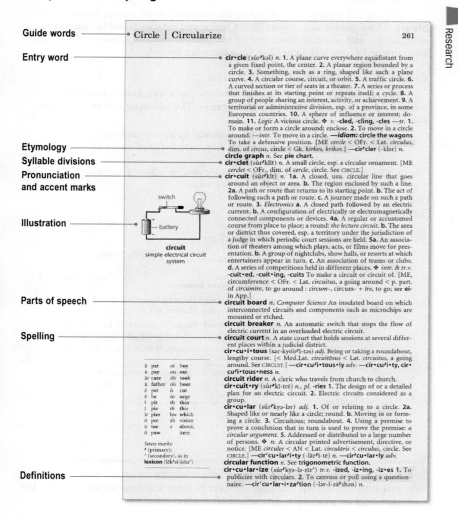

Circle | Circularize 261

Research

cir·cle (sûr′kəl) *n.* **1.** A plane curve everywhere equidistant from a given fixed point, the center. **2.** A planar region bounded by a circle. **3.** Something, such as a ring, shaped like such a plane curve. **4.** A circular course, circuit, or orbit. **5.** A traffic circle. **6.** A curved section or tier of seats in a theater. **7.** A series or process that finishes at its starting point or repeats itself; a cycle. **8.** A group of people sharing an interest, activity, or achievement. **9.** A territorial or administrative division, esp. of a province, in some European countries. **10.** A sphere of influence or interest; domain. **11.** *Logic* A vicious circle. ❖ *v.* **-cled, -cling, -cles** —*tr.* **1.** To make or form a circle around; enclose. **2.** To move in a circle around. —*intr.* To move in a circle. —*idiom:* **circle the wagons** To take a defensive position. [ME *cercle* < OFr. < Lat. *circulus,* dim. of *circus,* circle < Gk. *kirkos, krikos.*] —**cir′cler** (-klər) *n.*
circle graph *n.* See **pie chart.**
cir·clet (sûr′klĭt) *n.* A small circle, esp. a circular ornament. [ME *cerclet* < OFr., dim. of *cercle,* circle. See CIRCLE.]
cir·cuit (sûr′kĭt) *n.* **1a.** A closed, usu. circular line that goes around an object or area. **b.** The region enclosed by such a line. **2a.** A path or route that returns to its starting point. **b.** The act of following such a path or route. **c.** A journey made on such a path or route. **3.** *Electronics* **a.** A closed path followed by an electric current. **b.** A configuration of electrically or electromagnetically connected components or devices. **4a.** A regular or accustomed course from place to place; a round: *the lecture circuit.* **b.** The area or district thus covered, esp. a territory under the jurisdiction of a judge in which periodic court sessions are held. **5a.** An association of theaters among which plays, acts, or films move for presentation. **b.** A group of nightclubs, show halls, or resorts at which entertainers appear in turn. **c.** An association of teams or clubs. **d.** A series of competitions held in different places. ❖ *intr. & tr.v.* **-cuit·ed, -cuit·ing, -cuits** To make a circuit or circuit of. [ME, circumference < OFr. < Lat. *circuitus,* a going around < p. part. of *circuīre,* to go around : *circum-,* circum- + *īre,* to go; see **ei-** in App.]
circuit board *n. Computer Science* An insulated board on which interconnected circuits and components such as microchips are mounted or etched.
circuit breaker *n.* An automatic switch that stops the flow of electric current in an overloaded electric circuit.
circuit court *n.* A state court that holds sessions at several different places within a judicial district.
cir·cu·i·tous (sər-kyōō′ĭ-təs) *adj.* Being or taking a roundabout, lengthy course. [< Med.Lat. *circuitōsus* < Lat. *circuitus,* a going around. See CIRCUIT.] —**cir·cu′i·tous·ly** *adv.* —**cir·cu′i·ty, cir·cu′i·tous·ness** *n.*
circuit rider *n.* A cleric who travels from church to church.
cir·cuit·ry (sûr′kĭ-trē) *n., pl.* **-ries 1.** The design of or a detailed plan for an electric circuit. **2.** Electric circuits considered as a group.
cir·cu·lar (sûr′kyə-lər) *adj.* **1.** Of or relating to a circle. **2a.** Shaped like or nearly like a circle; round. **b.** Moving in or forming a circle. **3.** Circuitous; roundabout. **4.** Using a premise to prove a conclusion that in turn is used to prove the premise: *a circular argument.* **5.** Addressed or distributed to a large number of persons. ❖ *n.* A circular printed advertisement, directive, or notice. [ME *circuler* < AN < Lat. *circulāris* < *circulus,* circle. See CIRCLE.] —**cir′cu·lar′i·ty** (-lăr′ĭ-tē) *n.* —**cir′cu·lar·ly** *adv.*
circular function *n.* See **trigonometric function.**
cir·cu·lar·ize (sûr′kyə-lə-rīz′) *tr.v.* **-ized, -iz·ing, -iz·es 1.** To publicize with circulars. **2.** To canvass or poll using a questionnaire. —**cir′cu·lar·i·za′tion** (-lər-ĭ-zā′shən) *n.*

Labels (left margin):
- Guide words
- Entry word
- Etymology
- Syllable divisions
- Pronunciation and accent marks
- Illustration
- Parts of speech
- Spelling
- Definitions

Pronunciation key:
ă pat   oi boy
ā pay   ou out
âr care ŏŏ took
ä father ōō boot
ĕ pet   ûr urge
ē be   th thin
ĭ pit   th this
ī pie   hw which
îr pier zh vision
ŏ pot   ə about,
ō toe   item
ô paw

Stress marks:
′ (primary);
′ (secondary); as in
lexicon (lĕk′sĭ-kŏn′)

circuit
simple electrical circuit system

Give students time to examine the entries on the Sample Dictionary Page and to recognize how the elements on this page correspond to the bulleted items on SE page 380. Also discuss these additional elements in the entries:

- illustration labels and captions
- stress marks that accompany the pronunciation key
- irregular plural spellings (for example, the plural form of *circuitry, pl. -ries*)
- additional forms of the entry word at the end of the entry (*circularity, n.* and *circularly, adv.* at the end of *circular* entry)
- specific field in which the word has an applicable meaning (for example, *Logic* in definition 11 of the *circle* entry, *Electronics* in definition 3 of the *circuit* entry, *Computer Science* in the *circuit board* entry)
- explanation of the meaning of the word in figurative context (*idiom: circle the wagons* at the end of the *circle* entry)

English Language Learners

Point out the boldface numbers that are a part of certain entries on the dictionary page, and be sure students understand that the numbers represent the different senses or meanings of the entry word. Discuss the term *multiple meaning word,* and explain that dictionary entries provide all the meanings of a word. When students are reading and writing, they may need to consult a dictionary to find the different meanings a word might have.

Have students look at the definitions for *circuit,* and discuss the fact that each numbered definition has more than one lettered definition. Point out the close relationship among the lettered definitions.

Tell students they can use the *Readers' Guide* format to record their source information. By doing so at the time they locate the source, they will have all the information they need to find the source again and to cite the source accurately in their paper.

The subject entries for the *Readers' Guide to Periodical Literature* also list related articles on a specific topic. Students should look online to find these cross-references, using the library's databases. After they locate and decide to use an article, they should record the source information and make reference to the first article.

382

Using Periodical Guides

Periodical guides are located in the reference or periodical section of the library. These guides alphabetically list topics and articles found in magazines, newspapers, and journals. Some guides are printed volumes, some are CD's, and some are on library Web sites. Ask your librarian for help.

Readers' Guide to Periodical Literature

The *Readers' Guide to Periodical Literature* is a well-known periodical reference source and is found in most libraries. The following tips will help you look up your topic in this resource:

- Articles are always listed alphabetically by author and topic.
- Some topics are subdivided, with each article listed under the appropriate subtopic.
- Cross-references refer to related topic entries where you may find more articles pertinent to your topic.

Sample *Readers' Guide* Format

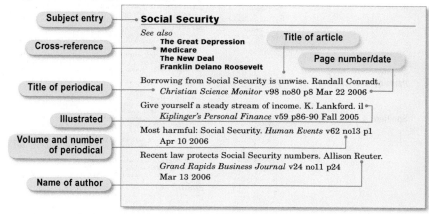

Tip

When you find a listing for your topic, write down the name and issue date of the magazine and the title and page numbers of the article. Your librarian may get the periodical for you, or you may need to find it yourself.

Research Writing
MLA Research Paper

Historians do more than tell what happened during a particular time period. Historians carry out careful research about a person, a place, or an event and then attempt to put their findings into perspective.

Like a historian, when you write a research paper, you need to do more than present the information that you have gathered. You need to analyze the data and present your own interpretation of its impact or importance.

One important aspect of American history is presidential policy. Each presidential administration creates its own policies in a number of areas, from foreign relations to economics. Most of these policies tend to produce both positive and negative effects. In this chapter, you'll learn all the steps necessary to write a research paper that analyzes a particular policy enacted by a president of the United States.

Writing Guidelines

Subject: A presidential policy
Form: Research paper
Purpose: To research a presidential policy and analyze its effectiveness
Audience: Classmates

"Self-confidence is the first requisite to great undertakings."

—Samuel Johnson

MLA Research Paper

Objectives

- demonstrate an understanding of the purpose, form, and content of an MLA research paper
- write responsibly and avoid plagiarism
- paraphrase, use quoted material, and use guidelines for in-text citations
- plan, draft, revise, edit, and publish an MLA research paper

Explain that the MLA, or Modern Language Association, was established in 1883. Its goal was to examine how the humanities should be taught in the United States. One result of its efforts was a set of rules for students to use to format research papers. Among other things, the rules set forth a method for acknowledging sources (parenthetical citations within the text and a works-cited page).

Explain that an MLA research paper is a piece of writing that uses standard MLA formatting to cite information assimilated into the paper from reliable resources. The MLA documentation style rules are widely used in colleges and professional organizations.

Technology Connections

Use this unit's Interactive Whiteboard Lesson to introduce research writing.

Interactive Whiteboard Lessons

Research Paper

Provide students with a printed copy of your guidelines and requirements for their MLA research paper, and suggest that they keep this copy in their **writer's notebook** *(see below)*. If you maintain a classroom Web site, consider publishing the guidelines and requirements on the site as a backup for students, tutors, and parents. You might also make available a reliable MLA site, such as http://owl.english. purdue.edu, at which students can find formatting guidelines.

Discuss the formatting of the sample title page and the outline, as well as the organization of information in the outline. Point out that the sample outline is an example of a sentence outline. (Students will learn more about creating a sentence outline on SE page 401.)

If your title page and outline requirements differ from those shown on SE page 384, display your requirements and discuss the differences with students.

384

Research Paper

While browsing a book of photographs from the Great Depression, Shawna Lopez became interested in this critical period in American history. She decided to write a paper about a presidential policy called the New Deal designed to help Americans get through this troubled time. You will find Shawna's paper on the next eight pages of this chapter. The margin notes point out important features of organization and formatting.

Roosevelt's New Deal:
Success or Failure?

Shawna Lopez
Mr. Collins
Language Arts
March 9, 2011

Title Page
Center the title about one-third of the way down the page. Center author information two-thirds of the way down.

Outline
Center the title one inch from the top of the page. Double-space throughout. Include the outline after the title page and before the first page of the paper.

. Roosevelt's New Deal: Success or Failure?

<u>Thesis Statement:</u> Although its success was incomplete, the New Deal saved the United States from collapsing into chaos and gave the nation's citizens the hope they needed to survive.

I. In the 1920s, the U.S. economy roared ahead like a powerful automobile, but beneath the shiny exterior, the economy was corroding.
  A. The value of stocks rose rapidly, and investors grew wealthy.
  B. Workers couldn't afford to buy consumer goods, so businesses cut back on production.
  C. Farm prices lagged, and many farmers lived in poverty.
II. In October 1929, the U.S. economy suddenly collapsed.
  A. The stock market dropped drastically, and investors rushed to sell their shares.
  B. Within weeks, the value of U.S. stocks had dropped by one-third.
  C. Banks had begun to fail, taking their customers' savings with them.
  D. President Herbert Hoover mistakenly believed that the economy would correct itself without government help.

Note: Not all teachers require a title page or an outline. If yours does, follow the guidelines above, or use specific instructions provided by your teacher.

Teaching Tip: Writer's Notebook

Students primarily use a writer's notebook to explore their thoughts on learning, to reflect on their experiences as a writer, and to jot down ideas for future writing assignments. Students can also use their notebook to store writing guidelines, instructions for document preparation, writing schedules, and other important information about writing that they can access throughout the year.

If students use a three-ring binder for their notebook, they should set aside a section for storing handouts. Students who use another type of writer's notebook or keep an electronic notebook can store this information in a folder.

✳ For more information on a writer's notebook, see SE page 2.

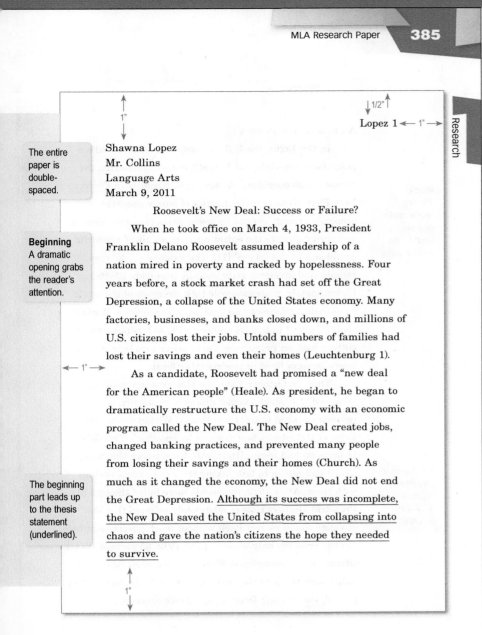

Research

↓ 1/2" ↑

Lopez 1 ← 1" →

Shawna Lopez
Mr. Collins
Language Arts
March 9, 2011

Roosevelt's New Deal: Success or Failure?

When he took office on March 4, 1933, President
Franklin Delano Roosevelt assumed leadership of a
nation mired in poverty and racked by hopelessness. Four
years before, a stock market crash had set off the Great
Depression, a collapse of the United States economy. Many
factories, businesses, and banks closed down, and millions of
U.S. citizens lost their jobs. Untold numbers of families had
lost their savings and even their homes (Leuchtenburg 1).

← 1" →

As a candidate, Roosevelt had promised a "new deal
for the American people" (Heale). As president, he began to
dramatically restructure the U.S. economy with an economic
program called the New Deal. The New Deal created jobs,
changed banking practices, and prevented many people
from losing their savings and their homes (Church). As
much as it changed the economy, the New Deal did not end
the Great Depression. Although its success was incomplete,
the New Deal saved the United States from collapsing into
chaos and gave the nation's citizens the hope they needed
to survive.

1"

The entire paper is double-spaced.

Beginning
A dramatic opening grabs the reader's attention.

The beginning part leads up to the thesis statement (underlined).

Have students read the research paper from
beginning to end. Encourage them to read for
content, as they will be asked to answer some
content-related questions in the **Respond to
the reading** on SE page 392. Tell them to keep
these questions in mind as they read:

- What is the topic of the research paper?
- What idea about the topic does the writer
  analyze?
- Does the writer sound knowledgeable and
  interested in the topic?
- Can you follow the flow of ideas and the
  writer's logic?
- How well has the writer analyzed the topic?

Have students take note of the formatting
elements in the paper, including margin widths,
paragraph indents, headings, page numbers,
and citations in parentheses.

English Language Learners

Read and discuss each page
of the sample research paper
with students. Direct their
attention to the headings,
explaining that they give clues
about the main idea of the
sections. As they read, have
students use each heading and
the details in the paragraphs
to identify the main idea for
each section.

Work through the Research Paper on SE pages 385–392 with students, using the margin notes as a guide to analyzing the content and form of the paper, as well as the writer's application of the traits of writing (Ideas, Organization, Voice, Word Choice, and Sentence Fluency).

Use the following points to discuss ideas in the paper. Have students examine the paper to find examples of each point.

- The writer captures the reader's attention and provides necessary background information about the topic. (See the beginning.)
- The writer identifies the topic—the policy known as the New Deal—and the focus of the paper—despite shortcomings, the New Deal was beneficial to the country. (See the thesis statement.)
- The writer uses enough informative details to support the thesis. (See the middle sections.)
- The writer draws parallels to the thesis and summarizes her findings. (See the conclusion and ending.)
- The writer incorporates facts and ideas from outside sources throughout the paper and provides a complete list of those sources. (See the in-text citations and the Works Cited page.)

386

Lopez 2

An Economic Meltdown

In the 1920s, the U.S. economy roared ahead like a powerful automobile, but beneath the shiny exterior, the economy was corroding. According to Kennedy in <u>Freedom from Fear</u>, "Nearly three decades of barely punctuated economic growth, capped by seven years of unprecedented prosperity, gave to the entire country, an air of masterful confidence in the future" (11). The value of stocks rose rapidly, and investors grew wealthy (Kennedy 10–15). Unfortunately, businesspeople took too much of the profit from their businesses and paid workers too little. Workers couldn't afford to buy consumer goods, so businesses began cutting back on production. Farm prices also lagged, and many farmers lived in poverty (Hartford).

Then, in October 1929, the U.S. economy suddenly collapsed. The stock market dropped drastically, and investors rushed to sell their shares. Within weeks, the value of U.S. stocks had dropped by one-third. The Great Depression had begun (Hartford). Even before this time, banks had begun to fail, taking their customers' savings with them. After 1929, thousands more failed (Badger 31). President Herbert Hoover mistakenly believed that the economy would correct itself without much government help, but the economy only worsened. By 1932, 25 percent of U.S. citizens were unemployed. Many had lost their homes and didn't have the food they needed to survive (Heale). As time passed, the nation's Depression became an economic and

Middle
The first middle section explains the need for the political policy.

The source of paraphrased information is cited in parentheses.

English Language Learners

If students have difficulty with the automobile simile in the first sentence, explain that the body of a car may have patches of rust beneath its shiny paint. In a similar way, the booming economy in the 1920s seemed strong but was falling apart in ways that people weren't able to see or notice at first.

Lopez 3

psychological problem. With national spirits at a new low, the country turned to Franklin Roosevelt for help. They put their faith in Roosevelt—and his New Deal.

The New Deal

In the first phase of the New Deal, Roosevelt addressed one of the nation's most pressing problems—the soundness of the banks. Panicked by bank failures, people had made "runs" on banks, pulling out their savings and draining the banks of needed funds. This caused even more failures (Badger 31). To stop this chain reaction, Roosevelt declared a "banking holiday" and closed all the banks. He then presented Congress with legislation to make banks stronger (Friedel 95). When the first banks reopened on March 13, people began to return their money (Hartford). The nation's psychology had begun to shift from despair to hope. Healing had begun.

Roosevelt understood that people needed financial relief, and that a flow of cash would jump-start the economy. In 1933, he introduced the National Industrial Recovery Act (NIRA). Congress approved giving him unprecedented legislative power to make laws to solve the nation's economic woes. With this act he authorized a number of new agencies that put people to work. The Tennessee Valley Authority hired workers to build electrical dams in the rural South. The Civilian Conservation Corps, or CCC, put people to work in forests, planting trees and building roads and shelters. The wages were low—just $30 per month in the CCC (Church), but as with the restructuring of the banks,

When a source has page numbers, the appropriate numbers are included in the citation.

Examples are included to clarify key points.

Use the following points to discuss the organization of the paper. Have students point out specific details from the research paper.

- The writer grabs the reader's attention from the beginning, with dramatic and interesting facts about the state of the country and the economy when FDR became president.
- Headings throughout help organize the paper visually and provide clues about the content of each section.
- The first group of middle paragraphs describes events leading up to the New Deal. (See An Economic Meltdown.)
- The next group of middle paragraphs describes the successes of the New Deal. (See The New Deal.)
- The final groups of middle paragraphs describe events that led to the ultimate demise of the New Deal. (See Bumps in the Road and The End of the New Deal.)
- The conclusion summarizes the analysis and presents the writer's ideas.

Struggling Learners

Help students comprehend "The New Deal" section by recording key events on a time line. Distribute photocopies of the reproducible Time Line (TE page 821), and work with students to list important events mentioned in the report. Also point out signal phrases, such as *first phase, this caused,* and *he then presented,* to help students understand the chronological order of events.

Use these points to discuss how the writer achieved a knowledgeable and authoritative voice in the paper. Have students point out additional specific details in other parts of the research paper.

- The writer uses specific facts and details, including the names of important acts and administrative boards, to explain the successes and failures of the New Deal. (See Bumps in the Road.)
- The writer supports an original thesis with facts, statistics, and the ideas of experts, creating a knowledgeable, authoritative voice.

388

Lopez 4

the psychological effect was critical. People who had lost hope and self-esteem once again became breadwinners, and their confidence began to return.

The New Deal helped citizens in other ways, too. The Home Owners Loan Act and the Farm Credit Act helped Americans refinance their mortgages and save their homes and farms (Mintz). The Social Security Act established a system by which workers paid money into a government fund that would provide them with a pension when they retired (Leuchtenburg 133). This pension secured the future for senior citizens, among those most vulnerable to economic downturns. The importance of Social Security was more than its economic benefits. Providing a future for the nation's elderly helped promote a feeling of national security that was critical during a very uncertain time.

Bumps in the Road

The newfound hope was real, but NIRA's Title 1 was in trouble. Title 1 attempted to create jobs and increase salaries by regulating labor practices, wages, and prices. It set maximum work hours per week, which forced businesses to hire more workers. It also set minimum wages and guaranteed the right of workers to form unions. Although these were all noble goals, the process to achieve those goals was coercive, cumbersome, and often unequally applied.

> Each paragraph includes a topic sentence, followed by supporting details.

> Headings guide the reader from section to section.

English Language Learners

Before reading the page, review vocabulary that may be unfamiliar to students:

- breadwinners (people who earn money for their families)
- pension (money set aside for workers to use after they retire)
- economic downturns (difficult times for people to earn or save money)
- coercive (forced)
- cumbersome (unmanageable)

Lopez 5

Other aspects of the NIRA proved equally problematic. The board that administered the act, the National Recovery Administration (NRA), churned out so many regulations that they became impossible to enforce, and even to understand. Many business owners and labor groups manipulated the regulations to their favor whenever possible, while other businesses simply ignored them (Black 303). The massive regulatory machine also helped turn many businesspeople against the New Deal. In 1935, the Supreme Court ruled against the NIRA. Historian Frank Friedel stated, "Chief Justice Hughes was devastating. He held that Roosevelt's code-making [lawmaking] authority was indeed an 'unconstitutional delegation of legislative power'" (161).

The Agricultural Adjustment Act (AAA) met a similar fate. Created to help farmers, the AAA paid farmers to reduce production, which in theory would cause farm prices to rise. Farmers would then make more for the crops they sold. AAA payments came from taxes on companies that processed and sold agricultural products. In fact, the AAA only succeeded in raising farm prices temporarily, and farmers continued to struggle (Black 307–8). In addition, processors hated paying the tax required by the act. They filed suit, and in 1936, the Supreme Court declared the AAA unconstitutional, saying that the agency had no authority to make laws (Black 328–29).

> A quotation is integrated into the paper to create an authoritative voice.

> Smooth-reading sentences make the paper very "readable."

Research

Have students notice the use of specific nouns and active verbs on this page and discuss how they help create the paper's authoritative voice. Have students identify other examples throughout the paper.

Word Choice
- The writer uses specific nouns to identify important groups, for example, *business owners, labor groups, farmers, processors.*
- The writer uses vivid verbs to express strong actions, for example, *churned out, manipulated, hated,* and *declared.*
- The writer includes a quotation by an expert on the New Deal.

Discuss the effect of using this quotation.

English Language Learners

Some students may have difficulty understanding the expression *massive regulatory machine.* Explain that the NIRA "churned out," or quickly produced, a number of business-related regulations, much as a machine in a factory mass-produces a product. Point out that the NIRA was such a large, complex act that enforcement was virtually impossible.

Have students notice these elements that contribute to sentence fluency and to the overall cohesiveness of the paper. Then have students point out additional examples in other parts of the paper.

Sentence Fluency

- The writer used a varied mix of sentence lengths and sentence constructions. (See the first paragraph.)
- The writer used **repetition** *(see below)* to link parallel ideas between paragraphs. (See the last sentence of the first paragraph and the first sentence of the following paragraph.)

390

Lopez 6

The End of the New Deal

By 1937, the New Deal had begun to improve the U.S. economy. Unemployment fell to about 12 percent, the lowest in years. Impressed by the improvements, Roosevelt cut back on government spending for New Deal programs (Black 428). This turned out to be a big mistake. By early 1938, the economy was sinking again. The unemployment rate rose to 22.5 percent, and the stock market had taken a major slide. Quickly, Roosevelt reversed position, and the economy began to respond (Black 435–36). Employment rose, and so did industrial production. However, the Depression still gripped the United States, and it would take a bigger force than the New Deal to create an economic boom.

During the 1930s, a depression also gripped Europe. In Germany, the poor economic conditions helped fascist leader Adolph Hitler rise to power (Mintz). In September 1939, Hitler's Germany initiated a world war by invading Poland. In December 1941, after being attacked by Japan, the United States entered the war. Soon U.S. factories converted to production of tanks, planes, bombs, and other war materials. By 1943, employment boomed, and factories were rolling again. The Depression was over, and the United States would enter one of its most productive periods ever (Hartford).

Conclusion

While the New Deal provided jobs for many people and allowed many families to keep their homes and farms,

Statistics help to paint a clear picture.

Dates help the reader follow the main points.

Teaching Tip: Repetition

Remind students that they can use repetition to link ideas between sentences and between paragraphs. Doing so can enable students to create a unified research paper, in which important ideas flow smoothly from sentence to sentence within a paragraph, and from paragraph to paragraph within a whole essay. Tactics for producing repetition include

- using a key word or phrase in consecutive sentences to connect and emphasize ideas, and
- repeating a key word or phrase at the end of one paragraph and in the beginning of the next paragraph.

* For more about the effect of repeating key words in sentences, see SE page 297.

MLA Research Paper **391**

Research

Lopez 7

it did not succeed in ending the Great Depression. Those who criticize the New Deal often fail to account for its major achievement: It saved the United States from complete collapse. In Europe, the German government lapsed into fascism, largely as a result of a depression there. In the United States, the same might have happened except for Roosevelt and the New Deal. The programs of the New Deal restored the citizens' faith that a democratic, capitalistic system could respond to their needs in the worst of economic times. This restored faith helped democracy and free enterprise to survive. The New Deal also created a new United States, one that would provide a safety net for the old, the infirm, and the suffering, and helped to prevent another economic and social tragedy from happening.

Perhaps just as important, the New Deal helped to convince people of the value of shared sacrifice and innovative vision. Both would prove critical in bringing the nation through another crisis—World War II. Conditioned by years of working together and following the leadership of Franklin Delano Roosevelt, U.S. citizens would meet the challenge of the war as a nation largely unified and willing to make the sacrifices necessary to defeat fascism. Once again, President Roosevelt would ask his nation to follow his creative leadership and make sacrifices for the common good. Once again, Roosevelt would help to kindle the faith and hope so critical to survival in a time of national crisis.

The conclusion includes the analysis and ideas of the writer.

Ending Parallel ideas bring the paper to an effective close.

Have students focus on how the writer accomplishes the following goals in the ending:

- to summarize main points used in the research paper (The New Deal helped people, although it did not end the Depression.)
- to analyze the effectiveness of the policy (The New Deal probably saved the United States from complete collapse, restored the people's faith in a democratic society, and provided a safety net for the needy.)
- to offer a personal view about the policy (The New Deal prepared U.S. citizens to unite and make sacrifices to defeat fascism in World War II.)

Explain to students that the most recent MLA style guidelines (see http://owl.english.purdue.edu) accept both underlining and italics for book titles. The Works Cited page on SE page 392 uses italics, the correct style when the paper is typed. Students composing on computers should get in the habit of italicizing the titles of printed works.

 Respond to the reading.

Ideas & Organization 1. Possible choices:
- successful—saved banks; gave people hope; put people to work; provided refinancing for mortgages; established pension (Social Security)
- fell short—achieving goals was coercive and cumbersome; too many regulations; farmers continued to struggle; the Great Depression did not end

2. The writer believes the New Deal saved the country from total economic disaster and chaos, and prepared the nation for the next major crisis—World War II.

3. chronological order of events

Voice 4. The voice is convincing. The writer provides a wealth of factual information and shows how the New Deal restored people's faith in a democratic, capitalistic society that was capable of meeting the needs of all its citizens.

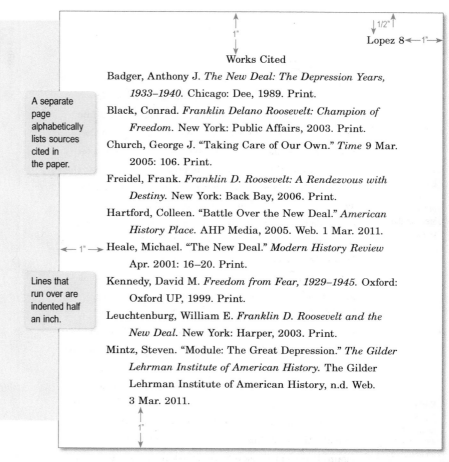

392

Lopez 8

Works Cited

Badger, Anthony J. *The New Deal: The Depression Years, 1933–1940.* Chicago: Dee, 1989. Print.

Black, Conrad. *Franklin Delano Roosevelt: Champion of Freedom.* New York: Public Affairs, 2003. Print.

Church, George J. "Taking Care of Our Own." *Time* 9 Mar. 2005: 106. Print.

Freidel, Frank. *Franklin D. Roosevelt: A Rendezvous with Destiny.* New York: Back Bay, 2006. Print.

Hartford, Colleen. "Battle Over the New Deal." *American History Place.* AHP Media, 2005. Web. 1 Mar. 2011.

Heale, Michael. "The New Deal." *Modern History Review* Apr. 2001: 16–20. Print.

Kennedy, David M. *Freedom from Fear, 1929–1945.* Oxford: Oxford UP, 1999. Print.

Leuchtenburg, William E. *Franklin D. Roosevelt and the New Deal.* New York: Harper, 2003. Print.

Mintz, Steven. "Module: The Great Depression." *The Gilder Lehrman Institute of American History.* The Gilder Lehrman Institute of American History, n.d. Web. 3 Mar. 2011.

A separate page alphabetically lists sources cited in the paper.

Lines that run over are indented half an inch.

 Respond to the reading. Now that you have read the sample research paper, answer the following questions.

Ideas & Organization (1) Name two ways in which the New Deal was successful—and two ways in which it fell short. (2) Why does the writer think the New Deal was important? (3) In a general way, how is the paper organized?

Voice (4) Is the voice of the paper convincing? Why or why not?

Advanced Learners

Have students find specific examples of factual information and reasoning in the report that help establish its authoritative voice. Have students present their findings, describing precisely how the examples they identify work to create the voice in the report.

Prewriting

In order to develop an effective research paper, you'll need to carry out a great deal of planning and research. During the prewriting stage, you will need to select an appropriate topic, gather facts and details about it, establish a thesis or focus, organize your data for writing, and so on.

Research

Keys to Effective Prewriting

1. For your topic, choose a significant presidential policy to analyze.

2. Make a list of questions you want to answer about the policy.

3. Use a gathering grid to organize your research questions and answers. Use note cards to keep track of longer answers. (See pages 397–398.)

4. Cite the sources of any information you paraphrase or quote.

5. Keep track of the publication details of all your sources. (See page 399.)

6. Gather enough information to offer a clear and complete analysis of your topic.

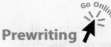

Prewriting

Keys to Effective Prewriting

Remind students that during the prewriting stage in the writing process the writer selects a topic, gathers details, and decides how to organize those details.

The Keys to Effective Prewriting list lays out the process students will be guided through on SE pages 394–401.

One way to monitor students' progress and to ensure that they are budgeting their time well over the course of the assignment is to require them to have topics approved. Then, have them submit prewriting materials and first drafts in stages, according to an established schedule.

Point out that the possibility always exists that students will realize, at some point during prewriting or writing, that they have chosen an unworkable topic. They may need to refocus the topic or select a new topic. In such circumstances, students should understand that they can request extra time without being penalized if they adhere to whatever guidelines you establish for requesting deadline extensions.

 Technology Connections

Students can use the added features of the Net-text as they explore this stage of the writing process.

Write Source Online Net-text

Prewriting Selecting a Topic

When searching for significant presidential policies, students might consider policies that affect the following areas, all of which impact any administration:

- education
- the environment
- civil rights
- immigration
- commerce and trade
- employment and wages
- health care
- taxes and tariffs

Focus on the Traits

Ideas

Emphasize the importance of selecting a topic that truly interests students. Remind them that they are going to be involved with this topic for a long time as they do research, gather and organize information, write, and revise. Although they should not expect to have extensive knowledge of the policy at this stage, they should at least be curious about it and want to learn more. This level of curiosity and interest will help students accomplish their goals and complete the assignment successfully.

394

Prewriting Selecting a Topic

To search for a topic, Shawna listed three U.S. presidents that she had studied, plus a significant policy that each one enacted. She also noted a few key points about each policy.

Topics List

Franklin Roosevelt
New Deal
- response to the Depression
- jump-started the economy
- gave people hope

John F. Kennedy
Alliance for Progress
- help for Latin America
- growth of industry
- land reform

Lyndon Johnson
Great Society
- response to poverty
- focused on civil rights
- expanded Social Security

Prewrite

Make a topics list. Create a list like the one above identifying two or three presidents and a significant policy enacted by each one. If necessary, refer to a textbook, your classroom notes, or the Internet for ideas. Also note a few key points about each policy that you identify. Then choose the policy you find most interesting as the topic of your paper.

Focus on the Traits

Ideas Choose a policy that truly interests you. Also consider the availability of information about your choice. You will need a thorough understanding of the policy in order to develop an effective analysis.

Struggling Learners

Have students choose a policy related to an era that they are currently studying in a history or government class. Point out that by researching a policy related to the era they are studying, students will reinforce learning and better understand the material they are learning in the other class.

MLA Research Paper 395

Sizing Up Your Topic

A paper analyzing a presidential policy should cover these main areas.

- **The policy:** Identify the policy, its reason for being, and its goals.
- **The successes:** Examine aspects of the policy that succeeded.
- **The failures:** Explain the ways in which the policy fell short.
- **Conclusion:** Summarize the main features of the policy. Then share your overall analysis of it.

Researching Your Topic

To prepare for writing her paper on the New Deal, Shawna did some quick research about the policy. She took notes on what she found.

Research Notes

What was the New Deal?

- The New Deal was a far-reaching economic program created in response to the Great Depression.
- Its goals were to end the Depression and put the U.S. on a better economic footing.

What were some of its successes?

- Roosevelt's "banking holiday" kept many banks from failing.
- The Tennessee Valley Authority and the Civilian Conservation Corps used government funds to put people to work.
- The Home Owners Loan Act and the Farm Credit Act helped save people's homes and farms.

What were some of its failures?

- The National Industrial Recovery Act was too complicated.
- The Agricultural Adjustment Act only succeeded temporarily.

How effective was the New Deal?

- It was only partially successful in ending the Great Depression.
- It saved the U.S. democratic, capitalistic system.

Shawna's initial research convinced her that her topic would provide enough information to support a research paper. Further, she realized that the successes and failures of the New Deal would make it a compelling topic.

Prewrite

Size up your topic. Do some quick research on your topic using the Internet or another reliable basic resource. Can you find sufficient information to support a research paper? If not, consider another topic.

Prewriting Sizing Up Your Topic

You may want to present the information in this Prewriting section in conjunction with the Writing Responsibly section that is found on SE pages 417–424.

Point out that the bulleted items at the top of this page state the main goals of their research paper. These items are also the source of the questions for the Research Notes that follow.

Some students can get bogged down at this initial stage doing too much research to answer the first question. As a result, they may not realize that their topic is unsuitable for the assignment until after they have put in a lot of time. To help students overcome the tendency to do too much research at this point, suggest that they model their notes exactly on the sample Research Notes, even copying the pattern of the responses, if doing so facilitates their work.

Advise students that if they cannot easily find at least two successes and two failures of the policy, they should choose another topic.

English Language Learners

Explain that *size up* means "to evaluate or measure something." Tell students that sizing up a topic means being sure there is enough information to make an interesting paper. Direct students' attention to the four bullets at the top of the page. Point out that preliminary research should give them enough information to fulfill the first three categories. Remind them that the last category contains the overall analysis and summary of the policy, or the conclusion. Point out that the analysis can wait until they have gathered and thoroughly examined all of their research.

Struggling Learners

Some students may be overwhelmed by the amount of information needed to get started on the research paper. Modify the assignment by limiting the number of sources; locating shorter, easier-to-read sources; or finding sources that are heavier on graphics and contain simpler text.

Prewriting Using a Gathering Grid

Unless students are **working on a computer** *(see below),* they will discover that most of their notes are too long to fit in the gathering grid. As a result, they may fail to appreciate the value of the grid. Explain that a gathering grid has definite benefits. Foremost, it organizes all their information in one place. Beyond that, a gathering grid enables students

- to see at a glance how much information they have available to address each main point of their research paper;
- to see quickly those ideas for which they need to find more supporting information;
- to identify easily the source of each fact, detail, and quotation; and
- to note if facts are supported by more than one source.

396

Prewriting Using a Gathering Grid

To help organize the information that you gather, use a graphic organizer such as a gathering grid. Shawna created a gathering grid to organize her research about the New Deal. In the left-hand column, she listed questions she wanted to answer. Across the top, she listed resources that answered those questions. For answers too long to fit in the grid, Shawna used note cards. (See page 397.) A portion of Shawna's grid is shown below.

Gathering Grid

THE NEW DEAL	Franklin D. Roosevelt and the New Deal (book)	"The New Deal" (magazine article)	The New Deal: The Depression Years, 1933–1940 (book)
Why was the policy created?	See note card 1.		
What were its successes?	TVA built dams for flood control and electricity.	Civilian Conservation Corps	Banking holiday People putting money back in banks
What were its failures?	NIRA was declared unconstitutional.	AAA was struck down by Supreme Court in 1936.	

Prewrite

Create a gathering grid. List questions in the left-hand column of your grid. Across the top, list sources you will use. Fill in the grid with answers you find. Use note cards for longer, more detailed answers.

Teaching Tip: Working on a Computer

Some students may choose to use the table feature on their word processing program to create a gathering grid. The obvious advantage of this is that cells in the table can expand automatically to fit the size of the note. Additionally, students can revise notes during research and cut-and-paste notes into a paper. Teachers and students who are familiar with using tables and grids can provide instruction for using this feature on the classroom computer.

Take this opportunity to remind students who are working on a computer

- to save their work frequently,
- to make a backup copy and print out a copy of their work after each session, and
- to password protect their file. This will prevent other users from accessing the file and accidentally deleting it.

Research

Creating Note Cards

A gathering grid works well for short answers, but when your answers are longer, it's better to use note cards. Number each note card and write a question at the top. Then answer the question with a list, a quotation, or a paraphrase. (See page 398.) At the bottom, identify the source, including the page number if appropriate.

Note Cards

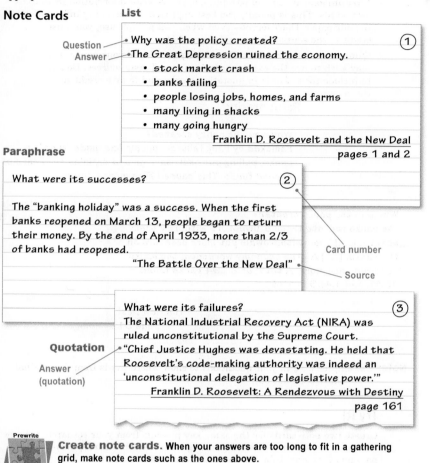

List

Question —
Answer —

Why was the policy created? ①
The Great Depression ruined the economy.
• stock market crash
• banks failing
• people losing jobs, homes, and farms
• many living in shacks
• many going hungry
Franklin D. Roosevelt and the New Deal
pages 1 and 2

Paraphrase

What were its successes? ②

The "banking holiday" was a success. When the first banks reopened on March 13, people began to return their money. By the end of April 1933, more than 2/3 of banks had reopened.
"The Battle Over the New Deal"

Card number

Source

What were its failures? ③
The National Industrial Recovery Act (NIRA) was ruled unconstitutional by the Supreme Court.

Quotation

Answer (quotation)

"Chief Justice Hughes was devastating. He held that Roosevelt's code-making authority was indeed an 'unconstitutional delegation of legislative power.'"
Franklin D. Roosevelt: A Rendezvous with Destiny
page 161

Prewrite
Create note cards. When your answers are too long to fit in a gathering grid, make note cards such as the ones above.

Prewriting Creating Note Cards

Students may have developed their own method for labeling note cards. For example, they may assign each question on their gathering grid a number, and then label all the cards that correspond to that question with that number and a letter of the alphabet, as shown below.

■ (First question on gathering grid) #1
■ (First two note cards that answer Question #1) #1-a, #1-b

Tell students that regardless of the method they use to label note cards, they should be sure to choose a method that will be helpful and clear to them when it's time to create an outline and draft their paper. They also should make sure that they add the corresponding card number (or other label) to their gathering grid.

English Language Learners

Some students may benefit from seeing all of their research at a glance. Instead of transferring information to note cards, suggest that they write out answers on the back of their gathering grid or create their grid on the computer.

Prewriting Avoiding Plagiarism

Some students may overuse quotations, stringing them together to fill a paper. Strongly caution students against doing this. Tell them that while well-chosen quotations can reinforce and enhance their ideas—for example, the Friedel quotation on SE page 389—too many quotations overpower the writer's ideas. Additionally, using the words of others without explanation can confuse the reader.

Encourage students to skim the sample research paper on SE pages 385–392, noting how and where quotations are used. Also suggest that students aim for a similar number of quotations for a paper of this length.

398

Prewriting Avoiding Plagiarism

Plagiarism means using someone else's words or ideas without giving them credit. Plagiarism is intellectual thievery and must always be avoided. As you write down facts and ideas during your research, take care to note their source and indicate whether the note is a paraphrase or a quotation.

- **Paraphrase:** When you paraphrase, you rewrite information in your own words. This is usually the best approach for including information in your paper. Don't forget—even when you paraphrase, you must give credit to the source of the paraphrased idea.

- **Quote exact words:** To add authority or color to your paper, you may wish to use the exact words from one of your sources. Be sure to include these words in quotation marks and to give credit to the source.

Paraphrasing

Why was the policy created?
Panicked by bank failures, people had made "runs" on banks, pulling out their savings and draining the banks of needed funds. This caused even more failures.

The New Deal
page 31

Quoting Exact Words

Why was the policy created?
"As banks ran into trouble, investors withdrew their assets. [. . .] Their withdrawals put more pressure on the banks. [. . .] As the economy worsened, the banks suffered once more. A total of 2,294 banks failed in 1931, and 1,453 in 1932."

The New Deal
page 31

Note: Use ellipses [. . .] in your quotations to show where words from the original source have been left out.

Try It!

Create two note cards for the same key passage from your research. On one card, *quote* a sentence from the passage. On the other card, *paraphrase* the passage. Give credit for the source on each card.

Struggling Learners

Some students may be inclined to rely more heavily on quotations because paraphrasing requires a clear understanding of often complex text. Assist students by providing practice in paraphrasing short passages and limiting the length of quoted text students may use in their paper. Have students present their paraphrases orally to you so that you can help them refine the wording of their interpretations of important ideas.

MLA Research Paper 399

Keeping Track of Your Sources

Keep careful track of the sources you find. To document sources according to MLA style, you'll generally need the following information for each type of source:

- **Book:** Author's name. *Title.* City: publisher, year of publication. Print.
- **Magazine:** Author's name. "Article title." *Magazine name* date: page numbers. Medium of publication.
- **Television:** "Episode title." *Program title.* Network. Call letters of local station, city, date of broadcast. Television.
- **E-mail Interview:** Name of person interviewed. E-mail Interview. date.
- **Internet:** Author's name (if listed). "Article title." *Title of Web site.* Name of sponsoring institution, date of posting or last update. Web. Date of access.
- **Newspaper:** Author's name. "Article title." *Newspaper name* date, edition (if listed): page numbers. Print.

Research

MLA-Formatted Source Notes

Book
Black, Conrad. Franklin Delano Roosevelt: Champion of Freedom. New York: Public Affairs, 2003. Print.

Magazine
Church, George J. "Taking Care of Our Own: The New Deal Probed the Limits of Government." Time 9 Mar. 2005: 106. Print.

Television Program
"F.D.R." The American Experience. PBS. WGBH, Boston, 28 Apr. 2006. Television.

E-mail Interview
Lavell, James. E-mail Interview. 25 Mar. 2011.

Internet
Powell, Jim. "Fresh Debate About FDR's New Deal." Individual Liberty, Free Markets, and Peace. Cato Institute, 2 Dec. 2003. Web. 3 Oct. 2011.

Newspaper
Ringle, Ken. "FDR's Monumental Place in History." Washington Post 2 May 2006: A1. Print.

Prewrite

List sources. Keep a list of your sources, using the information above as your guide. Whenever you use a new source, add it to your list.

English Language Learners

Some students may find it difficult to analyze and match sources to formats while researching. Simplify the task by having students bookmark the source page of online sources and then jot down the online address on their grid. For printed reference works, have students photocopy the title and copyright pages. If students don't have access to a photocopy machine, suggest they write down the book's call number in their grid so they can locate the source later. Once students are ready to create their MLA works-cited page (SE page 407), have them use the information to document their sources.

Prewriting Keeping Track of Your Sources

Have students check the list of sources they have compiled so far against the information provided for each bulleted item. Tell students to circle in red any sources that are missing required information, or any that they have listed in a style that differs from the sample. Suggest that they fill in missing information or correct the listing as soon as possible so that, later, they can transfer each source to their final works-cited page.

Prewriting **Writing Your Thesis Statement**

If students are having trouble deciding on a special part of their topic to emphasize in their thesis statement, suggest that

- they take some time to review their research notes that address the successes and failures of the policy, and
- they decide whether they think the policy was effective or whether it failed (which should be reinforced by their research).

If students decide the policy was effective, the special part of their thesis statement should focus on its effectiveness, as in the thesis statement about the New Deal. If they decide the policy proved ineffective, the special part of their thesis statement should give an overall or major reason for the failure of the policy.

✱ For more about writing effective thesis statements, see SE page 592.

Prewriting **Writing Your Thesis Statement**

Once you've completed your research, it's time to write a thesis statement. Your thesis statement expresses the main idea or focus of your research, and it helps guide your writing. All of the other ideas in your paper should support the thesis. You can use the formula below to help you write your thesis statement.

an interesting topic		special part to emphasize		a thesis statement
the New Deal	**+**	saved the United States from collapsing into chaos and gave the nation's citizens hope	**=**	The New Deal saved the United States from collapsing into chaos and gave the nation's citizens the hope they needed to survive.

Sample Thesis Statements

Wind power (an interesting topic) **provides a viable energy source in the Plains states** (a special part to emphasize).

A cell that functions abnormally (an interesting topic) **can initiate a process that results in cancer** (a special part to emphasize).

The marketing of high-profile professional athletes (an interesting topic) **has become big business** (a special part to emphasize).

Prewrite

Create your thesis statement. Carefully review your research notes and choose a main point you want to make about your topic. Using the formula above, write a thesis statement for that idea.

English Language Learners

To help students decide which special part to emphasize to form their thesis statement, provide copies of the reproducible T-chart (TE page 823). Have students use their research to list successes of the policy on one side and failures on the other side. Then have them use the chart and the following questions to help them decide:

- Why was this policy enacted?
- How did this policy help (or harm) citizens of the United States?
- Was this policy carried out effectively?
- What were the results of this policy?

Outlining Your Ideas

An outline is a powerful tool for organizing and planning your research paper. The outline serves as a map or a blueprint to guide your writing. There are two main kinds of outlines: A topic outline lists ideas as words or phrases; a sentence outline lists the ideas as full sentences.

Below is the first part of a sentence outline for the paper on pages 385–392. The outline begins with a thesis statement. Next, it lists the main point (topic sentence), marked by a Roman numeral, for each middle paragraph. Below each main point is a list of supporting details identified by capital letters.

Sentence Outline

In an outline, if you have a Roman numeral I, you must have at least a Roman numeral II. If you have a capital letter A, you must have at least a capital letter B.

Thesis Statement

Thesis Statement: Although its success was incomplete, the New Deal saved the United States from collapsing into chaos and gave the nation's citizens the hope they needed to survive.

Major Points (I., II., etc.)

I. In the 1920s, the U.S. economy roared ahead like a powerful automobile, but beneath the shiny exterior, the economy was corroding.

A. The value of stocks rose rapidly, and investors grew wealthy.

Supporting Ideas (A., B., C., etc.)

B. Workers couldn't afford to buy consumer goods, so businesses cut back on production.

C. Farm prices lagged, and many farmers lived in poverty.

Continue . . .

II. In October 1929, the U.S. economy suddenly collapsed.

A. The stock market dropped drastically, and investors rushed to sell their shares.

B. Within weeks, the value of U.S. stocks had dropped by one-third.

C. Banks had begun to fail, taking their customers' savings with them.

Prewrite

Create your outline. Write a sentence outline for your paper, using the main points and details from your research. Be sure that each topic sentence (I., II., III., . . .) supports the thesis statement, and that each detail (A., B., C., . . .) supports its topic sentence. Use your outline as a guide for writing your first draft.

Prewriting Outlining Your Ideas

Have students compare the first part of the sample sentence outline to the first part of the research paper on SE pages 385–386. This will help them see how a sentence outline can provide them with a framework for each paragraph in their paper. Students should note the following:

- The beginning (SE page 385) ends with the thesis statement from the outline. Details in this section lead up to this thesis statement, which gives direction to the essay.

- Each Roman numeral becomes a topic sentence for a paragraph on SE page 386. In this outline, the writer has taken the time to compose complete and strong topic sentences that did not need to be revised in the paper.

- Each of the detail sentences (represented by capital letters) appears in order in the paragraph. These are slightly revised for the paper to create a smooth, natural flow from sentence to sentence.

- Additional details, not in the outline, support the topic sentences and make the writer's ideas more complete.

✱ For more about creating an outline, see SE page 591.

Struggling Learners

Help students organize their outline by having them follow these steps:

- List the major points.
- Code each major point with a different colored highlighter.
- Review notes once for each color, and mark all information for that point.
- Use the color-coded notes as a road map for the outline.

Writing

Keys to Effective Writing

Remind students that the writing stage is when they get to write, or draft, their ideas on paper.

The Keys to Effective Writing list lays out the process students will be guided through on SE pages 403–407.

Encourage students to take this opportunity to review and organize all their prewriting materials to make sure they are complete and easily accessible to them when they start to write.

Technology Connections

Students can use the added features of the Net-text as they explore this stage of the writing process.

✸ *Write Source Online* **Net-text**

402

Writing

Now that you have organized your research and prepared an outline, it's time to write your first draft. Don't worry about getting everything perfect in the first draft; you'll have a chance to improve your writing later. For now, just get your ideas down on paper in a way that makes sense to you. The following points will help you.

> **Keys to Effective Writing**
>
> 1. In the beginning part, grab your reader's attention, introduce your topic, and present your thesis statement.
>
> 2. In the next section, explain the presidential policy and why it was created.
>
> 3. Next explore the successes of the policy.
>
> 4. Follow with a discussion of the policy's failures.
>
> 5. In the final section, analyze the effectiveness of the policy.
>
> 6. Cite the sources of any ideas you paraphrase or quote and list those sources alphabetically on a works-cited page.

Starting Your Research Paper

The opening part of your paper should grab your reader's attention, introduce your topic, and present your thesis statement. Here are two ways to begin:

- Open with a dramatic situation.
  When he took office on March 4, 1933, President Franklin Delano Roosevelt assumed leadership of a nation mired in poverty and racked by hopelessness.
- Start with an interesting fact.
  By 1932, more than one-quarter of the population of the United States was unemployed.

Beginning Paragraphs

Beginning
The beginning paragraphs open with a dramatic situation.

When he took office on March 4, 1933, President Franklin Delano Roosevelt assumed leadership of a nation mired in poverty and racked by hopelessness. Four years before, a stock market crash had set off the Great Depression, a collapse of the United States economy. Many factories, businesses, and banks closed down, and millions of U.S. citizens lost their jobs. Untold numbers of families had lost their savings and even their homes (Leuchtenburg 1).

As a candidate, Roosevelt had promised a "new deal for the American people" (Heale). As president, he began to dramatically restructure the U.S. economy with an economic program called the New Deal. The New Deal created jobs, changed banking practices, and prevented many people from losing their savings and their homes (Church). As much as it changed the economy, the New Deal did not end the Great Depression. <u>Although its success was incomplete, the New Deal saved the United States from collapsing into chaos and gave the nation's citizens the hope they needed to survive.</u>

The opening ends with a thesis statement (underlined).

Write

Write your beginning paragraphs. Using one of the approaches above, grab the reader's interest, introduce your topic, and state your thesis.

Research

Writing **Starting Your Research Paper**

Offer these options for beginning a research paper.

- Open with a memorable quotation about the policy by the president who enacted it.
- Start with a quotation by an expert on the president, the policy, or the times in which the policy was created.
- Begin with an anecdote, or a brief interesting story, that relates to the policy or to the people affected by it.
- Open with a thought-provoking question about some aspect of the policy.

Struggling Learners

Point out that the beginning paragraph introduces the topic with facts that connect the first sentence (attention grabber) with the last sentence (thesis statement). When writing their opening paragraphs, have students first develop their first and last sentences. Then have them write sentences that contain facts to fill in the paragraph and focus the paper.

Advanced Learners

Have students use the other options as the basis for writing alternate beginnings for the sample paper. Have students share their beginnings with each other and explore how each method grabs the reader's attention. Students' beginnings might resemble the following:

- The stock market crash of 1929 triggered a chain reaction of economic derailments that forced factories and banks to close, pushed unemployment rates to dizzying heights, and drained the savings of many American families.
- The Great Depression lived up to its name—an abyss of the economy in ruins.

Writing Developing the Middle Part

Give students time to review the middle paragraphs in the sample paper. Encourage them to pay particular attention to the following elements:

■ the unified structure of each paragraph—beginning with a topic sentence (underlined) that is followed by sentences that contain different **levels of details** (see below) that help explain the topic sentence

■ the use of dates to create a chronological pattern of organization

■ the smooth integration of quotations and facts

■ the variety of sentence lengths and sentence patterns

■ the use of the active voice as opposed to the passive voice

404

Writing Developing the Middle Part

The middle of your research paper should include ideas and details that support your thesis statement. Each middle paragraph should cover one main idea. Use your sentence outline to guide your writing.

Middle Paragraphs

Middle
The first middle section explains why the political policy was created.

An Economic Meltdown

In the 1920s, the U.S. economy roared ahead like a powerful automobile, but beneath the shiny exterior, the economy was corroding. According to Kennedy in Freedom from Fear, "Nearly three decades of barely punctuated economic growth, capped by seven years of unprecedented prosperity, gave to the entire country, an air of masterful confidence in the future" (11). The value of stocks rose rapidly, and investors grew wealthy (Kennedy 10–15). Unfortunately. businesspeople took too much of the profit from their businesses and paid workers too little. Workers couldn't afford to buy consumer goods, so businesses began cutting back on production. Farm prices also lagged, and many farmers lived in poverty (Hartford).

The details in each paragraph support its topic sentence (underlined).

Then, in October 1929, the U.S. economy suddenly collapsed. The stock market dropped drastically, and investors rushed to sell their shares. Within weeks, the value of U.S. stocks had dropped by one-third. The Great Depression had begun (Hartford). Even before this time, banks had begun to fail, taking their customers' savings with them. After 1929, thousands more failed (Badger 31). President Herbert Hoover mistakenly believed that the economy would correct itself without much government help, but the economy only worsened. By 1932, 25 percent of U.S. citizens were unemployed. Many

Teaching Tip: Levels of Details

Remind students that a well-constructed paragraph usually contains three levels of detail.

● Level 1: A controlling sentence that identifies the topic.
● Level 2: Clarifying sentences that support and explain the topic sentence.
● Level 3: A final concluding sentence that adds more details.

Have students point out the three levels of details found in the sample middle paragraphs on SE page 404–405.

✱ For more information about using three levels of detail in a paragraph, see SE page 110.

English Language Learners

Have students read each of their middle paragraphs to an English-proficient partner. Then ask the pair to discuss whether they think the paragraphs (1) explain the need for the policy, and (2) explain its successes and failures.

MLA Research Paper **405**

Research

had lost their homes and didn't have the food they needed to survive (Heale). As time passed, the nation's Depression became an economic and psychological problem. With national spirits at a new low, the country turned to Franklin Roosevelt for help. They put their faith in Roosevelt—and his New Deal.
The New Deal

In the first phase of the New Deal, Roosevelt addressed one of the nation's most pressing problems—the soundness of the banks. Panicked by bank failures, people had made "runs" on banks, pulling out their savings and draining the banks of needed funds. This caused even more failures (Badger 31). To stop this chain reaction, Roosevelt declared a "banking holiday" and closed all the banks. He then presented Congress with legislation to make banks stronger (Friedel 95). When the first banks reopened on March 13, people began to return their money (Hartford). The nation's psychology had begun to shift from despair to hope. Healing had begun.

Roosevelt understood that people needed financial relief, and that a flow of cash would jump-start the economy. In 1933, he introduced the National Industrial Recovery Act (NIRA). Congress approved giving him unprecedented legislative power to make laws to solve the nation's . . .

The next middle section describes the policy.

Sentences are arranged so the reader can easily follow the ideas.

Write

Write your middle paragraphs. Keep these tips in mind as you write.

1. Use a topic sentence and supporting details in each paragraph.
2. Refer to your outline (page 401) and the keys on page 402 for direction.
3. Add parenthetical references to credit all sources. (See pages 426–428.)

Point out that writers often have their own methods for staying organized as they write. For example, the student writer underlined the topic sentences in the middle paragraphs. Suggest that students underline or highlight their topic sentences when they draft their middle paragraphs.

- Underlining or highlighting can help them keep the main idea of the paragraph in mind as they add detail sentences.
- If they choose to exchange papers with a partner during revising, the partner can easily identify the main idea of a paragraph, and then check that all the details in the paragraph support this main idea.

Remind students to remove the underlining when they create their final draft.

Writing Ending Your Research Paper

To help students better understand how they can use the bulleted guidelines to write their ending, have them point out where the writer of the sample paper

- reminds the reader of the thesis of the paper (paragraph 1, sentence 2);
- reviews the key points (provided jobs, did not end the Great Depression, restored citizens' faith in a democratic, capitalistic system, created a new United States); and
- leaves the reader with something to think about (paragraph 2, sentence 1).

406

Writing Ending Your Research Paper

Your ending should sum up your research and bring your paper to a thoughtful close. You should . . .

- remind the reader of the thesis of your paper,
- review your key points, and
- leave the reader with something to think about.

Ending Paragraphs

Ending
The conclusion summarizes the paper's main points and shares the writer's views on the policy's effectiveness.

The writer considers how the policy may have prepared the nation for its next great challenge.

Conclusion

While the New Deal provided jobs for many people and allowed many families to keep their homes and farms, it did not succeed in ending the Great Depression. Those who criticize the New Deal often fail to account for its major achievement: It saved the United States from complete collapse. In Europe, the German government lapsed into fascism, largely as a result of a depression there. In the United States, the same might have happened except for Roosevelt and the New Deal. The programs of the New Deal restored the citizens' faith that a democratic, capitalistic system could respond to their needs in the worst of economic times. This restored faith helped democracy and free enterprise to survive. The New Deal also created a new United States, one that would provide a safety net for the old, the infirm, and the suffering, and helped to prevent another economic and social tragedy from happening.

Perhaps just as important, the New Deal helped to convince people of the value of shared sacrifice and innovative vision. Both would prove critical in bringing the nation . . .

Write

Write your ending. Draft your ending paragraph(s) using the guidelines above.

English Language Learners

Clarify the structure of the conclusion and have students use it as a model, if necessary. Point out the following:

- The first sentence summarizes the weakness (opposing viewpoint).
- The second sentence summarizes the major achievement and counters the first sentence (thesis point of view).
- The remaining sentences provide details related to the achievements of the New Deal.

Explain that addressing the shortcomings of the New Deal assures the reader that the research paper is balanced.

MLA Research Paper **407**

Creating Your Works-Cited Page

The purpose of a works-cited page is to let your reader find and read the sources you used. The examples on this page—an incomplete list—show the standard MLA format for common types of sources. Also see the guidelines on pages **429–436**.

Sample Works-Cited Entries

Book

Black, Conrad. *Franklin Delano Roosevelt: Champion of Freedom.*
New York: Public Affairs, 2003. Print.

Magazine

Church, George J. "Taking Care of Our Own: The New Deal Probed
the Limits of Government." *Time* 9 Mar. 2005: 106. Print.

Television Program

"F.D.R." *The American Experience.* PBS. WGBH, Boston. 28 Apr.
2006. Television.

Interview

Lavelle, James. E-mail interview. 25 Mar. 2011.

Internet

Mintz, Steven. "Module: The Great Depression." *The Gilder Lehrman
Institute of American History.* The Gilder Lehrman Institute of
American History. n.d. Web. 3 Mar. 2011.

Newspaper

Ringle, Ken. "FDR's Monumental Place in History." *Washington Post*
2 May 2006: A1. Print.

Write

Create your works-cited page. Check your paper and your source
notes (page **399**) to see which sources you actually used. Then follow these
directions.

1. Format your sources using the guidelines above and on pages **429–436**.
   (Use a sheet of paper or note cards.)

2. Create your works-cited page, listing sources in alphabetical order.
   (See page **392**.)

Writing Creating Your Works-Cited Page

Consider introducing the Documenting Research section of this unit (SE pages 425–438) now, before asking students to create a works-cited page for their report. This will ensure that students are aware of the specific guidelines for documenting different types of sources, and will help prevent the need for lengthy revisions on their works-cited page later.

Revising

Keys to Effective Revising

Remind students that the revising stage is their opportunity to think about refinements they might not have considered when they were drafting.

The Keys to Effective Revising list lays out the process students will be guided through on SE pages 409–411.

Encourage students to put aside their paper for a day or two before they attempt to revise. During that period, they may think of

- a more interesting and more engaging beginning,
- a better way to phrase an idea,
- a better word to convey an idea or a feeling, or
- the solution to a problem that they had in a particular section.

 Technology Connections

Have students use the Writing Network features of the Net-text to comment on each other's drafts.

 Write Source Online **Net-text**

Revising

In the first draft of your research paper, you connect all of your ideas. During revising, you make sure that the ideas are clear and well supported, the organization is logical, the voice sounds knowledgeable, the words are specific and accurate, and the sentences are varied and flow smoothly.

Keys to Effective Revising

1. Read your draft aloud to yourself or to a friend. Note any parts of the draft that sound unclear or unconvincing.

2. Review your thesis statement to be sure that it states the main point about your topic.

3. Be sure that your beginning engages the reader and that the ending includes your own analysis.

4. Check to see that the middle explains the need for the policy as well as its successes and failures.

5. Make sure your voice is knowledgeable and convincing.

6. Check for effective word choice and a smooth flow of sentences.

Improving Your Writing

There are always ways to improve a first draft. Shawna made a number of important revisions to improve the ideas, organization, voice, word choice, and sentence fluency in her research paper.

Research

A sentence beginning is varied.

A transition is inserted.

A transitional sentence improves clarity.

Word choice is strengthened.

Two sentences are combined for fluency.

A bracketed clarification is added.

Bumps in the Road

The newfound hope was real, but NIRA's Title 1 was in trouble. Title 1 attempted to create jobs and increase salaries by regulating labor practices, wages, and prices. *It* ~~Title 1~~ set maximum work hours per week, which forced businesses to hire more workers. It also set minimum wages and guaranteed the right of workers to form unions. *Although* These were all noble goals, ~~yet~~ the process to achieve those goals was coercive *and* cumbersome, often unequally applied. Other aspects of the NIRA proved equally problematic. The board that administered the act, the National Recovery Administration (NRA), ~~made~~ *churned out* so many regulations that they became impossible to enforce, and even to understand. Many business owners and labor groups manipulated the regulations to their favor whenever possible *, while* Other businesses simply ignored them (Black 303). The massive regulatory machine also helped turn many businesspeople against the New Deal. In 1935, the Supreme Court ruled against the NIRA. Historian Frank Friedel stated, "Chief Justice Hughes was devastating. He held that Roosevelt's code-making *[lawmaking]* authority was indeed an 'unconstitutional delegation of legislative power' " (161).

Revising Improving Your Writing

Although students are constantly being encouraged to read aloud their writing (item 1 in the Keys to Effective Revising on SE page 408), many ignore this advice or are embarrassed to follow it. Emphasize the benefits of reading a draft aloud. Explain that when students read aloud their writing, the following problems, which may be overlooked when reading silently, suddenly stand out:

- awkwardly constructed sentences
- ideas that should be joined by combining sentences
- repeated sentence patterns, especially sentences with simple subject-verb construction
- sentence fragments or run-ons
- words and phrases that are unnecessarily repeated
- vague or incomplete thoughts
- details that are out of order

English Language Learners

Discuss the transitional sentence that was added with students. Point out that *other aspects* and *equally problematic* are signal phrases that more NIRA Title 1 weaknesses will be discussed. Point out that the transition sentence also reminds readers that some weaknesses have already been discussed.

After having students read through all the revisions that are shown on SE pages 409–410, ask them to evaluate the effectiveness of Shawna's revisions, based on the margin notes and their own reaction to the revisions.

- Which revisions were most helpful in enabling you to follow the writer's ideas?
- Which revisions resulted in greater clarity?
- Which revisions convince you that the writer is interested in her topic?
- Which revisions convince you that the writer is knowledgeable about her topic?
- What other revisions do you think the writer could have made to improve her writing?

410

Wording is changed to improve voice.

An idea is moved for better organization.

An important idea is added.

met a similar fate.

The Agricultural Adjustment Act (AAA) ~~was also bad in ways.~~ Created to help farmers, the AAA paid farmers to reduce production, which in theory would cause farm prices to rise. Farmers would then make more for the crops they sold. In fact, the AAA only succeeded in raising farm prices temporarily, and farmers continued to struggle (Black 307-8). AAA payments came from taxes on companies that processed and sold agricultural products. In addition, processors hated paying the tax required by the act. They filed suit, and in 1936, the Supreme Court declared the AAA unconstitutional, saying that the agency had no authority to make laws (Black 328-29).

Revise

Revise your writing. Carefully review your first draft for ideas, organization, voice, word choice, and sentence fluency. Make any changes needed to improve your paper.

English Language Learners

Review the following vocabulary terms with students:

- adjustment (a change made to correct existing circumstances)
- fate (outcome; doom)
- production (making of things)
- in theory (in the abstract; conjecture)
- processed (prepared; treated)
- filed suit (brought a lawsuit)
- unconstitutional (in opposition to the Constitution of the United States)

Revising Using a Checklist

On a piece of paper, write the numbers 1 to 14. If you can answer "yes" to a question below, put a check mark next to that number. If not, continue to work on that part of your research paper.

Revising Checklist

Ideas

_____ **1.** Have I chosen an interesting presidential policy to write about?

_____ **2.** Do I state my thesis clearly?

_____ **3.** Have I included enough details to support my thesis?

_____ **4.** Do I give credit for ideas that I have paraphrased or quoted from other sources?

Organization

_____ **5.** Does my beginning paragraph capture the reader's interest and introduce my topic?

_____ **6.** Do my first middle paragraphs explain the need for the policy?

_____ **7.** Do my next middle paragraphs explore the successes and failures of the policy?

_____ **8.** Does my ending include a summary and my own analysis of the policy's effectiveness?

Voice

_____ **9.** Does my voice sound knowledgeable and engaging?

_____ **10.** Does my voice sound natural?

Word Choice

_____ **11.** Have I used specific nouns and active verbs?

_____ **12.** Do I avoid unnecessary modifiers?

Sentence Fluency

_____ **13.** Have I used a variety of sentence lengths and constructions?

_____ **14.** Do my sentences flow smoothly?

Revising Using a Checklist

After investing hours of time and energy working on their research paper, students may be tempted to check off every item in the Revising Checklist. To encourage students to assess their revised draft deeply and honestly,

- have students complete the checklist, giving careful consideration to each question before answering;
- then have partners read the revised draft along with the checklist answers; and
- have partners tell whether they agree or disagree with the writer's responses and why.

Struggling Learners

Some students may feel stymied when editing still results in a "no" answer to one or more of the checklist questions. Pair these students with writing partners who can help with editing issues related to Organization, Word Choice, and Sentence Fluency.

Grammar Connection

Active and Passive Verbs, Mood of Verbs

- **Proofreader's Guide** pages 722 (+), 724–725
- *GrammarSnap* Active and Passive Voice

Punctuating a Research Paper

- *SkillsBook* pages 35–36, 37

Sentence Review

- **Proofreader's Guide** pages 738–757 (+)
- *SkillsBook* pages 181–184

- *GrammarSnap* Kinds of Sentences: Declarative, Interrogative, Imperative, Exclamatory; Sentence Types: Compound, Complex, and Compound-Complex Sentences

Brackets, Ellipses, Parentheses

- **Proofreader's Guide** pages 638–639, 642–643, 644–645

Editing

Keys to Effective Editing

Point out to students that they owe it to themselves and to the hours of work that they have done to make sure that their paper is as error free as possible. Also point out that errors in spelling, punctuation, capitalization, and grammar are usually the first ones that readers notice, and that such errors can distract readers from giving serious consideration to the ideas in a paper.

Technology Connections

Students can use the added features of the Net-text as they explore this stage of the writing process.

Write Source Online **Net-text**

Editing

When you have finished revising your research paper, all that remains is to check it for conventions in spelling, punctuation, capitalization, and grammar.

Keys to Effective Editing

1. Read your paper aloud and listen for words or phrases that may be incorrect.

2. Use a dictionary, a thesaurus, and the "Proofreader's Guide" in the back of this book.

3. Look carefully for errors in punctuation, capitalization, spelling, and grammar.

4. Check your paper for proper formatting and for accuracy of citations. (See pages 384–392, 407, and 426–436.)

5. If you use a computer, edit on a printed copy. Then enter your changes on the computer.

6. Use the editing and proofreading marks on the inside back cover of this book.

Checking for Conventions

After revising the first draft of her paper, Shawna checked the new version for punctuation, capitalization, spelling, and grammar errors. She also asked a classmate to look it over.

A spelling error is corrected.

An unnecessary punctuation mark is deleted.

An error in verb tense is corrected.

A capitalization error is marked.

An abbreviation is properly punctuated.

The End of the New Deal

By 1937, the New Deal had begun to improve the U.S. economy. Unemployment fell to about 12 percent, the lowest in years. ~~Impresed~~ *Impressed* by the improvements, Roosevelt cut back on government spending for New Deal programs (Black, 428). This turned out to be a big mistake. By early 1938, the economy was sinking again. The unemployment rate rose to 22.5 percent, and the stock market had taken a major slide. Quickly, Roosevelt reversed position, and the economy ~~begun~~ *began* to respond (Black 435–36). Employment rose, and so did industrial production. However, the Depression still gripped the United States, and it would take a bigger force than the New Deal to create an economic boom.

During the 1930s, a depression also gripped Europe. In Germany, the poor economic conditions helped fascist leader Adolph Hitler rise to power (Mintz). In September 1939, Hitler's Germany initiated a World War by invading Poland. In December 1941, after being attacked by Japan, the United States entered the war. Soon US factories converted to production of tanks, planes, bombs, and

Point out that writers may often make the same mistakes with conventions again and again, from one piece of writing to the next. For example, one writer may inevitably place the end mark punctuation outside the end quotation mark. In the sample paper, the writer seems to have trouble distinguishing between compound nouns and compound proper nouns (world war and Great Depression).

Habitual mistakes may be difficult to catch during revising. To help students catch such mistakes, offer the following suggestions:

- Having a partner double-check for conventions is a good way to find these errors.
- Students can also look over edited drafts of previous assignments for errors they made in the past.
- Finally, they should look over teacher-corrected copies of final copies.

other war materials. By 1943, employment boomed, and factories were rolling again. The Depression was over, and the United States would enter one of its most ~~productve~~ *productive* periods ever (Hartford).

Another spelling error is corrected.

Conclusion

While the New Deal provided jobs for many people and allowed many families to keep their homes and farms, it did not succeed in ending the great Depression. Those who criticize the New Deal often fail to account for its major achievement: It saved the United States from complete collapse. In Europe, the German government lapsed into fascism, largely as a result of a depression there. In the United States, the same might have happened except for Roosevelt and the New Deal. The programs of the New Deal restored the citizens' faith that a democratic, capitalistic system could respond to their needs in the worst of economic times. This restored faith helped democracy and free enterprise to survive. The New Deal also created a new United States, one that would provide a safety net for the old, the infirm, and the suffering, and helped to prevent another economic and social tragedy from happening.

A capitalization error is marked.

An apostrophe is added to indicate possession.

Edit

Check your work for conventions. To begin, use your computer's spell-checker and grammar-checker to search your work for errors. Then print a clean copy of your paper and read it again to catch any errors the computer may have missed. Also ask a classmate to check over your paper.

Editing **Using a Checklist**

On a piece of paper, write the numbers 1 to 12. If you can answer "yes" to a question, put a check mark next to that number. If not, continue editing for that convention.

Editing Checklist

Conventions

PUNCTUATION

_____ **1.** Do I correctly punctuate compound and complex sentences?

_____ **2.** Have I correctly cited sources in my research paper?

_____ **3.** Do I use quotation marks around all quoted words from my sources?

_____ **4.** Do I use italics (or underlining, if handwriting) and quotation marks correctly for titles of works?

_____ **5.** Have I correctly formatted a works-cited page?

CAPITALIZATION

_____ **6.** Have I capitalized proper nouns and adjectives?

_____ **7.** Do I begin each sentence with a capital letter?

SPELLING

_____ **8.** Have I spelled all words correctly?

_____ **9.** Have I double-checked words my spell-checker may have missed?

GRAMMAR

_____ **10.** Do I use the correct forms of verbs (*he saw*, not *he seen*)?

_____ **11.** Have I used the right words (*there, their, they're*)?

_____ **12.** Do my subjects and verbs agree?

Editing **Using a Checklist**

Direct students' attention to the fourth item under Punctuation. Remind them to use italics and quotation marks correctly for titles of works in their essays and works-cited pages. For handwritten essays and works-cited pages, students may underline titles of works that would otherwise be italicized.

✳ For more about italics and underlining, see SE page 636.

Struggling Learners

Refer students who need extra help with spelling and using the right words to SE pages 678–699. Point out that this section can also help students to double-check words that the spell-check function on the computer may have missed.

Grammar Connection

Subjects and Predicates Review
- **Proofreader's Guide** pages 738 (+), 740 (+)
- *SkillsBook* page 120

Sentence Problems Review
- *SkillsBook* pages 165, 173–174

Subject-Verb Agreement and Pronoun-Antecedent Review
- **Proofreader's Guide** pages 752–753 (+), 754–755 (+), 756–757 (+)
- *SkillsBook* pages 143, 147, 148

- *GrammarSnap* Subject-Verb Agreement with Compound Subjects, Subject Verb Agreement with Indefinite Pronouns, Pronoun-Antecedent Agreement

Using the Right Word
- **Proofreader's Guide** pages 678–696 (+)
- *SkillsBook* pages 63–64

Shifts in Construction
- *SkillsBook* pages 172, 180

Publishing
Sharing Your Paper

If possible, have students present their research papers during a time when there is a heightened focus on the presidency and presidential policies. For example, students might present

- during a presidential campaign,
- during the month of February and the celebration of Presidents' Day,
- around the anniversary of a famous presidential policy, or
- when a policy of the current president is enacted or makes the news for positive or negative reasons.

Creating a Title

Most students will want a creative title. Point out that some policies, such as the New Deal, will lend themselves to clever titles. Students should try to create a title that best suits their thesis, content, and conclusion.

⚡ Technology Connections

Remind students that they can use the Writing Network features of the Portfolio to share their work with peers.

☀ *Write Source Online* **Portfolio**

☀ *Write Source Online* **Net-text**

416

Publishing Sharing Your Paper

When your editing is finished, make a neat final copy of your research paper and proofread it again before sharing it. Make extra copies for family members and friends if you wish. A research paper can also serve as the basis for a speech, a multimedia presentation, or a Web page. (See pages 439–449.) You worked hard on your paper, so find the best way to share your writing.

> **Publish**
> **Make a final copy.** To format your paper, use the following guidelines. (Also see pages 91–95 for instructions about designing on the computer.) Create a neat final copy to share.

Focusing on Presentation

- Use blue or black ink and double-space the entire paper.
- Write your name, your teacher's name, the class, and the date in the upper left corner of page 1.
- Skip a line and center your title; skip another line and start your writing.
- Indent every paragraph and leave a one-inch margin on all four sides.
- Write your name and the page number in the upper right corner of every page.
- If your teacher requires a title page and outline, follow his or her instructions. (See page 384.)
- If possible, type rather than handwrite your research report.

Creating a Title

Give your paper a title that will attract the reader's attention and provide some information about the topic. Try one of these approaches.

- Ask a question:
  Roosevelt's New Deal: Success or Failure?
- Be creative:
  The Big Deal About the New Deal
- Use an idea from your paper:
  The Deal That Saved the Nation
- Use compelling words:
  The New Deal = Relief + Hope

Advanced Learners

Have students discuss whether they think the student writer chose the best possible title for her paper (SE page 385). Have them review each title and discuss the merits of each. Challenge them to reach a consensus and to support their final choice with strong reasons.

417

Writing Responsibly

When you write a report based on research you've carried out, it's important to acknowledge your sources. Whether you use direct quotations or simply paraphrase another author's ideas, you commit plagiarism if you do not cite your source. The consequences of stealing copyrighted material vary, but in any case, plagiarism is wrong.

Citing your sources isn't difficult. Additionally, it shows that you've actually done your research, which adds authority to your writing. This chapter will answer your questions about using sources and avoiding plagiarism to produce a responsibly written research paper.

- Using Sources
- Avoiding Plagiarism
- Writing Paraphrases
- Using Quoted Material

"Next to the originator of a good sentence is the first quoter of it."
—Ralph Waldo Emerson

Writing Responsibly

Objectives
- understand how to use research to explore a topic
- know why to avoid plagiarism and how to avoid unintentional plagiarism
- learn how to paraphrase a source
- learn the conventions for using direct quotations

Remind students that an effective, well-written research paper contains a balance of directly quoted sources and paraphrased or summarized source information.

Give students a few minutes to review the research paper they just wrote to see how well they balanced the use of sources.
- Suggest that they skim their paper, noting the number of sources they used.
- Tell them to jot down how many times they used direct quotations, and how many times they paraphrased or summarized information.
- Would they say their paper displays a balance of directly quoted sources and paraphrased or summarized sources? How might they improve the balance?

Using Sources

If you introduce this chapter before students research and write their paper (SE pages 383–416), students can apply the guidelines on this page to that topic, and they can use that topic to complete the **Try It!** activity.

If you introduce this chapter after students have completed their paper, have them use their completed paper for the **Try It!** activity. As an alternative, students can use a topic they are exploring for another class or one that they might like to research and write about in the future.

Using Sources

What does *research* mean? Research means "searching out answers to questions."

Beginning Your Research

- **Consider your topic.** What do you already know about your topic? If you had to write your paper right now, what would you write?
- **Begin with the basics.** An encyclopedia or a Web search will turn up basic information. Use these sources for an overview of the topic.
- **Ask questions.** What do you wonder about your topic? Make a list of questions; then consider what sources you will search to find answers.

Reflecting on Your Research

- **Think about what you have read.** How has your initial research affected your thinking about the topic? What new questions do you have as a result of your reading?
- **Refine your topic, if necessary.** What new questions and ideas have occurred to you? Should you broaden or narrow your topic?

Doing Further Research

- **Focus your efforts.** Look for answers to your new questions.
- **Use the best sources.** Use trustworthy books, periodicals, and Web sites to find answers to your questions. Also consider conducting surveys, arranging personal interviews, and writing letters to experts.

Try It!

Whom could you interview for more information on your topic? Write three or four specific questions for this person, aiming for insight that you wouldn't find in other sources.

Presenting Your Results

- **Make the topic your own.** Your research paper should not just repeat other people's ideas. First and foremost, it should present your own thoughts and understanding of the topic.
- **Paraphrase or quote appropriately.** To support your ideas, paraphrase or quote credible sources as needed. References to other sources should be used only to enhance or support your own thinking.
- **Credit your sources.** Let your reader know the source of each idea you summarize or quote.

Advanced Learners

As students conduct further research, challenge them to include as many types of sources as possible. Have students review SE page 407 and skim the six most common types of sources. Challenge students to include one or two for each of the six categories.

Research

Avoiding Plagiarism

You owe it to your sources and your reader to give credit for others' ideas in your research paper. If you don't, you may be guilty of *plagiarism*—the act of presenting someone else's ideas as your own. (See the following pages for examples.) Cite every piece of information you borrow unless you're sure that the information is common knowledge.

Forms of Plagiarism

- **Submitting another writer's paper:** The most blatant form of plagiarism is to put your name on someone else's work (another student's paper, an essay bought from a "paper mill," the text of an article from the Internet, and so on) and turn it in as your own.
- **Using copy-and-paste:** It is unethical to copy phrases, sentences, or larger sections from a source and paste them into your paper without giving credit for the material.
- **Neglecting necessary quotation marks:** Whether it's just a phrase or a larger section of text, if you use the exact words of a source, they must be put in quotation marks and identified with a citation.
- **Paraphrasing without citing a source:** Paraphrasing (rephrasing ideas in your own words) is an important research skill. However, paraphrased ideas must be credited to the source, even if you reword the material entirely.
- **Confusing borrowed material with your own ideas:** While taking research notes, it is important to identify the source of each idea you record. That way, you won't forget whom to credit as you write your paper.

Other Source Abuses

- **Using sources inaccurately:** Be certain that your quotation or paraphrase accurately reflects the meaning of the original. Do not misrepresent the original author's intent.
- **Overusing source material:** Your paper should be primarily your words and thoughts, supported by outside sources. If you simply string together quotations and paraphrases, your voice will be lost.
- **"Plunking" source material:** When you write, smoothly incorporate any information from an outside source. Dropping in or "plunking" a quotation or paraphrased idea without comment creates choppy, disconnected writing.
- **Relying too heavily on one source:** If your writing is dominated by one source, the reader may doubt the depth and integrity of your research.

Avoiding Plagiarism

Provide examples of facts and details that are common knowledge and do not require in-text citations. For example, point out

- the dates used throughout the sample Research Paper on SE pages 385–392, and
- the reference on SE page 390 to the economic conditions in Germany that led to the rise of Hitler. Emphasize that the writer's description lies in the realm of common knowledge and can be supported by a variety of reliable sources. It is not a paraphrase of another's ideas or information from a specific source.

Remind students that they must list all of the sources that they used for factual information on their works-cited page.

Original Article

Computer technology has made it easy to copy short excerpts of text from several different sources and paste these excerpts into one's paper without crediting the sources. Remind students that the technology that makes plagiarizing easy for lazy writers also makes detecting the plagiarism easy for you (and other teachers). Use the following strategies as necessary.

- Point out that you know students' unique writing style, vocabulary, and voice.
- You are aware of their writing skills and the level of improvement they have achieved.
- If you suspect that an idea is not their own or that they have used someone else's words, you can type some or all of those words into a search engine to determine the true source.

420

Original Article

The excerpt below is from an original article about peer-to-peer music sharing. Take note of the examples of plagiarism that follow on the next page.

> **"Face the Music" by Claire Baughn**
>
> **. . . Anyone who uses computer technology like peer-to-peer (P2P) networking to share copyrighted music faces being sued by the music industry.** What the industry is finding out, however, is that prosecuting people who use widely available technology isn't stopping the activity. Recording companies need to understand that **they cannot regulate file-sharing technology the way they regulate the sale of physical objects such as tapes and CD's.**
>
> Members of the Recording Industry Association of America (RIAA) are recording companies trying to protect their financial interests. The RIAA terms P2P networking as "online piracy" even while admitting that the sharing enabled by digital technology has numerous advantages. Unfortunately, RIAA members think that more people sharing music means fewer people buying it, so they are targeting P2P services and their users with copyright infringement lawsuits.
>
> There's no question that copyright is an important part of music; **those who write and perform music deserve to profit from their work.** But are musicians really being hurt by P2P's and other file-sharing devices? A recent study shows that the music industry is affected very little. Researchers from Harvard University have published a study showing that sharing music on P2P networks has no effect on CD sales. In fact, **not only does P2P sharing not *hurt* musicians—it actually *helps* some artists promote their music.** These musicians avoid the industry middleman, delivering their music directly to the consumer. They make music because they love it—not to become rich.
>
> **Money is an important factor, but the consumer's right to privacy may be the most emotional part of the issue. Privacy is guaranteed by implication in the Bill of Rights (protected by a number of amendments), and it should apply to Internet users as much as to anyone else. However, the RIAA's approach to discouraging the downloading of copyrighted material requires Internet service providers (ISP's) to identify individuals whose Internet addresses indicate music sharing.** (In a number of cases, the ISP's are colleges and universities, drawing them into the fray, as well.) In one instance, Dawnell Leadbetter's ISP gave up her identity to RIAA, and the association threatened her with a lawsuit . . .

Advanced Learners

Challenge students to do some preliminary research on copyright infringement and its history during the past twenty-five years. Ask them to write a short paragraph that provides an overview and then a paragraph that explains how plagiarism and copyright infringement are similar and different.

Research

Examples of Plagiarism

Below are the three common types of plagiarism, sometimes committed on purpose and sometimes by accident. The plagiarized text is shown in bold type.

> 🚫 **Using copy-and-paste**
>
> - In this sample, the writer pastes in two sentences from the original article without using quotation marks or a citation.
>
>   In the land of the free, it's ironic that **anyone who uses computer technology like peer-to-peer (P2P) networking to share copyrighted music faces being sued by the music industry.** These companies seem to forget who made them wealthy in the first place—and, too bad for them, but **they cannot regulate file-sharing technology the way they regulate the sale of physical objects such as tapes and CD's.**

> 🚫 **Neglecting necessary quotation marks**
>
> - In the sample below, the writer cites the source of the exact words that she uses from the original article, but she doesn't enclose these words in quotation marks.
>
>   There are good reasons for musicians to copyright what they produce. In a recent article on P2P networking, Claire Baughn acknowledges this fact: **Those who write and perform music deserve to profit from their work** ("Face"). She goes on to say, however, that **not only does P2P sharing not *hurt* musicians—it actually *helps* some artists promote their music.** Why would the music industry have a problem with it?

> 🚫 **Paraphrasing without citing a source**
>
> - Below, the writer accurately paraphrases (restates) a passage from the original article, but she includes no citation.
>
>   **Probably the most emotional part of the issue is that of privacy, which is protected by law. Apparently, the RIAA disputes that this protection extends to Internet users, for the group has been demanding that Internet service providers identify music sharers.** It's an outrageous abuse of power.

Examples of Plagiarism

Conscientious students will do everything possible to avoid plagiarism, but emphasizing the seriousness of this issue is appropriate and beneficial. Make sure students are aware of the policy and administrative consequences of plagiarism in your class, the school, and the district.

Advanced Learners

Have students compile a list of their own reasons for crediting original sources. Have them share their ideas with the class. Students probably have definite views on the issue as it relates to music downloads. Making the connection between music downloads and literary sources can help the class understand the significance of plagiarism.

Writing Paraphrases

To help students better understand the distinction between a paraphrase and a summary, provided these additional tips.

A paraphrase

- is often longer than the original text (although it may be shorter);
- presents ideas in the same order as they are presented in the original text; and
- represents an interpretation of the writer's ideas, without changing the basic meaning of the author's ideas.

A summary

- is shorter than the original text,
- restates only the most important ideas, and
- demonstrates an understanding of the key ideas in the text but does not include an interpretation.

Writing Paraphrases

There are two ways to share information from another source: (1) quote the source directly or (2) paraphrase the source. When you quote directly, you include the exact words of the author and put quotation marks around them. When you paraphrase, you use your own words to restate someone else's ideas. In either case, you must cite your source. To paraphrase, follow the steps below.

1. **Skim the selection first** to get the overall meaning.
2. **Read the selection carefully,** paying attention to key words and phrases.
3. **List the main ideas** on a piece of paper.
4. **Review the selection** again.
5. **Write your paraphrase**; restate the author's ideas using your own words.
   - Stick to the essential information. Drop anecdotes and details.
   - Put quotation marks around key words or phrases taken directly from the source.
   - Arrange the ideas into a smooth, logical order.
6. **Check your paraphrase** for accuracy by asking these questions: *Did I keep the author's ideas and viewpoints clear in my paraphrase? Have I quoted where necessary? Have I cut out enough of the original? Too much? Could another person understand the author's main idea by reading my paraphrase?*

FYI

A *quotation*, a *paraphrase*, and a *summary* are all ways of referencing a source.

- **Quoting:** A *quotation* states the words of a source exactly. Quoting should be used sparingly in a research paper so that your writing doesn't sound like a patchwork of other people's statements. Use a quotation only when the exact words of the source are essential.

- **Paraphrasing:** In a *paraphrase*, you recast an idea from a source into your own words. Paraphrasing demonstrates that you understand the idea, and it maintains your voice within your paper. Paraphrasing is more commonly used than quoting or summarizing.

- **Summarizing:** A *summary* is a condensed version of an entire source. In a research paper, there is seldom any need to summarize an entire work unless that work is the subject of the paper. For example, you might summarize the plot of *King Lear* in a research paper about that play.

English Language Learners

When students take notes from sources, have them write their major points in short outlines or lists. This strategy will help them avoid accidental plagiarism from copying details verbatim because they are not able to put them in their own words.

Paraphrases

The original passage below is from *Life in a Medieval City,* a book by Edwin Benson. Below it are two sample paraphrases, properly cited.

Writing Responsibly **423**

Research

Original Passage

> The rooms in the houses were quite small, with low ceilings. The small windows, fitted with wooden shutters or glazed with many small panes kept together with strips of lead, lighted the rooms but poorly. The interior walls were of timbering and plaster, often white- or colour-washed. The ventilation and hygienic conditions generally were far from good, as may be imagined from a consideration of the smallness of the houses, the compactness of the city, . . . and especially the primitive system of sanitation, which was content to use the front street as a main sewer. . . .
>
> Rooms were furnished with chairs, tables, benches, chests, bedsteads, and, in some cases, tub-shaped baths. Carpets were to be found only in the houses of the very wealthy. The floors of ordinary houses were covered with rushes and straw. The spit was a much used cooking utensil. Tablecloths, knives, and spoons were in general use, but not the fork before the fifteenth century. At one time, food was manipulated by the fingers. York was advanced in table manners, for it is known that a fork was used in the house of a citizen family here in 1443. . . .

Basic Paraphrase with Quotation

> According to Benson, houses had small rooms and small windows that offered little natural light. Dried straw covered the floors (only the very wealthy had carpets). Basic furniture occupied each room, and in the kitchen were tablecloths, knives, and spoons—"but not the fork before the fifteenth century," although in York "it is known that a fork was used in the house of a citizen family here in 1433." Sanitation at the time was practically nonexistent; the street also served as a sewer (32–33).

Basic Paraphrase

> According to Benson, houses had small rooms and small windows that offered little natural light. Dried straw covered the floors (only the very wealthy had carpets). Basic furniture occupied each room, and in the kitchen were tablecloths, knives, and spoons (but no forks). Sanitation at the time was practically nonexistent; the street also served as a sewer (32–33).

Paraphrases

Use the Original Passage on SE page 423 to give students practice in applying the numbered steps on SE page 422 to write paraphrases.

■ Have students conceal the sample paraphrases at the bottom of the page with a half sheet of paper.

■ Then ask them to write two paraphrases for the original passage, which comes from pages 32–33 of the book by Edwin Benson. The first paraphrase should include a quotation, and the second paraphrase should not.

■ Have students compare their paraphrases to the two sample paraphrases at the bottom of the page and discuss similarities and differences.

Struggling Learners

Locate a short passage in a content-area textbook for students to use to practice writing a basic paraphrase. Then have students read their paraphrase to the group and compare the similarities in understanding and interpretation. Have students exchange their writing to check that the paraphrases are properly cited.

Using Quoted Material

Point out that using the cut-and-paste function on their computer is an effective way to copy direct quotations accurately into their paper. If they choose to do this, however, they must make sure to

- follow the guidelines on SE page 424 for punctuating quoted material or setting it off from the rest of the text,
- cut-and-paste only the quoted material they want to use, and
- cite properly the source in parentheses after the quotation.

424

Using Quoted Material

A quotation can be a single word or an entire paragraph. Choose quotations carefully, keep them as brief as possible, and use them only when they are necessary. When you do quote material directly, be sure that the capitalization, punctuation, and spelling are the same as that in the original work. Clearly mark changes for your reader: (1) changes within the quotation are enclosed in brackets [like this]; (2) explanations of sources are enclosed in parentheses after the closing quotation marks, but before the closing punctuation (like this).

Short Quotations

If a quotation is four typed lines or fewer, work it into the body of your paper and put quotation marks around it.

Long Quotations

Quotations of more than four typed lines (40 words in APA) should be set off from the rest of the writing by indenting each line one inch (about 10 spaces) and double-spacing the material. When quoting two or more paragraphs, indent the first line of each paragraph an additional quarter inch (about three spaces). Do not use quotation marks. (See 632.3.)

Note: Place the parenthetical reference after the final punctuation mark of the quotation. Generally, a colon is used to introduce quotations set off from the text. (See 620.4.)

Quoting Poetry

When quoting up to three lines of poetry (or lyrics), use quotation marks and work the lines into your writing. Use a diagonal (/) to show where each line of the poem ends. For quotations of four lines or more, indent each line one inch (about 10 spaces) and double-space the same as the rest of the text. Do not use quotation marks.

Note: To show that you have left out a line or more of verse in a longer quotation, make a line of spaced periods the approximate length of a complete line of the poem.

Partial Quotations

If you want to leave out part of the quotation, use an ellipsis to signify the omission. An ellipsis (. . .) is three periods with a space before and after each one. (See page 642.)

Note: Do not take out something that will change the author's original meaning.

Documenting Research

Most academic disciplines have their own manuals of style for research paper documentation. The style manual of the Modern Language Association *(MLA Handbook for Writers of Research Papers),* for example, is widely used in the humanities (literature, philosophy, history, and so on), making it the most popular manual in high school and college writing courses. (For complete information about MLA style, refer to the latest version of the *MLA Handbook.*) For papers in social sciences and social studies, the documentation style of the American Psychological Association (APA) is often used.

This chapter will provide you with guidelines for citing sources in both the MLA and APA styles. *Remember:* Always follow your teacher's directions, which may include special requirements or exceptions for the use of either documentation style. Because these styles continue to evolve, it is important to make sure you are using the most recent versions.

- **Guidelines for In-Text Citations**
- **MLA Works-Cited List**
- **APA Reference List**

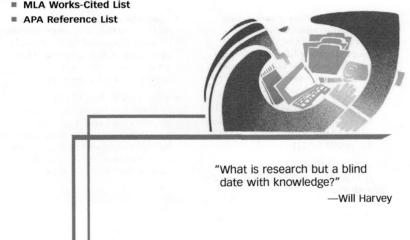

"What is research but a blind date with knowledge?"

—Will Harvey

Documenting Research

Objectives

- learn guidelines for in-text citations for an MLA paper and an APA paper
- learn standard MLA formatting to create a works-cited list
- learn standard APA formatting to create a reference list

Encourage students to review all the standard MLA and APA formats listed on SE pages 426–438 before they have to create a works-cited page or a reference list for a paper. Suggest that they have all their source information on hand so that they can determine which formatting standard applies to each of their sources.

Remind students that the MLA and APA styles continue to evolve, and it is important for students to confirm that they are using the most recent versions.

Guidelines for In-Text Citations

If possible, have available the latest editions of the *MLA Handbook* and the *Publication Manual of the American Psychological Association* (APA) for students to consult when crediting sources in the body text of their paper and on a works-cited page or reference list.

Focus attention on the fourth bulleted item in the list of Points to Remember. (Place your parenthetical citation at the end of a sentence, before the end punctuation.) Tell students that, even knowing this, their natural inclination may be to place the parenthetical citation after the end punctuation. Because of this, they should be sure to double-check during editing that all their parenthetical citations come before the end punctuation.

426

Guidelines for In-Text Citations

The simplest way to credit a source is to insert the information in parentheses after the words or ideas taken from that source. These in-text citations (often called "parenthetical references") refer to the "Works Cited" page at the end of an MLA paper or the "References" page concluding an APA paper.

Points to Remember

- Make sure each in-text citation clearly points to an entry in your reference list or list of works cited. Use the word or words by which the entry is alphabetized.
- Keep citations brief and integrate them into your writing.
- When paraphrasing rather than quoting, make it clear where your borrowing begins and ends. Use stylistic cues to distinguish the source's thoughts ("Kalmbach points out . . . ") from your own ("However, I believe . . . ").
- Place your parenthetical citation at the end of a sentence, before the end punctuation.
- Do not offer page numbers when citing complete works. If you cite a specific part, give the page number, chapter, or section, using the appropriate abbreviations (p. or pp., chap., or sec.). Do not, however, use p. and pp. in MLA parenthetical citations.

MLA	APA
• Place the **author's last name** (or, if unavailable, the first word or two of the title) and/or **page number** (if available) in parentheses following the cited text, except when these items have been included in the text.	• Place the **author** (or title), **date of the source,** and **page number** (if any), separated by commas, in parentheses, following the cited text, unless these items have been included in the text.
• For inclusive **page numbers** larger than 99, give only the two digits of the second number (113–14, not 113–114).	• **Titles** are italicized or placed in quotation marks. APA style requires that only first words and proper nouns in some titles be capitalized on the References page; however, this is not the case in the body of the paper.
• Italicize **titles** of books; place quotation marks around titles of articles.	

Model In-Text Citations

MLA	APA

A Work by One Author

Genetic engineering was dubbed "eugenics" by a cousin of Darwin's, Sir Francis Galton, in 1885 (Bullough 5).	Bush's 2002 budget was based on revenue estimates that "now appear to have been far too optimistic" (Lemann, 2003, p. 48).

A Work by Two or Three Authors

Students learned more than a full year's Spanish in ten days using the complete supermemory method (Ostrander and Schroeder 51).	Love changes not just who we are, but who we can become, as well (Lewis, Amini, & Lannon, 2000, p. 25).

Note: For APA, this format also applies to a work by up to five authors. After the first citation, list only the first author followed by *et al.* (meaning "and others").

A Work by Many Authors

This format applies to a work by four or more authors in MLA format or six or more authors in APA format. List only the first author followed by *et al.*

Communication on the job is more than talking; it is "inseparable from your total behavior" (Culligan et al. 111).	Among children 13 to 14 years old, a direct correlation can be shown between cigarette advertising and smoking (Lopez et al., 2004, p. 75).

An Anonymous Work

When there is no author listed, give the title or a shortened version of the title as it appears on the works-cited or reference page.

Statistics indicate that drinking water can make up 20 percent of a person's total exposure to lead (*Information* 572).	. . . including a guide to low-impact exercise (*Staying Healthy*, 2004, p. 30).

Research

Model In-Text Citations

Use the model in-text citations on SE pages 427–428 to discuss the differences between MLA and APA formatting for in-text citations. The main difference students should note is the inclusion of the comma and the date of publication in the APA style.

Have students skim any research assignments they are currently working on to make sure that, based on the information provided on these two pages, they credit sources correctly within the text.

If students still have questions about any of the formatting rules presented here, remind them that they also can get more information about other documentation styles on the Web sites of libraries and many major universities with writing labs.

Try It!
Answers

Possible Answers

With his superior military skills and his unfailing and passionate belief in his cause, Napoleon inspired his meager army to ward off larger, more powerful European armies for two years. In 1814, after he found himself besieged by the allied forces of four nations, Napoleon reluctantly admitted defeat [MLA] (Benezet). [APA] (Benezet, 1918).

Personal Communications

For an MLA paper, this parenthetical reference is the same as that for a publication with one author. In an APA paper, cite letters, e-mail messages, phone conversations, and so on as "personal communication" with their full date.

MLA	APA
. . . concern for the wetland frog population (Barzinji).	. . . hiring this spring (R. Fouser, personal communication, December 14, 2004).

A Work Referred to in Another Work

In MLA, use the abbreviation *qtd. in* (quoted in) before the source in your reference. For APA, credit the source by adding *as cited in* within the parentheses.

Quoting Prose

In MLA format, when you are quoting any sort of prose that takes more than four typed lines, do not use quotation marks. Instead, indent each line of the quotation one inch (ten spaces) and put the parenthetical citation (the pages and any chapter or other numbers) outside the end punctuation mark of the quotation.

> **Allende describes the flying machine that Marcos has assembled:**
>> **The contraption lay with its stomach on terra firma, heavy and sluggish and looking more like a wounded duck than like one of those newfangled airplanes they were starting to produce in the United States. There was nothing in its appearance to suggest that it could move, much less take flight. (12; ch. 1)**

Note: In APA format, quotations of 40 or more words are handled similarly, although the block of lines is indented only 5 spaces, and the abbreviation p. or pp. is included in the parenthetical reference.

Try It!

Paraphrase the passage below and refer to the source in a parenthetical citation in both MLA and APA styles.

> **"For two years Napoleon held (Europe) at bay, making up for his lack of soldiers by his marvelous military skill and by the enthusiasm which he never failed to arouse in his troops. In 1814, however, surrounded by the troops of Austria, Prussia, Russia, and England, he had to confess himself beaten."**

Source: *The World War and What Was Behind It* by L. P. Benezet, published 1918; not paginated

MLA Works-Cited List

The works-cited section of your report lists all of the sources you have referred to in your text. It does not include sources you may have read but did not refer to in your paper. Begin your list on a new page.

List each entry alphabetically by author's last name. If there is no author, use the first word of the title (disregard *A, An, The*). Use a single space after all punctuation in a works-cited entry.

List only the city for the place of publication. If several cities are listed, give only the first.

Additionally, note that publishers' names should be shortened by omitting articles *(a, an, the)*, business abbreviations *(Co., Inc.)*, and descriptive words *(Books, Press)*. Cite the surname alone if the publisher's name includes the name of one person. If it includes the names of more than one person, cite only the first of the surnames. Abbreviate "University Press" as UP. Also use standard abbreviations whenever possible. Lastly, note the medium of publication. The medium for all "hard copy" material is *Print*.

Books

Basic Format

Author's last name, First name. *Book Title*. City: Publisher, year of publication. Medium of publication.

Opie, John. *Ogallala: Water for a Dry Land*. Lincoln: U of Nebraska P, 1993. Print.

Add page numbers if the citation is to only a part of the work. In the rare instance that a book does not state publication information, use the following abbreviations in place of information you cannot supply:

n.p.	No place of publication given	n.p.	No publisher given
n.d.	No date of publication given	n. pag.	No pagination given

A Work by Two or Three Authors

Haynes, John Earl, and Harvey Klehr. *In Denial: Historians, Communism, & Espionage*. San Francisco: Encounter, 2003. Print.

List the authors in the same order as they appear on the title page. Reverse only the name of the first author.

A Work by Four or More Authors

Schulte-Peevers, Andrea, et al. *Germany*. Victoria: Lonely Planet, 2000. Print.

Research

MLA Works-Cited List

Make sure students take the time to read the introduction on SE page 429 as it contains important guidelines and tips for creating an MLA works-cited page.

Students will note that the MLA standard formats are separated into types of sources (Books, Periodicals, Online Sources, and Other Sources). Explain that this organization makes it easier for them to find the format that applies to the different types of sources they may have used in a paper.

Make sure, however, that students understand that sources on a works-cited page are not separated by types. They are listed together and arranged alphabetically. Have students look at the sample works-cited page on SE page 392 to illustrate this.

Students working on a computer can use their software's sort feature to alphabetize their sources automatically.

Point out that it is improbable that students will ever have to use every type of source shown on SE pages 429–436 in any one research paper. They should, nonetheless, tab these pages and write the Web site addresses of online style resources in their writer's notebook for easy reference whenever they are assigned expository writing.

430

Two or More Books by the Same Author

List the books alphabetically according to title. After the first entry, substitute three hyphens for the author's name.

Dershowitz, Alan M. *Rights from Wrongs.* New York: Basic, 2005. Print.

---. *Supreme Injustice: How the High Court Hijacked Election 2000.* Oxford: Oxford UP, 2001. Print.

An Anonymous Book

Chase's Calendar of Events 2010. Chicago: Contemporary, 2010. Print.

A Single Work from an Anthology

Mitchell, Joseph. "The Bottom of the Harbor." *American Sea Writing.* Ed. Peter Neill. New York: Library of America, 2000. 584–608. Print.

An Article in a Familiar Reference Book

It is not necessary to give full publication information for familiar reference works (encyclopedias, dictionaries). List the edition and publication year. If an article is initialed, check the index of authors for the author's full name.

Lum, P. Andrea. "Computed Tomography." *World Book.* 2000 ed. Print.

A Government Publication

State the name of the government (country, state, and so on) followed by the name of the agency. Most federal publications are published by the Government Printing Office (GPO).

United States. Dept. of Labor. Bureau of Labor Statistics. *Occupational Outlook Handbook 2000–2001.* Washington: GPO, 2000. Print.

When citing the *Congressional Record,* write *Cong. Rec.,* give the date, page numbers, and medium of publication.

Cong. Rec. 5 Feb. 2002: 5311–15. Print.

A Pamphlet, Brochure, Manual, or Other Workplace Document

Treat any such publication as you would a book.

Grayson, George W. *The North American Free Trade Agreement.* New York: Foreign Policy Assn., 1993. Print.

If publication information is missing, list the country of publication [in brackets] if known. Beyond that, use n.p. and n.d. as for a book.

Pedestrian Safety. [United States]: n.p., n.d. Print.

Research

One Volume of a Multivolume Work

Cooke, Jacob Ernest, and Milton M. Klein, eds. *North America in Colonial Times.*
Vol. 2. New York: Scribner's, 1998. Print.

Note: If you cite two or more volumes in a multivolume work, give the total number
of volumes after each title. Offer specific references to volume and page
numbers in the parenthetical reference in your text, like this: (2:112–14).

Salzman, Jack, David L. Smith, and Cornel West. *Encyclopedia of African-American
Culture and History.* 5 vols. New York: Simon, 1996. Print.

An Introduction, a Preface, a Foreword, or an Afterword

To cite the introduction, preface, foreword, or afterword of a book, list the
author of the part first. Then identify the part by type, with no quotation marks
or italics, followed by the title of the complete book. Next, identify the author of
the work, using the word *By.* (If the book author and the part's author are the
same person, give just the last name after *By.*) For a book that gives cover credit
to an editor instead of an author, identify the editor as usual. List any page
numbers for the part being cited, and, finally, the medium of publication.

Barry, Anne. Afterword. *Making Room for Students.* By Celia Oyler. New York: Teachers
College, 1996. Print.

Lefebvre, Mark. Foreword. *The Journey Home.* Ed. Jim Stephens. Madison: North
Country, 1989. ix. Print.

Second and Subsequent Edition

An edition refers to the particular publication you are citing, as in the third
(3rd) edition.

Joss, Molly W. *Looking Good in Presentations.* 3rd ed. Scottsdale: Coriolis, 1999. Print.

An Edition with Author and Editor

The term *edition* also refers to the work of one person that is prepared by
another person, an editor.

Shakespeare, William. *A Midsummer Night's Dream.* Ed. Jane Bachman. Lincolnwood:
NTC, 1994. Print.

Emphasize the importance of recording source
information correctly and completely when
students do their research so that when the
time comes to transfer that information to their
works-cited page, they will be able to do so
accurately.

Suggest that at the completion of any research-
based writing project, students keep an extra
copy of the works-cited page. Tell students to
store this record in a special folder for easy
reference. Some students may wish to cut
apart the various types of sources, creating an
organized list for each different type of resource
(books, periodicals, online sources, and other
sources).

Periodicals

As students recognize various sources they have used on SE pages 429–436, remind them to use the list as a resource.

- Point out that students are not expected to memorize any of these formats.
- The goal of the list is simply to familiarize them with the different types of sources they may use and reference in a research paper.
- When it's time to list a particular source, they can return to these pages, find the type of source that matches their type of source, and then create a citation, using the example provided as a model.

Periodicals

Basic Format

Author's last name, First name. "Article Title." *Periodical Title*
   date: page numbers. Medium of publication.

Stearns, Denise Heffernan. "Testing by Design." *Middle Ground*
   Oct. 2000: 21–25. Print.

An Article in a Weekly or Biweekly Magazine

List the author (if identified), article title (in quotation marks), publication title (italicized), full date of publication, page numbers, and medium of publication for the article. Do not include volume and issue numbers.

Goodell, Jeff. "The Uneasy Assimilation." *Rolling Stone* 6 Dec. 2001: 63–66. Print.

An Article in a Monthly or Bimonthly Magazine

As for a weekly or biweekly magazine, list the author (if identified), article title (in quotation marks), and publication title (italicized). Then identify the month(s) and year of the issue, followed by page numbers for the article. However, do not give volume and issue numbers. Finally, list the medium of publication.

"Patent Pamphleteer." *Scientific American* Dec. 2001: 33. Print.

An Article in a Scholarly Journal

Some scholarly journals are paginated by issue. Most are paginated continuously throughout in a single volume. However a journal is paginated, you should include the same information in your source citation. List the author, then the journal title, and then the volume number followed by a period. Then list the issue number, the year of publication (in parentheses), followed by a colon, and the page numbers of the article (not just the pages you used). Conclude your citation with the medium of publication.

Chu, Wujin. "Costs and Benefits of Hard-Sell." *Journal of Marketing Research* 32.2
   (1995): 97–102. Print.

Note: For articles that are continued on a nonconsecutive page, regardless of the publication type, add a plus sign (+) after the first page number.

Research

A Printed Interview

Begin with the name of the person interviewed.

Cantwell, Maria. "The New Technocrat." By Erika Rasmusson. *Working Woman* Apr. 2001: 20–21. Print.

If the interview is untitled, use *Interview* (no italics) in place of the title.

A Newspaper Article

Bleakley, Fred R. "Companies' Profits Grew 48% Despite Economy." *Wall Street Journal* 1 May 1995, Midwest ed.: 1. Print.

If a local paper does not name the city, add it in brackets (no italics).

To cite an article in a lettered section of the newspaper, list the section and the page number (A4). If the sections are numbered, however, use a comma after the year (or the edition); then indicate sec. 1, 2, 3, and so on, followed by a colon and the page number (sec. 1: 20). An unsigned newspaper article follows the same format:

"Bombs—Real and Threatened—Keep Northern Ireland Edgy." *Chicago Tribune* 6 Dec. 2001, sec. 1: 20. Print.

A Newspaper Editorial

If an article is an editorial, put *Editorial* (no italics) after the title.

"Hospital Power." Editorial. *Bangor Daily News* 14 Sept. 2004: A6. Print.

A Review

Begin with the author (if identified) and title of the review. Use the notation *Rev. of* (no italics) between the title of the review and that of the original work. Identify the author of the original work with the word *by* (no italics). Then follow with publication data for the review.

Olsen, Jack. "Brains and Industry." Rev. of *Land of Opportunity*, by Sarah Marr. *New York Times* 23 Apr. 1995, sec. 3: 28. Print.

An Article with a Title or Quotation Within Its Title

Morgenstern, Joe. "Sleeper of the Year: *In the Bedroom* Is a Rich Tale of Tragic Love." *Wall Street Journal* 23 Nov. 2001: W1. Print.

Note: Use single quotation marks around the shorter title if it is a title normally punctuated with quotation marks.

Students may benefit from seeing examples of citations that differ from the examples shown, but that are mentioned in the text on SE pages 432–433. These include

- articles that are continued on a nonconsecutive page,
- an untitled interview,
- a local paper that does not name the city,
- a review of a work by an editor or a translator, and
- a title normally punctuated with quotation marks within the longer title of an article.

If possible, display examples of these types of citations from actual research papers by former students or from published research papers found in professional journals. Alternately, you can ask volunteers to find and share examples of these kinds of citations.

Online Sources

Online encyclopedias often provide information at the end of an article that explains exactly how to cite the article. Students can cut-and-paste this information into their notes, but they will have to check the formatting to make sure the citation conforms to standard MLA formatting before using it for their works-cited page.

434

Online Sources

When you perform research on the Web, you may find yourself accessing a wide variety of documents. You might need to source scholarly journals, encyclopedias, archives of print publications, and other multimedia resources. The format for most online sources is similar to other media.

It is important to note that MLA style does not require the URL's of Web sources to be included in works-cited lists. URL's often change, and some are so long they cannot be retyped or pasted into a works-cited list without considerable difficulty. You need to include URL information only if the reader will not be able to locate the Web source without it or if your teacher specifically requires it. If a URL is needed, include it immediately following the date of access in angle brackets, ending with a period

Note: If you must include a line break in a long URL, do so only after a slash, and do not add a hyphen. For a particularly complicated address, give the URL of the site's search page instead.

Basic Format

Author's last name, First name. "Title." *Site Title.* Site sponsor, date of posting or last update. Medium of publication. Date accessed. <URL, if required>.

Tenenbaum, David. "Dust Never Sleeps." *The Why Files.* U of Wisconsin, Board of Regents. 28 July 1999. Web. 26 April 2011. <http://whyfiles.org/shorties/air_dust.html>.

Note: If certain details are not available, go on to the next item in the entry.

An Article in an Online Magazine or Newspaper

If you are not including print-publication data, format your citation like the examples above. Include the author's name; the article title in quotation marks; the name of the Web site (often the same as the magazine or newspaper) in italics; the publisher or sponsor of the site; and the date of publication. Add the medium of publication and the date of access.

Dickerson, John. "Nailing Jello." *Time.* Time, 5 Nov. 2001. Web. 9 Dec. 2010.

An Article in an Online Reference Work

Unless the author of the entry is identified, begin with the entry name in quotation marks. Follow with the usual online publication information.

"Eakins, Thomas." *Britannica Concise Encyclopedia.* Encyclopædia Britannica, 2004. Web. 26 Sept. 2010.

Documenting Research **435**

Research

An Article in an Online Database

When you use a library to access an online database, add the name of the database (in italics), the medium of publication, and the date of access.

Davis, Jerome. "Massacre in Kiev." *Washington Post* 29 Nov. 1999, final ed.: C12. *LexisNexis.* Web. 30 Nov. 2010.

An Online Multimedia Resource: Painting, Photograph, Musical Composition, Film or Film Clip, Etc.

After the usual information for the work being cited, indicate the title of the database or Web site, the medium of publication (*Web*), and the date of access.

Goya, Francisco de. *Saturn Devouring His Children.* 1819–1823. Oil on canvas. Museo del Prado, Madrid. *Artchive.* Web. 13 Dec. 2010.

An E-Mail Communication

Identify the author of the e-mail; then list the "Subject" line of the e-mail as a title, in quotation marks. Next, include a description—usually *Message to the author* (no italics), meaning the author of the paper. Finally, give the date of the message and the medium of delivery.

Barzinji, Atman. "Re: Frog Populations in Wisconsin Wetlands." Message to the author. 1 Jan. 2011. E-mail.

A Discussion Group or Blog Posting

Identify the author of the work, the title of the posting in quotation marks, the Web site name in italics, the publisher, and the posting date. Follow with the medium of publication and the date of access.

Handel, Sarah. "'12346' Is Not a Good Password." *Blog of the Nation.* Nat'l Public Radio, 7 Oct. 2009. Web. 1 Nov. 2010.

An Untitled Work

For an online source without an obvious title, include the name of the person who created the site, a description such as *Home page* (no italics) the publisher/sponsor or N.p., the date of the last update (if given), the medium of publication, and the date you accessed the site.

Jimenez, Leslie. Home page. N.p., 3 Mar. 2011. Web. 23 Oct. 2011.

Note: You may wish to include a URL with an untitled source because such sources could be difficult for your reader to locate. Remember to place the URL in angle brackets, as in the example on the previous page.

Call attention to the URL at the end of the Basic Format example given for Online Sources. Remind students that they will need to include URL information only if a reader will not be able to locate the source without it or if the URL is requested by the teacher. Remind students to be careful when copying long and complicated URLs to make sure that they don't leave out letters, words, numbers, or characters from the address. One way to ensure that their URL references are accurate is to highlight and copy addresses directly from the browser box on the Web sites. They can then paste the addresses into their notes or directly into their works-cited list. Encourage students to double check all URLs that they copy.

Other Sources: Primary, Personal, and Multimedia

If students cannot remember the exact title of a TV or radio program, urge them not to guess at it. Suggest, instead, that they look in a media program guide to check the title or go to the broadcaster's Web site to find the title. Students can also contact local television or radio stations for specific information.

Other Sources: Primary, Personal, and Multimedia

The following examples of works-cited entries illustrate how to cite sources such as television or radio programs, films, live performances, and other miscellaneous sources.

A Television or Radio Program

"Another Atlantis?" *Deep Sea Detectives*. The History Channel. 13 June 2005. Television.

A Film

The director, distributor, the year of release, and the medium consulted follow the title. Other information may be included if pertinent.

The Aviator. Dir. Martin Scorsese. Perf. Leonardo DiCaprio. Miramax Films, 2004. Film.

A Video Recording

Cite a DVD, filmstrip, slide program, or video cassette just as you would a film, but include the specific medium of reception.

Safe Boating is No Accident. JOI Home Video, 2010. DVD.

An Audio Recording

Cite the medium of reception or format, such as CD, LP, MP3 file, or audiocassette. To cite a specific song, place its title in quotation marks before the title of the recording.

Welch, Jack. *Winning.* Harper Audio, 2005. CD.

An Interview by the Author (Yourself)

Brooks, Sarah. Personal interview. 15 Oct. 2010.

A Cartoon or Comic Strip (in Print)

Luckovich, Mike. "The Drawing Board." Cartoon. *Time* 17 Sept. 2001: 18. Print.

A Lecture, a Speech, an Address, or a Reading

If there is a title, use it. Otherwise, use a descriptive label (Lecture, Address, Keynote speech, Reading) at the end of the citation.

Annan, Kofi. Acceptance of Nobel Peace Prize. Oslo City Hall, Oslo, Norway. 10 Dec. 2001. Speech.

Research

APA Reference List

The reference list begins on a separate page and includes all retrievable sources cited in a paper. List the entries alphabetically by author's last name. If no author is given, then list by title (disregarding *A, An,* or *The*).

Leave a single space after all end punctuation marks. Quotation marks are not used for article titles; italicize other titles. Capitalize only the first word (and any proper nouns) of book and article titles and subtitles; capitalize the names of periodicals in the standard upper- and lowercase manner.

Books

Basic Format

Author's last name, Initials. (year). *Book title.* Location: Publisher.

Guttman, J. (1999). *The gift wrapped in sorrow: A mother's quest for healing.* Palm Springs, CA: JMJ.

Note: Give the city of publication alone if it is well known. Otherwise, include the state. Include the state or province and the country if outside the United States.

A Book by Two or More Authors

Lynn, J., & Harrold, J. (1999). *Handbook for mortals: Guidance for people facing serious illness.* New York: Oxford UP.

List up to six authors; abbreviate subsequent authors as "et al." List all authors' names in reverse order. Separate authors' names with commas, and include an ampersand (&) before the last.

An Anonymous Book

If an author is listed as "Anonymous," treat it as the author's name. Otherwise, follow this format:

American Medical Association essential guide to asthma. (2003). New York: American Medical Association.

A Single Work from an Anthology

Nichols, J. (2005). Diversity and stability in language. In B. D. Joseph & R. D. Janda (Eds.), *The handbook of historical linguistics* (pp. 283–310). Malden, MA: Blackwell.

An Article in a Reference Book

Lewer, N. (1999). Non-lethal weapons. In *World encyclopedia of peace* (pp. 279–280). Oxford: Pergamon.

APA Reference List

After students have a chance to read the introduction and skim the different APA formats, ask them to explain the main differences between the listing of books and periodicals in an MLA style works-cited list and in an APA style reference list. Students should note the following.

- In MLA style, the titles of books and periodicals are italicized. The titles of articles are enclosed in quotation marks.
- In APA style, the titles of books and periodicals are italicized. The titles of articles are not enclosed in quotation marks.

To make sure students understand the point of the **Note** at the bottom of the page, have them revise the basic journal reference at the top of the page. Tell them to write a citation that would indicate they had read an exact duplicate of Silberman's print article online. The entry would read as follows:

Silberman, S. (2001, December). The geek syndrome. [Electronic version] *Wired,* 9(12), 174–183.

Periodicals

Basic Format

Author's last name, Initials. (year, Month day). Article. *Periodical,* vol. (issue), pages.

Silberman, S. (2001, December). The geek syndrome. *Wired, 9*(12), 174–183.

A Journal Article, Two Authors

Newman, P. A., & Nash, E. R. (2005). The unusual southern hemisphere stratosphere winter of 2002. *Journal of the Atmospheric Sciences, 62*(3), 614–628.

A Journal Article, More Than Six Authors

Watanabe, T., Bihoreau, M-T., McCarthy, L., Kiguwa, S., Hishigaki, H., Tsaji, A., et al. (1999, May 1). A radiation hybrid map of the rat genome containing 5,255 markers. *Nature Genetics, 22,* 27–36.

A Journal Article, Paginated by Issue

When the page numbering of the issue starts with page 1, the issue number (not italicized) is placed in parentheses after the volume number.

Lewer, N. (1999, summer). Nonlethal weapons. *Forum, 14*(2), 39–45.

A Newspaper Article

For newspapers, use "p." or "pp." before the page numbers; if the article is not on continuous pages, give all the page numbers, separated by commas.

Stolberg, S. C. (2002, January 4). Breakthrough in pig cloning could aid organ transplants. *The New York Times,* pp. 1A, 17A.

Online Sources

Basic Format

Author's last name, Initials. (year, Month day). Article. *Periodical, vol.* (issue), pages if available. doi: digital object identifier or Retrieved from URL

Volz, J. (2000, January). Successful aging: the second 50. *Monitor on Psychology, 31*(1). Retrieved from http://www.apa.org/monitor/jan00/cs.html

Note: If you have read an exact duplicate of a print article online, simply use the basic journal reference, but add [Electronic version] after the title of the article.

Making Oral Presentations

The last time you heard a speech was probably . . . today! Teachers give oral presentations every day. Usually the purpose of their talks is to inform or to demonstrate, but other presentations may attempt to persuade. Whatever the purpose of an oral presentation, it succeeds because of three key factors: familiarity with the material, preparation, and practice.

This chapter offers guidelines and tips for oral presentations. You'll learn how to organize your material, how to bring it to life with visual aids, and how to practice your way to a smooth, effective delivery.

- **Planning Your Presentation**
- **Creating Note Cards**
- **Considering Visual Aids**
- **Practicing Your Speech**
- **Delivering Your Presentation**
- **Evaluating a Presentation**
- **Preparing a Multimedia Report**
- **Multimedia Report Traits Checklist**

"A speech is poetry: cadence, rhythm, imagery, sweep! A speech reminds us that words, like children, have the power to make dance the dullest beanbag of a heart."

—Peggy Noonan

Copy Masters

T-chart (TE p. 448)

Making Oral Presentations

Objectives
- select a topic and details for a multimedia report
- plan, write, revise, and edit a multimedia report

Invite students to respond to the quotation from Peggy Noonan on SE page 439. Since most students dread the idea of making oral presentations, be prepared for some predictably negative and probably humorous responses. Use the following questions to spark the discussion.

- Have you ever thought of a speech as poetry?
- Have you ever heard a speech that made you conscious of the power of language? When?
- If you had to compare a speech to something, what would it be and why?
- What was your first reaction when you learned that you had to make an oral presentation? Why?

Planning Your Presentation

Suggest that students work with a partner to complete the **Try It!** activity.

- Tell students to **select a research paper** *(see below)* that they have completed in the recent past.
- Have partners read aloud the report so that students can review it as if they were in an audience. (Partners can take turns reading aloud reports for each other.)
- Tell students to write down any questions that come to mind as they listen to the report.
- Tell students to take notes about any ideas in the report that could be better explained or enhanced with visuals aids.

Planning Your Presentation

To transform a research paper into an oral presentation, you need to consider your purpose, your audience, and the content of your paper.

Determining Your Purpose

Your purpose is your reason for giving a presentation.

- **Informative** speeches educate by providing valuable information.
- **Persuasive** speeches argue for or against something.
- **Demonstration** speeches show how to do or make something.

Considering Your Audience

As you think about your audience, keep the following points in mind.

- **Be clear.** Listeners should understand your main points immediately.
- **Anticipate questions** the audience might have and answer them. This helps keep the audience connected.
- **Engage your listeners** through thought-provoking questions, revealing anecdotes, interesting details, and effective visuals.

Reviewing Your Research Paper

During an oral report, obviously your audience cannot go back and listen again to earlier statements, so you must be sure to share your ideas clearly from beginning to end. Review your paper to see how the different parts will work in an oral presentation. Use the following questions as a review guide.

- Will my opening grab the listeners' attention?
- What are the main points that listeners need to know?
- How many supporting details should I include for each main point?
- What visual aids can I use to create interest in my topic? (See page **444**.)
- Will the ending have the proper impact on the listeners?

Try It!

Choose a research paper you've completed. Review it as if you were a member of an audience, hearing the ideas in a presentation. What questions might this audience have about the topic? List them on a sheet of paper and then provide an answer for each one.

Teaching Tip: Selecting a Research Paper

If students have recently completed their research paper on the effectiveness of a presidential policy (SE pages 383–416), they will probably want to select it for their oral presentation. Point out that one advantage of selecting this paper is that the ideas are still fresh in their mind. Students also probably still have all their research materials and source information available, which will be helpful if they want to revise and rework sections of the paper.

Students are free to select another research paper they have completed in the past if they are still interested in the topic, and if you agree that the paper will make an interesting oral presentation.

Making Oral Presentations **441**

Research

Adapting Your Paper

To create a more effective oral presentation, you may need to rewrite certain parts of your paper. The new beginning below grabs the listeners' attention by using short, punchy phrases. The new ending makes a more immediate connection with the beginning.

Written Introduction (page 385)

When he took office on March 4, 1933, President Franklin Delano Roosevelt assumed leadership of a nation mired in poverty and racked by hopelessness. Four years before, a stock market crash had set off the Great Depression, a collapse of the United States economy. Many factories, businesses, and banks closed down, and millions of U.S. citizens lost their jobs. . .

Oral Introduction

Imagine the changed lives of so many people following the stock market crash of 1929. The Great Depression left families without jobs, savings, even homes. Now imagine the incredible responsibility of the new president four years later. When he took office on March 4, 1933, Franklin Delano Roosevelt . . .

Written Conclusion (pages 390–391)

While the New Deal provided jobs for many people and allowed many families to keep their homes and farms, it did not succeed in ending the Great Depression. Those who criticize the New Deal often fail to account for its major achievement: It saved the U.S. from complete collapse. . . .

Oral Conclusion

The New Deal did not halt the Depression, but it improved the nation's morale for years to come. When the U.S. was drawn into World War II, the country met the challenge, largely because of the mind-set established by the New Deal. People knew the value of shared sacrifice and innovative vision and heeded Roosevelt's requests to benefit the common good. Ultimately, the New Deal fostered the recovery of a nation's hope—not once, but twice.

Adapting Your Paper

Have students point out the details in the Oral Introduction that make it effective as an oral presentation. (It starts by asking listeners to imagine what it was like when the stock market crashed. This immediately involves listeners in the topic. Then it asks listeners to imagine what President Roosevelt faced when he took office. This helps create sympathy for Roosevelt, who had to find a way to help the nation.)

Next, have students explain how the Oral Conclusion makes an immediate connection with the Oral Introduction. (The Oral Conclusion starts by claiming that the New Deal didn't end the depression but did improve the nation's morale. This statement connects to the introduction; it also encourages listeners to focus on the good accomplished by the New Deal.)

Creating Note Cards

Have students refer to the sample note cards on SE page 397 as you review the guidelines for creating note cards.

Suggest that students look through any prewriting and writing materials that they may have saved to find earlier drafts of the beginning and ending paragraphs of their research paper. Ideas that they discarded in these earlier versions may be appropriate for an oral introduction or an oral conclusion. Encourage students to try out different introductions and conclusions in a group to find out which are most effective.

"Eloquence is in the assembly, not merely in the speaker."
—William Pitt

Creating Note Cards

If you are giving a prepared speech rather than an oral reading of your paper, you should use note cards to remind you of your main ideas. The guidelines below will help you make effective cards.

Note-Card Guidelines

Write out your entire introduction and conclusion on separate note cards. For the body of your speech, write one point per card, along with specific details.

- Place each main point at the top of a separate note card.
- Write supporting ideas on the lines below the main idea, using key words and phrases to help you remember specific details.
- Number each card.
- Highlight any ideas you want to emphasize.
- Mark the places that call for visual aids.

Three Main Parts to Consider

As you prepare your note cards, keep the following points in mind about the three parts of your oral presentation: the introduction, body, and conclusion.

- **The introduction** should grab the listeners' attention, identify the topic and the focus of your presentation, and provide any essential background information about the topic. (See pages 440–441.)
- **The body** should contain the main points from your paper and present details that will hold your listeners' attention. Remember to note the visual aids that you plan to use.
- **The conclusion** should restate your focus and leave the listeners with a final thought about your topic. (See pages 440–441.)

Try It!

Using one of your recent research papers, adapt the introduction and conclusion for an oral report. Write your complete beginning and ending on separate note cards.

Making Oral Presentations **443**

Note Cards

Below are the note cards Shawna used for her oral presentation about the New Deal.

Introduction   1

photo: Depression-era suffering

    Imagine the changed lives of so many people following the stock marke[t] crash of 1929. The Great Depression left families without jobs, savings, even homes. Now imagine the incredibl[e] responsibility of the new president fou[r] years later. When he took office on Ma[rch]

The Great Depression   2

photo: another Depression-era picture

– 1920s: U.S. economy out of control, in need of new political policy
– 25 percent of working population unemployed by 1932
– many without enough food or homes

The New Deal   3

photo: TVA workers

– Roosevelt's economic program to restructure economy
– banks being made stronger
– legislation to help people refinanc[e] mortgages, save homes
– Social Security to provide for retirement

Unsuccessful programs   4

– NIRA's attempt to regulate labor practices
– too much red tape with NRA; regulations manipulated
– AAA not helping farmers enough

Later years of New Deal   5

chart: unemployment statistics '37–'43

– economic recovery led to funding cut in 1937
– position reversed in '38 due to sinking economy
– economic boom created when U.[S.] entered WWII

Conclusion   6

    The New Deal did not halt the Depression, but it improved the nation's morale for years to come. When the U.S. was drawn into World War II, the country met the challenge, largely because of the mind-set established by the New Deal. People knew the value of shared sacrifice and innovative vision and heeded Roosevelt's . . .

Research

Note Cards

Remind students that during an oral presentation, note cards should be used as prompts, not reading material. Except for writing out the introduction and conclusion completely, students should not write exactly what they will say word for word on any of the other note cards. They should also keep their notes brief, limiting them to key words and phrases.

Some students may prefer using larger note cards to make their notes easier to read. Whatever the size, caution them not to use brightly colored cards, as they can distract the audience. Instead, they should highlight cues on the cards.

English Language Learners

Have students use this page as a model for writing their note cards. Point out that each section of the report is self-contained on a single note card.

Considering Visual Aids

Point out that while a limited number of strong visual aids can enhance students' presentations, too many or inappropriate visual aids can have the opposite effect.

Tell students to keep these ideas in mind as they select and create visuals to use in their oral presentation.

- Speakers have to manipulate visuals as they speak. If a visual is irregular or unwieldy in any way, the speaker may drop it and disrupt the speech.
- If the speaker stops the flow of the presentation to display a new visual, both the speaker and the audience are going to be distracted.
- If the visual does not relate directly to an idea being presented, the audience may wonder about how the visual fits in and miss information.

444

Considering Visual Aids

Consider using visual aids during your speech. They can make your presentation clearer and more meaningful. Here are some examples.

Posters	can include words, pictures, or both.
Photographs	illustrate what you are talking about.
Charts	explain points, compare facts, or give statistics.
Maps	identify or locate specific places being discussed.
Objects	show important items related to your topic.
Computer slides	project your photographs, charts, and maps onto a screen and turn your speech into a multimedia presentation. (See pages 448–449.)

Indicating When to Present Visuals

Write notes on your note cards to indicate where a visual aid would be helpful. Shawna considered the following visuals for her presentation about the New Deal.

- **photo of Depression-era unemployment lines**
- **photo of TVA workers on a dam project**
- **chart showing unemployment statistics 1937–1943**

Try It!

Identify two or three visual aids you could use in your presentation. Explain when and how you would use each one.

Tip

When creating visual aids, keep these points in mind.

- **Make them big.** Your visuals should be large enough for everyone in the audience to see.
- **Keep them simple.** Use labels and short phrases rather than full sentences.
- **Make them eye-catching.** Use color, bold lines, and simple shapes to make the contents clear and interesting.

Advanced Learners

Review the three tips with students, and challenge them to locate examples in print and online of effective visuals. Have students present their findings to the class and use the tips to justify their reasoning. As an extension, have them also look for examples they think do not meet the criteria.

Making Oral Presentations **445**

Practicing Your Speech

Practice is the key to giving an effective oral presentation. Knowing what to say and how to say it will help eliminate those butterflies speakers often feel. Here are some hints for an effective practice session.

- **Arrange your note cards in the proper order.** This will eliminate any confusion as you practice.
- **Practice in front of a mirror.** Check your posture and eye contact and be sure your visual aids are easy to see.
- **Practice in front of others.** Friends and family can help you identify parts that need work.
- **Record or videotape a practice presentation.** Do you sound interested in your topic? Are your voice and message clear?
- **Time yourself.** If your teacher has set a time limit, practice staying within it.
- **Speak clearly.** Do not rush your words, especially later when you are in front of your audience.
- **Speak up.** Your voice will sound louder to you than it will to the audience. If you sound too loud to yourself, you are probably sounding just right to your audience.
- **Work on eye contact.** Look down only to glance at a card.
- **Look interested and confident.** This will help engage your listeners.

Practice Checklist

To review each practice session, ask yourself the following questions.

_____ **1.** Did I appear at ease?
_____ **2.** Could my voice be heard and my words understood?
_____ **3.** Did I sound as though I enjoyed and understood my topic?
_____ **4.** Were my visual aids interesting and used effectively?
_____ **5.** Did I avoid rushing through my speech?
_____ **6.** Did I include everything I wanted to say?

Try It!

Practice your presentation. Give your speech to family or friends. Also consider videotaping your speech.

Research

English Language Learners

To help students feel comfortable speaking in front of their peers, schedule individual practice presentations followed by constructive feedback, based on the practice checklist at the bottom of the page. Hold as many practice sessions as time allows.

Practicing Your Speech

Watching a video of a practice presentation is an excellent way for students to identify missteps in their presentation. If possible, arrange for students to record practice presentations by reserving equipment in advance and asking volunteers to operate it. Then set up a schedule so that all students who want to record their practice speech will have an opportunity to do so.

In order to make their practice sessions as useful as possible, have students also read and apply the guidelines for voice control and body language on SE page 446.

Delivering Your Presentation

If students have had an opportunity to record their practice session, have them review their video one last time before they deliver their presentation to the class. Tell students to check to see how well they have applied the guidelines for controlling their voice and maintaining eye contact. Encourage them also to note where they could still strive for improvement, such as using visuals. Students should strive to make these adjustments before they deliver their speech.

Delivering Your Presentation

When you deliver a speech, concentrate on your voice quality and body language. They communicate as much as your words do.

Controlling Your Voice

Volume, tone, and *pace* are three aspects of your formal speaking voice. If you can control these, your listeners will be able to follow your ideas.

- **Volume** is the loudness of your voice. Imagine that you are speaking to someone in the back of the room and adjust your volume accordingly.
- **Tone** expresses your feelings. Be enthusiastic about your topic and let your voice show that.
- **Pace** is the speed at which you speak. For the most part, speak at a relaxed pace.

Tip

You can make an important point by slowing down, by pausing, by increasing your volume, or by emphasizing individual words.

Considering Your Body Language

Your body language *(posture, gestures,* and *facial expressions)* plays an important role during a speech. Follow the suggestions given below in order to communicate effectively.

- **Assume a straight but relaxed posture.** This tells the audience that you are confident and prepared. If you are using a podium, let your hands rest lightly on the surface.
- **Pause before you begin.** Take a deep breath and relax.
- **Look at your audience.** Try to look toward every section of the room at least once during your speech.
- **Think about what you are saying** and let your facial expressions reflect your true feelings.
- **Point to your visual aids** or use natural gestures to make a point.

Try It!

Deliver your presentation. As you do, be sure to control your voice and exhibit the proper body language.

English Language Learners

As part of their effort to control the rate of their presentation and to reduce the possibility of losing their place, have students put down their note cards when they introduce and position their visuals. Remind students to point to the elements on their visuals as they speak in order to help them highlight ideas they want to emphasize.

Evaluating a Presentation

You can use an evaluation sheet to rate a classmate's speech. Circle the best description for each trait. Then offer at least one positive comment and one helpful suggestion.

Peer Evaluation Sheet

Speaker _____ Evaluator _____

1. Vocal Presentation

Volume:
Clear and loud   Loud enough   A little soft   Mumbled

Pace:
Relaxed   A little rushed or slow   Rushed or slow   Hard to follow

Comments:
    a. _____
    b. _____

2. Physical Presentation

Posture:
Relaxed, straight   A bit stiff   Fidgeted a lot   Slumped

Eye contact:
Excellent contact   Some contact   Quick glances   None

Comments:
    a. _____
    b. _____

3. Information

Thought provoking   Interesting   A few points   Not informative

Comments:
    a. _____
    b. _____

4. Visual Aids

Well used   Easy to follow   Not clear   None

Comments:
    a. _____
    b. _____

Evaluating a Presentation

Encourage students to create their own **Peer Evaluation Sheets** *(see below)*, using the one shown here as a model. You can also create a template on the classroom computer. Students can then print out a new copy whenever they are asked to evaluate a classmate's speech.

Tell students to rely on the following to form their evaluations:
- their personal reaction to the ideas and presentation of the speech
- the descriptions for volume, tone, pace, and body language on SE page 446 for evaluating both Vocal Presentation and Physical Presentation
- the bulleted items in the Tip box at the bottom of SE page 444 for evaluating the effectiveness of visual aids.

Teaching Tip: Peer Evaluation Sheets

Remind students that peer evaluation sheets, and peer responding in general, are valuable only if carried out honestly and fairly.

- Peer evaluations can help students recognize what they have done well, which instills confidence and provides motivation to do better.

- Peer evaluations provide students with concrete ideas for improvement, giving writers options for revising their work.

* For more about peer responding, see SE pages 121–126.

Preparing a Multimedia Report

Have students read the sample Planning Script. Then ask them to explain how the writer plans to use slides and sounds at different stages of the oral presentation.

Distribute photocopies of the reproducible T-chart (TE page 823) for students to use to create a planning script for their multimedia report. Suggest that students refer to the Revising Checklist on SE page 449 to understand the overall goals for this task. Make sure students realize that they are basically creating a planning board, or map, for introducing the video and audio materials they will use during their presentation. They will use their oral report as the actual script.

Preparing a Multimedia Report

You can enhance an oral report by using electronic aids such as slides and sound. In order to use these effectively, you must plan exactly how each will fit into your speech.

Here is a planning script for a multimedia report on the New Deal. What will be *seen* appears in the "Video" column, and what will be *heard* appears in the "Audio" column. (Note that the speaker's directions are general, not the actual script.)

Planning Script

Video	Audio	
1. **Title Screen:** "Roosevelt's New Deal: Success or Failure?"	SOUND:	Music (fades and rises appropriately in subsequent slides)
2. **Slide 2:** Depression-era photo	SPEAKER:	Introduction
3. **Slide 3:** Photo of unemployment lines	SPEAKER:	Explanation of Great Depression
4. **Slide 4:** Photo of TVA workers on dam project	SPEAKER:	Explanation of how the New Deal helped restructure economy
5. **Slide 5:** Acronyms (+ meanings) of failed programs	SPEAKER:	Explanation of failed programs
6. **Slide 6:** Chart of unemployment statistics 1937–1943	SPEAKER:	Explanation of New Deal's later years
7. **Slide 7:** Photo of people donating scrap metal to war effort	SOUND:	Music up Conclusion

Multimedia Report Traits Checklist

Use the following checklist to help you improve your multimedia report. When you can answer "yes" to all of the questions, your report is ready.

Research

Revising Checklist

Ideas

_____ **1.** Have I included the main ideas of my research paper in my multimedia report?
_____ **2.** Have I effectively supported my main ideas?
_____ **3.** Does each slide or sound bite suit the audience and the purpose of the paper?

Organization

_____ **4.** Do I state the topic in my introduction?
_____ **5.** Do I include the main points in the body?
_____ **6.** Do I restate my focus in the conclusion?

Voice

_____ **7.** Do I sound interested and enthusiastic?
_____ **8.** Is my voice clear, relaxed, and expressive?

Word and Multimedia Choices

_____ **9.** Are the words and pictures on each slide easy to see and read?
_____ **10.** Have I chosen the best audio and video clips?

Presentation Fluency

_____ **11.** Does my oral report flow smoothly from point to point?

Conventions

_____ **12.** Is each slide free of errors in grammar, spelling, capitalization, and punctuation?

Multimedia Report Traits Checklist

If possible, provide one or two additional examples of other multimedia reports for students to evaluate, using the Multimedia Report Traits Checklist. Then have them review their own report to determine if it is ready to share. When students have completed the revising checklist and answered "yes" to all the questions, provide a schedule for them to present their multimedia report to the class.

Check that all the electronic equipment that students will need to create and present a multimedia report is in satisfactory working order, and that students are familiar with the operation of this equipment. Build in time and assistance for students to use available technology to create slides and sound bites for their report and incorporate them into their presentation.

Advanced Learners

Have students work with partners to develop a rubric based on the Multimedia Report Traits Checklists and have them develop criteria for each score point (1 to 6) based on the checklist questions. Then have each group share their results for the assigned trait and combine the information to form one rubric.

Have students practice using the rubric to score their multimedia reports. Point out that they should be prepared to justify the ratings they assign for each trait and offer suggestions for improvement for traits that do not meet the highest criteria.

Writing Across the Curriculum Overview

Common Core Standards Focus

Writing 4: Produce clear and coherent writing in which the development, organization, and style are appropriate to task, purpose, and audience.

Writing 5: Develop and strengthen writing as needed by planning, revising, editing, rewriting, or trying a new approach, focusing on addressing what is most significant for a specific purpose and audience.

Language 2: Demonstrate command of the conventions of standard English capitalization, punctuation, and spelling when writing.

Writing Forms

- learning log
- cause-effect essay
- directions
- informative essay
- editorial-cartoon response
- document-based essay
- article summary
- statistical argument
- response to a prompt
- explanatory essay
- career review
- research report
- performance review
- résumé
- proposal
- memo
- e-mail message
- news release

Focus on the Traits

- **Ideas** Including a variety of details and sufficient information to make the ideas clear and complete for the reader
- **Organization** Presenting information in the best order so that it is clear and easy to follow
- **Voice** Developing an appropriate voice that sounds knowledgeable, appropriate, engaging, informative, confident, positive, or persuasive
- **Word Choice** Defining or explaining scientific terms, unfamiliar terms, and technical terms
- **Sentence Fluency** Writing sentences that flow smoothly
- **Conventions** Checking for errors in punctuation, capitalization, spelling, and grammar

Technology Connections

 Write Source Online
www.hmheducation.com/writesource

- *Net-text*
- *Bookshelf*
- *GrammarSnap*
- *Portfolio*
- *Essay Scoring*
- *Writing Network features*
- *File Cabinet*

 Interactive Whiteboard Lessons

Unit Pacing

Writing in Science: 2–4.5 hours

This section presents **a cause-effect essay, directions, and a response to an expository prompt**. Collaborate with teachers from other content areas to assign these forms. Following are some of the topics that are covered:

- Taking classroom and reading notes
- Writing learning-log entries
- Researching the causes and effects of scientific phenomena
- Guidelines for writing a set of how-to directions
- Responding to an expository prompt

Writing in Social Studies: 1.5–3.5 hours

This section presents **an informative essay, an editorial-cartoon response,** and **a document-based essay**. Collaborate with teachers from other content areas to assign these forms. Following are topics that are covered:

- Following tips for taking notes
- Making a personal connection to learning in a learning log
- Guidelines for writing an informative essay
- Responding to an editorial cartoon
- Analyzing a series of documents in order to write an essay

Writing in Math: 2–4.5 hours

This section presents **an article summary, a statistical argument,** and **a response to a math prompt**. Collaborate with teachers from other content areas to assign them. Following are some of the topics that are covered:

- Summarizing an article containing statistics and figures and creating a graph to illustrate the data
- Writing a persuasive essay with statistical supporting evidence
- Following guidelines to respond to a math prompt
- Other forms of writing in math

Writing in the Applied Sciences: 2–4.5 hours

This section presents **an explanatory essay, a career review,** and **a response to a prompt**. Collaborate with teachers from other content areas to assign these forms. Following are some of the topics that are covered:

- Including a sketch or diagram when taking classroom notes
- Setting up a learning log
- Using a graphic organizer to arrange supporting details for an explanatory essay
- Selecting a job or career area and writing an analysis of it
- Responding to a prompt
- Other forms of practical writing

Writing in the Arts: 1.5–3 hours

This section presents **a research report, a performance review,** and **a response to an art prompt**. Collaborate with teachers from other content areas to assign them. Following are some of the topics that are covered:

- Using tips to take notes for art or music class
- Creating two-column learning-log entries
- Writing a research report related to an area of art or music
- Reviewing a performance
- Writing a short essay in response to a prompt about art or music

Writing in the Workplace: 2.5–4 hours

This section presents **a résumé, a proposal, a memo, an e-mail message,** and **a news release**. Collaborate with teachers from other content areas to assign these forms. Following are topics that are covered:

- Parts of a business letter
- Preparing a letter for mailing
- Writing a résumé
- Writing a proposal to fix a problem, address specific needs, or make improvements
- Writing a memo to ask and answer questions, describe procedures, give short reports, or remind others about deadlines and meetings
- Writing an e-mail message to communicate quickly
- Writing a news release to submit information to the media

Teacher's Notes for Writing Across the Curriculum

This overview of writing across the curriculum includes some specific suggestions for the unit.

Writing Focus

Writing in Science (pages 451–462)

Most science writing will take the form of classroom notes, reading notes, lab reports, or learning logs. Some essay tests and responses to expository prompts may also be part of science class. All of these are reviewed in this chapter.

Writing in Social Studies (pages 463–476)

Class notes and a learning log are covered in this chapter. In addition, guidelines are given to help students write informative essays, responses to editorial cartoons, and document-based essays.

Writing in Math (pages 477–486)

Even though most math writing is in the form of notes, learning logs, or word problems, this chapter reviews math-article summaries, statistical arguments, and responses to math prompts.

Writing in the Applied Sciences (pages 487–496)

Applying science to everyday life makes learning more exciting for many students. In this chapter, a sample essay about a high-protein diet uses science to explain why such a diet has risks. A career review and a response to a prompt are also modeled.

Writing in the Arts (pages 487–506)

Sample classroom notes, a learning log, a research report, a performance review, and a response to an art prompt are featured in this chapter.

Writing in the Workplace (pages 507–521)

The majority of your students will become professional writers. How so? They will earn their living, in part, by writing memos, e-mail messages, advertising copy, and résumés. This chapter offers guidelines and samples for the types of workplace writing students will do now and in the future.

Academic Vocabulary

Read aloud the academic terms, as well as the descriptions and questions. Model for students how to read one question and answer it. Have partners monitor their understanding and seek clarification of the terms by working through the meanings and questions together.

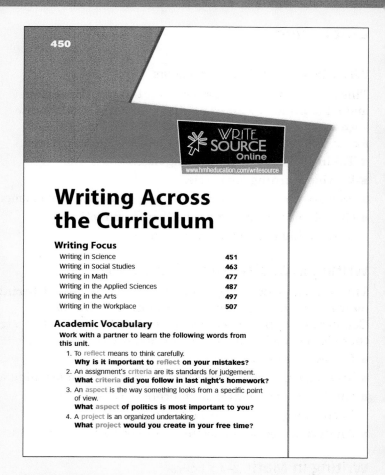

Academic Vocabulary

Work with a partner to learn the following words from this unit.

1. To reflect means to think carefully.
   Why is it important to reflect on your mistakes?
2. An assignment's criteria are its standards for judgement.
   What criteria did you follow in last night's homework?
3. An aspect is the way something looks from a specific point of view.
   What aspect of politics is most important to you?
4. A project is an organized undertaking.
   What project would you create in your free time?

Minilessons

Editorial Cartoons
Writing in Social Studies

■ **READ** pages 468–469 in your textbook. Then **CHOOSE** an issue and **DRAW** your own cartoon (use the example on page 469 as a guide). **EXCHANGE** papers with a classmate and **INTERPRET** each other's cartoons.

Statistics can lie.
Writing in Math

■ **FREEWRITE** for five minutes about what the saying "Statistics can lie" means to you. **USE** examples from your own life. **SHARE** your ideas with a partner or the class.

Fighting Infection
Writing in the Applied Sciences

■ **WRITE** a paragraph explaining why the overuse of antibiotics has become a problem. **SAVE** your work as a possible idea for a research paper.

What Is It?
Writing in the Arts

■ **SEARCH** the Internet, an art book, or an encyclopedia to find a picture of Chicago's Picasso (an unnamed work by Picasso) located in Daley Plaza in Chicago. **WRITE** a paragraph that describes the artwork and interprets what it means to you.

451

Writing in Science

Writing in Science

Writing is central to science. It allows scientists to express their hypotheses, to record their observations, and to communicate their conclusions. Writing gives structure to the scientific method and allows scientists to share what they've learned with others.

In science classes—biology, chemistry, physics, botany, geology, astronomy, and oceanography—you can make discoveries about the natural world and learn ways to explore it further. Writing about the practical applications of science in your everyday life requires research skills, accurate observations, and clear explanations.

This chapter covers the types of writing that will help you in your science classes and in applying scientific principles to everyday tasks. Research papers and responses to prompts allow you to share what you've learned with your teacher and others, while practical writing allows you to apply what you've learned to your life.

- ■ **Taking Classroom Notes**
- ■ **Taking Reading Notes**
- ■ **Keeping a Learning Log**
- ■ **Writing Guidelines: Cause-Effect Essay**
- ■ **Writing Guidelines: Directions**
- ■ **Writing Guidelines: Response to an Expository Prompt**

"Aerodynamically, the bumble bee shouldn't be able to fly, but the bumble bee doesn't know it so it goes on flying anyway."

—Mary Kay Ash

Objectives

- ● practice taking class and reading notes for science
- ● keep a learning log for science
- ● learn the form and content for a cause-effect essay and for writing directions that describe a scientific process
- ● understand how to analyze and respond to an expository prompt for science

The lessons on the following pages provide samples of writing students might do in a science class. Assigning these forms of writing will depend on

- ■ the skill level of your students,
- ■ the subject matter they are studying in science classes, and
- ■ the writing goals of your school, district, or state.

Taking Classroom Notes

Refer students to the detailed guidelines for taking classroom notes on SE pages 528–530.

Emphasize the importance of going back to reread and study class notes, and encourage students to do so within a day of taking the notes. This critical step—which many students skip—will greatly improve their mastery of the topic. Talk about the kinds of things students might do as they review their class notes:

- Tidy up messy handwritten notes.
- Find answers to questions they wrote down during class that weren't answered.
- Research answers to new questions that arise as they study the notes.
- Look for illustrations online that they can print out and add to their notes to clarify concepts—this is especially helpful if a student's own drawing is not as clear as it could be.
- Compile a glossary of specialized terms related to the topic to help them expand their vocabulary.

452

Taking Classroom Notes

Taking good notes helps you remember key lecture points, understand new material, and prepare for tests and writing assignments. Here are a few tips.

Before you take notes . . .

- **Set up your notes** in a three-ring binder so you can insert handouts. A spiral notebook with a pocket is another option.
- **Date each entry** in your notebook and write down the topic.
- **Organize each page.** A two-column format with lecture information on the left and questions on the right works well.

As you take notes . . .

- **Listen for key words.** Pay attention to information that comes after phrases like *for example, as a result,* or *most importantly.*
- **Use your own words** as much as possible.
- **Write down questions** as they occur to you.
- **Draw pictures** or quick sketches to capture complex ideas.

After you've taken notes . . .

- **Reread your notes** after class to add any information needed to make the notes clear.
- **Study your notes** to prepare for tests and exams.

The date and topic are noted.	**March 6, 2011 – First law of thermodynamics and conservation of energy**

First law of thermodynamics:
- Applies principle of conservation of energy
- Conservation of Energy = Energy can be transferred from one system to another in many forms. However, it cannot be created or destroyed. Total energy of an isolated system remains constant.

Main points are underlined.

Key points:
- Fundamental principle of all science, especially physics and chemistry
- Change in internal energy is equal to heat transferred into the system minus energy used in work by the system.
- Can also be stated positively if W (work) is defined as the work done on the system instead of work done by the system.

Dashes set off subpoints.

Formulas:
- $\Delta U = Q - W$, with ΔU = changes in internal energy, Q = heat added to the system, and W = work done by the system.
- Einstein stated that energy and matter are interchangeable, the quantity of energy and matter in the universe being fixed. $E = MC^2$
- Energy (E) is equal to matter (M) times the square of a constant (C).

Struggling Learners

Point out that transitions that indicate a cause-and-effect relationship are often used in science texts. Encourage students to look for these transitions as they take notes:

- Transitions that indicate a cause include *since, because, due to*, and *for this reason.*

- Transitions that indicate an effect include as *a result, consequently, therefore,* and *hence.*
- Reinforce understanding of such transitions by reading the following sentences aloud and having students identify each cause and effect.

1. *Since* copper is a good conductor, it is often used in electrical wires.
2. Dr. Jonas Salk developed the polio vaccine in the mid-1950s; *subsequently,* the incidence of polio dropped significantly.
3. Fossil fuels are limited natural resources, *hence* the development of alternative fuels.

Taking Reading Notes

Note taking can increase your understanding of reading assignments. Here are some tips on taking reading notes.

Before you take notes . . .

- **Write the date, book title, chapter, and topic** before each entry.
- **Organize each page.** For a two-column format, put your notes on the left and your thoughts and questions on the right.
- **Quickly skim the assigned text.** Read the title, introduction, headings, and chapter summaries. Look at graphics, charts, and examples.

As you take notes . . .

- **Write down headings or subtopics** and key details under each.
- **Use your own words** to help you understand the material better.
- **Summarize graphics.** Write down or sketch out main ideas.
- **List vocabulary words** and look up definitions later.

After you've taken notes . . .

- **Review your notes.** When you're done reading, write down any other questions you have. Research the answers and add them to your notes.

Questions and thoughts are listed in the second column.

Nov. 12, 2011: <u>Modern Physics</u>, Chapt. 12, Sec. 3 Radioactive Decay

Many nuclei are radioactive or unstable. They eventually decay—emit a particle, transform one nucleus into another, or change to a lower energy state—until a stable nucleus is reached.

– Nucleon number [r= total number of nucleons (neutrons + protons)] must be the same before and after a decay.

– <u>Alpha decay</u>: Nucleus with too many protons—excessive repulsion. Emit a helium nucleus to reduce the repulsion.

– <u>Beta decay</u>: Neutron/proton ratio too great in the nucleus—instability. Neutron turns into a proton and an electron, and electron is emitted.

– <u>Gamma decay</u>: Nucleus is at too high an energy. The nucleus falls down to a lower energy state, emitting a high-energy photon called a gamma particle.

In Beta decay, what if the neutron/proton ratio is too small?

1. positron emission
   A proton turns into a neutron and a positron—a positively charged electron. The positron is emitted.

2. electron capture
   The nucleus "captures" an electron, which turns a proton into a neutron.

Why is radioactive decay important?

When the unstable nuclei of atoms decay and release particles, the result is radiation. Some high-level radiation can cause tissue damage, cancers, and even death.

English Language Learners

Encourage students to keep a log of key vocabulary terms for each chapter of an assigned science text. Logs should note the term, its definition, and, if possible, an illustrative drawing. Students might also choose to make an audiotape of a chapter's key vocabulary.

Taking Reading Notes

Refer students to the detailed guidelines for taking reading notes on SE page 531.

Encourage students to take notes whenever they have reading assignments—even in classes other than the sciences. This kind of note taking can also be helpful when researching an essay topic.

Remind students that the key to success with these, or any other notes, is to focus on the main ideas. Provide suggestions to supplement the tips on the page.

- After skimming the text, consider the purpose of the assignment. What does the teacher want students to learn? What should they watch for as they read?
- Distill the information down to its essence. Examples, quotations, and anecdotes can often be omitted.
- Don't write down explanations that are already familiar. Either refer to them briefly or leave them out.
- Instead of copying detailed charts or graphics, cross-reference the reading. That is, write down the pages where they be found.

Keeping a Learning Log

Talk about the differences between class and reading notes, and learning logs.

- Study notes are usually compiled during a lecture, discussion, or reading assignment.
- Entries in learning logs are usually written after taking notes.
- Note taking is expository writing—its purpose is to follow the organization of the material to record and explain the main concepts.
- Writing in a learning log is narrative writing—its purpose is to reflect on new concepts to make connections to personal experience.

454

Keeping a Learning Log

A learning log is a specialized journal you use to reflect on things you are learning in class. In a learning log, you write about new concepts by connecting them to previous learning or personal experience. Here are some tips for keeping a learning log.

Before you make an entry . . .

- **Set up your learning log** in a binder or notebook.
- **Write the topic and date of each entry** so that you can find it easily.
- **Leave wide margins** so you have room for your own thoughts and questions.

As you make an entry . . .

- **Summarize key concepts** and develop meaningful comparisons.
- **Apply new ideas** to things you already know.
- **Think about questions** you may have about the subject.
- **Predict how the new ideas may prove helpful** in the future.
- **Make personal connections** by explaining what the ideas mean to you.

After you've made an entry . . .

- **Review your entries** periodically to see how your thoughts have been developing.
- **Research any questions** you have and write down the answers.
- **Continue your reflections** by writing new observations in the margins.

Tip

You can use an approach called "stop and write" in your learning log. Stop in the middle of your reading or at the end of a class discussion and write down your thoughts about what you've just learned. This can show how well you understand the science topics you are studying. Your learning-log entries can also help you prepare for exams by showing you which concepts are the most difficult for you.

Try It!

Follow the guidelines above to set up your own learning log. When you have a few minutes during class, stop and write, reflecting on what you are learning. Make personal connections with the ideas.

Struggling Learners

To encourage the habit of using learning logs, set aside class time for students to "stop and write" in their learning logs. If possible, share this strategy with members of your school's science department, and suggest that they provide several minutes for writing at the end of each class.

Learning-Log Entries

Here are some sample learning-log entries made by a student taking a meteorology class. The student thinks about the ideas discussed in class, analyzes them, and applies the theories to current weather trends.

Science

The date and topic are given, and ideas from the class are reviewed.

Sept. 28, 2011—El Niño

El Niño is the name for unusually warm ocean temperatures off the coast of Peru. It usually begins around the end of December and lasts several weeks. It has been known to last almost a year. Fish die in the warm waters and the jet stream shifts. El Niño causes warm winters in normally cold states and lots of rain in southern states. Now I understand why we sometimes have hardly any snow. In fact, we sometimes have more rain than snow. Of course, this means ice on the lakes is probably not safe.

Sept. 29, 2011—El Niño

Questions are listed, and answers from the teacher and other sources are added.

During an El Niño, normal trade winds weaken. Warmer western Pacific water then flows east to Peru. This is the fifth-largest fishing ground in the world. The cold, deep waters are rich in nutrients. This water does not cycle upward during an El Niño. I didn't know that the fish caught off Peru are ground up into meal for poultry. When there are fewer fish because of El Niño, feed prices go up and so does the price of chicken. I don't pay much attention to chicken prices. For me, the strange winter weather is disappointing because I enjoy winter sports.

Q. What impact does El Niño have on U.S. weather?

A. In El Niño winters, temperatures are usually warmer in the north central states and cooler than normal in the Southeast and Southwest.

Q. When was the last strong El Niño?

A. We looked this up online on the National Oceanic and Atmospheric Web site. A strong El Niño was visible as warm water spreading from the western Pacific to the eastern Pacific during 1997.

Learning-Log Entries

Ask students to read the sample learning-log entries carefully and to comment on how the writer has organized the information. Possible responses:

- In the left column, the student begins by describing a bit of interesting factual information from the class.
- Also in the left column, the student adds a variety of personal responses to the factual information described.
- In the right column, the student asks questions related to the entry and records the answer to the questions.

Note that students do not have to follow the same organization. Instead, they should feel free to develop their own ways of reflecting on what they are learning. Point out also that it is not necessary to include detailed explanations of factual information (unless they want to), since this information should be included in their notes.

English Language Learners

The learning-log entries contain multiple-meaning terms. Review the definitions of these terms as they apply to the writing:

- *rich* (adjective): plentiful
- *ground* (noun): an area of land used for a special purpose
- *ground* (past tense of the verb *grind*): to crush into small pieces or a fine powder
- *feed* (noun): food for farm animals

Writing Guidelines

Cause-Effect Essay

Remind students that a cause-effect essay is a form of expository writing. Refer them to the expository unit (SE pages 163–217) for step-by-step guidance in writing an essay in this style.

Review the cause-effect graphic organizers on SE pages 64 and 586, and encourage students to use one of them when they plan an essay.

456

Writing Guidelines Cause-Effect Essay

In your science classes, you may be called on to research the causes and effects of scientific phenomena. Your focus can be on one cause and one main effect, multiple causes and effects, one effect and its many causes, and so on. Follow these guidelines.

Prewriting

- **Select a topic.** If your teacher doesn't assign a specific topic, review your class notes, learning log, and textbook for ideas. Think about topics you have discussed in class. Choose a topic with a number of causes and/or effects.
- **Gather details.** Research your topic so that you understand it thoroughly. List the topic's cause and effects, or the central effect and its causes. (Consider using a graphic organizer. See page **64**.)
- **Outline your essay.** Write a thesis statement that names your topic. Then write down the cause and effects, in order of importance. Include important supporting details.

Writing

- **Connect your ideas.** Create a beginning that introduces the topic and leads to your thesis statement. Follow your outline as you write the middle of your essay. Include the details you gathered in your research. Conclude by explaining what you learned.

Revising

- **Review your writing.** Review your first draft for *ideas, organization,* and *voice*. Ask yourself these questions: *Does my essay focus on the cause and its effects? Does it include plenty of scientifically valid details? Does my voice sound knowledgeable and appropriate?*
- **Improve your style.** Check your *word choice* and *sentence fluency*, asking these questions: *Have I correctly used and defined any scientific terms? Do my ideas flow smoothly?* Use the rubric on pages **198–199** as a final revising guide.

Editing

- **Check for conventions.** Read your revised essay, looking for errors in spelling, punctuation, and grammar.
- **Prepare a final copy.** Make a neat final copy of your cause-effect essay and proofread it one last time.

Advanced Learners

Have students find examples of cause-effect essays written by high school students and published in science magazines and journals or on reliable Web sites. Have them compile a list of interesting writing topics related to science. Distribute the list to the class.

Cause-Effect Essay

In this essay, Janet Ledman discusses the causes and effects of flu epidemics in human populations.

Science

The beginning introduces the topic and leads to the thesis statement (underlined).

The first middle paragraph discusses the cause.

The second middle paragraph examines current effects.

Avian Influenza (Bird Flu)

Medical science has solved many riddles in the last 50 years, leading to the defeat of major diseases such as polio and smallpox. On the other hand, as the number of people and the ease of travel between countries increases, the threat of a pandemic (worldwide epidemic) is very real. Currently, health centers around the world are striving to head off such a crisis. Many are concerned that the world is heading for a catastrophic outbreak of avian influenza, often called bird flu.

In several countries, particularly in China, millions of people raise chickens, turkeys, and ducks. Unfortunately, these people often live surrounded by these birds. That means that any serious illness that affects the birds has access to the humans. The proximity of a human population that lacks sufficient hygiene raises the danger level. If mutation occurs, this bird virus could well move from simply infecting birds to infecting people, who then infect other people. This is what happened in the great flu epidemic of 1918 that killed an estimated 50 million people worldwide.

The effects of current strains of avian influenza are severe. For birds, a highly infectious form of the flu usually means death. The loss of these flocks impacts local economies. When humans are infected, fever, sore throat, pneumonia, and acute respiratory distress can easily overwhelm and kill. Young adults, normally able to fight flu, seem to be especially vulnerable. In Hong Kong, eighteen people were infected and six died. Authorities believe they halted the spread of the illness by killing 1.5 million domestic chickens and turkeys. Disease control centers around the world have sent out similar reports of people stricken with the bird flu. If the virus manages to mutate so that human-to-human transmission is possible, death will stalk the world.

Cause-Effect Essay

After students have read the essay, discuss its organization, asking questions as needed. For example:

- *How does the thesis statement address the main idea of cause and effect?* It says that avian flu (cause) could lead to catastrophe (effect).
- *How would you describe the order of information?* It reflects the order of the flu's widening impact, starting with the physical symptoms and going on to describe increasingly serious problems, ending with the possible economic collapse of entire countries.
- *What does each middle paragraph contribute to the essay?*
  1. describes conditions in which the flu can spread
  2. describes the flu symptoms, first for birds, then people
  3. describes how countries will try to contain the flu, if it strikes
  4. describes the economic catastrophe that could result from the pandemic

English Language Learners

Define the following terms for students before they read the essay:

- catastrophic (widely and suddenly disastrous)
- proximity (being near or next to)
- hygiene (conditions and practices that promote health and wellness)
- mutation (an alteration or a change in form)

- infectious (capable of causing illness)
- transmission (the process of sending from one person or thing to another)
- stalk (to pursue by tracking)
- quarantining (keeping in isolation to prevent the spread of disease)
- implementing (putting into effect, starting)

- contagion (the spreading of a disease)
- fragile (easily destroyed or damaged)
- dilemma (predicament, problem)

Focus on the trait of voice. How does the writer establish a knowledgeable, reliable-sounding voice in the essay? Possible responses:

■ The writer uses specialized terms such as *pandemic, avian influenza, mutation,* and *acute respiratory distress.*

■ The writer cites statistics to support her argument (50 million people died in 1918, 1.5 million birds were slaughtered in Hong Kong).

■ The writer avoids using overly emotional words and focuses instead on describing possible scenarios.

✱ For more about using statistics in writing, see SE page 56.

Ledman 2

The last two middle paragraphs discuss the possible effects of a pandemic on families, communities, and nations around the world.

At first, an outbreak will mean quarantining individuals and whole families. In the United States, the emphasis on personal freedom and rights will make implementing such action more difficult. But if officials do not act soon enough, the flu will spread. If the local quarantines fail, communities and surrounding areas will be closed off, conceivably restricting travel throughout entire states. Imagine National Guard troops on patrol, preventing anyone from entering or leaving an area the size of a state! Schools and colleges will be closed. Large public gatherings will be banned. People will not go to movies or eat at restaurants. Should the contagion rage in spite of these efforts, nations may close their borders to protect themselves. Those needing help could end up isolated, left to die or recover on their own. Dealing with the millions of patients and deaths would be just the beginning.

Companies, both large and small, would be impacted. The fragile airline industry may cease to exist or be severely scaled back. Trade, particularly of agricultural products, would suffer. Some countries dependent on outside sources for goods and/or food could well collapse into anarchy. Of course, places that cater to tourists would be big losers. During the four months it takes to develop a vaccine to fight the spread of the virus, avian influenza could do untold damage.

The ending summarizes the dilemma for the medical community.

Health officials face a dilemma. Do they act now, spending valuable time and resources to prepare for a pandemic that may not happen, or do they wait? If the flu virus mutates and begins a human-to-human journey, the world will suffer. The risk is too great to ignore, so research concerning avian influenza and its successful treatment will continue.

▶ **Try It!**

Write a cause-effect essay. Select a topic that interests you and follow the writing guidelines on page 456.

Struggling Learners

Refer students to the two cause-effect organizers in their book (SE pages 64 and 586). Encourage students to use one of the organizers during the prewriting stage when collecting and organizing details for their cause-effect essays.

Writing Guidelines Directions

Writing in Science **459**

You may also have the opportunity to write about science outside of school. For example, you may be asked to write a set of how-to directions based on scientific knowledge you've learned in class. While this type of writing is more informal than academic writing, it still requires careful attention to detail. Follow these writing guidelines.

Prewriting

- **Focus on the purpose** of your writing task.
- **Jot down the key points** you want to make.
  Write out the steps in the process that need to be explained.

Writing

- **Keep your main purpose in mind** as you write.
- **Use examples and specific details** to support and explain each step.
- **Keep your audience in mind.** For example, if you are writing instructions for someone who's doing a project for the first time, you cannot assume anything. Fully explain the names and functions of various ingredients or tools, where supplies are kept, and basic safety precautions.
- **Sum up.** Give the reader tips about where to get additional information if needed.

Revising

- **Improve your writing.** Review your first draft for *ideas, organization,* and *voice.* Ask these questions: *Are my directions clear and complete? Do they follow a logical sequence? Have I included only important details?*
- **Improve your style.** Evaluate your *word choice* and *sentence fluency,* asking these questions: *Have I used specific nouns and active verbs? Are technical terms explained? Do my directions read smoothly?*

Editing

- **Check for conventions.** Proofread your writing for errors in punctuation, capitalization, spelling, and grammar. *Remember:* Even a few errors affect the credibility of your information.
- **Prepare a final copy.** Make a neat final copy for your audience.

Writing Guidelines

Directions

Note that written directions are a form of expository writing. That is, they explain how to do something. Have students suggest different types of directions they have encountered. If possible, provide samples of these for them to examine. Ideas include the following:

- recipes
- instructions for how to assemble an object from a kit
- procedures for a science experiment (in a lab report)
- directions to a location

English Language Learners

Remind students that transitions are used to connect sentences within a paragraph, or to connect one paragraph to another. Explain that transitions that show time are often used to describe the steps in a process. Direct students to SE page 595 and have them review the list of words that show time.

Struggling Learners

Provide students with copies of the process diagram graphic organizer (SE pages 65 and 587). Encourage them to use the graphic when gathering details on a process or a cycle.

Directions

After students have read the sample, note that the writer chose to present the directions in the form of prose. Note how he **used transitions** *(see below)* to help the reader understand the order of the steps in the process.

Discuss additional strategies students might make use of in their own projects to ensure that they present the directions as clearly as possible. Possible responses:

- Use a numbered or bulleted list to make the steps stand out.
- Provide diagrams or illustrations to clarify complicated instructions.

❋ For more about process organization, see SE page 587.

460

Directions

Miguel entered a contest in which he was required to write directions for building a model bridge. He relied on the concepts he had learned in his physics class.

The **beginning** introduces the topic and lists the necessary materials.

The **middle** explains how to build the bridge and describes its strengths.

The **ending** gives final directions and recommends testing the finished project.

Building a Truss Bridge

A truss bridge is a type of bridge commonly used by railroads. The following materials are needed to construct a model truss bridge: quarter-inch and half-inch square pine sticks and sixteenth-inch-thick plywood. The necessary tools include a coping saw and woodworkers' glue.

To build the base, place two half-inch pine sticks, each 20 1/2 inches long, four inches apart. Attach them to each other on the ends with four-inch lengths of half-inch pine.

Next, to form the trusses, use the quarter-inch pine to build six equilateral triangles with four-inch sides, and four equilateral triangles with three-inch sides. Set one of the smaller triangles (point up) in front of you. Then place in a row three larger triangles (points up) next to the first one. Finish the row with another small triangle (point up). Now place a 3 1/2-inch piece of the smaller dimension pine from the top of the first small triangle to the top of the first large triangle and from the top of the third large triangle to the top of the second small triangle. Place a four-inch piece of pine from the top of the first large triangle to the top of the second large triangle and then from the top of the second to the top of the third large triangle.

Carefully glue the triangles together as they are now laid out. Glue small squares of the plywood on top of each of the connecting points. These mimic the plates used in real bridges to both connect and add strength to a joint. Now construct a second truss in the same way.

Finally, attach one truss to each side of the base structure built earlier. Connect the joint points on the tops of the two trusses using long enough pine pieces to form triangles. Allow the glue to dry on the model bridge and then test its strength. Constructed properly, the bridge should support a fair amount of weight. Trusses are an effective way to support the load that a roadbed must carry. The triangles, which cannot be pushed out of shape, make the trusses strong.

Teaching Tip: Use Transitions

Review the idea of using transitions to connect ideas, focusing on those that indicate time. Have students point out the transitions used in the sample, which include the following:

- Next
- Then
- Now
- Finally

❋ For more about transitions, see SE pages 595–596.

English Language Learners

For practice in understanding transitions that show time, have students make a list of such terms contained in Miguel's essay. Then have students use at least three of the transitions in a short paragraph explaining how to start a car.

Writing Guidelines Response to an Expository Prompt

On a science test, you may be asked to write a response to an expository prompt. This sort of test question is a great way to evaluate your knowledge and understanding of a scientific concept. Use the following tips to make the best of the limited time you will have to respond.

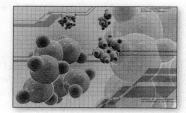

Science

Before you write . . .

- **Understand the prompt.** Review the STRAP questions listed on page 212. Remember that an expository prompt asks you to explain something or to share information.
- **Use your time wisely.** Plan a few minutes for making notes or filling in a graphic organizer before you begin writing, the main portion of time for the actual writing, and another few minutes at the end to check over your response.

As you write . . .

- **Decide on a focus or thesis for your essay.** Keep this main idea or purpose in mind during your writing.
- **Be selective.** Working from your notes, use examples and explanations that directly support your focus.
- **End in a meaningful way.** Close your essay by restating your main idea in a new way.

After you've written your response . . .

- **Check for completeness.** Use the STRAP questions on page 216 as a guide to revision.
- **Check for correctness.** Correct any errors in punctuation, capitalization, spelling, and grammar.

Tip

Many students feel nervous when taking a test, and that is only natural. However, by taking time to plan your response before you begin writing, you can relax and write with confidence.

Writing Guidelines

Response to an Expository Prompt

One good way for students to gain confidence in writing in a timed setting is for them to get plenty of practice. Consider holding regular "essay prompt clinics."

- Ask students' science teachers to provide essay prompts related to material being covered in their class. (You might also use prompts from curriculum areas other than science.)
- Work through the process of responding to the prompts, stage by stage (analyzing the prompt, planning the essay, writing, and editing).
- When students begin to get a sense of how to pace themselves, have them practice the entire process of responding to a prompt.
- After each session, have students discuss their experience.
  - ☐ How much time did they devote to each stage?
  - ☐ Which graphic organizer did they use?
  - ☐ What would they change about their approach for next time?
  - ☐ What worked best?

Response to an Expository Prompt

Have students answer the STRAP questions for the sample prompt.

- **Subject:** how displacement of water allows objects to float
- **Type:** essay
- **Role:** student
- **Audience:** teacher
- **Purpose:** to explain

Point out that the beginning of the sample essay immediately addresses one of the questions in the prompt, rather than using an attention-grabbing opening, such as an anecdote. Note that while students may certainly consider using a more dramatic opening, their main goal in a timed situation should be to answer the prompt fully and accurately, using as many details as they can that demonstrate their mastery of the topic. One of the best ways to do this is to get straight to the point.

462

Response to an Expository Prompt

One student analyzed the following prompt using the STRAP questions (page 212), made a quick list of details about the topic, and then wrote the response below.

Prompt

Two identical pieces of steel are placed in the water. One is shaped like a boat and the other is flat. What happens to each piece of steel? Why did this happen? How can this knowledge be put to practical use? Explain.

The **introduction** proposes an answer to the first part of the prompt.

In the **middle**, the student supports his answer by explaining a scientific principle.

The **ending** explains the practical use of the principle.

Displacement

Steel is more dense than water. This means that a flat piece of steel placed in the water will sink. But that same piece of steel formed into a large enough boat will float.

More than 2,200 years ago, Archimedes, a Greek mathematician, noticed that a liquid pushes up on an object placed in it with a force equal to the weight of the liquid displaced by the object. Since the density of a flat piece of steel is greater than the water it displaces, which means it weighs more, the steel will sink.

If a shipbuilder, on the other hand, uses that same amount of steel to build a boat shape of the right size, the boat will be less dense than the water it displaces. This happens because a boat is mostly air with a steel skin. The boat settles into the water, pushes away the amount of water equal to the weight of the boat, and finally floats.

A liquid denser than water, like mercury, would need less volume displaced for the ship to float. A lighter liquid, like alcohol, would need a much greater volume displaced to float the ship.

With this knowledge, shipbuilders can determine the best materials to use in a ship, and how much volume displacement is necessary to float that ship in either freshwater or seawater.

Try It!

Find a science-related prompt and write a response. Use the guidelines on page 461.

463

Writing in Social Studies

When you write in social studies, you may be asked to create an essay or other response based on information found in a variety of documents—texts, charts, graphs, maps, photos, and so on. In order to accomplish such a task, you'll need to quickly analyze the documents and summarize important information. You'll also need to organize your information carefully and write a response that satisfies the assignment's criteria.

This chapter models several types of writing you may be asked to do in your social studies classes, including an informative essay, responding to an editorial cartoon, and responding to a series of documents. You'll also find helpful tips for taking notes; keeping a learning log; and planning, writing, and editing a social studies response.

- ■ Taking Classroom Notes
- ■ Keeping a Learning Log
- ■ Writing Guidelines: Informative Essay
- ■ Writing Guidelines: Response to an Editorial Cartoon
- ■ Writing Guidelines: Document-Based Essay

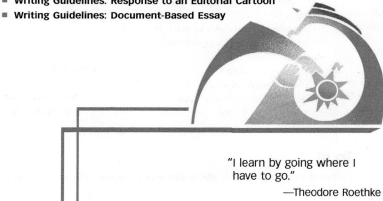

"I learn by going where I have to go."

—Theodore Roethke

Writing in Social Studies

Objectives

- • practice taking classroom notes for social studies
- • keep a learning log for social studies
- • apply the writing process and traits of writing to an informative report, an editorial-cartoon response, and a document-based essay

The lessons on the following pages provide samples of writing students might do in social studies classes. Assigning these forms of writing will depend on

- ■ the skill level of your students,
- ■ the subject matter they are studying in different social studies classes, and
- ■ the writing goals of your school, district, or state.

Taking Classroom Notes

Refer students to the detailed guidelines for taking classroom notes on SE pages 528–530.

Focus on the idea of condensing information. Encourage students to become familiar with abbreviations that will make this process easier. Have the class brainstorm a list of **common abbreviations** (*see below*). For example

- about: *re* (Latin term—*a book about birds* would be written *a book re: birds*)
- and: *&* or *+*
- answer: *ans.*
- because: *b/c*
- for example: *i.e.* or *e.g.* (common Latin terms)
- number: *no.* or *#*
- should be: *s/b*
- with and without: *w/* and *w/o*

Other shortcut techniques include the following:

- Use initials for names that are repeated—after first writing down the full name.
- Use symbols, such as asterisks, to highlight important items and question marks to identify items for investigation.
- Leave out words such as *a, an,* and *the,* provided the meaning is clear without them.

464

Taking Classroom Notes

Good note taking is a skill worth learning. Effective notes can help you understand a topic better, prepare for tests, and do better on writing assignments. Here are some tips for taking effective notes in class.

Before you take notes . . .

- **Write the topic and date** at the top of each page.
- **Do any assigned reading** before coming to class.

As you take notes . . .

- **Listen carefully and write down** the main ideas.
- **Copy what the teacher writes** on the board or on an overhead.
- **Condense information.** Write phrases and lists, not full sentences.
- **Use your own words** as much as possible.
- **Note new or unfamiliar terms** and add a definition later.

After you've taken notes . . .

- **Review your notes** as soon as possible.
- **Find answers to any questions** you still have.

Classroom Notes

The date and topic are noted.

Underlined headings organize notes.

Dashes set off facts and details.

May 12, 2011
Student Activism During the 1960s and 1970s
<u>Reasons for Activism</u>
– Protests against Vietnam War
– Civil rights for African Americans, Latinos, and Native Americans
– Campaign to win right to vote at age 18
– Concerns about the environment
<u>Results</u>
– Helped end Vietnam War
– Helped win civil rights
– Gave 18-year-olds the vote
– Started Earth Day

activism: campaigning for political or social change

Try It!

Follow the tips and sample above the next time you take notes in class.

Teaching Tip: Common Abbreviations

Point out that students who do a lot of instant messaging may already have developed a very useful way of condensing information for notes. Encourage them to adapt their instant messaging techniques to the task of note taking for classes.

Keeping a Learning Log

A learning log is a specialized notebook in which you can reflect on the facts, ideas, and social studies themes you learn about in the classroom. Writing in your learning log can help you clarify your understanding of a topic. It can also help you connect what you've learned in class to your everyday life.

Before you make an entry . . .

- **Write the date and topic** on the page each time you make an entry.

As you make an entry . . .

- **Summarize key concepts** and compare them to more familiar ideas.
- **Connect to the material** by explaining what it means to you.

After you've made an entry . . .

- **Review your entries** to see how well you understand the class material.

Learning Log

The writer makes a personal connection to the topic.

> May 12, 2011
> Student Activism in the 1960s and '70s
> Today we talked about student activism in the 1960s and '70s. I had heard a bit about student protests against the Vietnam War, but I wasn't aware of their extent. Today I also learned more about student activism in other areas, such as civil rights and the environment.
> Our classroom discussion about student activism made me think about the Friends of the North Branch Watershed group at our school. They are a group of students who are working to help clean up the North Branch River. Saturday they are holding their annual river cleanup. I think I will go to the event and use it as the topic of my descriptive social studies essay.

► Try It!

Keep a learning log for one of your classes. Concentrate on understanding topics and making a personal connection to what you learn.

Social Studies

Keeping a Learning Log

Suggest that students consider storing their learning-log entries in the same notebook as their class notes, directly following the notes for the session they're reflecting on. The benefits of developing this habit include the following:

- Students will not need a separate notebook for the log.
- Students can more easily cross-reference ideas from the class notes.
- Students are more likely to review their notes as they prepare for writing the learning-log entry.
- The log entry can serve as a personal summary of that class session.

English Language Learners

Students may have the misconception that classroom discussions must be recorded verbatim. Stress that when you summarize, you use your own words to write down the key points of the discussion. Have students read the article and summary on SE pages 544 and 545 to see how the summary focuses on main points only.

Advanced Learners

As an alternative to the **Try It!** activity, have students create a learning log about student activism today. What are issues students are concerned about? What kinds of actions are they taking, and how? What results has the activism had?

Writing Guidelines

Informative Essay

Remind students that an informative essay is an essay that tells—informs—readers about a specific topic.

- Students should explain the topic in a detailed, organized way, addressing pros and cons, if applicable.
- They should *not* express their personal opinion about it.

Newspaper stories can be considered informative essays because their goal is to provide an unbiased account of a newsworthy event.

Note that an informative essay is a form of expository writing. Refer students to the expository unit (SE pages 163–217) for step-by-step guidance in writing an essay in this style.

466

Writing Guidelines Informative Essay

Prewriting

- **Select a topic.** Your teacher will often assign a topic. If not, choose a topic you would personally like to learn more about—a specific event, person, place, or issue that relates to your course work.
- **Gather details.** Learn all you can about your topic. Get some background information from books and Web site articles. Study maps, graphs, and charts. This background information will help you write a clear and interesting description.
- **Outline your essay.** Organize your notes carefully, keeping related details together. If you are recalling an event, consider organizing your details in chronological order. If you are providing information about a place, a person, or an issue, consider organizing your details by order of location, order of importance, or by some other logical order.

Writing

- **Connect your ideas.** Start by introducing your topic. Engage the reader with an anecdote or interesting detail. In the middle paragraphs, develop the topic using a clear and effective method of organization. Write an ending that sums up your essay.

Revising

- **Improve your writing.** Review your first draft for *ideas, organization,* and *voice.* Then revise to make your ideas clear and your voice engaging and informative.
- **Improve your style.** Check for *word choice* and *sentence fluency.* Make sure your sentences flow smoothly and unfamiliar terms are explained.

Editing

- **Check for conventions.** Proofread your essay carefully. You may also wish to ask a friend to read it. Correct all errors in punctuation, capitalization, spelling, and grammar.
- **Prepare a final copy.** Make a neat final copy of your informative essay. Proofread this copy again before sharing it.

Informative Essay

In this essay, a student writes about an environmental issue after personally taking part in a cleanup event and interviewing a few of the participants.

The **beginning** captures interest with an anecdote.

The **middle** shares background information that explains the thesis.

The **ending** sums up the issue with current details.

Cleaning Up a "Tired" River

Seventeen-year-old Janice Hart spent last Saturday morning doing something she'd never imagined she'd do: hauling discarded tires and other debris out of the North Branch River. "I never thought of myself as an environmentalist," she said. When students clean up a river, they make a difference, and when they bring the problem to public attention, they can inspire change.

Hart, a senior at Ridgefield's Hamilton High School, was taking part in the annual cleanup sponsored by the Friends of the North Branch Watershed. The group, which was founded by Hamilton High students, is dedicated to cleaning up the river—and keeping it that way. More than thirty group members showed up on Saturday and spent eight hours making the river cleaner.

The history of human damage to the North Branch is a long one. In the early 1900s, William Hamilton's paper mill spewed waste into the river. Later, other factories moved in and dumped more pollutants. But by the 1970s, most of the factories had closed down, and new laws forced the remaining ones to clean up. Today, the river is cleaner than it's been, but it's far from perfect.

According to Elena Redmond, president of Friends of the North Branch, the group hauls tons of trash out of the river each year. And most of that, she says, comes from one source—discarded tires. "It's a big problem," Redmond said Saturday, pointing to a growing heap of tires on the bank of the river. "Landfills charge a fee for disposal. Rather than pay the fee, people dump tires in the river."

That may be about to change. For the past year, Redmond said, the group has been lobbying the state legislature to create a new tire-deposit law. Under the proposed law, tire buyers would put down a $5 deposit for every tire they buy, and they'd get their deposit back by returning the tires for recycling.

In just a few weeks, the Friends' bill will be voted on by the legislature. That's more evidence of the power of student activism. "Maybe someday," Redmond said, "heaps of tires will become an endangered species."

Informative Essay

Point out that the informative essay covers the topic in detail by answering the 5 W's and H questions. Write the question cues on the board and have students call out details from the essay that correspond to the questions.

- Who?—student members of the group Friends of the North Branch Watershed
- What?—volunteer cleanup
- Where?—North Branch River
- When?—last Saturday; also, in a larger sense, annually
- Why?—although laws prevent factories from polluting the river as they did in the past, people still dump trash there
- How?—reduce pollution by cleaning up the river; also prevent pollution in the first place by advocating new legislation

Struggling Learners

When students write an informative essay, some of them will find it helpful to use a graphic organizer during the prewriting stage. Refer students to the line diagram graphic organizer (SE page 65). Model how this tool can be used to collect and organize details for an informative essay by completing the graphic for the essay on SE page 467.

Writing Guidelines

Response to an Editorial Cartoon

Point out that in order to understand an editorial cartoon, it is important for students to be familiar with the news that inspired it. This means that as part of the gathering details aspect of prewriting, they should read articles from current papers about the topic. This is a good idea even if they already have general knowledge of the issue, because the articles will provide them with specific details, such as names, quotations, and statistics that might strengthen their response.

Remind students that a response to an editorial cartoon is created in the same way as a response to literature. Refer them to the response to literature unit (SE pages 275–339) for step-by-step guidance in writing an essay in this style.

468

Writing Guidelines Response to an Editorial Cartoon

Editorial cartoons use a powerful combination of words and images to comment on important, timely issues. Often, these cartoons employ exaggerated representations called caricatures to help make their point. Editorial cartoons may also include symbols, labels, and brief captions. The following guidelines can help you to interpret and respond to an editorial cartoon.

Prewriting

- **Analyze the cartoon.** Review both the visual and text elements of the cartoon carefully. If you are not sure what a particular element means, ask for help.
- **Gathering details.** On a separate piece of paper, list the different elements of the cartoon. Write a brief description next to the element. (The two examples below relate to the cartoon on the next page.)

  Amounts of money: The CEO has much more money than the employee.
  Faces: The CEO is smiling; the employee is not.

- **Plan your response.** After identifying the cartoon's main point, include that idea in a topic sentence. Then decide which details of the cartoon you will use to support your topic sentence.

Writing

- **Connect your ideas.** Start with your topic sentence. Then write body sentences that include supporting details from the cartoon. End with a sentence that restates the main point of the cartoon.

Revising

- **Improve your writing.** Review what you've written. Ask yourself if you have clearly explained the point of the cartoon. If necessary, revise to make your explanation clearer.
- **Improve your style.** Check for *word choice* and *sentence fluency*.

Editing

- **Check for conventions.** Review your response and correct any errors in punctuation, capitalization, spelling, and grammar.
- **Prepare a final copy.** Make a clean final copy of your response.

Advanced Learners

Remind students that an editorial cartoon uses a combination of words and images to send a powerful message on a timely topic. Then challenge students to create their own editorial cartoons incorporating hand-drawn art or computer-generated illustrations.

Response to an Editorial Cartoon

Writing in Social Studies **469**

A student named Ellie Jacobs took some time to analyze the following editorial cartoon. Afterward, she wrote the response that appears below.

Social Studies

"Big Business, 2006: Isn't it nice to share?"

Isn't It Nice to Share?

This editorial cartoon makes a clear point about today's large corporations: The CEO's receive an unfairly large share of the profit compared to the average employee. In the cartoon, a well-dressed CEO sits on a huge pile of money. This is his share, and he is dressed to prove it. In contrast, a ragged worker holds his share—a tiny fraction of the CEO's. The fact that the CEO is smiling and the worker frowning only adds impact to the point—one is happy with the situation, the other unhappy. The sarcastically toned caption reads, "Isn't it nice to share?" This implies, of course, that sharing in this fashion is neither nice nor right. The CEO gets far more than a fair share.

Try It!

Find an editorial cartoon in a national or local newspaper. Use the guidelines on page 468 and the sample above to help you write a response to the cartoon.

Response to an Editorial Cartoon

Discuss literary techniques that are commonly used in editorial cartoons. Possible responses:

- analogy—comparison of two things based on something they have in common (In the sample, the CEO's idea of sharing is analogous to sitting on a pile of large bills and handing your employee a penny.)
- symbolism—the use of images to stand for ideas (such as the pile of money and the coin in the sample)
- hyperbole—exaggeration to make a point
- irony—a statement that implies the opposite of its literal meaning (as the caption in the sample)

Encourage students to become familiar with as many literary terms as they can and to use them in their responses. Using these specialized terms will help them to create a knowledgeable voice.

✱ For more literary techniques see SE pages 600–601.

Writing Guidelines

Document-Based Essay

Review the sample documents *(see below)* on the following pages as a group. Before looking at the response to each task, have students cover it and discuss possible responses. They can then compare their responses with the sample responses.

Suggest that when students are assigned a document-based essay, they approach it as follows:

- Read the overall essay prompt and answer the STRAP questions for it (see SE page 461).
- Skim all documents, noting their forms, titles, and general content.
- For each document, analyze the prompt, read the document at least twice, and then plan and write an answer.
- Review the essay prompt.
- Plan the essay, based on the documents provided and students' own knowledge.
- Draft, revise, and edit the essay.

Writing Guidelines Document-Based Essay

In social studies class, you may be asked to analyze and respond to a series of documents. The documents may include excerpts from books, magazines, Web pages, diaries, or other text sources. Visual documents, such as photographs, maps, editorial cartoons, tables, graphs, or time lines, may also be included.

Often, you will be asked to analyze the documents and write an essay based on them. On some occasions, you may be asked to gather information from a document and present it in a new form, such as a graph or table. In either situation, you must quickly and accurately analyze the documents and prepare your response. Here are some guidelines that will help you.

Prewriting

- **Read all the information thoroughly.** In addition to the documents, review the introduction to the topic and your responses to any questions about each document.
- **Be sure you understand the prompt.** Focus on cue words such as *compare*, *explain*, and *define* that indicate the type of thinking and writing that is expected.
- **Analyze each document.** Consider how the documents relate to any questions you must answer—and to each other. Be aware of documents that present opposing views.
- **Organize your facts.** Use a graphic organizer to plan your response. Create an outline that gathers information from all the documents and your own prior knowledge.

Writing

- **Write your introductory paragraph.** Restate the question as a thesis statement.
- **Write the body of your essay.** Use each main point as the topic sentence of a paragraph that explains the idea. Be sure to follow your outline.
- **Write a concluding paragraph.** Briefly restate your position.

Revising

- **Improve your style.** Check for *word choice* and *sentence fluency*.

Editing

- **Check for conventions.** Proofread your essay carefully. Then correct any errors in punctuation, capitalization, spelling, and grammar.
- **Prepare a final copy.** Make a neat final copy of your essay.

Teaching Tip: Review Sample Documents

Students will benefit from the opportunity to review even more documents than those provided. If possible, bring in a wide assortment of other kinds of research for students to analyze as a group. This will

- provide them with valuable practice analyzing documents,

- expose them to different ways of interpreting a single document, and
- give them a sense of the variety of documents available to conduct their own research.

Documents

Introduction: Activist students played an important role in the politics of the 1960s and 1970s. One important issue was the campaign to lower the minimum voting age from 21 to 18. In 1971, the states ratified an amendment to the Constitution, giving Americans 18 years of age and older the right to vote.

Writing in Social Studies **471**

Social Studies

Document One

Give Us the Right to Vote!

Every day on the battlefield in Vietnam, young Americans are fighting and dying in service to their nation. Some put their lives on the line by choice. Others had no choice, being drafted into the military and forced to serve. Young men aged 18–20 are considered mature enough to carry weapons in a war zone, mature enough to face an enemy in battle, mature enough to sustain wounds and even die for their country. Yet the very country we serve will not allow us the right to vote.

Beyond protesting for the causes we believe in—causes like environmental protection and civil rights—we are not allowed to participate in the political process. If given a chance, we can bring in new ideas and new energy to help change our country and the world for the better. For this reason, we call upon the United States to lower the voting age to 18. Give us the right to vote NOW! We should be allowed to help elect the leaders whose decisions affect our very lives.

Source: "Give Us the Right to Vote!" pamphlet, 1970

Task: Summarize the main reasons 18–20-year-olds felt they were entitled to vote.

Summary: In 1970, many 18–20-year-olds were being sent to fight in Vietnam. Some young people believed that because they served their country in this way, they deserved the right to vote. They believed that if they could vote, they could make their country—and the world—a better place.

> Only the most important information is included in the summary.

Documents

Review the concept of summarizing with students. Remind them that a summary
- uses their own words, and
- describes the main idea of the original passage.

Note that the writer also could have chosen to answer the question more briefly, by using phrasing from the prompt. For example:

The main reasons 18–20-year-olds felt they were entitled to vote were that many people under age 21 were already (1) fighting in Vietnam—some of them drafted to serve in a war they didn't support—and (2) actively involved in U.S. politics and eager to have their ideas heard.

✳ Guidelines for summarizing are available on SE page 546.

✳ For more about rephrasing a prompt as part of a response, see SE page 556.

English Language Learners

Point out the transition word *because* in the third line of the sample task response. Explain that transitions that conclude and summarize are often used when analyzing and responding to a series of documents. Direct students to SE page 596, and review the list of words used to conclude or summarize.

Suggest that when responding to a poster, students use the guidelines for responding to an editorial cartoon (SE page 468). Note that students should try to use specific details from the picture to support their ideas. For the sample, a writer could mention the following:

- The young man is surrounded by a massive American flag.
- The man's uniform show he's in the military, even though this isn't stated.
- The subject appears to be calling out, though his message is open to interpretation.

In reviewing document three, emphasize the importance of reading the prompt carefully. Note that it asks students to

- describe trends *from 1972 to 1996* (dates must be noted with care—a chart could cover a wider time frame than the prompt asks students to consider), and
- use *fractions and ratios* (to show their familiarity with two ways to describe numbers, and their ability to read charts and graphs).

Document Two

Old Enough to Die.
Old Enough to Vote.

Poster: Old Enough to Die. Old Enough to Vote.

Task: Explain how this poster might be an effective way to support the campaign for voting rights for people 18 and over.

The poster would be effective because it states the case simply and powerfully. Putting a human face on the argument helps to build support for young people who want to vote.

Source: Voting Rights Archive

Document Three

Americans Age 18–21 Voting for President, 1972–1996

Year	% Who Registered	% Who Voted	% of Total Voters
1996	45.6	31	3.21
1992	44.9	33.2	3.29
1988	44.9	33.2	3.49
1984	47	36.7	4.05
1980	44.7	35.7	4.71
1976	47.1	38	5.3
1972	36.4	20.8	3.81

Source: Federal Elections Commission

Task: Explain the trend in young people's voting patterns from 1972 to 1996. Use fractions and ratios in your explanation.

From 1972 to 1996, the participation of young voters generally declined. At the peak in 1976, almost half of those 18-21 registered to vote, and the group that did go to the polls represented 1 out of 20 voters for that election. But after that, participation dropped off. In 1996, fewer than one-third of those 18-21 voted, representing 1 out of 30 votes cast.

Writing in Social Studies **473**

Social Studies

Document Four
Margin of Victory in U.S. Presidential Elections, 1972–1996

Year	% Voting Republican	% Voting Democratic	Winning Party
1996	40.72	49.23	Democratic
1992	37.45	43.01	Democratic
1988	53.77	45.65	Republican
1984	58.77	40.56	Republican
1980	50.75	41.01	Republican
1976	48.02	50.08	Democratic
1972	60.67	37.52	Republican

Source: Federal Elections Commission

Task: Calculate the greatest and smallest margins of victory for presidential elections between 1972–1996.

Statistics are used to make some generalizations.

The greatest margin of victory was in 1972, with the Republican camp defeating the Democrats by 23.15 percent of the total vote. The smallest margin was in 1976, with the Democrats defeating the Republicans by only 2.08 percent.

Document Five

"Bad politicians are sent to Washington by good people who don't vote."
—William E. Simon, former secretary of the United States Treasury

Task: How does this quotation relate to the argument over lowering the voting age?

Inference is used to make the connection.

There are two ways to connect this to the debate: (1) When very few of the informed young people vote, bad politicians may be voted into office. (2) If more informed young people voted, better politicians may get elected.

Remind students of the importance of reading the headings on charts and graphs carefully in order to be clear about the data. For instance, in document four, note that although all other documents have to do with young people's right to vote, this chart shows the total numbers of voters, of any age, in the presidential elections. Students must acknowledge this accordingly if they use information from the chart in their essay.

Ask students to read the excerpts carefully and then to respond to the sample answer. Can they suggest improvements to it? Possible responses:

- Choose words more carefully. The excerpts don't tell how many young people voted over the past 30 years (only in 1996 and 1998), so to say that the number of young voters is *lower than ever* may not be accurate.

- Analyze the reading in more depth. Although there was a presidential election in 1996, the 1998 elections were not for the presidency. Fewer people of all ages tend to vote in non-presidential elections. Therefore, comparing numbers for those two years does not, in itself, prove that the number of young voters is declining.

- Avoid overly general language. It is too vague to say that *people try to convince this age group to vote*. However, it would be accurate to say that the Society of American Voters tries to persuade them to vote.

474

Document Six

Excerpt 1

In 1996, only 8 million of the approximately 24 million voters under the age of 25 actually voted. In the 1998 elections, that number went down to 4,320,000, only 18 percent of eligible young voters. Why are these numbers so low? Shouldn't we have more votes from young people? If people aged 18–24 truly want to exercise their power and be taken seriously by politicians, the percentages of voter turnout on election day must increase dramatically. How can we motivate the youth of America to vote more often?

Excerpt 2

EVERY VOTE COUNTS

In order for your voice to be heard in our government, you must express your preferences by voting. Do elected officials adequately represent your interests and values? If you disagree with the way the government is currently being run, you have the chance to vote officials out of office and elect new ones. This is the heart of democracy. For America to become a better place, all of its citizens must participate in choosing our government.

Source: Society of American Voters, Y-Vote Project

Task: What does this document tell you about young people's interest and participation in politics today, more than 30 years after they won the right to vote?

Thirty years after winning the right to vote, the number of young people who vote is lower than ever. Although people try to convince this age group to vote, not many are listening, which limits young people's potential to change the world.

Document-Based Essay

Writing in Social Studies **475**

In this essay, a student draws on information presented in the six original documents.

> **Task: Extended Essay**
> **Using all six documents and your own knowledge about this topic, write an essay explaining why young people thought they should be able to vote and how they worked to win their campaign. Be sure to express your opinion about progress toward the goal of "changing the world for the better."**

Social Studies

Documents 1, 2, and 5
The opening provides background about winning the vote and states the thesis.

Fighting for the Right to Vote

In the 1960s, America's young people faced a dilemma. Spurred by the Vietnam War, the civil rights movement, and concerns over the environment, many young people became involved in politics. However, because the minimum voting age was 21, the influence these people could have over the political direction of the United States was limited. Young people could—and did—publicly state their position on the issues, but they could not vote to elect politicians who shared their views. Working together and using aggressive campaign strategies, young activists lowered the voting age to 18. Since then, their poor turnout at the polls has limited their goal of "changing the world" by voting.

Documents 1 and 2
The main issues surrounding the campaign for the vote are explained.

Perhaps no issue drove the campaign for the vote more directly than the Vietnam War. During the war, thousands of Americans age 18–20 served in the military, and thousands were wounded or killed. Some of these soldiers volunteered to serve in the military, but many were drafted into the military and legally required to serve. Many young people resented the fact that while 18- to 20-year-olds could be required to fight and die for their country, they did not have the right to vote. So they began a campaign to lower the minimum voting age to 18.

The campaign to win the vote featured appeals to other Americans to recognize the sacrifices young people were making for their country and the potential contributions young voters could make to the political system. Young

Document-Based Essay

Have students review the rubric for expository writing on SE pages 198–199. How would they rate this essay? Possible responses:

- **Ideas**—The thesis (more young people need to vote to effect political change) is supported with details. Specifics, such as who was elected in 1972 and 1976 (Richard Nixon and Jimmy Carter), could be added.
- **Organization**—The organization is clear; the first two middle paragraphs focus on why young activists wanted to vote, and the last middle paragraph tells what happened after they were allowed to do so.
- **Voice**—The voice sounds interested and knowledgeable.
- **Word choice**—Some specialized terms are used (*civil rights, drafted, suffrage*); some words convey the writer's opinion (*ominously, only 18 percent . . . bothered, lack of participation . . . harms*).
- **Sentence Fluency**—Sentence forms and lengths vary.
- **Conventions**—No errors.

✳ For more about using a traits-based rubric, see SE pages 33–45.

English Language Learners

Define the following terms for students before they read the essay:

- aggressive (assertive, bold)
- activists (individuals engaged in a certain activity or undertaking)
- appeals (earnest or urgent requests)
- stark (harsh in appearance, grim)
- suffrage (right or privilege to vote in public elections)
- ominously (threateningly)
- gubernatorial (relating to a governor)
- revitalize (to impart new life or vigor to after a decline)

To complete the section, assign students a practice document-based essay. As appropriate, compile the documents and write the prompts, or work with a teacher in another curriculum area to create them. Let students know whether or not you plan to grade this essay. Students may benefit from working through the process in depth, and then collaborating with a group of peers to respond to one another's work.

Remind students that a document-based essay is a research essay. Refer them to the research unit (SE pages 371–449) for detailed guidance for writing in this style.

476

Documents 1 and 2 The campaign tactics are detailed.

Documents 3, 4, and 6 Statistics from graphs and a Web site detail voting participation by young people.

Documents 5 and 6 The conclusion restates the thesis and looks at efforts to improve the situation.

campaigners used pamphlets, posters, and other printed materials to plead their case. The tone of these materials was aggressive, and even dramatic. One pamphlet demanded, "Give us the right to vote NOW!" A poster used an illustration of a brave soldier to put a human face on the sacrifice being made by young American soldiers.

The campaign to win the vote was successful, with the voting age lowered in 1971 to age 18. Off to a slow start in the 1972 election, the young voters did arrive at the polls in 1976 and made a difference. That year, the Democratic candidate won by a slim 2.08 percent margin. Some believe that the young people's vote made this victory possible. Their voting record since shows that the potential promised during the suffrage campaign has not been realized. Overall, in presidential elections from 1972 to 1996, fewer than half of eligible 18- to 21-year-olds have voted. More ominously, the number of 18- to 21-year-olds going to the polls has steadily declined. In the 1998 congressional and gubernatorial elections, only 18 percent of young people bothered to vote.

The lack of participation among young voters harms efforts to make America a better place. As former secretary of the United States Treasury William E. Simon once remarked, "Bad politicians are sent to Washington by good people who don't vote." Those who hope that young people can revitalize the American political system have not given up. Campaigns such as Rock the Vote and Y-Vote are working to encourage young people to vote. If these new campaigns succeed, the potential for young voters to change the world may be realized.

Essay Checklist

_____ **1.** Do all the ideas in my essay relate to my thesis statement?
_____ **2.** Do I cover all the requirements outlined in the task?
_____ **3.** Do I summarize my main points in the conclusion?
_____ **4.** Do I refer to information from all my documents?
_____ **5.** Do I include some of my own knowledge about this topic?
_____ **6.** Have I checked my punctuation, grammar, and spelling?

Writing in Math

When it comes to math, writing is one of the most valuable learning tools you have at your disposal. And as the math becomes more challenging—trigonometry, calculus, advanced algebra—the more essential and helpful writing becomes. Writing, in fact, helps you clarify your thinking and gain mastery over your math course work.

Keeping a learning log, writing summaries, forming statistical arguments—all of these forms of writing will sharpen your ability to distill the meaning of mathematical concepts. When you write in a learning log, you should write freely, sorting out your thoughts about new topics. When you write summaries or arguments, you should be more analytical, carefully displaying your understanding. This chapter will help you with all of your writing in math, from learning log entries to responding to math prompts.

- **Taking Classroom Notes**
- **Keeping a Learning Log**
- **Writing Guidelines: Article Summary**
- **Writing Guidelines: Statistical Argument**
- **Writing Guidelines: Response to a Math Prompt**
- **Other Forms of Writing in Math**

"It is impossible to be a mathematician without being a poet in soul."

—Sophia Kovalevskaya

Writing in Math

Objectives

- practice taking classroom notes for math
- keep a learning log for math
- apply the writing process and traits of writing to an article summary and a statistical argument
- practice responding to a math prompt
- learn other forms of math writing

The lessons on the following pages provide samples of writing students might do in a math class. Assigning these forms of writing will depend on

- the skill level of your students,
- the subject matter they are studying in different math classes, and
- the writing goals of your school, district, or state.

Taking Classroom Notes

Refer students to the detailed guidelines for taking classroom notes on SE pages 528–530.

Encourage students to form study groups or choose study partners for their math class. Students can meet regularly to

- review and compare class notes,
- ask and answer questions, and
- work through problems together.

Note that this strategy is especially effective for students who feel less confident with mathematics, but it can even help those who are comfortable with the subject. (Cooperative study is an effective way to learn any subject.)

Taking Classroom Notes

Using your own words to write down math steps and formulas can help you understand and remember them. Here are some note-taking tips.

Before you take notes . . .

- **Use a three-ring binder to store your notes** so that you can add handouts, work sheets, tests, and so on.
- **Write the date, textbook pages, and topic** at the beginning of each entry.

As you take notes . . .

- **Write down what your teacher puts on the board or overhead.** This information often contains math concepts, definitions, math terms, formulas, and important examples.
- **Put concepts in your own words.** Also write down questions you have about the material.
- **Draw pictures.** Use diagrams to help you visualize the problem.

After you've taken notes . . .

- **Find the answers** to your questions.
- **Study your notes** before the next class and again before exams.

Notes

January 16, 2011

Definition Logarithm (log): $\log_b b^x = x$

A logarithm indicates a relationship with exponents. Once the pattern is recognized, problems become much easier to handle.

Example 1: $\log_7 z = 2$
  This would be the same as $7^2 = z$.
  Since $7^2 = 49$, then $z = 49$.

Example 2: $\log_y 81 = 4$
  This would be the same as $y^4 = 81$.
  Since $3^4 = 81$, then $y = 3$.

Example 3: $\log_2 8 = x$
  This would be the same as $2^x = 8$.
  Since $2^3 = 8$, then $x = 3$.

Keeping a Learning Log

Writing in Math **479**

A learning log allows you to write about what you are learning, think through new concepts, ask questions, and find answers.

Before you write . . .

- **Set up the log.** Use a section of your three-ring binder so you have your learning log together with your notes.
- **Write the date and topic** at the beginning of each entry.
- **Leave wide margins** for writing questions and answers.

As you write . . .

- **Reflect on what you learn** by writing about what you understand and what is still confusing to you.
- **Summarize key concepts** and think about how they connect to your own experiences and to other ideas you have learned in math.

After you've written . . .

- **Answer any questions** you may still have about the topic.
- **Review your log** before a test or when you study a new topic.

Learning Log

January 16, 2011

Some Properties of Logarithms

1. $\log(ab) = \log a + \log b$
Example:
$\log(12) = \log(3 \cdot 4) = \log 3 + \log 4$

2. $\log\left(\dfrac{a}{b}\right) = \log a - \log b$
Example:
$\log 4 = \log\left(\dfrac{20}{5}\right) = \log 20 - \log 5$

Logarithms and exponents are related. Logarithm properties actually come from exponent properties.

How to remember properties:

1. When multiplying the same variable, add the exponents: $a^m \cdot a^n = a^{m+n}$. Taking the log of a product is the same as adding the log of each factor.

2. To divide the same variables, subtract the exponents: $\dfrac{a^m}{a^n} = a^{m-n}$. Taking the log of a quotient is the same as subtracting the log of each part.

In any base, the following rules apply: $\log(ab) = \log a + \log b$; $\log(a/b) = \log a - \log b$; $\log(1/a) = -\log a$; $\log a^b = b \log a$; $\log 1 = 0$ and $\log 0$ is undefined.

Keeping a Learning Log

Talk about the various topics students might write about in a learning log for math.

- One of the most effective ways to learn math is through the action of doing the problems. Students could document their experiences with solving problems—ideas on how to approach them, successes and frustrations, breakthroughs they experience in solving problems.
- The learning log is a good place to document what students discuss with study partners.
- If students notice that what they are learning in math applies to their everyday experiences, they should also include this information in the log (for example, when planning for an event; figuring out the budget; estimating the number of sandwiches, drinks, and other supplies needed; comparing prices per unit when shopping; calculating how much can be purchased while staying within the budget).

As with all learning logs, students will find that reflecting on the topic in this way helps them to achieve a deeper understanding of the subject they are studying.

Writing Guidelines

Article Summary

Review this and the following page before having students write their own summary. If possible, allow them several days to find a suitable article that interests them. Suggest that they look at articles in financial and science magazines or the business and science sections of the newspaper.

Note that the instructions under Writing describe a single-paragraph summary, with

- a topic sentence,
- body sentences, and
- a closing sentence.

For most articles, one paragraph should be sufficient for a summary, especially if an additional graphic element, such as the bar graph that accompanies the sample on SE page 481, is provided.

Review the types of graphs and charts students might consider to illustrate their summary.

✱ For information about the parts of a basic paragraph, see SE pages 578–579.

✱ For information about adding graphics, see SE page 95.

480

Writing Guidelines Article Summary

Many magazine articles and news stories include statistics and mathematical concepts. Use the following guidelines when summarizing a math-related article.

Prewriting

- **Select an article.** Find an article that presents figures and statistics to support the story.
- **Read the article.** Try to get an overall feeling for the topic. Then reread it carefully, paying attention to the details.
- **Find the focus.** Write down the main idea of the article.
- **Gather details, including math-related points.** Select only the most important details that support the main idea of the article.

Writing

- **Write your first draft.** State the main point of the article in your topic sentence. Then provide supporting details. End with a sentence that summarizes your thoughts.

Revising

- **Improve your writing.** Review your first draft for *ideas*, *organization*, and *voice*. Ask yourself the following questions: *Have I clearly presented the focus of the article? Have I included the most important supporting details? Have I explained any use of mathematical concepts in the article? Is my summary clear?*
- **Improve your style.** Check your *word choice* and *sentence fluency*. Ask yourself the following questions: *Have I used specific nouns and verbs? Does my summary read smoothly?*

Editing

- **Check for conventions.** Edit your revised draft, correcting any errors in punctuation, capitalization, spelling, and grammar.
- **Prepare a final copy.** Make all corrections and write a neat final draft.

Try It!

Find an article containing statistics and figures. Using the guidelines above and the sample on the next page, write a summary and create a graph to illustrate the data.

Advanced Learners

Have students write directions explaining how to create a computer-generated graph in a document, using a computer in the library or media center. Stress the need to identify every step of the process in user-friendly language. Provide copies of the final directions to students learning the task.

Math-Related Article

A student read the following article and wrote a brief summary, including a graph to illustrate the statistics in the article.

Employment Increase Misleading

A look at the 2009 employment picture of Grange County shows good news and bad news.

According to figures from the State Department of Revenue, employment in Grange County increased .86 percent, from 106,972 in December of 2008 to 107,895 in December of 2009. Most of the growth was due to new businesses located in new malls in the towns of Terrell, Point Leon, and Jasper. At first glance, this appears to be a positive trend; however, other factors make the picture less than perfect.

First, it must be noted that most of the new businesses are retail outlets or fast-food chains. Nearly half of workers at these businesses earn no more than minimum wage, many working less than full-time, with no benefits.

Next, while many new jobs have been introduced, many have been lost, due to businesses either moving or closing. The most significant impact was felt by the loss of Yarrow Graphics, accounting for a loss of 297 jobs.

In addition, some local companies closed in the face of new competition. Among them was Point Leon's Main Street Grocery. Owner Jim

Hawkins cited an inability to compete with the Mega Bite discount grocery that opened in the town's new mall. Of Main Street's 92 employees, 51 found jobs at the new store, earning significantly less at Mega Bite.

In December of 2008, only 20,774 workers in Grange County were earning minimum wage, while the next year that group rose a startling 47 percent to 30,448. The number of workers earning between $6 and $10 per hour saw a smaller increase of 4 percent, from 32,369 to 33,620. Meanwhile, the number of workers earning higher wages dropped. The largest decrease came in workers earning between $10 and $20 per hour. Their numbers fell from 41,649 in 2005 to 33,804 in 2009—a staggering 19 percent drop. Numbers of those earning more than $20 per hour also fell, a less startling but still significant 18 percent, from 12,180 to 10,023 jobs.

While the county has enjoyed a rise in employment, taxable income has not enjoyed a proportionate rise, tempering any economic celebration.

Article Summary

More Jobs, Not Better Jobs

The article "Employment Increase Misleading" reports on the current employment picture in Grange County. While the number of jobs has increased, salaries have decreased. Both the increase and decrease can be blamed on the types of new businesses in the area. Companies offering high-paying jobs have either relocated or closed down, while new businesses offering low-paying or minimum-wage jobs have proliferated. (See the graph.) Local workers have had to settle for lower pay than they had been earning. So while more people are working, they are earning less.

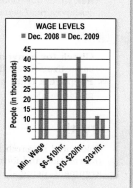

WAGE LEVELS
■ Dec. 2008 ■ Dec. 2009

Math-Related Article and Article Summary

After students have read both the article and the sample summary, ask them to assess the summary according to the traits of ideas, organization, voice, and word choice.

Ideas

- The summary clearly explains the main idea expressed in the original.
- The original article is acknowledged by title in the summary.

Organization

- The paragraph has a clear topic sentence, body sentences, and closing sentence.
- The summary paragraph provides verbal explanation; supporting statistics are presented in the accompanying bar graph.

Voice—The summary captures the tone of the original article.

Word choice—The writer uses her own words in the summary.

Writing Guidelines

Statistical Argument

Remind students that in addition to **crafting an interesting argument** *(see below)*, they are responsible for choosing reliable statistics, copying them down correctly, and using them responsibly. Possible problems with statistics include the following:

- Using outdated numbers—Statistics should always be as current as possible.
- Using data from a biased source—Such data are likely to be unreliable. Reputable research agencies are the best sources.
- Ignoring conflicting data—Students should take care to examine statistics from both sides of the argument. It isn't responsible to cite only numbers that support the thesis if other studies suggest another conclusion.
- Misinterpreting data—It's important to understand the information. For example, if a study finds that 52% of people who eat chocolate like milk chocolate best, it doesn't mean that 52% of the whole population likes milk chocolate.

482

Writing Guidelines Statistical Argument

Use the guidelines below to help you write a persuasive essay containing statistical supporting evidence.

Prewriting

- **Select a topic.** Think about a timely, statistic-driven topic related to your school or community: student dropout rate, state test scores, sports statistics, student volunteer activity, and so on. Choose a topic that interests you and will interest your reader.
- **Gather information.** Research your topic, using reliable sources of information. Take notes on key facts and figures.
- **Form an opinion.** State an opinion about the topic after reviewing your notes.

Writing

- **Write your first draft.** Introduce your topic and state your opinion. In your middle paragraphs, use your facts and statistics to support your position. Write an ending that restates your opinion.

Revising

- **Improve your argument.** Consider your *ideas, organization,* and *voice.* Ask these questions: *Is my position clear? Have I developed a convincing argument using statistics? Is my argument well organized? Does my voice sound confident?*
- **Improve your style.** Check your *word choice* and *sentence fluency.* Ask these questions: *Have I defined any unfamiliar terms? Do my sentences read smoothly?*

Editing

- **Check for conventions.** Correct any errors in punctuation, capitalization, spelling, and grammar.
- **Prepare a final copy.** Make a neat final copy of your argument and proofread it.

 Try It!

Select and research a timely, statistic-driven topic to write about. Gather information and form an opinion about the topic. Then write your argument, using statistics to make your point.

Teaching Tip: Crafting an Interesting Argument

Some students may be doubtful that writing based on statistics can be interesting. However, the book *Freakonomics,* by coauthors Steven D. Levitt and Stephen J. Dubner, contains many vivid and entertaining examples of writings on statistics-driven topics. Have students read examples from the book (or other articles written by the same authors) to get a sense of how statistics can be interesting.

Statistical Argument

Writing in Math **483**

The student writing the following persuasive essay uses statistics to emphasize the need for after-school programs.

Math

Happily Ever After

The **beginning** includes statistics to introduce the topic.

According to the U.S. Department of Labor, of the more than 28 million kids whose parents work outside the home, as many as 15 million have no prearranged supervision after school. Further, Child Trends Research reports that more than 4 million kids—10 percent of children between the ages of 6 and 12—are totally on their own until their parents get home from work. After-school programs are necessary for the safety of the entire community and the future of this country.

The **opinion** statement is underlined.

After-school programs have been proven to decrease crime and violence. According to studies by the organization Fight Crime: Invest in Kids, the time period between 3:00 p.m. and 6:00 p.m. is considered a "danger zone," with higher rates of violent crimes committed by children. After instituting an after-school program in the San Diego Public Schools, authorities noted a 13.1 percent reduction in after-school arrests, as well as an 11.7 percent reduction in juvenile violent crime.

In the **middle** part, statistics help support the opinion.

Students who participate in after-school programs do better in school and are less likely to drop out. They are also more likely to continue their education after high school. In addition, research shows they are less likely to engage in risky activities such as drinking, drugs, sex, and violent acts.

Finally, after-school programs save money. Research shows that every dollar invested in an after-school program saves taxpayers $3 in truancy and court costs, as well as the expense of students repeating a grade. A Brandeis University study reported that parents of unsupervised children miss an average of eight days of work per year and make more errors due to situations involving their children. After-school programs help eliminate these situations.

The **ending** restates the opinion.

After-school activity programs are crucial to protecting not only children, but society in general. When people realize the importance of such programs, they may begin shaping a new world.

Statistical Argument

Have students review the rubric for persuasive writing on SE pages 254–255 before reading and responding to the sample essay. Afterward, focus on the related traits of voice and word choice.

- Note that the generous use of statistics helps to establish an authoritative tone. Numbers are a convincing way to support an argument (even in essays that are not required to be based on statistics).
- Point out that while the writer clearly expresses his opinion (more after-school programs should be created), he avoids using loaded words or overly emotional language.
- The use of language specific to the topic, such as *juvenile violent crime* and *truancy*, helps to make the writer sound knowledgeable.

✴ For a definition of loaded words, see SE page 599.

English Language Learners

Define the following terms before students read the argument:

- prearranged (arranged in advance)
- supervision (the act of directing or watching over someone)
- instituting (setting into operation)
- reduction (the act of lessening or decreasing)
- engage (to participate or become involved)
- truancy (state of being absent without permission)
- crucial (of supreme importance, critical)

Writing Guidelines

Response to a Math Prompt

Focus on the information under *As you write* and emphasize the importance of students showing all their work when they respond to a math prompt.

- Remind students that sometimes teachers will give partial credit to students who approach a problem in a certain way, even if their final answer is wrong, so it's important for the teacher to be able to follow their whole sequence of thoughts.
- Note also that they are less likely to make errors if they take care to document each step of the problem instead of trying to solve parts of it in their heads.

Writing Guidelines Response to a Math Prompt

Math prompts propose word problems. You are asked to respond in writing in addition to showing your mathematical calculations and your answers. First you must analyze the prompt and decide what you are supposed to do. Then you respond one step at a time. Follow these guidelines.

Before you write . . .

- **Read the prompt.** Read carefully and watch for key words such as *find, solve, justify, demonstrate,* or *compare.* Then carry out the requested actions only. Be aware that some prompts have more than one part.
- **Gather details and data.** Write down any values, assumptions, or variables provided in the prompt.

As you write . . .

- **Build your solution.** Respond to each part of the prompt. Jot down formulas or equations and sketch brief diagrams if they will help solve the problem. Make the necessary calculations to get an answer and show all of your work.

After you've written a first draft . . .

- **Improve your response.** Reread the prompt after you do your calculations. If the problem has more than one part, be sure you have answered every part. Work the problem in another way to check that your solution is correct.
- **Check for conventions.** Check your solution for errors in punctuation, capitalization, spelling, and grammar.
- **Prepare a final copy.** Make a neat copy of your solution.

Response to a Math Prompt

The following math prompt contains more than one part. The writer provides a solution using words, numbers, and a diagram.

> *What is the probability of getting a sum of seven on two dice? First explain what is meant by probability and then solve the problem.*

Probability

Probability refers to the number of times the desired result occurs out of the total number of possible outcomes. This problem asks for the number of ways to get a sum of seven on two dice out of all of the possibilities when we roll two dice.

To solve this problem, I need to know the total possible results when throwing two dice (first number indicates result on first die and second number is result on second die):

1,1	1,2	1,3	1,4	1,5	(1,6)
2,1	2,2	2,3	2,4	(2,5)	2,6
3,1	3,2	3,3	(3,4)	3,5	3,6
4,1	4,2	(4,3)	4,4	4,5	4,6
5,1	(5,2)	5,3	5,4	5,5	5,6
(6,1)	6,2	6,3	6,4	6,5	6,6

This gives thirty-six possible results when throwing two dice. Looking at all of the possibilities, there are only six ways to get a sum of seven: 1+6, 2+5, 3+4, 4+3, 5+2, and 6+1. Therefore, the probability of getting a sum of seven would be 1 to 6: $\dfrac{sum}{total} = \dfrac{6}{36} = \dfrac{1}{6}$.

Try It!

Find a math prompt and write a response. Choose a practice prompt from your textbook or one recommended by your teacher. Follow the guidelines on page **484**.

Math

Response to a Math Prompt

As a group, review the prompt and sample response, drawing students' attention to important details.

- Emphasize the importance of reading the prompt carefully. For example, a student who rushed to start working on the question in sentence 1, without reading sentence 2, would overlook the critical instruction to define the word *probability* before solving the problem.
- Note that the prompt response is a type of expository writing. It is structured as directions (see SE pages 459–460), describing in chronological order how to solve the problem.
- Point out that the writer uses the first-person pronoun *I* in the response to describe what he did.
- Encourage students to try to include a diagram, along with the verbal explanation and numbers, whenever it will help to clarify their thought process in a math prompt.

Struggling Learners

Students may feel overwhelmed responding to a grade-appropriate math prompt while simultaneously striving to improve their writing skills. Modify the **Try It!** activity by presenting a below-level math prompt, such as the following:

Rosa is putting a border along the walls of a room that is 14 feet long and 10 feet wide. The border is sold by the yard. Describe the process Rosa should use to determine how many yards of border she needs. *(Process descriptions will vary; 16 yards)*

Other Forms of Writing in Math

Note that the position paper and research prompts are designed for longer writing projects, while the other four prompts are suitable for shorter pieces. If possible, have students practice writing a full-length math-related essay, in addition to working on an assortment of short pieces. You can use the prompts on the page if they apply to students' current math classes. Alternatively, coordinate with math teachers to devise prompts in a variety of forms, such as those suggested.

As students start work on a prompt, make sure they identify the style of writing needed and consult the relevant unit in the SE for more guidance. For example:

- Definition, compare-contrast, and process essay prompts—refer to the expository unit (SE pages 163–217)
- Narrative prompt—refer to the narrative unit (SE pages 141–161)
- Position paper—refer to the persuasive unit (SE pages 219–273)
- Research prompt—refer to the research unit (SE pages 371–449)

486

Other Forms of Writing in Math

Definition

Calculus—Write a detailed expository paragraph defining a vector and explaining its function in math.

Narrative

Any Math—Tell about a time you couldn't understand a mathematical principle and how you finally found a way to make it clear.

Compare and Contrast

Algebra—Compare and contrast real numbers and imaginary numbers. Include descriptions, properties, and functions.

Position Paper

Any Math—Defend or oppose the requirement of three years of math to get into college.

Process

Geometry—Explain the process you would use to figure the number of bricks you would need to build a wall around your backyard.

Research

Statistics—Calculate the probability of your favorite baseball team going to the World Series this year. Figure in the statistics of past seasons and each player's performance numbers, along with variables such as injuries, possible trades, and so on.

Struggling Learners

Students may have the misconception that responding to a math prompt does not involve a prewriting stage. Stress the importance of collecting and organizing one's ideas prior to creating a first draft. Provide students with copies of graphic organizers suited for use with math prompts, such as a definition diagram, a Venn diagram, and a process diagram.

Advanced Learners

Challenge students to write a math prompt that calls for one type of response described under the heading *Other Forms of Writing in Math*. Then have students trade prompts and write suitable responses.

487

Writing in the Applied Sciences

Thoughtful logic is at the heart of all scientific thinking and writing. Let's say you need to replace a light switch. You ask questions about what you need to do, and then you search for answers. Whether you go online, read a manual, or ask for advice, in the hands-on world of applied science, it is critical to know every step. Your safety may be at stake. Whenever you are asked to explain something, focus on being clear and complete.

In this chapter, you will learn about writing directions, essays of explanation, and even letters of complaint. Apply the solid logic of science and the clarity of good research to all your writing.

- ■ Taking Classroom Notes
- ■ Keeping a Learning Log
- ■ Writing Guidelines: Explanatory Essay
- ■ Writing Guidelines: Career Review
- ■ Writing Guidelines: Response to a Prompt
- ■ Other Forms of Practical Writing

"Knowledge is of two kinds. We know a subject ourselves, or we know where we can find information upon it."

—Dr. Samuel Johnson

Writing in the Applied Sciences

Objectives
- practice taking classroom notes for applied science
- keep a learning log for applied science
- apply the writing process and traits of writing to an explanatory essay and a career review
- practice responding to an applied science prompt
- learn other forms of writing in the applied sciences

The lessons on the following pages provide samples of writing students might do in a family and consumer science or technical education class. Assigning these forms of writing will depend upon
- ■ your students' skill level,
- ■ the subject matter students are studying in the applied sciences, and
- ■ the writing goals of your school, district, or state.

Taking Classroom Notes

Focus on the first item under As you take notes . . . and the idea that students should not only date each entry but also number the pages. Point out that this will ensure that they can keep their notes organized, if they need to remove pages temporarily or if the pages accidentally come loose from the binder.

- The easiest system is to number pages consecutively, picking up where they left off at the end of the previous class.
- Alternatively, students could begin each class with page number 1, in which case, they should write the topic and the date with the page number.
- To insert pages (such as class handouts) into their numbered notes, students should assign the new pages the same number as the previous page, plus a letter. For example, each sheet of a three-page handout inserted after page 7 would be numbered 7a, 7b, and 7c.

Taking Classroom Notes

Note taking can help you keep your projects organized and on track.

Before you take notes . . .

- **Keep a separate notebook for each class,** or use a three-ring binder with tabbed dividers for separate sections.
- **Divide your paper into two columns.** Use one for notes and the other for questions or drawings.

As you take notes . . .

- **Date each entry** and keep the pages in order.
- **Briefly jot down teacher instructions** as they are given in class.
- **Draw diagrams** and use graphics to organize details.

After you've taken notes . . .

- **Review your notes** with a partner and highlight main ideas.
- **Study your notes** before beginning a project or before taking a test.

January 9, 2011   Replacing a Switch

Shut off power to the circuit at the fuse box by removing the fuse or pushing the circuit breaker switch to off. Use a current tester at the light switch to be sure the power is off.

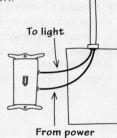

To light

From power

- Remove switch plate.
- Remove switch from the wall box.
- Loosen screws and remove wires keeping track of which wire is attached to the top screw.
- Attach wires to the new switch. Be sure each wire is underneath each screw head and tighten the screws.
- Fold the wires into the wall box and tighten screws that hold the switch in the box.
- Attach switch plate.

Turn the power back on at the fuse box and test the light.

Try It!

Take notes in an applied-sciences class. Try to include a sketch or diagram in your notes.

Applied Sciences

Keeping a Learning Log

A learning log is a journal for recording and reflecting on what you learn in a class.

Before you write . . .

- **Use a separate section in your notes** or a separate notebook.
- **Leave space** for writing questions and answers later on.

As you write . . .

- **Date each entry** and keep the pages in order.
- **Write about what you experienced,** what you learned, what worked and what didn't, and ask questions.
- **Consider your next steps.** Write about how the material connects with other things you have learned, and where it might lead.

After you've written . . .

- **Use your log as a supplement** to your notes to review for a test.
- **Write the answers to questions** you had in class or during a project.

Learning Log

October 6, 2011   Cooking Class

The five basic ingredients you need for making bread are flour, yeast, water, shortening, and salt. The flour's protein is called gluten, which traps air bubbles. The gluten combines with the flour's starch to create the texture of the bread. Some recipes add sugar to help get the yeast working, but there's some sugar in the flour that activates the yeast. Fat coats the gluten molecules, makes the finished bread softer, and helps it brown. Water or other liquids react with the gluten and the starch and create steam that makes the bread soft and high. Salt adds flavor and also strengthens the gluten.

Some breads call for eggs, which give a light texture, and sugar, which contributes to browning and flavor. Other ingredients can add nutrients and flavor.

My aunt told me to put a pan of water in the oven as the bread bakes so the crust doesn't get hard.

The more times the bread is punched down and allowed to rise, the higher and softer the bread will be.

► Try It!

Set up a learning log in a notebook. Be sure to date each entry.

Keeping a Learning Log

Students may find keeping a learning log for applied science classes to be an extremely fruitful writing project. This is because the topic naturally integrates

- factual knowledge acquired in the classroom with
- practical application to everyday life.

Encourage students to make their learning logs as **creative** (see below) as they wish, including poetry, drawings (both technical and creative), and personal narrative. Remind them that thinking about their newly acquired knowledge in different ways can help them master it more completely.

Teaching Tip: Creative Learning Logs

Suggest readings that might inspire students to make their learning logs more creative. Possibilities include the following:

- *The Notebooks of Leonardo da Vinci,* Leonardo da Vinci and Irma Richter (Editor)
- *John James Audubon, Writings and Drawings* (contains excerpts from his journals)
- *A Natural History of the Senses* and other works by Diane Ackerman, a poet who also wrote about the natural sciences

---

English Language Learners

Provide students with an opportunity to educate classmates about their cultures. Invite them to demonstrate the steps they follow when preparing a favorite traditional food. Encourage students to include some terms from their first language during the demonstration.

Writing Guidelines

Explanatory Essay

Focus on the last two bullets under Prewriting, noting that students' choice of graphic organizer will depend on the system of organization they use for their essay. For example:

■ If asked to explain a step-by-step process, students might use a time line or a process diagram.

■ Another organizer suited to topics involving a sequence of events is the cause-effect organizer. For example, this is useful for the essay on SE page 491, the topic of which focuses on the idea of *What happens when* _____.

■ For explanations that do not involve sequence, students should arrange details in the logical order that best supports their thesis. Good organizers for displaying assorted ideas related to a topic include cluster diagrams, line diagrams, and definition diagrams.

✳ For a variety of graphic organizers, see SE pages 64–65.

✳ For more about the cluster diagram, see SE page 213.

Writing Guidelines Explanatory Essay

An explanatory essay states a thesis and then provides details that clarify and explain the position given.

Prewriting

■ **Select a topic.** If your teacher does not assign a specific topic, review your notes, manual, or textbook for ideas. For example, in a metals fabrication class, you might explain why it is important to prevent electrode contamination.

■ **Gather details.** Use a graphic organizer to help you arrange your supporting details. Include facts, examples, and anecdotes to support your claims.

■ **Plan and organize.** Decide in which order to present your support points. How are they related? Decide on a pattern for moving smoothly from one topic to the next.

Writing

■ **Connect your ideas.** Introduce your points and their connection in the beginning paragraph. Then present each point, covering one completely before moving on to the next.

Revising

■ **Improve your writing.** Examine your work for *ideas, organization,* and *voice.* Rework any ideas that are unclear or incomplete.

■ **Improve your style.** Look at your *word choice* and *sentence fluency* and make any changes necessary to improve clarity and flow.

Editing

■ **Check for conventions.** Look for errors in spelling, punctuation, and grammar.

■ **Make a neat final copy.**

Explanatory Essay

For her nutrition class, Hanae explained the dangers of a high-protein diet.

The beginning introduces the topic and leads to the thesis statement (underlined).

The middle gives reasons that support the thesis.

The ending wraps up and makes a final statement.

More Than Weight Loss with High-Protein Diets

High-protein diets, which emphasize meat, eggs, seafood, and cheese, have become popular. However, while this type of diet produces quick weight loss, research shows its dangers far outweigh the benefits.

A 1988 publication called "Nutrition and Health in the United States" was published by the Surgeon General, and it discouraged high-protein diets because of the high levels of protein and saturated fat consumed. When carbohydrates needed for complete synthesis of fat are eliminated from the diet, the body faces a challenge: how to burn excess amounts of fat.

Fewer carbohydrates create problems. Fewer high-fiber plant foods combined with an increase in high-fat foods means increased cholesterol levels. Without the high-fiber plant foods, potassium, calcium, and magnesium are reduced and sodium levels rise, increasing the risk of high blood pressure that can lead to heart disease or a stroke. With fewer carbohydrates to help retain body fluids, the body risks dehydration. That strains the kidneys. When excess protein accumulates in the kidneys and is not adequately diluted, a person may develop kidney stones, kidney failure, or gallbladder disease.

The American Heart Association links high-protein diets and osteoporosis, rheumatoid arthritis, and even multiple sclerosis. Most high-protein foods are acidic. The body tries to maintain its alkaline pH balance. To do so, it dissolves bone into phosphorus and calcium to counteract the acid. This bone degeneration is the first step to osteoporosis. The kidneys excrete this bone material, potentially resulting in kidney stones.

Any weight-loss program should improve rather than jeopardize an individual's health. The best diet strategy is to eat a healthy diet, balance protein and carbohydrates, and increase physical activity.

Try It!

Write an essay of explanation. Select and explain one aspect of a topic.

Explanatory Essay

Challenge students to identify areas in need of improvement in the sample essay and to suggest improvements that could be made, identifying the writing trait that corresponds to their suggestions.

Ideas
- The writer could cite a more current source than the 1988 report.
- The writer could include some statistics to support the position.
- The addition of anecdotes or quotations would enhance the reader's interest in the piece.

Organization—The topic sentence for paragraph 4 suggests that the reader will learn how diet might cause osteoporosis, rheumatoid arthritis, and multiple sclerosis; however, the paragraph focuses only on osteoporosis.

Sentence fluency—The writer could have more clearly formulated some sentences. For example, the beginning of paragraph 3 (*Fewer carbohydrates create problems*) expresses the idea incompletely. It would be better to say *Consuming fewer carbohydrates creates problems.*

Conventions—The clause *That strains the kidneys*, paragraph 3, line 8, should be part of the previous sentence and should be followed by a period (not a comma).

English Language Learners

Make sure students can define these terms before they read the sample essay:

- emphasize (to stress or focus attention on)
- consumed (eaten or taken into the body)
- synthesis (combining single elements to form a whole)
- retain (to keep or hold in a particular place or position)
- dehydration (process by which water is removed from a body)
- diluted (reduced the concentration of a substance)
- counteract (to oppose or lessen the effect of)
- degeneration (a state of decline in form or function)

Writing Guidelines

Career Review

Most seniors will benefit from writing a career review. The writing can help them clarify their interests and goals, and may even help some of them choose a college or other path after graduation. When selecting a topic, suggest that students follow one of these strategies:

■ Choose the career they currently intend to pursue.

■ Profile the career of someone they admire.

■ Profile an extremely unusual career.

If possible, announce a career day toward the end of the semester, during which students present their review to their peers and faculty. Afterward, have volunteers collect all essays in a binder to circulate among interested students and their families.

✳ For more about making oral presentations, see SE pages 439–449.

492

Writing Guidelines Career Review

A career review is a specific type of essay of analysis. It includes the job's requirements, such as education or physical stamina, future advancement possibilities, benefits, and salary.

Prewriting

■ **Present your topic.** Explain which job you are analyzing. Remember your purpose. What important factors do you need to consider?

■ **Gather details.** Include details about the requirements, benefits, and future of the job, mentioning anything that makes the career stand out or fall short.

■ **Plan and organize.** Cover each area of the career point by point before moving on to the next.

Writing

■ **Include a clear beginning.** Explain why you are examining this topic.

■ **Write the middle.** Analyze the different areas of the topic, point by point.

■ **End with a final comment.** Wrap up by sharing one final insight about the topic.

Revising

■ **Improve your writing.** Look for *ideas, organization,* and *voice.* Consider all aspects of the topic.

■ **Improve your style.** Look for smooth sentences. Let your interest in the topic show through.

Editing

■ **Check for conventions.** Look for and correct any errors in spelling, punctuation, or grammar.

■ **Make a clean final copy.**

Advanced Learners

Challenge students to compile a list of "Top Ten Jobs of the Future." Have them research current predictions of industries that will likely experience the greatest growth and identify specific jobs associated with each industry. Invite students to share their findings on career day and include their report in the class career binder.

Career Review

Leon's careers class explores the duties and requirements of different careers. Here is his review of a radiology technician career.

Applied Sciences

The **beginning** explains the topic.

Becoming a Radiology Technician

With the aging population in this country, the number of health-related jobs is growing. A top job of the future is that of a radiology technician.

Radiology technicians, or radiographers, have a variety of duties. First of all, they need people skills, as they prepare people for X-rays and explain procedures. If diagnostic dye is used, sometimes technicians must mix the contrast medium as well as administer it to the patient. To administer X-rays, technicians set the level of radiation and the right distance between the machine and the area to be X-rayed. Fine adjustments create the correct angle, density, and contrast for the film to show clear images that allow doctors to make exact diagnoses.

The **middle** covers different aspects of the job.

Technical training is required. High school courses in science and computers are a good start. Specialized training is offered in technical schools, colleges, hospitals, and the military. Two-year associate degrees and bachelor's degrees are favored by hospitals. Teaching and administrative positions require four-year degrees.

Most jobs are in hospitals, although positions are also available in doctors' offices, diagnostic imaging centers, and outpatient care centers. Technicians work 40 hours or more per week. In 2007, salaries for radiographers varied between $38,000 to $55,000, but some earn as much as $72,000. Those trained in more complex radiological imaging, such as CT scans and MRI's, find the highest paying jobs.

The **ending** offers a summary and a final insight.

In summary, the job of radiology technician appears to be interesting, challenging, and important. It's clear that this is a promising career that can make a difference.

Try It!

Select a job or career area and write an analysis of it. Include as much detail as you can and give an opinion about the job.

Career Review

Point out that the sample provides an informative, objective overview of the job of radiology technician. Explain that approaching such a topic from a more personal point of view would also be appropriate. To do so, students could include

■ anecdotes or advice gleaned from people in the occupation,
■ quotations from interviews with people on the job,
■ students' own thoughts and plans about following the career path, and
■ education, training, and skills requirements for this career.

Emphasize that whether students approach the topic objectively or subjectively, certain questions must be answered in any career review. Challenge them to come up with a list of these. Possible responses:
■ What is the occupation called?
■ What does a person with this job actually do?
■ What skills and training are required?
■ Where do people with this job work?
■ What are the time and education commitments of the job?
■ How much are people in the field currently paid?

English Language Learners

Before students begin the **Try It!** activity, review the information essential to a career review by having pairs answer the questions above about the sample review. Possible responses:

- What is the occupation called? (radiology technician)
- What does a person with this job actually do? (see details in paragraph 2)
- What skills and training are required? (see details in paragraph 3)
- Where do people with this job work? (hospitals, doctors' offices, diagnostic imaging centers, and outpatient care centers)

Struggling Learners

To assist students in planning their career analysis for the **Try It!** activity, have them use the STRAP technique to plan their review (see SE page 212) and after they write their first draft, have them use STRAP to revise (see SE page 216)

Writing Guidelines

Response to a Prompt

Acknowledge that having a time limit can be one of the more anxiety-provoking aspects of writing tests. Suggest that the best way to handle the problem of writing within the time limit is for students to

- come to tests well prepared so they don't waste time struggling to recall information;
- practice responding to a variety of prompts in a timed setting to improve time spent in the planning and writing stages;
- become familiar with a variety of graphic organizers so they can quickly sketch the right one when they need it during a test; and
- study conventions rules and make a habit of using them correctly whenever they write so they need to spend less time worrying about them during tests.

✳ For more about budgeting time for on-demand writing, see SE page 575.

Writing Guidelines Response to a Prompt

Before you write . . .

- **Know your time limit.** Set limits for yourself to allow time for prewriting, writing, and revising.
- **Examine the prompt.** Look for key words that will help you determine the following elements:
  - **Subject** What is the topic of your writing?
  - **Purpose** Will you explain, inform, analyze, or persuade?
  - **Focus** What aspect of the subject should you examine?
  - **Form** How will you format your response? As an essay? A letter? A poem? A story?
- **Plan your response.** Write your thesis or opinion statement and use a brief outline or graphic organizer.

As you write . . .

- **Write an effective opening paragraph.** Use a hook to grab your reader's attention. Then introduce your topic and include your thesis statement.
- **Develop the middle.** Develop a clear topic sentence for each paragraph. Support each main point with details, including examples and paraphrases. If you are allowed to look at notes or texts, include quotations and statistics.
- **Write a strong closing paragraph.** Restate your thesis and offer a final thought. If you are writing a persuasive piece, include a call to action.

After you've written a first draft . . .

- **Read through your work.** Add, cut, or move your details to make your work stronger. Be aware of any time limitation, making the most necessary changes first.
- **Check for conventions.** Correct any errors you find.

Response to a Prompt

Teresa wrote a response to the following prompt in her life-skills class.

> *Your landlord has neglected to repair a leaky faucet, a running toilet, and a broken light fixture in your apartment. Write a letter of complaint convincing the landlord to take care of the problems.*

Applied Sciences

The beginning opens with a positive statement and the thesis (underlined).

Dear Mr. Miller:

First of all, I want to tell you I enjoy my apartment. It's so spacious, and the neighbors are great. However, I still have the leaking faucet and running toilet in the bathroom and the broken light fixture in the kitchen. Although I mentioned them when I first moved in last month, nothing has been done to fix them. <u>I must complain about the slow response and ask you again to please repair these problems.</u>

The middle gives the main points as topic sentences.

The water situation is most serious. The constant dripping is annoying and expensive. I checked my bill with my neighbors, and neither of their bills is as high as mine. They don't have leaks.

The broken kitchen light fixture is also a problem. Without a window in the kitchen, the main fixture is my only light except the stove hood, and it does not light the sink area.

The ending restates the thesis (underlined) and adds a final statement.

<u>Please take care of these problems.</u> They represent both cost and possible safety issues. Because they were noted as needing fixing on my initial move-in sheet, I ask you to fix them as soon as possible. I do not want to have to contact the Tenants' Union for assistance.

Thank you for your attention to this matter.

Sincerely,

Teresa Hernandez

Try It!

Write a letter of complaint for a real or fictitious situation.

Teaching Tip: Detailed Reasons

Note that the student writer filled in a lot of supporting details to make her point. For example, she mentions the leaking faucet, running toilet, and a broken light in the kitchen. She also mentions speaking to her neighbors about their bills. Tell students that they should not hesitate to create supporting details like these if a test prompt presents a hypothetical situation such as this one.

Response to a Prompt

Remind students that a letter of complaint is a form of persuasive writing (see SE pages 219–273); its purpose is to persuade the recipient to take action to address a problem. Have students use the sample to identify the elements of a letter of complaint.

- **Ideas**—The writer clearly describes the complaint and gives **detailed reasons** *(see below)*.
- **Organization**—Each middle paragraph focuses on a reason: the water problems are expensive; the kitchen does not have enough light.
- **Voice**—A positive statement helps establish a reasonable tone. Overall, the voice should be polite but firm: *Please take care of these problems*.
- **Word Choice**—The writer avoids loaded or attacking words, and also avoids an accusatory tone: *I must complain about the slow response* (not, *You are so slow to respond*).
- **Sentence Fluency**—Transitions clarify the reasons for the complaint: *First of all, However, Because*.
- **Conventions**—The letter should be error free.

Other Forms of Practical Writing

To expand on the information given about other forms of practical writing, bring in a selection of published practical writings for students to examine. Numerous examples of practical writing are available. Sources include the following:

- cooking magazines
- health and nutrition publications
- craft, woodworking, and hobby books and magazines
- home repair and decorating publications
- automobile restoration publications
- organic gardening magazines

Encourage students to become aware of practical writing in their daily lives. They will begin to notice how often they encounter it, and they can begin to take note of effective strategies to use in their own work.

496

Other Forms of Practical Writing

Process Essay

Architectural Drafting—Explain how to measure a kitchen for new cabinets and countertops.

Essay of Classification

Textile Arts—Explain the different types of needlework and give an example of each.

Essay of Analysis

Auto Mechanics—Analyze the pros and cons of a hydrogen-powered engine and consider its current feasibility for the mass market.

Essay of Explanation

Home Decorating—Explain the various uses of ceramic tile in the home and how to choose the right type of tile for each situation.

Problem-Solution Essay

Advanced Metals Fabrication—Explain the problems encountered by using a contaminated electrode in welding and explain how to repair it.

Persuasive Essay

Health—Write a paper that persuades people they do not need to fear or avoid those who are HIV positive.

Comparison-Contrast Essay

Classic Cooking—Compare the cuisines of Italy and Greece and explain reasons for the differences and similarities.

Struggling Learners

Students may benefit from a review of the traits of a comparison/contrast essay.

- To compare items, explain how they are alike.
- Transitions such as *likewise, as, in the same way, similarly, both,* and *also* compare ideas.

- To contrast items, explain how and in which ways they differ.
- Transitions such as *on the other hand, but, however, although, yet, nevertheless, still,* and *otherwise* contrast ideas.

Advanced Learners

Have students work in small groups to determine the **S**ubject, **P**urpose, and **A**udience of each of the different prompts. Have students also identify any graphic organizers that they think would be useful for planning a response for each prompt.

✳ For more about STRAP, see SE page 212.

Writing in the Arts

Archaeologists have found that even before there was language, there was art. Cave paintings told stories and related experiences. But art is more than basic communication. Mahatma Gandhi once said, "True art takes note not merely of form but also of what lies behind." Art is not just visual or aural; it is cerebral, stirring great thoughts as well as deep emotions—thoughts and emotions you can explore and write about.

When you write about art, you can examine your reactions to it and analyze why a piece affects you the way it does. You can examine art's effect on history or its reflection of a particular time period. This chapter will help you write about art in learning logs, essays, and reports. You will also learn to respond to an art prompt, using your thoughts and emotions to analyze and critique. In writing about art, you will soon gain a better understanding of yourself and others.

- Taking Classroom Notes
- Keeping a Learning Log
- Writing Guidelines: Research Report
- Writing Guidelines: Performance Review
- Writing Guidelines: Response to an Art Prompt

"I try to apply colors like words that shape poems, like notes that shape music."

—Joan Miro

Writing in the Arts

Objectives
- practice taking classroom notes for arts classes
- keep a learning log for an arts class
- apply the writing process and traits of writing to an art or music-related research report and a performance review
- practice responding to an art prompt

The following pages provide samples of writing students might do in an art or music class. Assigning these forms of writing will depend on
- the skill level of your students,
- the subject matter they are studying in arts classes, and
- the writing goals of your school, district, or state.

Taking Classroom Notes

Encourage students to be open to using different note-taking techniques for art classes. For example:

- For a drawing class, consider using a sketchbook, rather than lined paper. That way, they will have plenty of clear space for drawings and can jot down any other notes in the space around the pictures.
- Consider taking notes on large sticky pads, then attaching them to the pages of their textbook. (Each sticky note should be dated, for future reference.)
- Those who find that they need to compile a list of vocabulary words related to the topic can use a pocket-sized notebook. They can then divide each page into two columns and write the word on the left and its definition on the right.
- Keep a combination class-notes-and-learning-log notebook (SE page 499).

498

Taking Classroom Notes

In art and music classes, you usually work with a variety of art materials or practice for instrumental or vocal performances. However, it may occasionally be necessary to take notes in class. (See pages 528–530 for more information.)

Take notes when . . .

- **your teacher writes information on the board or overhead.**
  Taking notes helps make important information part of your own thinking. Be sure to write down new vocabulary words as well as names, dates, and key phrases.

- **you have a demonstration in class.**
  Your class may view slides of art pieces or listen to recordings of various musical styles. Taking notes will help you organize and remember the various works.

- **you have a guest speaker or performer.**
  Professional artists may visit your class and demonstrate or discuss their work. Your notes can help you think about the presentation. You may want to jot down questions you'd like to ask after the presentation.

Tip

- Date each entry and give it a topic heading so you can find it quickly when reviewing.

- List new vocabulary words. Leave room for adding definitions or examples later.

- Write down hints or examples to help jog your memory about a name, a term, or a concept.

- Draw sketches that may help you remember works of art.

- Mark a spot in your notes with a question mark if something confuses you. Ask about it later.

- Divide note pages into two columns with one side wider than the other. Put notes on one side and questions on the other.

- Work with a "study buddy." You can compare notes, go over questions, and review for tests together.

Keeping a Learning Log

In project-based classes such as art, dance, theater, and music, a learning log can help you keep track of and reflect on your progress. Andre wrote the following entries for a beginning class in watercolor painting. On the left side, he made notes about what the teacher talked about. On the right side, he added comments.

Learning Log

April 2, 2011	
In watercolor painting, what is left out can be as important as what is put on the paper. White paper showing through is often part of the composition. Different brushstrokes and washes create different effects.	Mr. Kirke showed us watercolor paintings of flowers that incorporated white space and used different types of washes.
April 5, 2011	
A flat wash is an important basic technique. 1. Clip a sheet of paper on a board. 2. Have plenty of clean water in jars. 3. Brush a band of color across the top. 4. Brush a second band in the opposite direction, picking up the fluid paint at the base of the previous stroke. 5. Continue laying in bands of the same color, working quickly and tilting the board to keep the leading edge wet. 6. Use a dry brush to pick up the excess color along the bottom of the wash.	Mr. Kirke let us experiment with using watercolors. I found out why it is important to let the one layer dry before applying more paint. When I started doing a tree on top of a flat wash for the sky, the painting got muddy because the blue wash wasn't quite dry. Unlike oil paints, you can't slather on watercolors over wet paint because the colors will run together.
April 12, 2011	
Use this technique on paper that is already wet with a background color. The color will spread more slowly as the paper dries. 1. First dampen the paper. 2. Touch the color onto the paper with the tip of a large brush. 3. Clean brush carefully between colors.	We worked on wet-on-wet techniques. I started with gray, giving the effect of a stormy sky. The technique is more complicated and interesting when applying two colors. I tried blending green and yellow to make a distant, hazy, yellow-green woods.

Arts

▶ Try It!

Set up a learning log for your drama, art, or music class. Keep one side for notes or instructions and the other side for your own comments.

Keeping a Learning Log

Note that the sample learning log combines traditional class notes (on the left) with personal thoughts (on the right). Students may find this a good format for note taking in arts classes.

Emphasize the benefits of documenting personal reactions to and thoughts about art. Because artworks are so often created to evoke a personal, aesthetic response, as well as an intellectual one, journal writing can be the best way to engage fully with the subject matter on both levels. Encourage students to include items such as the following:

- photocopies or postcards of artwork
- their own sketches
- poems and other creative reactions to the art
- lists of other artists mentioned during class whom they might want to explore
- accounts of their experiences with art outside of class

Writing Guidelines

Research Report

Have students refer to the research unit on SE pages 371–449 as they work on this essay.

If possible, coordinate this assignment with students' art or music teachers so that their topics correspond to what they are studying in class.

Alternatively, you can have students choose an arts-related topic that interests them personally. They may appreciate the chance to focus on a topic of their own choosing, independent of a school syllabus. As a result, they may approach in a more rigorous manner a subject they might previously have thought about only casually.

While students are selecting their topics, schedule conferences to discuss and, if necessary, help refine their ideas or narrow their topic before they begin writing.

Writing Guidelines Research Report

You may be asked to write a research report in your art or music class. You may decide to write about a famous painter or analyze a trend in music. The following guidelines will help you create a research report.

Prewriting

- **Choose a subject.** If your teacher doesn't provide a specific subject, list artworks, artists, musical trends, or other ideas that interest you.
- **List what you already know** about the subject as well as questions that you have.
- **Conduct research** about the subject. Check school or public library catalogs for books, look through magazines, and explore Web sites.
- **Write a thesis statement.** Review your research notes. Then write a thesis statement that clearly identifies the specific topic and focus for your research paper.
- **Plan and organize.** Outline your paper, putting details in the most appropriate order—for example, you may put key points in spatial order, chronological order, or order of importance.

Writing

- **Connect your ideas.** Introduce your topic, give background information, and state your thesis.
- **In the middle paragraphs,** support the thesis statement with specific details. Finally, summarize what you have learned or what you have to say about the topic.

Revising

- **Improve your writing.** Check your *ideas, organization,* and *voice.* Ask these questions: *Have I created a clear thesis? Have I supported it with a variety of details? Are my details in the best order? Do I sound knowledgeable?*
- **Improve your style.** Check your *word choice* and *sentence fluency.* Ask these questions: *Have I explained any technical terms? Do my sentences flow smoothly?*

Editing

- **Check for conventions.** Look for errors in spelling, punctuation, and grammar.
- **Prepare your final copy.** Proofread your research paper before turning it in.

Research Report

You can learn about the arts by studying how different artistic expressions reflect different periods and events throughout history. Tamika Sanders had been studying the migration of African Americans to the northern United States in her history class. She discovered that African American painter Jacob Lawrence had created a series of paintings called *The Great Migration,* and she decided, with permission from both teachers, to make that the topic of a report for her art and history classes.

Arts

Tamika Sanders
Mrs. Southwell
History
May 12, 2011

The Great Migration

The **beginning** presents the thesis statement of the report (underlined).

Painter Jacob Lawrence used art to tell stories—usually through a series of paintings on panels. <u>In the *Migration* series, which he started in 1940, Lawrence used the technique to capture the story of African Americans moving north after the turn of the century.</u>

The **middle** of the report discusses Lawrence's background and the influences that affected his art.

Lawrence began his career as an artist during the Depression in the Works Progress Administration's federal arts program. He said his style of telling stories through a series of paintings was influenced by African storytelling traditions, Mexican mural painters, and American cartoon strips (Black Genius). He often laid out his designs like a modern storyboard (Whitney). Before the *Migration* series, he had created historical painting series on Harriet Tubman, John Brown, and Frederick Douglass.

The *Migration* series was inspired by the people Lawrence grew up with. Although he had never been to the South before beginning his work, almost everyone in his neighborhood and family had moved north during the previous 50 years. His parents were part of the migration, with his mother settling in Harlem, where Lawrence grew up (Washington).

Arriving in the North, many blacks found new education opportunities and more jobs, but often experienced new forms of discrimination and injustice as well. To tell this story in paintings, Lawrence used

Research Report

After students have read the sample report, ask them to note different aspects of the subject that the writer brought out in her discussion of the topic. Remind students that they can discover these aspects by asking the 5 W's and H questions (see TE page 467 and SE page 65). Possible responses:

- biographical information (Who is the artist? When was he active? Where did he live?)
- the inspiration and historical background for the artwork (Why did he make the art?)
- a description of the artwork—or, in this case, a series of paintings (What does it look like?)
- a discussion of the artist's style in general (How did the artist create his work?)

English Language Learners

Define the following terms for students before they read the sample research report:

- migration (movement from one country or region to another)
- technique (a planned procedure used to accomplish a complex task)

- mural (a painting applied directly to a wall)
- discrimination (treating others differently based on a preconceived idea)
- urban (of or located in a city)
- distorted (exaggerated or misshapen)
- motifs (decorative figures or designs)

Advanced Learners

Have students research other American artists of the period and think about what focus they would give to a report about the artist. For example, they might focus on how the work affected techniques that artists use today.

Draw students' attention to the writer's use of an interesting quotation to conclude the essay. Explain that using a quotation can be a good ending strategy because the quotation can not only support the thesis of the essay (in this case, the idea that Lawrence used his painting to tell the story of African Americans' move northward) but also

■ contribute an interesting perspective on the topic—such as Lawrence's enthusiastic appreciation for every American's experience, not just that of African Americans;

■ give readers an opportunity to hear the actual voice of someone involved with the topic; and

■ provide a decisive, vivid closing, rather than allowing the essay simply to taper off.

✳ For more ideas for shaping great endings, see SE page 597.

502

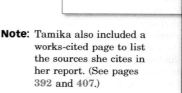

Sanders 2

bold colors, the geometric forms and shapes of his urban home, and intentionally distorted figures to illustrate the universal nature of the migrants' experiences.

The paintings cover all aspects of the move north. The first panel shows a crowd of stylized figures moving forward toward abstract railroad departure gates labeled "Chicago," "New York," and "St. Louis." Another painting in the series shows a quick, vivid arc of railroad track reflecting the industry where many of the immigrants found employment. Yet another shows well-dressed, haughty, long-time northern black residents, who often looked down on the poorly dressed, new rural immigrants.

As in many of his other series paintings, Lawrence repeated motifs, shapes, and words. In the *Migration* series, he repeated the images of a single large spike, chain links, hands, and a hammer to show the continuity in the lives, experiences, and struggles of the immigrants (Whitney).

The *Migration* series made Lawrence commercially successful, but to him, telling the story and the history was most important. "We have a tremendous history," he told a writer, "and I'm not just talking about the black, but the American people. . . . It's all one story. Exploring the American experience is a beautiful thing" (Black Genius).

The **ending** concludes with a summary of the impact of Lawrence's work.

Note: Tamika also included a works-cited page to list the sources she cites in her report. (See pages **392** and **407**.)

Writing Guidelines Performance Review

You may be asked to write about the arts by reviewing a specific performance. On the other hand, you may enjoy a performance so much that you want to share your thoughts with others through a blog, on your own Web site, or in a letter.

While this type of writing is more informal, or personal, than most academic writing, you should follow basic writing guidelines. A reader will respect your evaluation if your writing shows clarity and insight, so be sure to maintain your focus throughout the review.

Prewriting

- **Focus on what you want to say.**
- **Make notes** on your impressions of an art show or a concert.
- **Write a thesis statement.** Review your notes and state your focus.
- **Plan and organize.** Outline key points you want to make in your review.

Writing

- **Write freely,** always keeping your main idea in mind. Use your outline as a basic writing guide.
- **Use examples to support your points.** Whether the reader agrees with you or not, supporting your point of view with solid evidence is important and will gain the reader's respect.
- **Keep your audience in mind** in terms of what you need to explain.
- **Write a strong ending.** Sum up why the topic is important enough for you to write about.

Revising

- **Improve your writing.** Check your *ideas, organization,* and *voice.* Ask these questions: *Have I created a clear thesis? Have I supported it with a variety of details? Are my details in the best order? Do I sound knowledgeable?*
- **Improve your style.** Check your *word choice* and *sentence fluency.* Ask these questions: *Have I explained any technical terms? Do my sentences flow smoothly?*

Editing

- **Check for conventions.** Look for errors in spelling, punctuation, and grammar.
- **Prepare your final copy.** Proofread your review before sharing it.

Writing Guidelines

Performance Review

Collect or find online a selection of performance reviews of films, plays, television programs, dance performances, musical performances, and the like for students to examine. Also, have students find a published review to share with the class.

In addition to reading current reviews from local and national newspapers and magazines, students might enjoy seeing works by famous critics of the past such as the following:

- Lester Bangs (rock music)
- Pauline Kael (film)
- George Jean Nathan (theater)
- Dorothy Parker (theater and books)
- Edwin Denby (dance)
- George Bernard Shaw (art, music, and theater)

Performance Review

Discuss the aftereffects of negative reviews to stress how important it is that a reviewer have integrity. Points to consider include the following:

- Negative reviews can result in poor ticket sales or a lowered attendance at events or venues.
- Many publications consider it their responsibility to subscribers to publish critical or negative reviews. This calls into question the reviewer's independence.
- If a performance is not praised, some publications won't publish a review of it, which conveys the same message about the reviewer's autonomy.
- Future performances and bookings can be canceled, and the reputations of the performers can be damaged, even ruined, as the result of negative reviews.

504

Performance Review

Greg's school newspaper asked him to write a review about an African dance and drum troupe for the print edition of the paper and for the Web site. Greg took notes at the concert and then wrote about what he learned and about his reaction to the performance itself.

The **beginning** explains who the group is and gives the writer's reaction to the performance.

The **middle** describes the performers, the drums, and the sounds of the event.

The **ending** invites others to discover the group and learn about the special drums.

Feel the Rhythm

Now I know exactly what people mean when they say "you have to feel the rhythm." The pounding rhythm of beating drums and stomping feet went right down to my bones at the performance by African Steps. This dance and drum troupe from King High School shook the rafters in our auditorium during their Black History Month appearance on February 15.

African Steps weaves music and dance together seamlessly. The dancers wear ankle bells and shell bracelets so their movements become part of the pounding rhythm. The drummers' hands dance across the skins, flowing into the choreography.

If you think of drums as simple instruments, you would change your mind after hearing the complex interplay of the many different styles of drums African Steps uses—from pounding bass rhythms to more subtle, almost melodic tones. In introducing themselves, the drummers explained each drum's role. The djembe, for example, has a wide range of sound. It's a hollow drum made from a tree trunk and covered with goatskin. The drum hangs on straps from the musician's shoulders. It's played with the hands only. The kpanlogo gives a smooth but earthy tone.

The powerful, joyful rhythms had even the teachers in the back of the auditorium tapping their feet and swaying. This performance, and the explanations the dancers and drummers gave about the different pieces they performed, helped me appreciate African culture through music and dance. Don't miss the chance to share the experience.

Writing Guidelines Response to an Art Prompt

You may be asked to write a short essay in response to a prompt about art or music as a class assignment or as part of a test. Responding to a prompt allows you to express what you have learned about a specific work of art or style of music. Here are guidelines for responding to an art prompt.

Before you write . . .

- **Understand the prompt.** Read the prompt and focus on what you are asked to do. Should you explain, compare, describe, or persuade?

- **Gather your details.** If permitted, review your notes and research materials. Highlight or jot down important details. Note sources for quotations or facts. If you aren't permitted to use notes or research materials, jot down key facts that you remember about the topic.

- **Organize your details.** Check the prompt for clues that will help you organize your response. For example, if the prompt asks you to describe the jazz classic *Take Five* and discuss how improvisation reshapes the music, you might begin with a general description of the piece and then discuss specific musical themes that serve as springboards for improvisation. You could mention how specific instruments and performers develop the basic themes in creative variations.

As you write . . .

- **Write freely.** Use your notes as a guide and try to include all your main ideas. Many short responses are just one paragraph long. If your prompt calls for an essay, use a new paragraph for each main point.

After you've written a first draft . . .

- **Improve your writing.** Read your draft and cut any details that don't fit the prompt. Add information that will clarify your ideas or help answer the prompt. Make your response as complete as possible.

- **Improve your style.** Check your *word choice* and *sentence fluency* so that your response reads smoothly.

- **Check for conventions.** Look for errors in spelling, punctuation, and grammar.

Writing Guidelines
Response to an Art Prompt

Emphasize that more than with other types of prompts, an art prompt often asks the writer to include a personal opinion as part of the response. This usually means there is not necessarily a right or wrong answer, which on a test can be unsettling to some students.

Explain to students that the key to success in this situation is to
- state the opinion clearly,
- include accurate facts and background information, and
- use appropriate specialized language to convey knowledge and interest in the topic.

Students who keep detailed learning logs in art (see SE page 499) may have an advantage over other students in stating their opinion because they will have had more practice expressing their ideas in writing.

Response to an Art Prompt

After students **analyze the prompt** (*see below*) and read the response, ask them to focus on the writer's word choices. How does she use words to create an effective response? Possible responses:

- Even before she explicitly addresses her opinion in the last paragraph, the writer hints at her position in word choices such as *underestimate his technical skills* and *misinterpreted*.
- The writer establishes an informed tone through the use of specialized terms such as *form, technique, mass, expressionist, abstract,* and *cubism*.
- The writer maintains vigor and interest in her response by using strong, specific modifiers, nouns, and verbs—for example, *pure color; heavy, fluid pigments; obsessed;* and *emotional intensity.*

506

Response to an Art Prompt

In a two-part response, Jasmine discusses the style of artist Paul Cezanne.

Answer the following questions in one or more paragraphs: (1) Why did some consider Cezanne's work primitive? (2) Is the term appropriate in referring to Cezanne's work?

Response #1

Paul Cezanne, a nineteenth-century French painter, is sometimes called the father of modern art. At the time, both his critics and his supporters often used the term "primitive" to refer to his work.

Cezanne's use of pure color with simple brushstrokes and heavy, fluid pigments led many to underestimate his technical skills as an artist and compare his works to those of untutored, "primitive" artists. In addition, his figures were often distorted as he experimented with ways to put down on canvas what his eye was seeing. This approach was often misinterpreted as that of an artist lacking in basic drawing skills. He was obsessed with form and technique rather than with subject. As a result, the public often didn't understand his paintings.

Response #2

Cezanne's early experimental paintings may be called primitive in technique, but as he came closer and closer to putting down on canvas what he saw in nature, he began to use space, mass, and color in a very sophisticated way. Some of his early works, full of emotional intensity, laid the groundwork for the expressionist movement. By the late 1900s, his paintings became more abstract, with buildings and figures evolving into geometric forms. These works set the stage for cubism.

First, the writer explains who Cezanne was and what factors led some to define his work as primitive.

Then the writer gives specific examples.

Next, the writer argues that the term "primitive" isn't appropriate for most of the artist's work.

Try It!

Respond to a short-essay prompt your teacher will supply about a topic you are studying. Write a one- or two-paragraph answer.

Teaching Tip: Analyze the Prompt

Students will benefit from applying the STRAP questions. Have students work as a group to do this with the sample prompt.

- **Subject:** Paul Cezanne's work
- **Type:** one or more paragraphs
- **Role:** art student
- **Audience:** reader with knowledge of art/teacher
- **Purpose:** to explain (the term *primitive*) and persuade (express a personal opinion about whether Cezanne's work was primitive)

Writing in the Workplace

In the workplace, every bit of correspondence reflects the business and the professionalism of the people working there. Despite the changing landscape of business communication, good writing skills remain the bedrock for career success. Whatever the task—writing an e-mail message, a memo, a report, a presentation, or a proposal—it's important to communicate clearly and quickly in this environment.

Even if you remain a student for several more years, you'll find yourself using forms of workplace communication. You'll write letters and e-mail messages; you'll develop multimedia presentations; you'll create your résumé. In this chapter, some of the many forms of business writing are covered, along with tips and techniques to strengthen your skills.

- ▪ **Business Letter**
- ▪ **Writing Guidelines: Résumé**
- ▪ **Writing Guidelines: Proposal**
- ▪ **Writing Guidelines: Memo**
- ▪ **Writing Guidelines: E-Mail Message**
- ▪ **Writing Guidelines: News Release**

"In business you get what you want by giving other people what they want."

—Alice Foote MacDougall

Writing in the Workplace

Objectives

- • understand the form and content of a business letter
- • understand the contents and purpose of a letter of inquiry and a letter of application
- • apply the writing process and traits of writing to a résumé, a proposal, a memo, an e-mail message, and a news release

The lessons on the following pages provide samples of writing students might do in an effort to procure employment or in the actual workplace. Assigning these forms of writing will depend on

- ▪ the skill level of your students, and
- ▪ the writing goals of your school, district, or state.

Parts of a Business Letter

Review the parts of a letter listed on the page. Explain that these elements have been established by long-standing convention. Comment on the items listed, as appropriate.

- Inside address—Emphasize the importance of using the recipient's correct name and spelling it correctly. Using the wrong name or spelling may misdirect the letter or reflect so poorly on the writer that the letter is not taken seriously.
- Body—Note that the body of a business letter should get right to the point, stating the facts quickly, without a long introduction or creative language. This enables readers of the letter to understand quickly what's needed and shows that you respect their time.
- Notes—Explain that initials are only included as necessary.

Parts of a Business Letter

Writers use business letters to request information, apply for a job, or file a complaint. The basic format of an effective letter is similar whether it is sent through the regular mail or delivered via e-mail.

- The **heading** includes the writer's complete address, either on company stationery, in a computer template, or typed out manually. The heading also includes the day, month, and year. If the address is part of the letterhead, place only the date in the upper left corner.
- The **inside address** includes the recipient's name and complete address. If you're not sure who should receive the letter or how to correctly spell someone's name, you can call the company to ask. If a person's title is a single word or very short, include it on the same line as the name, preceded by a comma. If the title is longer, put it on a separate line under the name.
- The **salutation** is the greeting. For business letters, use a colon following the recipient's name, not a comma. Use *Mr.* or *Ms.* followed by the person's last name, unless you happen to be well acquainted with the person. Do not guess at whether a woman prefers *Miss* or *Mrs.* If the person's gender is not obvious from the name, one acceptable solution is to use the full name in the salutation. For example, *Dear Pat Johnson.* If you don't know the name of the person who will read your letter, use a salutation such as one of these:
  - Dear Manager:
  - Dear Sir or Madam:
  - Attention: Human Resources Department
  - Attention: Personnel Director
- The **body** is the main part of the letter. It is organized into three parts. The beginning states why you are writing, the middle provides the needed details, and the ending focuses on what should happen next. In a business letter, double-space between the paragraphs; do not indent. If the letter is longer than one page, on subsequent pages put the reader's name at the top left, the page number in the center, and the date at the right margin.
- The **complimentary closing** ends the message. Use *Sincerely* or *Yours truly*—followed by a comma. Capitalize only the first word.
- The **signature** makes the letter official. Leave four blank lines between the complimentary closing and your typed name. Write your signature in that space.
- The **notes** tell who authored the letter (uppercase initials and a colon), who typed the letter (lowercase initials), who received a copy (after *cc:*), and what enclosures are included (after *Enclosure* or *Encl:*).

Letter of Inquiry or Request

Plains Union High School offers advertising space in the programs they produce for the school's concerts and plays. Mandisa Kwafume, student liaison for the parents' Band Boosters Club, wrote this letter to solicit more advertising revenue from the business community. (The inside address would change depending on the business owner being contacted.)

Writing in the Workplace **509**

Workplace

Heading

Plains Union High School Band Boosters Club
676 Highway R
Dry Plains, TX 78112
October 6, 2011

Four to Seven Spaces

Inside address

Rex Neinheus
Area Aquatics
1322 Main Street
Dry Plains, TX 78113

Double Space

Salutation

Dear Mr. Neinheus:

Double Space

Body

The writer explains why she is writing, provides needed details, and suggests a next step.

I am writing on behalf of the Plains Union High School Band Boosters Club. Perhaps you are aware that the high school presents several concerts and plays throughout the year. Did you also know that many local businesses advertise in the programs for these events? Here is your opportunity to join them.

Purchasing an ad in one or more of the programs is a smart business move. The performers' family and friends—most of whom live in the area—read the programs and notice the businesses advertising in them. They'll make an effort to patronize a business that supports the school through advertising.

Enclosed you will find an insertion order for any size advertisement you care to place. You may provide camera-ready copy, or we will be happy to design something for you. Please be sure to indicate which program(s) you prefer for your ad; a checklist is provided.

Thank you for supporting the arts at Plains Union High School.

Complimentary closing

Double Space

Sincerely,

Signature

Mandisa Kwafume   Four Spaces

Mandisa Kwafume, Student Liaison

Double Space

Initials Copies Enclosure

MK: jb
cc: Ms. Felicia Goodman, President
Encl: insertion order

Letter of Inquiry or Request

Point out that many business letters use elements of persuasive writing (SE pages 219–273) by calling on the reader to take action based on information included in the letter. The purpose of a letter of inquiry is to persuade the reader to respond to the writer's questions or requests.

Point out that, unlike the conclusion of an essay, the last paragraph of a letter of inquiry or request does not need to restate the ideas expressed in the opening. Thanking the reader for her or his time and assistance is sufficient. The last paragraph (as in the sample on SE page 510) can also advise the reader as to when and where to contact the writer.

English Language Learners

Have students cover the sample letter with a sheet of paper, leaving only the margin notes/labels exposed. Then have them describe or give examples of what would appear in each part. Discuss any difficulties students have.

Letter of Application

Review the sample, commenting on the writer's application of the traits of writing.

- **Ideas**—In the introduction, the writer lists all enclosed documents. (This information is repeated in the notes.)
- **Organization**—The writer focuses each middle paragraph on one reason for his interest in the internship.
- **Voice**—The writer's voice becomes more personal in paragraph 3 (*myself included*). The writer states his personal interest in the internship.
- **Word Choice**—Encourage students to avoid overusing the first-person pronoun *I* at the start of sentences, a common issue in letters. The writer should rewrite several sentences to avoid this.
- **Sentence Fluency**—Note that the writer uses mostly long sentences—a natural result of trying to pack many details into a small space. Suggest that students try to vary sentence lengths in their letters.
- **Conventions**—There are **no errors** (*see below*).

510

Letter of Application

Lou Roberts wrote the following letter to apply for a summer science research internship position.

24 Hampshire Street
Skones, MT 59781
October 21, 2011

Brian Allman, Director
Office of Biomedical Studies
Medical College of Butte
540 Kings Row
Butte, MT 59702

Dear Mr. Allman:

*The **opening** introduces the writer as well as the purpose of the letter.*

Please find enclosed my official application for your High School Summer Research Internship Program, as well as the names and contact information for two references. I believe I am qualified for this internship and would love the opportunity to work with the mentors at the Medical College of Butte. Allow me to outline my research interests and career goals.

*The **middle** paragraphs discuss background, qualifications, and long-range goals.*

My interest in biochemistry and cell biology began in my high school science classes this past year. In these classes, we planned and executed several research experiments related to allergic reactions. Investigating the physiology behind these "overreactions" of the immune system proved fascinating.

This internship would be the first step in my ultimate goal of becoming an immunologist. I want to help people who suffer from allergies (myself included) to manage and treat their conditions. Although this career demands intensive training, I can't think of a better introduction to it than this internship.

*The **closing** adds information and thanks the reader.*

If you have any specific questions for me, please e-mail me at lrbts@email.net or call me at (406) 555-0515. Thank you for your consideration, and I hope to hear from you soon.

Sincerely,

Lou Roberts

Lou Roberts

Encl: application, references

Teaching Tip: No Errors

Emphasize the importance of finding and correcting all errors in a business letter. Allowing errors to go undetected could suggest to the recipient that the writer is careless or unprofessional. Encourage students always to proofread their letters carefully and to have at least one trusted reader review them before sending.

Suggest that one helpful way to proofread a piece is to read it from the last sentence to the first sentence. This can allow the reader to concentrate more fully on each sentence outside of its context.

Advanced Learners

Have students research summer internship positions available in your community, focusing on internships related to their desired career paths. Have students draft a letter of application for one position. After peer review, have students create and send their final drafts.

Preparing a Letter for Mailing

Letters sent through the mail will get to their destinations faster if they are properly addressed and stamped. Always include a ZIP code.

Addressing the Envelope

Place the return address in the upper left corner, the destination address in the center, and the correct postage in the upper right corner. Some word processing programs will automatically format the return and destination addresses.

LOU ROBERTS
24 HAMPSHIRE STREET
SKONES MT 59781

MR BRIAN ALLMAN
OFFICE OF BIOMEDICAL STUDIES
MEDICAL COLLEGE OF BUTTE
540 KINGS ROW
BUTTE MT 59702

There are two acceptable forms for addressing the envelope: the traditional form and the form preferred by the postal service.

Traditional Form	Postal Service Form
Liam O'Donnell	LIAM O'DONNELL
Macalester College	MACALESTER COLLEGE
Admissions Office	ADMISSIONS OFFICE
1600 N. Grand Ave.	1600 N GRAND AVE
St. Paul, MN 55105-1801	ST PAUL MN 55105-1801

Following U.S. Postal Service Guidelines

The official United States Postal Service guidelines are available at any post office or online at www.usps.org.

- Capitalize everything in the address and leave out commas and periods.
- Use the list of common state and street abbreviations found in the *National ZIP Code Directory* or on page **660** of this book.
- Use numbers rather than words for numbered streets (for example, 42ND AVE or 9TH AVE NW).
- If you know the ZIP + 4 code, use it.

Preparing a Letter for Mailing

Discuss different methods for addressing envelopes for business letters.

- Most word-processing programs have special templates that allow users to input addresses and print them out on envelopes. If possible, show students how this is done, using a class computer and printer.
- Alternatively, students could print the addresses on labels and stick them onto the envelope. Again, special templates for this are available with many word-processing programs.
- Finally, using a typewriter is a quick way to address a single envelope.

Writing Guidelines

Résumé

Many students will already have created a résumé. If possible, have them bring these to class so that they can work on updating and improving them as they follow the guidelines.

Explain that students will usually have to write a *cover letter* to accompany the résumé they send to a potential employer. The cover letter can be very much like the letter of application on SE page 510. In the cover letter, students should

- note that they are enclosing a résumé,
- state the position they are applying for,
- explain how they found out about the organization or the job,
- give a brief account of their qualifications (dealt with in greater detail on the résumé), and
- add any other brief, relevant details that give the reader a sense of their personality and goals.

Writing Guidelines Résumé

The purpose of a résumé is to interest an employer so he or she will call you for an interview. Instead of simply telling about yourself in a letter, use a special résumé format to highlight your skills, knowledge, work experience, and education, especially as they relate to the position for which you're applying. Prepare a basic version of your résumé. Then, depending upon the requirements of each position, customize your objective and your abilities to match the employer's expectations.

Prewriting

- **Think about your abilities,** experiences, and accomplishments.
- **Gather details** that will create a complete picture of you. Include classes or training taken outside of school, achievements, and other experience such as volunteer work, club duties, and so on.

Writing

- **Use a traditional résumé format** and organize the information into these parts:
  - Personal contact information
  - Objective
  - Qualifications
  - Specific work experience
  - Education
  - References (Be sure to get permission from each person you wish to use as a reference. It's a good idea to let them know each time you apply for a job so they will be prepared for a phone call.)

Revising

- **Improve your writing** by asking yourself these questions: *Have I included specific, accurate, and complete information? Have I given the most important information first? Have I used a business-like writing style? Have I used words appropriate to the reader? Have I defined any unfamiliar technical terms?*

Editing

- **Check for errors** in punctuation, mechanics, and grammar.
- **Ask someone else** to look over your résumé as well.

Publishing

- **Use text features** such as boldface, columns, bullets, and white space to make your résumé attractive and readable.

Struggling Learners

Students may have difficulty identifying which of their abilities and personal experiences are appropriate for a résumé and the type of work they are looking for. If necessary, schedule individual conferences with students to help them focus their list.

Advanced Learners

Have students compile a list of three individuals they could use as references. Have students contact each person to obtain permission for inclusion in a reference list. Encourage students to keep a record of vital information about each reference, such as the person's preference for form of address (title) and means of contact (home and/or business address, home and/or cell phone number, e-mail address). Remind students to thank their references and to advise and update them each time they apply for a job.

Résumé

A strong résumé isn't generic. Here is how one student presented himself in his search for summer employment on a landscaping crew.

The **beginning** provides contact information and the objective.

The **middle** lists key details.

The **ending** notes that references are available.

Workplace

Delmer Sobodian

250 Lowe Avenue • Sherwood Heights, MI 49065
Phone 517-555-1662   E-mail delsob@themailstop.com

Objective: Seeking full-time summer employment on a
landscaping crew.

Qualifications:
- Experienced with landscaping materials and plants
- Team worker
- Fast learner
- Good physical condition

Experience: *May–October and winter holiday season 2009*

Garcia's Gardens & Gifts
Part-time yard worker and cashier. Became
familiar with different kinds of plants, trees,
and shrubs and their care.

October 2008 – March 2009

Shop A Lot supermarket
Part-time stocker and cashier. Often worked
with heavy loads.

Education: Will graduate from Cayman High School in
June; plan to attend Tuyo Community College
this fall to work on a degree in horticulture.

Member of my school's chapter of the National
FFA Organization; assisted in yearly sale of
native-species plants to raise funds for our
chapter.

References: Available upon request.

Résumé

Explain that students should try to keep their résumé to a single page because it enables any prospective employer to see their qualifications and experience at a glance.

Emphasize that students should always take care to be precise and succinct; they should never add unnecessary words. Point out, too, that there is almost an absence of voice in a résumé: a résumé is an objective, concise listing of qualifications. Also, point out that an e-mail address is not required. They may include one if they open their e-mail regularly. Have students note the strategies the writer used in the sample to keep it concise.

- The writer's contact information (address, phone, e-mail) is presented in two lines instead of four.
- The writer purposely uses sentence fragments instead of full sentences.
- The writer leaves out small words, such as articles, that aren't needed for clarity (*assisted in yearly sale*).
- The writer has set margins narrower than for most other documents; this enables him to fit the information on the page.

Struggling Learners

Have students complete their résumé independently. Then they should ask a partner or you to check the organization, the information, and their wording, using the sample on SE page 513 as a guide.

Writing Guidelines

Proposal

Point out that the heading given under Writing is essentially a memo heading (see SE pages 516–517). A writer would use this format when the recipient of the proposal works within the same organization or is already expecting the proposal. Otherwise, the writer would appropriately omit the memo-style heading, give the proposal a title, and submit it along with a cover letter that explains

- who the writer is,
- how the writer heard of the project,
- the writer's interest in the work, and
- that a proposal is enclosed.

514

Writing Guidelines Proposal

People write proposals to fix problems, address specific needs, or make improvements. A proposal may be a simple letter suggesting the addition of a new microwave to the lunchroom or a complex report recommending establishment of a company day-care center.

Prewriting

- **Consider your audience** by thinking about who will receive your proposal and what you want that person to understand.
- **Determine your purpose** and jot down what you want your proposal to accomplish. What action are you proposing?
- **Gather details** based on what your reader needs to know in order to make a decision. Gather necessary supporting information.

Writing

- **Prepare a heading** that includes the following information:

To:	The reader's name
From:	Your first and last name
Date:	The month, day, and year
Subject:	A concise summary of the proposal

- **Organize the body** into three parts:

Beginning:	State what you are proposing and why.
Middle:	Provide details such as financial costs and other required resources. Write out key points and information supporting them. Show how the action will benefit the organization.
Ending:	Summarize what actions need to be taken next or what recommendations you are making.

Revising

- **Improve your writing.** Ask yourself these questions: *Is my proposal clear and logical? Is my purpose obvious? Have I provided sufficient information and detail to convince the reader that action is needed? Do I have an effective beginning, middle, and ending? Do I provide information to support my recommendations? Have I used a positive, persuasive tone? Have I explained any unfamiliar terms? Does my proposal read smoothly?*

Editing

- **Check for conventions.** Be sure punctuation, grammar, and mechanics are correct.
- **Prepare a final copy.** Proofread the final copy of your proposal.

Proposal

Alec Guiterrez works part-time for Roccoco's, a local restaurant. He drafted this proposal to create a Web site for the restaurant.

> The **beginning** states the rationale.

To: Juliet Barnes

From: Alec Guiterrez

Date: May 20, 2011

Subject: Web site for Roccoco's

Rationale:
More and more, people who need information about a place of business turn to the Internet. Without a Web site, a restaurant like Roccoco's is missing out on business. People looking on the Net for a place to eat won't find out about us. People who see our ad in the papers don't have a Web address for more information.

> The **middle** provides important details.

We can boost our credibility—and our business—with a Web site that I am willing to create. The restaurant's financial outlay will be minimal. I ask only that you pay me my normal wage for the time I spend on it. Other than that expense, there will be an annual charge for a domain name and a monthly charge for an Internet service provider to host the site. The following are approximate costs:

Initial outlay

Site creation: 8 hours @ $6.75	$54
Domain name registration:	12
	$66 total

Monthly maintenance

Site maintenance: 1.5 hours @ $6.75	$10
ISP hosting:	10
	$20 total

> The **ending** makes recommendations.

Recommendations:
As you can see, this is a very reasonable cost for the benefits. With a presence on the Web, Roccoco's can easily inform customers of our location, highlight specials, and offer coupons.

Ms. Barnes, I am sure this is the right direction for Roccoco's. I designed my own Web site and would like the opportunity to create one for Roccoco's. I am happy to answer any questions you may have.

Workplace

Proposal

Explain that many proposals in the workplace are presented in a multimedia presentation. Challenge students to think of additional elements that could be used, along with the basic written proposal, to make a persuasive case for this particular project. Answers might include the following:

- Show the Web site the student created for himself to convince the restaurant owner of the high quality of his work.
- Show other restaurant Web sites as examples of what could be done for her business.
- Display any other relevant designs the student has created (these might include sketches).
- Present research statistics about how Web sites improve sales for restaurants, and create charts to demonstrate this.

✱ For more about preparing and giving multimedia presentations, see SE pages 448–449.

Writing Guidelines

Memo

Emphasize that memos are used *within an organization*. Information sent to recipients outside of the organization should always be formatted as a business letter (see SE page 508).

Discuss the word *memo,* which is short for *memorandum,* Latin for "to be remembered." When the writing is clear, succinct, and error free, the recipient is more likely to remember the contents and respond promptly, if necessary. In most instances, memos should be no longer than a page.

Writing Guidelines Memo

Memos are short messages in which you ask and answer questions, describe procedures, give short reports, and remind others about deadlines and meetings. Memos are important to the flow of information within any organization. Many routine memos in schools and workplaces are distributed electronically, with hard copies posted on bulletin boards or sent by interoffice mail.

Prewriting

- **Consider your audience** by thinking about who will receive your memo and why.
- **Determine your purpose** and jot down your reason for writing the memo.
- **Gather necessary details** based on what your reader needs to know.

Writing

- **Prepare the heading** by typing "Memo" and centering it. Use a preprinted memo form or include a heading that contains the following information:

  Date: The month, day, and year
  To: The reader's name
  From: Your first and last name (You may initial it before sending.)
  Subject: The memo's topic in a clear, simple statement

- **Organize the body** into three parts:

  Beginning: State why you are writing the memo.
  Middle: Provide all the necessary details. Consider putting the most important points in a list rather than writing them out.
  Ending: Focus on what happens next—the action or response you would like from the reader or readers.

Revising

- **Improve your writing** by asking yourself these questions related to *ideas, organization, voice, word choice,* and *sentence fluency: Is my topic clear? Is my purpose obvious? Do I have an effective beginning, middle, and ending? Have I used a positive, friendly tone? Have I explained any unfamiliar terms? Does my memo read smoothly?*

Editing

- **Check for conventions.** Correct any errors in punctuation, grammar, and mechanics.
- **Prepare a final copy** of your memo and proofread it before distributing it.

English Language Learners

Point out the relationship of the word *memo* to the words *remember, memory, memoir,* and *memorial.* Explain that one purpose of a memo is to remind people in the workplace of meetings.

Memo

Ben Braun, an assistant to the personnel director, typed up this memo about his company's monthly staff improvement meetings.

The heading identifies the date, recipients, sender, and subject.

The beginning states why you are writing.

The middle shares the necessary details.

The ending makes a call for action.

Memo

Date: October 22, 2011

To: Inter-Tech Staff

From: Ben Braun, Assistant to the Personnel Director

Subject: New Technology

Our next staff meeting will be held on Thursday, November 18, at 9:00 a.m. in the new training center.

The guest at that meeting will be Dr. G. F. Hollis, a professor at City Technical College. She will speak on the latest technology and how we can expect it to affect us and our work.

Dr. Hollis is planning a winter-term training program that will cover all facets of office technology and communication. Those attending the meeting will receive additional information on the program.

Please sign up with me before the end of the day on Tuesday, November 6, if you plan to attend the meeting.

► Try It!

Draft a memo to a group of which you are a member. Follow the guidelines on the previous page and the model above.

Memo

Ask students to look for other examples of memos and bring them in to share with the class. If possible, have them obtain examples from family members who send or receive memos at work, as well as school-related memos or memos from extracurricular organizations.

Students may also be interested in seeking out some of the many historical memos available online. A large number of letters and memoranda related to events in modern U.S. history are available through the National Security Archive maintained by George Washington University (www.gwu.edu/~nsarchiv).

Writing Guidelines

E-Mail Message

Nearly all students will be familiar with e-mail and will use it primarily for casual online exchanges with friends and family. Explain that for business or other professional purposes, students should compose e-mails as carefully as they would a business letter.

Focus on writing the subject line of the e-mail. Emphasize that it should be

- brief (ideally no more than three or four words) yet
- descriptive of the contents (a subject such as *hello*, for example, would give the recipient no clue to the contents).

Discuss why a clear, concise subject line is important.

- It is easier for recipients who don't know the sender to recognize that the e-mail is legitimate and not spam (unsolicited commercial e-mail).
- A well-written subject line helps to clarify the writer's purpose, priority, and subject matter.
- It helps both sender and recipient to **file the e-mail** (*see below*).

518

Writing Guidelines E-Mail Message

Electronic mail is a fast, convenient way to communicate in the workplace. It saves paper and allows many people to share information simultaneously. Increasingly, e-mail is used not only within the office, but also to communicate with customers and business partners.

Prewriting

- **Consider your audience** and your purpose for sending the message.
- **Gather details** based on what the reader needs to know.

Writing

- **Organize the body** into three parts:

  Beginning: Complete your e-mail header, making sure your subject line is clear. Expand on the subject in the first sentences of your message. Get right to the point.

  Middle: Supply all the details of your message while keeping your paragraphs short. Double-space between paragraphs. Try to limit your message to one or two screens and use numbers, lists, and headings to organize your thoughts.

  Ending: Let your reader know what follow-up action is needed and when; then end politely.

Revising

- **Improve your writing** by asking yourself these questions: *Is my message accurate, complete, and clear? Do I have an effective beginning, middle, and ending? Is my tone appropriate for the topic and the reader?*
- **Improve your style.** Ask yourself these questions related to *word choice* and *sentence fluency*: *Have I used clear, everyday language? Does my message read smoothly?*

Editing

- **Check for conventions.** Correct any errors in grammar, punctuation, and mechanics before sending your e-mail.

Tip

- Never use all capital letters in an e-mail message; people feel you are shouting at them.
- Follow grammar conventions.
- Proofread. Because e-mail is so fast, it's easy to dash off a message and overlook a typo or a missing word.

Teaching Tip: File E-Mail

Emphasize the importance of devising a system for organizing e-mail. Discuss strategies for creating and maintaining files, and encourage students to experiment with their e-mail programs to discover other ideas. Helpful ideas include the following:

- Create project and personal folders for mail they wish to keep, and move e-mails from the Inbox to the appropriate folders as soon as possible.
- Create folders called *Immediate Response, Answer Soon,* and *Consider.* Move any message requiring a response to one of those three folders. Regularly check the response folders to answer mail as needed.
- Use spam filters to prevent junk e-mail from cluttering the Inbox.

E-Mail Message

Writing in the Workplace 519

Following an unpleasant experience at a local automobile dealership, Emiko Tikaram decided to contact the manufacturer directly to voice her concerns. She copied the general manager of the dealership, as well.

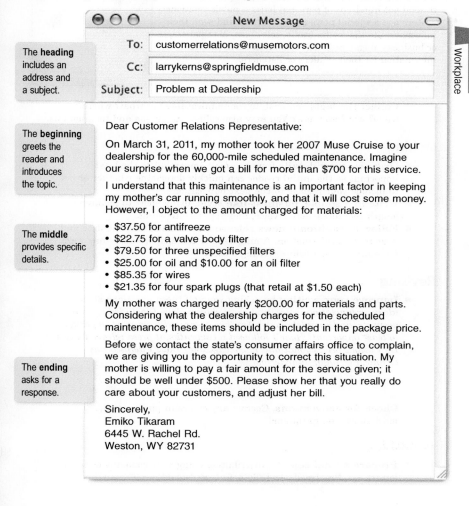

The heading includes an address and a subject.

The beginning greets the reader and introduces the topic.

The middle provides specific details.

The ending asks for a response.

Workplace

To: customerrelations@musemotors.com

Cc: larrykerns@springfieldmuse.com

Subject: Problem at Dealership

Dear Customer Relations Representative:

On March 31, 2011, my mother took her 2007 Muse Cruise to your dealership for the 60,000-mile scheduled maintenance. Imagine our surprise when we got a bill for more than $700 for this service.

I understand that this maintenance is an important factor in keeping my mother's car running smoothly, and that it will cost some money. However, I object to the amount charged for materials:

- $37.50 for antifreeze
- $22.75 for a valve body filter
- $79.50 for three unspecified filters
- $25.00 for oil and $10.00 for an oil filter
- $85.35 for wires
- $21.35 for four spark plugs (that retail at $1.50 each)

My mother was charged nearly $200.00 for materials and parts. Considering what the dealership charges for the scheduled maintenance, these items should be included in the package price.

Before we contact the state's consumer affairs office to complain, we are giving you the opportunity to correct this situation. My mother is willing to pay a fair amount for the service given; it should be well under $500. Please show her that you really do care about your customers, and adjust her bill.

Sincerely,
Emiko Tikaram
6445 W. Rachel Rd.
Weston, WY 82731

E-Mail Message

Point out that the sample e-mail is a letter of complaint (see SE page 495). Ask students to identify how the writer uses the traits of writing effectively, and to suggest improvements.

Ideas—The writer explains her position clearly and uses details to support it. In addition, she could have included

- her mother's name, to help the recipient locate the records;
- a street address, to give the recipient another way to contact her; and
- the retail prices of all materials (except *unspecified filters*), to reinforce further her argument.

Organization—The beginning, middle, and ending are clearly defined. The writer uses a list to make the point concisely.

Voice & Word Choice—The voice is polite and serious. The writer does not use inflammatory language.

Sentence Fluency—The writer varies her sentences to hold the recipient's attention.

Conventions—The writer uses standard grammar, capitalization, and spelling rules. There are no errors.

Advanced Learners

Students commonly ignore grammar conventions when composing personal e-mail or text messages. Reinforce this difference by having students write an e-mail to a friend that explains an experience similar to the one described in the sample message. Afterward, have them compare the contents of their personal e-mail and the sample e-mail. How are they similar? Where do they differ? Have students discuss why it is important to use standard English when writing e-mails in the academic setting or workplace.

Writing Guidelines

News Release

After discussing the page, have students work in small groups to come up with several upcoming school events about which they would want to inform the public. Examples might include a class car wash, a musical or theatrical event, or college recruiting sessions.

Have students collect all the pertinent facts related to the event. Then have groups assign different members to complete the various tasks discussed on the page: writing, revising, editing, and publishing.

Students can explore different media outlets, including the school bulletin, local newspaper, or local radio station, as recipients for their news releases.

520

Writing Guidelines **News Release**

A business may want to provide information to potential clients and an organization may want to inform the general public. Because it isn't practical to send out hundreds of personal letters, public-relations writers use a special news release format and send their information to the media (radio, television, newspapers, or business magazines). The media, in turn, publish the information for their readers or listeners.

Prewriting

- **Collect the facts** you wish to communicate—who? what? where? when? why? and how? You may also collect quotations and testimonials.

Writing

- **Organize your details** from the most important to the least important so the initial reader can quickly determine whether or not to include your release in the next publication.
- **Write in a simple, business-like style,** using short to medium-length sentences, active voice, and appropriate words.
- **Follow a traditional news release format** including the date and your contact information. A magazine or newspaper editor may want more information before writing a story.

Revising

- **Improve your writing** by asking yourself these questions about *ideas, organization, voice,* and *word choice*: *Have I included specific, accurate, and complete facts? Are they organized from most important to least important? Have I followed a conventional press release format? Do I sound professional and knowledgeable? Have I defined any technical or unfamiliar terms?*

Editing

- **Check for conventions.** Correct any errors in punctuation, mechanics, and grammar.

Publishing

- **Prepare a final copy** for distribution using your company or school letterhead. Proofread carefully before you send it.

News Release

Andy Frick prepared this news release to inform area readers and listeners of his high school's spring jazz concert featuring a special guest.

The heading identifies key information.

The beginning identifies the topic.

The middle provides additional details.

The ending gives purchasing information.

Writing in the Workplace **521**

Workplace

Orleans High School
4500 East Field Drive • Hunt, NV 89035
(705) 555-8876   Fax (705) 555-8880

For Immediate Release   Contact:
February 24, 2011   Andy Frick, (705) 555-2560

HUNT, NV—Orleans High School presents its annual spring jazz concert on March 18 with a special guest appearance by renowned recording artist Lucy Kane. The concert at the school's auditorium, 4500 East Field Drive, will also feature the Voices of Jazz choral group and the Orleans Jazz Band. The theme of the concert will be "Fresh as a Spring Daisy."

Saxophonist Lucy Kane has performed nationally as a solo artist and as a member of several jazz ensembles for nine years. She states, "Whenever I am approached to perform at a high school, I make a special effort to appear. It's so important for students to see what a career in music can be."

Art Rankin, head of the music department at Orleans, says, "We were thrilled when Ms. Kane indicated she was available. Jazz fans throughout the region always enjoy her shows."

Tickets for the concert are available at the school; ticket prices are $10.00 in advance and $12.00 the day of the show. Proceeds will go toward the Orleans High School music department's efforts to purchase a new grand piano.

END

News Release

Draw students' attention to the opening paragraph of the sample, and remind them of the instruction on the previous page to begin with the most important information. Emphasize that for a news release, the most important information consists of all the details readers will need should they decide to attend the event.

Note also that summarizing the opening paragraph in the closing paragraph is not necessary. It is best to avoid repetition of any kind in a news release for two reasons: first, the emphasis is on conveying information in an economical way, and second, the summary could introduce accidental errors.

Finally, point out the word *END* at the bottom of the page, and explain that this is standard journalistic practice for indicating the end of the news release. (Some papers use other codes such as *-30-* or ###. Students may wish to investigate their local paper's practice.)

English Language Learners

Some students will benefit from additional discussion of the purpose and form of a news release. Have students copy a news release about a favorite sports figure, celebrity, or television show posted on the Internet. Then have them label the heading, beginning, middle, and ending of the document. On the back of the paper, have students write three questions that can be answered by reading the release. Have students trade papers, read the news release, and answer each other's questions.

The Tools of Learning Overview

Common Core Standards Focus

> **Writing 10:** Write routinely over extended time frames (time for research, reflection, and revision) and shorter time frames (a single sitting or a day or two) for a range of tasks, purposes, and audiences.

Skills

- listening and speaking in class
- taking class notes, reading notes, meeting minutes
- reading critically to gain a clearer understanding of reading assignments
- summarizing and paraphrasing

Tools and Techniques

- note taking
- SQ3R

Test Taking

- test preparation
- four basic types of objective tests (true/false, matching, multiple-choice, and fill-in-the-blanks)
- essay tests
- standardized tests
- exit and entrance exams

Technology Connections

 Write Source Online
www.hmheducation.com/writesource

- **Net-text**
- **Bookshelf**
- **GrammarSnap**
- **Portfolio**
- **Essay Scoring**
- **Writing Network features**
- **File Cabinet**

 Interactive Whiteboard Lessons

Unit Pacing

Listening and Speaking: 25 minutes

This section instructs students on how to improve their listening and speaking skills in the classroom. Following are some of the topics that are covered:

- Knowing why you're listening
- Listening for the facts
- Putting the speaker's ideas into your own words
- Using basic strategies to become a better speaker
- Following basic guidelines to carry on productive discussions

Taking Notes: 45–60 minutes

This section has a dual goal: to help students recognize the value of good note taking and to help them learn how to take good notes. Following are some of the topics that are covered:

- Following guidelines for taking clear, organized notes
- Setting up and reviewing notes
- Taking reading notes
- Taking meeting minutes

Critical Reading: 90 minutes

In this section students are shown how to read critically in order to understand reading assignments and tests. Following are some of the topics that are covered:

- Surveying the reading
- Questioning the material
- Reading and reciting the information out loud
- Reviewing the material
- Reading fiction and poetry

Summarizing and Paraphrasing: 1.5 hours

This section shows students how to write concise summaries and accurate paraphrases. Following are some of the topics that are covered:

- Understanding what an effective summary includes
- Following guidelines for summarizing an article
- Understanding how a paraphrase differs from a summary
- Following strategies for paraphrasing a paragraph

Taking Tests: 1–1.5 hours

This section helps students understand the test-taking process. Following are some of the topics that are covered:

- Following a test-prep cycle
- Tips to use when taking a test
- How to take objective tests (true/false, matching, multiple-choice, fill-in-the-blanks)
- Understanding essay test prompts
- Understanding the kinds of questions on standardized tests

Taking Exit and Entrance Exams: 1–1.5 hours

This section helps students prepare for high-stakes writing exams. Following are some of the topics that are covered:

- Samples questions for practice in checking for conventions, revising sentences, revising paragraphs, and editing
- Responding to writing prompts
- Using the STRAP questions to analyze a prompt
- Budgeting time for on-demand writing

Teacher's Notes for the Tools of Learning

This overview of the tools of learning includes some specific teaching suggestions for the unit. The description of each chapter will help you decide which parts of the unit to teach.

Writing Focus

Listening and Speaking (pages 523–526)

Some students have trouble listening in class, while others have trouble speaking. Both listening and speaking in class are valuable communication tools for school and the workplace.

Taking Notes (pages 527–532)

Students risk losing a lot of information if they don't learn how to take good notes. A good note-taking system is important as well, so that facts are easily retrieved. Notes for class, reading notes, and minutes of meetings are modeled in this chapter.

Critical Reading (pages 533–542)

Reading makes up a major portion of home assignments, and students need strategies to succeed as readers. The SQ3R technique is explained to help students comprehend nonfiction texts. Special tips are also given for those reading fiction and poetry.

Summarizing and Paraphrasing (pages 543–550)

Students will, at times, need to summarize and paraphrase for research papers and essay tests. The chapter includes material so that students can practice both of these types of writing.

Taking Tests (pages 551–560)

Even in 12th grade there are a surprising number of students who struggle through tests because they don't know the best way to approach exams. This chapter includes sample tests and explains how to deal with each kind (objective and essay).

Taking Exit and Entrance Exams (pages 561–575)

This chapter helps students successfully handle an exit or entrance exam by telling them what to expect and giving them helpful strategies and techniques to use. A special section on time management is also included.

Academic Vocabulary

Read aloud the academic terms, as well as the descriptions and questions. Model for students how to read one question and answer it. Have partners monitor their understanding and seek clarification of the terms by working through the meanings and questions together.

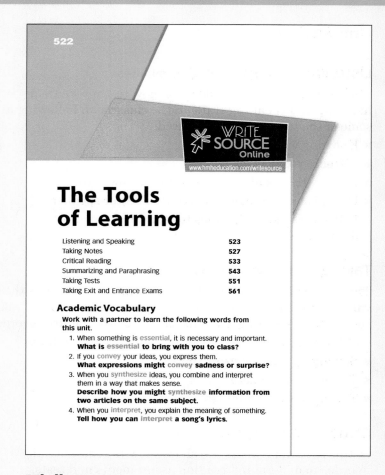

Academic Vocabulary

Work with a partner to learn the following words from this unit.

1. When something is essential, it is necessary and important.
   What is essential to bring with you to class?
2. If you convey your ideas, you express them.
   What expressions might convey sadness or surprise?
3. When you synthesize ideas, you combine and interpret them in a way that makes sense.
   Describe how you might synthesize information from two articles on the same subject.
4. When you interpret, you explain the meaning of something.
   Tell how you can interpret a song's lyrics.

Minilessons

Hear Ye, Hear Ye . . .   Listening and Speaking

- **LISTEN** as your teacher reads a brief news story from a newspaper, a news magazine, or the Internet. **WRITE** down answers for the 5 W's and H. **DISCUSS** the answers in class.

Design Clues   Critical Reading

- **PAGE** through your *Write Source* text. **IDENTIFY** elements that help the reader to read and understand the text (titles, headings, subheadings, margin notes, graphics, bulleted lists, color coding, icons, and so on).

Capturing Voice   Summarizing and Paraphrasing

- **PARAPHRASE** the persuasive paragraph "Control the Pet Population" on SE page 583. **MAINTAIN** the author's voice.

"I loved tests . . ."   Taking Tests

- **FREEWRITE** in response to the quotation by Suzanne Farrell on SE page 551. **EXPLAIN** your current attitude toward tests. Then **CONSIDER** how you could cultivate more of Ms. Farrell's attitude.

Listening and Speaking

Strong listening and speaking skills are the essence of effective communication. As you mature, you probably find these skills gaining importance in your everyday life. Good speaking skills allow you to communicate clearly with teachers, classmates, bosses, and coworkers. Solid listening skills help you understand lectures and take good notes.

The groundwork of learning is listening. It requires you to synthesize a speaker's main ideas and to evaluate and organize information. Speaking is vital, too. With it, you can convey ideas and feelings, explain, argue, persuade, inform, and even entertain. In this chapter, you will learn to improve your listening and speaking skills. As they improve, so will your ability to communicate effectively.

- **Listening in Class**
- **Speaking in Class**
- **A Closer Look at Listening and Speaking**

"I like to listen. I have learned a great deal from listening carefully. Most people never listen."

—Ernest Hemingway

Listening and Speaking

Objectives
- learn how to become a better listener in class
- develop skills for participating in a group
- improve listening and speaking skills

Discuss the Ernest Hemingway quotation that appears at the bottom of the page.
- Do you agree or disagree with Hemingway's statement that most people never listen? Explain.
- Do you think you're a good listener? Why or why not?
- What are some obstacles to your being a good listener?
- What responsibilities do speakers have to their listening audience?
- What responsibilities do listeners have?

Listening in Class

Ask students to explain the difference between hearing and listening. (Students should understand that hearing refers to the physical act of taking in sound through the ears while listening involves thinking about what is heard for the purpose of understanding.)

Distribute photocopies of the reproducible 5 W's chart (TE page 822). Suggest that students use the graphic organizer to identify important facts and details the next time they have to take notes in class.

If possible, for the **Try It!** activity, play a video of a television documentary and have students take notes. Afterward, schedule individual **writing conferences** (*see below*) to review students' notes and discuss ways to improve their note-taking techniques.

524

Listening in Class

To listen well, you need to go beyond just "hearing" what a speaker says. Listening takes practice and effort. These tips will help you become a better listener.

- **Know why you're listening.** What is the speaker's message? Will there be an exam? Are you being asked to complete an assignment?
- **Listen for facts.** The 5W and H questions—*who? what? when? where? why?* and *how?*—will help you identify the most important information.
- **Take notes.** As you hear important information, write it in your notebook. Also write down questions and comments in the margins. Review and complete your notes as soon after class as possible.
- **Put the speaker's ideas into your own words.** Paraphrase the speaker's key points when you take notes. Add your own comments.

Try It!

Practice your listening skills by taking notes in class or while viewing a documentary on television. Put the speaker's ideas into your own words. Use the margins in your notebook to add your questions and comments.

Multiple Intelligences

- Theory created by Harvard Prof. Howard Gardner — *Are there more faculties than just these 8?*
- A person's intelligence is made up of multiple <u>faculties</u> that can work alone or together.
- Faculties = inherent powers & abilities. — *Does everyone have all 8 faculties?*
- Gardner's 8 Faculties (a.k.a. "Intelligences"): Musical, Bodily-Kinesthetic, Logical-Mathematical, Linguistic, Spatial, Interpersonal, Intrapersonal, Naturalist. — *See handout for definitions*
- They provide 8 different pathways to teaching and learning. — *and examples of faculties.*

Teaching Tip: Writing Conferences

Whether students are going on to college or transitioning straight into the business world, many of them will benefit from knowing how to take readable, useful notes. Schedule one-on-one meetings with individual students to review their notes and to help them determine where they should focus their efforts for improvement. Use the notes from the **Try It!** activity or samples of notes students have taken in other classes to evaluate whether students can

- identify important information,
- summarize and paraphrase (see SE page 543–550), and
- ask relevant questions and make thoughtful comments about the material.

Encourage students to review their notes frequently, not only for the purpose of studying but also to evaluate whether the notes are actually helping them to learn.

Speaking in Class

Speaking in a group discussion is an important skill to master. A meaningful discussion depends on cooperation. These basic strategies will help you and your classmates become better speakers.

Before you speak . . .

- **Listen** carefully and take notes.
- **Think** about what others are saying.
- **Wait** until it's your turn to speak.
- **Plan** how you can add something positive to the discussion.

As you speak . . .

- **Use a loud, clear voice.**
- **Avoid repeating** what's already been said.
- **Support your ideas** with examples, facts, or anecdotes.
- **Maintain eye contact** with others in the group or class.

Tip

- Focus your comments on ideas, not on personalities.
- Ask meaningful questions.
- When necessary, summarize specific ideas brought up in the discussion.
- Mention another person's comments and expand on them constructively.

Try It!

Exercise your group discussion skills by taking part in the following "panel discussion" activity.

1. As a class, brainstorm discussion topics from current events or as directed by your teacher. Make a list of the topics.
2. Divide into groups (panels) of four or five. Each panel chooses one topic from the list and takes a turn discussing the topic for 10 to 15 minutes, with the class acting as an audience. There is no preparation time; participants should speak spontaneously about the issue.
3. Following each discussion, the audience analyzes the discussion based on the strategies on this page.

Speaking in Class

Learning to trust one's ideas, opinions, and judgments may be the biggest task that students face in becoming better speakers. In fact, a lack of confidence prevents some students from speaking during group discussions.

- Remind students that everyone should be given time to form their ideas and speak without interruption, and that everyone's ideas should be respected.
- During small-group discussions, group members should appoint a moderator who encourages everyone to contribute to the discussion and ensures that no one student dominates the discussion.
- For the **Try It!** activity, encourage total participation by checking that each panel chooses a topic that is familiar to everyone on the panel.

English Language Learners

In order to improve listening and speaking skills in a small-group setting, students may benefit from repeating what has already been said, as this practice reinforces both concepts and language. Form a small group and lead a discussion on a topic that students can easily grasp. Have students contribute to the discussion by either presenting a new idea or repeating an idea that has already been presented. They can try to repeat the idea word for word and then restate the idea in their own words.

Struggling Learners

Modify the **Try It!** activity for those who have difficulty speaking extemporaneously. Read aloud a short current-events article. Give students a few minutes to think about what you have read. Then reread the article and discuss any questions they have before asking them to state their opinion or share an insight.

A Closer Look at Listening and Speaking

While students do not have to sit "at attention" during class, slouching, slumping, or turning away from the speaker are signs that they are no longer listening. Tell students to maintain good posture when they listen and speak.

Encourage students to do some research before class to identify some of the greatest speakers of all time and to discover what traits made them great communicators. Invite students to share what they learn with the class. In addition to the guidelines for good speakers listed, students may discover that good speakers

- know what their audience cares about and wants to hear,
- do not hesitate to give the audience something new or controversial to think about,
- limit main ideas to three or four so that the audience doesn't get bored or overwhelmed,
- leave the audience with a challenge or new thought, and
- have prepared and practiced their speech.

526

A Closer Look at Listening and Speaking

Improving your listening and speaking skills will help you increase your confidence and effectiveness as a communicator. Follow these basic guidelines to carry on productive conversations and discussions.

Good listeners . . .	Good speakers . . .
<ul><li>think about what the speaker is saying.</li><li>stay focused so that they are prepared to respond thoughtfully.</li><li>pay attention to the speaker's tone of voice, gestures, and facial expressions.</li><li>interrupt only when necessary to ask questions.</li></ul>	<ul><li>speak loudly and clearly.</li><li>maintain eye contact with their listeners.</li><li>emphasize their main ideas by changing the tone and volume of their voice.</li><li>respect their audience by explaining and clarifying information that may be confusing.</li><li>use gestures and body language effectively to enhance their message.</li></ul>

▶ Try It!

Role-playing is an excellent way to practice listening and speaking skills. Try role-playing using this "read-question-answer" activity.

1. Imagine that you are a well-known author speaking to a group of students. Choose an excerpt from a book or a poem you have written. Read it to the group.
2. Have listeners take notes, jotting down questions and comments about "your" writing and the content of the excerpt.
3. Following the reading, role-play a question-answer session in which listeners ask questions and you answer extemporaneously (unrehearsed).

English Language Learners

Students may miss important information while listening because they are asked to do several tasks at once (reading, responding, writing). Have students tape-record the "read" part of the **Try It!** activity. Afterward, they should replay the tape to take notes in preparation for the "question-answer" part of the activity.

527

Taking Notes

Think of the volume of information your brain takes in each day. In this age of technology, information comes at you at a record pace. If you don't jot down the important things, you run the risk of not remembering them at all. This is why good note-taking skills are so important. Notes allow you to sort, organize, and process information.

Active listening and purposeful note taking are critical skills for students to master. Taking good notes can help you learn more efficiently, prepare for exams, and save time. In this chapter, you will learn how to sharpen your note-taking skills while listening to a lecture, reading a text, and attending a meeting.

- **Taking Classroom Notes**
- **Taking Reading Notes**
- **Taking Meeting Minutes**

"The pen is the tongue of the mind."

—Miguel de Cervantes

Taking Notes

Invite volunteers to share classroom notes that they used, or tried to use, to review material or to study for a test. Based on their experience, have them evaluate the notes for their effectiveness.
- Were the notes legible?
- Were the notes organized? Explain.
- Were the notes complete? If not, how much important information was missing? Were students able to find the missing information easily? Why or why not?

Taking Classroom Notes

The guidelines for taking notes are appropriate for taking notes during any kind of presentation. Remind students that if their teachers have established different guidelines for taking notes, however, they should follow those guidelines instead.

Students who shared and evaluated class notes (TE page 527) and found them ineffective, hard to follow, or incomplete should use the same notes to complete the **Try It!** activity.

Ask students what clues they listen for or watch for in order to identify the speaker's important ideas. (Possible responses: The speaker pauses before making an important point. The speaker repeats a key word or an important phrase for emphasis. The speaker uses visuals, proximity, or body language.)

528

Taking Classroom Notes

Your teacher may give a lecture to explain an important subject, introduce a new topic, or help the class review for a test. The following tips will help you take clear, organized lecture notes.

Guidelines for Class Notes

1. **Write the topic and date at the top of each page.** If you use loose-leaf paper, number each page as well.

2. **Listen carefully.** This is the key to taking good notes. If you are busy writing, you may miss important clues. For example, if a teacher says, "There are five steps you need to follow," listen for the five steps. Also listen for key words such as *first, second, next,* or *most importantly.*

3. **Use your own words.** You can't write down everything your teacher says. Instead, try to put the main points into your own words. You can fill in the details later.

4. **Begin taking notes right away** or you may miss something important. It's hard to catch up while taking notes.

5. **Write quickly, but neatly.** Your notes won't be helpful if you can't read them.

6. **Condense information.**
   - Use lists, phrases, and abbreviations (*p=page, ex=for example*).
   - Skip the small, unnecessary words, such as articles (*a, an, the*).
   - Shorten some words (*intro* for *introduction, chap* for *chapter*).
   - Use numbers and symbols (*1st, 2nd, +, =*).
   - Develop a personal shorthand (*w=with, w/o=without*).

7. **Draw sketches and diagrams** to explain a concept quickly.

8. **Copy important information** your teacher writes on the board.

9. **Ask your teacher** to explain something you don't understand, to repeat something, or to please slow down.

Try It!

Review some of your recent class notes while thinking of the guidelines above. How could you improve your note-taking skills? Explain.

English Language Learners

Students may have trouble identifying important information and writing it down without getting behind. Help students become better note takers by slowing your rate of speech and pausing between sentences and ideas. Also, establish a hand signal for students to cue a speaker when they need more time.

Setting Up Your Notes

Keep your notes in a notebook, preferably one for each subject. You can also take notes on loose-leaf paper kept in a three-ring binder, which lets you add and remove pages as needed. Write only on one side of the paper. This makes it easier to read and find portions of your notes.

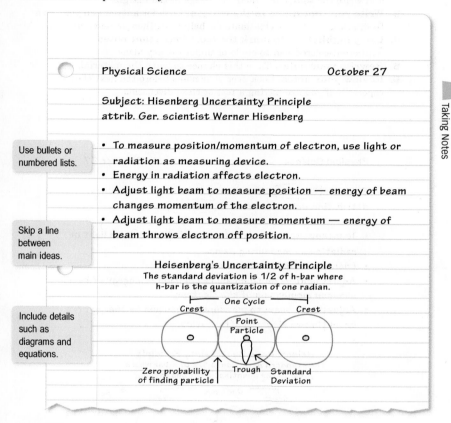

Use bullets or numbered lists.

Skip a line between main ideas.

Include details such as diagrams and equations.

Physical Science   October 27

Subject: Hisenberg Uncertainty Principle
attrib. Ger. scientist Werner Hisenberg

• To measure position/momentum of electron, use light or radiation as measuring device.
• Energy in radiation affects electron.
• Adjust light beam to measure position — energy of beam changes momentum of the electron.
• Adjust light beam to measure momentum — energy of beam throws electron off position.

Heisenberg's Uncertainty Principle
The standard deviation is 1/2 of h-bar where
h-bar is the quantization of one radian.

One Cycle
Crest   Point   Crest
               Particle

Zero probability   Trough   Standard
of finding particle   Deviation

FYI

Note taking helps you listen better in class, organize your ideas more effectively, and remember more of what you hear.

Setting Up Your Notes

Many of your students learned to use a computer keyboard before they learned to read or write. Many students probably prefer taking notes on a laptop. Students should check with their individual teachers to find out if **using a computer** *(see below)* to take classroom notes is permitted.

Remind students that the purpose for taking notes is to review material presented in class. If they use a different style of note taking from that shown on the page, have them defend the style they use. If they can find and use their notes on the spot—say, for a recent class presentation—then their notes are set up effectively.

Teaching Tip: Using a Computer

While using a computer to take notes can make the notes more useful and accessible to students, it does have risks. To avoid losing their notes through technology failure, students should keep these tips in mind:

• Save work frequently.
• Make backup copies on CD or on a separate hard drive.

• Print out notes after each session. If a file becomes corrupted, past notes won't be lost.
• Protect your note files with a password so that no one else who uses the computer has access to them.

English Language Learners

Discuss how a speaker's tone, pitch, volume, and expression can give cues about which information is most important. Have students flag what they think are the most important sections of their notes as reminders for when they organize their notes.

Reviewing Your Notes

Students may wonder what to highlight and what not to highlight, since they probably tried to write down key ideas and important details in the first place. If students find themselves highlighting almost every word in their notes when they review, then they will need to develop another strategy for recognizing salient information in their notes.

Point out that in the sample notes, the student didn't highlight the first bullet because the idea expressed is amplified in the following bullets. The student also didn't highlight the repeated words *Adjust light beam to*, but did highlight the words that explain the reasons for adjusting the light beam.

If students need additional guidance deciding what to highlight when they review, suggest that they make sure to highlight

- new ideas not expressed or explained anywhere else in the notes,
- definitions of key terms,
- reasons for specific events, and
- key dates and names.

Reviewing Your Notes

As you read over your notes, do the following:

1. **Circle and correct spelling errors.**
2. **Underline unfamiliar terms.** Look them up in a dictionary or glossary and write the words and their meanings in the margin.
3. **Write your questions in the margin.** Look for answers on your own first, ask a teacher or classmate for help next, then jot down answers.
4. **Use a highlighter to mark the most important notes,** a different-colored pen to circle or underline key ideas.
5. **Rewrite your notes.** Take this chance to learn the material.
6. **Review your notes.** Look over your notes before the next class, especially if you are having a test or class discussion.

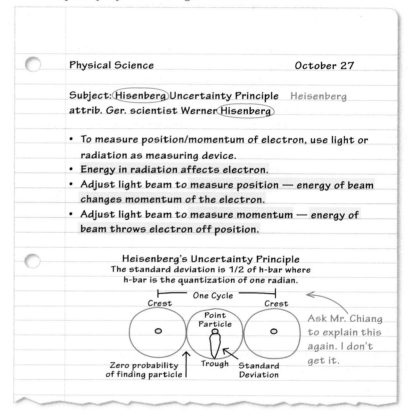

Taking Reading Notes

Taking notes while you read an assignment is easier than taking notes during a lecture. You can stop to write at any time, which means you can write more neatly and carefully. Here are some tips for taking reading notes.

Guidelines for Reading Notes

1. **Preview the assignment.** Look through your assignment to see what your reading is about. Look at the title, introduction, headings, and chapter summary. Also look at any pictures, maps, or graphics. (See page **95**.)

2. **Quickly read the entire assignment** once before taking notes. This gives you an overview of the material and allows you to pick out the main ideas.

3. **Take notes while reading a second time.** Read the material slowly, taking notes as you go along. Stop at new ideas or words.

   - **Write down the important information.**
   - **Put notes in your own words.** Don't just copy passages from the book. You learn more when you rewrite ideas in your words. (See pages **543–550** for more information on summaries and paraphrases.)
   - **Use headings or subtitles.** Headings and subtitles help to organize your notes. Write down the important information under each heading or subtitle.
   - **Include notes about pictures, charts, and illustrations.** You can also make quick sketches of these visual elements.
   - **Use graphic organizers.** (See pages **64–65**.)
   - **List and define any new words.** Look up each word in the glossary or in a dictionary. Write down the appropriate meaning in your notes. Also write down the number of the page where the word is located. This way you can easily find it again.

4. **Learn more.** See "Critical Reading" on pages **533–542** for more information on taking reading notes.

 Try It!

For your next reading assignment, take notes using the tips above.

Taking Reading Notes

Have students complete the **Try It!** activity in class. This will give you an opportunity to circulate among them to answer any questions they have about applying the guidelines for taking reading notes, or any other questions they have about the note-taking process.

- Have on hand a variety of magazines, books, and textbooks in which you have bookmarked possible reading selections.
- After students have selected a reading selection, tell them to quickly skim the selection to get a general idea of the **text construction and organization** *(see below)*.
- Next, have students turn to SE pages 64–65 to choose a graphic organizer to use to take notes when they read. Students can recreate the graphic organizer on their own paper. You can also provide photocopies of the reproducible Time Line, T-chart (for the Evaluation Collection Grid), 5 W's Chart, Venn Diagram, or Sensory Chart (TE pages 821–825).

Teaching Tip: Text Construction and Organization

Being able to recognize at a glance how text is constructed and organized can be key to taking good reading notes. Discuss different text structures that writers use to organize information, such as

- sequence,
- cause and effect,
- compare and contrast, and
- main idea and details.

Point out that once students recognize the specific text structure, they can organize their notes to reflect this structure. For example, if the selection is a chronicle of events leading up to a major event (sequence), students could use a sequence flow chart or a time line to take notes. If the selection compares and contrasts two or three topics, students could use a Venn diagram to record notes.

English Language Learners

Modify the **Try It!** activity by choosing a reading assignment that contains simpler sentence structures, fewer technical or specialized words, pictures and captions, less text on a page with a sufficient amount of white space, and subheads and other text features that organize text.

Taking Meeting Minutes

Encourage students who belong to school groups and clubs to bring in examples of meeting minutes from those organizations. (Students should check with the teacher or other adult who supervises the organization to make sure that these minutes can be shared.)

- Have students compare their sample minutes to the guidelines and sample minutes shown.
- Ask students to suggest different ways each group or club could improve their minute-taking techniques.
- Encourage students to volunteer to take the minutes the next time the group or club meets. If the group has an appointed secretary, suggest that students volunteer to take over the secretary's duties for one meeting and follow the guidelines when creating the minutes.

532

Taking Meeting Minutes

Recording the minutes of a meeting is another form of note taking. Minutes must be well organized and include everything from who is present to what is discussed and decided. Always report minutes in an objective (impersonal) voice. To record minutes during a meeting, you must listen carefully and write down information accurately. The following guidelines will help.

Guidelines for Taking Minutes

- Begin with the organization's name, the date, location, and topic of the meeting.

- Record what time the meeting begins.

- List those present (or absent). Indicate who led the meeting and who recorded the minutes.

- Note "old business" (from a previous meeting) that is discussed or resolved.

- Note "new business" (plans or decisions to be handled in the current meeting).

- Record any votes taken and their results.

- Record when the meeting is adjourned.

> **Longview High School Spanish Club Minutes**
> **Date:** November 26, 2011
> **Location:** Room 221 (Señor Ares, Faculty Advisor)
> **Topic:** Spring Trip
> **Meeting Time:** 2:15 P.M.–3:15 P.M.
>
> **Attending**
> Aslea Barron, Mary Canady, Chad Cooling, Megan Dilley (chair), Sheree Hewerdine, Raina Hawkins (recording), Tom Garcia
>
> **Absent**
> Taresha Young
>
> **Old Business**
> Mr. Machado, president and CEO of CityCorp Printing, visited our club last Monday. We gave him a plaque to thank his company for funding our spring trip to Mexico.
>
> Señor Ares reported that all travel arrangements have been made. He announced that we will visit Mexico City, Taxco, and Acapulco.
>
> A meeting for Spanish Club members and their parents was scheduled for February 9, 2012, at 7:00 PM in the school cafeteria.
>
> **New Business**
> At our next meeting on February 2, Tom will share his research about Mexico City's Museo Nacional de Antropologia.
>
> At the February 9 meeting, Ruth Phillips, RN, will speak to students and parents about health requirements for the trip.
>
> All signed permission slips must be returned to Señor Ares by February 15. We will take a field trip on March 6 to have our passport photos taken.

Tip

When you take minutes to tell what was discussed and decided upon by a group, record only the main points, not all the details. Be sure to accurately record any votes or official action taken.

Critical Reading

Many assignments require you to understand and interpret printed material and apply what you read. This is called *critical reading*. It means looking beyond the actual words to examine, question, and test the content. Successful critical reading enhances clarity and comprehension, allowing you to better understand the writer's message.

Critical reading requires several important steps. These include *surveying* an assigned reading, *questioning* what you read, *taking notes* about the text, and *reviewing* what you've read. In this chapter, you will learn to read critically to gain a clearer understanding of your reading assignments as well as any reading that you must do on tests.

- ■ **Critical Reading: SQ3R**
- ■ **Before You Read**
- ■ **As You Read**
- ■ **After You Read**
- ■ **Reading Fiction**
- ■ **Reading Poetry**

"Reading is to the mind what exercise is to the body. It is wholesome and bracing for the mind to have its faculties kept on the stretch."

—August Hare

Critical Reading

Objectives
- use the five steps of the SQ3R method for reading nonfiction critically
- learn strategies for reading fiction
- learn strategies for reading poetry

To introduce this chapter, write the phrase *critical reading* on the board.
- ■ Have students look up the word *critical* in the dictionary and tell its different meanings. (Possible responses: **1** having the tendency to point out what is wrong with something or someone; **2** related to the thoughtful analysis or careful judgment of something; **3** at a serious or dangerous stage—as with a disease; **4** very important)
- ■ Ask students which meaning they think applies to the phrase *critical reading* (**2** related to the thoughtful analysis or careful judgment of something).
- ■ Then have students suggest times when they practice critical reading. (Possible responses: to understand an idea so that they can discuss it in class, to answer questions on a test, to write a report)

Critical Reading: SQ3R

Remind students that any time they stop to write an idea on paper, the act of writing itself will reinforce the idea and help them to recall it later. That's why it's important to incorporate some form of note taking into each part of the SQ3R strategy.

Review the use of a K-W-L Chart with students. Point out that this is a good kind of organizer to use with the SQ3R strategy because it can be used before, during, and after reading. Explain that the letters *K, W,* and *L* stand for the following ideas.

- *K* = What I **know** about the topic before I read
- *W* = What I **want** to learn about the topic as I read
- *L* = What I **learned** about the topic

Because they often have long reading assignments on complex topics, students must develop a reading strategy that works for them. The strategy should help them make important connections with the text, and their written notes should assist them in their review of the material.

534

Critical Reading: SQ3R

An effective reading technique for all types of nonfiction is the SQ3R method. SQ3R stands for the five steps in this reading process: *survey, question, read, recite,* and *review.* These five steps are explained below and on the following pages.

Before you read . . .

- **Survey** Preview the reading assignment for its general content. Begin by reading the first and last paragraphs. Then read titles, subtitles, headings, and subheadings to see what is being covered. Take note of illustrations and any terms in bold or italic type.

- **Question** Ask yourself what you already know about the topic of the reading. Write down questions you still need answered. To get started, you could turn the text's titles, subtitles, headings, and subheadings into questions. Asking questions keeps you actively involved while reading.

As you read . . .

- **Read** Read slowly and carefully. Look for the main idea in each paragraph, section, or chapter. Try to answer questions you have already identified. At different points, also ask these questions: *What does this mean? How does it connect with previous material? What will come next?* Take notes as you go along. Take the time to read difficult parts slowly. Reread them if necessary.

- **Recite** Test your comprehension of the material by summarizing the main points out loud. Summarizing (reciting) in this way is one of the most valuable parts of SQ3R. After you read a page, section, or chapter, try to answer the 5 W and H questions (*who? what? where? when? why?* and *how?*) about that part. Reread any parts as needed.

After you read . . .

- **Review** Assess your knowledge by reviewing your notes. See how well you understand the entire reading assignment. Ask yourself these questions: *Have all my questions been answered? Can I summarize each main section? Can I summarize or outline the whole assignment?* Consider outlining the material (or using another type of graphic organizer) to help you remember what you have read.

Note: Critical reading means looking beyond surface details and thinking carefully about the information that is presented.

Advanced Learners

Challenge students to use the SQ3R technique with an article of interest from a scholarly journal. Have students locate a journal from a library or an online source, such as Project Muse, to complete the activity. Examples include *Steinbeck Studies, The Yale Journal of Criticism, Journal of Online Law, Philosophy East and West,* and *Human Rights Quarterly.*

Before You Read

Try to get the big picture of each assignment as you begin to read. The tips that follow will help you get started.

Surveying the Reading

To begin, survey the text for a general understanding of the main points.

- **Scan** chapter titles, subtitles, headings, and boldfaced type.
- **Identify the purpose of the material:** to inform, to persuade, to entertain.
- **Read** the first and last paragraphs.
- **List** the topic and the main points as best you can.

Sample Survey Notes

Below, Samantha surveys the beginning of an article about "senior slump." She writes her notes on a copy of the article.

Critical Reading

Are You Suffering from Senior Slump?

You've made it to your senior year, and your plans for next year are in place. Now you can just relax and coast. If you believe this, you may be suffering from "senior slump"—a belief that your education is nearly over and you can relax. Many high school seniors suffer from this condition and pay a high price.

Senior slump can be harmful because the final months before graduation can impact your future. If a college has accepted you, it can request and review your grades at any time during your senior year. If your grades slip, you may be asked to explain why. Poor grades in your senior year can mean entering college on probation, or not entering at all.

Another symptom of senior slump is loading up on electives instead of taking challenging honors classes. Whether your plans include college, work, or the military, much is expected of a high school graduate. If you slack off, it will probably come back to haunt you.

While a senior slump is inadvisable, so is crashing and burning. Try to balance your senior year. Challenge yourself to keep your grades up, spend quiet periods planning for next year, and find some time to relax and have fun.

Purpose:
To inform

Topic:
Senior slump

Key Points:
- Seniors can fall into a slump.
- Grades may drop, so don't slack off.
- Poor grades can keep you from getting into college or force you to enter on probation.
- Taking easy courses won't prepare you for the future.
- Balance is the key.

Before You Read

Provide small groups of students with photocopies of three short reading selections, each with a different purpose (to inform, to persuade, and to entertain). Ask members of each group to work together to create survey notes for each article, following the style as shown for Sample Survey Notes.

When students have finished, have the groups come together to share and compare their notes for each article. Ask them to explain how they identified each author's purpose and how deciding on the purpose helped them to organize their notes.

Questioning the Material

Provide photocopies of the reproducible 5 W's Chart (TE page 822) for students to list questions during the **Try It!** activity.

Point out the possibility that not all questions students have will be answered as they read. If this is the case, they might try rephrasing the question or checking additional resources after they read to find the answers. Making that extra effort to go beyond the reading material will provide them with a better understanding of the topic and a more complete and more satisfying learning experience.

Questioning the Material

After you have surveyed the entire text, ask questions about the reading. Use the following guidelines:

- **List what you already know about the topic.**
- **List questions that you still want answered.** Also ask the 5 W and H questions.
- **Turn headings and main points into questions.** For example, you may reword a chapter titled "Defining and Pursuing a Liberal Education" into *"What is a liberal education? Do I want to pursue a liberal education?"*

Below, Samantha formed questions about the main points of the sample article. Next to her questions she noted things she already knew about the topic.

	Already know:
1. Am I in a senior slump?	Senior slump can
2. Will the college penalize me if my grades slip from A's to B's?	lead to poor grades.
3. When is it all right to choose some fun electives?	It can affect my college acceptance
4. How can I keep myself challenged?	and my performance
5. What can I do to balance my senior year?	during freshman year.
6. Whom can I talk to about the way I feel?	
	I need to keep my brain in shape.
	Balancing learning and relaxation is key.

Try It!

Choose a reading assignment you've been given recently. Survey the text and write down any questions you have about the material.

As You Read

Once you have surveyed the assignment and formed questions about it, you are ready to read carefully. Try to turn your reading into a conversation with the text. Respect what the writer has to say, even as you question certain parts, and stay open to the unexpected.

Reading (and Taking Notes)

Always have a goal in mind when you read. Follow these guidelines as you read the material and answer the questions you listed.

- **Read slowly** so that you don't miss anything.
- **Reread parts** that seem challenging.
- **Write down key concepts.** (These are often in bold.)
- **Define key concepts** using context or a dictionary.
- **Record any additional questions** you may have.
- **Keep the following questions in mind** as you read: *What does this mean? How does it connect with what I already know about the topic? What will probably come next?*

 Try It!

Read your chosen assignment critically. Take careful notes as you go along, using the guidelines above.

Reciting Material Out Loud

After you complete the entire reading, it's time to reinforce what you have learned. Repeating information out loud is an effective way to evaluate how well you understand it. Use the following guidelines:

- **Recite the key points** without looking at your notes.
- **Answer the 5 W and H questions** *(who? what? where? when? why? and how?)* about the material.
- **Ask (and answer) your other questions** about the topic.
- **Identify any new questions** that occur to you.

Try It!

Recite what you have learned from your reading assignment. Use the guidelines above to help you complete this step.

As You Read

Focus on the questions in the last bulleted item under Reading (and Taking Notes). Point out that these are good questions to ask during all types of reading because answering them requires using proven reading strategies.

- *What does this mean?* Strategy: monitoring comprehension. Students clarify their understanding by rereading a selection, reviewing text features, reading more slowly, reading ahead, looking for context clues, and/or asking and answering questions about the text.
- *How does it connect with what I already know about the topic?* Strategy: making connections. Students can make connections with ideas presented earlier in the text, with ideas from other texts, and with what they know from their own experiences.
- *What will probably come next?* Strategy: making predictions. Students combine what they know and what they learn as they read to make an informed guess about what information will be presented next. Predictions do not have to be correct, but they do have to be logical and based on the text.

After You Read

Students should recognize that if they consistently use the SQ3R method for reading assignments, they can almost ensure that they will gain a greater understanding of the material. Encourage students to make a conscientious effort to use the SQ3R strategy. Point out that although it does require a greater commitment on their part, the benefits are undeniable.

- Students will be able to participate more fully in class discussions because they have a greater understanding of the topic. Some teachers consider class participation when determining final grades.
- Students will remember the material more easily and accurately, which is important at test time.
- Students will be able to draw on what they have learned when asked to write about a topic.

After You Read

Having completed the first four steps in the SQ3R method, you should review the reading. Reviewing will help you see how well you understand the material.

Reviewing the Material

A final review of your reading will make the information part of your own thinking. Use the following guidelines:

- **Go over your notes** one section at a time.
- **Keep searching for answers** if you have any unanswered questions.
- **Ask for help** if you cannot figure something out on your own.
- **Add illustrations or graphic organizers** to your notes to make complex ideas clearer.
- **Summarize the reading** at the end of your notes.

In the example below, Samantha wrote a summary paragraph for the article about senior slump. She also wrote some final thoughts about the material in the margin.

Sample Summary

"Are You Suffering from Senior Slump?"—Summary

This article defines "senior slump" as the belief that your education is nearly over so you can relax. The symptoms of senior slump are letting your grades slip and not challenging your mind. The cure is a balanced senior year that includes equal parts learning, thinking, and relaxation.

I need more information about senior slump and what to do about it.

I know that I'm not taking my senior year seriously.

This article made me aware that I need to make some changes.

Try It!

Review your reading assignment. Go over your notes and summarize the assignment. Be sure to include the main ideas and write any final thoughts in the margin.

Reading Fiction

Fiction uses imagined characters and events to reveal what is very often authentic or true about real life. This makes fiction a notable way to learn. Here are some tips for reading fiction.

Before you read . . .

- **Learn something about the author** and his or her other works.
- **React thoughtfully** to the title and opening pages.

As you read . . .

- **Identify** the following story elements: *setting, tone, main characters, central conflict,* and *theme.*
- **Predict** what will happen next.
- **Write** your reactions to the short story or novel in a reading journal as you go along.
- **Think** about the characters and what they do. *What motivates the characters? Have you encountered people similar to these characters? Have you faced situations similar to the ones faced by the main characters? Would you have reacted in the same way?*
- **Consider** how the author's life may have influenced the story.
- **Notice** the author's style and word choice. *How effectively has the author used literary devices? Did the author use particular words or phrases to suit a certain audience?*
- **Discuss** the story with others who are reading it.

After you read . . .

- **Consider** how the main character changes during the course of the story. Often, this is the key to understanding a work of fiction.
- **Determine** the story's main message or theme; then decide how effectively this message is communicated.

> ## Try It!
>
> Use the information above as a guide to help you better understand and enjoy the next short story or novel you read.

Critical Reading

Reading Fiction

Ask students if they have ever read a short story or novel that every one else loved, but that they didn't like at all.

- Did they feel comfortable saying they didn't like it? Why or why not?
- What was it about the story or book that they didn't like?

Point out that **using a reading journal** (*see below*) can give students the opportunity to explore their feelings and reactions to a book without worrying about justifying their responses to anyone else. As they continue to practice responding to literature, they will gain confidence in their analyses and be more willing to offer their viewpoint during a discussion.

✱ For more on analyzing and responding to literature, see SE pages 274–339.

Teaching Tip: Using a Reading Journal

If students are not keeping a reading journal, encourage them to start doing so now to write about the poems, books, and stories that they read for assignments and their own pleasure.

Reading-journal entries usually include the following:

- the title and author of the work
- a brief summary of the work, including the theme

- comments about characters, events, author's style
- the reader's thoughts, feelings, impressions, and opinions of the work as a whole

Students can use their journal to record their response, prepare for a discussion of the work, review for a test, and collect ideas for their own creative writing. Suggest that they preserve the journal from year to year for future reference.

Reacting to Fiction

Read aloud a short excerpt from a story or novel students have read.

- Give students time to discuss the excerpt and then make notes that reveal their reaction to it.
- Invite students to share their notes and discuss their response to the excerpt.
- If students have questions that aren't answered in the excerpt, have them suggest ways that they could find the answer. (For example, use a dictionary to find an unfamiliar word.)
- Help readers see that even when they agree with the majority opinion, they are responsible for defending their reasoning. Also point out that they may form an opinion early in the reading, only to reverse it by the end of a story, either due to the writing itself or because the reader experienced something in life that changed the opinion. Any change in position likewise needs to be defended.

540

Reacting to Fiction

The excerpt below is from Mary Shelley's classic novel *Frankenstein*. The margin notes reveal one student's reactions, which he wrote on a photocopy of the story. He makes observations, asks questions, and attempts to define a confusing term.

I'm not sure what "Prometheus" means. The best definition I found is "a Titan who stole fire from Olympus and gave it to mankind."

Why did he hold back and not destroy the cottage and its people?

Great descriptive writing

I feel sorry for the monster. The anger he feels toward his creator and all mankind comes through the strongest in this paragraph.

Frankenstein, or The Modern Prometheus
by Mary Wollstonecraft (Godwin) Shelley

Cursed, cursed creator! Why did I live? Why, in that instant, did I not extinguish the spark of existence which you had so wantonly bestowed? I know not; despair had not yet taken possession of me; my feelings were those of rage and revenge. I could with pleasure have destroyed the cottage and its inhabitants and have glutted myself with their shrieks and misery.

When night came I quitted my retreat and wandered in the wood; and now, no longer restrained by the fear of discovery, I gave vent to my anguish in fearful howlings. I was like a wild beast that had broken the toils, destroying the objects that obstructed me and ranging through the wood with a stag-like swiftness. Oh! What a miserable night I passed! The cold stars shone in mockery, and the bare trees waved their branches above me; now and then the sweet voice of a bird burst forth amidst the universal stillness. All, save I, were at rest or in enjoyment; I, like the arch-fiend, bore a hell within me, and finding myself unsympathized with, wished to tear up the trees, spread havoc and destruction around me, and then to have sat down and enjoyed the ruin.

But this was a luxury of sensation that could not endure; I became fatigued with excess of bodily exertion and sank on the damp grass in the sick impotence of despair. There was none among the myriads of men that existed who would pity or assist me; and should I feel kindness towards my enemies? No; from that moment I declared everlasting war against the species, and more than all, against him who had formed me and sent me forth to this insupportable misery.

The sun rose; I heard the voices of men and knew that it was impossible to return to my retreat during that day. Accordingly I hid myself in some thick underwood, determining to devote the ensuing hours to reflection on my situation.

English Language Learners

Students may become frustrated by the lengthy sentences in the excerpt. Help students digest the material by breaking complex sentences into simple and compound sentences. Also review the meanings of the following words from the excerpt:

- extinguish (put out)
- wantonly bestowed (immorally given)
- glutted (filled up beyond capacity)
- gave vent (declared, voiced aggressively)
- mockery (ridicule)
- fatigued (very tired)

Reading Poetry

You may not understand a poem completely in one reading, especially if it is lengthy or complex. In fact, each time you read a poem, you will probably discover something new about it. Reacting to poetry in a reading journal will help you to appreciate it more. Here are some strategies for reading poetry.

First Reading

- **Read the poem** at your normal reading speed to gain an overall first impression.
- **Jot down brief notes** about your immediate reaction to the poem.

Second Reading

- **Read the poem again**—out loud, if possible. Pay attention to the sound of the poem.
- **Note examples of sound devices** in the poem—alliteration, assonance, rhyme (see pages **368–369**). Finding a poem's phrasing and rhythm can help you discover its meaning.
- **Observe** the punctuation, spacing, and special treatment of words and lines.
- **Think** about the theme of the poem.

Third Reading

- **Identify** the type of poem you're reading. Does this poem follow the usual pattern of that particular type? If not, why not?
- **Determine** the literal sense or meaning of the poem. What is the poem about? What does it seem to say about its topic?
- **Look** for figurative language in the poem. How does this language—metaphors, similes, personification, symbols—support or add to the meaning of the poem? (See pages **600–601** and **368–369**.)

Try It!

Use the strategies above the next time you read a poem, especially one you need to write about as an assignment.

Reading Poetry

The greatest challenge for any reader in trying to determine the meaning of a poem is interpreting the figurative or symbolic language that the poet uses to convey the message.

Explain that poets, like authors of fiction, often explore similar themes from one work to the next. Poets may also use the same symbolic object to convey a theme in multiple poems. Therefore, the more students know about a poet's works, the easier it may be for them to interpret the symbolic language and unlock the meaning of a poem. Encourage students to learn as much as they can about the poet before they read and react to a poem. Unless the poem appears in isolation (as a writing prompt or in a test), students should read the poet's biographical information that accompanies the poem. Often this information provides an analysis of the poem and/or reveals the poem's theme and imagery.

Struggling Learners

To assist students in reading poetry critically, choose several simple poems and focus on one literary device, such as tone, figurative language, or imagery, to analyze. As a group, read through the poem several times before students make observations, ask questions, and write comments.

Advanced Learners

Have pairs choose a poem that contains several elements of figurative language. Then have them create a three-column chart, one column for each reading. After each reading, have pairs discuss the poem and jot responses in the appropriate column. Then have students share their responses with others.

Reacting to Poetry

To introduce this page and extend the **Try It!** activity, provide students with a copy of Shakespeare's "Sonnet 18" before they read the student notes that accompany the poem.

■ Take a few minutes to discuss the form of a traditional English sonnet (see reference below).

■ Have students write their observations, questions, reactions to word choices, and other personal responses to "Sonnet 18."

■ Have students compare their notes to the sample student notes, and discuss the similarities and differences with classmates.

✳ For more about understanding sonnets, see SE page 362.

542

Reacting to Poetry

"Sonnet 18" is a poem by William Shakespeare. The notes on the copy of the poem below show one student's reaction to it. The student makes observations, asks questions, reacts to word choice, and so forth. Whenever you read a challenging poem, try to react to it in several different ways.

Sonnet 18
by William Shakespeare

Theme: the stability of love

Shall I compare thee to a summer's day?
Thou art more lovely and more temperate:
Rough winds do shake the darling buds of May,
And summer's lease hath all too short a date:

Everything changes. Summer always comes to an end.

Sometime too hot the eye of heaven shines,
And often is his gold complexion dimm'd;
And every fair from fair sometime declines,
By chance, or nature's changing course untrimm'd;

I wonder what this poem would sound like written in modern language?

But thy eternal summer shall not fade,
Nor lose possession of that fair thou ow'st;
Nor shall Death brag thou wander'st in his shade,
When in eternal lines to time thou grow'st:

So long as men can breathe, or eyes can see,
So long lives this, and this gives life to thee.

This is an English sonnet:
14 lines
3 quatrains
1 final rhyming couplet

The last quatrain and couplet mean that, unlike summer, this person's beauty won't fade. It lives on because of this sonnet.

Try It!

Write freely for 5 to 10 minutes when you finish reading a poem. Include any thoughts or feelings you have about the poem. Relate it to other poems you have read.

543

Summarizing and Paraphrasing

Summarizing and paraphrasing are useful writing techniques. Using your own words to reduce and restate another writer's thoughts forces you to pull out the essentials from the reading—the main points, the key details, or the thread of the argument. It also stretches your ability to comprehend, analyze, and synthesize information—all important thinking skills.

Reports, term papers, and other types of academic writing often require you to summarize and paraphrase. As you apply these important writing skills, you will find that they help you to understand even the most challenging reading material. In this chapter, you will read examples of both kinds of writing and have an opportunity to practice writing your own summaries and paraphrases.

- ■ **Original Article and Summary**
- ■ **Guidelines for Summarizing**
- ■ **Strategies for Paraphrasing**
- ■ **Original Paragraphs and Paraphrases**
- ■ **Paraphrasing a Paragraph**

"The most valuable of all talents is that of never using two words when one will do."
—Thomas Jefferson

Summarizing and Paraphrasing

Objectives
- learn guidelines for summarizing a reading selection
- learn strategies for paraphrasing a paragraph
- practice summarizing and paraphrasing

A **summary** tells the main points of an excerpt or a whole selection. A summary
- ■ retells only the most important ideas from the original text,
- ■ is mostly a rewording but may contain key words and phrases from the original text, and
- ■ is always shorter than the original text.

A **paraphrase** retells a reading selection in other words. A paraphrase
- ■ includes the reader's interpretation of key points of the selection,
- ■ captures the tone and meaning of the original selection, and
- ■ may or may not be shorter than the original selection.

Original Article and Summary

Provide time for students to read the sample article. Ask them to jot down the main idea of the article and the key details the writer uses to support that main idea. Suggest that students draw on what they have learned as writers about the basic structure of an essay and effective expository writing to identify the main idea of the article and key supporting details.

✳ For more about the basic parts of an essay, see SE page 590. For more about constructing an expository essay, see SE pages 176–180.

Invite students to share the ideas they jotted down, and have a volunteer list them on the board, eliminating duplicates. Then work with students to determine which ideas belong in a summary of the article. Remind students that if they were actually writing a summary, they would probably combine and synthesize many of these ideas to make the summary shorter.

Leave the list of ideas on the board so that students can compare their ideas to the ideas in the sample summary on SE page 545.

544

Original Article and Summary

The following article is about the counterculture movement in the United States that took place in the 1960s.

The Antiwar Movement—Counterculture of the '60s

"All we are asking is give peace a chance." This mantra was chanted and sung in countless antiwar rallies in the 1960s. In a nation divided by the Vietnam War, thousands of American youth protested the war through rallies, demonstrations, and concerts for peace. They were soundly opposed to the conflict in southeast Asia, and the strength of their conviction created a rising counterculture in the United States.

This new culture rebelled against the traditional values of middle-class society. It exhibited its rebellion through long hair, rock music, and peaceful resistance. "Hippies" and "flower children" formed a community in the Haight-Ashbury neighborhood in San Francisco. Fed up with what they called "the establishment," they adopted the slogan "turn on, tune in, and drop out."

In the 1960s, young adults in the United States were more outspoken than at any other time in the nation's history. They took their protests to college campuses in major U.S. cities. They demonstrated at the Capitol in Washington, D.C., and near the White House. They gathered in San Francisco, with numbers exceeding fifty thousand, to participate in what they called the "Summer of Love," urging peace and nonconformity.

Before long, radical counterculture subgroups formed across the country. These groups planned and participated in more and more demonstrations in protest to the war, the bombing of Cambodia, and the draft. Their politics were described as the "new left," and it was common for police, and even the National Guard, to break up their demonstrations using riot gear and tear gas.

Peaceful protests against the war declined as more overt civil disobedience entered into the picture in an attempt to gain national attention. The counterculture movement of the sixties had fallen victim to more violence in its resolution for peace.

English Language Learners

Explain that the word *counterculture* is made up of *counter* (opposing) and *culture* (society). Point out that opposing cultures, or countercultures, challenge mainstream beliefs of the dominant culture. For example, at the beginning of the period of the American Revolution, those opposed to British rule went against the dominant culture in the colonies at the time.

Summary

The following is a student summary of the preceding article. Pay close attention to the three main points: the topic sentence, the body, and the closing sentence. (See side notes.)

The **topic sentence** expresses the main idea.

Each sentence in the **body** summarizes one or even two paragraphs from the article.

The **closing sentence** shares the article's concluding thoughts.

The Antiwar Movement—Counterculture of the '60s

In the 1960s, thousands of youth in the United States protested the Vietnam War. They formed a counterculture that rebelled against the war and traditional middle-class values. Their protests included peaceful demonstrations on college campuses and at the Capitol and the White House in Washington, D.C. Later, radical subgroups formed and engaged in more demonstrative protests as a way to get attention. Police often used riot gear and tear gas to break up the demonstrations. **Ironically, the counterculture movement of the 1960s had turned more violent in its quest for peace.**

Summarizing (sidebar)

Respond to the reading. Answer the following questions.

Ideas (1) What details from the original article are included in the summary? (2) What kinds of details are not included?

Organization (3) How is the summary paragraph organized?

Voice & Word Choice (4) Compare the first sentence of the summary with the first paragraph of the original. Which is simpler? Which offers more detail?

Summary

Students should notice that the sample summary is about one-third the length of the original article on SE page 544.

Respond to the reading.

Answers

Ideas 1. The most important details are included in the summary. These details tell about the thousands of young protestors to the Vietnam War in the 1960s, the counterculture they formed, the peaceful nature and specific locations of important demonstrations, the radical subgroups that formed later, and how police responded to their violent protests.
2. Less-important details are omitted. These include details about specific kinds of protests (rallies, demonstrations, concerts), nicknames ("hippies," "flower children,"), slogans, and other background information.

Organization 3. chronological order

Voice & Word Choice 4. The opening sentence of the summary is simpler than the original. The first paragraph of the original article provides background information and details that help explain how the antiwar movement of the 1960s began. The summary just states the fact that it happened.

Guidelines for Summarizing

Review the basic parts of a paragraph, including the topic sentence, the body, and the closing sentence. Remind students to apply what they have learned about writing effective paragraphs and the traits of writing when they write a summary paragraph.

✳ For more about basic paragraph skills, see SE pages 577–588.

Remind students that they should not mark up the original article. They should create an outline for their note taking and follow the organization in the original article. They should also follow your guidelines for documenting sources in their summary. Otherwise, they may be guilty of plagiarism.

✳ For more on avoiding plagiarism and documenting sources, see SE pages 419 and 425–438.

Guidelines for Summarizing

Follow these guidelines whenever you are asked to write a summary.

Prewriting

- **Select an article on a topic that interests you** or relates to a subject you are currently studying. Make a photocopy of the article if possible.
- **Read the article once,** quickly. Then read it again, underlining passages (if working with a photocopy) or taking notes on the key details.
- **Think about the article.** Identify and write down the main idea. For example, here is the main idea of the sample article:

    > In the 1960s, youth in the United States shaped a counterculture in response to the Vietnam War.

Writing

- **Write a topic sentence** that states the main idea of the article.
- **Write body sentences** that communicate the most important ideas of the article in your own words.
- **Conclude** by reminding your reader of the main point of the article. (*Remember:* A summary should not contain your personal opinions.)

Revising and Editing

Read and revise your summary and make necessary changes. Also edit for conventions. Ask yourself the following questions:

Ideas	*Do I correctly identify the article's main idea in my topic sentence? Do my body sentences contain only the most important details from the article?*
Organization	*Are the ideas in my paragraph arranged in the same order as the original article?*
Voice	*Does my voice sound informed and interested?*
Word Choice	*Have I used my own words for the most part? Are there terms that need to be defined?*
Sentence Fluency	*Have I varied sentence structures and lengths?*
Conventions	*Have I eliminated all errors in punctuation, spelling, and grammar?*

Struggling Learners

Viewing summary information in the form of a graphic organizer is helpful for some students. Create a summary graphic organizer, like the one here, and fill in the first box with the topic sentence, the middle boxes with body sentences, and the last box with the closing sentence.

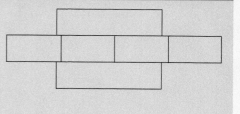

Summarizing an Article

The following article is about creating content for the Internet.

Content Creators

An individual is a content creator if he or she creates something and shares it on the Internet. Half of all teens who use the Internet (about 17 million between the ages of 12 and 17) are content creators. They regularly produce Web pages and blogs and post their original artwork, stories, and videos online.

The possibilities for creating digital content have increased dramatically with advancing technology. High-speed Internet connections combined with digital publishing software make it easy to create, remix, and share content. These tools allow teens to manipulate text, images, video, and audio files and share them on Web pages that they create for themselves and others.

Blogs are the most popular way for teens to share content. A blog is a Web log, a kind of Web page that serves as an online journal where thoughts and ideas are exchanged. One in four online teens (about 4.5 million) has created a personal blog. And 38 percent of all online teens read them. Most teen blog creators are very Internet savvy, and approximately 9 out of 10 report creating content to help adults do something online that the adults could not do themselves.

Web pages and blogs are just the beginning. Technology and teens go hand in hand. Today's teen content creators will be tomorrow's digital inventors. The possibilities for creating and sharing on the Internet are endless.

Try It!

Summarize the article above. Write a summary paragraph about this article, using the guidelines provided on page **546**.

Summarizing an Article

If you think students will benefit from a group approach to the **Try It!** activity, follow these steps.

- Have students read the article.
- Ask students to apply the prewriting guidelines on SE page 546 to the article. Suggest that they use self-stick tags and notes to mark key details and the main idea.
- Then have students share their ideas and decide together which of their ideas reflect the most important ideas in the article and should appear in a summary. Suggest that students list these details on the board.
- Next, have students work together to develop a topic sentence that they can use to begin their summary.
- Have students individually write their summaries, following the guidelines for writing on SE page 546.
- Have partners exchange summaries for the revising and editing steps. Encourage students to offer partners ideas for improvements if they answer "no" to any of the revising and editing questions.

English Language Learners

The meaning of *content* may be confusing to some students because it is pronounced two different ways to indicate different meanings. Explain that in some languages, such as Spanish, an accent mark is placed over the stressed syllable to differentiate between two words spelled the same way. For example, *papá* (father) and *papa* (potato) have the same spelling but two entirely different meanings. Point out that *content*, in which the first syllable is stressed, means "subject matter of a written work" as used in the article. Explain that *content*, in which the second syllable is stressed, means *satisfied*.

Struggling Learners

Help students write effective summaries by having them test their topic sentences as follows:

- Read it to a partner.
- Ask your partner to tell you in his or her own words what the main idea is.
- If your partner is not correct, clarify your topic sentence.

Strategies for Paraphrasing

Students should be extremely careful when choosing synonyms from a thesaurus.

- Remind students that not all synonyms convey the same **connotation** *(see below)*.
- Words with a different connotation can not only change the meaning but also affect the tone of a text.
- As an example, point out the word *exhibit* in the boxed text at the bottom of the page. Using a thesaurus, students might encounter the word *spectacle*. While the word *spectacle* has a dictionary meaning similar to *exhibit*, the synonym *spectacle* connotes something highly entertaining, usually in a garish way. This meaning does not fit the serious, matter-of-fact tone of the original text.

Ask students to explain why the first paraphrase for the original news report about the snow leopard has an inappropriate voice. (The word *roars* makes this paraphrase sound more like a catchy magazine headline than informative text. By omitting the word *rare,* the writer leaves out a vital piece of information and changes an important idea in the original text.)

548

Strategies for Paraphrasing

A paraphrase is a type of summary. It is effective for clarifying or explaining the meaning of an important passage that you would like to use in your research. While a summary is shorter than the original text and condenses the text's meaning, a paraphrase can be longer than the original material. A paraphrase *interprets* the key point of the original. Use the following strategies as a guide when you paraphrase.

Follow a plan: In order to complete an effective paraphrase, you must follow a series of important steps. There are no shortcuts.

- **Review the entire passage.** This will help you identify the main point and purpose of the material.
- **Carefully read the passage.** If necessary, reread parts that seem especially important or challenging.
- **Write your paraphrase.** Be sure your interpretation is clear and complete. For the most part, use your own words. (See below.)
- **Check your paraphrase.** Be sure that you have captured the tone and meaning of the passage.

Use your own words: Avoid the original writer's words as much as possible. Exceptions include key words such as *critical* and *perfection,* or proper nouns such as Arrowhead High School. (See the paraphrases on page 549.)

- **Consult a dictionary.** Refer to a dictionary to help you think of new ways to express certain terms or ideas.
- **Refer to a thesaurus.** When needed for clarification, use synonyms in place of words in the original text. For example, if the writer is describing a *realm,* a thesaurus will suggest synonyms such as *empire* and *kingdom.* Pick the synonym that fits the context of the passage.

Capture the original voice: In a paraphrase, you should try to communicate the original writer's opinions and feelings. Read the examples that follow.

Original News Report

The National Zoo has acquired a rare snow leopard, scheduled to arrive in March. It will be on display in the Big Cats exhibit beginning April 16th.

- **Paraphrase with inappropriate voice:** National Zoo roars into March with the addition of a snow leopard.
- **Paraphrase with proper voice:** In March, the National Zoo will add a rare snow leopard to its Big Cats exhibit.

Teaching Tip: Connotations

Students may benefit from a refresher of the definitions of *connotation* and *denotation*.

- *Connotation* is the feeling that a specific word creates for the reader.
- *Denotation* is the precise dictionary meaning of a word.

Caution students to make sure that the words they choose to replace a writer's original language have the appropriate connotation.

✳ For more on the connotations and denotations of words, see SE pages 188–189.

Advanced Learners

Challenge students to find several news articles in newspapers or news magazines and write paraphrases of the leads (opening sentences) that provide all the information and maintain the tone of the original writing.

Original Paragraphs and Paraphrases

The following expository paragraph discusses the author Edgar Allan Poe.

> Poe was a tireless critic of his own work, and both his standards of workmanship and his critical precepts have been of great service to his careless countrymen. He turned out between four and five short stories a year, was poorly paid for them, and indeed found difficulty in selling them at all. Yet he was constantly correcting them for the better. His best poems were likewise his latest. He was tantalized with the desire for artistic perfection. He became the pathbreaker for a long file of men in France, Italy, England, and America. He found the way and they brought back the glory and the cash.
>
> Bliss Perry, *The American Spirit in Literature*

A student shows her understanding of the paragraph:

> Poe wrote several stories a year, but he had a hard time selling them. He was paid poorly for the ones that he did sell. Poe was perpetually critical of his own works, and he worked tirelessly toward perfection. His hard work paid off with his last poems, which were his best. Other writers imitated Poe's style, and they were the ones who earned more money and fame.

The following text is part of a sports review in a high school newspaper.

> This school year, Phillips Rey High School, located in Phelps, entered District Six in the South-State Interschool Athletic Association, allowing its teams to compete in district and state playoffs. Phillips Rey has been in Eagle Township for more than 50 years, establishing a solid athletic presence. The strength of its girls' basketball team was proven last Wednesday when the team beat our Arrowhead girls' team 48-37. The Arrowhead team easily won first place in last year's SSIAA playoffs, but with Phillips Rey in District Six, our girls will have to fight hard to hang on to the traveling trophy.

A student reflects the writer's enthusiasm in her paraphrase of the review:

> This year, Phillips Rey High School joined the District Six South-State Interschool Athletic Association. Phillips Rey's teams will now compete with our Arrowhead High School teams. Phillips Rey has a long history of athletic excellence. Last Wednesday, its girls' basketball team beat our Arrowhead girls' team 48-37. The Arrowhead girls had no problem taking first place in last year's SSIAA playoffs, but to hang on to their traveling trophy, they will have to play hard to beat Phillips Rey.

Summarizing

Original Paragraphs and Paraphrases

Assign students to small groups and challenge them to write an original paraphrase for the paragraph about Poe, following the guidelines on SE page 548.

- Before writing, have each group identify the main point of the paragraph, its purpose, and its voice and tone (*purpose:* to inform; *main point:* Edgar Allen Poe was a prolific but poorly paid writer who provided later writers with a path to success; *voice and tone:* knowledgeable and serious).
- Next, have the group list the key words and phrases (Possible choices: *tireless critic, critical precepts, poorly paid, difficulty selling them, constantly correct for the better, best poems his latest, pathbreaker, glory and the cash*).
- Then have students work together to compose an original paraphrase.
- Finally, have them compare their paraphrase with the sample student paraphrase. How is it similar? How is it different? Which do they prefer? Why?

Paraphrasing a Paragraph

Explain the inclusion of author's point of view in the directions for the **Try It!**, since the strategies for paraphrasing on SE page 548 refer to voice and tone. Point out that the voice and tone of a piece of writing convey the author's point of view toward the topic.

Remind students that since they are expected to use their own words in a paraphrase, none of their paraphrases for these paragraphs will be exactly the same. However, the meaning and the voice and tone of all their paraphrases should match that of the original paragraphs. Suggest that before students write their paraphrase they write a one-sentence summary of the original paragraph at the top of their paper and another sentence that explains the voice and tone, or author's point of view toward the subject. Tell them to refer to these sentences as they write their paraphrase.

To assist students in recognizing the author's point of view of the paragraph they choose, remind them to examine

- the use of specific nouns, verbs, adjectives and adverbs; and
- the facts, details, and examples that support the ideas.

550

Paraphrasing a Paragraph

Each sample paragraph below has a main idea and a distinct author's voice.

It was plain that unless Lincoln could unite the various classes of the North, his utter failure would be a foregone conclusion. He saw this clearly. His first move was selecting his cabinet. He chose not only from various geographical divisions of the country but also from diverse political divisions of the party. It was not his purpose to have secretaries that would mimic himself, but able and representative men of various political opinions. At the outset, this did not meet with approval. Later, its wisdom was apparent. In the more than 100 years of United States administration history, there has never been an abler or a purer cabinet.

The system of democracy is not unique to the United States. The freedom to choose leaders is an important part of human rights and democracy around the world. It is so important that the U.S. government has made supporting human rights and democracy a major part of its relationships with other countries. The State Department works directly to help countries have free and fair elections. Sometimes the State Department also works with the United Nations to aid the voting process. By supporting democracies around the world, the United States makes the world safer and more prosperous. The world's people are all better off when they have the freedom to make their own choices, to work for a better life, and to live without fear.

On January 29, 1863, General Grant took command of the army intended to operate against Vicksburg, Mississippi, the last place held by the rebels on the Mississippi, and the only point at which they could cross the river and keep up communication with their armies in the southwest. It was the first high ground below Memphis, was very strongly fortified, and was held by a large army under General Pemberton. The complete possession of the Mississippi was essential to the federal government because the control of that great river would cut the Confederacy in two.

Try It!

Using the guidelines on page 548, paraphrase one of the paragraphs above. Include the main idea and the author's point of view in your own words.

Struggling Learners

If students find it difficult to identify the author's voice to complete the **Try It!** activity, point out words and phrases that have specific connotations associated with them. Remind students that connotation is the key to unlocking a distinct voice.

In the first paragraph, the author is a strong admirer of Lincoln. This is conveyed by the juxtaposition of *utter failure* and *wisdom* and many other words (*plain, foregone conclusion, clearly, not only . . . but also,* and so on).

In the second paragraph, the intensifier *so* after the repetition of *important* and the phrase *better off* underscore the author's emphasis.

In the third paragraph, words such as *command, last, only point, first, strongly fortified, complete,* and *essential* lend a feeling of intensity, urgency, and momentousness to the writer's voice.

551

Taking Tests

Tests are a part of school life. They help instructors see how well you understand a subject and where you need more work. Unfortunately, tests are stressful because they are usually connected with grades, and that stress can work against you. However, if you know how to take a test, you can ease that stress, perform better, and give a more accurate picture of your knowledge and understanding.

Taking a test is like any other challenge in life: If you are prepared, you will do well. This chapter will help you understand the different kinds of tests and the best way to prepare for each. Once you understand that tests are not meant to trick you, but rather to evaluate your understanding, you will be better able to prepare for them.

- **Preparing for a Test**
- **Test-Taking Tips**
- **Taking Objective Tests**
- **Taking Essay Tests**
- **Taking Standardized Tests**

"I loved tests because it was another form of competing, a healthy competition."

—Suzanne Farrell

Taking Tests

Objectives
- understand how to prepare for tests
- learn about the types of objective tests
- learn how to read and respond to writing prompts
- learn strategies for taking standardized tests

Invite students to share how they prepare for tests, to offer any tips they may have for overcoming the anxiety that accompanies taking tests, and to outline their own test-taking strategies. Entertain some less-than-serious responses, which can go a long way toward alleviating the feelings of stress and anxiety that afflict some students at the mere mention of test taking.

Preparing for a Test

Ask students if they have heard the terms *proactive* and *preventive* and to explain how these terms could apply to the steps for preparing for a test. If necessary, have students look up the words in a dictionary.

Students should point out that both *proactive* and *preventive* suggest taking action in the present in order to avoid problems in the future. The steps in the test-prep cycle that are shaded in green are pretest strategies that students can use to avoid anxiety and ensure success.

552

Preparing for a Test

When preparing for a test, you should anticipate its content. Usually, you can expect a test to cover what you've learned in class. Take good notes during lectures and review them often. Also keep your graded assignments so you can look them over later. Following the cycle below will help you improve your test scores.

Test-Prep Cycle

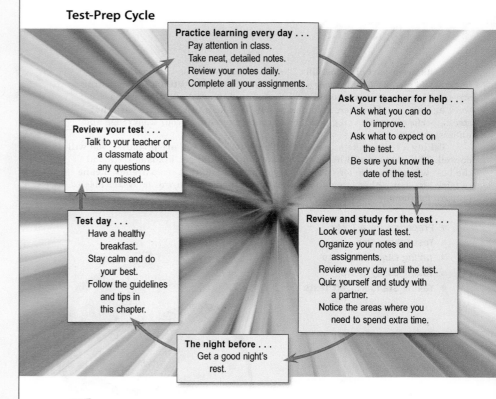

Practice learning every day . . .
Pay attention in class.
Take neat, detailed notes.
Review your notes daily.
Complete all your assignments.

Ask your teacher for help . . .
Ask what you can do to improve.
Ask what to expect on the test.
Be sure you know the date of the test.

Review your test . . .
Talk to your teacher or a classmate about any questions you missed.

Review and study for the test . . .
Look over your last test.
Organize your notes and assignments.
Review every day until the test.
Quiz yourself and study with a partner.
Notice the areas where you need to spend extra time.

Test day . . .
Have a healthy breakfast.
Stay calm and do your best.
Follow the guidelines and tips in this chapter.

The night before . . .
Get a good night's rest.

Try It!

Think of the ways you prepared for your last test. Did you leave out any of the above steps? See if you can improve your test scores by following this test-prep cycle.

English Language Learners

Suggest that students discuss test material with their study partners or in a group. Students can readily cement meaning by talking with others about the content, because they rely on their own words instead of parroting back sentences from their notes.

If students have difficulty discussing a certain part of the text, suggest that they review the material until they can explain it in their own words. They can also ask another student to explain it first and then put the explanation into their own words.

Struggling Learners

Suggest that students make review cards. Have them write a definition on the front and a related test question on the back. For example: "Edgar Allen Poe (1809–1849), an American writer known for his haunting poetry and short fiction, crafted and perfected the psychological thriller genre." The question on the reverse would be: "Who was Edgar Allen Poe?"

Test-Taking Tips

- **Listen carefully** as your teacher gives directions, makes any corrections, or provides other information. Stay focused while your teacher is talking; otherwise, you might miss important comments such as these:

"Make this change in number three."

"You have 30 minutes to finish the test."

"Write your answer to the final question on the back of the test sheet."

- **Put your name on the test right away.**
- **Take a quick look at the entire test.** This will help you decide how much time to spend on each section or question.
- **Begin the test.** Read the instructions before answering each set of questions. Do exactly what they tell you to do.
- **Read each question carefully.** Be sure you understand the question completely before answering it.
- **Answer all of the questions you are sure of first.** Then go back to the other questions and do your best to answer each one. Keep track of the time as you work on the more difficult questions.
- **Check over your answers when you finish the test.** If you skipped any really difficult questions, try to answer them now.

Try It!

Review these tips right before your next test and then put them into practice. Upon completion of the test, determine how closely you followed this advice.

Advanced Learners

Have students discuss strategies they use to help themselves study or retain information. Have one student in the group jot down the students' test tips on a list and then have the group rank the tips from most important to least important. Post the list for the rest of the class.

Test-Taking Tips

Have students use the test-taking tips to prepare for their next test. Afterward, invite students to discuss how closely they followed the tips. Ask them if they can conclude that these tips improved the test-taking experience for them, and if they think following these tips helped their grade. Challenge students who did not use the tips (or who think the tips did not help) to offer tips that might help more next time.

Taking Objective Tests

Read and discuss the four kinds of objective tests shown on SE pages 554–555 and the helpful tips for taking these kinds of tests.

Point out that if students are good test takers, they probably already apply all or most of these tips. However, there are other tips that can also prove helpful.

- For true/false statements, remember that two negatives make a positive. In other words, the negatives cancel out each other. If a statement has two negatives, cross out the negatives and reread the statement to see if it is true or false, for example,

It is ~~unlikely~~ ice will ~~not~~ melt when the temperature rises above 32 degrees.

- For matching tests with letters, make sure that you write the letter of the answer choice (a, b, c, and so on). Under pressure, it's easy to write the letter that begins the text of the answer instead.

554

Taking Objective Tests

Tests often have four different types of objective questions: true/false, matching, multiple-choice, and fill-in-the-blanks.

True/False

In a true/false test, you decide if a statement is correct or incorrect. Most true/false questions focus on the details, so read each statement carefully.

- **Look for absolutes and qualifiers.** Statements with absolutes such as *always, never, all,* and *none* are often false. Statements that use qualifiers such as *often, rarely,* and *seldom* are more likely to be true.

  False Nearsightedness is *always* hereditary in nature.
  (Nearsightedness is *often* hereditary in nature.)

  True As weather conditions change, warm, moist air associated with the Gulf Stream *often* provides a source of moisture for rainfall.

- **Test each part.** If even a single word or phrase in a statement is false, then the entire statement is false.

  False The Gulf Stream is a warm, rapid, relatively narrow ocean current that flows along the west coast of the United States.
  (The Gulf Stream flows along the *east* coast of the United States.)

- **Watch for statements that contain more than one negative word.** Words such as *don't, can't, doesn't,* and *wasn't* can confuse, so be sure you know what the statement means.

  True It is unlikely ice will not melt when the temperature rises above 32 degrees F.

Matching

In matching tests, you match items in one column to those in another column.

- **Read both columns before answering any questions.** This helps you find the best match for each item.
- **Match the items you know first.** If each answer is used only once, cross out the letter or number after you've used it.
- **Find grammar clues.** For example, plural subjects need plural verbs.

Match each word with its meaning.

~~1~~. animus	__2__	a lack of oxygen in the lungs
~~2~~. asphyxia	_____	those who argue in defense of a doctrine
3. apologists	__1__	a motivating force

Multiple-Choice

In multiple-choice questions, you choose the right answer from several possibilities.

- **Read each question carefully.** Usually, you will be asked to choose the best answer. Sometimes your choices may include "all of the above" or "none of the above."

  1. In *Frankenstein,* who is accused of murdering Victor's younger brother?
     A. Victor   C. Justine
     B. Alphonse   D. none of the above

- **Anticipate the answer.** Before reading the choices, try to answer the question or complete the sentence.
- **Read all the choices before you answer.** It's tempting to choose the first answer that seems close, but there may be another choice that is better.
- **Consider "all of the above" and "none of the above" answers carefully.** If there is even one choice that you know to be incorrect, do not choose "all of the above." If there is one choice you know to be correct, do not choose "none of the above."
- **Eliminate the wrong or unlikely choices first.**

  2. The first telegraph signal was successfully sent in _____.
     A. 1866   C. 1799 *(too early)*
     B. 1940 *(too late)*   D. 1902 *(first radio signal across the Atlantic)*

Fill-in-the-Blanks

Fill-in-the-blanks questions require you to complete the missing parts of a statement.

- **Check the number of blanks.** Often, there is one for each word.

  1. The "backbone" of the North American continent is the *continental divide*.

- **Check for grammar clues.** If there is an *a* before the blank, the answer should begin with a consonant. If there is an *an* before the blank, the answer should begin with a vowel.

  2. A polygon of eight sides and eight angles is an *octagon* .

◄ Try It!

Which types of objective questions are the most difficult for you? Use these tips to help you on your next test.

Tests

Remind students that while these tips for taking objective tests are helpful, the best way to reduce anxiety and improve test scores is to follow the steps of the test-prep cycle described on SE page 552.

Some teachers favor one type of objective test over another. Students usually learn early in the year what type of test to expect in each class. Encourage students to ask all of their teachers for information about upcoming tests, to use the test-taking tips in this section, and to prepare for each test in advance.

English Language Learners

Students may find it difficult to complete fill-in-the-blank items that fall inside a sentence. They may find it easier to answer items in which the blank falls at the end of the sentence because they can use the rest of the sentence to build context. If possible, modify test items so blanks fall at the end of the sentence.

Struggling Learners

To assist students in answering a question in which the blank occurs near the beginning of a statement, suggest that they rephrase the statement as a question. For example, The _____ _____ is a large current of fast-moving, warm water that flows along the east coast of the United States. Ask: *What current flows along the east coast of the United States?* (Gulf Stream)

Advanced Learners

Have volunteers create some true/false, matching, and multiple-choice questions on a topic that the class is studying or is otherwise familiar with, along with tips on how to prepare for answering such questions. Post the tips as a class reference.

Taking Essay Tests

Tell students that every time they respond to a prompt, they are engaging in one or more of six basic **levels of thinking** *(see below)*: recall, understand, apply, analyze, synthesize, evaluate. Each of the key words listed is a clue to the level of thinking they will use to answer the prompt.

- Define, Identify, Review (Recall)
- Describe, Explain, Summarize (Understand)
- Illustrate, Prove (Apply)
- Cause, Compare, Contrast (Analyze)
- Evaluate (Evaluate)

Also note that none of the key words on the list refers to *synthesize*. Synthesizing is bringing together information from more than one source, using key words such as *create* and *predict,* not on the list.

Try It!
Answers

Possible Answers

1. Macbeth is a tragic hero because his tragic flaws of greed and overconfidence lead to his downfall.
2. Before killing Duncan, Macbeth has a vision of a dagger floating in the air, leading him to the bedroom where the king is sleeping.

556

Taking Essay Tests

Many students feel that essay questions are the hardest type because, unlike other questions, possible answers are not given. Essay-test prompts require you to show how facts and supporting details are connected. The next few pages offer tips for taking an essay test.

Understanding and Restating the Prompt

- **Read the question carefully.**
- **Underline the key words** that explain what you are being asked to do. Here are some key words and their explanations.

    Compare . . . . . Tell how things are alike.
    Contrast . . . . . Tell how things are different.
    Cause . . . . Describe how one thing has affected another.
    Define . . . . Give a clear, specific meaning for a word or an idea.
    Describe . . . . . Use sensory details to explain how something looks, sounds, and so on.
    Evaluate . . . . . Make a value judgment supported by facts or examples.
    Explain. . . . . . . Use details and facts to tell what something means or how it works, or give reasons that tell why.
    Identify . . . . . . Answer the question using one or more of the 5 W's.
    Illustrate . . . . . Use examples to show how something works or why it's important.
    Prove . . . . Use facts and details to tell why something is true.
    Review. . . . . . . Create an overall picture of the topic.
    Summarize . . . Tell the main idea and key points about the topic.

- **Rephrase the prompt into a thesis statement.** It often works well to drop the key word from your thesis statement.

    Prompt: Explain why Macbeth plans to have Banquo and his son, Fleance, murdered.

    Thesis statement: Macbeth plans to murder Banquo and Fleance because he doesn't want Fleance to become king.

Try It!

Turn each essay-test prompt below into a thesis statement.

1. Explain what makes Macbeth a tragic hero.
2. Describe the vision Macbeth sees before he kills Duncan.

Teaching Tip: Levels of Thinking

Review how to use different levels of thinking when writing a response for an essay prompt.

- **Recall**—supply details, identify or define key terms, remember main points
- **Understand**—explain how something works, give reasons for something, summarize or paraphrase

- **Apply**—consider how to use the information, reorganize information
- **Analyze**—make comparisons and contrasts, point out what is important, categorize items, identify cause-and-effect relationships, describe a process

- **Synthesize**—combine ideas from different sources, use information in a creative work, use information to make informed predictions
- **Evaluate**—state an opinion, discuss advantages and disadvantages, suggest a course of action based on findings

Planning a One-Paragraph Response

Tests may include one or more prompts that call for a paragraph response rather than a full-length essay. The following guidelines will help you write an effective one-paragraph response to a prompt.

- **Read the prompt carefully.** Underline the key words and phrases.
- **Identify what you are asked to do** (explain, compare, prove, define).
- **Plan your response.**
  1. Turn the prompt into a topic sentence.
  2. Include at least three supporting details. Keep your topic sentence in mind as you select supporting details.

Prompt

Define and give an example of mutualism.

Planning Notes

Topic sentence: Mutualism is the relationship between two different species of interdependent organisms in which each benefits from the other.

Supporting details:
1. Example: relationship between fruit-bearing plants and fruit-eating birds
2. Fruit provides nutrition for birds
3. Fruit contains seeds that pass through bird's digestive system
4. Bird distributes seeds in waste so plant can reproduce

Paragraph Response

Mutualism

Mutualism is the relationship between two different species of interdependent organisms in which each benefits from the other. A good example of mutualism is the relationship between fruit-bearing plants and fruit-eating birds. When a bird eats fruit, it receives nutrition. The fruit contains seeds that pass through the bird's digestive system. The seeds are distributed in the bird's waste, allowing the fruit-bearing plant to reproduce.

Planning a One-Paragraph Response

After students have had a chance to read the instruction and review the prompt, planning notes, and sample response, ask them to evaluate the response based on the guidelines listed at the top of the page.

- How do you know from the planning notes that the student read and understood the prompt? (The planning notes show a clear topic sentence that contains a definition of *mutualism* and an example to support the definition.)
- Does the response have a clear topic sentence that restates the prompt and defines *mutualism*? (Yes. The topic sentence defines *mutualism* as "the relationship between two different species of interdependent organisms in which each benefits from the other.")
- Does the response include at least three supporting details? What are they? (Yes. The first detail provides an example of mutualism: the relationship between fruit-eating birds and fruit-bearing plants. Three more details explain the interdependence between the birds and the plants.)

English Language Learners

Some students may benefit from creating a "Prompt List." Have them record the key words featured on SE page 556 in their writer's notebook, and ask them to think of examples for each, such as the following:

- **Define** democracy.
- **Evaluate** whether the Supreme Court decision was fair.
- **Review** the parts of the circulatory system.
- **Summarize** Heisenberg's Uncertainty Principle.

Struggling Learners

Some students may have encountered difficulty understanding writing prompts. Have students read prompts from past tests and then restate each prompt in their own words to check for understanding. Have them use the list of key words on SE page 556 to identify the key words in each prompt.

Planning an Essay Response

Explain that if students take the time to properly plan an essay response, it will be easier to write a focused response. For a timed response, they should budget about one-fourth of the total time allowed to plan the response.

■ Point out to students that they can use a full-sentence outline like the one shown, a topic outline, or an organized list to plan their response to a prompt.

✳ For more about outlining, see SE page 591.

■ Before or instead of creating an outline, students can use a variety of graphic organizers to gather ideas for an essay response. For example, to gather ideas for the sample prompt on this page, students could use a Venn Diagram or a T-chart. Both these organizers can help students identify similarities and differences between two topics.

✳ For more graphic organizers students can use to plan a response, see SE pages 64–65 and 213.

558

Planning an Essay Response

Some essay prompts require you to respond with a full-length essay. The following tips will help you write a clear, well-organized response essay.

■ **Read the prompt** and restate it as a thesis statement.
■ **Plan your response** by outlining details that support your thesis.
■ **Write your essay answer.** Include your thesis statement in your opening paragraph. Each main point of your outline becomes the topic sentence for a body paragraph. In the final paragraph, write a meaningful conclusion that shows you truly understand the topic.

Prompt

Contrast how a writer might use dramatic monologue and soliloquy.

Planning Notes

<u>Thesis Statement:</u> Although both techniques involve a single speaker, soliloquy and dramatic monologue have different purposes and effects in literature.

I. A soliloquy and a monologue are both spoken by single characters.
  A. In a soliloquy, the speaker thinks out loud and is usually alone.
  B. An example of a soliloquy is Juliet's balcony speech from Romeo and Juliet.
  C. In a dramatic monologue, the speaker speaks to someone who remains silent.
  D. An example of a dramatic monologue is the duke's speech in the Robert Browning poem "My Last Duchess."
II. Soliloquies and dramatic monologues have specific purposes.
  A. Writers often use soliloquies to reveal a character's thoughts.
    1. Juliet reveals her feelings for Romeo.
    2. When Romeo learns Juliet's feelings, the plot can be advanced.
  B. A dramatic monologue shows how a character relates to others.
    1. The duke tries to prove he would be a good husband. . . .
    2. His words show how he dominated his first wife.

Advanced Learners

Have each student try a different graphic organizer as an alternative to the outline. Have them compare and contrast the results and discuss the advantages and disadvantages of each one. Then post the most successful alternatives for class reference.

Essay Response

The following essay response follows the outline on the previous page. The thesis statement appears at the beginning of the response. The final paragraph is a meaningful conclusion that shows that the writer clearly understands the topic.

Speaking All Alone

Although both techniques involve a single speaker, soliloquy and dramatic monologue have different purposes and effects in literature.

A soliloquy and a dramatic monologue are both spoken by single characters. In a soliloquy, the speaker thinks out loud and is usually alone. One of the most famous soliloquies occurs in Romeo and Juliet when Juliet speaks from her heart near the start of the balcony scene. During a dramatic monologue, a character speaks to someone who remains silent. In Robert Browning's poem "My Last Duchess," the duke talks about his former wife to another man, whose reactions we do not hear.

Soliloquies and dramatic monologues have specific purposes. Writers often use soliloquies to reveal a character's thoughts. In the balcony scene, Juliet says things to herself that she would not tell anyone else. She is embarrassed when Romeo speaks and reveals his presence. We (and Romeo) know her true thoughts, and the romance picks up speed.

A dramatic monologue shows how a character relates to others. The duke in "My Last Duchess" is talking to a man who has been sent to find out whether the duke would be a good husband. Instead of showing himself to be a considerate man, the duke brags about how he dominated his first wife. His words reveal a totally unlikable character.

Literary characters can be interesting for what they say. Soliloquy and dramatic monologue are two methods that writers use to tell the reader what their characters are really like. Even though only one character is speaking in both cases, the effects can be critical to the plot.

Try It!

Plan and respond to the following prompt: Aldous Huxley said, "Technological progress has merely provided us with more efficient means for going backward." Do you agree or disagree? Support your opinion with two examples from history or from your own observations or experiences.

Essay Response

Students will learn about using STRAP questions to analyze a prompt on SE pages 569–573. However, you may wish to introduce that strategy now and discuss how students can use it to plan and respond to the prompt for the **Try It!** activity.

- **Subject:** What topic should I write about? (the effects of technological progress on society)
- **Type:** What form of writing should I create? (essay)
- **Role:** (student, any member of society)
- **Audience:** (teacher)
- **Purpose:** (analyze and evaluate)

* For more about using the STRAP questions to analyze a prompt, see SE pages 212–216.

English Language Learners

Review unfamiliar vocabulary before students begin the **Try It!** activity:

- technological progress (improvements in technology)
- efficient (effective, useful)
- means (ways, resources)
- going backward (heading toward a time or place that is not as advanced)

Struggling Learners

Reading and responding to an entire page of text may be difficult for some students. Simplify the task by suggesting that students read and respond to one paragraph at a time.

Taking Standardized Tests

Point out that these guidelines for taking standardized tests are meant to reduce anxiety. Although it may be obvious, the less stressed and anxious students feel, the greater their chances are of completing the test successfully. Offer these additional tips.

- Students should not expect to know the answer to every question immediately. Some questions will require more thought than others, but as suggested on this page, after one minute they should move on to the next question.
- If students decide to skip a question, suggest that they circle the corresponding number on the answer sheet. This will ensure that they can find the question easily if they have time at the end to come back to it. It will also prevent them from accidentally using those answer choices to mark the answer to the next question.

Taking Standardized Tests

At certain times throughout your formal education, you will be required to take standardized tests. The guidelines below will help you take these tests.

Before the test . . .

- **Know what to expect.** Ask your teacher what subjects will be covered on the standardized test, what format will be used, and what day the test will be given.
- **Get a good night's rest.** Also be sure to eat breakfast before any test.
- **Be prepared.** Bring extra pens, pencils, and erasers. Make sure to have enough blank paper for notes, outlines, or numerical calculations.

During the test . . .

- **Listen to the instructions and carefully follow directions.** Standardized tests follow strict guidelines. You will be given exact instructions on how to fill in information and supply answers.
- **Pace yourself.** In general, don't spend more than one minute on an objective question; move on and come back to it later.
- **Keep your eyes on your own work.** Don't worry if others finish before you.
- **Match question numbers to answer numbers.** If you skip a question in the question booklet, be sure to skip the corresponding number on your answer sheet. After answering every few questions, double-check the question number against your answer sheet.
- **Answer every question.** As long as there is no penalty for incorrect answers, you should always answer every question. First eliminate all the choices that are obviously incorrect and then use logic to make your best educated guess.
- **Review your answers.** If you have time left, be sure that you've answered all the questions and haven't made any accidental mistakes. In general, don't change an answer unless you are sure that it's wrong. If you need to change an answer, erase the original answer completely.

After the test . . .

- **Be sure you have filled in all information correctly.**
- **Erase any unnecessary marks before turning in your test.**

Taking Exit and Entrance Exams

Teachers and administrators use exit and entrance exams to assess your ability to use skills and strategies in a subject area such as English or mathematics. Many school districts use exit exams to determine if students are qualified to graduate from high school. Scores on entrance exams such as the SAT and ACT help college admissions departments determine whether a student meets a school's admission standards.

Most exit and entrance exams include components designed to test your writing skills. When you take an entrance or exit exam, you may be asked to respond to writing prompts and answer objective questions that test your revising and editing skills. In this chapter, you'll learn strategies and skills that will help you succeed on the writing portion of exit and entrance exams.

- Questions About Conventions
- Sentence-Revision Questions
- Paragraph-Revision Questions
- Editing Questions
- Responding to Writing Prompts
- Responding to Prompts About Literature
- Budgeting Time for On-Demand Writing

"Beware the man who knows the answer before he understands the question."

—C. M. Manasco

Taking Exit and Entrance Exams

Objectives
- practice answering questions about conventions, sentence-revision questions, paragraph-revision questions, and editing questions
- learn to use STRAP questions to analyze, plan, and write a response to a prompt
- learn how to budget time for on-demand writing

If your district or state requires exit exams for graduation, find out if past tests are available online. If this service is available, suggest that students visit the appropriate Web site to view the tests and to get an idea of the kinds of questions they might be expected to answer at testing time. Scoring guides, rubrics, and sample answer keys are also usually provided with the test so that students can see examples of exemplary short responses and essay responses.

If past tests are available in print form, be sure to have several copies on hand for students to examine.

Advanced Learners

Have students discuss the meaning of the quotation at the bottom of the page. After the discussion, challenge students to write a statement of their own in which the Manasco quotation acts as the underlying theme. Invite them to publish their quotes on the school Web site.

Questions About Conventions

Give students time to complete the **Exercise** activity on their own. Have them jot down the answers on a separate sheet of paper, and tell them to circle any items that were difficult to answer.

Strongly recommend that they complete the activity without looking at the answer key on SE page 563 so that they get a good idea of what kinds of convention questions give them trouble. They should address those issues before they actually have to take a test.

562

Questions About Conventions

Some questions on exit and entrance exams ask you to edit sentences for conventions: punctuation, capitalization, spelling, and grammar. Read each question and its possible answers carefully. The following examples are typical conventions questions.

Exercise

Read the text in *italics* and follow the directions in bold. (Answers appear on the bottom of page 563.)

1. *Dover High School starts the last week in* <u>*August and*</u> *Seth Jones High School begins the first week in September.*
   The best punctuation for the underlined section is

   A. August, and
   B. August and
   C. August. and
   D. NO CHANGE

2. *Charise says that her three* <u>*brothers-in-law*</u> *hope to start a Web-based company that will market their ideas.*
   The correct spelling for the underlined noun is

   A. brother-in-laws
   B. brothers'-in-law
   C. brothers-in-laws
   D. NO CHANGE

3. *The customs agent looked at the passport and asked the man,* <u>*How long will you be staying in New York?*</u>
   The correct punctuation for the underlined section is

   A. "How . . . New York"?
   B. "how . . . New York"?
   C. "How . . . New York?"
   D. NO CHANGE

4. *The decision to change the import* <u>*tariff*</u> *on wool products was not* <u>*spontaneus,*</u> *for it came after five months of* <u>*extensive*</u> *research and debate.*
   Which underlined word is spelled incorrectly?

   A. tariff
   B. spontaneus
   C. extensive
   D. All three are correct.

5. *None of the 85 people on the boat <u>were</u> willing to get into the water once the shark was sighted.*

The correct choice for the underlined word is

A. was
B. are
C. is
D. NO CHANGE

6. *After hiking more than four miles out of the way due to a washed-out trail, the tired group of campers <u>couldn't hardly take</u> another step.*

The correct way to write the underlined section is

A. could hardly take
B. couldn't take
C. Both A and B
D. NO CHANGE

Tip

When you answer multiple-choice questions, be sure to do the following:

- **Read the question completely.** Do not try to answer a question until you understand all of its parts.

- **Read all answers.** Sometimes there is more than one correct answer, or there is no correct answer. The correct response may be "All of the above," "None of the above," or "A and B."

- **Eliminate obviously wrong answers.** Cross out answers you know are incorrect before making your choice.

- **Don't guess.** Most entrance exams will penalize incorrect answers as a way to discourage guessing.

Answer Key

1. The focus is punctuation (compound sentences), and the answer is **A**.
2. The focus is spelling, and the answer is **D**.
3. The focus is punctuation (dialogue), and the answer is **C**.
4. The focus is spelling, and the answer is **B**.
5. The focus is grammar (verb tense and subject-verb agreement), and the answer is **D**.
6. The focus is grammar (double negatives), and the answer is **C**.

Review the answers to the **Exercise** activity with students. For each response, ask students to explain the punctuation, capitalization, spelling, or grammar rule that they used to make the correct choice. If students are not sure why a particular answer is correct or incorrect, refer them to the Proofreader's Guide (see SE pages 605–759).

English Language Learners

Students may use double negatives in their writing because the construction is grammatically correct in their first language. For example, in Spanish, the expression *no tengo nada* ("I don't have nothing") is standard usage. Help make students aware of the difference between this rule in their first language and in English.

Sentence-Revision Questions

The sentence problems that appear in the **Exercise** activity on SE pages 564–565 are addressed throughout the book. Before students complete the activity, recommend that they review the strategies for correcting these problems.

✳ For misplaced modifiers, see SE page 88.

✳ For run-on and rambling sentences, see SE page 87.

✳ For fragments, see SE page 86.

✳ For incomplete or unclear comparisons, see SE page 190.

✳ For how to avoid redundancy, see SE page 79.

✳ For rules related to restrictive and nonrestrictive clauses and phrases, see SE page 612, item 612.2.

✳ For sentence combining, see Varying Sentence Lengths, on SE page 82.

564

Sentence-Revision Questions

Some sentence-revision questions test your ability to revise, combine, clarify, and correct sentences.

Exercise

Read the following sentences and choose the best revision or NO CHANGE. (Answers are on the bottom of page 565.)

1. *Demonstrating a new out-of-bounds play, we sat on the bleachers to watch the basketball coach.*
   - **A.** To watch the basketball coach, we sat on the bleachers demonstrating a new out-of-bounds play.
   - **B.** We sat on the bleachers to watch the basketball coach demonstrating a new out-of-bounds play.
   - **C.** Watching the basketball coach demonstrating a new out-of-bounds play, we sat on the bleachers.
   - **D.** NO CHANGE

2. *On Saturday morning, Thomas ate breakfast and then he put the finishing touches on his science project and then he walked to Dunn's Hardware to start his new job.*
   - **A.** Thomas ate breakfast . . . his science project. Then he walked . . . job.
   - **B.** Thomas ate breakfast. Then he put . . . project. He walked . . . job.
   - **C.** Thomas ate breakfast, put the . . . project, and then walked . . . job.
   - **D.** NO CHANGE

3. *Before we started our workout. We jogged around the track.*
   - **A.** Before we started our workout, we jogged around the track.
   - **B.** We jogged around the track, before we started our workout.
   - **C.** We jogged around the track before we started our workout.
   - **D.** Both A and C

4. *Caroline won more trophies than any other team member.*
   - **A.** Caroline won the most trophies.
   - **B.** Caroline won more trophies than any other team member won.
   - **C.** Caroline won even more trophies than any other team member.
   - **D.** NO CHANGE

5. *The thunderstorm roared through town, soaking the clothes on the line and leaving them dripping wet.*

   A. soaking the clothes on the line and leaving them dripping.
   B. soaking the dripping wet clothes on the line.
   C. leaving the clothes on the line dripping.
   D. NO CHANGE

6. *The girls' soccer team happy to have new uniforms will play in the post-season tournament.*

   A. The girls' soccer team, happy to have new uniforms will play . . . tournament.
   B. The girls' soccer team happy to have new uniforms, will . . . tournament.
   C. The girls' soccer team, happy to have new uniforms, will . . . tournament.
   D. NO CHANGE

7. *The new passenger plane is huge. The plane has two levels for passengers. It can hold as many as 850 people.*

   A. The huge new passenger plane has two levels for passengers and can hold as many as 850 people.
   B. The new passenger plane is huge and has two levels for passengers. It can hold as many as 850 people.
   C. The new passenger plane is huge. It has two levels for passengers and can hold as many as 850 people.
   D. NO CHANGE

Answer Key

1. The focus is misplaced modifiers, and the answer is **B**.
2. The focus is rambling sentences, and the answer is **C**.
3. The focus is fragments and combining, and the answer is **D**.
4. The focus is incomplete comparisons, and the answer is **B**.
5. The focus is avoiding redundancy, and the answer is **C**.
6. The focus is restrictive and nonrestrictive clauses and phrases, and the answer is **C**.
7. The focus is combining sentences, and the answer is **A**.

Remind students that they have practiced and assessed the trait of sentence fluency for every writing assignment in this book. The guidelines, examples, and rubrics have helped them recognize sentence problems and improve their writing. This experience should give them confidence whenever they have to answer sentence-revision questions on a test.

Have students compare their **Exercise** responses to those in the answer key. Make sure students understand why each of the correct responses is the best choice.

Paragraph-Revision Questions

Suggest that students read through the entire text one time. Then have them read through the text again, jotting down suggestions or revising the text to improve its organization of ideas and sentence fluency.

Discuss students' ideas for revising before asking them to answer the questions on SE page 567.

Paragraph-Revision Questions

Some questions test paragraph-revising skills. The key to success is to carefully read and reread the sample paragraph.

Exercise

Read the following text and answer the questions on page 567. (Answers are on the bottom of page 567.)

(1) After World War II, the United States and the Soviet Union engaged in the cold war, the cold war was a protracted political struggle over who would become the dominant world power. *(2)* The two countries competed in a variety of venues. *(3)* Their most dramatic competition was the so-called "space race," the battle to see who could attain supremacy in the exploration of outer space.

(4) In 1957, Russia's launch of *Sputnik 1,* the world's first artificial satellite, shocked the world. *(5)* Suddenly the launch of Sputnik created fears that the Soviet Union would develop space weaponry that would give it a military edge. *(6)* These weapons have rarely been used. *(7)* The launch also shook the United States to its core. As the first nation to develop nuclear weapons, the United States had enjoyed military superiority because of nuclear weapons.

(8) The United States developed its own space program. *(9)* Soon, the program began to focus on an almost unbelievable goal— taking human passengers to the moon and bringing them back. *(10)* The program developed to reach the moon was known as *Apollo. (11)* The first Apollo mission ended in tragedy during a launch simulation when the command module caught fire on the launchpad, killing all three members of the crew. *(12)* Subsequent tests proved successful, and in 1969, *Apollo 11* landed two U.S. astronauts on the moon. *(13)* Around the world, millions watched the event live on television.

(14) Several lunar landings gave the United States a key victory in the space race, but another program helped maintain U.S. dominance. *(15)* In 1981, the United States launched the first reusable space shuttle, signaling the next phase in space exploration. *(16)* More importantly, the United States and the Soviet Union finally began to cooperate on space exploration.

1. *Which part of sentence 1 should be deleted?*

   A. After World War II
   B. engaged in the cold war
   C. the cold war was
   D. NO CHANGE

2. *Which of the following would make the best addition to the beginning of sentence 8?*

   A. In response to *Sputnik,*
   B. The Soviets fought back,
   C. First of all,
   D. In conclusion,

3. *Which of the following sentences should be deleted?*

   A. Sentence 2
   B. Sentence 6
   C. Sentence 11
   D. Sentence 15

4. *Which revision would improve this essay?*

   A. Switch sentence 5 with sentence group 7.
   B. Switch sentence 1 with sentence 3.
   C. Switch sentence 11 with sentence 15.
   D. Switch sentence 15 with sentence 16.

5. *Which sentence would make the best conclusion to this passage?*

   A. The moon would never again be explored.
   B. Space exploration was no longer important.
   C. The *Apollo* program was no longer significant.
   D. The space race was over, but the exploration of space would continue.

Exit and Entrance Exams

Answer Key

1. The focus is correcting comma splices, and the answer is **C**.
2. The focus is effective use of transitions, and the answer is **A**.
3. The focus is details appropriate to the topic sentence, and the answer is **B**.
4. The focus is clear organization, and the answer is **A**.
5. The focus is closings, and the answer is **D**.

Complete the paragraph-revision questions together. Tell students to cover the Answer Key at the bottom of the page, and ask them to explain in their own words why they chose each answer.

After completing the questions and discussing the responses, have volunteers take turns reading aloud the text with the revisions in place in order to hear how these revisions affect the coherence and cohesiveness of the text.

When students are answering a paragraph-revising question on an actual test, suggest that they take the time to read the paragraph with each of the revision choices in place and listen for which choice actually improves the text.

English Language Learners

Students may have difficulty understanding why *A* is the most effective transition for the second question. Point out that the transition *In response* is used to signal a reply to something that has already happened, such as Russia's launch of *Sputnik 1* in the second paragraph on PE page 566.

Editing Questions

Point out that test writers are aware of the most common mistakes test takers make when writing. As a result, tests usually have questions that include these common mistakes.

* Encourage students to look over the list of ten common errors students are likely to find in their writing (SE pages 130–131). Students can keep these problems and their solutions in mind when they do the **Exercise** activity.

Have students jot down answers to each of the items in the activity without looking at the explanations and responses in the Answer Key. Then have students check their answers. Take a survey to find out how many students got all the answers correct. If students can't explain why a correct answer is correct, or why an incorrect answer is wrong, have them find the appropriate rule in the Proofreader's Guide (SE pages 604–763).

568

Editing Questions

Some tests assess your editing skills by asking you to spot problems in writing. (See the tip on page 563.)

Exercise

Choose the underlined word or words that should be edited or choose LEAVE AS IS. (Answers appear at the bottom of the page.)

1. *Jerome, Baker, or Steve <u>are</u> not ready <u>to board</u> the train <u>for</u> New York.*
                   A   **B**   **C**
   D. LEAVE AS IS

2. *Jumping <u>off the fence</u>, Kale <u>he</u> landed badly <u>and</u> twisted his ankle.*
              A   **B**   **C**
   D. LEAVE AS IS

3. *The massive size of the <u>huge</u> volcanic cloud <u>blotted</u> out the sun for <u>three</u> days.*
                 A   **B**   **C**
   D. LEAVE AS IS

4. *<u>After</u> practice, Bill <u>timidly</u> asked the director if he found <u>his</u> playbook.*
     A   **B**   **C**
   D. LEAVE AS IS

5. *<u>For the summer</u>, Jim plans to play baseball, <u>movies</u>, and go <u>swimming</u>.*
         A   **B**   **C**
   D. LEAVE AS IS

6. *After his friends described the roof at the new ballpark, <u>Mr.</u> Abar*
                                           A
   <u>decided</u> he should probably go watch the opening of the roof himself.
     B   **C**
   D. LEAVE AS IS

Answer Key

1. The focus is subject-verb agreement, and the answer is **A**.
2. The focus is double subjects, and the answer is **B**.
3. The focus is wordiness or redundancy, and the answer is **A**.
4. The focus is indefinite pronoun reference, and the answer is **C**.
5. The focus is parallel structure, and the answer is **B**.
6. The focus is ineffective writing, and the answer is **C**.

English Language Learners

Discuss why the last item represents ineffective writing. Point out that *he should watch* is a more effective phrase than *he should <u>probably go</u> watch*. Have students review "waffle words" on SE page 244, if necessary.

Responding to Writing Prompts

Some state and district exit exams require you to respond to a writing prompt in the form of an essay, a narrative, or a letter. You may be prompted to write from your own experience, or you may be asked to read one or two short passages and respond to them. These exams are usually timed, but some states and districts give students as much time as they need.

College entrance tests such as the ACT and SAT also include a timed writing section. The prompts on these tests ask you to support your point of view on a topic. The essays are evaluated on clarity, consistency, level of detail, and appropriateness. While correctness is important, evaluators understand that you are working within a limited time frame.

When you respond to a prompt, start by analyzing the prompt so that you know exactly what the test requires you to write. One way to analyze a prompt is to answer the following **STRAP questions** about it.

> <u>S</u>ubject: What topic (career, service, community) should I write about?
> <u>T</u>ype: What form (essay, letter, editorial, article, report) of writing should I create?
> <u>R</u>ole: What position (student, son or daughter, friend, employee) should I assume as the writer?
> <u>A</u>udience: Who (teacher, parents, friends, community members, employer) is the intended reader?
> <u>P</u>urpose: What is the goal (persuade, respond, evaluate, explain, tell, describe) of my writing?

Exercise

Analyze the following prompts by answering each STRAP question. (Note: If a prompt does not answer a question specifically, use your best judgment to answer.)

1. You have just learned that you can graduate in December. You have the option of taking additional classes and graduating in June or graduating early and beginning course work in a trade school or college. Which would you choose? Write a letter to the faculty and principal explaining your decision and asking for their support.

2. The school's budget has to be cut due to a revenue shortfall. As part of a student-faculty committee, your job is to propose the possible elimination of several sports. Write an essay explaining which sports should be cut and why. Use sound logic.

Responding to Writing Prompts

If this is the first time students are using the STRAP questions to analyze a prompt, take time to carefully go over the meaning of each letter in the acronym.

 For more about using the STRAP questions to analyze a prompt, see SE pages 212–216.

Exercise Answers

Possible Answers

1. **Subject:** early graduation
   Type: letter
   Role: student
   Audience: faculty and principal of school
   Purpose: explain (decision) and persuade (to provide support)

2. **Subject:** cuts to sports program because of limited revenues
   Type: essay
   Role: member of student-faculty committee
   Audience: students, faculty
   Purpose: explain (which sports to cut and why)

Advanced Learners

Have students choose one of the **Exercise** prompts and plan out their written response, using an outline or an alternative graphic organizer.

Have students then analyze their plan to determine what STRAP questions they have clearly included in it. It is possible that not all STRAP questions are overtly a part of the plan. If not, have students ask themselves which ones are missing and why. Remind them to keep these more subtle aspects of their response in mind when they are writing.

Reviewing a Prompt and Response

Remind students that they should draw on all of their essay-writing skills and experience to write a response to a prompt. Offer this advice:

- Follow the steps in the writing process, including prewriting, writing, revising, and editing.
- Apply the first five writing traits (ideas, organization, voice, word choice, and sentence fluency) as you write and revise. Check the conventions of punctuation, capitalization, spelling, and grammar when you edit.
- Write a **beginning** that introduces the topic and contains a thesis statement, **middle paragraphs** that support the thesis, and an **ending** that summarizes the main points and leaves the reader with something to think about.

Reviewing a Prompt and Response

The following prompt is similar to what you would find on an entrance or exit exam. Review it and the student response.

Sample Prompt

Former Green Bay Packers coach Vince Lombardi knew a lot about teamwork. According to Lombardi, "People who work together will win, whether it be against complex football defenses, or the problems of modern society." Drawing on your own experience, write an essay for your classmates explaining how a project you worked on benefited from teamwork.

STRAP Answers and Quick List

The student writer analyzed the prompt using the STRAP questions, wrote his position, and created a quick list. (See page 213 for other useful graphic organizers.)

Subject: Value of teamwork	**Position:** Teamwork makes a big project go smoothly.
Type: Essay of exposition	– The benefit concert demanded more than I could handle alone.
Role: Student	– I needed volunteers for the many tasks.
Audience: Classmates	– A dedicated group got the job done.
Purpose: Explain a personal experience.	

Sample Response

Next, the student developed his response. He paid as much attention to each part—the beginning, the middle, and the ending—as time permitted.

The **beginning** leads to a position statement (underlined).

Teamwork at Work

After volunteering at the Mendon Brook Food Bank last summer, I decided to organize a classical concert to benefit the facility. I thought it would be something I could accomplish on my own, but doing the project taught me a valuable lesson: Sometimes it takes more than one person to get the job done. The food bank benefit concert succeeded because a talented group of people combined their skills and worked as a team.

At first, I thought that I could easily organize the benefit concert by myself. As a member of the school orchestra, I had played violin in concerts for six years. I felt confident playing in public and had even performed in several benefit concerts. In addition, I knew other musicians who could help me realize my plan.

As I began to work, I realized the project was too big for just one person. It takes more than music to make a concert happen. I was able to put together a group of musicians and choose selections to perform, but I needed to find a venue, generate publicity, and even provide catering for people who attended. I quickly became overwhelmed and asked some friends and relatives for help.

My friend Carla, who is a fantastic writer and artist, handled the publicity like a professional. James, who had a summer job at a local college, found a hall we could use for free. Anna and her mother, who both love to cook, took charge of the catering. My dad found volunteers from work to serve as ushers. As the project progressed, we all ended up pitching in to do a little of everything.

In the end, the benefit concert was a great success, raising $700 for the Mendon Brook Food Bank. I also benefited because I learned the value of teamwork. The next time I need to tackle a project, I'll try the team approach. When it comes to doing a big job, the skills and energy of a group of people accomplish more than one person could ever accomplish alone.

Middle paragraphs share examples of teamwork to support the main idea.

The **ending** restates the lesson learned through this experience.

Exit and Entrance Exams

Exercise

Use the STRAP questions to analyze the following prompt. Then create a position statement and quick list and begin your response. Finish writing, revising, and editing in the time your teacher provides.

Imagine that the Senate wants to require that all people serve their country prior to pursuing college or a career. Would you support compulsory two-year service to the country for graduating seniors? The service could be community- or military-based. Write a letter to your senator supporting your position.

After students have had a chance to read the sample response, ask them if they think the student successfully responded to the prompt and why. (Most students will probably agree the student has written a well-constructed essay that clearly explains how a project he worked on—a classical concert to benefit a food bank—succeeded because of the combined efforts and talents of a large group of people, including his fellow musicians, several friends, and his dad.)

Exercise Answers

Possible Answers

- **Subject:** two-year compulsory service to the country for graduating seniors
- **Type:** letter
- **Role:** graduating senior
- **Audience:** my senator
- **Purpose:** explain a position on a controversial topic

Position statements and quick lists will vary.

Responding to Prompts About Literature

Provide students with these additional tips for writing responses to literature prompts.

- Be aware of the time you have available. Be sure to allow some time at the end to revise and edit.
- Use the STRAP questions to be sure you understand the prompt.
- Circle the key ideas in the prompt and read the literature with these important ideas in mind.
- Take notes that will help you form a solid thesis statement.
- Jot down your own insights about the work as they come to you.

✳ For extensive instruction, examples, and practice about responding to prompts about literature, see SE pages 323–339.

572

Responding to Prompts About Literature

Prompts may be based on literature that you have read prior to the exam or on selections that you read during the test. Here are some tips on writing responses to literature.

- **Write a thesis (focus) statement.** Reword the prompt so that it applies to the literature you're writing about.
- **Briefly outline your main points.** Support your thesis statement with convincing details.
- **Avoid summarizing the literature.** Follow your outline; don't simply retell a story or paraphrase a poem.
- **Include comments on the author's techniques.** Point out literary devices (symbols, repetition, metaphors, word choice) that reveal the author's purpose.
- **Make direct references to the text.** Quote or paraphrase important excerpts to support your analysis.

Sample Prompt and Response

> *Time and mortality are common themes in literature. The two poems that follow both deal with these themes, and each also says something about art itself. In "When I Have Fears That I May Cease to Be," John Keats writes about a poet's anxiousness to capture his thoughts on paper. In "Languages," Carl Sandburg describes how all languages change with time. Discuss what these two poems, taken together, have to say about time and human expression.*

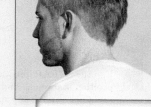

When I Have Fears That I May Cease to Be

When I have fears that I may cease to be
Before my pen has glean'd my teeming brain,
Before high piled books, in charact'ry,
Hold like rich garners the full-ripen'd grain;
When I behold, upon the night's starr'd face,
Huge cloudy symbols of a high romance,
And think that I may never live to trace
Their shadows, with the magic hand of chance;
And when I feel, fair creature of an hour!
That I shall never look upon thee more,
Never have relish in the faery power
Of unreflecting love!—then on the shore
Of the wide world I stand alone, and think
Till Love and Fame to nothingness do sink.
—John Keats (1795–1821)

English Language Learners

Work with students to help them understand Keats's poem. Read the title and discuss its literal meaning (the poet fears death). Then read the poem, stopping after each line, providing definitions for unfamiliar words. Then read the poem again, focusing on how the poet describes what he will miss if he were to die before he had written, read, and loved enough. Tell students that John Keats (1795–1821) wrote prolifically but died at the age of 25 of tuberculosis.

Struggling Learners

Many students may struggle with the meanings of the poems. Before reading them, have students turn ahead to SE page 574 and read the sample response to provide them with some scaffolding. Once students have read the analysis, have them read each poem carefully and discuss the central theme (mortality).

Taking Exit and Entrance Exams **573**

Languages

There are no handles upon a language
Whereby men take hold of it
And mark it with signs for its remembrance.
It is a river, this language,
Once in a thousand years
Breaking a new course
Changing its way to the ocean.
It is mountain effluvia
Moving to valleys
And from nation to nation
Crossing borders and mixing.
Languages die like rivers.
Words wrapped round your tongue today
And broken to shape of thought
Between your teeth and lips speaking
Now and today
Shall be faded hieroglyphics
Ten thousand years from now.
Sing—and singing—remember
Your song dies and changes
And is not here to-morrow
Any more than the wind
Blowing ten thousand years ago.

—Carl Sandburg (1878–1967)

Exit and Entrance Exams

STRAP Answers and Quick List

<u>S</u>ubject: Time and human
expression in
"When I Have
Fears . . ." and
"Languages"
<u>T</u>ype: Essay
<u>R</u>ole: Reader
<u>A</u>udience: Testers
<u>P</u>urpose: Analyze

<u>Position</u>: Both poems are positive
statements about eternity.
1. Keats feels the tension of limited time.
 – Too many ideas, eternal "symbols,"
   mortal love
 – He takes comfort in eternity.
2. Sandburg describes continual change.
 – Languages change and die like rivers.
 – Sing because today will soon be gone.

Point out to students that people don't always agree about the meaning of a poem. Interpretations of symbolic and figurative language and of the author's purpose in using these literary devices can differ from one analysis to the next. However, as long as students use logical reasoning, support their ideas with direct references to the text, and apply the traits of good writing to their analysis, their response will be successful.

It is possible that students will be asked to write about a poem that they don't understand, at least not on their first reading.

- Point out that the prompt will often provide clues to the theme of the poem and other ideas explored in the poem. For an example of this, students can look at the sample prompt on SE page 572, which states the themes in the poems and how the two poets treat these themes.
- Tell students to take their time and read the poem several times. As they read and reread the poem, they may be surprised at how the meaning of the poem begins to reveal itself.

Sample Response

Have students note the use of ellipsis points in the response. Remind students that ellipsis points indicate to the reader that words have been left out of a direct quotation from the literary work. Tell students that when they are deciding what to leave out of a quoted reference, they need to be sure that the text will still make sense to readers who may not have the poem in front of them. Students should also be careful to choose only those quotations that support their analysis.

574

Sample Response

Following his quick list, the student wrote a response that quoted and paraphrased passages from the two poems.

Inevitable Change

The **beginning** introduces both poems and ends with a thesis statement (underlined).

John Keats' famous sonnet "When I Have Fears That I May Cease to Be" may seem extremely dark and pessimistic. It may seem to end on an especially negative note about the pointlessness of effort in the face of eternity. Likewise, Carl Sandburg's "Languages" might be interpreted as a depressing recognition of mortality in the face of endless change. Upon careful reading, however, these two works reveal something different. <u>Both poems are actually positive statements about life and eternity.</u>

The first **middle** paragraph discusses one poem.

Keats' opening line "When I have fears . . . " begins in tension. The first three quatrains reveal fear that there won't be time to write all the thoughts of his "teeming brain," to explore "huge . . . symbols of a high romance," and to enjoy simple, "unreflecting love." In the final couplet, Keats' answer to these fears is to "stand alone" on the "shore of the wide world" until all tension fades. The suggestion is that it fades in the face of eternity.

The next **middle** paragraph discusses the other poem.

Similarly, Sandburg's poem ends with a statement that may seem bleak. He says, "Your song . . . / . . . is not here to-morrow" and compares it to "the wind / Blowing ten thousand years ago." Within the context of the whole poem, however, we can see that Sandburg celebrates life. He describes language as a living river, unable to be controlled. He says, "Sing—and singing—remember." What we are to remember is that life itself is change.

The **ending** revisits the thesis statement.

Together, these two poems reveal that eternity need not be frightening. It is only when people fear their mortality that they either grow tense at the shortness of time—as in Keats' poem—or try to resist change—as in Sandburg's. By accepting their mortality, the authors suggest, people become free to sing and love and explore and grow—to enjoy to the fullest their time on earth.

English Language Learners

Point out the key phrase *taken together* in the sample prompt on SE page 572. Help students understand the sample response by using a graphic organizer or a list to record the common features in both poems. Pause periodically to record the similarities. Review the information in the graphic organizer once the reading has been completed.

Advanced Learners

Have students choose two poems for the purpose of analyzing similar elements across texts. Have them compare the poems using one or more of the following:

- theme
- tone
- writing style/author's purpose
- symbols
- subject matter

Budgeting Time for On-Demand Writing

Responding to a prompt in an "on-demand" writing environment requires a special set of skills. The following tips can help you create your best response.

Before you write . . .

- **Know how much time you have.** Structure your response according to the clock. Use an accelerated approach for a 30-minute response, but take more time with prewriting and revising if you have 60 or 90 minutes.
- **Analyze the prompt.** Answer the STRAP questions so that you know exactly how to respond. Here are a sample prompt and one student's analysis:

What does it mean to be a humble person? What kind of person is humble? Write an essay defining humility and how it relates to the life of a student.

Subject: Humility
Type: Essay of definition
Role: Student
Audience: Tester
Purpose: To define

- **Plan your response.** Write your thesis or opinion statement and use a brief outline or graphic organizer to plan your writing.

During your writing . . .

- **Write an effective beginning paragraph.** Capture your reader's attention, introduce the topic, and state your thesis.
- **Develop the middle part.** Begin each paragraph with a topic sentence (main point) that supports your thesis. Each topic sentence should pertain to and explain your thesis. Use a variety of details, including quotations, paraphrases, and analyses. For persuasive writing, answer a major objection to your opinion.
- **Write a strong ending paragraph.** Complete your writing by providing a final thought or by restating your thesis. For persuasive writing, consider a call to action.

After you've written a first draft . . .

- **Read your work.** Watch for places where adding, cutting, or moving details will make your work stronger.
- **Check for conventions.** Correct any errors you find.

Budgeting Time for On-Demand Writing

Tell students to use these formulas for budgeting time for on-demand writing assignments.

For a 30-minute response:
- 5 to 10 minutes prewriting
- 15 to 20 minutes writing
- 5 minutes revising and editing

For a 45-minute response:
- 10 to 15 minutes prewriting
- 20 to 25 minutes writing
- 5 to 10 minutes revising and editing

For a 60-minute response:
- 15 minutes prewriting
- 30 to 35 minutes writing
- 10 to 15 minutes revising and editing

English Language Learners

Point out the key words *defining* and *relates to* in the prompt. Tell students that these are clues that their response needs two parts. Explain that first students must define, or give the meaning of, the word *humility*. After that, they must explain how humility relates to, or is meaningful to, the life of a student.

Struggling Learners

Point out that the accelerated approach for a 30-minute response will differ in many ways from 60- or 90-minute responses. Tell students that even with less time, they will benefit from using a graphic organizer to plan their ideas and write their first draft. If time allows, they can revise and edit. Point out that evaluators of essay tests take into consideration the time constraints that are imposed on students.

Writing Paragraphs Level 12 *Write Source* (One Week)

Day	Writing and Skills Instruction	Student Edition		SkillsBook	Write Source Online
		Main Pages	Resource Units*		
1–3	**Basic Paragraph Skills** (Models)	577–583			
	(Topic Sentences)	579			
	(Types and Patterns)	580–588			
	Revising Skills:				
	Editing Skills: • Abbreviations, Numbers		658–659, 660–661, 662–663	45, 46	
	• Apostrophes		628–629, 630–631	25, 26, 27, 28	
4–5	**Basic Essay Skills**	589–603			

* These units are also located in the back of the *Teacher's Edition*. Resource Units include "Basic Elements of Writing" and "Proofreader's Guide."
(+) This activity is located in a different section of the *Write Source Student Edition*. If students have already completed this activity, you may wish to review it at this time.

Academic Vocabulary

Read aloud the academic terms, as well as the descriptions and questions. Model for students how to read one question and answer it. Have partners monitor their understanding and seek clarification of the terms by working through the meanings and questions together.

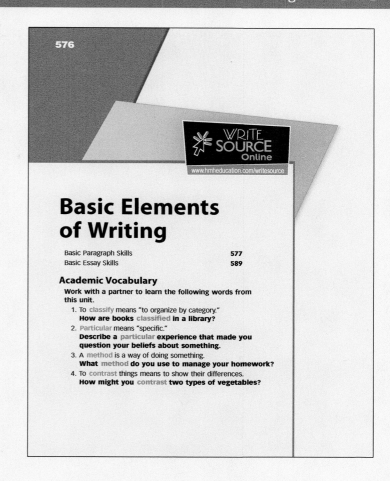

576

WRITE SOURCE Online
www.hmheducation.com/writesource

Basic Elements of Writing

Academic Vocabulary

Work with a partner to learn the following words from this unit.

1. To classify means "to organize by category."
   How are books classified in a library?
2. Particular means "specific."
   Describe a particular experience that made you question your beliefs about something.
3. A method is a way of doing something.
   What method do you use to manage your homework?
4. To contrast things means to show their differences.
   How might you contrast two types of vegetables?

Basic Paragraph Skills

When it comes to writing well, you must remember these two words: support and organization. You need to select details that support your main point, and you need to organize those details effectively. That's where the simple, time-honored tradition of paragraphing comes into play. Paragraphs help you organize your thoughts and make it easier for the reader to follow your line of thinking.

In this chapter, you will examine the four basic types of paragraphs. Each has a specific purpose, and each requires a particular type of thinking. Then you will look at examples of different ways you can organize your paragraphs to make them most effective. Learning how to write effective paragraphs will give you control of all your academic writing—from essays to research papers.

- The Parts of a Paragraph
- Types of Paragraphs: Narrative, Descriptive, Expository, and Persuasive
- Patterns of Organization: Classification, Comparison-Contrast, Cause-Effect, Process, and Climax

"I often have to write a hundred pages or more before there's a paragraph that's alive."

—Philip Roth

The Parts of a Paragraph

A basic paragraph contains three parts: a topic sentence, body sentences, and a closing sentence. Each detail in the body supports the topic sentence. The following expository paragraph provides information about hot-air ballooning.

Topic Sentence

Body

Closing Sentence

Hot-Air Ballooning

Based on the simple scientific principle that hot air rises, hot-air ballooning has been a popular pastime for more than two centuries. While the idea of a lighter-than-air vehicle had been around since Archimedes, the first functional balloon was created in France in 1783 by brothers Joseph and Etienne Montgolfier, who sent a duck, a chicken, and a sheep into the air for a brief but historical ride. Later that year, the first manned trip was taken by physicist Pilatre de Rozier and the Marquis Francois d'Arlandes, who glided over Paris for 28 minutes. Today's balloons have changed little from those early models, with the balloon envelope designed to trap hot air and lift the structure into the air. The envelope is formed from many strips, called *gores*, pieced together to create a rounded shape. The Montgolfiers' envelope was made of paper, but later balloons were created of silk, and today's models are usually made of ripstop nylon. The tapered bottom edge is open, with a fireproof skirt attached. Early balloons were kept aloft by burning a mixture of straw and manure, but today, propane tanks are used, suspended just below the skirt. Beneath the tanks hangs a basket, usually made of wicker, and large enough for passengers and extra propane tanks. Hot-air ballooning fell out of favor in the nineteenth century with the advent of gas balloons, which could travel farther. Then, in the mid-twentieth century, traditional ballooning had a renaissance. Today people enjoy peaceful scenic rides as well as the sport of balloon racing. Whatever the purpose, balloon enthusiasts throughout the world enjoy gliding on air.

Respond to the reading. What is the main idea of this paragraph? What specific details in the body support this idea? Name two or three of them.

A Closer Look at the Parts

Every paragraph, whether written to stand alone or to be part of a longer piece of writing, has three parts.

The Topic Sentence

Every topic sentence should do two things: (1) give the specific topic of the paragraph and (2) present a specific feature or feeling about the topic. When writing your topic sentence, you could use the following formula as a guide.

a specific topic (*hot-air ballooning*)

+ a particular feature or feeling about the topic (*has been a popular pastime for more than two centuries*)

= an effective topic sentence (*Hot-air ballooning has been a popular pastime for more than two centuries.*)

Tip

You can add phrases or clauses to your topic sentence as long as the basic sentence contains the main point your paragraph will explore.

Based on the simple scientific principle that hot air rises, **hot-air ballooning has been a popular pastime for more than two centuries.**

The Body

Each sentence in the body of the paragraph should support the topic sentence while adding new details about the topic.

- Use specific details to make your paragraph interesting.
  Early balloons were kept aloft by burning a mixture of straw and manure.

- Use the method of organization that best suits your topic: classification, order of importance, chronological order, and so on.

The Closing Sentence

The closing sentence ends the paragraph. It may restate the topic, summarize the paragraph, or provide a link to the next paragraph.

Whatever the purpose, balloon enthusiasts throughout the world enjoy gliding on air.

Basic Elements

Answers

Respond to the reading.

Main idea: Hot-air ballooning has been popular for more than 200 years.

Details:

- descriptions of balloon materials
- facts about the first workable hot-air balloon in France (1783)
- information about gas balloons winning favor over hot-air balloons in the nineteenth century
- the renaissance of traditional ballooning

Grammar Connection

Apostrophes

- **Proofreader's Guide** pages 628–629, 630–631
- *SkillsBook* pages 25, 26, 27, 28

Types of Paragraphs

There are four basic types of paragraphs: *narrative, descriptive, expository,* and *persuasive.*

Narrative Paragraph

A **narrative paragraph** tells a story. It may draw from the writer's personal experience or from other sources of information. A narrative paragraph is almost always organized chronologically, or according to time.

Topic Sentence

Body

Closing Sentence

A Good Start

Working in a day care center wasn't my idea of an ideal job, but it was the only one I had been offered, so I steeled myself for a summer surrounded by crazy kids. I was surprised to find the basement was relatively quiet. About eighteen kids of varying ages filled various areas of the main room. Some were building small projects, some were reading, and others were softly practicing musical instruments. I was taken to a back room with high, sunny windows. There, nine little kids were busy around a long table, engrossed in planting a minigarden in long wooden trays. I was an assistant supervisor, and soon we were giggling away, "hoeing" rows with our fingers and carefully planting tiny tomato and pepper seeds. One little girl shyly pulled on my shirt. Her neatly cornrowed hair sparkled in the sunlight as she softly asked me to help her plant some beans. I held a little jar over some newspaper as she carefully poured in some dirt. Then we selected some beans from a small pile. As she gently wriggled them down between the glass and the dirt, she explained that this way we could watch them grow. When we were finished, she gave me a smile and a hug. As we admired our work, I said to myself that this summer might be fun.

 Respond to the reading. What is the tone of the story (sad, humorous, angry, and so on)? What details help make the story interesting? Amusing?

 Write a narrative paragraph. Write a narrative paragraph in which you share your first job interview or your first tryout for an activity.

Descriptive Paragraph

A **descriptive paragraph** gives the reader a detailed picture of a person, a place, an object, or an event. This type of paragraph should contain a variety of sensory details—specific sights, sounds, smells, tastes, and textures.

Topic Sentence

Body

Closing Sentence

The Garden on the Balcony

In the middle of the city, high above the traffic and pollution, my mother has created a little bit of country on our apartment's balcony. When I step out through the sliding door, I feel as though I have been transported to a secret garden. The sounds of traffic are muffled, creating a soft background that mingles with the lively Tejano music my mom plays. On the left, a wall divides our balcony from our neighbor's. There, my mother has leaned a trellis and planted pots of climbing vines. In the summer, purple and pink trumpet-shaped flowers create a gorgeous cascade of color. In the fall, the leaves glow red. My dad built a slender table that hugs part of the safety wall along the front of the balcony, and there my mother has her herb garden, unusual pots containing lacy-leafed plants that fill the air with savory smells of basil and chive. Along the floor are large and small planters my sister created in her pottery class at the Y. Some overflow with bushy greenery; others contain bright geraniums. On the right, along our other wall, huddles our small gas barbecue. My father hung a board on that wall to hold garden tools and barbecue utensils. Nearby, two small lawn chairs flank a tiny, round wooden table. Two more chairs are folded against the wall, ready for a family dinner. On a stifling summer day, our balcony is our garden in the sky.

 Respond to the reading. Does this description create a clear picture of the place being described? Which two or three details are particularly effective?

 Write a descriptive paragraph. Describe someone you see in public. Use sensory details to let the reader know exactly how this person "appears" to you.

Basic Elements

Answers

Respond to the reading.

The tone of this paragraph is humorous and touching.

Interesting details:

- children planting minigardens
- the little girl who wanted the writer's help

Amusing detail:

- children giggling as they use their fingers to "hoe" the trays of soil

Answers

Respond to the reading.

Yes, there is a clear picture of the balcony garden the writer's mother has made.

Details:

- the wall on the left with the trellis and climbing vines
- the purple and pink blossoms
- the table
- the herb garden in "unusual" pots

Expository Paragraph

An **expository paragraph** shares information about a specific topic. It presents facts, gives directions, defines terms, explains a process, and so on. An expository paragraph may use classification, comparison-contrast, cause-effect, problem-solution, or chronological organization.

Topic Sentence

Hadrian's Wall

Hadrian's Wall was a monumental undertaking, a stone border that stretched across the northern part of England. Roman emperor Hadrian initiated the building of the wall in 122 C.E. The brick and turf wall ran 75 miles from east to west and took 10 years to complete. The wall varied from 8 to 10 feet in depth and from 13 to 16 feet in height. A turret used for signaling was placed each mile along the wall. Fourteen full-sized forts were eventually added along the wall, each housing up to 1,000 troops and employing gates to allow passage to the other side. The importance of the wall changed after Hadrian's death in 138 C.E. when the new emperor, Antoninus Pius, built his own wall—the Antonine Wall—about 100 miles north. In 164 C.E., emperor Marcus Aurelius once again utilized Hadrian's Wall, and it remained in use until the Roman withdrawal from Britain around the fourth century. Although some might argue the wall was built to separate Scotland from England, in fact, the wall is south of the Scottish border. Actually, the wall marked the northern border of the Roman Empire at the time and had several other practical purposes as well. For one, it was an effective warning to northern barbarians not to challenge Rome. It also kept soldiers occupied and provided trade opportunities for the locals. Through the years, stones were taken to build other structures, and today the wall is in disrepair. However, Hadrian's Wall is still a tourist destination, an impressive reminder of an ancient, changing Britain.

Body

Closing Sentence

Respond to the reading. What is the main point of the above paragraph? Give three examples of details used to support that idea.

Write an expository paragraph. Write a paragraph that gives information about a topic. Include plenty of details to support your topic sentence.

Persuasive Paragraph

A **persuasive paragraph** expresses an opinion and tries to convince the reader that the opinion is valid. To be persuasive, a writer must include effective supporting reasons and facts.

Topic Sentence

Control the Pet Population

Spaying or neutering is a humane way to treat the growing problem of unwanted animals in the United States. These simple operations can eliminate aggressive behavior and roaming, reducing the risk that a pet may be hit by a car or injured in a fight with another animal. While "fixing" a pet may make it gentler, it will not eliminate the protective behavior desired of watchdogs. Some say that fixing a cat or dog will make it fat and lazy, but it doesn't—overfeeding and lack of exercise do that. Spaying or neutering a pet may actually protect the animal's health, reducing or eliminating the risk of various cancers. Altered pets, in fact, live long, healthy lives. Perhaps the most compelling reason for altering a pet is to reduce the number of unwanted animals that fill pounds and humane societies. According to the American Humane Society, one dog or cat can be responsible for thousands of puppies or kittens born within a seven-year period. Controlling the pet population can reduce the numbers of homeless dogs and cats that roam city streets and the countryside, just trying to survive. These abandoned animals often revert to the wild, posing a threat or nuisance similar to the one posed by coyotes. It's cruel and even dangerous to allow animals to continue having unwanted litters. If people spay or neuter their pets, we can create a healthier, safer world for domestic animals.

Body

Closing Sentence

Basic Elements

Respond to the reading. What are three main reasons offered for the writer's opinion? Which of these reasons is the most important?

Write a persuasive paragraph. Write a paragraph presenting your opinion. Include at least three strong reasons to support your argument.

Answers

Respond to the reading.

Main point: The writer gives a description and brief history of Hadrian's Wall in England.

Details:

- the wall was 8 to 10 feet thick and 13 to 16 feet high
- construction of the wall took 10 years
- in spite of the general disrepair, it is still a tourist attraction.

Grammar Connection

Abbreviations, Numbers

- **Proofreader's Guide** pages 658–659, 660–661, 662–663
- **SkillsBook** pages 45, 46

Answers

Respond to the reading.

Three main points that support the writer's opinion about spaying/neutering:

1. it eliminates aggressive behavior and roaming
2. it reduces the risk of some cancers
3. unwanted litters are avoided

The final point is the most important.

Patterns of Organization

On the next five pages, sample paragraphs show basic patterns of organization. Reviewing these samples can help you organize your own writing.

Classification Order

Classification is used when you need to divide or break down a topic into categories. The line diagram below helps to organize the topic of plastics.

Line Diagram

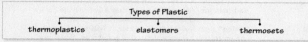

Types of Plastic

thermoplastics   elastomers   thermosets

Types of Plastic

Topic Sentence

Since the first plastic, cellulose nitrate, was developed more than 100 years ago, this durable material has become an integral part of daily life. Three structurally different plastics are created by chemically changing natural materials or by synthesizing raw materials.

Body

The three types are characterized by their molecular structure, which determines how each type reacts to heat. *Thermoplastics* have a branched molecular structure that forms the weakest bond. Pliable at normal temperatures, they melt into a sticky mess with high heat (packaging). Durable *elastomers* have a crosslink structure that allows for flexibility. Once shaped through heating, however, they cannot be reshaped but retain flexibility (tires). *Thermosets,* the most tightly structured plastics, are very hard, with a tightly woven molecular structure that resists reshaping once they are cured. This type of plastic is used to make everything from outlet covers to computer shelves. Different

Closing Sentence

types of plastics, each designed to meet different needs, all play key roles in today's world.

Respond to the reading. How is the topic classified in this paragraph? What are two things that you learned about the topic?

Comparison-Contrast Order

Organizing by **comparison** allows you to show the similarities or differences between two subjects. A Venn diagram effectively organizes this type of paragraph.

Venn Diagram

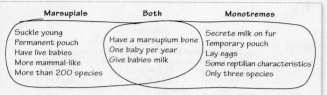

Marsupials	Both	Monotremes
Suckle young	Have a marsupium bone	Secrete milk on fur
Permanent pouch	One baby per year	Temporary pouch
Have live babies	Give babies milk	Lay eggs
More mammal-like		Some reptilian characteristics
More than 200 species		Only three species

Marsupials and Monotremes

Topic Sentence

Australia's marsupials and monotremes are very different from each other. Both types of mammals give birth to one baby per year and possess a marsupium bone that supports a pouch. However, the similarities end there. The

Body

monotreme does not possess a permanent pouch, nor does it suckle its young the way marsupials do. It secretes the milk onto its fur, and the baby laps it up. Marsupials give birth to live, undeveloped babies that grow within the mother's pouch; monotremes lay eggs. Physically, monotremes are reptilian-like with horizontal limb orientation, outward-turned rear feet, and the ability to regulate their body temperature. Marsupials have a more vertical bone structure and are warm blooded. There are only three species of monotremes—the platypus and the long- and short-nosed echidna—and they are found only in Australia and New Guinea. There are more than 200 species of marsupials, some of which are found in South America. One species,

Closing Sentence

the opossum, is native to North America. Marsupials and monotremes are amazing and unusual mammals that are very different from each other.

Respond to the reading. How many differences between the two topics are identified? Name them.

Answers

Respond to the reading.

The topic of plastics is classified according to different molecular structures and their reactions to heat.

Details learned:

- packaging materials are made of *thermoplastics*, which melt at high temperatures
- tires are made of *elastomers*, which are especially flexible
- shelving is made of hard plastic called a *thermoset*

Answers

Respond to the reading.

Seven differences between marsupials and monotremes are discussed:

1. Marsupials have a permanent pouch while monotremes' pouches are temporary.
2. The marsupial nurses its babies, but the monotreme secretes milk that the baby laps up from its mother's fur.
3. Marsupials bear live offspring and monotremes lay eggs.
4. Marsupials have a vertical bone structure, while monotremes have a horizontal limb orientation.
5. Marsupials are warm-blooded, while monotremes can regulate their body temperature.
6. There are more than 200 species of marsupials but only three species of monotremes.
7. Marsupials are found in North and South America, but monotremes are found only in Australia and New Guinea.

Cause-Effect Order

The **cause-effect** organizational pattern allows you to discuss the effects of a particular event or happening (the cause). The paragraph below discusses one cause (laughter) and its effects.

Cause-Effect Organizer

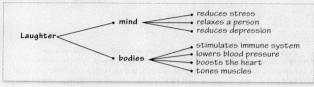

The Health Benefits of Laughter

Topic Sentence

A sense of humor can be one of the most powerful forces in our lives, affecting both the mind and the body. Laughter perks up brain function by stimulating the release of chemicals called *endorphins*. These chemicals relax a person, alleviate stress, reduce depression, and provide an overall sense of well-being. Endorphins do more than just make people feel good. Research shows that these chemicals, stimulated by laughter, have an even more important effect on the body. They can help the body deal with pain and even stimulate the immune system. Patients with a positive attitude and a well-developed sense of humor actually get well faster than those who flounder in pain and self-pity. Laughter can positively affect a person in other ways as well, lowering blood pressure and improving heart health. Laughing can even tone muscles. People who laugh hard may experience a side ache. That's because laughing actually stimulates the muscles. Although not a substitute for a real workout, belly laughs provide healthy exercise. So that old saying, "Laughter is the best medicine," may be true.

Body

Closing Sentence

 Respond to the reading. What are two ways laughter can affect us? Give two supporting details for each.

Process Organization

Process organization uses a step-by-step approach to explain a process. You start by introducing the topic and then follow with an appropriate series of steps.

Process Diagram

The Process of Cheese Making

Step 1: bacteria culture added to milk to produce lactic acid
Step 2: milk separates and rennet stirred in
Step 3: curds cut and drained, solids heated
Step 4: curds salted and put in press
Step 5: cheese coated with wax

Cheese Making

Topic Sentence

Cheese making was a chore for pioneers, but today many people enjoy making cheese. Although the process has been modernized, cheese is still made by souring and curdling milk and then separating liquids from the solids. To begin, warm milk is "ripened" by the addition of a bacterial culture. This starter culture produces lactic acid in the milk, which facilitates the separation of the milk into curds (solids) and whey (liquid). Then rennet, a chemical derived from either an animal or vegetable source, is stirred into the mixture to further coagulate the milk solids. Once the curds are set, they are cut into smaller pieces and drained, and the solids are heated gradually until firm. The curds are drained again and then salted and put into a cheese press to squeeze out the remaining whey. During the pressing process, the cheese is turned regularly to facilitate drying. Once the cheese has dried, it may be coated with a special wax to preserve it. Some cheeses can be eaten right away while others are best left to age for better flavor. With a little effort and know-how, anyone can make delicious homemade cheese.

Body

Closing Sentence

Basic Elements

 Respond to the reading. What transitional words or phrases are used to connect ideas? Name three.

 ## Answers

Respond to the reading.

Laughter can affect both our minds and our bodies.

Details:

- laughter releases endorphins that give us a sense of well-being and alleviate stress
- laughter lowers blood pressure and tones muscles, leading to better health

Answers

Respond to the reading.

Transitional words or phrases:

- Although
- To begin
- Then
- Once the curds are set
- During the pressing process
- Once the cheese has dried

Climax Organization

Climax (specific to general) is a method of organization in which the specific details lead up to an important summary statement. (If a topic sentence is used, it is placed at the end.) The paragraph below shows the excitement building as the writer waits for a concert to begin.

Details List

Leading up to a concert

- house lights dimmed
- multicolored spotlights begin
- sound builds
- feet stamping, hand clapping, whistling
- guitar blasts
- flash of light, shower of sparks

Anxiously Waiting

Opening Sentence

As the lights dimmed in the amphitheater, multicolored spotlights began to circle overhead, bouncing off the ceiling and swirling over the heads of the crowd. The sound began to build. At first, it sounded like thunder rumbling in the distance, but soon it grew to a deafening

Body

roar. People all around were stamping their feet, clapping their hands, and whistling through their fingers to show that they were ready for the show to begin. The crowd noise was soon drowned out by a blast of bass guitar and drums that seemed to come out of nowhere. Behind a blinding

Summary Topic Sentence

flash of light and a shower of glittering sparks, the band appeared on stage and began to play. At last, the concert had begun.

 Respond to the reading. What types of details does the writer use to build to the climax? Give two examples of effective details.

Basic Essay Skills

As you take more advanced classes, you will find that most of your writing assignments are in the form of essays—from essay tests to responses to literature. In these essays, you will explain, argue, or describe your thinking on a particular topic. The approach you take in each essay will depend on the guidelines established by your instructor and on your own judgment about how the topic should be presented. You may decide a traditional, straightforward approach works best, or you may find a more creative approach effective.

No matter which approach you take, developing an essay can be a challenge. You must have a good understanding of your topic and confidence in your position on that topic. Then you must develop your ideas so that your reader can clearly understand your thinking. The information in this chapter serves as a basic guide to essay writing.

- Understanding the Basic Parts
- Outlining Your ideas
- Writing Thesis Statements
- Creating Great Beginnings
- Developing the Middle Part
- Using Transitions
- Shaping Great Endings
- Key Terms, Techniques, and Forms

"Writing is the best way to talk without being interrupted."

—Jules Renard

 Answers

Respond to the reading.

The writer uses sensory details:

- multicolored spotlights bouncing off the ceiling and swirling over the heads
- sounded like thunder rumbling
- shower of glittering sparks

Understanding the Basic Parts

Each part of an essay—the beginning, middle, and ending—plays an important role. To develop your writing, refer to the suggestions below and to the sample essays earlier in this book.

Beginning **Your opening paragraph should capture the reader's attention and state your thesis.** Here are some ways to capture your reader's attention:

- Tell a dramatic or exciting story (anecdote) about the topic.
- Ask an intriguing question or two.
- Provide a few surprising facts or statistics.
- Provide an interesting quotation.
- Explain your personal experience or involvement with the topic.

> **Beginning**
> Middle
> Ending

Middle **The middle paragraphs should support your thesis statement.** They provide information that fully explains the thesis statement. For example, in an essay about the changes in the cartoon animation industry, each middle paragraph could focus on one main trend in that industry. Follow your own outline while writing this section.

> Beginning
> **Middle**
> Ending

Ending **Your closing paragraph should summarize your thesis and leave the reader with something to think about.** Here are some strategies for creating a strong closing:

- Review your main points.
- Emphasize the special importance of one main point.
- Answer any questions the reader may still have.
- Draw a conclusion and put the information in perspective.
- Provide a significant final thought for the reader.

> Beginning
> Middle
> **Ending**

Outlining Your Ideas

Once you've established a general pattern of development, you're ready to organize the main points and supporting details that you will cover in your essay. To help you organize this information, it may be wise to use a list, a topic outline, or a sentence outline.

Topic Outline

An outline is an orderly listing of related ideas. In a **topic outline**, each new idea is stated as a word or phrase rather than as a complete sentence. Before you start, write your working thesis statement at the top of your paper to keep you focused on the subject of your essay. Do not attempt to outline your opening and closing paragraphs unless specifically asked to do so.

Introduction
  I. Effects of malnutrition on the body
      A. Extreme weight loss and stunted growth
      B. Frequent infections
      C. Less resistance to diseases
  II. Extreme forms of malnutrition
      A. Marasmus
      B. Kwashiorkor
  III. Effects of malnutrition on development
      A. Limited ability to walk and to talk
      B. Stunted intellectual development
      C. Effects continuing into adulthood
Conclusion

Sentence Outline

A **sentence outline** contains more detail than a topic outline, and each new idea is expressed as a complete sentence. A sentence outline is often required for longer essays or research papers.

Introduction
  I. Genetic engineering is a form of biotechnology.
      A. Scientists can manipulate genes.
      B. Genes can be copied and moved to cells in other species.
      C. Scientists can recombine genes and clone entire organisms.
  II. Genetic engineering affects animal and plant breeding.
      A. Past species-improvement efforts proved unpredictable.
      B. Now development time is cut dramatically with better results.
      C. Animals are potential chemical factories, and new animals can be created and patented.
  III. Genetic engineering is feared by some.
      A. Dangerous organisms could be released.
      B. Public confidence in scientists has been undermined.
Conclusion

Basic Elements

Writing Thesis Statements

In most cases, a thesis statement takes a stand or expresses a specific feature or feeling about your topic. An effective thesis statement gives you the necessary direction to develop your essay.

Using a Formula

a specific topic *(multicultural education)*

+ a particular feature or feeling about the topic *(is vital to a society made up of many different peoples)*

= an effective thesis statement *(Multicultural education is vital to a society made up of many different peoples.)*

Sample Thesis Statements

Writing Assignment: Examine a psychological theme in a novel.
Specific Topic: *Animal Dreams*
Thesis Statement: In *Animal Dreams* by Barbara Kingsolver (**topic**), a woman's search for personal identity is juxtaposed with her father's identity loss to Alzheimer's (**particular feature**).

Writing Assignment: Defend a strongly held principle.
Specific Topic: The use of chemicals in food production
Thesis Statement: The use of chemicals in food production (**topic**) needs to be more stringently regulated (**particular stand**).

Writing Assignment: Review a music concert.
Specific Topic: The rap group Word
Thesis Statement: The rap group Word (**topic**) combines a powerful message with an infectious rhythm (**particular feeling**).

Thesis Checklist

Be sure that your thesis statement . . .

_____ identifies a limited, specific topic,

_____ focuses on a particular feature or feeling about the topic,

_____ can be supported with convincing facts and details, and

_____ meets the requirements of the assignment.

Creating Great Beginnings

▶ Beginning
Middle
Ending

The opening paragraph of an essay should grab the reader's attention, introduce your topic, and present your thesis. Try one of these approaches to start an opening paragraph:

- **Start with an interesting fact.**
  Recently, the question has come up about whether astronauts ever really did walk on the moon.

- **Ask an interesting question.**
  What if the government had set up an elaborate hoax to make people think astronauts had landed on the moon?

- **Start with a quotation.**
  "The body of physical evidence that humans did walk on the moon is simply overwhelming." So says Dr. Robert Park, Director of the Washington office of the American Physical Society and a known critic of NASA's manned space program.

Trying a Beginning Strategy

If you have trouble coming up with a good opening paragraph, follow the step-by-step example below.

First sentence: Grab the reader's attention with an opening sentence (see approaches above).

Recently, the question has come up about whether astronauts ever really did walk on the moon.

Second sentence: Give some background information about the topic.

The creators of a television exposé show suggest that the whole moon landing was really staged in a movie studio.

Third sentence: Introduce the specific topic of the essay in a way that builds up to the thesis statement.

However, this criticism has not gone unchallenged by NASA scientists.

Fourth sentence: Give the thesis statement of the paper (see page 592).

The fact is, there is overwhelming evidence to support the country's claims that astronauts have in fact walked on the moon.

Developing the Middle Part

The middle part of an essay is where you do most of the work. In this part, you develop the main points that support your thesis statement.

Use your outline or other planning notes as a guide when you write this section. However, new ideas may pop into your head as you go along. You may incorporate these ideas into your draft or make a note to research the ideas later.

Advancing Your Thesis

Keep these points in mind as you explain and develop your thesis statement.

- **Cover your main points.** Develop each main point in a paragraph or series of paragraphs.
- **Give background information.** If necessary, provide some history to put the topic in context.
- **Define terms.** Clarify any terms that your reader is not likely to know.
- **Order the main points.** Present the main ideas in a logical order (according to your outline).

Testing Your Ideas

When you write the middle part of an essay, you're testing your first thoughts about your topic. Here are some ways to test your ideas as you write.

- **Raise questions.** Anticipate any questions the reader may have about your topic.
- **Consider alternative ideas.** Take inventory of your thesis as you go along: Do you need to strengthen or rethink it? Also look at your main points from different angles.
- **Answer objections.** Address different points of view about your topic.

Building a Coherent Structure

Each middle paragraph should include main points and details that logically develop your thesis.

- **Develop one paragraph at a time.** Start a new paragraph whenever you shift to another main idea about the topic.
- **Connect your main points.** Use transitional phrases to link each new paragraph with the preceding one. (See page 595.)

Using Transitions

Transitions can be used to connect one sentence to another sentence within a paragraph, or to connect one paragraph to another within a longer essay or report. The lists that follow show a number of transitions and how they are used. Each colored list is a group of transitions that could work well together in a piece of writing.

Words used to show location

above	around	between	inside	outside
across	behind	by	into	over
against	below	down	near	throughout
along	beneath	in back of	next to	to the right
among	beside	in front of	on top of	under

Above	In front of	On top of
Below	Beside	Next to
To the left	In back of	Beneath
To the right		

Words used to show time

about	before	in the end	second	today
after	during	later	soon	tomorrow
as soon as	finally	meanwhile	then	until
at	first	next	to begin	yesterday

First	To begin	Now	First	Before
Second	To continue	Soon	Then	During
Third	To conclude	Eventually	Next	After
Finally			In the end	

Words used to compare things

also	both	like	one way
as	in the same way	likewise	similarly

In the same way	One way
Also	Another way
Similarly	Both

Words used to contrast (show differences)

| although | even though | on the other hand | still |
| but | however | otherwise | yet |

On the other hand	Although
Even though	Yet
Still	Nevertheless

Words used to emphasize a point

| again | for this reason | to emphasize | truly |
| especially | in fact | to repeat | |

| For this reason | Truly | In fact |
| Especially | To emphasize | To repeat |

Words used to conclude or summarize

| all in all | because | in conclusion | therefore |
| as a result | finally | lastly | to sum it up |

| Because | As a result | To sum it up | Therefore |
| In conclusion | All in all | Because | Finally |

Words used to add information

additionally	and	finally	moreover
again	another	for example	next
along with	as well	for instance	other
also	besides	in addition	

For example	For instance	Next	Another
Additionally	Besides	Moreover	Along with
Finally	Next	Also	As well

Words used to clarify

| for example | for instance | in other words | that is |

| For instance | For example |
| In other words | Equally important |

Shaping Great Endings

Beginning
Middle
► **Ending**

The closing paragraph of a paper should summarize your thesis and leave the reader with something to think about. When writing your closing paragraph, use two or more of the following approaches:

- **Review** your main points.
- **Emphasize** the special importance of one main point.
- **Answer any questions** the reader may still have.
- **Draw a conclusion** and put the information in perspective.
- **Provide a significant final thought** for the reader.

Trying an Ending Strategy

If you have trouble coming up with an effective closing paragraph, follow the step-by-step example below.

First sentence: Reflect on the topic. Start by reflecting on the material presented previously about the topic.

> The moon landing was real and was an important milestone in the history of the United States space program.

Second sentence: Add another point. Include a final point of interest that you didn't mention before.

> If the landing had been merely a hoax, other countries such as Russia and China could have easily prepared their own "moon landing," but they didn't.

Third sentence: Emphasize the most important point. Stress the importance of one or more key points that support the thesis.

> The information gathered by the moon astronauts, along with the rocks they brought home, proved invaluable to modern technology.

Fourth sentence: Wrap up the topic or draw a conclusion. Add one final thought about the topic or draw a conclusion from the points you've presented in the writing.

> The moon walk was real—as real as the new industries and materials developed during its planning, and as real as the pride people still feel when they remember those remarkable astronauts who took that first "giant leap for mankind."

Basic Elements

Learning Key Writing Terms

The next two pages include important terms related to writing. Refer to these pages whenever you have a question about the vocabulary associated with any part of the writing process.

Balance   Arranging words or phrases in a way that gives them equal importance

Body   The main part of a piece of writing, containing details that support or develop the thesis statement

Brainstorming   Collecting ideas by thinking freely about all the possibilities; used most often in groups

Central idea   The main point of a piece of writing, often stated in a thesis statement or a topic sentence

Closing sentence   The summary or final sentence in a piece of writing

Coherence   The logical arrangement of ideas that makes them clear and easy to follow

Dialogue   Written conversation between two or more people

Emphasis   Giving great importance to a specific idea in a piece of writing

Exposition   Writing that explains and informs

Figurative language   Language that goes beyond the normal meaning of the words used, often called "figures of speech"

Focus (thesis)   The specific part of a topic that is written about in an essay

Generalization   A general statement that gives an overall view rather than focusing on specific details

Grammar   The rules that govern the standard structure and features of a language

Idiom   A phrase or an expression that means something different from what the words actually say

The answer was really out in left field. (This means the answer was not even close to being correct.)

Next year you'll sing a different tune. (This means you'll think differently.)

Jargon   The special language of a certain group or occupation

The weaver pointed out the fabric's unique warp and woof.

Computer jargon: byte   icon   server   virus

Limiting the subject   Narrowing a general subject to a more specific one

Literal   The actual dictionary meaning of a word; language that means exactly what it appears to mean

Loaded words   Words slanted for or against the subject

The new tax bill helps the rich and hurts the poor.

Logic   Correctly using facts, examples, and reasons to support a point

Modifiers   Words, phrases, or clauses that limit or describe another word or group of words

Objective   Writing that gives factual information without adding feelings or opinions (See *subjective*.)

Poetic license   A writer's freedom to bend the rules of writing to achieve a certain effect

Point of view   The position or angle from which a story is told (See page 350.)

Prose   Writing in standard sentence form

Purpose   The specific goal of the writing

Style   The author's unique choice of words and sentences

Subjective   Writing that includes the writer's feelings, attitudes, and opinions (See *objective*.)

Supporting details   Facts or ideas used to sustain the main point

Syntax   The order and relationship of words in a sentence

Theme   The main point or unifying idea of a piece of writing

Thesis statement   A statement of the purpose, or main idea, of an essay

Tone   The writer's attitude toward the subject

Topic   The specific subject of a piece of writing

Topic sentence   The sentence that carries the main idea of a paragraph

Transitions   Words or phrases that connect or tie ideas together

Unity   A sense of solidarity in writing in which each sentence helps to develop the main idea

Usage   The way in which people use language (*Standard* language follows the rules; *nonstandard* language does not.)

Voice   A writer's personal tone or feeling that comes across in a piece of writing

Basic Elements

Using Writing Techniques

Experiment with some of these techniques in your own essays and stories.

Allusion	A reference to a familiar person, place, thing, or event **Mario threw me my mitt. "Hey,** Babe Ruth, **you forgot this!"**
Analogy	A comparison of similar ideas or objects to help clarify one of them **The mind of a bigot is like the pupil of the eye: The more light you shine on it, the more it will contract.** —Oliver Wendell Holmes, Jr.
Anecdote	A brief story used to illustrate or make a point **It is said that the last words John Adams uttered were "Thomas Jefferson survives." Ironically, Jefferson had died just a few hours earlier. Both deaths occurred on July 4, 1826—the 50th anniversary of the Declaration of Independence shepherded by the two great men.** (This ironic anecdote intensifies the importance of both men in our nation's history.)
Colloquialism	A common word or phrase suitable for everyday conversation but not for formal speech or writing "Cool" **and** "rad" **are colloquialisms suggesting approval.**
Exaggeration	An overstatement or a stretching of the truth to emphasize a point (See *hyperbole* and *overstatement*.) **We opened up the boat's engine and sped along at a** million miles an hour.
Flashback	A technique in which a writer interrupts a story to go back and relive an earlier time or event **I stopped at the gate, panting.** Suddenly I was seven years old again, and my brother was there, calling me "chicken" from the edge of the stone well. **Then I opened my eyes and heard only the crickets chirping. The years, the well, and my brother were gone. I turned back to the road, determined to get home before nightfall.**
Foreshadowing	Hints about what will happen next in a story **As Mai explained why she had to break their date, she noticed Luke looking past her.** Turning, she saw Meg smiling—at Luke.
Hyperbole	(hi-púr-bə-lĕ) Exaggeration used to emphasize a point **The music was** loud enough to make your ears bleed.
Irony	An expression in which the author says one thing but means just the opposite **As we all know,** there's nothing students love more than homework.

Juxtaposition	Putting two words or ideas close together to create a contrasting of ideas or an ironic meaning **Ah, the** sweet smell **of** fuel emissions!
Local color	The use of details that are common in a certain place
Metaphor	A figure of speech that compares two things without using the words *like* or *as* **The sheep were** dense, dancing clouds **scuttling across the road.**
Overstatement	An exaggeration or a stretching of the truth (See *exaggeration* and *hyperbole*.) **If I eat one more piece of turkey,** I will burst!
Oxymoron	Connecting two words with opposite meanings **small fortune cruel kindness original copy**
Paradox	A true statement that says two opposite things **As I crossed the finish line dead last, I felt a surge of triumph.**
Parallelism	Repeating similar grammatical structures (words, phrases, or sentences) to give writing rhythm We cannot undo, we will not forget, **and** we should not ignore the pain of the past.
Personification	A figure of speech in which a nonhuman thing is given human characteristics **The computer spit out my disk.**
Pun	A phrase that uses words that sound the same in a way that gives them a funny effect **I call my dog Trousers because he** pants **so much.**
Simile	A figure of speech that compares two things using *like* or *as* **Her silent anger was** like a rock wall, **hard and impenetrable.**
Slang	Informal words or phrases used by a particular group of people **cool it hang out shoot the breeze**
Symbol	A concrete object used to represent an idea
Understatement	The opposite of exaggeration; using very calm language to call attention to an object or an idea **The accident was fairly minor; I only broke both arms and legs.**

Basic Elements

Knowing the Different Forms

Finding the right form for your writing is just as important as finding the right topic. When you are selecting a form, be sure to ask yourself whom you're writing for (your *audience*) and why you're writing (your *purpose*).

Anecdote	A brief story that helps to make a point
Autobiography	A writer's story of his or her own life
Biography	A writer's story of someone else's life
Book review	An essay offering an opinion about a book (not to be confused with *literary analysis*)
Cause and effect	An examination of an event, the forces leading up to that event, and the effects following the event
Character sketch	A brief description of a specific character showing some aspect of that character's personality
Descriptive writing	Writing with sensory details that allow the reader to clearly visualize a person, a place, a thing, or an idea
Editorial	A letter or an article offering an opinion, an idea, or a solution
Essay	A thoughtful piece of writing in which ideas are explained, analyzed, or evaluated
Expository writing	Writing that explains something by presenting its steps, causes, or kinds
Eyewitness account	A report giving specific details of an event
Fable	A short story that teaches a lesson or moral, often using talking animals as the main characters
Fantasy	A story set in an imaginary world in which the characters usually have supernatural powers or abilities
Freewriting	Spontaneous, rapid writing to explore your thoughts about a topic of interest
Historical fiction	An invented story based on an actual historical event
Interview	Writing based on facts and details obtained through speaking with another person
Journal writing	Writing regularly to record personal observations, thoughts, and ideas
Literary analysis	A careful examination or interpretation of some aspect of a piece of literature

Myth	A traditional story intended to explain a mystery of nature, religion, or culture
Novel	A book-length story with several characters and a well-developed plot, usually with one or more subplots
Personal narrative	Writing that shares an event or experience from the writer's personal life
Persuasive writing	Writing intended to persuade the reader to follow the writer's way of thinking about something
Play	A form that uses dialogue to tell a story, usually meant to be performed in front of an audience
Poem	A creative expression that may use rhyme, rhythm, and imagery
Problem-solution	Writing that presents a problem followed by a proposed solution
Process paper	Writing that explains how a process works, or how to do or make something
Profile	An essay that describes an individual or re-creates a time period
Proposal	Writing that includes specific information about an idea or a project that is being considered for approval
Research report	An essay that shares information about a topic that has been thoroughly researched
Response to literature	Writing that is a reaction to something the writer has read
Science fiction	Writing based on real or imaginary science and often set in the future
Short story	A short fictional piece with only a few characters and one conflict or problem
Summary	Writing that presents the most important ideas from a longer piece of writing
Tall tale	A humorous, exaggerated story about a character or an animal that does impossible things
Tragedy	Literature in which the hero fails or is destroyed because of a serious character flaw

Basic Elements

Proofreader's Guide

Academic Vocabulary

Work with a partner to learn the following words from this unit.

1. Something indefinite doesn't have precise limits or boundaries.
   When might your plans for the day be indefinite?
2. If you omit something, you leave it out.
   Tell about a time you omitted part of a story.
3. A principle is a basic truth, law, or assumption.
   What are some of the principles of student government?
4. A component is one of the parts of a whole.
   What is one component of a short story?

Marking Punctuation

Period

605.1 At the End of a Sentence

Use a **period** at the end of a sentence that makes a statement, requests something, or gives a mild command.

> (Statement) **The man who does not read good books has no advantage over the man who can't read them.**
>
> —Mark Twain
>
> (Request) **Please bring your folders and notebooks to class.**
>
> (Mild command) **Listen carefully so that you understand these instructions.**

Note: It is not necessary to place a period after a statement that has parentheses around it and is part of another sentence.

> **My dog Bobot** (I don't quite remember how he acquired this name) **is a Chesapeake Bay retriever—a hunting dog—who is afraid of loud noises.**

605.2 After an Initial or an Abbreviation

Place a period after an initial or an abbreviation (in American English).

> **Ms.   Sen.   D.D.S.   M.F.A.   M.D.   Jr.   U.S.   p.m.   a.m.**
> **Edna St. Vincent Millay   Booker T. Washington   D. H. Lawrence**

Note: When an abbreviation is the last word in a sentence, use only one period at the end of the sentence.

> **Jaleesa eyed each door until she found the name Fletcher B. Gale, M.D.**

605.3 As a Decimal Point

A period is used as a decimal point.

> **New York City has a budget of** $46.9 **billion to serve its** 8.1 **million people.**

Exclamation Point

605.4 To Express Strong Feeling

Use the **exclamation point** (sparingly) to express strong feeling. You may place it after a word, a phrase, or a sentence.

> **"When I was a child," Marci told her son, "we didn't have cell phones, voicemail, or cable TV.** Imagine that!**"**

Punctuation

Academic Vocabulary

Read aloud the academic terms, as well as the descriptions and questions. Model for students how to read one question and answer it. Have partners monitor their understanding and seek clarification of the terms by working through the meanings and questions together.

Related Skills Activities

- **SkillsBook**
  Pretest: Punctuation, pp. 3–4
  End Punctuation, p. 5
  Run–On Sentences, p. 159

Question Mark

606.1 Direct Question

Place a **question mark** at the end of a direct question.

> How should I do this? I wondered. Am I supposed to give my dog his medication with a treat? Should I hide it in his food?

> Where did my body end and the crystal and white world begin?
> —Ralph Ellison, *Invisible Man*

When a question ends with a quotation that is also a question, use only one question mark, and place it within the quotation marks.

> On road trips, do you remember driving your parents crazy by asking, "Are we there yet?"

Note: Do not use a question mark after an indirect question.

> When I went backstage on opening night, I asked Mr. Mayans where my costume was.

> Marta asked me if I finished my calculus homework yet.

606.2 To Show Uncertainty

Use a question mark within parentheses to show uncertainty.

> This summer marks the 20th season (?) of the American Players Theatre.

606.3 Short Question Within a Sentence

Use a question mark for a short question within parentheses.

> We crept so quietly (had they heard us?) past the kitchen door and back to our room.

Use a question mark for a short question within dashes.

> He woke up at 4 a.m. with his heart beating fast—who hasn't had a nightmare, at one time or another?—but he soon forgot the dream and went back to sleep.

Grammar Practice

Periods, Exclamation Points, and Question Marks

 For each line in the paragraphs below, write where periods, exclamation points, or question marks are needed. Write the word preceding each mark. (Write "none" if no marks are needed.)

1   Herme was persistent about going after the job that he wanted

2   "A wildland firefighter" his mother exclaimed "Why did you choose a job

3   like that"

4   "Actually, Ma," Herme answered, "someday I want to be a smoke jumper,

5   like T J Brookes"

6   His mother got that "I'm going to win this argument" look on her face "A

7   smoke jumper" she cried out "I don't think so Mrs Wagero, down at the church,

8   she told me all about Terrance, Jr, the smoke jumper He still almost gives his

9   mama a heart attack every time he fights one of those wildfires No You will

10 *not* be a smoke jumper"

11 Herme picked up his backpack, kissed his mother good-bye, and headed

12 for the door The state employment office opened at eight The starting pay for

13 a tech trainee was just $700 an hour, but to Herme the low wage was worth

14 it—just to train as a wildland firefighter,

15 that was enough

Model

Model the following sentences to practice punctuating a sentence with a tag question (a short question at the end of a statement) correctly.

That's the Russian faith all over, isn't it? . . . Surely that's Russian, isn't it?
—Fyodor M. Dostoevsky, *The Brothers Karamazov*

Punctuation

Related Skills Activities

- **SkillsBook**
  End Punctuation, p. 5

Answers

line 1: wanted.	*line 8:* Jr.
line 2: firefighter!	jumper.
exclaimed.	*line 9:* wildfires.
line 3: that?	No!
line 4: none	*line 10:* jumper.
line 5: T. J. Brookes.	*line 11:* none
line 6: face.	*line 12:* door.
line 7: jumper!	eight.
out.	*line 13:* $7.00
so.	*line 14:* none
Mrs.	*line 15:* enough.

Comma

608.1 Between Two Independent Clauses

Use a **comma** between two independent clauses that are joined by a coordinating conjunction (*and, but, or, nor, for, yet, so*).

> I want to teach English in Latin America, but I need to study Spanish for at least another year before I can apply.

Note: Do not confuse a sentence containing a compound verb for a compound sentence.

> I had to erase my drawing and start all over.

608.2 To Separate Adjectives

Use commas to separate two or more adjectives that *equally* modify the same noun. (Note: Do not use a comma between the last adjective and the noun.)

> Bao's eyes met the hard, bright lights hanging directly above her.
> —Julie Ament, student writer

A Closer Look

To determine whether adjectives modify equally—and should, therefore, be separated by commas—use these two tests:

1. Shift the order of the adjectives; if the sentence is clear, the adjectives modify equally. (In the example below, *hot* and *smelly* can be shifted and the sentence is still clear; *usual* and *morning* cannot.)

2. Insert *and* between the adjectives; if the sentence reads well, use a comma when the *and* is omitted. (The word *and* can be inserted between *hot* and *smelly*, but *and* does not make sense between *usual* and *morning*.)

> Matty was tired of working in the hot, smelly kitchen and decided to take her usual morning walk.

608.3 To Separate Contrasted Elements

Use commas to separate contrasted elements within a sentence. Often the word or phrase that is set off is preceded by *not*.

> Since the stereotypes were about Asians, and not African Americans, no such reaction occurred.
> —Emmeline Chen, "Eliminating the Lighter Shades of Stereotyping"

Grammar Practice

Commas 1

- Between Independent Clauses
- To Separate Adjectives
- To Separate Contrasted Elements

 Indicate where commas are needed in the following sentences by writing the commas along with the words that surround them.

1. The newspaper printed a correction that Dr. Ellen Ochoa is Hispanic not Hawaiian.

2. Ellen was the first Hispanic female astronaut and she was also the inventor of optical analysis systems.

3. Her mother was a determined hardworking single parent who earned a college degree while raising five children.

4. Ellen possesses a powerful never-ending commitment to learn.

5. She is most often recognized as an astronaut not as an inventor.

6. Ellen completed a brief vigorous training program before her first shuttle ride.

7. "Usually it takes quite a bit longer but I got lucky," she said.

8. Ellen was accepted into the space program in 1991 and in 1993 she completed her first shuttle mission.

9. Few people know that she is also a talented experienced flutist.

10. Ochoa says, "Many doors opened for me when I completed college and I encourage all Latinas to seek out interesting challenging careers."

Model

Model the following sentence to practice using commas to separate adjectives.

> She had a quiet, unthreatening way about her that made older, uglier, fatter people take to her despite her beauty.
> —Maeve Binchy, *Scarlet Feather*

Related Skills Activities

- **Sentence Fluency**
  Check for Comma Splices, p. 87

- *SkillsBook*
  Commas with Coordinating Conjunctions, p. 7
  Commas in a Series and to Separate Equal Adjectives, p. 8
  Commas to Set Off Contrasted Elements, p. 11
  Comma Splices 1 and 2, pp. 160–161

- *GrammarSnap*
  Common Uses of Commas

Answers

1. Hispanic, not
2. astronaut, and
3. determined, hardworking
4. powerful, never-ending
5. astronaut, not
6. brief, vigorous
7. longer, but
8. 1991, and
9. talented, experienced
10. college, and
    interesting, challenging

Comma (continued)

610.1 To Set Off Appositives

A specific kind of explanatory word or phrase called an **appositive** identifies or renames a preceding noun or pronoun.

Benson, our uninhibited and enthusiastic Yorkshire terrier, **joined our family on my sister's fifteenth birthday.**

—Chad Hockerman, student writer

Note: Do not use commas with *restrictive appositives*. A restrictive appositive is essential to the basic meaning of the sentence.

Sixteen-year-old student Ray Perez **was awarded an athletic scholarship.**

610.2 Between Items in a Series

Use commas to separate individual words, phrases, or clauses in a series. (A series contains at least three items.)

The chef bought organic broccoli, spinach, and corn **at the farmers market.** (words)

I found a space, paid the rent, and set up my office **for my new business.** (phrases)

Note: Do not use commas when all the words in a series are connected with *or, nor,* or *and*.

He had his car cleaned and waxed and vacuumed out.

610.3 After Introductory Phrases and Clauses

Use a comma after an introductory participial phrase.

Determined to finish the sweater by Friday, **my grandmother knit night and day.**

Use a comma after a long introductory prepositional phrase or after two or more short ones.

In the oddest places and at the strangest times, **my grandmother can be found knitting madly away.**

Note: You may omit the comma if the introductory phrase is short.

Before breakfast **my grandmother knits.**

Use a comma after an introductory adverb (subordinate) clause.

After the practice was over, **Tina walked home.**

Note: A comma is not used if an adverb clause *follows* the main clause and is needed to complete the meaning of the sentence.

Tina practiced hard because she feared losing.

However, a comma is used if the adverb clause following the main clause begins with *although, even though, while,* or another conjunction expressing a contrast.

Tina walked home, even though it was raining very hard.

Grammar Practice

Commas 2

- To Set Off Appositives
- Between Items in a Series
- After Introductory Phrases and Clauses

 Indicate where commas are needed in the following sentences by writing the commas along with the words that surround them. If no commas are needed, write "none needed."

1. The idea of contact lenses the common substitute for glasses has been around for hundreds of years.

2. Leonardo da Vinci the Italian artist inventor and scientist sketched ideas for contacts in 1508.

3. More than a hundred years later Rene Descartes the French mathematician suggested placing a lens directly on the eye.

4. Though the idea had been around for centuries it was 1887 before the first contact lenses were produced.

5. The first glass lenses were made by F. A. Muller a German glassblower.

6. After centuries of ideas and experimentation today's contact wearers have their choice of hard soft or gas-permeable lenses.

7. Today about 90 percent of contacts sold in the United States are soft lenses.

8. Remi has a pair each of blue green and hazel lenses to suit her varying moods.

Model

Model the following sentences to practice using commas between items in a series, after introductory phrases, and to set off appositives.

Bill Post ran forward, gathered his little family in his arms for a moment, and then quickly ushered them toward the safety of the house.
—Thomas Steinbeck, "The Night Guide"

A few days before the shooting, Director Yu, a lecturer at a cinema school in Shanghai, gave Huping a small book to read.
—Ha Jin, "A Tiger-Fighter Is Hard to Find"

Related Skills Activities

- **Word Choice**
  Asyndeton, p. 80

- *SkillsBook*
  Commas to Set Off Contrasted Elements and
  Appositives, p. 11
  Commas in a Series and to Separate Equal Adjectives,
  p. 8
  Commas After Introductory Phrases and Clauses, p. 9

- *GrammarSnap*
  Common Uses of Commas
  Commas After Introductory Words, Phrases, and Clauses

Answers

1. lenses, the
   glasses, has
2. Vinci, the
   artist, inventor, and scientist, sketched
3. later, Rene Descartes, the
   mathematician, suggested
4. centuries, it
5. Muller, a
6. experimentation, today's
   hard, soft, or
7. none needed
8. blue, green, and

Comma *(continued)*

612.1 To Enclose Parenthetical Elements

Use commas to separate parenthetical elements, such as an explanatory word or phrase, within a sentence.

> **They stood together,** away from the pile of stones in the corner, **and their jokes were quiet, and they smiled rather than laughed.**
>
> —Shirley Jackson, "The Lottery"
>
> **Allison meandered into class,** late as usual, **and sat down.**

612.2 To Set Off Nonrestrictive Phrases and Clauses

Use commas to set off **nonrestrictive** (unnecessary) clauses and participial phrases. A nonrestrictive clause or participial phrase adds information that is not necessary to the basic meaning of the sentence. For example, if the clause or phrase (in red) were left out in the two examples below, the meaning of the sentences would remain clear. Therefore, commas are used to set them off.

> **The Altena Fitness Center and Visker Gymnasium,** which were built last year, **are busy every day.** (nonrestrictive clause)
>
> **Students and faculty,** improving their health through exercise, **use both facilities throughout the week.** (nonrestrictive phrase)

Do not use commas to set off a **restrictive** (necessary) clause or participial phrase, which helps to define a noun or pronoun. It adds information that the reader needs to know in order to understand the sentence. For example, if the clause and phrase (in red) were dropped from the examples below, the meaning wouldn't be the same. Therefore, commas are *not* used.

> **The handball court** that has a sign-up sheet by the door **must be reserved.**
> The clause identifies which handball court must be reserved. (restrictive clause)
>
> **Individuals** wanting to use this court **must sign up a day in advance.** (restrictive phrase)

A Closer Look

Use *that* to introduce restrictive (necessary) clauses; use *which* to introduce nonrestrictive (unnecessary) clauses. When the two words are used in this way, the reader can quickly distinguish necessary and unnecessary information.

> **The treadmill** that monitors heart rate **is the one you must use.**
> (The reader needs the information to find the right treadmill.)
>
> **This treadmill,** which we got last year, **is required for your program.**
> (The main clause tells the reader which treadmill to use; the other clause gives additional, unnecessary information.)

Grammar Practice

Commas 3

- To Enclose Parenthetical Elements
- To Set Off Nonrestrictive Phrases and Clauses

 Indicate where commas are needed in the following sentences by writing the commas along with the words that surround them. If no commas are needed, write "none needed."

1. The classic *Star Trek* series the one with Kirk and Spock was on television for only three seasons.

2. The show which was created by Gene Roddenbery was canceled because of low ratings.

3. Fans called "Trekkies" wanting the show to return waged a letter-writing campaign.

4. The show returned in syndicated reruns and became very popular.

5. *Star Trek* movies some great and others not so great led to a new television series: *Star Trek: The Next Generation.*

6. The new show known for its Shakespearean references starred Patrick Stewart as Captain Jean-Luc Picard.

7. The series that stars William Shatner and Leonard Nimoy remains popular with *Star Trek* fans.

8. Vendors sell merchandise everything you can think of with a *Star Trek* logo at conventions.

Model

Model the following sentence to practice using commas to set off nonrestrictive clauses.

> I . . . developed a very practiced smile, which I call my "Noh smile" because it resembles a Noh mask whose features are frozen.
>
> —Arthur Golden, *Memoirs of a Geisha*

Punctuation

Related Skills Activities

- ***SkillsBook***
  Commas with Nonrestrictive Phrases and Clauses 1 and 2, pp. 12–13

- ***GrammarSnap***
  Common Uses of Commas

Answers

1. series, the
   Spock, was
2. show, which
   Roddenberry, was
3. "Trekkies," wanting
   return, waged
4. none needed
5. movies, some
   great, led
6. show, known
   references, starred
7. none needed
8. merchandise, everything
   logo, at

Comma *(continued)*

614.1 To Set Off Dates

Use commas to set off items in a date.

On September 30, 1997, my little sister entered our lives.

He began working out on December 1, 2010, but quit by May 1, 2011.

However, when only the month and year are given, no commas are needed.

He began working out in December 2010 but quit by May 2011.

When a full date appears in the middle of a sentence, a comma follows the year.

On June 7, 1924, my great-grandfather met his future wife.

614.2 To Set Off Items in Addresses

Use commas to set off items in an address. (No comma is placed between the state and ZIP code.)

Mail the box to Friends of Wildlife, Box 402, Spokane, Washington 20077.

When a city and state (or country) appear in the middle of a sentence, a comma follows the last item in the address.

Several charitable organizations in Juneau, Alaska, pool their funds.

614.3 In Numbers

Use commas to separate numerals in large numbers in order to distinguish hundreds, thousands, millions, and so forth.

1,101   25,000   7,642,020

614.4 To Enclose Titles or Initials

Use commas to enclose a title or initials and names that follow a surname (a last name).

Letitia O'Reilly, M.D., is our family physician.

Hickok, J. B., and Cody, William F., are two popular Western heroes.

614.5 Before Tags

Use a comma before a tag, which is a short statement or question at the end of a sentence.

He's the candidate who lost the election, isn't he?

You're not going to like this casserole, I know.

614.6 Following Conjunctive Adverbs and Transitional Phrases

Use a comma following conjunctive adverbs such as *however, instead,* and *nevertheless,* and transitional phrases such as *for example, in fact,* and *as a result.* (Also see **618.2**.)

Jaleel is bright and studies hard; however, he suffers from test anxiety.

Pablo was born in the Andes; as a result, he loves mountains.

Grammar Practice

Commas 4

- To Set Off Dates
- To Enclose Titles
- Before Tags
- Following Conjunctive Adverbs and Transitional Phrases

 Indicate where commas are needed in the following sentences by writing the commas along with the words that surround them. If no commas are needed, write "none needed."

1. Cori Ramos is planning to attend USC this fall right?

2. I'm looking forward to graduation; however I'll miss high school and my friends.

3. The article written by Sanjay Singh M.D. is about fibromyalgia treatments.

4. On August 24 2006 many astronomers announced that Pluto is not a planet.

5. Many people were upset by the decision; in fact there is a strong movement to restore Pluto's status.

6. Special-effects technology is improving all the time; furthermore there is a need for specialists in this field.

7. Maya Angelou Ph.D. will speak at my sister's graduation ceremony.

8. My cousin started biking competitively in April 2000.

9. He didn't expect to lose did he?

10. He looked forward to winning at least second place; after all he had trained so long and hard.

Model

Model the following sentence to practice using a comma before a tag.

Though both sentences have a certain on-the-money ring to them, the first one sounds better, doesn't it?

—June Casagrande, *Grammar Snobs Are Great Big Meanies*

Related Skills Activities

- **SkillsBook**
  Other Uses for Commas 1 and 2, pp. 14–15
  Conjunctive Adverbs, p. 102

- **GrammarSnap**
  Common Uses of Commas

Answers

1. fall, right
2. however, I'll
3. Singh, M.D., is
4. 24, 2006, many
5. in fact, there
6. furthermore, there
7. Angelou, Ph.D., will
8. none needed
9. lose, did
10. after all, he

Comma *(continued)*

616.1 To Set Off Dialogue

Use commas to set off the speaker's exact words from the rest of the sentence. (It may be helpful to remember that the comma is always to the left of the quotation mark.)

> "It's like they knew we were coming," **said Maria, pointing at the dozens of people standing on the dock.**

616.2 To Set Off Interjections

Use a comma to separate an interjection or a weak exclamation from the rest of the sentence.

> Hey, **how do you expect me to remember all these numbers?**
>
> Wow, **I had no idea that she wears contacts.**

616.3 To Set Off Interruptions

Use commas to set off a word, a phrase, or a clause that interrupts the movement of a sentence. Such expressions usually can be identified through the following tests: (1) They may be omitted without changing the meaning of a sentence. (2) They may be placed nearly anywhere in the sentence without changing its meaning.

> George, well, **he's happy with what he can get.**
>
> **The safest way to cross this street**, as a general rule, **is with the light.**

616.4 In Direct Address

Use commas to separate a noun of direct address from the rest of the sentence. A *noun of direct address* is the noun that names the person(s) spoken to.

> **"You wouldn't understand yet**, son, **but your daddy's gonna make a transaction. . . . "**
> —Lorraine Hansberry, *A Raisin in the Sun*
>
> Quineisha, **why aren't you answering your phone?**

616.5 For Clarity or Emphasis

You may use a comma for clarity or for emphasis. There will be times when none of the traditional rules call for a comma, but one will be needed to prevent confusion or to emphasize an important idea.

> **It may be that those who** do most, dream most. (emphasis)
> —Stephen Leacock
>
> **What the crew** does, does **affect our voyage.** (clarity)

Grammar Practice

Commas 5

- To Set Off Dialogue
- To Set Off Interjections
- To Set Off Interruptions
- In Direct Address
- For Clarity or Emphasis

 Indicate where commas are needed in the following sentences by writing the commas along with the words that surround them.

1. What now dear reader shall we make of our telescope?
   —Johannes Kepler

2. The world as a rule does not live on beaches and in country clubs.
   —F. Scott Fitzgerald

3. Whatever you do do with all your might.
   —Marcus Tullius Cicero

4. As the poet said "Only God can make a tree."
   —Woody Allen

5. Don't criticize what you don't understand son.
   —Elvis Presley

6. "Now I have asked you a question my friend" said Mr. Jaggers.
   —Charles Dickens, *Great Expectations*

7. Well all I know is what I read in the papers.
   —Will Rogers

 Model

Model the following sentences to practice using a comma to set off an interruption, to set off dialogue, and in direct address.

> **On the Web, right now, Clark was hunting for someplace to buy roofing.**
> —Alice Munro, "The Runaway"
>
> **"General, sir,"** Mortenson shouted, **"I think we're heading the wrong way."**
> —Greg Mortenson and David O. Relin, *Three Cups of Tea*

Related Skills Activities

- **SkillsBook**
  Other Uses for Commas 1 and 2, pp. 14–15

- **GrammarSnap**
  Common Uses of Commas

Answers

1. now, dear reader, shall
2. world, as a rule, does
3. do, do
4. said, "Only
5. understand, son
6. question, my friend," said
7. Well, all

Semicolon

618.1 To Join Two Independent Clauses

Use a **semicolon** to join two or more closely related independent clauses that are not connected with a coordinating conjunction. (Independent clauses can stand alone as separate sentences.)

> He never brags about being a gifted writer; his books speak for themselves.

> The forest was quiet; not a creature made a sound as the red-tailed hawk circled above.

Note: When independent clauses are especially long or contain commas, a semicolon may punctuate the sentence, even though a coordinating conjunction connects the clauses.

> We waited all day in that wide line, tired travelers pressing in from all sides; and when we needed drinks or sandwiches, I would squeeze my way to the cafeteria and back.

618.2 With Conjunctive Adverbs and Transitional Phrases

A semicolon is used *before* a conjunctive adverb or transitional phrase (with a comma after it) when the word connects two independent clauses in a compound sentence.

> Many actors move to New York City hoping to make it big; however, they often discover that the fierce competition for acting jobs makes it less likely for them to succeed.

Common Conjunctive Adverbs

also, besides, finally, however, indeed, instead, meanwhile, moreover, nevertheless, next, still, then, therefore, thus

Common Transitional Phrases

after all, as a matter of fact, as a result, at any rate, at the same time, even so, for example, for instance, in addition, in conclusion, in fact, in other words, in the first place, on the contrary, on the other hand

618.3 To Separate Groups That Contain Commas

A semicolon is used to separate groups of words that already contain commas.

> Every Saturday night my little brother gathers up his things—goggles, shower cap, and snorkel; bubble bath, soap, and shampoo; tapes, stereo, and rubber duck—and heads for the tub.

Grammar Practice

Semicolons

- To Join Two Independent Clauses
- With Conjunctive Adverbs
- To Separate Groups That Contain Commas

 Indicate where a semicolon is needed in the following sentences by writing the semicolon along with the words that surround it.

1. Everyone is talking about the weather they wonder why significant weather events are happening more frequently.

2. Weather is news these days—hurricanes, cyclones, and tornadoes flash floods, droughts, and tsunamis even snow in the deep South.

3. Unusual weather events have always been a part of the earth's climate consider January 1997, when snow fell near the bridge between Florida's mainland and the Keys.

4. In 2006, El Niño raised water temperatures in the Pacific Ocean moveover, it affected many countries.

5. Wetter conditions than normal affect Chile, Peru, and Ecuador southern Brazil and northern Argentina and Mexico's northwest states.

6. Earth is warming this may be the reason for the unusual weather events.

7. As the climate grows warmer, evaporation will increase therefore, there will be heavier rainfalls.

8. Higher ocean temperatures might change the path of hurricanes look for them to track more often through the Caribbean or to make landfall along the east coast of the United States.

Model

Model the following sentence to practice using a semicolon to join two independent clauses.

> The trees echoed with birdsong; a warm southeasterly breeze carried the sweetness of lime blossom.
> —Michelle Paver, *Spirit Walker*

Punctuation

Related Skills Activities

- **Sentence Fluency**
  Check for Comma Splices, p. 87

- *SkillsBook*
  Semicolons, pp. 17–18
  Comma Splices, pp. 161–162

- *GrammarSnap*
  Semicolons

Answers

1. weather; they
2. tornadoes; flash
   tsunamis; even
3. climate; consider
4. Ocean; moreover
5. Ecuador; southern
   Argentina; and
6. warming; this
7. increase; therefore
8. hurricanes; look

Colon

620.1 After a Salutation

Use a **colon** after the salutation of a business letter.

Dear Judge Parker: **Dear Governor Whitman:**

620.2 Between Numerals Indicating Time

Use a colon between the hours, minutes, and seconds of a number indicating time.

8:30 p.m. **9:45 a.m.** **10:24:55**

620.3 For Emphasis

Use a colon to emphasize a word, a phrase, a clause, or a sentence that explains or adds impact to the main clause (also see 650.3).

One goal of space exploration is to find the element essential to the support of human life: water.

620.4 To Introduce a Quotation

Use a colon to formally introduce a quotation, a sentence, or a question.

Directly a voice in the corner rang out wild and clear: "I've got him! I've got him!"

—Mark Twain, *Roughing It*

620.5 To Introduce a List

A colon is used to introduce a list.

He is a successful politician: attractive, articulate, and well-funded.

A Closer Look

Do not use a colon between a verb and its object or complement, or between a preposition and its object.

Incorrect: Min has: a snowmobile, an ATV, and a canoe.
Correct: Min has plenty of toys: a snowmobile, an ATV, and a canoe.
Incorrect: I watch a TV show about: cooking wild game.
Correct: I watch a TV show about a new subject: cooking wild game.

620.6 Between a Title and a Subtitle

Use a colon to distinguish between a title and a subtitle, volume and page, and chapter and verse in literature.

Encyclopedia Americana IV: 211 Psalm 23:1–6 *Bass: A Handbook of Strategies*

Grammar Practice

Colons

- After a Salutation
- Between Numerals Indicating Time
- For Emphasis
- To Introduce a Quotation
- To Introduce a List
- Between a Title and Subtitle

 Indicate where a colon is needed in the following sentences by writing the colon along with the words or numbers that surround it.

1. Darnell found the following items in his backpack two notebooks, some dirty socks, his cell phone charger, a comb, and a twenty-dollar bill.

2. Last weekend, Salli bought the DVD of *The Chronicles of Narnia The Lion, the Witch, and the Wardrobe.*

3. Dad reminded me of the inevitable "Real life begins after graduation."

4. The letter began, "Dear Mr. Parker Welcome to Lingston University!"

5. Tanisha plans to take the 813 a.m. train to Chicago; she'll arrive home tonight at 745.

6. Malcolm Gladwell's book *The Tipping Point How Little Things Can Make A Big Difference* is about sudden, unexpected changes in our society.

7. I have a lot to do on Saturday attend my brother's softball game, help Mom clean the basement, and install some new software on my computer.

8. Kennedy couldn't stop herself from thinking about Juan Was he just using "work" as an excuse to not see her?

Model

Model the following sentence to practice using colons to introduce a list.

It's more than just the way I look: refugee-skinny with absolutely no chest to speak of, hair the color of dirt, connect-the-dot freckles on my cheeks that, let me tell you, do not fade with lemon juice or sunscreen or even, sadly, sandpaper.

—Jodi Picoult, *My Sister's Keeper*

Related Skills Activities

- ***SkillsBook***
  Colons 1 and 2, pp. 19–20

 ## Answers

1. backpack: two
2. *Narnia: The*
3. inevitable: "Real
4. Parker: Welcome
5. 8:13
   7:45
6. *Point: How*
7. Saturday: attend
8. Juan: Was

Test Prep!

Read the following paragraphs. Write the letter of the correct way to punctuate each underlined part from the choices given on the next page. If it is already correct, choose "D."

My best friend, Ty, asked me if I wanted to try my hand at filmmaking? It
(1)   **(2)**
seemed like such a monumental task. It takes years to make a film, doesn't it?
(3)
Following some wheedling on his part Ty convinced me to join his filmmaking club.
(4)
    The first thing I discovered was that short films can take various forms
(5)
documentaries, narrative fiction, music videos, narrative poetry and even political
(6)
campaign ads. I decided that making a short film is a lot like writing a short

story or an essay the principles even follow the traits of writing. First, you sort
(7)
through all your amazing creative ideas, and then you choose one as the subject of
(8)
your film. You write a script, organize your ideas, and find the appropriate voice;

then you revise and edit. Hey; I can do that!
(9)
    Ty and I came up with an idea that required a day trip to the nation's

capital Washington D.C. We would interview our U.S. senator and the topic would
(10)   **(11)**
be the importance of teen voting. Our plan was to emphasize that teens not just
(12)
older voting Americans play an important role in all elections.

    On April 11 2006 we conducted the interview. We had planned everything
(13)
ahead of time, as a result the filmmaking went even better than we had
(14)
expected. The senator helped our script by improvising the ending: "In just five
(15)
minutes, one person can change the country—even the world." He liked our film

so much, that he plans to use it in his next election campaign!
(16)
    Filmmaking, which I thought would be hard turned out to be one of
(17)
the most enjoyable experiences of my senior year. In fact, I plan to take some

filmmaking classes in college this fall. Perhaps I'll even choose it as my major!
(18)

1
 (A) My best friend Ty
 (B) My best friend, Ty
 (C) My best friend Ty,
 (D) correct as is

2
 (A) filmmaking; It
 (B) filmmaking. It
 (C) filmmaking, it
 (D) correct as is

3
 (A) a film doesn't it?
 (B) a film, doesn't it.
 (C) a film doesn't it.
 (D) correct as is

4
 (A) on his part,
 (B) on his part.
 (C) on his part;
 (D) correct as is

5
 (A) various forms, documentaries,
 (B) various forms; documentaries
 (C) various forms: documentaries,
 (D) correct as is

6
 (A) poetry and,
 (B) poetry, and
 (C) poetry, and,
 (D) correct as is

7
 (A) essay, the
 (B) essay the,
 (C) essay; the
 (D) correct as is

8
 (A) amazing, creative ideas
 (B) amazing, creative ideas,
 (C) amazing creative ideas
 (D) correct as is

9
 (A) Hey,
 (B) Hey:
 (C) Hey?
 (D) correct as is

10
 (A) capital, Washington D.C.
 (B) capital Washington, D.C.
 (C) capital, Washington, D.C.
 (D) correct as is

11
 (A) senator, and
 (B) senator, and,
 (C) senator and,
 (D) correct as is

12
 (A) teens, not just older voting Americans
 (B) teens, not just older voting Americans,
 (C) teens not just older voting Americans,
 (D) correct as is

13
 (A) April 11, 2006
 (B) April 11 2006,
 (C) April 11, 2006,
 (D) correct as is

14
 (A) time, as a result,
 (B) time; as a result,
 (C) time; as a result
 (D) correct as is

15
 (A) ending;
 (B) ending
 (C) ending,
 (D) correct as is

16
 (A) so much that
 (B) so much that,
 (C) so much, that,
 (D) correct as is

17
 (A) Filmmaking which I thought would be hard
 (B) Filmmaking which I thought would be hard,
 (C) Filmmaking, which I thought would be hard,
 (D) correct as is

18
 (A) my major?
 (B) my major;
 (C) my major,
 (D) correct as is

Punctuation

Related Skills Activities

■ **SkillsBook**
Review: End Punctuation, p. 6
Review: Commas 1, p. 10
Review: Commas 2, p. 16
Review: Semicolons and Colons, p. 21
Posttest: End Punctuation, p. 187
Posttest: Commas, p. 188
Posttest: Semicolons and Colons, p. 189

■ **GrammarSnap**
Common Uses of Commas
Commas After Introductory Words, Phrases, and Clauses

Answers

1. D
2. B
3. D
4. A
5. C
6. B
7. C
8. B
9. A
10. C

11. A
12. B
13. C
14. B
15. D
16. A
17. C
18. D

Hyphen

624.1 In Compound Words

Use the **hyphen** to make some compound words.

great-**great-grandfather**   maid-**in-waiting**   three-**year-old**

624.2 To Create New Words

Use a hyphen to form new words beginning with the prefixes *self-, ex-, all-,* and *half-.* Also use a hyphen to join any prefix to a proper noun, a proper adjective, or the official name of an office. Use a hyphen before the suffix *-elect.*

self-**contained**   ex-**governor**   all-**inclusive**   half-**painted**
pre-**Cambrian**   mid-**December**   president-**elect**

Use a hyphen to join the prefix *great-* only to the names of relatives.

great-**aunt,** great-**grandfather** (correct)   **great-hall** (incorrect)

624.3 To Form an Adjective

Use a hyphen to join two or more words that serve as a single adjective (a single-thought adjective) before a noun.

Marisa, who volunteers at the soup kitchen on her days off, is a big-hearted **woman.**

Use common sense to determine whether a compound adjective might be misread if it is not hyphenated. Generally, hyphenate a compound adjective that is composed of . . .

- a phrase   heat-and-serve **meal**   off-and-on **relationship**
- a noun + adjective   oven-safe **handles**   book-smart **student**
- a noun + participle (*ing* or *ed* form of a verb)   bone-chilling **story**

624.4 To Join Letters and Words

Use a hyphen to join a capital letter or lowercase letter to a noun or participle. (Check your dictionary if you're not sure of the hyphenation.)

T-**shirt**   Y-**turn**   G-**rated**   x-**axis**

A Closer Look

When words forming the adjective come after the noun, do not hyphenate them.

In real life I am large and big boned.

When the first of these words is an adverb ending in *-ly,* do not use a hyphen.

delicately prepared **pastry**

Also, do not use a hyphen when a number or a letter is the final element in a single-thought adjective.

class B **movie**

Grammar Practice

Hyphens 1

- In Compound Words
- To Create New Words
- To Form an Adjective
- To Join Letters and Words

 For each sentence below, correctly write the words that should be hyphenated. Some sentences contain more than one hyphenated word.

1. The three year old Detroit based store is going out of business.

2. My great great uncle was an all or nothing sort, a self made man who earned his fortune in land speculation during the 1840s.

3. Some thought provoking arguments were raised in this award winning film.

4. My brother in law got a small business loan to open his restaurant.

5. Senator elect Ricchio spoke last night at the Italian American club.

6. The race car driver approached the S curve at an unsafe speed.

7. Dana's great grandpa is a self sufficient, fun loving person.

8. He decided to take Web based lessons to learn how to play the banjo.

9. Saied has a ten dollar credit on his prepaid phone card.

10. Tovah bought a yellow V neck T shirt at the mall.

Model

Model the following sentences to practice using hyphens to form adjectives and to create new words.

The stones which Deucalion threw sprang up as full-grown men, strong, and handsome, and brave.
—James Baldwin, "The Flood"

He did look cautiously behind it first, as if he half-expected to be terrified with the sight of Marley's pigtail sticking out into the hall.
—Charles Dickens, *A Christmas Carol*

Punctuation

Related Skills Activities

- ***SkillsBook***
  Hyphens, p. 22

Answers

1. three-year-old
   Detroit–based
2. great-great uncle
   all-or-nothing
   self-made
3. thought-provoking
   award-winning
4. brother-in-law
   small-business
5. Senator-elect
   Italian-American
6. race-car
   S-curve
7. great-grandpa
   self-sufficient
   fun-loving
8. Web-based
9. ten-dollar
10. V-neck
    T-shirt

Hyphen *(continued)*

626.1 Between Numbers and Fractions

Use a hyphen to join the words in compound numbers from *twenty-one* to *ninety-nine* when it is necessary to write them out (see 658.3).

Use a hyphen between the numerator and denominator of a fraction, but not when one or both of those elements are already hyphenated.

four-tenths   five-sixteenths   (7/32) seven thirty-seconds

626.2 In a Special Series

Use hyphens when two or more words have a common element that is omitted in all but the last term.

The ship has lovely two-, four-, or six-person cabins.

626.3 To Join Numbers

Use a hyphen to join numbers indicating the life span of a person or the score in a contest or a vote.

We can thank Louis Pasteur (1822–1895) for pasteurized milk.
In the 2007 Rose Bowl, USC defeated Michigan 32–18.

626.4 To Prevent Confusion

Use a hyphen with prefixes or suffixes to avoid confusion or awkward spelling.

re-create (not *recreate*) the image   re-cover (not *recover*) the sofa

626.5 To Divide a Word

Use a hyphen to divide a word, only between its syllables, at the end of a line of print. Always place the hyphen after the syllable at the end of the line—never before a syllable at the beginning of the following line.

Guidelines for Dividing with Hyphens

1. Always divide a compound word between its basic units: **sister-in-law,** not **sis-ter-in-law.**

2. Avoid dividing a word of five or fewer letters: **paper, study, July.**

3. Avoid dividing the last word in a paragraph.

4. Never divide a one-syllable word: **rained, skills, through.**

5. Never divide a one-letter syllable from the rest of the word: **omit-ted,** not **o-mitted.**

6. When a vowel is a syllable by itself, divide the word after the vowel: **epi-sode,** not **ep-isode.**

7. Never divide abbreviations or contractions: **shouldn't,** not **should-n't.**

8. Never divide the last word in more than two lines in a row.

Grammar Practice

Hyphens 2

- Between Numbers and Fractions
- In a Special Series
- To Join Numbers
- To Prevent Confusion
- To Divide a Word

 For each sentence below, correctly write the word(s) that should be hyphenated or are incorrectly hyphenated.

1. The unusual foliage has a shelllike coating.

2. Your assignment is to write an 800 to 1,000 word persuasive essay.

3. Say what you will, but I believe these arguments about money have stra-ined our relationship.

4. Even one thirty second of an inch error in measurement will result in an inaccurate reading.

5. Cut the board into two, four, and six inch lengths.

6. Dr. Mahan's degree is in chemistry, but he is always ready with one histo-rical fact or another to explain his lessons.

7. Two thirds of the crowd left when the score was 33 10 in the fourth quarter.

8. My boss asked me to resign the form after rereading sections 5 7.

9. Prior to the exam, the proctor gave this instruction: "You will need to o-mit question number six from your answers due to a printing error."

10. Sergei wrote of yesterday's Moscowwide electrical outage in his e-mail.

11. By 2015, more than one half of the world's population will live in urban areas.

12. Ramona created six and eight sided paper snowflakes.

Model

Model the following sentence to practice using hyphens in a special series.

Two-, three-, and four-column notebooks are available at the bookstore.

Related Skills Activities

 SkillsBook
Hyphens, p. 22

Answers

1. shell-like
2. 800- to 1,000-word
3. strained
4. one thirty-second
5. two-, four-, and six-inch
6. his-torical *or* histori-cal
7. Two-thirds
   33–10
8. re-sign
   5–7
9. omit
10. Moscow-wide
11. one-half
12. six- and eight-sided

Apostrophe

628.1 In Contractions

Use an **apostrophe** to show that one or more letters have been left out of a word group to form a contraction.

hadn't – **o** is left out   they'd – **woul** is left out   it's – **i** is left out

Note: Use an apostrophe to show that one or more numerals or letters have been left out of numbers or words in order to show special pronunciation.

class of '12 – **20** is left out   g'day – **ood** is left out

628.2 To Form Singular Possessives

Add an apostrophe and *s* to form the possessive of most singular nouns.

Spock's **ears**   Captain Kirk's **singing**   the ship's **escape plan**

Note: When a singular noun ends with an *s* or a *z* sound, you may form the possessive by adding just an apostrophe. When the singular noun is a one-syllable word, however, you usually add both an apostrophe and an *s* to form the possessive.

San Carlos' **government** (or) San Carlos's **government** (two-syllable word)
Ross's **essay** (one-syllable word)   the class's **field trip** (one-syllable word)

628.3 To Form Plural Possessives

The possessive form of plural nouns ending in *s* is usually made by adding just an apostrophe.

students' **homework**   bosses' **orders**

For plural nouns not ending in *s*, an apostrophe and *s* must be added.

children's **book**   men's **department**

A Closer Look

It will help you to punctuate correctly if you remember that the word immediately before the apostrophe is the owner.

girl's **guitar** (*girl* is the owner)   boss's **order** (*boss* is the owner)
girls' **guitars** (*girls* are the owners)   bosses' **order** (*bosses* are the owners)

628.4 To Show Shared Possession

When possession is shared by more than one noun, use the possessive form for the last noun in the series.

Hoshi, Linda, and Nakiva's **water skis** (All three own the same skis.)
Hoshi's, Linda's, and Nakiva's **water skis** (Each owns her own skis.)

Grammar Practice

Apostrophes 1

- In Contractions
- To Form Singular Possessives
- To Form Plural Possessives
- To Show Shared Possession

 For each sentence, write the contraction for or the possessive form of the word or words in parentheses.

1. *(Ravi, Simone, and Lucas)* biology classes went on a field trip together.

2. They had to take two buses because everyone *(would not)* fit on one.

3. *(Mount Ranier)* Sunrise Area was the destination for the *(students)* trip.

4. Simone said, "*(I have)* never been here before. I hope *(it will)* be fun!"

5. The *(classes)* assignment was to observe and investigate an *(alpine ecosystem)* fragility.

6. The *(teachers)* lesson plans provided excellent insight into the *(mountain)* ecological systems.

7. *(Ravi and Simone)* shoes *(were not)* appropriate for a three-mile hike.

8. Ravi wished *(he had)* worn hiking boots.

9. *(Mr. Sullivan and Mrs. Ling)* first-aid kit was put to good use.

10. *(It is)* a good thing that *(they are)* always prepared; the kids *(would have)* suffered without bandages for their blisters.

Model

Model the following sentences to practice using apostrophes to form singular and plural possessives.

Take each man's censure, but reserve thy judgment.
—William Shakespeare, *Hamlet*

The notion that nutmeg could ward off the plague survived longer than many another old wives' tales.
—Simon Winchester, *Krakatoa*

Related Skills Activities

Answers

1. Ravi's, Simone's, and Lucas's
2. wouldn't
3. Mount Ranier's
   students'
4. I've
   it'll
5. classes'
   alpine ecosystem's
6. teachers'
   mountain's
7. Ravi's and Simone's
   weren't
8. he'd
9. Mr. Sullivan and Mrs. Ling's
10. It's
    they're
    would've

Apostrophe (continued)

630.1 To Show Possession with Indefinite Pronouns

Form the possessive of an indefinite pronoun by placing an apostrophe and an *s* on the last word (see 704.1 and 706.3).

everyone's   anyone's   somebody's

It is everybody's responsibility to keep his or her locker orderly.

In expressions using *else,* add the apostrophe and *s* after the last word.

This is somebody else's mess, not mine.

630.2 To Show Possession in Compound Nouns

Form the possessive of a compound noun by placing the possessive ending after the last word.

the secretary of the interior's (singular) agenda
her lady-in-waiting's (singular) day off

If forming a possessive of a plural compound noun creates an awkward construction, you may replace the possessive with an *of* phrase. (All four forms below are correct.)

their fathers-in-law's (plural) birthdays
or the birthdays of their fathers-in-law (plural)
the ambassadors-at-large's (plural) plans
or the plans of the ambassadors-at-large (plural)

630.3 To Express Time or Amount

Use an apostrophe and an *s* with an adjective that is part of an expression indicating time or amount.

a penny's worth   two cents' worth   this morning's meeting
yesterday's news   a day's wage   six months' pay

630.4 To Form Certain Plurals

Use an apostrophe and *s* to form the plural of a letter, a number, a sign, or a word discussed as a word.

B – B's   C – C's   8 – 8's   + – +'s   *and* – *and's*

Ms. D'Aquisto says our conversations contain too many *like's* and *no way's.*

Note: If two apostrophes are called for in the same word, omit the second one.

Follow closely the *do's* and *don'ts* (not *don't's*) on the checklist.

Grammar Practice

Apostrophes 2

- To Show Possession with Indefinite Pronouns
- To Show Possession in Compound Nouns
- To Express Time or Amount
- To Form Certain Plurals

 Write each underlined word in the following paragraphs with the apostrophe placed correctly.

Each day, I drink about five **(1)** <u>dollars</u> worth of coffee. You might share **(2)** <u>everyone elses</u> opinion that I drink too much coffee, but that's not true—no **(3)** <u>ifs, ands or buts</u> about it! I buy only one cup of coffee a day, and it's always one of the **(4)** <u>Super 20s</u> at Sergio's Coffee Shop. (Each specialty cup of coffee holds 20 ounces.)

The shop is staffed by Sergio's family members, and these **(5)** <u>Italian Americans</u> cooking is superb. Sergio uses his **(6)** <u>sister-in-laws</u> recipes for the special coffee drinks, and she works in the shop as a barista. Her Almond Joy Super 20 (I love it!) is a flavored latte that's **(7)** <u>everybodys</u> favorite. Some of the other Super 20 flavors are **(8)** <u>Cs in 3s</u> (cappuccino with chocolate and caramel syrups) and **(9)** <u>Anyones</u> Guess, which is **(10)** <u>todays</u> flavor of the day.

Model

Model the following sentences to practice using apostrophes to express time or amount and to show possession with indefinite pronouns.

I never did a day's work in my life. It was all fun.

—Thomas Edison

Everybody's business is nobody's business, and nobody's business is my business.

—Clara Barton

Related Skills Activities

- ***SkillsBook***
  Apostrophes in Contractions and Plurals, p. 25

Answers

1. dollars'
2. everyone else's
3. *if*'s, *and*'s, or *but*'s
4. Super 20's
5. Italian Americans'
6. sister-in-law's
7. everybody's
8. C's in 3's
9. Anyone's
10. today's

Quotation Marks

632.1 To Set Off Direct Quotations

Place **quotation marks** before and after the words in direct quotations.

"Please give the liver and onions a try," she said. "I think you'll like it."

In a quoted passage, put brackets around any word or punctuation mark that is not part of the original quotation. (See 644.1.)

If you quote only part of the original passage, be sure to construct a sentence that is both accurate and grammatically correct.

Much of the restructuring of the Postal Service has involved "turning over large parts of its work to the private sector."

632.2 Placement of Punctuation

Always place periods and commas inside quotation marks.

"Well, that's a relief," said Isabel. "I thought we wouldn't make it to the theater in time for the previews."

Place an exclamation point or a question mark *inside* quotation marks when it punctuates the quotation and *outside* when it punctuates the main sentence.

"Am I dreaming?"   Had she heard him say, "Here's the key to your new car"?

Always place semicolons or colons outside quotation marks.

I wrote about James Joyce's "The Dead"; I found it thought provoking.

632.3 For Long Quotations

If you quote more than one paragraph, place quotation marks before each paragraph and at the end of the last paragraph (Example A). If a quotation has more than four lines on a page, you may set it off from the text by indenting 10 spaces from the left margin (block form). Do not use quotation marks either before or after the quoted material, unless they appear in the original (Example B).

Example A   **Example B**

Grammar Practice

Quotation Marks 1

■ To Set Off Direct Quotations
■ Placement of Punctuation
■ For Long Quotations

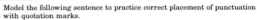 Indicate where quotation marks are needed in the following paragraphs by writing the quotation marks along with the words and other punctuation after or before them. (Use ellipses to show omitted words in your answers.)

1   I couldn't believe what I held in my hands. It was a yellowed letter that
2   I'd discovered tucked among the pages of an old scrapbook in our attic. Mom,
3   look at this, I said. It's a love letter. I handed her the fragile page filled with
4   the following almost illegible scrawl.

5   This letter brings the same old theme, which instead of growing old
6   by telling only grows brighter. This proves that my love for you is
7   stronger with each passing day. My happiness can not be any greater
8   than since I met you, my darling Ella. Being apart from you, far
9   across the sea, seems like an eternity to me. I long to see your smile
10   again, to hold your hands, and to look into your beautiful eyes.

11   Mom sighed. This letter is from your great-grandfather to his wife, Ella,
12 she said. Grandma told me once that Grandpa Doty had written her some
13 wonderful letters. She also told me how they fell in love.

14   It really was a love-at-first-sight story. Ella and William, a soldier, met a
15 few weeks before he was scheduled to leave for England. It was during World
16 War I, and many soldiers were dying in the war overseas. The day before he
17 shipped out, they ran off and got married against their parents' wishes.

18   William wrote to Ella almost every day, and I wouldn't be surprised if
19 we find more letters up here. Now I can't wait to go through all this old stuff!
20 Mom said.

21   I can't either, I answered. All of a sudden, cleaning the attic was a
22 treasure hunt instead of a chore.

Model

Model the following sentence to practice correct placement of punctuation with quotation marks.

It is not a lucky word, this name "impossible"; no good comes of those who have it so often in their mouths.
—Thomas Carlyle

Punctuation

Related Skills Activities

■ *SkillsBook*
Quotation Marks with Dialogue 1, 2, and 3, pp. 30–32
Punctuation Used in Research Papers, pp. 35–36

Answers

lines 2–3: "Mom . . . this," I said. "It's . . . letter."

lines 11–12: "This . . . Ella," she said. "Grandma . . .

line 14: "It . . .

lines 18–20: "William . . . stuff!" Mom said.

line 21: "I . . . either," I answered.

Quotation Marks *(continued)*

634.1 Quotation Marks Within Quotations

Use single quotation marks to punctuate a quotation within a quotation. Use double quotation marks if you need to distinguish a quotation within a quotation within a quotation.

> "For tomorrow," said Mr. Botts, "read 'Unlighted Lamps.'"
> Sue asked, "Did you hear Mr. Botts say, 'Read "Unlighted Lamps"'?"

634.2 For Special Words

You may use quotation marks (1) to distinguish a word that is being discussed, (2) to indicate that a word is unfamiliar slang, or (3) to point out that a word is being used in a special way.

> (1) As any English teacher will tell you, the word "whom" is rarely used correctly.
> (2) I . . . asked the bartender where I could hear "chanky-chank," as Cajuns called their music.
> —William Least Heat-Moon, *Blue Highways*
> (3) Tom pushed the wheelchair across the street, showed the lady his "honest" smile . . . and stole her purse.

Note: You may use italics (underlining) in place of quotation marks in each of these three situations. (See 636.3.)

634.3 To Punctuate Titles

Use **quotation marks** to punctuate titles of songs, poems, short stories, one-act plays, lectures, episodes of radio or television programs, chapters of books, unpublished works, electronic files, and articles found in magazines, newspapers, encyclopedias, or online sources. (For punctuation of other titles, see 636.2.)

> "Santa Lucia" (song)
> "The Chameleon" (short story)
> "Twentieth-Century Memories" (lecture)
> "Affordable Adventures" (magazine article)
> "Dire Prophecy of the Howling Dog" (chapter in a book)
> "Dancing with Debra" (television episode)
> "Miss Julie" (one-act play)

Note: Punctuate one title within another title as follows:

> "Clarkson's 'Breakaway' Hits the Waves"
> (title of a song in title of an article)

Grammar Practice

Quotation Marks 2

- Quotation Marks Within Quotations
- For Special Words
- To Punctuate Titles

 Write the word or words that should be enclosed in quotation marks in the following sentences.

1. Parker's poem entitled North to Midnight was accepted for publication in the national magazine *Know It!*

2. Tremain said, Did you see that ridiculous *Enquirer* article, Pterodactyls Found Alive in Tanzanian Cave?

3. The real estate agent used words like spacious, open, and airy to describe the home's sunroom.

4. Dad says that I should check out the drum solo in the song Away by an old rock group called Rain Sign.

5. Melissa's essay was titled The Natural State and told of the clear lakes, streams, and abundance of natural wildlife in Arkansas.

6. Rob asked, Have you read *Walden Pond* for English class?

7. His favorite episode of *Deadliest Catch* is Race Against the Ice.

8. Employees at the soda bottling company are subject to pop quizzes.

Model

Model the following sentences to practice using quotation marks within quotations.

> In my new pen pal's latest e-mail, he wrote about his musical tastes: "The Beatles are my all-time favorite band, and my favorite Beatles songs are probably 'Paperback Writer' and 'Hey Jude.' I like lots of newer bands, too, though."
> "I was lucky," said Jane. "The proctor announced, 'Put your pencils down,' just as I was filling in the last answer."

Related Skills Activities

- **SkillsBook**
  Punctuation Used in Research Papers, p. 35
  Italics (Underlining) and Quotation Marks, p. 33

Answers

1. "North to Midnight"
2. "Did . . . 'Pterodactyls . . . Cave'?"
3. "spacious," "open," "airy"
4. "Away"
5. "The Natural State"
6. "Have . . . class?"
7. "Race Against the Ice."
8. "pop"

Italics (Underlining)

636.1 Handwritten and Printed Material

Italics is a printer's term for a style of type that is slightly slanted. In this sentence, the word *happiness* is printed in italics. In material that is handwritten or typed on a machine that cannot print in italics, underline each word or letter that should be in italics.

> *My Ántonia* is the story of a strong and determined pioneer woman.
> (printed)
>
> Willa Cather's <u>My Ántonia</u> describes pioneer life in America.
> (typed or handwritten)

636.2 In Titles

Use italics to indicate the titles of magazines, newspapers, pamphlets, books, full-length plays, films, videos, radio and television programs, book-length poems, ballets, operas, paintings, lengthy musical compositions, sculptures, cassettes, CD's, legal cases, and the names of ships and aircraft. (For punctuation of other titles, see 634.3.)

> *Newsweek* (magazine) *Cold Sassy Tree* (book)
> *Shakespeare in Love* (film) *Law & Order* (television program)
> *Caring for Your Kitten* (pamphlet) *Hedda Gabler* (full-length play)
> *Chicago Tribune* (newspaper) *The Thinker* (sculpture)

636.3 For Special Uses

Use italics for a number, letter, or word that is being discussed or used in a special way. (Sometimes quotation marks are used for this reason. See 634.2.)

> I hope that this letter *I* on my report card stands for *incredible* and not *incomplete*.

636.4 For Foreign Words

Use italics for foreign words that have not been adopted into the English language; also use italics for scientific names.

> The voyageurs—tough men with natural *bonhomie*—discovered the shy *Castor canadensis*, or North American beaver.

636.5 For Emphasis

Use italics for words that require particular emphasis.

> I guess it really *was* worth it to put in extra study time.

Grammar Practice

Italics (Underlining)

- In Titles
- For Special Uses
- For Foreign Words
- For Emphasis

 Write and underline the word or words that should be italicized in the following sentences.

1. In algebra, we use the letters Z, Q, R, and C respectively to represent integers, rational, real, and complex numbers.

2. Giana hugged the queen—quite a faux pas, she later learned.

3. I enjoy planning trips to places I read about in National Geographic magazine.

4. Vinny did say that he would be late, remember?

5. Robin wrote a humorous opera called Diary of a Soccer Mom's Daughter.

6. Did you mix up the words bring and take?

7. "Not now!" Amber cried when her computer froze in the middle of a message.

8. She would have to call her cousin in New York about some tickets for the show Rent.

Model

Model the following sentence to practice using italics (underlining) for emphasis.

> "As yet," cried the stranger—his cheek glowing and his eye flashing with enthusiasm—"as yet, I have done *nothing*."
> —Nathaniel Hawthorne, "The Ambitious Guest"

Related Skills Activities

- **SkillsBook**
  Italics (Underlining) and Quotation Marks, p. 33

Answers

1. *Z, Q, R,* and *C*
2. *faux pas*
3. *National Geographic*
4. *did*
5. *Diary of a Soccer Mom's Daughter*
6. *bring*
   take
7. *now*
8. *Rent*

Parentheses

638.1 To Set Off Explanatory Material

You may use **parentheses** to set off explanatory or added material that interrupts the normal sentence structure.

> **Benson (our dog) sits in on our piano lessons (on the piano bench), much to the teacher's surprise and amusement.**
>
> —Chad Hockerman, student writer

Note: Place question marks and exclamation points within the parentheses when they mark the added material.

> **Ivan at once concluded (the rascal) that I had a passion for dances, and . . . wanted to drag me off to a dancing class.**
>
> —Fyodor Dostoevsky, "A Novel in Nine Letters"

638.2 With Full Sentences

When using a full sentence within another sentence, do not capitalize it or use a period inside the parentheses.

> **Because the weather in the mountains can be unpredictable (it sometimes hails in the summer), make sure you bring a poncho and warm clothes.**

When the parenthetical sentence comes after the period of the main sentence, capitalize and punctuate it the same way you would any other complete sentence.

> **They kiss and hug when they say "hello," and I love this. (In Korea, people are much more formal; they just shake hands and bow to each other.)**
>
> —Sue Chong, "He Said I Was Too American"

Note: For unavoidable parentheses within parentheses (. . . [. . .] . . .), use brackets. Avoid overuse of parentheses by using commas instead.

Diagonal

638.3 To Show a Choice

Use a **diagonal** (also called a *slash* or *forward slash*) between two words, as in *and/or*, to indicate that either is acceptable.

> **Press the load/eject button.**
> **Don't worry; this is indoor/outdoor carpet.**

638.4 When Quoting Poetry

When quoting more than one line of poetry, use a diagonal to show where each line of poetry ends. (Insert a space on each side of the diagonal.)

> **"Let not the wind / Example find, / To do more harm than it purposeth."**
>
> —John Donne, from "A Valediction: Of Weeping"

Grammar Practice

Parentheses and Diagonals

- To Set Off Explanatory Material
- With Full Sentences
- To Show a Choice
- When Quoting Poetry

 For the following sentences, write the word or words that should be enclosed in parentheses or divided by a diagonal. (Include parentheses or diagonals.)

1. Thai food have you tried it? is gaining popularity.

2. Old-style Thai cooking features the foods of a "waterborne lifestyle." This means ingredients like aquatic animals, plants, and herbs.

3. Americanized Thai food a unique blend of flavors is influenced by centuries-old Eastern and Western cultures.

4. Choose a curry dish and or a spiced salad to begin your meal.

5. Thai food everything is served in bite-sized pieces never needs a knife.

6. The server provides his her patrons with just a fork and a spoon.

7. You might want to try Khao Phat and Phat Thai one of the popular rice and noodle dishes when you visit a Thai restaurant.

 Rewrite the haiku poem below as if you were quoting it in the text of an essay.

8. Moored to the heavens
The wistful moon and bound stars
Dream about dancing.

Model

Model the following sentence to practice parentheses to set off explanatory material.

> **We asked people in the street (outside the Palladium Theatre, as it happens, at about 5 p.m.) if they used proper punctuation when sending text messages.**
>
> —Lynne Truss, *Eats, Shoots and Leaves*

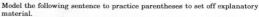

Punctuation

Related Skills Activities

- ***GrammarSnap***
  Punctuating Parenthetical Elements with Commas, Dashes, or Parenthesis

Answers

1. (have you tried it?)
2. (This means ingredients like aquatic animals, plants, and herbs.)
3. (a unique blend of flavors)
4. and/or
5. (everything is served in bite-sized pieces)
6. his/her
7. (one of the popular rice and noodle dishes)
8. "Moored to the heavens / The wistful moon and bound stars / Dream about dancing."

Dash

640.1 To Indicate a Sudden Break

Use a **dash** to indicate a sudden break or change in the sentence.

Near the semester's end—and this is not always due to poor planning—**some students may find themselves in a real crunch.**

Note: Dashes are often used in place of commas. Use dashes when you want to give special emphasis; use commas when there is no need for emphasis.

640.2 To Set Off an Introductory Series

Use a dash to set off an introductory series from the clause that explains the series.

A good book, a cup of tea, a comfortable chair—**these things always saved my mother's sanity.**

640.3 To Set Off Parenthetical Material

You may use a dash to set off parenthetical material—material that explains or clarifies a word or a phrase.

A single incident—a tornado that came without warning—**changed the face of the small town forever.**

640.4 To Indicate Interrupted Speech

Use a dash to show interrupted or faltering speech in dialogue.

> **Sojourner: Mama, why are you—**
> **Mama: Isabelle, do as I say!**
> —Sandy Asher, *A Woman Called Truth*

640.5 For Emphasis

Use a dash to emphasize a word, a series, a phrase, or a clause.

After several hours of hearing the high-pitched yipping, Petra finally realized what it was—coyote pups.

After years of trial and error, Belther made history with his invention—the unicycle.

Grammar Practice

Dashes

- To Indicate a Sudden Break
- To Set Off an Introductory Series
- To Set Off Parenthetical Material
- For Emphasis

 A word, a phrase, or a clause follows each sentence below. Rewrite the sentences to include those words, set off by one or two dashes.

1. The strange sound came from Old Ike's cornfield; I couldn't tell if it was human, or not. (*a low, guttural groaning*)

2. One would never guess that this colorful bird is considered a pest in Australia. (*the rainbow lorikeet*)

3. The members of Lemuel's band, Elixer K8, finally reached their long-sought-after goal. (*hearing their song played on the radio*)

4. That's all I need for a relaxing day on the beach. (*a cold drink, sunscreen, my MP3 player, and a good book*)

5. At 8:00 p.m. Saul arrived to take Trina to the prom. (*almost two hours late*)

6. Tony Akgulian spoke out in favor of a citywide graduation party sponsored by the Downtown Association. (*fifth-district alderman*)

7. Jarvis borrowed his brother's leather jacket to wear at the audition. (*the "lucky" jacket*)

8. Edward had applied to these prestigious schools. (*Princeton, Harvard, and Yale*)

 Model

Model the following sentence to practice using dashes to set off parenthetical material.

When I first beheld this apparition—for I could scarcely regard it as less—my wonder and my terror were extreme.

—Edgar Allan Poe, "The Black Cat"

Related Skills Activities

- ***SkillsBook***
  Dashes, p. 23

- ***GrammarSnap***
  Punctuating Parenthetical Elements with Commas, Dashes, or Parentheses

Answers

1. The strange sound—a low, guttural groaning—came from Old Ike's cornfield; I couldn't tell if it was human, or not.
2. One would never guess that this colorful bird—the rainbow lorikeet—is considered a pest in Australia.
3. The members of Lemuel's band, Elixer K8, finally reached their long-sought-after goal—hearing their song played on the radio.
4. A cold drink, sunscreen, my MP3 player, and a good book—that's all I need for a relaxing day on the beach.
5. At 8:00 p.m.—almost two hours late—Saul arrived to take Trina to the prom.
6. Tony Akgulian—fifth-district alderman—spoke out in favor of a citywide graduation party sponsored by the Downtown Association.
7. Jarvis borrowed his brother's leather jacket—the "lucky" jacket—to wear at the audition.
8. Princeton, Harvard, and Yale—Edward had applied to these prestigious schools. *or* Edward had applied to these prestigious schools—Princeton, Harvard, and Yale.

Ellipsis

642.1 To Show Omitted Words

Use an **ellipsis** (three periods with one space before and after each period) to show that one or more words have been omitted in a quotation.

(Original)

We the people of the United States, in order to form a more perfect Union, establish justice, insure domestic tranquility, provide for the common defense, promote the general welfare, and secure the blessings of liberty to ourselves and our posterity, do ordain and establish this Constitution for the United States of America.

—Preamble, U.S. Constitution

(Quotation)

"We the people . . . in order to form a more perfect Union . . . establish this Constitution for the United States of America."

642.2 At the End of a Sentence

If words from a quotation are omitted at the end of a sentence, place the ellipsis after the period that marks the conclusion of the sentence.

"Studies serve for delight, for ornament, for ability. . . . So every defect of the mind may have a special receipt."

—Sir Francis Bacon, from "Of Studies"

Note: If the quoted material is a complete sentence (even if it was not complete in the original), use a period, then an ellipsis.

(Original)

I am tired; my heart is sick and sad. From where the sun now stands I will fight no more forever.

—Chief Joseph of the Nez Percé

(Quotation)

"I am tired. . . . From where the sun now stands I will fight no more forever."

or

"I am tired. . . . I will fight no more. . . . "

642.3 To Show a Pause

Use an ellipsis to indicate a pause.

I brought my trembling hand to my focusing eyes. It was oozing, it was red, it was . . . it was . . . a tomato!

—Laura Baginski, student writer

Grammar Practice

Ellipses

- To Show Omitted Words
- At the End of a Sentence
- To Show a Pause

For the following paragraph, select the least important information to replace with ellipses. Write the shortened paragraph on your paper.

1   Have you ever tried making a tasty, cheesy, wonderful, homemade pizza
2 from scratch? Making a pizza is easy to achieve, especially if you use a bread
3 machine. Combine the following easy-to-find ingredients in the pan of the
4 bread machine: 3 1/2 cups flour, 1 cup warm water, 2 tablespoons dry yeast,
5 2 tablespoons honey (you can leave this ingredient out if you want to; it's
6 entirely up to you), 1/4 cup olive oil, and about 1/2 teaspoon of salt (more or
7 less, to your preferred taste). Set the machine to the "dough only" setting and
8 push the start button. When it is ready, place the dough on a wood cutting
9 board or another flat surface. Throw some flour on the surface and flatten the
10 dough with your hands or a sturdy rolling pin. Work it until it's the size of the
11 pan you plan to cook it on (a round pizza pan or a cookie sheet works well).
12 Rub a little olive oil onto the pan and then press the dough evenly into the
13 pan. Prick some small holes in the crust with a fork. This will help to keep it
14 from bubbling up while cooking, and it also helps to hold the sauce, as well.
15 Top the crust with pizza sauce, a lot of tasty mozzarella cheese, and whatever
16 other kinds of toppings that you like on your pizza. Bake the pizza in a
17 400-degree oven until the crust is light brown. Enjoy eating your pizza!

Exercise

For each of the following situations, write a sentence or two in which you use an ellipsis to show a pause.

Your best friend has asked a special person to the prom dance. You want to know if the answer was "yes."

You are surprised by the contents of a letter that you've just read.

Punctuation

Answers

Answers will vary.

Have your ever tried making a . . . pizza from scratch? Making a pizza is easy . . . if you use a bread machine. Combine the following . . . ingredients in the pan . . . : 3 1/2 cups flour, 1 cup warm water, 2 tablespoons dry yeast, 2 tablespoons honey . . . , 1/4 cup olive oil, and about 1/2 teaspoon of salt. . . . Set the machine to . . . "dough only" . . . and push . . . start. . . . When it is ready, place the dough on . . . flat surface. Throw some flour on the surface and flatten the dough . . . until it's the size of . . . a round pizza pan or a cookie sheet. . . . Rub a little olive oil onto the pan and then press the dough evenly into the pan. Prick some small holes in the crust with a fork. . . . Top . . . with pizza sauce, . . . mozzarella cheese, and . . . other . . . toppings. . . . Bake . . . in a 400-degree oven until the crust is light brown. Enjoy. . . !

Brackets

644.1 To Set Off Clarifying Information

Use **brackets** before and after words that are added to clarify what another person has said or written.

> "It [his hand] began to itch after he touched the poison ivy by mistake."

Note: The brackets indicate that the words *my hand* are not part of the quotation but were added for clarification.

644.2 Around an Editorial Correction

Place brackets around an editorial correction inserted within quoted material.

> "Brooklyn alone has 8 percent of lead poisoning [victims] nationwide," said Marjorie Moore.
> —Donna Actie, student writer

Note: The brackets indicate that the word *victims* replaced the author's original word.

Place brackets around the letters sic (Latin for "as such"); the letters indicate that an error appearing in the material being quoted was made by the original speaker or writer.

> "When I'm queen," mused Lucy, "I'll show these blockheads whose [sic] got beauty and brains."

644.3 To Set Off Added Words

Place brackets around comments that have been added to a quotation.

> "Congratulations to the astronomy club's softball team, which put in, shall we say, a 'stellar' performance." [groans]

Punctuation Marks

´	Accent, acute	,	Comma	( )	Parentheses
`	Accent, grave	†	Dagger	.	Period
,	Apostrophe	—	Dash	?	Question mark
*	Asterisk	/	Diagonal/Slash	" "	Quotation marks
{ }	Brace	¨ (ü)	Dieresis	§	Section
[ ]	Brackets	...	Ellipsis	;	Semicolon
^	Caret	!	Exclamation point	~	Tilde
(c)	Cedilla	-	Hyphen	__	Underscore
^	Circumflex	...	Leaders		
:	Colon	¶	Paragraph		

Grammar Practice

Brackets

- To Set Off Clarifying Information
- Around an Editorial Correction
- To Set Off Added Words

 Follow the directions for each activity below.

1. In the following quotation, the speaker is talking about solar flares. Rewrite the quotation, using that word in brackets to clarify the quotation.

   > "Early records indicate that the sun went through a period of inactivity in the late seventeenth century," Dr. Johnson explained. "Very few were seen from about 1645 to 1715."

2. Quote the following statement and show that the error was made by the original author, Jean le Fleur.

   > Many belief that the "Kennedy curse" began with the death of Joseph Kennedy during World War II.

3. In the following quotation, replace the speaker's use of the word *motorsport* with the words *auto racing*. Place brackets around your editorial correction.

   > According to David Carls, a local race-car enthusiast, "Motorsport is probably the world's most popular spectator sport because everybody dreams of being able to drive a car that fast—legally."

4. Use brackets to add the writer's comment, a yawn, to these sentences.

   > All of this endless talk about a referendum is getting old. Put it on a ballot and take it to the people!

Model

Model the following sentence to practice using brackets to set off clarifying information.

> He [a physicist] is an atom's way of knowing about atoms.
> —George Wald

Punctuation

Answers

1. "Early records indicate that the sun went through a period of inactivity in the late seventeenth century," Dr. Johnson explained. "Very few [solar flares] were seen from about 1645 to 1715."

2. Jean le Fleur asserts, "Many belief [*sic*] that the 'Kennedy curse' began with the death of Joseph Kennedy during World War II."

3. According to David Carls, a local race-car enthusiast, "[Auto racing] is probably the world's most popular spectator sport because everybody dreams of being able to drive a car that fast—legally."

4. All of this endless talk about a referendum is getting old. [yawn] Put it on a ballot and take it to the people!

Test Prep!

From the choices given on the next page, write the letter of the correct way to punctuate each underlined part of the following essay. If it is already correct, write "D."

Ms. Hoffman, my art history teacher, said, "The origin of stained glass is a mystery." "Most likely, the technique came from making jewelry and mosaics. For 50
_____ (1)
years, 1050 1100 C.E., a monk wrote instructions for making stained glass windows".
_____ (2) _____ (3)
I couldn't wait to hear the monks' instructions. I've always been fascinated
_____ (4)
by how adding just a little bit of metallic salts or oxides to liquid glass creates the
beautiful colors. I had read a book called *Stained Glass Basics* and learned that gold
_____ (5) _____ (6)
makes a brilliant cranberry color, cobalt makes blue, silver makes yellows-golds,
_____ (7)
and copper makes green and, surprisingly, brick red. Yet I didn't know how to put it
_____ (8)
together to create a piece of art. What would I learn from this monk about his 'new'
art form—a stained glass window?
_____ (9)
"These old instructions are still followed today," Ms. Hoffman continued.
"Here is what they say; "To assemble these windows, first mark their lengths and
_____ (10) _____ (11)
breadths on a wooden board. Then draw scrollwork, or anything else that pleases you,
and select colors to add. Cut the glass with a grozing iron (a tool with a hardened
_____ (12)
steel point—and fit the pieces together. Enclose them with cames [narrow lead
strips,] and solder them on both sides. Surround the window with a wooden frame
_____ (13)
strengthened with nails and set it up in the place you wish.' "
_____ (14)
At this point, Ms. Hoffman asked, "Have you ever seen real stained glass in
anyones' home? It can increase the value of a house dramatically." I volunteered that
_____ (15)
I had seen a recreation of Van Gogh's painting "Irises" in a house in Rome, Virginia.
_____ (16) _____ (17)
(The house had become a museum in the 1970s). Stained glass can add not only
_____ (18)
beauty but also value to windows in any building.

1 Ⓐ mystery." Most
   Ⓑ mystery. Most
   Ⓒ mystery. "Most
   Ⓓ correct as is

2 Ⓐ 1050—1100 C.E.
   Ⓑ 1050 / 1100 C.E.
   Ⓒ 1050–1100 C.E.
   Ⓓ correct as is

3 Ⓐ windows."
   Ⓑ windows'.
   Ⓒ windows.'
   Ⓓ correct as is

4 Ⓐ cound'nt wait to hear the monks'
   Ⓑ could'nt wait to hear the monk's
   Ⓒ couldn't wait to hear the monk's
   Ⓓ correct as is

5 Ⓐ "Stained Glass Basics"
   Ⓑ 'Stained Glass Basics'
   Ⓒ "Stained Glass Basics,"
   Ⓓ correct as is

6 Ⓐ gol-d
   Ⓑ g-old
   Ⓒ This word should not be divided.
   Ⓓ correct as is

7 Ⓐ yellows golds
   Ⓑ yellows—golds
   Ⓒ yellows/golds
   Ⓓ correct as is

8 Ⓐ Yet I di'dnt
   Ⓑ Yet I did'nt
   Ⓒ Yet: I didn't
   Ⓓ correct as is

9 Ⓐ "new" art form—a
   Ⓑ "new" art form [a
   Ⓒ 'new' art form (a
   Ⓓ correct as is

10 Ⓐ they say: 'To
   Ⓑ they say: "To
   Ⓒ they say; 'To
   Ⓓ correct as is

11 Ⓐ len-gths
   Ⓑ le-ngths
   Ⓒ This word should not be divided.
   Ⓓ correct as is

12 Ⓐ a tool with a hardened steel point)
   Ⓑ —a tool with a hardened steel point—
   Ⓒ Either "A" or "B" is correct.
   Ⓓ correct as is

13 Ⓐ narrow lead strips,)
   Ⓑ (narrow lead strips)
   Ⓒ [narrow lead strips),
   Ⓓ correct as is

14 Ⓐ wish."
   Ⓑ wish.'"
   Ⓒ wish.'
   Ⓓ correct as is

15 Ⓐ anyones's home
   Ⓑ anyone's home
   Ⓒ anyones home
   Ⓓ correct as is

16 Ⓐ recreation of Van Goghs'
   Ⓑ re-creation of Van Goghs'
   Ⓒ re-creation of Van Gogh's
   Ⓓ correct as is

17 Ⓐ Irises
   Ⓑ 'Irises'
   Ⓒ Irises
   Ⓓ correct as is

18 Ⓐ 1970s.
   Ⓑ 1970s.)
   Ⓒ [1970s].
   Ⓓ correct as is

Punctuation

Related Skills Activities

■ **SkillsBook**
Review: Hyphens and Dashes, p. 24
Review: Apostrophes, p. 29
Review: Quotation Marks and Italics (Underlining), p. 34
Posttest: Hyphens and Dashes, p. 190
Posttest: Quotation Marks and Italics (Underlining), p. 191
Posttest: Punctuation, p. 193v

Answers

1. B
2. C
3. A
4. C
5. D
6. C
7. C
8. D
9. A

10. A
11. C
12. C
13. B
14. D
15. B
16. C
17. C
18. B

Checking Mechanics

Capitalization

648.1 Proper Nouns and Adjectives

Capitalize proper nouns and proper adjectives (those derived from proper nouns). The chart below provides a quick overview of capitalization rules. The pages following explain some specific rules of capitalization.

Capitalization at a Glance

Names of people	Alice Walker, Matilda, Jim, Mr. Roker
Days of the week, months	Sunday, Tuesday, June, August
Holidays, holy days	Thanksgiving, Easter, Hanukkah
Periods, events in history	Middle Ages, the Battle of Bunker Hill
Official documents	Declaration of Independence
Special events	Elgin Community Spring Gala
Languages, nationalities, religions	French, Canadian, Islam
Political parties	Republican Party, Socialist Party
Trade names	Oscar Mayer hot dogs, Pontiac Sunbird
Official titles used with names	Mayor John Spitzer, Senator Feinstein
Formal epithets	Alexander the Great

Geographical names

Planets, heavenly bodies	Earth, Jupiter, the Milky Way
Continents	Australia, South America
Countries	Ireland, Grenada, Sri Lanka
States, provinces	Ohio, Utah, Nova Scotia
Cities, towns, villages	El Paso, Burlington, Wonewoc
Streets, roads, highways	Park Avenue, Route 66, Interstate 90
Landforms	the Rocky Mountains, the Sahara Desert
Bodies of water	Yellowstone Lake, Pumpkin Creek
Buildings, monuments	Elkhorn High School, Gateway Arch
Public areas	Times Square, Sequoia National Park

Grammar Practice

Capitalization 1

■ Proper Nouns and Adjectives

 For each sentence below, write the word or words that should be capitalized.

1. Charles the bald was the youngest son of louis the pious, emperor and king of the franks.

2. The fugitive slave law of 1793 provided the return of runaway slaves to their owners.

3. Swahili, also known as "kiswahili," is a complex language spoken in east africa.

4. To avoid using the word "crock-pot," a registered trademark, use "slow cooker" instead.

5. The swallows day parade is an annual event in orange county, california.

6. The dixie highway stretched as far north as ontario, canada, and reached as far south as florida city, florida.

7. Lake powell, lake mead, and lake nassar are all man-made lakes.

8. In which u.s. city can you find the united nations secretariat building?

9. It is located in the turtle bay neighborhood (in the borough of manhattan) in new york city.

10. The building was featured in the movies *the pink panther strikes again* and *the interpreter*.

Model

Model the following sentence to practice capitalizing proper nouns and adjectives.

It was early February, in the middle of the peaceful lull that settles over Venice every year between New Year's Day and Carnival.

—John Berendt, *The City of Fallen Angels*

Mechanics

Related Skills Activities

■ **Word Choice**
Using General and Specific Nouns, p. 74

■ **SkillsBook**
Capitalization 1, 2, and 3, pp. 41–43

■ **GrammarSnap**
Capitalization of Proper Nouns and Adjectives

Answers

1. Bald
   Louis the Pious
   Franks
2. Fugitive Slave
   Law
3. "Kiswahili"
   East Africa
4. "Crock-Pot"
5. Swallows Day
   Parade
   Orange County,
   California
6. Dixie Highway
   Ontario, Canada
   Florida City,
   Florida
7. Lake Powell
   Lake Mead
   Lake Nasser

8. U.S.
   United Nations
   Secretariat
   Building
9. Turtle Bay
   Manhattan
   New York City
10. *The Pink
    Panther
    Strikes Again
    The Interpreter*

Capitalization *(continued)*

650.1 First Words

Capitalize the first word of every sentence, including the first word of a full-sentence direct quotation.

> **Jane was nervous and excited. In a trembling voice, she whispered to her brother, "Did you see that cougar? it was on the trail just behind us." At that moment, they heard a noise behind them.**

650.2 Sentences in Parentheses

Capitalize the first word in a sentence enclosed in parentheses, but do not capitalize the first word if the parenthetical appears within another sentence.

> **Shamelessly she winked at me and grinned again. (That grin! She could have taken it off her face and put it on the table.)**
>
> —Jean Stafford, "Bad Characters"
>
> **Damien's aunt (she's a wild woman) plays bingo every Saturday night.**

650.3 Sentences Following Colons

Capitalize the first word in a complete sentence that follows a colon when (1) you want to emphasize the sentence or (2) the sentence is a quotation.

> **When we quarreled and made horrible faces at one another, Mother knew what to say: "Your faces will stay that way, and no one will marry you."**

650.4 Sections of the Country

Capitalize words that indicate particular sections of the country; do not capitalize words that simply indicate direction.

> **Mr. Johnson is from the Southwest.** (section of the country)
>
> **After moving north to Montana, he had to buy winter clothes.** (direction)

650.5 Certain Religious Words

Capitalize nouns that refer to the Supreme Being, the word *Bible,* the books of the Bible, and the names for other holy books.

> **God   Jehovah   the Lord   the Savior   Allah   Bible   Genesis**

650.6 Titles

Capitalize the first word of a title, the last word, and every word in between except articles (*a, an, the*), short prepositions, and coordinating conjunctions. Follow this rule for titles of books, newspapers, magazines, poems, plays, songs, articles, films, works of art, photographs, and stories.

> ***Washington Post***   **"The Diary of a Madman"**   ***Nights of Rain and Stars***

Grammar Practice

Capitalization 2

- First Words
- Sentences in Parentheses
- Sentences Following Colons
- Sections of the Country
- Certain Religious Words
- Titles

 Find the word or word groups that are not correctly capitalized in the following paragraphs. Write the line number in which each error appears, followed by the corrected word(s).

1   There was a cavernous rumble. Reed said, "over there!" He was pointing

2   at a giant supercell. (these rotating thunderstorms can spawn tornadoes.) I felt

3   a huge adrenaline rush as we watched the storm ramble toward us from the

4   Southwest.

5   Soon enough, the expected happened: a black rope slithered down from

6   the wall cloud. I shouted, "we have a tornado!" Reed, a seasoned storm chaser

7   from the midwest, grabbed my arm, and we bolted for his truck.

8   I thanked god that I was assigned to chase with Reed. as a

9   filmmaker, I was excited to see his photogrammetric analysis of the

10   storm. (Tornado photogrammetry is the use of film or video to

11   determine wind speed.) Some of his weather photography was featured

12   in a recent edition of *national geographic* magazine.

13   The tornado was gone as abruptly as it had appeared. the wind had died

14   down, and an eerie green atmosphere blanketed the Area. Reed started his

15   truck, ready to pursue the next storm to hit this area of the deep south.

Model

Model the following sentence to practice capitalizing sections of the country.

> **The Avalon Peninsula is the easternmost prow of North America—a vaguely H-shaped chunk of land that is very nearly an island itself.**
>
> —Scott Weidensaul, *Return to Wild America*

Mechanics

Related Skills Activities

- ***SkillsBook***
  Capitalization 1, 2, and 3, pp. 41–43

- ***GrammarSnap***
  Capitalization of Proper Nouns and Adjectives

Answers

line 1: Over
line 2: These
line 4: southwest
line 5: A
line 6: We
line 7: Midwest
line 8: God
       As
line 12: *National Geographic*
line 13: The
line 14: area
line 15: Deep South

Capitalization (continued)

652.1 Words Used as Names

Capitalize words like *father*, *mother*, *uncle*, and *senator* when they are used as titles with a personal name or when they are substituted for proper nouns (especially in direct address).

> **We've missed you, Aunt Lucinda!** (*Aunt* is part of the name.)
> **I hope Mayor Bates arrives soon.** (*Mayor* is part of the name.)

A Closer Look

To test whether a word is being substituted for a proper noun, simply read the sentence with a proper noun in place of the word. If the proper noun fits in the sentence, the word being tested should be capitalized; otherwise, the word should not be capitalized.

> **Did Mom (Sue) say we could go?** (*Sue* works in this sentence.)
> **Did your mom (Sue) say you could go?** (*Sue* does not work here.)

Note: Usually the word is not capitalized if it follows a possessive —*my, his, your*—as it does in the second sentence above.

652.2 Letters

Capitalize the letters used to indicate form or shape.

> **U-turn   I-beam   S-curve   T-shirt   V-shaped**

652.3 Organizations

Capitalize the name of an organization, an association, or a team.

> **Lake Ontario Sailors   American Indian Movement   Democratic Party**

652.4 Abbreviations

Capitalize abbreviations of titles and organizations. (Some other abbreviations are also capitalized. See pages 660–662.)

> **AAA   CEO   NAACP   M.D.   Ph.D.**

652.5 Titles of Courses

Capitalize words like *sociology* and *history* when they are used as titles of specific courses; do not capitalize these words when they name a field of study.

> **Who teaches History 202?** (title of a specific course)
> **It's the same professor who teaches my sociology course.** (a field of study)

Note: The words *freshman*, *sophomore*, *junior*, and *senior* are not capitalized unless they are part of an official title.

> **Rosa is a senior this year and is in charge of the Senior Class Banquet.**

Grammar Practice

Capitalization 3

- Words Used as Names
- Letters
- Organizations
- Abbreviations
- Titles of Courses

Find the words that are incorrectly lowercased in the following memo. Write the line number along with the words that should be capitalized.

1	**Date:**	December 8, 2011
2	**To:**	senator Robert Flanagan
3	**From:**	Mayor Dana Stepanski of Rockdale
4	**Subject:**	Update on Rerouting r.r. 27

5   Representatives from madd (mothers against drunk driving) have
6 gathered 2,500 signatures in support of rerouting the s-curve on Rural Route
7 27. Monica Curtis, ph.d, president of the Rockdale chapter of MADD and
8 chairperson of the environmental and safety department at McKay College,
9 presented our city council with the petition.

10   Professor Curtis teaches the highway traffic safety course at the college.
11 She pointed out that r.r. 27 has had more accidents than any other state
12 highway in River Rock County. The petition addresses the issue of accidents
13 on the S-curve in 2008-2009. As you know, there have been six fatalities on the
14 curve, and the highway investigation committee reports seventeen accidents
15 there in 2008-2009.

16   This issue needs to be addressed. Please let me know when you are
17 available to meet with me to develop a proposal to present to governor Billingsly.

Model

Model the following sentence to practice capitalizing titles of courses.

> **I love math, so I can't wait to take Calculus II in college next year.**

Related Skills Activities

- **SkillsBook**
  Numbers and Abbreviations 1 and 2, pp. 45–46

Answers

line 2: Senator
line 4: R.R.
line 5: MADD (Mothers Against Drunk Driving)
line 6: S-curve
line 7: Ph.D.
line 8: Environmental and Safety Department
line 10: Highway Traffic Safety
line 11: R.R.
line 14: Highway Investigation Committee
line 17: Governor

Plurals

654.1 Most Nouns

Form the **plurals** of most nouns by adding *s* to the singular.

cheerleader – cheerleaders
sign – signs
crate – crates

654.2 Nouns Ending in *sh, ch, x, s,* and *z*

Form the plurals of nouns ending in *sh, ch, x, s,* and *z* by adding *es* to the singular.

lunch – lunches   dish – dishes   mess – messes   fox – foxes

Exception: When the final *ch* sounds like *k*, add an *s* (*monarchs*).

654.3 Nouns Ending in *y*

The plurals of common nouns that end in *y*—preceded by a consonant—are formed by changing the *y* to *i* and adding *es*.

fly – flies   jalopy – jalopies

Form the plurals of nouns that end in *y*—preceded by a vowel—by adding only an *s*.

donkey – donkeys   monkey – monkeys

Note: Form the plurals of all proper nouns ending in *y* by adding *s* (*Kathys*).

654.4 Nouns Ending in *o*

The plurals of nouns ending in *o*—preceded by a vowel—are formed by adding an *s*.

radio – radios   rodeo – rodeos   studio – studios   duo – duos

The plurals of most nouns ending in *o*—preceded by a consonant—are formed by adding *es*.

echo – echoes   hero – heroes   tomato – tomatoes

Exception: Musical terms always form plurals by adding *s*.

alto – altos   banjo – banjos   solo – solos   piano – pianos

654.5 Nouns Ending in *ful*

Form the plurals of nouns that end in *ful* by adding an *s* at the end of the word.

two tankfuls   three pailfuls   four mouthfuls

Note: Do not confuse these examples with *three pails full* (when you are referring to three separate pails full of something) or *two tanks full*.

654.6 Compound Nouns

Form the plurals of most compound nouns by adding *s* or *es* to the important word in the compound.

brothers-in-law   maids of honor   secretaries of state

Grammar Practice

Plurals 1

- Most Nouns
- Nouns Ending in *sh, ch, x, s,* and *z*
- Nouns Ending in *y*
- Nouns Ending in *o*
- Nouns Ending in *ful*
- Compound Nouns

 Write the correct plurals of the underlined word or words in each sentence.

1. Ten local <u>artist</u> will present their renderings of <u>church</u> at Gallery One.
2. The <u>Knight of Columbus</u> are sponsoring the exhibit.
3. Two husband-wife <u>duo</u> will show their joint <u>work</u> of art.
4. The <u>Buchinsky</u> will exhibit their sculptures called "The Three <u>Faithful</u>."
5. These works feature <u>mystery</u> associated with historical <u>mosque</u>.
6. Carol and Franco Diaz will show religious folk art created from Mexican <u>box</u>.
7. <u>*Echo in Time*</u> and other paintings by Margaret Cliffton can be found in the <u>hallway</u> of the gallery.
8. Visitors can view a demonstration of fabric art using <u>chintz</u>.
9. They will also be able to sign up for art <u>class</u> at the gallery.
10. A highlight of the exhibit will be Fr. Anthony Spinozza's pen-and-ink <u>drawing</u> of Roman <u>church</u> from early <u>century</u>.
11. Several art <u>studio</u> will be open for tours Sunday afternoon.
12. Jacob Barr will entertain at the event with his original piano <u>solo</u>.

Model

Model the following sentences to practice using the plurals of nouns ending in *sh* and *ch*.

We would often be sorry if our wishes were gratified.
—Aesop

It is just the little touches after the average man would quit that make the master's fame.
—Orison Swett Marden

Mechanics

Related Skills Activities

- ***SkillsBook***
  Pretest: Plurals and Spelling, pp. 47–48
  Plurals 1 and 2, pp. 49–50

Answers

1. artists
   churches
2. Knights of Columbus
3. duos
   works
4. Buchinskys
   Faithfuls
5. mysteries
   mosques
6. boxes
7. *Echoes in Time*
   hallways
8. chintzes
9. classes
10. drawings
    churches
    centuries
11. studios
12. solos

Plurals *(continued)*

656.1 Nouns Ending in *f* or *fe*

Form the plurals of nouns that end in *f* or *fe* in one of two ways: If the final *f* sound is still heard in the plural form of the word, simply add *s*; but if the final *f* sound becomes a *v* sound, change the *f* to *ve* and add *s*.

Plural ends with *f* sound: roof – roofs; chief – chiefs
Plural ends with *v* sound: wife – wives; loaf – loaves

Note: Several words are correct with either ending.
Plural ends with either sound: hoof – hooves/hoofs

656.2 Irregular Spelling

A number of words form a plural by taking on an irregular spelling.

crisis – crises	child – children	radius – radii
criterion – criteria	goose – geese	die – dice

Note: Some of these words are acceptable with the commonly used *s* or *es* ending.

index · indices/indexes   cactus – cacti/cactuses

Some nouns remain unchanged when used as plurals.

deer   sheep   salmon   aircraft   series

656.3 Words Discussed as Words

The plurals of symbols, letters, numbers, and words being discussed as words are formed by adding an apostrophe and an *s*.

Dad yelled a lot of *wow's* and *yippee's* when he saw my A's and B's.

Note: You may omit the apostrophe if it does not cause any confusion.

the three R's or Rs   YMCA's or YMCAs

656.4 Collective Nouns

A collective noun may be singular or plural depending upon how it's used. A collective noun is singular when it refers to a group considered as one unit; it is plural when it refers to the individuals in the group.

The class was on its best behavior. (group as a unit)
The class are preparing for their final exams. (individuals in the group)

If it seems awkward to use a plural verb with a collective noun, add a clearly plural noun such as *members* to the sentence (changing the noun to an adjective), or make the collective noun the object of a preposition that follows the plural noun.

The class members are preparing for their final exams.
The students in the class are preparing for their final exams.

Grammar Practice

Plurals 2

- Nouns Ending in *f* or *fe*
- Irregular Spelling
- Words Discussed as Words
- Collective Nouns

 Write the correct plurals of the underlined word or words in each sentence.

1. Football is a game of four quarters and two <u>half</u>.

2. Early colonists shouted *<u>huzzah</u>* instead of *<u>hurray</u>*.

3. <u>Chef</u> sometimes use bay <u>leaf</u> to season soups and stews.

4. Scientists found <u>fungus</u> and <u>bacterium</u> in the samples.

5. How many English words contain two <u>u</u> in a row?

6. <u>Man</u>, <u>woman</u>, and <u>child</u> waited in line for the latest Harry Potter book.

7. I determine if I want to read certain books by first reading <u>synopsis</u>.

8. On our drive through the country, we saw <u>deer</u>, <u>sheep</u>, and <u>sheaf</u> of wheat.

9. "All the <u>and</u> and <u>but</u> in this sentence should give you a clue, Dave," said the teacher, "that it's a run-on."

10. Have you ever wondered why <u>goose</u> have no <u>tooth</u>?

 For each sentence below, choose the correct pronoun (in parentheses).

11. The committee gathered *(their, its)* luggage at the airport.

12. The committee presented *(their, its)* findings at the convention.

 ## Exercise

Write one or two sentences using the plurals of all the following words.

index, phenomenon, thief, life, offspring

Related Skills Activities

- ***SkillsBook***
  Plurals 1 and 2, pp. 49–50

Answers

1. halves
2. *huzzah*'s
   hurray's
3. Chefs
   leaves
4. fungi
   bacteria
5. *u*'s
6. Men
   women
   children
7. synopses
8. deer
   sheep
   sheaves
9. *and*'s
   but's
10. geese
    teeth
11. their
12. its

Numbers

658.1 Numerals or Words

Numbers from one to nine are usually written as words; numbers 10 and over are usually written as numerals. However, numbers being compared or contrasted should be kept in the same style.

8 to 11 years old   eight to eleven years old

You may use a combination of numerals and words for very large numbers.

1.5 million   3 billion to 3.2 billion   6 trillion

If numbers are used infrequently in a piece of writing, you may spell out those that can be written in no more than two words.

ten   twenty-five   two hundred   ten thousand

658.2 Numerals Only

Use numerals for the following forms: decimals, percentages, chapters, pages, addresses, phone numbers, identification numbers, and statistics.

26.2   8 percent   Highway 36   chapter 7
pages 287–89   July 6, 1945   44 B.C.E.   a vote of 23 to 4

Always use numerals with abbreviations and symbols.

8%   10 mm   3 cc   8 oz   90° C   24 mph   6' 3"

658.3 Words Only

Use words to express numbers that begin a sentence.

Fourteen students "forgot" their assignments.

Note: Change the sentence structure if this rule creates a clumsy construction.

Clumsy: *Six hundred thirty-nine teachers were laid off this year.*

Better: This year, 639 teachers were laid off.

Use words for numbers that come before a compound modifier if that modifier includes a numeral.

They made twelve 10-foot sub sandwiches for the picnic.

658.4 Time and Money

If time is expressed with an abbreviation, use numerals; if it is expressed in words, spell out the number.

4:00 A.M. (or) four o'clock

If an amount of money is spelled out, so is the currency; use a numeral if a symbol is used.

twenty dollars (or) $20

 ## Grammar Practice

Numbers

- Numerals or Words
- Numerals Only
- Words Only
- Time and Money

 For each sentence below, write the underlined numbers the correct way. If a number is already correctly presented, write "correct."

1. The <u>two-thousand-and-four</u> tsunami was the deadliest in history.
2. It struck at <u>seven-fifty-three</u> a.m. local time on December 26.
3. Initial estimates of the death toll neared <u>300,000</u> people.
4. The earthquake that caused it registered <u>nine-point-one</u> on the Richter scale.
5. The quake lasted between <u>500</u> and <u>six hundred</u> seconds.
6. The tsunami created waves up to <u>thirty</u> meters (<u>100</u> feet).
7. <u>Sixty-six</u> percent of the fishing fleet was destroyed in coastal areas.
8. Energy released by the quake equaled about as much as the United States typically uses in <u>11</u> days.
9. The quake caused the earth to wobble on its axis about <u>1</u> inch in the direction of <u>one-hundred forty-five</u> degrees east longitude.
10. <u>16</u> coral-reef atolls crushed by sea waves could be uninhabitable for decades.
11. <u>Three billion dollars</u> in aid was provided by world countries.
12. Many children aged <u>six to 18</u> contributed aid to victims.

Model

Model the following sentences to practice using numbers and numerals correctly.

In the future, everyone will be famous for 15 minutes.
—Andy Warhol

Fifteen years ago, Congress took a significant step in implementing national health insurance for the aged with the establishment of Medicare.
—Select Committee on Aging, "Medicare: A Fifteen-Year Perspective"

Related Skills Activities

- ***SkillsBook***
  Numbers and Abbreviations 1 and 2, pp. 45–46

Answers

1. 2004
2. 7:53
3. correct
4. 9.1
5. correct
   600
6. 30
   correct
7. correct
8. correct
9. one
   145
10. Sixteen
11. correct
12. 6 to 18

Abbreviations

660.1 Formal and Informal Abbreviations

An **abbreviation** is the shortened form of a word or phrase. Some abbreviations are always acceptable in both formal and informal writing:

Mr.   Mrs.   Jr.   Ms.   Dr.   a.m. (A.M.)   p.m. (P.M.)

Note: In most of your writing, you do not abbreviate the names of states, countries, months, days, or units of measure. However, you may use the abbreviation *U.S.* after it has been spelled out once. Do not abbreviate the words *Street, Company,* and similar words, especially when they are part of a proper name. Also, do not use signs or symbols (%, &, #, @) in place of words. The dollar sign, however, is appropriate with numerals ($325).

660.2 Correspondence Abbreviations

United States

	Standard	Postal
Alabama	Ala.	AL
Alaska	Alaska	AK
Arizona	Ariz.	AZ
Arkansas	Ark.	AR
California	Calif.	CA
Colorado	Colo.	CO
Connecticut	Conn.	CT
Delaware	Del.	DE
District of Columbia	D.C.	DC
Florida	Fla.	FL
Georgia	Ga.	GA
Guam	Guam	GU
Hawaii	Hawaii	HI
Idaho	Idaho	ID
Illinois	Ill.	IL
Indiana	Ind.	IN
Iowa	Iowa	IA
Kansas	Kan.	KS
Kentucky	Ky.	KY
Louisiana	La.	LA
Maine	Maine	ME
Maryland	Md.	MD
Massachusetts	Mass.	MA
Michigan	Mich.	MI
Minnesota	Minn.	MN
Mississippi	Miss.	MS
Missouri	Mo.	MO
Montana	Mont.	MT
Nebraska	Neb.	NE
Nevada	Nev.	NV
New Hampshire	N.H.	NH
New Jersey	N.J.	NJ
New Mexico	N.M.	NM
New York	N.Y.	NY
North Carolina	N.C.	NC
North Dakota	N.D.	ND
Ohio	Ohio	OH
Oklahoma	Okla.	OK
Oregon	Ore.	OR
Pennsylvania	Pa.	PA
Puerto Rico	P.R.	PR
Rhode Island	R.I.	RI
South Carolina	S.C.	SC
South Dakota	S.D.	SD
Tennessee	Tenn.	TN
Texas	Texas	TX
Utah	Utah	UT
Vermont	Vt.	VT
Virginia	Va.	VA
Virgin Islands	V.I.	VI
Washington	Wash.	WA
West Virginia	W.Va.	WV
Wisconsin	Wis.	WI
Wyoming	Wyo.	WY

Canadian Provinces

	Standard	Postal
Alberta	Alta.	AB
British Columbia	B.C.	BC
Labrador	Lab.	NL
Manitoba	Man.	MB
New Brunswick	N.B.	NB
Newfoundland	N.F.	NL
Northwest Territories	N.W.T.	NT
Nova Scotia	N.S.	NS
Nunavut		NU
Ontario	Ont.	ON
Prince Edward Island	P.E.I.	PE
Quebec	Que.	QC
Saskatchewan	Sask.	SK
Yukon Territory	Y.T.	YT

Addresses

	Standard	Postal
Apartment	Apt.	APT
Avenue	Ave.	AVE
Boulevard	Blvd.	BLVD
Circle	Cir.	CIR
Court	Ct.	CT
Drive	Dr.	DR
East	E.	E
Expressway	Expy.	EXPY
Freeway	Fwy.	FWY
Heights	Hts.	HTS
Highway	Hwy.	HWY
Hospital	Hosp.	HOSP
Junction	Junc.	JCT
Lake	L.	LK
Lakes	Ls.	LKS
Lane	Ln.	LN
Meadows	Mdws.	MDWS
North	N.	N
Palms	Palms	PLMS
Park	Pk.	PK
Parkway	Pky.	PKY
Place	Pl.	PL
Plaza	Plaza	PLZ
Post Office Box	P.O. Box	PO BOX
Ridge	Rdg.	RDG
River	R.	RV
Road	Rd.	RD
Room	Rm.	RM
Rural	R.	R
Rural Route	R.R.	RR
Shore	Sh.	SH
South	S.	S
Square	Sq.	SQ
Station	Sta.	STA
Street	St.	ST
Suite	Ste.	STE
Terrace	Ter.	TER
Turnpike	Tpke.	TPKE
Union	Un.	UN
View	View	VW
Village	Vil.	VLG
West	W.	W

661.1 Other Common Abbreviations

abr. abridged; abridgment
AC, ac alternating current
ack. acknowledge; acknowledgment
acv actual cash value
A.D. in the year of the Lord (Latin *anno Domini*)
AM amplitude modulation
A.M., a.m. before noon (Latin *ante meridiem*)
ASAP as soon as possible
avg., av. average
BBB Better Business Bureau
B.C. before Christ
B.C.E. before the Common Era
bibliog. bibliographer; bibliography
biog. biographer; biographical; biography
C 1. Celsius 2. centigrade 3. coulomb
c. 1. circa (about) 2. cup
cc 1. cubic centimeter 2. carbon copy
CDT, C.D.T. central daylight time
C.E. of the Common Era
chap. chapter
cm centimeter
c.o., c/o care of
COD, C.O.D. 1. cash on delivery 2. collect on delivery
co-op. cooperative
CST, C.S.T. central standard time
cu., c cubic
D.A. district attorney
d.b.a. doing business as
DC, dc direct current
dec. deceased
dept. department
DST, D.S.T. daylight saving time
dup. duplicate
DVD digital video disc
ea. each
ed. edition; editor
EDT, E.D.T. eastern daylight time
e.g. for example (Latin *exempli gratia*)
EST, E.S.T. eastern standard time
etc. and so forth (Latin *et cetera*)
ex. example
F Fahrenheit
FM frequency modulation
F.O.B., f.o.b. free on board
ft foot
g 1. gram 2. gravity
gal. gallon
gloss. glossary
GNP gross national product
hdqrs, HQ headquarters
HIV human immunodeficiency virus
Hon. Honorable (title)
hp horsepower
HTML hypertext markup language
Hz hertz
ibid. in the same place (Latin *ibidem*)
id. the same (Latin *idem*)
i.e. that is (Latin *id est*)
illus. illustration
inc. incorporated
IQ, I.Q. intelligence quotient
IRS Internal Revenue Service
ISBN International Standard Book Number
Jr. junior
K 1. kelvin (temperature unit) 2. Kelvin (temperature scale)
kc kilocycle
kg kilogram
km kilometer
kn knot
kW kilowatt
l liter
lat. latitude
lb, lb. pound (Latin *libra*)
l.c. lowercase
lit. literary; literature
log logarithm
long. longitude
Ltd., ltd. limited
m meter
M.A. master of arts (Latin *Magister Artium*)
Mc, mc megacycle
M.C., m.c. master of ceremonies
M.D. doctor of medicine (Latin *medicinae doctor*)
mdse. merchandise
mfg. manufacturing
mg milligram
mi. 1. mile 2. mill (monetary unit)
misc. miscellaneous
ml milliliter
mm millimeter
mpg, m.p.g. miles per gallon
mph, m.p.h. miles per hour
MS 1. manuscript 2. Mississippi 3. multiple sclerosis
Ms., Ms title of courtesy for a woman
MST, M.S.T. mountain standard time
neg. negative
N.S.F., n.s.f. not sufficient funds
oz, oz. ounce
PA 1. public-address system 2. Pennsylvania
pct. percent
pd. paid
PDT, P.D.T. Pacific daylight time
PFC, Pfc. private first class
pg., p. page
P.M., p.m. after noon (Latin *post meridiem*)
P.O. 1. personnel officer 2. purchase order 3. postal order; post office 4. (also p.o.) petty officer
pop. population
POW, P.O.W. prisoner of war
pp. pages
ppd. 1. postpaid 2. prepaid
PR, P.R. 1. public relations 2. Puerto Rico
P.S. post script
psi, p.s.i. pounds per square inch
PST, P.S.T. Pacific standard time
PTA, P.T.A. Parent Teacher Association
qt. quart
RF radio frequency
RN registered nurse
R.P.M., rpm revolutions per minute
R.S.V.P., r.s.v.p. please reply (French *répondez s'il vous plaît*)
SASE self-addressed stamped envelope
SCSI small computer system interface
SOS 1. international distress signal 2. any call for help
Sr. 1. senior (after surname) 2. sister (religious)
ST standard time
St. 1. saint 2. strait 3. street
std. standard
syn. synonymous; synonym
TBA to be announced
tbs, tbsp tablespoon
TM trademark
tsp teaspoon
UHF, uhf ultra high frequency
UPC universal product code
UV ultraviolet
V 1. *Physics:* velocity 2. *Electricity:* volt 3. volume
V.A., VA Veterans Administration
VHF, vhf very high frequency
VIP *Informal:* very important person
vol. 1. volume 2. volunteer
vs. versus
W 1. *Electricity:* watt 2. *Physics:* (also w) work 3. west
whse., whs. warehouse
wkly. weekly
w/o without
wt. weight
yd yard (measurement)

Mechanics

Related Skills Activities

■ *SkillsBook*
Numbers and Abbreviations 1 and 2, pp. 45–46

Acronyms and Initialisms

662.1 Acronyms

An **acronym** is a word formed from the first (or first few) letters of words in a phrase. Even though acronyms are abbreviations, they require no periods.

radar	radio detecting and ranging
CARE	Cooperative for American Relief Everywhere
NASA	National Aeronautics and Space Administration
VISTA	Volunteers in Service to America
LAN	local area network

662.2 Initialisms

An **initialism** is similar to an acronym except that the initials used to form this abbreviation are pronounced individually.

CIA	Central Intelligence Agency
FBI	Federal Bureau of Investigation
FHA	Federal Housing Administration

662.3 Common Acronyms and Initialisms

ADD	attention deficit disorder
AIDS	acquired immunodeficiency syndrome
AKA	also known as
ATM	automatic teller machine
BMI	body mass index
CD	compact disc; certificate of deposit
DMV	Department of Motor Vehicles
ETA	estimated time of arrival
FAA	Federal Aviation Administration
FCC	Federal Communications Commission
FDA	Food and Drug Administration
FDIC	Federal Deposit Insurance Corporation
FEMA	Federal Emergency Management Agency
FTC	Federal Trade Commission
FYI	for your information
GPS	global positioning system
HDTV	high-definition television
IRS	Internal Revenue Service
IT	information technology
JPEG	Joint Photographic Experts Group
LCD	liquid crystal display

LLC	limited liability company
MADD	Mothers Against Drunk Driving
MRI	magnetic resonance imaging
NASA	National Aeronautics and Space Administration
NATO	North Atlantic Treaty Organization
OPEC	Organization of Petroleum-Exporting Countries
OSHA	Occupational Safety and Health Administration
PAC	political action committee
PDF	portable document format
PETA	People for the Ethical Treatment of Animals
PIN	personal identification number
PSA	public service announcement
ROTC	Reserve Officers' Training Corps
SADD	Students Against Destructive Decisions
SUV	sport utility vehicle
SWAT	special weapons and tactics
TDD	telecommunications device for the deaf

Grammar Practice

Abbreviations, Acronyms, and Initialisms

 Write the correct abbreviation for the underlined word or words.

1. Find the <u>universal product code</u> on this <u>digital video disc</u>.

2. Luis lives at 1279 <u>North</u> Bethesda <u>Circle</u>, Watch Hill, <u>Rhode Island</u>.

3. During the awards ceremony, the <u>master of ceremonies</u> introduced the <u>very important persons</u>.

4. The program begins at 8:00 <u>ante meridiem, eastern daylight time</u>.

5. The National 4-H <u>headquarters</u> is in Washington, <u>District of Columbia</u>.

6. All books have an <u>International Standard Book Number</u>.

7. <u>Mister</u> Jenkins took a class to learn <u>hypertext markup language</u>.

8. My grandfather is in a <u>Veterans Administration</u> hospital in <u>Iowa</u>.

9. Anwar Singh, <u>doctor of medicine</u>, spoke about the <u>human immunodeficiency virus</u>.

10. Under "time" for next week's meeting, someone had written "<u>to be announced</u>."

11. Look for a maximum <u>pounds per square inch</u> stamp on your tires before adding air.

12. The <u>longitude</u> of Tuscaloosa, <u>Alabama</u>, is 87.62 degrees; the <u>latitude</u> is 33.23 degrees.

> **Model**
>
> Model the following acronyms and initialisms to come up with your own abbreviations. (Write at least one acronym and one initialism.)
>
> BOYS — Bradford Orchid and Yam Society
> JUSTICE — Jesuit University Students Together in Concerned Empowerment
> ZFF — Zephyr Flower Flats
> DHS — Department of Homeland Security

Related Skills Activities

■ **SkillsBook**
Numbers and Abbreviations 2, p. 46

Answers

1. UPC	7. Mr.
DVD	HTML
2. N.	8. V.A. *or* VA
Cir.	IA
RI	9. M.D.
3. M.C.	HIV
VIP's	10. TBA
4. A.M.	11. psi *or* p.s.i.
EDT	12. long.
5. hdqrs *or* HQ	AL
D.C.	lat.
6. ISBN	

Spelling Rules

664.1 Write *i* before *e*

Write *i* before *e* except after *c*, or when sounded like *a* as in *neighbor* and *weigh*.

relief   receive   perceive   reign   freight   beige

Exceptions: There are a number of exceptions to this rule, including these: *neither, leisure, seize, weird, species, science.*

664.2 Words with Consonant Endings

When a one-syllable word *(bat)* ends in a consonant *(t)* preceded by one vowel *(a)*, double the final consonant before adding a suffix that begins with a vowel *(batting)*.

sum—summary   god—goddess

Note: When a multisyllabic word *(control)* ends in a consonant *(l)* preceded by one vowel *(o)*, the accent is on the last syllable *(con trol')*, and the suffix begins with a vowel *(ing)*—the same rule holds true: Double the final consonant *(controlling)*.

prefer—preferred   begin—beginning
forget—forgettable   admit—admittance

664.3 Words with a Silent *e*

If a word ends with a silent *e*, drop the *e* before adding a suffix that begins with a vowel. Do not drop the *e* when the suffix begins with a consonant.

state—stating—statement   like—liking—likeness
use—using—useful   nine—ninety—nineteen

Exceptions: *judgment, truly, argument, ninth*

664.4 Words Ending in *y*

When *y* is the last letter in a word and the *y* is preceded by a consonant, change the *y* to *i* before adding any suffix except those beginning with *i*.

fry—fries—frying   hurry—hurried—hurrying   lady—ladies
ply—pliable   happy—happiness   beauty—beautiful

When *y* is the last letter in a word and the *y* is preceded by a vowel, do not change the *y* to *i* before adding a suffix.

play—plays—playful   stay—stays—staying
employ—employed

Important reminder: Never trust your spelling even to the best spell-checker. Use a dictionary for words your spell-checker does not cover.

Grammar Practice

Spelling 1

Find the 12 words that are misspelled in the following paragraph and write them correctly. (Each misspelled word is in the "Commonly Misspelled Words" list on pages 666–667.)

1   A playright is a person who writes dramatic literture. Sophocles and
2   Euripides, ancient Greeks, created some of the earleist plays around the
3   fifth century B.C.E. The dramatic forms of comedy and traggedy are usualy
4   studied in asociation with the life of William Shakespeare. He was a brilliant
5   writer during England's Elizabethan period. Shakespeare's works have
6   withstood the test of time. Performances of his plays are still presented by
7   modern-day proffesional theater groups in America and abroad. Undoutably,
8   the works of these early authors were instramental in influencing the creation
9   of modern drama.

Model

Model the following sentences to practice using the spelling rules that deal with adding a suffix.

A playwright lives in an occupied country. And if you can't live that way, you don't stay.
—Arthur Miller

It's discouraging to think how many people are shocked by honesty and how few by deceit.
—Noel Coward

Mechanics

Related Skills Activities

■ *SkillsBook*
Plurals and Spelling, pp. 47–48
Spelling 1 and 2, pp. 51–52v

Answers

line 1: playwright
         literature
line 2: ancient
         earliest
line 3: tragedy
         usually
line 4: association
         brilliant
line 6: performances
line 7: professional
         Undoubtedly
line 8: instrumental

Commonly Misspelled Words

A

abbreviate
abrupt
absence
absolute (ly)
absurd
abundance
academic
accelerate
accept (ance)
accessible
accessory
accidentally
accommodate
accompany
accomplish
accumulate
accurate
accustom (ed)
ache
achieve (ment)
acknowledge
acquaintance
acquired
across
address
adequate
adjustment
admissible
admittance
adolescent
advantageous
advertisement
advisable
aggravate
aggression
alcohol
alleviate
almost
alternative
although
aluminum
amateur
analysis
analyze
anarchy
ancient
anecdote
anesthetic

annihilate
announce
annual
anonymous
answer
anxious
apologize
apparatus
apparent (ly)
appearance
appetite
applies
appreciate
appropriate
approximately
architect
arctic
argument
arithmetic
arrangement
artificial
ascend
assistance
association
athlete
attendance
attire
attitude
audience
authority
available

B

balance
balloon
bargain
basically
beautiful
beginning
believe
benefit (ed)
biscuit
bought
boycott
brevity
brilliant
Britain
bureau
business

C

cafeteria
caffeine
calculator
calendar
campaign
canceled
candidate
catastrophe
category
caught
cavalry
celebration
cemetery
certificate
changeable
chief
chocolate
circuit
circumstance
civilization
colonel
colossal
column
commercial
commitment
committed
committee
comparative
comparison
competitively
conceivable
condemn
condescend
conference
conferred
confidential
congratulate
conscience
conscientious
conscious
consequence
consumer
contaminate
convenience
cooperate
correspondence
cough
coupon

courageous
courteous
creditor
criticism
criticize
curiosity
curious
cylinder

D

dealt
deceitful
deceive
decision
defense
deferred
definite (ly)
definition
delicious
descend
describe
description
despair
desperate
destruction
development
diameter
diaphragm
diarrhea
dictionary
dining
disagreeable
disappear
disappoint
disastrous
discipline
discrimination
discuss
dismissal
dissatisfied
dissect
distinctly
dormitory
doubt
drought
duplicate
dyeing
dying

E

earliest
efficiency
eighth
elaborate
eligible
eliminate
ellipse
embarrass
emphasize
employee
enclosure
encourage
endeavor
English
enormous
enough
enrichment
enthusiastic
entirely
entrance
environment
equipment
equipped
equivalent
especially
essential
eventually
exaggerate
examination
exceed
excellent
excessive
excite
executive
exercise
exhaust (ed)
exhibition
exhilaration
existence
expensive
experience
explanation
exquisite
extinguish
extraordinary
extremely

F-G

facilities
familiar
fascinate
fashion
fatigue (d)
feature
February
fiery
financially
flourish
forcible
foreign
forfeit
fortunate
forty
fourth
freight
friend
fulfill
gauge
generally
generous
genuine
glimpse
gnarled
gnaw
government
gradual
grammar
gratitude
grievous
grocery
guard
guidance

H

happiness
harass
harmonize
height
hemorrhage
hereditary
hindrance
hoping
hopping
hospitable
humorous

hygiene
hymn
hypocrisy

I-J

ignorance
illiterate
illustrate
imaginary
immediately
immense
incidentally
inconvenience
incredible
indefinitely
independence
indispensable
industrial
industrious
inevitable
infinite
inflation
innocence
inoculation
inquiry
installation
instrumental
intelligence
interesting
interfere
interrupt
investigate
irregular
irresistible
issuing
itinerary
jealous (y)
jewelry
journal
judgment

K-L

knowledge
laboratory
laugh
lawyer
league
legacy
legalize
legitimate
leisure

liaison
license
lightning
likable
liquid
literature
loneliness

M-N

maintenance
maneuver
manufacture
marriage
mathematics
medieval
memento
menagerie
merchandise
merely
mileage
miniature
miscellaneous
mischievous
misspell
moat
mobile
mortgage
multiplied
muscle
musician
mustache
mutual
mysterious
naive
nauseous
necessary
neither
neurotic
nevertheless
ninety
nighttime
noticeable
nuclear
nuisance

O-P

obstacle
obvious
occasion
occupant
occupation

occurred
occurrence
official
often
omitted
opinion
opponent
opportunity
opposite
optimism
ordinarily
organization
original
outrageous
pamphlet
parallel
paralyze
partial
particularly
pastime
patience
peculiar
pedestal
performance
permanent
permissible
perseverance
personal (ly)
personality
perspiration
persuade
petition
phenomenon
physical
physician
picnicking
planned
playwright
plead
pneumonia
politician
ponder
positively
possession
practically
precede
precious
preference
prejudice
preparation
presence
prevalent
primitive

privilege
probably
proceed
professional
professor
prominent
pronounce
pronunciation
protein
psychology
puny
purchase
pursuing

Q-R

qualified
quality
quantity
questionnaire
quiet
quite
quizzes
recede
receipt
receive
recipe
recognize
recommend
reference
referred
regard
regimen
religious
repel
repetition
residue
responsibility
restaurant
rheumatism
rhythm
ridiculous
robot
roommate

S

sacrifice
salary
sandwich
satisfactory
scarcely
scenic

schedule
scholar
science
secretary
seize
separate
sergeant
several
severely
sheriff
shrubbery
siege
signature
signify
silhouette
similar
simultaneous
sincerely
skiing
skunk
society
solar
sophomore
souvenir
spaghetti
specific
specimen
statue
stomach
stopped
strength
strictly
submission
substitute
subtle
succeed
success
sufficient
supersede
suppose
surprise
suspicious
symbolism
sympathy
synthetic

T-U

tariff
technique
temperature
temporary
tendency

thermostat
thorough (ly)
though
throughout
tongue
tornado
tortoise
tragedy
transferred
tremendous
tried
trite
truly
unanimous
undoubtedly
unfortunately
unique
unnecessary
until
urgent
usable
usher
usually

V

vacuum
vague
valuable
variety
vengeance
versatile
vicinity
villain
visibility
visual

W

waif
Wednesday
weird
wholly
width
women
wrath
wreckage

Y

yesterday
yield
yolk

Related Skills Activities

- ■ **SkillsBook**
  Spelling 3 and 4, pp. 53–54

Steps to Becoming a Better Speller

1. Be patient.
Becoming a good speller takes time.

2. Check the correct pronunciation of each word you are attempting to spell.
Knowing the correct pronunciation of a word can help you remember its spelling.

3. Note the meaning and history of each word as you are checking the dictionary for pronunciation.
Knowing the meaning and history of a word provides you with a better notion of how the word is properly used, and this can help you remember its spelling.

4. Before you close the dictionary, practice spelling the word.
Look away from the page and try to "see" the word in your mind. Then write it on a piece of paper. Check your spelling in the dictionary; repeat the process until you are able to spell the word correctly.

5. Learn some spelling rules.
For four of the most useful rules, see page 664.

6. Make a list of the words that you often misspell.
Select the first 10 and practice spelling them.

STEP A: Read each word carefully; then write it on a piece of paper. Check to see that you've spelled it correctly. Repeat this step for the words that you misspelled.

STEP B: When you have finished your first 10 words, ask someone to read them to you as you write them again. Then check for misspellings. If you find none, congratulations! (Repeat both steps with your next 10 words, and so on.)

7. Write often.

Grammar Practice

Spelling 2

  For each quotation below, fill in the letters to spell the correct word from the list of "Commonly Misspelled Words" (pages 666–667).

1. Television is instantaneous and s____u__t_____s: Everyone gets the message at the same time.
—William J. Donnelly

2. It takes time to p_____e men to do even what is for their own good.
—Thomas Jefferson

3. The g____r l____ stump has as tender a bud as the sapling.
—Henry David Thoreau

4. Only strong personalities can endure history; the weak ones are e__t___g_____d by it.
—Friedrich Nietzsche

5. The day is but a Scandinavian night; the winter is an a _ c ____ c summer.
—Henry David Thoreau

6. I have noted that persons with bad j____g_____t are most insistent that we do what they think best.
—Lionel Abel

7. R____e_____n is tedious.
—Mason Cooley

8. No l__g__c__ is so rich as honesty.
—William Shakespeare

9. S_____ is counted sweetest by those who ne'er succeed.
—Emily Dickinson

10. No guest is so welcome in a friend's house that he will not become a n_____a_____ after three days.
—Titus Maccius Plautus

Model

Model the following sentence to practice using the spelling rule for writing *i* before *e*.

Time folded in on itself then. What is left lies in clear yet disjointed pieces in my head.
—Sue Monk Kidd, *The Secret Life of Bees*

Mechanics

Answers

1. simultaneous
2. persuade
3. gnarled
4. extinguished
5. arctic
6. judgment
7. repetition
8. legacy
9. success
10. nuisance

Test Prep!

Write the letter of the correct way to express each underlined part from the choices given on the next page. If it is already correct, choose "D."

See if you can form any <u>theorys</u> about what these <u>peoples</u>, events, and things
        (1)   **(2)**
have in common: Elvis Presley, wildflowers, rock 'n' roll, the Civil War, <u>legendes of the</u>
<u>west</u>, the <u>nineteen ninety-two</u> Summer Olympics, and dinosaurs. If you can't make a
    (3)
       (4)
connection, don't <u>despair</u>. The answer is that all of them are on the <u>united states</u>
      (5)   **(5)**
<u>postal service (USPS)</u> list of the 10 most popular commemorative postage stamps in
    (6)
U.S. history.

In 1893, <u>postmaster General John Wanamaker</u> was reprimanded for <u>issueing</u>
          (7)   **(8)**
the first commemorative stamps. Congress protested that the stamps, celebrating
the <u>world columbian exposition</u>, were <u>unneccessary</u>. Though he <u>recieved</u> criticism,
     (9)   **(10)**   **(11)**
Wanamaker believed that the stamps would be popular. He was <u>right: people</u>
                                      (12)
<u>(hundreds</u> of them) stood in line to buy the stamps. Collectors came with <u>handfuls</u> of
cash to purchase the stamps as an investment. Two billion of the Columbian stamps
                                         (13)
were sold for <u>$40 million dollars</u>. Today, one of these <u>4-¢</u> stamps is worth up to $88.
          (14)   **(15)**
Commemorative stamp collection remains one of the most popular collection <u>hobby</u> in
                                           (16)
the world.

1
  (A) theoreys
  (B) theories
  (C) theoryes
  (D) correct as is

2
  (A) people
  (B) persones
  (C) people's
  (D) correct as is

3
  (A) Legendes of the West
  (B) legends of the west
  (C) legends of the West
  (D) correct as is

4
  (A) nineteen 92
  (B) 19 ninety-two
  (C) 1992
  (D) correct as is

5
  (A) dispair
  (B) dispare
  (C) despare
  (D) correct as is

6
  (A) United States postal service
      (USPS)
  (B) United States Postal Service
      (U.S.P.S.)
  (C) United States Postal Service
      (USPS)
  (D) correct as is

7
  (A) Postmaster General John
      Wanamaker
  (B) Postmaster general John
      Wanamaker
  (C) postmaster general John
      Wanamaker
  (D) correct as is

8
  (A) ishuing
  (B) issuing
  (C) isueing
  (D) correct as is

9
  (A) world Columbian exposition
  (B) world Columbian Exposition
  (C) World Columbian Exposition
  (D) correct as is

10
  (A) unnecessary
  (B) uneccessary
  (C) unecesary
  (D) correct as is

11
  (A) receivied
  (B) received
  (C) resieved
  (D) correct as is

12
  (A) right: people (100's
  (B) right: People (100's
  (C) right: People (hundreds
  (D) correct as is

13
  (A) handsful
  (B) handsfuls
  (C) handfulls
  (D) correct as is

14
  (A) $40 million
  (B) 40 million $
  (C) 40,000,000 $
  (D) correct as is

15
  (A) four-¢
  (B) four-cent
  (C) 4-cent
  (D) correct as is

16
  (A) hobbeys
  (B) hobbys
  (C) hobbies
  (D) correct as is

Mechanics

Related Skills Activities

■ **SkillsBook**
Review: Capitalization, p. 44
Review: Plurals and Spelling, pp. 55–56
Posttest: Capitalization, p. 194
Posttest: Plurals and Spelling, p. 195
Posttest: Numbers, Abbreviations, and Acronyms, p. 196

■ **GrammarSnap**
Capitalization of Proper Nouns and Adjectives

Answers

1. B
2. A
3. C
4. C
5. D
6. C
7. A
8. B

9. C
10. A
11. B
12. C
13. D
14. A
15. B
16. C

Understanding Idioms

Idioms are phrases that are used in a special way. You can't understand an idiom just by knowing the meaning of each word in the phrase. You must learn it as a whole. For example, the idiom *bury the hatchet* means "to settle an argument," even though the individual words in the phrase mean something much different. This section will help you learn some of the common idioms in American English.

apple of his eye	Eagle Lake is the apple of his eye. (something he likes very much)
as plain as day	The mistake in the ad was as plain as day. (very clear)
as the crow flies	New London is 200 miles from here as the crow flies. (in a straight line)
at a snail's pace	My last hour at work passes at a snail's pace. (very, very slowly)
axe to grind	The manager has an axe to grind with that umpire. (disagreement to settle)
bad apple	There are no bad apples in this class. (bad influences)
beat around the bush	Don't beat around the bush; answer the question. (avoid getting to the point)
benefit of the doubt	Everyone has been given the benefit of the doubt at least once. (another chance)
beyond the shadow of a doubt	Beyond the shadow of a doubt, this is my best science project. (for certain)
blew my top	When I saw the broken statue, I blew my top. (showed great anger)
bone to pick	Alison had a bone to pick with the student who copied her paper. (problem to settle)
brain drain	Brain drain is a serious problem in some states. (the best students moving elsewhere)
break the ice	The nervous ninth graders were afraid to break the ice. (start a conversation)
burn the midnight oil	Devon had to burn the midnight oil to finish his report. (work late into the night)

bury the hatchet	My sisters were told to bury the hatchet immediately. (settle an argument)
by the skin of her teeth	Sumey avoided an accident by the skin of her teeth. (just barely)
champing at the bit	The skiers were champing at the bit to get on the slopes. (eager, excited)
chicken feed	The prize was chicken feed to some people. (not worth much money)
chip off the old block	Frank's just like his father. He's a chip off the old block. (just like someone else)
clean as a whistle	My boss told me to make sure the place was as clean as a whistle before I left. (very clean)
cold shoulder	I wanted to fit in with that group, but they gave me the cold shoulder. (ignored me)
crack of dawn	Ali delivers his papers at the crack of dawn. (first light of day, early morning)
cry wolf	If you cry wolf too often, no one will believe you. (say you are in trouble when you aren't)
dead of night	Hearing a loud noise in the dead of night frightened Bill. (middle of the night)
dirt cheap	A lot of clothes at that store are dirt cheap. (inexpensive, costing very little money)
doesn't hold a candle to	That award doesn't hold a candle to a gold medal. (is not as good as)
drop in the bucket	The contributions were a drop in the bucket. (a small amount compared to what's needed)
everything from A to Z	That catalog lists everything from A to Z. (a lot of different things)
face the music	Todd had to face the music when he broke the window. (deal with the punishment)
fish out of water	He felt like a fish out of water in the new math class. (someone in an unfamiliar place)
fit for a king	The food at the athletic banquet was fit for a king. (very special)

Idioms

flew off the handle	**Bill** flew off the handle **when he saw a reckless driver near the school.** (became very angry)
floating on air	**Celine was** floating on air **at the prom.** (feeling very happy)
food for thought	**The boys' foolish and dangerous prank gave us** food for thought. (something to think about)
get down to business	**After sharing several jokes, Mr. Sell said we should** get down to business. (start working)
get the upper hand	**The wrestler moved quickly on his opponent in order to** get the upper hand. (gain the advantage)
give their all	**Student volunteers** give their all **to help others.** (work as hard as they can)
go fly a kite	**Charlene stared at her nosy brother and said, "**Go fly a kite.**"** (go away)
has a green thumb	**Talk to Mrs. Smith about your sick plant. She** has a green thumb. (is good at growing plants)
has a heart of gold	**Joe** has a heart of gold. (is very kind and generous)
hit a home run	**Rhonda** hit a home run **with her speech.** (succeeded, or did well)
hit the ceiling	**When my parents saw my grades, they** hit the ceiling. (were very angry)
hit the hay	**Exhausted from the hike, Jamal** hit the hay **without eating supper.** (went to bed)
in a nutshell	**Can you,** in a nutshell, **tell us your goals for this year?** (in summary)
in one ear and out the other	**Sharl, concerned about her pet, let the lecture go** in one ear and out the other. (without really listening)
in the black	**My aunt's gift shop is finally** in the black. (making money)
in the nick of time	**Janelle caught the falling vase** in the nick of time. (just in time)
in the red	**Many businesses start out** in the red. (in debt)
in the same boat	**The new tax bill meant everyone would be** in the same boat. (in a similar situation)

iron out	**Joe will meet with the work crew to** iron out **their complaints.** (solve, work out)
it goes without saying	It goes without saying **that saving money is a good idea.** (it is clear)
it stands to reason	It stands to reason **that your stamina will increase if you run every day.** (it makes sense)
keep a stiff upper lip	Keep a stiff upper lip **when you visit the doctor.** (be brave)
keep it under your hat	Keep it under your hat **about the pop quiz.** (don't tell anyone)
knock on wood	**My uncle** knocked on wood **after he said he had never had the flu.** (did something for good luck)
knuckle down	**After wasting half the day, we were told to** knuckle down. (work hard)
learn the ropes	**It takes every new employee a few months to** learn the ropes. (get to know how things are done)
leave no stone unturned	**The police plan to** leave no stone unturned **at the crime scene.** (check everything)
lend someone a hand	**You will feel good if you** lend someone a hand. (help someone)
let the cat out of the bag	**Tom** let the cat out of the bag **during lunch.** (told a secret)
let's face it	Let's face it. **You don't like rap.** (let's admit it)
look high and low	**We** looked high and low **for Jan's dog.** (looked everywhere)
lose face	**In some cultures, it is very bad to** lose face. (be embarrassed)
needle in a haystack	**Trying to find a person in New York is like trying to find a** needle in a haystack. (something impossible to find)
nose to the grindstone	**With all of these assignments, I have to keep my** nose to the grindstone. (work hard)
on cloud nine	**After talking to my girlfriend, I was** on cloud nine. (feeling very happy)
on pins and needles	**Emiko was** on pins and needles **during the championship game.** (feeling nervous)

Idioms

out the window	Once the rain started, our plans were out the window. (ruined)
over and above	Over and above the required work, Will cleaned up the lab. (in addition to)
pain in the neck	Franklin knew the report would be a pain in the neck. (very annoying)
pull your leg	Cary was only pulling your leg. (telling you a little lie as a joke)
put his foot in his mouth	Lane put his foot in his mouth when he answered the question. (said something embarrassing)
put the cart before the horse	Tonya put the cart before the horse when she sealed the envelope before inserting the letter. (did something in the wrong order)
put your best foot forward	When applying for a job, you should put your best foot forward. (do the best that you can do)
red-letter day	Sovann had a red-letter day because she did so well on her math test. (very good day)
rock the boat	I was told not to rock the boat. (cause trouble)
rude awakening	Jake will have a rude awakening when he sees the bill for his computer. (sudden, unpleasant surprise)
save face	His gift was clearly an attempt to save face. (fix an embarrassing situation)
see eye to eye	We see eye to eye about the need for a new school. (are in agreement)
shake a leg	I told Mako to shake a leg so that we wouldn't be late. (hurry)
shift into high gear	Greg had to shift into high gear to finish the test in time. (speed up, hurry)
sight for sore eyes	My grandmother's smiling face was a sight for sore eyes. (good to see)
sight unseen	Liz bought the coat sight unseen. (without seeing it first)
sink or swim	Whether you sink or swim in school depends on your study habits. (fail or succeed)

spilled the beans	Suddenly, Kesia realized that she had spilled the beans. (revealed a secret)
spring chicken	Although Mr. Gordon isn't a spring chicken, he sure knows how to talk to kids. (young person)
stick to your guns	Know what you believe, and stick to your guns. (don't change your mind)
sweet tooth	Chocolate is often the candy of choice for those with a sweet tooth. (a love for sweets, like candy and cake)
take a dim view	My sister will take a dim view of that movie. (disapprove)
take it with a grain of salt	When you read that advertisement, take it with a grain of salt. (don't believe everything)
take the bull by the horns	It's time to take the bull by the horns so the project gets done on time. (take control)
through thick and thin	Those two girls have remained friends through thick and thin. (in good times and in bad times)
time flies	Time flies as you grow older. (time passes quickly)
time to kill	Grace had time to kill, so she read a book. (extra time)
to go overboard	The class was told not to go overboard. A $50.00 donation was fine. (to do too much)
toe the line	The new teacher made everyone toe the line. (follow the rules)
tongue-tied	He can talk easily with friends, but in class he is usually tongue-tied. (not knowing what to say)
turn over a new leaf	He decided to turn over a new leaf in school. (make a new start)
two peas in a pod	Ever since kindergarten, Lil and Eve have been like two peas in a pod. (very much alike)
under the weather	Guy was feeling under the weather this morning. (sick)
wallflower	Cho knew the other girls thought she was a wallflower. (a shy person)
word of mouth	Joseph learns a lot about his favorite team by word of mouth. (talking with other people)

Idioms

Using the Right Word

a lot ■ *A lot* (always two words) is a vague descriptive phrase that should be used sparingly.

> You can learn a lot about the world just by reading.

accept, except ■ The verb *accept* means "to receive" or "to believe"; the preposition *except* means "other than."

> The principal accepted the boy's story about the broken window, but she asked why no one except him saw the ball accidentally slip from his hand.

adapt, adopt ■ *Adapt* means "to adjust or change to fit"; *adopt* means "to choose and treat as your own" (a child, an idea).

> After a lengthy period of study, Malcolm X adopted the Islamic faith and adapted to its lifestyle.

affect, effect ■ The verb *affect* means "to influence"; the verb *effect* means "to produce, accomplish, complete."

> Ming's hard work effected an A on the test, which positively affected her semester grade.

The noun *effect* means the "result."

> Good grades have a calming effect on parents.

aisle, isle ■ An *aisle* is a passage between seats; an *isle* is a small island.

> Many airline passengers on their way to the Isle of Capri prefer an aisle seat.

all right ■ *All right* is always two words (not *alright*).

allusion, illusion ■ *Allusion* is an indirect reference to someone or something; *illusion* is a false picture or idea.

> My little sister, under the illusion that she's movie-star material, makes frequent allusions to her future fans.

already, all ready ■ *Already* is an adverb meaning "before this time" or "by this time." *All ready* is an adjective meaning "fully prepared."

Note: Use *all ready* if you can substitute *ready* alone in the sentence.

> Although I've already had some dessert, I am all ready for some ice cream from the street vendor.

Grammar Practice

Using the Right Word 1

accept, except; affect, effect; aisle, isle; already, all ready

 Find the words that are used incorrectly. Write the line number followed by the right word.

1   Parnel, feeling a bit depressed, is watching TV: an ancient movie from
2 the 1950s in which the wealthy escape to the Isle of Capri. Here's the dashing
3 Cary Grant, breakfasting on a veranda overlooking a lush valley. There's his
4 lovely lady Audrey Hepburn, all ready growing restless with the relaxation.
5 Cary knows, of course, it is up to him to effect a change in her attitude, and
6 sets about doing so. Getting Audrey to except this life of leisure won't be easy,
7 but, darn it, he's determined!
8   Obviously, the movie has a big affect on Parnel. He dreams he is Cary,
9 except with better-looking hair. He is making his way down the isle of a small
10 jet, which is all first class. He finds himself at the open door, all ready to jump
11 out. Cary/Parnel checks to make sure his parachute is secure; even dreaming,
12 he does not want to think about how skydiving
13 without a parachute will affect his looks. He
14 jumps . . . he falls gently . . . he screams as
15 he . . . hears his alarm clock.

◤ Model

Model the following sentences to practice using the verbs *affect* and *effect* correctly.

> If we dreamed the same thing every night, it would affect us as much as the objects we see every day.
> —Blaise Pascal

> Frankly, I do not know how to effect a permanency in American foreign policy.
> —Franklin D. Roosevelt

Related Skills Activities

■ ***SkillsBook***
Pretest: Using the Right Word, p. 57
Using the Right Word 1, p. 58

Answers

line 4: already
line 6: accept
line 8: effect
line 9: aisle

altogether, all together ■ *Altogether* means "entirely." The phrase *all together* means "in a group" or "all at once."

"There is altogether too much gridlock," complained the Democrats. All together, the Republicans yelled, "No way!"

among, between ■ *Among* is typically used when speaking of more than two persons or things. *Between* is used when speaking of only two.

The three of us talked among ourselves to decide between going out or eating in.

amount, number ■ *Amount* is used for bulk measurement. *Number* is used to count separate units. (See also *fewer, less.*)

A substantial amount of honey spilled all over a number of my CD's.

annual, biannual, semiannual, biennial, perennial ■ An *annual* event happens once every year. A *biannual* or *semiannual* event happens twice a year. A *biennial* event happens every two years. A *perennial* event is one that is persistent or constant.

Dad's annual family reunion gets bigger every year.
We're going shopping at the department store's semiannual white sale.
Due to dwindling attendance, the county fair is now a biennial celebration.
A perennial plant persists for several years.

anyway ■ Do not add an *s* to *anyway*.

ascent, assent ■ *Ascent* is the act of rising or climbing; *assent* is "to agree to something after some consideration" (or such an agreement).

We completed our ascent of the butte with the assent of the landowner.

bad, badly ■ *Bad* is an adjective. *Badly* is an adverb.

This apple is bad, but one bad apple doesn't always ruin the whole bushel.
In today's game, Sumey passed badly.

base, bass ■ *Base* is the foundation or the lower part of something. *Bass* (pronounced like *base*) is a deep sound or a musical instrument. *Bass* (pronounced like *class*) is a fish.

A car's wheel base is the distance between the centers of the front and rear wheels.
Luther is the bass player in his bluegrass band.

beside, besides ■ *Beside* means "by the side of." *Besides* means "in addition to."

Mother always grew roses beside the trash bin. Besides looking nice, they also gave off a sweet smell that masked odors.

Grammar Practice

Using the Right Word 2

among, between; amount, number; annual, biannual, semiannual, biennial, perennial; ascent, assent; beside, besides

 In each paragraph below, find the word or words that are used incorrectly. Then write the right word(s) correctly. If there are no incorrect words, write "none."

1. Among serious gardeners here in Watertown, the biennial sale at Garden Emporium—every March and October—is anticipated most. It offers the widest assortment of spring and fall perennials in the area, including a good amount of jonquils and hostas. Besides that, they also offer volume discounts.

2. When it comes to choosing among one automaker's model and another manufacturer's car, buyers have their work cut out for them. Some makes are so similar that it's hard to tell them apart, even when they're right beside each other. In such a case, though, it's the dollar amount on the window sticker that will help the car shopper decide.

3. It was getting difficult to organize the pinecone collectors' convention each year, so we decided to make it a biennial event instead. We were sure the members of the Cone Collectors of America would assent to this change; they had been "pining" for it for years!

4. Jorge's assent in the amateur golf rankings is the result of consistent practice. He is now positioned between Dave Vasquez, the regional leader, and Marty White, winner of last year's Daily Cup tournament. Jorge's goal is to make it to the Jetar-Bettim Annual Tourney, to be held in Carson, Nevada, this year.

Model

Model the following sentences to practice using the words *amount* and *number* correctly.

Talent isn't genius, and no amount of energy can make it so.
—Louisa May Alcott

Civilization is built on a number of ultimate principles . . . respect for human life, the punishment of crimes against property and persons, the equality of all good citizens before the law . . . or, in a word, justice.
—Max Nordau

Right Word

Related Skills Activities

■ *SkillsBook*
Using the Right Word 1, p. 58

Answers

1. biannual *or* semiannual
number
2. between
3. none
4. ascent

board, bored ■ *Board* is a piece of wood. *Board* is also an administrative group or council.

> The school board approved the purchase of fifty 1- by 6-inch pine boards.

Bored is the past tense of the verb "bore," which may mean "to make a hole by drilling" or "to become weary out of dullness."

> Watching television bored Joe, so he took his drill and bored a hole in the wall where he could hang his new clock.

brake, break ■ *Brake* is a device used to stop a vehicle. *Break* means "to separate or to destroy."

> I hope the brakes on my car never break.

bring, take ■ *Bring* suggests the action is directed toward the speaker; *take* suggests the action is directed away from the speaker.

> Bring home some garbage bags so I can take the trash outside.

can, may ■ *Can* suggests ability while *may* suggests permission.

> "Can I go to the mall?" means "Am I physically able to go to the mall?"
> "May I go to the mall?" asks permission to go.

capital, capitol ■ The noun *capital* refers to a city or to money. The adjective *capital* means "major or important." *Capitol* refers to a building.

> The state capital is home to the capitol building for a capital reason. The state government contributed capital for its construction.

cent, sent, scent ■ *Cent* is a coin; *sent* is the past tense of the verb "send"; *scent* is an odor or a smell.

> For forty-one cents, I sent my girlfriend a mushy love poem in a perfumed envelope. She adored the scent but hated the poem.

cereal, serial ■ *Cereal* is a grain, often made into breakfast food. *Serial* relates to something in a series.

> Mohammed enjoys reading serial novels while he eats a bowl of cereal.

chord, cord ■ *Chord* may mean "an emotion" or "a combination of musical tones sounded at the same time." A *cord* is a string or a rope.

> The guitar player strummed the opening chord to the group's hit song, which struck a responsive chord with the audience.

chose, choose ■ *Chose* (choz) is the past tense of the verb *choose* (chooz).

> Last quarter I chose to read Chitra Divakaruni's *The Unknown Errors of Our Lives*—a fascinating book about Indian immigrants.

Grammar Practice

Using the Right Word 3

brake, break; cereal, serial; chord, cord; chose, choose

Write the correct choice from those given in parentheses.

1. Ms. Alford drove to the dealership to have her *(brake, break)* system inspected.

2. During a service call, most computer manufacturers require that you state the *(cereal, serial)* number of your product before they will answer any questions.

3. It is now possible for new parents to save the blood from the umbilical *(chord, cord)* that once connected their baby to his or her mother.

4. Aunt Margaret gave me two options for dinner; then she told me to *(choose, chose)* the one I'd like to make!

5. Nasim is going to *(brake, break)* a leg if he continues to snowboard without the proper equipment.

6. *(Cereal, Serial)* is an important ingredient in dog food, but it should not be the first in the list of ingredients.

7. The power *(chord, cord)* is commonly used in rock music.

8. Mae *(choose, chose)* from among dozens of fresh fruits and vegetables at the farmers' market.

9. *(Cereal, Serial)* dramas became known as "soaps" because detergent manufacturers often sponsored them.

10. You can *(brake, break)* the record for consecutive pogo-stick jumps by bouncing 177,738 times.

Model

Model the following sentences to practice using the words *chord* and *cord* correctly.

> [A] chord in music is analogous to a word in language.
> —Sigmund Spaeth

> No cord or cable can draw so forcibly, or bind so fast, as love can do with a single thread.
> —Robert Burton

Right Word

Related Skills Activities

■ *SkillsBook*
Using the Right Word 2, p. 59

Answers

1. brake
2. serial
3. cord
4. choose
5. break
6. Cereal
7. chord
8. chose
9. Serial
10. break

coarse, course ■ *Coarse* means "rough or crude"; *course* means "a path or direction taken." *Course* also means "a class or a series of studies."

> Fletcher, known for using coarse language, was barred from the golf course until he took an etiquette course.

complement, compliment ■ *Complement* refers to that which completes or fulfills. *Compliment* is an expression of admiration or praise.

> Kimberly smiled, thinking she had received a compliment when Carlos said that her new Chihuahua complemented her personality.

continual, continuous ■ *Continual* refers to something that happens again and again with some breaks or pauses; *continuous* refers to something that keeps happening, uninterrupted.

> Sunlight hits Iowa on a continual basis; sunlight hits Earth continuously.

counsel, council ■ When used as a noun, *counsel* means "advice"; when used as a verb, it means "to advise." *Council* refers to a group that advises.

> The student council counseled all freshmen to join a school club. That's good counsel.

desert, dessert ■ The noun *desert* (dĕz´ ərt) refers to barren wilderness. *Dessert* (dĭ zûrt´) is food served at the end of a meal.

> The scorpion tiptoed through the moonlit desert, searching for dessert.

The verb *desert* (dĭ zûrt´) means "to abandon"; the noun *desert* (dĭ zûrt´) means "deserved reward or punishment."

> The burglar's hiding place deserted him when the spotlight swung his way; his subsequent arrest was his just desert.

die, dye ■ *Die* (dying) means "to stop living." *Dye* (dyeing) is used to change the color of something.

different from, different than ■ Use *different from* in a comparison of two things. *Different than* should be used only when followed by a clause.

> Carlos is quite different from his brother.
> Both are different than they were as children.

farther, further ■ *Farther* refers to a physical distance; *further* refers to additional time, quantity, or degree.

> Alaska extends farther north than Iceland does.
> Further information can be obtained in an atlas.

fewer, less ■ *Fewer* refers to the number of separate units; *less* refers to bulk quantity.

> Because we have fewer orders for cakes, we'll buy less sugar and flour.

Grammar Practice

Using the Right Word 4

complement, compliment; continual, continuous; desert, dessert; different from, different than; fewer, less

 Write the correct choice from those given in parentheses.

1. *(Continually, Continuously)* rising at 5:30 a.m. to get to school by 7:00 is not my ideal way of life.

2. The stray dog would *(desert, dessert)* us after we fed him a few times.

3. How are tostadas *(different from, different than)* sopes?

4. Not all women consider being whistled at a *(complement, compliment)*.

5. Aunt Lulu would always let me eat *(desert, dessert)* first.

6. Generally speaking, a hybrid vehicle burns *(fewer, less)* gallons of gas over the same distance than a gas-only vehicle does.

7. Min braids cornrows *(different from, different than)* Rae Lin does.

8. We've had *(fewer, less)* sunshine this month than in any other this year.

9. Mr. Allen's neighbors began to worry about the *(continual, continuous)* music—the same CD—blaring from his apartment.

10. The hoodia plant grows wild only in the Kalahari *(Desert, Dessert)* of Africa.

11. My red jacket would be the perfect *(complement, compliment)* to your outfit!

12. Is a medal a fair *(desert, dessert)* for breaking a record in the Olympics?

Model

Model the following sentences to practice using the words *complement* and *compliment* correctly.

> There may be as much nobility in being last as in being first, because the two positions are equally necessary in the world, the one to complement the other.
> —José Ortega Y Gasset

> We were told our campaign wasn't sufficiently slick. We regard that as a compliment.
> —Margaret Thatcher

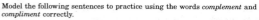

Right Word

Related Skills Activities

■ *SkillsBook*
Using the Right Word 2, p. 59

Answers

1. Continually
2. desert
3. different from
4. compliment
5. dessert
6. fewer
7. different than
8. less
9. continuous
10. Desert
11. complement
12. desert

flair, flare ■ *Flair* refers to style or natural talent; *flare* means "to light up quickly" or "burst out" (or an object that does so).

> Ronni was thrilled with Jorge's flair for decorating—until one of his strategically placed candles flared, marring the wall.

good, well ■ *Good* is an adjective; *well* is nearly always an adverb. (When *well* is used to describe a state of health, it is an adjective: He was happy to be *well* again.)

> The CD player works well.
> Our team looks good this season.

heal, heel ■ *Heal* means "to mend or restore to health." A *heel* is the back part of a foot.

> Achilles died because a poison arrow pierced his heel and caused a wound that would not heal.

healthful, healthy ■ *Healthful* means "causing or improving health"; *healthy* means "possessing health."

> Healthful foods build healthy bodies.

hear, here ■ You *hear* with your ears. *Here* means "the area close by."

heard, herd ■ *Heard* is the past tense of the verb "hear"; *herd* is a large group of animals.

hole, whole ■ A *hole* is a cavity or hollow place. *Whole* means "complete."

idle, idol ■ *Idle* means "not working." An *idol* is someone or something that is worshipped.

> The once-popular actress, who had been idle lately, wistfully recalled her days as an idol.

immigrate, emigrate ■ *Immigrate* means "to come into a new country or environment." *Emigrate* means "to go out of one country to live in another."

> Martin Ulferts immigrated to this country in 1882. He was only three years old when he emigrated from Germany.

imply, infer ■ *Imply* means "to suggest or express indirectly"; *infer* means "to draw a conclusion from facts." (A writer or speaker implies; a reader or listener infers.)

> Dad implied by his comment that I should drive more carefully, and I inferred that he was concerned for both me and his new car.

Grammar Practice

Using the Right Word 5

flair, flare; good, well; idle, idol; imply, infer

 Write the correct choice from those given in parentheses.

1. The groupings of pampas grass definitely add *(flair, flare)* to Jacinda's flower garden.

2. Tempers *(flaired, flared)* as it became evident that the "contest" was a hoax and there would be no winners.

3. After five months of winterlike conditions, it felt *(good, well)* to soak up some sun in the park.

4. I didn't sleep so *(good, well)* last night; nightmares plagued me.

5. Uncle Isaac's old jalopy has sat *(idle, idol)* in the barn for 15 years.

6. A dozen candles surrounded the *(idle, idol)* on the small altar.

7. Does wearing torn jeans *(imply, infer)* a lack of funds to purchase nicer clothing?

8. Satish *(implied, inferred)* from his boss's cold stare that he was in trouble.

9. Because Mia wasn't feeling *(good, well)*, she opted out of going to the mall with her friends.

10. The group stranded on a pleasure boat shot a *(flair, flare)* into the sky in hopes that rescuers would come.

Model

Model the following sentences to practice using the words *idle* and *idol* correctly.

> There is one piece of advice, in a life of study, which I think no one will object to; and that is, every now and then to be completely idle—to do nothing at all.
> —Sydney Smith

> There is a strange and mighty race of people called the Americans, who are rapidly becoming the coldest in the world because of this cruel, man-eating idol, lucre.
> —Edward Dahlberg

Right Word

Related Skills Activities

■ **SkillsBook**
Using the Right Word 3, p. 60

Answers

1. flair
2. flared
3. good
4. well
5. idle
6. idol
7. imply
8. inferred
9. well
10. flare

insure, ensure ■ *Insure* means "to secure from financial harm or loss." *Ensure* means "to make certain of something."

To ensure that you can legally drive that new car, you'll have to insure it.

it's, its ■ *It's* is the contraction of "it is." *Its* is the possessive form of "it."

It's hard to believe, but the movie *Shrek* still holds its appeal for many kids.

later, latter ■ *Later* means "after a period of time." *Latter* refers to the second of two things mentioned.

Later that year we had our second baby and adopted a stray kitten. The latter was far more welcomed by our toddler.

lay, lie ■ *Lay* means "to place." *Lay* is a transitive verb. (See 716.1.)

Lay your books on the big table.

Lie means "to recline," and *lay* is the past tense of *lie*. *Lie* is an intransitive verb. (See 716.1.)

In this heat, the children must lie down for a nap. Yesterday they lay down without one complaint. Sometimes they have lain in the hammocks to rest.

lead, led ■ *Lead* (lēd) is the present tense of the verb meaning "to guide." The past tense of the verb is *led* (lĕd). The noun *lead* (lĕd) is a metal.

We were led along the path that leads to an abandoned lead mine.

learn, teach ■ *Learn* means "to acquire information." *Teach* means "to give information."

I learn better when people teach with real-world examples.

leave, let ■ *Leave* means "to allow something to remain behind." *Let* means "to permit."

Would you let me leave my bike at your house?

lend, borrow ■ *Lend* means "to give for temporary use." *Borrow* means "to receive for temporary use."

I told Mom I needed to borrow $18 for a CD, but she said she could only lend money for school supplies.

like, as ■ When *like* is used as a preposition meaning "similar to," it can be followed only by a noun, pronoun, or noun phrase; when *as* is used as a subordinating conjunction, it introduces a subordinate clause.

You could become a gymnast like her, as you work and practice hard.

medal, meddle ■ *Medal* is an award. *Meddle* means "to interfere."

Some parents meddle in the awards process to be sure that their kids get medals.

Grammar Practice

Using the Right Word 6

insure, ensure; it's, its; lay, lie; lend, borrow; medal, meddle

 Find the words that are used incorrectly. Write the line number followed by the right word.

1   Mr. and Mrs. Hartleson entered the bank together. They desperately

2   needed to borrow $10,000 to cover some overdue payments. They could no

3   longer lay low—they had to take action now to insure their stake in the new

4   condo development in which they had invested.

5   "Please let me handle this," said Mrs. Hartleson to her spouse. "You can

6   insure my success in this endeavor if you promise not to meddle."

7   If Mr. Hartleson was offended, he did not show it. "That's fair," he said.

8   "I know you are laying your professional reputation on the line here." Then he

9   added, "Its obvious that you'll deserve a medal if you pull this off." He patted

10   her on the back.

11   They were uneasy; if the bank would not borrow them the money, they

12   would be in serious financial trouble. Mr. Hartleson had recently been forced

13   to take a cut in pay, and although Mrs. Hartleson herself was a banker, this

14   time she was on the other side of the fence. *This* bank—and it's loan officers,

15   who looked decidedly unfriendly today—was going to sit in judgment. Anxious

16   sweat formed on the back of her neck.

Model

Model the following sentences to practice using the words *lend* and *borrow* correctly.

We don't inherit the earth from our ancestors; we borrow it from our children.

—David Brower

Parents lend children their experience and a vicarious memory; children endow their parents with a vicarious immortality.

—George Santayana

Right Word

Related Skills Activities

■ ***SkillsBook***
Using the Right Word 3, p. 60

Answers

line 3: lie
line 6: ensure
line 9: It's
line 11: lend
line 14: its

metal, mettle ■ *Metal* is a chemical element like iron or gold. *Mettle* is "strength of spirit."

> Grandad's mettle during battle left him with some metal in his shoulder.

miner, minor ■ A *miner* digs for valuable ore. A *minor* is a person who is not legally an adult. A *minor* problem is one of no great importance.

moral, morale ■ A *moral* is a lesson drawn from a story; as an adjective, it relates to the principles of right and wrong. *Morale* refers to someone's attitude.

> Ms. Ladue considers it her moral obligation to go to church every day.
> The students' morale sank after their defeat in the forensics competition.

passed, past ■ *Passed* is a verb. *Past* can be used as a noun, an adjective, or a preposition.

> That old pickup truck passed my sports car! (verb)
> Many senior citizens hold dearly to the past. (noun)
> Tilly's past life as a circus worker must have been . . . interesting. (adjective)
> Who can walk past a bakery without looking in the window? (preposition)

peace, piece ■ *Peace* means "tranquility or freedom from war." *Piece* is a part or fragment.

> Grandma sits in the peace and quiet of the parlor, enjoying a piece of pie.

peak, peek, pique ■ A *peak* is a high point. *Peek* means "brief look" (or "look briefly"). *Pique*, as a verb, means "to excite by challenging"; as a noun, it is a feeling of resentment.

> The peak of Dr. Fedder's professional life was his ability to pique children's interest in his work. "Peek at this slide," he said to the eager students.

pedal, peddle, petal ■ A *pedal* is a foot lever; as a verb, it means "to ride a bike." *Peddle* means "to go from place to place selling something." A *petal* is part of a flower.

> Don Miller paints beautiful petals on his homemade birdhouses. Then he pedals through the flea market every weekend to peddle them.

personal, personnel ■ *Personal* means "private." *Personnel* are people working at a particular job.

plain, plane ■ *Plain* means "an area of land that is flat or level"; it also means "clearly seen or clearly understood."

> It's plain to see why settlers of the Great Plains had trouble moving west.

Plane means "flat, level"; the noun *plane* is a tool used to smooth the surface of wood.

> I used a plane to make the board plane and smooth.

Plane also means "a level of existence or consciousness."

Grammar Practice

Using the Right Word 7

metal, mettle; peak, peek, pique; personal, personnel; plain, plane

 Write the correct choice from those given in parentheses.

1. "A *(plain, plane)* 'yes' or 'no' will suffice," admonished the defense attorney.

2. My illness is of a rather *(personal, personnel)* nature, and I'd rather not discuss it.

3. There is nothing that can *(peak, peek, pique)* my curiosity like an unfamiliar word.

4. It takes unusual *(metal, mettle)* to persevere despite harsh conditions.

5. As a child, Dale would *(peak, peek, pique)* down through the stairway railings, watching the people at his parents' parties.

6. Adding sand to paint transforms the wall from a *(plain, plane)* surface to a more interesting, texturized one.

7. Whereas many kitchen appliances used to be made of *(metal, mettle)*, today they are more likely to be plastic.

8. Just as Terry reached what he thought was the *(peak, peek, pique)* of his endurance, he got a second wind.

9. You must go to the *(personal, personnel)* office down the hall to report an on-the-job injury.

10. Abi left the meeting in a *(peak, peek, pique)* following Nathan's presentation of her idea as his own.

Model

 Model the following sentences to practice using the words *plain* and *plane* correctly.

> Man cannot live on the human plane; he must be either above or below it.
> —Eric Gill

> Any woman who has brains and willing hands finds twenty remunerative occupations open to her where formerly she would have found merely the inevitable two—plain sewing, or the dull little boys.
> —Clara Lanza

Right Word

Related Skills Activities

■ **SkillsBook**
Using the Right Word 4, p. 61

Answers

1. plain
2. personal
3. pique
4. mettle
5. peek
6. plain
7. metal
8. peak
9. personnel
10. pique

poor, pour, pore ■ *Poor* means "needy or pitiable." *Pour* means "to cause to flow in a stream." A *pore* is an opening in the skin.

> Tough exams on late spring days make my poor pores pour sweat.

principal, principle ■ As an adjective, *principal* means "primary." As a noun, it can mean "a school administrator" or "a sum of money." *Principle* means "idea or doctrine."

> His principal concern is fitness. (adjective) The principal retired. (noun)
> During the first year of a loan, you pay more interest than principal. (noun)
> The principle of *caveat emptor* is "Let the buyer beware."

quiet, quit, quite ■ *Quiet* is the opposite of "noisy." *Quit* means "to stop." *Quite* means "completely or entirely."

quote, quotation ■ *Quote* is a verb; *quotation* is a noun.

> The quotation I used was from Woody Allen. You may quote me on that.

real, really, very ■ Do not use *real* in place of the adverbs *very* or *really*.

> Mother's cake is usually very (not *real*) tasty, but this one is really stale!

right, write, wright, rite ■ *Right* means "correct or proper"; it also refers to that which a person has a legal claim to, as in copyright. *Write* means "to inscribe or record." A *wright* is a person who makes or builds something. *Rite* refers to a ritual or ceremonial act.

> Write this down: It is the right of the shipwright to perform the rite of christening—breaking a bottle of champagne on the stern of the ship.

ring, wring ■ *Ring* means "encircle" or "to sound by striking." *Wring* means "to squeeze or twist."

> At the beach, Grandma would ring her head with a large scarf. Once, it blew into the sea, so she had me wring it out.

scene, seen ■ *Scene* refers to the setting or location where something happens; it also may mean "sight or spectacle." *Seen* is a form of the verb "see."

> Serena had seen her boyfriend making a scene; she cringed.

seam, seem ■ *Seam* (noun) is a line formed by connecting two pieces. *Seem* (verb) means "to appear to exist."

> The ragged seams in his old coat seem to match the creases in his face.

set, sit ■ *Set* means "to place." *Sit* means "to put the body in a seated position." *Set* is transitive; *sit* is intransitive. (See 716.1.)

> How can you just sit there and watch as I set all these chairs in place?

Grammar Practice

Using the Right Word 8

principal, principle; quote, quotation; real, really, very;
right, write, wright, rite

 In each paragraph below, find the word or words that are used incorrectly. Then write the right word(s) correctly. If there are no incorrect words, write "none."

1. Given the circumstances, uttering the quote from last night's *Daily Show* may not have been appropriate—but it *was* really funny. Unfortunately, it tends to lose its humor when you have to write it 50 times as a punishment from the principal.

2. Mario has had several real good stories published. Eventually he would like to be a well-known playwrite, but for now his principle concern is finishing a novel begun last year. He hopes to have it published by his twenty-first birthday.

3. Once a month, Jim performs a right of cleansing in which he drinks only water, rests, does yoga, and meditates for a full day. He says this ritual is based on the principle that regular "bathing" should apply not only to the outside of the body, but to its insides and to the mind, as well. He hasn't talked me into trying it myself, but it certainly hasn't seemed to do *him* any harm.

4. In any writing in which you quote another person's words, it is only right to acknowledge the source. To not do so is to steal—a real transgression in the world of publishing. Avoid plagiarism: Be sure to cite your quotations.

Model

Model the following sentences to practice using the words *principal* and *principle* correctly.

> I remember one dinner for which I had relied upon a form of ice as the principal feature of the dessert.
> —Julia Ward Howe

> The first principle of a free society is an untrammeled flow of words in an open forum.
> —Adlai Stevenson

Right Word

Related Skills Activities

■ *SkillsBook*
Using the Right Word 4, p. 61

Answers

1. quotation
2. really *or* very
   playwright
   principal
3. rite
4. none

sight, cite, site ■ *Sight* means "the act of seeing"; a *sight* is what is seen. *Cite* means "to quote" or "to summon," as before a court. *Site* means "location."

In her report, the general contractor cited several problems at the downtown job site. For one, the loading area was a chaotic sight.

sole, soul ■ *Sole* means "single, only one"; *sole* also refers to the bottom surface of the foot. *Soul* refers to the spiritual part of a person.

As the sole inhabitant of the island, he put his heart and soul into his farming.

stationary, stationery ■ *Stationary* means "not movable"; *stationery* refers to the paper and envelopes used to write letters.

steal, steel ■ *Steal* means "to take something without permission"; *steel* is a type of metal.

It takes nerves of steel to brazenly steal another's possessions in broad daylight.

than, then ■ *Than* is used in a comparison; *then* tells when.

Abigail shouted that her big brother was bigger than my big brother. Then she ran away.

their, there, they're ■ *Their* is a possessive personal pronoun. *There* is an adverb used to point out location. *They're* is the contraction for "they are."

They're a well-dressed couple. Do you see them there, with their matching jackets?

threw, through ■ *Threw* is the past tense of "throw." *Through* means "from beginning to end."

Through seven innings, Danielle threw just seven strikes.

to, too, two ■ *To* is a preposition that can mean "in the direction of." *To* is also used to form an infinitive. (See **726.2**.) *Too* means "also" or "very." *Two* is a number.

vain, vane, vein ■ *Vain* means "valueless or fruitless"; it may also mean "holding a high regard for oneself." *Vane* is a flat piece of material set up to show which way the wind blows. *Vein* refers to a blood vessel or a mineral deposit.

The vain prospector, boasting about the vein of silver he'd uncovered, paused to look up at the turning weather vane.

vary, very ■ *Vary* means "to change." *Very* means "to a high degree."

Though the weather may vary from day to day, generally, it is very pleasant.

Grammar Practice

Using the Right Word 9

sight, cite, site; stationary, stationery; than, then; vain, vane, vein

Select the correct word from the list above to complete each sentence.

1. With so many other means to send messages these days, is _____ obsolete?

2. A _____ from the leg is often used in heart bypass surgery.

3. A journalist may be out of a job if he or she does not _____ sources precisely.

4. The road curves around a large, _____ boulder.

5. According to the _____ atop the roof, the wind is coming from the north today.

6. Masafumi started to jack up the car, but _____ he remembered that he had to loosen the lug nuts first.

7. A person who accurately predicts future events is said to have "second _____."

8. Some might mistake someone with a high level of self-confidence for a _____ person.

9. An affordable _____ for a home is becoming increasingly hard to find.

10. Rather _____ taking the bus to school every day, Jasmine rides her bike when she can.

▶ Model

Model the following sentences to practice using the words *sight* and *site* correctly.

If the sight of the blue skies fills you with joy, if a blade of grass springing up in the fields has power to move you, if the simple things of nature have a message that you understand, rejoice, for your soul is alive. —Eleonora Duse

Studying the mass of his manuscript was something like excavating the site of ancient Troy. —Edward Aswell

Right Word

Related Skills Activities

■ **SkillsBook**
Using the Right Word 5, p. 62

Answers

1. stationery
2. vein
3. cite
4. stationary
5. vane
6. then
7. sight
8. vain
9. site
10. than

vial, vile ■ A *vial* is a small container for liquid. *Vile* is an adjective meaning "foul, despicable."

It's a vile job, but someone has to clean these lab vials.

waist, waste ■ *Waist* is the part of the body just above the hips. The verb *waste* means "to spend or use carelessly" or "to wear away or decay"; the noun *waste* refers to material that is unused or useless.

Her waist is small because she wastes no opportunity to exercise.

wait, weight ■ *Wait* means "to stay somewhere expecting something." *Weight* refers to a degree or unit of heaviness.

ware, wear, where ■ *Ware* refers to a product that is sold; *wear* means "to have on or to carry on one's body"; *where* asks "in what place?" or "in what situation?"

The designer boasted, "Where can anybody wear my ware? Anywhere."

way, weigh ■ *Way* means "path or route." *Weigh* means "to measure weight" or "to have a certain heaviness."

My dogs weigh too much. The best way to reduce is a daily run in the park.

weather, whether ■ *Weather* refers to the condition of the atmosphere. *Whether* refers to a possibility.

Due to the weather, the coach wondered whether he should cancel the meet.

which, that ■ Use *which* to refer to objects or animals in a nonrestrictive clause (set off with commas). Use *that* to refer to objects or animals in a restrictive clause. (For more information about these types of clauses, see 612.2.)

The birds, which stay in the area all winter, know where the feeders are located. The food that attracts the most birds is sunflower seed.

who, whom ■ Use *who* to refer to people. *Who* is used as the subject of a verb in an independent clause or in a relative clause. *Whom* is used as the object of a preposition or as a direct object.

To whom do we owe our thanks for these pizzas? And who ordered anchovies?

who's, whose ■ *Who's* is the contraction for "who is." *Whose* is a pronoun that can show possession or ownership.

Cody, whose car is new, will drive. Who's going to read the map?

your, you're ■ *Your* is a possessive pronoun. *You're* is the contraction for "you are."

Take your boots if you're going out in that snow.

Grammar Practice

Using the Right Word 10

waist, waste; which, that; who, whom; who's, whose; your, you're

 For each numbered sentence, write the correct choice from the words given in parentheses.

(1) If *(your, you're)* like the average American, you generate about four pounds of garbage each day. **(2)** While some of it gets recycled or incinerated, most of the country's *(waist, waste)* ends up in landfills. **(3)** These burial sites for anything *(which, that)* can't be recycled are filling up fast as people produce more trash, and environmental problems sometimes follow.

(4) *(Who's, Whose)* the culprit? **(5)** It's not just one group of people *(who, whom)* share responsibility for America's growing trash predicament. Of course, individuals and organizations should try to reuse and recycle as much as they can. **(6)** A growing problem, however, is companies promoting disposable goods, *(which, that)* ultimately end up in a landfill. **(7)** It's *(your, you're)* choice whether to buy such items, so avoid them when possible.

(8) *(Who's, Whose)* job is it to make sure a landfill is safe? Although the federal Environmental Protection Agency's regulations must be met, each state has its own laws. Elected municipal officials also legislate actions related to landfills, so be sure to vote for those **(9)** *(who, whom)* you trust with the environment.

Model

Model the following sentences to practice using the words *who's* and *whose* correctly.

Show me a man who proposes on bended knee and I'll show you a man who's overcompensating.

—Laurien Berenson, *Hot Dog*

He felt that his whole life was some kind of dream, and he sometimes wondered whose it was and whether they were enjoying it.

—Douglas Adams, *The Hitchhiker's Guide to the Galaxy*

Right Word

Related Skills Activities

■ **SkillsBook**
Using the Right Word 5, p. 62

Answers

1. you're
2. waste
3. that
4. Who's
5. who
6. which
7. your
8. Whose
9. whom

Test Prep!

Write the letter of the line in which a word is used incorrectly. If all the words are correct, choose "D."

1.
(A) Did you break this hammer? Perhaps Mr.
(B) Schultz, who's a carpenter, would be kind
(C) enough to borrow us one of his old ones.
(D) All are used correctly.

2.
(A) Though it's a bit scary to think about now,
(B) Anna's fall was real funny when it
(C) happened. I hope she's already feeling better.
(D) All are used correctly.

3.
(A) Rather than an impersonal e-mail, I prefer
(B) a handwritten letter on pretty stationery.
(C) It peaks my curiosity, and I tear it open to read!
(D) All are used correctly.

4.
(A) We hope our school's new principal will
(B) affect a permanent change in the students'
(C) attitudes, which are quite negative lately.
(D) All are used correctly.

5.
(A) With this product, in order to ensure the
(B) the right result, apply it anytime
(C) except when the ground is wet.
(D) All are used correctly.

6.
(A) I'm trying to eat less calories, but this
(B) dessert looks fabulous—and it is the
(C) perfect complement to your wonderful dinner!
(D) All are used correctly.

7.
(A) Yesterday Tim wasted no time in his
(B) careful assent up the steep roof,
(C) scrambling to the peak to repair the flapping shingles.
(D) All are used correctly.

8.
(A) My kindergarten teacher, who I adored,
(B) had a flair for comforting little children.
(C) She was different from the other adults at school.
(D) All are used correctly.

9.
(A) If your hoping to change my mind with
(B) these compliments, I'm afraid they are
(C) given in vain. I'm not changing my mind.
(D) All are used correctly.

10.
(A) Gene was glad he chose to give up his
(B) isle seat on the airplane; there was
(C) definitely less noise where he ended up.
(D) All are used correctly.

11.
(A) The amount of exercise you do directly
(B) affects your health. Some people find this
(C) known fact a bit difficult to accept.
(D) All are used correctly.

12.
(A) The box of cereal you are looking for is
(B) among the Oaty-O's and the Weety-
(C) Flakes. Those Ricey-Puffs sure taste good!
(D) All are used correctly.

13.
(A) Terell's car needed brake work. He told
(B) the tow-truck driver, "It's by Bell's Diner
(C) —the blue car which is parked nearest the door."
(D) All are used correctly.

14.
(A) Dad once demonstrated his metal by
(B) rescuing a kid at a construction site.
(C) That's why he's the only idol in my life.
(D) All are used correctly.

15.
(A) "What a sight!" Mr. Clayton said. "This
(B) place is a real mess. You—" he said,
(C) pointing at me, "lie your books down and give me a hand."
(D) All are used correctly.

16.
(A) Must you continually refer to the
(B) unusually high number of flamingos
(C) here? After all, we're on an isle where they are common.
(D) All are used correctly.

17.
(A) Just because I do well in science and
(B) math, do not imply that I want to be an
(C) engineer. Besides, I'm actually looking into cosmetology.
(D) All are used correctly.

18.
(A) Are you familiar with the famous quote
(B) about idle hands? Although I agree with
(C) it in principle, I do admit to occasional laziness.
(D) All are used correctly.

Right Word

Related Skills Activities

- **SkillsBook**
  Review: Using the Right Word, p. 63
  Posttest: Using the Right Word, p. 197
  Final Proofreading Posttest—Parts 1 and 2, pp. 198–201

Answers

1. C	**10.** B
2. B	**11.** D
3. C	**12.** B
4. B	**13.** C
5. D	**14.** A
6. A	**15.** C
7. B	**16.** D
8. A	**17.** B
9. A	**18.** A

Parts of Speech

Words in the English language are used in eight different ways. For this reason, there are eight parts of speech.

700.1 Noun

A word that names a person, a place, a thing, or an idea
> Governor Smith-Jones Oregon hospital religion

700.2 Pronoun

A word used in place of a noun
> I you she him who everyone these neither
> theirs themselves which

700.3 Verb

A word that expresses an action or a state of being
> float sniff discover seem were was

700.4 Adjective

A word that describes a noun or a pronoun
> young big grim Canadian longer

700.5 Adverb

A word that describes a verb, an adjective, or another adverb
> briefly forward regally slowly better

700.6 Preposition

The first word or words in a prepositional phrase (which functions as an adjective or an adverb)
> away from under before with for out of

700.7 Conjunction

A word that connects other words or groups of words
> and but although because either, or so

700.8 Interjection

A word that shows strong emotion or surprise
> Oh no! Yipes! Good grief! Well, . . .

Parts of Speech

Noun

A **noun** is a word that names something: a person, a place, a thing, or an idea.
> governor Oregon hospital Buddhism love

Classes of Nouns

The five classes of nouns are *proper*, *common*, *concrete*, *abstract*, and *collective*.

701.1 Proper Noun

A **proper noun** names a particular person, place, thing, or idea. Proper nouns are always capitalized.
> Jackie Robinson   Brooklyn   World Series
> Christianity   Ebbets Field   Hinduism

701.2 Common Noun

A **common noun** does not name a particular person, place, thing, or idea. Common nouns are not capitalized.
> person woman president park baseball government

701.3 Concrete Noun

A **concrete noun** names a thing that is tangible (can be seen, touched, heard, smelled, or tasted). Concrete nouns are either proper or common.
> child   Grand Canyon   music
> aroma   fireworks   Becky

701.4 Abstract Noun

An **abstract noun** names an idea, a condition, or a feeling—in other words, something that cannot be touched, smelled, tasted, seen, or heard.
> New Deal greed poverty progress freedom awe

701.5 Collective Noun

A **collective noun** names a group or a unit.
> United States   Portland Cementers   team   crowd   community

Related Skills Activities

- ***SkillsBook***
  Pretest: Nouns, p. 69
  Types of Nouns, p. 70
  Classes of Nouns, p. 71
  Specific Nouns, p. 74

- ***GrammarSnap***
  Nouns
  Capitalization of Proper Nouns and Adjectives

Forms of Nouns

Nouns are grouped according to their *number, gender,* and *case.*

702.1 Number of a Noun

Number indicates whether the noun is singular or plural.

A **singular noun** refers to one person, place, thing, or idea.

actor   stadium   Canadian   bully   truth   child   person

A **plural noun** refers to more than one person, place, thing, or idea.

actors   stadiums   Canadians   bullies   truths   children   people

702.2 Gender of a Noun

Gender indicates whether a noun is masculine, feminine, neuter, or indefinite.

Masculine:

uncle   brother   men   bull   rooster   stallion

Feminine:

aunt   sister   women   cow   hen   filly

Neuter (without gender):

tree   cobweb   amoeba   closet

Indefinite (masculine or feminine):   president   plumber   doctor   parent

702.3 Case of a Noun

Case tells how nouns are related to other words used with them. There are three cases: *nominative, possessive,* and *objective.*

- A **nominative case** noun can be the subject of a clause.

  Humberto's car broke down again. That incompetent mechanic created additional problems when he tried to fix it.

  A nominative noun can also be a predicate noun (or predicate nominative), which follows a "be" verb (*am, is, are, was, were, be, being, been*) and renames the subject. In the sentence below, *type* renames *Mr. Cattanzara.*

  Mr. Cattanzara was a different type than those in the neighborhood.
  —Bernard Malamud, "A Summer's Reading"

- A **possessive case** noun shows possession or ownership.

  The inspector's approval meant that the restaurant could finally reopen.

- An **objective case** noun can be a direct object, an indirect object, or an object of the preposition.

  Marna always gives Mylo science fiction books for his birthday.

  (*Mylo* is the indirect object and *books* is the direct object of the verb "gives." *Birthday* is the object of the preposition "for.")

Grammar Practice

Nouns

- Classes of Nouns
- Number of a Noun
- Case of a Noun

 For each underlined noun, classify it as *proper* or *common* and *singular* or *plural.* Also indicate whether it is a *collective* noun and identify its case as *nominative, possessive,* or *objective.*

1. <u>Maddy</u>, my cat, is extremely overweight, but she is on a special <u>diet</u> now.

2. The life sciences <u>faculty</u> at Lee's school have judged our science <u>fair</u> for years.

3. Did your <u>father</u> ever see <u>Herb's</u> guitar?

4. We've had great <u>luck</u> to have six gorgeous <u>days</u> in a row!

5. This type of <u>iguana</u> is wild in <u>Mexico</u>.

6. My <u>niece</u> loves to see marching <u>bands</u> in city parades.

7. Juanita cooks <u>dinner</u> for her family on every <u>Thursday</u>.

8. <u>Ladybugs</u> must be squeezing in through cracks in the window <u>frame</u>.

9. His <u>computer's</u> hard drive is corrupt and needs replacing, according to the guy in the <u>Information Technology Department</u>.

10. Perhaps the <u>games</u> that his <u>son</u> installed caused the problem.

Model

Model the following sentences to practice using abstract nouns in the objective case.

Politics is made up largely of irrelevancies.
—Dalton Camp

She tells enough white lies to ice a wedding cake.
—Margot Asquith

Related Skills Activities

- **SkillsBook**
  Function of Nouns, p. 72
  Nominative, Possessive, and Objective Cases of Nouns, p. 73

- **GrammarSnap**
  Nouns

 ## Answers

1. Maddy—proper, singular, nominative
   diet—common, singular, objective

2. faculty—common, singular, collective, nominative
   fair—common, singular, objective

3. father—common, singular, nominative
   Herb's—proper, singular, possessive

4. luck—common, singular, objective
   days—common, plural, objective

5. iguana—common, singular, objective
   Mexico—proper, singular, objective

6. niece—common, singular, nominative
   bands—common, plural, objective

7. dinner—common, singular, objective
   Thursday—proper, singular, objective

8. ladybugs—common, plural, nominative
   frame—common, singular, objective

9. computer's—common, singular, possessive;
   Information Technology Department—proper, singular, objective

10. games—common, plural, nominative
    son—common, singular, nominative

Pronoun

A **pronoun** is a word used in place of a noun.

> I, you, she, it, which, that, themselves, whoever, me, he, they, mine, ours

The three types of pronouns are *simple, compound,* and *phrasal.*

> Simple: I, you, he, she, it, we, they, who, what
> Compound: myself, someone, anybody, everything, itself, whoever
> Phrasal: one another, each other

All pronouns have **antecedents**. An antecedent is the noun that the pronoun refers to or replaces.

> Mr. O'Connor **is a popular teacher. Hundreds of students have taken** his **class on American Literature.** He **always makes the class interesting, and students work extra hard for** him.
>
> (*Mr. O'Connor* is the antecedent of *his, he,* and *him.*)

Note: Each pronoun must agree with its antecedent. (See page 756.)

704.1 Classes of Pronouns

The six classes of pronouns are *personal, reflexive and intensive, relative, indefinite, interrogative,* and *demonstrative.*

Personal

I, me, my, mine / we, us, our, ours
you, your, yours / they, them, their, theirs
he, him, his, she, her, hers, it, its

Reflexive and Intensive

myself, yourself, himself, herself, itself, ourselves, yourselves, themselves

Relative

what, who, whose, whom, which, that

Indefinite

all	both	everything	nobody	several
another	each	few	none	some
any	each one	many	no one	somebody
anybody	either	most	nothing	someone
anyone	everybody	much	one	something
anything	everyone	neither	other	such

Interrogative

who, whose, whom, which, what

Demonstrative

this, that, these, those

Grammar Practice

Pronouns 1

■ Antecedents

 Find the pronoun in each sentence below. Write the pronoun—labeled as *simple, compound,* or *phrasal*—and its antecedent.

1. Dominique carefully chose the ingredients for her salad.

2. Bonita and Lora took down each other's phone number.

3. Gesturing at the pot of rice and beans, Claude said, "Is that for lunch?"

4. The toddlers—twins, by the look of things—grabbed the toy from the child-care provider and proclaimed, "Do ourselves!"

5. Uh-oh, the cell phone is displaying gibberish on its screen.

6. The honor-roll students lined up, and each one approached the stage to receive an award.

7. Dr. Lopez encouraged the crowd: "Everyone here has the potential to make a difference!"

8. Petra decided to change the tire herself.

9. Some of the lug nuts were rusty, and Petra had difficulty loosening them.

10. Petra positioned the jack and raised it up to the car's frame.

◀ Model

Model the following sentences to practice using compound and phrasal pronouns.

> The most important thing is to be whatever you are without shame.
> —Rod Steiger

> Hearing voices no one else can hear isn't a good sign, even in the wizarding world.
> —J. K. Rowling, *Harry Potter and the Chamber of Secrets*

Related Skills Activities

■ **SkillsBook**
Pretest: Pronouns, p. 76

■ **GrammarSnap**
Pronoun-Antecedent Agreement

Answers

1. her—simple, Dominique
2. each other's—phrasal, Bonita and Lora
3. that—simple, pot
4. ourselves—compound, toddlers
5. its—simple, cell phone
6. each one—phrasal, students
7. everyone—compound, crowd
8. herself—compound, Petra
9. them—simple, lug nuts
10. it—simple, jack

Pronoun (continued)

706.1 Personal Pronouns

A **personal pronoun** can take the place of any noun.

Our coach made her point loud and clear when she raised her voice.

- A **reflexive pronoun** is formed by adding *-self* or *-selves* to a personal pronoun. A reflexive pronoun can be a direct object, an indirect object, an object of the preposition, or a predicate nominative.

  Miss Sally Sunshine loves herself. (direct object of *loves*)

  Tomisha does not seem herself today. (predicate nominative)

- An **intensive pronoun** is a reflexive pronoun that intensifies or emphasizes the noun or pronoun it refers to.

  Leo himself taught his children to invest their lives in others.

706.2 Relative Pronouns

A **relative pronoun** relates or connects an adjective clause to the noun or pronoun it modifies.

Students who study regularly get the best grades. Surprise!

The dance, which we had looked forward to for weeks, was canceled.

(The relative pronoun *who* relates the adjective clause to *students; which* relates the adjective clause to *dance*.)

706.3 Indefinite Pronouns

An **indefinite pronoun** refers to unnamed or unknown people or things.

I wonder why anybody would want to travel around the world alone; if you know anybody who has done this, I would love to meet him or her.

(The antecedent of *anybody* is unknown.)

706.4 Interrogative Pronouns

An **interrogative pronoun** asks a question.

"Who gave you my name? Why are you calling me? What do you want from me?"

706.5 Demonstrative Pronouns

A **demonstrative pronoun** points out people, places, or things without naming them.

This shouldn't be too hard.   That looks about right.

These are the best ones.   Those ought to be thrown out.

Note: When one of these words precedes a noun, it functions as an adjective, not a pronoun. (See 728.1.)

That movie bothers me. (*That* is an adjective.)

Grammar Practice

Pronouns 2

- Personal Pronouns
- Reflexive and Intensive Pronouns
- Relative Pronouns
- Indefinite Pronouns
- Interrogative Pronouns
- Demonstrative Pronouns

 Write down the 15 pronouns in the paragraphs below and label their class.

1   In March 1989, a geomagnetic storm caused a malfunction in Quebec's
2 power grid. In only a minute and a half, a complete blackout that left 6 million
3 people without power disrupted critical services (transportation, fire and police
4 protection)—and everything else—for nine hours.
5   What is a geomagnetic storm? You may have heard of it as a solar storm.
6 These storms are responsible for the incredible light displays known as the
7 auroras, but they also cause temporary disruptions of radio transmissions,
8 navigation systems, and, as evidenced above, power grids. This is how it
9 happens: A solar eruption causes an incredible solar wind shock wave that
10 strikes Earth's magnetic field a day or so later. The shock waves change the
11 electric currents in the atmosphere, which, in turn, are attracted to electric
12 transmission lines. The added current in the lines overheats transformers,
13 causing them to fail.
14   The utility companies themselves are not to blame since the storms can't
15 be prevented. Instead, they have plans to ride out the storms. That may not
16 be the best strategy, but the companies' only existing alternative is installing
17 complex, costly devices to block the extra current. With any luck, nobody will
18 have to cope with a solar storm causing a large-scale blackout.

 Model

Model the following sentences to practice using demonstrative pronouns.

I was thought to be 'stuck up.' I wasn't. I was just sure of myself. This is and always has been an unforgivable quality to the unsure.

—Bette Davis

Related Skills Activities

- **Sentence Fluency**
  Expanding Sentences, p. 83

- *SkillsBook*
  Reflexive and Intensive Pronouns, p. 80
  Relative Pronouns, p. 81
  Indefinite, Interrogative, and Demonstrative Pronouns, p. 82

- *GrammarSnap*
  Subject-Verb Agreement with Indefinite Pronouns

 ## Answers

line 2: that—relative
line 4: everything—indefinite
line 5: What—interrogative
         You—personal
         it—personal
line 7: they—personal
line 8: This—demonstrative
         it—personal
line 9: that—relative
line 11: which—relative
line 13: them—personal
line 14: themselves—intensive
line 15: they—personal
         That—demonstrative
line 17: nobody—indefinite

Forms of Personal Pronouns

The form of a personal pronoun indicates its *number* (singular or plural), its *person* (first, second, third), its *case* (nominative, possessive, or objective), and its *gender* (masculine, feminine, or neuter).

708.1 Number of a Pronoun

Personal pronouns are singular or plural. The singular personal pronouns include *my, him, he, she, it.* The plural personal pronouns include *we, you, them, our.* (*You* can be singular or plural.) Notice in the caption below that the first *you* is singular and the second *you* is plural.

"Larry, you need to keep all four tires on the road when turning. Are you still with us back there?"

708.2 Person of a Pronoun

The **person** of a pronoun indicates whether the person, place, thing, or idea represented by the pronoun is speaking, is spoken to, or is spoken about.

■ **First person** is used in place of the name of the speaker or speakers.

"We can't pick up the phone every time it rings," said my mother; "I don't like being interrupted if I'm in the middle of something. They can wait until I call them back."

■ **Second person** pronouns name the person or persons spoken to.

"If you let me borrow your binoculars, will you show me again how to use them?" Robert said.

■ **Third person** pronouns name the person or thing spoken about.

She had hardly realized the news, further than to understand that she had been brought . . . face to face with something unexpected and final. It did not even occur to her to ask for any explanation.

—Joseph Conrad, "The Idiots"

Grammar Practice

Pronouns 3

■ Number of a Pronoun
■ Person of a Pronoun

 Identify the person and number of each underlined pronoun.

1. "You should rent the first season of *Friends* on DVD," Pasha said when she heard that I had never seen it.

2. We read *Things Fall Apart*, by Chinua Achebe, in our Contemporary Literature class.

3. She got to the gym just in time to see her boyfriend sink the winning basket.

4. "Will you call us if you're running late?" the parents asked the teens.

5. I am eager to try scuba diving in the ocean this summer.

6. Luisa, when are you picking them up at the airport?

7. Whether or not they called him to go to the movie, he was going to see it.

8. I can't believe that Li Ming didn't invite them to opening night.

9. "You have until Friday to complete your term papers," Mr. Weatherby told his students.

Model

 Model the following sentence to practice using first- and third-person pronouns correctly.

I had been encouraged early on by my mother and my grandmother to be a high achiever, and I got hooked on the accolades they showered on me.

—Dana Buchman, *A Special Education*

Related Skills Activities

■ **SkillsBook**
Number and Person of Personal Pronouns, p. 77

■ **GrammarSnap**
Pronoun-Antecedent Agreement

Answers

1. You—second person singular
   she—third person singular
   I—first person singular
2. We—first person plural
   our—first person plural
3. She—third person singular
   her—third person singular
4. you—second person plurals
   us—first person plural
5. I—first person singular
6. you—second person singular
   them—third person plural
7. they—third person plural
   him—third person singular
   it—third person singular
8. I—first person singular
   them—third person plural
9. You—second person plural
   your—second person plural

Parts of Speech

710.1 Case of a Pronoun

The **case** of each pronoun tells how it is related to the other words used with it. There are three cases: *nominative, possessive,* and *objective.*

■ A **nominative case** pronoun can be the subject of a clause. The following are nominative forms: *I, you, he, she, it, we, they.*

I like life when things go well. You must live life in order to love life.

A nominative pronoun is a *predicate nominative* if it follows a "be" verb (*am, is, are, was, were, be, being, been*) or another linking verb (*appear, become, feel,* etc.) and renames the subject.

"Oh, it's only she who scared me just now," said Mama to Papa, glancing over her shoulder.

"Yes, it is I," said Mai in a superior tone.

■ **Possessive case** pronouns show possession or ownership. Apostrophes, however, are not used with personal pronouns. (Pronouns in the possessive case can also be classified as adjectives.)

But as I placed my hand upon his shoulder, there came a strong shudder over his whole person.

—Edgar Allan Poe, "The Fall of the House of Usher"

■ An **objective case** pronoun can be a direct object, an indirect object, or an object of the preposition.

The kids loved it! We lit a campfire for them and told them old ghost stories.
(*It* is the direct object of the verb *loved. Them* is the object of the preposition *for* and the indirect object of the verb *told.*)

Number, Person, and Case of Personal Pronouns

	Nominative	Possessive	Objective
First Person Singular	I	my, mine	me
Second Person Singular	you	your, yours	you
Third Person Singular	he	his	him
	she	her, hers	her
	it	its	it
	Nominative	Possessive	Objective
First Person Plural	we	our, ours	us
Second Person Plural	you	your, yours	you
Third Person Plural	they	their, theirs	them

710.2 Gender of a Pronoun

Gender indicates whether a pronoun is masculine, feminine, or neuter.

Masculine: he him his   Feminine: she her hers

Neuter (without gender): it its

Grammar Practice

Pronouns 4

■ Case of a Pronoun
■ Gender of a Pronoun

 Identify each underlined pronoun as *nominative, possessive,* or *objective.* If the pronoun is gender specific, write its gender, too.

(1) My sister-in-law Julie and (2) I went shopping for my brother's birthday present. He's into snowboarding, and Julie wanted to get (3) him a new board before (4) they went on (5) their vacation to the mountains. Snowboarding is a sport that Julie knows (6) nothing about, so (7) she called (8) her amazing brother-in-law (that would be (9) me) to help her shop.

When (10) we got to the sporting goods store, I asked Julie, "How much do (11) you want to spend?"

She said, "I want to get (12) your brother a good quality board, but (13) it should be one that really stands out."

Just then, I saw (14) it, and I pointed it out to Julie. (15) Its jazzy, yellow design screamed at (16) us from across the aisle. (I wished that it were (17) mine.) Julie looked at it closely and said, "(18) It is perfect! Let's get it for him."

Model

Model the following sentences to practice using nominative- and objective-case pronouns.

Computers are useless. They can only give you answers.   —Pablo Picasso

There was a definite process by which one made people into friends, and it involved talking to them and listening to them for hours at a time.

—Rebecca West

Related Skills Activities

■ *SkillsBook*
Functions of Pronouns, p. 78
Nominative, Possessive, and Objective Cases of Pronouns, p. 79

■ *GrammarSnap*
Nominative, Possessive, and Objective Cases of Pronouns

Answers

1. possessive
2. nominative
3. objective, masculine
4. nominative
5. possessive
6. objective, neuter
7. nominative, feminine
8. possessive, feminine
9. nominative
10. nominative
11. nominative
12. possessive
13. nominative, neuter
14. objective, neuter
15. possessive, neuter
16. objective
17. possessive
18. nominative, neuter

Test Prep!

For each underlined word (or words), write the letter of the part of speech from the choices given on the next page.

The world is becoming smaller as more people are able to reach faraway places
(1)
in a relatively short time. Air travel, once reserved for the "jet set," is now a ubiquitous

form of transportation, available to just about anyone, anywhere. Fortunately, air travel
(2)
is one of the safest modes of transportation, as well, thanks to air traffic controllers.
(3)   (4)
With the growing number of aircraft in the skies, the primary job of an
(5)
air traffic controller (ATC) is very important: He or she prevents planes from
(6)   (7)
getting too close to each other. With the assistance of computer software and radio

contact with pilots, an ATC keeps track of several aircraft simultaneously, thereby

ensuring safe distances between them. ATC's also provide weather information
(8)
and navigation directions to pilots when necessary.

What does it take to become an ATC? Excellent spatial perception is mandatory,
(9)   (10)
as are superior vision, hearing, and speaking skills. The position can involve a great

deal of stress, so having a healthy mind and body is a definite advantage. The Federal
(11)
Aviation Administration (FAA), the agency responsible for hiring and training ATC's,

administers physical and psychological tests to all applicants.

In the United States, there are only 14 colleges that offer ATC education.
(12)
Graduates of these programs receive 15 weeks of training at an FAA facility in
(13)
Oklahoma City, after which they get on-the-job training. Experienced controllers are
(14)   (15)
among the highest-paid federal employees, earning more than $102,000 annually.

The volume of air traffic today places a heavy demand on the air traffic
(16)
control system, and weather conditions play a big role in its smoothness. Being
(17)
part of this important service isn't for everyone. Those who thrive on challenge,
(18)
however, will find air traffic control a dream job.

1
Ⓐ proper noun, neuter gender
Ⓑ common noun, neuter gender
Ⓒ common noun, indefinite gender
Ⓓ proper noun, indefinite gender

2
Ⓐ relative singular pronoun
Ⓑ intensive third-person pronoun
Ⓒ indefinite plural pronoun
Ⓓ indefinite singular pronoun

3
Ⓐ indefinite neuter pronoun
Ⓑ common noun, indefinite gender
Ⓒ demonstrative pronoun, masculine gender
Ⓓ common noun, neuter gender

4
Ⓐ proper noun, indefinite gender
Ⓑ common noun, indefinite gender
Ⓒ abstract plural noun
Ⓓ concrete plural noun

5
Ⓐ abstract singular noun
Ⓑ concrete singular noun
Ⓒ abstract plural noun
Ⓓ concrete plural noun

6
Ⓐ singular noun, indefinite gender
Ⓑ plural noun, indefinite gender
Ⓒ singular masculine noun
Ⓓ singular feminine noun

7
Ⓐ objective case feminine pronoun
Ⓑ nominative case pronoun, feminine gender
Ⓒ indefinite feminine pronoun
Ⓓ intensive feminine pronoun

8
Ⓐ plural first-person pronoun
Ⓑ singular third-person pronoun
Ⓒ plural pronoun, objective case
Ⓓ plural pronoun, nominative case

9
Ⓐ interrogative pronoun, objective case
Ⓑ singular third-person pronoun
Ⓒ plural pronoun, objective case
Ⓓ interrogative pronoun, possessive case

10
Ⓐ abstract noun, objective case
Ⓑ abstract noun, nominative case
Ⓒ concrete noun, objective case
Ⓓ concrete noun, nominative case

11
Ⓐ proper singular noun
Ⓑ proper plural noun
Ⓒ concrete noun, objective case
Ⓓ abstract noun, objective case

12
Ⓐ indefinite pronoun, nominative case
Ⓑ relative pronoun, nominative case
Ⓒ indefinite pronoun, objective case
Ⓓ relative pronoun, objective case

13
Ⓐ concrete noun, possessive case
Ⓑ collective noun, nominative case
Ⓒ plural noun, antecedent of "they"
Ⓓ abstract noun, antecedent of "these"

14
Ⓐ proper noun, objective case
Ⓑ concrete noun, nominative case
Ⓒ plural noun, antecedent of "they"
Ⓓ abstract proper noun

15
Ⓐ personal pronoun, first person
Ⓑ personal pronoun, third person
Ⓒ intensive pronoun, third person
Ⓓ relative neuter pronoun

16
Ⓐ concrete noun, nominative case
Ⓑ concrete noun, objective case
Ⓒ abstract noun, nominative case
Ⓓ abstract noun, objective case

17
Ⓐ personal pronoun, objective case
Ⓑ indefinite pronoun, possessive case
Ⓒ personal pronoun, possessive case
Ⓓ demonstrative pronoun, nominative case

18
Ⓐ personal pronoun, objective case
Ⓑ indefinite pronoun, possessive case
Ⓒ personal pronoun, possessive case
Ⓓ demonstrative pronoun, nominative case

Related Skills Activities

■ *SkillsBook*
Review: Nouns, p. 75
Review: Pronouns, p. 83
Posttest: Nouns, p. 202
Posttest: Pronouns, p. 203

■ *GrammarSnap*
Nouns
Pronoun-Antecedent Agreement
Nominative, Possessive, and Objective Cases of Pronouns

Answers

1. B
2. D
3. A
4. C
5. D
6. A
7. B
8. C
9. A

10. B
11. A
12. B
13. C
14. A
15. B
16. D
17. C
18. D

Verb

A **verb** is a word that expresses action (*run, carried, declared*) or state of being (*is, are, seemed*).

Classes of Verbs

714.1 Linking Verbs

A **linking** verb links the subject to a noun or an adjective in the predicate.
> In the outfield, the boy felt confident.
> He was the best fielder around.

Common Linking Verbs						
is	are	was	were	be	been	am

Additional Linking Verbs						
smell	seem	grow	become	appear	sound	
taste	feel	get	remain	stay	look	turn

Note: The verbs listed as "additional linking verbs" function as linking verbs when they do not show actual action. An adjective usually follows these linking verbs. (When they do show action, an adverb or a direct object may follow them. In this case, they are action verbs.)
Linking: This fruit smells rotten.
Action: Maya always smells fruit carefully before eating it.

714.2 Auxiliary Verbs

Auxiliary verbs, or helping verbs, are used to form some of the **tenses** (718.3), the **mood** (724.1), and the **voice** (722.2) of the main verb. (In the example below, the auxiliary verbs are in red; the main verbs are in blue.)

> The road to the hospital was obscured by sheets of rain that were whipping along the ground. The streetlights had gone out, and it was impossible to see the curb where the water was gushing like a river.

Common Auxiliary Verbs							
is	was	being	did	have	would	shall	might
am	were	been	does	had	could	can	must
are	be	do	has	should	will	may	

Grammar Practice

Verbs 1

- Linking Verbs
- Auxiliary Verbs

 Label each underlined verb in the paragraph below as a *linking verb*, an *auxiliary verb*, or *neither*.

Laisha **(1)** is a real estate agent. She **(2)** has decided to have an addition to her house built. Although the addition **(3)** is going to cost a lot of money, Laisha **(4)** feels good about it. She **(5)** has no experience working with contractors, so she **(6)** will read as much as she can about it beforehand. She **(7)** does not want to seem like an easy target for unscrupulous businesses. She will **(8)** sound authoritative and **(9)** appear as though she's done this before. She will not **(10)** be weak in any negotiations. She **(11)** looks forward to the experience as one that **(12)** can improve her job skills.

Model

> Model the following sentences to practice using linking and auxiliary verbs correctly.

> **The hallmark of creative people is their mental flexibility.**
> —Roger von Oech, *A Kick in the Seat of the Pants*

> **Our ability to delude ourselves may be an important survival tool.**
> —Jane Wagner

Related Skills Activities

- **Word Choice**
  Understanding Action and Linking Verbs, p. 75

- ***SkillsBook***
  Pretest: Verbs, p. 84
  Main Verbs and Auxiliary Verbs, p. 85
  Linking Verbs, p. 86

- ***GrammarSnap***
  Verb Tense Overview

Answers

1. linking
2. auxiliary
3. auxiliary
4. linking
5. neither
6. auxiliary
7. auxiliary
8. linking
9. linking
10. linking
11. neither
12. auxiliary

716.1 Action Verbs: Transitive and Intransitive

An **intransitive verb** communicates an action that is complete in itself. It does not need an object to receive the action.

> The boy flew on his skateboard. He jumped and flipped and twisted.

A **transitive verb** (red) is an action verb that needs an object (blue) to complete its meaning.

> The city council passed a strict noise ordinance.
> Raul takes pictures for the student paper.

While some action verbs are only transitive *or* intransitive, some can be either, depending on how they are used.

> He finally stopped to rest. (intransitive)
> He finally stopped the show. (transitive)

716.2 Objects with Transitive Verbs

- A **direct object** receives the action of a transitive verb directly from the subject. Without it, the transitive verb's meaning is incomplete.

  > The boy kicked his skateboard forward. (*Skateboard* is the direct object.)
  > Then he put one foot on it and rode like a pro.

- An **indirect object** also receives the action of a transitive verb, but indirectly. An indirect object names the person *to whom* or *for whom* something is done. (An indirect object can also name the thing *to what* or *for what* something is done.)

  > Ms. Oakfield showed us pictures of the solar system.
  > (*Us* is the indirect object.)
  > She gave Tony an A on his project.

Note: When the word naming the indirect receiver of the action is in a prepositional phrase, it is no longer considered an indirect object.

> Ms. Oakfield showed pictures of the solar system to us.
> (*Us* is the object of the preposition *to*.)

Grammar Practice

Verbs 2

- Transitive and Intransitive Verbs
- Direct and Indirect Objects

 For each underlined verb, indicate whether it is transitive or intransitive. For transitive verbs, write the direct object, too. If there is an indirect object, write and label it, as well.

For Dad's birthday, Mom and I **(1)** are giving him a gift he won't easily forget: a skydiving lesson. A small local airport **(2)** offers lessons from certified instructors. The plane **(3)** will fly at about 10,000 feet, and Dad will tandem-jump with the instructor. Then will come the scary part: free-falling! (Even though the free fall **(4)** lasts only about 45 seconds, I bet it will seem longer.) Once the instructor **(5)** releases the parachute, they will **(6)** float for about five minutes before reaching the ground.

If Dad **(7)** likes skydiving enough to do more jumps, he **(8)** can jump by himself eventually. For the first dozen or so jumps, however, an instructor **(9)** must supervise his efforts. He or she **(10)** shows students important things—such as the location of the pull cord for the reserve parachute.

Model

Model the following sentences to practice using transitive verbs with direct and indirect objects.

> Always acknowledge a fault. This will throw those in authority off their guard and give you an opportunity to commit more.
> —Mark Twain

> From the day I arrived until the day I left, she would tell me some pearl of wisdom that usually went in one ear and out the other.
> —Patti LaBelle and Laura Randolph Lancaster,
> *Patti's Pearls: Lessons in Living Genuinely, Joyfully, Generously*

Related Skills Activities

- ***SkillsBook***
  Direct and Indirect Objects, p. 92

- ***GrammarSnap***
  Transitive and Intransitive Verbs

Answers

1. transitive, gift, IO him
2. transitive, lessons
3. intransitive
4. intransitive
5. transitive, parachute
6. intransitive
7. transitive, skydiving
8. intransitive
9. transitive, efforts
10. transitive, things, IO students

718

Forms of Verbs

A verb has different forms depending on its *number, person, tense, voice,* and *mood.*

718.1 Number of a Verb

Number indicates whether a verb is singular or plural. In a clause, the verb (in blue below) and its subject (in red) must both be singular or both be plural.

- **Singular**
  One large island floats off Italy's "toe."
  Italy's northern countryside includes the truly spectacular Alps.
- **Plural**
  Five small islands float inside Michigan's "thumb."
  The Porcupine Mountains rise above the shores of Lake Superior.

718.2 Person of a Verb

Person indicates whether the subject of the verb is first, second, or third person (is speaking, is spoken to, or is spoken about). The form of the verb usually changes only when a present-tense verb is used with a third-person singular subject.

	Singular	Plural
First Person	I sniff	we sniff
Second Person	you sniff	you sniff
Third Person	he/she/it sniffs	they sniff

718.3 Tense of a Verb

Tense indicates time. Each verb has three principal parts: the *present, past,* and *past participle.* All six tenses are formed from these principal parts. The past and past participle of regular verbs are formed by adding *ed* to the present form. For irregular verbs, the past and past participle are usually different words; however, a few have the same form in all three principal parts.

718.4 Simple Tenses

- **Present tense** expresses action that is happening at the present time, or action that happens continually, regularly.
  In September, sophomores smirk and joke about the "little freshies."
- **Past tense** expresses action that was completed at a particular time in the past.
  They forgot that just ninety days separated them from freshman status.
- **Future tense** expresses action that will take place in the future.
  They will recall this in three years when they will be freshmen again.

Grammar Practice

Verbs 3

- Number of a Verb
- Person of a Verb
- Simple Tenses of a Verb

 Find the verbs in the following sentences. Write each, followed by its person and number and its tense.

1. I think of Leonardo da Vinci as an artist, but he was quite an inventor, as well.
2. He created designs for a diving suit, a revolving bridge, and a helicopter.
3. Can you imagine such intelligence?
4. Flocks of starlings race after the lawn mower, seeking a meal of the bugs set loose by the blades.
5. Mahender attends Blakely School for the Blind.
6. The radio station will feature an interview with Otto at 3:00 this afternoon.
7. You look as red as a ripe tomato!
8. Alfonso and Lela will call me when they are ready to go.
9. After I brushed my teeth, Rachelle offered me a warm brownie.
10. The British Virgin Islands attract tourists from around the world.
11. Jaime, please fold your clothes and put them away.
12. The summer solstice will occur at 11:59 p.m. on June 20, 2013.

 Model

Model the following sentences to practice using verbs of different number, person, and tense in the same sentence.

Home runs win a lot of games, but I never understood why fans are so obsessed with them.
　　　　　　　　　　　　　　　　　　　—Hank Aaron

Always go to other people's funerals; otherwise, they won't come to yours.
　　　　　　　　　　　　　　　　　　　—Yogi Berra

Related Skills Activities

- **SkillsBook**
  Simple Tense Verbs, p. 89

- **GrammarSnap**
  Verb Tense Overview

Answers

1. think—first person singular, present
   was—third person singular, past
2. created—third person singular, past
3. can imagine—second person singular, present
4. race—third person plural, present
5. attends—third person singular, present
6. will feature—third person singular, future
7. look—second person singular, present
8. will call—third person plural, future
   are—third person plural, present
9. brushed—first person singular, past
   offered—third person singular, past
10. attract—third person plural, present
11. fold and put—second person singular, present
12. will occur—third person singular, future

Forms of Verbs *(continued)*

720.1 Perfect Tenses

■ **Present perfect tense** expresses action that began in the past but continues in the present or is completed in the present.

Our boat has weathered **worse storms than this one.**

■ **Past perfect tense** expresses an action in the past that occurred before another past action.

They reported, wrongly, that the hurricane had missed **the island.**

■ **Future perfect tense** expresses action that will begin in the future and be completed by a specific time in the future.

By this time tomorrow, the hurricane will have smashed **into the coast.**

720.2 Irregular Verbs

Common Irregular Verbs and Their Principal Parts

Present Tense	Past Tense	Past Participle	Present Tense	Past Tense	Past Participle	Present Tense	Past Tense	Past Participle
am, be	was, were	been	go	went	gone	shrink	shrank	shrunk
begin	began	begun	grow	grew	grown	sing	sang, sung	sung
bite	bit	bitten	hang (execute)	hanged	hanged	sink	sank, sunk	sunk
blow	blew	blown				sit	sat	sat
break	broke	broken	hang (suspend)	hung	hung	slay	slew	slain
bring	brought	brought				speak	spoke	spoken
buy	bought	bought	hide	hid	hidden, hid	spring	sprang, sprung	sprung
catch	caught	caught	know	knew	known			
choose	chose	chosen	lay (recline)	laid	laid	steal	stole	stolen
come	came	come	lead	led	led	strive	strove	striven
dive	dove	dived	leave	left	left	swear	swore	sworn
do	did	done	lie (recline)	lay	lain	swim	swam	swum
draw	drew	drawn				swing	swung	swung
drink	drank	drunk	lie (deceive)	lied	lied	take	took	taken
drive	drove	driven				teach	taught	taught
eat	ate	eaten	lose	lost	lost	tear	tore	torn
fall	fell	fallen	make	made	made	throw	threw	thrown
fight	fought	fought	ride	rode	ridden	wake	waked, woke	waked, woken
flee	fled	fled	ring	rang	rung			
fly	flew	flown	rise	rose	risen	wear	wore	worn
forsake	forsook	forsaken	run	ran	run	weave	weaved, wove	weaved, woven
freeze	froze	frozen	see	saw	seen			
get	got	gotten	shake	shook	shaken	wring	wrung	wrung
give	gave	given	show	showed	shown	write	wrote	written

These verbs are the same in all principal parts: *burst, cost, cut, hurt, let, put, set,* and *spread.*

Grammar Practice

Verbs 4

■ Perfect Tense Verbs
■ Irregular Verbs

 Write the past participle of the verb in parentheses to complete each sentence. Indicate whether the verb is *present perfect, past perfect,* or *future perfect.*

1. Melford hadn't *(see)* the cat in a while; he assumed that she had *(lie)* in a patch of sunlight for most of the afternoon.

2. I'm sure I have *(eat)* at this restaurant before, since I have never *(sit)* in a booth like this anywhere else!

3. By the time this batter will have *(swing)* at another pitch, the guy on second base will have *(run)* to third.

4. Colleen has *(lead)* her niece's scout troop for three years, and she's *(do)* a great job.

5. The vase, teetering on the edge of the shelf for so long, had finally *(fall)* and *(break)* into little pieces.

6. Odds are that Noney will have *(catch)* some serious tanning-booth rays before she heads to Florida this spring; she has *(grow)* rather fond of her skin's orangey glow.

7. D'Shawn had *(choose)* Melanie's watercolor painting over the others because he liked the way she had *(draw)* bare trees over the colors in dark ink.

8. Dad has *(lay)* his last brick; by tomorrow he will have *(throw)* out the trowel that he used for so many years.

Model

Model the following sentences to practice using irregular perfect tense verbs correctly.

A person who talks fast often says things she hasn't thought of yet.
—Caron Warner Lieber

The only ones among you who will be really happy are those who have sought and found how to serve.
—Albert Schweitzer

Related Skills Activities

■ **SkillsBook**
Perfect Tenses, p. 90
Irregular Verbs 1 and 2, pp. 93–94

■ **GrammarSnap**
Verb Tense Overview

Answers

1. seen—past perfect
   lain—past perfect
2. eaten—present perfect
   sat—present perfect
3. swung—future perfect
   run—future perfect
4. led—present perfect
   done—present perfect
5. fallen/broken—past perfect
6. caught—future perfect
   grown—present perfect
7. chosen—past perfect
   drawn—past perfect
8. laid—present perfect
   thrown—future perfect

722.1 Continuous Tenses

■ A **present continuous tense** verb expresses action that is not completed at the time of stating it. The present continuous tense is formed by adding *am, is,* or *are* to the *-ing* form of the main verb.

Scientists are learning **a great deal from their study of the sky.**

■ A **past continuous tense** verb expresses action that was happening at a certain time in the past. This tense is formed by adding *was* or *were* to the *-ing* form of the main verb.

Astronomers were beginning **their quest for knowledge hundreds of years ago.**

■ A **future continuous tense** verb expresses action that will take place at a certain time in the future. This tense is formed by adding *will be* to the *-ing* form of the main verb.

Someday astronauts will be going **to Mars.**

This tense can also be formed by adding a phrase noting the future *(are going to)* plus *be* to the *-ing* form of the main verb.

They are going to be performing **many experiments.**

722.2 Voice of a Verb

Voice indicates whether the subject is acting or being acted upon.

■ **Active voice** indicates that the subject of the verb is, has been, or will be doing something.

For many years Lou Brock held **the base-stealing record.**

Active voice makes your writing more direct and lively.

■ **Passive voice** indicates that the subject of the verb is being, has been, or will be acted upon.

For many years the base-stealing record was held **by Lou Brock.**

Note: With a passive verb, the person or thing creating the action is not always stated.

The ordinance was overturned. **(Who did the overturning?)**

Tense	Active Voice		Passive Voice	
	Singular	Plural	Singular	Plural
Present	I see	we see	I am seen	we are seen
	you see	you see	you are seen	you are seen
	he/she/it sees	they see	he/she/it is seen	they are seen
Past	I/he saw	we/they saw	I/it was seen	we/they were seen
	you saw	you saw	you were seen	you were seen
Future	I/you/he will see	we/you/they will see	I/you/it will be seen	we/you/they will be seen

Grammar Practice

Verbs 5

■ Continuous Tenses
■ Voice of a Verb

 In each sentence below, identify the verb in the underlined group of words as *present continuous, past continuous,* or *future continuous.*

1. The students <u>are going to be creating</u> their own Web page designs.

2. Aliyya and her brother, Haani, <u>are working in their family's restaurant.</u>

3. <u>Construction workers were finally repaving</u> the pothole-filled road.

4. <u>Rufus and I are looking forward to</u> the first game of the season.

5. <u>You will be graduating soon.</u>

6. In my programming course, <u>I am learning</u> how to create lifelike animations.

7. <u>Darius was leaning against the wall,</u> waiting his turn in the long line.

8. Wolf <u>spiders were building an intricate web</u> on our front porch.

9. <u>Will they be laying their eggs</u> there soon?

10. Those <u>spiders aren't going to be catching many bugs</u> in that web.

Model

 Model the following sentences, but change the passive voice to the active voice.

> [A] calm is not desirable in any situation in life. . . . Man was made for action and for bustle too, I believe.
> —Abigail Adams

> The wise are instructed by reason; ordinary minds by experience; the stupid, by necessity; and brutes by instinct.
> —Cicero

> I am prepared to meet my Maker. Whether my Maker is prepared for the great ordeal of meeting me is another matter.
> —Winston Churchill

Related Skills Activities

■ *SkillsBook*
Active and Passive Voice, p. 91

■ *GrammarSnap*
Verb Tense Overview
Active and Passive Voice

Answers

1. future continuous
2. present continuous
3. past continuous
4. present continuous
5. future continuous
6. present continuous
7. past continuous
8. past continuous
9. future continuous
10. future continuous

Parts of Speech

724.1 Mood of a Verb

The **mood** of a verb indicates the tone or attitude with which a statement is made.

■ **Indicative mood** is used to state a fact or to ask a question.

> Sometimes I'd yell questions at the rocks and trees, and across gorges, or yodel, "What is the meaning of the void?" The answer was perfect silence, so I knew.
>
> —Jack Kerouac, "Alone on a Mountain Top"

■ **Imperative mood** is used to give a command.

"Whatever you do, don't fly your kite during a storm."
—Mrs. Abiah Franklin

■ **Subjunctive mood** is not as commonly used in English as it once was; however, careful writers may choose to use it to express the exact manner in which their statements are meant.

Use the subjunctive *were* to express a condition that is contrary to fact.

> If I were finished with my report, I could go to the movie.

Use the subjunctive *were* after *as though* or *as if* to express an unreal condition.

> Mrs. Young acted as if she were sixteen again.

Use the subjunctive *be* in "that" clauses to express necessity, legal decisions, or parliamentary motions.

> "It is moved and supported that no more than 6 million quad be used to explore the planet Earth."
>
> "Ridiculous! Knowing earthlings is bound to help us understand ourselves! Therefore, I move that the sum be amended to 12 million quad."
>
> "Stupidity! I move that all missions be postponed until we have living proof of life on Earth."

Grammar Practice

Verbs 6

■ Mood of a Verb

 Write whether each statement shows *indicative, imperative,* or *subjunctive* mood.

1. If I were eighteen, I could vote in the November election.
2. Stop at my house after school and pick up Jana's homework.
3. Have you heard that Matthias got a job at Gordon's garage?
4. Be certain the air conditioning is operating by tomorrow!
5. Because someone else called in sick today, I'm working until ten tonight.
6. Pedro acts as if he were a shoo-in for the lead role.
7. Notice how Dot sands the table with fine-grain sandpaper.
8. Why do you like the idea of earlier start times for high schools?
9. I've decided to enroll in a technical college this fall.
10. Get off the freeway at the next exit.
11. The vice principal peered at the boys as though they were criminals.
12. Before you leave the house, make sure you empty the dishwasher and put the dishes away.
13. Tino proposed to his parents that he be permitted to be out until 1:00 a.m. on weekends.
14. Please take the garbage out.

 Model

Model the following sentences to practice using the imperative mood.

> Do not try to fight a lion if you are not one yourself.
> —African Proverb

> Never chase a lie. Let it alone, and it will run itself to death.
> —Lyman Beecher

Answers

1. subjunctive
2. imperative
3. indicative
4. imperative
5. indicative
6. subjunctive
7. imperative
8. indicative
9. indicative
10. imperative
11. subjunctive
12. imperative
13. subjunctive
14. imperative

Verbals

A **verbal** is a word that is derived from a verb but does not function as a verb in a sentence. Instead, a verbal acts as another part of speech—noun, adjective, or adverb. There are three types of verbals: *gerunds*, *infinitives*, and *participles*. Each is often part of a verbal phrase.

726.1 Gerunds

A **gerund** is a verb form that ends in *ing* and is used as a noun.

Swimming is my favorite pastime. (subject)
I began swimming at the age of six months.
(direct object)
The hardest part of swimming is the resulting sore muscles.
(object of the preposition of)
Swimming in chlorinated pools makes my eyes red.
(gerund phrase used as a subject)

726.2 Infinitives

An **infinitive** is a verb form that is usually introduced by *to*; the infinitive may be used as a noun, an adjective, or an adverb.

Most people find it easy to swim. (adverb modifying an adjective)
To swim the English Channel must be a thrill. (infinitive phrase as noun)
The urge to swim in tropical waters is more common. (infinitive phrase as adjective)

726.3 Participles

A **participle** is a verb form ending in *ing* or *ed* that acts as an adjective.

The workers raking leaves are tired and hungry.
(participial phrase modifying *workers*)
The bags full of raked leaves are evidence of their hard work.
(participle modifying *leaves*)
Smiling faces greeted my father when he returned from a business trip.
(participle modifying *faces*)

Note: The past participle of an irregular verb can also act as an adjective.
That rake is obviously broken.
It's a known fact that leaves make good compost.

Grammar Practice

Verbals

- Gerunds
- Infinitives
- Participles

 Label each underlined phrase in the following paragraphs as a *gerund phrase*, a *participial phrase*, or an *infinitive phrase*. Also state the function of each infinitive phrase (*noun, adjective, or adverb*).

You may have heard the term "hijab" in the news lately. **(1)** Derived from the Arabic word "hajaba," the word means "to hide from view." In the religion of Islam, passages in the holy book refer to the requirement for women **(2)** to cover their heads and bodies. Today, some people—**(3)** Muslims included—find hijab a controversial matter.

On one side of the issue are tradition and pride. Many women who observe hijab are comfortable with **(4)** making the statement about their religious identity. **(5)** To maintain their religious beliefs is more important than **(6)** fitting in to any other society. They are of the opinion that their way of dress forces others **(7)** to judge them for their intelligence and ability rather than for their looks and sexuality.

Some Muslim communities interpret hijab more loosely. Although **(8)** covering the entire body is not strictly enforced, families and the culture itself still expect women to dress modestly. Usually **(9)** consisting of long-sleeved shirts or dresses, long skirts or pants, and a scarf over the hair, this attire is acceptable to many **(10)** working Muslim women.

Model

Model the following sentences to practice using an infinitive as a noun.

To fulfill a dream, to be allowed to sweat over lonely labor, to be given the chance to create is the meat and potatoes of life. The money is the gravy.
—Bette Davis, *The Lonely Life*

What would you attempt to do if you knew you could not fail?
—Robert Schuller

Related Skills Activities

- **Sentence Fluency**
Expanding Sentences, p. 83

- ***SkillsBook***
Gerunds, Infinitives, and Participles, p. 87

Answers

1. participial phrase
2. infinitive phrase, adjective
3. participial phrase
4. gerund phrase
5. infinitive phrase, noun
6. gerund phrase
7. infinitive phrase, adverb
8. gerund phrase
9. participial phrase
10. participial phrase

Adjective

An **adjective** describes or modifies a noun or a pronoun. The articles *a, an,* and *the* are also adjectives.

> The young **driver peeked through** the big **steering wheel.**
> (*The* and *young* modify *driver*; *the* and *big* modify *steering wheel*.)

728.1 Types of Adjectives

A **proper adjective** is created from a proper noun and is capitalized.

> In Canada (proper noun), **you will find many cultures and climates.**
> Canadian (proper adjective) **winters can be harsh.**

A **predicate adjective** follows a form of the "be" verb (or other linking verb) and describes the subject.

> Late autumn seems grim **to those who love summer.** (*Grim* modifies *autumn*.)

Note: Some words can be either adjectives or pronouns (*that, these, all, each, both, many, some,* and so on). These words are adjectives when they come before the nouns they modify; they are pronouns when they stand alone.

> Jiao made both **goals.** (*Both* modifies *goals*; it is an adjective.)
> Both **were scored in the final period.** (*Both* stands alone; it is a pronoun.)

728.2 Forms of Adjectives

Adjectives have three forms: *positive, comparative,* and *superlative.*

- The **positive form** describes a noun or a pronoun without comparing it to anyone or anything else.
  > The first game was long **and** tiresome.
- The **comparative form** (*-er, more,* or *less*) compares two persons, places, things, or ideas.
  > The second game was longer **and** more tiresome **than the first.**
- The **superlative form** (*-est, most,* or *least*) compares three or more persons, places, things, or ideas.
  > The third game was the longest **and** most tiresome **of all.**

Note: Use *more* and *most* (or *less* and *least*)—instead of adding a suffix—with many adjectives of two or more syllables.

Positive	Comparative	Superlative
big	bigger	biggest
helpful	more helpful	most helpful
painful	less painful	least painful

Parts of Speech

Grammar Practice

Adjectives

- Types of Adjectives
- Forms of Adjectives

 Write the adjectives (not including articles) in each of the following sentences. Label *proper, predicate, comparative,* and *superlative* adjectives. (Some adjectives will have two labels.)

1. The new warehouse seems much larger than the old one.
2. I hope to scale Mt. Everest—the highest mountain in the world.
3. African sunsets on the Serengeti Plain are gorgeous.
4. Of all the bands, One Step Back was the most enjoyable.
5. Hunter looks handsome in his royal blue tuxedo.
6. Shineece's Chihuahua is smaller than any dog I have ever seen.
7. Olga crocheted long, multicolored scarves for both grandmothers.
8. Didn't second-hour geometry class seem longer than usual?
9. The Chinese culture was brought to life through Shaiming's amazing presentation.
10. The highway worker's bright orange vest really made her stand out against the gray-brown background of the bare trees lining the country road.

 Model

Model the following sentences to practice using adjectives well.

> His solid belly filled the stretched sack of his maroon cardigan sweater. . . .
> —Tom Bissell, *God Lives in St. Petersburg*

> Miss Bart was discerning enough to know that the inner vanity is generally in proportion to the outer self-depreciation.
> —Edith Wharton, *The House of Mirth*

Related Skills Activities

- **Word Choice**
  Recognizing Problems with Adjectives, p. 78

- *SkillsBook*
  Pretest: Adjectives and Adverbs, p. 96
  Types of Adjectives, p. 97
  Effective Adjectives, p. 98
  Forms of Adjectives, p. 99

- *GrammarSnap*
  Adjectives, Comparative and Superlative

Answers

1. new
   larger—pred.,
   comp.
   old
2. highest
   superlative
3. African—
   proper
   gorgeous
   predicate
4. most
   enjoyable—
   pred., super.
5. handsome—
   predicate
   blue
6. smaller—pred.,
   comp.
   any

7. long
   multicolored
   both
8. second-hour
   longer—pred.,
   comp.
9. Chinese—
   proper
   amazing
10. highway
    bright
    orange
    gray-brown
    bare
    country

Adverb

An **adverb** describes or modifies a verb, an adjective, or another adverb.

She sneezed loudly. (*Loudly* modifies the verb *sneezed*.)

Her sneezes are really **dramatic.** (*Really* modifies the adjective *dramatic*.)

The sneeze exploded very **noisily.** (*Very* modifies the adverb *noisily*.)

An adverb usually tells *when, where, how,* or *how much.*

730.1 Types of Adverbs

Adverbs can be cataloged in four basic ways: *time, place, manner,* and *degree.*

Time (These adverbs tell *when, how often,* and *how long.*)

today, yesterday   daily, weekly   briefly, eternally

Place (These adverbs tell *where, to where,* and *from where.*)

here, there   nearby, beyond   backward, forward

Manner (These adverbs often end in *ly* and tell *how* something is done.)

precisely   effectively   regally   smoothly   well

Degree (These adverbs tell *how much* or *how little.*)

substantially   greatly   entirely   partly   too

Note: Some adverbs can be written with or without the *ly* ending. When in doubt, use the *ly* form.

slow, slowly   loud, loudly   fair, fairly   tight, tightly   quick, quickly

730.2 Forms of Adverbs

Adverbs of manner have three forms: *positive, comparative,* and *superlative.*

- The **positive form** describes a verb, an adjective, or another adverb without comparing it to anyone or anything else.

  Model X vacuum cleans well **and runs** quietly.

- The **comparative form** (-*er, more,* or *less*) compares how two things are done.

  Model Y vacuum cleans better **and runs** more quietly **than model X does.**

- The **superlative form** (-*est, most,* or *least*) compares how three or more things are done.

  Model Z vacuum cleans best **and runs** most quietly **of all.**

Irregular Forms		
Positive	Comparative	Superlative
well	better	best
fast	faster	fastest
remorsefully	more remorsefully	most remorsefully

Grammar Practice

Adverbs

- Types of Adverbs
- Forms of Adverbs

 Write the adverbs in each of the following sentences (some sentences have more than one). Identify each as an adverb of *time, place, manner,* or *degree.* For an adverb of manner, also identify it as *positive, comparative,* or *superlative.*

1. Of all the board members, the mayor reacted most enthusiastically to our proposal.

2. P. J. sat there lazily while I foolishly hauled his boxes to the car alone.

3. Jason rode his motorbike clear across the course in minutes.

4. An immense cargo carrier roared deafeningly overhead.

5. Yesterday, my brother discovered that I'd accidentally dented his pickup truck.

6. I observed an affectionate side of Arnell when he spoke very gently to his nephew.

7. The speaker shared a very interesting anecdote.

8. His was one of the most finely planned science projects at the fair.

9. I performed well on last year's SAT's, but I slipped behind on my final exams.

10. Mr. and Mrs. O'Leary indulgently had their colorful tropical drinks delivered poolside.

 Model

Model the following sentences to practice using comparative and superlative adverbs.

People always call it luck when you've acted more sensibly than they have.

—Anne Tyler, *Celestial Navigation*

Practice shows that those who speak the most knowingly and confidently often end up with the assignment to get the job done.

—Bill Swanson, *Swanson's Unwritten Rules of Management*

Related Skills Activities

- **SkillsBook**

  Pretest: Adjectives and Adverbs, p. 96

  Adverbs, p. 101

  Conjunctive Adverbs, p. 102

  Effective Adverbs, p. 103

  Forms of Adverbs, p. 104

  Adverbs vs. Alternatives, p. 105

- **GrammarSnap**

  Adjectives, Comparative and Superlative

 ## Answers

1. most enthusiastically—manner, superlative
2. there—place
   lazily—manner, positive
   foolishly—manner, positive
   alone—manner, positive
3. clear—degree
4. deafeningly—manner, positive
   overhead—place
5. Yesterday—time
   accidentally—manner, positive
6. very—degree
   gently—manner, positive
7. very—degree
8. most finely—manner, superlative
9. well—manner, positive
   behind—place
10. indulgently—manner, positive
    poolside—place

Preposition

A **preposition** is the first word (or group of words) in a prepositional phrase. It shows the relationship between its object (a noun or a pronoun that follows the preposition) and another word in the sentence. The first noun or pronoun following a preposition is its object.

To make a mustache, Natasha placed the hairy caterpillar under **her** nose.
(*Under* shows the relationship between the verb, *placed*, and the object of the preposition, *nose*.)

The drowsy insect clung obediently to **the girl's upper** lip.
(The first noun following the preposition to is *lip*; *lip* is the object of the preposition.)

732.1 Prepositional Phrases

A **prepositional phrase** includes the preposition, the object of the preposition, and the modifiers of the object. A prepositional phrase functions as an adverb or as an adjective.

Some people run away from caterpillars.
(The phrase functions as an adverb and modifies the verb *run*.)

However, little kids with inquisitive minds **enjoy their company.**
(The phrase functions as an adjective and modifies the noun *kids*.)

Note: A preposition is always followed by an object; if there is no object, the word is an adverb, not a preposition.

Natasha never played with caterpillars before. (The word *before* is not followed by an object; therefore, it functions as an adverb that modifies *played*, a verb.)

Common Prepositions

aboard	before	from	of	save
about	behind	from among	off	since
above	below	from between	on	subsequent to
according to	beneath	from under	on account of	through
across	beside	in	on behalf of	throughout
across from	besides	in addition to	onto	till
after	between	in back of	on top of	to
against	beyond	in behalf of	opposite	together with
along	by	in front of	out	toward
alongside	by means of	in place of	out of	under
along with	concerning	in regard to	outside of	underneath
amid	considering	inside	over	until
among	despite	inside of	over to	unto
apart from	down	in spite of	owing to	up
around	down from	instead of	past	upon
aside from	during	into	prior to	up to
at	except	like	regarding	with
away from	except for	near	round	within
because of	for	near to	round about	without

Parts of Speech

Grammar Practice

Prepositions

■ Prepositional Phrases

 For each underlined prepositional phrase, indicate whether it functions as an adjective or an adverb.

Nearly all my life, **(1)** except the last three years, was spent **(2)** at home. I never traveled much, and in fact, never expected to become a traveler, and above all an unwilling heroine **(3)** in the North-West troubles. I had several sisters and brothers. I was the eldest **(4)** of the family, and as such, **(5)** for many years had to devote my time **(6)** to household cares. My school days seem now the pleasantest period **(7)** of my early life.

From *Two Months in the Camp of Big Bear* by Theresa Gowanlock and Theresa Delaney

If this journey had taken place **(8)** during my days **(9)** of study and happiness, it would have afforded me inexpressible pleasure. But a blight had come **(10)** over my existence, and I only visited these people **(11)** for the sake of the information they might give me **(12)** on the subject in which my interest was so terribly profound. Company was irksome to me; when alone, I could fill my mind **(13)** with the sights of heaven and earth; the voice of Henry soothed me, and I could thus cheat myself **(14)** into a transitory peace.

From *Frankenstein* by Mary Wollstonecraft Shelley

Model

 Model the following sentence to practice using prepositional phrases effectively.

One minute you're pedaling along a highway, and the next minute, boom, you're face-down in the dirt.
— Lance Armstrong, *It's Not About the Bike*

Related Skills Activities

■ **Sentence Fluency**
Expanding Sentences, p. 83

■ *SkillsBook*
Pretest: Prepositions, Conjunctions, and Interjections, p. 107
Prepositions and Interjections, p. 108

■ *GrammarSnap*
Prepositions

Answers

1. adverb
2. adverb
3. adjective
4. adverb
5. adverb
6. adverb
7. adjective
8. adverb
9. adjective
10. adverb
11. adverb
12. adjective
13. adverb
14. adverb

Conjunction

A **conjunction** connects individual words or groups of words. There are three kinds of conjunctions: *coordinating, correlative,* and *subordinating.*

734.1 Coordinating Conjunctions

Coordinating conjunctions usually connect a word to a word, a phrase to a phrase, or a clause to a clause. The words, phrases, or clauses joined by a coordinating conjunction are equal in importance or are of the same type.

> She knew it would be **difficult to go to college** and **scary to live in a new town,** but **she had a lot of support from her family.**

> (*And* connects the two parts of a compound predicate; *but* connects two independent clauses that could stand on their own.)

734.2 Correlative Conjunctions

Correlative conjunctions are conjunctions used in pairs.

> They were not only **exhausted by the day's journey** but also **sunburned.**

734.3 Subordinating Conjunctions

Subordinating conjunctions connect two clauses that are *not* equally important, thereby showing the relationship between them. A subordinating conjunction connects a dependent clause to an independent clause in order to complete the meaning of the dependent clause.

> **A brown trout will study the bait** before **he eats it.** (The clause *before he eats it* is dependent. It depends on the rest of the sentence to complete its meaning.)

Kinds of Conjunctions

Coordinating: and, but, or, nor, for, yet, so

Correlative: either, or; neither, nor; not only, but also; both, and; whether, or

Subordinating: after, although, as, as if, as long as, as though, because, before, if, in order that, provided that, since, so that, that, though, till, unless, until, when, where, whereas, while

---

Note: Relative pronouns (706.2) and conjunctive adverbs (618.2) can also connect clauses.

Interjection

An **interjection** communicates strong emotion or surprise. Punctuation—a comma or an exclamation point—sets off an interjection from the rest of the sentence.

> Oh no! **The TV broke.** Good grief! **I have nothing to do!** Yikes, **I'll go mad!**

Grammar Practice

Conjunctions

 Write the 14 conjunctions you find in the following paragraph and label them *coordinating, subordinating,* or *correlative.* (Write both correlative conjunctions as one answer.)

1   A very special baby was born on July 17, 1990. His given name was
2   Matthew Joseph Thaddeus Stepanek, but everyone knew him as "Mattie."
3   Mattie was special; not only was he born with a rare neuromuscular disease,
4   but he also was destined to become a well-known peacemaker and poet.
5   Mattie used a wheelchair to get around because he was unable to walk. He
6   also needed a ventilator so he could breathe. The pain and discomfort of his
7   illness never stopped him from writing and speaking about world peace.
8   Although he was often very ill in his short life (he died on June 22, 2004), he
9   neither complained nor wanted people to feel sorry for him. Before his death,
10 he published eight books of poetry, and five made it to the *New York Times*
11 best-seller list. Mattie also appeared on numerous talk shows to discuss his
12 philosophies about peace efforts and global tolerance. After he died, former
13 President Jimmy Carter delivered the eulogy at his funeral (the two had
14 been friends since 2002, bonding over their passion for peacemaking). Carter
15 said that he had known many kings and queens, but Mattie was the most
16 extraordinary person he had ever met. Matthew Joseph Thaddeus Stepanek
17 was indeed a remarkable young man, and he left us with these final thought-
18 provoking words: "Remember to play after every storm."

 Model

Model the follow sentences to practice using interjections effectively.

> Oh no! Look out! That car is going too fast.

> "This is fantastic!" Mr. Rumsfeld blurted. "I've got a laser pointer! Holy mackerel!"
> —Eric Schmitt, *The New York Times*

Related Skills Activities

- **Sentence Fluency**
  Check for Commas Splices, p. 87

- **SkillsBook**
  Pretest: Conjunctions, p. 107
  Prepositions and Interjections, p. 108
  Coordinating Conjunctions, p. 109
  Commas Splices 1 and 2, pp. 160–161

- **GrammarSnap**
  Subordinating Conjunctions
  Common Uses of Commas

Answers

line 2: but, coordinating
line 3: not only, but also, correlative
line 4: and, coordinating
line 5: because, subordinating
line 6: so, subordinating
       and, coordinating
line 7: and, coordinating
line 8: Although, subordinating
line 9: neither, nor, correlative
line 10: and, coordinating
line 12: and, coordinating
        After, subordinating
line 15: that, subordinating
        and, coordinating
        but, coordinating
line 17: and, coordinating

Test Prep!

For each underlined word or group of words, write the letter of the answer that best describes it from the choices given on the next page.

Each year, tens of thousands of <u>United States</u> citizens lose a limb or are
(1)
born without one. Until fairly recently, their choices <u>were</u> limited to getting by
(2)
without the limb <u>or</u> using a bulky, sometimes ugly artificial limb. Today, however,
(3)
many congenital or accidental amputees <u>experience</u> an improved quality of life
(4)
<u>as a result</u> of advances in the design of prosthetic limbs.
(5)

Someone who needs an artificial limb cannot <u>simply</u> go to the store and
(6)
buy one. The socket for each prosthetic—the part that fits onto the body—<u>must</u>
(7)
be custom made. A patient usually obtains a new <u>limb</u> through consultation with
(8)
a doctor; a prosthetist, who fits the limb; and a physical therapist, who helps the
patient with exercises that strengthen the specific muscles <u>used</u> to move the limb.
(9)
<u>Since</u> the weight of prosthetics is <u>important</u>, newer limbs <u>are made</u> mostly
(10)   (11)   (12)
of plastic and lightweight metal. One of the greatest advances in prosthetic
technology is the use of myoelectricity, which allows electrical signals from the
patient's muscles <u>to move</u> the limb. Computerized components <u>further</u> enhance its
(13)   (14)
range of motion and responsiveness. <u>Offering</u> even greater freedom for amputees
(15)
in the near future is the goal of "biohybrid" limbs. Currently <u>in development</u>,
(16)
these limbs will merge artificial components with human tissue, permanently
affixing the limb to the body.

Amputees—whether by birth, accident, or war—will <u>always</u> face obstacles in
(17)
their lives. But doctors, engineers (biomedical, chemical, electrical, and mechanical),
and prosthetic manufacturers have given these <u>people</u> a higher degree of normalcy.
(18)
They help people with limb loss avoid an additional loss: that of independence.

1
- (A) abstract noun
- (B) proper noun
- (C) proper adjective
- (D) predicate adjective

2
- (A) auxiliary verb
- (B) linking verb
- (C) intransitive verb
- (D) verbal

3
- (A) correlative conjunction
- (B) coordinating conjunction
- (C) subordinating conjunction
- (D) interjection

4
- (A) transitive verb
- (B) intransitive verb
- (C) participle
- (D) present perfect verb

5
- (A) verbal
- (B) subordinating conjunction
- (C) prepositional phrase functioning as adjective
- (D) prepositional phrase functioning as adverb

6
- (A) adjective
- (B) adverb of degree
- (C) adverb of manner
- (D) adverb of time

7
- (A) auxiliary verb
- (B) linking verb
- (C) transitive verb
- (D) intransitive verb

8
- (A) adverb of manner
- (B) abstract noun
- (C) indirect object
- (D) direct object

9
- (A) transitive verb
- (B) auxiliary verb
- (C) participle
- (D) gerund

10
- (A) subordinating conjunction
- (B) correlative conjunction
- (C) coordinating conjunction
- (D) preposition

11
- (A) proper adjective
- (B) predicate adjective
- (C) adverb of manner
- (D) adverb of degree

12
- (A) participial phrase
- (B) gerund phrase
- (C) active voice verb
- (D) passive voice verb

13
- (A) intransitive verb
- (B) transitive verb
- (C) infinitive
- (D) participle

14
- (A) adverb of manner
- (B) adverb of degree
- (C) adverb of time
- (D) adjective

15
- (A) gerund
- (B) transitive verb
- (C) participle
- (D) auxiliary verb

16
- (A) prepositional phrase functioning as adverb
- (B) prepositional phrase functioning as adjective
- (C) subordinating conjunction
- (D) interjection

17
- (A) adverb of manner
- (B) adverb of place
- (C) adverb of degree
- (D) adverb of time

18
- (A) adjective
- (B) direct object
- (C) indirect object
- (D) participle

Related Skills Activities

- ■ **SkillsBook**
  Review: Verbs 1, p. 88
  Review: Verbs 2, p. 95
  Review: Adjectives, p. 100
  Review: Adverbs, p. 106
  Review: Prepositions, Conjunctions, and Interjections, p. 112
  Review: Parts of Speech Activities, pp. 113–114
  Posttest: Verbs, p. 204
  Posttest: Adjectives and Adverbs, p. 205
  Posttest: Prepositions, Conjunctions, and Interjections, p. 206
  Final Parts of Speech Posttest—Parts 1 and 2, pp. 207–210

- ■ **GrammarSnap**
  Verb Tense Overview
  Adjectives, Comparative and Superlative
  Prepositions
  Subordinating Conjunctions

Answers

1. C	10. A
2. A	11. B
3. B	12. D
4. A	13. C
5. D	14. B
6. C	15. A
7. A	16. B
8. D	17. D
9. C	18. C

Understanding Sentences

Constructing Sentences

A **sentence** is made up of one or more words that express a complete thought. Sentences begin with a capital letter; they end with a period, a question mark, or an exclamation point.

> **What should we do this afternoon? We could have a picnic. No, I hate the ants!**

Using Subjects and Predicates

A sentence usually has a subject and a predicate. The subject is the part of the sentence about which something is said. The predicate, which contains the verb, is the part of the sentence that says something about the subject.

> We write **from aspiration and antagonism, as well as from experience.**
> —Ralph Waldo Emerson

738.1 The Subject

The **subject** is the part of the sentence about which something is said. The subject is always a noun; a pronoun; or a word, clause, or phrase that functions as a noun (such as a gerund or a gerund phrase or an infinitive).

> Wolves **howl.** (noun)
> They **howl for a variety of reasons.** (pronoun)
> To establish their turf **may be one reason.** (infinitive phrase)
> Searching for "lost" pack members **may be another.** (gerund phrase)
> That wolves and dogs are similar animals **seems obvious.** (noun clause)

- A **simple subject** is the subject without its modifiers.
  > Most wildlife biologists **disapprove of crossbreeding wolves and dogs.**
- A **complete subject** is the subject with all of its modifiers.
  > Most wildlife biologists **disapprove of crossbreeding wolves and dogs.**
- A **compound subject** is composed of two or more simple subjects.
  > Wise breeders and owners **know that wolf-dog puppies can display unexpected, destructive behaviors.**

738.2 Delayed Subject

In sentences that begin with *There* or *It* followed by a form of the "be" verb, the subject comes after the verb. The subject is also delayed in questions.

> **There was** nothing **in the refrigerator.** (The subject is *nothing*; the verb is *was*.)
> **Where is my** sandwich? (The subject is *sandwich*; the verb is *is*.)

Grammar Practice

Constructing Sentences 1

- Simple, Complete, and Compound Subjects
- Delayed Subjects

 Write the complete subject of each independent clause (and each dependent clause in a complex or compound-complex sentence). Circle the simple subject or subjects.

(1) In 1953, General Motors introduced an automobile destined to become one of the most popular cars in American history. **(2)** It was the Chevrolet Corvette. **(3)** It wasn't the Corvette's performance that was striking; the design sold the car. **(4)** You could only buy the '53 "Vettes" in white, and all were convertibles. **(5)** The red vinyl interior, soft black top, and red rims around the whitewall tires defined the design. **(6)** There was nothing else like it on the road. **(7)** The suggested retail price for the base model amounted to about $3,500.

(8) GM created only 300 of the '53 Corvettes, but the limited number was unintentional. **(9)** The powerful corporate giant got a late start building the cars. **(10)** A temporary manufacturing plant in Flint, Michigan, was the production site. **(11)** The plant and assembly line required time to set up, so workers were able to make just 300 cars before the start of the 1954 model year.

(12) About 225 of the '53 Corvettes still exist today, representing the rarest of all model-year Corvettes. **(13)** Whoever owns one of these automobiles holds a valuable collector's piece worth more than $105,000. **(14)** There is a nice little sum!

 Model

Model the following sentence to practice using a compound subject.

> **Junipero Serra, the Majorca-born missionary who headed the effort, and his small band of Franciscan followers built a chain of missions from San Diego in the south to San Rafael in the north.**
> — H. W. Brands, *The Age of Gold*

Related Skills Activities

- **Sentence Fluency**
  Use Inverted Sentences, p. 85

- *SkillsBook*
  Pretest: Subjects and Predicates, p. 117
  Using Subjects and Predicates 2, p. 119

- *GrammarSnap*
  Complete Sentences and Sentence Fragments

Answers

Students will circle the boldfaced words.

1. **General Motors**
2. the **Chevrolet Corvette**
3. the Corvette's **performance**; **that**; the **design**
4. **You**; **all**
5. The red vinyl **interior**, soft black **top**, and red **rims** around the whitewall tires
6. nothing **else** like it
7. The suggested retail **price** for the base model
8. **GM**; the limited **number**
9. The powerful corporate **giant**
10. A temporary manufacturing **plant** in Flint, Michigan
11. The **plant** and **assembly line**; **workers**
12. About **225** of the '53 Corvettes
13. **Whoever**
14. a nice little **sum**

740.1 Predicates

The **predicate** is the part of the sentence that shows action or says something about the subject.

> **Giant squid** do exist.

- A **simple predicate** is the verb without its modifiers.
  > **One giant squid** measured nearly 60 feet long.

- A **complete predicate** is the simple predicate with all its modifiers.
  > **One giant squid** measured nearly 60 feet long.
  > (*Measured* is the simple predicate; *nearly 60 feet long* modifies *measured*.)

- Compound and complex sentences have more than one predicate.
  > **The sperm whale** has an enormous head that is approximately a third of its entire length.
  > **A whale** is a mammal, but a squid is a mollusk.

- A **compound predicate** is composed of two or more simple predicates.
  > **A squid** grasps its prey with tentacles and bites it with its beak.

Note: A sentence can have a **compound subject** and a **compound predicate**.
  > Both sperm whales and giant squid live and occasionally clash in the deep waters off New Zealand's South Island.

- A **direct object** is part of the predicate and receives the action of the verb. (See 716.2.)
  > **Sperm whales sometimes eat** giant squid.
  > (The direct object *giant squid* receives the action of the verb *eat* by answering the question *whales eat what?*)

Note: The **direct object** may be compound.
  > In the past, whalers harvested oil, spermaceti, and ambergris from slain sperm whales.

740.2 Understood Subjects and Predicates

Either the subject or the predicate may be "missing" from a sentence, but both must be clearly **understood**.

> Who is in the hot-air balloon?
> (*Who* is the subject; *is in the hot-air balloon* is the predicate.)

> No one.
> (*No one* is the subject; the predicate *is in the hot-air balloon* is understood.)

> Get out of the way!
> (The subject *you* is understood; *get out of the way* is the predicate.)

Grammar Practice

Constructing Sentences 2

■ Simple, Complete, and Compound Predicates

 Write the complete predicate of each sentence. Circle the simple predicate or predicates. In sentences with a direct object, underline it.

1. Danica Patrick finished fourth in the 2005 Indianapolis 500.

2. She led for 19 laps and became the first woman driver ever to lead the race.

3. Her car stalled in the pits about halfway through the 500-mile race.

4. She restarted the car but dropped to the middle of the field.

5. Her fourth-place finish was the highest ever for a female driver.

6. Danica won the 2005 title of Rookie of the Year.

7. At 10 years old, Danica began racing go-carts.

8. Today Danica drives Indy cars for the Rahal-Letterman racing team.

9. In the 2006 Indy race, Danica finished in eighth place.

10. Think about how exciting that would have been!

 Model

Model the following sentence to practice using a compound predicate.

> When I get bored, I drive downtown and get a great parking spot, then sit in my car and count how many people ask me if I'm leaving.
> —Steven Wright

Related Skills Activities

- ***SkillsBook***
  Pretest: Subjects and Predicates, p. 117
  Using Subjects and Predicates 1 and 2, pp. 118–119

- ***GrammarSnap***
  Complete Sentences and Sentence Fragments

Answers

Students will circle the boldfaced words.

1. **finished** <u>fourth</u> in the 2005 Indianapolis 500
2. **led** for 19 <u>laps</u> and **became** the first woman driver ever to lead the race
3. **stalled** in the pits about halfway through the 500–mile race
4. **restarted** the <u>car</u> but **dropped** to the middle of the field
5. **was** the highest ever for a female driver
6. **won** the 2005 <u>title</u> of Rookie of the Year
7. At 10 years old . . . **began** racing go–carts
8. Today . . . **drives** Indy <u>cars</u> for the Rahal–Letterman racing team
9. In the 2006 Indy race . . . **finished** in eighth place
10. **Think** about how exciting . . . **would have been**

Using Phrases

A **phrase** is a group of related words that function as a single part of speech. The sentence below contains a number of phrases.

> Finishing the race will require biking up some steep slopes.

finishing the race (This gerund phrase functions as a subject noun.)

will require (This phrase functions as a verb.)

biking up some steep slopes (This gerund phrase acts as an object noun.)

742.1 Types of Phrases

- An **appositive phrase,** which follows a noun or a pronoun and renames it, consists of a noun and its modifiers. An appositive adds new information about the noun or pronoun it follows.

  > **The Trans-Siberian Railroad,** the world's longest railway, **stretches from Moscow to Vladivostok.** (The appositive phrase renames *Trans-Siberian Railroad* and provides new information.)

- A **verbal phrase** is a phrase based on one of the three types of verbals: *gerund, infinitive,* or *participle.* (See 726.1, 726.2, and 726.3.)

  - A **gerund phrase** consists of a gerund and its modifiers. The whole phrase functions as a noun.

    > **Spotting the tiny mouse** was easy for the hawk.
    > (The gerund phrase is used as the subject of the sentence.)
    > **Dinner escaped by** ducking under a rock.
    > (The gerund phrase is the object of the preposition *by.*)

  - An **infinitive phrase** consists of an infinitive and its modifiers. The whole phrase functions either as a noun, an adjective, or an adverb.

    > To shake every voter's hand **was the candidate's goal.**
    > (The infinitive phrase functions as a noun used as the subject.)
    > **Your efforts** to clean the chalkboard **are appreciated.**
    > (The infinitive phrase is used as an adjective modifying *efforts.*)
    > **Please watch carefully** to see the difference.
    > (The infinitive phrase is used as an adverb modifying *watch.*)

  - A **participial phrase** consists of a past or present participle and its modifiers. The whole phrase functions as an adjective.

    > Following his nose, **the beagle took off like a jackrabbit.**
    > (The participial phrase modifies the noun *beagle.*)
    > **The raccoons,** warned by the rustling, **took cover.**
    > (The participial phrase modifies the noun *raccoons.*)

Sentences

Grammar Practice

Constructing Sentences 3

- Appositive Phrases
- Verbal Phrases

 Identify each underlined phrase as an *appositive, gerund, infinitive,* or *participial* phrase. (One phrase below will have two correct answers.)

1. The citizens approved a referendum for <u>increasing library funds</u>.

2. Kai, <u>my best friend for ten years</u>, will be my college roommate.

3. Ping went to the mall <u>to buy a dress</u> for the prom.

4. James dreams about <u>becoming an ER doctor</u>.

5. <u>To avoid burning the burgers</u>, Ryan watched them closely.

6. Paul Anka, <u>the dog on the television show *Gilmore Girls*</u>, is named after a famous teen idol.

7. The student <u>chosen as valedictorian</u> will speak at the graduation ceremony.

8. <u>Camping in the woods</u> at this time of year is dangerous.

9. The camper <u>clearing the snow from the site</u> is building up a good appetite.

10. The best exercise, <u>walking every day</u>, costs only the price of a good pair of shoes.

Model

Model the following sentence to practice using a gerund phrase.

> For me, singing sad songs often has a way of healing a situation.
> —Reba McEntire

Related Skills Activities

- **Sentence Fluency**
  Expanding Sentences, p. 83

- *SkillsBook*
  Pretest: Phrases, p. 121
  Gerunds, Infinitives, and Participles, p. 87
  Verbal Phrases, p. 122
  Prepositional and Appositive Phrases, p. 123
  Using Phrases Like a Pro, p. 124

- *GrammarSnap*
  Commas After Introductory Words, Phrases, and Clauses
  Appositives
  Participial Phrases

Answers

1. gerund
2. appositive
3. infinitive
4. gerund
5. infinitive, gerund
6. appositive
7. participial
8. gerund
9. participial
10. gerund and appositive

Sentences

Using Phrases *(continued)*

■ A **verb phrase** consists of a main verb preceded by one or more helping verbs.
   Snow has been falling **for days.** (*Has been falling* is a verb phrase.)

■ A **prepositional phrase** is a group of words beginning with a preposition and ending with a noun or a pronoun. Prepositional phrases function mainly as adjectives and adverbs.

   Reach for that catnip ball behind the couch.
   (The prepositional phrase *behind the couch* is used as an adjective modifying *catnip ball.*)

   Zach won the wheelchair race in record time.
   (*In record time* is used as an adverb modifying the verb *won.*)

■ An **absolute phrase** consists of a noun and a participle (plus the participle's object, if there is one, and any modifiers). An absolute phrase functions as a modifier that adds information to the entire sentence. Absolute phrases are always set off with commas.

   Its wheels clattering rhythmically over the rails, **the train rolled into town.** (The noun *wheels* is modified by the present participle *clattering.* The entire phrase modifies the rest of the sentence.)

Using Clauses

A **clause** is a group of related words that has both a subject and a predicate.

744.1 Independent and Dependent Clauses

An **independent clause** presents a complete thought and can stand alone as a sentence; a **dependent clause** (also called a *subordinate clause*) does not present a complete thought and cannot stand alone as a sentence.

   Sparrows make nests in cattle barns (independent clause) **so that they can stay warm during the winter** (dependent clause).

744.2 Types of Dependent Clauses

There are three basic types of dependent clauses: *adverb, noun,* and *adjective.*

■ An **adverb clause** is used like an adverb to modify a verb, an adjective, or an adverb. Adverb clauses begin with a subordinating conjunction. (See 734.3.)
   If I study hard, **I will pass this test.** (The adverb clause modifies the verb *will pass.*)

■ A **noun clause** is used in place of a noun.
   However, the teacher said that the essay questions are based only on the last two chapters. (The noun clause functions as a direct object.)

■ An **adjective clause** modifies a noun or a pronoun.
   Tomorrow's test, which covers the entire book, **is half essay and half short answers.** (The adjective clause modifies the noun *test.*)

Grammar Practice

Constructing Sentences 4

■ Verb Phrases
■ Prepositional Phrases
■ Absolute Phrases
■ Dependent Clauses
■ Independent Clauses

 For each underlined group of words, write whether it is a *verb phrase,* a *prepositional phrase,* or an *absolute phrase.*

1. Mara did not find the resources needed for the assignment.

2. The school year nearly finished, Hannah and Sally made plans for the summer.

3. My sister will meet us at the coffee shop at three o'clock.

4. After the race, Huan beelined for the water fountain, his chest heaving.

5. He was having difficulty breathing.

 For each underlined group of words, write whether it is an *independent clause* or a *dependent clause.* If it is a dependent clause, also identify its type.

6. Nobody except Jaleesa knows where the party will be.

7. She took the job so that she could pay her college tuition.

8. Ms. Klema has been giving me extra help, and my grades are improving.

9. The house that we used to live in was sold.

10. My back hurts so much because I fell yesterday.

◀ Model

Model the following sentence to practice using prepositional phrases effectively.

At the house, a small white gate opened from the lane into a country garden, which in summer would shine with bunched roses and morning glories and tresses of sweet pea.

—Frank Delaney, *Ireland*

Related Skills Activities

■ **SkillsBook**
Using Absolute Phrases, p. 125
Using Phrases Like a Pro, p. 124
Pretest: Clauses, p. 127
Independent and Dependent Clauses, p. 128
Creating Adverbs Clauses, p. 129
Creating Adjective Clauses, p. 130

■ **GrammarSnap**
Adverb Clauses
Adjective Clauses
Noun Clauses
Commas After Introductory Words, Phrases, and Clauses

Answers

1. verb phrase, prepositional phrase
2. absolute phrase, prepositional phrase
3. verb phrase, prepositional phrase
4. prepositional phrase, absolute phrase
5. verb phrase
6. dependent clause, noun
7. dependent clause, adverb
8. independent clause
9. dependent clause, adjective
10. independent clause

746

Using Sentence Variety

A **sentence** may be classified according to the type of statement it makes, the way it is constructed, and its arrangement of words.

746.1 Kinds of Sentences

The five basic kinds of sentences are *declarative, interrogative, imperative, exclamatory,* and *conditional*.

- **Declarative sentences** make statements. They tell us something about a person, a place, a thing, or an idea. Although declarative sentences make up the bulk of most academic writing, there are overwhelmingly diverse ways in which to express them.

  The Statue of Liberty stands in New York Harbor.
  For over a century, it has greeted immigrants and visitors to America.

- **Interrogative sentences** ask questions.

  Did you know that the Statue of Liberty is made of copper and stands more than 150 feet tall?
  Are we allowed to climb all the way to the top?

- **Imperative sentences** make commands.

  You must purchase a ticket.

  They often contain an understood subject (*you*) as in the examples below.

  Go see the Statue of Liberty.
  After a few weeks of physical conditioning, climb its 168 stairs.

- **Exclamatory sentences** communicate strong emotion or surprise.

  Climbing 168 stairs is not a dumb idea!
  Just muster some of that old pioneering spirit, that desire to try something new, that never-say-die attitude that made America great!

- **Conditional sentences** express wishes ("if . . . then" statements) or conditions contrary to fact.

  If I could design a country's flag, I would use six colors behind a sun, a star, and a moon.
  I would feel as if I were representing many cultures in my design.

747

Grammar Practice

Kinds of Statements

 Write the kind of statement each sentence makes: *declarative, interrogative, imperative, exclamatory,* or *conditional*.

1. A superstition is an illogical belief that comes from fear or ignorance.

2. You should hear some of these unusual, old superstitions!

3. If you carry a hoe into the house, you should carry it out walking backward to avoid bad luck.

4. Always close a front door with your face toward it.

5. Do you believe that an apple a day keeps the doctor away?

6. Seeing a single crow is unlucky, but seeing two means good luck.

7. Have you heard that a dead beetle tied around the neck is a cure for whooping cough?

8. When eating a fish, start at the tail and work toward the head.

9. We are what we believe ourselves to be.

10. If you believe in superstition, it will always follow you.

 Sentences

Model

Model the following conditional statements.

Rome, after all, had more than half a dozen aqueducts: if one failed, the others could make up the deficit.

—Robert Harris, *Pompeii*

If you don't know where you are going, any road will get you there.

—Lewis Carroll

Related Skills Activities

- **SkillsBook**
  Pretest: Sentences, p. 133
  Kinds of Sentences, p. 134

- **GrammarSnap**
  Kinds of Sentences: Declarative, Interrogative, Imperative, Exclamatory

Answers

1. declarative
2. exclamatory
3. conditional
4. imperative
5. interrogative
6. declarative
7. interrogative
8. imperative
9. declarative
10. conditional

748.1 Types of Sentence Constructions

A sentence may be *simple, compound, complex,* or *compound-complex.* It all depends on the relationship between independent and dependent clauses.

■ A **simple sentence** can have a single subject or a compound subject. It can have a single predicate or a compound predicate. However, a simple sentence has only one independent clause, and it has no dependent clauses.

> **My** back aches.
> (single subject; single predicate)
> **My** teeth **and my** eyes hurt.
> (compound subject; single predicate)
> **My** throat **and** nose feel **sore and** look red.
> (compound subject; compound predicate)
> I must have caught the flu **from the sick kids in class.**
> (independent clause with two phrases: *from the sick kids* and *in class*)

■ A **compound sentence** consists of two independent clauses. The clauses must be joined by a comma and a coordinating conjunction or by a semicolon.

> **I usually don't mind missing school,** but **this is not fun.**
> **I feel too sick to watch TV;** **I feel too sick to eat.**

Note: The comma can be omitted when the clauses are very short.

> **I wept** and **I wept.**

■ A **complex sentence** contains one independent clause (in black) and one or more dependent clauses (in red).

> When I get back to school, **I'm actually going to appreciate it.**
> (dependent clause; independent clause)
> **I won't even complain about math class,** although I might be talking out of my head because I'm feverish.
> (independent clause; two dependent clauses)

■ A **compound-complex sentence** contains two or more independent clauses (in black) and one or more dependent clauses (in red).

> **Yes, I have a bad flu, and** because I need to get well soon, **I won't think about school just yet.**
> (two independent clauses; one dependent clause)
> **The best remedy for those** who suffer with flu symptoms **is plenty of rest and fluids, but the chicken soup** that Grandma makes for me **always helps, too.**
> (two independent clauses; two dependent clauses)

Grammar Practice

Types of Sentence Constructions

 Identify each of the following sentences as a *simple, compound, complex,* or *compound-complex* sentence.

1. The Tomb of the Unknowns is guarded 24 hours a day, 365 days a year, in all kinds of weather.

2. The Third United States Infantry is labeled "The Old Guard."

3. "The Old Guard" guards the tomb, and it follows strict rules.

4. Its procedure is precise.

5. A sentinel, man or woman, marches 21 paces past the tomb.

6. He makes a crisp 90-degree turn; he faces east for 21 seconds.

7. The sentinel makes another 90-degree turn, and then he faces north and stands for 21 seconds.

8. He quickly moves his rifle.

9. He places its barrel on his shoulder, facing away from the tomb, to show that he stands between the tomb and any threat.

10. After this procedure is completed, it is repeated, and this goes on 24 hours each day.

11. The Tomb of the Unknowns, located in Arlington National Cemetery, contains the remains of several unknown American soldiers.

12. The unknown soldiers were killed in both World Wars, the Korean War, and the Vietnam War.

Model

Model the following sentence to practice forming a compound sentence.

> **Windows rattled and floors shook; the sound was a giant hand shaking Lydia Kilkenny's sleeping shoulders.**
> —Myla Goldberg, *Wickett's Remedy*

Sentences

Related Skills Activities

■ **SkillsBook**
Writing Simple and Compound Sentences, p. 135
Writing Complex and Compound–Complex Sentences, p. 136

■ **GrammarSnap**
Sentence Types: Compound, Complex, and Compound-Complex Sentences
Restrictive/Nonrestrictive Clauses for Combining Sentences
Participle Phrases

Answers

1. simple
2. simple
3. compound
4. simple
5. simple
6. compound
7. compound
8. simple
9. complex
10. compound–complex
11. simple
12. simple

750.1 Arrangements of Sentences

Depending on the arrangement of the words and the placement of emphasis, a sentence may also be classified as *loose, balanced, periodic,* or *cumulative.*

- A **loose sentence** expresses the main thought near the beginning and adds explanatory material as needed.

    We hauled out the boxes of food and set up the camp stove, **all the time battling the hot wind that would not stop, even when we screamed into the sky.**

    The earliest television shows were like radio with pictures—**much more talking and fewer visual effects.**

- A **balanced sentence** is constructed so that it emphasizes a similarity or a contrast between two or more of its parts (words, phrases, or clauses).

    The wind in our ears drove us crazy **and** pushed us on.
    (The similar wording emphasizes the main idea in this sentence.)

    Some people dislike contemporary art because they do not understand **it;** perhaps that is because they do not understand **the point of art.**

- A **periodic sentence** is one that postpones the crucial or most surprising idea until the end.

    Following my mother's repeated threats to ground me for life,
    I decided it was time to propose a compromise.

    A writer can do what most people cannot—tell absolute truths and absolute lies.

- A **cumulative sentence** places the general idea in the middle of the sentence with modifying clauses and phrases coming before and after.

    With careful thought and extra attention to detail, I wrote out my plan for being a model teenager, a teen who cared about neatness and reliability.

    After several months, Mark became more comfortable teaching English to Chinese students,especially when he began to learn Chinese.

Note: Writers often experiment with arrangement in order to have a variety of sentences in a particular piece of writing. Remember, however, that the arrangement of a sentence indicates the importance of the ideas within it. Don't rearrange sentences so much that your original emphasis is lost.

Grammar Practice

Arrangements of Sentences

 Classify each of the following sentences as *loose, balanced, periodic,* or *cumulative.*

(1) Although she knew little about her ancestors, Soo Jin found genealogy intriguing. **(2)** Last summer, at a family reunion, she got a surprise. **(3)** A distant cousin presented her with her great-grandmother's diary, which was written in Korean. **(4)** Soo Jin was ecstatic, anticipating the family stories this book held.

(5) With great care, Soo Jin opened this heirloom from her ancestry, something she thought she would never do. **(6)** Until now, Soo Jin had not worried about learning Korean. **(7)** She hoped that someone at the reunion could read it, but she was disappointed. **(8)** She needed to find a translator, someone to unlock the diary's secrets.

(9) As it turned out, Mrs. Kim, a volunteer at the youth center, read Korean, and she helped Soo Jin. **(10)** Together, they enjoyed translating the diary.

Model

 Model the following balanced and cumulative sentences.

The experience left me troubled; I knew there was something wrong but not quite what it was.
—Tim Flannery, *The Weather Makers*

While she watched, the snake nosed up into the exact corner between the cupboards and in an instant disappeared, as if it had been sucked up by vacuum tube.
—Christina Adam, *Any Small Thing Can Save You*

Related Skills Activities

- ### *SkillsBook*
  Arranging Sentences 1 and 2, pp. 157–158

Answers

1. periodic
2. periodic
3. loose
4. loose
5. cumulative
6. periodic
7. balanced
8. loose
9. balanced
10. periodic

Sentences

Getting Sentence Parts to Agree

Agreement of Subject and Verb

A verb must agree in number (singular or plural) with its subject.

The student was proud of her quarter grades.

Note: Do not be confused by words that come between the subject and verb.

The manager, as well as the players, is required to display good
sportsmanship. (*Manager*, not *players*, is the subject.)

752.1 Compound Subjects

Compound subjects joined by *or* or *nor* take a singular verb (when they are singular subjects).

Neither Bev nor Kendra goes to the street dances.

Note: When one of the subjects joined by *or* or *nor* is singular and one is plural, the verb must agree with the subject nearer the verb.

Neither Yoshi nor his friends sing in the band anymore. (The plural subject *friends* is nearer the verb, so the plural verb *sing* is correct.)

Compound subjects connected with *and* require a plural verb.

Strength and balance are necessary for gymnastics.

752.2 Delayed Subjects

Delayed subjects occur when the verb comes before the subject in a sentence. In these inverted sentences, the delayed subject must agree with the verb.

There are many hardworking students in our schools.
There is present among many young people today a will to succeed.
(*Students* and *will* are the true subjects of these sentences, not *there*.)

752.3 "Be" Verbs

When a sentence contains a form of the "be" verb—and a noun comes before and after that verb—the verb must agree with the subject, not the *complement* (the noun coming after the verb).

The cause of his problem was the bad brakes.
The bad brakes were the cause of his problem.

752.4 Special Cases

Some nouns that are **plural in form but singular in meaning** take a singular verb: *mumps, measles, news, mathematics, economics, gallows, shambles.*

Measles is still considered a serious disease in many parts of the world.

Some nouns that are plural in form but singular in meaning take a plural verb: *scissors, trousers, tidings.*

The scissors disappear whenever I need them.

Grammar Practice

Agreement of Subject and Verb 1

 For each sentence, write the correct verb from the choice given in parentheses.

1. Neither the school board nor the superintendent *(have, has)* made a decision.

2. On our flight to Italy *(was, were)* several athletes from Team USA.

3. There *(is, are)* too many abandoned animals at the shelter.

4. Someone who adopts one of these animals *(saves, save)* it from an uncertain fate.

5. *(Is, Are)* you interested in adopting a shelter dog?

6. Dwayne or his sisters *(is, are)* going to college in Montana.

7. Great—there *(go, goes)* our train to Chicago!

8. *(Were, Was)* Nina's parents asking about the trip?

9. The Downtown Committee *(is, are)* planning a fall harvest fair.

10. Kandi, Robyn, or Lyndsay *(have, has)* a laptop you might borrow.

11. I can't understand why the soda machines *(are, is)* gone.

12. My dad, as well as his golf partner, *(was, were)* asked to play in the tournament.

 Model

Model the following sentences to practice correct subject-verb agreement.

Her cheekbones were still high and strong, but the skin was parched and ruddy.
— Jeannette Walls, *The Glass Castle: A Memoir*

Blue jeans are the most beautiful things since the gondola.
—Diana Vreeland

Related Skills Activities

■ **SkillsBook**
   Pretest: Subject–Verb Agreement, p. 140
   Subject–Verb Agreement 1, p. 141
   Subject–Verb Agreement 2, p. 142

■ **GrammarSnap**
   Subject-Verb Agreement with Compound Subjects

Answers

1. has
2. were
3. are
4. saves
5. Are
6. are
7. goes
8. Were
9. is
10. has
11. are
12. was

Agreement of Subject and Verb *(continued)*

754.1 Collective Nouns

Collective nouns (*faculty, committee, team, congress, species, crowd, army, pair, squad*) take a singular verb when they refer to a group as a unit; collective nouns take a plural verb when they refer to the individuals within the group.

> **The favored** team **is losing, and the** crowd **is getting ugly.** (Both *team* and *crowd* are considered units in this sentence, requiring the singular verb *is*.)
> **The** pair reunite **after 20 years apart.**
> (Here, *pair* refers to two individuals, so the plural verb *reunite* is required.)

754.2 Indefinite Pronouns

Some **indefinite pronouns** are singular: *each, either, neither, one, everybody, another, anybody, everyone, nobody, everything, somebody,* and *someone.* They require a singular verb.

> Everybody is **invited to the cafeteria for refreshments.**

Some **indefinite pronouns** are plural: *both, few, many,* and *several.*

> Several like **trail-mix bars.** Many ask **for frozen yogurt, too.**

Some **indefinite pronouns** are singular or plural. (See page 250.)

Note: Do not be confused by words or phrases that come between the indefinite pronoun and the verb.

> One **of the participants** is (not *are*) **going to have to stay late to clean up.**

A Closer Look

Some **indefinite pronouns** can be either singular or plural: *all, any, most, none,* and *some.* These pronouns are singular if the number of the noun in the prepositional phrase is singular; they are plural if the noun is plural.

> Most **of the food complaints** are **coming from the seniors.**
> (*Complaints* is plural, so *most* is plural.)
> Most **of the tabletop** is **sticky.**
> (*Tabletop* is singular, so *most* is singular.)

754.3 Relative Pronouns

When a **relative pronoun** (*who, which, that*) is used as the subject of a clause, the number of the verb is determined by the antecedent of the pronoun. (The antecedent is the word to which the pronoun refers.)

> **This is one of the books** that are **required for geography class.**
> (The relative pronoun *that* requires the plural verb *are* because its antecedent, *books,* is plural.)

Note: To test this type of sentence for agreement, read the "of" phrase first.

> **Of the books** that are **required for geography class, this is one.**

Grammar Practice

Agreement of Subject and Verb 2

For each numbered sentence, write the correct verb from the choice given in parentheses.

(1) Imagine that you are a young person who *(live, lives)* in Florida during the first half of the twentieth century. **(2)** You are excited that one of your state's most famous athletes *(is, are)* Babe Didrikson. **(3)** Many girls your age *(credit, credits)* her as a role model. **(4)** Most of the local papers *(carry, carries)* stories about her versatile athletic abilities. **(5)** Because of Babe's basketball skills, her high school team *(play, plays)* in a women's national basketball championship. **(6)** Everyone *(is, are)* thrilled when she sets world records at the Olympics in the 80-yard dash and javelin throw.

(7) Babe's career *(don't, doesn't)* stop there. She pitches on a women's baseball team, and then she tries tennis. **(8)** This is one of the sports that *(is, are)* a problem for Babe. **(9)** The U.S. Lawn Tennis Association *(bar, bars)* her from the game because she plays too well. **(10)** By spring of 1934, Babe *(become, becomes)* famous as one of the top competitors on the professional golf circuit. **(11)** The Associated Press *(take, takes)* notice. **(12)** Its members *(vote, votes)* Babe Didrikson Zaharias the Top Woman Athlete of the Half Century (1900–1949).

Model

Model the following sentences to practice subject-verb agreement.

> **Everybody likes a compliment.**
> —Abraham Lincoln

> **Most of the luxuries and many of the so-called comforts of life are not only not indispensable, but positive hindrances to the elevation of mankind.**
> —Henry David Thoreau

Related Skills Activities

- **SkillsBook**
  Collective Nouns, p. 71
  Indefinite, Interrogative, and Demonstrative Pronouns, p. 82
  Subject–Verb Agreement 1 and 2, pp. 141–142
  Sentence Combining 1 and 2, pp. 151–153

- **GrammarSnap**
  Subject-Verb Agreement with Indefinite Pronouns

Answers

1. lives
2. is
3. credit
4. carry
5. plays
6. is
7. doesn't
8. is
9. bars
10. becomes
11. takes
12. vote

Agreement of Pronoun and Antecedent

A pronoun must agree in number, person, and gender with its *antecedent*. (The *antecedent* is the word to which the pronoun refers.)

> Cal **brought** his **gerbil to school.** (The antecedent of *his* is *Cal.* Both the pronoun and its antecedent are singular, third person, and masculine; therefore, the pronoun is said to "agree" with its antecedent.)

756.1 Agreement in Number

Use a **singular pronoun** to refer to such antecedents as *each, either, neither, one, anyone, anybody, everyone, everybody, somebody, another, nobody,* and *a person.*

> **Neither** of the brothers likes his (not their) **room.**

Two or more singular antecedents joined by *or* or *nor* are also referred to by a **singular pronoun.**

> **Either** Connie or Sue **left** her **headset in the library.**

If one of the antecedents joined by *or* or *nor* is singular and one is plural, the pronoun should agree with the nearer antecedent.

> **Neither the** manager **nor the** players **were crazy about** their **new uniforms.**

Use a **plural pronoun** to refer to plural antecedents as well as compound subjects joined by *and.*

> Jared **and** Carlos **are finishing** their **assignments.**

756.2 Agreement in Gender

Use a **masculine** or **feminine pronoun** depending upon the gender of the antecedent.

> Tristan **would like to bring** his **dog along on the trip.**
> Claire **is always complaining that** her **feet are cold.**

Use a **neuter** pronoun when the antecedent has no gender.

> **The ancient** weeping willow **is losing many of** its **branches.**

When a *person* or *everyone* is used to refer to both sexes or either sex, you will have to choose whether to offer optional pronouns or rewrite the sentence.

> A person **should be allowed to choose** her or his **own footwear.**
> (optional pronouns)
> People **should be allowed to choose** their **own footwear.**
> (rewritten in plural form)

Grammar Practice

Agreement of Pronoun and Antecedent

 For each sentence, write the correct pronoun from the choice given in parentheses.

1. Leah and Abdul made plans to go to *(their, her)* senior prom.
2. Sidnie helped her brother fill out *(his, their)* income tax form.
3. Most of the wall had crayon marks all over *(it, them).*
4. Each college-bound student should have received *(his or her, their)* application materials by now.
5. Francisco or Rory will babysit for *(their, his)* sister this Saturday night.
6. Chuck's new pants were too long, and he didn't know how to hem *(it, them).*
7. Most of the team's shirts had commemorative patches on *(it, them).*
8. Either Mr. Ramos or his son lost *(his, their)* drill at the work site.
9. My Princess Diana rosebush has black spots on *(its, her)* leaves.
10. I asked everyone to bring *(his or her, their)* ideas to the meeting.
11. Neither my motorcycle nor any bicycles had dents on *(it, them)* as a result of the hail.
12. Did anyone leave *(their, his or her)* cell phone at my house last night?

Model

Model the following sentences to practice pronoun-antecedent agreement.

> **A good person will resist an evil system with his or her whole soul.**
> —Mohandas Gandhi

> **Far away, there in the sunshine, are my highest aspirations. I may not reach them, but I can look up and see their beauty, believe in them, and try to follow where they lead.**
> —Louisa May Alcott

Related Skills Activities

- **SkillsBook**
  Pretest: Pronoun–Antecedent Agreement, p. 144
  Pronoun–Antecedent Agreement 1 and 2, pp. 145–146
  Making References Clear, p. 147–148
  Pronoun Shifts 1 and 2, pp. 178–179

- **GrammarSnap**
  Pronoun-Antecedent Agreement

Answers

1. their
2. his
3. it
4. his or her
5. his
6. them
7. them
8. his
9. its
10. his or her
11. them
12. his or her

Test Prep!

Write the letter or letters of the best answer or answers for each underlined part from the choices given on the next page.

Julian is a college student heading to the Gulf Coast, <u>the site of a devastating hurricane.</u> It's spring break, and <u>instead of partying and tanning on the beach, he decided to make a difference.</u> This is his first assignment <u>with the</u> "alternative break" movement.
(1) ... **(2)** ... **(3)**

<u>Colleges and volunteer organizations across the nation</u> encourage students to plan alternative breaks. Thousands of students <u>participate in the program</u> each year. They volunteer <u>to build houses</u> for low-income families, care for AIDS patients, tutor special-needs students, and more.
(4) ... **(5)** ... **(6)**

High school students <u>have been volunteering,</u> too. <u>If you read UCLA's survey of 260,000 college freshmen, the results might surprise you.</u> <u>Desiring to aid their communities,</u> 82 percent had volunteered during their senior year. <u>Volunteering weekly</u> was the goal of 70 percent of those surveyed. Overall, teens volunteered with an organization at nearly double the rate of adults.
(7) ... **(8)** ... **(9)** ... **(10)** ... **(11)**

If you were Julian, <u>how would you be helping?</u> Mucking out damaged homes, <u>clearing debris,</u> and putting tarps on roofs are just a few of the activities you might do. <u>What a huge help you would be to the victims of a hurricane!</u>
(12) ... **(13)** ... **(14)**

1 (A) gerund phrase (B) infinitive phrase (C) participial phrase (D) appositive phrase

2 (A) simple sentence (B) compound-complex sentence (C) compound sentence (D) complex sentence

3 (A) dependent clause (B) independent clause (C) absolute phrase (D) prepositional phrase

4 (A) compound subject (B) delayed subject (C) simple subject (D) complete subject

5 (A) simple predicate (B) complete predicate (C) compound predicate (D) dependent clause

6 (A) gerund phrase (B) infinitive phrase (C) participial phrase (D) appositive phrase

7 (A) gerund phrase (B) participial phrase (C) complete predicate (D) verb phrase

8 (A) complex sentence (B) compound sentence (C) conditional sentence (D) periodic sentence

9 (A) gerund phrase (B) infinitive phrase (C) participial phrase (D) appositive phrase

10 (A) gerund phrase (B) infinitive phrase (C) participial phrase (D) appositive phrase

11 (A) cumulative sentence (B) balanced sentence (C) periodic sentence (D) loose sentence

12 (A) declarative sentence (B) interrogative sentence (C) exclamatory sentence (D) conditional sentence

13 (A) gerund phrase (B) infinitive phrase (C) participial phrase (D) appositive phrase

14 (A) declarative sentence (B) interrogative sentence (C) exclamatory sentence (D) conditional sentence

Related Skills Activities

Answers

1. D		8. A, C	
2. C		9. C	
3. D		10. A	
4. A, D		11. C	
5. B		12. B, D	
6. B		13. A	
7. D		14. C	

Diagramming Sentences

A **graphic diagram** of a sentence is a picture of how the words in that sentence are related and how they fit together to form a complete thought.

760.1 Simple Sentence with One Subject and One Verb

Chris fishes.

| subject | verb |

760.2 Simple Sentence with a Predicate Adjective

Fish are delicious.

| subject | verb | predicate adjective |

760.3 Simple Sentence with a Predicate Noun and Adjectives

Fishing is my favorite hobby.

| subject | verb | predicate noun | adjective | adjective |

Note: When possessive pronouns (*my, his, their,* etc.) are used as adjectives, they are placed on a diagonal line under the word they modify.

760.4 Simple Sentence with an Indirect and Direct Object

My grandpa gave us a trout.

| subject | verb | direct object | adjective | indirect object | adjective |

Note: Articles (*a, an, the*) are adjectives and are placed on a diagonal line under the word they modify.

Grammar Practice

Sentence Diagramming 1

 Diagram the following sentences.

1. Jerry MacDonald studies ancient fossils.
2. The New Mexico desert is his workplace.
3. His discoveries are incredible!
4. The Paleozoic Trackways Project was his best find.
5. Jerry dug.
6. He unearthed interesting tracks.
7. He showed some colleagues his discovery.
8. The tracks were prehistoric.
9. They gave us a new understanding.
10. Paleontology is exciting!

Half a truth is often a great lie.

—Benjamin Franklin

Model

Model the following proverbs to practice writing simple sentences with direct objects.

The early bird catches the worm.
The big thieves hang the little ones.

 Answers for page 761

1.  Jerry MacDonald | studies | fossils \ ancient

2. desert | is \ workplace / The / New Mexico \ his

3. discoveries | are \ incredible \ His

4. Paleozoic Trackways Project | was \ find \ The \ his \ best

5. Jerry | dug

6. He | unearthed | tracks \ interesting

7. He | showed | discovery / colleagues \ his \ some

8. tracks | were \ prehistoric \ The

9. They | gave | understanding \ us \ a \ new

10. Paleontology | is \ exciting

Diagramming Sentences (continued)

762.1 Simple Sentence with a Prepositional Phrase

I like fishing by myself.

762.2 Simple Sentence with a Compound Subject and Verb

The team and fans clapped and cheered.

762.3 Compound Sentence

The team scored, and the crowd cheered wildly.

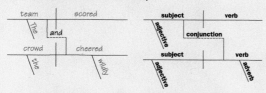

762.4 Complex Sentence with a Subordinate Clause

Before Erin scored, the crowd sat quietly.

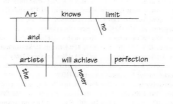

Grammar Practice

Sentence Diagramming 2

 Diagram the following sentences.

1. Jamar completed the first leg of the triathlon.
2. Landon and his dad explored caves with a guide.
3. In our high school, the principal has the toughest job.
4. The guard on duty at the mall always wears a uniform.
5. I will be tired when I get home from the game.
6. Geeta and Melissa went to the sale and bought some shoes.
7. You can grow awesome flowers, but it takes a "green thumb."
8. Some students are unprepared and so do not have control over their futures.
9. Hector went for a swim in the lake.
10. Lauren laughed, but her dad frowned.

Art knows no limit, and the artists will never achieve perfection.

—Bente Borsum

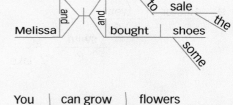

Model

Model the following sentences to practice writing compound and complex sentences.

If at first you don't succeed, you're running about average.

—M. H. Alderson

I think, therefore I am.

—Rene Descartes

Answers for page 763

1.
2.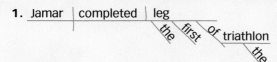
3.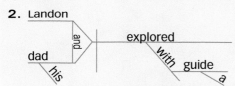
4.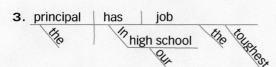

5.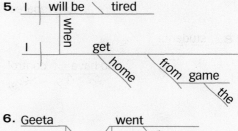
6.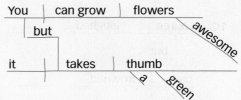

Answers 8–10 are on page 764.

(continued from page 763)

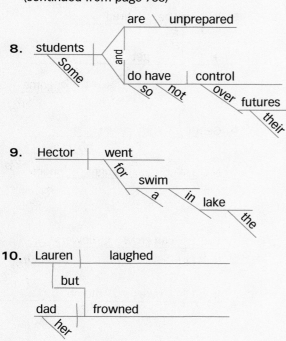

ASSESSMENT SHEET AND RUBRICS

BENCHMARK PAPERS

GRAPHIC ORGANIZERS

GETTING STARTED

INDEX

Assessment Sheet

 **Directions** Use one of the rubrics listed below to rate a piece of writing. Circle the rubric your teacher tells you to use. If you need information about assessing with a rubric, see pages 40–45 in your *Write Source* book.

- ■ **Narrative Rubric (pages 150–151)**
- ■ **Expository Rubric (pages 198–199)**
- ■ **Persuasive Rubric (pages 254–255)**
- ■ **Response to Literature (pages 310–311)**

Title _____

____ **Ideas**

____ **Organization**

____ **Voice**

____ **Word Choice**

____ **Sentence Fluency**

____ **Conventions**

Evaluator_____

Rubric for Narrative Writing

Ideas

6 The narrative shares a memorable event. Details bring the essay to life.

5 The writer shares an interesting experience. Specific details help maintain interest.

4 The writer tells about an interesting experience. Details need to show, not tell.

3 The writer should focus on one event. Some details do not relate to the essay.

2 The writer should focus on one experience. More details are needed.

1 The writer should select an experience and provide details.

Organization

6 The structure of the narrative makes it enjoyable and easy to read.

5 The narrative has a clear beginning, middle, and ending. Transitions are helpful.

4 For the most part, the narrative is organized. Most of the transitions are helpful.

3 The order of events must be corrected. More transitions are needed.

2 The beginning, middle, and ending all run together. The order is unclear.

1 The narrative must be organized.

Voice

6 The writer's voice captures the experience for the reader.

5 The writer's voice sounds natural. Dialogue helps hold the reader's interest.

4 The writer's voice creates interest in the essay, but dialogue needs to sound more natural.

3 The writer's voice can usually be heard. More dialogue is needed.

2 The voice is weak. Dialogue is needed.

1 The writer sounds uninvolved or disinterested in the essay.

Word Choice

6 The writer's excellent word choice creates a vivid picture of the event.

5 Specific nouns, verbs, and modifiers create clear images and feelings.

4 Some stronger nouns, verbs, and/or modifiers would create a clearer picture.

3 More specific nouns, verbs, and modifiers would paint a clearer picture of the event.

2 Better words are needed. Words are overused or too general to paint a clear picture.

1 The writer has not considered word choice or has used words incorrectly.

Sentence Fluency

6 The sentences are skillfully written to hold the reader's interest.

5 The sentences are skillfully written, show variety, and are easy to understand.

4 The sentences are varied, but some should flow more smoothly.

3 A better variety of sentences is needed. Sentences do not flow smoothly.

2 Many incomplete or short sentences make the writing choppy.

1 Few sentences are written well. Help is needed.

Conventions

6 The narrative has no errors in spelling, grammar, or punctuation.

5 The narrative has one or two errors in spelling, grammar, or punctuation.

4 The narrative has a few minor errors in punctuation, grammar, or spelling.

3 The narrative has several errors.

2 Numerous errors make the narrative hard to read and confusing.

1 Help is needed to find errors and make corrections.

6-Point

Rubric for Expository Writing

Ideas
6 The ideas in the essay are compelling from start to finish.
5 The essay is informative with a clear thesis and specific details.
4 The essay is informative with a clear thesis. More specific details are needed.
3 The thesis of the essay should be clearer, and more specific details are needed.
2 The topic should be narrowed or expanded. Many more specific details are needed.
1 The writer should select a new topic.

Organization
6 The essay shows thoughtful use of an organizational pattern. Transitions are strong.
5 The beginning interests the reader. The middle supports the focus. The ending works well. Transitions are used.
4 The essay is divided into a beginning, a middle, and an ending. Some transitions are used.
3 The beginning or ending is weak. The middle needs a paragraph for each main point. More transitions are needed.
2 The beginning, middle, and ending all run together. Paragraph breaks and transitions are needed.
1 The essay should be reorganized.

Voice
6 The writing voice is lively, engaging, and memorable.
5 The writer's voice sounds knowledgeable and confident. It fits the audience.
4 The writer's voice sounds knowledgeable most of the time and fits the audience.
3 The writer sometimes sounds unsure, and the voice needs to better fit the audience.
2 The writer sounds unsure. The voice needs to fit the audience.
1 The writer needs to learn about voice.

Word Choice
6 Word choice is vivid and precise. Special terms are defined or explained.
5 Specific nouns and action verbs make the essay clear and informative.
4 Some nouns and verbs could be more specific.
3 Too many general words are used. Specific nouns and verbs are needed.
2 General or missing words make this essay difficult to understand.
1 The writer needs help finding specific words.

Sentence Fluency
6 Sentences are carefully crafted. Sentences flow naturally and vary in type and length.
5 The sentences have flair and flavor, and the reader will enjoy them.
4 Most of the sentences read smoothly, but some are short and choppy.
3 Short, choppy sentences need to be rewritten to make the essay read smoothly.
2 Many sentences are choppy or incomplete and need to be rewritten.
1 Most sentences need to be rewritten.

Conventions
6 Editing shows mastery of conventions. The essay is error free.
5 The essay has one or two errors.
4 The essay has some errors in punctuation, spelling, or grammar.
3 Several errors confuse the reader.
2 Many errors make the essay difficult to read.
1 Help is needed to make corrections.

6-Point

Rubric for Persuasive Writing

Ideas

6 The position is convincingly presented and supported; it compels the reader to act.

5 The position is convincingly supported and defended.

4 Most reasons support the writer's position. An important objection is addressed.

3 More supporting reasons and a more convincing response to an objection are needed.

2 A clearer position statement is needed. Better support for the position must be provided.

1 A new position statement and reasons are needed.

Organization

6 All parts of the essay work together to build a very thoughtful, convincing position.

5 The opening states the position, the middle provides clear support, and the ending reinforces the position.

4 Most parts of the essay are organized adequately except for one part.

3 Some parts of the essay need to be reorganized.

2 The beginning, middle, and ending run together.

1 The organization is unclear and incomplete.

Voice

6 The writer's voice is completely confident, knowledgeable, and convincing.

5 The writer's voice is confident, knowledgeable, and convincing in the main.

4 The writer's voice is respectful, but needs to sound more persuasive or knowledgeable.

3 The writer's voice needs to be more persuasive and respectful.

2 The writer's voice sounds too emotional and unconvincing.

1 The writer needs to learn about voice in persuasive writing.

Word Choice

6 The writer's choice of words makes a powerful case and helps persuade the reader.

5 The writer's choice of words makes a powerful case.

4 The writer avoids inflammatory (unfair) words but needs to remove some qualifiers.

3 The writer needs to change some inflammatory words and remove some qualifiers.

2 The words do not create a clear message. Some inflammatory words are used.

1 Word choice for persuasive writing has not been considered.

Sentence Fluency

6 The sentences flow smoothly throughout the strong essay.

5 The sentences spark the reader's interest in the essay.

4 Variety is seen in both the types of sentences and their beginnings.

3 Variety is seen in most of the sentences.

2 More variety is needed in the beginnings or kinds of sentences used.

1 Sentence fluency has not been considered.

Conventions

6 The writing is error free.

5 The writing has one or two errors.

4 Grammar and punctuation errors are few. The reader is not distracted by the errors.

3 Several distracting grammar and punctuation errors confuse the reader.

2 Frequent errors make the essay difficult to read.

1 Nearly every sentence contains errors.

Rubric for Response to Literature

Ideas

6 The ideas show a complete understanding of the reading and form a compelling analysis.
5 The ideas show a complete understanding of the reading.
4 The essay has a clear focus statement. Unnecessary details need to be cut.
3 The focus statement is too broad. A variety of details is needed.
2 The focus statement is unclear. More details are needed.
1 The essay needs a focus statement and details.

Organization

6 All the parts work together to create an insightful essay.
5 The organization pattern fits the topic and purpose. All parts of the essay are well developed.
4 The organization pattern fits the topic and purpose. A part of the essay needs better development.
3 The organization fits the essay's purpose. Some parts need more development.
2 The organization doesn't fit the purpose.
1 A plan needs to be followed.

Voice

6 The voice expresses interest and complete understanding and engages the reader.
5 The voice expresses interest and complete understanding.
4 The voice expresses interest but needs to show more understanding.
3 The voice needs to be more interesting and express more understanding.
2 The voice does not show interest in or an understanding of the topic.
1 The writer needs to understand how to create voice.

Word Choice

6 The word choice is precise and colorful and reflects a thorough understanding of the reading.
5 The word choice, including the use of figures of speech, creates a clear message.
4 The word choice is clear, but more figures of speech would improve the essay.
3 The word choice is too general, and more figures of speech are needed.
2 Little attention was given to word choice.
1 The writer needs help with word choice.

Sentence Fluency

6 The sentences in the essay are skillfully written and create a clear flow of ideas.
5 The sentences flow well and make the ideas plain.
4 No sentence problems exist. More sentence variety is needed.
3 A few sentence problems need to be corrected.
2 The essay has many sentence problems.
1 The writer needs to learn how to construct sentences.

Conventions

6 Grammar and punctuation are correct, and the copy is free of errors.
5 Grammar and punctuation are correct in the main, with one or two errors.
4 The essay has a few careless errors in punctuation and grammar that do not interfere with the reader's understanding.
3 The errors in the essay confuse the reader.
2 The number of errors make the essay hard to read.
1 Help is needed to make corrections.

5-Point

Rubric for Narrative Writing

Use this rubric for guiding and assessing your narrative writing. Refer to it whenever you want to improve your writing using the six traits.

Ideas

5 The writer shares an interesting experience. Specific details help maintain interest.
4 The writer tells about an interesting experience. Details should show, not tell.
3 The writer should focus on one event. Some details do not relate to the essay.
2 The writer should focus on one experience. More details are needed.
1 The writer should select an experience and provide details.

Organization

5 The narrative has a clear beginning, middle, and ending. Transitions are helpful.
4 For the most part, the narrative is organized. Most of the transitions are helpful.
3 The order of events must be corrected. More transitions are needed.
2 The beginning, middle, and ending all run together. The order is unclear.
1 The narrative must be better organized.

Voice

5 The writer's voice sounds natural. Dialogue helps hold the reader's interest.
4 The writer's voice creates interest in the essay, but dialogue should sound more natural.
3 The writer's voice usually can be heard. More dialogue is needed.
2 The voice is weak. Dialogue is needed.
1 The writer sounds uninvolved or disinterested in the essay.

Word Choice

5 Specific nouns, verbs, and modifiers create clear images and feelings.
4 Some stronger nouns, verbs, and/or modifiers would create a clearer picture.
3 More specific nouns, verbs, and modifiers would paint a clearer picture of the event.
2 Better words are needed. Many are overused or too general to paint a clear picture.
1 The writer has not considered word choice or has used words incorrectly.

Sentence Fluency

5 The sentences are skillfully written, show variety, and are easy to understand.
4 The sentences are varied, but some should flow more smoothly.
3 A better variety of sentences is needed. Sentences do not flow smoothly.
2 Many incomplete or short sentences make the writing choppy.
1 Few sentences are written well. Help is needed.

Conventions

5 The narrative has no errors in spelling, grammar, or punctuation.
4 The narrative has a few minor errors in punctuation, grammar, or spelling.
3 The narrative has several errors.
2 Numerous errors make the narrative hard to read and confusing.
1 Help is needed to find errors and make corrections.

5-Point

Rubric for Expository Writing

Use this rubric for guiding and assessing your expository writing. Refer to it to help you improve your writing using the six traits.

Ideas

5 The essay shows a clear relationship between thesis and supporting evidence.

4 The essay presents a clear topic and thesis. More support is needed.

3 The essay shows some understanding of the topic and thesis. More support is needed.

2 The topic and thesis should be more focused. The essay needs specific support that relates to the topic.

1 The topic should be reworked and a new thesis formed.

Organization

5 The essay uses an effective organizational pattern. Transitions are strong.

4 The essay follows an organizational pattern. Transitions could be stronger.

3 The essay does not follow an organizational pattern. Key points need separate paragraphs and transitions.

2 The beginning, middle, and ending parts need to be made clear.

1 The essay must be rewritten using an organizational plan.

Voice

5 Voice is appropriate for the topic, purpose, and audience and sounds knowledgeable.

4 Voice fits the audience and sounds knowledgeable in most places.

3 Voice sounds uneven. It should match topic, purpose, and audience.

2 Voice sounds as if the writer does not have a good understanding of the subject.

1 Voice does not show confidence.

Word Choice

5 Word choice is vivid and precise. Special terms are defined or explained.

4 Word choice is effective. Words are not repeated and special terms are defined.

3 Word choice is adequate. Some overused words could be replaced.

2 Word choice needs to be more precise, and overused words need to be replaced.

1 The writer needs help choosing stronger words throughout.

Sentence Fluency

5 Sentences are carefully crafted. Sentences flow naturally and vary in type and length.

4 Sentences flow well and are varied in type and length.

3 Sentences are basic. More variety is needed in sentence type and length.

2 Too many sentences are simple and begin the same way.

1 Most sentences need to be rewritten.

Conventions

5 Editing shows mastery of conventions. The essay is error free.

4 Editing is effective, but a few errors in grammar, spelling, or punctuation remain.

3 Control of conventions is basic. Errors sometimes get in the way of understanding.

2 Many corrections are needed to make the essay less confusing.

1 The writer needs help to understand and edit conventions.

5-Point

Rubric for Persuasive Writing

Use the following rubric for guiding and assessing your persuasive writing. Refer to it whenever you want to improve your writing using the six traits.

Ideas
5 The position is convincingly presented and supported; it compels the reader to act.
4 Most of the reasons support the writer's position. An objection is addressed.
3 More supporting reasons and a more convincing response to an objection are needed.
2 A clearer position statement is needed. Better support for the position must be provided.
1 A new position statement and reasons are needed.

Organization
5 All parts of the essay work together to build a very thoughtful, convincing position.
4 The opening states the position, the middle provides clear support, and the ending reinforces the position.
3 Most parts of the essay are organized adequately except for one part.
2 Some parts of the essay need to be reorganized.
1 The organization is unclear and incomplete.

Voice
5 The writer's voice is persuasive, knowledgeable, and respectful.
4 The writer respects the audience but needs to sound more persuasive or knowledgeable.
3 The writer's voice needs to be more persuasive and respectful.
2 The writer's voice sounds too emotional and unconvincing.
1 The writer needs to learn about voice in persuasive writing.

Word Choice
5 The writer's choice of words makes a powerful case and helps persuade the reader.
4 The writer avoids unneeded modifiers but needs to remove some repetition.
3 The writer needs to change modifiers and remove some repetition.
2 The words do not create a clear message. Some words are repeated.
1 Word choice for persuasive writing has not been considered.

Sentence Fluency
5 The sentences flow smoothly throughout the strong essay.
4 Variety is seen in the types of sentences used and in their beginnings.
3 Variety is seen in most of the sentences.
2 More variety is needed in the beginnings or kinds of sentences used.
1 Sentence fluency has not been considered.

Conventions
5 The writing is error free.
4 Grammar and punctuation errors are few. The reader is not distracted by the errors.
3 Distracting grammar and punctuation errors are seen in a few sentences.
2 Frequent errors make the essay difficult to read.
1 Nearly every sentence contains errors.

5-Point

Rubric for Response to Literature

Use this rubric for guiding and assessing your writing. Refer to it whenever you want to improve your writing using the six traits.

Ideas
5 The essay has a clear focus statement and necessary supporting details.
4 The essay has a clear focus statement. Unnecessary details need to be cut.
3 The focus statement is too broad. A variety of details are needed.
2 The focus statement is unclear. More details are needed.
1 The essay needs a focus statement and details.

Organization
5 The organization pattern fits the topic and purpose. All parts of the essay are well developed.
4 The organization pattern fits the topic and purpose. A part of the essay needs better development.
3 The organization fits the essay's purpose. Some parts need more development.
2 The organization doesn't fit the purpose.
1 A plan needs to be followed.

Voice
5 The voice expresses interest and complete understanding. It engages the reader.
4 The voice expresses interest but needs to show more understanding.
3 The voice needs to be more interesting and express more understanding.
2 The voice does not show interest in or an understanding of the topic.
1 The writer needs to understand how to create voice.

Word Choice
5 The word choice, including the use of quotations, creates a clear message.
4 The word choice is clear, but better quotations would improve the essay.
3 The word choice is too general, and quotations are needed.
2 Little attention is given to word choice.
1 The writer needs help with word choice.

Sentence Fluency
5 The sentences are skillfully written and keep the reader's interest.
4 No sentence problems exist. More sentence variety is needed.
3 A few sentence problems need to be corrected.
2 The essay has many sentence problems.
1 The writer needs to learn how to construct sentences.

Conventions
5 Grammar and punctuation are correct, and the copy is free of all errors.
4 The essay has one or two errors that do not interfere with the reader's understanding.
3 The essay has a few careless errors in punctuation and grammar.
2 The errors in the essay confuse the reader.
1 Help is needed to make corrections.

4-Point

Rubric for Narrative Writing

Use this rubric for guiding and assessing your narrative writing. Refer to it whenever you want to improve your writing using the six traits.

Ideas
4 The writer shares an interesting experience. Specific details help maintain interest.
3 The writer tells about an interesting experience. Details should show, not tell.
2 The writer should focus on one event. More details are needed.
1 The writer should select an experience and provide details.

Organization
4 The narrative has a clear beginning, middle, and ending. Transitions are helpful.
3 For the most part, the narrative is organized. Most of the transitions are helpful.
2 The order of events must be corrected. More transitions are needed.
1 The beginning, middle, and ending all run together. The narrative must be better organized.

Voice
4 The writer's voice sounds natural. Dialogue helps hold the reader's interest.
3 The writer's voice creates interest in the essay, but dialogue should sound more natural.
2 The writer's voice is weak. More dialogue is needed.
1 The writer sounds uninvolved or disinterested in the essay.

Word Choice
4 Specific nouns, verbs, and modifiers create clear images and feelings.
3 More specific nouns, verbs, and modifiers would paint a clearer picture of the event.
2 Better words are needed. Words are overused or too general to paint a clear picture.
1 The writer has not considered word choice or has used words incorrectly.

Sentence Fluency
4 The sentences are skillfully written, show variety, and are easy to understand.
3 The sentences are varied, but some should flow more smoothly.
2 A better variety of sentences is needed. Sentences do not flow smoothly.
1 Few sentences are written well. Help is needed.

Conventions
4 The narrative has no errors in spelling, grammar, or punctuation.
3 The narrative has several errors.
2 Numerous errors make the narrative hard to read and confusing.
1 Help is needed to find errors and make corrections.

4-Point

Rubric for Expository Writing

Use this rubric for guiding and assessing your expository writing. Refer to it to help you improve your writing using the six traits.

Ideas
4 The essay shows a clear relationship between thesis and supporting evidence.
3 The essay shows some understanding of the topic and thesis. More support is needed.
2 The topic and thesis should be more focused. The essay needs specific support that relates to the topic.
1 The topic should be reworked and a new thesis formed.

Organization
4 The essay uses an effective organizational pattern. Transitions are strong.
3 The essay follows an organizational pattern. Transitions could be stronger.
2 The essay does not follow an organizational pattern. Key points need separate paragraphs and transitions.
1 The essay must be rewritten using an organizational plan.

Voice
4 Voice is appropriate for the topic, purpose, and audience and sounds knowledgeable.
3 Voice fits the audience and sounds knowledgeable in most places.
2 Voice sounds uneven. It should match topic, purpose, and audience.
1 Voice does not show confidence.

Word Choice
4 Word choice is vivid and precise. Special terms are defined or explained.
3 Word choice is effective. Words are not repeated and special terms are defined.
2 Word choice is adequate. Some overused words could be replaced.
1 Word choice needs to be more precise and overused words need to be replaced.

Sentence Fluency
4 Sentences are carefully crafted. Sentences flow naturally and vary in type and length.
3 Sentences flow well and are varied in type and length.
2 Sentences are basic. More variety is needed in sentence type and length.
1 Too many sentences are simple and begin the same way.

Conventions
4 Editing shows mastery of conventions. The essay is error free.
3 Editing is effective, but a few errors in grammar, spelling, or punctuation remain.
2 Control of conventions is basic. Errors sometimes get in the way of understanding.
1 Many corrections are needed to make the essay less confusing.

4-Point

Rubric for Persuasive Writing

Use the following rubric for guiding and assessing your persuasive writing. Refer to it whenever you want to improve your writing using the six traits.

Ideas

4 The position is convincingly presented and supported; it compels the reader to act.

3 Most of the reasons support the writer's position. An objection is addressed.

2 More supporting reasons and a more convincing response to an objection are needed.

1 A clearer position statement is needed. Better support for the position must be provided.

Organization

4 All parts of the essay work together to build a very thoughtful, convincing position.

3 The opening states the position, the middle provides clear support, and the ending reinforces the position.

2 Some parts of the essay need to be reorganized.

1 The organization is unclear and incomplete.

Voice

4 The writer's voice is persuasive, knowledgeable, and respectful.

3 The writer respects the audience but needs to sound more persuasive or knowledgeable.

2 The writer's voice needs to be more persuasive and respectful.

1 The writer needs to learn about voice in persuasive writing.

Word Choice

4 The writer's choice of words makes a powerful case and helps persuade the reader.

3 The writer avoids unneeded modifiers but needs to remove some repetition.

2 The writer needs to change modifiers and remove some repetition.

1 The words do not create a clear message. Some words are repeated.

Sentence Fluency

4 The sentences flow smoothly throughout the strong essay.

3 Variety is seen in the types of sentences used and in their beginnings.

2 Variety is seen in most of the sentences.

1 More variety is needed in the beginnings or kinds of sentences used.

Conventions

4 The writing is error free.

3 Grammar and punctuation errors are few. The reader is not distracted by the errors.

2 Distracting grammar and punctuation errors are seen in a few sentences.

1 Frequent errors make the essay difficult to read.

4-Point

Rubric for Response to Literature

Use this rubric for guiding and assessing your writing. Refer to it whenever you want to improve your writing using the six traits.

Ideas
4 The essay has a clear focus statement and necessary supporting details.
3 The essay has a clear focus statement. Unnecessary details need to be cut.
2 The focus statement is unclear. More details are needed.
1 The essay needs a focus statement and details.

Organization
4 The organization pattern fits the topic and purpose. All parts of the essay are well developed.
3 The organization pattern fits the topic and purpose. A part of the essay needs better development.
2 The organization fits the essay's purpose. Some parts need more development.
1 The organization doesn't fit the purpose.

Voice
4 The voice expresses interest and complete understanding. It engages the reader.
3 The voice expresses interest but needs to show more understanding.
2 The voice needs to be more interesting and express more understanding.
1 The voice does not show interest in or an understanding of the topic.

Word Choice
4 The word choice, including the use of quotations, creates a clear message.
3 The word choice is clear, but better quotations would improve the essay.
2 The word choice is too general, and quotations are needed.
1 Little attention is given to word choice.

Sentence Fluency
4 The sentences are skillfully written and keep the reader's interest.
3 No sentence problems exist. More sentence variety is needed.
2 A few sentence problems need to be corrected.
1 The essay has many sentence problems.

Conventions
4 Grammar and punctuation are correct, and the copy is free of all errors.
3 The essay has one or two errors that do not interfere with the reader's understanding.
2 The essay has a few careless errors in punctuation and grammar.
1 The errors in the essay confuse the reader.

Narrative Rubric Checklist

Title _____

_____ Ideas
- Is the narrative about making the right decision for the wrong reason?
- Is background information provided?
- Does the narrative include specific details and dialogue?

_____ Organization
- Does the beginning interest the reader?
- Does the middle include a series of actions that build to the climax?
- Does the ending show what was learned?

_____ Voice
- Does the writing sound natural?
- Does the dialogue sound realistic?

_____ Word Choice
- Does the writing contain vivid verbs and specific nouns?
- Does it contain descriptive modifiers?

_____ Sentence Fluency
- Do the sentences flow smoothly?
- Is the writing free of fragments and rambling sentences?

_____ Conventions
- Does the narrative avoid careless errors?
- Is the dialogue correctly punctuated?

Expository Rubric Checklist

Title _____

____ Ideas
- Does my essay include a clear thesis statement?
- Do I support my thesis with a variety of details?

____ Organization
- Does my overall structure work well?
- Have I used signal words to make my structure clear?

____ Voice
- Are most of my sentences active?
- Do I use third-person point of view consistently?

____ Word Choice
- Do I use words with the appropriate connotation?
- Do I use words with the correct denotation?

____ Sentence Fluency
- Are all my series parallel?
- Are my comparisons clear and complete?

____ Conventions
- Do I use correct punctuation, capitalization, spelling, and grammar?

Persuasive Rubric Checklist

Title _____

____ ## Ideas
- Does my essay include a clear position statement?
- Do I support my position with reasons and details?
- Do I avoid logic errors?

____ ## Organization
- Does the beginning introduce the topic and state the position?
- Does the middle support my position?
- Does my ending restate the position and offer a final thought?

____ ## Voice
- Do I use the right level of language?
- Do I connect with the reader?

____ ## Word Choice
- Have I used only necessary modifiers?
- Have I avoided repeating words too often?

____ ## Sentence Fluency
- Do I use long sentences effectively?
- Do I use short sentences effectively?

____ ## Conventions
- Have I avoided most errors in punctuation, capitalization, spelling, and grammar?

Response-to-Literature Rubric Checklist

Title _____

____ **Ideas**
- Do I have a clear thesis statement?
- Do I use effective details?

____ **Organization**
- Does the beginning state the thesis?
- Does the middle focus on major elements?
- Does the ending expand the theme?

____ **Voice**
- Is my voice suitably analytical?
- Is my voice compelling as I narrate the plot?

____ **Word Choice**
- Have I used correct literary terminology?
- Have I focused on symbols?

____ **Sentence Fluency**
- Do my sentences read smoothly?

____ **Conventions**
- Have I followed the rules of English?

Narrative Writing

My Escape from Vietnam

1   During the summer of 1987, I had just finished the assessment

2   test for junior high and was ready to take the high school entrance

3   test. My family and I were aware, however, that it would be rather

4   difficult for me to continue my education and lifestyle under the

5   Communist government. My father had worked for the South

6   Vietnamese government before the Communist takeover in 1975,

7   a fact that would not be looked upon favorably by the new regime.

8   Moreover, current policy dictated a mandatory two-year stint in the

9   army on reaching age seventeen. I found this fact quite unsettling,

10   for most seventeen-year-olds I knew had been sent to Cambodia only

11   to return with a missing arm or leg. My parents could not imagine

12   seeing me in army fatigues, so they arranged for my older sister and

13   me to escape from Vietnam.

14   We made our first escape attempt in early May of 1987, leaving

15   at daybreak so as not to arouse suspicion. My parents gave us

16   some cash, food, and gold that we concealed in our waistbands. We

17   planned to use the precious commodity for necessities when we got to

18   Thailand.

19   As I had never taken a major trip away from home, I was quite

20   saddened saying good-bye to our parents, watching tears stream

21   down their faces. My parents asked us to be careful, take care of each

22   other, and write them immediately when we got to Thailand. I was

23   too young to understand the significance of the trip, but looking back,

24   I realize that it had a huge impact on my future.

25   When that first escape attempt proved unsuccessful, we returned

26   to Vietnam and waited for another opportunity. Weeks later, my

27   father, a younger brother, an uncle, and a cousin accompanied my

28   sister and me to the harbor of Phnom Penh. It was raining cats and

29   dogs and a powerful wind blew against our movement. Lightning and

30   thunder were on our side as they guided and silenced our footsteps.

31   Upon reaching the harbor, we discovered that we would have

32   to swim 200 yards to reach our boat to freedom. We watched others

33   jump into the angry ocean and move away from the shore. Our family

34   remained on land because my father was the only one of us who

35   knew how to swim. Driven by a determination to find a better life for

36   his children, my father put my brother on his shoulders and walked

37   his way to the boat. The sight of the strong waves pushing my father

38   back and forth, causing him to swallow mouthfuls of seawater, moved

39   me to tears. After depositing my brother on the big boat, my father

40   came back, put me on his shoulders, and began his second trip. I

41   could feel my father's trembling movements, stopping sometimes for

42   the unwelcome waves or gasping for the nonexistent air as his whole

43   body went underwater. There were times when I thought he would

44 let go of me and come up for air, but he kept going until we finally

45 reached the boat. He deposited me next to my brother and then

46 made his last trip to get my sister. As I watched him, I prayed that

47 something would keep my father and sister from the hungry mouth

48 of the ocean. My prayers were answered because my father and sister

49 made their way to the boat a few moments later. As we headed to

50 Thailand, strong waves shook the boat vigorously causing all of us to

51 vomit repeatedly. I could feel and taste the bitter, sour stomach juice

52 on my tongue and my mouth. I remember thinking that death would

53 be nicer than going through this.

54   We did finally reach Thailand and the events that occurred

55 during our journey there represent a turning point in my life. I now

56 realize that freedom is precious; I do not take it for granted. My

57 experience also demonstrated the depth of parents' love for their

58 children. I am thankful every day for being the recipient of such love.

Narrative Rubric Checklist

Title ___*My Escape from Vietnam*_____

_4_ Ideas

- Is the narrative about a meaningful experience?
- Is background information provided?
- Does the narrative include specific details and dialogue?

_6_ Organization

- Does the beginning interest the reader?
- Does the middle include a series of actions that build to the climax?
- Does the ending show what was learned?

_4_ Voice

- Does the writing sound natural?
- Does the dialogue sound realistic?

_6_ Word Choice

- Does the writing contain vivid verbs and specific nouns?
- Does it contain descriptive modifiers?

_6_ Sentence Fluency

- Do the sentences flow smoothly?
- Is the writing free of fragments and rambling sentences?

_6_ Conventions

- Does the narrative avoid careless errors?
- Is the dialogue correctly punctuated?

OVERALL COMMENTS

- Your writing focuses on a turning point in your life. You provide the reader with background information that explains the need for your life-threatening escape. However, your writing lacks dialogue, which would help build suspense and provide more specific details about your journey.

- Your writing begins with an interesting opening that causes a reader to want to learn whether you successfully escape your native land. In your middle paragraphs, you build suspense that leads to a harrowing climax. In your ending, you reflect on what you have learned.

- Your writer's voice sounds quite natural. However, your essay lacks dialogue that would "show" readers what you and your family members felt and thought during your journey.

- Your narrative includes specific nouns, active verbs, and descriptive modifiers. Including figures of speech in your writing (lightning and thunder were on our side . . .) makes readers feel as if they are traveling alongside you.

- Throughout your writing, you used long and short sentences effectively. As a result, your essay flows smoothly and holds the reader's attention.

- Your narrative lacks errors in spelling, grammar, and punctuation.

Narrative Writing

Learning to Express Our Love

1   My brother Ross and I never got along, and we fought all the
2 time. I have many memories of all the times we yelled at each other.

3   Ross was always a ringleader, he did not like me so no one else
4 could either. Ross, my sister Janna, and their friends played a game
5 called ditch her. When I heard the words "ditch her," I knew what
6 was going to happen. They would get on their bikes and take off until
7 they ditched me. They were all a few years older, so I never caught
8 up. I would go home crying. Ross and Janna would usually be in
9 trouble when they got home, which made them hate me more.

10   Ross never wanted to be where I was or doing the same thing I
11 was thats because I was a tomboy and liked to play outside with the
12 neighborhood boys. They played football 24 hours a day, seven days
13 a week. Many of the guys liked it when I played, but of course Ross
14 hated it and if he was playing, he would quit and go sit inside.

15   Many of Ross's words impacted my life. Many of them I will
16 never forget. We said a great deal of harsh words to each other. There
17 is no way to take any of them back. I really did love my brother. But,
18 I could not show it. He did not like me. So, I acted like I did not like
19 him either. Many times I laid in bed wondering when we would get
20 along. I tried to think of when the first time would be when he would
21 give me a hug. I thought and hoped that he would give me a hug at

22 his high school graduation. My hope came true a couple of months

23 before his graduation. Ross played basketball and in his senior year

24 they won the state championship. He gave me a hug after they won,

25 the first hug that I can remember! He also gave me a hug at his

26 graduation from high school and at my graduation from grade school.

27 I could not believe it!

28   When Ross went to college, we finally started getting along.

29 There was one incident which turned everything around. My sister

30 Janna and I had a tournament softball game and my parents had not

31 been at a game for a while. I was looking all over for them but I could

32 not find them. My little sister Jill was there and told Janna that our

33 parents were not coming because something had happened. We knew

34 something was wrong but we did not know what. We found after the

35 game that Ross and his girlfriend Angie had a car accident!

36   Ross was in an accident! I could not believe it! The ride home

37 was the longest ride ever. We did not know how badly they were hurt.

38 All we knew was that Angie was rushed to the hospital. My aunt and

39 uncle took me and my sisters home. We cried the whole way home. I

40 was so scared! I will never forget the moment I walked into our house

41 that night. Ross was sitting on a stool by the phone talking to Angie's

42 mom and dad, who were in the hospital with her. He was crying like I

43 have never seen a guy cry before. Their he sat on the stool with blood,

44 cuts and stitches on his head. Tears ran down his face. The sight

45 brought another flow of tears to my eyes. It hit me that he could

46 have been gone and I knew right then how much I loved him! Many

47 times we do not appreciate the things we have until they are gone, or

48 almost gone! When Ross got off the phone, I gave him an enormous

49 hug and said "I love you!" It came from the bottom of my heart. I still

50 feel that love today, and I always will!

51   The next day in church I cried threw every song. I had finally

52 realized how much Ross meant to me. I was so thankful that his life

53 was spared!

Narrative Rubric Checklist

Title __*Learning to Express Our Love*__

__4__ Ideas

- Is the narrative about a meaningful experience?
- Is background information provided?
- Does the narrative include specific details and dialogue?

__3__ Organization

- Does the beginning interest the reader?
- Does the middle include a series of actions that build to the climax?
- Does the ending show what was learned?

__4__ Voice

- Does the writing sound natural?
- Does the dialogue sound realistic?

__2__ Word Choice

- Does the writing contain vivid verbs and specific nouns?
- Does it contain descriptive modifiers?

__2__ Sentence Fluency

- Do the sentences flow smoothly?
- Is the writing free of fragments and rambling sentences?

__3__ Conventions

- Does the narrative avoid careless errors?
- Is the dialogue correctly punctuated?

OVERALL COMMENTS

- The backstory of your essay provides the reader with background information about your uncomfortable relationship with Ross. This helps the reader recognize the impact of the accident. However, including more specific details and additional dialogue would *show* readers how your feeling about your brother changed.

- While your opening *does* introduce the situation, it does not draw the reader in. Your middle develops the story line in a rather uneventful manner. In your ending, you *do* reveal what you have learned from the experience.

- Your voice sounds flat in some places. Adding dialogue, as well as personal thoughts and feelings, will help readers understand how your feelings about your brother changed.

- Your writing contains words that are overused or too general to paint a clear picture of your relationship (thing, liked, hug). Your essay lacks specific nouns, verbs, modifiers, and figures of speech that would make your writing more engaging to readers.

- While you have varied your sentence beginnings, your narrative contains rambling sentences (paragraph 3) and also many short, choppy sentences. These make the narrative hard to read.

- Your writing contains quite a few errors in punctuation, grammar, and spelling. These errors should be corrected.

© Houghton Mifflin Harcourt Publishing Company

Expository Writing

The Almond Story

1   Ancestors. Everyone has them. However, people aren't the only

2   ones who have ancestors; many items have come to this country from

3   far-off lands. One such item that has become very familiar to me is

4   the almond. These strange little nuts have quite a story.

5   The almond, a fruit related to peaches, plums, and cherries, is

6   known for the tasty nut found inside the fruit. Much like peanuts,

7   almonds are very versatile and can be eaten in many different forms.

8   They are delicious right off the tree, but they are also good candied,

9   chocolate covered, blanched, roasted, salted, or even garlic flavored.

10   Almonds are a prime ingredient in many kitchens around the world

11   and also in food manufacturing. Almond butters and oils enhance a

12   variety of dishes.

13   Aside from just being delicious, almonds are very nutritious as

14   well. Formerly thought of as high in fat, recent studies have shown that

15   they contain little fat and no cholesterol. Almonds are rich in vitamin E

16   and protein as opposed to many other flavorings and snack foods.

17   This history of the almonds extends to Biblical times when

18   they were a main ingredient in the breads served to the Egyptian

19   pharaohs. In the 1700s the Franciscan padres brought almonds from

20   Spain to their missions in California. They were brought mostly

21   as decorations for the missions along the El Camino Real which

22 stretched from San Diego in the south to Sonoma in the north.

23 The coastal missions did not provide good growing conditions for

24 the almonds, and they were not grown successfully inland until

25 hundreds of years later. After research and crossbreeding methods

26 had developed, it was well into the twentieth century before the

27 almonds growing in the Sacramento and San Joaquin Valleys could

28 be considered an industry.

29 Almonds are best grown in climates characterized by hot dry

30 summers and rainy winters. Thus the Central Valley in California

31 provides the ideal growing conditions. In fact, California grows 70

32 percent of the world's almonds. More than 400,000 acres of almond

33 trees grown in the state, making it California's most important crop.

34 When the almond hit California's Central Valley, the industry

35 became important to my own family. Almonds have been our

36 livelihood since the 1940s. My great-grandfather decided to start his

37 own farm when almonds became a popular crop in our area in the late

38 1930s. He passed his successful business to my grandfather, who now

39 shares it with my dad and my uncles. Our whole family now seems to

40 be a part of the business. And it is a beautiful business to be in.

41 Almond tress bud and blossom in late winter to early spring.

42 The blossoms of the almond tress are amazing beautiful and sweet

43 smelling. When I go over the overpass into town, the amazing blanket

44 of white I see in front of me fills me with awe. When I'm standing in

45 the orchard, it is incredible to hear the bees pollinating busily and

46 smell the nectar they produce. Because of this beauty, the blossoming

47 time of year is the favorite for most in California.

48 Once the beautiful petals drop, the leaves grow and the fruit

49 appears. In July, the outside (or hull) hardens and beings to split.

50 Between mid to late August and October, the split in the hull widens,

51 the shell is exposed, and this allows the nut to dry. When the hull

52 opens completely, the almonds are knocked from the tress manually

53 or by a "shaker" machine that shakes the tree's trunk with almost

54 seismic force. After the almonds are swept into a cart, they are

55 transported to a machine that separates the leaves, hull, shell, and

56 nut.

57 The nut isn't the only useful part of the almond after the

58 harvest. The hulls are used as feed for dairies, and the shells can

59 be used as bedding in corrals or barns. Almonds also come in many

60 different varieties that are separated and graded, and often used for

61 different purposes such as cooking, blanching and slicing.

62 The almond's origins and harvesting processes probably don't

63 cross people's minds when they snack on one. When my dad brings

64 home a can of honey roasted almonds, I rarely think of the growing

65 and hulling process. Many people do not see an almond for anything

66 more than a tasty snack, but when you look deeper, you realize it

67 represents so much more.

Expository Rubric Checklist

Title *The Almond Story*

_4_ Ideas

- Does my essay include a clear thesis statement?
- Do I support my thesis with a variety of details?

_5_ Organization

- Does my overall structure work well?
- Have I used signal words to make my structure clear?

_5_ Voice

- Are most of my sentences active?
- Do I use third-person point of view consistently?

_6_ Word Choice

- Do I use words with the appropriate connotation?
- Do I use words with the correct denotation?

_6_ Sentence Fluency

- Are my series parallel?
- Are my comparisons clear and complete?

_4_ Conventions

- Do I use correct punctuation, capitalization, spelling, and grammar?

OVERALL COMMENTS

- Your writing shows great understanding of the topic—almonds. However, your thesis statement could be stronger. What is it about the almond's story that you are trying to highlight? Is it the beauty of the plant, its varied uses, or its history?

- Your essay uses an effective organizational pattern. Your transitions are appropriate.

- Your voice sounds knowledgeable and fits your audience. With the exception of paragraphs that describe your personal experiences with the almond plant, your writing employs third-person point of view.

- Throughout your essay, you use words with appropriate connotations and correct denotations.

- Your writing contains a variety of sentence types. In the second paragraph, you included a parallel series (also good candied, chocolate covered, blanched, roasted, salted, or even garlic flavored).

- Your essay has several careless errors in punctuation, grammar, and spelling.

Expository Writing

Why Rome Fell

1   At its peak, the Roman Empire would have been a good place to

2   live. At its best, Rome was like modern America. For its time, that it.

3   There was running water. The Romans also had public and private

4   baths. There were centers of learning and great works of art. The

5   road system that spanned the empire gave meaning to the saying,

6   "All roads lead to Rome." Yet the Roman Empire fell due to the

7   decline of morals.

8   All of the reasons had a common denominater—poor morals.

9   Due to the breakdown in morals, decay got into every other part of

10   Rome. The military system broke down. This caused several things

11   to happen. With not enough dedicated citizens to fight, the Romans

12   began to use barbarians in the army. There were even some emperers

13   who were of partly German blood. The Emperers was murdered after

14   holding the position for only a short while. The Praetorian Guard

15   was supposed to act as the body guard for the emperer. If the guard

16   did not like the current emperer, they would kill him for that reason

17   as well. The imoral institution of slavery flourished. Why pay a man

18   to do a job that a slave can do at not cost? After all, they only had to

19   pay once to buy the slave. After the job was completed, they could sell

20   the slave for a profit. Poverty was widespread for two reasons. First,

21   the slaves taking the jobs of freemen and the small-time farmers not

22   being able to compete with the great plantations. Since people used

23   slaves to do all the work, they were able to sell grain for extremely

24   low prices. Because of the low prices, the small farmer could not

25   make a profit. So small farmers would move to the city in hopes of

26   finding work. There were no jobs. Slaves had taken all available

27   work.

28   Greed also spread to their social lives. Romans wanted to party

29   without having to pay the consequences. They got addicted to drugs.

30   Alcohol was widespread. And they slept with all sorts of people.

31   Because of choosing to live such imoral lives, they would contract

32   horrible diseases. They did not want to accept the responsibility for

33   the decisions they made. The Romans lost all value for life. They

34   loved to watch the gladiators fight to death. They treated them like

35   idols. Like we do to movie stars and athletes. The people of Rome

36   wanted violance, torture, and death for fun! Criminals and Christians

37   died from wild beasts. Romans enjoyed watching pain being given to

38   others.

39   Maybe if the Romans had not become so wicked, their empire

40   would have lasted longer.

Expository Rubric Checklist

Title **_Why Rome Fell_**

_3_ Ideas

- Does my essay include a clear thesis statement?
- Do I support my thesis with a variety of details?

_3_ Organization

- Does my overall structure work well?
- Have I used signal words to make my structure clear?

_4_ Voice

- Are most of my sentences active?
- Do I use third-person point of view consistently?

_3_ Word Choice

- Do I use words with the appropriate connotation?
- Do I use words with the correct denotation?

_2_ Sentence Fluency

- Are my series parallel?
- Are my comparisons clear and complete?

_2_ Conventions

- Do I use correct punctuation, capitalization, spelling, and grammar?

OVERALL COMMENTS

- Your essay shows a general understanding of the topic. However, your thesis statement needs greater focus.

- Your essay contains many specific details, all of which contributed to the fall of Rome. However, you could have organized your essay more effectively by combining like ideas into shorter paragraphs.

- Your voice sounds knowledgeable and fits your audience. You consistently use third-person point of view. Some of your sentences should be revised from passive voice to active voice.

- You generally use words with appropriate connotations and correct denotations. However, your writing contains words that are overused or too general (great, supposed to). You should replace these stagnant terms with specific nouns, verbs, and modifiers.

- More variety is needed in sentence type and length. Your essay contains many short sentences that interfere with the flow of your writing.

- Your essay contains numerous errors in subject-verb agreement and spelling (emperers, imoral, violance). These errors make your writing confusing and difficult to read.

Persuasive Writing

Creatine Crazy

1   Walk into any fitness club today, and you will find someone who

2 is taking creatine, a training supplement that has become popular

3 with athletes. For the last decade, athletes around the world have

4 been taking it to gain muscle mass. If athletes work out regularly,

5 follow a good diet, and take creatine, they'll get results. But are

6 bigger muscles worth it? For high school athletes, the answer is *no*

7 because creatine presents too many risks.

8   One of the concerns with high school athletes are the overload

9 creatine use creates. To help build muscles, the body actually produces

10 creatine naturally—at the rate of 2 to 3 grams a day. The problem is

11 that the athletes who take supplemental creatine start with a loading-

12 up phase, taking 20 to 25 grams a day for a week. Then they follow

13 with an eight-week cycle of 5 grams a day. In other words, athletes on

14 the supplement start by taking more than seven times the natural

15 daily amount before dropping down to twice the daily amount.

16   In the short term, creatine use may be more harmful than people

17 believe. The harmful side effects may include diarrhea, dehydration,

18 nausea, muscle strains and increased blood pressure. While these

19 harmful side effects are rare, at least one local high school football

20 player was taken to the hospital for dehydration from using creatine,

21 or "power powder" as it is often called.

22   Doctors are even more concerned about possible long term

23 problems. As Dr. Michael Colgan, a clinical nutritionist, states in

24 *Today's Health* magazine, "Taken in doses of more than 25 grams

25 per day, creatine can crucify (torture) your kidneys, and there's also

26 evidence that is can contribute to muscle cramping and the tearing of

27 connective tissues" (67). Experts worry about the kidneys having to

28 filter extra creatine, and some believe that the body might actually

29 stop producing creatine naturally.

30   Even knowing the possible harmful effects, more and more

31 high school athletes are using creatine. Why? They feel tremendous

32 pressure to become bigger, stronger, and faster. George Hurley, a

33 football coach from Newbury Park High in California, said in a recent

34 interview in *Sportz* magazine, "Kids come to the conclusion that if

35 the guy next to me in the weight room is doing creatine and I'm not

36 doing it, he is ahead of me" (117). The result is that teen athletes

37 believe they must take creatine to compete in high school sports, and

38 to have any chance of competing at the next level.

39   Few young athletes (or parents) take the time to weight the

40 pros and cons of their decision about creatine. They fail to consider

41 that very few high school athletes go on to play in college, and even

42 fewer will play professionally. They don't understand that they are

43 risking a lifetime of health problems for a short-term gamble at the

44 big leagues. They don't listen to the cautions that come their way. For

45   example, the National Federation of High School Sports Medicine

46   had stated in its *NFSM Journal* that "school personnel and coaches

47   should not dispense any drug, medication, or food supplement except

48   with extreme caution" (42). Adults responsible for young athletes

49   should not promote the use of creatine in their schools.

50   Today, teenage athletes are under a lot of stress. There is way too

51   much emphasis placed on performing well in a society that seems to

52   eat, sleep, and breath sports. Coaches, administrators, and parents

53   should de-emphasize winning at all costs and keep teens away from

54   supplements like creatine, at least until more is known about them.

55   Young athletes should be encouraged to rely on their natural talents

56   and strength so that sports are fair and safe for everybody. Creatine

57   may make athletes stronger, but it won't necessarily makes them

58   better, and in the long run, it really isn't worth the risk.

Persuasive Rubric Checklist

Title *Creatine Crazy*

_6_ Ideas

- Does my essay include a clear position statement?

- Do I support my position with reasons and details?

- Do I avoid logic errors?

_6_ Organization

- Does the beginning introduce the topic and state the position?

- Does the middle support my position?

- Does my ending restate the position and offer a final thought?

_6_ Voice

- Do I use the right level of language?

- Do I connect with the reader?

_4_ Word Choice

- Have I used only necessary modifiers?

- Have I avoided repeating words too often?

_5_ Sentence Fluency

- Do I use long sentences effectively?

- Do I use short sentences effectively?

_4_ Conventions

- Have I avoided most errors in punctuation, capitalization, spelling, and grammar?

OVERALL COMMENTS

- The last sentence of paragraph 1 clearly states your position statement. You support your position with logical reasons bolstered with documented facts. In addition, an important objection to your position is countered convincingly.

- Your middle paragraphs support your position, presenting your reasons in order of importance. Your ending restates your position and offers your readers a final thought.

- Your voice is persuasive and respects your audience. You sound confident in your position regarding the use of creatine.

- Some parts of your essay contain unneeded modifiers (tremendous pressure . . . ; . . . harmful side effects). You should revise your essay and remove these extra, repetitive terms.

- Your essay contains sentences that are varied in type and beginnings. This makes the essay flow smoothly.

- Your essay has a few careless errors in punctuation, grammar, and spelling. These should be revised.

Persuasive Writing

Environmental Pollution

1   In the time that it will take to read this essay (about five

2   minutes), about two thousand children around the world will die

3   from air and water pollution. Pollution is a problem throughout the

4   entire world, and it can be reduced and eventually prevented. Air

5   pollution, water pollution, and the filling up of landfills are all issues

6   everybody deals with every day.

7   Air pollution is everywhere, whether it is in a smoky restaurant,

8   behind a running car, or in a smoggy city. One fifth of the people

9   in the world are exposed to hazardous levels of air pollutants. The

10 exhaust fumes from cars are a huge contributor to outdoor pollution.

11 These fumes negatively help with the greenhouse effect, which allows

12 sunlight to come into the atmosphere, but lets no heat out. Outdoor

13 pollution from cars can be helped by people driving less. Driving

14 less will conserve energy, which is one of the best ways to help the

15 environment. Conserving energy reduces the air pollution made by

16 power plants, which makes the air cleaner.

17   Air pollution is also caused by tobacco smoke in restaurants and

18 other buildings. A simple way to decrease exposing yourself to this

19 kind of pollution is to stay away from smoke. These are two simple

20 things that everyone can do to make a huge difference in the fight

21 against air pollution.

22   Along with air pollution, water pollution is another dangerous

23   type of pollution. Throughout the world about five million people die

24   every year from drinking polluted water. Water can be contaminated

25   by sewage, toxic chemicals, metals, and oils. This contamination can

26   affect bodies of water and ground water as well. Water contamination

27   is often caused by improper separation of waste water from clean

28   drinking water. In some parts of the world, water carrying human

29   waste can flow into drinking water, which also causes cholera and

30   dysentery. About ten percent of the groundwater across our nation

31   has been contaminated. Maybe this is why so many people drink only

32   bottled water. In some cases, solutions to water pollution problems

33   can be as simple as buying water filters, but some third world

34   countries need to create a whole new system to purify water. Other

35   solutions like buying products that are safe for the environment are

36   things that everyone can do.

37   Pollution in the water is connected with the overfilling of

38   landfills. Every day in the United States there are one hundred

39   sixty million tons of garbage. This is about three and a half pounds

40   per person. Many landfills are overflowing, causing coastal and

41   metropolitan areas to dump their waste into nearby oceans, thus

42   causing water pollution. The dumping of the trash also puts toxic

43   hospital waste into oceans. This includes hospital needles infected

44   with the AIDS virus. The dumping of this infected waste could help

45 spread the virus to many innocent victims. Many landfills in the

46 United States are starting to fill up quickly. Many people are trying

47 to find solutions that will slow the filling of landfills. Recycling is

48 one major factor that could help reduce the overfilling of landfills.

49 Seventy-five percent of the waste in landfills is recyclable. Recycling

50 keeps garbage out of landfills, doesn't generate pollution, and keeps

51 people from using our diminishing raw materials. Recycling is

52 one simple thing that everyone can do to reduce the overfilling of

53 landfills, and it is also good for the environment.

54   Every five minutes over two thousand innocent children die from

55 something that can be prevented and cured—pollution. Forty percent

56 of the deaths in the world can be attributed to environmental factors.

57 Air and water pollution are at the top of the list of killers. Driving

58 less, using water filters, conserving energy, using environmentally

59 friendly products, and recycling can and will make a difference.

Persuasive Rubric Checklist

Title *Environmental Pollution*

__3__ Ideas

- Does my essay include a clear position statement?
- Do I support my position with reasons and details?
- Do I avoid logic errors?

__2__ Organization

- Does the beginning introduce the topic and state the position?
- Does the middle support my position?
- Does my ending restate the position and offer a final thought?

__2__ Voice

- Do I use the right level of language?
- Do I connect with the reader?

__3__ Word Choice

- Have I used only necessary modifiers?
- Have I avoided repeating words too often?

__5__ Sentence Fluency

- Do I use long sentences effectively?
- Do I use short sentences effectively?

__6__ Conventions

- Have I avoided most errors in punctuation, capitalization, spelling, and grammar?

OVERALL COMMENTS

- The first sentence of your essay grabs the reader's attention. However, the topic of your essay is too broad. You should revise your writing to focus on a specific type of pollution.

- While your essay contains a wealth of information about pollution, its organization pattern is unclear. Your writing should be restructured to create a clear beginning, middle, and end.

- Your voice shows that you are knowledgeable about environmental pollution. However, in many instances, your voice becomes quite emotional and conveys a message of panic to the reader.

- Your beginning and closing repeat verbatim an alarming statistic. You also repeat statements regarding the link between car exhausts and air pollution. You should revise your essay and remove this repetition.

- Your essay contains sentences that are varied in type and beginnings. This makes the essay flow smoothly.

- Your writing is error free!

Response to Literature

The Beast of Fear

1 In William Golding's novel *Lord of the Flies*, the boys allow

2 themselves to be terrorized by a beast they create in their minds

3 because deep down they want it to exist. By creating a physical object

4 to represent everything they are afraid of, the boys can base their

5 fears on something external and distant, rather than on something

6 close and personal.

7 When they first arrive on the island, the boys have many

8 implied fears: fear of being left on the island, fear of being on their

9 own without adult assistance, and fear of what may be occurring in

10 the war (World War II) from which they have fled. As a result, they

11 all embrace the concept of the beast, for it is a way to externalize

12 their fears. What the boys want is something they can fear in good

13 conscience, some evil that does not stem from their own personal

14 experience. So they place their fear outside themselves and believe in

15 a beast.

16 Jack sums up the reason why externalized fear is so much

17 easier to deal with than internal fear when he says, "If there was a

18 snake we'd hunt it and kill it." It's a simple question of power. The

19 boys never would have thought that they were responsible for the

20 appearance of the beast, but they did believe that they could be

22 responsible for its demise or destruction. If the beast is something

© Houghton Mifflin Harcourt Publishing Company

23 that can be destroyed, there is the potential that everything can turn

24 out all right, the possibility that all the evil that the boys perceive

25 on their island can be purged with the removal of this one creature.

26 In one sense, Jack's cause is a noble one: purifying his world of evil.

27 However, he goes about looking for the beast in all the wrong places,

28 and as a result, the boys commit several horrible crimes. In fact,

29 part of Golding's message is that "to fancy thinking the beast was

30 something you could hunt and kill" is really catering to the true inner

31 beast itself.

32   The development of the beast in *Lord of the Flies* is not an

33 unusual one. We are always looking for a beast or a scapegoat

34 to destroy to solve our problems. And, as the Nazis set out to

35 exterminate the Jews, and Stalin the freedom of the individual, the

36 boys create the beast as a safety net, an outside evil that protects

37 them from the knowledge of their true nature as fallen creatures, or

38 "beasts," themselves.

Response-to-Literature Rubric Checklist

Title _**The Beast of Fear**_

__4__ Ideas

- Do I have a clear thesis statement?
- Do I use effective details?

__6__ Organization

- Does the beginning state the thesis?
- Does the middle focus on major elements?
- Does the ending expand the theme?

__6__ Voice

- Is my voice suitably analytical?
- Is my voice compelling as I narrate the plot?

__4__ Word Choice

- Have I used correct literary terminology?
- Have I focused on symbols?

__6__ Sentence Fluency

- Do my sentences read smoothly?

__6__ Conventions

- Have I followed the rules of English?

OVERALL COMMENTS

- Your essay has a clear thesis statement. You also include many specific examples to support your main points. Including more direct quotations from the text would have made your paper even stronger.

- The beginning of your essay clearly identifies your thesis. Your middle paragraphs further develop this theme. Your ending expands the theme to other historical events.

- Your voice expresses interest and in-depth understanding of the selection.

- You do an exemplary job of exploring the meaning of the beast symbol. In your analysis, however, you fail to incorporate literary terminology into your essay.

- Your writing contains a variety of sentence types and beginnings. As a result, your essay flows smoothly and is easy to read.

- Your writing is free of spelling, grammar, or punctuation errors.

Response to Literature

Huck Finn: The Relationship Between Huck and Jim

1   Ethnic background, social status, or even age do not prove to be a
2 factor in the friendship of Huck Finn and Jim. The two very different
3 characters serve not only as companions but as friends throughout
4 the novel. It seems as if differences in the many categories that
5 usually make up friendship showed no signs of affecting the
6 relationship between Huck and Jim. While Huck and Jim had no
7 different pasts and no different futures, the two found each other
8 on a level of friendship. The same level that doesn't pay attention to
9 race, domestic abuse, or even silly superstitions. True friendship was
10 found between the unlikely characters of Huck and Jim.

11   Quite possibly, the best way to describe the relationship between
12 Huck and Jim is to describe it as one of differences, yet seeking a
13 common goal. Truthfully speaking, the two characters were coming
14 from opposite lines of the social spectrum. While Huck was living a
15 life of freedom (though he didn't think much of it), Jim was confined
16 to the evils of slavery. Whereas Jim never lived a day in his life with
17 certain freedoms, Huck enjoyed the freedoms on a regular basis. Even
18 though Jim was a slave and Huck was free, both looked farther into
19 the future to goals which they hoped to reach. While both lived in
20 different social classes, they both strived for limits, looked 'down the
21 river'.

22 The relationship grew as the two found their own destiny. The true

23 similarities between the two characters come to life in the realization

24 that they both were looking for their destiny together, on the river.

25 Jim had run away from slavery, attempting to catch a boat from Cairo,

26 IL up through the free states of New York. Huck had run away from

27 the uniformity of Southern lifestyle. He had escaped the mandatory

28 church services, abuse from his father, and constant hassles from Miss

29 Watson. Huck wants to think on his own, establish his own opinions,

30 live for himself. With Jim and Huck both escaping their own societies,

31 they meet together on a Mississippi River raft, symbolically speaking,

32 the united carriage toward their own individual freedom.

33 Matters of race, social standing, and age all play a roll in how

34 Jim and Huck are different in many ways. However, the united dream

35 towards individual freedom, that they both share, helps them overcome

36 certain obstacles along the way. The relationship is aided in the fact

37 that Huck's quick mouth often times was enough to get the two out of

38 close calls along the river. In addition, it was Jim's knowledge in fixing

39 the raft that helped the two stay afloat. Their hand in hand, symbiotic

40 relationship only aided in the two finding their own freedom.

41 Jim and Huck shared few qualities. They didn't talk alike, act

42 alike, or dress alike. However, the fact that they gave each other true

43 friendship made their relationship a positive step towards each of

44 them finding their own individual freedom.

Response-to-Literature Rubric Checklist

Title _Huck Finn: The Relationship Between Huck and Jim_

_2_ Ideas

- Do I have a clear thesis statement?

- Do I use effective details?

_3_ Organization

- Does the beginning state the thesis?

- Does the middle focus on major elements?

- Does the ending expand the theme?

_4_ Voice

- Is my voice suitably analytical?

- Is my voice compelling as I narrate the plot?

_2_ Word Choice

- Have I used correct literary terminology?

- Have I focused on symbols?

_5_ Sentence Fluency

- Do my sentences read smoothly?

_4_ Conventions

- Have I followed the rules of English?

OVERALL COMMENTS

- The first paragraph of your essay contains a clear thesis statement. However, you fail to support your thesis statement with effective details. Including specific examples from the text that show how Huck and Jim grow into their unique friendship would strengthen your essay.

- While your beginning does state your thesis, your middle paragraphs basically restate the same information. Your ending paragraph, which expands the theme, should be developed more.

- Your voice shows that you are knowledgeable about the selection. However, in an attempt to be analytical, you sometimes sound bored and unnatural.

- Your writing does not include literary terms that reveal your understanding of the selection. In addition, you fail to include quotations that connect your analysis to the text.

- Your writing contains a variety of sentences designed to keep the reader's interest.

- Your essay has a few minor errors in mechanics. Reading your paper aloud will help to catch these errors.

Editing and Proofreading Marks

Use the symbols and letters below to show where and how your writing needs to be changed. Your teachers may also use these symbols to point out errors in your writing.

Symbols	Meaning	Example	Corrected Example
≡	Capitalize a letter.	George orwell wrote *1984*.	George Orwell wrote *1984*.
/	Make a capital letter lowercase.	His novel explores life without personal Freedom.	His novel explores life without personal freedom.
⊙	Insert (add) a period.	*1984* focuses on a parallel world in the future It is . . .	*1984* focuses on a parallel world in the future. It is . . .
⬭ or *sp.*	Correct spelling.	Winston Smith tries to escape the (tyrany.)	Winston Smith tries to escape the tyranny.
⟋	Delete (take out) or replace.	His every movement is scrutinized.	His every move is scrutinized.
∧	Insert here.	Winston and Julia create a plan. *(complicated)*	Winston and Julia create a complicated plan.
∧ ∧ ∧ (, : ;)	Insert a comma, a colon, or a semicolon.	Together they profess their allegiance against the Party.	Together, they profess their allegiance against the Party.
∨ ∨ ∨ (' " ")	Insert an apostrophe or quotation marks.	OBrien is not a member of the Brotherhood.	O'Brien is not a member of the Brotherhood.
? ! ∧ ∧	Insert a question mark or an exclamation point.	Broken, Winston screams, "Not me"	Broken, Winston screams, "Not me!"
¶	Start a new paragraph.	¶Winston is a changed man after he . . .	Winston is a changed man after he . . .
∼	Switch words or letters.	Julia admits ultimately her betrayal.	Julia ultimately admits her betrayal.

© Houghton Mifflin Harcourt Publishing Company

Time Line

Topic: _____

5 W's Chart

Topic: _____

Who?	
What?	
When?	
Where?	
Why?	
How?	

T-Chart

Topic:

Venn Diagram

Subject A

Differences

Similarities

Subject B

Sensory Chart

Subject: _____

Sights	Sounds	Smells	Tastes	Textures

Details Chart

Quick List

1. **First Point:**

   -

   -

2. **Second Point:**

   -

   -

3. **Third Point:**

   -

   -

© Houghton Mifflin Harcourt Publishing Company

Scavenger Hunt 1: Find It!

Directions Find the following information in your book by turning to the pages listed in parentheses.

1. Types of support you can use to develop main points in your writing (pages 108–109)

_____

_____

2. What STRAP stands for (page 212)

_____

3. A writing technique that connects two words with opposite meanings (page 601)

_____

4. Types of sentence constructions (page 748)

_____

5. How to keep a learning log in art class (page 499)

_____

_____

6. When to use long and short sentences (pages 246–247)

_____

_____

7. Forms of plagiarism (page 419)

_____

_____

8. Purposes for adjusting voice in your writing (page 69)

_____

_____

9. Patterns of organization (pages 584–588)

_____

_____

10. How to avoid repeating a word too often (page 245)

_____

_____

Scavenger Hunt 2: What Is It?

© Houghton Mifflin Harcourt Publishing Company

> **Directions** Find the answers to the following questions using the index in the back of the book.

1. What is asyndeton?

   _____

2. What is enjambment?

   _____

3. What types of writing prompts can be found on college applications?

   _____

4. What is deductive writing?

   _____

5. What are understood subjects and predicates?

   _____

6. What is backstory?

   _____

   _____

7. What are the best fonts to use for main text and headings?

   _____

8. What does SQ3R stand for?

   _____

9. What is internal dialogue?

   _____

10. What is "plunking" source material?

    _____

11. What are verbals?

    _____

    _____

12. What are cliches?

    _____

Getting to Know *Write Source*

Locate the pages in *Write Source* where answers to the following learning tasks can be found. Both the index and the table of contents can help you.

_____ **1.** Your teacher reminds you to focus on the traits of writing in your next writing assignment. You need to make sure you understand the traits.

_____ **2.** You are applying for a job. You need to know how to write a résumé.

_____ **3.** You are writing an MLA research paper. You need to know how to create a works-cited page.

_____ **4.** Your teacher tells you to use a rubric to guide, revise, and edit your writing as well as to assess it. You need to know how to use a rubric for these purposes.

_____ **5.** You are supposed to take notes while you read an assignment. You need some guidelines for taking reading notes.

_____ **6.** Before you write a sonnet, your teacher reminds you to use either the English form or the Italian form. You need to understand the forms of sonnets.

_____ **7.** You're not sure whether to use the word *lay* or *lie* in the story you're writing. You need to know which is the right word to use.

_____ **8.** You have a hard time participating in class discussions. You need some tips for speaking in class.

_____ **9.** Your assignment is to write an essay of evaluation. You need to see a model of one.

_____ **10.** Your teacher suggests using a graphic organizer during prewriting. You need to see examples of graphic organizers.

Getting-Started Activity Answers

Scavenger Hunt 1: Find It!

1. There are several types of support you can use to develop main points in your writing, including explaining, describing, arguing, reflecting, and analyzing.

2. STRAP stands for Subject, Type, Role, Audience, and Purpose.

3. An oxymoron is a writing technique that connects two words with opposite meanings.

4. Simple, compound, complex, and compound-complex are the types of sentence constructions.

5. A good way to keep a learning log in art class is to make a two-column chart. On the left, make notes about what the teacher talked about. On the right side, add your own comments.

6. Use long sentences to convey a wealth of information about a complex issue. Use short sentences to make an important point.

7. There are several forms of plagiarism: submitting another writer's paper, using copy-and-paste, neglecting necessary quotation marks, paraphrasing without citing a source, and confusing borrowed material with your own ideas.

8. Adjust your voice in your writing when relating an experience, sharing information, or persuading a reader.

9. Several patterns of organization include classification order, comparison-contrast order, cause-effect order, and process organization.

10. You can avoid repeating a word too often by employing one of the following strategies: replace the word with an appropriate synonym; replace the word with a pronoun, making sure the antecedent is clear; and rewrite sentences to avoid the word.

Scavenger Hunt 2: What Is It?

1. Asyndeton is presenting a series with no conjunctions at all (p. 80).

2. Enjambment is carrying sentences from line to line and ending them inside a line (p. 364).

3. Open-ended prompts, influences in your life, and general subject prompts are all types of writing prompts that can be found on college applications (p. 161).

4. Deductive writing is leading the reader to your conclusion by presenting a main idea, or thesis, and then supporting it with specific details (p. 62).

5. Understood subjects and predicates may be missing from the sentence, but they are usually already known or implied. When giving a command like "Get out of the way," the understood subject would be "you" (p. 740).

(CONTINUED)

Getting-Started Activity Answers

6. In expository writing, backstory is the events that occurred before the experience begins (p. 147).

7. In most cases, a serif font is best for the text, and a sans serif font works for any headings (p. 92).

8. SQ3R stands for the five steps in the critical reading process: survey, question, read, recite, and review (p. 534).

9. Internal dialogue shows the thoughts of your main character (p. 348).

10. "Plunking" source material is dropping in a quotation or paraphrased idea without comment (p. 419).

11. Verbals are words that are derived from a verb but do not function as a verb in a sentence (p. 726).

12. Cliches are overused phrases that give the reader nothing new (p. 79).

Getting to Know *Write Source*

1. 48

2. 512–513

3. 407

4. 38–45

5. 531

6. 362–365

7. 720.2

8. 525–526

9. 259–266

10. 64–65

Index